CONTEMPORARY HUMAN RESOURCE MANAGEMENT

TEXT AND CASES

CONTEMPORARY HUMAN RESOURCE MANAGEMENT

Text and Cases

Fourth Edition

Tom Redman and
Adrian Wilkinson

PEARSON

Harlow, England • London • New York • Boston • San Francisco • Toronto • Sydney
Auckland • Singapore • Hong Kong • Tokyo • Seoul • Taipei • New Delhi
Cape Town • São Paulo • Mexico City • Madrid • Amsterdam • Munich • Paris • Milan

PEARSON EDUCATION LIMITED
Edinburgh Gate
Harlow CM20 2JE
Tel: +44 (0)1279 623623
Fax: +44 (0)1279 431059
Website: www.pearson.com/uk

First published 2001 (print)
Second edition published 2006 (print)
Third edition published 2009 (print)
Fourth edition published 2013 (print and electronic)

ISBN: 978-0-273-75782-5 (print)
         978-0-273-75786-3 (ebook)
         978-0-273-78051-9 (eText)

British Library Cataloguing-in-Publication Data
A catalogue record for the print edition is available from the British Library
Library of Congress Cataloging-in-Publication Data
A catalog record for the print edition is available from the Library of Congress

10 9 8 7 6 5 4 3 2 1
16 15 14 13 12

Print edition typeset in [Minion Pro 10/12] by 73
Print edition printed and bound by Rotolito Lombarda, Italy
NOTE THAT ANY PAGE CROSS REFERENCES REFER TO THE PRINT EDITION

To Erin and Aidan
and
Rachel and Rosie

CONTENTS

PART 1
FUNDAMENTALS OF HUMAN RESOURCE MANAGEMENT

PART 2
CONTEMPORARY THEMES AND ISSUES

CASE STUDIES AND EXERCISES

EDITORS

Tom Redman is Professor of Human Resource Management and Director of Research at the University of Durham Business School. Before joining Durham Business School, Tom was a Professor of Human Resource Management at the University of Sheffield. Prior to this he was Professor of Human Resource Management at the University of Teesside. Tom has also spent 10 years in industry, in quality, production and HR management positions (mainly with Royal Worcester Porcelain) prior to re-entering academic life. His books include *Managing Managers* (Blackwell, 1993) and *Managing with TQM: Theory and Practice* (Macmillan, 1998) and *The SAGE Handbook of Human Resource Management* (Sage, 2009). He is a Fellow of the Chartered Institute of Personnel and Development.

Adrian Wilkinson is Professor and Director of the Centre for Work, Organisation and Wellbeing at Griffith University, Brisbane, Australia. Prior to his 2006 appointment, Adrian worked at Loughborough University in the United Kingdom where he was Professor of Human Resource Management from 1998 to 2006. Adrian has also worked at the Manchester School of Management at the University of Manchester Institute of Science and Technology. He holds Visiting Professorships at Loughborough University, the University of Sheffield and the University of Durham, and is an Academic Fellow at the Centre for International Human Resource Management at the Judge Institute, University of Cambridge. Adrian has written/edited 20 books, over 100 articles in refereed journals, and numerous book chapters. His books (with co-authors) include *Making Quality Critical* (Routledge, 1995); *Managing Quality and Human Resources* (Blackwell, 1997); *Managing with TQM: Theory and Practice* (Macmillan, 1998); *Understanding Work and Employment: Industrial Relations in Transition* (Oxford University Press, 2003); *Human Resource Management at Work* (5th edition, Chartered Institute of Personnel and Development, 2012); *The SAGE Handbook of Human Resource Management* (Sage, 2009); *The Oxford Handbook of Participation in Organisations* (Oxford University Press, 2010); *The Research Handbook of The Future of Work and Employment Relations* (Elgar, 2011); *The Future of Employment Relations* (Palgrave, 2011); *The Handbook of Comparative Employment Relations* (Elgar, 2011); and *The International Handbook of Labour Unions* (Elgar, 2012). He is a Fellow and Accredited Examiner of the Chartered Institute of Personnel and Development in the UK and a Fellow of the Australian Human Resource Institute. Adrian was appointed as a British Academy of Management Fellow in 2010. In 2011 he was elected as an Academician of the Academy of Social Sciences in recognition of his contribution. Adrian was Chief Editor of the *International Journal of Management Reviews* from 2004–9 and is an Associate Editor for *Human Resource Management Journal*.

CONTRIBUTORS

Peter Ackers	Professor of Industrial Relations and Labour History, Loughborough University Business School
Deirdre Anderson	Lecturer in Organisational Behaviour, Cranfield School of Management
Aline Bos	Assistant Professor, Utrecht University School of Governance, Utrecht University, The Netherlands
Paul Boselie	Professor, Utrecht University School of Governance, Utrecht University, The Netherlands
Nick Bacon	Professor of Human Resource Management, Cass Business School
Michelle Barker	Professor of Management, Griffith Business School
Sara Branch	Research Fellow, Key Centre for Ethics, Law, Justice and Governance, Griffith University
Samantha Callan	Honorary Research Fellow, School of Clinical Sciences and Community Health, College of Medicine and Veterinary Medicine, Edinburgh University, and Chairman in Residence (Family, Early Years and Mental Health) at the Westminster based think tank, Centre for Social Justice
Cathy Cassell	Professor of Organisational Psychology, Manchester Business School
Alistair Cheyne	Senior Lecturer in Organisational Psychology, Loughborough University Business School
David Collings	Professor of Human Resource Management, Dublin City University Business School
Laurie Cohen	Professor of Organisational Behaviour, Nottingham University Business School
Michael Dickmann	Professor of International Human Resource Management, Cranfield University
Tony Dundon	Lecturer in Human Resource Management, Department of Management, National University of Ireland, Galway
Amal El-Sawad	Lecturer in Human Resource Management, Associate Professor of Human Resource Management at Zayed University, Abu Dhabi, United Arab Emirates
Mark Gilman	Senior Lecturer in Industrial Relations and Human Resource Management at Kent Business School
Dulini Fernando	Research Associate, Centre for Professional Work and Careers, Loughborough University
Irena Grugulis	Professor of Employment Studies, Management School, Durham University
Philip Hancock	Professor of Work and Organisation, Essex Business School
Gail Hebson	Lecturer in Employment Studies, Manchester Business School
William Hunter	Senior Lecturer in Human Resource Management, University of Sunderland
Donald Hislop	Senior Lecturer in Organisational Behaviour, Loughborough University Business School
Louise Hopper	Group Head of Human Resources, Mother Holdings Ltd
Sue Hutchinson	Associate Professor of Human Resource Management, University of West of England
Scott Hurrell	Lecturer in Work and Employment Studies, University of Stirling
Stewart Johnstone	Lecturer in Human Resource Management, University of Newcastle
Clare Kelliher	Professor of Work and Organisation, Cranfield University
Ashlea Kellner	Research Fellow, Centre for Work, Organisation and Wellbeing, Griffith University
Gill Kirton	Professor in Employment Relations and Human Resource Management, Queen Mary, University of London
Nick Kinnie	Reader in Human Resource Management, School of Management, University of Bath

John Loan-Clarke   Senior Lecturer in Organisational Development, Loughborough University Business School

Anne McCormack   Lecturer, University of Strathclyde

Miral Metawie   Doctoral Student, Kent Business School

Olav Muurlink   Research Fellow, Centre for Work, Organisation and Wellbeing, Griffith University

Alankrita Pandey   Department of Management, University of Texas at Arlington

David Peetz   Professor of Employment Relations, Griffith Business School

Sheryl Ramsay   Senior Lecturer in Management, Griffith Business School

Doug Renwick   Lecturer in Human Resource Management, University of Sheffield Management School

Bradley Saunders   Doctoral Student, Loughborough University

Dora Scholarios   Professor of Work Psychology, Strathclyde University

Dhara Shah   Doctoral Student, Griffith Business School

Ed Snape   Professor, Department of Management, Hong Kong Baptist University

Ruth Smyth   Head of HR, Alexander Mann Solutions

Juani Swart   Professor of Human Capital, School of Management, University of Bath

David Thompson   Associate Professor, Department of Management, Hong Kong Polytechnic

Keith Townsend   Senior Research Fellow, Griffith Business School

Melissa Tyler   Professor of Work and Organisation, Essex University Business School

Steven Vincent   Professor of Human Resource Management, Leeds University Business School

Geoffrey Wood   Professor of International Business at Warwick Business School, University of Warwick

Xiaozheng Zhang   Lecturer, Business School, Nottingham Trent University

Yajaun Zhan   Independent Consultant

ACKNOWLEDGEMENTS

As with any book, the list of acknowledgements is extensive, but these are the most important: Thanks to our editor Gabrielle James.

As usual, our family and friends make a major contribution, and Tom and Adrian are grateful to their families for their support while the book was being written.

Publisher's acknowledgements

We are grateful to the following for permission to reproduce copyright material:

Figures

Figure 2.4 from *People Management and Performance*, Oxford: Routledge (Purcell, J., Kinnie, N., Swart, J., Rayton, B. and Hutchinson, S. 2009) p. 15, Figure 1.2; Figure 3.2 adapted from *The Equality Act: What's new for employers?*, London: ACAS (2011) p. 2, © Crown Copyright, contains public sector information licenced under the Open Government Licence v1.0; Figure 11.1 from P. Almond and O. Tregaskis, International HRM, in, *Human Resource Management: A contemporary approach*, 6th ed., p. 649 (Beardwell, J. and Claydon, T. 2010), © Pearson Education Limited 2001, 2010; Figure 11.2 adapted from A typology of international human resource management strategies and processes, *International Journal of Human Resource Management*, Vol. 17 (4), pp. 580–601 (Dickmann, M. and Muller-Camen, M. 2006), reprinted by permission of the publisher Taylor & Francis Ltd., http://www.tandf.co.uk/journals; Figure 11.3 adapted from H. De Cieri and P. Dowling, Strategic human resource management in multinational enterprises: theoretical and empirical developments, in, *Research in Personnel and Human Resource Management: Strategic human resources in the twenty-first century, 4th Supplement* (Wright, P.M., Dyer, L.D. and Boudreau, J.W. (Eds) 1999), Stamford, CT: JAI Press, Emerald Group Publishing Ltd.; Figure 11.5 from *Global Careers*, London: Routledge (Dickmann, M. and Baruch, Y. 2011) p. 120, Figure 5.4, republished with permission of Taylor & Francis Group LLC – Books, permission conveyed through Copyright Clearance Center, Inc.; Figure 11.6 adapted from Expatriate selection, training and career-pathing: A review and critique, *Human Resource Management*, Vol. 26 (3), pp. 331–45 (Mendenhall, M., Dunbar, E. and Oddou, G. 1987), John Wiley & Sons, Copyright © 1987 Wiley Periodicals, Inc. A Wiley Company; Figure 11.7 from A. Haslberger, Expatriate adjustment: a more nuanced view, in, *International Human Resource Management – A European Perspective*, 2nd ed., p. 138, Figure 7.1 (Dickmann, M., Brewster, C. and Sparrow, P. (Eds) 2008), London: Routledge; Figure 16.1 from G.C. McMahon, A. Pandey and B. Martinson, To downsize human capital: A strategic human resource perspective on the disparate outcomes of downsizing, in, *Downsizing: Is less still more?*, p. 139, Figure 5.2 (Cooper, C.L., Pandey, A. and Quick, J.C. (Eds) 2012), Cambridge, UK: Cambridge University Press; Figure 17.1 from M. Marchington, Employee involvement: patterns and explanations, in, *Participation and Democracy at Work: Essays in honour of Harvie Ramsay* (Harley, B., Hyman, J. and Thompson, P. (Eds) 2005), London: Palgrave, used with permission of the editors; Figure 20.1 from United we stand, or else? Exploring organizational attempts to control emotional expression by employees on September 11, 2001, *Journal of Organizational Change Management*, Vol. 16 (5), pp. 534–46 (Driver, M. 2003), p. 542, Figure 1, Emerald Group Publishing Ltd.; Figure 21.1 from Part-time employment, in, *OECD Factbook 2011–2012: Economic, Environmental and Social Statistics*, © OECD 2011, http://dx.doi.org/10.1787/factbook-2011-60-en; Figure 21.2 from Eurostat (online data code: ifsa_etpga), © European Communities, 1995–2010; Figure 22.1 from mobbing.ca, http://www.mobbing.ca, Bobbie Osborne (Photographer) and Anton Hout (Designer), reprinted with permission of Anton Hout of Overcome Bullying Canada; Figure 22.3 from Workplace Mobbing Australia, www.workplacemobbing.com/mobbing.html, Linda Shallcross (designer), reproduced with permission of Linda Shallcross of Workplace Mobbing Australia

Tables

Table 1.3 from *Human Resource Champions*, Harvard Business School Press, Boston, MA (Ulrich, D. 1998) pp. 20–21, Copyright © 1998 by the Harvard Business School Publishing Corporation, all rights reserved, reprinted with permission of Harvard Business School Press; Table 3.1 from *Recruiting and Training Among Large National Employers*, Institute for Employment Studies and IFF Research on behalf of Learning and Skills Council (Bates, P., Johnson, C. and Gifford, J. 2008) p. 33; Table 3.2 from IDS HR Study 865, Competency Frameworks, March 2008, p. 17, www.idshrstudies.com, table reprinted by kind permission of Income Data Services; Table 3.3 from *Resourcing and Talent*

Planning (2011) p. 16, CIPD, with the permission of the publisher, the Chartered Institute of Personnel and Development, London (www.cipd.co.uk); Table 4.1 adapted from *Staffing Organizations: Contemporary practice and theory*, 3rd ed., Mahwah, N.J.: Lawrence Erlbaum Associates (Ployhart, R.E., Schneider, B. and Schmitt, N. 2006) p. 380, Table 7.3, republished with permission of Taylor and Francis Group LLC, Books, conveyed through Copyright Clearance Center, Inc.; Table on page 157 from A. Fuller and L. Unwin, Expansive learning environments: integrating organisational and personal development, in, *Workplace Learning in Context*, p. 130; Table 6.1 from *Financial Participation: The role of governments and social partners*, European Foundation for the Improvement of Living and Working Conditions, 2004, Wyattville Road, Dublin 18, Ireland (Pendleton, A. and Poutsma, E. 2004); Figure 8.1 (Rainbird, H., Fuller, A. and Munro, A. (Eds) 2004), London and New York: Routledge; Table 6.1 from *Financial Participation: The role of governments and social partners*, European Foundation for the Improvement of Living and Working Conditions, 2004, Wyattville Road, Dublin 18, Ireland (Pendleton, A. and Poutsma, E. 2004); Table 6.2 adapted from J. Arrowsmith, H. Nicholaisen, B. Bechter and R. Nonell, The management of variable pay in banking: forms and rationale in four European countries, in, *Challenges in European Employment Relations: Employment regulation, trade union organization, equality, flexicurity*, pp. 201–40 (Blanpain, R. and Dickens, L. (Eds) 2008), © 2008 Kluwer Law International B.V., The Netherlands, republished with permission of Wolters Kluwer Law & Business (Aspen Publishers, Inc.), conveyed through Copyright Clearance Center, Inc.; Table 8.2 after *OECD Employment Outlook: 2004 Edition*, based on Table 3.3, Trade union density and collective bargaining coverage in OECD countries, 1970–2000; Table 8.3 from K. Hamann and J. Kelly, Varieties of capitalism and industrial relations, in, *The Sage Handbook of Industrial Relations*, pp. 129–48 (Blyton, P., Bacon, N., Fiorito, J. and Heery, E. (Eds) 2008), London: Sage. Copyright © 2008 Sage Publications Ltd., reproduced by permission of Sage Publications, London, Los Angeles, New Delhi and Singapore; Table 8.4 from Workplace industrial relations in Britain 1980–2004, *Industrial Relations Journal*, Vol. 38 (4), pp. 285–302 (Blanchflower, D.G., Bryson, A. and Forth, J. 2007), Copyright © John Wiley and Sons; Table 10.1 from *Leadership for Competitive Advantage* (Georgiades, N. and Macdonnell, R. 1998) p. 174, Copyright © John Wiley and Sons Ltd.; Table 11.1 from *Managing Across Borders: The transnational solution*, Random House Business Books (Bartlett, C. and Ghoshal, S. 1989),; Table 11.2 adapted from N.J. Adler and F. Ghadar, Strategic human resource management: a global perspective, in, *Human Resource Management: An international comparison*, p. 240, Table 1 (Pieper, R. 1990), New York: de Gruyter, © 1990 De Gruyter; Table 11.4 from The coffee-machine system: how international selection really works, *International Journal of Human Resource Management*, Vol. 10 (3), pp. 488–500 (Harris, H. and Brewster, C. 1999), reprinted by permission of the publisher Taylor & Francis Ltd., http://www.tandf.co.uk/journals and; Table 11.5 adapted from *International Human Resource Management*, London: CIPD (Harris, H., Brewster, C. and Sparrow P. 2003) p. 146, with the permission of the publisher, the Chartered Institute of Personnel and Development, London (www.cipd.co.uk); Table 11.6 adapted from *Global Careers*, London: Routledge (Dickmann, M. and Baruch, Y. 2011) p. 194, republished with permission of Taylor & Francis Group LLC – Books, permission conveyed through Copyright Clearance Center, Inc.; Table 11.7 adapted from *Global Careers*, London: Routledge (Dickmann, M. and Baruch, Y. 2011) p. 234, republished with permission of Taylor & Francis Group LLC – Books, permission conveyed through Copyright Clearance Center, Inc.; Table 11.8 adapted from *Global Careers*, London: Routledge (Dickmann, M. and Baruch, Y. 2011) p. 40, republished with permission of Taylor & Francis Group LLC – Books, permission conveyed through Copyright Clearance Center, Inc.; Table 16.1 from Strategies for successful organization downsizing, *Human Resource Management*, Vol. 33 (2), pp. 189–211 (Cameron, K.S. 1994), p. 197, Table II, John Wiley and Sons, Copyright © 1994 Wiley Periodicals, Inc., A Wiley Company; Table 18.2 adapted from Finders, keepers? Attracting, motivating and retaining knowledge workers, *Human Resource Management Journal*, Vol. 13 (4), pp. 23–44 (Horwitz, F., Heng, C. and Quazi, H. 2003), John Wiley & Sons; Table 22.1 from Bullying: From the playground to the boardroom, *Journal of Leadership and Organizational Studies*, Vol. 12 (4), pp. 1-11 (Harvey, M. G., Heames, J. T., Richey, R. G. and Leonard, N. 2006), Copyright © 2006 Baker College, reprinted by permission of SAGE Publications.

Text

Extract on page 124 from Using situational interviews to assess engineering applicant fit to work group. Job and organizational requirements, *Engineering Management Journal*, Vol. 18, pp. 27–35 (Maurer, S.D. 2006), 1 September, reproduced with permission of American Society for Engineering Management in the format textbook and 'other' book via Copyright Clearance Center; Case Study 5.3 from The rise of the 'network organisation' and the decline of discretion, *Human Resource Management Journal*, Vol.13 (2), pp.45–59 (Grugulis, I., Vincent, S. and Hebson, G. 2003), Copyright © 2003 John Wiley & Sons; Box 5.5 from Big, bad welfare: welfare reform politics and children, *The Progressive*, Vol.58 (8), pp. 18–21 (Conniff, R. 1994), used with permission; Box 6.1 from *Managing Reward: Job Evaluation and Grading. One stop guide*, Reed Business Information Ltd. (Childs, M. 2004) www.xperthr.co.uk; Box 12.1 from *Culture's Consequences: Comparing values, behaviors, institutions and organizations across nations*, 2nd ed., Thousand Oaks, California: Sage Publications (Hofstede, G. 2001) p. 29, ISBN 0–8039–7323–3

© Geert Hofstede B.V., quoted with permission; Case Study 12.1 from Human resource management practice and institutional constraints: The case of Mozambique, *Employee Relations: An International Journal*, Vol.27 (4), pp.369–85 (Webster, E. and Wood, G. 2005), © Emerald Group Publishing Limited all rights reserved; Box 17.1 from *Information and Consultation of Employees (ICE)* *Regulations 2004*, Department for Business, Innovation and Skills, DTI 2006, © Crown copyright, contains public sector information licensed under the Open Government Licence v1.0

In some instances we have been unable to trace the owners of copyright material, and we would appreciate any information that would enable us to do so.

PART 1

FUNDAMENTALS OF HUMAN RESOURCE MANAGEMENT

CHAPTER 1

HUMAN RESOURCE MANAGEMENT: A CONTEMPORARY PERSPECTIVE

Tom Redman and Adrian Wilkinson

Introduction

This book is about human resource management and is concerned with the way in which organisations manage their people. In this introductory chapter we discuss our own approach to the study of HRM and the rationale underpinning the ordering and presentation of material in the book. Our aim is to chart the broad terrain of a rapidly developing field of study in order to prepare the reader for the more finely grained treatment of specific HRM topics to be found in the individual chapters. In particular, we examine the rise of HRM, the effects of the changing context of work on HRM, what HRM involves the strategic nature of HRM practice, its impact on organisational performance and the changing role of the HRM function. The chapter concludes with a consideration of our views on the audience at which the book is targeted and some thoughts on how it may best be used.

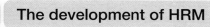 The development of HRM

The roots of HRM can be found in the emergence of industrial welfare work from the 1890s, as organisations driven by a mix of humanitarian, religious and business motives began to provide workplace amenities such as medical care, housing and libraries. In addition, employment offices were established to deal with hiring, payroll and record keeping. When scientific management emerged, the principles of science were also to be applied to the management of people as well as the management of production. We see here the shift from direct systems of management (personal supervision, traditional paternalism and simple piecework systems) to more technical systems of management and bureaucratic forms of employment (Gospel 2005, 2009). From here the HRM function came to life, responsible for establishing modern personnel methods (Kaufman, 2007, 2010), and we have seen a growing professionalisation of the role. However, it has been often seen as largely an administrative function and as dealing with the 'labour problem' rather than contributing to strategic goals. This is the backcloth for the rise of the new HRM.

The past 20 years or so have seen the rise of what has been called the human resource management (HRM) new orthodoxy (Bacon, 2003; Boxall *et al.*, 2007; Guest, 1998; Marchington and Wilkinson, 2012; Torrington *et al.*, 2011; Wilkinson *et al.*, 2009). In the mid-1980s in the UK, and earlier in the US, the term 'HRM' became fashionable and gradually started to replace others such as 'personnel management', 'industrial relations' and 'labour relations'. The practitioners of people management are no longer personnel officers and trainers but are HR managers and human resource developers (and importantly, line managers). The 1990s saw the launch of new journals and the flourishing of university courses in HRM. The then Institute of Personnel Management, the main professional body for personnel practitioners, relaunched its journal *People Management,* but subtitled it *'the magazine for human resources professionals'*. The millennium has now witnessed the professional body receiving a Royal Charter to become the Chartered Institute of Personnel and Development. The new HRM bandwagon was well and truly rolling.

Early contributions on the implications of the rise of HRM were concerned to define it and to compare it with the more traditional approach to personnel management (e.g. Guest, 1987). HRM was in turn both heralded as 'a new era of humane people oriented employment management' (Keenoy, 1990: 375) and derided as a 'blunt instrument to bully workers' (Monks, 1998), especially with the decline of collective bargaining and the reduced influence of trade unions (Nolan and Wood, 2003; Wilkinson, 2008). There has been considerable ambiguity in the use of the term, with various commentators using 'HRM' as simply a more modern label for traditional personnel management, as a 're-conceptualising and re-organising of personnel roles', or as a new and distinctive approach, attempting to develop and utilise the potential of human resources to the full in pursuit of an organisation's strategic objectives. It is the promise that is held by this latter view that has most excited practitioners and attracted the attention of management academics (Marchington and Wilkinson, 2012; Storey, 2007).

There has long been a debate over whether HRM is no more than a relabelling of personnel management, the 'old wine in new bottles' critique, or something more fundamental (Gennard and Kelly, 1997; Legge, 1995). As we have noted, traditionally, personnel management is often characterised as having little focus on broader business links and being overly concentrated on the activities of personnel professionals, unions and a range of operational techniques. Thus personnel management was seen as a low-level record-keeping and 'people maintenance' function. The HRM stereotype, in contrast, is characterised as being much more concerned with business strategy, and linkages with HR strategy, taking the view that HR is a, if not *the,* most important organisational resource. Thus there has been much talk of an HRM 'revolution'.

The new HRM?

Storey conceptualises HRM as being about: beliefs and assumptions, strategic qualities, the critical role of managers and key levers (see Table 1.1). The definition of HRM by Storey emphasises a particular set of policies now identified with 'high-commitment management' or 'high-performance work systems':

> Human resource management is a distinctive approach to employment management which seeks to achieve competitive advantage through the strategic deployment of a highly committed and capable workforce, using an integrated array of cultural, structural and personnel techniques. *(Storey, 1995: 5)*

In contrast, a broader definition is provided by Boxall and Purcell:

> HRM includes anything and everything associated with the management of employment relationships in the firm. We do not associate HRM solely with a high-commitment model of labour management or with any particular ideology or style of management. *(Boxall and Purcell, 2000: 184).*

Bacon (2003) points out that if HRM is defined exclusively as high-commitment management then the subject marginalises itself to the discussion of a relatively small number of distinct companies since many organisations pursue a 'low-wage path'. The above 'exclusive' definition thus identifies HRM in contrast to other forms of labour management (industrial relations or traditional personnel management), whereas the second inclusive definition covers all forms of labour management (Bacon, 2003: 73).

Table 1.1 The new HRM model

---

1 **Beliefs and assumptions**

- That it is the human resource which gives competitive edge.
- That the aim should not be mere compliance with rules, but employee commitment.
- That therefore employees should, for example, be very carefully selected and developed.

2 **Strategic qualities**

- Because of the above factors, HR decisions are of strategic importance.
- Top management involvement is necessary.
- HR policies should be integrated into the business strategy – stemming from it and even contributing to it.

3 **Critical role of managers**

- Because HR practice is critical to the core activities of the business, it is too important to be left to personnel specialists alone.
- Line managers are (or need to be) closely involved as both deliverers and drivers of the HR policies.
- Much greater attention is paid to the management of managers themselves.

4 **Key levers**

- Managing culture is more important than managing procedures and systems.
- Integrated action on selection, communication, training, reward and development.
- Restructuring and job redesign to allow devolved responsibility and empowerment.

Source: Storey, 2007: 9

Slippage between these two differing definitions, the new HRM according to Storey and HRM as a more generic term, is the cause of considerable confusion, generating more heat than light in debates on HRM and its meaning. However, although evolution is less exciting than revolution, Torrington *et al.*,'s (2002) view was that HRM is merely the next stage in the development of personnel management is persuasive. Torrington (1993), a staunch defender of 'good' personnel management, has also suggested that much of what is now labelled 'HRM' may be seen much more simply as longstanding good people management practice, while what was less effective has been relegated to remain, rather unfairly it seems, with the 'personnel management' brand.

Similarly Lewin (2008) defines HRM as the attraction, retention, utilisation, motivation, rewarding and disciplining of employees in organisations – in short, the management of people at work. This seems a good definition, which is broad and less subject to fashion. However, he also notes that HRM as a label conveys the shift in terms of a greater emphasis on people as a resource whose active management can positively contribute to organisational success. In this sense HRM has an aspirational quality.

The changing context of work

Things are happening in employment that are neither a cause nor an effect of HRM but which could have some impact on it. These include the intensification of work, the choices of work location provided by technology and the divisive nature of a society in which many are idle and impoverished while many others are seriously over-worked. *(Guest, 1998: 51)*

Even the more 'upbeat' HRM work such as that of Storey (1992) indicates that changes in the arena of HRM did not come from initiatives designed directly to do this. Change was driven by broader organisational initiatives, and thus personnel specialists have not been seen as the key drivers of change. Similarly Wood's (1999) work on high-commitment practices suggests that innovations in HRM tend to accompany changes in production systems and that innovations on humanistic grounds are unrealistic. Thus in part HRM can be seen as a consequence of managing in 'uncharted territory' with new rules governing the employment relationship (Beardwell, 1998; Wilkinson and Townsend, 2011a,b).

In the main, developments in HRM, as we argue above, have been driven by large-scale organisational changes as employers adjust to a much more competitive global economic environment (Sisson, 2010). To meet some of the challenges posed by intense competition, organisations have been downsized, delayered and decentralised (Nolan, 2011; Wilkinson, 2005). Organisations are now less hierarchical in nature; have adopted more flexible forms; and have been subjected to continuing waves of organisational change programmes such as total quality management, business process re-engineering, performance management, lean production, learning organisations and a seemingly relentless series of culture change initiatives.

But we need to be careful: there is a danger that accounts of change in organisations are always portrayed as major paradigm-shifting events when the reality is rather different. The rhetoric of organisational change often relies too heavily on hype from unrepresentative examples (Beynon, *et al.*, 2002; Thompson and O'Connel Davidson, 1995). Managers, it seems, often perceive themselves to be in the midst of massive organisational change. Eccles and Nohira's (1992) historical account of post-Second World War management traces how it has been the norm rather than the exception for practitioners and writers to view their organisational environment as turbulent and characterised by transformative change or, as Sorge and van Witteloostuijn (2004) put it, the nature of the change hype changes regularly just as flu viruses mutate over time.

Nevertheless, it appears that the type of staff employed and the way they are organised has also undergone change. Employees are often now more likely to be female, work part-time, away from the workplace (e.g. home working and mobile working) mediated by technology (e.g. hot desking, telework), and be subcontractors, consultants, temps and interims. The boundaries between work and home are much more blurred (Walsh, 2009) and employment now has to be managed across organisational boundaries, public, private, partnerships, franchises, agencies and other forms of inter-firm contractual relations which have a major impact on work and employment (Grimshaw *et al.*, 2010; Marchington *et al.*, 2011a,b).

Pressures have not been restricted to the private sector and we have seen the rise of the so-called 'new public management' with its emphasis on economy and efficiency (Bach, 2008; Exworthy and Halford, 2002; Pollit and Bouchert, 2011). The public sector has undergone many similar changes, with new organisational forms emerging in wake of 'marketisation', compulsory competitive tendering , 'best value' and more recently the challenges of maintaining HRM practices in an era of 'austerity' (Bach and Givan, 2010; Grimshaw *et al.*, 2010). For example, the civil service has experienced delayering, market testing and citizens' charters as well as the creation of next-step agencies, and most recently has been targeted for major downsizing and restructuring. The NHS has seen the creation of internal markets and the introduction of performance league tables and patients' charters.

Some of these changes are seen as facilitating more discretion for staff while at the same time retaining control of performance. Here the relevance of HRM comes to the fore; new forms of work and organisation demand new HRM strategies and practices. The new work context also brings new HRM challenges; not the least of these derives from the impact of such changes on the stresses and strains involved in working under such conditions. Here the growing literature on stress at work paints a rather disconcerting picture of organisational life in the new workplace. Typical of this work is the series of surveys of safety reps by the TUC (2007). These show that the number of workers suffering from stress has steadily increased over the series. The main reasons cited for stress are increased workloads, change at work, staff cuts, long hours, and bullying and job insecurity. Interestingly, given the changes highlighted above, it is the public sector where the highest stress levels are found. The TUC surveys find nearly two-thirds (64 per cent) of public sector workers complained of stress at work, compared to less than half (48 per cent) in the private sector. Stress is still problematic in the workplace with the latest UK estimates based on analysis by the Health and Safety Executive (HSE, 2012) of the Labour Force Survey showing that the total number of cases of stress in 2010/11 was 400,000 out of a total of 1,152,000 for all work-related illnesses. The industries that reported the highest rates of work-related stress in the last three years, were as we note above subject to major organisational changes, were health, social work, education and public administration.

It is perhaps hardly surprising that much research reports a decline in organisational commitment at work. Taylor (2003) notes a significant deterioration has taken place among workers in relation to personal commitment to their company. Despite all the HRM rhetoric there is no widespread belief in any sense of obligation to the firms who employ them. Green's research (2005) shows a significant downturn in job satisfaction since the early 1990s, despite rising wage levels and a generally tight labour market. Green notes that employees are receiving less control and autonomy, and have to cope with more targets, rules and greater stress. Therefore, a high workload allied to little control over work is liable to cause stress.

While HRM practices (e.g. employee assistance programmes, workplace counselling schemes etc.) are used in some organisations to provide a more supportive environment, there is evidence that they may only ease rather than cure the impact of workplace stress. Thus, the general picture may be rather bleak. Indeed, HRM practices may have added considerably to the stresses of modern worklife with the increased use of such practices as performance management systems, contingent pay and flexibilisation. For example, in relation to flexibility, reports from the Citizens' Advice Bureau find numerous accounts of worker exploitation, with unilateral changes in contracts and forced reduction in hours and pay.

Recent times have also witnessed the return of 'zero hours contracts', particularly in retailing, whereby employers do not guarantee that any work will be offered, but should they require labour the employee is expected to be available. The impact of organisational change on employees has been so considerable that commentators now argue that there is a need to radically reconstruct the nature of the 'psychological contract' between employer and employee (Brotherton, 2003; Guest, 2007). The search is now on for new deals for new times (Herriot and Pemberton, 1995) as trust has been fractured (Dietz *et al.*, 2011).

These concerns have led to engagement being the latest idea to take root in the world of HRM (Alfes *et al.*, 2010; MacLeod and Clarke, 2009; Saks, 2006; Wilkinson and Fay, 2011; Wilkinson *et al.*, 2012). The CIPD define it as 'a combination of commitment to the organisation and its values, plus a willingness to help out colleagues. It goes beyond job satisfaction and is not simply motivation. Engagement is something the employee has to offer: it cannot be "required" as part of the employment contract' (CIPD, 2012: 1). A Watson Wyatt study (2009) indicated that a company with highly engaged employees achieves a financial performance that is four times better than those with poor engagement. Other reports also report on the potential gains of engaged staff, with Gallup finding that more highly engaged staff take an average of 2.5 sick days per year whereas disengaged staff take on average 6.2 days per year (Harter *et al.*, 2006). The concept has not been without criticism. Welbourne (2011) observes the beauty of employee engagement is that it can be everything (positive) to everybody. As she points out, employee engagement speaks to something most managers believe, that is when employees go 'above and beyond' the call of duty then organisations fare better.

In the UK, the Macleod report entitled *Engaging for Success* (Macleod and Clarke, 2009) was designed to open a national discussion on the subject but the assumption behind this was not to debate the merits of the idea but to work out how best to implement it given a recognition that one size does not fit all. Trust in management job satisfaction and involvement in decision-making are seen as the basic building blocks for employee engagement (Purcell, 2010). From the UK WERS data not all employees appear engaged and, indeed, the number who are 'fully engaged', defined as scoring highly on every dimension, is often less than one in five. On a scale of 1–5, where one is 'fully disengaged' and five is 'fully engaged' with three meaning 'neither engaged nor disengaged', the expectation would be that the bulk of employees in a well functioning firm would be 'engaged' (i.e. score 4) and the median score would be over 3. Lower levels of engagement are also more likely to be found where there is perceived unfairness in rewards, where there is bullying and harassment and where people believe they are stuck in their jobs and feel isolated from open communications. All this clearly has implications for line managers (Purcell, 2010: 4).

One issue relates to the reciprocity of engagement. One can see why employers would like to get employees working harder or smarter because they are engaged, but what is the return for employees? Or what can employers provide to support employees better? Another neglected dimension is whether engagement will always be good. Can staff be too engaged for their own good ? (Marchington and Wilkinson, 2012: 352–5.).

Clearly more research is needed in this area. A strong central theme of HRM in these accounts is that of linking the people management practice to business strategy, and we examine this in the next section of this chapter.

Strategy and HRM

HR scholars have been calling for a stronger focus on the human resources inside the firm and how they are managed (Boselie and Paauwe, 2009), but as Morris and Snell point out (2009: 85) mainstream strategy scholars are also beginning to acknowledge that they need to focus on 'micro-level' factors; the value proposition of a firm is seen as relying more on knowledge and service activities, and so strategic management depends very much on what people know and how they behave. As Morris and Snell note, because no other resource possessed by a firm has free will or heterogeneity of ideas, products and services often originate in individuals. This makes the human resources within the firm, and how they are managed, a potentially unique source of strategic leverage. The increase in differentiated workforces poses added cultural, geographical and competency gaps (Becker and Huselid, 2009; see Marchington and Wilkinson, 2012: 5). Despite this call, it is rare for texts on strategy to pay much attention to HRM issues; for example, Johnson *et al.*, (2011) devote only a handful of pages to managing human resources while Grant (2010) allocates just one page to HRM in his discussion of resources and capabilities.

Meanwhile the study of HRM has adopted a cross-functional approach and expanded its breadth of analysis beyond the staple concerns of selection, training, reward etc. (Paauwe, 2004). In particular, one stream of research, strategic human resource management (SHRM), has emerged as being particularly influential in this respect. In essence SHRM theory posits that an organisation's human resource assets are potentially the sole source of sustainable competitive advantage. Much of the work in this area draws from the resource-based theory (RBT) of the firm (Allen and Wright, 2007; Barney, 1991, 1995; Boxall and Purcell, 2003, 2008, 2011). Here RBT suggests that competitive advantage depends ultimately on an organisation having superior, valuable, rare, non-substitutable resources at its disposal and that such resources are not easily imitated by others. The non-imitable nature of resources is a key aspect, otherwise competitors would be able to replicate and the advantage would rapidly disappear.

The subtleties of the human resource value creation process, however, are extremely difficult for competitors to imitate. The ambiguities and complexities associated with even the 'strongest' of organisational cultures, and how HRM practices are related to culture, are considerable and cannot be easily teased out by would-be imitators. Equally, any competitive advantage located in a codified and explicit set of HRM practices is also much less likely to be non-imitable than one based on the complex interaction of HRM policies and an organisation's 'social architecture' (Mueller, 1996). By social architecture, Mueller is referring to skill formation activities, cooperative behaviour and the tacit knowledge that organisations possess. Thus the value creation process arising from HRM competencies does appear to meet the criteria set out by RBT and consequently a growing body of empirical and theoretical work has emerged on SHRM (see Boxall and Purcell, 2003; Guest, 2011; Paauwe, 2009 for reviews of this literature). Thus RBT perhaps helps us explain some of the contradictions in HRM, and provides answers to questions such as that posed by Guest and King (2001: 11), namely, 'if good people management is self-evidently beneficial to organisations, why do not more of them adopt it?' One particular concern in applying the RBT to HRM is that it lacks a theory of the employment relationship because it assumes that internal resources do not have interests which may conflict or require negotiated alignments (Bacon, 2003: 80).

A recurrent theme in the SHRM literature is that organisations need to 'match' their human resource strategies to their business strategies, so that the former contribute towards the successful implementation of the latter (Becker and Huselid, 2009; Boxall, 1992; Lengnick-Hall and Lengnick-Hall, 1988; Martin-Alcazar *et al.*, 2005; Miller, 1987; Schuler and Jackson, 1989). A number of sectoral and company-level studies have shown how organisations facing change in their competitive environment have responded with new business strategies, which in turn have required a transformation in the organisations' approach to the management of staff (see for example, Boxall and Steenveld, 1999; Snape *et al.*, 1993).

This approach, the so-called 'matching model' by Boxall (1992), argues for a fit or match between business strategy and a human resource strategy, which fosters the required employee attitudes and behaviour. In this sense, human resource strategy flows from the initial choice of business strategy (Purcell, 1989). Furthermore, to the extent that changes in the corporate environment evoke a particular business strategy response, human resource strategies can also be seen as being strongly influenced by environmental change (Hendry *et al.*, 1988). As Sparrow and Hilltrop (1994: 628) argue, 'HRM strategies are all about making business strategies work'. A closely related body of work has recently called for a *configurational* approach to SHRM. Here it is argued that it is the pattern of HRM practices that supports the achievement of organisational goals and that, in line with the contingency approach, fit with strategy is vital to explaining the HR – performance nexus. The configurational approach takes the best-fit view a step further in that it argues that there are a number of specific ideal types that provide both horizontal fit between HR practices, and vertical fit between HR practices and business strategy (Ferris *et al.*, 1999). The configuration of practices which provides the tightest fit is then seen as being ideal for the particular strategy. Although this work is still in its relative infancy, there has been some theorising on the nature of the 'ideal types' of configurations for customer, operations or product-led organisations etc. (Martin-Alcazar *et al.*, 2005; Sheppeck and Militello, 2000).

Nevertheless, there is an issue as to how far human resource strategies can simply be 'matched' with the requirements of a changing business strategy (Bacon, 2008). As Boxall (1992: 68) notes, much of the 'matching' literature has implicitly assumed that employee attitudes and behaviour can be moulded by management strategy in the pursuit of strategic fit. However, human resource outcomes cannot be taken for granted, and whatever the merits of the view that personnel managers must increasingly see themselves as 'business managers', it is important to recognise that personnel management and industrial relations are about more than simply selecting the appropriate fit with a given business strategy. Thus the best-fit approach can be criticised for failing to acknowledge the importance of social norms and legal rules in the search for alignment (Paauwe and Boselie, 2007). Indeed, the notion of fit is somewhat static and an inappropriate metaphor in a fast-changing corporate world.

Moreover, as Boxall and Purcell note (2003: 197), inconsistent application of well-designed HR policies often undermines their desired impact. This is very evident in the work of Gratton *et al.*, (1999) and their study of seven leading-edge UK organisations. Hence, according to Boxall and Purcell 'there is no such thing as *the* single HR practice of the firm. It is more accurate to imagine the HR practices of the firm as norms around which there is variation due to the idiosyncratic behaviour of line managers' (2003: 198). Truss (2001) notes the importance of 'agency', thus we should not assume that simply having a particular human resource policy will necessarily lead to a desired outcome. Problems of implementation and interpretation occur alongside people's sometimes unpredictable responses and actions.

Performance and HRM

For years, HR professionals have yearned for evidence to show that people were really the most important asset a company had and that good HR practice delivered in terms of organisational performance. By the mid-1990s their prayers appeared to have been answered in that a growing number of studies appeared to demonstrate just that. For example, in research undertaken on behalf of the then Institute of Personnel and Development in the UK, the Sheffield Effectiveness Programme (based on 100 small and medium-sized enterprises (SMEs) in manufacturing) concluded that people management is not only critical to business performance but is also much more important than an emphasis on quality, technology, competitive strategy or R&D in terms of influence on the bottom line. Thus according to Patterson *et al.*, (1998), this finding in one sense validates the oft-quoted claims of CEOs that people are the most important asset but is also paradoxical in that it is one aspect of business that is the most neglected:

> Overall, the results of this study clearly indicate the importance of people management practices in influencing company performance. The results are unique, since no similar study has been conducted, comparing the influence of different types of managerial practices upon performance. If managers wish to influence the performance of their companies, the results show that the most important area to emphasise is the management of

> people. This is ironic, given that our research has also demonstrated that emphasis on HRM practices is one of the most neglected areas of managerial practice within organisations. *(Patterson et al., 1998: 21)*

These findings have been replicated in the public sector. In a well-cited study of the NHS, UK, West *et al.*, (2002) reported that practices associated with high-performance work systems (HPWS), particularly the extent and sophistication of appraisal systems, the extent of teamworking and the quality and sophistication of training, were associated with lower patient mortality. However, research studies sponsored by the Chartered Institute of Personnel Development (CIPD) have also underscored the broad scale of the implementation problems of 18 'high-commitment' practices in 237 UK companies. Only 1 per cent used more than three-quarters of the practices, 25 per cent used more than half and 20 per cent used fewer than a quarter (Guest, 2000). These findings and others have become a source of increasing concern to both HR practitioners and academics (Caldwell, 2004).

There are various terms used in these studies, for example high-performance management, high-commitment management, best practice HRM, high-involvement management, but each share a common message: the adoption of HRM practices pays in terms of where it matters most, the bottom line (Applebaum *et al.*, 2000; Bamber *et al.*, 2009; Huselid 1995; see also Kinnie and Swart, Chapter 2 of this volume). An exhaustive review by Ichniowski *et al.*, (1996: 299) concluded that a

> collage of evidence suggests that innovative workplace practices can increase performance, primarily through the use of systems of related practices that enhance worker participation, make work design less rigid and decentralise managerial tasks.

They also note that individual work practices have no effect on economic performance but

> the adoption of a *coherent and integrated system* of innovative practices, including extensive recruiting and careful selection, flexible job definitions and problem-solving teams, gainsharing-type compensation plans, employment security and extensive labour–management communication, substantially improves productivity and quality outcomes.

The general argument is that piecemeal take-up of HR practices means that many managements miss out on the benefits to be gained from a more integrated approach (Marchington and Wilkinson, 2012). Thus such collections of reinforcing HR practices have begun to be referred to as a 'bundle', and the task of HR managers is to identify and implement such HR systems.

However, this appears to be rather more easily prescribed than achieved (Guthrie *et al.*, 2011; Lewin, 2011; Pfeffer and Veiga, 1999). Many authors produce lists of HR practices which should be included in these bundles. Unfortunately, there is yet little consistency and we still await a definitive prescription of the best 'bundle'. Boselie *et al.*, (2005), Wall and Wood (2005) and Storey (1992) identified aspects such as integrated selection systems, performance-related pay, harmonisation, individual contracts, teamworking and learning companies. Pfeffer (1994: 30–59) provides a list of 16, which includes employment security, selectivity in recruitment, incentive pay, employee ownership, participation and empowerment, teamworking, training and skill development, wage compression and promotion from within. These are held together under an overarching philosophy with a long-term commitment and a willingness to engage in consistent measurement of whether or not high standards are being achieved. Dyer and Reeves (1995) counted 28 HR practices across four studies of the human resource – performance link, of which only one practice, formal training, was common to all. Similarly, Becker and Gerhart (1996) found 27 practices, none of which was common across five studies of the human resource management – performance link. Delaney *et al.*, (1989) identified 10 practices, Huselid (1995) 13, Wood (1999) 17, while Delery and Doty (1996) appear quite miserly in comparison in only identifying seven strategic practices. All this must seem at the very least confusing to the practitioner but, more than this, there appear to be some quite contradictory notions in the various lists (Wall and Wood, 2005). For example, on the one hand formal grievance systems appear in some bundles as an indicator of best practice but are associated in others with trade unionism and thus seen as part of the bureaucratic 'personnel management' approach.

Aside from the inconsistencies in the HRM bundle, the best practice and universalistic approach has received considerable criticism. Purcell, for example, is wary of the claim for a universal application:

> The claim that the bundle of best practice HRM is universally applicable leads us into a utopian cul-de-sac and ignores the powerful and highly significant changes in work, employment and society visible inside organisations and in the wider community. The search for bundles of high commitment work practices is important, but so too is the search for understanding of the circumstances of where and when it is applied, why some organisations do and others do not adopt HCM, and how some firms seem to have more appropriate HR systems for their current and future needs than others. It is only one of many ways in which employees are managed, all of which must come within the bounds of HRM. *(Purcell, 1999: 36)*

Reviews of the HRM-performance relationship (Boselie *et al.*, 2005; Combs *et al.*, 2006; Guest, 2011; Lewin, 2011; Macky and Boxall, 2007; Paauwe, 2009; Sengupta and Whitfield, 2011; Whitfield and Poole, 1997: 757) point out that there are unresolved issues of causality – largely because few studies use longitudinal data, problems of the narrow base of the work undertaken, and concerns that much of the data is self-reported by single management respondents, neglect of the actual implementation of practices, as well as doubts about measures of performance which are used. Even if the data does indicate a link, we lack understanding of the processes involved and the mechanisms by which practices translate into desired outcomes. Equally problematic is the implicit assumption that a particular bundle of practices is feasible for all organisations. Some organisational structures and cultures will provide major difficulties in implementing certain HRM practices, for example high-involvement practices in highly bureaucratic and formal organisations will be particularly problematic. The notion of a reinforcing bundle of practices also cannot be fully convincing given the variation in the bundles noted above. It cannot yet be dismissed that the different HR practices have a differential impact on firm performance. The best practice approach thus appears somewhat of a black box and many questions remain as yet unanswered. Why is there a linkage? What is it about having these practices that delivers performance? What is the process by which these outcomes have occurred? It is unlikely, say, that the very act of introducing practices X, Y and Z will deliver benefits directly. Much will depend on the context of its introduction, the way it is implemented and the support provided etc.

As Pass notes,

> the mechanisms involved in the 'causal chain' are rarely specified and are, in general, based upon assumptions or beliefs in 'employee outcomes' of commitment, motivation and increased competence. As a result, a 'black box' has been created with organisations left wondering 'how it works' – they are, instead, prescribed to follow a make believe scenario whereby they borrow Dorothy's ruby slippers from the Wizard of Oz (the appropriate bundle of HR practices), click them together three times and then arrive at their destination (high organisational performance with happy workers). *(Pass, 2004: 1)*

Some of the HRM advocates are now adopting a more modest tone. Storey (2007: 17) for example admits that 'HRM is no panacea; no set of employment practices ever will be. However, as a persuasive account of the logic underpinning choice in certain organisations and as an aspirational pathway for others, it is an idea worthy of examination'. Guest (2011) concludes that after two decades of extensive research, we are still unable to answer core questions about the relationship between human resource management and performance.

This is largely the result of limited longitudinal research to address the linkages between HRM and performance via the management of HR implementation. As he observes 'many of the basic questions remain the same and after hundreds of research studies we are still in no position to assert with any confidence that good HRM has an impact on organisational performance' (Guest, 2011: 11).

Some writers (e.g. Godard, 2004: 371) argue that the conflicts embedded in the structure of the employment relationship may limit the effectiveness of the high-performance paradigm for employers, and render it highly fragile, and it is this that may explain its variable adoption depending on workplace context. These same conflicts may also explain why high-performance practices are often implemented in ways that tend to have negative effects for workers and unions. In other words, it may be in the interests of only a minority of employers to adopt high-performance management and, even when it is adopted, it may not have positive implications for workers or their unions. Thus there is a need to recognise that there may not be a universal coincidence of interests here, in which what is good for employers is also always good for workers and their unions (Blyton *et al.*, 2011; Dundon and Rollinson, 2011). Equally, others such as Lewin (2008, 2011) have suggested a dual theory of HRM – while some groups of employees are best managed through what he terms high-involvement management, others may be best not seen as an asset on which expenditure will yield a positive economic return, and are managed via a low-involvement model. The former applies to core employees only. The key question here sees concerns over the best balance of core and peripheral staff (an answer which is likely to differ by industry) although he notes that the ratio of perphieral to core employees has grown markedly in the USA and in other developed nations over the last quarter of a century.

 ## The changing role of HRM

Despite the growing recognition of the importance of effective people management for organisational success as discussed above, there are still a number of concerns about the future for HRM. (Farndale and Brewster, 2005; Farnham, 2010; Guest and Conway, 2011; Sparrow *et al.*, 2010). At a surface level the HRM function seems to be in good health. The CIPD now claims over 135,000 members (CIPD, 2012) and Workplace Employment Relations Survey (WERS) data shows that the proportion of workplaces with personnel specialists, defined as managers whose job titles contain personnel, HR or industrial, employee or staff relations and who spend at least a quarter of their time on such matters, has been rising. In 2004, the percentage of workplaces that employed a personnel specialist was up from 14 per cent in 1984 and 20 per cent in 1998 (Cully *et al.*, 1999; Kersley *et al.*, 2006). However, worries about the effectiveness of the HR function linger on.

According to Peter Drucker, there has been a tendency in the past for the HR department to be seen as something of a 'trash can' function, a repository for all those tasks which do not fit neatly anywhere else:

> Personnel administration . . . is largely a collection of incidental techniques without much internal cohesion. As personnel administration conceives the job of managing worker and work, it is partly a file-clerk's job, partly a housekeeping job, partly a social worker's job and partly fire-fighting to head off union trouble or to settle it . . . the things the personnel administrator is typically responsible for . . . are necessary chores. I doubt though that they should be put together in one department for they are a hodge-podge . . . They are neither one function by kinship of skills required to carry out the activities, nor are they one function by being linked together in the work process, by forming a distinct stage in the work of the managers or in the process of the business. *(Drucker, 1961: 269–70; quoted in Legge, 1995: 6)*

Table 1.2 Functions performed by the HR department

Job analysis

Human resource planning

Recruitment and selection

Training and development

Pay and conditions of employment

Grievance and disciplinary procedures

Employee relations and communications

Administration of contracts of employment

Employee welfare and counselling

Equal opportunities policy and monitoring

Health and safety

Outplacement

Culture management

Knowledge management

Talent management

Table 1.2 lists some of the key functions that HR departments now provide. In part, Drucker's critique that the HR function lacks coherence has been moderated by some recent organisational changes (Sparrow *et al.*, 2010). In particular, the practice of outsourcing saw many of the more peripheral HR responsibilities, such as catering arrangements and security, subcontracted to specialist firms. Equally, the practice of decentralising HR responsibility from corporate central departments to business-unit-level departments, shared-services, and further still to line management has seen much 'streamlining' of HR responsibilities. However, perhaps more worrying for the HR function is that these trends have also seen some traditional core personnel areas, such as recruitment, training and employee welfare management, also outsourced to HR consultants. In some accounts these trends have been seen as part of a 'crisis' as HR struggled for legitimacy and status in cost-conscious times (Clark and Clark, 1990; Parry, 2011; Sparrow *et al.*, 2011).

Others have interpreted the increasing use of consultants as reflecting a sign that HR is now seen as being much more important and thus merits additional investment. Management consultants are argued to be an important conduit along which new and more sophisticated HR practices flow between organisations. However, some recent trends suggest that a 'crisis' of interpretation may be more in tune with the facts. In particular, the reduction of the HR domains appears to have been taken one step further and there is now a considerable debate on the benefits of outsourcing the entire HR function. In part, such changes have been driven by further cost pressures in a period of corporate downsizing, but more worrying for the HR function is that outsourcing may also have been fuelled by senior management concerns about the quality and responsiveness of in-house HR functions (Greer *et al.*, 1999).

For example, from one of the CIPD's own studies of a survey of senior executives, non-HR managers rated the HR profession poorly, seeing it as 'bureaucratic' and 'isolated from the outside world' (Guest and King, 2001). Perhaps more worrying is that this 'news' does not appear to be new to the HR profession. The survey canvassed the views of over 3,000 HR managers in the UK and found that:

- just a quarter think HR is respected by other managers, is seen as a key function of senior management, or has strong input at board level;
- 85 per cent agree that the profession 'struggles to get a voice at the highest level in organisations' and a similar number admit that it is 'often overlooked by executives'.

Yet, when asked to rate themselves and the contribution they make, the respondents have been more diametrically opposed:

- over 85 per cent of HR managers believe that HR will be vital to the continued success of an organisation;
- over 75 per cent of respondents believe HR has a strategic business focus and acts as internal consultant and enabler.

In short, there is a large gap between what HR professionals see as their role and how other managers in the organisation see it (Haggerty and Wright, 2009; Hird *et al.*, 2010; Kulik and Perry, 2008). Thus the rising recognition that HR issues are vitally important in organisations has, paradoxically, not been all good news for the HR department given its 'Cinderella' image. It seems that many senior managers may be of the view that people management is far too important to be left to the HR department. Thus in a *Fortune* article one commentator urged CEOs to 'Blow the sucker [HR] up' (Stewart, 1996). While others have not been as forthright as this, the HR function appears to be at a dangerous crossroads, with some suggesting ascendancy to a full 'business partner' while others predict a painful demise (Keegan and Francis, 2010). On the one hand the ascendancy school sees the rise of HR following hard on the success of SHRM and the creation of competitive advantage for organisations. In contrast, the formula for demise often involves the failure of HR to understand the broader business agenda. The literature typically sees a need for the 'reinvention' of HR along such lines and that HR must simply evolve or die. However, Ulrich (1997) has also warned that the literature is replete with premature death notices of the HR function.

What then is the 'formula' for HR success? First, in addressing this question there is a real danger in slipping into unrealistic, wishful thinking – of which there is already an ample supply in the prescriptive HR literature. Second, there is rather more consistency in the literature on what the future for HR should *not* be based on, than that on what it should be. Thus Rucci (1997) has suggested that the worst-case scenario for HR survival is a department that does not promote change, does not identify leaders, does not understand the business, does not know customers, does not drive costs and does not emphasise values. According to Pfeffer (1998: 195), 'if human resources is to have a future inside organisations, it is not by playing police person and enforcer of rules and policies, nor is it likely to be ensured by playing handmaiden to finance'.

In contrast, there are a wide variety of suggestions for what the HR department should do in the future. The future agenda according to Brockbank (1997) is that a successful HR department needs to be involved in framing not only HR strategy but also business strategy, promoting growth rather than downsizing, and building more credible relationships with key shareholders and board members. Beer and Eisenstat (1996) emphasise the need for a comprehensive HR vision and that in the future HR managers will require coordination skills across functions, business units and borders following the increased globalisation of business, and general management, communication leadership, creativity and entrepreneurship competencies. Research by Eichinger and Ulrich (1995) on the top priorities that HR professionals believe need to be addressed in the future emphasises organisational redesign, attracting new leaders, customer focus, cost containment, rejecting fads, addressing diversity and becoming a more effective business partner with their line management customers. Ulrich, (1998; Ulrich *et al.*, 2007) also reports the results of survey research on the key competencies managers believe will be necessary for future success in HR roles – see Table 1.3. The ability to manage culture and change coupled with personal credibility is seen as critical.

According to Hamel (2005), HR has to lead the way in making businesses more like communities and less bureaucratic in the quest for business resilience. HR is seen as having a historic opportunity to create organisations 'in which people can bring all their humanity to work every day'. This would involve breaking down traditional hierarchies and creating forums where everyone can analyse where things have gone wrong, and offer '1,000 wacky ideas'. 'As long as it's mostly bureaucracy, there will be an upper limit on human effort,' he said. 'Resilience depends on initiative, creativity and passion.' However, HR would first have

Table 1.3 Key competencies of HR professionals

Relative importance to effectiveness	%
Understanding of business	14
Knowledge of HR practices	17
Ability to manage culture	19
Ability to manage change	22
Personal credibility	27

Source: Ulrich, 1998: 20–1. Reprinted by permission of Harvard Business School Press. Copyright © 1998 by the Harvard Business School Publishing Corporation; all rights reserved.

to get managers to 'escape the denial trap', and look at the world 'in the way it is, and not in the way we want it to be' (Millar, 2004).

Thus a key theme in much of the work is that HR needs to earn its place at the top, i.e. senior management (Pritchard, 2010). One danger in these accounts is that the emphasis is very much on the strategic and business aspects of the HR role. In particular, the 'bread and butter' issues of effectively managing the recruitment, selection, appraisal, development, reward and involvement of staff have been rather pushed to the periphery. What is interesting about Table 1.3 is the relatively low rating of knowledge of HR practices. There is thus a real concern that HR managers could be neglecting 'the basics' in their search for legitimacy and status with senior managers (Wright and Snell, 2005). In short, HR could be accused of ignoring employees. Indeed, HR 'futurologists', it seems, need to be reminded of Giles and Williams' (1991) rejoinder to accept that the HR role is to serve their customers and not their egos. In short, is there a danger that the senior management and shareholder customers will be getting rather better service than the 'employee customer' in the HR department of the future. Such a view is shared by Francis and Keegan (2006), who note that the employee champion role is shrinking because HR professionals have been encouraged to aspire to the role of strategic or business partner.

Lewin (2008: 1) argues that it is not just about being a business partner:

There are many other roles and purposes that HR functions and those who lead these functions serve in modern business enterprises including complying with human resource/labor regulation (newer and older regulation), enforcing organisational and employment policies and practices, measuring employee performance, providing services and assistance to employees, maintaining employee personnel files, monitoring workplace safety, handling employee relocation. With this menu of potential duties and responsibilities, it is understandable that many HR functions in modern business enterprises are considered to be largely operational functions rather than strategic functions. But if the claim that business enterprises increasingly compete on the basis of their intellectual capital is at all valid, then the main challenge regarding HRM in the 21st Century is for HR functions and leaders to keep their eye on the prize of a strategic role in these enterprises while also performing the necessary operational role.

Perceived from the perspective of HR practitioners, 'progress' in implementing HRM is an unfinished process. The six areas where practitioners believe most policy progress has been made are the areas they consider less important (Table 1.4). Caldwell (2004: 211) argues that a plausible interpretation of this is to suggest that the idea of 'most progress' tends to correlate with the easier to deliver, softer and less high-level strategic aspects of HRM. Improvements in employee communications, for example, are achievable through the relatively low-level interventions associated with 'traditional' personnel management. In contrast, the areas where 'least progress' appears to have been made towards implementation seem to be associated with the more strategic aspects of HRM. For example, the shift towards treating people as assets, and witness the interest in talent management (Scullion and Collings, 2010).

Table 1.4 Policy importance and progress in implementing HRM

Most important, least progress
Managing people as assets which are fundamental to the competitive advantage of the organisation
Developing a close fit of personnel policies, procedures and systems with one another
Creating a flatter and more flexible organisation capable of responding more quickly to change
Encouraging team working and cooperation across internal organisational boundaries
Creating a strong customer-first philosophy throughout the organisation
Increasing line management responsibility for personnel management and HR policies

Least important, most progress
Improving employee involvement through better internal communication
Aligning HRM policies with business planning and corporate strategy
Empowering employees to manage their own self-development and learning
Developing reward strategies designed to support a performance-driven culture
Developing the facilitating role of managers as enablers
Building greater employee commitment to the organisation

Source: Caldwell, 2004: 200 (www.blackwell-synergy.com).

Productivity improvements and competitiveness requires that HRM becomes an integral aspect of strategic decision-making at the highest level.

Thus one of our aims in the presentation of material in this book has been to balance the discussion in terms of both employee expectations and management expectations of the HR function. For example, in accounts of topics such as downsizing, involvement and participation, performance management, reward, flexibility etc. the aim has been not only to examine critically HR's strategic role in the process, but also to review the impact of these practices on employees. The last section of this chapter now discusses in more detail the layout of the book and some suggestions on its use.

 ## The book

This book has been written primarily as a text for students of business and management who are studying HRM. It aims to be critical but pragmatic: we are wary of quick fixes, slogans, prescriptive checklists and bullet points of 'best practice'. The authors are all prominent researchers and draw from a considerable depth of research in their field. Each chapter provides a critical review of the topic, bringing together theoretical and empirical material. The emphasis is on analysis and insight, and areas of growing significance are also included in each chapter. At the same time we wish to look at the implications of HRM research and theory development for practice and to do so in a readable, accessible manner. The book does not assume prior knowledge on the part of the reader, but seeks to locate issues in a wider theoretical framework. It is suitable for MBAs, and for undergraduates who these days may be doing business studies as well as degrees in engineering, humanities, social sciences etc. As such, this is appropriate for modular degree courses.

Each chapter is accompanied by a combination of case studies and/or exercises for students. The intention is that students should be actively involved in the study of HRM. We believe that in this sense the book is unique in the UK, where the trend has been for the publication of separate text and case books. Our aim in combining these elements in a single volume is to permit a smoother integration of the topic material and supporting cases and exercises. In all chapters the authors have provided both text and cases, although in some we also include additional material from other authors. The cases and exercises are of different lengths, level and type in order to serve different teaching and learning purposes, e.g. a long case study for students to read and prepare prior to seminars/tutorials as well as shorter cases and exercises which can be prepared in the session itself. The aim is to provide a good range of up-to-date, relevant material based upon actual HRM practice.

The book is divided into two parts; the first one, the 'Fundamentals of HRM', examines the core elements of HR practice (see Table 1.2 above). In this section there are chapters on the HRM-performance link; selection and recruitment, performance appraisal, employee development, reward, industrial relations, line managers and corporate culture. The second half of the book, 'Contemporary Themes and Issues', addresses some key areas of rising importance in HRM practice. Here there are chapters on international and comparative HRM, careers, downsizing, participation, ethics, work–life balance, emotion, flexibility, bullying, knowledge management and diversity management.

CASE STUDY 1.1

HUMAN RESOURCE MANAGEMENT AND PRIVATE EQUITY IN THE PUBLIC DOMAIN: JUST SHOW ME THE MONEY!

ALINE BOS AND PAUL BOSELIE

Introduction

The focus of this case is on the impact of private equity (PE) interventions on human resource management in a hospital. In its simplest form, private equity firms buy a profitable company and sell it three to seven years later for more than it paid. The gain is the sum of the capital gain on resale and the operating profit realised meanwhile (Folkman et al., 2009; Robbins et al., 2008). Such an intervention constitutes an important organisational event that usually heralds major organisational transformations (Boselie and Koene, 2010), including reorganisations, increased job insecurity, unemployment and significant effects on employee outcomes such as organisational commitment, employee trust in top management and job stress. A PE intervention is closely related to the investor buy-out, the later often representing single investors with substantial personal investments (Boselie and Koene, 2010). There is a substantial body of literature on PE interventions in the private sector (Wright and Bruining, 2008). However, little is known about the impact of PE in the public sector or for the semi-public organisations that make up the bulk of the public sphere in Western countries (Kickert, 2001). As private organisations performing public functions, they are positioned somewhere between a pure government agency and a commercial firm (Rainey, 1991). Given that PEFs are known for their aggressive, commercial operations, this trend raises questions about the effects on public service workers, because public organisations differ in some aspects from the private sector. First, public sector organisations are in many cases partly financed by public funds. Second, services delivered by these organisations are seen as essential services, which have to be highly accessible and transparent. Finally, public service workers are often seen as being motivated by contributing to society and not by financial aspects (Vandenabeele, 2007).

The central question in this case study is therefore: What is the impact of PE interventions on human resource management (HRM) in public organisations? The PE intervention is aimed at increasing organisational performance. But it is not always clear how this is achieved, who will be involved in the process, how PE will affect human resource practices (for example recruitment and selection, employee development and compensation) and whether increasing performance also includes increasing employee well-being and societal well-being. The last goal (societal well-being) is in particular relevant for organisations operating in the public domain. The aim of this case is to provide insights on both content and process through a case study analysis of a public organisation on the impact of private equity on HRM. Sub-questions that are linked to the central research question are:

- What is the actual involvement and participation in decision making of different stakeholders such as works councils?
- What is the potential impact of private equity on HRM practices?
- What is the potential impact of private equity on HRM outcomes?

The case starts with the context, then, PE and HRM are further defined. Next, the central questions will be elaborated by describing the case: the PE involvement in a Dutch hospital and its HRM effects. Finally, a conclusion and the lessons learned are formulated.

Setting the stage

The subject of PE involvement in child day-care and healthcare organisations is a relatively new development and one that receives significant media attention in the Netherlands. TNS NIPO and the iBMG of Erasmus University recently found – in a survey of 1,100

Dutch citizens, including healthcare workers – that private investments are preferred to cuts in healthcare. This research also found that economists have positive expectations of private investments in healthcare. In 2013, the Dutch law will enable the distribution of profits in public organisations such as hospitals. Almost every Dutch hospital has recently consulted with private equity firms (PEFs) (Castelijns et al., 2011). The interventions of PEFs in the healthcare are rising (Boer and Croon, 2011; Stevenson and Grabowski, 2008). The phenomenon poses strategic challenges for the public sector and its organisations. The shifting capital flows will change the control and ownership of public services (e.g. van der Steen et al., 2010). More generally, existing research on the impact of PEFs has mainly been carried out in the UK and the US, and little in the Netherlands where the impact of these firms is already significant: the Dutch Association of Investment Companies (NVP) has stated that the private equity sector in the Netherlands is responsible for 6 per cent of private sector employment. Dutch companies receive €816 million of private equity firms. Total assets under management of Dutch private equity firms is estimated at €23.3 billion, invested in 1,300 companies, of which 80 per cent of Dutch companies (NVP, 2010).

Private equity

The market for private equity firms is growing significantly. A PEF invests money in organisations not quoted on a stock market in exchange for a periodic management fee and a share in profits. Typically within three to seven years, the firms sell their investment (Robbins et al., 2008). PEFs can act aggressively and are considered to have an extremely commercial outlook. PEFS often buy under-performing organisations using high levels of debt (generally up to 70 or 75 per cent). After the transaction this debt is transferred to the organisation that has been taken over. The Dutch private retail company KBB, for example, (with warehouse chains Bijenkorf, Vroom & Dreesman, and HEMA) was bought by a consortium of PEFs. After the take-over the property (stores and building ground) of KBB was sold to a leasing firm. The individual stores then had to rent their location and property back from this leasing company. With this transaction the PEF got back more than 50 per cent of the initial investment. The leasing construction also puts additional incentives on the individual stores for increasing performance levels. A financial advantage for the PEF is that high costs at store level decrease profits and therefore reduces taxes.

As the assets of PEFs grow faster than they can invest, PEFs seek to expand to a broader playground. First, they are increasingly operating outside the original UK and US markets. Second, firms have changed their focus from blue-collar to white-collar services (Guo et al., 2009). Third, PEFs are diversifying from private (Wright and Bruining, 2008) to public organisations (van der Steen et al., 2010). At the same time, an increasing number of public organisations are struggling with their financial performance. They have to balance the economics of their organisation with their public duties (Boselie, 2010).

Since PEFs can be seen as an extreme expression of private values, investment by PEFs in public organisations raises questions at the heart of the debate on public values – such as accessibility, transparency and citizenship – versus private values – such as consumerism, profitability and competition (Benington and Moore, 2011; Bozeman, 1993; Pollitt, 1988). This debate has been especially strong since the rise of New Public Management ideas in the 1980s (Hood, 1991). Some authors argue that a decline in public sector values is occurring due to the adoption of private sector values (Kernaghan, 2003; Maesschalck, 2004), and that this has critical implications for the identity, legitimacy and motivation of public service (Haque, 2001). Combining public and private values can promote opportunistic behaviour and stimulate the neglect of duties (Karré, 2011).

PEFs are particularly interested in the child day-care and the healthcare sectors (Robbins et al., 2008) as these are growth markets, with potential efficiency improvements and room for new financial resources given governmental budget cuts. In the Netherlands, PEFs have already invested in semi-public organisations such as Catalpa (child day-care, 2,300 employees).

In the private sector private equity firms tend to buy under-performing companies from the public stock market. After the transition the company is no longer subject to transparency creating new opportunities for alternative control mechanisms to achieve organisational goals (mainly defined in financial terms). The Chief Executive Officer (CEO) is often replaced although usually little changes within the first year of the take over. This might be a strategic distraction to avoid negative media attention. After one or two years the new owners will often start initiatives to increase performance and will also start reorganisations that usually lead to selling parts of the organisation. After six to eight years the private equity firms usually have sold all the parts of the organisation.

From a pure theoretical perspective there are roughly two possible strategies that can emerge after a private equity intervention: An upward agency strategy or a downward agency strategy (Wright and Bruining, 2008). The upward agency strategy represents additional investments in the organisation because of untapped resources that can contribute to organisational success. In the past these upward agency strategies often emerged when a mother company sold a business unit with a lot of market potential that was not considered to be part of the core business of the mother company. A private equity intervention was then a relief for the business unit creating new opportunities for market development (e.g. Bruining and Wright, 2002). The HRM implications of an upward agency strategy might be recruitment and selection of new employees and substantial training and development. The downward agency strategy represents cost reduction strategies immediately after the take over by a private equity firm. This is often the case when the organisation is under-performing. The HRM implications might be a vacancy stop, training and development only when a direct link with organisational performance can be shown, cutting employee benefits and performance-related pay linked to financial performance. Empirical research shows both strategies can emerge in the case of private equity interventions (Wright and Bruining, 2008). It is, however, very difficult to predict which strategy a PEF is going to pursue.

Human resource management (HRM)

Human resource management (HRM) involves management decisions related to policies and practices which together shape the employment relationship and are aimed at achieving individual, organisational and societal goals (Boselie, 2010). This definition builds on a typical continental European perspective on HRM. In this perspective multiple stakeholders are taken into account (including trade unions, works councils, government, management, employees, financiers and shareholders), the organisational context plays an important role (so-called contextual or situational factors), and performance is defined according to a multidimensional construct focused on (1) organisational performance (for example productivity and quality), (2) individual well-being (for example job satisfaction and work–life balance) and (3) societal well-being (for example employment). The Dutch society can be characterised by industrial relations with general acceptance of multiple stakeholders such as trade unions and works councils (Paauwe, 2004). Another key characteristic of the Dutch context is the relevance and impact of institutional mechanisms (in particular labour legislation) on human resource management (Paauwe and Boselie, 2003). The explicit incorporation of multiple stakeholders and contextual (institutional) factors in studying HRM therefore makes sense. Dominant Anglo-Saxon HRM perspectives, mainly from the USA, tend to take a more unitarist view focused on shareholder value and including a limited number of stakeholders. Private equity firms represent investment companies that tend to embrace Anglo-Saxon principles in their operations and activities. In other words, PEFs are interested in money while targeting organisations. PEFs are therefore sometimes called 'barbarians' (Boselie and Koene, 2010).

THE DUTCH HOSPITAL REMBRANDT VAN RIJN

ALINE BOS AND PAUL BOSELIE

In this case study we focus on a Dutch hospital. Mergers and acquisitions from the 1990s onwards resulted in less than 100 general hospitals in the Netherlands in 2011. On average these hospitals employed 5,000 people. The New Health Insurance Act of 2006 has put enormous pressure on healthcare organisations to increase service quality and reduce costs. Given the ageing population of many western countries such as the Netherlands, the Dutch hospitals are confronted with multiple challenges that are interlinked:

- the ageing population increases healthcare demands because more older citizens require more care and cure services;
- the baby boom generation is about to retire and only few young people are willing and able to work in healthcare;
- the Dutch government is forced to cut costs on healthcare causing limited financial resources for healthcare organisations, their employees and their activities.

The increased pressure for improved organisational performance has led to increased competition among Dutch hospitals, reflected in for example yearly rankings published in popular newspapers.

The general Rembrandt van Rijn hospital employs around 1,600 people including 300 medical specialists and 1,300 nurses and medical support staff. Almost half of the medical specialists within the hospitals are self-employed, which is a typical characteristic of the Dutch healthcare sector. These self-employed specialists have a powerful position within the organisation and are represented at the highest level, without being formally employed by the organisation.

After privatisation of the municipal Rembrandt van Rijn hospital in 1998, the deficits ran up to over €7 million in 2002. The Dutch Minister of Health announced the closure of the hospital, but the Second Chamber in Dutch Parliament prevented the minister from doing so. By 2007, the hospital was nearly bankrupt. The two-tier board of the hospital Rembrandt van Rijn was confronted with major financial losses. Regular financiers such as banks and insurance companies are no longer willing to finance the hospital without very strict conditions.

In 2007, the board members got in touch with an external investor who was working for a PEF and interested in investing in the hospital. The investor expressed willingness to invest substantially in the Rembrandt van Rijn hospital on the condition that the PEF got ownership of the hospital. Dutch legislation has recently changed and the national government stimulates entrepreneurship, commercialisation and privatisation in the public sector. With new ownership from outside the two-tier board hopes to create a momentum for major organisational change and opportunities for improving performance through new managerial approaches (for example a new performance management system).

The case of PEF and the Hospital Rembrandt van Rijn has three phases:

1st the pre-bid phase in which a possible private equity intervention is announced.
2nd the actual private equity intervention and direct consequences.
3rd the period of two to six years after the private equity intervention.

We will briefly describe each phase and focus on the key questions of this chapter.

1. The pre-bid phase: Barbarians at the gate or El Salvador?

The initial meetings between the two-tier board of the hospital and representatives of the PEF are top secret to avoid negative publicity and internal turbulence. At this stage the two board members need to decide whom to involve. It is decided to actively involve a senior legal officer. After several secret meetings the board members decide to make a public announcement that the hospital is seriously looking for alternative investors and is investigating the possibility of private equity involvement. For most employees the news is not immediately picked up and taken seriously. After a stream of negative announcements over the past two years about low performance levels and after years of relatively low-ranking positions in Dutch hospital lists (e.g. the AD hospital top-100) most employees are aware of the sense of urgency for a major organisational change. For them a private equity intervention is too abstract and difficult to assess. From here on all members of the management team (the level below the two-tier board) are also involved in the negotiation process with the private equity firm. Now, the manager of the research and treatment department, the manager of clinical, the manager of administrative department and the manager of the general and technical service are involved. Medical specialists, the medical staff, are consulted and the supervisory board is informed as well.

The HR director, who is part of the management team, is able to convince the board that from this moment on the works council of the hospital should be informed on a regular basis. The director also suggests informing the client council of the hospital. Although there is no legal requirement for this information sharing, the HR director makes a strong plea for this type of works councils' and client councils' involvement to maintain effective employment relationships in times of turbulence. As the media picks up the story of a possible private equity intervention in the public domain this starts up a hot debate about the nature of the private equity firm's intentions and possible negative impact of such an intervention for the quality of healthcare, the position of the employees and the public values of a Dutch hospital in general, such as accessibility. From this moment on employee trust levels decline dramatically, in particular with regard to employees' trust in management. Top management response to all the commotion is putting emphasis on the sense of urgency and the opportunity a private equity intervention creates for organisational renewal.

2. The actual private equity intervention

After almost a year of negotiations it looks like nothing is going to change. The financial performance of the hospital is even more pressing. Representatives of the private equity firm propose a bonus package for the top management (two-tier board) arguing that these bonuses are necessary to retain top managers during and after the private equity intervention process. As soon as the media finds out about this pay proposal the PEF is accused of bribing top managers to make the ownership change happen. While this type of bonus intervention for top management is common in private equity interventions, given the healthcare context and its public values this proposal feeds scepticism about the PEF's true intentions with the hospital. Employee trust in top management decreases even further.

The two-tier board sticks to the plan and pursues the process of an actual intervention. They now decide to organise group meetings for all employees within the hospital. There are two main goals for these road shows. First, the meetings provide a platform for employees to share their emotions, frustrations and feelings of insecurity. Second, the board members can use the opportunity to show leadership and emphasise the sense of urgency for a radical change. Without new investments the hospital is most likely to go bankrupt within one or two years.

The HR director's main concern at this stage of the actual PE intervention is the retention of highly motivated and qualified employees. Both medical specialists and nurses represent the human capital of the Rembrandt van Rijn hospital. Major employee turnover rates could disturb and damage the continuity of healthcare activities.

3. The period after the private equity intervention

The private equity intervention is completed. The works council involvement at an early stage in the process now pays off. In the actual transition of ownership the works council's trust in top management supports creating the new deal with the PEF. Much to everybody's surprise, the first 12 months after the take over nothing really changes. After a year one of the board members makes use of an early retirement arrangement and the vacancy is filled by a top manager connected to the PEF. This manager has prior experience in a US private company. As soon as this person is appointed things are starting to change rapidly. A new performance management system, based on General Electric's Six Sigma system, is introduced to increase efficiency, improve service quality and stimulate innovation. The human resource practices linked to this new performance system include:

- training and development of nurses aimed at improving productivity (more clients per hour) and increasing customer satisfaction scores;
- individual scorecards and team scorecards with weekly and monthly outcome measures such as

customer satisfaction, employee absence rates, productivity outcomes and peer evaluations of job performance;
- bonuses for excellent teams up to one additional month pay for every team member.

At the same time, some major reorganisations are planned to make drastic cutbacks:

- all hospital volunteers are dismissed, because in fact they are old and need a lot of care themselves, which distracts the medical professionals from their patients;
- the level of middle management is removed. The board now directly speaks with medical professionals;
- new and financially attractive forms of medical service are introduced, such as an influenza clinic and a stop smoking clinic;
- all contracts with interim-managers and external advisors are terminated;
- all temporary contracts are terminated and those workers can only continue working for the hospital when they work for a special flex company that employs contingent workers in healthcare;
- Multiple disciplines within the hospital are labelled as non-core business activities (for example psychology) and these functions and departments are outsourced.

For the healthcare sector, the hospital uses unconventional methods, a top-down management style and private sector competitive strategies. This causes conflict with the works council, with other hospitals and even with the local government.

Conclusion

Four years after the private equity intervention organisational performance has improved, in particular with regard to productivity and service quality levels. When the PEF entered the organisation, there was a deficit of €4.3 million. After six years, the annual profits are around €5.0 million. The Rembrandt van Rijn hospital is no longer at the bottom of the Dutch hospital ranking in the newspapers, but in the middle. In the AD newspaper hospital top-100, the hospital jumped from place 99 in 2007 to the 49th place in 2011.

1 With regard to the three central questions at the beginning of this case, we can conclude that the Dutch hospital executed a quite intentional strategy of involving stakeholders. Starting with secret meetings between the hospital board and the PEF, more and more stakeholders get involved. A legal officer, a HR director, middle management, the medical

staff, the works council and client council are one after the other consulted in the first phase. In the second phase, when the deal is actually made, all employees are involved. We can conclude that different stakeholders become involved in early phases, which fits the European stakeholder perspective and turns out to be a good strategy when the deal is actually made.

2 Concerning the HRM practices, goal setting through performance management has become a central theme. Through the new performance management system, the linkage between organisational goals, team goals and individual employee goals has become much clearer for all actors involved. Nurses and medical specialists, for example, now have a much better understanding of the value and goal of specific training programmes. The HR function and its HR professionals have played an important role in the implementation and communication of the new performance management system.

3 The HRM outcomes of these interventions and HRM practices are not clear yet. Employee satisfaction levels from the yearly employee surveys still show moderate scores. Employees appear reasonably satisfied about their job but less happy with their organisation. While employee trust levels have gone up the general employee trust in management is still relatively low.

The private equity intervention has led to more focus on the actual core business. The downside of the private equity intervention is that many good healthcare workers have left the organisation. Both medical specialists and nurses voluntarily left the hospital. In the Amsterdam region it was not difficult for them to find a new job in another hospital. Because of the financial and performance orientation of the private equity form, the Rembrandt van Rijn hospital now has the reputation of a good general hospital providing good cure and care services. But the hospital is not considered a high-quality and highly specialised organisation from the workers' perspective.

Lessons learned

The case study shows the relevance of different stages or phases in the process of organisational change related to a private equity intervention. It also reveals the importance of dynamics and the notion of time. In our HRM approaches we must therefore be aware of the fact that organisational challenges are in a state of flux and hardly static or stable. In this case, for example, upward as well as downward strategies are executed; each strategy needs a different approach and specific HR-interventions. This also shows us the relevance of both content and underlying processes related to HRM issues given organisational changes. The HRM discipline is often implicitly focused on the content of static issues. This private equity intervention highlights the impact of processes and dynamics. The case study also emphasises the role of top management in the change process. The road shows are important for stressing leadership support of the organisational changes made and for employees' trust in the strategic decisions being made. The involvement of works councils and client council, mainly through information sharing, paid off in later stage of the private equity process. Building a strong relationship with social partners (e.g. works councils, client councils and trade unions) can contribute to optimally managing organisational change processes particularly in highly institutionalised contexts such as the Netherlands (Boselie, 2010). Finally, the case highlights the relevance of perceptions and sentiments of those involved. Emotions, feelings of insecurity, employee distrust in management, turnover intentions, dissatisfaction and low commitment levels are partly inevitable in times of major organisational change. Human resource management (HRM) or good people management can contribute to decrease these negative attitudes and perceptions with an active role of the HR function and its HR professionals in PE interventions.

Questions

1 What are the advantages and disadvantages of works council and client council involvement at an early stage of a private equity intervention from the top management perspective and from the individual employee perspective?

2 What kind of human resource policies and practices can be applied to retain valuable employees (highly qualified and motivated workers) during a process of a major organisational change? Are there any differences in strategies between public and private organisations?

3 Why is it important that the two board members actively participate in a road show in which they personally explain the private equity situation?

4 What is the impact of a General Electric inspired performance management system on professionals (nurses and medical specialists) in a hospital?

5 How does the new performance management affect organisational commitment, occupational commitment and team commitment of employees within the hospital?

6 What is the impact of outsourcing disciplines on employees who are being outsourced and employees who may stay?

7 In order to attract and retain talented workers, organisations need to build, strengthen and maintain their corporate identity. A concept that refers to this phenomenon is 'employment branding'. Given the background of the PE intervention in the Rembrandt van Rijn hospital, what human resource management strategy and policy can be developed to contribute to the 'employment branding' of the organisation?

8 What kind of qualities and competencies do HR professionals need for adding value to the organisational change process caused by a private equity intervention?

9 What kind of concrete HR practices can be applied to minimise the negative effects on a private equity intervention on employee attitudes and perceptions? Also explain why?

CASE STUDY 1.2
GROWING UP FAST – HOW GAZELLES MANAGE HRM

OLAV MUURLINK, ADRIAN WILKINSON, DAVID PEETZ AND KEITH TOWNSEND
GRIFFITH BUSINESS SCHOOL, GRIFFITH UNIVERSITY, BRISBANE, AUSTRALIA

Introduction

Like the creatures grazing the open grasslands of Africa, firms known as 'gazelles' are not just fast (in this case, fast growing), but hard to hunt down. That's partly because they are rare. Relatively early estimates suggested they make up just 4 per cent of firms (Birch,

1979), and if anything, these estimates seem to have overshot the mark. Birch's work brought this small cluster of fast-growing firms into prominence, because he claimed that these relatively small and young firms captured the lion's share of net jobs growth in the economy. Generally, gazelles are defined by their percentage of sustained growth, either in turnover or employment, but some definitions guarantee the gazelle minority status, defining the breed as the crème-de-la-crème, gazelles simply being the fastest-growing firms in a population (Henrekson and Johansson, 2009), and while their role as jobs generators has been heavily questioned (Davis *et al.*, 1996), gazelles are undoubtedly a fascinating laboratory in which to study HRM.

These high-growth firms can create severe pressure on the management of people. They tend to be innovative in the way they handle people, and they are certainly innovative in products and service as they seek to rapidly carve out a niche in the economy, but such innovations come at a cost for staff and management (Janssen *et al.*, 2004). As the organisation – or subunit – grows beyond a certain size, inconsistencies in treatment, exacerbated by the creation of a management chain, and an increasingly depersonalised management, gives rise to incentives for more systematic HR policies and procedures to prevent mistakes. In cases where sub-units attempt to replicate parent company policy, there may be strains between generic parent expectations and specific local conditions. Nevertheless, formalising HR structures can also help to retain expertise and ensure that foundation levels of commitment are maintained. For example, in order to recruit staff, rather than relying on word-of-mouth and existing contacts, greater use is made of sophisticated methods for recruitment and selection, training, performance review and pay and reward. As the need for specialist expertise becomes more apparent across the whole organisation, so too does the pressure to employ professional HR services internal to the organisation. If HRM is still informal and ad hoc, an increasing number of problems are bound to emerge because HR policies – such as grievance and discipline procedures or pay systems – are applied inconsistently. The result is policy made on the run by the managers by whom everything has to be funnelled through them, enmeshing them with all HR issues.

Two routes to success . . . or failure?

Becoming a gazelle in the midst of the global financial crisis (GFC) is no mean feat, but the route to success for the two companies we will examine, New Leaf Supermarkets and Freshcoat, with a growth from zero to around 100 staff in four years at the height of the GFC came by very different means. Australia, where both companies were situated, was a unique case in terms of GFC response, in that the federal government had a substantial war chest with which to stimulate declining economic growth. Nevertheless, Dun and Bradstreet

numbers showed a 48 per cent increase in small business failures in 2010–11 and an extraordinary 95 per cent fall in the number of start-ups (Dun and Bradstreet, 2012). However, neither New Leaf nor Freshcoat took advantage of federal munificence, and instead trod much more conventional paths to success. But that is where the similarity ends.

New Leaf began as a university project for its founding CEO, who was asked by some friends, who were supermarket managers, for assistance in responding to an impending takeover of the company that employed them, a takeover that threatened their job security. The accidental nature of the company's birth contrasted with the very deliberate manner in which the principals executed their plan to enter the supermarket industry, gradually buying up cheap or under-valued assets, some in remote rural locations, and adding value to their new outlets with low-cost makeovers and a new service orientation. 'We were, I suppose, hungry to acquire more stores, and put some volume into the business and establish a support office, and get all the resources that we needed,' recalled the CEO. Ultimately, this hunger proved costly.

At first, the tactic of developing some skills, such as human resource management – using intensive training for a former grassroots supermarket supervisor who became HRM manager – and importing others, such as the former finance manager of a significant airport retailing chain, seemed to work. The company and the brand gained peer respect. While the company, like the CEO leading it, was remarkably young, it demonstrated all the attributes of a mature firm. It had a solid hard-working head office, relatively sober attitudes to cost, and hid its cost-cutting measures (such as its paint-brush and broom-stick approach to refurbishing stores) well enough to disguise the cash-flow difficulties associated with rapid growth in a competitive industry. The Australian supermarket industry is almost internationally unique in that a colossal 80 per cent of the Australian retail groceries market is dominated by just two players, Woolworths and Coles, companies so large (despite the relatively small Australian market) that they are both within the top 25 retailers in the world. Against a background of two Goliaths, New Leaf was very much a David. When New Leaf made a play for a high-profile (but failing) fruit and vegetable retailer, it was a signal of intent. Due diligence dragged on, and in what may well have been a case of the power of sunk costs detailed in Teger and Cary's *Too Much Invested to Quit* (1980), despite niggling concerns, New Leaf sealed the deal. 'Every day literally a skeleton jumps out of the closet,' the CEO admitted, months later. Later the same year, the company had fallen into administration. The outlets associated with the fruit and vegetable retailer all closed, with staff laid off. Some of the original New Leaf sites remained open, under new management. The dream was over less than four years after it began.

The founder of Freshcoat was the highly successful sales manager of a company making cladding for an Australia-wide market, but harboured dreams of owning the business he worked for. It was a dream he thought he shared with his employers, who were approaching retirement age. That dream was dashed when his employers suddenly sold the firm to a third party, leaving the sales manager fuming – and motivated. He immediately set to work. The day the announcement was made was the day he was about to take annual leave. He never returned. Instead of sunning on the beach, he secured a large contract, using skills in costing that he had built up at his former employers. Suddenly, without a single employee to its name, the company had a big order on its books. He assembled a team, including the factory foreman of his former employer, who became one of the minority partners at Freshcoat. He stumbled on a disused heavy industry factory in a commercial suburb not far from his home, and within four years had over 100 staff, including a factory fitted with the latest in computer-aided manufacturing equipment (all leased) and highly paid tradespeople fitting cladding to client's projects. In contrast to New Leaf, this growth came without the usual paraphernalia of middle management. The company had no HR manager, no in-house finance manager, no payroll office, and no dedicated health and safety officer. The company's highly driven founder and his second-in-charge – the factory foreman – fulfilled multiple roles, but conceded that the pressure had come at significant cost to their mental health and family relationships. Again, from the outside, Freshcoat's success attracted media attention. The company was chosen for some of the most high-profile, and highly visible structures in the fast-growing mining state of Queensland, and at the time of this case study, it was on the cusp of moving into purpose-built new premises close to its old headquarters.

So, we have two companies – one retail, one manufacturing – both initiated by individuals with drive and vision, and following a plan executed with very different approaches to human resource management.

New Leaf's approach was highly conventional. It borrowed standard policies from retail industry groups, and modified them to fit. It instituted formal policies, and personnel management systems that mimicked the approach of much larger firms. Its approach was partly guided by the formal business education of the company's founder and CEO, and partly by the industry in which it operated. The supermarket industry worldwide is low margin. It employs staff generally on minimum wages. In Australia, the rights of minimum wage earners are carefully scrutinised and enforced by federal and state frameworks, including bodies with power to force compliance. Freshcoat's approach to entry-level factory floor staff, relatively unskilled and doing repetitive tasks guiding mechanised processes, was similarly bound by legislation, however, the company operated in a relatively higher margin industry – Queensland's booming building industry – which allowed the managers to give staff above-award wages and conditions. With a highly casualised staff typical of supermarkets, New Leaf's operators had no such luxury, and subsequently experienced high levels of turnover in entry-level staff.

Freshcoat's turnover problems had an entirely different origin. In both its working principals, Freshcoat's management lacked both real managerial experience and formal business training. The factory manager confessed that turnover in the first year of operation – remarkably, 150 per cent – was due to his own experience at managing staff on this scale. 'I was very – it was zero tolerance. "Mate, you're not doing your job. Go,"' the young manager admitted. For staff and management, the psychological consequences were severe. Once the company stabilised and the young managers grew in confidence and experience, a very different climate came over the company. With both companies still young enough to be driven by the vision of their founders, like New Leaf, Freshcoat had a paternalistic flavour to the way it treated staff. Both companies showed greater interest in the day-to-day non-working lives of staff than is typical at larger firms. However, unlike New Leaf, Freshcoat had the resources to take this paternalism further. One of its staff – a promising athlete with a potential Olympic career in front of him – was given sponsorship and time off for training, and another staff member, struggling to get his life together, was given a whole suite of assistance, including driving lessons from one of the managers, to help him purchase his first car.

There are high levels of government intervention in the Australian industrial relations landscape, but in recent years, successive conservative and Labour governments have introduced widespread reform characterised by increasing flexibility in employer–employee relationships. Freshcoat took advantage of one of these reforms to introduce a unique Enterprise Bargaining Agreement for its shop floor staff, featuring a 45-hour week (as opposed to 38-hour week) standard, with overtime extending it to a maximum of 48 hours. For the hours between 38 and 45, no overtime was paid, but instead, staff were given a higher standard wage, with guaranteed nine hours of 'overtime' built into their pay packet. The theory was that in quiet periods, the staff would be allowed to work less than 45 hours and still collect the full wage, but in a gazelle firm such as Freshcoat, organisational slack is a rare 'problem', and staff revealed this rarely eventuated.

Outside the shop floor, Freshcoat introduced what was dubbed 'The System', a graded hierarchy that offered staff a clear-cut career progression path – for staff with the 'right' attitude. 'Ones' were senior managers, 'Fives' were entry-level staff with no supervision responsibility. With the Queensland building industry booming, demand for tradespeople, such as those working in Freshcoat's field operations, was high, and wages were far higher than awards established during much bleaker times. Because of lack of tradespeople, Freshcoat, like many similar industries, had a high emphasis on training, with even the second-in-charge at the firm enrolling himself in a trade apprenticeship, by way of example.

At New Leaf, the motivation to train staff was different. With access to a pool of non-skilled, often casual staff, New Leaf needed to train its staff in order to compete with its competitors on customer service. It was in the midst of planning its own internal Training Academy, complete with a working checkout aisle and cash register, when the chain collapsed. The purchase of the fruit and vegetable chain that eventually triggered its downfall had been more than simply a financial and logistical challenge. The acquisition target had been left floundering for many months before the takeover, and morale was desperately low. 'You walk into any one of the [newly acquired stores] and it's like walking into a morgue,' the CEO admitted. Staff hurriedly covered their uniforms as soon as they left work. 'They're not proud of where they work.' Even though New Leaf had bought the target chain – essentially little more than a series of leased stores with years of television advertising to give the group some market heft – for its 'goodwill', it quickly realised that there was none attached to the brand. New Leaf created a new brand, with new store livery, layouts and uniforms. The results in terms of store morale were excellent, and while the stores experienced a surge in sales that went beyond the honeymoon period, it proved to be a case of too little, too late for New Leaf.

In terms of recruitment, for the vast majority of staff, both firms chose informal methods, despite the formal training of New Leaf's senior management. New Leaf used in-store signs to recruit the majority of staff, targeting people interested in casual work within each store's catchment area. It's low cost approach to recruitment extended to more senior staff, with the company introducing a database of existing staff and their skills, with the intent of promoting internally wherever possible into managerial roles, within store, and within the group. Freshcoat's attitude to recruitment was similarly ad hoc, employing contacts of existing staff, or 'walk ins' coming through the factory door seeking work. Its informal approach was, however, driven as much by the lack of time to devote to more formal recruitment on the part of the overworked principals and a desire to employ characters with the 'right stuff', as the factory foreman put it, as to save money.

Conclusions

While this case merely gives a snapshot of the hectic, high-pressure early years of two gazelle firms, it gives an insight into how different HR practice looks in high growth SME firms.

While managers of SMEs tend to rank HR high in their priority order, the cases of Freshcoat and New Leaf demonstrate that as firms move off the blueprint stage and rapidly grow, foundation managers quickly become overwhelmed with the commercial implications of growth, focusing instead on satisfying customers, sourcing working capital and ensuring cashflow. While HR in gazelles may not always be characterised by a high degree of formal, structured HR, and clearly, Freshcoat proves that growth without a focus on policies is possible, the managers of these growing firms expressed repeatedly an appreciation of the value of policy as offering a life raft of stability in a sea of uncertainty. Entrepreneurial gazelles may be founded on a basis of personalised vision of individual managers (Cocca and Alberti, 2010), with managers tending to retain close control and personal connections with staff, but this level of personalisation comes at a cost. Managers in the two companies admitted to being glad, on occasion, to be able to arbitrate fraught decisions by reference to a standard operating procedure. In Freshcoat, where such policies were relatively absent, the managers had to frequently arbitrate on HRM issues an *ad hoc* basis, and clearly suffered greater stress than the managers at New Leaf – even though Freshcoat was thriving commercially, and New Leaf was about to hit the kind of reef that gazelles are vulnerable to.

Questions

1 In what way do these cases illustrate the role of organisational slack in mediating approaches to HRM problems?
2 What special challenges and opportunities does the growth experienced by a gazelle firm imply for the HRM manager?
3 What advantages and disadvantages would Freshcoat have experienced, if it had introduced formal HRM policies earlier in its lifecycle?

Bibliography

Alfes, K., Truss, C., Soane, E.C., Rees, C. and Gatenby, M. (2010) *Creating an Engaged Workforce*, London: CIPD.

Allen, M. and Wright, P. (2007) 'Strategic management and HR', in Boxall, L.P., Purcell, I.J. and Wright, P. (eds) *The Oxford Handbook of Human Resource Management,* Oxford: Oxford University Press.

Appelbaum, E., Bailey, T., Berg, P. and Kalleberg, A. (2000) *Manufacturing Competitive Advantage: The Effects of High Performance Work Systems on Plant Performance and Company Outcomes*, New York: Cornell University Press.

Bach, S. (2008) 'Public sector HRM', in Wilkinson, A., Bacon, N. Redman, T. and Snell, S. (eds) *The SAGE Handbook of Human Resource Management*, London: Sage.

Bach, S. and Givan, R. (2010) 'Regulating employment conditions in a hospital network: the case of the private finance initiative', *Human Resource Management Journal*, Vol.20, No.4, 424–39.

Bacon, N. (2003) 'Human resource management and industrial relations', in Ackers, P. and Wilkinson, A. (eds) *Understanding Work and Employment: Industrial Relations in Transition,* Oxford: Oxford University Press.

Bacon N. (2008) 'Management strategy and industrial relations' in Blyton, P., Heery, E., Bacon, N. and Fiorto, J. (eds) *The SAGE Handbook of Industrial Relations,* Thousand Oaks, CA: Sage.

Bamber, G., Gittell, J., Kochan, T. and Von Nordenflycht, A. (2009) *Up in the Air: How Airlines can Improve Performance by Engaging their Employees*, Ithaca, NY: Cornell University Press.

Barney, J. (1991) 'Firm resources and sustained competitive advantage', *Journal of Management,* Vol.17, No.1, 99–120.

Barney, J. (1995) 'Looking inside for competitive advantage', *Academy of Management Executive,* Vol.9, No.4, 49–61.

Beardwell, I. (ed.) (1998) *Contemporary Industrial Relations,* Oxford: Open University Press.

Becker, B. and Gerhart, B. (1996) 'The impact of human resource management on organizational performance: progress and prospects', *Academy of Management Journal,* Vol.39, 779–801.

Becker, B.E. and Huselid, M.A. (2009) 'Strategic human resource management: Where do we go from here?' in Wilkinson, A., Bacon, N., Redman, T. and Snell, S. (eds) *The SAGE Handbook of Human Resource Management*, London: Sage.

Beer, M. and Eisenstat, R. (1996) 'Developing an organisation capable of implementing strategy and learning', *Human Relations,* Vol.49, No.5, 297–619.

Benington, J. and Moore M.H. (eds) (2011) *Public Value, Theory and Practice,* New York: Palgrave Macmillan.

Beynon, H., Grimshaw, D., Rubery, J. and Ward, K. (2002) *Managing Employment Change, The New Realities of Work,* Oxford: Oxford University Press.

Birch, D. (1979) *The Job Generation Process*, University of Illinois at Urbana-Champaign's Academy for Entrepreneurial Leadership Historical Research Reference in Entrepreneurship.

Blyton, P., Heery, E. and Turnbull, P. (eds) (2011) *Reassessing the Employment Relationship,* Basingstoke: Palgrave Macmillan.

Boer and Croon (2011) *Overnames in de NL Gezondheidszorg*, Amsterdam: Boer & Croon.

Bolton, C. and Houlihan, M. (eds) (2007) *Searching for the Human in Human Resource Management,* London: Palgrave Macmillan.

Boselie, P. (2010) *Strategic Human Resource Management. A Balanced Approach*, Berkshire: McGraw-Hill.

Boselie, P. and Koene, B. (2010) 'Private equity and human resource management: "Barbarians at the gate!" HR's wake-up call?' *Human Relations,* Vol.63, No.9, 1297–319.

Boselie, P. and Paauwe, J. (2009) 'HRM and the resource based view', in Wilkinson, A., Bacon, N., Redman, T. and Snell, S. (eds) *The SAGE Handbook of Human Resource Management*, London: Sage.

Boselie P., Dietz G. and Boon C. (2005) 'Commonalities and contradictions in HRM and performance research', *Human Resource Management Journal,* Vol.15, No.3, 67–94.

Boxall, P. (1992) 'Strategic human resource management: beginnings of a new theoretical sophistication?', *Human Resource Management Journal,* Vol.2, No.3, 60–79.

Boxall, P. and Purcell, J. (2000) 'Strategic human resource management: where have we come from and where should we be going?' *International Journal of Management Reviews*, Vol.2, No.2, 183–203.

*Boxall, P. and Purcell, J. (2003) *Strategy and Human Resource Management,* London: Palgrave.

Boxall, P. and Purcell, J. (2008) *Strategy and Human Resource Management,* Basingstoke: Palgrave Macmillan.

Boxall, P. and Purcell, J. (2011) *Strategy and Human Resource Management,* New York: Palgrave Macmillan.

Boxall, P. and Steenveld, M. (1999) 'Human resource strategy and competitive advantage: a longitudinal study of engineering consultancies', *Journal of Management Studies,* Vol.36, No.4, 443–63.

Boxall P., Purcell, J. and Wright, P. (eds) (2007) *The Oxford Handbook of Human Resource Management,* Oxford: Oxford University Press.

Bozeman, B. (1993), *Public Management,* San Francisco, CA: Jossey-Bass.

Brockbank, W. (1997) 'HR's future on the way to a presence', *Human Resource Management,* Vol.36, No.1, 65–69.

Brotherton, C. (2003) 'Industrial relations and psychology', in Ackers, P. and Wilkinson, A. (eds) *Understanding Work and Employment: Industrial Relations in Transition,* Oxford: Oxford University Press.

Bruining, H. and Wright, M. (2002) 'Entrepreneurial orientation in management buyouts and the contribution of venture capital', *Venture Capital: An International Journal of Entrepreneurial Finance,* Vol.4, 147–68.

Caldwell, R. (2004) 'Rhetoric, facts and self-fulfilling prophecies: exploring practitioners' perceptions of progress in implementing HRM', *Industrial Relations Journal,* Vol.35, No.3, 196–215.

Castelijns, E., van Kollenburg, A. and Oh, L. (2011) *Second Opinion, Ziekenhuisstrategieën Tegen het Licht,* Utrecht: Berenschot.

CIPD (2012) *Annual Report*, London: Chartered Institute of Personnel Development.

Clark, I. and Clark, T. (1990) 'Personnel management and the use of executive recruitment consultancies', *Human Resource Management Journal,* Vol.1, No.1, 46–62.

Cocca, P., and Alberti, M. (2010). 'A framework to assess performance measurement systems in SMEs', *International Journal of Productivity and Performance Management,* Vol.59, No.2, 186–200.

*Combs, C., Lui Y., Hall, A. and Ketchen, D. (2006) 'How much do high performance work systems matter? A meta-analysis of their effects on organizational performance', *Personnel Pyschology*, Vol.59, No.3, 501–28.

Cully, M., Woodland, S., O'Reilly, A. and Dix, G. (1999) *Britain at Work,* London: Routledge.

Davis, S.J., Haltiwanger, J., and Schuh, S. (1996) 'Small business and job creation: dissecting the myth and reassessing the facts', *Small Business Economics,* Vol.8, No.4, 297–315.

Delaney, J.T., Lewin, D. and Ichniowski, C. (1989) *Human Resource Policies and Practices in American Firms,* Washington, DC: US Government Printing Office.

Delery, J. and Doty, D. (1996) 'Modes of theorizing in strategic human resource management: tests of universalistic, contingency and configurational performance predictions', *Academy of Management Journal,* Vol.39, No.4, 802–35.

Dietz G., Martins, A. and Searle, R. (2011) 'Trust, HRM and the employment relationship', in Wilkinson, A. and Townsend, K. (eds) *The Future of Employment Relations,* London: Palgrave Macmillan, 141–64.

Drucker, P. (1961) *The Practice of Management,* London: Mercury.

Dun and Bradstreet (2012) 'Small business failures up 48%', *Dun and Bradstreet Insight,* Autumn 2012, No.4.

Dundon, T. and Rollinson, D. (2011) *Understanding Employment Relations*, (2nd edn), London: McGraw Hill.

Dyer, L. and Reeves, T. (1995) 'Human resource strategies and firm performance: what do we know and where do we need to go?', *International Journal of Human Resource Management,* Vol.6, 656–70.

Eccles, R. and Nohira, N. (1992) *Beyond the Hype: Rediscovering the Essence of Management,* Boston, MA: Harvard Business School Press.

Eichinger, B. and Ulrich, D. (1995) 'Are you future agile?', *Human Resource Planning,* Vol.18, No.4, 30–41.

Exworthy, M. and Halford, S. (2002) *Professionals and the New Managerialism in the Public Sector,* Buckingham: Open University Press.

Farndale, E. and Brewster, C. (2005) 'In search of legitimacy: personnel management associations worldwide', *Human Resource Management Journal*, Vol.15, No.3, 33–48.

Farnham, D. (2010) *Human Resource Management in Context: Strategy, Insights and Solutions,* London: CIPD.

Ferris, G.R. Hochwarter, W.A., Buckley, M.R., Hamell-Cook, G. and Frink, D.D. (1999) 'Human resource management: some new directions', *Journal of Management,* Vol.25, No.3, 385–415.

Folkman, P., Froud, J., Williams, K. and Johal, S. (2009), Private equity: levered on capital or labour?', *Journal of Industrial Relations,* Vol.51, No.4. 517–27.

Francis, H. and Keegan, A. (2006) 'The changing face of HRM: in search of balance', *Human Resource Management Journal*, Vol.16, No.3, 231–49.

Gennard, J. and Kelly, J. (1997) 'The unimportance of labels: the diffusion of the personnel/ HRM function', *Industrial Relations Journal,* Vol.28, No.1, 27–42.

Giles, E. and Williams, R. (1991) 'Can the personnel department survive quality management?', *Personnel Management,* April, 28–33.

Godard, J. (2004) 'A critical assessment of the high-performance paradigm', *British Journal of Industrial Relations,* Vol.42, No.2, 349–78.

Gospel, H. (2005) 'The management of labour and human resources', in Jones G. and Zeitlin J. (eds) *The Oxford Handbook of Business History,* Oxford: Oxford University Press.

Gospel, H. (2009) 'Human resource management: a historical perspective', in Wilkinson, A., Bacon, N., Redman, T. and Snell, S. (eds) *The SAGE Handbook of Human Resource Management*, London: Sage.

Grant, R. (2010) *Contemporary Strategy Analysis*, (7th edn), Oxford: Blackwell.

Gratton, L., Hope Hailey, V., Stiles, P. and Truss, C. (1999) *Strategic Human Resource Management,* Oxford: Oxford University Press.

Green, F. (2005) 'Why is work effort becoming more intense?' *Industrial Relations: A Journal of Economy and Society,* Vol.43, No.4, 709–41.

Greer, C.R., Youngblood, S.A. and Gray, D.A. (1999) 'Human resource management outsourcing: the make or buy decision', *Academy of Management Executive,* Vol.13, No.3, 85–96.

Grimshaw, D., Rubery, J. and Marchington, M. (2010) 'Managing people across hospital networks in the UK: multiple employers and the shaping of HRM', *Human Resource Management Journal*, Vol.20, No.4, 407–23.

Guest, D. (1987) 'Human resource management and industrial relations', *Journal of Management Studies,* Vol.24, No.5, 503–21.

Guest, D. (1998) 'Beyond HRM: Commitment and the contract culture', in Marchington, M. and Sparrow, P. (eds) *Human Resource Management: The New Agenda,* London: Pitman.

*Guest, D. (1999) 'Human resource management: The workers' verdict', *Human Resource Management Journal,* Vol.9, No.3, 5–25.

Guest, D. (2000) 'Piece by piece', *People Management,* 20 July, 26–31.

Guest, D. (2007) 'Human resource management and the worker: towards a new psychological contract?', in Boxall, P., Purcell, J. and Wright, P. (eds) *Oxford Handbook of Human Resource Management,* Oxford: Oxford University Press.

Guest, D. (2011) 'Human resource management and performance: still searching for some answers', *Human Resource Management Journal*, Vol.21, No.1, 3–13.

Guest, D. and Conway, N. (2011) 'The impact of HR practices, HR effectiveness and a "strong HR system" on organisational outcomes: a stakeholder perspective', *International Journal of Human Resource Management*, Vol.22, No.8, 1686–702.

Guest, D. and King, Z. (2001) 'Voices from the boardroom report: state of the profession survey', *Personnel Today,* 10–11.

Guo, S., Hotchkiss, E.S., and Song, W. (2009) *Do Buyouts (Still) Create Value?* Manuscript, Boston College.

Guthrie, J., Flood, P., Liu, W., MacCurtain, S. and Armstrong, C. (2011), 'Big hat, no cattle? The relationship between use of high-performance work systems and managerial perceptions of HR departments', *International Journal of Human Resource Management*, Vol.22, No.8, 1672–85.

Haggerty, J. and Wright, P. (2009) 'Strong situations and firm performance: a proposed reconceptualisation of the role of the HR function', in Wilkinson, A., Bacon, N., Redman, T. and Snell, S. (eds) *The SAGE Handbook of Human Resource Management*. London: Sage.

Haque, M.S. (2001) 'The diminishing publicness of public service under the current mode of governance', *Public Administration Review,* Vol.61, No.1, 65–82.

Hamel, G. (2005) *The Future of Management*, Cambridge, MA: Harvard Business School Press.

Harter, J.K., Schmidt, F.L., Killham, E.A. and Asplund, J.W. (2006). *Q12 Meta-Analysis*, Omaha, NE: Gallup.

Hendry, C., Pettigrew, A. and Sparrow, P. (1988) 'Changing patterns of human resource management', *Personnel Management,* November, 37–41.

Henrekson, M. and Johansson, D. (2009) 'Gazelles as job creators: a survey and interpretation of the evidence', *Small Business Economics,* Vol.35, No.2, 227–44.

Herriot, P. and Pemberton, C. (1995) *New Deals: The Revolution in Management Careers,* London: Wiley.

Hird, M., Sparrow, P. and Marsh, C. (2010) 'HR structures: are they working?', in Sparrow, P., Hird, M., Hesketh, A. and Cooper, C. (eds) *Leading HR,* London: Palgrave Macmillan.

Hood, C. (1991) 'A public management for all seasons?', *Public Administration*, Vol.69, 3–19.

HSE (2012) *Health and Safety Executive: Stress Statistics*, London: HSE.

Huselid, M. (1995) 'The impact of human resource management practices on turnover, productivity and corporate financial performance', *Academy of Management Journal,* Vol.38, No.3, 635–72.

Ichniowski, C., Kochan, T., Levine, D., Olsen, C. and Strauss, G. (1996) 'What works at work: overview and assessment', *Industrial Relations,* Vol.35, No.3, 299–333.

Janssen, O., Van de Vliert, E. and West, M. (2004) 'The bright and dark sides of individual and group innovation: a special issue introduction', *Journal of Organizational Behavior,* Vol.25 No.2, 129–45.

Johnson G., Whittington, R. and Scholes, K, (2011) *Exploring Corporate Strategy*, (8th edn), London: Prentice Hall.

Karré, P.M. (2011) *Head and Tails: Both Sides of the Coin. An Analysis of Hybrid Organizations in the Dutch Waste Management Sector,* Den Haag: Eleven International Publishers.

Kaufman, B. (2007) 'The development of HRM', in Boxall, L.P., Purcell L.J. and Wright, P. (eds) *Oxford Handbook of Human Resource Management*, Oxford: Oxford University Press.

Kaufman, B. (2010) *Hired Hands or Human Resources: Case Studies of HRM Programs and Practices in Early American Industry,* Ithaca, NY: Cornell University Press.

Keegan, A. and Francis, H. (2010) 'Practitioner talk: the changing text-scape of HRM and emergence of HR business partnership', *International Journal of Human Resource Management*, Vol.21, No.6, 873–98.

Keenoy, T. (1990) 'HRM: rhetoric, reality and contradiction', *International Journal of Human Resource Management,* Vol.1, No.3, 363–84.

Kernaghan, K. (2003) 'Integrating values into public service: the values statement as centerpiece', *Public Administration Review,* Vol.63, No.6, 711–19.

Kersley, B., Alpin, C., Forth, J., Bryson, A., Bewley, H., Dix, G. and Oxenbridge, S. (2006) *Inside the Workplace: Findings from the 2004 Workplace Employment Relations Survey,* Abingdon: Routledge.

Kickert, W.J.M. (2001) 'Public management of hybrid organizations: governance of quasi-autonomous executive agencies', *International Public Management Journal,* Vol.4, No.2, 135–50.

Kochan, T., McKersie, R. and Cappelli, P. (1983) 'Strategic choice and industrial relations theory', *Industrial Relations,* Vol.23, No.1, 16–39.

Kulik, C. and Perry, E. (2008) 'When less is more: the devolution of HR's strategic role and construed image', *Human Resource Management*, Vol.47, No.3, 541–58.

Legge, K. (1995) *Human Resource Management: Rhetorics and Realities,* Basingstoke: Macmillan.

Lengnick-Hall, C.A. and Lengnick-Hall, M.L. (1988) 'Strategic human resources management: a review of the literature and a proposed typology', *Academy of Management Review,* Vol.13, No.3, 454–70.

Lewin, D. (2008) 'HRM in the 21st century', in Wankel, C. (ed.) *Handbook of 21st Century Management,* London: Sage.

Lewin, D. (2011) 'High performance human resources', in Wilkinson, A. and Townsend, K. (eds) *The Future of Employment Relations*. London: Palgrave Macmillan.

Macky, K. and Boxall, P. (2007) 'The relationship between "high-performance work practices" and employee attitudes: an investigation of additive and interaction effects', *International Journal of Human Resource Management*, Vol.18, No.4, 537–67.

MacLeod, D. and Clarke, N. (2009) *Engaging for Success: Enhancing Performance through Employee Engagement,* London: Department for Business, Innovation and Skills.

Maesschalck, J. (2004) 'The impact of the new public management reforms on public servants' ethics: towards a theory', *Public Administration*, Vol.82, No.2, 465–89.

Marchington, M. and Wilkinson, A. (2012) *Human Resource Management at Work* (5th edn), London: CIPD.

Marchington, M., Rubery, J. and Grimshaw, D. (2011a) 'Alignment, integration and consistency in HRM across multi-employer networks', *Human Resource Management*, Vol.50, No.3, 313–39.

*Marchington, M., Hadjivassiliou, K., Martin, R. and Cox, A. (2011b) 'Employment relations across organisational boundaries', in Wilkinson, A. and Townsend, K. (eds) *The Future of Employment Relations,* London: Palgrave Macmillan.

Martin-Alcazar, F., Romero-Fernandez, P. and Sanchez-Gardey, G. (2005) 'Strategic human resource management: integrating the universalistic, contingent, configurational and contextual perspectives', *International Journal of Human Resource Management*, Vol.16, No.5, 633–59.

Millar, M. (2004) 'HR must reduce bureaucracy to reduce business resilience', *Personnel Today,* 2 November 2004, 2.

Miller, P. (1987) 'Strategic industrial relations and human resource management: distinction, definition and recognition', *Journal of Management Studies,* Vol.24, No.4, 347–61.

Monks, J. (1998) 'Trade unions, enterprise and the future', in Sparrow, P. and Marchington, M. (eds) *Human Resource Management: The New Agenda,* London: FT/Pitman.

Morris, S. and Snell, S. (2009) 'The evolution of HR strategy: adaptations to increasing global complexity', in Wilkinson, A., Bacon, N., Redman, T. and Snell, S. (eds) *The SAGE Handbook of Human Resource Management,* London: Sage.

Mueller, F. (1996) 'Human resources as strategic assets: an evolutionary resource based theory', *Journal of Management Studies,* Vol.33, No.6, 757–85.

Nederlandse Vereniging van Participatiemaatschappijen (NVP)/Dutch Association of Investment Companies (2010) *De Nederlandse Private Equity Market in 2009, Ondernemend Vermogen*, Amsterdam: NVP.

Nolan, P. (2011) 'Money, markets, meltdown: the 21st-century crisis of labour', *Industrial Relations Journal*, Vol.42, No.1, 2–17.

Nolan, P. and Wood, S. (2003) 'Mapping the future of work', *British Journal of Industrial Relations*, Vol.41, No.2, 165–74.

*Noon, M. and Blyton, P. (2002) *The Realities of Work,* London: Palgrave.

Paauwe, J. (2004). *HRM and Performance: Achieving Long Term Viability*, New York: Oxford University Press.

Paauwe, J. (2009) 'HRM and performance: achievements, methodological issues and prospect', *Journal of Management Studies*, Vol.46, No.1, 129–42.

Paauwe, J. and Boselie, P. (2003) 'Challenging "strategic HRM" and the relevance of the institutional setting', *Human Resource Management Journal*, Vol.13, No.3, 56–70.

Paauwe, J. and Boselie, P. (2007) 'HRM and societal embeddedness', in Boxall, P., Purcell, J. and Wright, P. (eds) *The Oxford Handbook of Human Resource Management,* Oxford: Oxford University Press.

Parry, E. (2011) 'An examination of the e-HRM as a means to increase the value of the HR function', *International Journal of Human Resource Management*, Vol.22, No.5, 1146–62.

Pass, S. (2004) 'Looking inside the "Black Box": employee opinions of HRM/HPWS and Organisational Performance', BUIRA Conference, Nottingham University, 1–3 July.

Patterson, M., West, M., Hawthorn, R. and Nickell, S. (1998) 'Impact of people management practices on business performance issues', *Issues in People Management, No.22*, London: Institute of Personnel Management.

Pfeffer, J. (1994) *Competitive Advantage Through People,* Boston, MA: Harvard Business School Press.

*Pfeffer, P. (1998) *The Human Equation,* Boston, MA: Harvard Business School Press.

Pfeffer, J. and Veiga, J.F. (1999) 'Putting people first for organizational success', *The Academy of Management Executive,* Vol.13, No.2, 37–48.

Pollitt, C. (1988) 'Bringing consumers into performance measurement', *Policy and Politics*, Vol.16, 77–87.

Pollit, C. and Bouchert, G. (2011) *Public Management Reform: A Comparative Analysis of New Public Management Governance and the Neo-Weberain State,* Oxford: Oxford University Press.

Pritchard, K. (2010) 'Becoming an HR strategic partner: tales of transition', *Human Resource Management Journal*, Vol.20, No.2, 175–88.

Purcell, J. (1989) 'The impact of corporate strategy on human resource management', in Storey, J. (ed.) *New Perspectives on Human Resource Management,* London: Routledge.

Purcell, J. (1999) 'Best practice and best fit: chimera or cul-de-sac?', *Human Resource Management Journal,* Vol.9, No.3, 26–41.

Purcell, J. (2001) 'The meaning of strategies in human resource management', in Storey, J. (ed.) *Human Resource Management: A Critical Text* (2nd edn), London: Routledge.

Purcell, J. (2010) *Building Employee Engagement*, ACAS policy discussion paper. Available at: www.acas.org.uk.

Rainey, H.G. (1991) *Understanding and Managing Public Organizations*, San Francisco, CA: Jossey-Bass.

Robbins, C.J., Rudsenske, T. and Vaughan, J.S. (2008) 'Private equity investment in health care services', *Health Affairs*, Vol.27, No.5, 1389–98.

Rucci, A.J. (1997) 'Should HR survive? A profession at the crossroads', *Human Resource Management,* Vol.36, No.1, 169–75.

Saks, A.M. (2006) 'Antecedents and consequences of employee engagement', *Journal of Managerial Psychology*, Vol.21, No.7, 600–19.

Schuler, R.S. and Jackson, S.E. (1989) 'Determinants of human resource management priorities and implications for industrial relations', *Journal of Management,* Vol.15, No.1, 89–99.

Scullion, H. and Collings, D. (2010) 'Global talent management', *Journal of World Business*, Vol.45, 105–8.

Sengupta, S. and Whitfield, K. (2011) 'Ask not what HRM can do for performance but what HRM has done to performance', in Blyton, P., Heery, E. and Turnbull, P. (eds) *Reassessing the Employment Relationship,* London: Palgrave Macmillan.

Sheppeck, M.A. and Militello, J. (2000) 'Strategic HR configurations and organizational performance', *Human Resource Management,* Vol.39, No.1, 5–16.

Sisson, K. (2010) *Employment Relations Matter.* Available online at: http://www2/warwick.ac.uk/fac/soc/wbs/research/irru.

Snape, E., Wilkinson, A. and Redman, T. (1993) 'Human resource management in building societies: making the transformation?', *Human Resource Management,* Vol.3, No.3, 43–60.

Sorge, A. and van Witteloostuijn, A. (2004) 'The (non)sense of organizational change: an essay about universal management hypes, sick consultancy metaphors, and healthy organization theories', *Organization Studies,* Vol.25, 1205–31.

Sparrow, P. and Hilltrop, J. (1994) *European Human Resource Management in Transition,* London: Prentice Hall.

Sparrow, P., Hird, M., Hesketh, A. and Cooper, C. (2010) *Leading HR,* London: Palgrave Macmillan.

Sparrow, P., Scullion, H. and Farndale, E. (2011) 'Global talent management: new roles for the corporate HR function?' in Scullion, H. and Collings, D. (eds) *Global Talent Management,* New York: Routledge.

Stevenson, D.G. and Grabowski, D.C. (2008) 'Private equity investment and nursing home care: is it a big deal? *Health Affairs*, Vol.27, No.5, 1399–408.

Stewart, T. (1996) 'Taking on the last bureaucracy', *Fortune Magazine,* 105–8.

Storey, J. (1992) *Developments in the Management of Human Resources,* Oxford: Blackwell.

Storey, J. (ed) (1995) *Human Resource Management: A Critical Text,* London: Routledge.

*Storey, J. (ed) (2001) *Human Resource Management: A Critical Text,* (2nd edn), London: Routledge.

Storey, J. (ed) (2007) *Human Resource Management* (4th edn), London: Routedge.

Taylor, R. (2003) *Britons World of Work: Rights and Realities,* Swindon: ESRC.

Teger, A.I., and Cary, M. (1980) *Too Much Invested to Quit*, New York: Pergamon Press.

Thompson, P. and O'Connel Davidson, J. (1995) 'The continuity of discontinuity: Managerial rhetoric in turbulent times', *Personnel Review,* Vol.24, No.4, 17–33.

Torrington, D. (1993) 'How dangerous is human resource management?', *Employee Relations,* Vol.15, No.5, 40–53.

Torrington, D., Hall, L. and Taylor, S. (2002) *Human Resource Management,* London: FT/ Prentice Hall.

Torrington, D., Hall, L., Taylor, S. and Atkinson, C. (2011) *Human Resource Management*, (8th edn), London: FT Prentice Hall.

Truss, C. (2001) 'Complexities and controversies in linking HRM with organizational outcomes', *Journal of Management Studies,* Vol.38, No.8, 1121–49.

TUC (2007) *Survey of Safety Representatives,* London: Trades Union Congress.

Ulrich, D. (1997) *Tomorrow's Human Resource Management,* New York: Wiley.

Ulrich, D. (1998) *Human Resource Champions,* Boston, MA: Harvard Business School Press.

Ulrich, D., Brockbank, W., Johnson, D. and Younger, J. (2007) 'Human resource competencies: responding to increased expectations', *Employment Relations Today*, Vol.34, No.3, 1–12.

Vandenabeele, W. (2007) 'Towards a theory of public service motivation: An institutional approach', *Public Management Review*, Vol.9, No.4, 545–56.

van der Steen, M., Dicke, W., Karré, P.M. and van Twist, M. (2010), *De Weg van het Geld. Hoe Kapitaalstromen zich Verleggen en wat dat Betekent voor de Zeggenschap over Publieke Ddienstverlening*, Den Haag: Boom Lemma Uitgevers.

Wall, T.D. and Wood, S.J. (2005) 'The romance of human resource management and business performance and the case for big science', *Human Relations*, Vol.58, No.4, 429–62.

Walsh, J. (2009) 'Work life balance', in Wilkinson, A., Bacon, N., Snell, S. and Redman, T. (eds) *The SAGE Handbook of Human Resource Management*, London: Sage.

Watson Wyatt (2009) *Continuous Engagement: The Key to Unlocking the Value of Your People During Tough Times*, Work Europe Survey 2008–2009, London: Watson Wyatt.

Welbourne, T. (2011) 'Engaged in what? So what? A role-based perspective for the future of employee engagement', in Wilkinson, A. and Townsend, K. (eds) *The Future of Employment Relations: New Paradigms, New Approaches*. London: Palgrave Macmillan.

West, M., Borrill, C., Dawson, J., Scully, J., Carter, M., Anelay, S., Patterson, M. and Waring, J. (2002) 'The link between the management of employees and patient mortality in acute hospitals', *International Journal of Human Resource Management,* Vol.13, No.8, 1299–311.

Whitfield, K. and Poole, M. (1997) 'Organizing employment for high performance', *Organization Studies,* Vol.18, No.5, 745–64.

Wilkinson, A. (2005) 'Downsizing, rightsizing or dumbsizing? Quality, human resources and the management of sustainability', *Total Quality Management,* Vol.16, No.58/9, 1079–88.

Wilkinson, A. (2008) 'Industrial relations', in Clegg, S. and Bailey, J. (eds) *Encyclopaedia of Organizational Studies,* London: Sage, 652–3.

Wilkinson, A. and Fay, C. (2011) 'New times for employee voice?' *Human Resource Management*, Vol.50, No.1, 65–74.

Wilkinson, A. and Townsend, K. (2011a) 'The changing face of work and industrial relations', pp. 1–10, in Townsend, K. and Wilkinson, A. (eds) *Research Handbook on Work and Employment Relations,* Cheltenham: Edward Elgar.

Wilkinson, A. and Townsend, K. (eds) (2011b) *New Directions in Employment Relations,* Basingstoke: Palgrave.

Wilkinson, A., Dundon, T. and Marchington, M. (2012) 'Employee involvement and voice', in Bach, S. and Edwards, M. (eds) *Managing Human Resources,* Oxford: Blackwell.

Wilkinson, A., Bacon, N., Redman, T. and Snell, S. (2009) 'The field of human resource management', in Wilkinson, A., Bacon, N., Redman, T. and Snell, S. (eds) *The SAGE Handbook of Human Resource Management,* London: Sage.

Wilkinson, A., Bacon, N., Snell, S. and Redman, T. (eds) (2009) *The SAGE Handbook of Human Resource Management,* London: Sage.

Wood, S. (1999) 'Human resource Management and performance', *International Journal of Management Reviews,* Vol.1, No.4, 367–413.

Wright, M. and Bruining, H. (2008) 'Private equity and management buy-outs: international trends, evidence and policy implications', in Wright, M. and Bruining, H. (eds) *Private Equity and Management Buy-outs*, Cheltenham/Northampton: Edward Elgar.

Wright, P. and Snell, S.A. (2005) 'Partner or guardian? HR's challenge in balancing value and values', *Human Resource Management*, Vol.44, No.2, 177–82.

---

*Useful reading

CHAPTER 2
HUMAN RESOURCE MANAGEMENT AND ORGANISATIONAL PERFORMANCE: IN SEARCH OF THE HR ADVANTAGE

Nicholas Kinnie and Juani Swart

Introduction

Research into the links between HR practices and organisational performance has become one of the main areas, some would say *the* main area of study, in the field of Human Resource Management (Purcell and Kinnie, 2007). The claims made, especially in the mid-late 1990s, for the impact of HR practices on business performance raised the profile of the issue among practitioners and policy makers. However, debate rages among academics over these claims and their theoretical, empirical and methodological underpinnings. Indeed, Guest (2011: 3), in a recent review, notes that after 20 years of extensive research we are 'knowledgeable but not much wiser' about the links between HR and performance.

While some authors regard the evidence as the Holy Grail they have been searching for, others question the basis of the research (Legge, 2001). They say the research is too narrowly focused on business performance at the expense of other important measures such as employee well-being and corporate responsibility (Delaney and Godard, 2001; Janssens and Steyaert, 2009; Marchington and Grugulis, 2000). Others warn of the risks of methodological weaknesses and confusion which cast doubt on the robustness of the relationship between HR and performance (Paauwe, 2009; Purcell, 1999; Wright *et al.,* 2005).

It is not difficult to see the reasons for the increased interest in the field. Senior managers were looking for ways to improve their performance by becoming more flexible and responsive in markets that became increasingly competitive because of globalisation and deregulation (Becker and Gerhart, 1996; Boxall and Purcell, 2011). The rise of the knowledge economy where firms rely almost completely on their human and intellectual capital for their competitive advantage elevated the importance of people management still further (Swart, 2007). In this context, managers of HR saw the opportunity to demonstrate their contribution to the business more convincingly than in the past (Wright *et al.,* 2005). Some researchers in the field, it has been suggested, were motivated by the desire to demonstrate the policy relevance of their research (Legge, 2001).

It is against this background that we aim in this chapter to:

- place the debate over HR and performance in the wider context of strategy and HRM;
- Identify a suitable framework for analysing the HR and performance research;
- Review the research and evidence in this field critically;
- Consider the implications of cross-boundary ways of organising work for the links between HR and performance;
- Provide case study examples.

Strategy and HRM

We first need to place the HR and performance debate in its wider context of the links between strategy and HRM. These debates have consumed many person hours and we are consequently able only to scratch the surface.[1] We will, however, briefly discuss the various perspectives on strategy.[2]

The adoption of sets of HR practices is often thought to be strategic only if:

1   it contributes to organisational performance,[2] and in doing so
2   is aligned with the strategy of the organisation.

This leads us to question what strategy is and just what the variations in the alignment between the HR practices and the business strategy might be.

Boxall and Purcell (2011: 40) follow Mintzberg (1994) and differentiate between the firm's strategic plan and its strategy. They ask whether an organisation, especially a small organisation, which does not have a strategic plan and strategic objectives, can be said to have a strategy. The existence of a strategy and the ability to strategise will, of course, differ from industry to industry. In some industries the market conditions change at a faster rate than others: some are characterised by novel and complex problems while others are more predictable.

We need first to understand the ways in which HR strategy might vary (Swart *et al.,* 2004). The principal source of variation is the predictability of, and knowledge about, the environment. At one extreme, organisations will have a clear sense of how the environment may evolve. The environment in, for example, the public sector and industries with large capital costs of configuration change such as the energy industry, tends to be more stable or at least more predictable. At the other extreme, firms do not know whether their environment will change rapidly nor what may trigger a change in the environment. For example, research and technology firms may not be able to predict what the next wave of scientific discovery may be. Firms respond to uncertainty in demand by creating a spread of responses at as low a cost as is practicable in order to capture the demand that eventually emerges (Powell and Wakeley, 2003).

Each of these types of environment presents a different strategic paradigm and requirement for competence development (see Figure 2.1). First, the left-hand position represents the classic perspective which views strategy as a plan or a set of strategic objectives (Ansoff, 1965; Porter, 1985). Success or failure, according to this school of thought, is determined internally through operational detail of the strategic plan (Whittington, 2001). The more stable and predictable environment allows for environmental diagnosis, scenario-planning, gap analysis and forecasts with their relevant action plans. This approach to strategy

---

[1]Those looking for a more in-depth treatment are advised to consult Boxall and Purcell (2011).
[2]The link between HR and performance as it relates to strategy will not be discussed in this section as most of the chapter is dedicated to this exploration.

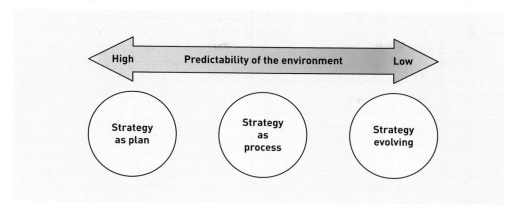

Figure 2.1
The strategy continuum

has been criticised severely in recent years, mainly because of the dynamic nature of global markets which call for flexibility. This raises the further question as to whether it is possible first, to write a strategic plan and second, to implement this as planned (Boxall and Purcell, 2011).

As we move along the continuum we arrive at a point which sees strategy as process. According to this viewpoint the strategy process changes continually as a result of ongoing learning across the organisation and is therefore more adaptable throughout its enactment.

According to Pettigrew (1973) strategy as a process is influenced by individual and collective cognitions and the interplay of power and politics at every organisational level. This approach is essentially more fluid with an emphasis on the enactment of strategy, as expressed through behaviours and cognitions. It is therefore more about *seeing* strategy than *planning* strategy.

This perspective can be illustrated by taking the example of a call centre whose customer relationship processes need to change considerably due to technological development and labour market shifts. The call centre may not know exactly how this technological development could impact upon its processes but a strategy can be enacted through developing relationships with the originators of advanced technologies (in response to technological change and in preparation for customer demands) and as customers make their decisions.

Finally, the other extreme of the continuum represents an evolutionary approach to strategy (Foss, 1994; Loasby, 1991; Powell and Wakeley, 2003). Here organisations operate in near-chaotic environments where change is typically too fast, too unpredictable and too implacable to anticipate and pre-empt and the advice is to concentrate on day-to-day viability while trying to keep options open (Whittington, 2001: 37). The strategic responses in these environments are characterised by a random generation of a spread of responses (since prediction is futile), together with a cost sensitive trialling of these responses and a planned retention of knowledge gained by that trialling. If we recall the example of the research and technology organisation that develops several research innovations to an unexpected buyer demands, we can see that the organisation can 'keep its options open' through the design and initial development of several offerings. These are then exposed to developments in the market, both through professional networks, scientific partnerships and through market testing. Through the process of gauging responses to possible compounds, for example, the organisation can learn more about its environment and therefore develops an ability to enact future strategies and reinvests the knowledge gained in the development process.

Each of the points on the continuum in Figure 2.1 has implications for competence development. The key focus for the first position is on the development of core competence that will enable the enactment of the strategic plan. Competence development is, therefore, specific and relatively narrow. The focus on competence development is more broadly defined at the mid-point in the continuum where there are several options to a relatively familiar but changing environment. For example, the focus could be on customer service or technology development but given the uncertainty it is impossible to define exactly which core competence will be needed to successfully compete in the marketplace. Finally, the right-hand position calls for a development of a more generic meta-competence that is related to multiple-offering development, trial analysis and fast response once the source of change is known. The level of the competence development is therefore higher compared with the previous two cases and the focus is even wider.

This continuum takes a knowledge-based view to strategy and represents the strategic paradigms accordingly. Several other methods of representation are possible including the strategic freedom perspective. Firms at each point along the continuum may experience various degrees of client pressure or influence upon their strategic choice. A large firm such as Toyota may not be in a position to plan for every eventuality but given its dominant position within its local network it has a greater degree of freedom of strategic choice (Kinnie *et al.*, 2005). Boxall and Purcell (2011: 50) argue it is important to steer between 'hyper-determinism' on the one hand and 'hyper-voluntarism' on the other. Firms therefore neither completely control their environment nor are they completely controlled by it. This is a general statement; we need to be aware of the varying degrees of freedom within and between industries that operate within each of the strategic paradigms. This has implications for the ways human resources are deployed and developed to achieve sustainable competitive advantage.

In this section we have considered the variety of forms that the links between strategy and HR might take. In particular, we have differentiated between three different links between strategy and HR by referring to a continuum based on the predictability of and knowledge about the environment. Having set the context through the consideration of strategy and HR we now turn our attention to how HR practices are linked to organisational performance.

HR and organisational performance: our approach and some background

Our aim is not to simply describe and evaluate all the available research in the field. This is a self-defeating task because the reader will quickly become lost in a mass of detail. Indeed, there are already a number of excellent detailed reviews to be found elsewhere (Becker and Gerhart, 1996; Becker and Huselid, 2006; Boselie *et al.*, 2005; Boxall and Purcell, 2011; Combs *et al.*, 2006; Delery and Doty, 1996; Guest, 2011; Huselid and Becker, 2000; Lepak, *et al.*, 2006; Paauwe, 2009; Purcell, 1999; Purcell and Kinnie, 2007; Purcell *et al.*, 2009; Wall and Wood, 2005; Wright and Gardener, 2000; Wright *et al.*, 2005). One recent review of the research (Wall and Wood, 2004) examined the 26 most cited studies published since 1994 and identified a number of characteristic features. Half were based in the industrial sector, most used a single respondent and were cross-sectional in design. Just over half the measures of performance were self-reported and were from the same source as the HRM measures.

We take a thematic approach to the research referring to key studies as illustrations. More importantly, we use a much needed theoretical framework based on the concept of Human Resource Advantage (Boxall, 1996; 1998; Boxall and Steeneveld, 1999) to guide us through the maze of research findings. We use this framework to examine the research thematically in the following way. The next major section outlines the concept of HR advantage and explains how it will be used to structure our analysis of the impact of HR policy and practice.[3] This is followed by an examination of the research into the two forms of

---

[3]Following Lepak *et al.* (2006: 221) we define HR policies as expressing the broad HR aims in particular areas, e.g. the commitment to pay for performance, whereas HR practices are the specific organisational actions designed to achieve specific outcomes e.g. profit sharing, individual appraisal related pay.

HR advantage referred to as Human Capital Advantage (HCA) and Organisational Process Advantage (OPA). The chapter concludes by considering the theoretical, methodological and practical implications of our discussion. Before all of this we need to give some of the background to our discussion.

Background to the research

There has been a long-standing, almost intuitive view that the performance of an organisation was affected by the way its employees are managed. Indeed, this was virtually an unstated assumption behind much of the early research into Scientific Management, the Hawthorne studies and Total Quality Management movement. However, much of this early work lacked a strategic focus (Golding, 2004; Legge, 1978).

Research in the US in the early-to-mid 1980s looked in a more focused way at the possible links between HR and performance. The texts by Beer *et al.* (1985) and by Fombrun *et al.* (1984) were thought to be particularly influential and in some ways represented a major leap forward in the area. These studies were not, however, based on empirical research and there were no attempts at this stage to measure performance in any well defined or systematic way (Truss, 2001: 1122).

It is only relatively recently that studies have explicitly focused on the performance issue and the data has been available and shown a positive relationship between the presence of key HR practices and organisational performance. Much of the recent interest can be traced back to the work of Huselid (1995) and Pfeffer (1994; 1998) in the US (which itself can be linked back to Peters and Waterman (1982)). The key work is that by Huselid (1995) who sought to measure the contribution of HR to performance in much more well defined and precise ways than in the past. Drawing on a survey of 968 US firms and taking financial performance (although other outcome measures were also used for example employee turnover and retention) as his dependent variable he used sophisticated statistical techniques to consider the impact of high performance work systems. Huselid found that 'the magnitude of the returns for investments in High Performance Work Systems is substantial'. Indeed, 'A one standard deviation increase in such practices is associated with a relative 7.05% decrease in (labour) turnover, and on a per employee basis, $27,044 more in sales and $18,641 and $3,814 more in market value and profits, respectively' (Huselid, 1995: 667). More recently, Huselid and Becker (2000: 851) claimed that 'Based on four national surveys and observations in more than 2,000 firms, our judgement is that the effect of a one standard deviation change in the HR system is 10–20% of a firm's market value.'

Research by Patterson *et al.* (1997) in the UK came up with similar findings. Drawing on research in 67 UK manufacturing businesses studied over time they found that 18 per cent of the variation in productivity and 19 per cent of profitability could be attributed to people management practices. These were a better predictor of company performance than strategy, technology and research and development.

Following the early research there have been over 100 studies looking at the links between HR and performance and many of these have focused on the links between HR practices and performance. Boselie *et al.* (2005) report that there were 104 articles in the area in refereed journals between 1994 and 2003. Despite this extensive effort the goal of establishing a clear link between HR practices and performance still seems some way off. As Purcell and Kinnie (2007: 533) noted 'numerous review papers… have found this field of research often wanting in terms of method, theory and the specification of HR practices to be used when establishing a relationship with performance outcomes'. Becker and Huselid (2006: 921) put the same point in a slightly different way, 'Despite the remarkable progress the field of SHRM may be at a cross-roads.'

These studies have stimulated an intense debate surrounding the very nature, purpose and outputs of the research (Hesketh and Fleetwood, 2006; Janssens and Steyaert, 2009; Keenoy, 1997; Legge, 1995; Paauwe, 2009;). However, before we explore the findings of this research in more detail we need to establish our framework for analysis.

Human resource advantage

Research in the field has often been criticised for an excessive emphasis on the quantitative analysis of data collected by the survey method. For example, when commenting on the early research Guest (1997: 264) noted that 'While these studies represent encouraging signs of progress, statistical sophistication appears to have been emphasized at the expense of theoretical rigour. As a result the studies are non-additive, except in a very general way.' Wood (1999: 408) in turn argued that 'The empirical work . . . has concentrated on assessing the link between practices and performance with increasing disregard for the mechanisms linking them.' Consequently Guest argued (1997: 263) 'if we are to improve our understanding of the impact of HRM on performance, we need a theory about HRM, a theory about performance and a theory about how they are linked'.

The work by Peter Boxall and his colleagues provides a way forward with their development of the concept of Human Resource Advantage (HRA) (Boxall, 1996; 1998; Boxall and Purcell, 2011; Boxall and Steeneveld, 1999). HRA is the series of policies, practices and processes that together contribute to the competitive advantage of the organisation. This advantage is comprised of a Human Capital Advantage (HCA) and an Organisational Process Advantage (OPA). There are various forms of capital which are critical to organisational performance (including human, social, structural, organisational, client and network capital – see Figure 2.2 for further details) and our discussion focuses on the generation of HCA which involves developing superior practices in key areas such as recruitment, selection, training and team building designed to ensure the best people are employed and these staff develop high levels of skill. However, HCA is unlikely to generate competitive advantage in the practices themselves because they are easily copied (Mueller, 1996). It is the processes and routines required to put these practices into operation as intended that are more difficult to replicate and form the OPA (Boxall, 1996: 67). These processes, such as team-based learning and cross-functional cooperation, develop over time, are socially complex and causally ambiguous (Boxall and Purcell, 2011: 103–4).

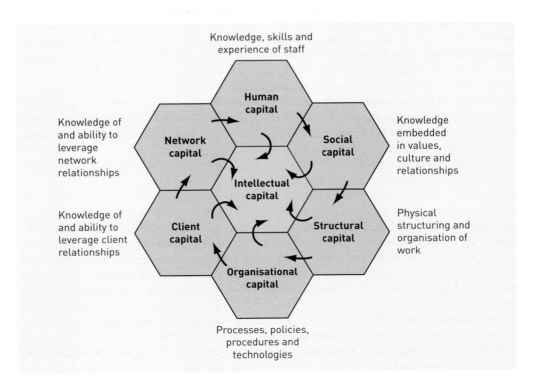

Figure 2.2
Forms of capital

Sources: Kinnie *et al.*, 2006; Swart, 2006.

Both HCA and OPA can generate competitive advantage, but they are most effective when they are combined together. The form of HR advantage is likely to change as the firm grows through the establishment, mature and renewal contexts (Boxall, 1998). Thus 'While knowledge of individual HR practices is not rare, the knowledge of how to create a positively reinforcing blend of HR philosophy, process, practice and investment *within* a particular context is likely to be very rare' (Boxall and Purcell, 2003: 86). This 'social architecture' is created and re-created at all levels in the firm and is therefore especially difficult to imitate (Mueller, 1996: 177).

For our purposes this creates a dual focus on the design and content of HR practices *and* the role of line managers and employees in putting these into action. We use this framework as a way of organising our discussion of the links between HR and performance. We look first at the research conducted into the influences shaping the HR practices that comprise the HCA. This can be broken down into two schools of thought typically referred to as 'best practice' and 'best fit'. Attention is then turned to studies of OPA looking at the role of employees and line managers.

Human capital advantage

Research into the impact of HR practices on performance can be divided into two groups. First, those who argue that a set of HR practices can be identified which can be applied in a wide variety of circumstances and will have a positive effect on business performance. The second view is that the effectiveness of HR practices depends on the external and internal context of the organisation. We review each of these using illustrations from the principal studies.

Best practice

There is a long history of researching individual best practices, for example psychology based research into psychometric testing (Boxall and Purcell, 2011: 86–7). What is new is the concept of looking for a combination or 'bundle' of practices which need to be combined together (Guest, 1997 Huselid, 1995; Lepak, *et al.*, 2006: 218; MacDuffie, 1995). Making changes to individual practices will, it is argued, have a very limited effect whereas making changes together will have a more powerful effect. This suggests there is a set of practices which can and should be adopted by firms which will lead to improvements in performance. In practical terms not only must firms become aware of these practices, but they also need support from top-level managers to adopt these practices. Researchers have also highlighted the need to avoid what they referred to as 'deadly' combinations, for example the introduction of individual performance pay and teamworking (Delery, 1998).

The terms for these bundles vary, indeed there is an array of acronyms used which seem designed to confuse the practitioner and the academic including HR System, High Commitment Management (HCM), High Performance Work Systems (HPWS), High Involvement Management (HIM).

These approaches seek to identify a distinctive set of successful HR practices that can be applied successfully to all organisations irrespective of their setting. Pfeffer (1994, 1998) developed a list of 16 best practices which were subsequently reduced to seven (1998). The seven practices are: employment security, selective hiring, self-managed teams/teamworking, high compensation contingent on organisational performance, extensive training, reduction of status differentials and sharing information.

Huselid (1995) argued that there needs to be an integrated system of work practices to fit the particular needs of the organisation. This research involved collecting data relating to the number of practices the firm employs by means of a postal questionnaire completed by a single respondent representing the company as a whole. The resulting analysis produced impressive results linking the number of practices and various forms of performance – typically profit and market value.

Research by Guest *et al.* (2003) drawing on a survey of 366 UK firms produced rather more mixed results. They found that increased use of HR practices was associated with lower labour turnover and higher profit per employee, but not with higher productivity. However, once profitability in earlier years is taken into account these associations ceased to be significant (Guest *et. al.*, 2003: 306). Thus the association between HR practices and organisational performance is confirmed, but there is no evidence to show that the presence of HR practices causes a change in performance (Guest *et. al.*, 2003: 307). Wright *et al.,* (2005) also found that virtually all of their significant correlations disappeared when controlling for past performance.

This type of research has a number of advantages because it focuses the debate on the role of HR practices but also raises various problems (Boxall and Purcell, 2011: 90–4; Purcell, 1999). Two kinds of problems have been identified: methodological and theoretical (Paauwe, 2009). Let us look at methodological problems first.

Methodological problems

Perhaps the easiest way of summarising the criticisms of this research is to pose a series of questions.

What is the direction of causation? It is possible that the direction of causation is in the opposite direction to that which is proposed since it may be only the successful firms that can afford these HCM practices (Guest *et. al.*, 2003: 309). Indeed, Wright *et al.* (2005: 432–3) argued for exercising 'extreme caution in inferring a direct causal impact on performance.' They suggest that dual causation provides a possible explanation for what they have observed: business units that perform well invest more in HR practices which pay off in terms of improved performance. There is also the possibility that respondents might believe that HR practices are good simply because the performance of their organisation is good (Gerhart, 1999: 42; Wright and Gardener, 2000: 8). Moreover, it is highly likely that there will be multiple causes of any improvement in performance and it is very difficult to unpick these satisfactorily.

What measures should be used? The measures of performance are typically narrowly focused on financial criteria with very few studies examining the broader issue of employee attitudes and well-being (Janssens and Steyaert, 2009). Similarly, there are issues over the extensiveness of HR practices: should they, for example, apply to all employees or only a selection? One study may examine whether the organisation has self-managed teams (i.e. yes or no), while another may look at the proportion of employees working in a self-managed team. Linked to this is the profound problem, discussed in more detail when we look at organisational process advantage, which has either been ignored or side-stepped by much of this research that the practices that are being so carefully counted are not actually implemented in practice.

How should the data be collected, analysed and presented? Many studies rely on postal surveys where the main problem is mis-reporting by single respondents who have limited knowledge of the extent and use of the practices themselves (Gerhart, 1999). Much of the research makes use of highly sophisticated statistical techniques that produce results that are hard for the practitioner, as well as many students and academics, to understand.

Theoretical problems

As we have mentioned there have been strong criticisms of the lack of theoretical development. This poses another set of questions which need to be addressed. Best practice for whom? Is there room for an employee voice in this discussion or is the emphasis simply on the perspective of shareholders and managers? (Boxall and Purcell, 2011: 85–6). Marchington and Grugulis (2000: 1105–6) consider the impact of these practices on employees and argue that these practices, such as teamwork or performance-related pay,

> which appear superficially attractive may not offer universal benefits and empowerment but actually lead to work intensification and more insidious forms of control; in other words quite different and more worrying interpretations from that portrayed in the 'upbeat' literature – such as that by Pfeffer.

They are in short 'nice words and harsh realities'.

Ramsey *et. al.* (2000) investigated the labour process explanation which argues that improvements in productivity are the result of the intensification of work using the data from the Workplace Employee Relations Survey (Cully *et al.,* 1999). However, they could not find support for either the labour process or the high commitment management explanations.

More generally the absence of an independent employee voice is noted (Marchington and Grugulis, 2000: 1119) reflecting more generally a set of unitarist assumptions underpinning Pfeffer's work. Thus emphasis tends to be on the psychology-based techniques such as recruitment and selection, training, performance appraisal and pay rather than those based on pluralist assumptions, for example employee involvement practices and collective bargaining.

Which practices should be included? It is relatively easy to spot so called 'bad' practices, for example the use of unstructured selection interviews or a poorly conducted performance appraisal. However, it is difficult to get agreement on what the good practices are, apart from the most obvious statements such as the need for careful planning. The lists of practices themselves vary (Boxall and Purcell, 2011: 90) and there is no agreement on what constitutes the best practices, such that 'studies of so-called high performance work systems vary significantly as to the practices included and sometimes even as to whether a practice is likely to be positively or negatively related to high performance' (Becker and Gerhart, 1996: 784). Guest and Hoque (1994), for example, list 23 practices, MacDuffie (1995) has 11 items and Pfeffer has seven. Marchington and Grugulis (2000: 1114) note that employment security is included by Pfeffer but not by a number of other authors; similarly the importance of employee voice varies: some include it but Pfeffer does in a very limited way. Arthur (1994) gives low emphasis to variable pay whereas Huselid (1995) and MacDuffie emphasise this (Truss, 2001: 1124). Consequently, both Boxall and Purcell (2011) and Youndt *et al.* (1996: 839) argue there is a need for this kind of research to be more selective in the way findings are presented.

Do you need all of these practices and are they all equally important? The argument put forward by MacDuffie (1995), based on bundles of HR practices, suggests that these practices need to be combined and just taking one or two are likely to be ineffective. Marchington and Grugulis (2000: 1112–5) argue that in practice we often find weak links between these practices or simply contradictory practices – one person's job security might be at the expense of another person's whether in the employing firm or a subcontractor.

Are all employees treated in the same way? Are these practices just reserved for a minority of supposedly core employees or are they applied to all (Marchington and Grugulis, 2000: 1117)? This is not just an issue of differences between manual and staff employees but applies more widely in times of the decline of the internal labour market and the externalisation of the workforce through sub-contracting and network relations. Early work into the 'flexible firm' suggested that employees would be treated differently based on how central they were to the core of the firm (Atkinson, 1984). More recent work by Lepak and Snell (1999), discussed below, also addresses this issue. There is also growing evidence that certain practices are more effective or at least more worthwhile for specific groups of employees (Becker and Huselid, 2011) which offers support for the contingency approach to HRM.

What is the level and unit of analysis? The question of the level and unit of analysis is an important one (Paauwe, 2009). In some cases the research has been carried out at the level of the corporate head office (Huselid, 1995) where the gap between HR practices, the employees they are intended for and performance is wide. Other research has collected data at the level of the business unit where the gap between the HR policy and performance data is narrowed (Wright *et. al.*, 2003). This issue is addressed to some extent by the sectoral studies discussed below.

If these practices are so effective why are they not used more widely? Evidence from the Workplace Employee Relations Survey (Cully *et. al.*, 1999) found that only 14 per cent of workplaces used HCM and while in the US (Osterman, 1994), only 35 per cent of firms used two or more HCM practices, a finding confirmed by Gittleman *et al* (1998). Guest *et. al.* (2000) found that only 1 per cent of their firms used three-quarters of 18 progressive practices and 20 per cent use less than a quarter. It is possible that just putting practices in on their own does not change very much leading to a loss of enthusiasm because of the difficulty in identifying results.

More generally Guest *et al.* (2000) tell us that there were relatively few firms in their survey that had an HR strategy and a long tail of firms who did not. They found that while two-thirds of firms rely on people as their source of competitive advantage only about 10 per cent gave people a priority above that of marketing and finance and in most companies people are not viewed by top managers as their most important asset.

How important is the context? Both national context where customers, laws, cultures and styles vary (Boxall and Purcell, 2011: 90–1) and organisational sectoral contexts pose questions about the suitability of these practices, although multinational companies will attempt to standardise their practices across countries (Boxall and Purcell, 2011: 92–3). There may well be circumstances where employers simply cannot afford these practices, most commonly in labour intensive organisations, where arguably the difficulty of controlling costs is greatest (Marchington and Grugulis, 2000: 1117).

To sum up, we can see from these questions that although the best practice view has gained a great deal of publicity because of the simplicity of the message it has also attracted widespread criticism. Indeed, Purcell (1999) has characterised research in this area as leading into a *cul-de-sac* where no forward progress is possible. Many of the critics argue that what works in one organisational setting, for example a small knowledge intensive firm, will be quite different to what is effective in another, for example a low cost manufacturing company, or an NHS Trust. This leads them to argue that in order to maximise performance managers must tailor their HR policies and practices to the contexts within which they are working – a view typically referred to as 'best fit'.

Best fit

This perspective is derived from the contingency view that argues that the effectiveness of HR practices depends on how closely they fit with the external and internal environment of the organisation. Business performance, it is argued, improves when HR practices mutually re-inforce the choice of competitive strategy. This is the concept of vertical integration between the competitive strategy, the objectives of the firm, the HR practices and individual objectives (Fombrun *et. al.*, 1984; Wright *et. al.*, 1994) and it helps to explain lack of diffusion because the appropriate practices will depend on the context.

There are different views on the importance of particular contexts: some stress the stage in the life cycle whereas others draw attention to the 'outer context' of the competitive strategy or the 'inner context' of existing structures and strategy (Hendry and Pettigrew, 1992). It is also important to note that it is not just the 'stage of growth/life cyle' which is important but also the size of the organisation. That is to say, a mature, small organisation would require a very different set of HR practices from those required by a mature multinational corporation.

Some authors (Baird and Meshoulam, 1988; Kochan and Barocci, 1985) argue that there needs to be a fit between the HR practices and the stage in the business life cycle. They suggest that the HR practices needed during the start-up phase are quite different from those needed during growth, maturity and decline. However, most organisations will have a series of products that are at different stages in their life cycles producing the situation familiar to many managers whereby certain parts of their business are growing whereas others are shrinking, producing quite different pressures on HR practices.

However, perhaps the best known examples of this perspective draw on analysis (Porter 1980) of the sources of competitive advantage (Miles and Snow, 1978; 1984; Schuler and Jackson, 1987) which argues that HR practices work best when they are adapted to the competitive strategy. Miles and Snow (1984) identify three types of strategic behaviour and link these to various HR practices: 'Defenders' will have narrow, relatively stable products and will emphasise internal, process-oriented training and internal pay equity; 'Prospectors' have changing product lines and rely more on innovation leading to the use of external recruitment, results-oriented compensation and external pay equity; 'Analysers' have changing and stable product lines leading them to use internal and external recruitment and pay equity measures and process-oriented performance appraisal.

Schuler and Jackson (1987) and Jackson and Schuler (1995) developed these approaches where they identified the different competitive strategies of organisations and the role behaviours which were needed with each of them. They drew attention to the different kinds of behaviours needed for innovation, quality enhancement and cost reduction and the types of HR practices which are needed to achieve these. For example a strategy based on cost leadership will result in minimal levels of investment in human capital with low standards for recruitment and poor levels of pay and training. In contrast a strategy based on innovation calls for HR practices that encourage risk taking and cooperative behaviour. Youndt *et al.* (1996) and Delery and Doty (1996) provide some support for this perspective.

The 'best fit' approach is well illustrated in studies carried out in a single sector where most firms are operating within the same industrial context. For example, Arthur (1994) demonstrated how steel mini-mills firms pursuing cost leadership business strategies adopted cost minimisation command and control type approaches. Those seeking product and quality differentiation pursued HCM or HPWS approaches with emphasis on training, employee problem solving, team working, higher pay, higher skills and attempts to create a work community. Batt and Moynihan (2004) found that HR practices emphasising investment in employees were more successful in the parts of the industry that required employees to exercise their discretion when they examined call centres in the US telecommunications industry.

Thompson (2000) carried out two surveys of firms in the UK aerospace industry. In 1997 he found that establishments with higher levels of value added per employee tended to have higher penetration of innovative working practices among their non-management employees. These workplaces were more likely to engage in specialist production for niche markets and employed a richer mix of technical and professional employees. Later work in 1999 revealed 'compelling evidence that firms introducing a greater number of high performance work practices have much improved business performance' (Thompson, 2000: 10). Firms moving from less than five to more than six innovative practices made a 34 per cent gain in value added per employee.

Other research has highlighted the influence of the network of relationships within which firms, especially knowledge intensive and professional service firms are working (Beaumont *et. al.*, 1996; Donnelly, 2011; Kinnie and Swart, 2012; Sinclair *et. al.*, 1996; Swart and Kinnie, 2003; Swart *et al.*, 2007). Firms form relationships with clients, suppliers and collaborators who will seek to influence the HR practices pursued by the focal firm both directly and indirectly (see Box 2.1 and Figure 2.3). These external parties influence HR practices directly, for example through shaping recruitment and selection criteria or through requiring certain types of training to be conducted, or indirectly by setting performance targets that can be reached only by adopting, for example, team-based forms of work organisation (Kinnie and Parsons, 2004). We explore these and other challenges emanating from this cross-boundary working below.

Box 2.1 HRM in practice   Tocris Cookson

Tocris Cookson, with 60 employees, is a specialist chemical company with experience in the synthesis of a wide variety of compounds. They employ teams of skilled chemists (mainly at post-doctoral level) and operate from one site in the UK and one site in the USA. HR practices in Tocris Cookson can be understood only in the context of the network in which they operate (see Figure 2.3 below).

Tocris Cookson's key clients are life science researchers at universities or other research institutes. In order to build these clients relationships and make the compounds they need to maintain very strong ties with large pharmaceutical companies, patent lawyers and academics in the field. Pharmaceutical firms often have patents on some of the chemicals that need to be synthesised, however these could lapse in an 8–10 year period. If a 'cool chemical is spotted' the patent rights need to be negotiated with the relevant firm. A senior manager in Tocris Cookson said, 'once our key to success was developing compounds, now it is building relationships'.

Relationships with universities also need to be maintained to:

(i) update employees' skills in the pharmacological discipline;
(ii) build client relationships, where the universities are often users of the compounds made;
(iii) build an external recruitment pool by making top performing research chemists aware of the business.

The process of building external relationships was regarded as 'an art' which could only be mastered over several years of experience: first as a doctoral chemist, then as a post-doctoral researcher and finally as a negotiator with major pharmaceutical firms.

Tocris Cookson recruits its employees during a post-doctoral placement at the company and this is often their first full-time employment. Managers regard this as a threat because of the majority of their workforce is young, highly qualified and mobile (single). The threat is managed through the strong organisational culture, which employees describe as a family or home away from home.

Most formalised HR practices originated from an elaborate HR policy, which was written by the part-time HR manager. The drive toward more formalised HR systems coincided with the company objective of 'becoming more corporate'. Within the set of formalised practices, performance management was central to other HR practices both practically, given its links to reward and development, and politically, because it influenced the career development of this group of knowledge workers. Furthermore, the performance appraisal process was questioned by research chemists and there was a push to develop an in-house system because it is particularly difficult to appraise the outcome of research. This resulted in sets of HR practices evolving from formalised practices that may have originated outside the firm to sets of practices that grew from within the community of knowledge workers.

Labour markets are also important because firms in certain industries and geographical areas find they have to compete much more intensively than others. Tight labour markets, for example where call centres are concentrated, will put pressure on particular HR practices such as recruitment and selection and reward (Kinnie *et al.*, 2000).

Others argue that HR practices need to fit with and complement other important strategies and structures within the organisation. Organisational size will be important – larger firms will have complex internal structures often with multiple layers and more generally just the resources needed to fund certain approaches, for example a formalised salary structure or recruitment scheme. The manufacturing strategy of the firm also needs to be taken into account (Baron and Kreps, 1999; Boxall and Purcell, 2011: 83; Purcell, 1999).

The best fit approach has been subject to extensive review (see Boxall and Purcell, 2011: 71–85; Purcell, 1999: 32 for further details). Perhaps the most basic point of all is the assumption that firms have a competitive strategy with which HR practices can fit (Legge, 1995; Ramsey *et al.*, 2000). The second and related point is that it is possible to typify the firms in the way that has been suggested. Purcell (1999) suggests this is unlikely for a variety of reasons. In practice, organisations may pursue a mix of competitive strategies for example

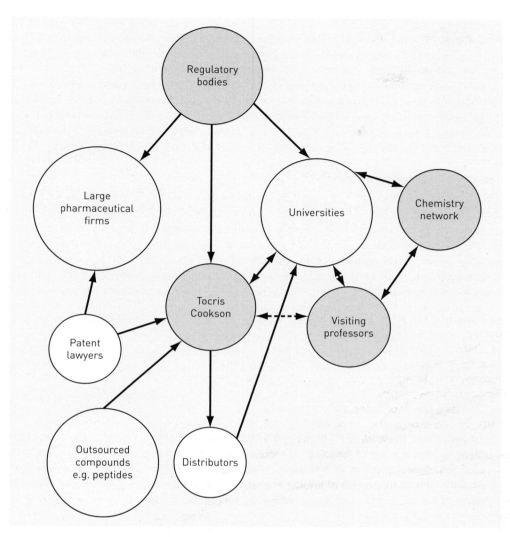

Figure 2.3
Tocris Cookson
network

seeking both cost leadership and differentiation leading to confusion over the most appropriate HR practices. Even if the firm does have a strategy, this view assumes that the one they have is the most appropriate for them. This may not be the case if firms do not have sufficient knowledge of their external environment or if they have misinterpreted the information that they have gathered.

Multiple contingencies

Perhaps the biggest problem is that most firms exist within complex external environments with multiple contingencies that cannot all be isolated or identified. There are particular problems with modelling the influences, with understanding what happens if the influences do not all pull in the same direction and with coping with change (Purcell, 1999: 34). This raises the issue of the dynamic fit between policy and context: if the external environment changes should firms keep changing their practices to fit the market circumstances? There are strong arguments against this because HR practices are quite slow to change. Consequently, Purcell (1999) has argued that firms seeking a best fit are effectively chasing a 'chimera'.

In response to criticisms of the best fit approach Wright and Snell (1998) argue for the need to have both fit and flexibility (Boxall and Purcell, 2011: 84). This is not just the ability to move from one best fit to another, but to be able to adapt to the situation where the need to change is virtually continuous. 'Flexibility provides organisations with the ability to modify current practices in response to non-transient changes in the environment' (Wright and Snell, 1998: 757). In particular, there is a need to achieve fit between the HR system and the existing competitive strategy while at the same time achieving flexibility in a range of skills and behaviours needed to cope with changing competitive environments.

More broadly, there may be some characteristics of successful organisations that are impossible to model, usually referred to as idiosyncratic contingency or causal ambiguity (Purcell, 1999: 35). These are the patterns and routines of behaving or the cultural norms that have been built up slowly over a long period associated with success. It may simply not be possible to disentangle what exactly are the key factors in success when looking at a large complex organisation.

Treating employees differently

The need to respond to external pressures creates problems of treating employees with consistency of treatment especially over time (Baron and Kreps, 1999). In reality, it is likely that a combination of practices will be needed depending on external circumstances: as products grow and decline there may need to be redundancies for some employees but also the need to retain good employees and to develop them (Boxall and Purcell, 2011: 79–82).

In response to some of these criticisms we have seen the development of the HR architecture model (Lepak and Snell, 1999). This is based on the configurational view which argues that it is unlikely that a company will use a single approach for all its employees (Becker and Huselid, 2011). It suggests that the best fit approach is too simple because there is a need to focus on combination or patterns of practices which are needed – putting horizontal fit together with vertical fit (Delery and Doty, 1996). Most organisations employ different groups of employees who will need to be treated differently and in effect there are different configurations of practices for different types of employees.

The Lepak and Snell model of HR architecture expresses these ideas in a more accessible form. They argue that,

> To date most strategic HRM researchers have tended to take a holistic view of employment and human capital, focusing on the extent to which a set of practices is used across all employees of a firm as well as the consistency of these practices across firms. We believe that the most appropriate mode of investment in human capital will vary for different types of capital. (*Lepak and Snell, 1999: 32; Lepak et al., 2011*).

Their model distinguishes between employees on the basis of the value they create for the organisation (the extent they contribute towards the creation of competitive advantage) and the extent to which their knowledge and skills are specific to that organisation (uniqueness).

This approach represents a step forward but also raises various questions. In particular there is the issue of consistency here: if an employer wishes to pursue an inclusive culture-based approach why should they treat employees differently? If certain activities are externalised there is a danger that the core competences of an organisation will be lost. There is also a moral issue here – why should different groups be treated differently?

Recent work (Purcell *et al.*, 2009) has examined this is in a slightly different way looking at the attitudinal outcomes such as organisational commitment and job satisfaction for different occupational groups (see Box 2.2 for further details).

Box 2.2 HRM in practice   Influences on the attitudes of different occupational groups

Much of the research assumes that the set of HR practices adopted will have the same effect on all employees who work for the organisation. We investigated this, drawing on an analysis of data drawn from the *Workplace Employee Relations Survey, 2004* (Kersley, 2006). We found[6] (Purcell *et. al.* 2009)

---
[6]We focused on the largest occupational group in each workplace.

that a different practice mix is associated with high levels of organisation commitment for different occupations. There are some practices (satisfaction with the work itself and with the level of managerial support) which seem to have a consistently positive influence on employee commitment across virtually all of the employee groups. However, there were other aspects of the work experience which were distinctively associated with particular work groups. Sales and customer service workers' commitment seemed to be closely tied to the flexibility of the job, whereas the role of line managers was unimportant. Pay satisfaction was important for skilled, personal service and elementary workers while teamwork was important only for the commitment of skilled and personal service employees. The role line managers was important for all employees other than sales and customer service work. Variables for job stress, career opportunities, job involvement and training were not associated with employee commitment. Further details of the most important HR practices for each group are given below (the shaded areas indicate that there are negative correlations between the HR practice and employee commitment).

Lower skill employees: elementary
Satisfaction with work itself
Satisfaction with pay
Trust managers

Lower skill employees: operatives
Expect long-term employment
Satisfaction with achievement
Relationships with managers
Job security
Satisfaction with work itself
Trust managers
Zero hours
Job sharing
PBR
Selection by performance tests

Sales
Zero hours
Satisfaction with work itself
Able to reduce FT to PT hours
Job security guarantee

Skilled workers
Zero hours contracts
Satisfaction with achievement
Satisfaction with pay
Satisfaction with work itself
Teamworking
Job challenge
Trust managers
Able to work term-time only
5 days training
Satisfaction with job security
Employee unease

Professionals
Ability to change work patterns
Select via performance tests
Satisfaction with work itself
Satisfaction scope to use initiative
Trust managers
Ability to work same hours
Zero hours contracts

In summary, we have considered the best practice and best fit approaches towards the generation of human resource advantage and examined the criticisms which have been made of these. It is possible, however, that these approaches can be reconciled. Boxall and Purcell (2011: 95–6) conclude that some general principles can be established, for example, on selection interviewing, but that practices themselves are likely to be influenced by best fit considerations at national and organisational levels. This combination of views remains, however, incomplete, because it is still looking only at the formal practices and we now need to consider how these practices are actually used.

Organisational process advantage

The key theme running throughout our discussion has been that the acquisition of HR advantage depends on developing both a capital and a process advantage (Purcell, 1999: 36; Boxall and Purcell, 2011: 17). We need to therefore understand how HR practices are actually translated into operation before we can begin to thoroughly understand the links between HR and performance. It is important to look at the routines and processes, or using another language, both the formal and informal practices which make up the day-to-day realities of organisational life.

Studying OPA is much more difficult than looking at practices because these processes are often tacit and intangible; they are immune to data collection by postal questionnaire and analysis by sophisticated statistical packages. In fact, OPA is only seen most clearly when it is absent, when things go wrong: there is infighting between departments, poor knowledge sharing within and between project teams, or people do not work to their full potential. The concept of OPA is derived from research carried out into the resource-based view (RBV) of strategy.

Resource-based view

This draws attention to the intangible assets of the firm which make up its distinctive competencies and organisational routines (Purcell, 1999: 35). The resource-based view (RBV) has developed from business strategy literature that competitive advantage is based on what is difficult to imitate not on what can be copied. There is a need to develop an exclusive form of fit. This is particularly important for knowledge intensive firms that rely almost entirely on their human and intellectual capital for their success and is effectively rebalancing an over dependence on the Porter approach (Boxall and Purcell 2011: 97–100). It also emphasises the importance of know-how-in-action (Swart, 2011) of human capital as a resource and re-introduces the human aspect of human resource strategy (Wright and McMahan, 2011).

The RBV involves looking at the internal resources of the firm and considering the ways in which HR can maximise their contribution to development of competitive advantage. This focuses on how human resources can become scarce organisation specific and difficult to imitate (Barney, 1991; Barney and Wright, 1998) and draws on the research into core competencies (Hamel and Prahalad, 1994).

In particular this view involves looking at how HR can develop the following (Barney and Wright, 1998; Golding, 2004: 51):

Value – how does the firm seek to distinguish itself from its competitors? What part does HR play in this?

Rarity – is the firm doing something with its employees that its competitors are not?

Inimitable – casual ambiguity means that the unique history of each firm makes it difficult to ascertain what causes the advantage and therefore make it difficult to copy.

Non-substitutability – these internal resources are integrated into coherent systems so advantage is sustainable and cannot be substituted by other resources.

Research into the resource-based view tends to be associated with unpredictable environments and emphasises what is distinctive. However, we need to remember that firms also need to have the base line characteristics right before developing distinctive characteristics, what Hamel and Prahalad (1994) and Boxall (1996) refer to as 'table stakes', the resources and skills needed simply to play the game. Once these have been established it is the differences between firms which are important. Truss (2001) notes one of the problems with the RBV is its emphasis on the importance of synergy and fit between the various elements of the HR system and asks how compatible is a systems-based approach with flexibility (Becker and Gerhart, 1996: 789).

Becker and Huselid (2006: 901) note, however, that 'the attention given to the independent influence of "implementation" in the strategy literature offers an opportunity to make the theoretical HR-performance link more concrete'. Indeed, they recall that Barney (2001: 54) notes that 'the ability to implement strategies is by itself a resource that can be a source of competitive advantage'. This also relates to the original conceptualisation of the RBV which emphasises the importance of managerial enactment and decision making.

If we are to examine the implementation issues in the HR context we need to consider what has come to be known as the 'black box' research.

Application to HR: examining the 'black box'

Becker and Gerhart (1996: 793) noted the importance of examining the implementation of HR practices when they argued that 'future work on the strategic perspective must elaborate on the black box between a firm's HR systems and the firm's bottom line'. Moreover, 'more effort should be devolved to finding out what managers are thinking and why they make the decisions they do' (1996: 794). This suggests we need to understand how and why HR practices influence performance and to move away from basic input–output models which have policy inputs on the left-hand side of the model and outcomes on the right-hand side (Becker and Huselid, 2006).

When we begin to look inside the 'black box' we find that there are differences between the espoused practices and the practices in use (Elorza *et al.*, 2011). Truss (2001) highlights the importance of the informal processes that exist alongside the formal practices drawing on her research in Hewlett Packard. There were clear gaps between what the company claimed they were doing and what was actually experienced by employees 'in areas such as appraisals and training and development the results obtained were not uniformly excellent; in fact some were highly contradictory' (Truss, 2001: 1143). Although the formal HP appraisal procedures rewarded employees' performance against targets related to the company's objectives 'informally what counted was visibility and networking if people wanted to further their careers' (Truss, 2001: 1144). Despite espousing the value of training less than half said they got the training they needed to do their job, fewer than half felt the appraisal system was working well and less than one third felt their pay was fair. 'These are all examples of a strong disconnect between the "rhetoric" of human resource management as expressed by the human resource department, and the reality as experienced by employees' (Truss, 2001: 1143). This 'highlights the importance of the informal organisation as mediator between policy and the individual' (Truss: 2001: 1144).

These findings were repeated in a study of 12 organisations where there was a clear gap between formal HR policy statements and actual practice in areas such as performance appraisals, training, involvement and communication (Purcell *et al.*, 2003, 2009). For example in organisations which claimed to have formal employee involvement schemes (such as team briefs) for all their employees, not all staff were aware of the existence of these initiatives and an even lower proportion of employees claimed to have been practically involved in such schemes (Hutchinson and Purcell, 2003: 36).

Research into formal and informal practices (Brown, 1972, 1973; Terry, 1977) has a long tradition in the industrial relations literature and sheds important light on contemporary concerns about the key processes involved. This makes a focus solely on formal practices inappropriate, and in particular we need to consider the role of the 'individual manager as agent, choosing to focus his or her attention in varying ways' (Truss, 2001: 1145). We consider this by looking at discretionary behaviour. However, we first need to examine the role of employees when engaging in discretionary behaviour.

Employee discretionary behaviour

The importance of employee discretionary behaviour has been highlighted by research in the US steel, clothing and medical equipment industries (Appelbaum *et al.*, 2000). Drawing evidence from shop floor employees and managers as well as a study of formal HR practices, Appelbaum and her colleagues found that the willingness of employees to engage in discretionary behaviour depended on the creation of opportunities to participate, skill development and motivation and incentives (Appelbaum *et al.*, 2000: 118–20).

Their most important finding was that the positive effects of HPWS on plant performance were felt through increased discretionary effort by employees and an improved knowledge accumulation. These practices had a different effect on performance in different industries (Appelbaum *et al.*, 2000: 227). In steel there was evidence that quality and employment security raised 'up time' by 8 per cent, incentives by 13 per cent and work organisation by 14 per cent and HPWS as a whole by 17 per cent (Appelbaum *et al.*, 2000: 108). In clothing, modular production involving self-directed teams reduced sewing time by 94 per cent and led to substantial cost savings. In medical equipment, the opportunity to participate is closely linked to value added per dollar and profits and quality (Appelbaum *et al.*, 2000: 108). The likelihood of employees engaging in this discretionary behaviour is also influenced by the role of line managers.

Role of line managers in bringing practices to life

Recent research has examined how the discretionary behaviour of managers, especially first line managers contributes towards the development, or absence, of an organisational process advantage.

Over the last decade numerous studies have observed how line managers have played a more prominent role in the delivery of HR practices such as performance management, team leadership and communications as an increasing number of people management activities have been devolved to them (Hutchinson and Wood, 1995; Larson and Brewster, 2003; Renwick, 2000). The important role of line managers has been identified by Marchington and Wilkinson (2002: 232–7) and earlier work on the 'forgotten supervisor' (Child and Partridge, 1982; Thurley and Wirdenius, 1973) and the role of the line manager in the emergence of informal practices (Armstrong and Goodman, 1979; Brown, 1972, 1973; Terry, 1977).

Recent studies (Purcell and Hutchinson, 2007; Purcell *et al.*, 2003, 2009) show that the way line managers implement and enact HR practices by 'bringing them to life' and show leadership strongly influences employees' attitudes. Employees' perceptions of line management behaviour (in terms of how they carry out their HR activities such as responding to suggestions from employees) was the most important factor in explaining variations in both job satisfaction and job discretion – or the choice people have over how they do their jobs. There is also evidence that a pattern can be traced between line manager activities, employee attitudes and the performance of comparable business units and in changes over time.

Bartel (2000) examined these issues in the banking industry in Canada and found that when controlling for environment and branch and managerial effects that the HR environment (as measured by the quality of feedback and communications) has a significant positive effect on loan sales. Although there were common HR practices, it was clear that there was discretion over how these were applied. One standard deviation increase in managerial effectiveness accounts for a 16–26 per cent increase in loan sales. Thus the discretion exercised by branch managers has a direct effect on performance through the education and motivation of branch staff.

These differences between 'espoused' and 'enacted' practices can be partly attributed to the line manager for a variety of reasons (Hutchinson and Purcell, 2003; Marchington, 2001; McGovern *et al.*, 1997; Purcell and Hutchinson, 2007). Line managers may suffer from work overload partly because of organisational restructuring and the demise of the middle manager and simply lack the time to carry out all their duties. They may have inadequate training on how to operate the practices, lack commitment to them (Marchington, 2001), be doubtful about the claimed benefits, or simply be ignorant of what is expected of them.

In an attempt to analyse this role, Purcell *et al.* (2009) develop a model which places the discretionary behaviour exercised by line managers at the centre of the analysis, as shown in Box 2.3 and Figure 2.4. In particular, it sees the link between HR practices and performance as being the interaction between line manager behaviour and employee attitudes and behaviour. Line managers are important because of the key role they play in the generation of operational process advantage: most employees experience work through their contacts with their immediate team and their team leader.

Box 2.3 HRM in practice   HR causal chain model

Many attempts to link HR policy and performance pay insufficient attention to the linking mechanisms. We draw on the work of Appelbaum *et al.* (2000) MacDuffie (1995) and Wright and Nishii (2004) to identify the key causal steps in the chain from intended HR practices to performance outcomes (Purcell *et al.,* 2009).

The model has the following key features:

- *Intended HR practices* are those designed by senior management to be applied to most or all of the employees and concern employees' ability, motivation and opportunity to participate. These practices will be influenced by the articulated values of the organisation and found in the HR manual or the appropriate web pages. These also include the ways work is structured and organised since this has an impact on employee attitudes and behaviour.
- *Actual HR practices* are those which are actually applied, usually by line managers. There may often be a substantial difference between the espousal and the enactment of HR practices in an organisation (Hutchinson and Purcell, 2003).
- *Experienced HR practices* requires that attention is focused on how employees experience and then judge the HR practices that are applied to them. What they perceive may be different, or the same, as intended and may be judged through a lens of fairness and organisational justice.
- *Attitudinal outcomes* include attitudes employees hold toward their job, and their employer and/or levels of morale or motivation. This especially includes employees' willingness to cooperate and their overall satisfaction with their job.
- *Behavioural outcomes* flow in the main from these attitudinal dimensions. This can be learning new methods of working, engaging in behavior which is beyond that required, such as organisational citizenship behaviour (OCB) (Coyle-Shapiro *et al.,* 2004), or seen in levels of attendance and remaining in the job (or their opposites).
- *Performance outcomes* can be distal or proximal and can be restricted to short-term definitions of performance or can be expanded to include measures of effectiveness.

More precisely the model draws attention to:

- The need to distinguish between intended HR and actual HR practices as experienced by employees;
- The key role played by line managers in the interpretation and implementation of HR practices;
- The link between experienced practices and employee attitudes and behaviours;
- The choice of performance measures that have meaning and significance for the companies and are close to the employee attitudinal data;
- The importance of organisational culture.

The key role played by line managers opens up further lines of inquiry concerning how these line managers are themselves managed. Research (Hutchinson and Purcell, 2003) suggests that the key factors influencing line managers' commitment and job satisfaction and their willingness to engage in discretionary behaviour are their relationships with their line managers and the existence of career opportunities. In addition, work–life balance, the ability to discuss problems with their managers and job security are associated with organisational commitment, while involvement is linked with job satisfaction (Hutchinson and Purcell, 2003: 48; Hutchinson and Purcell, 2007).

More broadly this suggests that the values and culture of the organisation can be a form of organisational process advantage. There are positive links between this form of OPA and organisational commitment, for example, employees in firms which exhibit 'strong values' or who have a clear, well established Big Idea have higher levels of commitment compared to employees in firms without these values (Purcell *et al.*, 2003, 2009). Box 2.4 provides more details of this. This supports the argument made by Barney (1986: 656) some time ago that 'Firms with sustained superior … performances typically are characterised by a strong set of core managerial values that define the way they conduct business.'

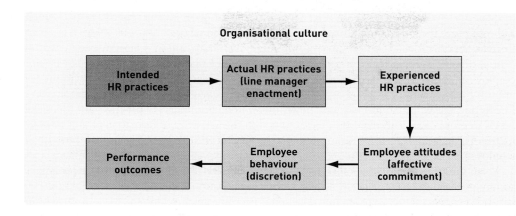

Figure 2.4
HR causal chain
model

Source: Purcell *et al.*,
2009.

Box 2.4 HRM in practice   The Big Idea

In some companies it is not just the senior managers but also employees at all levels who identify strongly with the values and mission of the organisation. We came to call this 'the Big Idea' since it seemed there was something simple or easy to explain that captured the essence of the firm and clearly informed or enthused HR policy and practice. The essence of this is:

'A clear sense of mission underpinned by values and a culture expressing what the firm is and its relationship with its customers and employees'.

The Big Idea had a number of attributes:

- **Embedded** – it was embedded throughout the organisation, for example quality in Jaguar;
- **Connected** – it connected, and derived from the same root, the way customers were treated and employees managed, for example mutuality in Nationwide;
- **Enduring** – it was enduring, not a flash in the pan, not the product of a board discussion on an away day and had clear historical roots, for example a long standing commitment to 'have fun and make money' in AIT;
- **Collective** – it was encapsulated in routines about the way work was done and people behaved. In that sense it was collective, combining people in processes and routines in the sense of a taken for granted, everyday activity as seen in Nationwide;
- **Measured and managed** – it was measured and managed often using broad measures of performance as we found in Selfridges.

Source: Purcell *et al.*, 2009.

Changing ways of working: the challenge to linking HR practices and organisational performance

Our discussion of the links between HR and performance needs to be placed within the context of contemporary ways of organising. Recent changes present a series of challenges to those seeking to connect HR practices and organisational performance (Capelli, 2008). As organisations operate within the knowledge-based economy they are typically part of complex networks made up of various parties such as clients, suppliers and partners (Alvesson, 2004; Kinnie and Swart, 2012; Kinnie *et al.*, 2006; Swart, 2007). They rely not only on their own human capital to generate valuable outputs such as client solutions but they are increasingly reliant upon inter-organisational resources to create sustained competitive advantage. Work tends to be organised into projects which span the boundaries of the firm and employees are engaged intensively in network-based activities.

This presents challenges to linking HR practices and organisational performance which are even more profound than those found in more traditional organisations where it is easier to create a single focus of employee commitment. Firms may find they employ people whom cannot directly manage (outsourced) and conversely they manage people whom they do not employ (in-sourced). In this context we therefore need to reassess our notion of the boundary of both the firm and of HR and adapt the HRM models accordingly to ensure that they are fit-for-purpose within and across that newly understood boundary. In practice, HR therefore needs to cross organisational boundaries to match the activities of human capital it is seeking to manage. This has implications at both the level of the organisation and the individual employee.

From the organisational perspective, the focus of the HRM model is therefore no longer simply on seeking to manage employees within organisational boundaries. Success now depends on being able to leverage human capital (Wright and McMahan, 2011) both within and across organisational boundaries. This presents a profound challenge to both HR and line managers. In practice, they have to manage (i) staff who are employed by their firm but over whom they do not have control – which is often found in a matrix context; (ii) agency and self-employed staff and (iii) staff working for partners, suppliers and clients who are collaborating on a project. This challenges many of the taken-for-granted assumptions about the use of traditional HR practices such as reward and performance management. In a cross-boundary environment many of these authority-based levers are simply irrelevant. Instead, HR and line managers find they have to rely on the management of lateral rather than hierarchical relationships – something for which they may be ill-equipped by traditional management training and development programmes. Similar challenges exist in organisations which rely heavily on the work of volunteers such as charities. Again, few of the traditional HR instruments are relevant here and emphasis is placed on developing commitment to the organisation through attachment to values, beliefs and principles.

Employees working across organisational boundaries interact with a series of representatives from external parties including clients, partners and suppliers. This creates the opportunity for them to become committed to these parties rather than to the organisation which employs them (Kinnie and Swart, 2012). Indeed, these parties may be competing for the commitment of these employees. Furthermore, in some cases, such as consulting, we might refer to employees occupying a liminal space where they are 'betwixt and between' organisations (Tempest and Starkey, 2004). They are at the limits of existing social structures which breeds ambiguity for those spanning organisational boundaries (Tushman and Scanlan, 1981). Whereas more traditional employees could tie their identity to their organisation the 'networked citizen' anchors their identity in their 'skill' and thus puts employability before loyalty to an organisation. Employees occupying this liminal space may experience a sense of freedom but also insecurity and an absence of trust. Lacking traditional organisational ties they may find themselves floating between their firm and their client, but anchored to neither. This in turn may reduce their willingness to engage in extra role behaviour towards their employer. We can identify four types of situations where employees are operating in this cross-boundary environment.

The first type is where organisations operate in a relatively traditional environment but find they are interacting extensively with clients who are vital to their success: a situation typically found in marketing and advertising agencies. These firms seek to leverage a strong set of organisational values and culture which form the foundation of the portfolio of HR practices. Work is usually organised in a series of project teams based around the client campaign. Projects teams may be anything from 2–25 people and may last for a few weeks to several years. Various groups of employees belong to project teams including creative staff such as art directors and copywriters, account handlers, planners and strategists. Some employees will be members of multiple project teams. Interaction with the client will vary – in some instances it will be frequent and intense, in others relatively intermittent. Managers, including those in HR, face a series of challenges in these circumstances. First, they have to ensure that all the project teams are adequately resourced – not always an easy task when the demands from clients fluctuate. Second, they have to balance the needs of all the relevant parties: the clients, the employees and the need for the firm to achieve their financial targets. In particular, they have to encourage the employees to put the interests of the clients first, but at the same time staying loyal to the firm. The example of Mother (see Case study 2.1) provides excellent insights into the way in which this is achieved.

The second type is the situation where a firm employs people whom they do not manage; this is commonly found in outsourcing organisations. In this situation a firm will provide services such as facilities management, IT and HR to a series of clients. In some instances this may involve the employees of the firm working on the client site and alongside client employees. Indeed, the firm employees will be providing a service directly to managers from the client firm. Thus the client finds it is managing people whom it does not employ. This presents a serious challenge to generating organisational commitment: the firm employees will experience the client site on a day-to-day basis and may have relatively little contact with their employer. The case of Alexander Mann Solutions (see Case study 2.2) provides a good example of how this situation can be managed successfully.

The third type is where firms collaborate together to produce a particular project output. Professionals from individual firms, such as engineers, independent contractors and regulators often collaborate in a network where they work as an integrated project team. One such example is where defence contractors may collaborate to build a new warship. The individual partners may work together on a shared physical site and will often share domain knowledge such as naval engineering. The nature of this networked way of working often requires long-term commitment to the integrated project team. The advantage for the individual firm is that their employees will gain exposure to cutting-edge industry knowledge which could then be integrated into the firms. The danger is, however, that the integrated project team becomes such a focal point for the professionals and their knowledge consequently becomes so specialised that it cannot be integrated into their firm.

The final type of networked working is the most advanced and the core characteristic is the sophisticated nature of integration of the various network parties. The professionals from the various firms will work together so closely that a separate, partly virtual, organisation will be established to direct their interaction. The Marks and Spencer case study (see Case study 2.3) provides a good example of this kind of networked activity where a series of management structures and HR practices were developed to hold the network together. Individuals would therefore identify with their employing organisation, but would also hold a very strong identification with the separate networked organisation. In this context, the cross-boundary team represents an organisation in its own right and would have sets of HR practices that exist at the level of the network and therefore ensures the sustainability of the cross-boundary organisation. The advantage of this advanced form of networking is the efficiency and the 'ease' of collaboration which it facilitates via the shared identity which it establishes. The risk is that employees may seek employment opportunities with other collaborators in the network. This may lead to a loss of human capital for the employing firm.

Conclusions and implications

We have examined research into the links between HR and performance using the concept of HR advantage. This has highlighted the importance of gaining both a human capital and a process advantage. Our discussion has implications for method, theory and practice.

The methodological debates referred to here are likely to continue. The approach based on the sophisticated analysis of quantitative data collected by questionnaires is likely to remain popular, especially where it is supported by a wider research tradition and higher education infrastructure as in the US. However, the implication of this discussion is that this approach is unlikely to gain insights into the organisational processes that are clearly crucial to successful organisations. Indeed, Becker and Huselid (2006: 915) argue that,

A clearer articulation of the 'black box' between HR and firm performance is the most pressing theoretical and empirical challenge in the SHRM literature. This requires a new emphasis on integrating strategy implementation as the central mediating variable in the HR-performance relationship.

These critical processes and routines can only be effectively examined by means of the case study approach. However, the problems of generalisability of case study findings will remain. One possible way forward is the collection of a combination of quantitative and qualitative data perhaps within a restricted number of industries (Paauwe, 2009).

A whole series of theoretical issues are thrown up by our discussion. Perhaps the most basic issues of all revolve around questions such as: What do we mean by performance? Whose performance? How do we measure this? Delaney and Godard (2001) have argued it is time for the research to move outside the narrow confines of financial performance. Not only should the narrow measures of organisational performance be broadened, but also concern should be given to wider measures such as employee well-being. This also points to the need to move away from the assumption that all employees are treated in the same way. Becker and Huselid (2006: 908) argue that research needs to focus on the level of the business process because this is where strategic value is created, not at the level of the firm. This, in turn, means greater attention needs to be given to the differentiation of HR practices to support these business processes which again takes us back to the importance of implementation since 'Designing an HR system with greater differentiation is not the problem. The challenge is motivating line managers to implement these systems' (Becker and Huselid, 2006: 919).

We also need to explore the concept of HR advantage in more detail, particularly the sources of organisational process advantage or disadvantage. We need to understand more clearly why gaps between espoused and operational policy emerge and what the consequences of this are for all parties. If line managers are critical to this, we need to know more about how they are managed and what factors influence their attitudes and behaviour. This raises the much broader issue of widening the focus of study away from human resource management to people management (Purcell and Kinnie, 2007: 543). From the tendency to study formal HR practices to a range of factors that impinge directly on the employee experience of work and which trigger discretionary behaviour. This would include the role of line managers in the operation of policy, the cultural context and work organisation and job design.

The policy implications of this discussion are profound. The 'best fit–best practice' debate has largely been sidelined by the realisation that both fit and flexibility are needed. The most likely way of getting this is by employing staff who carry out the HR practices most closely to the way that they were intended. More generally, the implication is that simply developing the appropriate practices is not in itself going to be enough because HR advantage also depends on how these practices are implemented. Consequently, looking for a link between HR practices and performance is a misguided activity because the main focus needs to be on the links between policy, practices, processes, implementation and performance.

This focus on process has potential benefits for HR specialists because these processes have to be carefully developed internally and cannot simply be copied from a textbook in the way that practices might be. Here the HR practitioner role becomes key because the development of what we might call 'best processes' can become a core competence which is embedded within the thinking and acting of the organisation such that it cannot be imitated or outsourced.

CASE STUDY 2.1

MOTHER LONDON

NICHOLAS KINNIE AND LOUISE HOPPER[4]

Background

Mother London is a creative organisation employing around 280 people and part of Mother Holdings which has 20 companies with around 700 people including freelancers. Established in 1996, Mother works with around 40 clients including a number of high-profile brands. It is independently owned by its seven partners who include the three founding partners. Mother's main outputs are producing commercials for television, and cinema as well experience events and some online output. Not experienced an experience event is the actual term – highly participative marketing events. It has also developed creative ideas in addition to traditional advertising including an award winning feature film, graphic novels and various 'house projects' such as the 'uncarriable carrier bags'. It has an extremely high reputation for its creative output and was recently voted Agency of the Decade by *Campaign* magazine.

Core principles

Mother is characterised by a series of core principles which reflect the beliefs of its founders and have a profound effect on how it is managed and structured and the relationships it has with its employees and clients.

Quality of creative output

Creativity is the essence of Mother. The quality of the creative output is at the heart of everything that Mother produces. In the words of one of the founding partners, 'it's what comes out of the door that matters' while another senior manager said 'Mother stands for creativity'. Since its foundation, Mother has become the destination brand for creative people who are attracted by the opportunity to work alongside people who have a high reputation for creativity and to work with well known clients.

Holy Trinity of values

This emphasis on the quality of output is reflected in what is referred to as the 'Holy Trinity' within Mother – essentially a statement of values which underpins how they work. It is these values which set their priorities and drive their relationships with employees and clients. These values are:

- Produce high quality creative output;
- Have fun;
- Make money;

Ways of organising

Mother have a distinct way of organising and working with clients which is unlike other creative and advertising agencies. In many other agencies there will be a group of staff known as Account Handlers or Client Services (sometimes referred to as the 'suits') which act as the 'go-between' between the creative staff (the T-shirts) and the client representatives. Mother has dispensed with this group preferring that their creative staff, their strategists and their producers have direct contact with clients.

Ways of working

Mother is characterised by a highly collaborative style of working which involves both specialists and non-specialists being involved in the creative process. In particular, there is a high degree of flexibility and permeability between the various skill groups. Staff often perform multiple roles and will move frequently between different teams. Moreover, a problem-solving approach is adopted which often involves multiple solutions being developed of which one is selected.

Joint ownership of creativity

In an industry which is often accused of pandering to the highly individualistic prima donnas who build personal portfolios at the expense of others, Mother promotes joint ownership of creative output. Rewards and recognition are attributed to Mother collectively rather than to individuals.

Brand teams

The brand teams are at the heart of the creative process and are responsible for running campaigns and managing relationships with clients. These teams are dedicated to a particular client, brand or campaign and are typically composed of:

---

[4]Group Head of HR, Mother Holdings Ltd.

- **Creatives** – these include copywriters, art directors and Creative Directors;
- **Strategists** – who are responsible for the development of strategy;
- **'Mothers'** – who co-ordinate the team activities;
- **'Nannies'** – who manage the relationships and logistics of the team.

These Brand Teams then work with a series of internal and external parties in order to produce work for clients. These include the television editing suite, Finance, HR and Office Management, each of which has a Discipline Head, and with a whole set of external television producers.

However, it is the way Mother works with clients which is particularly distinctive. Members of the brand teams work alongside the client representatives to focus on the problem; they see the client as part of the solution to the shared problem rather than the problem. In the words of one senior manager 'our way of working is designed to work *with* the client rather than *for* the client...agencies are often seen to be at the beck and call of clients whereas we are not afraid to turn around and say no.'

Forms of capital

We can consider the key resources, or forms of capital, upon which Mother draws to develop its creative output. In particular we can consider their human, social and organisational capital.

Human capital

The core principles of Mother mean that they are completely reliant upon the quality of their human capital for their success, indeed they can be said to adopt a 'talent-or people-centric approach'. The staff themselves have very high reputations in the industry built up over many years and they are highly skilled and experienced. They tend to employ staff who have gained some experience elsewhere and are attracted to work at Mother because of the people who already work there. In the words of one senior manager, 'they need to have a passion for creativity, they need to be inquisitive, be up for a challenge, have an edge about them and a conviction about what they do'. However, they also need to be 'tenacious and get stuff done. They need to be right and left brain people. And although they need to be ambitious – they also need to have humility.'

Social capital

The core principles and especially the 'Holy Trinity' of values mean that the culture of the organisation plays a key part in Mother's success. The fit with the organisation culture, which gives priority to creativity, is absolutely essential; in essence this commitment is the glue that holds Mother together. Without this it would be impossible to convert the knowledge, skills and experience of its staff into valuable client outputs. The result is a high level of emotional attachment to the work produced.

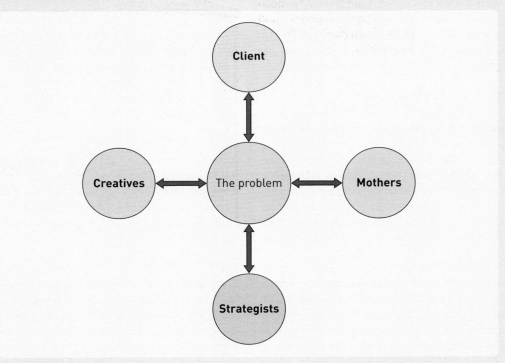

Figure 2.5 Ways of working with clients

Organisational capital

The structures, procedures and processes also reflect the core principles of Mother. The organisation structure itself is relatively flat with only three levels, but more importantly there is a high level of interaction between the partners and more junior staff. One distinctive characteristic is the way in which staff are physically located. Not only is the work space open plan, but many staff are not physically located within what in a more traditional organisation would be their function or department. The Head of HR is just as likely to be sitting next to a creative as someone from Finance. Moreover, staff are rotated between their allocated spaces every eight weeks to allow a wide range of relationships to be formed and contribute to the development of social capital.

People management practices

People management responsibilities are shared between three groups of staff: Discipline Heads; the HR team and the Partners. These practices make a direct contribution to the success of Mother.

Resourcing

External recruitment is mostly in the hands of each Head of Discipline who work with the Partners to identify suitable staff. Although some use is made of agencies, most newcomers are recruited through the extensive personal networks of senior staff. The selection process involves the Heads of Discipline and the Partners with most emphasis placed on the applicant's portfolio of work. A cultural fit is also extremely important and considered when hiring. The HR team deal with the unsolicited applications and internships.

The internal allocation of creative staff is made by the Head of Creative Resource in collaboration with the Partners. The task here is to balance the needs of the employees for interesting and challenging work and the clients who want to work with the best possible staff. Senior staff are very aware of the risk of their best staff being poached by competitors.

Training and development

There is a mix of formal and more informal training opportunities. Although a budget is set aside for formal training for each employee there are no formal, routine training programmes. Instead, bespoke training is arranged for employees as needed. Much more emphasis is placed on the opportunity for relatively junior staff to work alongside much more senior staff. Employees learn by working with other experienced people, by being challenged by new creative tasks and from clients. In particular, great care is taken to identify the training and development needs of individual staff. One of the resource managers said, 'I take great care to find out what they want to do, what are their aspirations, do they want to write a book or a blog?'

Performance management and rewards

There is an annual system for appraising performance to be carried out by the line managers. This meeting involves discussion of the previous year's performance and changes to the reward package. However, any changes in salary have to be approved by one of the Partners. The benefits package is very strong with very good provision for insurance and time off.

Questions for discussion

1 In what ways have the different forms of capital contributed to the success of Mother?

2 Explain the role of people management practices in supporting these forms of capital.

3 What risks and problems might Mother encounter in the future in the people management area and how might these be overcome?

CASE STUDY 2.2

ALEXANDER MANN SOLUTIONS

NICHOLAS KINNIE, RUTH SMYTH[5]

Background

Alexander Mann Solutions (AMS) provides Recruitment Process Outsourcing (RPO) and consultancy services to 45 major clients. They were the first to introduce the concept of RPO in 1996 and are now the leading global provider of these services employing approximately 1,500 people. They have won a series of awards over the years, most recently the HROA Baker's Dozen Customer Satisfaction Award.

Mission and structure

AMS provides talent and resourcing capability for organisations, based on the shared belief that people are the foundation for success. They deliver this through innovative and measurable outsourcing and consulting services. In practice, the services provided can be grouped into three areas:

- Outsourced recruitment and selection services;
- Management of internal resourcing and contingent workforces;
- Consulting advice in areas such as employer branding, external and internal resourcing, talent management, executive search and outplacement and redeployment.

They provide these services to clients in various sectors including: Investment Banking, Retail Banking & Financial Services, Consulting Services, IT & Telco, Healthcare, Defence & Engineering and FMCG. The geographical breakdown of numbers of employees is as follows:

Table 2.1 Geographical location of employees

Region	Number of employees
UK	800
Continental Europe (excluding the UK)	470
Asia-Pacific	180
Americas	50

Employees are located on one of four sites (see Figure 2.6):

- Client sites providing day-to-day recruitment and selection services, where about 40 per cent of their employees are located;
- Global Services Centres (in Krakow, UK, Manila and Cleveland, OH) providing extensive back-office services such as security checks and organising interview schedules and assessment centres (15 per cent of the workforce);
- Regional Offices providing recruitment and selection services to clients (39 per cent of the workforce);
- UK office central functions including HR, resourcing, finance, commercial, legal, marketing facilities and technology (6 per cent of the workforce).

A very high proportion of AMS staff are therefore working for clients either directly or indirectly. AMS employees based on client sites are working alongside client staff on a daily basis and are surrounded by their branding. One client-based senior manager said, *'You are pretty much totally immersed with the client. Everything about your employment, bar your pay packet, is client-focused, your business card, your laptop, your client office. My contact with the world outside of (the client) is minimal.'* The risk here is that AMS employees may become more committed to their client than to their employer. Indeed, in some instances AMS can seem very remote and abstract.

Role types

The following roles are typically found within each of the client teams:

- **Head of Client Services** – has overall responsibility for relationships and delivery of all resourcing services to one or more clients;
- **Manager** – is responsible for the day-to-day management of the client relationship and service delivery;
- **Principal Specialist** – responsible for delivering day-to-day services to hiring managers and dealing with candidates.

---

[5]Head of HR, Alexander Mann Solutions.

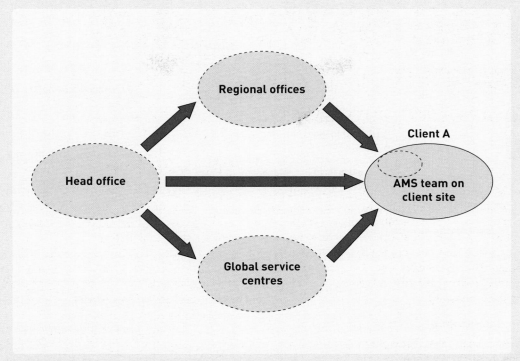

Figure 2.6 Alexander Mann Solutions – location of staff

- **Specialist** – is involved in the day-to-day resourcing activities for the client;
- **Administrator/Coordinator** – provides back-up and support to the Specialist and Principal Specialists.

Client teams can vary in size from over 100 people for a large account to just two or three for a smaller one.

People Strategy

The People Strategy seeks to make the employee value proposition of 'inspiring people' a reality for all employees. In particular the People Capital specialists aim to support the AMS vision and mission by driving business transformation and delivering operational excellence through the provision of innovative global programmes. In particular the key priorities are to create a high-performance culture within AMS by:

- Creating a positive and inclusive environment;
- Strengthening the leadership capability;
- Identifying and nurturing talent;
- Rewarding achievement and delivering high performance;
- Making a positive difference to global and local communities;
- Ensuring flexibility and choice.

People capital structure

There is a global team, based in six territories (UK, US, Australia, Poland, Philippines, China) of approximately 20 HR and training professionals. The HR Business Partner (HRBP) model is adopted, with the HRBP providing specific sector or geography specific support, who are in turn supported by an HR operations team (administration, technology, reporting etc.), as shown below. Most of the Operations support is provided from Poland and the Philippines.

Particular emphasis is given to the professional development of AMS employees. Indeed, the firm facilitates professional development by encouraging employees to move between different clients on a regular basis – typically after two years with a client. This is designed to allow employees to learn new skills, acquire knowledge about a range of sectors and add well-known brands to their CV. One client manager said, *'without ever having to jump into another organisation I am getting the exposure and contacts, and just working with clients in different industries is quite rare'*. Another more junior client-based employee said, *'I have had variety …you might work on something for 6 months and then it is something else, you always feel as if you are doing something a bit different.'* While a team manager commented that *'There is always the opportunity to*

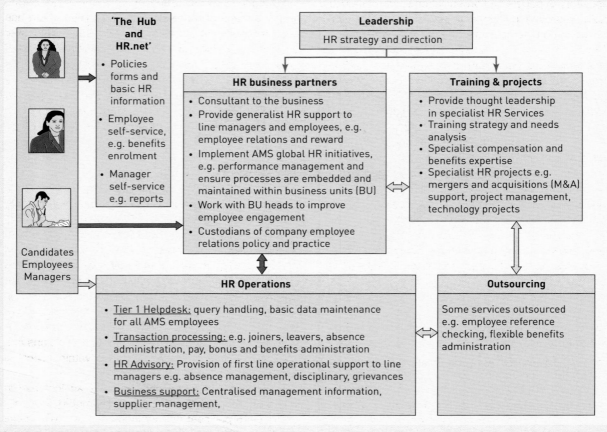

Figure 2.7 People capital structure in AMS

take yourself off one client site and go and work another site, so that was always a big draw for me, the fact that I am part of a bigger organisation that has other opportunities.'

This also has benefits for clients because they have the benefit of staff who have a range of experiences upon which they can draw and these staff themselves have a network of talent that they can consult if a difficult problem emerges.

Research into employee attitudes

AMS has carried out a series of surveys in order to improve their understanding of employee attitudes and behaviours. These surveys (known as Pulsepoint) have formed the basis for the development of an action plan setting targets to be achieved before the next survey.

Findings from the first survey

There were key findings in the areas of employee commitment and professional and career development.

Employee commitment.

There were two important findings. First, it was found that employee commitment was positively related to

willingness to stay in the organisation. Second, the organisational commitment of employees on client sites was lower than those elsewhere.

Professional and career development

The key findings were that the satisfaction of professional development needs within the organisation was positively related to willingness to stay and managers with 3–4 years' experience have unmet training and development needs.

Subsequent actions that were taken and their outcomes

A series of actions were taken to improve employee commitment, communications and involvement and professional development opportunities.

Employee commitment, communications and involvement

A series of actions were taken to improve employee commitment including: first, a substantial enhancement of the corporate induction process to improve the frequency and content of the programme; second, the introduction of the knowledge exchange, an online repository of people and organisational information and finally improved guidance to senior managers when managing communications.

In addition, various actions were taken to improve communications with and involvement opportunities for employees. This included members of the Leadership Team visiting over 400 employees on client sites in 2010; extensive in-house communications regarding AMS achievements including the Pulsepoint results through *The Point*, a hard copy in-house magazine, and CheckPoint, which involved making leadership team video webcasts available to all employees and the initiation of the Global Inspiring Teamwork award. Furthermore, all members of the Leadership Team are now measured on the results from the Pulsepoint surveys and Heads of Client Services have to develop action plans in collaboration with the people capital team to address areas of concern ensuring a high level buy-in to these issues.

Impact of these changes

These changes contributed to a number of improvements in employee attitudes and behaviours. First, there were important changes in employee attitudes. Employee commitment (scale 1–7) increased from 4.93 (2009) to 5.27 (2011), an 8 per cent improvement and employees' intention to quit reduced from 3.20 (2009) to 2.94 (2011) an 11 per cent reduction. This contributed towards a reduction in employee turnover leading to substantial cost savings.

In terms of organisational performance more generally, there has been a substantial growth of the business following the successful acquisition of two major clients and one major client re-signing. In addition, there has been a significant increase in employment with over 500 permanent hires in 2010 and an additional 220 new employees taken on between September 2010 and February 2011. These changes also contributed to the winning of two awards: the Baker's Dozen – the main accreditation award for RPO outsourcing and the corporate partner of the year by AMS's UK Charity of the Year.

Professional development

A series of actions were taken which sought to improve opportunities for professional development within AMS. These included increasing technical and soft skills training by 15 per cent, increasing the management development programmes by 45 per cent especially in the areas of performance management and coaching and a significant increase in the number of senior managers who attended the AMS Leadership Academy. In addition, there was an improvement in the agility of HR processes in response to employee and manager feedback which allowed localised promotion decisions and performance management decisions within accounts and functions.

The impact of these changes was an increase in the proportion of the workforce promoted internally from 10–15 per cent and an increased ability to move positions within AMS to improve skill development leading to 240 moves in 2010. In addition, the Investors in People Bronze Award was obtained along with the Polish Investors in Human Capital Award.

Questions

1 What are the main challenges faced by AMS when seeking to strengthen employee commitment to the organisation?

2 Consider the possible actions that AMS might have made to strengthen organisational commitment?

3 Why have AMS made the changes, as detailed in the case, to their HR practices?

4 What evidence is there that these changes have had a positive influence on organisational performance?

CASE STUDY 2.3

MARKS AND SPENCER ONE TEAM

NICHOLAS KINNIE AND JUANI SWART

Marks and Spencer is a major UK-based retailer employing over 78,000 people with over 700 stores in the UK. Our detailed focus within Marks and Spencer is on the establishment of a logistical network, known as One Team, which provides a best practice example of the operation of HR practices at the level of the network. In this case the various stakeholders in the network acknowledged the need to establish network level skills, relationships and processes to improve performance. In order to do this they critically developed HR practices at the level of the network.

The network is composed of Marks and Spencer and its third party logistical and fulfillment solutions partners (referred to as the 3PLs) who supply warehousing and merchandising facilities. In 2010 Marks and Spencer, led by Jason Keegan, Head of Logistics – Strategic Network, teamed up with its 3PLs, including DHL, NDL, Wincanton, Tesam Distribution, IDS, CML and The Elite Group, to form One Team.

The shared aims of the One Team network are to work together to improve the performance of Marks and Spencer and the network by sharing knowledge and best practice between the parties. In particular they seek to build a highly competitive retail network, achieve high levels of customer satisfaction, generate significant cost savings and establish a common culture. Although the network was instigated by Marks and Spencer, the 3PLs have participated extensively in the operation of One Team. The network has implemented a number of common practices and a shared approach to human capital management. In order to do this they have structured their decision-making and created HR practices at the level of the network.

There are two key managerial structures which are integral to the operation of One Team. First, a Steering Group was established jointly by senior Marks and Spencer staff and each of the 3PLs. This group takes overall responsibility for the direction and strategy of One Team and establishes a common purpose among the members. Meetings take place face to face monthly usually at 3PL sites around the country. Second, five work-streams were established to take responsibility for particular aspects of One Team activities including Values and Behaviours, Marketing and Communications, Collaboration, Customer Focus and Developing Talent.

These involve managers below the Steering Group from Marks and Spencer and the 3PLs acting semi-autonomously, but reporting to the Steering Group regularly with plans for action to contribute to One Team. Both of these managerial structures are vital to supporting the development of shared knowledge and skills. Moreover, they also provide the infrastructure for the continuation of this cross-boundary organisation and they also offer important development opportunities for staff at all levels.

Senior Marks and Spencer managers saw the enhancement of talent management throughout One Team as one of their clear objectives and the principal responsibility of the Developing Talent work-stream. The work-stream facilitates this by advertising all relevant job vacancies across all members of One Team via the shared website, discussed below. This encourages staff to move between 3PLs and Marks and Spencer in ways they would not have done previously. Indeed, this provides Marks and Spencer with the opportunity to identify future talent and to retain this within the network. Employees have the opportunity for career development in ways that they would not otherwise have been aware.

Key internal resourcing decisions were also made over which staff would be allocated to the work-streams. Critically, these staff were identified according to their role suitability and were drawn from a variety of levels and might just as easily include a team leader as a senior manager from a 3PL site. Once they became members of these work-streams the staff had clear opportunities to develop their personal skills and knowledge in a number of respects. First, each work-stream had a high degree of autonomy over how they achieved their objectives. Consequently, the members found they had the freedom to develop new ideas and to innovate. Second, since the members of the work-stream were drawn from multiple levels in One Team, junior staff could find themselves working alongside quite senior staff from Marks and Spencer and other 3PLs in a way they would not do normally. Apart from the knowledge and skills development opportunities, these staff had career benefits because they had a chance to 'get themselves noticed'. It is important to note that the developmental opportunities now extended beyond the boundaries of each organisation and existed at the level of the network.

Alongside these more informal development opportunities there are also a series of formal training and development activities at the level of the network. These activities are focused on One Team and not the 3PLs and aim to develop multi-level agility and to encourage the sharing of knowledge and best practices. For instance, training needs analysis within One Team showed that in order for One Team to function more effectively at the team level there was a need for members of the 3PLs to understand their inter-personal styles and managerial approaches in greater detail. A process was implemented across the network wherein which each individual's preferred communication style was identified and each team was made aware of its particular team member configuration. This enabled improved communication within the cross-boundary team as well as enhanced social relationships.

Performance management and reward practices were also established at the level of the network. Efficiency targets were established for each site and performance was measured weekly. Each site has complete knowledge of its own performance and the performance of others within the league table which was established. This provides a strong incentive to improve performance which is highly visible throughout One Team. Once these targets were set, each local manager sought to make changes to improve their performance. Often this led to changes in working practices which led to improvements in efficiency and performance against target. These improvements could then be shared throughout the network either in the work-streams or via the website.

There were also One Team reward mechanisms to recognise the contribution of individual employees. Every month an employee was recognised for their outstanding contribution and these were then entered into a quarterly competition. The rewards linked to being the 'employee of the month' included travel and entertainment benefits; all of which were linked to personal pride in having displayed One Team values and behaviours. This network-level practice provided a financial and recognition incentive for employees to identify with the network and therefore they were willing to share rather than hoard their knowledge.

Perhaps one of the key drivers in the multi-dimensional agility model is the involvement and participation practices that exist at the level of the network. There are a series of practices designed to encourage all members to adopt a One Team perspective and to strengthen the relationships at all levels. First, six regional champions were established who meet face-to-face regularly to build relationships and share knowledge. Second, various social activities take place between members of the sites at all levels to build awareness of One Team and make contacts. Third, employees at all levels have the opportunity to contribute to the One Team suggestion scheme for efficiency savings discussed above. Fourth, the One Team website mentioned previously has multiple purposes. Not only does it allow the job vacancies to be advertised, but it also provides for social network and activities between members of One Team at multiple levels. Finally, all employees are encouraged to wear the One Team uniform rather than the uniform of the 3PL that they work for.

In summary, One Team provides a sophisticated example of infrastructure, managerial practices and HR practices which operate across all the member organisations at the level of the network. Critically, these practices impact upon all levels of seniority within the partners and Marks and Spencer. It is not only senior staff who are involved, junior staff also have opportunities to develop their career, improve their knowledge and exercise decision-making discretion in ways that would not be available to them within their 3PL. Moreover, these structures and practices are multistranded. They are not solely focused on cost savings and efficiencies and recognise that shared values and behaviours and relationships hold the key to the knowledge sharing which in turn is the life blood of productivity improvements.

It is important to understand that this HRM model, which exists at the level of the network, results in the development of flexible human capital, which can be effectively deployed across the network as well as within the individual firms. These efficiencies have resulted in very significant cost-savings, multi-stranded talent development and have generated further networked ways of working. This HRM model therefore supports a positive spiral of networked benefits.

Questions

1 What were the key forms of human, social and organisational capital generated in One Team?
2 What role did HR practices play in supporting these forms of capital?
3 In the future:
   a How might the network be developed further?
   b What obstacles might be encountered to further development?
   c How might these obstacles be overcome?

Bibliography

Alvesson, M. (2004) *Knowledge Work and Knowledge Intensive Firms*, Oxford: Oxford University Press.

Ansoff, H.I. (1965) *Corporate Strategy,* Harmondsworth: Penguin.

Appelbaum, E., Bailey, T. and Berg, P. (2000) *Manufacturing Advantage: Why High-Performance Systems Pay Off*, Ithaca, NY: ILR Press.

Armstrong, P. and Goodman, J. (1979) 'Management and supervisory custom and practice', *Industrial Relations Journal*, Vol.10, No.3, 12–24.

Arthur, J. (1994) 'Effects of human resource systems on manufacturing performance and turnover', *Academy of Management Journal*, Vol.37, No.3, 670–87.

Atkinson, J. (1984) 'Manpower strategies for flexible organisations', *Personnel Management,* August' 28–31.

Baird, L. and Meshoulam, I. (1988) 'Managing two fits of strategic human resource management', *Academy of Management Review,* Vol.13, No.1, 116–28.

Barney, J.B. (2001) 'Is the resource-based theory a useful perspective for strategic management research? Yes', *Academy of Management Review*,Vol.26, No.1, 41–56.

Barney, J. (1986) 'Organizational culture: can it be a source of competitive advantage?' *Academy of Management Review*, Vol.11, No.3, 656–65.

Barney, J. (1991) 'Firm resources and sustained competitive advantage', *Journal of Management,* Vol.17, No.1, 99–120.

Barney, J. and Wright, P. (1998) 'On becoming a strategic partner: the role of human resources in gaining competitive advantage', *Human Resource Management*, Vol.37, No.1, 31–46.

Baron, J. and Kreps, D. (1999) 'Consistent human resource practices', *California Management Review,* Vol.41, No.3, 29–53.

Bartel, A.P. (2000) 'Human resource management and performance in the service sector: the case of bank branches', *NBER Working Paper Series*, Cambridge, MA : National Bureau of Economic Research,

Batt, R. and Moynihan, L. (2004) 'The viability of alternative call centre models', in Deery, S. and Kinnie, N. (eds) *Call Centres and Human Resource Management,* Basingstoke: Palgrave.

Beaumont, P.B., Hunter, L.C. and Sinclair, D. (1996) 'Customer-supplier relations and the diffusion of employee relations change', *Employee Relations*, Vol.18, No.1, 9–19.

Becker, B. and Gerhart, B. (1996) 'The impact of human resource management on organizational performance: progress and practice', *Academy of Management Journal*, Vol. 39, No.4, 779–801.

Becker, B. and Huselid, M. (2006) 'Strategic human resource management: where do we go from here?' *Journal of Management*, Vol. 32, No.6, 898–925.

Becker, B.E., and Huselid, M.A. (2011) 'Bridging micro and macro domains: workforce differentiation and strategic human resource management', *Journal of Management*, Vol.37, No.2, 421–8.

Beer, M., Spector, B., Lawrence, P. Quinn Mills, D. and Walton, R. (1985) *Human Resource Management: A General Manager's Perspective*, New York: Free Press.

Berg, P. (1999) 'The effects of high performance work practices on job satisfaction in the United States Steel Industry', *Relations Industrielles*, Vol.54, No.1, 111–34.

Berg, P., Appelbaum, E., Bailey, T. and Kalleberg, A. (1996) 'The performance effects of modular production in the apparel industry', *Industrial Relations*, Vol.35, No.3, 356–73.

Boselie, P., Dietz, G. and Boon, C. (2005) 'Commonalities and contradictions in research on human resource management and performance', *Human Resource Management Journal*, Vol.15, No.3, 67–94.

Boselie, P., Paauwe, J. and Jansen, P. (2000) 'Human resource management and performance lessons from the Netherlands', *International Journal of Human Resource Management'* Vol.12, No.7, 1107–25.

Boxall, P. (1992) 'Strategic human resource management: beginnings of a new theoretical sophistication?' *Human Resource Management Journal*, Vol.2, No.3, 60–79.

Boxall, P. (1994) 'Placing HR strategy at the heart of business success', *Personnel Management*, Vol.26, No.7, 32–5.

Boxall, P. (1995) 'Building the theory of comparative HRM', *Human Resource Management Journal*, Vol.5, No.5, 5–17.

Boxall, P. (1996) 'The strategic HRM debate and the resource-based view of the firm', *Human Resource Management Journal*, Vol.6, No.3, 59–75.

Boxall, P. (1998) 'Achieving competitive advantage through human resource strategy: towards a theory of industry dynamics', *Human Resource Management Review*, Vol.8, No.3, 265–88.

Boxall, P. (1999) 'Human resource strategy and industry-based competition: a conceptual framework and agenda for theoretical development', in Wright, P., Dyer, L., Boudreau, J. and Milkovich, G. (eds) *Research in Personnel and Human Resource Management (Supplement 4: Strategic Human Resources Management in the Twenty-First Century)*, Stamford, CT & London: JAI Press.

Boxall, P. and Purcell, J. (2000) 'Strategic human resource management: where have we come from and where should we be going?', *International Journal of Management Reviews*, Vol.2, No.2, 183–203.

Boxall, P. and Purcell, J. (2003) *Strategy and Human Resource Management*, Basingstoke: Palgrave MacMillan.

Boxall, P. and Purcell, J. (2011) *Strategy and Human Resource Management* (3rd edn), Basingstoke: Palgrave MacMillan.

Boxall, P. and Steeneveld, M. (1999) 'Human resource strategy and competitive advantage: a longitudinal study of engineering consultancies', *Journal of Management Studies*, Vol.36, No.4, 443–63.

Brown, W. (1972) 'A consideration of custom and practice', *British Journal of Industrial Relations*, Vol.10, No.1, 42–61.

Brown, W. (1973) *Piecework Bargaining*, Oxford: Heinemann.

Cappelli, P. (ed.) (2008) *Employment Relationships*, Cambridge: Cambridge University Press.

Child, J. (1997) 'Strategic choice in the analysis of action, structure, organizations and environment: retrospect and prospect', *Organization Studies,* Vol.18, No.1, 43–76.

Child, J. and Partridge, B. (1982) *Lost Managers,* Cambridge: Cambridge University Press.

Combs, J., Yongmei, L., Hall, A. and Ketchen, D. (2006) 'How much do high performance work practices matter? A meta-analysis of their effects on organizational performance', *Personnel Psychology*, Vol.59, 501–28.

Coyle-Shapiro, J.A.M., Kessler, I. and Purcell, J. (2004) 'Exploring organizationally-directed citizenship behaviour: reciprocity of it's my job?', *Journal of Management Studies*, Vol.42, 85–106.

Cully, M., Woodland, S., O'Reilly, A. and Dix, G. (1999) *Britain at Work: as Depicted by the 1998 Workplace Employee Relations Survey*, Abingdon: Routledge.

Delaney, J.T. and Godard, J. (2001) 'An industrial relations perspective on the high performance paradigm', *Human Resource Management Review*, Vol.11, 395–429.

Delery, J. and Doty, H. (1996) 'Modes of theorising in strategic human resource management: tests of universalistic, contingency and configurational performance predictions', *Academy of Management Journal,* Vol.39, No.4, 802–35.

Delery, J. (1998) 'Issues of fit in strategic human resource management: implications for research', *Human Resource Management Review,* Vol.8, No.3, 289–309.

Donnelly, R. (2011).'The coalescence between synergies and conflicts of interest in a top consultancy firm: an analysis of the implications for consultants' attitudes and behaviours', *Human Resource Management Journal*, Vol.20, No.1, 60–73.

Dyer, L. and Reeves, T. (1995) 'Human resource strategies and firm performance: what do we know and where do we need to go?', *International Journal of Human Resource Management,* Vol.6, No.3, 656–70.

Dyer, L. and Shafer, R. (1999) 'Creating organizational agility: implications for strategic human resource management', in Wright P., Dyer, L., Boudreau, J. and Milkovich, G. (eds.) *Research in Personnel and Human Resource Management (Supplement 4: Strategic Human Resources Management in the Twenty-First Century)*, Stamford, CT and London: JAI Press.

Elorza, U., Aritzeta, A. and Ayestaran, S. (2011) 'Exploring the black box in Spanish firms: the effect of the actual and perceived system on employees' commitment and organisational performance', *International Journal of Human Resource Management,* Vol.22, No.7, 1401–22.

Fombrun, C., Tichy, N. and Devanna, M. (eds) (1984) *Strategic Human Resource Management*, New York: Wiley.

Foss, N.J. (1994) 'Realism and evolutionary economics', *Journal Social and Biological Systems,* Vol.17, No.1, 21–40.

Fox, A. (1974) *Beyond Contract: Work, Power and Trust Relations*, London: Faber.

Gerhart, B. (1999) 'Human resource management and firm performance: measurement issues and their effect on casual and policy inferences', in Wright, P., Dyer, L., Boudreau, J. and Milkovich, G. (eds) *Research in Personnel and Human Resource Management (Supplement 4: Strategic Human Resources Management in the Twenty-First Century)*, Stamford, CT and London: JAI Press.

Gittleman, M., Horrigan, M. and Joyce, M. (1998) '"Flexible" workplace practices: evidence from a nationally representative survey', *Industrial and Labor Relations Review,* Vol.52, No.1, 99–115.

Golding, N. (2004) 'Strategic human resource management', pp. 32–74, in Beardwell, I., Holden, L. and Claydon, T. (eds) *Human Resource Management. A Contemporary Approach* (4th edn), Harlow: Pearson Education.

Goshall, S. and Napahiet, J. (1998) 'Social capital, intellectual capital and the organizational advantage', *Academy of Management Review,* Vol.23, No.2, 242–66.

Gratton, L., Hope-Hailey, V., Stiles, P. and Truss, C. (1999a) 'Linking individual performance to business strategy: the people process model', *Human Resource Management,* Vol.38, No.1, 17–31.

Gratton, L., Hope-Hailey, V., Stiles, P. and Truss, C. (1999b) *Strategic Human Resource Management: Corporate Rhetoric and Human Reality*, Oxford: Oxford University Press.

Guest, D. (1987) 'Human resource management and industrial relations', *Journal of Management Studies,* Vol.24, No.5, 503–21.

Guest, D. (1995) 'Human resource management, trade unions and industrial Relations', in Storey, J. (ed.) *Human Resource Management: A Critical Text,* London: Routledge.

Guest, D. (1997) 'Human resource management and performance: a review and research agenda', *International Journal of Human Resource Management,* Vol.8, No.3, 263–76.

Guest, D. (1999) 'Human resource management and performance: the workers' verdict', *Human Resource Management Journal,* Vol.9, No.3, 5–25.

Guest, D.E. (2011) 'Human resource management and performance: still searching for some answers', *Human Resource Management Journal,* Vol.21, No.1, 3–13.

Guest, D. and Hoque, K. (1994) 'The good, the bad and the ugly: employment relations in new non-union workplaces', *Human Resource Management Journal*, Vol.5, No.1, 1–14.

Guest D., Michie, J., Conway, N. and Sheehan, M. (2003) 'Human resource management and corporate performance in the UK', *British Journal of Industrial Relations*, Vol.41, No.2, 291–314.

Guest, D., Michie, J., Sheehan, M. and Conway, N. (2000) *Effective People Management: Initial Findings of the Future of Work Study*, London: Chartered Institute of Personnel and Development.

Hall, L. and Torrington, D. (1998) 'Letting go or holding on: the devolution of operational personnel activities', *Human Resource Management Journal,* Vol.8, No.1, 41–55.

Hamel, G. and Prahalad, C. (1994) *Competing for the Future*, Boston, MA: Harvard Business School Press.

Hendry, C. and Pettigrew, A. (1992) 'Strategic choice in the development of human resource management', *British Journal of Management,* Vol.3, No.1, 37–56.

Hesketh, A. and Fleetwood, S. (2006) 'Beyond measuring the human resources – organizational performance link: applying criticalrealist meta-theory', *Organization*, Vol.13, No.5, 677–700.

Huselid, M. (1995) 'The impact of human resource management practices on turnover, productivity and corporate financial performance', *Academy of Management Journal*, No.38, No.3, 635–72.

Huselid, M.A. and Becker, B. (2000) 'Comment on "Measurement error in research on human resource management: how much error is there and how does it influence effect size estimates?" By Gerhart, Wright, McMahan and Snell', *Personnel Psychology*, Vol.53, No,4, 835–54.

Hutchinson, S., Kinnie, N., Purcell, J., Collinson, M., Scarbrough, H. and Terry, M. (1998) *Getting Fit, Staying Fit: Developing Lean and Responsive Organisations*, London: Institute of Personnel and Development.

Hutchinson, S., Kinnie, N., Purcell, J., Rees, C., Scarbrough, H. and Terry, M. (1996) *The People Management Implications of Leaner Ways of Working*, Issues in People Management No.15, London: Institute of Personnel and Development.

Hutchinson, S. and Purcell, J. (2003) *Bringing Policies to Life*, London: Chartered Institute of Personnel and Development.

Hutchinson, S. and Purcell, J. (2007) *The Role of Line Managers in People Management*, London: Chartered Institute of Personnel and Development.

Hutchinson, S. and Wood, S. (1995) *Personnel and the Line: Developing the New Relationship: The UK Experience,* London: Institute of Personnel and Development.

Ichniowski, C., Shaw, K. and Prennushi, G. (1995) 'The impact of human resource management practices on productivity', *Working Paper 5333,* Cambridge, MA: National Bureau of Economic Research.

Ichniowski, C., Kochan, T., Levine, D., Olson, C. and Strauss, G. (1996) 'What works at work: overview and assessment', *Industrial Relations,* Vol.35, No.3, 299–333.

Jackson, S. and Schuler, R. (1995). 'Understanding human resource management in the context of organizations and their environments', *Annual Review of Psychology,* Vol.46, 237–64.

Janssens, M. and Steyaert, C. (2009) 'HRM and performance: a plea for reflexivity in HRM studies', *Journal of Management Studies*, Vol.46, No.1, 143–55.

Keenoy, T. (1997) 'HRMism and the languages of re-presentation', *Journal of Management Studies*, Vol.34, No.5, 825–41.

Kersley, B., Alpin, C., Forth, J., Bryson, A., Bewley, H., Dix, G. and Oxenbridge, S. (2006) *Inside the Workplace: First Findings from the 2004 Workplace Employment Relations Survey,* Abingdon: Routledge.

Kinnie, N. and Parsons, J. (2004) 'Managing client, employee and customer relations: constrained strategic choice in the management of human resources in a commercial call centre', pp. 102–26, in Deery, S. and Kinnie, N. (eds) *Call Centres and Human Resource Management,* Basingstoke: Palgrave.

Kinnie, N. and Swart, J. (2012) 'Committed to whom? Professional knowledge worker commitment in cross boundary organisations', *Human Resource Management Journal,* Vol.2, No.1, 21–38.

Kinnie, N., Purcell, J. and Hutchinson, S. (2000) 'Human resource management in telephone call centres', in Purcell, K. (ed.) *Changing Boundaries*, Bristol: Bristol Academic Press.

Kinnie, N.J., Swart, J. and Purcell, J. (2005) 'Influences on the choice of HR systems: the network organisation perspective', *International Journal of Human Resource Management,* Vol.16, No.6, 1004–28.

Kinnie, N., Purcell, J., Hutchinson, S., Rayton, B. and Swart, J. (2005) 'Satisfaction with HR practices and commitment to the organisation: why one size does not fit all', *Human Resource Management Journal*, Vol.15 No.4, 9–29.

Kinnie, N., Swart, J., Lund, M., Morris, S., Snell, S. and Kang, S.-K., (2006) *Managing People and Knowledge in Professional Service Firms*, London: CIPD.

Kochan, T. and Barocci, T. (1985) *Human Resource Management and Industrial Relations*, New York: Basic Books.

Larsen, H.H. and Brewster, C. (2003) 'Line management responsibility for HRM: what is happening in Europe?', *Employee Relations*, Vol.25, No.3. 228–44.

Legge, K. (1978) *Power, Innovation, and Problem-solving in Personnel Management*, London: McGraw-Hill.

Legge, K. (1995) *Human Resource Management: Rhetorics and Realities,* Basingstoke: Macmillan.

Legge, K. (2001) 'Silver bullet or spent round? Assessing the meaning of the High performance commitment management/performance relationship', in Storey, J. (ed.) *Human Resource Management: A Critical Text* (2nd edn), London: Thompson Publishing.

Leonard, D. (1992) 'Core capabilities and core rigidities: a paradox in managing new product development', *Strategic Management Journal,* Vol.13, 111–25.

Leonard, D. (1998) *Wellsprings of Knowledge: Building and Sustaining the Sources of Innovation*, Boston, MA: Harvard Business School Press.

Lepak, D. and Snell, S. (1999) 'The strategic management of human capital: determinants and implications of different relationships', *Academy of Management Review,* Vol.24, No.1, 1–18.

Lepak, D., Takeuchi, R., and Swart, J. (2011) 'How organizations evaluate and maintain fit of human capital with their needs' pp.333–58, in *The Oxford Handbook of Human Capital*, Burton-Jones, A. and Spender' J.C. (eds) Oxford: Oxford University Press.

Lepak, D.P., Liao, H., Chung, Y. and Harden, E.E. (2006) 'A conceptual review of human resource management systems in strategic human resource management research', *Personnel and Human Resource Management*, Vol.25, 217–71.

Loasby, B.J. (1991) *Equilibrium and Evolution*, Manchester: University of Manchester Press.

Lowe, J., Delbridge, R. and Oliver, N. (1997) 'High-performance manufacturing: evidence from the automotive components industry', *Organization Studies,* Vol.18, No.5, 783–98.

MacDuffie, J.P. (1995) 'Human resource bundles and manufacturing performance: organizational logic and flexible production systems in the world auto industry', *Industrial and Labor Relations Review,* Vol.48, No.2, 197–221.

MacDuffie, J.P. and Pil, F.T. (1997) 'Changes in auto industry employment practices: an international overview', in Kochan I.A., Lansbury, R.D. and Macduffie, J.P. (eds) *After Lean Production: Evolving Employment Practices in the World Auto Industry*, Ithaca, NY: ILR Press.

Marchington, M. (2001) 'Employee involvement at work', in Storey, J. *Human Resource Management: A Critical text* (2nd edn), London: Thompson Publishing.

Marchington, M. and Grugulis, I. (2000) '"Best practice" human resource management: perfect opportunity or dangerous illusion?', *International Journal of Human Resource Management,* Vol.11, No.6, 1104–24.

Marchington, M. and Wilkinson, A. (2002) *People Management and Development.* London: Chartered Institute of Personnel and Development.

McGovern, P., Gratton, L., Hope-Hailey, V., Stiles, P. and Truss, C. (1997) 'Human resource management on the line?', *Human Resource Management Journal,* Vol.7, No.4, 12–29.

Miles, R. and Snow, C. (1978) *Organizational Strategy, Structure and Process,* New York: McGraw-Hill.

Miles, R. and Snow, C. (1984) 'Designing strategic human resources systems', *Organizational Dynamics*, Vol.13, No.1, Summer, 36–52.

Miles, R. and Snow, C. (1999) 'The new network firm: a spherical structure built on human investment philosophy', in Schuler, R. and Jackson, S. (eds) *Strategic Human Resource Management,* Oxford: Blackwell.

Miller, D. and Shamsie, J. (1992) 'The resource-based view of the firm in two environments: the Hollywood film studios from 1936 to 1965', *Academy of Management Journal,* Vol.39, No.3, 519–43.

Millward, N., Bryson, A. and Forth, J. (2000) *All Change at Work: British Employment Relations 1980–1998 as Portrayed by the Workplace Industrial Relations Survey Series*, London: Routledge.

Mintzberg, H. (1994) 'Rethinking strategic planning part 1: pitfalls and fallacies', *Long Range Planning*, Vol.27, No.3, 12–21.

Mueller, F. (1996) 'Human resources as strategic assets; an evolutionary resource-based theory', *Journal of Management Studies,* Vol.33, No.6, 757–85.

Osterman, P. (1987) 'Choice of employment systems in internal labor markets', *Industrial Relations,* Vol.26, No.1, 46–67.

Osterman, P. (1994) 'How common is workplace transformation and who adopts it?', *Industrial and Labor Relations Review,* Vol.47, No.2, 173–88.

Osterman, P. (2000) 'Work reorganization in an era of restructuring: trends in diffusion and effects on employee welfare', *Industrial and Labor Relations Review,* Vol.53, No.2, 179–96.

Paauwe, J. (2009) 'HRM and performance: achievements, methodological issues and prospects', *Journal of Management Studies*, Vol.46, No.1, 129–42.

Patterson, M., West, M., Hawthorn, R. and Nickell, S. (1997) 'Impact of people management practices on business performance', *Issues in People Management No. 22*, London: Institute of Personnel and Development.

Peters, T. and Waterman, R.H. (1982) *In Search of Excellence: Lessons from America's Best-Run Companies*, New York: Harper & Row.

Pettigrew, A.M. (1973) *The Politics of Organizational Decision Making*, London: Tavistock.

Pfeffer, J. (1994) *Competitive Advantage Through People*, Boston, MA: Harvard Business School Press.

Pfeffer, J. (1998) *The Human Equation: Building Profits by Putting People First*, Boston, MA: Harvard Business School Press.

Pfeffer, J. and Salancik, G.R. (1978) *The External Control of Organizations: A Resource Dependence Perspective*, New York: Harper & Row.

Pil, F.K. and MacDuffie, J.P. (1996) 'The adoption of high involvement work practices', *Industrial Relations,* Vol.35, No.3, 423–55.

Porter, M.E. (1980) *Competitive Strategy*, New York: Free Press.

Porter, M.E. (1985) *Competitive Advantage: Creating and Sustaining Superior Performance.* New York: Free Press.

Powell, J.H., and Wakeley, T. (2003) 'Evolutionary concepts and business economics: Towards a normative approach', *Journal of Business Research*, Vol.56, 153–61.

Prahalad, C. and Hamel, G. (1990) 'The core competence of the corporation', *Harvard Business Review,* Vol.68, No.3, May–June, 79–91.

Purcell, J. (1999) 'Best practice and best fit: chimera or cul-de-sac?', *Human Resource Management Journal,* Vol.9, No.3, 26–41.

Purcell, J. (2004) 'The HRM–performance link: why, how and when does people management impact on organisational performance?', John Lovett Memorial Lecture, University of Limerick. (Available from the author.)

Purcell, J. and Hutchinson, S. (2007) 'Front line managers as agents in the HRM–performance causal chain: theory, analysis and evidence', *Human Resource Management Journal,* Vol.17, No.1, 3–20.

Purcell, J. and Kinnie, N. (2007) 'Human resource management and business performance', in Boxall, P., Purcell, J. and Wright, P. (eds) *The Oxford Handbook of Human Resource Management,* Oxford: Oxford University Press.

Purcell, J., Kinnie, N., Hutchinson, S. Rayton, B. and Swart, J. (2003) *Understanding the People and Performance Link: Unlocking the Black Box*, London: Chartered Institute of Personnel and Development.

Purcell, J., Kinnie, N., Swart, J., Rayton, B. and Hutchinson, S. (2009) *People Management and Performance,* Oxford: Routledge.

Ramsay, H., Scholarios, D. and Harley, B. (2000) 'Employees and high-performance work systems: testing inside the black box', *British Journal of Industrial Relations,* Vol.38, No.4, 501–31.

Renwick, D. (2000) 'HR-line work relations: a review, pilot case and research agenda' *Journal of European Industrial Training*, Vol.24, Nos.2-4, 241–53.

Richardson, R. and Thompson, M (1999) 'The impact of people management practices on business performance: a literature review', *Issues in People Management,* London: Institute of Personnel and Development.

Schuler, R. and Jackson, S. (1987) 'Linking competitive strategies and human resource management practices', *Academy of Management Executive,* Vol.1, No.3, 207–19.

Schuler, R. (1989) 'Strategic human resource management and industrial relations', *Human Relations,* Vol.42, No.2, 157–84.

Schuler, R. (1996) 'Market-focused management: human resource management implications', *Journal of Market-Focused Management,* Vol.1, 13–29.

Sinclair, D., Hunter, L. and Beaumont, P.B. (1996) 'Models of customer–supplier relations', *Journal of General Management*, Vol.22, No.2 56–75.

Snell, S., Youndt, M. and Wright, P. (1996) 'Establishing a framework for research in strategic human resource management: merging resource theory and organizational learning', *Research in Personnel and Human Resources Management,* Vol.14, 61–90.

Snell, S., Lepak, D. and Youndt, M. (1999) 'Managing the architecture of intellectual capital: implications for human resource management', in Wright, P., Dyer, L., Boudreau, J. and Milkovich, G. (eds) *Research in Personnel and Human Resources Management: Strategic Human Resource Management in the Twenty-First Century,* Stamford, CT: JAI Press.

Swart, J. (2007) 'HRM and knowledge workers', in Boxall, P., Purcell, J. and Wright, P. (eds) *The Oxford Handbook of Human Resource Management,* Oxford: Oxford University Press.

Swart J. (2011) 'That's why it matters. The value generating properties of knowledge'. *Management Learning*. Vol.49, No.3, 319–32.

Swart, J. and Kinnie, N. (2001) 'Human resource advantage within a distributed knowledge system: a study of growing knowledge intensive firms', Paper presented at ESRC Seminar: 'The Changing Nature of Skills and Knowledge'. Manchester School of Management, September 2001. (Available from the authors.)

Swart, J. and Kinnie, N. (2003) 'Knowledge intensive firms: the influence of the client on HR systems', *Human Resource Management Journal*, Vol.13, No.3, 37–55.

Swart, J. and Kinnie, N. (2004) *Managing the Careers of Knowledge Workers*, London: Chartered Institute of Personnel and Development.

Swart, J. Kinnie, N. and Purcell, J. (2003) *People and Performance in Knowledge Intensive Firms*, London: Chartered Institute of Personnel and Development.

Swart, J., Kinnie, N. and Rabinowitz, J. (2007) *Managing Across Boundaries*, London: Chartered Institute of Personnel and Development.

Swart, J., Price, A., Mann, C. and Brown, S. (2004) *Human Resource Development: Strategy and Tactics*, London: Butterworth-Heinemann.

Tempest, S. and Starkey, K. (2004) 'The effects of liminality on individual and organizational learning', *Organization Studies,* Vol.25, No.4, 507–27.

Terry, M. (1977) 'The inevitable growth of informality', *British Journal of Industrial Relations*, Vol.15, No.1, 76–90.

Thompson, M. (2000) *Final Report: The Bottom Line Benefits of Strategic Human Resource Management, The UK Aerospace People Management Audit,* London: Society of British Aerospace Companies.

Thurley, K. and Wirdenius, H. (1973) *Approaches to Supervisory Development*, London: Institute of Personnel Management.

Truss, C. (2001) 'Complexities and controversies in linking HRM with organizational outcomes', *Journal of Management Studies*, Vol.38, No.1, 1121–49.

Tushman, M.L. and Scanlan, T.J. (1981) 'Characteristics and external orientations of boundary spanning individuals', *Academy of Management Journal*, Vol.24, No.1, 83–98.

Ulrich, D. (1997) 'Measuring human resources: an overview of practice and a prescription for results', *Human Resource Management,* Vol.36, No.3, 303–20.

Ulrich, D. (1998) *Human Resource Champions*, Boston, MA: Harvard Business School Press.

Wall, T.D. and Wood, S.J. (2004) 'The romance of human resource management and business performance, and the case for big science', *Human Relations*, Vol.58, No.4, 429–62.

Wall, T. and Wood, S. (2005) 'The romance of HRM and business performance, and the case for big science', *Human Relations,* Vol.58, No.4, 29–62.

Whittington, R. (2001) *What is Strategy – and Does it Matter?* (2nd edn), London: Thompson Learning.

Wood, S. (1996) 'High commitment management and payment systems', *Journal of Management Studies,* Vol.33, No.1, 53–77.

Wood, S. (1999) 'Human resource management and performance', *International Journal of Management Reviews,* Vol.1, No.4, 367–413.

Wood, S. and Albanese, P. (1995) 'Can we speak of high commitment management on the shop floor?' *Journal of Management Studies,* Vol.32, No.2, 215–47.

Wright, P. and Gardener, T.M. (2000) 'Theoretical and empirical challenges in studying the HR practice–firm performance relationship', paper presented at the Strategic Human Resource Management Workshop, European Institute for Advanced Studies in Management, Insead, March. (Available from the Center for Advanced Human Resource Studies Working Paper Series Number 00-04, Cornell University.)

Wright, P., and McMahan, G.C. (2011) 'Exploring human capital: putting human back into strategic management', *Human Resource Management Journal*, Vol.21, No.2, 93–104.

Wright, P. and Nishii, L.H. (2004) 'Strategic HRM and organizational behavior: integrating multiple levels of analysis'. Paper presented at the Erasmus University Conference 'HRM: What's Next?'

Wright, P. and Snell, S. (1998) 'Toward a unifying framework for exploring fit and flexibility in strategic human resource management', *Academy of Management Review,* Vol.23, No.4, 756–72.

Wright, P.M., Gardener, T.M. and Moynihan, L.M. (2003) 'The impact of HR practices on the performance of business units', *Human Resource Management Journal*, Vol.13, No.3, 21–36.

Wright, P., McMahan, G. and McWilliams, A. (1994) 'Human resources and sustained competitive advantage: a resource-based perspective', *International Journal of Human Resource Management,* Vol.5, No.2, 301–26.

Wright, P.M., Gardner, T., Moynihan, L.M. and Allen, M. (2005) 'The HR performance relationship: examining causal direction', *Personnel Psychology*, Vol.58, No.2, 409–46.

Wright, P., McCormick, B., Sherman, W. and McMahan, G. (1999) 'The role of human resource practices in petrochemical refinery performance', *International Journal of Human Resource Management,* Vol.10, No.4, 551–71.

Youndt, M., Snell, S., Dean, J. and Lepak, D. (1996) 'Human resource management, manufacturing strategy, and firm performance', *Academy of Management Journal,* Vol.39, No.4, 836–66.

CHAPTER 3
RECRUITMENT

Scott Hurrell and Dora Scholarios

Introduction

Recruitment is often neglected in the HRM literature. Most accounts combine the discussion of recruitment with selection, with greater emphasis on selection. However, the more effective organisations are at identifying and attracting a high quality pool of job applicants, the less important the selection stage of hiring becomes. According to some, recruitment is 'the most critical human resource function for organizational survival or success' (Taylor and Collins, 2000: 304).

Barber (1998: 5) provided one of the first dedicated reviews of recruitment,[1] defining it as 'practices and activities carried out by the organization with the primary purpose of identifying and attracting potential employees'. Emphasis is usually on filling a position from outside a firm (rather than internal appointments or promotion). An important recent development is the greater attention devoted to how individuals become applicants – or the attraction element (Searle, 2003). Sometimes referred to as an 'applicant perspective' (Billsberry, 2007), this acknowledges a two-way relationship between organisations and applicants, where applicant decision-making becomes an important factor shaping whether the recruitment process is successful or not. It is not just the efficiency of the organisation's procedures in identifying applicants which will ensure the desired outcome (a good match between the individual and the job), but also how potential applicants perceive and act on the opportunities offered. Thus, recruitment activities should 'enhance their [applicants'] interest in and attraction to the organization as an employer; and increase the probability that they will accept a job offer' (Saks, 2005: 48).

In this chapter, we use both an organisational and applicant perspective to understand recruitment. Our approach is represented in Figure 3.1. We begin with a summary of the context within which recruitment takes place (the external environment, organisational characteristics, and the nature of the job vacancy to be filled). We use the example of the UK context for illustrative purposes although also draw from international research to show the pressures impacting organisations globally. We show how each of these contextual drivers impacts recruitment activities, and emphasise the reasons why many organisations now pay more attention to the applicant perspective. This is the driving force behind many recent developments such as the growth in e-recruitment, the use of social networking sites and 'employer branding'.

---

[1]For other reviews, see Breaugh and Starke (2000), Rynes (1991), Rynes and Cable (2003) and Taylor and Collins (2000).

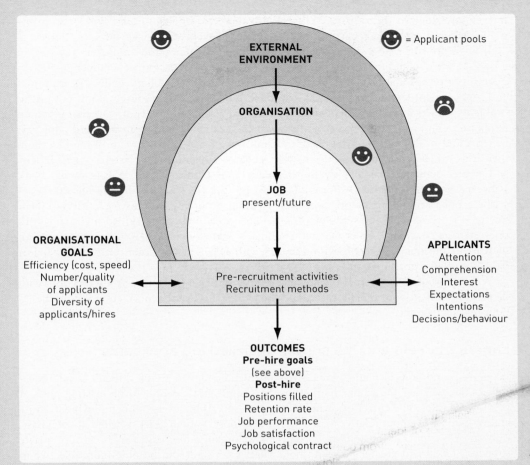

**Figure 3.1
Recruitment
framework**

The external environment

At one time, it was thought that the aim of recruitment was simply to maximise the size of the applicant group, which would then be reduced through a rigorous selection procedure for identifying the most qualified candidates. This assumed an abundant supply of qualified applicants and that those selected would accept the jobs offered. All recruiters had to do was advertise a job vacancy and appropriate candidates would apply and accept job offers. Although this approach may have sufficed for the job demands and labour force of the past, these assumptions are more tenuous in today's employment context. In this section, we consider how the organisation's external environment impacts recruitment.

The economy

The wider economy exerts a positive or negative effect on hiring activity through job growth and contraction. In 2012, most advanced economies are experiencing a declining demand for labour due to the global 'credit crunch', subsequent recession and ongoing debt crises within Eurozone countries. Record high unemployment rates are affecting some European countries (notably Spain, Ireland and Greece), as countries fail to recover post-financial crisis (OECD, 2011). In the US, despite stabilising unemployment rates, new job creation remains uneven and sluggish (BLS, 2012). With the private sector unable to offset job losses in the public sector, there is a lack of confidence among employers over the economic outlook.

It is hardly surprising, then, that recruitment consultancies and employers report that growth in the demand for labour has increased at the slowest pace since October 2009, with medical care, hospitality and financial services affected particularly badly (Recruitment and Employment Confederation (REC) and KPMG, 2011). Other sources point not just to problems with rising unemployment, but also to increasing numbers of workers relying on temporary employment, with involuntary part-time or short-term contracts and poor pay, benefits and health and safety (European Commission, 2011). At least until the recession, there was evidence for job creation in white-collar occupations, such as customer services, and greater demand for managerial/professional and technical skills (Wilson *et al.*, 2004). However, writers in the US (Autor *et al.*, 2006) and the UK (Goos and Manning, 2007) describe a polarised labour market, with job creation occurring in 'lousy' jobs (low-skilled/low-paid work referred to as 'McJobs') as well as 'lovely' jobs (high-skilled/high-paid work referred to as 'Macjobs'). Osterman and Shulman's (2008) book *Good Jobs America* shows an increase in 'the lousy-job sector' within the US, with 24 per cent of Americans working in low paid, low quality positions.

Worrying stagnation across the advanced economies suggests limited job creation, with demand mainly in poor quality work, and the prospect of future contraction within the labour market to come.

Labour markets and the supply of skilled job applicants

Economic conditions also affect the degree to which employers find it difficult to fill job vacancies, i.e. whether the labour market provides appropriate people to fill existing posts at going wage rates. The current slowing job market and rising levels of unemployment create an over-supply of labour relative to demand, and a 'looser' labour market (where there is basically an over-supply of job applicants). This allows organisations easier access to appropriate supplies of skill and greater power to hold salaries constant and become more selective in their hiring processes. Indeed, one recruitment survey reported 'historically low' pay inflation as employers used market conditions to keep wages depressed (REC and KPMG, 2011). For job applicants, of course, fewer job opportunities and greater competition for jobs exist. Applicants also have less bargaining power relative to employers, longer job search times and declining job security as they can easily be replaced by one of the 'reserve army' of unemployed.

The recent recession and current depression has led to a significant decline in the number of job vacancies, however where vacancies do occur these tend to be predominantly due to skills shortages (i.e. applicants with the correct skills cannot be identified). The generally loose nature of the labour market, however, means that few establishments are affected by skills shortage vacancies (SSVs). Indeed when examining the most recent data for the UK, only approximately 3 per cent of establishments reported SSVs[2] (UKCES, 2010). Skills shortages can still, none the less, affect particular establishments and in tighter labour market conditions (with fewer applicants for each job and low unemployment) problems with SSVs become more acute. In 'tight' labour markets, firms compete for qualified staff or have difficulties finding staff at all. Therefore they have to become more creative in finding job applicants, for example, through identifying non-traditional applicant groups or by offering additional incentives such as pay and benefits.

Since 2004, many European employers have benefited from an increase in labour mobility from eastern Europe. Taking the case of migration to the UK, figures released in 2011 revealed that the proportion of non-UK born workers had increased from 9 to 14 per cent of the total workforce since 2002 (ONS, 2011). Within this increase the biggest proportional rise was in those from the eight Eastern European and Baltic accession states (EUA8), joining the EU in 2004, whose share of UK employment grew 11 times (ibid.). Workers from

---

[2]This data is for England, Scotland and Northern Ireland only.

the EUA8 states are, however, much more likely than UK workers and other migrants to be found in 'low-skill' jobs such as postal workers, porters, waiting and bar staff. Just fewer than 40 per cent of EUA8 workers were found in such low-skill employment, compared to only approximately 10 per cent of UK workers. Migrants working in the UK from elsewhere in the EU were most likely to be found in highly skilled professional and senior managerial work. Thirty-six per cent of non A8EU migrants were found in such highly skilled work in 2011, compared with 29 per cent of migrants from outside of the EU and 27 per cent of UK born workers (ibid.). With respect to these higher-end skills, the UK health service has previously experienced particular difficulties in attracting critical care nurses, midwives, dentists and pharmacists and has looked to skilled migrants to fill these gaps. It has also made greater use of incentives likely to attract both career and family-oriented health professionals, such as access to high-quality learning and development and flexible working practices (e.g. Department of Health, 2007).

Skill supply is also affected by levels of educational attainment. The UK seems to be in a position where the skills which are being supplied do not always reflect those being demanded by employers, resulting in a skills deficit in important areas. More graduates are being produced than before – the graduation rate for the UK, the number of degrees awarded as a percentage of those of graduation age, is one of the highest in the OECD (Perryman, 2003). Yet, employers are concerned about the quality of technical graduates and levels of numeracy (Barber, et al., 2005). The few skills shortage vacancies that are reported in the UK have also typically been attributable to technical and practical skills and in intermediate level occupations such as skilled tradespeople and technical occupations (UKCES, 2010). Research has also shown that where establishments used more advanced production technologies skills shortages are higher, suggesting concentrated technical skills issues for particular employers (Haskel and Martin, 2001).

Even though more jobs now require a degree or higher qualifications, recent evidence suggests that graduates' skills are being under-utilised in many jobs. Conversely, unfilled vacancies due to inadequate qualifications and recruitment difficulties also exist. Furthermore, despite positive evidence regarding upskilling, a UK government skills survey reported an oversupply of workers for jobs that required some form of qualification, suggesting further mismatches between workers' skills and the jobs on offer (Felstead et al., 2007). Box 3.1 summarises some of these issues from the survey. Moreover, for those without the necessary skills for the Macjobs, opportunities will most likely be in the low-security, poorly paid Mcjobs.

BOX 3.1 HRM in practice — **Trends in qualifications used at work and skill supply (UK): 1986–2006**

- The proportion of jobs not requiring qualifications has fallen from two-fifths to under a third.
- The proportion of jobs requiring degrees or their equivalent rose from about 16 per cent in 1986 to around 22 per cent in 2006.
- The use of 'generic skills' has increased, including literacy, numeracy, technical know-how, problem-solving, checking, planning, 'influencing' skills and various forms of communication.
- A growing number of workers hold qualifications at a higher level than needed to do their job – 49 per cent of workers in 2006 compared to 35 per cent in 2001.
- There is an under-supply of workers for jobs that require no qualifications, compared to an over-supply of workers for jobs requiring at least some qualifications. This phenomenon is, however, mainly because the number of people without any qualifications in the labour market has fallen substantially during the period.
- There are mismatches between skills supply and skills required, especially in scientific, engineering and technical skills.

Source: Felstead et al., 2007.

Challenges of demographic and social change

The size and composition of the labour force is projected to change dramatically, with implications for employers' recruitment goals and practices. Immigration, an ageing population and more women seeking employment mean a far more diverse workforce. Some of these changes will address skill shortages (as with recent A8EU migration to several northern European economies). Others will exacerbate recruitment problems, especially once labour market conditions tighten. Changing retirement laws, such as the abolition of the Default Retirement Age in the UK, could also contribute to flattened recruitment levels and youth unemployment as people continue to work for longer (CIPD, 2011). Longer life expectancy and the transition of the 'baby boom' generation to this age group (Madouros, 2006) will contribute to the decline in 16–24 year olds and a rapid increase in the number of people aged 50 or over.

Given continuing skill shortages in some areas, organisations will increasingly turn to candidates from non-traditional 'talent pools', such as migrants, older workers or women who are currently carers wishing to return to work. This kind of targeted recruitment can be seen in some industries which continue to experience skill shortages. The youth-oriented ICT industry, for example, has been highlighted for the implicit age discrimination in its recruitment methods – the stereotypical attitudes of managers towards older workers or beliefs that older workers cannot keep pace with technological developments. Legislation which includes age among protected characteristics (see below) now makes such discrimination illegal. Many have drawn attention to the reorientation of recruitment and selection methods as a way of encouraging a more age diverse workforce which at the same time addresses skill shortages (see for example Healy and Schwarz-Woelzl, 2007).

Another trend is the changing priorities of job candidates and what attracts them to jobs and organisations. In one survey, the top attractions to a job listed by employees were holiday entitlement (43 per cent), location of work (47 per cent), flexible working and bonuses (39 per cent), and the company's workplace culture and environment (38 per cent) (YouGov, 2006). Development opportunities came relatively low down the list of priorities (cited by 28 per cent). In another survey of 1,000 people between 25 and 35, 75 per cent admitted to looking for a new job because their life needs were not being taken into consideration (The Future Laboratory, 2005), and, more recently, PricewaterhouseCoopers' (2010) global survey confirmed that flexible working arrangements, such as compressed hours, were more valued by employees across countries than other benefits such as bonuses or training and development.

This indicates increasing overlap between life and work for many job seekers, who are considering what jobs can offer them in terms of their prospects for work–life balance. This growing concern for work–life balance and flexible working patterns has been popularly linked to the working preferences of so-called 'Generation Y', born between approximately 1977 and the millennium (Armour, 2005). This generation, while driven, eager to learn and constantly seeking new challenges, are seen to be much more concerned with accommodating their non-work lives and ensuring that their employers' values (for example, on the environment) fit their own (ibid.; Murray, 2008). Similar evidence has been found in surveys of graduates during their first five years in the workplace (CIPD, 2006), and employers seem to be taking notice. In the 2007 Work–Life Balance Employer Survey, for instance, there was an increase since 2003 in the provision, and employee take-up of, flexible working arrangements like job sharing and compressed hours, while 42 per cent of employers cited flexible working as an advantage when recruiting (Hayward *et al.*, 2007). Box 3.2 illustrates how some of the most attractive global employers design their recruitment strategies with these job seekers in mind.

Employment legislation

Freedom from discrimination is viewed, internationally (in theory at least), as a fundamental right. European Union (EU) member countries have been forced towards compliance with EU legislation. One example is new UK legislation, passed between 2003 and 2006, to

Box 3.2 HRM in practice   Global companies' recruitment strategies

The power of the brand

A 'talent pipeline' recruitment strategy is followed by many global companies. This requires a talent attraction and employer branding strategy.

Examples of this in operation are provided by Universum's global talent attraction index which identifies 'The World's Most Attractive Employers 2011' based on 160,000 job seekers with business or engineering backgrounds (www.universumglobal.com). The Top 4 in 'business' employers are: Google, KPMG, PwC and Ernst & Young. In the IT/engineering category first again is Google, followed by IBM, Microsoft and BMW.

Major trends in top companies' recruitment strategies include an emphasis on:

- A 'new working-culture paradigm' – the relaxed and creative office – shown in the attractiveness of the software industry for Generation Y job seekers; and
- Work–life balance, which was the most attractive attribute offered by companies for both business and engineering job seekers.

Companies are also tapping into talent pools they have not considered before, as shown in the attractiveness of IT companies for job seekers with business backgrounds.

The talent pool strategy

Stahl *et al.*'s (2007) global study involving interviews with 263 HR professionals in 20 multinational corporations and 36 countries – including Infosys, Procter and Gamble, GlaxoSmithKline, Shell, Novartis, Nissan, IBM and IKEA – showed that many tend to follow a talent pool strategy – hiring the 'best' and *then* placing them in jobs. Key features of these companies' strategies are as follows:

- Recruit the best – highly selective with very low selection ratios (number hired divided by number of applicants). Many hire the top 1 per cent from thousands of applicants.
- Recruit for person–organisation or person–culture fit not for specific positions.
- Build relationships with potential candidates; e.g. use internet applications, ties with international universities, on-campus recruitment and internship programmes.
- Use global branding for name recognition and to understand what appeals to applicants e.g. professional freedom, learning opportunities, work–life balance.

comply with the 2000 EU Employment Directive (DTI, 2006), which outlaws discrimination on the grounds of age, sexual orientation, religion or belief, as well as updating disability discrimination legislation. The International Labour Organization (ILO), a specialist branch of the United Nations, also seeks to advance workers' rights and social justice (for further information see www.ILO.org). All member states of the ILO are obliged to 'respect, promote and realise' certain fundamental rights at work, one of which is the 'elimination of discrimination' (ILO, 1998). In the US, enforcement of federal laws prohibiting discrimination, on the basis of certain protected characteristics is one of the central functions of the Equal Employment Opportunities Commission (see www.eeoc.gov).

Employers potentially face legal action and employment tribunals if their recruitment practices are not compliant with legislation. The basic principle of employment legislation related to recruitment is that all individuals should be considered according to their merits and provided equality of opportunity. Discrimination in recruitment, selection or promotion is illegal, unless it can be 'objectively justified', such as where possession of a 'protected characteristic' (the legal bases on which discrimination claims may be brought such as race, sex or age) is considered a genuine occupational qualification (GOQ) for a particular job. An example of a GOQ may be the need to recruit a female doctor to work in a women only prison, for the comfort of the patients. This applies both to *direct* discrimination on the basis of a protected characteristic and *indirect* discrimination, where there is no intentional discrimination, but the practice disproportionately impacts members of particular groups. For example, recruiting through events targeted exclusively at all boys' schools would indirectly discriminate against women. Discrimination can also occur by *association* (i.e. when someone faces discrimination because they associate with someone who has a protected characteristic) or by *perception* (i.e. where someone is discriminated against as they are perceived as having a characteristic which they do not have, for example where someone appears to be older than they are).

For many years, the UK seemed to lag behind the US and other parts of Europe with respect to specific legislation. By far the most comprehensive change to employment legislation for a number of years was the introduction of the 2010 Equality Act (see Box 3.3).

BOX 3.3 HRM in practice — UK anti-discrimination legislation and the Equality Act 2010

Anti-discrimination laws in the UK relating to equal pay between men and women (1970) sex (1975) and race (1976) have been in existence for over 30 years. More recent legislation extends legal protection for discrimination to the protected characteristics of disability (1995); gender reassignment (1999); sexual orientation, religion or belief (2003); and age (2006). Protection against discrimination because of marriage has been in existence since the 1975 Sex Discrimination Act (SDA) but this was extended to same sex couples in civil partnerships from 2004. Discrimination on the grounds of maternity/pregnancy was also first introduced in the SDA with further specific provisions on discrimination during maternity leave introduced in 1999 and 2008. The 2010 Equality Act effectively harmonised the many existing pieces of discrimination legislation on the different protected characteristics into one place, extended existing protection in a number of areas and also introduced new stronger discrimination protection into law.

Sources: ACAS, 2011; Willey *et al.*, 2009.

Of particular importance for recruitment is the concept of 'positive action'. *Positive discrimination* or *affirmative action* when making hiring decisions (i.e. in selection) is controversial because of its justification of quota systems to redress existing discrimination or disadvantage for minority groups. *Positive action* with respect to recruitment emphasises ensuring equal access to opportunity.

If a group which shares a particular protected characteristic is under-represented in a job or workplace (e.g. low levels of ethnic minority police officers), or are felt to face a particular disadvantage, then employers can take voluntary positive action to increase this group's participation (such as targeted recruitment activity). The UK Equality Act places the burden on employers to be aware of the composition of their workforce, whether this proportionately reflects the composition of the wider labour market, and whether their HR practices, including recruitment methods, treat groups differently. For example, using our earlier example of ICT occupations, if an employer recognises under-representation of women and can attribute this to hiring procedures which mean women have fewer opportunities to apply for job vacancies (e.g. recruiting from undergraduate engineering courses where women are already under-represented), then positive action may be used. This action could take the form of a recruitment campaign that uses alternative channels to try to increase the number of applications from women (e.g. recruit from Masters IT conversion courses). Under the Equality Act, however, positive action could go further still to the actual selection decision and involve deliberately hiring a woman over a man for the job, but *only* if they were as qualified for the job as the man.[3]

---

[3]For positive action to be applied in a selection decision, the 2010 Equality Act requires (1) that a candidate with the protected characteristic is *as qualified as* other candidates for the post and (2) that there is evidence that people with the particular protected characteristic are under-represented or face particular difficulties in the workplace. If these

	Direct discrimination	Indirect discrimination	Discrimination by association	Discrimination by perception
Age				
Disability				
Gender reassignment				
Race				
Religion/belief				
Sex				
Sexual orientation				
Marriage/civil partnership				
Pregnancy/maternity				

Key:

PC covered prior to Equality Act	
PC covered as a result of Equality Act	
Characteristic still not covered in legislation	

Figure 3.2 Protected characteristics (PCs) and types of discrimination under the 2010 Equality Act
Source: Adapted from ACAS (2011).

The Equality Act also limits the use of pre-employment health checks (i.e. before a job offer is made) to: decide whether an applicant can carry out an essential job function, to aid the employer in making adjustments to the recruitment process, to monitor diversity and/or to aid in the employment of disabled people (ACAS, 2011). The Equality Act also impacts recruitment by: the extension of indirect discrimination to cover disability and gender reassignment (other protected characteristics were already covered by indirect discrimination); the extension of discrimination by association to cover age, disability, gender reassignment and sex (race, religion/belief and sexual orientation were already covered by discrimination by association prior to the Act); and the extension of discrimination by perception to cover disability, gender reassignment and sex (age, race, religion/belief and sexual orientation were already covered by discrimination by perception prior to the Act) (ibid.). Figure 3.2 presents an overview of the protected characteristics covered by the Equality Act, and the kinds of discrimination that apply to each characteristic.

Employers may decide to take positive action to avoid legal action or to manage the risk of costly tribunals. There is some evidence to suggest that employers do act on such legislation. Woodhams and Corby (2007), for example, showed an increase in the use of monitoring or positive action in recruitment (e.g. work introduction schemes), since the introduction of disability legislation in 1995 and 2003.

There are also arguments for a 'business case' in reducing discrimination during recruitment (Cassell, 2005), perhaps to gain access to a wider applicant pool, to project an image of a responsible employer or to harness the skills of a more diverse group of employees. In fact, examples of positive action recruitment efforts are now prominently publicised on many organisations' websites; for example, Sikh recruitment by the British Army or female officers in many police forces.

Monitoring job applicants by ethnicity, gender, age and disability, when used to ensure representativeness and check that all groups have equal chances at all stages of recruitment, is

---

are not met then any decision that takes a protected characteristic into account will in itself be discriminatory and unlawful. Employers must always consider the 'abilities, merits and qualifications of all the candidates (for a job)' using the protected characteristic only as a 'tie-breaker' (ACAS, 2011: p.8).

considered good practice (ACAS, 2006). However, equal opportunities policies and the practices to support them tend to be more common in public sector organisations, large workplaces, and those with HR specialists who seem to act as 'the guardians of equal opportunities' (Hoque and Noon, 2004: 497). McKay and Avery (2005) recommend caution in seeking numerical targets to satisfy diversity goals if workplace climates are not consistent with the principles of diversity. 'Otherwise firms will be apt to default on their implied recruitment promises, minority recruits will feel misled, and some form of backlash will be probable' (2005: 335). Hoque and Noon (2004), similarly, argued that policies introduced without the substantive practices to support them were nothing more than 'empty shell' policies, a situation which their evidence showed was more common in smaller private sector companies.

Other regulations affecting recruitment are less about avoiding discrimination and more about ensuring standards. These apply to the employment of particular groups, for instance ex-offenders, and specify procedures, like disclosure of previous convictions, to protect vulnerable people e.g. children (see for example, the Criminal Records Bureau). High profile cases have revealed that if the applicant had been vetted at the recruitment stage, it may have been possible to prevent a tragedy occurring. A further piece of legislation that impacts upon recruitment practices in the UK is the 1998 Data Protection Act (DPA) which gives job applicants the right to transparency in the collection of recruitment data in terms of what information is being collected about them and why (ICO, 2005). Other implications of the DPA include the secure and confidential handling of applicants' data by the recruiting organisation, that data collected during recruitment and selection should only be used for these purposes and that no more data is collected than is necessary for the recruitment and selection process (ibid.).

The discussion so far has focused on four aspects of the outer ring presented in Figure 3.1 – the external environment. We can summarise the effects of these pressures on recruitment as follows.

External environment		Impact on recruitment
		Skill needs and supply
Economy		Composition of the applicant pool
Labour market		Recruitment strategy and practice
Social change		• *equity and fairness of processes*
Legislation		• *degree of selectivity possible*
		• *monitoring & targeting applicants*

The organisation

Geographical location, industry sector and stage of growth or technological development can impact upon skill shortages and the ability to access appropriate applicants. Employers in areas of high unemployment, for instance, usually experience looser labour markets, while those in larger urban conurbations will benefit from a more heterogeneous and skilled labour force.

Some industry sectors have also been impacted more than others by globalisation, technological advances, changing business environments or legislation. Apart from the on-going financial crisis described earlier, for example, the financial sector had already experienced intensified competition and restructuring of business operations throughout the 1990s. These pressures resulted in a growth in the use of temporary labour to staff more flexible and continuous customer service functions (Marshall and Richardson, 1996). Although all organisations will be affected in some way by these external forces, some sectors, such as the public or health sector, have relatively more stable skill demands and supply. On the other hand, public sector organisations will be more likely to have systems in place, and be held accountable, for upholding employment legislation (Pearn, 1993). Indeed the UK Equality Act includes a specific *public sector equality duty* which states that public organisations have an obligation to advance equality of opportunity between people who share a protected characteristic and those who do not (EHRC, 2011).

Size

The one feature which has perhaps the most significant impact on how an organisation manages recruitment is its size. Large organisations are more likely to recruit on a regular basis, use more recruiting sources, have dedicated HR staff for recruitment, adopt diversity policies and practices, and derive their recruitment strategy from wider organisational and HR priorities (Barber *et al.*, 1999; Hoque and Noon, 2004; Olian and Rynes, 1984). Recruitment strategies in large organisations, therefore, tend to be more strategically driven and formalised. For example, diversity goals have had a significant impact on large-scale military or police force recruitment efforts, with more positive action to recruit ethnic minorities or women, and even the creation of a new role – the police community support officer – in an effort to increase the representativeness of public policing and respond to legislation on police reform (Johnston, 2006). Large companies in the private sector are also more likely to adopt diversity policies and set recruitment targets. Here, though, this strategy may have more to do with cultivating the company image of being a responsible employer, as well as reducing the risk of potential tribunal cases (Purcell *et al.*, 2002).

Most recruitment research has been directed at what happens in these large organisations; but small and medium-sized enterprises (SMEs) (those employing fewer than 250 employees) dominate most countries' economies. In the UK, 99 per cent of enterprises are classified as small (employing less than 50 employees) with a further 0.7 per cent classified as 'medium' (employing between 50 and 249 employees) (BIS, 2011). Most recruitment activity, therefore, is likely to be informal rather than guided by a formal structure or specialist HR staff.

Generally, recruitment presents greater challenges for smaller companies. SMEs have, on aggregate, lower labour productivity and lower capital/labour ratios, which results in a more constrained pool of resources to expand the workforce or dedicate to recruitment. Unlike the larger organisations illustrated above, small companies are less likely to have the resources to meet demands for a more diverse workforce in keeping with demographic changes (Gallagher and O'Leary, 2007). They are also less able to recruit from internal or national labour markets and are often thought to be disadvantaged by not having the promotional prospects offered by large firms to attract the best qualified staff (Cable and Graham, 2000; Vinten, 1998).

Research evidence confirms that smaller firms tend to rely on less formal methods of recruitment, such as word of mouth. This can lead to several problems, caused by restricting the potential supply of qualified recruits or reliance on unsuitable candidates, simply because they are convenient. Carroll *et al.*, (1999) showed how restricting the pool of recruits for childcare jobs to mainly young women eventually resulted in problems of high turnover due to disillusionment with the job. Such a restricted pool could also be viewed as discriminatory and illegal. This same research, however, also showed that informality and the use of trusted sources was seen as more cost effective in the short term.

Along the same lines, other research has shown that SMEs are better placed for utilising local labour markets and inter-firm networks – perhaps through these informal channels – and that this has some advantages in being able to adapt to recruitment problems. In a comparison of recruitment in small and large urban, suburban and rural hotels, Lockyer and Scholarios (2004) found that small hotels operated in a way that was more attuned to local labour market characteristics, and could therefore more easily identify and match potential employees with local customer expectations. Large hotels which were part of a chain operated a more bureaucratic approach, for example, relying on advertisements in national newspapers or, as we explore further in the next section, the outsourcing of recruitment to agencies. In many cases, this meant they were less effective at utilising local networks to fill vacancies.

Outsourcing and devolution of HRM

In larger organisations, the structure of HR functions and the responsibility for recruitment has shifted over the last few decades. This has occurred alongside important broader trends in HRM including the devolution of traditional HR roles and functions to line managers (Purcell and Hutchison, 2007; Renwick, 2006) and an upsurge in the number of companies claiming to implement Ulrich's HR partner model. The most recent version of the latter sees HR as a 'three-legged stool' consisting of strategic business partners (senior HR professionals working with business leaders), shared administrative service centres, and centres of HR expertise (see also Ulrich and Beatty, 2001).

Fewer than one-third of UK organisations has introduced the Ulrich model for their HR function in full (CIPD, 2007a). As a result, the recruitment function appears in various forms. For some, mostly in large multinationals, it is carried out by HR Partners or 'experts' as in the Ulrich model. Elsewhere it is undertaken by a shared service centre that provides routine administration and sometimes more tailored additional HR services. Shared service centres can be resourced by in-house staff or they can be outsourced to specialist third-party providers. Consequently, many companies have outsourced all or at least part of their HR functions, particularly those associated with recruitment. Some organisations have made the decision to outsource the recruitment function for particular grades of staff. For example, 81 per cent of organisations are thought to use agencies for recruiting temporary workers (CIPD, 2007a), while 11 per cent of private sector organisations consider them 'integral to attracting top talent', as in the case of executive search agencies (CIPD, 2011).

This strategy, which is often referred to as 'Recruitment Process Outsourcing' (RPO), is presented as a way of cutting costs, improving efficiency, for example, by reducing the length of the recruitment process, and also attracting high-quality applicants (CIPD, 2011). Before the economic recession and decline in recruitment levels, a vibrant business had emerged in RPO partnerships, particularly in the UK (*Personnel Today*, 10 July 2007). Many organisations still work only with preferred supplier lists of agencies which re-tender periodically to retain their contracts. The agency then carries out the whole recruitment process on behalf of the organisation.

Such partnerships between organisations and outsourcers have developed to such a level of sophistication that some research has presented them as a template for a 'new model of recruitment' which would accommodate recruitment at all levels of an organisation (Gallagher and O'Leary, 2007). This 'new model' would combine more personalised, 'high-value' approaches – high cost strategies designed to attract candidates for high-skilled positions – with more standardised processes for low-skilled positions taking advantage of the efficiency-gains offered by the use of new technologies. However, there seems to be a decrease in the use of agencies, with many employers viewing them as unaffordable, an unnecessary expense, and stopping use of them altogether (CIPD, 2011). Thus, while RPO still is a popular strategy, there is some evidence that companies are bringing recruitment back in-house. Some of these issues are explored in Case study 3.2.

In organisations which retain the recruitment function, often this is centralised as part of a support function for line managers. If the responsibility for HR, including recruitment, has been devolved to line managers, HR may have a role in supporting the line manager in identifying their recruitment needs, suggesting appropriate strategies, advising them about legislation, assisting in drawing up staff requirements and recommending appropriate methods. In the case of agency partnerships, this becomes one of setting, agreeing and monitoring the standard of service provided by the agency, which thus removes the more routine tasks from HR. Arguably, these different roles and responsibilities enhance, or at the very least change, the role of HR practitioners, and demand a different set of skills from that required to carry out administrative tasks. Ulrich and Brockbank (2005) have claimed that HR professionals will need to be 'credible activists', 'culture and change stewards', 'talent managers/organisational designers', 'strategy architects' and 'operational executers'.

Taking each of these organisational characteristics into account, the importance of the second layer of the model in Figure 3.1 can be summarised as follows.

The organisation	Impact on recruitment
Sector	Frequency
Location	Positions to be filled (*short-term/long-term, skill level*)
Growth	Global market for recruits
HR strategy	Strategic goals
Size	Formalisation of procedures
	Benefits package/career opportunities offered
	Entry requirements
	Responsibility for recruitment (*line manager, HR partnering, outsourcing, ad hoc*)

The job

We have already noted the changing nature of jobs and the effects this has on the skills demanded by employers. Recent research on the most valued attributes sought in job candidates shows that many companies are recruiting for 'motivation' or 'attitude', and that this is consistent across jobs with different levels of job quality (measured in terms of skill variety, autonomy and allowance for employee involvement) (see Table 3.1). This emphasises the increasing relevance of generic, transferable and customer-oriented competencies in all types of jobs.

Employers must also make a decision about whether the job should be allocated internally to existing employees or filled using externally resourced staff – either full-time, subcontracted,

Table 3.1 Main attributes that employers are looking for when recruiting, by job 'quality'

	Job quality			Total
	High	Medium	Low	
	%	%	%	%
Specific/technical skills	25	16	13	19
Generic skills	15	19	20	17
Particular qualification or level of qualification	9	13	9	10
Particular type or number of years of work	7	7	1	5
Motivation and/or attitude	41	45	56	47
Others	1	0	1	1
Don't know	0	0	2	1

Source: Bates *et al.*, 2008.

outsourced or temporary. This depends to a large extent on the expected employment relationship. Lepak and Snell (2002) describe a rational decision choice here with respect to the level of human capital required to perform the job. Jobs which require high skill and knowledge which is unique to the organisation (hence greater investment in training) are better managed as internal promotions or transfers, as these have implications for building a committed workforce. Jobs which do not require costly training and which can be performed at a lower skill level can be externalised with a view to a more short-term employment relationship.

There are of course detrimental effects of short-term employment strategies, with employers' under-investment in temporary employees affecting the employee's future employability once they are back on the job market (DFES, 2003; Kellard *et al.*, 2001) Under-investment in employees can also cause skills shortages on the external labour market as well as skills problems caused by staff turnover. It has been argued, for example, that if employers wish to utilise the flexible labour market they should be prepared to bear the costs involved with providing workers with the requisite skills, even if this involves spill-over effects to other organisations once the employee has left the firm (ibid.). Furthermore, many jobs that have short tenure (and high turnover) are often seen as poor quality, not least in terms of pay (Siebern-Thomas, 2005) and thus potentially unattractive to potential recruits. Indeed, prior to the A8 states joining, the UK was seen as having some of the worst-quality jobs in the EU (ibid.).

The distinction between high- and low-quality work highlights the distinction between core and peripheral workers (Boxall and Purcell, 2003). Those viewed as core to the success of a business are employed on a competitive salary and, in most cases, with a view to a long-term relationship. This longer-term investment is reflected in the resources dedicated to recruitment. For high-value graduate positions, for example, large companies tend to have dedicated recruitment programmes managed by in-house staff. Those of less long-term value to the organisation are either outsourced entirely or employed in less secure, short-term contracts. In some industries, such as the IT sector, temporary agency staff are also used to fill skills gaps in specialist, 'cutting edge' areas, as well as in less skilled areas, such as helpdesk roles (Purcell *et al.*, 2004). This allows the organisation to maximise workforce flexibility and operate more flexibly in unpredictable and competitive markets. (For further analysis of the human resource challenges of the use of temporary workers see Burgess and Connell, 2006.)

Pre-recruitment activities

The previous section illustrates the diverse recruitment conditions which organisations face. It is hard to imagine a single, 'best practice' approach to actual recruitment which would be appropriate for all situations. However, there are some generalisations which can be made about how organisations should prepare for recruitment. Detailed accounts of these activities can be found in other texts (e.g. Lees and Cordery, 2000; Marchington and Wilkinson, 2005; Torrington *et al.*, 2008). Here, we provide a brief review of two of the most fundamental pre-recruitment activities which are common across all situations – producing job descriptions and person specifications.

Job descriptions

Filling a vacancy begins with a process called job analysis. This should be 'a purposeful, systematic process for collecting information on the important work-related aspects of a job' (Gatewood and Feild, 1998: 245), and should define what is required to perform the job successfully. Early approaches were based on producing a list of task-based and worker-based attributes (e.g. McCormick, 1976) drawing from: interviews/surveys with job incumbents or supervisors, observation, past job descriptions or databases about occupational classifications. For example, a firefighter's job may involve the task of 'applying water or chemical agents to extinguish flames' but we need to know the essential worker (or personal) attributes, such as situational awareness or confidence and resilience in the face of pressure, to recruit the right person to carry out this task (Department for Communities and Local Government, 2009).

Various job analysis techniques have been proposed (e.g., Position Analysis Question-naire, Functional Job Analysis, Work Profiling System) each using a slightly different approach to breaking down jobs into specific dimensions and ranking the importance of each to job success. Campion's (1988) multi-dimensional model of job analysis and design attempted to draw together many of these earlier approaches to provide the most comprehensive description possible of what a job entails. This proposed that jobs should be described using all of the following dimensions: tasks; worker characteristics (e.g. knowledge, skills, abilities, personality, motivation, perceptual-motor requirements); job context (e.g. tools/equipment needed; degree of social interaction); the reward structure (e.g. benefits of teamwork or autonomy); and job demands (e.g. problem-solving, intensity, speed).

There are at least two notable points about current thinking on describing jobs. The first is that the components of a job, whether the tasks or the worker characteristics, cannot be separated from the organisational setting in which it takes place; hence the position of the job at the centre of the concentric circles in Figure 3.1. The notion of skill, for example, may reflect specific product markets or organisational strategies. Grugulis (2007) distinguishes skill as residing in the individual, the job and the setting. Two hotel workers may each possess similar individual skills in interpersonal communication, but the setting means that one uses these skills in the context of tightly prescribed standards and a script to guide their dealings with customers, while the other may have more autonomy and scope to use their discretion (see for example Hurrell et al., forthcoming). This has implications for job analysis methods, which some suggest should be refocused around the broader goals of work analysis rather than specific job tasks (Gatewood and Feild, 1998). It also impacts decisions about matching the work context with the preferences of potential applicant groups, perhaps targeting workers seeking short-term employment for low discretion jobs, and workers seeking long-term positions in high discretion jobs.

A second key point is that job descriptions should not be static or too narrow; they should take into account how jobs may change as a result of environmental drivers, such as technological advances or competitive pressures, and consider the interconnections between specific jobs and other organisational roles (Sanchez, 1994). As an example, organisational restructuring and delayering of middle-management levels has pushed many managerial responsibilities, such as problem-solving, on to non-managerial roles. Future-oriented (or strategic) job analysis, described as a way of planning for future jobs (Schneider and Konz, 1989), should intentionally include those involved in planning change in the organisation rather than relying on existing job incumbents as a source of information (see also Herriot and Anderson, 1997).

Person specifications and competency frameworks

Person specifications, which are derived from the job description, detail the personal qualities that workers require to perform the job. The exact nature of person specifications has been influenced greatly by the competency profiling approach. This identifies the worker-based attributes (knowledge, skill, ability, personality etc.), or competencies, which are required to reach a required level of performance (or competence). The difference between this and traditional approaches is that the emphasis is on observable behaviours.

This approach emerged from the work of McClelland (1976) and Boyatzis (1982) who, focusing initially on managers, identified the behaviours which differentiated high- and poor-performing individuals and linked these to key underlying personal qualities. In the UK, there was an equally strong movement towards a functional competence approach based on minimum standards of observable performance outcomes rather than inferring underlying personal attributes. One such example was the Management Charter Initiative (1990), which consulted professional bodies for management development in order to identify a framework of competences required by managers at various levels. Today, this tradition continues in approaches which specify Key Performance Indicators (KPIs), or what behaviours the individual should achieve. Companies may purchase 'off the shelf' frameworks, which can then be amended to suit their needs, or develop their own competency frameworks in-house or with consultants (IDS, 2008). This then might feed into the compilation of a competency dictionary which demonstrates each competency with positive and negative indicators (see Table 3.2 for an example related to the competency 'team spirited' and Marchington and Wilkinson (2005) for further examples). As with future-oriented job analysis, the competencies that organisations specify as the basis for recruitment and selection should be continually reviewed so that they can anticipate emerging and declining competency requirements (Robinson *et al.*, 2005).

Competency frameworks are evident in growing numbers of organisations. By 2010, two-thirds of 168 organisations responding to one UK survey used a competency framework to target their recruitment (Suff, 2010). Many companies identify 'core competencies' which are applied to all employees – for instance 'customer focus' and 'communication' – as well as specific competencies which may apply to different occupational groups. Typical competencies used are teamworking, communication, people management, customer service skills, team skills, results-orientation and problem-solving (ibid.), which indicates further that organisations are interested in recruiting for personal qualities as well as for specific technical skills and qualifications (see Table 3.2).

Returning again to Figure 3.1, we can now add further detail to how job requirements are likely to shape recruitment, as follows.

The job	Impact on recruitment
Current demands/skills	Person specification
Core/periphery	Changes to competency profile
Job/work analysis	'Future orientation' of job analysis
Future job demands	Effort in targeting applicant groups

Table 3.2 Example competency statement and associated behaviours

Team spirited

The way we pull together in an environment, which recognises and celebrates each other's strengths and contribution.

Positive behaviours	Negative behaviours
• Works effectively together to accomplish organisational goals	• Creates or tolerates an 'us and them' culture
• Builds positive working relationships with other teams and individuals	• Relies upon others to complete their work; doesn't take ownership
• Shows consideration for the needs of the team; thinks about how colleagues will be affected	• Doesn't build networks; see themselves as self-sufficient
• Happy to provide support to colleagues; doesn't wait to be asked	• Avoids dealing with conflict between teams

Source: *IDS HR Studies 865*, March 2008, 17.

Recruitment methods

As a result of the challenges discussed so far, organisations seem to be using more creative solutions, targeting diverse applicant groups and using internet channels to communicate to potential applicants alongside traditional methods, such as advertising, agencies and personal contacts. In 1989, the Institute of Personnel Management (IPM) reported that the majority of employers only advertised in regional or national press. Over 20 years on, e-recruitment has become the method of choice for many organisations, although, as we saw with the rise of outsourced recruitment and the use of flexible labour, agency recruitment is also popular (see Table 3.4). In this section, we summarise the most popular methods, moving between those which provide advantages in terms of the efficiency of recruitment (e-recruitment, agencies) and those which are directed more at attracting the attention of candidates (referrals, word-of-mouth, networks, and online social networking). We conclude with a strategy borrowed from marketing which aims to solve recruitment difficulties by directly targeting applicant perceptions – employer branding.

Internet recruitment and social networking

Job information and recruitment channels are increasingly found on company websites, portals which host vacancies for similar types of posts (e.g. graduate jobs) or publicly funded sites such as the UK's Jobcentre Plus, which is one of the most popular sites used by the internet population to search for work (Hasluck *et al.*, 2005). As shown in Table 3.4, according to a 2011 survey, 59 per cent of organisations regarded corporate websites as the most effective method for attracting applicants, and more in the public sector, surpassing the popularity of other traditional methods. Parry and Tyson (2008) found that, of approximately 400 companies using corporate websites for recruitment, the most commonly reported reason was cost-effectiveness (75 per cent) followed by ease of use for candidates (63 per cent). Other frequently reported reasons were the generation of a larger candidate pool, ease of use for the organisation, speed of hiring and company policy.

A recent trend is 'viral recruitment' where companies use social network sites such as Facebook or LinkedIn to target technologically literate Generation Y applicants (school leavers, students and recent graduates). Some creative examples pioneered by TMP Worldwide, an international recruitment consultant, include: the use of online digital music service Spotify to guide potential graduate recruits to Jaguar Land Rover's career website (winner of the 2010 Association of Graduate Recruiters' best website award for large recruiters); a global recruitment fair on the virtual world Second Life which allowed hundreds of global interviews; and the use of virtual gaming adverts to recruit graduates for jobs at the British Intelligence agency (GCHQ). Games such as Tom Clancy's Splinter Cell: Double Agent were chosen because of their secret service theme.

Use of the internet and social networking for recruitment is now accepted practice for employers to help target their recruitment or raise awareness of their brand (Tenwick, 2008). There are some drawbacks, however. Parry and Tyson (2008) followed up their survey with HR manager interviews in 15 organisations using online recruitment. The most common problem identified was receiving a large number of unsuitable applicants, thus making the filtering of candidates more resource intensive. Other problems included applications from overseas candidates who did not have suitable work permits, concern that certain applicant groups may not be reached and concern over the impersonal nature of online recruitment.

For applicants, the internet allows easier access to job networks, enabling them to match their skills with the needs of employers (Cabinet Office, 2004), and, in fact, for some may be the only job search medium. According to a survey of 400 graduate jobseekers by Reed Employment, 89 per cent looked at the web regularly for job opportunities while only 3 per cent consulted newspapers (*People Management*, 7 March 2008).

There are also some negative implications for candidates, though. Online methods may not be fully compliant with disability discrimination legislation and there are concerns about accessibility for socially excluded groups, such as the unemployed or less IT-literate (Cabinet Office, 2004; Digital Europe, 2003; Searle, 2006). Research has shown that younger people, the better educated and those already in work are more likely to carry out job searches online (Kuhn and Skuterud, 2000). As a result, equality legislation, generally, also promotes using traditional methods, such as application forms, and other ways of ensuring all groups have equal access to job information.

There is also increased reported use of employers using social networking sites to pre-screen applicants (as distinct from trying to attract applicants via social media). Broughton *et al.* (2011) cite a US survey of over 2,600 HR professionals, 45 per cent of whom checked applicants' social network profiles prior to hiring them. Although apparently less frequent in the UK, a further survey of almost 600 UK managers and directors revealed that approximately 20 per cent found information online about an applicant *which the applicant did not volunteer* (Viadeo, 2007 emphasis added). Furthermore, almost 60 per cent of these managers stated that such information did influence their hiring decisions, with HR managers especially likely to report that candidates were declined on the basis of information discovered through social networking sites.

These trends have several implications for applicants. First, there is the possibility of indirect age discrimination if someone is not hired based on information they post on social networking sites, as such sites are more likely to be used by younger job candidates. Second, there are also wider discrimination implications if any information on any of the protected characteristics discussed above are discovered through social network sites, and are subsequently used to filter applicants from the process. Third there is an issue around data protection legislation especially if information is sought covertly, although the public nature of social network sites potentially makes this a contentious issue. Finally there is an ethical issue regarding applicant privacy.

Perhaps given these issues, employers should follow the advice of one US consultancy to simply 'put in place a written policy that they will not use information from social networking sites to assess candidates' (Fishman and Morris, 2010: 4).

Agencies and headhunters

Fifty-nine per cent of employers, and more in manufacturing and production, and private services, report using agencies (Table 3.4). Surveys of UK employers indicate that the main reason for using agency employment is to fill temporary vacancies in administrative positions or some professional posts, such as teachers or dentists (Welfare, 2006). Although for employers this means a reduction in short-term labour costs, Forde and Slater (2006) argue that agency employment in many cases is also accompanied by low levels of commitment and greater job insecurity for employees.

A specific form of agency recruitment is carried out by executive search agencies or head-hunters which identify candidates for senior management or executive roles. This involves cold-calling targeted individuals with the intention of tempting them to apply for the post on offer, but can also involve the development of close relationships between the agency, the client and potential job seekers (Finlay and Coverdill, 2000). For such senior-level appointments, where discretion is required by both parties, headhunters are likely to remain the preferred route of recruitment over internet media.

Targeting applicant perceptions: referrals, networks, recruiters and incentives

Some methods are more directly focused on influencing the way that potential applicant perceive the job and their decision to apply, as in the targeted use of social networking sites described above. The 2011 CIPD survey of employers also showed that other 'informal' methods (such as employee referrals or word of mouth) are considered effective at attracting applicants by a quarter or more of employers (Table 3.3).

Employee referrals, for instance, have several apparent advantages. Candidates who have already been vetted by an employee, are usually a better fit with the company and job, and have a better understanding of the business, often possessing some of the tacit knowledge which is accumulated through experience (*Personnel Today*, 29 May 2007; Yakubovich, 2006). Employees feel that their reputation is at stake with a referral, which encourages them to refer only the highest-quality applicants. From the applicants' perspective, those referred receive valuable information about the job and organisation from their contacts. This 'realism' attracts people with more accurate expectations and better 'fit' to the job, allowing others to self-select out of the process at an early stage. Using referrals has also been shown to increase the recruit's commitment to the company and reduce turnover (Breaugh and Mann, 1984). The dangers of these informal methods, however, are that they can perpetuate existing social networks and working practices, hence acting as a barrier to change, as well as being open to challenge regarding their fairness (for example because of 'same as me' hiring decisions). Building networks is intended to create relationships with potential future employees. For example, employers create links with schools/colleges/universities, perhaps offering internships and work placements to students with the prospect of retaining them as permanent employees. Professional networking, especially through online sites such as LinkedIn, has been used increasingly for specialist IT staff, financial services and the media. This tool is used not only for job postings but also 'to build pipelines of possible future recruits' among those who are not actively looking for jobs (ComputerWeekly.com, 11 June 2010).

As well as affecting pre-hire concerns, such as enhancing the quality of applicants who ultimately apply for jobs, these informal methods are also thought to affect post-hire outcomes; for example, improving person–organisation fit in terms of employee and employer values and needs, future employee satisfaction and commitment, and increasing retention rates (Anderson *et al.*, 2001; Breaugh and Starke, 2000).

There has also been considerable research on how the characteristics of initial contacts affect potential applicants' first impressions of the organisation, and their subsequent decisions to apply. One area often studied is the crisis facing military recruitment in many nations (because of changing social values, the unpopularity of recent conflicts such as Iraq, or the job prospects themselves). Focusing on the Belgian armed services, Schreurs *et al.* (2005) found that the perceived warmth and competence of career counsellors in recruitment outlets made potential recruits more likely to apply. However, they were also less likely to apply the more information they were given, suggesting that this process may also have imparted more realistic (or negative) information about the potential job. This finding is consistent with the large body of research on realistic recruitment information which shows that this leads to more accurate expectations and lower voluntary turnover after hiring (Phillips, 1998).

Finally, financial incentives, such as increased pay or 'golden hellos', have been shown to increase the number of applications (Williams and Dreher, 1992). The latter especially are evident in many areas of the current UK job market – cash lump sums or interest free loans have been offered to new graduates in some areas of employment with hard-to-fill vacancies, such as teachers who indicate that they will accept a placement in any geographical area. However, those recruited through financial inducements rather than through voluntary attraction based on value fit or a realistic expectation of the job – a process influenced more often by the informal processes discussed above – may be less likely to feel attachment to and remain with the organisation (Taylor and Schmidt, 1983).

Employer branding

Taking the applicant perspective further, there has been a surge of interest in the image of the employer (Saks, 2005) and, in particular, 'branding' as a competitive attraction strategy.

Table 3.3 Most effective methods to attract applicants, by industry sector (%)

	2011 survey (all)	Manuf. & production	Private sector services	Public sector	Voluntary, community, not-for-profit	2010 survey (all)
Own corporate website	59	44	57	77	66	63
Recruitment agencies	54	77	62	22	30	60
Local newspaper ads	32	38	23	41	51	36
Employee referral scheme	29	33	38	5	14	35
Commercial job boards	27	33	29	14	29	33
Specialist journals/trade press	27	24	23	30	43	31
Speculative applications/ word-of-mouth	25	30	29	9	23	24
Jobcentre Plus	25	24	24	22	34	23
Professional networking (e.g. LinkedIn)	16	11	23	5	9	14
Search consultants	15	24	17	5	4	22
Links with schools/ colleges/universities	13	16	13	9	17	18
Apprenticeships	11	19	9	13	9	12
National newspaper ads	1	4	6	23	29	16
Secondments	11	7	8	21	12	11
Links with local organisations making redundancies*	7	13	5	7	9	–
Previous employees	5	6	7	2	1	5
Social networking sites (e.g. Facebook)	3	4	5	3	4	3

Source: CIPD, 2011. From *Resourcing and Talent Planning*, CIPD, with permission of the publisher the Chartered Institute of Personnel Development, London (www.cipd.co.uk).
Base: 604 (2011); 464 (2010).
*New item introduced in 2011.

As well as being a key feature of recruitment for the top global employers we highlighted in Box 3.2, many employers are increasingly viewing investment in a brand as a long-term strategy for recruiting when roles become available (TMP Worldwide, 2011). It seems to be more than a passing fad (CIPD, 2007b). Despite the current negative economic climate, nearly three-quarters of respondents in a 2011 survey of UK employers claimed to take action to improve their employer brand, for example, by introducing or extending flexible working/homeworking or introducing student placements (CIPD, 2011).

The concept implies that organisations should think beyond just recruitment for specific job vacancies, and focus on communicating information about their image and the whole employment package to potential applicants. This is especially important when there is competition for skilled labour, as applicant decision-making may be influenced by other job offers or informal information about a company; for example, negative comments on 'blogs' which may damage the employer 'brand' (*People Management*, 20 March 2008). One often-cited example is in graduate recruitment, where the primary reason given for difficulties filling some vacancies is graduates' perceptions of particular sectors, such as the voluntary sector (Association of Graduate Recruiters, 2008; Hurrell *et al.*, 2011).

Various sources of information, such as corporate websites, word-of-mouth, university sponsorship or publicity events can contribute to perceptions of a brand, particularly in conditions where organisations are competing to become the 'employer of choice'. High-profile publications are also influential. For example, more applications are submitted to companies ranked high in US business publications, such as Fortune's *100 Best Companies to Work For* (Cable and Turban, 2003) or the UK's *Sunday Times' Best Companies to Work For*. Companies ranked in Universum's *The World's Most Attractive Employers 2011* (see Box 3.2) are likely to enjoy the same benefits in terms of candidate attraction.

These surveys are based on ratings either by existing employees or job seekers on a number of attributes; for example, opportunities for personal growth, well-being/work–life balance, teamwork, 'giving something back', the way the company treats staff, and, fair pay and benefits. These can be described as a mix of instrumental and symbolic attributes. In their study of Belgian final year students and employees targeted by the banking industry, Lievens and Highhouse (2003) found that applicants' job choices were more likely to be influenced by companies' symbolic attributes, such as what the company stands for, than objective (or instrumental) attributes, such as pay or conditions. Sometimes these symbolic attributes can also be communicated more subtly as in the case of job applicants who are attracted to certain service sector employers because of an affinity with the 'style' of the company (see Hurrell and Scholarios, 2011).

The need for an applicant perspective

The 'war for talent' when demand for applicants exceeds supply (although admittedly less of a concern in the current climate) and the search for more engaged and committed employees has meant that a purely selective approach to hiring based on matching job and person characteristics is often inadequate for finding the 'right' employees. As we examine further in the next chapter, staffing may be viewed as an interactive social process where the applicant also has some power; e.g. whether to engage in the application process. This places greater importance on the perceptions of potential and actual applicants. In some situations companies will have to work harder to attract qualified applicants, maintain their interest in the company, and convince them that they should accept an offer of employment. As we saw in our analysis of the recruitment context, consideration of the applicant is important in situations where there are skills shortages and an inadequate supply of quality labour, or for some organisations, such as SMEs. Convincing applicants to accept job offers is, of course, likely to be less of a concern in current, looser, labour markets.

Applicant 'attraction' to organisations implies getting applicants to view the organisation as a positive place to work. A considerable amount of research has been generated on just how applicant views are formed, for instance, how they are affected by recruiter behaviour, what draws their attention to corporate websites, how do they process this information and how they use this to make decisions about the attractiveness of the organisation (e.g. Ehrhart and Ziegert, 2005; Zottoli and Wanous, 2000). This has provided information on the effectiveness of alternative recruitment sources, as well as investigating which sources provide the best employees in terms of post-hire outcomes such as better job performance and lower turnover. We have reviewed some of this research in our consideration of each recruitment method above. Case study 3.3 also considers the issue of 'fit' between applicants and the brand in more detail.

Conclusions

There is no 'best practice' recruitment approach, although methods which comply with equality legislation are a requirement. The model shown in Figure 3.1 demonstrates the factors which will impact recruitment outcomes, and hence the range of activities which organisations may adopt. The scarcity and criticality of the skills sought, decisions concerning the permanency of jobs, and, the impact on particular applicant groups are just a few of the issues discussed in this chapter which will determine how employers choose to attract job applicants. For some organisations, recruitment is planned, integrated into wider HR strategies, and a key concern of senior managers who wish to attract and retain committed people. For others, it remains a low priority task where ad hoc arrangements, sometimes through recruitment agencies, are made as the need arises. HR practitioners still have a role to play, but that role might range from one of simply sending out instructions in a service centre, to one of major strategic importance where specific expertise is required, as in the design and/or implementation of behavioural competency frameworks.

The 'applicant perspective' considers all recruitment methods as part of the developing relationship between applicants and organisations, which takes place in a changing external context. Recent interest in this approach has added considerably to earlier research which suggested that those hired through informal channels, such as referrals, would be different from those hired by formal methods, such as adverts or agencies. The former tended to be happier, more committed employees, with better fit to the needs of the organisation and less prone to turnover (see Barber, 1998 for a review). More recent ways of looking at the effects on applicants have recognised that all recruitment channels, including traditional adverts, online systems, and 'branding' efforts, send relevant messages to potential applicants which will affect their perceptions of the job/organisation and their intentions with respect to job search.

As well as trying to address objective recruitment goals, therefore, such as cost, the number of applications, diversity targets, or time taken to fill a vacancy, organisations will also gain from using methods which communicate accurate information and attractive images of the job to applicants. These have been shown to influence interest in the application process and willingness to apply. Taking all these factors into account should mean a greater chance of successful recruitment, both in the short-term with respect to recruitment goals and compliance with legislation, and in the longer-term, with respect to the performance and attitudes of future employees.

CASE STUDY 3.1

CHANGING RECRUITMENT AT MERCADO SUPERMARKETS

SCOTT HURRELL AND DORA SCHOLARIOS

Mercado's HR strategy is: 'to provide improved capability to become the best retail HR function and make Mercado a great place to work'. New HR processes were introduced in 2007 which meant that many of the functions involved in recruitment and selection were centralised in the 'HR Shared Service Centre'.

Previously, there were issues with in-store recruitment processes because staff were dealing with a large number of CVs and application forms and this was time-consuming and expensive. The number of applications at peak recruitment times, for example before Christmas, could be overwhelming, and this made them difficult to track on the old system. It was also recognised that the application screening process was not always robust, as department managers sometimes had to interview candidates who were not really suitable and this was not the best use of their time. Problems also existed in keeping up with the applicants' references. Eddie Pitt, the Grocery Manager in the Fenwick store raised the subject regularly in the weekly meeting of department managers.

> I am wasting so much of my time seeing people who just don't have what it takes to work here. I am not a HR Manager and I've got bigger priorities than looking at application forms and preparing for interviews that turn out to be a waste of my time and theirs. Some of them have no common sense and no interest in working for the company. We need to get more colleagues who have a real desire to work with us and who are going to help our customers.

Now, applications are made online only and not on paper. This means that stores no longer accept or receive paper application forms and do not write advertisements to display in-store. Application forms are no longer scored manually. Offer letters and contracts are produced centrally.

For the company, this is an attempt to have a consistent recruitment brand and experience for applicants. It is hoped that 'prospect pools' for specialist and hard to recruit roles can be developed and thereby assist HR planning and induction training. The centralised system

will also facilitate the production of management information, for example, recruitment reports and statistics.

The process begins with the store identifying the need to recruit; then it seeks authority to do this. The store then loads vacancy details onto the system, including interview slots and pay. Applicants browse the corporate web site then apply for a specific vacancy and do a test. The vacancy automatically closes when a pre-determined number of applicants have been successfully screened. The system then forwards the applicant to HR shared services, who arrange interviews directly with the applicants and then confirm the details. Eddie Pitt likes the new system so far, but it has taken a bit of time for him to learn how to put his vacancies on the website. 'I am more confident now that I have put three vacancies on. I had help and coaching from the store HR manager at first, but I did the last one by myself.'

From the store's perspective, it holds interviews at agreed times and returns notes to shared services, though the store ranks applicants and makes the decision. Eddie's colleague, the Bakery Manager, Jenny Jackson, was a bit unsure about setting aside interview times on a computer system. Her experience of her first interview arrangements has been positive.

> I was a bit cynical about how it would work when you are dealing with people a couple of hundred miles away. I thought I would prefer to keep the old system. The applicants turned up for my interviews and seemed to know a bit about the job and the company. I had to plan my time to fit in the interview but it was worth it. It is hard to find qualified bakers, so if this is going to help get people more quickly, then it will be a good thing.

HR Shared Services makes a verbal offer, then sends out a contract and invitation to induction. It also sends for references when necessary. It means that department managers have to ensure that their department has the right skills and should plan ahead with vacancy requirements. They are also responsible for making sure that interviews take place at the planned time. An additional function for stores is that they can contact a 'prospect pool', or those applicants who have expressed a desire to work in specific skilled roles, like bakery, then advise them to apply online. They can also identify applicants with the 'on hold' status who were successful but who were not offered a role. Stores can contact them and arrange a meeting to discuss a new vacancy. Jenny Jackson offered a job to a baker who was 'on hold' because he was second choice at the Paisley store.

> This saved me so much time. I was able to get an offer made and start the new baker within a week. Peter was well impressed by how quickly we got him started – he decided to come to us and turn down another job that he has been waiting to hear from for three weeks.

A key objective is to improve the applicant's experience. The applicant browses the site for suitable opportunities. Those wishing to apply then create a user account. If there are no suitable vacancies, they can register interest in certain roles. In order to comply with the Equality Act, applicants with special needs are referred directly from the website to Shared Services for assistance with their application.

Applicants normally apply online for vacancies and enter their details. They then complete a job-specific screening test online. If successful, they are contacted by Shared Services to arrange an interview, then attend the interview.

The challenges of implementing this change to existing practice from the store's perspective have been about communicating the change to all relevant staff (including customer service staff, who can provide some information to applicants in-store), training people who are directly involved in the process on the new system, and providing ongoing coaching support. Jean is a Customer Service Adviser. In the past, she kept a supply of application forms at the desk, but now she has to refer all those who enquire to the company website.

> At first, I felt that I could not really help people asking about jobs, but the briefing I was at in the store explained the new system to me. I now understand what they have to do and I know where to get more help advice for them if they need it.

This e-recruitment strategy is being monitored closely to determine its effectiveness from the point of view of the organisation. Measures are being taken of, for instance, the number of candidates registered, calls received and average call handling time at the Shared Service Centre, offers made, percentage of references processed, and average time taken to fill a vacancy from advert to verbal offer.

While the experiences in one branch have been positive, the pilot study in another small store has highlighted some issues. There are only five user names and passwords allocated to staff and this means that not all managers can be authorised to use the system. Inevitably, there are problems of uploading vacancies, arranging interviews and making appointments.

It is too early to assess the impact on candidates, but there have been some success stories like Peter. Managers are still adapting to the new approach. Eddie Jackson is keeping an open mind, but his experience so far is that the system is 'letting me concentrate on managing the people I have already – and spending less time on interviewing people who don't want to be part of Mercado'.

Questions

1   What do you think were the main drivers for the company to develop its e-recruitment strategy?

2   Is e-recruitment appropriate for all types of vacancies in a retail store?

3   What are the advantages of this approach?

4   What are the disadvantages?

5   Which other methods would you suggest?

6   How would you design a research project to evaluate the effectiveness of this example of e-recruitment from the point of view of the applicant?

7   To what extent has this new strategy 'improved capability to become the best retail HR function. . . and make Mercado a great place to work'?

8   The head of HR shared services has also suggested screening applicants through looking at their pages on social networking sites (where applicants have these). If you were a manager in Mercado would you recommend taking up this suggestion? What are the reasons for your decision?

CASE STUDY 3.2
OUTSOURCING RECRUITMENT AT BLUEBERRY

SCOTT HURRELL AND DORA SCHOLARIOS

This case highlights two different issues. First, it is an example of an outsourcing strategy adopted by a call centre, and second, it highlights some methods used to recruit for scarce skills. It is based on the authors' research with one of the largest global providers of Human Resources services (a Fortune Global 500 company) which provides career and staffing services for job seekers and employers, and with a technical customer services call centre for a multinational IT company.

Blueberry is a subsidiary of a multinational IT company based in the US (Globalchip) which established its European help desk three years ago. Currently, it directly employs 40 staff whose contracts are permanent. New recruits need to be fluent in a European language other than English and have technical competence (computer skills, some product knowledge) and customer service skills. The recruitment of individuals with these relevant technical and language skills has been very difficult. Currently, the Customer Service Unit includes fluent speakers of Spanish, French, Italian, Finnish, Dutch, German and Greek. The majority are non-UK nationals.

In the United States, the parent company, Globalchip, operates a similar help desk for Asia. When the Asian Help Desk was established, the strategy adopted, after much discussion and deliberation, was to outsource the whole unit to an agency (Succuro) which recruits the staff, employs them and manages them with respect to personal development, discipline and performance management. There is a very tight budget for salaries. Blueberry managers are responsible for the overall operation of the unit.

The HR Director of Blueberry's parent company asked the HR partner, Liz McDonald, who is responsible for liaising with the European Help desk, to identify the steps which would need to be taken to put a similar outsourced help desk in place. She was also asked to collaborate with her US colleague to determine the difficulties that Succoro currently face in recruiting individuals with the required skills and competencies.

Her enquiries have shown that Globalchip has a three-year contact with Succuro, which is due for renewal soon. A 'service-level agreement' was produced by the company, which clearly indicated what level of performance was expected of the agency, for instance, time to fill vacancies, provision of statistical data about the levels of absence and performance of agents.

Succoro is finding it increasingly difficult to recruit suitable people within the budget constraints. However, it is an important contract which it wants to retain. The agency has been performing well and exceeding the service-level agreement in some indicators. Succoro use an online application form, and then screen applicants in a telephone interview. Globalchip managers are involved in the final selection decision.

Liz McDonald is a member of her local HR network, which is a group of HR practitioners who meet every three months to share their knowledge and experience in order to help with their continuing professional development. One of the other members, Jim Gray, works for an agency which runs a similar operation for a mobile phone company in a different area of the UK. Jim Gray offered to share his experience of recruiting those with languages and technical skills.

> The main difficulty is trying to attract applicants to jobs which are paying a little below the average rate. Our agency cannot afford to use some of the more popular websites, because they are expensive. We need to use other ways of targeting people who might be willing to live and work in the UK – almost to sell the experience. We try to use networks, like websites for those who want to travel and work abroad, to advertise. We target social networking sites like Facebook and Gumtree. We are having real difficulties getting speakers of, for example, Dutch and Finnish to come to work here in our UK site.
>
> Jim added,

> It takes about eight weeks to fill a vacancy, though for some of the more common languages, there sometimes is a pool of applicants in our skills bank. We advertise on our website in the UK but have links posted in other national websites for our agency.

Liz is still investigating the implications of outsourcing for Blueberry.

Questions

1 How would outsourcing change the HR function?

2 What is a service-level agreement?

3 Which methods would you use to attract applicants to their international call centre in the UK?

4 To what extent is this an example of 'viral' recruitment?

5 Companies target applicants who are predominantly young people under 30 years old who use social network sites. Is this potentially discriminatory?

CASE STUDY 3.3

RECRUITMENT AND SKILLS GAPS IN FONTAINEBLEAU AND OXYGEN

SCOTT HURRELL AND DORA SCHOLARIOS

Fontainebleau and Oxygen are two leading multinational hotel chains that have branches throughout the world. Both hotels have a strong focus on customer service; however, two of their outlets represent contrasting fortunes in terms of the customer service skills of their workforce.

Although both hotels have strong service brands, the exact nature of these differ considerably. Oxygen managers and staff describe the hotel as 'young', 'fresh' and 'stylish'. The hotel building itself had won design awards and had a minimalist interior complemented by modern art prints. There was also an emphasis on informality when serving customers and employees were allowed a high degree of discretion over service encounters. Employees were also allowed some discretion over their appearance at work, although a designer uniform was supplied. As such there was a stated requirement for Oxygen employees to be 'stylish', 'funky' 'friendly' and 'individual'.

Fontainebleau has a much more formal service brand characterised by managers and employees as 'traditional' and 'professional'. This was reflected in the decor of the hotel, which was grandiose and opulent, with antique style furniture and complemented by classical art prints. Employees had to adhere to rigid brand standards when they served customers, reinforced through regular training, and were expected to interact with customers in a highly formal manner. Employees were expected to be 'polite', 'clean' and 'tidy'. Fontainebleau provided an industry standard uniform and strict guidelines existed over staff appearance.

Managers in one branch of Fontainebleau reported a number of *current* staff who were not fully proficient in customer service skills (known as skills *gaps*), with line managers reporting such problems in approximately 60 per cent of reception staff (although many were new employees) and 25 per cent of chefs, waiting staff and bar staff. The HR manager also reported that approximately 30 per cent of front-line staff lacked customer service skills. In Oxygen, however, no customer service skills gaps were reported. The Food and Beverage (F and B) Managers in the hotels (who recruited most front-line customer service staff) also reported contrasting incidence of skills *shortages* in *potential* employees during the recruitment process; Fontainebleau's F and B manager reported few customer service skills shortages while Oxygen's F and B manager reported that many applicants lacked the required customer service skills. The two hotels also had differing staff turnover rates, with Fontainebleau reporting a rate of 75 per cent in the previous year and Oxygen 42 per cent.

Both hotels used recruitment methods such as: internal advertising; recruitment websites; press adverts;

advertising in schools, colleges and universities; advertising in local job centres; accepting speculative enquiries; and accepting recommendations from current staff. Oxygen, however, relied more heavily on recruiting from university campuses and informal staff recommendations. The rationale for using informal recruitment methods also differed between the hotels, although managers in both saw their benefits. In Fontainebleau the HR manager believed that recruiting through recommendations of current employees fostered a happy work environment and good team spirit, while in Oxygen there was more emphasis on the fit between people and the establishment.

Formal job adverts also differed between the two establishments. While Fontainebleau's adverts tended to emphasise details about the job and benefits of working for the company, Oxygen's recruitment advertising emphasised the company's brand. One advertising campaign, for example, gave a picture of the inside of the hotel alongside words such as 'distinctive', 'unmistakable' and 'unique' before adding 'but enough about you' and then describing what Oxygen offered to

employees. This advert mirrored a customer advertising campaign, which had almost identical wording.

Fontainebleau's HR manager also noticed a problem that, 'Some of the managers would recruit...based on the fact that "OK that person's willing to do the job" and not necessarily concerned with what skills they have', prompting a move to a standardised, competency-based selection interview process. It became clear, however, that not all managers were using the competency-based interviews. In Oxygen the F and B manager emphasised 'cherry picking' applicants with the correct skills and while interviews were semi-structured, they were much less formal than in Fontainebleau. Oxygen managers also stated that interviews were viewed as a two-way process, intended to establish whether candidates' expectations '...married up with reality'. Oxygen also took applicants on an establishment tour as part of the recruitment process, with the reception manager reporting that he found this to be one of the most important features to allow candidates to assess the reality of their expectations of the hotel.

Questions

1 What might the different experiences of the two hotels' F and B departments in terms of customer service skills *shortages* and customer service skills *gaps* tell us about recruitment practices?

2 What other factors could potentially have led to Fontainebleau's customer service skills gaps?

3 What perspectives on recruitment, discussed during the chapter, can be used to analyse Oxygen's superior performance in terms of skills gaps and staff turnover?

4 Are there any apparent contradictions in terms of the recruitment approaches of the two hotels and their subsequent experiences with skills gaps?

5 Are there any potential drawbacks with Oxygen's approach to recruitment?

Bibliography

Advisory Conciliation and Arbitration Service (ACAS) (2006) *Recruitment and Induction, Advisory Booklet,* London: ACAS.

ACAS (2011) *The Equality Act – What's New for Employers*? London: ACAS.

Anderson, N., Born, M. and Cunningham-Snell, N. (2001) 'Recruitment and selection: applicant perspectives and outcomes', pp. 200–18, in Anderson, N., Ones, D., Sinangil H.K. and Viswesvaran, C. (eds) *Handbook of Industrial, Work, and Organizational Psychology: Volume 1 Personnel Psychology*, London: Sage.

Armour, S. (2005) 'Generation Y: they've arrived at work with a new attitude', *USA Today*, 11 June. Available at http://www.usatoday.com/money/workplace/2005-11-06-gen-y_x.htm.

Association of Graduate Recruiters (2008) *The AGR Graduate Recruitment Survey 2008: Winter Review.* Available at http://www.agr.org.uk.

Autor, D., Katz, L.F. and Kearney, M.S. (2006) *The Polarization of the US Labor Market*, NBER Working Paper No.1 2006. National Bureau of Economic Research, Cambridge, MA, USA.

Barber, A. (1998) *Recruiting Employees: Individual and Organisational Perspectives,* London: Sage.

Barber, A.E., Wesson, M.J., Roberson, Q.M. and Taylor, M.S. (1999) 'A tale of two job markets: organizational size and its effects on hiring practices and job search behaviour', *Personnel Psychology*, Vol.52, 841–67.

Barber, L., Hill, D., Hirsh, W. and Tyers, C. (2005) *Fishing for Talent in a Wider Pool: Trends and Dilemmas in Corporate Graduate Recruitment*, IES Report 421, Brighton: Institute for Employment Studies.

Bates, P., Johnson, C. and Gifford, J. (2008) *Recruitment and Training Among Large National Employers*, Brighton: Institute for Employment Studies and IFF Research on behalf of Learning and Skills Council.

Billsberry, J. (2007) *Experiencing Recruitment and Selection*, Chichester: John Wiley & Sons.

BIS (Department for Business Innovation and Skills) (2011) *Business Population Estimates for the UK and Regions 2011*. Available at http://www.bis.gov.uk/analysis/statistics/business-population-estimates.

BLS (Bureau of Labor Statistics) (2012) *Business Employment Dynamics – Fourth Quarter 2011*. Available at http://www.bls.gov/bdm/.

Boxall, P. and Purcell, J. (2003) *Strategy and Human Resource Management*, Basingstoke: Palgrave Macmillan.

Boyatzis, R.E. (1982) *The Competent Manager: A Model for Effective Performance,* New York: Wiley.

Breaugh, J.A. and Mann, R.B. (1984) 'Recruiting source effects: a test of two alternative explanations', *Journal of Occupational Psychology*, Vol.57, 261–7.

Breaugh, J. and Starke, M. (2000) 'Research on employee recruiting: so many studies, so many remaining questions', *Journal of Management*, Vol.26, 405–34.

Broughton, A., Higgins, T., Hicks, B. and Cox, A. (2011) *Workplaces and Social Networking: The Implications for Employment Relations*, London: ACAS.

Burgess, J. and Connell, J. (2006) 'Temporary work and human resources management: issues, challenges and responses', *Personnel Review*, Vol.35, No.2, 129–40.

Cabinet Office (2004) *Enabling a Digitally United Kingdom,* Report of the Digital Inclusion Panel.

Cable, D.M. and Graham, M.E. (2000) 'The determinants of organizational reputation: a job search perspective', *Journal of Organizational Behavior*, Vol.21, 929–47.

Cable, D.M. and Turban, D.B. (2003) 'The value of organizational image in the recruitment context: a brand equity perspective', *Journal of Applied Social Psychology*, Vol.33, 2244–66.

Campion, M.A. (1988) 'Interdisciplinary approaches to job design: a constructive replication with extension', *Journal of Applied Psychology*, Vol.73, 467–81.

Carroll, M., Marchington, M., Earnshaw, J. and Taylor, S. (1999) 'Recruitment in small firms: processes, methods and problems', *Employee Relations*, Vol.21, No.3, 236–50.

Cassell, C.M. (2005) 'Managing diversity', in Redman, T. and Wilkinson, A. (eds) *Contemporary Issues in Human Resource Management: Text and Cases* (2nd edn), Harlow: Pearson. Education.

CIPD (2006) *Graduates in the Workplace. Does a Degree Add Value?* London: Chartered Institute of Personnel and Development.

CIPD (2007a) *Recruitment, Retention and Turnover Survey,* London: Chartered Institute of Personnel and Development.

CIPD (2007b) *Employer Branding. The Latest Fad or the Future of HR?* London: Chartered Institute of Personnel and Development.

CIPD (2011) *Resourcing and Talent Planning,* London: Chartered Institute of Personnel and Development.

ComputerWeekly.com (11 June 2010) 'Will LinkedIn reshape the recruitment sector?' Available at http://www.computerweekly.com/news/1280097144/Will-LinkedIn-reshape-the-recruitment-sector.

Department for Communities and Local Government (2009) *National Firefighter Selection Process. Development of the National Firefighter Selection Tests: Psychological Report.* Available at www.communities.gov.uk.

Department for Education and Skills (DFES) (2003) *21st Century Skills: Realising Our Potential; Individuals, Employers, Nation,* Norwich: HMSO.

Department of Health (2007) *Additionality Shortage Professions List.* Available at www.dh.gov.uk.

Department of Trade and Industry (DTI) (2006) *Explanatory Memorandum to the Employment Equality (Age) Regulations 2006*. Available at http://www.legislation.gov.uk/uksi/2006/1031/pdfs/uksiem_20061031_en.pdf.

Digital Europe (2003) *European i2010 Initiative on e-Inclusion*, European Commission.

Ehrhart, K.H. and Ziegert, J.C. (2005) 'Why are individuals attracted to organizations?' *Journal of Management,* Vol.31, 901–19.

Equality and Human Rights Commission (EHRC) (2011) *The Essential Guide to the Public Sector Equality Duty*, London: EHRC.

European Commission (September 2011) *EU Employment and Social Situation Quarterly Review*, European Commission: Employment, Social Affairs and Inclusion.

Felstead, A., Gallie, D., Green, F. and Zhou, Y. (2007) *Skills at Work, 1996–2006,* Cardiff/Oxford: ESRC.

Finlay, W. and Coverdill, J. (2000) 'Risk, opportunism and structural holes: how headhunters manage clients and earn fees', *Work and Occupations*, Vol.27, No.3, 377–405.

Fishman, N. and Morris, J. (2010) *Recruiting with Social Networking Sites: What You DO Know Can Hurt You*, Cleveland, OH: EmployeeScreenIQ. Available at http://www.employeescreen.com/whitepaper_social_networking.pdf.

Forde, C. and Slater, G. (2006) 'The nature and experience of agency working in Britain: what are the challenges for human resource management?' *Personnel Review*, Vol.35, No.2, 141–57.

Gallagher, N. and O'Leary, D. (2007) *Recruitment 2020. How Recruitment is Changing and Why it Matters,* London: Demos.

Gatewood, R.D. and Feild, H.S. (1998) *Human Resource Selection* (4th edn), Fort Worth, TX: Dryden Press.

Goos, M. and Manning, A. (2007) 'Lousy and lovely jobs: the rising polarization of work in Britain', *Review of Economics and Statistics*, Vol.89, No.1, 118–33.

Grugulis, I. (2007) *Skills, Training and Human Resource Development: A Critical Text,* Basingstoke: Palgrave Macmillan.

Haskel, J. and Martin, C. (2001) 'Technology, wages, and skill shortages: evidence from UK micro data', *Oxford Economic Papers*, Vol.53, No.4, 642–58.

Hasluck, C., Mhonda, J., Winter, E., Durrant, C., Thompson, M., Dobbs, L. and Christou, G. (2005) *The Use and Development of Alternative Service Delivery Channels in Jobcentre Plus: A Review of Recent Evidence*, Research Report No.280, Department for Work and Pensions.

Hayward, B., Fong, B. and Thornton, A. (2007) *The Third Work-Life Balance Employer Survey: Executive Summary*. Employment Relations Research Series No.86, Department for Business, Enterprise and Regulatory Reform.

Healy, M. and Schwarz-Woelzl, M. (2007) *Recruitment Policies and Practices in the Context of Demographic Change: Critical Issues in the ICT Sector and Recommendations*, Study report of the mature@eu project Vienna: European Commission. Available at www.mature-project.eu/downloads.html.

Herriot, P. and Anderson, N. (1997) 'Selecting for change: how will personnel and selection psychology survive?', in Anderson, N.R. and Herriot, P. (eds) *International Handbook of Selection and Assessment,* London: Wiley.

Hoque, K. and Noon, M. (2004) 'Equal opportunities policy and practice in Britain: Evaluating the "empty shell" hypothesis', *Work Employment and Society*, Vol.18, No.3, 481–506.

Hurrell, S.A. and Scholarios, D. (2011) 'Recruitment and selection practices, person–brand fit and soft skills gaps in service organisations: the benefits of institutionalised informality', in Brannan, M., Parsons, E. and Priola, V. (eds) *Branded Lives: The Production and Consumption of Meaning at Work*, Cheltenham: Edward Elgar.

Hurrell, S. A., Scholarios, D. and Thompson, P. (forthcoming) 'More than a "Humpty Dumpty" term: Strengthening the conceptualization of soft skills', *Economic and Industrial Democracy*. Prepublished, 7 June 2012, DOI: 0143831X12444934.

Hurrell, S.A., Warhurst, C. and Nickson, D. (2011) 'Giving Miss Marple a makeover: graduates, skills shortages and the voluntary sector', *Non-Profit and Voluntary Sector Quarterly*, Vol.40 No.2, 336–55.

Incomes Data Services (IDS) (2008) *Competency Frameworks,* HR studies, 865. London: IDS.

Information Commissioner's Office (ICO) (2005) *Data Protection: Quick Guide to Employment Practices Code*, Wilmslow: ICO.

International Labour Organization (ILO) (1998) *The text of the Declaration and its follow-up*. Available at www.ilo.org/declaration/thedeclaration/textdeclaration/lang–en/index.htm.

Johnston, L. (2006) 'Diversifying police recruitment? The deployment of police community support officers in London', *The Howard Journal of Criminal Justice,* Vol.45, No.4, 388–402.

Kellard, K., Walker, R., Ashworth, K., Howard, M. and Liu, W.C. (2001) *Staying in Work: Thinking About a New Policy Agenda*, DFEE Research Report No. 264, Nottingham: DFEE.

Kuhn, P. and Skuterud, M. (2000) 'Job search methods: internet versus traditional', *Monthly Labor Review,* Vol.123, No.10, 3–11.

Lees, C.D. and Cordery, J.L. (2000) 'Job analysis and design', pp. 45–68, in Chmiel, N. (ed.), *Introduction to Work and Organizational Psychology,* Oxford: Blackwell.

Lepak, D.P. and Snell, S.A. (2002) 'Examining the human resource architecture: the relationships among human capital, employment, and human resource configurations', *Journal of Management*, Vol.28, 517–43.

Lievens, F. and Highhouse, S. (2003) 'The relation of instrumental and symbolic attributes to a company's attractiveness as an employer', *Personnel Psychology*, Vol.56, 75–102.

Lockyer, C.J. and Scholarios, D. (2004) 'Selecting hotel staff: why best practice doesn't always work', *International Journal of Contemporary Hospitality Management*, Vol.16, No.2, 125–35.

Madouros, V. (2006) 'Projections of the UK labour force, 2006–2020', *Labour Market Trends*, Newport: Office for National Statistics, January.

Management Charter Initiative (1990) *Occupational Standards for Managers*, Department of Employment and NFMED.

Marchington, M. and Wilkinson, A. (2005) *Human Resource Management at Work: People Management and Development,* London: CIPD.

Marshall, J.N. and Richardson, R. (1996) 'The impact of "telemediated services" on corporate structures: the example of "branchless" retail banking in Britain', *Environment and Planning A*, Vol.28, 1843–58.

McClelland, D.C. (1976) *A Guide to Job Competency Assessment,* Boston, MA: McBer and Company.

McCormick, E.J. (1976) 'Job and task analysis', pp. 651–96, in Dunnette M.D. (ed.), *Handbook of Industrial and Organizational Psychology*, Chicago, IL: Rand-McNally.

McKay P. and Avery D. (2005) 'Warning! Diversity recruitment could backfire', *Journal of Management Enquiry,* Vol.14, No.4, 330–6.

Murray, S. (2008) *StepStone Total Talent Report 2008*: *A report from the Economist Intelligence Unit.* Available at http://www.businessresearch.eiu.com/total-talent-report-2008.html.

OECD (Organization for Economic Co-operation and Development) (2011) 'Persistence of High Unemployment: What Risks? What Policies?' *OECD Economic Outlook*, Paris: OECD available from www.oecd.org/dataoecd/8/36/47656668.pdf.

Olian, J.D. and Rynes, S.L. (1984) 'Organizational staffing: integrating practice with strategy', *Industrial Relations*, Vol.23, No.2, 170–83.

ONS (Office for National Statistics) (2011) *Non-UK born workers – 2011.* Available at http://www.ons.gov.uk/ons/rel/lmac/non-uk-born-workers/2011/non-uk-born-workers.html.

Osterman, P. and Shulman, B. (2008) *Good Jobs America. Making Work Better for Everyone.* New York: Russell Sage Foundation.

Parry, E. and Tyson, S. (2008) 'An analysis of the use and success of online recruitment methods in the UK', *Human Resource Management Journal*, Vol.18, No.3, 257–74.

Pearn, M. (1993) 'Fairness in selection and assessment: a European perspective', in Schuler, H., Farr, J.L. and Smith, M. (eds) *Personnel Selection and Assessment: Individual and Organizational Perspectives,* Hillsdale, NJ: Lawrence Earlbaum.

Perryman, S. (2003) *The IES Annual Graduate Review: 2003 Update. Business as Usual? Trends in Student and Graduate Numbers*, Report 399, Brighton: Institute for Employment Studies.

Phillips, J.M. (1998) 'Effects of realistic job previews on multiple organizational outcomes: a meta-analysis', *Academy of Management Journal,* Vol.41, 673–91.

PricewaterhouseCooper (2010) *Managing Tomorrow's People: Where Will You be in 2020?*

Purcell, J. and Hutchinson, S. (2007) 'Front-line managers as agents in the HRM-performance causal chain: theory, analysis and evidence', *Human Resource Management Journal*, Vol.17, No.1, 3-20.

Purcell, J., Purcell, K. and Tailby, S. (2004) 'Temporary work agencies: here today, gone tomorrow?', *British Journal of Industrial Relations*, Vol.42, No.4, 705–25.

Purcell, K., Rowley, G. and Morley, M. (2002) *Recruiting From a Wider Spectrum of Graduates,* London: Council for Industry and Higher Education, May.

Recruitment and Employment Confederation (REC) and KPMG (2011) *News Release: Report on Jobs, October.* Available at http://www.kpmg.com/UK/en/IssuesAndInsights/Articles Publications/NewsReleases/Pages/Report-on-Jobs-Growth-of-staff-appointments-eases-further-in-September.aspx.

Renwick, D. (2006) 'Line managers', pp. 209–28, in Redman, T. and Wilkinson, A. (eds) *Contemporary Human Resource Management* (2nd edn), Harlow: Pearson Education.

Robinson, M.A., Sparrow, P.R., Clegg, C. and Birdi, K. (2005) 'Forecasting future competency requirements: a three-phase methodology,' *Personnel Review,* Vol.36, No.1, 65–90.

Rynes, S.L. (1991) 'Recruitment, job choice, and post-hire consequences', pp. 399–444, in Dunnette, M.D. (ed.), *Handbook of Industrial and Organizational Psychology* (2nd edn), Palo Alto, CA: Consulting Psychologists Press.

Rynes, S.L. and Cable, D. (2003) 'Recruitment research in the twenty-first century', pp. 55–76, in Borman, W.C., Ilgen, D.R. and Klimoski, R.J. (eds) *Handbook of Psychology, Volume 12, Industrial and Organizational Psychology*, Hoboken, NJ: Wiley.

Saks, A.M. (2005) 'The impracticality of recruitment research', pp. 47–72, in Evers, A., Anderson, N. and Voskuijl, O. (eds) *Handbook of Personnel Selection*, Oxford: Blackwell.

Sanchez, J.I. (1994) 'From documentation to innovation: reshaping job analysis to meet emerging business needs', *Human Resource Management Review*, Vol.4, No.1, 51–74.

Schneider, B. and Konz, A. (1989) 'Strategic job analysis', *Human Resource Management*, Vol.28, 51–63.

Schreurs, B., Derous, E., De Witte, K., Proost, K., Andriessen, M. and Glabeke, K. (2005) 'Attracting potential applicants to the military: the effects of initial face-to-face contacts', *Human Performance,* Vol.18, No.2, 105–22.

Searle, R. (2003) *Selection and Recruitment: A Critical Text,* London: Palgrave Macmillan and Milton Keynes: The Open University.

Searle, R. (2006) 'New technology: the potential impact of surveillance techniques in recruitment practices', *Personnel Review,* Vol.35, No.3, 336–51.

Siebern-Thomas, F. (2005) 'Job quality in European labour markets', in Bazen, S., Lucifora, C. and Salverda, W. (eds) *Job Quality and Employer Behaviour*, Basingstoke: Palgrave MacMillan.

Stahl, G., (2007) *Global Talent Management: How Leading Multinationals Build and Sustain their Talent Pipeline,* INSEAD.

Suff, R. (2010) 'Using competencies in HR practices: the 2010 IRS survey', *IRS Employment Review*, 23 August.

Taylor, M.S. and Collins, C.J. (2000) 'Organizational recruitment: enhancing the intersection of theory and practice', pp. 304–34, in Cooper, C.L. and Locke, E.A. (eds) *Industrial and Organizational Psychology: Linking Theory and Practice*, Oxford: Blackwell.

Taylor, M.S. and Schmidt, D.W. (1983) 'A process-oriented investigation of recruitment source effectiveness', *Personnel Psychology,* Vol.36, 343–54.

Tenwick, C. (2008) 'Generation Y requires a "viral" approach to recruitment'. *HRZone* 27 March. Available at http:///www.hrzone.co.uk.

TMP Worldwide (2011) *The Value of a Managed Employer Brand in an Increasingly Competitive Landscape*. tmp.worldwide. Available at www.tmpw.co.uk.

The Future Laboratory (2005) *Freestylers and Work,* London: Standard Life Bank.

Torrington, D., Taylor, S. and Hall, L. (2008) *Human Resource Management* (7th edn), Harlow: Pearson Education/Financial Times.

UK Commission for Employment and Skills (UKCES) (2010) *Ambition 2020: World Class Skills and Jobs for the UK*, London: UKCES.

Ulrich, D. and Beatty, D. (2001) 'From players to partners: extending the HR playing field', *Human Resource Management,* Vol.40, No.4, 293–307.

Ulrich, D. and Brockbank, W. (2005) 'Role call', *People Management,* 16 June, 24–8.

Viadeo (2007) *What Does Your NetRep Say About You? A Study of How your Internet Reputation Can Influence Your Career Prospects.* Available at http://www.viadeo.com/NetRep

Vinten, G. (1998) 'Skills shortage and recruitment in the SME sector', *Career Development International*, Vol.3, No.6, 238–42.

Welfare, S. (2006) 'A two-way process: informing and consulting employees', *IRS Employment Review,* No. 859, 17 November, 8–15.

Willey, B., Murton, A., Hannon, E., Mison, S. and Sachdev, S. (2009) *Employment Law in Context: An Introduction for HR Professionals* (3rd edn), Harlow: Pearson Education.

Williams, M.L. and Dreher, G.F. (1992) 'Compensation system attributes and applicant pool characteristics', *Academy of Management Journal*, Vol.35, 571–95.

Wilson, R., Homenidou, K. and Dickerson, A. (2004) *Working Futures: National Report 2003–4,* Warwick: Institute for Employment Research, University of Warwick.

Woodhams, C. and Corby, S. (2007) 'Then and now: disability legislation and employers' practices in the UK', *British Journal of Industrial Relations,* Vol.45, No.3, 556–80.

Yacubovich, V. (2006) 'Passive recruitment in the Russian urban labor market', *Work and Occupations*, Vol.33, No.3, 307–34.

YouGov (2006) *Has your Business got the X Factor?* London: Croner.

Zottoli, M.A. and Wanous, J.P. (2000) 'Recruitment source research: current status and future directions', *Human Resource Management Review*, Vol.10, No.4, 353–82.

CHAPTER 4
SELECTION

Dora Scholarios

Introduction

'Best-practice' employee selection is usually associated with the 'psychometric' model. This recommends rigorously developed psychometric tests, performance-based or work simulation methods, and the use of multiple methods of assessment, all designed to accurately measure candidates' knowledge, skills, abilities, personality and attitudes.

This view has dominated literature on selection. Its popularity is no doubt due to its emphasis on objectivity, meritocracy and efficiency, which are all evident in the story of selection, and indeed the emergence of HRM, over the last century. Industrialisation and mass manpower planning during the early twentieth century required a systematic way of matching the attributes of individuals to the requirements of jobs, and early psychological research on understanding and scaling individual differences (for example, the work of Alfred Binet or Raymond Cattell in the field of education) provided tools for military and commercial organisations faced with this massive scale problem of person–job fit. These early assessment efforts became gradually refined to show how organisations of all types could gain from systematic selection methods. By the 1980s, it had become a core element of competitive strategy, and an essential part of an organisation's strategic capability for adapting to competition (Hamel and Prahalad, 1989). Systematic selection is now regarded as one of the critical functions of HRM, essential for achieving key organisational outcomes (Storey, 2007), and a core component of what has been called a high commitment or high performance management approach to HRM (Marchington and Wilkinson, 2005; Pfeffer, 1998).

This chapter begins with a review of the principles of the psychometric model and the range of assessment methods available to organisations which follow this model. The chapter then considers whether organisations have adopted these methods. This leads to a more sceptical account of 'sophisticated' selection, and the possibility of alternative paradigms which move away from a techniques-driven approach. Three alternatives are covered: a 'best fit' approach; an 'interactive action-oriented' perspective (Newell, 2006); and a discourse view, which describes selection as a contested, rather than rational, process, muddied by multiple possible interpretations and interests. We conclude by examining what these alternative paradigms imply for selection practice and for HRM.

A brief overview of psychometric quality

> How do we identify people with knowledge, skill, ability and the personality to perform well at a set of tasks we call a job? Even more difficult, how do we do this before we have ever seen that person perform on the job? *(Ployhart et al., 2006: 10)*

This is the problem which gives the psychometric model its alias as the 'prediction' or 'predictivist' paradigm and takes up the majority of space in most textbooks on the subject of selection. Decisions whether to hire someone are usually based on their performance on a test assessing their suitability for the job – hence the prediction – but how do we make sure this test does what it is intended to do? Four standards are used to make this evaluation (more detail on each can be found in any textbook account of selection; e.g., Schmitt and Chan, 1998; Searle, 2003a).

1   The method of assessment must be *reliable*; i.e. accurate and free from contamination. Reliable methods have high physical fidelity with job performance itself, are standardised across applicants, have some degree of imposed structure and show consistency across multiple assessors. Work samples or simulations, which measure performance on a structured task reflecting behaviours used in the job are likely to have high reliability. Interviews are generally thought to have low reliability, although the use of panels, rather than individual decision makers, and structure and standardisation, like question–response scoring, have been shown to increase their reliability (McFarland *et al.,* 2004).

2   Selection methods must also be *valid* – relevant for the work behaviours they are meant to predict. At minimum, to be valid, assessment must be designed around a systematic job analysis and person specification for the job, and be reliable. For example, introducing structure into interviews also enhances their validity (Schmidt and Zimmerman, 2004). A valid method, though, should also show an association between scores on the assessment tool and desired job behaviours. This is often expressed as a correlation coefficient – known as a criterion-related validity coefficient – representing the relationship between scores on the predictor (or proposed selection method) and scores on a criterion (or proxy measure) of job performance. This correlation coefficient can range from 0 (chance prediction or no relationship) to 1.0 (perfect prediction). Table 4.1 summarises what values are considered to be low, moderate or high predictive validity coefficients for a range of selection methods.

3   *Subgroup predictive validity* should be the same for different applicant groups, such as men and women; i.e. the selection method should treat all groups the same. Members of one subgroup should not be selected disproportionately more or less often than members of another. The example of cognitive ability testing illustrates perfectly the trade-offs between predictive validity and different subgroup prediction. Psychometric tests which measure general cognitive ability (also known as general intelligence) provide the best predictors of future success in the workplace regardless of the specific job, with validity coefficients in the region of .60 (Schmidt and Hunter, 1998). However, some minority groups tend to score lower as a group on such tests, even though the tests themselves are not inherently unfair. In the US, this has been the case for blacks and Hispanics. As a result of this differential predictive validity, the US federal government has encouraged the search for alternatives to cognitive ability testing for hiring purposes in order to minimise adverse impact against historically and socially disadvantaged groups.

4   The selection method should have high *utility* for the organisation. This usually takes into account cost and potential return on investment so that methods with high validity which are not expensive to develop or administer will have higher utility. This also is affected by the hiring context; for example, the number of applications received for a job opening and the proportion of these who will be hired (the selection ratio).

The 'what' and 'how' of selection

Each of these four psychometric standards is concerned with how we should design the assessment tools, or selection methods, for determining people's suitability for jobs. Also relevant is what underlying individual characteristics we wish to capture with these methods, as a range of methods (the 'how') could be used to tap into a single underlying construct (the 'what'). For example, application forms, interviews and psychometric tests could all be used to measure personality, but with varying degrees of psychometric rigour.

One useful framework distinguishes between cognitive, non-cognitive and performance-based individual differences. Cognitive characteristics reflect intellectual processes, academic achievements and knowledge; non-cognitive characteristics include personality traits, motivation, past experience and qualifications; and performance-based characteristics refer to more hands-on behavioural examples of job performance. Each of these constructs represents the 'what' to be measured; the selection technique used to do this represents the 'how'.

Table 4.1 brings together the four psychometric standards and three types of individual differences to classify various selection methods. The table also indicates the general findings from research on user acceptability with respect to these methods, an issue to which we return later in the chapter. We discuss only some of these selection methods here. An important point to note from the discussion and Table 4.1 is that performance-based selection methods generally have higher reliability/validity, lower subgroup differences in predictive validity and higher user acceptability, all of which has resulted in their increasing popularity.

Table 4.1 The psychometric quality of alternative selection methods

Selection method	Psychometric quality			User acceptability
	Predictive validity[a]	Subgroup differences (Race/Gender)	Utility	
Cognitive				
Ability/aptitude test	High	Large/small	High	Moderate
Achievement/job knowledge test	High	Moderate/small	High	Favourable
Non-cognitive				
Personality test	Low/moderate	Small/small	Moderate	Unfavourable
Biographical information	Moderate	Small/small	Moderate	Unfavourable
Experience	Moderate	Small/small	Low	Moderate
Performance-based				
Work sample	Moderate/High	Small-moderate/small	Moderate	Favourable
Interview-unstructured	Low	Small/small	Moderate	Low
Interview-structured	High	Small/small	Moderate	Moderate
Situational judgement test	Moderate	Moderate/small	High	Favourable
Assessment centre	Moderate	Moderate/small[b]	Moderate	Favourable

Sources: Adapted from Ployhart *et al.*, 2006: Table 7.3 and Schmidt and Hunter, 1998.
Notes
[a] Descriptors for criterion-related validity coefficients are based on the following accepted ranges: 0.10 = Low; 0.20 = Moderate; 0.30 and above = High
[b] Descriptors reflect general findings. Subgroup differences tend to vary by exercise.

Cognitive ability

Psychometric tests are standardised instruments designed to measure individual differences, most commonly cognitive ability or aptitude, achievement or personality. Although there is some blurring between cognitive ability and aptitude, measures of ability focus more on current levels of skill in specific areas, such as arithmetic or verbal ability, while aptitude refers to one's potential to learn or acquire skill, regardless of past experience, and is often associated with a broader measure of intelligence. Ability may underlie aptitude – high logical reasoning ability may be required for computer programming aptitude. Also, aptitudes may be targeted at specific occupational areas – an aptitude for making inferences from numerical data contributes to performance in financial services occupations. Tests of achievement include school examinations, typing tests, or statutory professional examinations; e.g. for accountancy certification or where public safety may be at risk, as in the use of firefighting equipment or electrical safety.

During the 1980s, there was a flurry of influential research centred on tests of general cognitive ability (referred to as *g*), which include both ability and aptitude. Most test batteries measuring *g* consist of tests of numerical, verbal, reasoning and spatial ability, and emphasise future potential for learning or adapting to new situations. Research shows that tests of *g* provide the best way of predicting performance differences between job applicants in any type of job, with potentially high returns on investment (utility) for organisations. Using the statistical techniques of meta-analysis to aggregate the results from different studies, *g* has been found to be a strong predictor of various measures of job success, including supervisory ratings, production quantity and quality, and training performance (e.g., Hunter and Hunter, 1984). This has been shown to hold across different employment and cultural contexts. For example, Bertua *et al.* (2005) showed high validity for a range of UK jobs, and Salgado *et al.* (2003) did the same for ten European Commission countries.

Current thinking on the structure of ability distinguishes between tests which measure fluid intelligence, representing general reasoning ability across situations, and crystallised intelligence, which represents a culturally specific view of intelligence which develops as a result of specific experiences (Carroll, 1993). An example of how these tests are being used by graduate employers as a way of measuring fluid intelligence, and hence future potential, is described in Box 4.1. Today, over 70 specialised ability tests are available as aids to decision-makers.

That is not to say that *g* is now uncontroversially the psychometric test of choice in employment contexts. There are several areas of resistance. First, performance on a test does not necessarily reflect intelligence or the test-taker's best possible performance, but may depend on whether the individual is interested in doing well, where they focus their attention and how much effort they expend. This leads to the distinction between typical and maximal performance. Rather than focusing on predicting someone's maximal behaviour, like most tests of cognitive ability, some argue we should focus on finding out how a person typically performs a task in the actual job environment (Klehe and Anderson, 2005). Later sections in this chapter consider the role of personality tests as one way of predicting typical behaviour.

A second development is in tests measuring different kinds of 'intelligence'. This includes dimensions of creative and emotional intelligence which cannot be captured by linguistically based psychometric tests, but which some argue affect many aspects of work performance (Weisinger, 1998). Tacit knowledge, which represents practical knowledge of 'how' to do a job and is inferred from experience rather than academically acquired, has also received attention, especially in non-routine and unstructured jobs, such as management (Sternberg *et al.*, 1995). Tacit knowledge also underlies the increasing use of situational judgement tests, which we consider later under performance-based methods.

Finally, as shown in Table 4.1, cognitive ability testing suffers from high subgroup differences in predictive validity; i.e. it has adverse impact on members of minority racial groups. Even though the reliability, validity and utility of cognitive ability testing have all been shown – that is, they are free from any bias – their use is a liability to employers who are concerned

Box 4.1 HRM in practice   Psychometric testing for graduate jobs

A recent decline in the number of 'graduate' jobs due to the economic recession means that employers can now choose from a growing pool of graduates, many of whom have been in the job market for several years. Some sectors are expected to expand graduate recruitment in 2012 (IT/telecommunications, construction), but overall the average number of applications for each graduate job has doubled since 2009 (Association of Graduate Recruiters, 2012). More employers insist on a 2:1 degree as a minimum standard and more are using pre-screening processes, such as online ability tests which assess fluid intelligence, to differentiate graduates with the highest potential and save the costs of expensive, face-to-face assessment (Lawton et al., 2009).

SHL (www.shl.com) is a leading provider of sophisticated online assessment tools for graduate recruitment. Their *Verify Range of Ability Tests* includes measures of Inductive Reasoning, Numerical Reasoning, and Verbal Reasoning. Similarly, Cubiks (www.cubiks.com) is another international consultancy which provides online assessment tools for managerial and graduate roles. Their *Reasoning for Business* ability tests series also includes tests of Verbal, Numerical and Inductive Reasoning that cover different areas of business reasoning.

● Inductive reasoning tests the ability to draw inferences and understand the relationships between various concepts independent of acquired knowledge. This is relevant for roles dealing with new concepts and approaches, building strategies, and resolving complex, ambiguous and novel problems.
● Numerical reasoning measures the ability to make correct decisions or inferences from numerical or statistical data.
● Verbal reasoning measures the ability to evaluate the logic of various kinds of argument as presented in written form.

with maintaining a diverse workforce. Different applicant groups, for example, Caucasian, Hispanic, Asian and African Americans, tend to score differently on these tests, which can lead to substantially different hiring rates, especially as organisations become more selective (i.e. hire fewer applicants or increase their cut scores on selection methods). In the US, federal law has battled with the issue of minority group preference in hiring and university entrance admissions and whether selection procedures should be race-neutral or race-conscious (see, for example, Kravitz, 2008).

Internationally, the debate has tended to recommend careful design and validation of tests for particular groups (men/women, racial/cultural groups) to provide norm-referenced testing. If we remember the culturally specific element of intelligence (crystallised intelligence), though, we might question whether Western-designed tests are appropriate for other cultures' understanding of ability. Many multinational organisations face such issues when selecting staff who can work in any part of the world. There are interesting, unresolved dilemmas here with respect to culture-free and valid testing, as articulated by Searle (2003a: 189). Should we aim for generic measures which tap into fluid (cultural-neutral) intelligence, or should we acknowledge the importance of cultural differences in what abilities are valued and develop different tests for different parts of the world? Another alternative may be that multinationals devise their own tests, which are valid for predicting performance in specific roles which transcend geographical boundaries. We return later to the issue of global selection methods when we look at what organisation's actually do.

Personality

Personality is a non-cognitive characteristic. With respect to the value of personality tests, there is continuing debate about fakeability, generally low predictive validity (Table 4.1), and even about the very existence of such a thing as personality (see for example Dilchert *et al.*, 2006). Despite this, there has been a resurgence of interest focused especially on the Five Factor Model or the 'Big Five' dimensions. This claims that personality differences between people can be explained by five dimensions – Extraversion, Conscientiousness, Agreeableness, Neuroticism or Emotional Stability and Openness to Experience (Costa and McCrae, 1992). One of these in particular – Conscientiousness – has emerged as a valid predictor of many aspects of work performance. This combines hard work, thoroughness, self-control and dependability, and is shown to have higher validity when used to predict pro-social aspects of work performance (also known as discretionary behaviour), such as altruism and (inversely) turnover or theft (Salgado, 2002).

The most recent summaries conclude that personality tests are valid and useful when developers pay attention to possible moderators, such as social desirability effects or the specific task contexts which are being predicted (Viswesvaran *et al.*, 2007). For instance, there are a number of studies showing that the dimensions of Extraversion, Agreeableness and Neuroticism, predict customer service behaviours but, that in sales environments (closing a deal, for example), Agreeableness may be a disadvantage (Liao and Chuang, 2004).

Another application is in the use of personality tests to predict team performance. The aggregated score of team members on some of the Big Five personality dimensions, including the score of team leaders, is related to how well the team works together. Personality explains why homogeneous groups are more cohesive, while those which are heterogeneous are better at problem-solving (Moynihan and Peterson, 2004).

Ones *et al.* (2007) summarised the findings from accumulated validity studies and showed that the Big Five personality dimensions predict performance best for customer service, sales and managerial occupations. Although faking is a possibility, well-designed personality tests are most useful when used in combination with other information about the person and for specific work contexts. They also have lower adverse impact on women or racial minority groups than cognitive ability tests which is one reason given for their increased use alongside other methods (Shackleton and Newell, 1997).

Despite these developments, the debate about the role of personality testing in selection has continued, with prominent researchers arguing from both sides of the fence. One exchange occurred over two 2007 issues of the prestigious journal *Personnel Psychology* (see Morgeson *et al.*, 2007; Ones *et al.*, 2007; Tett and Christiansen, 2007).

Newer types of measures based on personality and other non-cognitive psychological constructs also are emerging. Two deserve mention here. First, emotional intelligence describes an individual's personal and social competence in managing their own and others' emotions, and is thought to be especially suited to predicting performance in roles requiring interpersonal interaction and leadership qualities (Zeidner *et al.*, 2004).

A second development is in the use of personality traits to form compound traits. These are 'custom-made' personality measures based on combinations of traits designed to predict job-relevant behaviour in a specific context. They offer higher levels of predictive validity. Integrity, for example, which is often rated by employers as one of the most important employee characteristics, is made up of measures of hostility, impulsiveness, trust and dutifulness; these have been used to predict dishonest behaviour with high validity. Other compound scales have been designed for predicting customer service, stress tolerance, violence and managerial potential (see Ones *et al.*, 2005).

Biographical information

Another non-cognitive characteristic is biographical information or biodata, where applicants describe retrospectively their past experience and work history. The assumption is that performance on past jobs predicts how someone will behave in future job situations as it reflects underlying personal qualities such as attitudes or motivation. Application forms designed to collect biodata tend to be used by the majority of organisations as their initial screening device, and are now commonly found only on line (Association of Graduate Recruiters, 2012; Hill and Barber, 2005).

In general, biodata has moderate to high predictive validity for predicting tenure and performance (Reilly and Chao, 1982). 'Hard', verifiable items, such as success in educational or occupational pursuits, tend to be more valid than 'soft' items related to values or aspirations, which are liable to faking (Lautenschlager, 1994). Selectors also must avoid using information haphazardly without consideration of the important qualities to be judged for the job opening. The general principle behind making biodata job-relevant involves a process called 'criterion keying' – linking responses to each item with either high- and low-performing groups of employees and being able to specify what responses are the most desirable. Furnham (1997), for example, explains that items which showed an applicant's emphasis on financial responsibility, early family responsibility and stability were all good differentiators of good and bad insurance salesmen.

Instruments known as Weighted Application Blanks or Biographical Information Blanks make the weighting of important items more objective and may reduce adverse impact against protected groups (Chapman and Webster, 2003). However, focusing on past accomplishments is clearly suited only to those with experience, which excludes much of the youth applicant pool. This is one reason why many graduate recruitment schemes are designed to assess aptitude (potential) or personal competencies rather than experience. Similarly, many organisations use qualifications as a way of screening out a large number of applicants, for example, by increasing the minimum level of qualifications required, from non-degree to degree. However, the requirement of a university degree may bear no relation to the knowledge, skills, abilities and personality characteristics actually required to do the job. For similar reasons, legislation addressing age and disability discrimination places any items from which this information could be inferred (e.g. age) at risk of legal challenge; i.e. the selection method would adversely impact particular subgroups, such as older or disabled applicants. Practices such as only accepting candidates who are 'first jobbers' or those who have graduated within a restricted number of years, which can be inferred from biodata, would all be considered discriminatory.

Performance-based methods

The third type of individual difference targeted by selection methods is performance itself. Performance-based tests and simulations focus on replicating a set of behaviours required on the job rather than an underlying psychological characteristic. The focus is on measuring present performance in order to predict future performance, although methods taking this approach can reflect varying degrees of complexity and physical fidelity to the actual tasks to be performed on the job, as shown in Table 4.1.

Work samples or job simulations are samples of the job, so represent 'high-fidelity' methods which focus primarily on assessing current skills and performance of actual tasks – what a person can actually do rather than what they 'know'. Unsurprisingly, compared to cognitive and non-cognitive measures, these methods have higher validity and less adverse impact for non-traditional candidates (e.g., women, minority ethnic groups) (Schmitt and Mills, 2001). Users, including managers and candidates, are generally more favourable towards performance-based methods. Selectors tend to pay more attention to observed behavioural information about a candidate than self-report data derived from personality or biodata, and candidates benefit from a realistic preview of the job itself. In a direct comparison of the psychometric qualities of a job simulation versus cognitive test for selecting insurance agents, Schmitt (2003) showed that while the simulation had lower validity (.36 versus .46 for the cognitive test), a higher proportion of capable minority individuals were selected using the simulation. Box 4.2 outlines the role simulation which was developed by Schmitt for these customer service agents.

Situational judgement tests have been called low fidelity simulations or 'white collar work samples' (Muchinsky, 1986). These typically ask applicants to select from several possible behavioural responses for a question about a work situation. This is essentially a test of judgement, which emerged originally as a measure of tacit knowledge or knowledge acquired through experience to complete everyday tasks. As there is no absolute correct answer, responses may vary depending on how the questions are designed, revealing some uncertainty about what is actually being measured. Ployhart and Erhart (2003) showed that asking people what they 'would do' in a certain situation tended to tap behavioural intentions, personality and past behaviour; asking what they 'should do' tapped job knowledge and cognitive ability. It may also be that 'would do' questions are more open to response distortion or faking – this remains an unresolved issue. Nevertheless, they have generally high validity, low subgroup differences, distinctiveness from other measures of past experience and job knowledge, and benefit from evolving delivery formats. New developments allowing multimedia, such as video-based clips, are better able to portray dilemmas or conflict encounters. As these become more powerful in representing the 'reality' of work, they may be able to increase fidelity for the assessment of judgement, prioritisation, decision-making or diagnostic skills (Olson-Buchanan and Drasgow, 2005) (see Box 4.2 for some examples).

Box 4.2 HRM in practice   Increasing realism through performance-based methods

Job simulations

Schmitt (2003) describes a role-play simulation which replicates a typical day in the life of a service representative at an insurance company. Typical tasks were questions from customers about insurance rates and the various coverage options and products available to current or potential customers. A computer programme first provided candidates with information about the company, how they should handle customer calls, and how to use several computerised databases to obtain information for customers. The candidates also had access to a policy-and-procedures manual and reference charts. Candidates had 30 minutes to review the material and to examine an abbreviated version of the customer database. The assessment began when two trained assessors made a series of 11 customer calls to the applicants. To respond appropriately to these calls, the applicants needed to draw together the information available to them, including the computerised databases, so that they could provide appropriate answers to the 'customer' queries. The assessors each used detailed scripts and took turns in playing the role of customer with the candidates. The assessor who was not role playing listened to the conversation and took detailed notes.

Situational judgement tests

Lievens and Coetsier (2002) describe a video-based physician–patient situational judgement test for medical school admissions in Belgium. Scripts were written and verified by Subject Matter Experts (professors) based on the identification of critical incidents, and videos were filmed with semi-professional actors, with the involvement of experienced physicians. In a follow up study (Lievens *et al.*, 2005), this test was shown to have validity for predicting medical school performance where interpersonal skill was important (e.g. situations involving patient interaction).

Situational interview

Maurer (2006) describes an engineering company's interview of technically qualified applicants for entry-level jobs. The aim of the interview was to assess their tendency to act in ways that 'fit' expected actions in critical job situations consistent with the values, goals and culture of the organisation and the work group. Incumbent project engineers created the following project management dilemma and rating criteria using a behaviourally anchored five-point scale:

> *Suppose that you are in charge of a large-scale equipment installation project that must be completed on time to avoid significant penalties for exceeding the expected due date. The six-month-long project is now about 75 per cent completed and your PERT analysis indicates that, at best, it will be finished about 2–3 days ahead of schedule. However, an installation supervisor who works for you has just informed you*

that there may be a delay in material delivery that could add 7–10 working days to the project. What would you do to deal with this situation?

1 = Poor. Ignore the situation since it is only a potential problem. Be prepared to deal with it when/if you hear that the delay is actually going to occur.

3 = Acceptable. Tell the supervisor that you expect them to deal with the problem. Remind the supervisor of the completion date and make it clear that you expect it to be met and that you want to be kept appraised of the situation.

5 = Excellent. Meet with the supervisor ASAP to determine the exact nature of the potential problem and formulate a plan for preventing or dealing with it. Set a follow-up procedure to make sure that the plan is being carried out.

The two points without specific anchors (i.e., the 2 and 4 points on the scale) would be used to evaluate answers that do not conform with all parts of the behavioural anchors. For instance, a response such as, 'Since it is not yet a problem, I would simply tell the supervisor to deal with it', would be a level '2' response since it contains parts of both the '1' and '3' anchors but does not comply with the full text of either.

Finally, structured interviews involve situational or behaviourally based assessments. The vast literature on the use of interviews for recruitment and selection highlights its various roles; e.g. as a way of selling the organisation to applicants or to prescreen applicants on minimum requirements. While the former involves a considerable amount of negotiation and subjective interaction – something we return to later in the chapter – the latter is based on simple, verifiable questions and is now frequently carried out by telephone. When interviews are used to assess more complex individual qualities, such as personality, knowledge, social skills or values which may or may not fit with the organisation, the need for reliable, valid techniques becomes much more apparent.

In short, structured interviews show high predictive validity (Table 4.1). Some examples of how structure can be introduced are by using a critical incident-based job analysis for designing the questions, using multiple, trained interviewers and raters, minimising any use of prior information, such as applicant test scores, or limiting follow-up, prompting or elaboration.

With respect to our current interest in assessing performance, the use of questions based on hypothetical situations (situational interviews), past behaviour or experience (behavioural interviews) or direct job knowledge questions (either knowledge of facts or of procedures) provide the greatest potential in terms of psychometric quality (see Box 4.2 for an example). Like situational judgement tests, these do not directly measure an applicant's ability to do the job so they have lower fidelity to the job than work samples or simulations. Interview questions are usually tied to specific competencies which have been identified in the job analysis, however, and this emphasis on job relevance has been found to allow assessors to focus more on knowledge, skills, abilities and other qualities more directly linked to actual performance rather than relying on inferences about underlying characteristics. Structured interviews are not correlated with cognitive ability or personality tests, so it has been argued that companies can significantly enhance the validity of their selection methods by adding a structured interview to their hiring process (Huffcutt and Youngcourt, 2007).

Mixed approaches

The emphasis on behaviour is also visible in the competency movement which dominates much of HRM. Competencies are transferable personal qualities, such as teamworking or business awareness, which draw from a range of skills, abilities, traits, job knowledge, experience and other qualities needed to perform a job effectively. Service orientation, for example, includes personality characteristics such as courtesy, consideration and tact

(Hogan *et al.*, 1984) but also behaviours displayed towards customers and colleagues during the service delivery process (Baydoun *et al.*, 2001). The focus here is on behavioural outputs – individuals' achievements or what they should be able to do. In theory, therefore, different combinations of underlying psychological characteristics may achieve the same outputs (i.e. display competence in the job), which is why the focus is more on performance than the underlying cognitive or non-cognitive construct. One well known generic competency framework is the Great Eight Competency Model (see Box 4.3).

Box 4.3 HRM in practice   Great Eight competency model

Tests of ability and personality have been shown to have moderate to good correlations with line-manager ratings of the following generic competencies. In other words, the tests have moderate to good predictive validity for these indicators of performance across a range of jobs.

- Leading and deciding;
- Supporting and cooperating;
- Interacting and presenting;
- Analysing and interpreting;
- Creating and conceptualising;
- Organising and executing;
- Adapting and coping;
- Enterprising and performing.

Source: Bartram (2005).

Of growing interest are 'future-oriented' behavioural competencies which go beyond immediate person–job fit. A typical example is in the selection of managers with leadership potential. Financial services firm HBOS uses a single behavioural competency framework based on 'leadership commitment' to guide selection across 18 different graduate schemes (e.g. HR, finance, IT, actuarial, corporate banking) and a range of methods, including online application forms, numerical and verbal reasoning tests, a telephone interview and teamwork and business scenario exercises (*People Management*, 4 October 2007).

Finally, an amalgam of many of these approaches is reflected in assessment centres which focus on a series of situational exercises designed to reveal various behaviourally based performance dimensions (Thornton and Mueller-Hanson, 2004). As they use multiple methods, multiple assessors and systematic scoring procedures for integrating candidate data, they are thought to provide good validity for many occupations. They have high favourability both with managers and candidates because of their face validity (their appearance of measuring job-related factors), and the range of exercises ensures lower adverse impact against under-represented groups. Some concern has been expressed about what assessment centres are actually measuring, despite the formalised systems and scoring. One critical account of graduate assessment centres (Brown and Hesketh, 2004) describes a high degree of active, impression management by candidates, especially by those who are identified as 'stars' (the most employable candidates on paper), or the 'players' who were able to produce 'flashes of the appropriate behavioural competencies' (2004: 173). There was also inevitable subjectivity on the part of assessors whose evaluations of candidates might be based not on the objective test scores, but on performance in coffee breaks or even opinions formed when 'watching from afar'. From a more psychometric slant, careful attention to how assessors are trained and how they conduct their final evaluations, as well as to the design of the exercises themselves, is essential for improving reliability and maximising the potential validity of this approach

(Lievens and Klimoski, 2001). Given their high cost, though, they are likely to have utility only for the highest skilled, and more valuable, potential employees; for example, managers or professionals.

Summary of trends

From the review so far, we can detect several important trends in selection practice which build on the four indicators of psychometric quality.

- *More reliable and valid assessment tools.* This can be achieved, for example, by: conducting detailed job analyses, introducing structure and standardisation, training assessors, carrying out validation studies, and making more use of statistical aggregation and correction techniques such as meta-analysis, across validity studies to increase the precision of the prediction task (for a review see Sackett and Lievens, 2008). Advances in these areas have resulted in increased confidence in the validity of many selection methods.
- *Greater use of high validity/low adverse impact assessment tools.* As seen in Table 4.1, biodata, structured behavioural and situational interviewing, situational judgement tests, work samples and assessment centres, have lower differential subgroup validity; i.e. they are less likely to adversely impact non-traditional applicant groups. Many selection processes use multiple methods in order to increase validity and lower adverse impact. For an example applied to call centre agents which combines biodata, psychometric cognitive or non-cognitive tests, and situational judgement tests see Konradt *et al.* (2003).
- *Increasing importance of assessing non-cognitive qualities.* Across all types of jobs, interest has grown in a wider spectrum of behaviours, such as organisational citizenship or adaptability. The challenge has been to design valid tools to target these qualities. Some personality tests have been shown to be good predictors of this type of behaviour, and situational interviews can be designed to assess behaviours such as helping colleagues or volunteering (Latham and Skarlicki, 1995).
- *Increasing use of bespoke simulations.* These provide valid behavioural indicators of qualities relevant to a particular job or organisation, along with low adverse impact and high user acceptability. These organisationally specific approaches reflect a growing strategic orientation which links selection to wider competencies, not just job-specific skills, which are essential for ensuring competitive advantage and dealing with strategic pressures, such as restructuring. Searle (2003a) argues:

  the use of these tools reflects an increasing sophistication and confidence among human resource professionals, who see the adoption of more complex and rigorous assessment and development practices as demonstrating this professional group's pivotal place in helping to shape organizations for the future. (2003a: 226)

- *Web-based delivery and scoring of assessment.* Internet testing is likely to increase even more as organisations are forced to handle more applicants for each position and try to screen out unsuitable applicants as efficiently and cheaply as possible. The early stages of selection for many jobs with high numbers of applicants now often consist of ability tests, situational judgement tests and multimedia simulations; for example, one bank created a numerical reasoning test which looked like the Bloomberg business television channel with key information scrolling along the bottom of the screen ('Guide to assessment', *People Management*, 8 October 2012). Predictive validity and positive applicant reactions are reported (Bartram, 2000) but questions remain about security, equality of access and the quality of applicants (Anderson, 2003). For this reason, some organisations use an unproctored internet test for pre-screening but a second (in-person) test sitting for the actual hiring decision (Lievens and Chapman, 2010).

What do organisations actually do?

Psychometric principles of good practice in the design and administration of assessment methods are endorsed by professional psychological and HR associations across the world, but most employers tend not to pay close attention.

Informal selection methods, such as responding to speculative applications, word-of-mouth and unstructured interviews, still dominate. Larger organisations with a dedicated HR function, and especially those in the public sector, are more likely to adopt a psychometric approach, especially for managerial or skilled/technical positions. Estimates place the use of personality or ability tests at around 40 per cent of Fortune 100 companies and all of the top 100 (Rothstein and Goffin, 2006). The most recent figures for the UK show use by about 38 per cent of large employers (CIPD, 2011). Salgado and Anderson (2002) conducted one of the few comparisons of test use across countries showing that Belgium, Britain, the Netherlands, Portugal and Spain were more likely to use ability or aptitude tests than France, Germany, Greece, Ireland or Italy. In the US, the figure is lower than even some of the latter group of countries at 20 per cent for tests of cognitive ability, perhaps because of their associated legal problems.

Performance-based and competency tests tend to be more common in public sector organisations than private sector enterprises, and for managerial and administrative/secretarial positions. For management roles, personal competency methods include the use of Weighted Applicant Blanks or interviews designed to assess leadership qualities or business awareness. Work samples or achievement tests for administrative/secretarial positions may assess clerical tasks or data manipulation. Their greater use in the public sector is because this sector has tended to do more to ensure that hiring practices are non-discriminatory and encourage diversity (Kersley *et al.*, 2006; Wolf and Jenkins, 2006).

A growing strategic issue for many large organisations managing multinational workforces is whether it is possible to apply a single selection system universally across countries, either for expatriate selection or for local recruits. Box 4.4 summarises the work of one influential US researcher and her colleagues in this area.

Box 4.4 HRM in practice   Global or local staffing?

Over the last decade or so, Ryan and her colleagues have studied the growing use of global staffing systems used by many multinational companies (MNCs) such as IBM, Motorola, Procter & Gamble, and Shell and whether there is convergence or divergence in selection practice across countries. In a book dedicated to the topic, Ryan and Tippins (2009) conclude that globalisation, efficiency and technology are the main driving forces behind increasing convergence towards 'sophisticated' selection systems – but the need for local cultural sensitivity to hiring staff remains. They introduce the problem with the case scenario below. We follow this with a summary of how their work has led to greater understanding of an issue which is central to global companies' staffing strategy.

Case scenario

The corporate HR Director and the corporate Manufacturing Director are debating whether to implement a global selection system for engineers in all the manufacturing plants or to allow each country to develop its own system tailored to the location's special needs. The Manufacturing Director feels that a good engineer needs to have the same skills no matter where in the world you go, and he wants the HR group to come up with a useful web-screening tool and interview protocol that can be implemented worldwide. The HR Director believes that cultural differences mean that different skills and characteristics are needed to perform the engineering job in different countries, and therefore each region needs to come up with its own system.

Consider some of the evidence gathered by these researchers summarised below. How would you respond in this situation?

The evidence base

- **Cultural values do matter**

  In 1999, Ryan and colleagues surveyed HR practitioners/senior managers in 959 organisations in 20 countries. Countries scoring high on the cultural value of uncertainty avoidance (feeling threatened by unknown situations), such as Belgium, Japan and Spain, made greater use of testing, used more test types, more standardised interviews and greater auditing of selection processes. This was thought to reflect a preference for structured methods which reduced uncertainty about an unknown individual.

- **Local autonomy matters**

  In 2003, interviews with local country MNC managers showed that it was important to allow local discretion in applying the global system. One Motorola manager commented, 'I think everybody wants local norms; they don't want to be compared to the United States, they want to be compared locally for selection. it's their applicant pool really from which they draw.' This led them to conclude that 'best practice' for global staffing systems should 'integrate global tools into local systems'.

- **But applicants' preferences are converging**

  In 2008 the research team turned attention to international applicants' perceptions of the fairness of different selection methods (including cognitive tests, personality, biodata and situational judgement tests). A global sample of over 1,000 undergraduates were asked to rate their perceptions of selection tools used by a particular MNC for an entry-level management job. There were no differences due to country, suggesting that cultural differences in candidates' perceived fairness are not a barrier to the global selection systems used by MNCs.

Sources: Ryan and Tippins, 2009: 5; Ryan et al., 1999, 2003, 2008.

Explaining practice

Selection is more than the application of assessment techniques. It is now accepted that selection can be thought of from at least three other perspectives which take into account the organisational and social hiring context (see also Iles, 1999): (1) selection as 'best-fit' for the organisation (as opposed to a normative, 'best practice' model); (2) selection as an interactive decision process involving multiple stakeholders; and (3) selection as discourse, where power and interests dominate what happens more than the validity and utility of assessment methods.

(1) Selection as 'best-fit': the organisation's perspective

In the study of HRM generally, there is often an assumption of similar needs across sectors, organisations, occupations and even countries, which leads to 'best practice' guidelines, such as those of the psychometric model. These guidelines, however, are formulated almost completely in a vacuum. Valid methods are held to always have high utility, but this assumes a low selection ratio (i.e., a low number hired relative to the number of applicants), that the cost of poor selection is high (as it may be in a top management or skilled position), and that the top performers can always be selected (i.e., the 'best' actually accept the job offer). The reality of staffing is that these conditions are not always met.

Table 4.2 Factors influencing selection practice and decisions

Economic pressures

Short-term financial impact

Skills supply and labour market tightness

Patterns of employment and turnover

Organisation size

Life cycle of the organisation

Long-term versus short-term performance orientation

Ownership (multinational, single owner, shareholder pressures)

Presence of HR

Experience/training of selectors

Time resource constraints

Long-term financial impact

High-skill (managerial/professional) occupations/vacancies

Career potential of position (internal labour markets, investment in training)

Competition and rate of change

Market segment/differentiation strategy

Organisation values

Social pressures

Legislative/institutional

Regulatory environment

Visibility/accountability of organisation

National culture

Entry standards/statutory requirements

Other stakeholders

Users

Applicants

Industry/profession

Test developers

Table 4.2 summarises a range of factors which shape selection practice. These are organised using Klehe's (2004) distinction between economic and social pressures as a way of illustrating the effects of the wider context of selection decisions and allow us to make predictions about when sophisticated (i.e. strategic/psychometric) approaches are likely to be adopted.

With respect to economic pressures, the higher the initial cost and development required, and the more dependent the organisation is on the approval of owners concerned with short-term financial impact, the less likely it will be to adopt sophisticated methods. Short-term resource considerations (e.g., the cost of more structured behavioural interviewing, training inexperienced assessors, relieving managers for multi-method assessment days or evaluating procedures) often outweigh the longer-term potential returns. This is why competency-based methods are more common for managers. Similarly, the fewer applicants the organisation has to choose from and the more dependent it is on filling the vacant post quickly the less likely the organisation is to invest heavily in its selection procedure. This may be the position of many SMEs, organisations located in suburban or rural areas, or sectors where there is high demand for key skills and skills shortages. The informality of unsolicited correspondence and face-to-face contact may be a more rational option for attracting suitable candidates where there is a small pool of qualified applicants or where the position must be filled quickly.

Social pressures are divided into two types in Table 4.2: legislative/institutional and stakeholder pressure. We consider the role of stakeholders in the next section. For now, it is possible to identify the direct effects of employment legislation on hiring practice. Employers are increasingly required by law in many countries to pay attention to psychometric principles. Public sector organisations are especially affected. In an examination of 400 Canadian federal selection discrimination cases, Terpstra and Kethley (2002) showed that the government sector was more likely to have had litigation brought against it than any other sector. This kind of accountability and risk encourages the use of multiple methods, greater standardisation and monitoring of selection procedures in order to ensure diversity (Jewson and Mason, 1986; Pearn, 1993). US federal legislation also goes further in placing a burden on employers to justify the job-relatedness of all selection measures, and this is one of the reasons why psychometric testing is used more in some European countries (the UK, Spain and Portugal) than in the US (Salgado and Anderson, 2002). UK employers, conversely to those in the US, perceive the rigour of a testing approach as a 'precautionary measure' which can protect them from legal challenge (Wolf and Jenkins, 2006).

In other ways, though, the institutional context in Europe, Australia and Asia is more restrictive in terms of labour relations and greater reliance on recruitment from educational systems or internal labour markets. Huo *et al.* (2002) speculated that a greater focus on individual candidate fit with cultural values in Australia was related to a recent tradition of joint consultation practice between employees and employers at the level of the enterprise.

In Box 4.5, we use this framework to illustrate the pressures faced in three different industry examples – hotels, construction companies and voluntary sector organisations. In these situations, cost, time and recruitment crises may be more salient than reliability and validity (Johns, 1993; Muchinsky, 2004). We return to these examples again in the next section.

(2) Selection as an interactive decision process

Social pressures can also originate from other stakeholders in the hiring process. This includes the selectors (managers, HR) who implement the procedures, institutional bodies which set guidelines for entry into occupations or who exert influence over assessment (e.g. professional associations) and applicants themselves. Searle (2003b) has argued that, with the growing use of online testing, test developers, whose interests are quite distinct from those of organisations and applicants, have become an increasingly powerful stakeholder because of the access they have to the results of testing processes. From this perspective, hiring is not just about the organisation choosing the right assessment tools for its needs, but involves an interactive process of information exchange and negotiation – a series of 'social episodes' (Herriot, 1989) – between the organisation and its wider environment. This impacts two general areas.

How methods are perceived by stakeholders

In Table 4.1, we introduced the idea of user acceptability as a counterweight to the psychometric ideals of reliability and validity. This refers to whether the method is perceived as credible, and hence whether managers or practitioners will actually use it, as well as how it is perceived by the candidates who are exposed to it. Performance-based methods are more favourable as users can clearly see the relevance of the assessment for the job itself. This means these methods are more likely to be adopted and used appropriately than less transparent, psychometric tests.

The participation of users in the development of selection methods is also important. Millmore (2003), in his exploration of what makes recruitment and selection strategic, talks

Box 4.5 HRM in practice Economic and social pressures on selection in three sectors

ECONOMIC PRESSURES ➡	SELECTION ⬅	SOCIAL PRESSURES

Example 1: HOTELS

Labour market (competition, shortages)
Short-term pressures to fill vacancies (casualisation, high turnover)
Market segmentation (chain, deluxe)
Resource pressures (only chains have centralised HR/train selectors)

Short-termist approach
Informal methods targeted at local transient labour market/unpredictability
Longer-term approach
Strategic alignment (high quality localised approach, combines standardisation with informal networks)
Emphasis on staff retention, permanent positions, person–culture fit

Applicant perceptions (low pay, poor prospects, antisocial hours, hard work, isolated locations)

Example 2: CONSTRUCTION (manual & skilled/technical workers)

Workflow (project-/network-based, local site decentralisation, flexibility due to design/supply variations)
Project ownership (network of subcontractors & professionals, local focus)
Labour market (skill shortages, limited training, competency-based skill certification voluntary)
Resources (working to contract, time, cost)
Change (rapid technological change, changing markets, multiskilling)

Larger firms more formalised ('skills identity card', HR functions)
Local variation even where formalised procedures existed (procedures called 'raindances')
Strong emphasis on probationary days (work simulations) and site manager local networks (time served on other jobs)
After technical ability, valued honesty, conscientiousness, adaptability

Applicant perceptions (dangerous work, masculine culture, antisocial hours)
Industry Industry Training Board common accreditation)
Customers (pressures for improved quality, cost reduction)
Firm-specific demands (work against industry standards)
Site manager (autonomous at local level)
Legislation (Health & Safety)

Example 3: VOLUNTARY SECTOR (front-line care and social services)

Resources (insecure funding, 'full cost recovery' problematic, increased scope due to work transition from public services, increasingly need to staff new business processes
Labour market (competition with private/public sector, shortage of high skill/graduates)
High attrition/turnover (unrealistic expectations)

Seek person–organisation fit
Social process/attraction strategies (ensure value congruence, provide applicant power/choices, realistic job/organisation previews)
Need for rebranding to attract wider applicant pool (flexible working, work–life balance, satisfaction, 'altruism payoff', underutilised graduates)

Applicant perceptions (uncompetitive salaries, insecurity, high emotional demands, women's work, need value-based high commitment, skills under-used)
Public perception (unprofessional, voluntary (unpaid), not a career, need for greater transparency)

Sources: Lockyer and Scholarios, 2004, 2007; Nickson et al., 2008.

about the involvement of multiple stakeholders as equal partners in the process and the involvement of all levels of management and peers in the design of the process (e.g. defining person specifications, panel interviews). This should lead to greater consensus about the qualities being sought and hence more reliable assessment. Local managers of MNCs discussed in Box 4.4 are also stakeholders who are key to effective implementation of the hiring process.

Applicants too should be considered equal partners. Schuler (1993) argued that applicants have the right to be treated with dignity, provided information about what is expected of them and on their performance, and involved in the process by providing their consent and even their own input. Millmore suggested providing, at least, information packs and feedback on performance at all stages of the selection process. Candidates should also have their privacy respected, for example, in questions asked in application forms or interviews, and the right to appeal decisions which they think are unfair. This introduces the idea of perceptions of fair treatment, or what is sometimes called procedural justice (Cropanzano and Wright, 2003). Some suggestions to improve fairness perceptions are to use a combination of methods, or modify how tests are administered. Box 4.6 summarises how job applicants across countries rate the fairness of selection methods.

Box 4.6 HRM in practice   Perceived fairness of selection methods

Job applicants across Europe, North America and Asia seem to rank their most and least favourable methods consistently. These rankings are shown from (1) 'most favourable' to (10) 'least favourable' below. How does this compare with your own experiences?

1 interviews
2 CVs/resumes
3 work sample tests
4 biographical information
5 written ability tests
6 personal references
7 personality tests
8 honesty/integrity tests
9 personal contacts
10 graphology

Source: Anderson and Witvliet, 2008.

Going even further than this, some would argue that individuals entering a position should be able to influence the job demands rather than being fitted for the job requirements, thus making selection a truly two-way process. Work sample tests, for example, tend to imply that there is agreement about a single correct way to perform the job; however, candidates could be given freedom to demonstrate other ways of performing the job successfully rather than confined to the taken-for-granted views which are demanded by the psychometric approach (Searle, 2003a: 233).

The important point here is that applicant exposure to the assessment method influences important outcomes – whether qualified applicants maintain interest in the job for which they are applying, whether they decide to continue to the next stage of the recruitment process, whether they accept the job if offered or even whether the method has 'negative psychological effects', such as lowering self-esteem (Anderson and Goltsi 2006: 237). Box 4.7 illustrates how university graduates seeking jobs in 2007 made such decisions. It suggests that companies who fail to consider perceptions may run the risk of losing qualified candidates to competitors. Of course, with the number of graduates applying for each job doubling since 2009 (e.g. 'Graduate gloom as 83 apply for every vacancy', *The Independent*, 28 June 2011), applicant perceptions may be of less interest to employers.

Box 4.7 HRM in practice   Candidates as customers

Prompted by a global skills shortage and employer recruitment crisis at the time, a 2007 study by Reed Consulting argued for a shift in how employers treated potential job candidates. Twenty-two per cent of 2,500 university graduates surveyed refused a job offer because they were unhappy with an organisation's recruitment process. Sixty-six per cent of job applicants didn't receive a response – making potential talent feel disregarded and devalued – and this was especially the case in the financial services sector which received high volumes of applications. The study also found that:

- more than one-third of graduates avoided products and services offered by a company that disappointed them in the recruitment process;
- 90 per cent of dissatisfied candidates told family and friends about their bad experiences, with serious implications for damaging both the consumer and employer brand;
- failure to respond to a recruitment hotline phone call in 30 seconds resulted in 29 per cent of applicants hanging up.

Would a similar survey now find the same results?

How applicants perceive the job or organisation

As we saw earlier (see Chapter 3), negative impressions may be caused by uninformative websites; disinterested recruiters; long, complicated application processes; or any message which communicates undesirable images of the employer brand (Van Hoye and Lievens, 2005). The early stages of selection can be used to build identification with the organisation and encourage only those who see a match with the values of the organisation to remain in the application process. In an example from a police force in a US midwest city, the interview stage provided a realistic preview of the job and prompted some candidates to withdraw from the process (Ployhart *et al.*, 2002). Of most relevance to organisations is how potential applicants perceive 'fit' between their own goals and what is offered by the job, including issues such as pay, working conditions, organisational values and reputation, and career options.

This is important for several reasons. First, if some applicant groups withdraw from the process more frequently than others, then potentially qualified candidates who are required to meet skill gaps are excluded. This seems to be the case for graduates who are not pursuing voluntary sector job vacancies because of the perceptions of what the job offers (see Box 4.5).

Second, this exclusion may adversely impact members of minority groups, such as women or blacks. These applicants withdrew disproportionately from the US police selection process indicated above. This also harms diversity staffing targets, an issue of some concern to police forces in many parts of the world who consider being representative of the community as essential to good policing.

Finally, in some employment situations, the balance of power lies with applicants rather than the organisation. The voluntary sector suffers recruitment difficulties because it competes with both the private and public sector for specialists and graduates (Box 4.5). At the other end of the labour market, the hospitality industry is often portrayed as being in competition with higher paying, 'cleaner', more flexible, temporary, part-time work offered by the likes of the call centre industry. Tackling negative perceptions of potential applicants may mean that informal methods of selection, such as personal interviews, are a better approach in these situations. Of course, problems of inequality, bias and limits on diversity which are associated with informality still have to be recognised.

A further purpose of selection is to build relationships between the organisation and future employees. The interview has high 'social validity' for both managers and candidates as it allows two-way communication and a richer environment for both to establish congruence or person–organisation 'fit'. Roe and van den Berg's (2003) survey suggested that European employers prefer interviews for this reason. In a similar vein, British Telecom replaced external assessors with their own managers in the final interviews at their graduate assessment centre in order to 'interface with the candidates themselves'(*Guardian*, 19 January 2008).

One last consequence of paying attention to social processes in selection is their 'socialisation impact' (Anderson, 2001). Methods which allow both parties to establish 'fit' will lead to employees who are more likely to be satisfied in their jobs, more committed to the goals of the organisation and less likely to leave. Again, a clear application of this is provided by the voluntary sector example in Box 4.5. Thus, as well as establishing hurdles, selection informs, attracts and increases the commitment of applicants to the job and organisation as the relationship progresses.

(3) Selection as discourse

A more radical view is that selection is a process which cannot easily be reduced to the quality of assessment tools and rational decision-making. The reference to discourse relates to the idea that there are many different ways of talking about (i.e. describing and understanding) selection. The choice of which discourse we focus on at a particular point in time will vary; for example, some may value meritocracy and hence use a discourse which focusses on developing neutral assessment techniques which are reliable and valid (a psychometric discourse), while others are more concerned with mutual respect, treating applicants in an ethical way and building relationships of trust (a social process or decision interactive discourse). These two examples, in fact, are often used to describe the quite different dominant discourses which guide actual selection practice in North America versus Europe, respectively (de Wolff, 1993). These selection discourses have become accepted by the culture as a result of societal values and guiding principles, established, for example, through legislation. Other discourses also may develop within organisations, clusters of organisations or professions as a result of other powerful forces. This may explain why 'blue-chip' multinational companies, who project themselves as global market leaders or 'good employers', often lead the way in adopting the most sophisticated, expensive and psychometrically sound selection systems, in order to be seen to comply with 'good practice' as presented by respected external bodies (e.g. those promoting equal opportunities legislation or human resource professionalism). This view goes as far as to argue that selection discourses, such as strict psychometric measurement, can be used as a way of making the management of people more explicitly controllable e.g. to further particular interests (Townley, 1989).

We use two examples here to illustrate this perspective and how it challenges the psychometric model (see also Iles, 1999). The first questions whether job suitability can be objectively reduced to an agreed set of individual knowledge, skills, abilities, and traits.

The 'good' firefighter. In one of the author's research studies, the qualities of a firefighter were mused over by the Fire Service's personnel officer. They have to be able to put up with long periods of monotony and boredom, but can suddenly be faced with emotional and harrowing situations. In many ways, the job is now so procedural things rarely go wrong (e.g. virtual reality of many of the city's buildings means that firefighters no longer enter smoke-filled buildings without knowing where they are going). In fact, they have to be able to follow instructions without questioning orders in what can be a militaristic culture. At the same time, they are looking for general ability and the ability to think strategically. As well as basic physical ability and practical tests, assessors are looking for evidence of person–culture fit (prior knowledge of the service, commitment to a career and serving the community) all of which is assessed through self-report questions on an application form (e.g. Why do you want to become a firefighter?) and interviews with senior officers. How can this complexity of demands be reduced to behaviours appropriate for every situation? Assessors often cannot agree on the suitability of candidates, and use other shortcuts, such as appearance, to justify their decisions, even though they all go through assessor training. 'State of the art' for firefighter selection recommends a combination of cognitive/mechanical and interpersonal/emotional skills tests (Blair and Hornick, 2005), but this 'all rounder' view may just be the latest construction of the 'good' firefighter, which contrasts to earlier beliefs that firefighters should be the 'bravest and strongest' (shown through physical ability), 'smartest' (cognitive testing), or have the 'right' person profile (personality testing). Some may argue that this is just another discourse of what is 'acceptable' reflecting society, and the historical and cultural influences of those who draw up the person specifications and make final decisions. The effects of this are illustrated in a study of a similar profession, police work, which showed how good performance is constructed in terms of a 'masculine crime fighting' discourse (as opposed to an equally valid service discourse which privileges skills associated with femininity) and prevents potentially qualified women from applying (Dick and Nadin, 2006).

The second example raises the question whether formalisation and legislation can ever eliminate the inherent subjectivity of hiring decisions. This challenges the assumption of the rational assessor.

Graduate assessment centres. Despite multiple assessors and careful exercise design, assessment centres have been portrayed as 'politically charged contexts', 'largely uncontrollable and permeated with problems of meaning', and a 'conspiracy of distortion' between assessors who rank subjectively while hiding behind a 'façade of systematic and scientific professionalism' (Knights and Raffo, 1990: 37). Brown and Hesketh's (2004) analysis of attempts to measure 'soft' competencies at graduate assessment centres showed that even after training on diversity issues, assessors were still inclined to resort to first impressions or compare people to the existing management in the company. In 'washing up sessions' some opinions held more sway than others (e.g. a particularly negative view of how one candidate described what she gained from her gap year) and simplistic heuristics were used to organise the information from each exercise about the candidates. Candidates were labelled 'stars', 'geeks', 'razors' and 'safe bets'. Value was attached to 'appearance, accent and appropriate behaviour' (2004: 161) tending to favour the social capital possessed by Oxbridge candidates, while finding ways to match these to the 'objectively defined' behavioural indicators.

Conclusions and implications for HRM

There has been a recent frenzy of activity to develop the most valid assessment tool for predicting a diverse range of work behaviours, with 'best practice' showing a gradual shift towards holistic assessments encompassing a mix of measures of cognitive, non-cognitive and performance qualities. The move to performance-based methods, with their lower adverse impact against under-represented groups, is particularly notable, as this seems to have accommodated the trend towards diversity as a strategic direction, whether among large private multinationals or the more publically accountable government sectors.

Beyond this, though, different ways of understanding selection have also gained strength. These expand on the non-rational, unplanned, informal, social and power bases of selection, leading to an alternative language for evaluating the outcomes of any hiring process. Diverse contexts dictate alternative logics from that of prediction or formality, suggesting more of a 'best fit' approach than a normative one. For instance, the employee attributes required may shift alongside an organisation's strategic goals, and firms facing staffing problems will shape their selection strategies in ways which they consider will attract the 'right type' of employees or enhance employee retention. The 'best practice' model of selection offered by the psychometric model assumes that the number of applicants exceeds the positions available, and that the best applicants will always accept the jobs they are offered. This is clearly not the case.

Selection can also be judged in terms of the quality of the social exchange between organisations and other stakeholders. The treatment of applicants, their perceptions and attitudes, take on a more important role in ensuring they find the job and organisation attractive and whether person–organisation 'fit' is achieved. Also important is the way that selection techniques are used to further interests which often are only tenuously linked to the psychometric paradigm's aspirations of objectivity and fairness. Each of these perspectives – 'best fit', social process and discourse – highlights the deficiencies of the psychometric model for achieving a comprehensive understanding of all aspects of the selection problem (cf. Herriot, 1993; Iles, 1999).

Within HRM, selection has been viewed as a core function essential for achieving key organisational outcomes; high performance, low levels of absenteeism and turnover, and high employee well-being and commitment have all been linked with 'selective hiring' (Storey, 2007). As argued in several HRM texts (Legge, 2005), however, the reality of strategic integration and practice seldom has matched the rhetoric, and this seems equally as applicable to the adoption of 'best practice' selection. Based on 'best fit' perspectives, expensive testing and bespoke assessment may only be reserved for higher value core employees that organisations wish to retain or those at senior levels (Kwiatkowski, 2003).

From the psychometric perspective, HR professionals (or those responsible for selection) should serve a monitoring function, ensuring that assessment methods are designed appropriately with a view to current legislation and practice developments and that relevant performance criteria (broad as well as job-specific) are used. Methods should be reappraised often and based on more frequent and focused validation programmes, although all this assumes that HR and HR issues are afforded an appropriate status and influence within the organisation. Interactive, social process perspectives may add to this the need to ensure that all stakeholders' views are accommodated in the design if not implementation of the assessment, and that selectors are encouraged to think of the applicant groups they wish to attract as potentially powerful decision-makers with their own views about the attractiveness of the organisation and the job. The increased devolution of HR functions to line managers may also suggest the need for an additional level of support in managing the complexities of the process (Whittaker and Marchington, 2003), although in many organisations, such as SMEs, this is rarely available. Nevertheless, these issues become particularly crucial if we acknowledge the discourse perspective's warnings of how persistent subjectivity, vested interests and less politically neutral forces are able to obstruct the ideal of creating meritocratic selection systems.

Case studies

Methods designed to reveal a service or sales orientation now form the basis of many hiring processes used in call centres. Baldry *et al.* (2007) described the following call centre selection processes.

CASE STUDY 4.1

MONEYFLOW

DORA SCHOLARIOS

One call centre in the financial services sector, Money-flow, dedicated 3 hours 20 minutes to each candidate for the position of Customer Advisor. At the time of this example, there was a vibrant employment market in the area and this call centre was competing against 15 other companies for qualified staff. The demand for staff was high, as many of those recruited often left after the two days training. Recruitment consultants were used to pre-select candidates for the company to interview. This recruitment agency was chosen because, in comparison to other agencies used, it seemed to understand the business and skill specifications required by the company and provide higher-quality candidates.

Stages of selection

1 A general register of candidates is developed (few active call centre workers were available given the buoyant employment situation for call centre work in the area).
2 Ads are placed locally and nationally, including in universities. Local ads for part-time work were aimed at encouraging returners to work.
3 Candidates asked to complete work history, details of present employment and a financial planning questionnaire (to eliminate credit risks). The company designed and validated a self-assessment application form for the call centre advisor role based on work profiling and critical incident methods. This captured five customer-oriented competencies (customer focus, fact finding, relating to customers, convincing, oral communication) and two related to contextual performance (independent facilitation, job dedication) (see Bywater and Green, 2005). It also acted as a realistic job preview to inform candidates of the sales component of the job and act as a self-selection tool.
4 Skills testing: tests of visual accuracy; spelling; key depressions; arithmetic; and alphanumeric skill. All these were provided by the company to the agency.
5 Interview (20–30 minutes) based on CV/work history. Sales skills explored further in the interview.
6 Telephone role play. 'You are a CA in a travel service.' Looking for questioning and listening skills as well as selling/additional sales.
7 Recruitment consultants send list of pre-selected candidates to the company to select for one hour interview with two team leaders. Depending on need, the agencies often put all candidates forward for interview without pre-selection.

Questions

1 What underlying psychological characteristics are being assessed at each stage?
2 Based on the information provided in Table 4.1, what do you think the overall psychometric quality of such a procedure might be? Take into account what you know about the criterion of successful performance for call centre agents might be, the use of both recruitment agencies and team leaders to carry out the assessment, and the wider labour market context of the call centre.
3 Is user acceptability an important factor in this selection process?

CASE STUDY 4.2

THEJOBSHOP

DORA SCHOLARIOS

Thejobshop is a growing city-based, multi-business outsourced call centre, which operates on behalf of 15 external clients. Outsourcing is attractive to organisations which have no call centre expertise and have the advantage of being able to set up a call centre in a very short period of time. Pay also tends to be lower in an outsourced call centre. The staffing numbers involved in a contract can range from approximately 200 to 3. There is some variation though in the extent to which client businesses retain autonomy over their operations. At the one extreme are 'co-sourcing' accounts, notably in the high-value operations, where the business retains greater controls over the service provided. These provide operators with distinct e-mail addresses and corporate slogans. At the other extreme are lower-value accounts where Thejobshop completely manages the operations on behalf of the client.

These differences are reflected in how selection is managed. Thejobshop try to keep the clients out of the selection process as much as possible as they feel they know what they are looking for, although some, like the bluechip IT company are more hands-on and want to shape the type of person employed to match their culture. Carco (a luxury car sales business) want 'tans and teeth' and 'young, happy and shiny' people, even though most of their customer base is older and would prefer someone older to speak to. They make regular visits on site.

The operations managers said:

> We perhaps show the client a half dozen who we feel are right and let them comment. We're looking for 'basic core competencies', although we try to tailor them for each set of interviews, for each individual client. We give clients the opportunity to give us details of the competencies they are looking for. For example, we asked DrinksNow to supply us with a list of the competencies they were looking for. They gave us a piece of A4 with a list of 8 points, that's all. A new financial sector client have identified their target customer group as 95 per cent female and mostly over the age of 35. They want the customer service agents to reflect this. The match between client, product and agent tends to happen naturally.

Agencies are used to prescreen on keyboard skills (paste and copy, data entry) and basic numerical and literacy skills because of the need to find people quickly, 60 people within days. If they are given a few weeks' notice they place their own adverts in the press and control the process. This is preferable as agencies often are less discriminating and just want 'bums on seats to get their cut'. They also tend to prefer people with previous call centre experience as they will be aware of the shift systems and nature of the work, so it won't be a shock.

CASE STUDY 4.3

ENTCOMM

DORA SCHOLARIOS

Entcomm, located in a small ex-industrial town near Glasgow, provides telecommunications and entertainment services for a large US multinational company. The call centre handles inquiries, billing, payments, new accounts and repairs maintenance. During a recent period of high-volume recruitment for 150 customer advi-sor posts it has found difficulties finding flexible staff. They advertise in local further education colleges and universities, and especially target training courses in IT for women returners, and over 50s. This addresses the problem of employing young part-timers (high turn-over) while achieving some flexibility in staffing to cover fluctuations in business. The vacancies are for 12–20 hours per week (4–6 hours per shift) in some cases finishing at 12.45am, and the starting pay £6 per hour.

There is a friend and family recruitment scheme where the employee receives £300 for a full-time member of staff found acceptable. Referrals still have to pass the tests though. The first filtering comes from a tele-screen interview which gives an initial indication of whether the prospective CSA has the required telephone manner and whether the shift preferences are compatible with the business needs. Keyboard skills are tested at this stage followed by two role-play exercises. These will involve one difficult customer (who may shout and scream) and one technical issue from a customer.

This procedure is outsourced to an agency who receive £350 per CSA they supply for the next stages of selection. The final interview is competency-based and conducted by team leaders and HR. A lot of emphasis here is put on why the recruits find this an attractive job e.g. entertainment sector, no cold calling. The interviews also include questions about coping with stressful situations building on the role play simulation. Existing employees talk about how they cope with difficult situations, and some are better than others. Jenny, an agent in her early twenties, commented, 'screaming customers I can cope with . . . one day though it was a really patronising customer and it just threw me completely . . . it was just the straw that broke the camel's back – I actually got up off the seat one day and I threw a booklet'. Cathy, who is in her 50s, was more resilient. 'I can let a customer scream away and let them rattle on until they are finished and then say now I'll help you . . . it's just my experience I suppose.'

Questions

1 Examine the economic and social pressure impacting selection in both Thejobshop and Entcomm. (Use the framework provided in Box 4.5 and Table 4.2.)

2 Explain the 'balance of power' in the selection process between employers, candidates and other stakeholders in each of the call centres.

3 Do these call centres operate a selection process which follows the psychometric process? Explain your answer.

4 What would the discourse perspective say about how the definition of the competent call centre employee in the three call centres (Moneyflow, Thejobshop and Entcomm)? How does this affect the process and outcomes of selection?

CASE STUDY 4.4

'YOU'RE EITHER ABERCROMBIE HOT – OR YOU'RE NOT'

DORA SCHOLARIOS

American clothing retail firm, Abercrombie & Fitch, has stores in the UK, Canada, Japan, Singapore, and throughout Europe, and is expanding rapidly, aiming to have stores worldwide by 2016. It has been ranked 241 in Deloitte's *Global Powers of Retailing*, 2012 and 651st in 2010's Fortune 1000, a list of the 1,000 largest American companies according to revenue.

Image is central to how the company sells its four brands – Abercrombie & Fitch, Abercrombie Kids, Hollister and Gilly Hicks. The first two target teens and young adults with an east-coast American slant; Hollister provides surfing-themed casual wear; and Gilly Hicks specialises in Australian-themed women's underwear. Investor materials describe the flagship

Abercrombie & Fitch brand as 'rooted in East Coast traditions and Ivy League heritage' and 'the essence of privilege and casual luxury'. The importance of these brand values to the company is shown in a recent effort to disassociate from the MTV reality show *The Jersey Shore* by paying the cast not to wear its clothes. The company claim their rowdy behaviour is 'contrary to the aspirational nature of our brand' (BBC News, 17 August 2011).

As described by one of the employees in the company's recruitment video employees are expected to be ambassadors for the brand. Job advertisements are for 'cool' and 'good looking' applicants (Human Resources News, 2010). A company spokesperson describes their advertisements as just 'aimed at attracting fun-loving and stylish people for the job' and as having no discriminatory intent.

This approach is consistent with the image they wish to portray of the company and brands they sell. The job description for sales assistants (called 'models') states: 'Models protect and project the image of the brand through personal style, providing customer service and maintaining presentation standards' (www.abercrombie.co.uk/anf/careers/model.html). Sales associates and managers reflect the 'casual, energetic and aspirational attitude of the brands'.

One manager described it as, 'You're either Abercrombie hot – or you're not.' Their 'look policy', which was revealed in a 2005 class action discrimination suit brought by 10,000 former job applicants and employees, stipulates that all employees 'represent Abercrombie & Fitch with natural, classic American style consistent with the company's brand' and 'look great while exhibiting individuality'. Workers must wear a 'clean, natural, classic hairstyle' and have nails which extend 'no more than a quarter inch beyond the tip of the finger'.

Attracting and selecting future leaders, 'models', and 'part-time impacts'

In the world of fashion retail, there is no shortage of young, willing workers attracted to the brand cachet of Abercrombie & Fitch. Drawing significantly from the part-time student workforce, many potential applicants, themselves, are 'brand advocates'. In fact, this is one of the qualities which the company looks for in potential employees. Social media sites such as Facebook and Twitter are used to build a following and a potential pool of self-selected potential applicants. Once hired, store managers emphasise to new hires that they were selected because of their looks – 'people see us and they want to be us' – and they are also given opportunities to be 'cast' as billboard models. Mystery shoppers ensure employees are adhering to company guidelines regarding their look. This 'image management' all has a strong

impact on future applicants' expectations of what an Abercrombie & Fitch employee should be like, and, in some at least, shapes the desire to be one of them.

The following extracts from online fora ('The Student Room' and 'Glassdoor') for discussing jobs and employers reveal potential applicants' perceptions of the company, and how this is shaped by current and past employees.

> I've applied for the model role for the Abercrombie & Fitch branch in London. Do I have to look all clean and fresh, with wavy beach hair?

> They invite everyone to the interview, and once you're there they'll analyse you in terms of looks and previous experience. Don't wear coloured nail varnish or obvious make-up; basically look like you've come off a beach and they'll take you.

> I wore a Hollister 'vintage' shirt, Abercrombie jeans and Adidas Ultrastar 2's and I was ever so slightly shocked in how 4 out of the 8 people wore black (which Abercrombie don't even sell.)

> I've had an interview for Hollister's and for Abercrombie & Fitch. I haven't heard from any of them yet. But both interviews went really well to [sic] my opinion. Also do you guys think that they hire black people? I am a model, black (chocolate skin) not too skinny and pretty. I am going to attach a picture to this but please let me know of what you think.

> This company stresses customer service, by using several different taglines, depending on where you're in the store [fitting room, front room, registers.] They clearly hire based on looks and personality. I have not seen anyone with acne or any overweight people yet.

The selection of graduates for their retail management programme is similar to most other multinational company graduate schemes. There is an emphasis on retail experience, demonstrated behavioural competencies, and a series of panel and one-to-one interviews. The Manager in Training programme is the first step towards becoming a 'store executive' (Assistant Manager and then Store Manager) and a future within the company.

> We hire nice, smart, talented people who are interested in building a career at Abercrombie & Fitch. We have a strong philosophy of promotion from within. All of our District Managers, Regional Managers, Directors – even the Senior Vice President of Stores – have gone through the Manager in Training program. With the growth of the company do-

mestically and internationally, career opportunities have never been better. (www.abercrombie.co.uk/anf/careers)

TARGETjobs, an online graduate jobs forum which provides potential applicants with Employer Insights and tips on how to get hired, describes the importance of demonstrating retail experience, details of when applicants have exceeded a set target, and experience of leading and organising others. Even for these positions, the advice from independent experts is to pay attention to style: 'given that all Managers in Training will be working on the shop floor around their merchandise, having some idea of the style of the stores in which they will be working will certainly help give off the right image'. Stores Recruiting Teams target Careers Fairs at specific universities, and online recruitment media are used to project the youthful, good-looking and fun company culture. Interviews are described on online careers fora as 'laid back', often taking place in a food court or walking around a mall, and involving one or two Store/District Managers.

For sales associates, applications are taken 'in store', which presents an early opportunity to screen out those who are not 'Abercrombie hot'. Store managers approach customers to encourage them to apply as potential employees. The company has created a 'look book', a collection of images for managers to refer to when hiring. A group interview usually includes questions such as 'What is your favourite thing about Abercrombie & Fitch, and what style, in your opinion, is the style of Abercrombie & Fitch?'; 'How would you handle it if your co-worker wasn't doing their job and you were left do to everything yourself?'; and 'What is your definition of diversity, and do you think it is important in the workplace?'

The role of 'model' mainly consists of saying hello to customers rather than folding clothes, replenishing stock or working the tills as in any other retail job. This is left to the part-time 'impact team'. The person specifications for these two roles are compared in Table 4.3. Past employees tell some interesting stories about the differences between the roles. Take for example, Luke, posting a response to a *BBC News Magazine* article on 'What is the Abercrombie look?' (26 June 2009).

> Whilst at uni I worked in the stockroom and as a shop floor maintainer (tidying stock). I was told on many occasions that I was not allowed to speak to the models and they were told they were not allowed to help maintain the look of the room. The amount of flirting is sickening and the favouritism between managers and models is enough to make you gag. Every year we get an intake of models who have just come off of the program shipwrecked and every time the superiority complex was quick

to kick in as the 'hotties' established themselves apart from the 'notties'.

Is this discrimination?

Direct linking of corporate and HR strategy is common in companies which reinforce a brand image through their employees. One well known example is Hooters, the American restaurant chain known for its scantily clad waitresses. The company's expectations of employees are stated up front in a written contract which all prospective employees must sign.

> I hereby acknowledge and affirm that the Hooters concept is based on female sex appeal and that the work environment is one in which joking and innuendo based on female sex appeal is commonplace. I also expressly acknowledge and affirm I do not find my job duties, uniform requirements or work environment to be intimidating, hostile or unwelcome.
>
> (*Guardian*, 11 April 2008)

According to a Hooters' spokesperson, 'All signing the document means is that we have taken the time to give [the waitress] the full picture of the Hooters concept' (ibid.). The company can claim that all applicants are fully aware of what will be expected of them and that its hiring policies simply tailor the employee qualities they are seeking according to the market demands of a solid (mostly male) customer base.

Abercrombie & Fitch may use the same argument to justify hiring based on its 'look policy'. However, it has come under legal pressure to reform its hiring practices. Class action lawsuits in the US have charged the company with discrimination against minorities and women. In *Gonzalez et al. v Abercrombie & Fitch* (14 April 2005), Latino, African American, Asian American and female job applicants or former employees (the plaintiffs) argued that they were either limited to low visibility, back-of-the-store type jobs or terminated because of their race or ethnicity. The settlement agreement applied to recruitment, hiring, job assignment, training and promotion of Abercrombie & Fitch, Hollister and Abercrombie Kids employees. This required, among other conditions:

- that the company abide by 'benchmarks' for hiring and promotion of the affected groups;
- a prohibition on targeting (predominantly white) fraternities, sororities and specific colleges for recruitment;
- advertising in publications which targeted minorities of both genders;
- Equal Employment Opportunity and Diversity Training for all employees with hiring authority;

Table 4.3 Abercrombie & Fitch sales assistant roles

Models	Part-time impact
What you need to bring to the job	*What you need to bring to the job*
Sophistication, aspiration, sense of style, diversity awareness, integrity, applied learning, outgoing personality and communication skills	Positive outlook, diversity awareness, integrity, applied learning, passion for the brand, work ethic and communication skills
Skills you will develop on the job	*Skills you will develop on the job*
Passion for the brand, multi-tasking, adaptability/ flexibility, attention to detail, product knowledge and customer focus	Multi-tasking adaptability flexibility, attention to detail, customer focus, adhering to company guidelines in personal appearance and rules of conduct, stockroom systems, scanning systems and merchandising

Source: http://www.abercrombie.co.uk/anf/careers.

- that managers' performance evaluations and bonuses should be based on making progress toward diversity goals; and
- marketing materials which reflect diversity.

They were even required to appoint a Vice President of Diversity. The company's recruitment pages now feature various ethnic minorities (see for example http://www.abercrombie.co.uk/anf/careers/model.html) and they publicise on their website that 'Diversity and inclusion are key to our organization's success. We are determined to have a diverse culture, throughout our organization, that benefits from the perspectives of each individual.' 'Diversity awareness' is a quality expected from all employees (see Table 4.3). The website advertises the company's success in embracing 'the conversation around diversity and inclusion'. For example, it cites the following facts: 'as of April 30th, 2010 . . . we are proud of [the fact that]:

- Our in-store workforce, as a whole is 50.22% people of color
- Our in-store models are 48.44% people of color
- Our in-store managers-in-training are 41.04% people of color'.

(www.abercrombie.co.uk/anf/careers/diversity.html)

The problem does not seem to have disappeared, however. In 2009, a sales assistant in one of their London stores sued for disability discrimination claiming she had been 'hidden' in a stockroom because her prosthetic arm did not fit with its 'look policy' (Pidd, 2009); and a Muslim US teenager claimed she was turned down for a sales position, because her hijab violated the 'look policy' for sales staff (Nasaw, 2009).

With recruitment targeting of job candidates by managers, it is hard to see how any kind of diversity targets for recruitment can be monitored. And managers are clearly encouraged to make decisions based on 'image norms', which are likely to apply in all selection methods, including interviews, as well as in the informal approaches to customers with 'the look' (Hurley Hanson and Giannantonio, 2006).

In a 2006 interview for Salon.com, Mike Jeffries, CEO, made the following statement about their corporate strategy:

> **Candidly, we go after the cool kids. We go after the attractive all-American kid with a great attitude and a lot of friends. A lot of people don't belong [in our clothes], and they can't belong. Are we exclusionary? Absolutely. Those companies that are in trouble are trying to target everybody: young, old, fat, skinny. But then you become totally vanilla. You don't alienate anybody, but you don't excite anybody, either.**

it may not be surprising, then, that their HR strategy, and specifically selection practice, mirrors the exclusivity of the brand.

Questions

1 How are each of the perspectives of selection presented in this chapter – psychometric, best-fit, interactive decision process and discourse – represented in the hiring process for (a) Managers in Training and (b) sales assistants (both 'models' and 'part-time impact' roles)?

2 Evaluate the selection process with respect to the four criteria of psychometric quality described at the start of the chapter. Can falling short on any of these criteria, in your opinion, be justified? Design a selection process for the sales associate roles in Table 4.3 using psychometric principles (start with a job analysis).

3 Identify as many examples of 'selection as an interactive decision process' in this case as you can. Should these processes be eliminated on the grounds they discriminate against particular groups, or can a case be made for retaining all or some of them?

4 How is the 'selection as discourse' perspective reflected in this case? Does this explain why the legal challenges to the company's hiring approach have not eliminated the problem?

Bibliography

Anderson, N. (2001) 'Towards a theory of socialization impact: selection as pre-entry socialization', *International Journal of Selection and Assessment,* Vol.9, Nos.1/2, 84–91.

Anderson, N. (2003) 'Applicant and recruiter reactions to new technology in selection: a critical review and agenda for future research', *International Journal of Selection and Assessment,* Vol.11, 121–36.

Anderson, N. and Goltsi, V. (2006) 'Negative psychological effects of selection methods: construct formulation and an empirical investigation into an assessment center', *International Journal of Selection and Assessment*, Vol.14, No.3, 236–55.

Anderson, N. and Witvliet, C. (2008) 'Fairness reactions to personnel selection methods: an international comparison between the Netherlands, the United States, France, Spain, Portugal, and Singapore', *International Journal of Selection and Assessment*, Vol.16, No.1, 1–13.

Association of Graduate Recruiters (2012) *The AGR Graduate Recruitment Survey 2012: Winter Review.* available at http://www.agr.org.uk.

Baldry, C.J., Bain, P.M., Taylor, P., Hyman, J.D., Scholarios, D. M., Marks, A., Watson, A.C., Gilbert, K., Gall, G. and Bunzl, D. (2007) *The Meaning of Work in the New Economy*, Basingstoke: Palgrave Macmillan.

Bartram, D. (2000) 'Internet recruitment and selection: kissing frogs to find princes', *International Journal of Selection and Assessment*, Vol.8, 261–74.

Bartram, D. (2005) 'The Great Eight competencies: a criterion-centric approach to validation', *Journal of Applied Psychology*, Vol.90, 1185–203.

Baydoun, R., Rose D. and Emperado, T. (2001) 'Measuring customer service orientation: an examination of the validity of the customer service profile', *Journal of Business and Psychology*, Vol.15, No.4, 605–20.

Bertua, C., Anderson, N. and Salgado, J. (2005) 'The predictive validity of cognitive ability tests: a UK meta-analysis', *Journal of Occupational and Organizational Psychology*, Vol.78, No.3, 387–409.

Blair, M.D. Hornick, C.W. (2005) 'Fire selection in the new millennium'. Paper presented at the 29th Annual Conference of the International Public Management Association Assessment Council. Orlando, FL.

Brown, P. and Hesketh, A. (2004) *The Mismanagement of Talent*, Oxford: Oxford University Press.

Bywater, J. and Green, V. (2005) 'Can scorable application forms predict task and contextual performance in call centre work?' *Selection & Development Review*, Vol.20, No.6.

Carroll, J.B. (1993) *Human Cognitive Abilities: A Survey of Factor-Analytic Studies*, Cambridge: Cambridge University Press.

Chapman, D.S. and Webster, J. (2003) 'The use of technologies in the recruiting, screening, and selection processes for job candidates', *International Journal of Selection and Assessment,* Vol.11, Nos.2–3, 113–20.

CIPD (2011) *Resourcing and Talent Planning,* London: Chartered Institute of Personnel and Development.

Costa, P.T. Jr. and McCrae, R.R. (1992) 'Normal personality assessment in clinical practice: the NEO Personality Inventory', *Psychological Assessment,* Vol.4, 5–13.

Cropanzano, R. and Wright, T.A. (2003) 'Procedural justice and organizational staffing: a tale of two paradigms', *Human Resource Management Review*, Vol.13, 7–39.

Dick, P. and Nadin, S. (2006) 'Reproducing gender inequalities? A critique of realist assumptions underpinning personnel selection research and practice', *Journal of Occupational and Organizational Psychology*, Vol.79, No.3, 481–98.

Dilchert, S., Ones, D.S., Viswesvaran, C. and Deller, J. (2006) 'Response distortion in personality measurement: born to deceive, yet capable of providing valid assessments?' *Psychology Science*, Vol.48, 209–25.

Furnham, A. (1997) *The Psychology of Behaviour of Work,* Hove: Psychology Press.

Hamel, G. and Prahalad, C.K. (1989) 'Strategic intent', *Harvard Business Review*, May–June, 63–74.

Herriot, P. (1989) 'Selection as a social process', pp. 171–8, in Smith, M. and Robertson, I.T. (eds) *Advances in Selection and Assessment,* Chichester: Wiley.

Herriot, P. (1993) 'Commentary: a paradigm bursting at the seams', *Journal of Organizational Behavior, Vol.14,* 371–5.

Hill, D. and Barber, L. (2005) *Is Graduate Recruitment Meeting Business Needs? Web Audit*, Brighton: Institute for Employment Studies.

Hogan, R.T., Hogan, J. and Busch, A. (1984) 'How to measure service orientation', *Journal of Applied Psychology*, Vol.69, No.1, 167–3.

Huffcutt, A.I. and Youngcourt, S.S. (2007) 'Employment interviews', 181–200, in Whetzel, D. and Wheaton, G. (eds) *Applied Measurement: Industrial Psychology in Human Resources Management,* Hillsdale, NJ: Lawrence Earlbaum.

Human Resources News (2010) 'Recruitment policy of Abercrombie and Fitch draws criticism', 7 April 2012. Available at http://www.humanresources-news.co.uk.

Hunter, J.E. and Hunter, R.F. (1984) 'Validity and utility of alternative predictors of job performance', *Psychological Bulletin, Vol.*96, 72–98.

Huo, Y.P, Huang, H.G. and Napier, N.K. (2002) 'Divergence or convergence: A cross-national comparison of personnel practices', *Human Resource Management Journal*, Vol.41, No.1, 31–44.

Hurley Hanson, A.E. and Giannantonio, C.M. (2006) 'Recruiters' perceptions of appearance: the stigma of image norms', *Equal Opportunity International*, Vol.25, No.6, 450–63.

Iles, P. (1999) *Managing Staff Selection and Assessment,* Milton Keynes: Open University Press.

Jewson, N. and Mason, D. (1986) 'The theory and practice of equal opportunities policies: liberal and radical approaches,' *Sociological Review*, Vol.34, No.2, 307–24.

Johns, G. (1993) 'Constraints on the adoption of psychology-based personnel practices: lessons from organizational innovation', *Personnel Psychology,* Vol.46, No.3, 569–92.

Kersley, B., Alpin, C., Forth, J., Bryson, A., Bewley, H., Dix, G. and Oxenbridge, S. (2006) *Inside the Workplace: Findings from the 2004 Workplace Employment Relations Survey*, Abingdon: Routledge.

Klehe, U. (2004) 'Choosing how to choose: institutional pressures affecting the adoption of personnel selection procedures', *International Journal of Selection and Assessment*, Vol.12, No.4, 327–42.

Klehe, U.–C. and Anderson, N. (2005) 'The prediction of typical and maximum performance', in Evers, A., Smit-Voskuijl, O. and Anderson, N. (eds) *Handbook of Personnel Selection*, Oxford: Blackwell.

Knights, D. and Raffo, C. (1990). 'Milkround professionalism in personnel recruitment: myth or reality?' *Personnel Review,* Vol.19, No.1, 28–37.

Konradt, U., Hertel, G. and Joder, K. (2003) 'Web-based assessment of call center agents: development and validation of a computerized instrument' *International Journal of Selection and Assessment,* Vol.11, Nos.2–3, 184–93.

Kravitz, D.A. (2008) 'The diversity–validity dilemma: beyond selection – the role of affirmative action', *Personnel Psychology*, Vol.61, 173–93.

Kwiatkowski, R. (2003) 'Devolving HR responsibility to the line: threat, opportunity or partnership?', *Journal of Managerial Psychology,* Vol.18, No.5, 245–61.

Latham, G.P. and Skarlicki, D.P. (1995) 'Criterion-related validity of the situational and patterned behavior description interviews with organizational citizenship behavior', *Human Performance,* Vol.8, 67–80.

Lautenschlager, G.J. (1994) 'Accuracy and faking of background data', in Stokes, G.S., Mumford, M.D. and Owens, W.A. (eds) *Biodata Handbook,* Palo Alto, CA: Consulting Psychologists Press, 391–419.

Lawton, D., Baum, N., Feltham, R. and Stirling, E. (2009) *Online Testing*. The AGR Briefing Paper Series.

Legge, K. (2005) *Human Resource Management: Rhetorics and Realities,* Basingstoke: Palgrave Macmillan.

Liao, H. and Chuang, A. (2004) 'A multilevel investigation of factors influencing employee service performance and customer outcomes', *Academy of Management Journal*, Vol.47, 41–58.

Lievens, F. and Chapman, D. (2010) 'Recruitment and selection', pp. 133–54, in Wilkinson, A. (ed.) *The SAGE Handbook of Human Resource Management*, London: Sage.

Lievens, F. and Coetsier, P. (2002) 'Situational tests in student selection: an examination of predictive validity, adverse impact, and construct validity', *International Journal of Selection and Assessment,* Vol.10, No.4, 245–57.

Lievens, F. and Klimoski, R.J. (2001) 'Understanding the assessment centre process: where are we now?', *International Review of Industrial and Organizational Psychology,* Vol.16, 246–86.

Lievens, F., Buyse, T. and Sackett, P.R. (2005) 'The operational validity of a video-based situational judgment test for medical college admissions: illustrating the importance of matching predictor and criterion construct domains', *Journal of Applied Psychology,* Vol.90, No.3, 442–52.

Lockyer, C. and Scholarios, D. (2004) 'Selecting hotel staff: why best practice doesn't always work', *International Journal of Contemporary Hospitality Management*, Vol.16, No.2, 125–35.

Lockyer, C. and Scholarios, D. (2007) 'The 'raindance' of selection in construction: rationality as ritual and the logic of informality', *Personnel Review*, Vol.36, No.4, 528–48.

Marchington, M. and Wilkinson, A. (2005) *Human Resource Management at Work: People Management and Development*, London: CIPD.

Maurer, S.D. (2006) 'Using situational interviews to assess engineering applicant fit to work group job and organizational requirements', *Engineering Management Journal*, 1 September.

McFarland, L.A., Ryan, A.M., Sacco, J.M. and Kriska, S.D. (2004) 'Examination of structured interview ratings across time: the effects of applicant race, rater race, and panel composition', *Journal of Management,* Vol.30, 435–52.

Millmore, M. (2003) 'Just how extensive is the practice of strategic recruitment and selection?', *Irish Journal of Management,* Vol.24, No.1, 87.

Morgeson F.P., Campion, M.A., Dipboye, R.L., Hollenbeck, J.R., Murphy. K. and Schmitt, N. (2007) 'Reconsidering the use of personality tests in personnel selection contexts', *Personnel Psychology*, Vol.60, No.3, 683–729.

Moynihan, L.M. and Peterson, R.S. (2004) 'The role of personality in group processes', pp. 317–45, in Schneider, B. and Smith, D.B. (eds) *Personality and Organizations,* Mahwah, NJ: Lawrence Erlbaum.

Muchinsky, P.M. (1986) 'Personnel selection methods', in Cooper, C. and Robertson, I. (eds) *International Review of Industrial and Organizational Psychology,* New York: Wiley.

Muchinsky, P.M. (2004) 'When the psychometrics of test development meets organizational realities: a conceptual framework for organizational change, examples, and recommendations', *Personnel Psychology,* Vol.57, 175–209.

Nasaw, D. (2009) 'Abercrombie and Fitch discriminated against US Muslim teen, lawsuit claims', *Guardian* [online], 18 September. Available at http://www.guardian.co.uk/world/2009/sep/18/abercrombie-fitch-muslim-discrimination.

Newell, S. (2006) 'Selection and assessment', pp. 65–98, in Redman, T. and Wilkinson, A. (eds) *Contemporary Human Resource Management,* (2nd edn), London: Pearson Education.

Nickson, D., Warhurst, C., Hurrell, S. and Dutton, E. (2008) 'A job to believe in: recruitment in the Scottish voluntary sector', *Human Resource Management Journal*, Vol.18, No.1, 18–33.

Olson–Buchanan, J.B. and Drasgow, F. (2005) 'Multimedia situational judgment tests: the medium creates the message', pp. 253–78, in Weekly, J.A. and Ployhart, R.E. (eds) *Situational Judgment Tests: Theory, Measurement*, London: Routledge.

Ones, D.S., Viswesvaran, C. and Dilchert, S. (2005) 'Personality at work: raising awareness and correcting misconceptions', *Human Performance,* Vol.18, 389–404.

Ones, D., Dilchert, S., Viswesvaran, C. and Judge, T.A. (2007) 'In support of personality assessment in organizational settings', *Personnel Psychology,* Vol.60, No.4, 995–1027.

Pearn, M. (1993) 'Fairness in selection and assessment: a European perspective', in Schuler, H., Farr, J.L. and Smith, M. (eds) *Personnel Selection and Assessment: Individual and Organizational Perspectives*. Hillsdale, NJ: Lawrence Erlbaum.

Pfeffer, J. (1998) *The human equation. Building profits by putting people first*, Boston: Harvard Business School Press.

Pidd, H (2009) 'Disabled student sues Abercrombie and Fitch for discrimination', *Guardian* [online], 24 June. Available at http://www.guardian.co.uk/money/2009/jun/24/abercrombie-fitch-tribunal-riam-dean.

Ployhart, R.E. and Erhart, M.G. (2003) 'Be careful what you ask for: effects of response instructions and the construct validity and reliability of situational judgment tests', *International Journal of Selection and Assessment*, Vol.11, No.1, 1–16.

Ployhart, R.E., McFarland, L.A. and Ryan, A.M. (2002) 'Examining applicants' attributions for withdrawal from a selection procedure', *Journal of Applied Social Psychology,* Vol.32, No.11, 2228–52.

Ployhart, R.E., Schneider, B. and Schmitt, N. (2006) *Staffing Organizations: Contemporary Practice and Theory.* Mahwah, NJ: Lawrence Erlbaum.

Reed Consulting (2007) *Candidates as Customer: Changing Attitudes to Recruitment*, London: Reed Consulting.

Reilly, R.R. and Chao, G.T. (1982) 'Validity and fairness of some alternative employee selection procedures', *Personnel Psychology*, Vol.35, No.1, 1–62.

Roe, R. and van den Berg, P. (2003) 'Selection in Europe: context, developments and research agenda', *European Journal of Work and Organizational Psychology*, Vol.12, No.3, 257–87.

Rothstein, M.G. and Goffin, R.D. (2006) 'The use of personality measures in personnel selection: what does current research support?', *Human Resource Management Review*, Vol.16, No.2, 155–80.

Ryan, A.M. and Tippins, N. (2009) *Designing and Implementing Global Selection Systems*, Chichester: Wiley–Blackwell.

Ryan, A.M., McFarland, L., Baron, H. and Page, R. (1999) 'An international look at selection practices: nation and culture as explanations for variability in practice', *Personnel Psychology,* Vol.52, 359–94.

Ryan, A.M., Wiechmann, D. and Hemingway, M. (2003) 'Designing and implementing global staffing systems: Part II—best practices', *Human Resource Management*, Vol.42, 85–94.

Ryan, A.M., Boyce, A.S., Ghumman, S., Jundt, D., Schmidt, G. and Gibby, R. (2008) 'Going global: cultural values and perceptions of selection procedures', *Applied Psychology: An International Review,* Vol.58, 520–56.

Sackett, P.R. and Lievens, F. (2008) 'Personnel selection', *Annual Review of Psychology*, Vol.59, 419–50.

Salgado, J.F. (2002) 'The Big Five personality dimensions and counterproductive behaviors', *International Journal of Selection and Assessment,* Vol.10, Nos.1/2, 117–25.

Salgado, J.F. and Anderson, N.R. (2002) 'Cognitive and GMA testing in the European Community: issues and evidence', *Human Performance*, Vol.15, 75–96.

Salgado, J.F., Anderson, N., Moscoso, S., Bertua, C. and De Fruyt, F. (2003) 'International validity generalization of GMA and cognitive abilities: a European Community meta-analysis', *Personnel Psychology*, Vol.56, No.3, 573–605.

Schmidt, F.L. and Hunter, J.E. (1998) 'The validity and utility of selection methods in personnel psychology: practical and theoretical implications of 85 years of research findings', *Psychological Bulletin*, Vol.124, No.2, 262–74.

Schmidt, F. and Zimmerman, R.D. (2004) 'A counterintuitive hypothesis about employment interview validity and some supporting evidence', *Journal of Applied Psychology*, Vol.89, No.3, 553–61.

Schmitt, N. (2003) 'Employee selection: how simulations change the picture for minority groups', *Cornell Hospitality Quarterly,* Vol.44, 25–32.

Schmitt, N. and Mills, A. (2001) 'Traditional tests and job simulations: minority and majority performance and test validities', *Journal of Applied Psychology*, Vol.86, No.3, 451–58.

Schmitt, N. and Chan, D. (1998) *Personnel Selection: A Theoretical Approach*, London: Sage.

Schuler, H. (1993) 'Social validity of selection situations: a concept and some empirical results', pp. 11–26, in Schuler, H., Farr, J.L. and Smith, M. (eds) *Personnel Selection and Assessment: Individual and Organizational Perspectives,* Hillsdale, NJ: Lawrence Erlbaum.

Searle, R.H. (2003a) *Selection and Recruitment: A Critical text,* Milton Keynes: The Open University.

Searle, R.H. (2003b) 'Organizational justice in e–recruiting: issues and controversies', *Surveillance and Society*, Vol.1, No.2, 227–31.

Shackleton, V. and Newell, S. (1997) 'International assessment and selection', in Anderson, N. and Herriot, P. (eds) *International Handbook of Selection and Assessment*, London: John Wiley & Sons.

Sternberg, R.J., Wagner, R.K., Williams, W.M. and Horvarth, J.A. (1995) 'Testing common sense', *American Psychologist*, Vol.50, No.11, 912–27.

Storey, J. (2007) 'Human resource management today: an assessment', in Storey, J. (ed.) *Human Resource Management: A Critical Text* (3rd edn), London: Thomson Learning.

Terpstra, D.E. and Kethley, R.B. (2002) 'Organizations' relative degree of exposure to selection discrimination litigation', *Public Personnel Management*, Vol.31, No.3, 277–92.

Tett, R.P and Christiansen, N.D. (2007) 'Personality tests at the crossroads: a response to Morgeson, Campion, Dipboye, Hollenbeck, Murphy, and Schmitt (2007)', *Personnel Psychology,* Vol.60, No.4, 967–93.

Thornton, G.C. III and Mueller-Hanson, R.A. (2004) *Developing Organizational Simulations: A Guide for Practitioners and Students*. Hillsdale, NJ: Lawrence Erlbaum.

Townley, B. (1989) 'Selection and appraisal: reconstituting "social relations"?', pp. 92–108, in Storey, J. (ed.), *New Perspectives on Human Resource Management,* London: Routledge.

Van Hoye, G and Lievens, F. (2005) 'Recruitment–related information sources and organizational attractiveness: can something be done about negative publicity?', *International Journal of Selection and Assessment*, Vol.13, No.3, 179–87.

Viswesvaran, C., Deller, J. and Ones, D.S. (2007) 'Personality measures in personnel selection', *International Journal of Selection and Assessment*, Vol.15, No.3, 354–8.

Weisinger, H. (1998) *Emotional Intelligence at Work,* San Francisco, CA: Jossey–Bass.

Whittaker, S. and Marchington, M. (2003) 'Devolving HR responsibility to the line: threat, opportunity or partnership'?, *Employee Relations*, Vol.25, No.3, 245–61.

Wolf, A. and Jenkins, A. (2006) 'Explaining greater test use for selection: the role of HR professionals in a world of expanded regulation', *Human Resource Management Journal*, Vol.16, No.2, 193–213.

Wolff, C.J. de (1993) 'The prediction paradigm' in Schuler, H., Farr, J.L. and Smith, M. (eds) *Personnel Selection and Assessment: Individual and Organizational Perspectives.* Hillsdale, NJ: Lawrence Erlbaum.

Zeidner, M., Matthews, G. and Roberts, R.D. (2004) 'Emotional intelligence in the workplace: a critical review', *Applied Psychology: An International Review*, Vol.53, No.3, 371–99.

CHAPTER 5

TRAINING AND DEVELOPMENT

Irena Grugulis

Introduction

Training, development and skills are key aspects of economic life. At the levels of the firm and the national economy training offers the hope of increased competitiveness through raising skill levels, productivity and 'value added'. For trade unions and professional associations, training enhances members' expertise, facilitating negotiations for pay and status. While for individuals, given that life chances are still heavily influenced by the job a person does and the wages they earn, education and training can increase knowledge and opportunities, give access to more highly rewarded work and reduce the prospect of unemployment. Small wonder then that consensus exists in this area, that governments encourage training through regulation or exhortation or that employers praise its importance in surveys. Yet despite this support, the levels and quality of vocational education and training in Britain are neither as high, nor as evenly distributed, as might be hoped. Excellent practice exists, but rarely 'trickles down' to less well-provided areas. This chapter, explores the positive reasons why both firms and individuals should invest in vocational education and training (VET), before going on to review the very different practices of market-based and regulated economies. It describes current practice in the UK and the implications of the increasing emphasis on soft skills and personal qualities, then concludes with explaining some of the *disadvantages* of training and development and the links between skill and performance. Throughout, it argues that, in common with other human resource practices, training should not be considered in isolation. Its effectiveness, or otherwise, hinges on the wider economic and organisational context.

Box 5.1 HRM in practice

I've actually got the convenor saying to me, 'we've got to watch this multi-skill thing, because it's too interesting for them'.

Source: Managing Director, GKN Hardy Spicer; cited in Hendry, 1993: 92.

 ## The case for training and development

The advantages of training and development are not illusory. Within organisations, it can equip workers to carry out tasks, monitor quality and manage complex products and services. Arthur's (1999) research into US steel mini-mills describes the way that switching between different types of steel or different shapes required close monitoring by melt-shop employees. The exact nature of changeover activities was difficult to predict and down-time was expensive so the quality and quantity of production relied heavily on the skills of operators and maintenance workers who had a considerable amount of discretion managing these shifts. Here, as elsewhere, quality products relied heavily on workers' expertise.

Training and development safeguards such productivity as well as supporting it, by preparing employees for future jobs and insulating firms from skills shortages. When jobs can be filled internally, firms are less dependent on the outside labour market and do not risk appropriate recruits not being available (or not being available at the price the organisation wishes to pay). Such security is welcome. According to Vivian *et al.* (2011: 7), even in the midst of recession, 3 per cent of UK employers had skill-shortage vacancies and 13 per cent reported internal skills gaps (in which not all employees are fully proficient at the work that they do). The problems reported as a result of these gaps include difficulties with customer service, delays developing new products and losing business to competitors.

Within firms, training and development is a key element of human resource management, indeed, Keep (1989) argues that it is the litmus test against which other aspects of management practice should be gauged. When firms compete on the basis of quality and adopt high-commitment work practices such as employee involvement, team-working or merit-based pay; developing employees is the key element in performance. It can raise the capacity of the individuals and groups employed, enabling them to participate meaningfully in systems where their contribution is encouraged (Keep and Mayhew, 1996). Arthur (1999) links the 'commitment'-oriented human resource practices in steel mini-mills to the strategic focus on quality and batch production, contrasting it with less developmental 'control' mechanisms in organisations where production was routine and where human resource practices focused on minimising labour costs.

Box 5.2 HRM in practice

McDonald's famously and relentlessly standardise every aspect of their product in order to eliminate the need for human input. The Operations and Training Manual (known to staff as 'the Bible') provides detailed prescriptions on every aspect of working life. Its 600 pages include full colour photographs illustrating the proper placement of ketchup, mustard and pickle on every type of burger, set out the six steps of counter service and even prescribe the arm motions that should be used in salting a batch of fries. Kitchen and counter technology reinforce these instructions as lights and buzzers tell workers when to turn burgers or take fries out of the fat, ketchup dispensers provide measured amounts of product in the requisite 'flower' pattern and lights on the till remove the need for serving staff to write out orders as well as prompting them to offer additional items.

For more information on this see Leidner, 1993; Ritzer, 1998.

In addition to these substantive factors, training and development also serves an important and very positive symbolic function. Everything that a firm does sends messages (of one kind or another) to its employees (one of the key elements of the positive side of HRM). Organisations that spend money on raising skills are, quite literally, investing in their workers.

Voluntarist and regulated approaches: international practice

While there is a consensus over the importance and value of training and development, this is not matched by any agreement on how best to encourage good practice. At a national level the two principal approaches are voluntarist (market based) and regulated (educational). Both the USA and Britain are broadly voluntarist. The principal assumption behind such systems is that organisations operate more effectively when unfettered by regulation. Market pressures (to remain competitive, produce quality goods and run efficiently) will ensure that, where training is appropriate, firms will invest in it and, in the absence of expensive and cumbersome official bureaucracy, investment can be accurately targeted to respond to market needs.

By contrast, in a regulated system, as in much of continental Europe, vocational education and training is supported by the state. Regulation may take a variety of forms. In France, employers are required to support training or pay a levy to the state while in Germany there is a system of extensive and rigorous apprenticeships for young people entering the labour market, coupled with 'licences to practice' for particular occupations. The assumption behind this approach is that vocational education and training is a public good and it is in the long-term interests of all to have a highly skilled workforce. However, left to themselves individual firms will prioritise profitability and may not invest in skills development or may fund only short-term and low-level training. Training and development is, after all, only one way of securing skilled workers and firms may choose to recruit workers trained elsewhere or de-skill production instead. By providing an appropriate infrastructure (or a system of levies, or by regulating practice) the state ensures robust skills development.

Both voluntarist and regulated approaches can be successful. Silicon Valley, California provides an excellent example of the way that skills can be developed in a market-based system. Silicon Valley is famously the site of a cluster of extremely high-tech computing firms. These are supported by the proximity of universities (University of California campuses in Berkeley, San Francisco, San Diego and Los Angeles and private institutions such as Stanford, USC and CalTech) that supply expert labour, share research and stimulate start-up companies. Stanford (whose graduates include William Hewlett and David Packard) even set up the first university science park to provide fledgling firms with support services. The infrastructure is conducive to growth with good local transport, international airport and a state-of-the-art telecommunications system and the availability of venture capital, low levels of regulation and limited penalties on bankruptcy encourage start-ups. These small, and often highly focused, firms prosper through interdependency forming partnerships with other organisations and participating in employer groups to pursue initiatives such as improving technical training in city colleges, that are to their mutual benefit. Individuals also collaborate through professional associations, continuing education courses and alumni associations. In firms there is little formal training but skills and expertise are developed through project work on cutting edge technical challenges. Even labour mobility, a point of concern elsewhere, assists knowledge diffusion here and increases personal and professional networks (Finegold, 1999).

Such an unstructured 'ecosystem' is very successful at developing and supporting the most expert who work at the cutting edge of their profession. However, the USA as a whole is far less successful in training and development for the majority and it is here that a more regulated system triumphs. The highly regarded German apprenticeship system is one of the best known routes to achieving vocational qualifications. Full apprenticeships last three years and trainees are taught technical skills in the classroom which are subsequently developed through participation in a series of problem-solving activities, graded in terms of difficulty. Care is taken to ensure that apprentices are exposed to a full range of different work situations with central training centres supplementing workplace experience and providing additional workplace settings for trainees to learn in; an arrangement which gives smaller employers the capacity to offer high-level training. Technical training is supplemented with knowledge of work control and design (manufacturing qualifications involve familiarity with costs, design and planning, and administration and production) and, in addition to this, all apprentices are required to continue to participate in further education for the duration of their vocational studies (Lane, 1989; Rubery and Grimshaw, 2003).

Nor, despite pessimism, the problems of unifying East and West Germany, economic problems and the rise of the service sector (Culpepper, 1999; Kirsch *et al.,* 2000) does this system appear to be in decline. Apprentice numbers peaked in the mid-1990s but the system overall has remained both strong and popular. New programmes developed for IT occupations attracted 48,859 apprentices in 2002, half of whom already held an *Abitur* (the prestigious academic school leaving qualification taken at 18). And many apprenticeships have taken advantage of the fact that those taking them are far better educated than before to raise the standards of their theoretical components (Bosch, 2010).

The German system is made possible by close, collaborative links between employers' associations, trade unions and regional governments cooperating on creating a system that works for the benefit of all. Indeed, Bosch and Charest (2010) argue that new apprenticeship programmes have only been successfully launched in countries such as Germany, Austria, Denmark, Switzerland and Norway, which have both strong trade unions and a tradition of corporatist cooperation between firms (though see Buchanan and Evesson, 2004a,b on the Australian experience). Taiwan is different, its economy is dominated by small and medium-sized enterprises (SMEs), that successfully resisted the introduction of a levy for vocational education and training in the 1970s. Yet, despite this it has managed to introduce extensive vocational skills development, increasing the amount of technical, vocational education and the numbers of scientists and engineers through the education system. Demand for education was for academic education (and this would have been cheaper to provide) but access to academic courses was officially restricted, more than half of school-children were channelled into technical training and, at university level, more courses were made available for scientists and engineers and new Institutes of Technology launched. Student numbers, textbooks and curricula were state controlled and this meant that Taiwan succeeded in both the growing low-cost industrial products for export and also managed the transition from this to higher value-added production across many if not all sectors without significant reported skills shortages (Green *et al.,* 1999).

Each system has its strengths and limitations. The 'high skills market-based eco-system' of Silicon Valley is highly responsive to developing new and expert skills in professionals working on cutting edge projects where qualifications rarely exist while regulation does mean that skilled workers are widely available with two-thirds of German workers holding intermediate qualifications or above. By contrast, in unregulated systems some occupations neglect training even when this is to their detriment. After construction was de-regulated in the USA, training levels fell dramatically – as did investment in physical capital and productivity (Bosch, 2003). There, young people who do not graduate from high school have little chance of finding a decent job with a middle-class income (Bailey and Berg, 2010). But not even regulation guarantees provision. Although German apprenticeships are highly regarded, economic pressures means that actual apprentice places are in decline and in former East Germany large numbers of young people are not integrated into the system.

Perhaps the most notable feature of these examples is that they are systemic, success here goes beyond the simple provision of high-quality training (indeed, in the US example, formal training is one of the least significant elements of skills development). The high-skills eco-system of Silicon Valley is made possible by the fact that recruits are already extremely highly educated on entry (and many of them are IT experts). In Germany, the existence of employers' associations, trade unions and vocational colleges that are prepared to collaborate; and in Taiwan the government's readiness to both pay for skills development and take decisions that may be unpopular with individual students and their families, facilitate good intermediate skills training.

This is an important point and a key element of the success of each of these approaches. It also has implications for attempts to identify and transplant 'best practice', which generally focus only on one narrow element of a successful system. Korea's attempt to replicate the German apprenticeship system is a case in point (Jeong, 1995). This had government support and experienced German advisors were engaged. But little financial support was available, the firms employing the apprentices provided little training, and used them as low-paid and low-skilled workers, few college tutors were sufficiently skilled to make up this deficit and seniority, rather than skill, remained the key element in promotion. As a result, the initiative failed. Since then job mobility has increased substantially and, as elsewhere, lifetime employment practices are being dismantled. Jobs are being created, but in recent years most have been in low-wage service sector jobs and many workers are overqualified for, and frustrated by, work. Vocational training is available, particularly for those workers who are unemployed or need to be redeployed, but it is not well integrated into occupations (Yoon and Lee, 2010). It seems that the lessons of the earlier failure have not be learned.

Vocational education and training means different things in different countries. As Bosch and Charest (2010: 1) note:

> Depending on the quality of the VET, the signals vocational certificates give to employers might differ from country to country. In some countries, they might signal competency to perform complex tasks autonomously in a broad occupational field; in others, however, they might signal that the holder is a low achiever in the school system and possesses only narrowly based skills for specific jobs.

In other words, vocational training is important but it needs to be understood as one part of a wider system of work and skills rather than as isolated initiatives. Training is only meaningful if it is integrated into work.

Training and development in the workplace

While there are many reasons to support training and development, and while both voluntarist and regulated approaches can work not every employer trains. Excellent provision exists, but is rather unevenly distributed and not all training is developmental. Indeed, despite increasing levels of government subsidy, training in the UK is in decline (Vivian *et al.,* 2011), particularly for high-skilled and professional workers (Mason and Bishop, 2010). According to the Labour Force Survey, 9.4 per cent of workers in Britain received either on- or off-the-job training (ONS, 2011b). But this experience of training (and particularly of the duration and content of training) varies greatly according to both occupation and sector. Employees in the public sector, younger workers, people who are new to the job and those working in professional or clerical occupations are far more likely to receive training than older workers in 'blue collar' jobs (Cully *et al.,* 1999). While 20.6 per cent of public sector workers, 17.1 per cent of managers and professionals and 13 per cent of service sector workers had received training, only 9 per cent of production workers and 8.7 per cent of men had done so (ONS, 2011b).

This is particularly significant when we step back from the data and recall what training is provided for. One of the main advantages of training and development was that it could enhance the skills base, equip workers with expertise and change the way that they worked.

Box 5.3 HRM in practice — **Expansive and restrictive approaches to training and development**

Systemic approaches to training and development can also be observed *within* firms. One manufacturer of bathroom showers, described by Fuller and Unwin (2004), took an *expansive* approach to development. It had a long-established apprenticeship programme and many ex-apprentices had progressed to senior management. Apprentices were rotated around different departments to gain wider knowledge of the business and improve their skills. They also attended college on day release, working towards knowledge-based qualifications which would give them access to higher education, went on residential courses designed to foster team-working and were involved with local charities through the company's apprenticeship association. Contrast this with the *restrictive* environment of a small steel polishing company where apprentices had been reluctantly taken on only when managers were unable to recruit qualified staff. After less than a year, the two apprentices who had learned on the job, had gained all the skills necessary for their work. There was no system of job rotation and formal training was limited to ten half-day courses on steel industry awareness (the sum total of apprentices' outside involvement) and an NVQ.

Source: Fuller and Unwin, 2004

←Approaches to workforce development→

Expansive	Restrictive
Participation in multiple communities of practice inside and outside the workplace	Restricted participation in multiple communities of practice
Primary community of practice has shared 'participative memory': cultural inheritance of workforce development	Primary community of practice has little or no 'participative memory': no or little tradition of apprenticeship
Breadth: access to learning fostered by cross-company experience	Narrow: access to learning restricted in terms of tasks/knowledge/location
Access to range of qualifications including knowledge-based VQ	Little or no access to qualifications
Planned time off-the-job including for knowledge-based courses and for reflection	Virtually all-on-job: limited opportunities for reflection
Gradual transition to full, rounded participation	Fast – transition as quick as possible
Vision of workplace learning: progression for career	Vision of workplace learning: static for the job
Organisational recognition of, and support for employees as learners	Lack of organisational recognition of, and support for employees as learners
Workforce development is used as a vehicle for aligning the goals of developing the individual and organisational capability	Workforce development is used to tailor individual capability to organisational need
Workforce development fosters opportunities to extend identity through boundary crossing	Workforce development limits opportunities to extend identity: little boundary crossing experienced
Reification of 'workplace curriculum' highly developed (e.g. through documents, symbols, language, tools) and accessible to apprentices	Limited reification of 'workplace curriculum' patchy access to reificatory aspects of practice
Widely distributed skills	Polarised distribution of skills
Technical skills valued	Technical skills taken for granted
Knowledge and skills of whole workforce developed and valued	Knowledge and skills of key workers/groups developed and valued

(Continued)

←Approaches to workforce development→

Expansive	Restrictive
Team-work valued	Rigid specialist roles
Cross-boundary communication encouraged	Bounded communication
Managers as facilitators of workforce and individual development	Managers as controllers of workforce and individual development
Chances to learn new skills/jobs	Barriers to learning new skills/jobs
Innovation important	Innovation not important
Multidimensional view of expertise	Uni-dimensional top-down view of expertise

Source: Taken from Fuller and Unwin (2004: 130).

So the content of training is also important. Workplace training can cover a multitude of activities. Graduate trainee accountants with major accountancy firms spend three years on a mixture of formal courses, guided work experience and personal study, leading to a prestigious professional qualification. By contrast, call centre workers can expect far more basic workplace training. In Callaghan and Thompson's (2002) study, one call centre worker, who had let his voice drop slightly during a conversation with a customer, was sent on a training course to teach him to keep intonation even and enthusiastic. Both of these activities count as training and both may increase organisational effectiveness, but the advantages they confer on workers are very different.

Box 5.4 HRM in practice   Can organisations learn?

In theory, training also allows organisations to adapt to changes in the business environment, however their success in this rests on their ability to learn, particularly their ability to learn from their mistakes. Unsurprisingly perhaps, few firms are adept at this (Keep and Rainbird, 2000). Baumard and Starbuck's (2006) revealing analysis of organisational failures demonstrates that, far from admitting to errors, managers concealed large failures until discovery was certain then blamed them on unusual circumstances or external factors. Small failures were seen as inevitable because they did not fit in with the rest of the organisation or because the initiatives were only 'experiments'. Politically necessary behaviours to ensure managerial success but guaranteed to curtail organisational learning.

Reinforcing this, the two types of training most commonly funded by employers are health and safety and induction (though they are not the majority of all training provided, see Shury et al., 2010), a factor that may explain why temporary workers are more likely to receive training than their permanent colleagues. Heyes and Gray (2003), in their survey of SMEs after the introduction of the National Minimum Wage, found that training spend had risen, but that this was because employers were hiring younger (and cheaper) workers rather than up-skilling existing staff. Clearly it is important that workplaces are healthy and safe places to be and that new recruits receive adequate induction. However, it is highly unlikely that such forms of training will affect productivity, product quality or individual career development.

Training and development may also serve a social function, helping workers to form friendships and distracting them from alienating work. Two call centres investigated by Kinnie *et al.* (2000) used employee teams, games and spot prizes to motivate employees. These organisations also had three-week induction and technical training, but their on-going investment was in activities described by one supervisor as 'fun and surveillance'. An interesting modern variant on Adam Smith's (1776/1993) approval of publicly funded education for the working poor, who engaged only in simple, de-humanising and repetitive tasks, the better to support a 'decent and orderly' (1993: 436) society.

Personal qualities and generic skills

The type of training identified by Kinnie and his colleagues, the focus on games and the development of 'soft' or generic skills is becoming more widespread. Indeed, soft skills were the most commonly mentioned skill needs by UK employers with management skills, customer handling, problem-solving, team-working and communication heading their list of requirements (Shury *et al.*, 2010: 138). In part this shift to soft skills reflects attempts to alleviate repetitive work, increase commitment or foster a particular organisational culture, but it also stems from the fact that workforce skills are increasingly being defined in attitudinal terms. The Department for Education and Employment's Skills Task Force included communication, problem-solving, team-working, an ability to improve personal learning and performance, motivation, judgement, leadership and initiative in its list of skills (Department for Education and Employment 2000: 24). The CBI's (1989) earlier suggestions included values and integrity and interpersonal skills; Whiteways Research (1995) extended this to cover self-awareness, self-promotion, political focus and coping with uncertainty. These are not isolated instances and some of the lists produced can be extremely long. In a study of managerial skills Hirsch and Bevan (1988) itemised 1,745 different qualities.

To a certain extent there is little here that is novel. Employers have always demanded appropriate qualities and attributes from their workers and work has always involved a mixture of soft and technical skills. It is, after all, not enough to know something, to be effective a worker must be able to put that into practice in their workplace. This may involve enlisting the assistance of others, negotiating for resources with line managers, fitting new processes into existing ones and considering the impact on current practice. Even when the skills demanded of workers are basic and tasks demand minimal engagement, workers are likely be required to 'get on' with one another and to 'fit in' (Steiger, 1993). Moreover, the increasing numbers of service jobs demand very different qualities of those who carry them out than manufacturing work. In services, the process of being served is as much a part of the purchase as any product being sold and customers may conflate their delight at service levels with their appreciation of the product (Korczynski, 2001, 2002). As a result, the way that employees look and feel and the impressions and emotions they provoke in others are important (see, among others Hochschild, 1983; Leidner, 1993). However, couching this in the language of skill causes a number of problems. Unlike formally accredited technical skills, it is not clear that soft skills are either transferable or give their holders power in the labour market. The communication skills needed to tell a customer which aisle the baked beans are in are very different from those needed to describe the rules of cricket or explain complex statistics. In each of these areas (just as for the exercise of judgement, leadership or problem-solving), efficacy demands technical and local knowledge, a factor neglected by the compilers of generic lists. This is particularly worrying since there is some evidence that organisations attempting to train their staff in soft skills are neglecting the technical aspects of work (Grugulis and Vincent, 2009).

Box 5.5 HRM in practice

During the first week [of a US state-funded training programme] about a dozen women and two men sit around a conference table at the Dane county job centre. The instructor, who introduces herself as Kelly, shows flashcards. One flashcard says, *You'll never amount to anything.*

'Has anybody ever heard this in your life?' she asks.

No response.

'Good! Because it's not true!'

She holds up another flashcard: *You can do anything you set your mind to.*

'How about this one, how often do we hear this?'

No one says anything.

This is day three of the two-week … session. The topic: communication. From Kelly's point of view, things aren't going so well. 'People aren't talking a lot', she says.

Several participants are clearly trying though. Kelly holds up a flashcard that says *I'm so proud of you.* 'How do we feel when someone says this to us?' she asks.

'Good?', one participant offers.

'Yeah!', says Kelly. She hands out pieces of paper and asks everyone to write down the names of two people who have had a positive influence on their lives.

'It's the person who believes in you', she says.

She writes 'belives' in magic marker on a flip chart, then crosses it out and writes 'beleives'.

'Don't tell her,' the woman in front of me whispers.

'What?', Kelly asks, 'Don't tell me what?'

'You still spelled "believes" wrong', someone says.

Kelly stares at the flip chart.

'It's I before E except after C', another participant explains.

'That's okay', the woman in front of me says. 'That's a hard one.'

After a short break, Kelly lists some more rules for good communication. 'Here are two of the hardest things to say in the English language', she says, and writes 'Thank you' and 'I'm sorry' on the flip chart … I interview some participants after class. 'I don't want to knock the programme or anything – maybe someone is getting their self-esteem raised', says one. . . . . 'But . . . they've given me an ultimatum: you either go to this class or it's your check.'

Source: Conniff (1994: 18–21); quoted in Lafer (2004: 121).

Then too, soft skills may be reciprocal and relational rather than individual. In his study of the skills required by US employers Lafer (2004) draws on research by Moss and Tilly (1996) in two warehouses in the same district of Los Angeles both of which employed present and past gang members. While managers in one complained of high turnover, laziness and dishonesty, in the second, which paid several dollars per hour more, managers had few complaints and turnover was a modest 2 per cent. As Lafer (2004: 117) argues:

traits such as discipline, loyalty and punctuality are not 'skills' that one either possesses or lacks; they are measures of commitment that one chooses to give or withhold based on the conditions of work offered.

Focusing on motivation as an individual skill presupposes that people are unaffected by their conditions of work or the way that they are treated. Factors once considered the responsibility of management or personnel are individualised such that the emphasis on control systems, job design, pay rates or being a 'good employer' becomes the straightforward problem of hiring the most appropriately 'skilled' people (Grugulis *et al.*, 2004; Keep 2001).

In workplaces it also seems to matter *who* exercises the skill, with soft skills being rated far more highly (as well as rewarded, see Dickerson and Green, 2002) when they are possessed by knowledge workers than by people with low or intermediates-skills. Grugulis and Vincent's (2009) study of high-skilled IT professionals and intermediate-skilled housing benefit caseworkers revealed that, while soft skills were rhetorically valued in both workplaces, it was the IT professionals who were able to secure status and pay for their soft skills, with soft skills developed in tandem with high-level technical skills. The housing benefit caseworkers found that soft skills *replaced* much technical training and was used to allocate women to gendered and career-limiting roles, despite their protests. Ironically, the very entrepreneurial qualities that the employer valued in the young IT professionals enabled them to avoid learning the details of the local system, which was so necessary to their employers, and concentrate instead on gaining expertise in software which could and did help them to move to better paid work elsewhere.

Nor is the exercise of soft skills particularly clear. Employers value them but often judge their presence or their absence through sexual and racial stereotypes. Women are favoured for call centres and reception desks. Asian women are not considered to be career minded and men's marital status may be taken as a proxy for their reliability (Collinson *et al.*, 1990; Hebson and Grugulis, 2005; Oliver and Turton, 1982). As Ainley (1994: 80) argues, 'at rock bottom, the real personal and transferable "skills" required for preferential employment are those of whiteness, maleness and traditional middle-classness'. It is difficult to escape from the conclusion that in some environments focusing on soft skills can be used to legitimise prejudice and reinforce disadvantage.

This is a conundrum. At one level most jobs clearly require a mixture of both technical and soft skills and, given the existing lack of recognition for women's skills, rhetorical support for their importance should advantage them. At another, as Bolton (2004) argues, these skills – regardless of their complexity – seem to be the exception to the normal laws of supply and demand in the sense that, no matter how much employers require them, they are seldom highly rewarded when not accompanied by high levels of technical skill. The advantages that soft skills offer seem precariously dependent on their being noted, appreciated and rewarded by senior management (Grugulis and Vincent, 2009). In isolation they provide workers with few of the labour market advantages of technical skills (Keep, 2001; Payne, 1999, 2000).

In part this is a systemic issue. A focus on soft skills (such as communication, loyalty or even punctuality) in low-level work confers few advantages on workers because it equips them only to perform low level tasks. Whereas an emphasis on team-working, problem-solving and responsibility for production integrated with technical skills in Thompson *et al.'s* (1995) cross-national comparisons of vehicle production provided employees with opportunities for progression. Similarly, in NUMMI's plant in Freemont, California soft skills are combined with the development of technical skills and workers are given a great deal of discretion to address workplace problems (Rothenberg, 2003). But, while integrating these generic qualities with challenging work may make them more 'skilful' and advantage those workers who possess or develop them, it does not overcome the tendency to read these virtues into gender, race, class, age or marital status.

The disadvantages of training and development

The overall picture of training and development is not clear cut. Some courses, qualifications and on-the-job training are excellent at developing workforce skills which can then be integrated into the way work is designed and controlled. But developmental provision is set alongside narrow qualifications and training courses that serve only to entertain. At one level, such behaviour is difficult to explain. If training and development is universally believed to have a positive impact then why are so few firms training and why are the ones that do train confining much of their activity to short courses, health and safety and induction? Equally, why do not individual employees respond to this by filling the gap themselves? Such lack of activity appears, at best, irrational.

However, there is an explanation. Training and development does not occur in a vacuum, rather it is one aspect of an organisation's activities and exists to support the other activities. As Keep and Mayhew (1999) argue, training is a third-order issue, following on from decisions about competitiveness, product specification and job design. For organisations that choose to compete on the basis of quality, highly-skilled workers are essential (and as Shury et al., 2010 point out, firms that do compete on quality provide more, and better funded training); for ones that compete on cost, they are an unjustifiable extravagance – and large sections of the British economy still compete on cost (Bach and Sisson, 2000). The second reason, and this is related to the first, is that many jobs are designed to be tightly controlled with employee discretion (and with it skill) taken away. One employer, interviewed by Dench et al. (1999) said that their ideal worker had two arms and two legs. When this is what jobs demand, it is difficult to see how training will help. Job design is not set in stone and it is perfectly possible to construct skilled work from the same jobs, the same market conditions and the same strategy. Boxall and Purcell (2011) provide an interesting example from two firms competing with one another in delivering bottled gas. British Oxygen decided to compete by using delivery drivers as key staff. Drivers were trained in customer relations, cab-based information systems and product knowledge, ensuring that customers were satisfied and encouraging them to trade up wherever possible. By contrast Air Products, a rival firm in the same industry facing the same pressures, decided to compete by outsourcing its haulage and distribution to an independent contractor. Their drivers were not expected to know anything about bottled gas beyond the standard health and safety guidelines. When large numbers of employers design jobs to be done without skill, pay low wages and workers with little purchasing power buy products of low price and low quality we have all the elements of what Finegold and Soskice describe as a 'low skills equilibrium' (1988).

Then too, it is instructive to consider the areas of job creation. In June 2011 82.5 per cent of UK jobs were in the service sector (ONS, 2011a). Service work includes many of the most highly skilled and knowledgeable workers such as medics, teachers and IT professionals but it also, and in far greater numbers, covers care workers, security staff and personal services, numbers of which are rising far faster. The sector as a whole is dominated by low-paid, part-time workers, few of whom are either highly skilled or allowed to exercise their skills in their work. This need not be the case (Bozkurt and Grugulis, 2011). McGauran's (2000, 2001) research into retail work in France and Ireland shows how French employers expect their workers to be experts in the products sold and French customers request advice on products and product care when shopping. However, it is not clear that this skilled variant of shop-work influences behaviour elsewhere. Rather, pressure for hyper-flexibility, described by Gadrey (2000: 26) as 'tantamount to a personnel strategy based on zero competence', zero qualifications, zero training and zero career, means that retail work is dominated by poorly paid part-time workers and the flexibility demanded of them is availability for shift work at short notice. In Germany, this is threatening long-established traditions of training and qualifications as employers avoid training employees, since this would make them expensive to hire, and rely instead on large numbers of low-paid staff supported by small numbers of highly skilled 'anchor' workers (Kirsch et al., 2000).

At an individual level too there are good and sound reasons for not taking up vocational training. Human capital theory is neither as straight forward, nor as axiomatic as some commentators argue. While some qualifications do indeed bring high returns, others do not and it is the low-level vocational qualifications that bring least reward (see, for example Grugulis, 2003). Then too, not all skills are equal and the status and labour market power of job holders influence the way their skills are perceived (Rubery and Wilkinson, 1994). In practice this means that women's work, even when technically and objectively more complex than men's, tends to be under-valued (Phillips and Taylor, 1986). Mechanistically assessing workers as a supply of skills neglects both this social construction and factors such as trust and motivation that are needed to put skills into practice at work (Brown, 2001). Human capital theory also individualises the responsibility for acquiring and developing skills. Nor is it clear that highly skilled workers create their own demand. As the UK skills survey consistently demonstrates, more than one-third of workers report that their skills are under-utilised in employment (Felstead *et al.,* 2007).

 Skill and performance

It seems, given the above, that the rewards from vocational training are neither as straightforward, nor as automatic, as some writers on human capital theory would like to believe. This is a key point and worth considering in a little more detail. After all, as noted at the start of the chapter, part of the implicit (and occasionally explicit) promise of skills development is a link with performance and productivity for individuals, organisations and nations. Skills should lead, in the words of the *Leitch Review* (2006) to prosperity for all.

In many instances, of course, they do. An expert and experienced worker performs better than an untried novice, in the USA, college graduates earn more than their peers with only high school qualifications and nations with better systems of education and vocational education and training out-do their competitors (Green, 2006; Nolan and Slater, 2003). However, these results are neither deterministic nor inevitable and it is worth considering three areas where the links are questionable: linking shop-floor and organisational performance, the varying points of analysis and performance in the service sector (for a more detailed discussion see Grugulis and Stoyanova, 2011).

Analysing performance

There are many excellent studies of the impact that variations in skills and work design have on productivity. The National Institute for Economic and Social Research (NIESR) has specialised, over many decades, in conducting comparative case studies in the same industry and controlling for technology wherever possible but where work is organised differently and workers' skills vary dramatically (see Prais, 1995 for an overview of these). Their conclusions are clear and positive: highly skilled workers can contribute more to the production process; technology can be better integrated; less supervision is required and higher-quality goods result. So far, so good.

Box 5.6 HRM in practice

Biscuits and skill: biscuit making in Britain and Germany
This is taken from a study of biscuit manufacture in ten British and eight German firms.

The type of biscuits produced varied greatly between the two countries, largely owing to national tastes and demand. In Britain, demand concentrated on relatively basic biscuits: either plain or with one simple coating of chocolate, cream or jam. In Germany, there was a much higher demand for decorated and multi-textured products (soft biscuits with jam filling in chocolate cases or layered variegated biscuits). Since this affected the type of biscuits that each firm produced, relative output figures were not easy to measure. On crude output figures, productivity per employee hour was 25 per cent higher in Britain than in Germany, largely because British firms produced large quantities of simple, low-quality biscuits. However, when these productivity figures were adjusted for quality, the British advantage disappeared with German firms 40 per cent more productive per employee hour.

In Germany 90 per cent of process workers were craft-trained bakers and could work in all of the main areas of operations (mixing, biscuit-forming and oven control). This multi-skilling meant that three-person teams could be responsible for at least two oven lines at the same time. In German firms, employees were focused in areas that added value to the product. Maintenance staff were highly qualified and, in addition to undertaking regular maintenance, they worked with supervisors to customise equipment and increase productivity. In Britain, no process workers and few supervisors were vocationally qualified. As a result, each individual production line needed a three-person team to cover mixing and baking since workers were narrowly trained and tended to stick to their own jobs. Few firms had any regular system of machine maintenance since shift work meant that equipment was rarely scheduled to stop but breakdowns were frequent and high staffing levels in areas such as wrapping were needed to sort out problems caused by equipment breakdown and malfunction. On the line, narrow training restricted the ability of shop-floor workers to anticipate problems (such as machine malfunctioning) and take appropriate action.

Source: Mason *et al.*, 1996.

However, as Cutler (1992) points out, this is performance at the level of the shop floor and not of the organisation. Between these two levels other factors such as currency movements, accounting conventions, the performance of the salesforce and the national economy can and do influence firm performance. Shop-floor skills are important, but they are not the only, nor even the most important, element in organisational performance.

There are difficulties too, in attempting to integrate positive returns for individuals, organisations and nations, not least because such returns may be mutually incompatible. Higher wages for individuals detract from organisational profits. Firm performance may be improved by the strategic implementation of a redundancy programme (to boost share price); national performance by *increasing* the number of people in work (Keep *et al.*, 2002). There is, as is frequently observed of the employment contract, only a *partial* coincidence of interest between these three parties. Some activities will indeed benefit all, but in many cases there is a zero sum game and increasing performance in one area results in penalties elsewhere.

Finally, and most confusingly, is the issue of the service sector, where existing assumptions about performance and productivity are regularly challenged. Here quality may be increased by, for example, a four-star hotel employing more unskilled staff to attend to guests, carry bags or advise on local restaurants. But this move may damage their overall performance since economists tend to measure productivity by reckoning on the number of employees taken to 'process' a guest. Equally, investing in employees' skills in areas such as customer service may not attract the sort of returns that the marketing textbooks promise, since customers tend to use a whole range of factors, not simply excellent service levels, when making purchasing decisions. As Keep and colleagues (2002) point out, SwissAir, which won awards for its customer service, went bankrupt, while Easyjet thrives.

So, skills can have a positive effect on performance at a whole range of levels but this is by no means guaranteed and might best be described as prosperity for some, rather than prosperity for all.

Re-thinking training and development

This chapter has deliberately extended the debate on training and development beyond the confines of formal courses and qualifications. These are important factors but, for students of HRM, they are only one aspect of a wider issue, the development of 'resourceful humans'. A knowledgeable workforce is the product, not of excellent training in isolation, but of a combination of a range of factors including training, job design, status, control systems and discretion. As Cockburn (1983) and Littler (1982) argue, skill reposes in the individual, in the job and in the social setting. In practice, this means that for development to be effective, individuals need enough discretion and challenge in their work to exercise their skills.

Given this, there are some reasons for optimism in Britain. Between 1986 and 2006 skills in work have risen against almost every indicator. Employers are demanding more (and more advanced) qualifications, training periods for jobs are rising and the amount of experience that employees need to do their work well is also rising (Felstead *et al.*, 2007). However, while this trajectory is encouraging, it starts from a low base and most work still demands few skills with 61 per cent of jobs requiring less than three months' training and 20 per cent less than one month's experience to do well (compared to 26 per cent which require more than two years, Felstead *et al.*, 2002). *iMac* jobs have not yet entirely replaced *McJobs* (Warhurst and Thompson, 1998).

This skills survey also reveals two extremely worrying developments. The first emerged in the 1990s as more individuals gained qualifications and workplace demand failed to keep pace. The most recent results show that at an aggregate level the number of workers holding level four qualifications (roughly equivalent to degree level, though here degrees themselves are treated as a separate group within this category) exceeds the number of jobs that require workers educated to level four (7.7 million jobs set against 8.8 million individuals). However, at the other end of the spectrum there are 7.4 million jobs which require no qualifications at all but only 2.4 million economically active people without qualifications (Felstead *et al.*, 2007: 24).

This under-utilisation of skills is apparent in Rainbird and Munro's (2003) research. Drawing on an extensive study of low-paid workers they found that rigid hierarchies, narrow job descriptions and cost constraints all acted as barriers that employees, who were often highly educated, skilled or anxious to progress, could not overcome. Nor was there any sign, despite the very significant differences that good managers could make, that this might change. Indeed, the structural innovations observed, such as contracting out by the public sector, often reduced employees' areas of influence and took away aspects of their work that were interesting or skilful.

The second area for concern is the sharp decline in discretion employees can exercise, a trend that was particularly marked for professional workers. In 1986, 72 per cent of professionals reported that they had 'a great deal' of choice over the way that they worked. By 2001 this figure had fallen to 38 per cent (Felstead *et al.*, 2002: 71; see also Evetts, 2002; Grugulis *et al.*, 2003). Yet discretion is a prerequisite for skills to be put into practice.

Discussion and conclusions

It has frequently been argued that training is the 'litmus test' of human resource management (Keep, 1989). The pivotal element of a system designed to harness the talents of those it employs (through well designed jobs, team working, employee involvement and other human resource practices) is ensuring that employees are developed for their roles. However, the reverse also applies and human resource practices are the test of training. There is little point in training and developing employees if the jobs they are to undertake are tightly controlled with no trust or discretion given. Skill is an aspect of jobs as well as a part of individuals and a highly skilled individual put in a job where they have little control, discretion or responsibility and which they have little power to change is likely to become frustrated. This means that, just as many excellent analyses of human resource management have queried the extent to which its ambitious rhetoric has been matched by its lived reality, so training and development needs to be subjected to the same scrutiny. Good training and development has the capacity to significantly change lives. It can equip people for more interesting, better paid and more demanding work; help to mitigate the discrimination in the labour market experienced by women and members of minority groups and provide an effective route out of poverty for people working in unskilled and low-paid jobs. However, just because some forms of training can do this does not mean that all can. Training and development is not straightforwardedly a 'good thing' – not all training is developmental and not all development is integrated into work. Before according our approval we really do need to examine what is involved in particular training systems, the effect it has on individuals and the way it is integrated into work. If this is not the case there is a danger that effort and resources will be put into systems which simply reinforce disadvantage and equip people only for minimum wage employment (Lafer, 2004) or horizontal movement between a range of low-skilled jobs (Grimshaw *et al.,* 2002).

CASE STUDY 5.1

DEVELOPING RESOURCEFUL HUMANS

IRENA GRUGULIS

This chapter showed the way that training and development may be systemic and linked to product strategies, job design, the way that work is controlled and the level of discretion workers can use. For each of the jobs listed below set out:

a. how people are trained to do the job;
b. what (if any) continuing development they have on the job (remember that a challenging job provides opportunities for development, just as formal training does);
c. how much discretion they can exercise;
d. what other human resource policies you would expect (on pay rates, involvement, career ladders, etc.);

e. what would happen to these jobs if recruits received more developmental training or were more highly educated.

A secondary school teacher
A call centre worker
An anaesthetist
An accountant
A gardener
A shop assistant
A junior manager in a chain restaurant
A bank cashier
A factory worker
A cleaner

CASE STUDY 5.2

SOFT SKILLS AT WORK

IRENA GRUGULIS AND STEVEN VINCENT

Soft skills and personal qualities are an increasingly important part of work with employees expected to show them in work and assessed on them at recruitment, appraisal and promotion. However, there have also been claims that judging soft skills may simply be an expression of individual and collective prejudice with gender, race and class used to stereotype workers. This case study provides descriptions of two groups of workers in different organisations who had varying experiences of soft skills. Read the descriptions and answer the questions below.

Benefit caseworkers in TCS

TCS was an outsourcing company with a contract with a London council to do housing benefit processing, work which required intermediate-level skills. The housing benefit caseworkers were expected to demonstrate customer focus, attitude, flexibility and endurance with managers condemning the '9 to 5' mentality of the public sector and new staff were screened for positive attitudes. Initial technical training was dramatically reduced and instead staff were taught about punctuality, personal presentation and attitude. A reception desk was set up to deal with customer claimants. The work involved was largely unskilled and staff had difficulty returning to the skilled work of claims processing after stints on reception. Despite protests, women were preferred for this task since the manager considered them naturally better at it and 16 of the 20 reception workers were women. In claims processing, new managers were chosen for their soft skills (and particularly whether they were considered 'TCS people') rather than their occupational knowledge and some had no experience of housing benefit at all. Performance was monitored by statistics and claims staff lost their professional discretion.

IT consultants in FutureTech

FutureTech provided outsourced computing and IT services to Govco, a large government department. Its workers were highly skilled and new entrants were all graduates. Consultants were expected to be customer-focused, flexible and to actively work towards ensuring harmony in the relationship between the two firms; while graduates were hired as enthusiastic self-starters who were responsible for their own learning and development. Extensive training was provided with most time devoted to improving technical knowledge, though much of the actual work was mundane. Long hours and weekend working were common. Some expatriate US managers on the staff made efforts to introduce motivational techniques and make the British workers more emotional, including encouraging them to stand up and applaud themselves.

Graduates were very technically skilled but most avoided learning the details of Govco's internal systems which were necessary for success internally but had little market value. Instead, they became adept at creating their own developmental opportunities and competing for projects which involved new software. Turnover increased from 2 to 9 per cent overall and was described as 'dysfunctionally high' for graduates.

Questions

1 What soft skills were required in the two organisations? What sort of balance was there between soft skills and technical skills?

2 What effect did this have on (a) the workers, (b) their work and (c) their employers? Whom did the soft skills benefit?

3 How does knowing about workers' technical skills help us to understand this?

4 Think about another job that you are familiar with. What soft skills and what technical skills are required? Do they advantage the employee or the employer?

5 What effect does an emphasis on soft skills have on workers?

For further details of this case study see Grugulis and Vincent (2009).

CASE STUDY 5.3

JOBS, DISCRETION AND SKILL

IRENA GRUGULIS, STEVEN VINCENT AND GAIL HEBSON

This case study explores two 'networks', an outsourced group of housing benefit caseworkers and production workers in a specialist chemicals company, and considers the effect that each network had on employee skills.

Total Customer Services (TCS) specialise in business operations outsourcing. With a turnover of over £200 million per year and more than 3,000 employees, TCS has one of the largest players in this emerging market and had a strategy of rapid expansion. It took over the management of the housing benefits office of a London borough as a loss-leader in order to break into an expanding area of outsourcing business. This housing benefits office had previously been under-performing and was identified as one of the worst boroughs in London. Here, claim processing was outsourced to improve the quality of service provided.

Scotchem is a pigment manufacturing plant. It is one of several UK-based chemical production facilities owned by Multichem, a large European multinational that specialises in developing and producing industrial chemicals. Pigments have been produced on the site for over 75 years and Scotchem is Multichem's centre of excellence in pigment manufacture. The company employs over 650 people on its unionised site and produces around 24,000 tonnes of pigment. A regular feature of this production process was that Scotchem collaborates with customers and suppliers in order to develop both processes and products for specific orders.

Both of these networks were organised, and gained their flexibility, in slightly different ways. In TCS claims processing was contracted out for seven years and initially contact between the council and TCS (with the exception of contract negotiation at senior level) took the form of council staff monitoring claims processed by TCS caseworkers. However, the original contract also set performance levels for TCS and these were not met. As a result, the council set a new series of targets and weekly meetings were held with senior TCS staff to discuss performance.

Scotchem's network is far more flexible, at least in terms of its relations with customers and suppliers. Since it produces chemicals in bulk and can both place and fill orders on a very large scale, many of its suppliers and customers are long-term, with 20- or 30-year relationships not uncommon. Formal contracts tended to be short-term, with quarterly negotiations used to set prices and agree approximate levels of consumption in order to manage work in progress. However, these agreements are part of very long-term relationships. As a result, a series of alliances and friendships have built up between various staff members, with informal contacts and tacit knowledge supplementing official agreements about cooperation.

Contracts, control and the decline of discretion

In theory, outsourcing only changes the responsibility for completing a task, not the task itself. In theory too, such a change may improve efficiency and effectiveness. The organisation that outsources may gain numerical flexibility, hiring staff only when needed, or secure access to expertise that it lacks internally. Yet these theories focus on organisational experience or expectations and assume that the way work is managed does not affect the way it is carried out. In practice, in TCS, outsourcing required a change in management structure which fundamentally altered the work processes. Such adjustments might have been predicted. There are, broadly, two distinct ways of controlling staff: 'status', in which employees are trusted to perform often ill-specified or 'extra-functional' activities (and through which they may gain certain rights), and 'contract', where tasks tend to be clearly specified and tightly controlled, completed at the order of employers (Streeck, 1987). Most employment relationships tend to be a fluid mixture of both, influenced by organisational structures, individuals and contexts. According to the prescriptive literature, liberation from bureaucratic control should increase an individual's autonomy; in practice, in TCS, the reverse was the case. Here the process of contracting meant that tasks were more strictly defined and monitored and employees were able to exercise less discretion.

Housing benefit staff had previously been responsible for seeing an entire claim through from start to finish, ensuring that the documentation was complete and correct and often exercising their professional judgement to condone minor omissions. Since forms were complicated and demanded repeated pieces of evidence, these omissions were reasonably common. Under TCS, once the work was contracted out, processing was reorganised so that caseworkers 'specialised' in one part of the claims process or worked in the newly set-up call centre for extended periods of time (instead of part of a shift, as had been the case under the local authority). Housing benefit is a complex area and regulations are subject to change, so this specialisation not only made processing claims less pleasurable by taking away caseworkers' feelings of 'ownership' and making their work less interesting, it also meant that skills declined. Staff were no longer aware of changes that occurred outside their own narrow remit. Their power to make decisions was also lost. Caseworkers were required only to ensure that the paperwork was complete before passing the form back to the local authority, rather than approving it as it stood.

> Under [the council] I had my own caseload, a set number of cases, surnames for a particular area, I go through all those cases from start to finish. If during the benefit period there was a change of circumstances it was my sole ability to do that case. I knew those cases. You could call the name and address and I could tell you what that entailed. We don't have that under [TCS]. What we have, it's even worse now … we come in and they give us this sheet and they say this is your work for the day. You don't really know the cases. Ten people could have touched that case since it came in before it gets to the person who finally pays the claim. So from the customer point of view it's not very helpful as they tend to receive letters from five or six different case workers – they say, who wrote to me?

> (TCS caseworker, female)

To a certain extent, this decline in discretion was an inevitable part of the contracting process. After all, tasks may be contracted out, but responsibility remains with the original organisation. This institutional separation of execution and authority has implications for work processes. While in-house staff might be controlled through trust, work undertaken by external bodies was regulated by 'contract'. Because local authorities must validate claims, council staff checked every detail of every form before authorising it. The in-house experts retained by the council found that the monitoring was as time-consuming and tedious for them as it was for the ex-colleagues they monitored.

Changing skills, changing workers

This decline in employees' discretion was also matched by changes in personnel. In TCS the initial work group was of skilled staff who had transferred over from the local authority, but these were supplemented by agency staff (25 from a workforce of 110) whose levels of skill and experience varied. Further, TCS itself hired and trained new recruits, but these were less qualified than the existing caseworkers and the training that they were given was greatly shortened.

Such increasingly active management was more a product of the subcontracting process than a reflection of changes in the skills base. The audit systems were imposed on all workers and even the most experienced and skilled staff, who had been accustomed to exercise discretion when working 'in-house', were subjected to higher levels of control as subcontractors. There was a reduction in the skills base that had existed prior to contracting out, but this reduction was a consequence, rather than a cause of, the increasing emphasis on audit. This reduction in skills was partly because the temporary nature of the agreements provided fewer incentives for organisations to develop and maintain employees' skills. TCS, which had a seven-year contract with the council, introduced a caseworker training programme, but they recruited less qualified people than the council had and their training programme then equipped workers with fewer technical skills since the redesigned work processes demanded fewer skills.

Scotchem and 'learning networks'

Scotchem's network was qualitatively different from TCS's outsourced work. Since it was one of the largest multinationals engaged in producing chemicals and pigments, several of its relationships with suppliers and customers were long-term. Specific contracts for services could be short, but they were repeated and inter-firm relationships could and did last 20 or 30 years. Many of these companies were competitors, but the size of their orders and the duration of the contacts meant that, here at least, market dependency resulted in the growth of trust. Officially, contact took the form of contracts for particular services; unofficially, it came close to a contract for service, allowing trust and status to develop.

In Scotchem, individual employees held permanent contracts and staff at all levels were expected to exercise responsibility and engage in 'extra-functional' activities. When a new plant was set up, one of the operatives commented that:

> We've been left with quite a free role to prioritise ourselves, and sort our own team out, what we do and who does it, left to our own responsibility for that . . . We know our responsibilities, we organise

ourselves. I think the ownership has come from – because we understand the business and the needs of the business.

These expectations were extended to work with other firms. Orders for pigment would often involve developing products or improving delivery and, to achieve this, Scotchem employees at all levels were required to collaborate with customers and suppliers, a working arrangement which included shop-floor employees who would test new processes and equipment before developments were finalised. Two of the most recent results of such inter-organisational collaborations are a complex automated loading facility for part of the Scotchem site, and larger and tougher bags for the powdered chemicals. Extensive collaboration with one preferred supplier in producing bag specifications has maximised benefits for both parties by significantly reducing leakage which might foul the loading equipment.

Each of these collaborations was formally governed through contract, and the information that could be revealed to competitors was restricted. However, the long-term relations between the firms and the friendships that often existed between employees meant that contracts were honoured more in breach than in observation. Exchanges generally went beyond permitted limits and several people commented that projects would not have succeeded were it not for both sides' generosity with information. Significantly too, contracts set out the aims of each collaboration and little attempt was made to specify or monitor detailed tasks.

Questions

1 What were the main differences between the way work was organised at TCS and at Scotchem?

2 What implications did this have for skill?

3 What impact would improving or increasing training have had in these companies?

4 How important is discretion (a) in these two case studies, and (b) as part of skill?

5 Given the evidence here, what are the implications of a general increase in outsourcing work?

Source: Grugulis *et al.*, 2003.

Bibliography

Ainley, P. (1994) *Degrees of Difference,* London: Lawrence and Wishart.

Arthur, J.B. (1999) 'Explaining variation in human resource practices in US steel mini-mills', 11–42, in Cappelli, P. (ed.) *Employment Practices and Business Strategy*, Oxford and New York: Oxford University Press.

Bach, S. and Sisson, K. (2000) 'Personnel management in perspective', pp. 3–42, in Bach, S. and Sisson, K. (eds) *Personnel Management*, Oxford: Blackwell.

Bailey, T. and Berg, P. (2010) 'The vocational and training system in the USA', pp. 271–94, in Bosch, G. and Charest J. (eds) *Vocational Training: International Perspectives*, New York and London: Routledge.

Baumard, P. and Starbuck, W.H. (2006) *Is Organisational Learning a Myth*? London: The Advanced Institute of Management Research.

Bolton, S.C. (2004) 'Conceptual confusions: emotion work as skilled work', pp. 19–37, in Warhurst, C., Grugulis, I. and Keep, E. (eds) *The Skills that Matter*, Basingstoke: Palgrave Macmillan.

Bosch, G. (2003) 'Skills and innovation – a German perspective, Paper presented at The Future of Work/SKOPE/Centre for Organisation and Innovation Conference on Skills, Innovation and Performance, 31 March to 1 April, Cumberland Lodge, Windsor Great Park.

Bosch, G. (2010) 'The revitalisation of the dual system of vocational training in Germany', pp. 136–61, in Bosch, G. and Charest, J. (eds) *Vocational Training: International Perspectives*, New York and London: Routledge.

Bosch, G. and Charest, J. (2010) 'Vocational training: international perspectives', pp. 1–26, in Bosch, G. and Charest, J. (eds) *Vocational Training: International Perspectives*, New York and London: Routledge.

Boxall, P. and Purcell, J. (2011) *Strategy and Human Resource Management*, Basingstoke: Palgrave Macmillan.

Bozkurt, O. and Grugulis, I. (2011) 'Why retail work demands a closer look', pp. 1–21 in Grugulis, I. and Bozkurt, O. (eds) *Retail Work*, Houndsmills: Palgrave Macmillan.

Brown, P. (2001) 'Skill formation in the twenty-first century', pp. 1–55, Brown, P., Green, A. and Lauder, H. (eds) in *High Skills: Globalization, Competitiveness and Skill Formation*, Oxford: Oxford University Press.

Buchanan, J. and Evesson, J. (2004a) 'Creating markets or decent jobs? Group training and the future of work', *Australia National Training Authority, NCVER*. Adelaide.

Buchanan, J. and Evesson, J. (2004b). 'Redefining skill and solidarity at work: insights from group training arrangements in Australia'. Paper presented at 22nd International Labour Process Conference, 5–7 April, Amsterdam.

Callaghan, G. and Thompson, P. (2002) 'We recruit attitude: the selection and shaping of routine call centre labour', *Journal of Management Studies,* Vol.39, No.2, 233–54.

CBI (Confederation of British Industry) (1989) *Towards a Skills Revolution: A Youth Charter*, London: CBI.

Cockburn, C. (1983) *Brothers: Male Dominance and Technological Change*, London: Pluto Press.

Collinson, D., Knights, D. and Collinson, M. (1990) *Managing to Discriminate*. London and New York: Routledge.

Conniff, R. (1994) 'Big bad welfare: welfare reform politics and children', *The Progressive,* Vol.58, No.8.

Cully, M., Woodland, S., O'Reilly, A. and Dix, G. (1999) *Britain at Work: As Depicted by the 1998 Workplace Employee Relations Survey*. London: Routledge.

Culpepper, P.D. (1999) 'The future of the high-skill equilibrium in Germany', *Oxford Review of Economic Policy,* Vol.15, No.1, 43–59.

Cutler, T. (1992) 'Vocational training and British economic performance: a further instalment of the "British Labour Problem"?', *Work, Employment and Society,* Vol.6, No.2, 161–83.

Dench, S., Perryman, S. and Giles, L. (1999) 'Employers' perceptions of key skills', *IES Report*. Sussex: Institute of Manpower Studies.

Department for Education and Employment (2000) 'Skills for all: research report from the National Skills Task Force', Suffolk: DfEE.

Dickerson, A. and Green, F. (2002) 'The growth and valuation of generic skills', *SKOPE Research Paper*, Oxford and Warwick: Universities of Oxford and Warwick.

Evetts, J. (2002) 'New directions in state and international professional occupations: discretionary decision making and acquired regulation', *Work, Employment and Society*, Vol.16, No.2, 341–53.

Felstead, A., Gaillie, G. and Green, F. (2002) *Work Skills in Britain 1986–2002*. Nottingham: DfES Publications.

Felstead, A., Gallie, D., Green, F. and Zhou, Y. (2007) *Skills at Work 1986–2006*. Oxford: SKOPE and ESRC.

Finegold, D. (1999) 'Creating self-sustaining, high-skill ecosystems', *Oxford Review of Economic Policy*, Vol.15, No.1, 60–81.

Finegold, D. and Soskice, D. (1988) 'The failure of training in Britain: analysis and prescription', *Oxford Review of Economic Policy*, Vol.4, No.3, 21–43.

Fuller, A. and Unwin, L. (2004) 'Expansive learning environments: integrating organisational and personal development', pp. 126–44, in Rainbird, H., Fuller, A. and Munro, A. (eds) *Workplace Learning in Context*, London and New York: Routledge.

Gadrey, J. (2000) 'Working time configurations: theory, methods and assumptions for an international comparison', pp. 21–30, in Baret, C., Lehndorff, S. and Sparks, L. (eds) *Flexible Working in Food Retailing: A Comparison Between France, Germany, the UK and Japan*, London and New York: Routledge.

Green, F. (2006) *Demanding Work: The Paradox of Job Quality in the Affluent Economy*, Princeton, NJ and Oxford: Princeton University Press.

Green, F., Ashton, D., James, D. and Sung, J. (1999) 'The role of the state in skill formation: evidence from the republic of Korea, Singapore and Taiwan', *Oxford Review of Economic Policy*, Vol.15, No.1, 82–96.

Grimshaw, D., Beynon, H., Rubery, J. and Ward, K. (2002) 'The restructuring of career paths in large service sector organisations: "delayering", up-skilling and polarisation', *Sociological Review*, Vol.50, No.1, 89–116.

Grugulis, I. (2003) 'The contribution of NVQs to the growth of skills in the UK', *British Journal of Industrial Relations*, Vol.41, No.3, 457–75.

Grugulis, I. and Stoyanova, D. (2011) 'Skill and performance', *British Journal of Industrial Relations*, Vol.49, No.3, 515–36.

Grugulis, I. and Vincent, S. (2009) 'Whose skill is it anyway? "Soft" skills and polarisation', *Work, Employment and Society*, Vol.23, No.4, 597–615.

Grugulis, I., Vincent, S. and Hebson, G. (2003) 'The rise of the "network organisation" and the decline of discretion', *Human Resource Management Journal*, Vol.13, No.2, 45–59.

Grugulis, I., Warhurst, C. and Keep, E. (2004) 'What's happening to skill', pp. 1–18, in Warhurst, C., Grugulis, I. and Keep, E. (eds) *The Skills that Matter*, Basingstoke: Palgrave Macmillan.

Hebson, G. and Grugulis, I. (2005) 'Gender and new organisational forms', pp. 217–385, in Marchington, M., Grimshaw, D., Rubery, J. and Willmott, H. (eds) *Fragmenting Work: Blurring Organisational Boundaries and Disordering Hierarchies*, Oxford: Oxford University Press.

Hendry, C. (1993) 'Personnel leadership in technical and human resource change', in Clark, C. (ed.) *Human Resource Management and Technical Change*, London: Sage.

Heyes, J. and Gray, A. (2003) 'The implications of the national minimum wage for training in small firms', *Human Resource Management Journal*, Vol.13, No.2, 76–86.

Hirsch, W. and Bevan, S. (1988) *What Makes a Manager?* Brighton: Institute of Manpower Studies, University of Sussex.

Hochschild, A.R. (1983) *The Managed Heart: Commercialization of Human Feeling*. Berkley, CA: University of California Press.

Jeong, J. (1995) 'The failure of recent state vocational training policies in Korea from a comparative perspective', *British Journal of Industrial Relations,* Vol.33, No.3, 237–52.

Keep, E. (1989) 'Corporate training strategies: the vital component?', pp. 109–25 in Storey, J. (ed.) *New Perspectives on Human Resource Management*, London: Routledge.

Keep, E. (2001) 'If it moves, it's a skill'. Paper presented at ESRC seminar on The Changing Nature of Skills and Knowledge, 3–4 September, Manchester.

Keep, E. and Mayhew, K. (1996) 'Evaluating the assumptions that underlie training policy', pp. 303–34 in Booth, A. and Snower, D.J. (eds) *Acquiring Skills*, Cambridge: Cambridge University Press.

Keep, E. and Mayhew, K. (1999) 'The assessment: knowledge, skills and competitiveness', *Oxford Review of Economic Policy,* Vol.15, No.1, 1–15.

Keep, E. and Rainbird, H. (2000) 'Towards the learning organisation?', pp. 173–94, in Bach, S. and Sisson, K. (eds) *Personnel Management: A Comprehensive Guide to Theory and Practice*, Oxford: Blackwell.

Keep, E., Mayhew, K. and Corney, M. (2002) 'Review of the evidence on the rate of return to employers of investment in training and employer training measures' *SKOPE Research Paper*. Universities of Oxford and Warwick, SKOPE.

Kinnie, N., Hutchinson, S. and Purcell, J. (2000) 'Fun and surveillance: the paradox of high commitment management in call centres', *International Journal of Human Resource Management,* Vol.11, No.5, 967–85.

Kirsch, J., Klein, M., Lehndorff, S. and Voss-Dahm, D. (2000) 'The organisation of working time in large German food retail firms', pp. 58–82, in Baret, C., Lehndorff, S., and Sparks, L. (eds) *Flexible Working in Food Retailing: A Comparison between France, Germany, the UK and Japan*, London and New York: Routledge.

Korczynski, M. (2001) 'The contradictions of service work: call centre as customer-oriented bureaucracy', pp. 79–101, in Sturdy, A., Grugulis, I. and Willmott, H. (eds) *Customer Service: Empowerment and Entrapment*, Basingstoke: Palgrave.

Korczynski, M. (2002) *Human Resource Management in Service Work*, Basingstoke: Palgrave.

Lafer, G. (2004) 'What is skill?', pp. 109–27, in Warhurst, C., Grugulis, I. and Keep, E. (eds) *The Skills That Matter*, Basingstoke: Palgrave Macmillan.

Lane, C. (1989) *Management and Labour in Europe*. Aldershot: Edward Elgar.

Leidner, R. (1993) *Fast Food, Fast Talk: Service Work and the Routinizations of Everyday Life*, Berkeley and Los Angeles, CA: University of California Press.

Leitch, S. (2006) 'Prosperity for all in the global economy – world class skills. Final report.' *Leitch Review of Skills*. London: The Stationery Office.

Littler, C. (1982) *The Development of the Labour Process in Capitalist Societies*, London: Heinemann.

Mason, G. and Bishop, K. (2010) 'Adult training, skills updating and recession in the UK: the implications for competitiveness and social inclusion' *LLAKES Research Paper*, London: Institute of Education.

Mason, G., Van Ark, B. and Wagner, K. (1996) 'Workforce skills, product quality and economic performance', pp. 175–98, in Booth, A. and Snower, D. J. (eds) *Acquiring Skills*, Cambridge: Cambridge University Press.

McGauran, A.-M. (2000) 'Vive la différence: the gendering of occupational structures in a case study of Irish and French retailing', *Women's Studies International Forum,* Vol.23, No.5, 613–27.

McGauran, A.M. (2001) 'Masculine, feminine or neutral? In-company equal opportunities policies in Irish and French MNC retailing', *International Journal of Human Resource Management,* Vol.12, No.5, 754–71.

Moss, P. and Tilly, C. (1996) 'Soft skills and race: an investigation into black men's employment problems', *Work and Occupations,* Vol.23, No.3, 252–76.

Nolan, P. and Slater, G. (2003) 'The labour market: history, structure and prospects', pp. 58–80, in Edwards, P. (ed.) *Industrial Relations: Theory and Practice*, Oxford: Blackwell.

Oliver, J.M. and Turton, J.R. (1982) 'Is there a shortage of skilled labour?', *British Journal of Industrial Relations,* Vol.20, No.2, 195–200.

ONS (2011a) *Release Edition Jobs*, Newport: Office for National Statistics.

ONS (2011b) *Training Statistics, Labour Force Survey*, Newport: Office for National Statistics.

Payne, J. (1999) 'All things to all people: changing perceptions of "Skill" among Britain's policy makers since the 1950s and their implications'. *SKOPE Research Paper No. 1*. Coventry: University of Warwick.

Payne, J. (2000) 'The unbearable lightness of skill: the changing meaning of skill in UK policy discourses and some implications for education and training', *Journal of Education Policy,* Vol.15, No.3, 353–69.

Phillips, A. and Taylor, B. (1986) 'Sex and skill', in Feminist Review (ed.) *Waged Work: A Reader*, London: Virago.

Prais, S. (1995) *Productivity, Education and Training: An International Perspective*, Cambridge: Cambridge University Press.

Rainbird, H. and Munro, A. (2003) 'Workplace learning and the employment relationship in the public sector', *Human Resource Management Journal,* Vol.13, No.2, 30–44.

Ritzer, G. (1998) *The McDonaldisation Thesis*, London: Sage.

Rothenberg, S. (2003) 'Knowledge content and worker participation in environmental management at NUMMI', *Journal of Management Studies,* Vol.40, No.7, 1783–802.

Rubery, J. and Grimshaw, D. (2003) *The Organization of Employment*, Basingstoke: Palgrave Macmillan.

Rubery, J. and Wilkinson, F. (1994) 'Introduction', in Rubery, J. and Wilkinson, F. (eds) *Employer Strategy and the Labour Market*, Oxford: Oxford University Press.

Shury, J., Winterbotham, M., Davies, B., Oldfield, K., Spilsbury, M. and Constable, S. (2010) *National Employer Skills Survey for England 2009: Main Report*, London: UKCES.

Smith, A. (1776/1993) *Wealth of Nations*, Oxford and New York: Oxford University Press.

Steiger, T.L. (1993) 'Construction skill and skill construction', *Work, Employment and Society,* Vol.7, No.4, 535–60.

Streek, W. (1987) 'The uncertainties of management in the management of uncertainty: employers, labour relations and industrial adjustment in the 1980s', *Work, Employment and Society,* Vol.1, No.3, 281–308.

Thompson, P., Wallace, T., Flecker, J. and Ahlstrand, R. (1995) 'It ain't what you do, it's the way that you do it: production organisation and skill utilisation in commercial vehicles', *Work, Employment and Society,* Vol.9, No.4, 719–42.

Vivian, D., Winterbotham, M., Shury, J., Davies, B. and Constable, S. (2011) '*UK Employer Skills Survey 2011: First Findings*', London: UKCES.

Warhurst, C. and Thompson, P. (1998) 'Hands, hearts and minds: changing work and workers at the end of the century', in Thompson, P. and Warhurst, C. (eds) *Workplaces of the Future*, London: Macmillan.

Whiteways Research (1995) *Skills for Graduates in the 21st Century*, London: Association of Graduate Recruiters.

Yoon, J.H. and Lee, B.-H. (2010) 'The transformation of the government-led vocational training system in Korea', pp. 162–86, in Bosch, G. and Charest, J. (eds) *Vocational Training: International Perspectives*, New York and London: Routledge.

CHAPTER 6
REWARD MANAGEMENT

Mark W. Gilman

Introduction

Regardless of whether it is to do with the amount(s) paid or the method of payment, as a core element of the employment relationship the payment of employees has always been surrounded by controversy, especially when one considers employees collective concern (Brown *et al*., 2003). Despite arguments that equilibrium pay levels are determined by Adam Smiths 'invisible hand' (Smith, 1986), traditionally pay has been examined against the objectives of recruitment, retention and motivation of employees (Kessler and Purcell, 1992). This raises the notion that pay is not just the price of labour determined by the interaction of market forces but also that employers, managers and many other actors play an important role in pay determination. More recently, for example, reward systems are argued to have far reaching aims and objectives. Nowhere is this starker than in debates concerning human resource management (HRM) where the role of employees is seen as crucial to the creation of an organisations competitive advantage. As part of this, pay and reward are seen as an integral element of strategic HRM. Also, in today's global economy, multinational corporations (MNCs) face the added problems of managing pay and reward across different national systems, cultures, institutions, legislation and collective bargaining regimes to say the least. As Dowling *et al*., (2008: 159) state, pay is increasingly seen as: a mechanism to develop and reinforce a global corporate culture, a primary source of corporate control, explicitly linking performance outcomes with associated costs, and the nexus of increasingly strident, sophisticated and public discourses on central issues of corporate governance in an international context.

It has long been known that variations in pay occur for a variety of reasons other than those stated by classical economic theories. In taking a prominent role in the search for incentives, employers, institutions, legislation, etc., determine the type and potency of variable pay. Therefore it is important to understand where variations in pay arise from and the nature of variable pay as an incentive to meeting various organisational objectives. This chapter will first examine why there are variations in pay by looking at pay setting arrangements in practice, international comparisons and economic explanations for such variations. Second, it will examine more recent reward systems that aim to pay for performance looking at what they are, the extent and growth, roles of the social partners and how strategic they are in relation to the organisations overall strategy.

Why pay systems vary

Historically there have always been different pay and reward systems operating as employers and employees struggle over the most appropriate method to suit their requirements. However, pay and reward systems also seem to have 'mimetic' (Paauwe, 2004) properties in that during certain periods, and in certain sectors, particular schemes have taken prominence over others. Having said this, there may be many considerations why an employer might want to vary their pay systems. First, employers may want to recognise an employee's ability or skill. If firms want to sort workers by ability, they will adopt pay systems that reward the most able and/or skilled. Second, they may want to consider the association between output and effort. If there is a clear relationship between effort and output it is easier to pay for performance, If not they may choose a day rate. Third, they may want to consider monitoring costs. Paying for performance is more feasible if monitoring costs are low. Fourth, they may have to consider the risk preferences of workers because 'risk averse' workers will be less willing to 'gamble' on pay related to performance, than a guaranteed set amount of pay. Fifth, employers may have to consider whether trade unions or employers associations are involved in deciding pay and what the effects of this may be. Sixth, fairness of the pay or system has to be taken account of. This is problematic because there are generally two notions of fairness that are involved: first, 'the rate for the job', in which it is only fair that employees doing the same job are paid the same rate of pay, and second, it is only fair that reward should reflect an employee's contribution or effort and hence their pay will vary accordingly. Finally, pay may be dependent on power. If labour is scarce, employees have more power and hence may be able to demand higher pay, if labour is plentiful, employers have more power and hence may be able to hold pay at lower rates.

Variations in pay can cause dispersion and compression. In reducing inequality of pay and bringing about fairness, institutions matter; particularly support for unions and collective bargaining. Institutions also reflect and influence the balance of power between labour (unions) and capital (employers). But it can be argued that there are costs and benefits to dispersion and compression. The cost of compression is that if top performers are underpaid, they may quit. The benefits of compression are that greater cooperation may be generated with less emphasis on individual performance and more on quality consciousness. The costs of dispersion may be conflict over perceived inequity. The benefits of dispersion may include the ability to use pay as a motivator and as a tool for attracting and retaining top performers: Whatever the case there may be spill-over effects for society and not just the organisation. In setting pay a number of forces have to be understood. It is these that we turn to in the next section.

Pay setting in practice

Not all pay systems rely on a direct relationship with performance. Time-based pay is a system where employees on similar grades receive the same pay, expressed in either hourly (waged) or salaried terms. Wages are distinguished by an hourly rate of pay, with a specified working week in terms of the normal expected hours. Under wage systems, earnings may consist of many elements including a basic rate, shift or overtime payments, bonuses and allowances (Drucker, 2000). Under time-based payment systems, employers control over pace and performance is reliant on either direct supervision or the willingness of employees to engage with the task. Hourly based pay often provides a base line from which other wage systems are developed. In comparison, within time-based pay arrangements, salaries are calculated on an annual basis and are normally paid monthly. Although traditionally blue-collar workers have been waged and white-collar worker salaried, there is no clear occupational classification which determines which categories of employees receive wages or salaries.

The ultimate question always asked is if you pay a worker by the hour, day, week or month how can you make sure that the employee is going to work at full capacity? Take the hypothetical example of a garage that maintains and repairs cars. Taking out overheads, profit, etc., let's imagine that a mechanic can maintain a car per day at a value of £50. Their employer might thus agree to pay the mechanic £50 per day (a weekly wage of 5×50 = £250). But if there were problems, such as materials/parts not delivered on time, broken tools/machinery, or other unforeseen problems, this may slow maintenance down to two cars every 2.5 days. The mechanic will still want paying £50 per day but the employer would only want to pay the mechanic £40 per day (4×50 = 200 divided by 5 days = £40) to reflect the fact that only four cars are maintained per week. Here the employer will want to pay only for the direct output (effort) whereas the employee may say that they still exert effort in attending work, and carrying out the job using different methods, even if they are not as productive as usual, etc.

Such situations are then interpreted as being one in which the employee will always want to work in a way which allows them to put in the minimum amount of effort for the highest amount of pay and the employer will want the maximum effort for the minimum amount of pay. Agency theory, therefore assumes that: it is difficult for the employer and employee to make a contract based on observed effort because monitoring is too difficult or expensive; the employee is averse to effort; the employee is also averse to risk; and by paying a worker for effort you will motivate them to work harder (Baron and Kreps, 1999). The consequence of this is that employers might want to find a pay system that better relates performance to effort: incentive or variable pay. The problem of incentive pay then becomes how to relate effort, output and the price of labour in the correct proportions.

Setting the price of labour not only has to take account of perceived levels of knowledge and effort but has also to take consideration of a number of interrelated factors to do with external and internal market factors, and in doing so a number of arrangements that act as intermediaries to the external and internal markets such as job evaluation and collective bargaining.

External market

For classical economic theory, the level of wages is the competitive outcome of the forces of the supply and demand for labour. In competitive markets for labour, workers in similar occupations and with similar skills should ultimately receive the same wage. No individual employee or individual firm has the market power to sustain deviations and pay decisions are made by studying the 'going rate'. In reality, empirical observations do not match such a theory and there have been many attempts to explain why this is (see Box 6.3). Nevertheless, it is still the case that organisations cannot survive if they do not pay attention to competitive labour market rates. More recently, external labour market pressures have become apparent in a number of developments in pay practices (Kessler, 2008): first, organisations are placing a greater weight on making sure that wages compare with the external market when determining pay; second, attention is increasingly being focused on how to cope with the uneven external market pressures such as differing regional or occupational rates of pay; third, responses to these external market pressures have emerged as organisations have sought to modernise their internal grading structures.

Internal market

It has long been recognised that employers can sometimes deliberately seek to shelter employees from the effects of the external labour market. This can especially be the case in large organisations where internal relativities are more important than just external relativities. Therefore an organisation may make decisions concerning pay through a system of internal labour markets: that is coherent wage and career structures internal to the firm (see Doeringer and Piore, 1971). Kessler (2008) argues that the importance of internal equity emerged more recently in at least three different forms. The first relates to attempts to regulate pay at the extremes of the labour market. Organisations have therefore had to deal with the governments attempts to deal with inequalities at senior management/director level and low pay via the National Minimum Wage. Second, is the question of internal equality in light of the continuing question of gender differences in pay? Finally, linked to the issue of pay process, organisations are increasingly attempting to give greater thought to the transparency underpinning pay determination.

Job evaluation

Internally developed pay systems can reward individuals who develop firm specific human capital and the method most often utilised to maintain these internal constancies is job evaluation. In determining the value of its jobs, however, an organisation will have to turn its consideration to both external and internal labour market equity (Kessler, 2008). This it does by using job evaluation. Job evaluation is a systematic process for establishing the relative worth of jobs within an organisation. Pay is then usually allocated to jobs in line with a grading structure developed in conjunction with the system of job evaluation. Job evaluation is not an exact science, but it can at the least bring a degree of objectivity to the decision-making process. There are a variety of schemes which fall under two main types (see Box 6.1). The first are 'analytical', where jobs are broken down into individual components, the second are 'non-analytical', where the job as a whole is assessed (Egan, 2004). Analytical schemes are thought to be used by 86 per cent of companies while non-analytical are only used by 14 per cent (IRS, 2007). In analytical schemes criteria are decided by the organisation and these factors are then used to evaluate jobs. The most commonly used are as follows (IRS, 1998):

- knowledge and skills;
- responsibility;
- problem-solving and decision-making;
- people management
- relationships and contacts.

In other schemes certain jobs may then be used as benchmarks to provide a basis of comparison for other jobs evaluated. Whichever schemes, a value is then created for the jobs and jobs are then placed within a grading structure which can either contain narrow bands to maintain jobs within small variations of pay or broad bands that allow for larger variations. An important issue to note, however, is that internal and external equity can often be in conflict (Kessler, 2008). An important method of dealing with such conflicting forces is the collective determination of pay.

Box 6.1 HRM in practice   Non-analytical job evaluation schemes

Ranking of whole jobs in order of 'size', complexity or business impact is the most straight forward method of job evaluation. The system works, as the title suggests, by listing jobs in their order of importance comparing one criterion or multiple criteria. However, using only one aspect of the job is more likely to distort outcomes. Once all jobs have been listed, the job evaluators will need to make decisions about the number of grades they would like to use in their organisation and then lines are drawn through the rank order at agreed break points, e.g., at each point where there is perceived to be a step difference in the size of jobs.

Job categorisation – sometimes termed job classification. This is more of a top-down approach whereby the categories, classes or grades are determined in advance and roles are slotted or placed into the category in which they are perceived to fit best. The Federal US Fair Labor Standards Act (FLSA) is in effect a simple form of job categorisation inviting employers to classify jobs as exempt or non-exempt (for overtime pay).

Paired comparison is, in many respects, a more rigorous approach to job ranking. Paired comparisons force the employer to make a choice between two factors or two whole jobs and arrive at more objective decisions about the relative worth of a job.

Analytical job evaluation schemes

Points factor is by far the dominant form of job evaluation, the Hay job evaluation method being the leading proprietary brand of 'points factor' schemes. The points factor method is a highly analytical approach to job evaluation, breaking down jobs into a number of factors against which points are allocated. It highlights the importance of focusing on the job rather than the person. This is because the factors are intended to be impersonal objective lenses through which a job is deconstructed into its component parts, each part scored independently, and then the values are added together to give a total points value to the re-assembled job.

Non-analytical job evaluation – the pros and cons

Pros	Cons
Straightforward to operate	No clear basis for grading or re-grading
No special 'technical' training is required to be a job evaluator	Quality of outcomes depends on evaluator's understanding of jobs
Relatively transparent and speedy	Not regarded as a scientific approach
More likely to result in 'felt fair' outcomes for those involved in process	Hard to justify outcomes to those who have not been involved in process

Analytical job evaluation – the pros and cons

Pros	Cons
Perceived to be a scientific method	Often regarded as too 'black-box'
Job evaluation panels are a means of involving trades unions in decisions	Panels are criticised for being time-consuming, expensive and bureaucratic
Trained evaluators are more likely to deliver objectives outcomes	Evaluators have to undertake quite extensive training
Judgements are more consistent and re-grading appeals are easier to handle	Despite the apparent objectivity of the process, subjectivity still plays a role

Source: Childs, 2004.

The collective determination of pay bargaining

In most countries to one extent or another, other than management prerogative, collective bargaining has been the most influential form of discussing and setting pay arrangements. It is a system of deciding pay through negotiation between employees (and their unions) and employers (and their associations). Sometimes even government can be involved either as employers within the public sector or as interested parties in the health of the economy. The form of collective bargaining utilised can depend on union structure, bargaining structure, government, ideology and power. One has to take into account that while unions are democratic organisations and behave in ways that are solidaristic to employees collective requirements, employers and their organisations are not. Yet, in reality the role of trade unions is seen as controversial and dependent on ones ideology and beliefs. For example, the process of collective bargaining can be viewed, on the one hand, as a 'distributive' relationship in which the parties acknowledge their mutual dependence and seek to coerce each other into an agreement on the distribution of a limited resource; a fixed-sum game, in which one party's gain is the other's loss. On the other hand, it can be seen as more 'integrative', more concerned with resolving problems facing them both and which may facilitate a win-win outcome being possible: a variable-sum game (Walton and McKersie, 1965).

The collective determination of pay and conditions became dominant throughout the twentieth century particularly in the post Second World War era and peaking in the early 1980s. For example, in the UK during the 1950s and 1960s, in the main, there was a split between blue-collar (manual) wage earners and white-collar (office and professional) salaried employees. Pay was largely based on seniority even where schemes were related to performance as with piecework and bonuses. Collective bargaining was widespread with rates for the job determined through national or industry wide agreements often via multi-employer bargaining. In the UK, those not covered by collective bargaining were covered by the Fair Wages Resolution and Statutory Wage Councils. Towards the end of the period, problems of 'wage drift' began to occur as employees sought to increase their rates of pay in line with the rising cost of living.

Consequently, during the 1960s and 1970s there were growing problems with increasing inflation and unemployment. Increasingly different types of incomes policies were attempted by successive governments in a bid to reduce inflation and unemployment. In the late 1960s the Donovan Commission reported two systems of wage determination working side by side: formal bargaining by trade unions and employers associations and informal bargaining being increasingly carried out between shop stewards and management at the organisational level (Hyman, 2003). Both Labour, through the 1969 White Paper 'In place of strife' and Conservative governments (The Industrial Relations Act 1971) attempted to regulate the reform of industrial relations (Dickens and Hall, 2003). The Donovan Report argued for the formalisation of industrial relations procedures at shop-floor level and the integration of shop stewards into the machinery of collective bargaining (Nolan and Slater, 2003). The formalising of such systems was supposed to lead to greater productivity, but only if workers believed that they would also gain some benefit in the form of increased rewards (Hyman, 2003). This period therefore experienced the reform of collective bargaining to the establishment level to allow for productivity agreements. The most famous of which was the agreement at the Fawley oil refinery (Flanders, 1964). Productivity agreements were also used in times of incomes policies to allow employers to award higher than average increases in pay if they had achieved higher than average productivity increases.

The 1980s saw the end of government policy aimed towards maintaining prices and full employment within the economy. The Thatcher government of 1979 saw trade unions and collective bargaining practices as the main cause of rising inflation and unemployment. Trade unions were 'rigidities in the market system stopping wages from finding their market rate'. To this end, many legal changes were made to curb the powers of the trade unions. The Fair Wages resolutions were revoked and replaced by compulsory competitive tendering and statutory wage councils were abolished.

By the end of the 1990s collective bargaining coverage had fallen from 71 per cent in 1984 to 41 per cent in 1998. Management prerogative was now widespread within pay determination. Performance-related Pay schemes were being increasingly introduced along with broad banding to allow for wider variation. At the end of the period of 18 years of Conservative governments, Tony Blair's 'New Labour' were elected, signalling the possibility that there might be changes to the way employment relations was viewed. For pay purposes, the most significant legal change during the period was the introduction of the UKs first legally binding National Minimum Wage (Gilman *et al.*, 2002).

By 2004, the most common form of pay determination was unilateral pay setting by management with 70 per cent of workplaces paying at least some of their employees in this way. On the other hand, only 27 per cent of workplaces set pay for at least some of their employees through collective bargaining with trade unions (Kersley *et al.*, 2006). So overall, although it had slowed down, there has been a continual decline in collective bargaining since the 1980s. There has also been a trend away from mixed methods of pay determination to the use of single pay determination with pay being set by management at workplace level: a growth from 32 per cent in 1998 to 43 per cent in 2004 within the private sector. Within the public sector there has also been an increase in the incidence of unilateral pay determination from 21 per cent in 1998 to 28 per cent in 2004 (Kersley *et al.*, 2006).

International comparisons

Not only do reward practices and rates of pay vary within a particular country, they can also vary significantly depending on which country you live and work in. Changes to pay setting arrangements have not been confined to the UK but are in fact an international phenomenon. Yet, despite the identification of some common trends, both in terms of the decentralisation of collective bargaining and the use of variable pay systems, consequences will differ significantly because employer practices, institutions, legislation, etc., can be very different to begin with. This is important for a number of reasons, in particular, because of the globalisation of the world economy. In an increasingly global economy this has huge significance for the pay and reward practices of MNCs. In order to manage the pay and reward of the whole organisation they must understand the differing national and regional systems. For example, in the USA there have traditionally been very low levels of collective bargaining. Where bargaining does take place, it is mainly at workplace level, although once concluded the agreement can be very comprehensive. There has also been extensive use of variable pay supported by confidentiality clauses to stop employees discussing earnings with each other. By contrast, if we look at Germany, pay bargaining predominantly takes place at the industry level. More recently, there has been pressure on this system with increasing options for more flexible workplace deals. In the German system non-union workers are also usually covered by collective agreements, although this practice is less widespread than it used to be. Employees still have some influence on the workplace through a dual system of representation not only through collective bargaining but also through works councils and supervisory boards.

Another aspect to take into account is the wide variations found in the distribution of pay across countries. For example, there are wide differences between the CEOs and the average salary of production workers as is highlighted below:

	1997	2002
USA	325:1	600:1
UK	18:1	20:1
Japan	15:1	15:1
Germany	13:1	14:1
Sweden	11:1	11:1
France	12:1	12:1

Source: Kakabadse *et al.*, 2005.

Why do such differences come about, and what effects do they have on outcomes? Taking the example of the UK, there are wide variations within local labour markets and within occupations. Some have estimated that the 'range of indeterminacy' even within local labour markets and occupations is in the order of 20 per cent of average earnings (Blanchflower *et al.*, 1990; Gilman *et al.*, 2002). Internationally, what underlies the enormous difference in pay equality is shown to have a high correlation with trade union density, the degree of centralisation of collective bargaining, and to some extent whether a social democratic type of government is in power (Vernon, 2006).

International reward management

In developing an international compensation policy MNCs will need to consider a number of objectives from its own and its employee's perspectives (Dowling *et al.*, 2008). First, the MNCs' objectives will want to consider whether the policy is consistent with its strategy, structure and needs. Second, it must recruit and retain staff in areas of greatest need. Third, it needs to facilitate the transfer of employees internationally. Fourth, it must be equitable and easily administered. From the employee's perspective it will want to consider a) the employee's need for financial protection in terms of benefits and living costs in other countries; b) that the employee is likely to expect financial advancement from a foreign assignment; c) that the employee will expect housing, education of children and other social issues to be covered. Taken together, the above thus raise the potential for many complexities and problems (Dowling *et al.*, 2008). The MNC will also have to consider the fact that, on the one hand, they have to be aware of the institutions, structures and actors in the different countries while, on the other hand, through factors such as globalisation, the increasing use of information technology, European social legislation, etc. that their practices in different countries are becoming more and more visible to other parties.

So, most MNCs face far more complex challenges when designing their reward systems. Depending on the nature of the MNC and/or its wider business strategy it may have very different objectives for various groups of employees. For example, it is well documented that a MNC will sometimes want to take advantage of cheaper labour costs and therefore be attracted to invest in countries where this is the case. But then again they will have to deal with reward packages for those employees who may move to work for subsidiaries in one country or another. Therefore it is often the case that MNC face's reward challenges across three main groups:

- parent country nationals (PNCs) – ethnocentric and geocentric
- locals or host country nationals (HCNs) – polycentric
- third country nationals (TCNs) – geocentric and regiocentric.

The way that MNCs manage rewards for these employees will also be influenced by their overall management styles for managing their overseas subsidiaries, which can be highlighted through Perlmutter's (1969) approaches: ethnocentric, polycentric, regiocentric or geocentric approach to staffing.

Ethnocentric multinational corporations expect their expatriate managers to transfer headquarters' cultures and philosophy by working in their host country's overseas operations. Communication and information is top-down and all strategic decisions are steered from corporate headquarters. Subsidiaries sell products designed and manufactured by parent with little or no local control.

In polycentric MNCs, managers from the host country manage subsidiaries with some co-ordination from headquarters on how the subsidiary should operate. Overseas subsidiaries take more responsibility adapting designs, products and operations to meet local needs. Subsidiaries are managed as independent units with 'hands off' control from headquarters.

Regiocentric MNCs would be organisanised simialar to polycentric ones but subsidiaries would be grouped into larger regional entities. Regions are consistent with natural boundaries, such as the Europe, America and Asia-Pacific.

Geocentric MNCs work on a global basis using the best techniques and processes from around the world and adapting these to suit. Technology is transferred rapidly to sell more or less the same product worldwide. The geocentric organisation will create a pool or cadre of international managers capable, in theory, of being employed anywhere in the world. The geocentric approach may lead to more compensation problems than the other approaches because it aims for a common worldwide culture.

Three of these four staffing approaches – ethnocentric, regiocentric and geocentric – rely on extensive use of expatriate managers (PCNs and TCNs).

A key consideration with the above is that while acknowledging the diversity in MNC working population and the need to reward practices that reflect this. The corporate strategy literature emphasises the need to have consistent and integrated policies. Therefore business strategy should not be considered in isolation from internal and external equity (Perkins and White, 2008). Strategic international reward may also be constrained by the national context e.g. culture social, regulation of work, legislation, TUs and employers' associations. All of these define the limits within which organisations can operate. These external forces/features

Box 6.2 HRM in practice   Approaches or policies to international compensation

There are three approaches or policies to international compensation. These policies are:

- **Home-based policy.** This policy links the base salary for PCNs and TCNs to the salary structure of the relevant home country. It aims to keep in place a relativity of rewards against those for PCN employees while providing enough benefit to compensate the employee for carrying out the foreign assignment. As Sheilds (2012) argues this approach would have to cover base salary, a foreign service inducement, allowances and benefits to keep parity in rewards and provide incentives for employees to work overseas.
- **Host-based policy.** The base salary is linked to the salary structure of the host country but supplementary allowances for cost of living, housing, schooling and so on are linked to the home country salary structure. If the host country pay rates are comparatively higher than the home country the company will have to bare this extra cost. If they are lower they will still have to maintain pay parity with the person's present salary, but this means that other managers in the host country will be on less pay.
- **Region-based policy.** This is something of a compromise between the home-based and host-based policies This approach is more typical of a geocentric strategy whereby employees are encouraged to become mobile on a regional or global scale. The consequence would be the need to develop a reward strategy that fits with the company's global strategy.

define the confines of the 'strategic space' within which approaches to reward are shaped and highlight that a balance must be struck between organisational uniformity and local conditions (Vernon, 2011).

Economic explanations for pay variations

For a long time economists did not have an explanation for these variations other than blaming them on rigidities and distortions to the market. But there have been growing attempts to establish theories which explain the day-to-day observations which differ significantly from classical theory. Some of these are explained in Box 6.3. The first three of these remain within the orthodox framework of competitive equilibrium, while the latter three seek to explain why employers may choose wage rates higher or lower than their competitors (Brown *et al.*, 2003).

Box 6.3 HRM in practice   Economic explanations for Variation

Sorted by ability

Marshall (1920) argued that the differences in earnings reflect the different productive capacities among a group. Marshall's famous example was that farm labourers in the north of England, he said, were more adept at 'putting roots into a cart' than their brethren from the south, and the wages paid reflected this difference in physical efficiency in 'about the same proportion'. The outcome of this theory is that each establishment will employ only the best, the worst or the average worker for each job and will pay them accordingly. But this still leaves unexplained important elements of inter-firm wage differentials (Abowd *et al.*, 1999).

Absence of perfect information

This explanation drops the neo-classical assumption that information is perfectly (and costlessly) available. Instead, employees incur (searching) costs in identifying the range of wages on offer within the labour market. These theories are essentially a specification of labour supply, rather than demand. They do not account for the empirical observation that wage offers are generally based on the job rather than on the individual and they 'fail to specify the behavioural and institutional processes which give rise to a particular structure of wage offers'.

Compensating differentials

Within this explanation, the wage or earnings, do not accurately measure the net compensation for each job. Instead, it leaves out non-wage items such as fringe benefits and doesn't account for the variability in working conditions. The consequence is that firms offering undesirable jobs need to improve the working conditions or offer wages above the market rate. However, this forgets the practical fact that wages are very highly positively correlated with the advantages of employment.

Monopsony

This explanation examines why some firms can pay below the market rate without losing their employees to competitors. Two options are that a single employer is sole purchaser of a type of labour within the local labour market. Employees find it more costly to find work elsewhere hence the employer is able to pay less than a competitor's rate. Second, even if employers can't attract the right number of employees, they may operate with vacancies because this represents a lower cost option than raising the wage.

Insider/outsider

This explains the importance of company specific influences on pay in terms of the advantages enjoyed by workers already in employment (insiders) over those on the external labour markets (outsiders). In these models, workers can only be paid above market-clearing levels because the firm itself is operating in imperfectly competitive markets and hence able to earn profits above the norm. Employees are able to use their bargaining power which comes from firm-specific skills. The wage level is thus indeterminate depending largely on the bargaining power of the employer and employee. Some empirical evidence supports this, but it does not explain why employers should pay over the market rate unless coerced by trade unions.

Efficiency wages

This explanation posits a causal relationship between the level of wages and an individual worker's productivity. Firms will maximise profits by paying workers in excess of the market clearing rate. In return, this induces a more productive workforce. The increments in productivity will yield a higher profit. The increased productivity arises via reduced monitoring (or shirking) costs; decreased turnover; and sociological considerations (e.g. morale, loyalty, etc.). All have at their core the proposition, not accepted in orthodox neo-classical analysis, that individuals can vary their effort and, hence, their output.

Source: Adapted from Brown *et al.*, 2003.

The above therefore raises the question that rather than the wage rate being market determined, there are in fact other factors involved including employees and their representatives (trade unions), employers and their representatives (employers associations) and government. Employers may want to vary the wage rate for a number of reasons including, prestige, competition, control, motivation, cost and change management. Yet they may also face constraints such as productive vs. allocative efficiency, discretion offered by product market conditions and discretion offered by production strategy, highlighting that pay is not an isolated device.

In fact, it was argued above that in balancing internal and external market factors management has been able to sustain variations in pay for a number of reasons. More recently, Kessler (2008) adds business strategy as one of the three fundamental principles on which pay systems and structures are founded (the others being external/internal equity as mentioned above). The major problem is that these three principles are often in competition and it is business strategy on which organisations are likely to place the emphasis, rather than equity.

Linking reward with business strategy is synonymous with the growth of HRM, especially its strategic versions, emphasising that reward is an integral part of the HRM cycle (Fombrum *et al.*, 1984). Strategic HRM focusses on the overall direction of the organisation in pursuit of its stated goals and objectives. Increasing the core competencies of the firm, in particular human resources, is one of the key elements in the success of the firm. The idea that people management can be a source of sustained competitive advantage calls for the integration of both HRM and business strategy (Chen and Hsieh, 2006). Schuler and Jackson (1987) also talk about the fact that HRM and the concentration on internal equity would result in lower salaries that would allow employees to become stockholders and have the freedom to choose the mix of rewards which might make up their pay package (Paauwe, 2004).

In linking reward with strategic HRM, two of the main keywords seen as integrally linked with variable pay in the 1980s/1990s were reward management and performance management. Both of these concepts are argued to be a move away from the static salary administration of the post-war period. Both do not necessarily have to include pay for performance as part of the process, yet for most it is seen as an essential reinforcement for the type of behaviours the organisation requires.

Reward management recognises that the motivation to improve must extend to all employees and not just high flyers. Second, they must be flexible and not tied to rigid salary structures and job evaluation schemes. There is both an implicit and explicit assumption that employees are the key to organisational success and that reward management is a means of helping to achieve the individual and organisational behaviour that a company needs if its business goals are to be met (Armstrong, 1996).

Performance management is a form of reward management and akin to what Lawler (1990) calls the 'new pay'. It is 'about the agreement of objectives, knowledge, skill and competence requirements and work development plans' (Armstrong 1996: 260). It mainly emphasises the importance of goal setting and feedback – reviewing performance in relation to agreed objectives. Fundamental is that it is not something handed down by employers, but rather all members of the organisation are regarded as partners. A CIPD (2005) survey highlighted that this approach is still strong with over 80 per cent reporting that the primary objective of their reward systems was to support business goals.

Kessler (2008) argues that recently a range of external and internal labour market pressures have encouraged the review and restructuring of pay around 'total reward' packages. Such packages allow for employer choice around flexible packages of both intrinsic and extrinsic reward as well as aligning external and internal pressures as will be outlined below.

Total reward

Recent developments have made it more important than ever for companies to make sure they have a strategic, holistic and integrated approach to reward (Chen and Hsieh, 2006). In order to distinguish themselves from other organisations in the labour market, it is necessary to offer more than just good salary. It is argued that that a 'one size fits all' approach will not succeed. Instead, each organisation needs a tailor-made system to address its particular needs. Total reward holds out the promise of recruiting and retaining better quality staff, reduced waste from staff turnover, better business performance and enhanced employer reputation. There are many different models, but all include a balance between pay, benefits, work–life balance, individual growth and development, a positive workplace and future opportunities. Provision of total reward demonstrates that the organisation takes into consideration the needs of the employee and is prepared to be flexible in meeting those needs. In return 'the employee is supposed to feel that they have some control over the various options from a range of benefits (Thompson, 2002). Therefore a strategic reward plan involving' total reward' can go beyond cash to include training, job redesign, flexible work, share options, etc. (Chen and Hsieh, 2006).

Therefore, in designing international total reward systems, the role of the HR reward manager becomes one of combining global data to develop appropriate compensation packages for the global workforce, using centralised systems to maintain some control, and linking global financial outcomes with regional costs (Burnett and Van Glinow, 2011). The objectives of the system would have to aim to maximise recruitment and retention of the appropriate staff, develop cost-effective reward policies, develop global reward practices and policies that are fair and consistent, and ensure consistency with business strategy. This is a tall order, but given the emphasis on the pay/performance link, an important area to be fully understood. We therefore turn our attention to understanding pay for performance in greater detail.

 ## Paying for performance: variable pay

Relating pay to performance has generated a tremendous amount of interest over the past three decades, but very little in the way of conclusive evidence. The recent growth of variable pay experienced in the UK is also an international phenomenon (Arrowsmith *et al.*, 2007). The defining feature of variable pay systems (VPS) is an explicit attempt to move away from time- or seniority-based pay to performance-related criteria. There are many different ways of paying for performance and there are also many different labels used for the various schemes: incentive pay, performance-related pay (PRP), variable pay, payment by results (PBR) are all labels commonly used. Although it is often the US that are seen as the leader in the promotion of variable pay, the UK is said to be among the leading European countries in the diffusion of VPS, with PBR long being a feature of the manufacturing sector (Arrowsmith *et al.*, 2007; Drucker, 2000).

Definitions of variable pay systems

Definitions of variable pay are problematic not least because more recently the term has become part of the rhetoric of 'new pay', a complete reward system prescribed for the modern, strategically minded organisation (see Lawler, 1990, 1995). In the UK sense, however, it is fair to say that the term is more often referred to under the umbrella of incentive pay. Incentive pay is described as a system of payment in which a proportion of earnings is related to either the level of worker effort (input) or the level of output (Gilman, 2001).

Given the more 'all encompassing' rationale which will be outlined below, it is probably better to refer to such schemes as VPS. VPS can therefore include systems which have a direct relationship with output such as payment by results. It is, however, also used to cover schemes in which workers may be encouraged to perform with only an indirect relationship with output (e.g. merit pay and performance-related pay). More recently, it is used to describe reward systems in which there is no necessary relationship at all with individual performance, but where workers are entitled to a share in the company's performance and profitability, such as profit-related pay and employee share ownership plans (i.e. financial participation (Gilman, 2001)).

Casey *et al.*, (1992) add a further dimension by distinguishing between those where the incentive is integrated into basic pay, such as PRP, and those where the incentive is clearly discernible from basic pay such as bonuses, profit-related pay and share ownership schemes. More recently, however, some PRP schemes include a non-consolidated bonus that is not included into basic pay. Bonuses can therefore fall into either or all of the three categories, and can either be consolidated into a person's wage or salary, or unconsolidated and paid as 'one-off' payments (Gilman, 2004).

Payment by results

This is a type of payment system sometimes used in a strict sense to indicate a system in which there is a direct relationship between pay and output (e.g. piecework). At other times, the term may be taken to refer to any system in which an element of pay is related to employee performance, and thus could include such items as attendance bonus. Piecework is a payment system in which an agreed sum of money is paid in exchange for a specified unit of work. There are two basic types: money piecework, which attaches a price to each piece of work, and, time piecework, in which a worker is given a fixed time to do a job but is paid the same amount if the job is finished early. The term piecework is sometimes, incorrectly, used more generally as a synonym for payment by results. Systems of payment by results were the most common form of payment for manual workers in British manufacturing. Evidence now points to a shift away from strict output-based systems especially for manual workers (Drucker, 2000).

Performance-related pay

Sometimes referred to as 'merit pay', it is probably worth spending more time explaining this type of VPS as it has undergone more change and been more closely related to the logic of strategic HRM than any of the others. Also, the principles underlying its introduction have been used as a justification for other developments in VPS.

PRP is a method of payment where an individual employee receives an increase in pay based wholly or partly on the regular and systematic assessment of individual performance. The payment of salary increments, bonus and other incentives is determined by a process of systematic performance appraisal. The performance measures may concern inputs or outputs, but generally focus on the achievement of specific individual objectives. In the public sector, governments have used them to make a direct link between a person's contribution to the standards of service provided and their reward. Linking pay to individual performance is seen to contribute to the traditional objectives of pay systems (recruitment, retention, motivation) but also to play a role in organisational change, particularly instilling a more 'entrepreneurial' culture (see Gilman, 2004; Heery, 1998; Marsden and French 1998; Marsden and Richardson, 1994). This objective appears to have influenced the development of such schemes in organisations following privatisation. Many organisations have experienced difficulties in setting performance criteria, assessing performance objectively, and in linking pay to performance, particularly where budget constraints limit the potential size of any reward. Individual performance-related pay systems have also been found to undermine teamworking.

The principle of PRP, or merit pay as it was known, has been well established since at least the late 1940s, in particular occupations and sectors, along with its counterpart job evaluation. There was basically no change in the nature of these schemes until their new lease of popularity in the 1980s (Fowler, 1988). Since then, five basic changes have been noted: There has been a move away from assessments based on personal qualities towards those assessed against working objectives (i.e. rewarding output rather than input); the schemes have been increasingly introduced into the public sector; there has been an extension of these schemes from their traditional area of managerial occupations downwards to all job categories in general; there has been a move away from a general two-part increase which included a cost of living increase and a performance-related element, towards a single increase based solely on performance; and these pay systems, it is claimed, are linked more closely to the overall business objectives of the organisation.

Despite the simplicity of the title 'PRP', it is extremely difficult to say what it is in a simple sentence given its many guises. Useful characterisations are as follows:

> a means of translating and transmitting market based organisational goals into personalised performance criteria whilst at the same time preserving the integrity of a coherent grading structure. *(Kessler and Purcell, 1992)*

> [A means whereby] an individual's increase in pay is determined solely or mainly through his/her appraisal or merit rating. *(Swabe, 1989)*

Storey and Sisson (1993) also differentiate between individual PRP which is measured through output criteria, and merit pay which is judged on behavioural traits. These descriptions, while embodying many of the sentiments involved with PRP, are mainly about different aspects of observed behaviours and are not applicable to all aspects and forms of PRP.

Thus, PRP can be characterised by the linking of an individual's increase in pay to an appraisal of their performance against the use of a set of predetermined criteria based on objectives, behaviours, competences or some combination of the three (Gilman, 2004).

PRP has obvious similarities with PBR schemes, but whereas PBR is measured by fixed output norms, PRP is measured by the attainment of previously set objectives or targets. Through these, effort within PRP is reconstituted to embrace not just levels of output, as is the case with PBR, but also the quality of that output and the level of discretion and initiative exercised by the individual. In emphasising the individual, appraisal becomes both a means of communicating with and to the individuals involved, while reward systems based on contribution to the organisations' objectives for sustainable competitive advantage are highly favoured by employers. Another point is that whereas PBR is mechanistic, PRP involves an amount of subjective speculation of performance.

Ways of determining PRP can also range from progression through set pay bands based on the attainment of certain criteria or performance targets/objectives (this is similar to progression based on seniority, which was common place in the public sector), to variable bonus payments that are utilised to target money to certain high-performing employees. Sometimes more than one type can run at the same time.

Financial participation

This is a term applied to various forms of employee profit-sharing and share ownership schemes which give employees a financial stake in the company for which they work. Under the prompting of the Finance Acts of 1978, 1980 and 1984, employee shareholding schemes have grown in the United Kingdom in recent years. A recent survey showed that just over 20 per cent of public and private companies practised at least some form of employee share ownership, although not necessarily for all their employees. They are subject to a number of limitations and restrictions under the Income Tax Act 2003 (Tew, 2008). Although seen by some as a form of workers' participation and industrial democracy, in most cases the numbers of shares involved are small, providing workers with no real shareholder power, and in some cases may involve the allocation of non-voting shares only.

Employee share ownership plan (ESOP): An idea brought into the UK from the US which provides a way for employees to obtain an equity stake in the company for which they work, that they would not otherwise be able to afford. A trust is established which purchases shares on behalf of employees, using money borrowed from a financial institution. The dividends on the preference shares are used to pay off the loan and the shares are then gradually released to the employees. They are still held in the trust but, if the scheme so allows, the employees can sell them. ESOPs have been used in connection with management and employee buy-outs of companies when new shares are acquired at the buy-out price.

Profit-sharing scheme: This form of financial participation has a long history but has received renewed attention in the past decade because of legislative encouragement and tax advantages. Approved profit-sharing (APS) schemes involve distribution of shares to employees free of charge. The shares are purchased by a trust established by the company and financed from company profits. The shares are allocated to individual employees and held by the trustees on their behalf for a minimum of two years. Since April 2003 such schemes have been largely replaced by employee share incentive plans (Tew, 2008).

Another scheme with tax advantages is **SAYE (save-as-you-earn)**, where an employee enters into a savings contract with the option to purchase shares at the end of the contract period at a price fixed previously. Both types of scheme must be open to all full-time employees who have been with the company for at least five years. In 1980, there were 184 APS and seven SAYE schemes. This had increased by June 1986 to 562 APS and 541 SAYE. There were also some 1,676 approved discretionary schemes (allowing companies to grant share options to selected employees, such as executives), and also non-approved schemes which do not enjoy the tax advantages.

Profit-related pay: This is an element in the total pay package which is related by some formula to the profitability of the company (or a unit thereof). Survey evidence indicates that some 20 per cent of private sector establishments had a cash-based profit-sharing scheme in 1984 and 15 per cent paid value added bonuses.

As with profit sharing, there were tax advantages for employees where the scheme was approved by the Inland Revenue. The intention of a profit-related pay scheme is that part of the employees' pay will move up or down according to the profits made by the company, thus making pay more responsive to company performance. As well as being seen as a way of improving individual performance and motivation through giving employees a direct interest in the success of the business, and as a means of fostering commitment to the company, profit-related pay is argued by its supporters to have employment implications in that labour costs will be automatically reduced when the company runs into difficulties (through the profit-related element), thus minimising the risk of layoff and redundancy. These claimed advantages of profit-related pay have yet to be substantiated by research findings.

Companies which have introduced financial participation generally express relatively long-term objectives such as making employees feel they are part of the company, increasing employee commitment and making employees profit conscious. Conversely, arguments against financial participation are: the double risk it involves for employees in tying their jobs and savings to the success of the same organisation; the recruitment inhibiting effects which may result from existing employees attempting to maximise their proportion of the profits; and the fear that employees, through their representatives rather than as shareholders, may demand a greater say than management is prepared to concede in the strategic decisions which can affect the company's profitability and consequently their pay.

The role of trade unions, employers associations and government in variable pay

Trade unions can feel threatened by the idea of variable pay as they see it as a move away from collective to individual pay arrangements. A survey of trade union policy (Heery and Warhurst, 1994) found that only 8 per cent of unions supported the idea of PRP, 69 per cent opposed it (although only 26 per cent of these were committed to resisting its introduction) and the rest had no policy or were pragmatic about it. Governments' determination to extend PRP into the public sector came despite union opposition to its proposals and a body of research evidence that casts doubt on its suitability and efficacy. According to Gunnigle *et al.* (1998), variable pay serves to increase the individualisation of the employment relationship and reduce the role of trade unions. Additionally, it poses a threat to fair treatment and procedural justice (Heery, 2000). The dominant response has been to attempt to secure collective agreements which regulate its operation (Heery and Warhurst, 1994), although this is not often possible with profit-related, share ownership and bonus schemes (Marginson *et al.*, 2007). The TUC have also supported wider share ownership and partnership.

Employer organisations have continually promoted variable pay schemes as a means of providing individuals with the motivation to improve their performance. PRP schemes are seen as a far more efficient way of controlling the total wage bill while differentiating between employee performance. Because profit-related and employee share schemes usually attract certain tax benefits they are seen as particularly cost-efficient forms of remuneration.

Governments have continuously promoted the idea of 'market forces' and 'individualisation' of the employment relationship, and have been determined to eliminate what they see as rigidities in the working of the labour market (Brown and Walsh, 1991). Pay, according to government sources, ought to be linked only to what companies can afford (as in profit-related pay schemes which have been encouraged through direct tax concessions) as well as to an individual's performance as in PRP. Like its predecessors, the Labour government (1997–2010) embraced the concept of variable pay. For example, PRP was promoted for both private and public sector employees. The Government's White Paper 'Modernising government', set out changes reflecting their reward agenda of linking pay to individual performance. The introduction of PRP for teachers was particularly controversial (Marsden, 2007; Payne, 2000). In principle, paying for measurable performance has become increasingly blurred. It has led many public sector bodies to consider alternative PRP schemes that incorporate team-based rewards and a wider assessment of employees' overall contribution to the business. The Makinson report (2000) noted, in particular, the damaging effects of perceived unfairness in the public sector organisations studied. It noted that although there was widespread acceptance of PRP in principle there was also much disenchantment with it in practice. Marsden (2007) also noted much the same effect with the PRP scheme for teachers.

Governments have at various times explicitly encouraged profit/share schemes through the provision of tax incentives. Also, public consciousness of share ownership was increased dramatically by the privatisation of state enterprises such as water, gas and electricity.

The coalition government elected in 2010 are still emphasising the link of pay and performance with several reviews underway (e.g. teachers and police).

Extent and growth of variable pay

There are no overall detailed figures available in the UK or elsewhere to signify the true extent of variable pay, largely because there is no commonly agreed definition of what it is. The 1990 Workplace Industrial Relations Survey (WIRS) and the 1998 and 2004 Workplace Employee Relations Survey (WERS), however, included data on incentive pay. Although overall comparisons can be made for some aspects, the structure of the questions differed within each survey making meaningful comparisons difficult.

In the 1990 data, 63 per cent of workplaces had at least one type of incentive scheme. By 1998, the figure was 58 per cent. Despite this, the authors (Millward *et al.*, 2000) argue that it would be safer to conclude that there was little overall change over the period. There were, however, changes in the way that incentive pay was used. In 1990, PBR schemes were more commonly used for manual rather than white-collar employees, whereas by 1998 the reverse was true. In 2004, 40 per cent of workplaces had incentive pay schemes: PBR was used in nearly one-quarter (23 per cent), Merit pay in 9 per cent and both in 7 per cent. While the above does not give an accurate picture of the extent over time, the panel survey highlighted an increase from 20 per cent in 1998 to 32 per cent in 2004. Evidence also suggests that larger workplaces and those without recognised unions continued to make greater use of incentive pay (Kersley *et al.*, 2006; Sharp, 2011). IRS (2006) report that 21 per cent of organisations used PBR and 44 per cent used cash bonuses while Geldman (2011) highlighted that three-quarters have bonus schemes. However, companies reported that there were problems with bonus schemes including: disappointment with the size of the bonus, lack of employee understanding and a weak link with performance. Although increasing performance was the main reason for the use of such schemes, the vast majority said that recruitment and retention would be seriously affected if they were withdrawn: raising questions concerning the exact rationale for continuing to use them.

The precise extent of the coverage of PRP is also problematic because official data sources such as the New Earnings Survey only include PRP among the 'catch all' category of 'incentive pay' (Casey *et al.*, 1992). Smaller surveys highlight that the proportion of companies using PRP varies between one-third (IRS, 1991) and one half (Casey *et al.*, 1992; IRS, 1991; WIRS, 1992). While the WERS 2004 survey only found a low presence of PRP for the largest occupational group, IRS (2006) and Sharp (2011) found that it was the most commonly used form of reward strategy with over half of organisations using it for at least some employees. Importantly, these surveys found that although this has been one of the most popular forms of pay system for the last decade, the use of such schemes seems to be on the decline.

Table 6.1 highlights that financial participation schemes in the EU tend to be prominent in France and the UK. In the UK, from the 1980s, both profit-related and share ownership schemes became far more widespread due to encouragement by consecutive Conservative

Table 6.1 Extent of financial participation schemes in the EU (selected countries)

Percentages of workplaces or organisations with profit-sharing or share ownership schemes

Country	Percentage of establishments with 50+ employees with profit sharing in 1996 (EPOC study)	Percentage of establishments with 50+ employees with share ownership in 1996 (EPOC study)	Percentage of organisations with 200+ employees with broad-based profit sharing in 1999 (CRANET study)	Percentage of organisations with 200+ employees with broad-based share ownership in 1999 (CRANET study)
Belgium	n/a	n/a	12	11
France	57	7	84	23
Germany	13	4	18	10
Italy	5	3	8	2
Netherlands	14	4	55	21
Portugal	6	3	17	2
Sweden	20	2	19	12
UK	40	23	30	30

Source: Pendleton and Poutsma, 2004.

governments via generous tax concessions. There was only a slight growth of profit-related schemes during the 1990s primarily in the manufacturing sector, among foreign-owned establishments and UK MNCs. The single most important characteristic of the extent of profit-related pay was the size of the workplace. At its peak in the mid-1990s, profit-related pay covered 4.1 million employees in 14,000 companies (IRS, January 1998). Recent studies find that profit-related pay is prominent in financial services and electricity, gas and water but disagree on its extent (15 per cent, IRS, 2006; 36 per cent, Kersley *et al.*, 2006).

Share ownership schemes declined over the 1990s particularly in the private service sector UK-owned companies while usage among foreign-owned companies increased. According to data from the Inland Revenue (IRS May, 2000): save-as-you-earn schemes were operated by 1,200 companies with 1.75 million participants; approved profit sharing was operated by 900 companies with 1.25 million participants; and company share option plans were operated by 3,700 companies with 400,000 participants. Recent figures (WERS, 2004) highlight that 21 per cent of organisations (19 per cent, IRS, 2006) had at least one share ownership scheme the most common of which was SAYE (13 per cent). Overall, with both share ownership and profit-related pay there had been little change in the number of organisations using them since 1998.

There were also differences in the overall utilisation of incentive schemes depending on sector highlighting its use to be most likely in sales and customer service and least likely in caring, leisure and personal services (Kersley *et al.*, 2006).

The nature of VPS

In the UK, profit-related schemes had their tax advantages phased out between 1996 and 2000, and have therefore declined in importance. Share schemes, however, continue to receive support from both government and the unions.

Most VPS work in a way that means an individual is unlikely to receive an overall decrease in pay. The worst scenario usually is that no increase or bonus would be awarded, although

Table 6.2 Profile of VPS in four countries

	Type of VPS	Coverage	Criteria	Frequency	Quantitative significance (% of earnings)
UKC1	Merit pay	All employees	Individual appraisal around Balanced Scorecard (BSC) – matrix removed 2004	Incorporated into monthly salary	Varies. 2006 pay pot = 4% but 3% dedicated towards market and minima uplifts. Leaves 1% available to managers to distribute according to performance.
	Bonus	Some 20 to 30 schemes covering all employees	Individual sales and BSC	Varies	5–6% for main retail workforce
	Share scheme	All employees	Free shares plus matching	Annually	3% salary (up to max. 3,000 shares)
	Flexible benefit package	All employees	Allowance to purchase benefits or take as cash	Annually	4%
NOC1	PRP – pay interview model	All, but varies who gets what	Competence, ability to co-operate, work performance (results), responsibilities, values	Pay interview annually. Incorporated into monthly salary on permanent basis	On average 1% annually (2005). Varies between individuals from no increase till substantial increases
	FP – profit-sharing scheme	All	No formal criteria, but based on company results. Discretionary decision by CEO/board	Payouts at retirement or if leaving the company	Ca. 3% of total wages allocated in 2005
	Ad hoc bonus for commercial banking unit (one time payments)	Employees in this unit	No criteria. Sum distributed to bank managers, who decide how to distribute	Was paid in 2005 (expected to be some arrangement for 2006 as well)	Limited information (2–3 per cent average?)
	PBR – bonus, used by i.e. business market department + international payments	All in units but only 125 of 7,000 employees	10 factors ranging from reducing loss till carrying out planned training. A total score set the total bonus pot.	Annually	0.5 – 1.0% on average; 5–10% for those in receipt depending on wage level and size of bonus (varies between €2,400 and €3,600)
ESC1	Merit pay (1991)	Discretionary, pay revision for technical staff (75% of total)	Pay band systems and bonus reference (internal and external equity criteria), individual skills appraisal. Discretionary and consolidated, non-pensionable	Incorporated into monthly salary	n.a.

(Continued)

Table 6.2 Profile of VPS in four countries (*Cont.*)

	Type of VPS	Coverage	Criteria	Frequency	Quantitative significance (% of earnings)
	Bonus (1991)	Individual bonus 8,149 employees; team 16,823	Management by results, reference bonus, individual score achievement, team performance appraisal and BSC. Discretionary, non-consolidable and non-pensionable	Annually	Individual: wage bill 8.2%, employee earnings 24.8%; Team: wage bill 5%; employee earnings 10.7%
	Extra bonus	High performance staff (score 150 +)	Reference bonus, results each business unit division, discretionary non-consolidable and non-pensionable	Annually	20–50% increase over ordinary bonus in employee earnings
	Commercial incentives	Those 10% branches in same classification with better results	Allowance to purchase benefits or take as cash, non-consolidable and non-pensionable	Annually	20% increase over ordinary bonus in employee earnings
ATS1	Performance pay (since 1993): savings from pay scheme reforms are redistributed as PP	100% all staff	Job evaluation factor and MBO with 4 criteria: job requirements, agreement on objectives, performance attitude, and exe-cutive functions	Monthly	10% wage bill
	Voluntary balance bonus (since 1993)	100%	Company success	Annually	3.5% wage bill Max. half month's pay
	Incentive system market (since 2000)	68.8% (market employees)	40% is paid as team bonus and 60% as individual bonus; latter discretionary by supervisors	Annually	1.5% of the premiums; 12% wage bill.
	Incentive system back office (since 1990)	31% (administrative employees)	Extraordinary performance, discretionary proposal by supervisors (max. 50% of employees), subject to managing board confirming who/amount	Annually	2% wage bill

Source: Adapted from Arrowsmith *et al.*, 2007.

in the case of share ownership schemes, depreciation is a possibility. The median budget for merit awards during 2011 was 2.7 per cent of the paybill while the median individual award was in the region of 2.2 per cent (Sharp 2011).

With PRP, schemes are usually introduced with unions then attempting to influence schemes in three main ways: to regulate the process of performance appraisal in a bid to ensure that management decision-making involves rules and procedures; to reduce the financial risk to employees covered by such schemes; and secure procedural rights to pursue appeals, have access to information concerning the running of the schemes and jointly review the schemes with management. Schemes and the amounts awarded are rarely the subject of negotiation. The increased importance of variable pay coincides with the decentralisation and decline in the extent of collective bargaining.

There is little or no information concerning the full extent of collective agreements over variable pay. If the extent of collective bargaining was taken as a general indication, by 1998 only 29 per cent of workplaces had their pay determined by collective bargaining.

A recent study (Arrowsmith *et al.*, 2007) highlighted the use of collective bargaining over variable pay systems in the Banking and Machinery & Equipment sectors of Austria, Norway, Spain and the UK. Comparing single employer bargaining (SEB) with multi-employers bargaining (MEB) it was found that variable pay in Spain and the UK were more employer-driven than in Norway. In Austria, there was a difference between the savings banks (sector agreements) and the commercial banks (no agreements). In banking, multiple variable pay schemes were apparent in the majority of companies. Individual performance-related pay is subject to collective regulation in all four countries, but with the exception of Spain, account for only a small proportion of earnings. Rather it was bonuses and profit-related pay that yielded larger quantitative significance and was in all four countries subject to less collective regulation. In Machinery & Equipment variable pay was more employer-driven in the UK than Austria or Norway. Variable pay was rarely accompanied by collective bargaining in the UK whereas in Norway it was at the company level and Austria at the Sector level. Table 6.2 highlights examples of typical VPS within the banking sector of four European countries different examples.

The international study mentioned above found that different types of VPS had differing effects on the individualisation of the employment relationship. Whereas PRP schemes were more collective in nature this was less the case for bonuses, share schemes and profit-related pay. Also, the strategic nature of VPS depended on factors such as the environment, structure and factors. For example, there was a bigger range of VPS in banking than in manufacturing with a higher percentage of earnings related to performance. Different strategies were used in the two sectors. In banking, strategy was emergent with intentions adapting over time to changing realities. In manufacturing, strategy was more deliberate with a premium placed on reward systems that respond to customer requirements brought about by intense competition (Arrowsmith *et al.*, 2007).

Pay for performance: How strategic is it?

Based on simplistic views

Variable pay schemes have attracted increasing attention throughout the past decades. In particular they have been seen to be linked with the concepts of human resource management (HRM), high performance work systems (HPWS) and quality systems such as total quality management (TQM). Like these concepts, the research into VPS has produced indeterminate results. But this has not stopped them from being prescribed by academics and specialists alike as the reward systems to solve the problems of the last three decades.

As well as its traditional use as a means of aiding the recruitment, retention and motivation of staff, VPS are said to hold out the promise of a direct link between effort and reward, and be a means of consolidating moves towards the creation of an internal labour market in line with other HRM/TQM techniques. Supporters even point to the fact that employees themselves have great difficulty in arguing against the logic of such schemes. It is also argued that such schemes are a fairer way of rewarding people as it is only 'fair' that reward should have a direct link with effort.

It is surprising that companies should place so much emphasis on particular pay systems without evidence as to whether they work or not, given that these schemes are rarely introduced independently and are usually argued to be part and parcel of other business goals and objectives to enhance competitiveness.

There have been various studies, mainly emanating from the US, which highlight the positive performance benefits of PRP (e.g. Lazear, 2000). It is interesting to note that whereas these examples are used to promote the use of PRP they actually turn out to be piecework systems rather than PRP or merit pay. The relative merits and pitfalls of piecework were studied intensely in the UK throughout the post-war period (see Brown, 1973) and do not need rehearsing here. The main point is that definition and terminology make it very difficult to have a serious discussion of the relative strengths and weaknesses of any VPS. To do so requires a deeper understanding of the different VPS on an international basis.

In the UK comprehensive studies within public sector organisations (Gilman, 2004; Heery, 1998; Marsden, 2004, 2007; Marsden and French, 1998; Marsden and Richardson, 1994;) tend to describe indeterminate results from PRP schemes in terms of performance but a widespread acceptance that such schemes lead to employee de-motivation. Thus leading some to argue that increased performance, where present, is more the result of work intensification than improved productivity. In Marsden's (2007) latest work he noted that the usual problems of line management bias in rating performance, poor quality appraisal and goal setting, etc., can be improved by involving employees and their representatives in the design of and improvements to such schemes. Belfield and Marsden (2003: 460) also argue that it 'is not so much the choice of pay system that drives organisational performance outcomes but the combination of pay system and monitoring environment'.

A recent international study by the OECD (see *TES*, 2009) of 23 countries concluded that schools around the world should introduce performance-related pay to reward good teaching and raise standards. Union officials argued that after being told by the majority of teachers that they lacked incentives to improve their teaching or be more innovative the report assumes without further evidence that performance-related pay will work. This is despite the fact that over the past decade, research is increasingly indicating that performance-related pay leads to the opposite of the desired outcomes when it is applied to any work involving cognitive rather than repetitive skill (Ariely *et al.*, 2005). Irlenbusch (2009) highlights that such schemes may reduce an employee's natural inclination to complete a task and derive pleasure from doing so. He finds that the provision of incentives can result in a negative impact on overall performance and that companies should be aware that the provision of performance-related pay could result in a net reduction of motivation across a team or organisation.

The problem according to Pink (2011) is that dominant concepts of motivation (based on the human desire to seek reward and avoid punishment) have survived largely unchallenged because they are easy to understand, simple to monitor and straightforward to enforce. But it has long been the case that intrinsic motivation – how creative a person feels – is the strongest and most pervasive driver. The trouble with schemes such as PRP is that they assume that we are all robotic wealth maximisers: 'Intrinsic motivation is of great importance for all economic activities. It is inconceivable that people are motivated solely or even mainly by external incentives' (2011: 28).

Pink (2011) argues that there are seven reasons why traditional carrot and stick approaches do not work:

1 They can extinguish intrinsic motivation.
2 They can diminish performance.

3   They can crush creativity.
4   They crowd out good behaviour.
5   They encourage cheating, shortcuts and unethical behaviour.
6   They become addictive.
7   They foster short-term thinking.

In the modern organisation where knowledge and using people as competitive advantage is key, it is argued that autonomy, mastery and purpose are essential drivers which any strategic reward scheme must incorporate.

This aligns with a recent study by Attwood (2012) which highlights that the top priority for many large organisations for 2012 is to review benefit packages, grading structures and salary benchmarking. The prime motivation is the recruitment and retention of the right people. Organisations are consistently looking at the external/internal match of their reward schemes emphasising the implementation of a reward strategy being a clear priority especially as they experience a lack of consistent approach to reward and no clear association with performance. Despite arguing that they set clear objectives, 75 per cent of organisations do not evaluate their pay for performance schemes. Even where evaluation is carried out it only takes the form of staff feedback. Furthermore, only a quarter of organisations offer internal training to staff concerning their schemes (Sharp 2011).

Discussion

It has been highlighted that reward is in fact an enormously complex issue which has to take account of three fundamental principles in determining systems and structures: internal equity, external equity and business strategy. In doing so it requires tools, such as job evaluation, and interacts with other interested parties, as in the collective determination of reward. Historically, there have been many changes introduced as the actors struggle with a combination of economic, political, social and technological pressures. These factors are intensified further when we include an examination of reward at international level.

Looking at the past 20 years, there is no doubt that variable pay has become much more important. In particular, VPS loom larger and have permeated further and further down the occupational ladder. There are also different types of VPS with many organisations preferring to use them in combinations rather than any one individual type. It was also highlighted that in different sectors and countries schemes take on a variety of forms due to factors such as competitive environment and institutional HRM arrangements. Simultaneously, collective bargaining over pay has declined significantly and coincided with a greater individualisation of the employment relationship. This is because incentives are argued to be most influential where they apply to the individual. Having said this however, over the past few years the negative effects of such schemes as PRP are leading both government and companies to look at ways of incentivising employees.

There is very little evidence of any positive effects for performance or employees especially in the case of PRP schemes. Most academic research shows that such schemes, on the whole, tend to have a demotivational rather than motivational effect. One of the main problems is the difficulty in balancing and maintaining salary structures whilst attempting to provide incentives. VPS do not seem to be meeting their traditional objectives but other objectives have been found:

- To signal a change in organisational culture;
- To bring about a restructuring of the employment relationship;
- To allow selective reward without increase in the pay bill;
- To decentralise collective bargaining;
- To marginalise trade unions;

- To allow closer financial control;
- To balance the lack of promotional opportunities with selective reward for development.

Different schemes may even have different goals. Arrowsmith *et al.*, (2007) found that bonus schemes were used as incentives, PRP was used for cost control and development (although these two are clearly in conflict) and profit-related pay to signal wider business goals and cultures. Some are now beginning to argue that PRP and other VPS are more about control with employers wanting to re-establish more control over the effort bargain. Despite the above, there is no shortage of commentators willing to extol the virtues of variable pay schemes. Companies have consistently chosen an approach of altering schemes in an attempt to rectify problems, without any fundamental changes to the principals involved: total reward presently being the flavour of the month.

So variable pay is presently confusing. While it is easy to discuss in broad terms, in reality the enormous variability and rhetoric surrounding such schemes has produced a state of uncertainty. More recently, companies are being advised to take a much more strategic approach to pay by utilising many different types of variable pay schemes in a way which 'fits' with the strategic intent of the company and its business plan. But as Arrowsmith and Sisson (1999) note, changes in pay arrangements reflect adjustments of management strategy in the light of intense competition, new production arrangements and key changes to the organisational context. All of these factors are likely to be personal to each organisation and lead to 'personal' outcomes concerning variable pay which fits with Kessler's (2008) argument that organisations are more likely to focus on business strategy than internal or external equity.

Strategic success for reward systems relies on a whole range of factors (Marginson *et al.*, 2007). The fact that integration of strategic HRM involves many practices (e.g. appraisal, training, corporate culture, etc.) combined with consideration of contingencies (technology, wider environment, etc.) means that it is difficult for any organisation to balance external and internal labour market factors whilst also offering the packages of VPS,

In offering systems under the label of 'total reward', organisations are clearly attempting to give themselves more flexibility to balance the three fundamental principles. The key question is what effects will this have on performance? The recent evidence from the US casts doubt on the continued use of pay for performance, especially where knowledge and creativity are important.

CASE STUDY 6.1

POLITICAL IMPLICATIONS FOR TOTAL REWARD STRATEGY: A CASE OF KENT COUNTY COUNCIL

M. METAWIE

Kent County Council (KCC) governs the majority of the county of Kent, and comprises twelve District Councils and more than 300 town and Parish Councils. The Council's headquarters are based in Maidstone. The overall population of the KCC area (excluding Medway), as estimated by the Office for National Statistics (ONS) in 2010, is 1.4 million. The largest local authority district is Canterbury with a population of 149,700 people, while the smallest is Dartford with a population of 92,000 people (KCC Research and Intelligence, 2012). KCC employs a total of 45,000 employees, including those working in schools, who account for almost two thirds of KCC's workforce (30,500 employees). KCC is further divided into four main directorates and one executive department. These are the Communities Directorate which has the largest number of KCC's workforce with 4,277 employees; Children, Families and Education (4,179 employees), Adult Services Directorate (3,777 employees), Environment and regeneration directorate (902 employees), and the Chief Executive's Department (1,870 employees). Sixty per cent of KCC's workforce are part-time employees and 80 per cent are female (KCC Reward Manager, 2006). KCC is controlled by the Conservative party (KCC, 2009). The continuance of conservative domination has been a main feature of Kent politics since the 1980s (Atkinson, 2001).

Trajectory of pay determination in KCC: economic and political implications

Prior to the 1980s, similar to the rest of the public sector, pay in KCC was characterised by centralised negotiations, through collective bargaining, at national level between the local authority and trade union representatives (Levinson, 1971). Increments and progressions in salary were linked to seniority and length of service. Since the economic recession of the 1970s and the election of the Thatcher Conservative Government in 1979, the government sought to control the expenditure of the public sector.

In local government in particular, there was increasing financial pressure through curbing expenditure, and in particular rate capping, on local authorities. In an attempt to increase flexibility and extend discretion to local bargaining, KCC was one of the first authorities to opt out of national agreements (Sheldrake, 1988) and replace the traditional incremental progression system by a performance-related pay system.

A nationally determined pay system was seen as inflexible, hindering the Council's ability to respond to the government's expenditure control strategy (Griffiths, 1990) and meet labour market conditions and demands. Employers in the area of Kent were faced with pressures to compete with the London labour market in terms of recruitment and retention, due to their proximity to London (White et al., 2001). KCC, along with a number of authorities in the south-east of England, sought the introduction of local agreements as a means of dealing with labour market pressure (Jackson et al., 1993). Additionally, traditional automatic incremental progression systems were seen as being too remote from the performance culture adopted by KCC (Griffiths, 1990). As a result, in 1990, KCC introduced 'Kent Pay Plus' as the new method of pay determination (Griffiths, 1990).

Kent Pay Plus was characterised by four main features. The first key feature of this system was the move away from local bargaining. Collective bargaining in general, was not seen as a relevant method of pay determination for the Council, as members of unions represented only one-third of the total workforce (KCC Reward Manager, 2006). Yet, the rights of recognised trade unions to negotiate conditions of service were maintained (Griffiths, 1990). The second feature was the introduction of a new flatter grading structure. The third feature of 'Kent Pay Plus' was that the Hay system of job evaluation at KCC was used to provide comparability of jobs at KCC with similar jobs in the region. Finally, there was a move towards a performance-based system and the introduction of PRP.

Joining the Kent Pay Plus system was entirely voluntary for employees (Griffiths, 1990). With regard to PRP, individual performance was based on individual appraisals and assessed against three levels of performance ratings whereby levels one and two resulted in no pay progression (KCC Reward Projects and Development Manager, 2006). According to the KCC Reward Projects and Development Manager (2006), the system was partially budget-driven and was influenced by whether managers did, or did not have, enough money to reward those who they thought deserved the top-level assessment rating. Additionally, there was limited guidance as to how to measure performance, resulting in a lack of clear measurement against which employees were assessed, and, a lack of high-level moderation of the assessment results. For instance, managers who felt their team did well could award them a level 2 increment, but may not have had clear action plans or performance targets against which they could measure the assessment. Decisions regarding pay were perceived by employees as being fairly arbitrary. According to employees who were employed by KCC during that period (1990–5), PRP created inequalities and failed to measure all aspects of the job, particularly for those in lower grades (KCC Reward Manager, 2006). Additionally, the system was seen as remote by those at the top of their grades because it lacked any additional rewards. Overall, PRP was seen to lack the consistency in measurement required of an appraisal system (KCC Reward Projects and Development Manager, 2006). As a result, not all managers engaged with the system, and it was abolished in 1996.

In 1996, KCC reverted back to the traditional, automatic, annual increments, where employee progression was based on length of service without linking to any formal performance review. The pay structure consisted of 12 grades for employees ranging from A to L (L–D included senior level employees and A–D included lower level employees – some jobs in grade D overlapped). The eradication of PRP at KCC coincided with the loss of Conservative party control over the council from 1993 to 1997. During that period the council was under the control of a coalition of Labour and Liberal Democrats. Three years after the Conservatives' regained control over the council, KCC sought further changes to its grading structure as well as pay determination methods. A new pay strategy – total reward strategy, was agreed in 2003 and introduced in 2005.

Total reward strategy: key features and objectives

KCC Total Reward Strategy has three key features. The first is the introduction of single status for former manual workers with the aim of harmonising pay and terms and conditions of employment between manual and non-manual workers. The second feature of the total reward strategy is the implementation of a new approach to job evaluation based on job families and profiles. The KCC Reward Manager explained that the purpose of developing job families is to enable individuals to compare their grades and roles across KCC and to see a bigger and clearer picture of their own progression within their 'family'. Linked to the new job evaluation system was the introduction of three additional grades, with the aim of shortening the length of, and minimising the overlap between, job grades. The number of pay bands changed from 12 grades (A – L) to 15 grades (KS1 – KS15) (see Figure 6.1).

Equating to each of these 15 grades were 15 job profiles. Job analysis and job evaluation defined the relative difference between grades based on four key areas: problem-solving and accountability, skills and knowledge, supervision and management, and competence. The third feature of the total reward strategy is the introduction of a new PRP system – TCP, the most fundamental element of the total reward strategy (KCC Reward Manager, 2006).

The KCC reward strategy had two main sets of objectives: recruitment, retention and recognition, and broad organisational change. Within the objective of broad organisational change, KCC sought structural and cultural change. With regard to structural change, KCC aimed to reduce bureaucracy, through the introduction of a new grading system and pay structure. With regard to cultural change, the total reward strategy was perceived as a tool for promoting a performance-oriented culture through shifting the focus from performance outcomes to performance input (KCC Reward Manager, 2006). TCP intended to achieve this shift through the integration of behavioural competencies into the performance assessment criteria of TCP (KCC TCP Guide, 2005).

The introduction of TCP: a phased approach

The decision to introduce TCP was unanimous among cabinet chief officer group (COG) and cabinet members (KCC Reward Projects and Development Manager, 2010). Following the decision to introduce TCP, an ongoing process of consultation, design and development began in 2001, to formulate the new reward strategy. KCC developed a partnership with recognised trade unions (e.g. Unison, General Municipal Boilermakers and Allied Trades Unions (GMB), Unite (formerly the Transport and General Workers' Union) and Amicus) to consult over the new reward strategy. This partnership approach, although viewed as a formal opportunity through which negotiations between unions

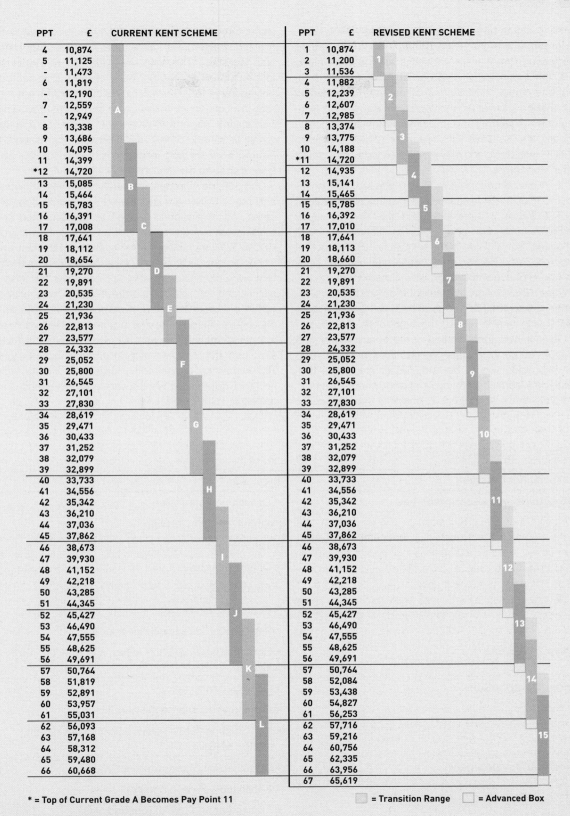

Figure 6.1 KCC revised pay structure

Source: KCC TCP Guide, 2005.

and KCC could take place, did not involve any written agreements (KCC Reward Manager, 2006). During negotiations, there were concerns among the unions about the individualistic nature of TCP, and in turn, about managers' capabilities of assessing individual performance. However, there was no opposition from the unions regarding the implementation of TCP. Additionally, the KCC Reward Manager (2006) explained that TCP was designed in a way which accommodated unions' concerns.

The implementation of TCP was phased. Actual replacement of the automatic incremental progressions with TCP began in April 2005 and was completed by April 2007. In the first phase of implementation, 5,000 employees from grade KS7 to grade KS15, and all supervisory and senior staff, were covered by TCP. Adopting a phased approach was aimed to 'fine tune' the system before final implementation, and to familiarise managers with TCP's operational processes before its extension to the rest of the workforce. To this regard, senior managers voiced some concern over the definition of performance criteria; they believed that more examples should be supplied to clarify the distinction between different levels of performance ratings. Moreover, a few managers expressed their concerns

about the time lag between the mid-year review and the total contribution assessment which they thought was too short. They explained that the nature of work in the Council, as in other parts of the public sector, involved some long-term projects of which the outcomes may require years to be seen and measured. This is particularly important given the absence of a profit target at the end of the year. These concerns were taken into account and feedback obtained on the above issues shaped the final strategy.

In 2006, new grades and pay scales were introduced and pay progression was based on contribution. In the same year, the second phase was implemented by extending the system to all staff on Kent scheme grades KS1 to KS7, including staff in schools. In the last phase of implementation, twenty presentations about the system were carried out involving more than 160 individuals. At the same time, communication was on-going within directorates through personnel and middle-line managers. Along with the communication campaign, appraisal training sessions were also carried out to ensure that the process of performance assessment in TCP would be consistently carried out by appraisers, and that appraisees were aware of the processes integrated in TCP.

Table 6.3 Total contribution assessment categories

Assessment Category	Elements
Objectives and Accountabilities	• Delivery to action plan
	• Effectiveness in job role
	• Targets
	• Quality standards
	• Budgetary control
	• Customer feedback
	• Peer group/360-degree feedback
Ways 2 Success	• Continuously improving in terms of how the job is done
Wider Contribution	• Contribution to team
	• Project work outside the normal job
	• Participation in KCC work activities not directly related to job role
Personal Development	• Achievement of development plan
	• Application of development
	• Attainment and use of required skills
	• Qualifications attained

Source: KCC TCP Guide, 2005.

The design and operation of total contribution pay (TCP)

TCP is based on an assessment of the individual's total contribution against their pre-determined targets and personal development plans. This assessment is conducted over three main stages of TCP: target-setting; performance assessment; and pay evaluation. The target-setting meeting takes place at the beginning of the year between February and April. During the meeting, employees and their managers should jointly identify and agree four key elements against which an individual's total contribution is assessed. These are: objectives and accountabilities; ways to success; wider contribution; and, personal development. The Reward Manager (2006) explained that 'performance targets within the categories of objectives and accountabilities, and personal development should be: Specific, Measurable, Achievable, Realistic, and Timed (SMART)'.

The second stage of TCP which is performance assessment involves on-going reviews of staff performance and development, with formal, twice-yearly reviews, supported by planned, regular, one-to-one meetings between managers and their subordinates throughout the year. The formal, twice-yearly reviews consist of a mid-year review and an end of year formal appraisal. Managers and their employees should agree

a date, at least two weeks prior to the mid-year review or end of year appraisal. The mid-year review takes place between July and September and should offer the opportunity for staff to receive feedback on their performance, and make improvements, if and where needed. However, it is not until the appraisal, carried out between December and January, that a formal discussion of progress against the personal action plan and personal development plan takes place.

During the appraisal, managers consider each assessment category within the context of total contribution. Although individual's performances within different grades should be assessed against the same performance criteria, including all of the above four performance indicators, the Reward Manager (2006) expected the focus to be on accountabilities for lower pay bands. He explained that the lower the grades, the more complicated it was to incorporate the council's overall business plan into individual's objectives because of the size and nature of the council. In this regard, he further argued (2006) that managers were expected to use their discretion to agree a sensible balance of the assessment categories with each of their employees. After the completion of the performance assessment, managers prepare and send an appraisal form containing a TCP rating recommendation, to a 'grandparent' to be signed off.

If on a full pay point

Contribution assessment	Position on incremental pay band		
	2 or more increments from the top	1 increment from the top	Top
Exceptional	2	1 + A	A
Excellent	1½	1 + ½A	½A
Good	1	1	0
Incomplete	½	½	0
Poor	0	0	0

If on a full pay point

Contribution assessment	Position on incremental pay band		
	2½ or more increments from top of pay band	1½ increments from top of pay band	½ increment from top of pay band
Exceptional	2	1½ + ½A	½ + A
Excellent	1½	1½	½ + ½A
Good	1	1	½
Incomplete	½	½	0
Poor	0	0	0

Like the previous Kent Scheme, TCP utilises the same overall pay budget, but distributes it differently to recognise individual's contributions. For additional flexibility, TCP enables progress on a scale of half increments up to a maximum of two increments each year. In addition, individuals who are at the top of their grades can receive up to one additional pay point as a one off award depending on their performance. TCP, hence, introduced five levels of performance rating using half increments to provide shades of contribution. The ratings hence are as follows:

A good rating can be the overall result of a combination of ratings for each category. However, an excellent rating should be the result of the combination of excellent rating in all criteria, or with the combination of exceptional rating. Similarly, an exceptional rating should be the result of the combination of exceptional performance rating in all assessment categories.

There are also cash and non-cash awards. Cash awards can be also used throughout the year to reward specific actions. These can also be considered as part of rewarding Total Contribution but managers should ensure that there is no double counting of an individual's contribution and should note any recognition of payments given earlier in the year. Managers can award individuals for a good piece of work with £500 depending on how instant that reward should be and its impact on employees' motivation. Awards higher than £500 have to be signed off by the grandparent. Non-cash awards include, for example, buying a bunch of flowers, or a box of chocolates.

After the manager's completion of their direct report's assessment, the documents are sent to their grandparent for review. This process is repeated up the reporting line to the top of the directorate. At this point, results between directorates are also compared together with an equalities assessment. This is a moderation process that is used to assess the distribution of the manager's assessment and compliance against quality standards. Ultimately, directorates need to collate results to assess the distribution of the assessment scores on a wider basis and implications for budget expenditure. To show management good faith, TCP provides the opportunity for individuals who disagree with the outcomes of their assessment to appeal against the assessment result to their grandparent through the appeal process.

Finally, the total reward package offers flexible benefits to all staff from buying and selling leave, health care, lifestyle screening, salary sacrificing to an employee discount rewards and benefits scheme. (Current offers include deals on finance, cars, gifts, days out, clothing, mobile phones, health & beauty, home & garden, holidays, entertainment, sport and fitness.) Employees can use those benefits and calculate their effects on their salaries using the online interactive reward statements. KCC expects the new reward strategy and the change in culture to grant employees the right to ask for their benefits.

Discussion questions

1 Discuss the implications of the external environment on pay determination in KCC.
  Here students can discuss the economic and political pressure placed on KCC. Students should also mention the role of collective bargaining and unions in the acceptance/rejection of PRP plans.
2 Considering the demographic profile of KCC's workforce, what do you think the impact of the system will be on internal alignment and equity?
  Students should examine how part-time workers and women can be disadvantaged by the system
3 Assess the alignment of TCP with the Council's strategy and culture.
  Students should highlight the difference between private and public sector culture. Did KCC adopt a best practice or best fit approach? How can the long term projects be measured? Wider contribution etc…
4 Compare KCC's old reward system Kent Pay Plus with the new Total Reward Strategy. How effective/ successful do you think the new system is?

There are four main differences: phased implementation; total reward package (raising awareness of employees benefits); input performance measures in TCP; and, moderation process. However, students should also note the possible negative implications of those four features of the new system. For example, how does conducting a statistical moderation affect performance assessment results, fairness? How can input measures be SMART? Etc….

CASE STUDY 6.2
DESIGNING REWARD SYSTEMS

MARK W. GILMAN

Despite there being many different reasons for the introduction of pay for performance essentially, for employers, it is about raising productivity. Yet companies use not only pay, but a diverse range of methods to do so, despite the fact that recent research argues that they are very rarely linked in a way which might be described as a 'productivity enhancing strategy'. This raises some interesting questions for the HR manager concerning which reward system is going to be more appropriate for the organisation and its employees, what are its components and how does it fit with other elements of the productivity increasing measures to ensure that one compliments the other.

In this chapter we have highlighted not only the differing combinations of rewards available but also some of the differing internal and external pressures faced when deciding how to pay employees. Despite this, it is still common for employers to concentrate on performance-related pay schemes as their major form of reward. While a number of employers say that they have had a positive experience of tying pay to performance, there are a number of pitfalls including encouraging different behaviours to those it was supposed to encourage. Below are a number of examples of recent schemes introduced by companies from a range of different sectors to meet a range of different priorities. The first, reintroducing an across the board increase, had a concern for overall pay equality; the second, despite being in the same industry, was moving in the opposite direction with a concentration on pay for performance; the third, had to deal with employee market power; the fourth with a lack of flexibility, the fifth with consistency across European operations and the final one not wanting to pay employees extra for what they should already be doing. In doing so companies were utilising similar schemes in different ways, attempting to balance internal and external factors and the requirements of the differing stakeholders.

Yorkshire Water implemented a new pay and performance management system in 1998, the scheme was considered ahead of its time and even credited with helping to turn the business round. It featured individual performance-related pay that offered employees the chance of consolidated merit awards, and formed the basis of a series of two-year pay deals.

However, unions representing the company's 2,200 skilled, technical and professional staff were unhappy with the individual performance element of the system. They were particularly concerned that an employee whose performance was poor in one year – leading to a zero pay increase – suffered not just in that year but for the remainder of their career and into retirement. Their calculations showed that a 40-year-old employee, who missed out on a pay rise in that one year, while colleagues got a 3 per cent rise, would lose between £30,000 and £40,000 in pay and pension.

As a result of this and other concerns, Yorkshire Water and its recognised unions have now negotiated a new agreement which came into effect in 2005. It will include an inflation-linked increase for all employees until 2010, and non-consolidated individual merit bonuses. These non-consolidated bonuses are paid quarterly, and their value is known in advance. For 2005/06, for example, each quarterly bonus is worth £250 to an 'over-achiever' and £150 to an 'achiever'. A system of consolidated bonuses is also available to those who consistently over-achieve, along with consolidated 'progression' increases. The move to the new scheme has been accepted by the unions, which say that their members are happier with the new approach.

Severn Trent Water operates 3,000 sites and employs around 5,000 staff. Frontline employees fall into two groups including head office staff and contact centre employees and process and maintenance workers. Reward practices were considered out of date, with little provision for the desired flexibility or link to performance. Performance-related pay had been attempted for some of these groups in the past but had proved unsuccessful. The HR department had to devise an alternative model that provided clear performance-related progression for staff but at the same time retained a banded pay framework.

The company employed the Hay Group to provide consultancy services, enabling them to gain valuable insights into other reward practices and options, but decided that they wanted to create their own pay model. In its first two years up to 2004 the scheme involved an across-the-board pay increase, as it had done previously, and a performance-related increase. It was made clear that the basic pay increase would not be an entitlement and was not guaranteed – employees still had to meet the specified performance criteria.

From 2006 a new framework was negotiated linking pay to company profit targets and improvements in safety performance and attendance levels. A published formula shows how the amount of money available for next year's pay increase can be enhanced by outperforming in all three areas.

In 2008, HR managers at **Yahoo Europe** were given the challenge of dampening down employee pay expectations. The company focused on rewarding only its best performers so that there were no expectations of linking pay to inflation or to what the employees themselves thought they were worth. The problem for the company was one in which global economic conditions are leading to recession but employees are well aware of their own value and hence perceive themselves to have a degree of market power to demand higher pay.

The company has introduced 'forced rankings', where managers have to identify who their best and worst performers are. The company have commented that a significant proportion of employees will get zero in this years pay round while performance will be rewarded more than normal. The company are hoping to get employees and managers to take accountability for their own performance and differentiate between strong and weak performance.

In 2002, insurance firm, **DAS Legal Expenses** decided on an overhaul of their pay scheme after line managers complained that the scheme offered little flexibility. The new scheme is based on an appraisal system built around four core values – excellence, respect, improvement and cooperation – which, when broken down to individual targets, provides managers with both structure and a degree of flexibility.

The scheme operates by scoring employees on a quarterly basis from 0 to 14 for each aspect of their performance, and weighting the scores according to the perceived importance of each aspect to the department in which they work. Results are then compiled over the course of a full year ahead of the next pay review date. Although the merit element of pay rises can then be determined according to appraisal ratings, the system also includes room for collective bargaining with the Amicus trade union over the pay rise sum to be allocated to each grading.

The scheme is generally judged to be a success because it provides clarity to employees about company goals and their contribution to achieving them, and because it gives senior managers regular performance metrics that rapidly show up problems.

At business travel management consultancy **Carlson Wagonlit**, merit pay is linked to a programme of performance reviews that take place at least once every year for each employee. A similar system operates for managers, who receive a bonus based on company and individual performance.

An intriguing aspect of the Carlson Wagonlit scheme is that the key competencies were developed by employees in the UK, rather than by consultants or the HR department, and have since been adopted for use throughout the company's European operations – although union resistance is likely to mean that these are not used to determine pay outside the UK.

Sterilisation products manufacturer **Isotron**, reviewed its reward systems after doubling its turnover and employee numbers in a takeover two years ago. Although it decided that performance-related pay was not right for it, the company does now have a performance-related bonus scheme. The company considered that rewarding managers with additional increases to their salary for jobs they were already paid to do was undesirable. Instead, they wanted to reward for increased responsibilities only.

There had been a prior subjectively allocated performance bonus, but the new bonus is decided via a performance review based on key values and reviewed by a senior manager. The company say that the scheme has involved a considerable culture shift in how pay and performance is viewed.

Source: Adapted from Attwood, 2005; IRS, 2004; *Personnel Today*, 2008.

Questions

1 Are the above companies utilising the appropriate reward system? Should they be using other rewards as part of their overall package? What would you advise for these companies?

2 Take an example of a company that you know and design a reward system explaining the reasons for your design and ensuring that it incorporates the company's culture, strategy, employees, etc. Would you use the same system for all employees within the company?

Bibliography

Abowd, J., Kramarz, F. and Margolis, D. (1999) 'High wage workers and high wage firms', *Ecomometrica,* Vol.67, No.2, 251–333.

Ariely, D., Gneezy, U., Lowenstein, G. and Mazar, N. (2005) 'Large stakes and big mistakes', Federal Reserve Bank of Boston Working Paper No.05–11, 23 July.

Armstrong, M. (1996) *Employee Reward*, London: Institute of Personnel and Development.

Arrowsmith, J. and Sisson, K. (1999) 'Pay and working time: towards organization-based Systems', *British Journal of Industrial Relations*, Vol.37, 51–75.

Arrowsmith, J., Nicholaisen, H., Bechter, B. and Nonell, R. (2007) 'The management of variable pay in banking: forms and rationale in four European countries'. Paper presented at the 8th European Congress of the International Industrial Relations Association, September, Manchester UK.

Atkinson, B. (2001). 'Politics', in Yates, N. (ed) *Kent in the Twentieth Century,* Woodbridge: The Boydell Press and Kent County Council.

Attwood, S. (2005) 'Performing flexible reward at Severn Trent Water', *IRS Employment Review*, No.834, October.

Attwood, S. (2012) 'Reward priorities in 2012: The XpertHR survey', *IRS Employment Review*, February.

Baron, J.N. and Kreps, D.M. (1999) *Strategic Human Resources: Frameworks for General Managers*, New York: Wiley & Sons.

Belfield, R. and Marsden, D.W. (2003) 'Performance pay, monitoring environments, and establishment performance', *International Journal of Manpower*, Vol.24, No.4, 452–71.

Blanchflower, D., Oswald, A. and Garrett, M. (1990), 'Insider power in wage determination', *Economica*, Vol.57, 143–70.

Brown, W.E. (1973) *Piecework Bargaining*, London: Heinemann.

Brown, W. and Walsh, J. (1991) 'Pay determination in Britain in the 1980s: the anatomy of decentralization', *Oxford Review Of Economic Policy*, Vol.7, No.1, 44–59.

Brown, W., Marginson, P. and Walsh, J. (2003) 'The management of pay as the influence of collective bargaining diminishes', pp.189–213, in Edwards, P.K. (ed.) *Industrial Relation's: Theory and Practice* (2nd edn) Oxford: Blackwell.

Burnett, M. and Von Glinow, M.A. (2011) 'Total rewards in the international context', in Harzing, A. and Pinnington, A.H. (eds) (2011) *International Human Resource Management*, (3rd edn), London: Sage.

Casey, B., Lakey, J. and White, M. (1992) *Payment Systems: A Look at Current Practice*. Employment Department Research Series No.5, London: Policy Studies Institute.

Chen, H.-M. and Hsieh, Y.-H.(2006) 'Key trends of the total reward system in the 21st century', *Compensation and Benefits Review*, Vol.38, 64–70.

Childs, M. (2004) *Managing Reward: Job Evaluation and Grading. One Stop Guide*. xperthr.co.uk.

CIPD (2005) *How to Stand Out From the Crowd*. Summary of Thompson, P. (2002) *Total Reward: Executive Briefing*. London: CIPD.

Dickens, L. and Hall, M. (2003) 'Labour law and industrial relations: a new settlement', pp.124–56, in Edwards P.K. (ed.) *Industrial Relations: Theory and Practice* (2nd edn), Oxford: Blackwell.

Doeringer, P.B. and Piore, M.J. (1971) *Internal Labor Markets and Manpower Analysis*, Lexington, MA.

Dowling, P.J., Festing, M. and Engle, A.D. (2008) *International Human Resource Management* (5th edn) London: Thomson Learning.

Drucker, J. (2000) 'Wage systems', pp.106–25, in Drucker, J. and White, G. (eds) *Reward Management*, London: Routledge.

Egan, J. (2004) 'Putting job evaluation to work: tips from the front line', *IRS Employment Review*, No.792.

Flanders, A. (1964) *The Fawley Productivity Agreements*. London: Faber & Faber.

Fowler, A. (1988) 'New directions in performance pay', *Personnel Management*, November, Vol.20, No.11.

Fombrum, C., Tichy, N.M. and Devanna, M. (eds) (1984) *Strategic Human Resource Management*, New York: John Wiley.

Geldman, A. (2011) 'Bonus schemes 2011: providing an incentive', *IRS Employment Review*, December.

Gilman, M. (2001) *Variable Pay: The Case of the UK*, Dublin: European Industrial Relations Observatory.

Gilman, M.W. (2004) *The Characteristics of Performance Related Pay*. Canterbury Business School working papers, No.59, March.

Gilman, M., Edwards, P., Ram, M. and Arrowsmith, J. (2002) 'Pay determination in small firms in the UK', *Industrial Relations Journal*, Vol.33, 52–67.

Griffiths, W. (1990) 'Kent County Council: a case of local pay determination'. *Human Resource Management Journal*, Vol.1, No.1, 100–7.

Gunnigle, P., Turner, T. and D'Art, D. (1998) 'Counterposing collectivism: performance related pay and industrial relations in greenfield sites', *British Journal of Industrial Relations*, Vol.36, 567–78.

Heery, E. (1998) 'A return to contract? Performance related pay in a public service', *Work Employment and Society,* Vol.12, No.1, 73–95.

Heery, E. (2000) 'Trade unions and the management of reward', pp. 54–83, in Drucker, J. and White, G. (eds) *Reward Management*, London: Routledge.

Heery, E. and Warhurst, J. (1994) *Performance Related Pay and Trade Unions: Impact and Response*, Kingston University, Occasional Paper Series, August.

Hyman, R. (2003) 'The historical evolution of British industrial relations', pp. 37–57, in Edwards, P.K. (ed.) *Industrial Relations: Theory and Practice* (2nd edn), Oxford: Blackwell.

Irlenbusch, B. (2009) 'When performance related pay backfires', *LSE,* June. Available at www2.lse.ac.uk/news And media/news/archives/2009/performance pay.aspx

IRS (1991) *Pay and Benefits Bulletin*, No.587, September.

IRS (1998) 'Barclays settles pay dispute', *Pay and Benefits Bulletin*, No.444, March.

IRS (1999) 'The end of the world is nigh: planning for the post-PRP age', *Pay and Benefits Bulletin*, No.464, January.

IRS (1999) 'Pay report', *Pay and Benefits Bulletin,* No.472, May.

IRS (1999) 'Pay prospects survey', *Pay and Benefits Bulletin,* No.483, November.

IRS (2000) 'Assessing the value of share ownership', *Pay and Benefits Bulletin*, No.496, May.

IRS (2004) 'Making merit work: one size doesn't fit all', *IRS Employment Review*, No.813.

IRS (2006) 'Pay prospects survey', *Pay and Benefits Bulletin,* No.852, November.

IRS (2007) 'Job evaluation is thriving, survey finds', *Employment Review*, No.667.

IRS (2007) 'Financial sector pay', *Employment Review*, No.668, August.

Jackson, M., Leopold, J. and Tuck, K. (1993) *The Decentralization of Collective Bargaining*, Macmillan: London.

Kakabadse, N.K., Kakabadse, A. and Kouzmin, A. (2005) 'Directors' Remuneration: the need for a geo-political perspective', *Personnel Review*, Vol.33, No.5, 561–2.

KCC Kent County Council (2009). *How the Council Works*. Available at http://www.kent.gov .uk/your_council/how_the_council_works.aspx [accessed 7 November 2009].

KCC Research and Intelligence Unit, (2012) Kent County Council: Facts and Figures, Available at http://www.kent.gov.uk/your_council/kent_facts_and_figures.aspx [accessed 2 February 2012].

KCC Reward Manager (2006) [Interview] Kent County Council, County Hall.

KCC Reward Project and Development Manager (2006) [Interview] Kent County Council, County Hall.

KCC (2005) *Total Contribution Pay Guide*, Kent County Council.

Kersley, B., Alpin, C., Forth, J., Bryson, A., Bewley, H., Dix, G. and Oxenbridge, S. (2006) *Inside the Workplace: Findings from the 2004 Workplace Employment Relations Survey,* Abingdon: Routledge.

Kessler, I. (2008) 'Reward choices: strategy and equity', pp.159–76, in Storey, J. (ed.) *Human Resource Management: A Critical Text* (3rd edn), London: Thomson Learning.

Kessler, I. and Purcell, J. (1992) 'Performance related pay objectives and application', *Human Resource Management Journal*, Vol.2, No.3,16–33.

Lawler, E.E. (1990) *Strategic Pay: Aligning Organizational Strategies and Pay Systems*, San Francisco, CA/Oxford: Jossey-Bass.

Lawler, E. (1995) 'The new pay: a strategic approach', *Compensation & Benefits Review*, July/August, Vol.27, No.4, 14–20.

Lazear, E.P. (2000) 'Performance pay and productivity' *American Economic Review*, Vol.90, 1346–61.

Levinson, H. (1971). *Collective bargaining by British local authority employees*. University of Michigan-Wayne State University: Institute of Labour and Industrial Relations.

Makinson, J. (Chair) (2000) *Incentives For Change: Rewarding Performance in National Government Networks*, London: Public Services Productivity Panel, HM Treasury.

Marginson, P., Arrowsmith, J. and Gray, M. (2007) 'Undermining or reframing collective bargaining? Variable pay in two sectors compared', Pay and Reward Conference (PARC), Manchester.

Marsden, D.W. (2004) 'The role of performance related pay in renegotiating the "effort bargain": the case of the British public service', *Industrial and Labor Relations Review,* Vol.57, No.3, April, 350–70.

Marsden, D.W. (2007) 'Individual employee voice: renegotiation and performance management in public services', *International Journal of Human Resource Management*, Vol.18, No.7, July,1263–78.

Marsden, D.W. and French, S. (1998) 'What a performance: performance related pay in the public services, Centre for Economic Performance Special Report', London: London School of Economics. Available at: www.cep.lse.ac.uk.

Marsden, D.W. and Richardson, R. (1994) 'Performing for pay? The effects of "merit pay" on motivation in a public service', *British Journal of Industrial Relations*, Vol.32, No.2, June, 243–62.

Marshall, A. (1920) *Principles of Economics: An Introductory Volume* (8th edn), London: Macmillan.

Millward, N., Bryson, A. and Forth, J. (2000) *All Change at Work*, London: Routledge.

Nolan, P. and Slater, G. (2003) 'The labour market: history, structure & prospects', pp. 58–80, in Edwards, P.K. (ed.) *Industrial Relations*: *Theory and Practice* (2nd edn). Oxford: Blackwell.

Paauwe, J. (2004) *HRM and Performance: Achieving Long Term Viability*, New York: Oxford University Press.

Payne, J. (2000) 'School teachers' review body gives green light to performance-related pay', EIRO online, UK0011100F.

Pendleton, A. and Poutsma, E. (2004) *Financial Participation: The Role of Governments and Social Partners*, Dublin: European Foundation for the Improvement of Living and Working Conditions.

Perkins, S.J. and White, G. (2008*) Employee Reward: Alternatives, Consequences and Contexts*, London: CIPD.

Perlmutter, H. (1969) 'The tortuous evolution of the multinational corporation', *Columbia Journal of World Business*, January–February, 9–18.

Personnel Today (2008) 'Yahoo staff face performance related pay', 12 February. Available at www.personneltoday.com/Articles/12/02/2008/44326/performance-related-pay-imposed-at-yahoo.htm.

Pink D.H. (2011) *Drive: The Surprising Truth about what Motivates Us,* Edinburgh: Canongate.

Schuler, R.S. and Jackson, S.E. (1987) 'Linking competitive strategies with human resource management practices', *Academy of Management Executive*, Vol.1, 209–13.

Sharp, R. (2011) 'Performance related pay: the XpertHR survey 2011', *IRS Employment Review*, September.

Sheldrake, J. (1988) 'The changing pattern of collective bargaining in local government', in Saran, R. and Sheldrake, J. (eds) *Public Sector Bargaining in the 1980s*, pp. 59–63, Aldershot, UK: Avebury

Shields, J. (2012) 'Reward management', in Kramer, R. and Syed, J. (eds) *Human Resource Management in a Global Context*, Basingstoke: Palgrave Macmillan.

Smith, A. (1986) *The Wealth of Nations*, Books 1–3. Harmondsworth: Penguin.

Storey, J. and Sisson, K. (1993) *Managing Human Resources and Industrial Relations,* Milton Keynes: Open University Press

Swabe, A.I.R. (1989) 'Performance related pay: a case study', *Employee Relations*, Vol.11, No.2, 17–23.

TES (2009) 'Performance-related pay would raise standards, international study claims', *TES magazine*, 19 June.

Tew, P. (2008) *Employment Law*, IRS.

Thompson, P. (2002) *Total Reward*, Executive briefing. London: CIPD.

2006. The determination of pay and other terms and conditions. In (eds)

Vernon, G. (2006) 'International pay and reward', in Edwards, T. and Rees, C. (eds) *International Human Resource Management: Globalization, National Systems and Multinational Companies*, Harlow: Pearson Education.

Vernon, G. (2011) 'International and comparative pay and reward', pp. 206–28, in Edwards, T. and Rees, C. (eds) *International Human Resource Management: Globalization, National Systems and Multinational Companies* (2nd edn), Harlow: Pearson Education.

Walsh, J. (1992) 'Internalization v decentralization an analysis of recent developments in pay'. Discussion paper, Leeds University School of Business and Economic Studies.

Walton, R.E. and McKersie, R.B. (1965) *A Behavioural Theory of Labor Negotiations*, New York: McGraw Hill.

White, G., Edmunds, M. and Druker, J., (2001) *Work and Employment Relations in Kent, Findings from the University of Greenwich/Acas Kent Employees Relations Survey.*

WERS 2004 – Workplace Employment Relations data set. Available at www.wers 2004.info/index.php.

WIRS, 1992 – Workplace Industrial Relations data set. Available at www.wers2004.info/index.php.

CHAPTER 7
PERFORMANCE APPRAISAL

Tom Redman

Introduction

The practice of performance appraisal has undergone many major changes over the past two decades. In the main, developments have been driven by large-scale organisational change (see Chapter 1) rather than theoretical advances in the study of performance appraisal. Particularly prominent here are the advent of downsizing, decentralisation and delayering, flexibilisation of the workforce, the move to team-working, wave after wave of culture change programmes and new managerial initiatives such as total quality management (TQM), business process re-engineering (BPR), competency, knowledge management and, in particular in the UK, Investors in People. The Workplace Employee Relations Survey (WERS) data reports that organisations that are recognised as an Investor in People were significantly more likely to have a performance appraisal scheme in use (Cully *et al.,* 1999; Kersley *et al.,* 2006). Changes in payment systems have also fuelled the growth and development of performance appraisal. Developments in integrated reward systems, harmonisation and the increased use of merit- and performance-based pay have been strongly associated with the growth of performance appraisal.

Two main implications for performance appraisal practice arise from the new organisational context. First, it would be clearly inappropriate to expect those appraisal schemes operating ten years or so ago to be effective in many organisations today (see Case Study 7.1 at the end of this chapter). Second, rather than new developments heralding the end of performance appraisal or diminishing its importance, they appear to have enhanced its contribution to helping achieve organisational objectives and have stimulated considerable experimentation and innovation in its practice. Performance appraisal, as we discuss below, has in fact become more widespread. It has grown to include previously untouched organisations and occupational groups. In particular, performance appraisal has moved down the organisational hierarchy to encompass manual, secretarial and administrative staff and part-time staff and from the private to the public sector. New forms of appraisal have also emerged. We thus now have competency-based appraisal systems, staff appraisal of managers, team-based appraisal, customer appraisals and '360°' systems. Old systems of performance appraisal have also been dusted down and have re-emerged in new forms (see Box 7.1).

This chapter's main aim is to critically review some of the key developments in the practice of performance appraisal. First, a brief history of performance appraisal is presented and current practice examined by considering how widespread it is, what it is used for, and its role as a managerial control tool within broader performance management systems. Second, we review some of the major innovations in the practice of performance appraisal. Third, some of the problems of performance appraisal in practice are considered; in particular, here we examine the compatibility of performance appraisal with TQM, continuous improvement and customer service initiatives. Finally, in light of the growing criticisms, we conclude by considering whether performance appraisal has a future in HRM practice.

Box 7.1 HRM in practice — Performance appraisal in hard times: ranking and yanking

A growing number of organisations are reported as having adopted a performance appraisal system in which best-to-worst ranking methods are used to identify poor performers. Such appraisal systems rank employees along a normal distribution curve in which the top 10 per cent typically receive an A grade or equivalent, the middle 80 per cent earn a B, and the bottom 10 per cent earn a C and dismissal if they do not improve.

Such systems gained popularity in the 1990s, and about a third of companies now use them in the US, up from 13 per cent in 1997, according to *Time* magazine (Fonda, 2003). The rationale for such performance systems is to punish the bottom as well as rewarding the top employees. The poor performers thus identified are first given help and a period of time to improve. If they fail to rise in the ranking, they must leave. The exit may be 'encouraged' with a redundancy package, but if the poor performer refuses to leave voluntarily, they face the possibility of termination without compensation. This strategy has become known as the 'rank and yank' system after the nickname given to the scheme by former Enron employees where it appears to have first emerged.

An example of the rank and yank appraisal is provided by Sun Microsystems. The company ranks its 43,000 employees into three groups. The top 20 per cent are rated as 'superior', the next 70 per cent as 'standard'. At the bottom is a 10 per cent band of 'under-performers'. The under-performers are told that they must improve and are provided with one-on-one coaches. The ultimate fate of these employees is clear from the CEO's view that these under-performers must be 'loved to death'. Informal variants of rank and yank appraisal systems seem to have emerged in some UK university departments in the run-up to the 2008 Research Assessment Exercise (RAE). The RAE ranks a department's research from subnational to world-class levels (0 to 4*). In some mock assessment exercises university managers have ranked the research output and esteem of employees on this grading system, with 4* performers receiving 'retention packages' while those rated 1* and 0 rated have been made to feel, in the words of one dean, 'very unloved and uncomfortable'.

The advocates of rank and yank believe that forced rankings make managers and supervisors take the unpleasant but tough decisions that otherwise they would seek to avoid as being too fraught with conflict. Some organisations see the forced ranking approach as a way to create a continuously improving workforce. The view is that an annual culling system produces a 'hotbed of over-achievers' who increase the overall calibre of an organisation. However, despite its obvious Darwinian managerial appeal, there are many problems with the system. First, someone must always fall into the lower or under-performing category, even if everyone has performed at a very high level. It is also possible that those rated as 'poor performers' in highly productive departments may contribute more to the overall progress of the organisation than those rated as 'good performers' in other low-performing departments. Forced ranking thus does little for teamwork and can encourage high levels of in-fighting and dysfunctional internal competition as employees seek to protect their own position at the expense of their co-workers. The legality of such dismissals in many countries must be open to question and some ranking and yanking systems have been abandoned in the US following legal challenge. It must also be questioned whether the level of churn induced by such a system with an annual culling is good for the stable employee networks required to produce innovation and creativity, and whether it justifies the increased administrative costs associated with replacement recruitment and training. However, it is not clear that 'yanked' employees have been always replaced and some critics have suggested that the schemes are thinly disguised smokescreens for downsizing or to get rid of older workers who often populate the lower rankings. Thus the US has also seen forced ranking systems subject to a rising number of age discrimination lawsuits.

Development of performance appraisal

Informal systems of performance appraisal have been around as long as people have worked together; it is a universal human tendency to make evaluations of our colleagues at work. Formal performance appraisals have a shorter but still considerable history. Grint (1993) traces it back to a third-century Chinese practice. In the UK, Randell (1989) identifies its first use via the 'silent monitor' in Robert Owen's textile mills. Here a multicoloured block of wood was hung over the employee's workspace with the front colour indicating the foreman's assessment of the previous day's conduct, from white for good through to black for bad. Owen also recorded a yearly assessment of employees in a 'book of character'.

Since these early developments, performance appraisal has become a staple element of HRM practice. Personnel managers themselves, however, have tended to be much keener on it than their line manager colleagues. Accompanying practitioner interest in performance appraisal has seen a mushrooming of academic research, notably by occupational psychologists. A key thrust of much of this research has been on improving performance appraisal's effectiveness and, in particular, its accuracy in assessing employee performance. We know rather less about a more strategic use of performance appraisal as an organisational change lever and managerial control tool. There is now a wealth of academic studies on performance appraisal. Computer literature searches on the topic show over 20 academic articles per month appearing with 'performance appraisal' in their titles. Despite the large and growing volume of research work on the subject, however, it is debatable how much influence such studies have had on the actual practice of performance appraisal. It seems that managers are peculiarly reluctant to heed the advice of researchers in this area of business practice and there is a persistent 'gap' between research and practice (Maroney and Buckley, 1992).

This lack of impact of research on practice is not simply a question of general managerial indifference to the academic researcher, especially when compared to the wide influence of consultants and popular management 'gurus'. Rather, one explanation is that little of the research has considered the implications for practitioners who are faced with a plethora of organisational constraints not encountered in the research laboratory. More damning perhaps is the view that much of the research has had little to offer HR managers, except for the recommendation to train appraisers, as it has generally been unable to provide much improvement in terms of accuracy at least, over the simplest of supervisory ratings systems.

The practice of performance appraisal

How widespread is performance appraisal?

Performance appraisal has become more widespread in Western countries. For example, surveys report performance appraisal in the US increasing from 89 per cent of organisations surveyed in the mid-1970s to 94 per cent by the mid-1980s (Locher and Teel, 1988). In large and medium-sized US organisations performance appraisal systems are now virtually universally present. Similar surveys in the UK by the Chartered Institute of Personnel and Development report increasing coverage of formal performance appraisal arrangements (Armstrong and Baron, 1998; CIPD, 2005; IPD, 1999; Long, 1986). Performance appraisal is also now more common in many other non-Western countries such as China (Chow, 1994; Snape *et al.*, 1998), Japan in the form of *Satei* (Endo, 1994); Africa (Arthur *et al.*, 1995) and India (Lawler *et al.*, 1995). Performance appraisal appears to be one of the most commonly adopted HR practices in high-performance work systems (ILO, 2002).

Appraisal is particularly prominent in some industrial sectors in the UK, such as financial services (IRS, 1999), and it has grown rapidly in the public sector of late. It is now widespread in schools, hospitals, universities, local authorities, the civil service, etc. For example, some 80 per cent of local authorities surveyed either operated or were currently introducing performance appraisal (IRS, 1995a). It has also grown from its main deployment in the middle of organisation hierarchies, particularly in middle management and professional occupations, to include a much broader group of manual and clerical employees (Kersley *et al.*, 2006). Increasingly it seems, in line with harmonisation policies, all employees in an organisation are included in the performance appraisal system. An IRS survey found that 39 per cent of organisations' appraisal applied to every employee (IRS, 1994) and a replication of the survey five years later found 75 per cent to do so (IRS, 1999). The coverage of employees in the public sector, given the relative infancy of many schemes, is still rather more limited than the private sector. The IRS found only 17 per cent of public sector organisations surveyed included all employees in the scheme. However, these claims can be misleading. Employers who include the growing numbers of 'contingent' or 'peripheral' workers, such as part-time and contract staff, in performance appraisal schemes appear to be the exception rather than the rule.

One suggestion from analysis of UK and Australian data on the extent of performance appraisal is that its coverage is strongly linked to expectations of job tenure. The longer the expected tenure of employees, the less important is the role of current remuneration and the more important is deferred pay and promotion. Thus the need for detailed monitoring via performance appraisals is required. Reducing tenure expectations thus promotes the use of performance appraisal (Addison and Belfield, 2008; Brown and Heywood, 2005).

How is appraisal conducted?

There is a wide range of methods used to conduct performance appraisals, from the simplest of ranking schemes through objective, standard and competency-based systems (see below) to complex behaviourally anchored rating schemes (see Snape *et al.*, 1994). The nature of an organisation's appraisal scheme is largely a reflection of its managerial beliefs (Randell, 1994), the amount of resources it has available to commit and the expertise it possesses. Thus smaller organisations with limited HR expertise tend to adopt simpler ranking and rating schemes while the more complex and resource-consuming systems, such as competency-based and 360° appraisal, are found mainly in larger organisations.

Most employers use only one type of appraisal scheme, often a 'hybrid form' of a number of methods, and a few companies even provide employees with a choice of methods in how they are appraised. The IRS surveys (IRS, 1994, 1999) found many organisations with more than one system of performance appraisal operating. The main reason behind multiple systems was the wish to separate out reward and non-reward aspects of appraisal, different systems for different occupational groups (e.g. managerial and non-managerial employees) and separate systems for different parts of the organisation.

What is it used for?

Organisations use performance appraisal for a wide range of different purposes. Surveys commonly report the use of performance appraisal for clarifying and defining performance expectations, identifying training and development needs, providing career counselling, succession planning, improving individual, team and corporate performance, facilitating communications and involvement, allocating financial rewards, determining promotion, motivating and controlling employees and achieving cultural change (Bowles and Coates, 1993; IDS, 2007; IRS, 1994, 1999).

Recent trends suggest that the more judgemental and 'harder' forms of performance appraisal are on the increase and that 'softer' largely developmental approaches are declining (Armstrong and Baron, 1998; CIPD, 2005; Gill, 1977; IPD, 1999; Long, 1986). Thus there has been a shift in performance appraisal away from using it for career planning and identifying future potential and increased use of it for improving current performance and allocating rewards. Here the arrival of flatter organisations has given rise to the need to uncouple, to some extent at least, performance appraisal and promotion, while competitive pressures have emphasised the need to incentivise improvements in short-term performance.

There are both advantages and disadvantages to such broad demands upon performance appraisal systems. A wide use helps to integrate various, often disparate, HRM areas into a coherent package of practices. For example, by providing a link between performance and rewards, and development needs and succession planning, more effective HRM outcomes are possible. However, it also gives rise to the common criticism that performance appraisal systems are simply too ambitious in that managers expect them to be able to accommodate a very wide range of purposes. The breadth of use thus results in appraisal becoming a 'blunt instrument that tries to do too much' (Boudreaux, 1994).

Further, many of the above purposes of appraisal are seen as being in conflict. Thus recording the past and influencing future performance is difficult to achieve in a single process. The danger is that appraisal, particularly given the trends identified above, concentrates on the past at the expense of the future performance, with a common analogy here being that this is rather like using the rearview mirror to drive future performance. Similarly, allocating rewards and identifying training needs are often seen as being incompatible objectives in a single appraisal scheme. The openness required for meaningfully assessing development needs is closed down by the need for the employee to 'explain away' performance problems in order to gain a merit rise. However, the danger of disconnecting reward allocation from appraisal is that appraisers and appraised would not treat the process as seriously because without it appraisal lacks bite and 'fires blank bullets' (Lawler, 1994). Increasingly, as we now examine, performance appraisal is used as one element of a much broader performance management system.

Performance management

Performance management, like many HRM innovations, is a US import that has been a major driver in the increased use of performance appraisal by British organisations (IDS, 2007). Performance management has been defined as 'systems and attitudes which help organizations to plan, delegate and assess the operation of their services' (LGMB, 1994: 6). Bevan and Thompson (1991) describe a 'textbook' performance management system thus:

- a shared vision of the organisation's objectives communicated via a mission statement to all employees;
- individual performance targets which are related to operating unit and wider organisational objectives;
- regular formal review of progress towards targets;
- a review process which identifies training and development needs and rewards outcomes;
- an evaluation of the effectiveness of the whole process and its contribution to overall organisational performance to allow changes and improvements to be made.

A principal feature of performance management is thus that it connects the objectives of the organisation to a system of work targets for individual employees. In such models of performance management, objective setting and formal appraisal are placed at the heart of the approach. The development of performance management systems has had major implications for performance appraisal. A key trend has been away from 'stand-alone' performance appraisal systems and towards individual appraisal becoming part of an integrated performance management system.

There is a growing critique of performance management systems. First, they are seen as adding more pressure to a short-term view among managers, which may well hamper organisational performance over the long term. Second, they are often proffered in a very prescriptive fashion, with many writers advocating a single best way for performance management, to the neglect of important variables such as degree of centralisation, unionisation, etc. This is in contrast to the actual practice of performance management in the UK, which is 'extremely diverse' (Fletcher and Williams, 1992). The real danger is that performance management systems cannot be simply 'borrowed' from one organisation and applied in another, as many advocates appear to suggest. Third, it is supposed to be line-management 'driven', but case studies of its practices report the motivating forces in organisations as being chief executives and HR departments with often questionable ownership and commitment from line managers (Fletcher and Williams, 1992). Fourth, there is a growing concern that performance management systems, because of their dedicated focus on improving the 'bottom line', have added unduly to the pressures and stresses of work–life for many employees. Many systems have been introduced with scant regard for employee welfare (see Box 7.1) and there is increasing concern that employees are now being performance managed to exhaustion (Brown and Benson, 2003) and burnout (Gabris and Ihrke, 2001). Last, and perhaps more damning, is the view that it is ineffective. The main driver of performance management is the improvement of overall organisational effectiveness. However, there is little support from various studies for the view that performance management actually improves performance. For example, Bevan and Thompson's (1991) survey of performance management in the UK found that there was no relationship between high-performing UK companies (defined as those demonstrating pre-tax profit growth over a five-year period) and the operation of a performance management system.

Performance appraisal as managerial control

With the decline of careers in the flat, delayered organisation, HRM techniques such as performance appraisal have become more important managerial tools in motivating and controlling the workforce. Appraisal is now seen by some commentators as being much more important in maintaining employee loyalty and commitment than in directly managing performance (Bowles and Coates, 1993). Its use provides managers with a major opportunity to reinforce corporate values and attitudes and thus it appeals as an important strategic instrument in the control process. Thus we find an increasing use of appraisal systems for non-managerial employees that are based on social, attitudinal and trait attributes (Townley, 1989). Employees are increasingly being appraised not only on 'objective' measures such as attendance, timekeeping, productivity and quality but also on more subjective aspects such as 'dependability', 'flexibility', 'initiative', 'loyalty', etc.

Analyses of performance appraisal, based upon the work of Foucault, have given particular emphasis to the power relations implicit in performance appraisal (Coates, 1994; Townley, 1993, 1999). For Townley, performance appraisal has the potential to act as the 'paper equivalent' of the panopticon with its 'anonymous and continuous surveillance' (1993: 232). Thus recent developments in appraisal, which have both broadened the range of and increased the number of appraisers, via 360° appraisal, upward appraisal and the use of external customers, have increased the potential for managerial control and the utilisation of the panoptical powers of performance appraisal. In such systems the employee is now continually exposed to the appraisers 'constant yet elusive presence' (Fuller and Smith, 1991: 11). Every customer, peer, subordinate and colleague is now also a potential appraiser. Thus it is hardly surprising that employees have nicknamed peer reviews of performance 'screw your buddy' systems of appraisal.

Managers themselves are not immune from the disciplinary 'gaze' of performance appraisal (see below). Managerial attitudes, especially at middle-management levels, have often been identified as a barrier to the introduction of new ways of managing, such as introducing employee involvement and empowerment. Upward appraisal of managers by staff is increasingly being used to link managerial behaviour more closely with corporate values and mission statements by incorporating questions on these into appraisal instruments which are completed by the employee (Redman and Snape, 1992). Thus at one and the same time organisations promote their required values to their employees and evaluate the commitment of their managers to these. Managers scoring badly in such appraisals are often 'culled' (see Redman and Mathews, 1995). Thus, for example, at Semco, the much-discussed Brazilian company, managers are upwardly appraised every six months using a scale up to 100. The results are then posted on a noticeboard and those who consistently under-perform are squeezed out or simply 'fade away'.

 ## Recent developments in performance appraisal

As we noted in the introduction, there have been many innovations in performance appraisal practice. In this section we discuss some of the more influential of these.

Upward appraisal

Upward appraisal is a relatively recent addition to performance appraisal practice in the UK. Although still far from common, the last decade or so has witnessed the introduction of upward appraisal in a range of UK companies. Upward appraisal is more common in the US and appears to have spread from US parent companies to their UK operations (e.g. at companies such as Federal Express, Standard Chartered Bank and AMEX) and from these to UK companies such as WH Smith, The Body Shop and parts of the UK public sector (see Redman and Mathews, 1995). Upward appraisal involves the employee rating their manager's performance via, in most cases, an anonymous questionnaire. The process is anonymous to overcome employees' worries about providing honest but unfavourable feedback on managerial performance. Anonymity limits the potential for managerial 'retribution' or what is termed the 'get even' factor of upward appraisal.

Advocates claim significant benefits for upward appraisal (Bettenhausen and Fedor, 1997; Redman and Snape, 1992), including improved managerial effectiveness and leadership through 'make-you-better feedback' and increased employee voice and empowerment. Equally, upward appraisal is seen as being more in tune with the delayered organisation where managerial spans of control are greater and working arrangements much more diverse. In such situations employees are in much greater contact with their manager than the manager's manager and thus traditional top-down boss appraisal is seen as being less effective. Upward appraisal, because of the use of multiple raters, is also seen as being more robust to legal challenge of performance judgements. Given the increasingly litigious culture in the UK and US, it is surprising that performance appraisal methods and the systems in which they are embedded are not attacked in the courts more often (Lee *et al.*, 2004).

Managers have been reported as not being especially fond of upward appraisal systems. In part this may stem from the career-threatening use of upward appraisal schemes in some organisations. For example, one of BP Exploration's objectives in introducing upward appraisal was to return to individual contribution roles those managers 'clearly not cut out to manage people' (Thomas *et al.*, 1992). Often it appears to the manager on the receiving end of upward appraisal that, according to Grint (1993), 'the honest opinions of subordinates look more like the barbs on a whale harpoon than gentle and constructive nudges'. Such a lack of managerial acceptance of upward appraisal, especially at middle and junior levels of management, may go some way to explaining its relatively low uptake in the UK after a flurry of activity in the early 1990s.

360° performance appraisal

The so-called 360° appraisals appear to be taking root and becoming an established form of appraisal in the UK (see Box 7.2). Dugdill (1994) traces the origins of 360° appraisal to the US army in the 1970s. Here military researchers found that peers' opinions were more accurate indicators of a soldier's ability than were those of superiors.

The term 360° is used to describe the all-encompassing direction of feedback derived from a composite rating from peers, subordinates, supervisors and occasionally customers. It is again normally conducted via an anonymous survey, although some recent innovations include the use of audio and videotape to record feedback answers. Some organisations also use online computerised data-gathering systems. There is a wide variation in what

---

Box 7.2 HRM in practice   360° appraisal at Northumbrian Water

Following the hot, dry summers and accompanying water shortages, adverse public relations and intense media interest, life has been particularly difficult for managers in the UK privatised water companies. One company, Northumbrian Water, has been helping its managers to cope with a range of management development practices, including 360° appraisal.

Northumbrian Water introduced a 360° feedback programme for its managers via a pilot group of 35 managers. A key reason behind the introduction was to provide data for the company's development centre for senior managers. The development centre was designed to enable managers to move to a position of managing their own career development. It was considered important that individual managers should have a view from their colleagues about their performance, potential and development needs in order to facilitate sound career decisions. The 360° appraisal instrument consists of a bank of questions asking respondents to comment on the effectiveness and performance of the appraised manager against three main categories: competence, style and role. Appraisers, for example, are asked to say how often they see the candidate behave in a particular fashion which is consistent with the behaviours listed for a senior manager. Space is also provided for open comments on the manager's performance and the company feels it is often these which prove the most enlightening.

The system is based upon a refined competency model originally developed in the early 1980s. The competency model was further developed following privatisation of the industry as the roles and styles of management appropriate to the company's new values were developed. For example, commercial awareness and customer care were not present in the original formulation. A study of HRM practices in the post-privatisation water industry considers Northumbria to have introduced the 'most dramatic changes' of all the companies (IRS, 1992).

The feedback forms are distributed to 10–12 of the managers' colleagues in some form of distribution, such as two above, five sideways and four below, by the individual manager. Internal customers are often part of the process but the company has yet to incorporate external customers. The forms are returned directly to the company's consultants, who produce a summary data booklet, discuss the results with the manager, and help prepare them for the development centre.

The main benefit the company perceives it has obtained from 360° feedback is in providing individual managers with vital insights into some of their shortcomings, which would otherwise remain unaddressed. Although it has been somewhat of a shock for some, managers are considered to be much more self-aware about their leadership qualities and are felt to be working better with their staff. Also, 360° appraisal is seen as making a valuable contribution in encouraging managers to engage in continuous professional development and encouraging an approach where performance problems can be positively tackled through training and development. The main problems the company has found with its implementation are that in the early programmes there was some difficulty in convincing managers that such feedback was of value because their development and career planning was within their own remit rather than that of their of boss. A few individuals also had great difficulty in accepting the feedback and searched for reasons to rationalise their opposition.

Source: Interviews with managers.

is appraised in 360° feedback. Many companies use fully structured questionnaires based upon models of managerial competency. Others, such as Dupont's use of 360° appraisal in its individual career management programme, employ a much less structured approach. Here appraisers respond to open questions, which ask for descriptions of the appraiser's 'major value-adding areas for the year'; summaries of the manager's strengths; descriptions of key improvement needs; and a call for other general comments. Unstructured systems of appraisal have advantages in tapping into key aspects of managerial performance. However, the danger of using an unstructured approach is that the popular but incompetent manager may well fare better than one who is highly effective but not particularly pleasant. Mostly the appraisers remain anonymous but some systems, such as Dupont's, leave the option open to the appraiser whether or not to add their name to the appraisal form. However, unless a composite rating only is presented to the manager, and this tends to counter the value of having multiple perspectives in 360°, it is very difficult to provide the immediate supervisor with anonymity.

It seems that 360° appraisal is edging away from a management development tool and towards a broader organisational role (Toegal and Conger, 2003). Increasingly, and controversially, it seems organisations are also experimenting with linking 360° and managerial remuneration. Given that 360° appraisal is now so popular for managers and professionals that some see it as replacing traditional performance appraisal systems, this trend to widening its remit raises some concerns. Toegal and Conger (2003) suggest that 360° appraisal is being 'overstretched' by including such broader administrative concerns and that these additions blunt its usage as a feedback tool. The solution, it seems, is to develop two distinct 360° appraisal tools, one for management development and one for performance feedback, a solution that, as we note above, could raise as many problems as it solves.

Rather a lot is claimed for 360° appraisal, and like many new initiatives we have seen a rash of articles announcing how it can 'change your life' (O'Reilly, 1995) and deliver competitive advantage for the organisation (London and Beatty, 1993). Because of its use of multiple raters with different perspectives, a sort of safety in numbers approach, it is often suggested that it provides more accurate and meaningful feedback. However, as Grint (1993) notes, this often simply replaces the subjectivity of a single appraiser with the subjectivity of multiple appraisers.

Undoubtedly, many organisations have gained some advantages from using it, particularly in management developmental terms. It has proved especially useful for providing feedback for senior managers who are often neglected at the top in appraisal terms. One key benefit of the broad group of appraisers used in 360° is that it can provide a more meaningful appraisal for employees with little contact with their workplace. In such situations traditional top-down appraisals are of little value. A strength of 360° is that management consultants proffering systems will tailor a basic questionnaire to meet the organisation's characteristics, such as culture, mission, business values and structure and management practices. It remains to be seen whether the benefits gained are outweighed by the considerable time, effort and costs involved. Indeed, it seems that some management consultants are 'gravy training' on the back of the current enthusiasm for 360°, with week-long feedback courses, facilitated by themselves, recommended to debrief managers.

Thus a number of questions remain unanswered about 360° appraisal, not least whether the data generated is accurate, valid and, more importantly, meaningful for the appraisee and whether the organisation stands to benefit from it. Ratings are only as good as the questions asked and often the interpretation of question wording is far from clear in many instruments. Such questions as 'Does the manager deal with problems in a flexible manner' are not uncommon in appraisal instruments. Items need to be clear, easy to understand and easy to rate given the raters' contact with the appraisee. One particular criticism of many 360° systems is that all raters are given the same instrument, despite the different nature of the contact with the appraisee. Some issues are clearly more visible to the rater from different vantage points and questionnaires should ideally be constructed accordingly. Items based on actual behaviours – key organisational competencies or critical incidents observed in the workplace indicative of superior performing managers – tend to be more effective. However, respondents will usually provide ratings on whatever questions are asked, whether or not they are in a position to do so.

There is also a certain tendency to produce overly bureaucratic systems. The danger here is that one common cause of failure generally in performance appraisal, that of requiring participants to fill in large quantities of paperwork, is being ignored. Making the feedback meaningful is also a challenge many users of 360° fail to rise to. To ensure meaningful feedback a process of self-appraisal, comparison against other managers' ratings and follow-up with facilitators and those who provided the ratings is the minimum required. Also there is an implicit expectation on the part of those providing the ratings that such feedback will lead to improvements and that managers will change their behaviour for the better. There is, however, yet little evidence that this actually occurs.

Lastly, many so-called 360° appraisal systems are actually far from an all-round view of managers; the external customer as a reviewer is often left out, but, as we discuss in the next section, customers are an increasingly heard voice in the assessment of employee performance.

Customer appraisal

TQM and customer care programmes are now very widespread in both the private and public sectors in the UK. One impact of these initiatives is that organisations are now increasingly setting employee performance standards based upon customer care indicators and appraising staff against these. A mix of 'hard' quantifiable standards such as 'delivery of a customer's first drink within two minutes' and soft qualitative standards such as 'a warm and friendly greeting', as used at one roadside restaurant chain, are now used in performance appraisal systems (IRS, 1995b). The use of service guarantees, which involve the payment of compensatory moneys to customers if the organisations do not reach the standards, has also led to a greater use of customer data in performance appraisal ratings.

Customer service data for use in appraising employees is gathered by a variety of methods. First, there is the use of a range of customer surveys, such as via the completion of customer care cards, telephone surveys, interviews with customers and postal surveys. Organisations are now using such surveys more frequently and are increasingly sophisticated in how they gather customer views. Second, there is a range of surveillance techniques used by managers to sample the service encounter. Here the electronic work monitoring of factory workers is being extended into the services sector. For example, customer service managers at contact centres spend considerable time and effort reviewing staff performance by recording staff–customer conversations and giving immediate feedback, as well as using the data for the regular formal review process.

Third, and even more controversial, is the increasing use of the so-called 'mystery' or 'phantom' shopping. For some commentators, customer service can only be really effectively evaluated at the boundary between customer and organisation and this view has fuelled the growth of mystery shopping as a data-capturing process. Here staff employed by a specialist agency purport to be real shoppers and observe and record their experience of the service encounter. It is now commonly used in banks, pub companies, insurance companies, supermarkets and parts of the public sector. Some local authorities evaluate the quality of telephone responses by employing consultants to randomly call the authority and assess the quality of the response (IRS, 1995b).

Mystery shopping is argued to give a company a rich source of data that cannot be uncovered by other means, such as customer surveys. Such surveys, although useful for some purposes, are often conducted many months after the service encounter and thus exact service problems are difficult to recollect. Mystery shopping is also seen as being particularly useful in revealing staff performance that causes customers to leave without purchasing. In many service sector organisations a natural consequence of the use of mystery shoppers has been to utilise the data in the performance evaluations of staff (Fuller and Smith, 1991). Although as yet relatively understudied, there are a number of concerns with mystery shopping, not least the psychometric quality of data collected in comparison to customer surveys. Few studies have addressed this issue, but work by Kayande and Finn (1999) report that mystery shopping provides 'reasonably reliable ratings' of performance and that such data can be produced at considerably less cost than customer surveys. All this suggests that mystery shopping is very likely to grow in use in the future.

However, these data-gathering methods are, as one could well expect, not very popular with staff. Employees often question the ethics of introducing mystery shoppers and feel that it represents a distinct lack of managerial trust in them (Shing and Spence, 2002). Thus employees describe shoppers in terms of 'spies' and 'snoopers' and react with hostility and 'shopper spotting' to their introduction. The introduction of mystery shopping for largely negative reasons of catching staff performing poorly only fuels such reactions. Cook (1993) advises that using them to reward staff for good performance rather than punish them for poor performance can help their acceptance. Staff who obtain good mystery shopping ratings should be rewarded and recognised, while those who obtain poor ones should use them as a source of identifying training needs.

In an increasing number of organisations internal service-level agreements are also being established. The introduction of compulsory competitive tendering and subsequently 'best value' has given considerable impetus to such agreements in the public sector. Often in such agreements there is an internal customer-service 'guarantee' stating the level and nature of services the supplier will provide. It thus has been a natural progression of such a development for organisations, such as at Federal Express, to incorporate performance data from service-level agreements into the appraisal process (e.g. Milliman *et al.,* 1995). A key advantage claimed for using internal customers in this way is that joint goal-setting helped provide both internal customer and provider with greater understanding of the roles that individuals and departments provide. It thus helps in breaking down internal barriers between departments.

Team-based appraisal

Work is increasingly being restructured into highly interdependent work teams, yet, despite this, performance appraisal often remains stubbornly based on the individual. In some cases teams are increasingly being given responsibility for allocating work tasks, setting bonuses, selecting new staff and even disciplining errant members. For such organisations it has thus been seen as entirely appropriate that performance appraisals should also be based upon and even conducted by the team themselves.

Two main variants of team appraisal can be identified. In some approaches the managers appraise the team as a whole. Targets are set, performance measured and assessments made, and rewards allocated as with traditional individual appraisals. The manager makes no attempt to differentiate one member from another in performance terms, in fact the creation of internal inequity with respect to rewarding performance is a deliberate aspect (Lawler, 1994). Equal ratings and rewards ensue for all of the team regardless of performance. The team are then encouraged to resolve internally any performance problems or competence deficiencies in order to facilitate overall team performance and development. Team members themselves may then provide informal awards or recognition of superior performance. The other main variant is whereby individual appraisals of each team member are still made but not by management. Rather, in a form of peer appraisal, team members appraise each other, usually via the use of anonymous rating questionnaires.

Competency-based appraisal

Interest in the concept of competency has been one of the major HR themes of recent times. Connock (1992) describes it as one of HRM's 'big ideas'. One consequence of this has been the attempt by some organisations to use the competency approach to develop an integrated human resource strategy. This has been particularly pronounced in HR practices targeted at managers but is also growing for non-managerial groups. A consequence of the development of organisational competency models has been that employers have increasingly extended their use from training and development, selection and reward into the area of appraisal. For example, the most widely reported innovation in performance appraisal systems during the recent past has been the linking of appraisals to competency frameworks (Abraham, 2001; IRS 1999).

The assessment of competencies in the appraisal process has a number of benefits. The evaluation of competencies identified as central to a good job performance provides a useful focus for analysing the progress an individual is making in the job rather than the static approach of many ability- or trait-rating schemes. Thus competency-based assessment is especially useful in directing employee attention to areas where there is scope for improvement. The use of competencies broadens appraisal by including 'how well is it done' measures in addition to the more traditional 'what is achieved' measures. It also helps concentrate the appraisal process on the key area of performance and effectiveness and provides a language for feedback on performance problems. This latter benefit overcomes one of the problems of traditional objective-based appraisal systems in which the appraiser is often at a loss as to how to counsel an employee on what they should do differently if the appraisal objectives have not been achieved. However, these benefits must be counterbalanced against the development and running costs involved and the wider critical debate surrounding the 'competency movement' in general.

 ## Problems of performance appraisal

Performance appraisals appear to be one human resource activity that everyone loves to hate. Carroll and Schneier's early (1982) research found that performance appraisal ranks as the most disliked managerial activity and there is little evidence that managerial views have changed. It is frequently suggested in the popular management literature that most managers would prefer to have a dental appointment than conduct a performance appraisal. Many appraisees, it seems, would also prefer this! According to Grint (1993: 64), 'rarely in the history of business can such a system have promised so much and delivered so little'.

Box 7.3 HRM in practice   Cronies and doppelgangers in performance appraisal

The search for accurate performance appraisals is a seemingly illusory one, with many pitfalls and distorting effects strewn in the appraiser's path. Some of the main ones are:

Halo effects. This is where one positive criterion distorts the assessment of others. Similarly the *horns effect* is where a single negative aspect dominates the appraisal rating.

Doppelganger effect is where the rating reflects the similarity between appraiser and appraised.

Crony effect is the result of appraisal being distorted by the closeness of the relationship between appraiser and appraised.

Veblen effect is named after the economist Veblen, who gave all his students the grade C irrespective of the quality of their efforts. Thus all those appraised received middle-order ratings.

Impression effect is the problem of distinguishing actual performance from calculated 'impression management'. The impression management tactics of employees can result in supervisors liking them more and thus rating their job performance more highly. Employees often attempt to manage their reputations by substituting measures of process (effort, behaviour, etc.) for measures of outcome (results), particularly when the results are less than favourable.

The critics of performance appraisal argue that it is expensive; causes conflict between appraised and appraiser; has limited value and may even be dysfunctional in the improvement of employee performance; and, despite the rhetoric, its use contributes little to the strategic management of an organisation. It is also argued to be riddled with so many distorting 'effects' that its accuracy in providing an indicator of actual employee performance must also be called into question (see Box 7.3). Some appraisal systems, especially the more judgemental, those tied into merit pay systems and those with forced distributions, are argued to be especially problematic in these respects. Thus for many writers performance appraisal is 'doomed' (Halachmi, 1993); a managerial practice 'whose time has gone' (Bhote, 1994; Fletcher, 1993) and whose end is often predicted (Roth and Ferguson, 1994).

Why does performance appraisal not work? One reason is that despite their widely held belief to the contrary, most managers are not naturally good at conducting performance appraisals. According to Lawler (1994: 17), it is an 'unnatural act' for managers, a result of which is that if they are not trained properly it is done rather poorly. Appraisal meetings are thus reported as being short-lived, ill-structured and often bruising encounters. Studies find that appraisers are ill-prepared, talk too much and base much of the discussion on third-party complaints, with many of the judgements made on 'gut feelings'. It is then of little surprise when we find reports of how it takes the average employee six months to recover from it.

Being subject to 'political' manipulation also discredits appraisals. Managers, it seems, frequently play organisational games with performance ratings (Snape *et al.*, 1994). Longenecker's (1989) research found that managers' appraisal ratings are often manipulated to suit various ends. Sometimes ratings were artificially deflated to show who was the boss; to prepare the ground for termination; to punish a difficult and rebellious employee; and even to 'scare' better performance out of the appraisee. One manager we interviewed described how he deflated the performance ratings of all new graduate trainees for their first few years of employment in order to 'knock some of the cleverness out of them' and show them that they 'did not know everything'. Equally, a poor performer may be given an excellent rating in order that they will be promoted up and out of the department and managers may inflate ratings in the hope that an exemplary set of appraisals reflects favourably on the manager responsible for such a high-performing team.

The move to more objective forms of performance appraisal, particularly encouraged by performance management models, and increasingly reported for managerial grades, is often argued to overcome some of the above 'subjective' problems. Legal challenges to personality- and trait-based performance appraisal schemes, particularly in North America and increasingly in the UK (Lee *et al.*, 2004), have also encouraged the move away from personality- and trait-based systems. However, the so-called objective-based schemes are not without difficulties. First, measurement is often difficult and, according to Wright (1991), 'there are a number of jobs where the meaningful is not measurable and the measurable is not meaningful'. The tendency is also to simplify measurement by focusing on the short rather than the long term. Second, since objectives are set for individual employees or teams under such systems it can be especially challenging to achieve equitable ratings. Equally problematical is that the actions of the employee may account for little of the variability in the outcomes measured (a key criticism of the quality gurus) and thus the extent to which they are achievable is not within the employee's control. This has posed real problems with appraisals in industries such as financial services, where the economic climate and general business cycle arguably affect outcomes far more than individual effort. The potential here is thus for employee demotivation and disillusionment, especially when many such systems are now linked to reward structures.

Kessler and Purcell (1992) identify a range of further specific problems with objective-based systems. These include the difficulty in achieving a balance between maintenance and innovator objectives; in setting objectives that cover the whole job so that performance does not get skewed to part of it; and the lack of flexibility to redefine objectives as circumstances change during the appraisal cycle. The introduction of performance appraisal into the public sector has also given rise to many concerns. In particular, there are worries about its potential to undermine professional autonomy, with this concern being strongly expressed by clinicians in the NHS. A more general concern is that such a 'managerialist' intervention would undermine the public service values and public accountability of employees (Redman *et al.*, 2000).

A range of more practical difficulties also results in problems with performance appraisal. Often the paperwork used to support the system can become excessive and give rise to a considerable bureaucratic burden for managers, particularly as spans of control grow. Some organisations have attempted to reduce this problem by designing paperless systems, requiring the employee to complete the bulk of the paperwork, or moving to a computer-based system. A real danger in many systems is that the paperwork dominates and the process is reduced to an annual 'cosy chat' and a ritual bureaucratic exercise devoid of meaning or importance for all concerned. Thus according to Barlow (1989: 503), the performance appraisal of managers is little more than the 'routinized recording of trivialities'. Appraisers and appraised go through the motions, sign off the forms and send them to a central personnel department who simply file them away rather than utilising the data in a meaningful way (Snape *et al.*, 1994). Given the lack of follow-up in many appraisal systems it is hardly surprising when they fall into disrepute and eventual decay.

Lastly, the growth of TQM and customer care programmes has triggered a considerable debate and a reassessment of the organisational value of appraisal. On the one hand there has been a high-profile barrage of criticism rejecting appraisal as being incompatible with TQM. In its strongest formulation it is suggested that managers face a stark choice between choosing either TQM or performance appraisal (Aldakhilallah and Parente, 2002). On the other hand, some have suggested that appraisal may play a key role in developing, communicating and monitoring the achievement of quality standards (Fletcher, 1993) and many organisations have been spurred by the introduction of TQM to revise their appraisal schemes in more customer-focused ways.

TQM has thus focused attention on some old as well as highlighting some new problems with performance appraisal. In relation to old problems some of the quality gurus, most notably Deming (1986), maintain that performance appraisal is inconsistent with quality improvement. He argues that variation in performance is attributable mainly to work systems rather than to variations in the performance of individual workers. Quality improvements are thus found mainly by changing processes rather than people, and the key is to develop cooperative teamwork. This, he claims, is difficult to do where the focus is on 'blaming' the individual, as in traditional appraisal, and where as a result there is a climate of fear and risk avoidance, and a concern for short-term, individual targets, all of which undermine the cooperative, creative and committed behaviour necessary for continuous improvement.

Deming is careful to argue, in rejecting performance appraisal, not that all staff perform equally well but that appraisers are incapable of disaggregating system effects from individual staff effects. Thus what is needed for TQM is a shift away from the traditional focus on results and individual recognition, towards processes and group recognition. The TQM critics also raise some new problems with performance appraisal, in particular that it 'disempowers' employees by reducing variety and increasing homogenisation of the workforce, while for meaningful customer care we need the 'empowered' employee.

Conclusions

Performance appraisal is now more widespread that at any time in its history and the organisational resources consumed by its practice are enormous. At the same time its critics grow both in number and in the ferocity of their attacks. It is thus tempting to adopt a somewhat sceptical view of the value of performance appraisal. Following the rise of TQM and the prominence of its, mainly American, management gurus it has become rather fashionable of late to reject performance appraisal outright. Pathological descriptions of performance appraisal as a 'deadly disease' and an 'organisational virus' are increasingly common.

However, it would appear that the danger here is that such views are often based on little more than anecdote rather than solid empirical research. For example, one survey of employer reasons for introducing appraisal systems in the UK found that in over a third of cases it was developed to provide support for quality management initiative (IRS, 1994). Our studies of managers' actual experience of being appraised finds many reporting its overall value to them and the organisation, with few suggesting it should be discarded altogether (e.g. Redman and Mathews, 1995; Redman *et al.*, 2000). Many of the criticisms are based upon a hard and uncompromising model of performance appraisal that is now less commonly found in practice, and the ineffective way that many organisations implement appraisal. The critics all too often have rather conveniently ignored many of the new developments we discuss above, which act to ameliorate some of these problems. Many of the problems of performance appraisal can be ironed out over time, as experience with its practice accumulates. Indeed, there is some evidence to suggest that employers who have utilised performance appraisal for longer report fewer problems (Bowles and Coates, 1993).

Further, performance appraisal's detractors are usually silent on what should replace it. A common response is to suggest this is an unfair question in that it is the organisational equivalent of asking, 'What would you replace pneumonia with?' (e.g. see *People Management* 13 July 1995: 15). The question of how to assesses individual performance, determine rewards and promotion, provide feedback, decide training and career needs and link business and individual goals without a performance appraisal system, however, cannot be so easily shrugged off.

Performance appraisal emerged in the first place to meet such needs and employees still need guidance in focusing their skills and efforts on important organisational goals and values. Hence we would suggest that performance appraisal will continue to have an important role in HRM practice. A good example here is that organisations often struggle to get managers committed to taking health and safety management as seriously as other aspects of their jobs. Tombs (1992) reports that 'safety leaders' in the chemical industry ensure that managers give safety management the attention it deserves by developing a 'safety culture', a key part of which is achieved by incorporating safety objectives into their performance appraisals. Thus the first objective of all ICI plant managers is always a safety one.

This is not to argue that the current practice of performance appraisal is unproblematic. Certainly some of the evidence presented above would suggest that there are many concerns with its application. However, these are persistent but certainly not insurmountable or terminal problems, and it is argued strongly that organisations should think very carefully before abandoning it altogether. Rather, the evidence would seem to support the view that the key task facing most organisations in the millennium is the upgrading, renewal and reinvention of performance appraisal such that it is more compatible with new business environments.

CASE STUDY 7.1

PERFORMANCE APPRAISAL AT NORTH TRUST

TOM REDMAN, ED SNAPE AND DAVID THOMPSON

Organisation background[1]

This case study examines the practice of performance appraisal in an NHS Trust hospital. North Trust (NT) is a whole district Trust in the northeast of England serving a community of a quarter of a million people. It provides 32 major healthcare services, including the full range of in-patient, day case and out-patient services alongside a comprehensive primary care service including health visiting and district nursing services. It employs some 2,200 'whole time equivalent' (WTE) staff. The Trust has recently been relatively successful, meeting all its financial targets thus far. However, at the time of the study – the late 1990s–mid 2000s – it was, similar to many other Trusts, experiencing increasing difficulties in meeting the demand for healthcare services within the constraints of its current resources.

The development of appraisal at NT

Appraisal at North Trust, a variant of the national Individual Performance Reviews (IPR) scheme, was first implemented for senior managers in 1988. Between 1988 and 1994 it was largely restricted to managerial and senior professional groups. In 1994 a review of IPR was conducted. An initial analysis found patchy coverage of IPR and a half-hearted commitment to it. Following the review a decision was taken to revise and re-launch the IPR scheme and 'roll it out' to a wider group of staff. There were two key influences underpinning this decision. First, a new chief executive with a much greater belief in the value of performance management was appointed. Second, a decision to pursue the Investors in People (IiP) award resulted in a decision to commit more time and effort to making IPR work. The next 18 months thus saw the revising of policy, the redesigning

of supporting paperwork, and the committing of major training resources to IPR.

Final written agreement was secured in March 1995 and the new policy and procedure were 'signed off' by the chief executive in June 1995. The key aims of IPR at NT were articulated in the new policy document as ensuring all staff understand the Trust's goals and strategic direction; are clear about their objectives, how these fit with the work of others and the organisation as whole and are aware of the tasks they need to carry out; are given regular feedback and explicit assessment of performance; and are developed to improve their performance. The revised policy document made an explicit commitment to implement IPR for all employees.

The revised IPR policy at NT placed greater emphasis on measurability as a key aspect of the setting of individual objectives. The policy document outlines the principles underpinning individual objective setting as following the acronym 'SMART'. Here objectives should be specific, measurable, agreed/achievable, realistic and time-bound, with the form of measurement for each objective to be agreed at the time that they are set. According to the CEO, when he first arrived, this aspect was perceived as being very weak in practice:

> **Most people didn't know what an objective was if it sat up and bit them on the backside. Objectives here tended to be half-a-dozen or so generalised statements with no measurable outcome, no timescale, no agreement about how something is to be judged and whether it has been done or not, with the result that there is little accountability.**

For the CEO the result of this was major problems in 'getting things done' at the Trust:

> **We don't have a performance culture here. This place was just great for talking about things. Only talking about things, not actually doing them.**

Thus a key aim for the CEO was to 'toughen up' IPR. This was to be attained in part by an increased emphasis on the evaluation of the achievement of work objectives and to encourage detailed measures to be

[1]This case study draws on four main sources of data: interviews with managers and professionals, a fully structured postal questionnaire administered to a sample of 270 managers and professionals, the analysis of internal documents and procedures manuals and, finally, the observation of training workshops on appraisal and several senior management meetings reviewing appraisal practice at the organisation (see Redman et al., 2000).

established for all new objectives. However, the CEO's view of the direction that IPR should go in did not seem to be shared by its 'owners': the personnel department. Here a softer, more developmental focus for IPR was envisioned:

> **What is important is the manager taking the time out to talk to the individual about how they are progressing. How they feel things are going. And talk about training and development. These things really help morale. Forget the form filling and objectives, and all the other bits. It is these things that really make the difference.**

In the remainder of this case study we describe the practice of performance appraisal in North Trust.

The IPR process

Mechanics

IPR at NT is designed to cascade downwards through the organisation. The business plan is formulated by December/January each year and reviews conducted during February and March for senior managers. The majority of appraisals for other staff take place during April and May. A minority of managers, because of the large number of appraisals they conducted, in one case over 50, scheduled the appraisals over the full year, which in effect largely undermined the direct link with business planning for the majority of their staff. However, linkages with the business plan, especially for lower levels of staff, were also difficult to discern in the accounts of the IPR reviews conducted by those managers who did these in phase with the business planning process. Here managers' descriptions of how they appraised healthcare assistants, porters, domestics, catering staff, laundry workers and nurses rarely mentioned anything other than the loosest of connections with the business plan.

The IPR policy specifies very much a 'top-down' process, noting that only occasionally might it be beneficial to involve another manager closely involved with the objectives being measured (such as a project manager). In practice, no examples of this were found. A particular problem reported by the interviewees was that of continuity of appraisers between appraisal cycles. Owing to high levels of managerial turnover, caused by resignations, promotions, transfers, secondments, etc. of both appraisees and appraisers, nearly a third of interviewees reported having different appraisers from one cycle to the next. This level of managerial change, because of the need for a close working relationship between manager and employee for appraisal to be effective (see below), was generally felt to limit IPR's potential. Interviewees described how continuity between appraiser and appraisee was important because reviews

were generally perceived as improving as both parties got to know each other better and the discussion became more useful and open.

Coverage

There was an uneven application and use of IPR. Despite the avowed intention of the new policy to 'roll out' IPR uniformly over the trust, its use appeared to be distinctly patchy. The personnel department estimated that only around 25–30 per cent of staff received a performance review and that below management levels 'huge swathes' of staff were not involved. One of the tools to encourage its greater uptake was that senior managers were now being given personal objectives in their own appraisals to introduce IPR for all their staff. However, this strategy alone did not seem sufficient in gaining their commitment to making IPR process effective. As one manager explains:

> **Appraisal for lower level staff is a 5-minute wonder, get it out of the way. The supervisors say . . . 'I have got to go through this with you. You haven't been too bad a lad this year have you. See you next year.' We get the odd constructive thing coming out of it but the main thing is that the director will be happy that he can report we have now appraised all the staff in our department when he has his next IPR.**

Such cynical attitudes were a source of irritation to the majority of managers who spent considerable time and effort on conducting IPRs in their departments. Here it was particularly resented that their managerial colleagues either did not conduct appraisals ('It's not fair that I have to do it if others don't'; 'Other staff feel they are missing out because they are not getting it') or gave mere lip service to them ('It brings the whole IPR process into disrepute and makes it much more difficult for me to get my staff to take it seriously').

Documentation

The standard Trust documentation was used for less than half of our interviewees' appraisals. The standard forms were felt to be too cumbersome and somewhat of an administrative chore, especially for use with employees at lower levels in the organisation. Thus those responsible for IPR often tailored the forms, usually reducing their length. A problem with some of the customised forms was that questionable performance categories, such as an appraisee's 'personality', featured prominently in these versions. In contrast, some professional groups found the forms rather too simplistic to capture the nature of their roles and again customised the standard forms to suit their needs. In a number of departments reviews were conducted without the aid of either customised or standard forms,

Table 7.1 How long did the appraisal interview last?

	%
Less than 30 minutes	11
Between 30 minutes and an hour	43
Between one and two hours	35
More than two hours	12

and in one case an appraiser admitted that this was because he had never got round to actually reading them.

The IPR encounter

The heart of the IPR process, and the main source of participants' evaluation of it as either a success or failure, is the face-to-face meeting between appraiser and appraisee. Here for IPR is its 'moment of truth'. Table 7.1 shows that the majority of our appraisees reported interviews of at least 30 minutes, with 47 per cent having interviews of more than an hour. Judging from Table 7.2, appraisers were not usually dominating the interviews. The impression gained is that the majority of appraisees were having a sufficiently long and participative appraisal interview, an encouraging finding when we note that those who reported longer and more participative interviews also tended to report greater satisfaction with the appraisal process.

Table 7.3 sets out the extent to which various issues were discussed during the appraisal, as reported by our appraisees. The main emphasis appears to be on the achievement and planning of work objectives and on the planning of training and development. Not surprisingly, given the absence of performance-related pay for most staff, pay and benefits were only discussed in any detail during the appraisal interview. Overall, the approach seems to be one of performance management and development rather than of judgement and reward allocation.

A strong theme in the accounts of those who were positive about the overall IPR process was the notion that the interview represented 'quality time' between manager and managed. For some it was an 'employee's right' to have meaningful 'one-on-one time' with their manager and:

> People value quality time to talk through with their immediate manager what they are doing, why they are doing it, and what they need to do in the future.

As we have seen, in these 'quality-time' appraisals, which were often between two to three hours' duration for managers, appraisees reported that a broad range of issues were discussed.

In contrast, the focus for lower-level grades was much more restricted and our in-depth interviews suggested that for such staff the time spent on the IPR interview varied between 10 and 45 minutes. Typical descriptions of the nature of appraisals for lower-grade staff were:

> I discuss with them how they have worked this year. I say 'You've been a bit slack in these things. You are bloody good at that. You are one of my key workers for this. But your time-keeping wants pulling up a bit and your general attitude is not what it should be.'

> To be honest there is very little to say to someone who feeds sheets into a machine five days a week. I have found it hard to think of positive things.

One manager reported the difficulty of getting lower-grade staff to relax during their appraisal because prior to IPR's introduction the only time such staff were called to her office was for a 'rugging'. Perhaps unsurprisingly, given such an approach, lower-grade staff were often

Table 7.2 During the appraisal interview approximately what proportion of the time did you and the appraiser talk?

	%
Mainly me (more than 75%)	13
Approximately 60% me	26
Approximately equal	48
Approximately 60% appraiser	12
Mainly the appraiser (more than 75%)	1

Table 7.3 To what extent were the following issues covered in your appraisal?

	3	2	1
	Thoroughly discussed	Briefly discussed	Not discussed at all
		%	
Your achievement of work objectives	63	32	5
Your future work objectives	65	31	4
Your personality or behaviour	17	42	42
Your skills or competencies	35	52	13
Your training and development needs	45	43	12
Your career aspirations and plans	30	43	27
Your pay or benefits	3	12	85
Your job difficulties	24	57	19
How you might improve your performance	16	40	44
How your supervisor might help you to improve your performance	15	45	40
Your personal or domestic circumstances	4	20	76

reported as being 'indifferent' to and 'uninterested' in the IPR process.

> It's the lower grades that feel 'Do I have to go through this again? I don't know why. I only want to do the job I'm doing and get my money at the end of the week.' These tend to be short interviews, most are less than 10 minutes.

Managers appeared to be coping with this lack of interest via a number of strategies. First, by renewing efforts in an attempt to encourage active staff participation and using developmental 'carrots'. Second, individual sceptics were labelled 'lost causes' and managers simply went through the motions in IPR and waited for such staff to leave. A more difficult problem was with 'clusters' of IPR-resistant employees. Here a coping strategy, often sold under the guise of self-development, appeared to be one of 'sharing the misery' more evenly with more junior managers and supervisors. The responsibility for conducting IPRs for 'difficult', 'obstructive' and 'awkward' staff was spread around the managerial team.

Generally, appraisees felt that their managers were good at giving performance feedback but fewer felt that they received regular feedback on their progress towards objectives (Table 7.4). The need for appraisal to be an ongoing, year-round exercise was emphasised in the IPR system (see below). It seems that at NT, significant minorities of appraisers were neglecting to

do the expected follow-up. Judging from our interviews, constructive feedback was especially welcomed by the appraisees in providing direction ('You realise you are getting there'; 'Gives me some comfort I am getting there') and helping to boost confidence ('You know what you are doing is being done correctly'). Critical feedback was also valued but not often received by the interviewees, who in part blamed appraisal training here, which overly emphasised the 'positive' nature of IPR. Around a third of interviewees said they often 'watered down' their feedback in the reviews to ensure a positive IPR event and 'harmony' within their work-teams. Appraisees, especially female managers, emphasised the value of constructive criticism and 'meaningful' appraisals, with cosy chats being seen as a waste of their time.

Sound personal relationships between appraiser and appraised were emphasised by our interviewees as being a necessary but not sufficient condition for the appraisal to be effective. The large majority of appraisees felt that their managers were professional enough not to reward favourites, were confident that appraisers were objective, felt they could talk freely, were confident enough to challenge their appraisal, and that keeping on good terms with their manager was not a requirement in order to obtain a good appraisal (see Table 7.4). However, this still leaves a minority of appraisers whose appraisal behaviour was less positively rated by appraisees. Thus, some interviewees reported a poor relationship with their manager, describing IPR reviews in

Table 7.4 Perceived supervisor behaviour

	5	4	3	2	1
	Strongly Agree	Agree	Neither agree nor disagree	Disagree	Strongly disagree
			%		
POSITIVE ASPECTS					
My supervisor is good at giving me feedback on my performance	7	51	19	19	4
I receive regular informal feedback from my supervisor regarding my progress towards agreed targets and objectives	4	37	19	30	9
My supervisor takes my appraisals very seriously	21	50	15	12	2
My supervisor takes my career aspirations very seriously	5	50	24	17	3
I am confident that my supervisor is as objective as possible when conducting appraisals	10	60	20	8	1
NEGATIVE ASPECTS					
I have to keep on good terms with my supervisor in order to get a good appraisal rating	2	10	21	52	14
Supervisors use appraisals to reward their favourites	2	6	16	54	23
I am not entirely happy about challenging my supervisor's appraisal of my performance	3	18	17	52	11
I found it difficult during my performance appraisal to talk freely with my supervisor about what I wanted to discuss	4	14	9	52	21

terms of conflict, verbal confrontation, point scoring and 'edging about the real issues'. At its worst, this came down to appraisers using IPR to list what the appraisee had done wrong or badly over the year. A few appraisers, particularly those in clinical posts, described the problems of achieving an appropriate environment for conducting appraisal in a busy, emergency-led hospital:

> When I had my IPR the phones were going, people were coming in and out of the office, the manager got called away. It spoke volumes to me about the value that was attached to IPR here.

> Conducting IPRs on nights, at 2am, when people are not at their best, is hardly conducive to a quality process.

Mini-reviews

The formal annual reviews are supported by 'mini-reviews'. The policy document sees these as a 'crucial element' of IPR, providing constant review and monitoring such that the annual review itself becomes 'mainly a confirmation of agreements made during the year' or, as the title of the IPR training video suggests, appraisees should experience *No Surprises*. However, these appear to be rather sporadic in practice and, as we saw in Table 7.4, only 41 per cent of survey appraisees said that they received regular feedback from their supervisor on their progress towards their objectives.

A few departmental heads formally scheduled three-monthly reviews for all employees. The norm for the mini-reviews was a six-monthly, informal discussion, with a minority of interviewees receiving only the annual appraisal. Below management and professional levels, the impression gained was that mini-reviews were extremely rare or very ad hoc and rushed at best – 'corridor and canteen chats' – with managers struggling to find the time to conduct even the annual appraisal for some groups. However, the interviewees themselves often stressed the value of mini-reviews not only in providing a measure of progress and attainment but in a general updating of performance objectives. Several interviewees reported requesting, and receiving, additional mini-reviews. Here mini-reviews were especially useful to fine-tune, and often to replace, personal objectives that had been rendered obsolete by a rapidly changing organisational environment. Given the current level of change and 'churn' in the NHS, we suggest that it may now be appropriate to consider it a 'high-velocity' environment requiring fast, strategic decision-making. In such circumstances static yearly objectives are clearly inappropriate. Interviewees reported how objectives set in April of one year were often irrelevant and obsolete by the following year. Mini-reviews allowed for individual objectives to be kept in line with changes in business strategy.

Objective setting

As we have seen, the increased emphasis on work objectives and measurability desired by the CEO is reflected in the issues covered in the appraisal process, with appraisees reporting that the achievement and planning of work objectives were the most thoroughly discussed issues in the appraisal process. Generally, appraisees found the emphasis on objectives a useful part of the IPR process. A picture that emerges from the survey findings is that objectives are generally clear, cover the most important parts of the job, and that appraisees are actively involved in the objective setting process (see Table 7.5). Interviewees reported being reassured they were on the 'right track', 'working along the right lines', 'on-line', and 'knowing where they stood' ('You might

Table 7.5 Objectives and feedback

	5	4	3	2	1
	Strongly agree	Agree	Neither agree nor disagree	Disagree	Strongly disagree
		%			
The goals that I am to achieve are clear	8	61	13	15	2
The most important parts of my job are emphasised in my performance appraisal	3	58	24	13	2
The performance appraisal system helps me understand my personal weaknesses	5	48	19	26	3
My supervisor allows me to help choose the goals that I am to achieve	13	65	10	10	1
The performance appraisal system helps me to understand my job better	3	37	27	31	1
The performance appraisal system gives me a good idea of how I am doing in my job	6	55	23	14	2

think You are doing a good job but you need someone to tell you that and vice versa') in their jobs. For example:

> Without IPR it would be so easy for you to drift and not do anything. It keeps you on your toes. It keeps you focused. You know exactly what you are aiming for. It makes you look at what you do and what the organisation's trying to achieve. If you didn't have appraisal it would be so easy just to not do anything. You'd just drift. It makes you think about where you are going and where you would like to be.

The setting of objectives provided direction in an increasingly complex and fast-moving organisational environment. The view of one manager was that by appraising her staff she:

> Gives them something to hang on to. The job description is so vast and we are facing so many changes. The objectives give direction. It's a stepping stone for them. They give staff guidance and something to aim for, something constructive to aim for.

Interviewees reported how they often tended to 'push' and 'challenge' themselves to make 'progress', attain 'personal development' and 'growth' via the objective-setting process.

The general view was that in this respect the objectives they set for themselves were more challenging (and interesting) than those produced by their managers. For example:

> Generally I can take them in my stride. There are one or two demanding ones but they are actually objectives I have brought forward myself. I probably tend to push myself harder than the organisation does.

> I always put a new really challenging one in each time, like reducing sickness absence. I tend to challenge myself.

However, for some interviewees their accumulated experience of objective setting had taught them not to challenge themselves 'too much' and restrict both the scope and the number of the objectives they set for themselves. Here we find managerial appraisees becoming sensitised to the objective-setting 'game'. For example:

> What I've learnt, as time goes by, is you've got to be careful, right at the outset, how you set your objectives because you can be over optimistic, unrealistic. There's a danger of sitting down and thinking of all the things you'd love to do, or ideally should do, forgetting that you've got lots of constraints and you couldn't in a month of Sundays achieve it. So I think quite a few of us have learnt

there is a skill in setting objectives which are reasonable and stand a chance of being achieved. I think that that bit is probably more important than anything else. There is nothing more demoralising than being measured against something which you yourself have declared as being in need of being done and finding that you couldn't possibly do it.

Some appraisees felt that objectives were 'imposed' on them but most accepted that this was 'just part of the job'. However, occasionally this caused some considerable irritation and anger, particularly in the clash with IPR's espoused developmental focus. One manager described 'ending up with nothing you really wanted to do' from his IPR and another described how when she pushed her appraiser to include a particular objective that she perceived as being a key issue for the department and which fitted well with her personal development needs, she was told 'either forget it or fit it into your own time'. The danger with imposing objectives on staff reluctant to accept them was that all that was achieved was lip service and half-hearted commitment, accompanied by subsequent 'fudge' in the appraisal review on the measures of achievement. For example:

> I've got to do them [objectives]. I don't not do them but I don't give them the commitment they need if I don't feel it's right. And it never gets picked up at the next appraisal.

Measuring achievement

The use of data in measuring and evaluating individual performance was reported by interviewees as being very reactive on the part of appraisers. Here if the appraisee did not produce data there tended to be very little use of anything other than informed opinion in assessing whether objectives had actually been achieved. An effect of this lack of data use appears to be that although a majority appraisees felt that IPRs represented an accurate measure of their performance, a substantial number were unclear on the standards used to evaluate performance (see Table 7.6).

Some appraisees were prolific in their use of data in the IPR process. Interviewees who had also undertaken NVQ management programmes described a considerable use of reports and the production of memorandums to measure their achievement of objectives. Here, it seems that the NVQ requirement to produce a portfolio causes managers to start to document their work – at least until they attain the award. Our findings suggest this new-found enthusiasm for the memorandum and report generated by NVQs found a further outlet in the IPR process. Further, such documentation and the generally greater level of preparation on the part of the appraisee

Table 7.6 Measuring performance

	5	4	3	2	1
	Strongly agree	Agree	Neither agree nor disagree	Disagree	Strongly disagree
			%		
My performance appraisal for this year represents a fair and accurate picture of my job performance	7	68	11	13	1
My supervisor and I agree on what equals good performance in my job	6	67	14	12	1
I know the standards used to evaluate my performance	2	40	26	29	4

enabled them to control, to a considerable extent, the content and outcomes of the IPR process. For example:

> I took lots of things along [to the IPR meeting]. One of my objectives was to set up team objectives on the ward. I copied examples of these objectives and took them along. I showed reports I had done on the empowerment of patients, and gave her copies of patients' meetings. I used information to show that I had done things. I used these things to prove to her that I had achieved them.

In contrast, other managers usually reported a much less documented measuring process under IPR. The effective use of documentation by this group of managers and professionals thus raises the issue of 'impression management' in the performance measurement process. Impression management is a process by which people attempt to create and sustain desired perceptions of themselves in the eyes of others. In the employment context such others are colleagues, peers, internal customers, clients and especially bosses. The theory of impression management suggests that employees attempt to control, sometimes consciously and sometimes unconsciously, information on themselves which positively shapes others' perceptions of them. The performance-appraisal process is a particular important arena for the creation of favourable impressions at work. The effective use of performance documentation on the part of appraisees thus appears to be a very powerful tool in the production of an overall favourable impression of their managerial capability. A number of appraisers appeared to be very aware of staff's attempts at impression management via the IPR process. Such

appraisers reported how they supplemented data from the IPR interview with views from an appraisee's peers and the 'grapevine'. Some declared that they were very wary of the accuracy of views offered by 'mouthy' and 'gobby' staff. For example:

> A nurse who's an extrovert, who does a lot of mouthing off, may give the impression that they are doing a really wonderful job and the lass who is quiet could be doing an even better job. But because she's not there selling herself, telling you how wonderful she is, she often loses out here.

> I am always wary of the gobby ones. Those who are always telling you how wonderful she is and how hard-worked she is.

It appears the key for managers in measuring individual performance under IPR was distinguishing between 'real' and 'created' performance achievements, the danger being that managers may actually measure an employee's ability to perform in the 'theatrical' rather 'task-oriented' sense.

Objectives and teamwork

The CEO was also keen to encourage wider sharing of objectives, particularly between managers. Here the IPR policy's emphasis on the confidential nature of the appraisal process and its individual nature was seen as discouraging the formal communication of personal objectives with others. The individualistic nature of IPR thus fitted rather uneasily with the considerable growth in teamwork across the trust. For example, according to one manager:

My boss knows how my objectives fit in with my colleagues, but I don't because I never see them.

The CEO was attempting to introduce change here by leading by example and then encouraging other managers to do the same. After setting objectives for his executive directors, all objectives for each manager, including his own, were circulated to the entire senior management team and also sent out to the clinical divisions. However, there generally did not seem to be much formal sharing of objectives among other managers and professionals. Many of our interviewees felt greater sharing of objectives would be valuable, not least in creating a better understanding of performance priorities within and between departments. On informal levels some staff were actively sharing objectives. One manager describes how she encourages this at team meetings with her managers and supervisors:

I'll say at meetings 'Have you looked at your IPR lately? Who's got that in their IPR? Somebody's got that in their IPR.'

Interviewees expressed how they found it easier to prepare their own objectives when their appraising manager provided copies of their own objectives in advance of the review process. Appraisees also reported that much of their work was now conducted in teams, and many felt that more team-based appraisals and the setting of team objectives would helpfully supplement the individualistic nature of IPR. For example:

I think IPR needs to achieve a better balance between individual performance and team performance. We need a much greater emphasis on team performance. Nowadays at NT we are all about teamwork. The IPR approach is too preoccupied with individual performance. It can become too narrow and it is often divisive.

A number also suggested that wider collaboration on the setting of objectives with other managers, project leaders, working parties, etc. would be beneficial in encompassing the full range of their activities.

IPR outputs

In this last section we report our findings on what the IPR process actually achieves. Here we structure our discussion under four main headings; management control; employee motivation; training and development; and rewards.

Management control

Clearly, as we discuss above, the setting and measuring of work objectives facilitates a direct form of managerial control over the labour process. Despite the rhetoric and policy of development, appraisers seemed to use IPR to exert their managerial authority. Occasionally, this was done in a very crude way. For example, a number of interviewees reported problems with managers waiting for the IPR to 'settle scores' for past conflicts. IPR was thus perceived as a vehicle by some appraisees for the line manager to 'tell me what I should be doing', and to 'tell me what I am not doing right in my job'. There is also evidence that IPR acts as a less manifest and more indirect form of managerial control. Here IPR appears to act as a vehicle to encourage 'self-discipline' and 'responsibility' among staff and thus to promote the reshaping of staff attitudes to fit new managerial values and beliefs in line with the changing form of work organisation. For example, even some of the sternest critics of IPR noted its subtle effects on them:

I achieve nothing from it. I suppose the main benefit is I actually discipline myself more with my time management. I think 'Oh, I have got to do so and so', and I chart out my work better so that I'll take all that in. I give myself deadlines for my work, saying 'I'll achieve that by March'.

The direction of control in the IPR process, however, is far from one way. Some managers described how their staff turned the IPR 'tables' on them:

The cooks use IPR to say 'This is why I cannot do my job. This is why I cannot achieve this objective.' And then they trot out a great list of problems with the job.

One manager described why he hated doing appraisals with lower-level staff because it reduced to 'a managerial witch-hunt and a general gripe and groan session about what I had or hadn't done over the year'. The manager became so fed up with being on the receiving end of this that he had written to all staff reminding them of the nature of the IPR process and asking for a more positive attitude and less moaning about perceived managerial inadequacies. However, the memorandum had only served to highlight his discomfort with the process and to increase the level of complaining behaviour from appraisees, such that he now admitted to merely 'going through the motions with IPR to get it over with as quickly as possible'.

Employee motivation

IPR, as we discuss above, was often perceived by appraisers and appraised as a good opportunity for managers and managed to talk meaningfully, and engage in 'quality time' together. Not only did IPR visibly and symbolically demonstrate to staff their value and importance to the organisation, but also that the manager personally cared about their well-being. In some of the accounts of appraisers there were classic human-relations descriptions of the IPR encounter going well beyond the boundaries of work relations. Here interviewees reported appraisals discussing broader personal and social issues and referred to this as 'getting to know your staff':

> IPR helps people in knowing where their professional career and their lives are going.

> It's your time that you devote to them. And some of them have aspirations that you wouldn't know about until you sit down and talk to them. You show that you are genuinely interested in them as people as well as nurses.

The language used to describe these encounters was often heavily redolent of the unitary ideology of human relations. Appraisees and appraisers stories were littered with references to 'progress', 'going forward together', 'participation', 'empowering the appraisee', 'boosting morale', 'becoming a proactive team', 'harnessing our collective energies' via IPR. Interviewees emphasised the importance of good communication, listening and being listened to particularly, as being a manager was often described as being a 'lonely job'. Thus some two-thirds of interviewees felt that they performed the duties of the post better and that IPR contributed positively to their personal motivation and job satisfaction:

> If they scrapped it tomorrow, I don't think I would go home in tears but I would miss it. It helps me keep going, helps me keep motivated. It gives me some comfort, considering all the problems we have at the moment – I've got a service with a lot of problems – that I am achieving what I am supposed to do in my job.

In contrast, other managers, again especially in relation to lower-level staff, were not convinced that IPR reviews delivered much other than a lot of 'hot air' and wasted time that could have been much more profitably employed doing other things. For example:

> I have 49 staff. Appraisal takes at least 30–40 minutes each. That's a lot of man-hours to get nothing out of it other than hot air.

> Senior management would like to think that if you appraise everybody it would instill in them some kind of belonging, some kind of corporate feeling. But for the rank and file they are just not interested.

Training and development

Despite the emphasis of IPR on training and development by the personnel department, as we can see from Table 7.3 the discussion of an appraisee's training needs takes second place to that on work objectives.

Some 12 per cent of appraisees reported that training and development issues were not discussed at all. The majority of those interviewed emphasised training and development as an output of the IPR process. All interviewees claimed to have discussed their own 'personal development plan' (PDP) during the interview. However, this was often reported to be a relatively unfocused and vague discussion. Indeed, few interviewees, under persistent probing, could actually give details of what was in their PDP. The impression gained was that the PDP title signified a much more formalised, more detailed and rather grander training and development document in theory at least if not in practice. Many of the interviewees described a rather mechanical process whereby training and development was discussed as a distinct, almost stand-alone issue. The appraiser was often perceived as running through a checklist of items to be covered in the interview, of which training and development was one, rather than the identification of training needs emerging from a grounded discussion of appraisee performance. The large majority of interviewees felt that much of the training and development that was taking place would still have occurred without the use of IPR but possibly less systematically and at a slower pace.

Managers reported problems with the IPR process – especially coupled with the decision to pursue the IiP award – giving rise to appraisees producing training and development 'wish lists'. Here the key difficulty was finding the training resources to fund costly external courses in the face of increasingly tight training budgets. The demand for degree and diploma courses – particularly among nursing staff – fuelled in part by IPR, was causing managers problems in maintaining staff commitment to the appraisal process, given few employees could be supported in this way. Managers described a coping strategy here of encouraging employees to consider alternative, and less costly, development activities such as short secondments, work shadowing and job exchanges. Interviewees were also critical of the personnel department pushing the current training 'flavour of the month' via the IPR process. At the time of our study this was reported as being the managerial NVQ programme running in-house in conjunction with a local university.

Rewards

The PRP element of IPR was not particularly popular with either appraisers or appraisees. Whereas the general view of IPR was that a majority of both appraisees and interviewees considered it to be an overall positive experience, at least for managers and professionals, the views expressed in relation to performance-related pay were largely all negative. A strong view from those receiving PRP was that it was a lot of 'hassle' for little reward; more influenced by quotas than real performance; did little to motivate yet was often demotivating; unfair; arbitrary; inequitable; highly subjective; bias laden; ineffective and detrimental to professionalism; created dysfunctional interpersonal competition; and undermined the developmental focus of IPR. For some, IPR was 'sullied' by its linkage with PRP. At best appraisees felt PRP might possibly work with better and more stringent guidelines, where performance targets were clear and easily measurable rather than subject to an assessment based on ratings, and when they got on well with their line manager. However, PRP also ensured that appraisals were treated seriously. Many of these issues are very familiar 'moans and groans' from the growing PRP literature. A particular problem identified at NT was that performance was highly dependent on team effort and that work was increasingly being re-organised along teamwork lines yet PRP was individually based. The team – individual conflict in PRP may be at least partially resolved by including teamwork objectives in the appraisal process but as we discuss above this was rarely done at NT. Thus:

> To achieve my objectives I have to rely on all my heads of departments. I have to rely on people outside our division to cooperate or to take things on board. It's a team effort yet I receive an individual

reward that's largely determined on things beyond my control.

Equally, those who did not receive PRP were not keen to be subject to it. This seems to contradict the view that PRP is like an extramarital affair where those with no experience of such things think they are missing out on something terribly exciting and rewarding while those who were involved simply felt miserable. For example:

> I don't need someone wielding a financial stick to tell me how to do my job or push myself.

> PRP wouldn't affect me in the slightest. A few hundred pounds is neither here nor there for me.

Only one of the non-PRP managers was concerned that he was not receiving PRP. In essence this stemmed from his belief that it was unfair for some managers to receive PRP while others (such as himself) did not, rather than any great desire to be subject to it himself:

> IPR was first introduced here for senior managers and was linked to their pay. Then they brought it down to other managers. This is not sour grapes, but when it got down to my level of management the pay was wiped out and just the appraisal was left.

Questions

1 Is IPR a failure at North Trust?
2 Should IPR be retained by the organisation? If you recommend retention, what changes would you advise? If you recommend it should be scrapped, what would you advise should replace it?
3 According to Wright (1991), a paradox of performance management systems is that the meaningful is rarely measurable and the measurable is rarely meaningful. What evidence is there to support such a criticism in North Trust?
4 A key for managers in measuring individual performance under systems of performance appraisal is distinguishing between 'real' and 'created' performance achievements. The danger is that managers may actually measure an employee's 'ability to perform in the theatrical rather than task oriented sense' (Randle and Rainnie, 1997). What evidence is there that this is a problem at North Trust? How can the problems of 'impression management' be minimised?
5 It has been suggested that the key challenge currently facing performance appraisal systems is their upgrading, renewal and re-invention such that they are more compatible with business environments. To what extent does IPR fit the business environment of the 'new, modern and dependable NHS' (Department of Health, 1997)?
6 Some analysts have suggested that the NHS is moving from a bureaucratic mode of organisation to a network mode of organising. What are the implications of such a development for IPR practice?

CASE STUDY 7.2

PERFORMANCE APPRAISAL AND QUALITY MANAGEMENT

Evaluation of performance, merit-rating, or annual review. It nourishes short-term performance, annihilates long-term planning, builds fear, demolishes teamwork, and nourishes rivalry and politics.

It leaves people bitter, crushed, bruised, battered, desolate, despondent, dejected, feeling inferior, some even depressed, unfit for work for weeks after receipt of rating, unable to comprehend why they are inferior. It is unfair, as it ascribes to the people in a group differences that may be caused entirely by the system they work in.

(Deming, 1986)

Using performance appraisal of any kind as a basis for reward of any kind is a flat out catastrophic mistake. It is a sure road to demoralising your workforce. Just don't do it.

(Scholtes, 1990)

Question

You are the HR manager at a manufacturing company. The Chief Executive has recently attended a conference where he was exposed to the ideas of the Deming and others on performance appraisal and quality improvement – see above. He suggests that the company should discontinue all the performance appraisal practices. How would you respond to this request?

Bibliography

Abraham, S., Karns, L., Shaw, K. and Mena, M. (2001) 'Managerial competencies and the managerial performance appraisal proves', *Journal of Management Development*, Vol.20, No.10, 842–52.

*Addison, J. and Belfield, J. (2008) 'The determinants of performance appraisal systems: a note', *British Journal of Industrial Relations*, Vol.46, No.3, 521–31.

Aldakhilallah, K. and Parente, D. (2002) 'Re-designing a square peg: total quality management performance appraisals', *Total Quality Management,* Vol.13, No.1, 39–51.

Armstrong, M. and Baron, A. (1998) *Performance Management,* London: IPD.

Arthur, W., Woehr, D.J., Akande, A. and Strong, M.H. (1995) 'Human resource management in West Africa: practices and perceptions', *International Journal of Human Resource Management,* Vol.6, No.2, 347–67.

*Barlow, G. (1989) 'Deficiencies and the perpetuation of power: latent functions in management appraisal', *Journal of Management Studies,* Vol.26, No.5, 499–517.

Bettenhausen, K.L. and Fedor, D.B. (1997) 'Peer and upward appraisals: a comparison of their benefits and problems', *Group and Organizational Management,* Vol.22, No.2, 236–63.

Bevan, S. and Thompson, M. (1991) 'Performance management at the crossroads', *Personnel Management,* November, 36–9.

Bhote, K.R. (1994) 'Boss performance appraisal: a metric whose time has gone', *Employment Relations Today,* Vol.21, No.1, 1–8.

Boudreaux, G. (1994) 'What TQM says about performance appraisal', *Compensation and Benefits Review,* Vol.26, No.3, 20–4.

Bowles, M.L. and Coates, G. (1993) 'Image and substance: the management of performance as rhetoric or reality', *Personnel Review,* Vol.22, No.2, 3–21.

*Brown, M. and Benson, J. (2003) 'Rated to exhaustion? Reactions to performance appraisal processes', *Industrial Relations Journal,* Vol.34, No.1, 67–81.

Brown, M. and Heywood, J.S. (2005) 'Performance appraisal systems: determinants and change', *British Journal of Industrial Relations*, Vol.43, 659–79.

Carroll, S.J. and Schneier, C.E. (1982) *Performance Appraisal and Review Systems: The Identification, Measurement, and Development of Performance in Organizations,* Glenview, IL: Scott, Foresman and Company.

Chow, I. (1994) 'An opinion survey of performance appraisal practices in Hong Kong and the Peoples' Republic of China', *Asia Pacific Journal of Human Resources,* Vol.32, 62–79.

CIPD (2005) *Performance Management,* Survey Report, London: Chartered Institute of Personnel and Development.

Coates, G. (1994) 'Performance appraisal as icon: Oscar-winning performance or dressing to impress?' *International Journal of Human Resource Management,* Vol.5, No.1, 165–91.

Connock, S. (1992) 'The importance of "big ideas" to HR managers', *Personnel Management,* Vol.21, No.11, 52–6.

Cook, S. (1993) *Customer Care,* London: Kogan Page.

CPCR (1995) *The Right Angle on 360-degree Feedback,* Newcastle: CPCR.

Cully, M., Woodland, S., O'Reilly, A. and Dix, G. (1999) *Britain at Work,* London: Routledge.

Deming, W.E. (1986) *Out of the Crisis: Quality, Productivity and Competitive Position*, Cambridge: Cambridge University Press.

Department of Health (1997) *The New NHS: Modern, Dependable,* London: The Stationery Office.

Dugdill, G. (1994) 'Wide angle view', *Personnel Today,* 27 September, 31–2.

Endo, K. (1994) '*Satei* (personal assessment) and interworker competition in Japanese firms', *Industrial Relations,* Vol.33, No.1, 70–82.

Fletcher, C. (1993) 'Appraisal: an idea whose time has gone?', *Personnel Management,* September, 34–8.

Fletcher, C. and Williams, R. (1992) 'The route to performance management', *Personnel Management,* 42–7.

Fonda, D. (2003) 'It's the B team's time to shine: under-appreciated corporate foot soldiers may be quick to bolt when the economy rebounds', *Time,* 15 September, 62–4.,

Fuller, L. and Smith, V. (1991) 'Consumers' reports: management by customers in a changing economy', *Work Employment and Society,* Vol.4, No.1, 1–16.

Gabris, G.T. and Ihrke, D.M. (2001) 'Does performance appraisal contribute to heightened levels of employee burnout?', *Public Personnel Management,* Vol.30, No.2, 157–72.

Gill, D. (1977) *Appraising Performance: Present Trends and the Next Decade*, London: IPD.

*Grint, K. (1993) 'What's wrong with performance appraisals? A critique and a suggestion', *Human Resource* Management*, Vol.3, No.3, 61–77.

Halachmi, A. (1993) 'From performance appraisal to performance targeting', *Public Personnel Management,* Vol.22, No.2, 323–44.

IDS (2007) *Performance Management*, HR Studies, London: Incomes Data Services.

ILO (2002) *Supporting Workplace Learning for High Performance Working,* Geneva: International Labour Organization.

IPD (1999) *Training and Development in Britain 1999,* IPD Survey Report, London: Institute of Personnel and Development.

IRS (1992) 'Industrial relations developments in the water industry', *Employment Trends,* No.516, 6–15.

IRS (1994) 'Improving performance? A survey of appraisal arrangements', *Employment Trends,* No.556, 5–14.

IRS (1995a) 'Survey of employee relations in local government', *Employment Trends,* No.594, 6–13.

IRS (1995b) 'The customer is boss: matching employee performance to customer service needs', *Employment Trends,* No.585, 7–13.

IRS (1999) 'New ways to perform appraisal', *Employment Trends,* No.676, 7–16.

Kayande, U. and Finn, A. (1999) 'Unmasking the phantom: a psychometric assessment of mystery shopping', *Journal of Retailing,* Vol.75, No.2, 135–217.

Kersley, B., Alpin, C., Forth, J., Bryson, A., Bewley, H., Dix, G. and Oxenbridge, S. (2006) *Inside the Workplace: Findings from the 2004 Workplace Employment Relations Survey,* London: Routledge.

Kessler, I. and Purcell, J. (1992) 'Performance related pay: objectives and application', *Human Resource Management Journal,* Vol.2, No.3, 16–33.

Lawler, E.E. (1994) 'Performance management: the next generation', *Compensation and Benefits Review,* May–June, 16–28.

Lawler, J.J., Jain, H.C., Ratnam, C.S.V. and Atmiyanandana, V. (1995) 'Human resource management in developing economies: a comparison of India and Thailand', *International Journal of Human Resource Management,* Vol.6, No.2, 320–46.

Lee, J., Havighurst, L. and Rassel, G. (2004) 'Factors related to court references to performance appraisal fairness and validity', *Public Personnel Management,* Vol.33, No.1, 61–77.

LGMB (1994) *Performance Management and Performance-Related Pay. Local Government Practice*, London: Local Government Management Board.

Locher, A.H. and Teel, K.S. (1988) 'Appraisal trends', *Personnel Journal,* Vol.67, No.9, 139–43.

London, M. and Beatty, R.W. (1993) '360-degree feedback as a competitive advantage', *Human Resource Management,* Vol.32, Nos 2–3, 353–72.

Long, P. (1986) *Performance Appraisal Revisited,* London: Institute of Personnel and Development.

Longenecker, C. (1989) 'Truth or consequences: politics and performance appraisals', *Business Horizons,* November–December, 76–82.

Maroney, B.P. and Buckley, P.P.M. (1992) 'Does research in performance appraisal influence the practice of performance appraisal? Regretfully not', *Public Personnel Management,* Vol.21, No.2, 185–96.

Milliman, J.F., Zawacki, R.A., Schulz, B., Wiggins, S. and Norman, C. (1995) 'Customer service drives 360-degree goal setting', *Personnel Journal,* June, 136–41.

O'Reilly, B. (1995) '360-degree feedback can change your life', *Fortune Magazine,* 17 October, 55–8.

Randell, G. (1994) 'Employee appraisal', in Sisson, K. (ed.) *Personnel Management: A Comprehensive Guide to Theory and Practice in Britain,* Oxford: Blackwell.

Randle, K. and Rainnie, A. (1997) 'Managing creativity, maintaining control: a study in pharmaceutical research', *Human Research Management Journal,* Vol.7, No.2, 32–46.

Redman, T. and Mathews, B.P. (1995) 'Do corporate turkeys vote for Christmas? Managers' attitudes towards upward appraisal', *Personnel Review,* Vol.24, No.7, 13–24.

Redman, T. and Snape, E. (1992) 'Upward and onward: can staff appraise their managers?', *Personnel Review,* Vol.21, No.7, 32–46.

*Redman, T., Snape, E., Thompson, D. and Ka-ching Yan, F. (2000) 'Performance appraisal in the National Health Service: a trust hospital study', *Human Resource Management Journal,* Vol.10, No.1, 1–16.

Roth, W. and Ferguson, D. (1994) 'The end of performance appraisals?', *Quality Digest,* Vol.14, No.9, 52–7.

Scholtes, P.(1990) 'An elaboration of Deming's teachings on performance appraisal', in *Performance Appraisal: Perspectives on a Quality Management Approach*, Gary N. McLean, Susan R. Damme and Richard A Swanson (eds). American Society for Training and Development, Alexandria: Va.

Shing, M. and Spence, M. (2002) 'Investigating the limits of competitive intelligence gathering: is mystery shopping ethical', *Business Ethics: A European Review,* Vol.11, No.4, 343–4.

Snape, E., Redman., T. and Bamber, G. (1994) *Managing Managers,* Oxford: Blackwell.

*Snape, E., Thompson, D., Ka-ching Yan, F. and Redman, T. (1998) 'Performance appraisal and culture: practice and attitudes in Hong Kong and Great Britain', *International Journal of Human Resource Management,* Vol.9, No.5, 841–61.

Thomas, A., Wells, M. and Willard, J. (1992) 'A novel approach to developing managers and their teams: BPX uses upward feedback', *Management Education and Development,* Vol.23, No.1, 30–2.

Toegel, G. and Conger, J. (2003) '360-degree feedback: time for reinvention', *Academy of Management Learning and Education,* Vol.2, No.3, 297–311.

Tombs, S. (1992) 'Managing safety: could do better . . .', *Occupational Safety and Health,* Vol.26, No.1, 9–12.

Townley, B. (1989) 'Selection and appraisal: reconstituting "social relations"', in Storey, J. (ed.) *New Perspectives on Human Resource Management,* London: Routledge.

Townley, B. (1993) 'Performance appraisal and the emergence of management', *Journal of Management Studies,* Vol.30, No.2, 221–38.

Townley, B. (1999) 'Practical reason and performance appraisal', *Journal of Management Studies,* Vol.36, No.3, 287–306.

Wright, V. (1991) 'Performance related pay', in Neale, F. (ed.) *The Handbook of Performance Management,* London: Institute of Personnel Management.

---

*Useful reading

CHAPTER 8
INDUSTRIAL RELATIONS

Nicolas Bacon

Introduction

The purpose of this chapter is to outline some of the key contemporary developments in industrial relations and consider the implications. The term 'industrial relations', when broadly defined, encompasses the study of all aspects of the employment relationship (see Heery *et al.*, 2008: 2); more narrowly defined, it has traditionally focused on those areas of the employment relationship in which managers deal with the representatives of employees rather than the direct management of individual employees (Edwards, 1995). Industrial relations systems involve a variety of actors including employers and managers, workers and workers' organisations (usually trade unions) and the state. Recently, greater attention has been paid to new actors in the industrial relations system to consider the impact of financial investors (for example, private equity), consultants and civil society organisations. Actors in the industrial relations system create rules to regulate work. Some of these are 'substantive rules', covering such issues as wages and working hours, and others are 'procedural rules', covering such matters as how to bargain, consult and resolve disputes over issues. Whether substantive or procedural rules are set unilaterally by employers, the extent to which the state decides to intervene and regulate employment, and the role of workers and trade unions in the process of establishing rules, are among the central industrial relations issues explored in this chapter. Although employers may set rules to try to maximise efficiency, other actors in the employment relationship may challenge employer decisions on a variety of grounds. The state or trade unions, for example, may feel that employer under-investment in training and skills will result in low levels of productivity and threaten economic performance. In addition, workers and the state are also particularly interested in the fairness of employment outcomes and seek to influence employer policies on a range of issues. On the issue of pay for example, trade unions may disagree with employer interpretations of what constitutes a fair day's work for a fair day's pay, the fair distribution of pay between workers producing work of equal value (men and women for example), and between workers and senior executive remuneration. In order to manage such differences of opinion and interests, employment practices in many organisations are often the result of joint regulation between employers and trade unions. Joint regulation of employer practices requires some degree of employee participation in managerial decision-making and it is appropriate to start by considering how managers react to this challenge to their authority.

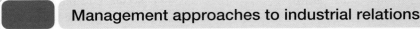

Management approaches to industrial relations

The suggestion that trade unions or the state should intervene, or intervene more, in regulating employment often provokes a strong negative response in many employers and managers. Many managers prefer to make unilateral employment decisions and protect the right to manage (frequently termed the management prerogative) from attempts by workers, unions and the state to intervene (Budd and Bhave, 2008). In defending the right to manage it is assumed that managers should act as the agents of shareholders and make decisions purely in the shareholders' interests, rather than balancing shareholders' rights against the interests of a broader range of stakeholders. These assumptions applied to industrial relations are termed 'frames of reference' (Fox, 1966: 1974), which describe managers' often deeply held assumptions towards a labour force and the rights of workers, trade unions or the state to influence management decisions. Three separate frames of reference can be identified: unitarism, pluralism and radical. A manager with one frame of reference will differ from a manager with an alternative frame of reference in terms of their beliefs about the nature of organisations, the role of conflict and the task of managing employees. Managers holding a unitarist frame of reference believe that the natural state of organisations is one of harmony and cooperation. All employees are thought to be on the same team, pulling together for the common goal of organisational success. Managers need to prevent conflict arising from misunderstandings that result if they fail to adequately communicate organisational goals to employees. Any remaining conflicts are attributed to mischief created by troublemakers. In contrast, a pluralist frame of reference recognises that organisations contain a variety of sectional groups who legitimately seek to express their divergent interests. The resulting conflict that arises is considered inevitable and the task of managers is to establish a system of structures and procedures to institutionalise conflict and establish a negotiated order. The radical critique of pluralism is not, strictly speaking, a frame of reference for understanding management views of the employment relationship. It draws upon Marxist explanations of workplace conflict as inevitable given the broader historical and social struggle between opposing social classes.

There are no simple methods to assess whether managers hold one frame of reference or another – individual managers may have a complex range of views, and of course managers may hold different views in different countries. In Britain, as typical of liberal market economies, most managers: oppose sharing power with unions; prefer unilateral managerial decision-making; express a preference for flexible labour markets; and oppose government involvement in wage setting (Poole *et al.*, 2005). As trade union power has declined, managers have also felt less need for the state to intervene to restrict union power (Poole *et al.*, 2005).

Answers to another question frequently posed to managers indicate that a majority of workplace managers do not have a single frame of reference. Most managers directly responsible for industrial relations issues in Britain (62 per cent) express 'neutral' views about union membership, with 21 per cent 'in favour' and 17 per cent 'not in favour' of union membership by employees in their workplace (Kersley *et al.*, 2006: 112–13). However, unitarist preferences emerge when the same managers are asked more explicitly whether they prefer to manage employees directly or through unions. For example, 79 per cent of managers surveyed agreed with the statement 'we would rather consult directly with employees than with unions' (Kersley *et al.*, 2006: 50). Consequently, management approaches to industrial relations are often characterised as mixing and matching unitarist and pluralist beliefs (Edwards *et al.*, 1998). Many managers hold such views because it reflects the reality of employees' need for representation to protect their interests from employers, or a pragmatic acceptance that in some industries unions are powerful and employees will only regard rules as legitimate if their representatives participate in management decisions. Encouraging or deterring employees from joining unions appears to be particularly important, as employers' attitudes towards unions are positively associated with union presence in the workplace (Kersley *et al.*, 2006: 114) and union membership across Europe (Schnabel and Wagner, 2007), and this is also likely to be the case outside Europe.

Frames of reference are also important because they are one aspect of the broader management style adopted towards the workforce. The approach taken to industrial relations is often linked to broader work organisation and human resource management issues (Fox, 1974; Purcell and Ahlstrand, 1994; Purcell and Sisson, 1983; Storey and Bacon, 1993; for a review see Bacon, 2008). An important question is whether employers enforce managerial prerogatives in order to introduce high-performance work practices and compete on the basis of investments to increase employee knowledge, skills and abilities (Bacon, 2003). Or, in contrast, are managers avoiding unions in order to compete on the basis of reducing employment costs? Before considering this in more detail, however, employers cannot devise effective industrial relations approaches without carefully considering the views of their employees, and the next section explores this issue.

Why employees join unions

A widespread criticism of management during the 1960s and 1970s, a point which still holds today, is that employees may not feel that everyone shares the same goals in their workplace and they may reject unitarist assumptions. In many workplaces employees talk of 'us' and describe managers as 'them', believing that there are two sides with at least partially conflicting interests (Clegg, 1979). Thus, many employees feel that workers and managers are at times on different sides, rather than feeling that work is like playing for a football team, where all groups supporting a club are on the same side and pursuing a common goal (Ramsey, 1975).

Many employees therefore join trade unions because they feel their interests differ from those of their employers. Trade unions have approximately 320 million members worldwide, which amounts to between one-fifth and one-quarter of the global labour force (Visser, 2003). Significant variation exists between countries. For instance, Russia, Ukraine and Belarus (58 per cent) and China (42 per cent) have high rates of union membership; around one-quarter (26 per cent) of European workers are union members; whereas a smaller proportion of workers in North America (13 per cent) and Asia (10 per cent) belong to unions. It is therefore important that managers understand why employees join trade unions.

Employees join unions for a wide range of reasons (Schnabel, 2003: 19). They may join a union because they feel dissatisfied with their work situation (termed the frustration–aggression thesis). Joining a union may bring benefits such as higher wages that outweigh the costs of membership (a rational choice explanation). Alternatively, employees may be encouraged to join by the traditions and opinions of their work group (an interactionist explanation). In a study across 18 EU countries, in addition to the aforementioned relationship between employers' attitudes towards unions and whether union members are present in the workplace, the probability of union membership is also affected by workplace characteristics, personal characteristics and an individual's attitudes (Schnabel and Wagner, 2007). The types of workplace, the personal characteristics of the labour force and individual attitudes may, of course, vary between countries. Alongside other factors, these characteristics and attitudes help explain national differences in levels of union membership. In addition, state support for unions, the union role in social insurance schemes, and national political history, are also important explanations of differences in national levels of union membership. To illustrate in more detail, some of the factors identified in the study of 18 EU countries just mentioned were important in a survey of almost 11,000 union members in the UK (Waddington and Whitston, 1997). In the UK survey, employees revealed that they continued to join unions for collective protection and to improve their terms and conditions (Table 8.1). These findings are in line with studies suggesting that workers' perceptions of 'them' and 'us'

Table 8.1 The reasons employees give for joining unions

Support if I had a problem at work	72%
Improved pay and conditions	36%
Because I believe in trade unions	16%
Free legal advice	15%
Most people at work are members	14%

Source: Waddington and Whitston, 1997: 521.

are still strong, even though managers over the past 20 years have attempted to increase levels of employee commitment through a wide range of initiatives described in other chapters in this book (see Coupland *et al.*, 2005; D'Art and Turner, 1999; Kelly and Kelly, 1991).

The decline of joint regulation

The degree of joint regulation of industrial relations is not of course fixed, but changes in response to global and national economic, social and political pressures. In a majority of countries union membership has fallen over the past 20 years, especially in Europe and North America. Increased market competition, for example, has reduced the willingness of employers to recognise and negotiate with trade unions in many, but not all, countries (Brown, 2008). Table 8.2 shows the extent of decline in union density – the proportion of employees who are union members – in 20 OECD countries. In different European regions and in liberal market economies, union density has declined, although it has declined only marginally in northern Europe (Denmark, Finland, Norway and Sweden) and has declined most steeply in liberal market economies (Australia, Canada, Ireland, New Zealand, the UK and the US).

Declining union density is only one indication of joint regulation and it is also important to consider trends in collective bargaining coverage – the proportion of employees whose terms and conditions of employment are set by collective bargaining. Reflecting the comments made above about the impact of national economic and political differences on unionisation, Table 8.3 shows that the most dramatic decline in collective bargaining coverage has occurred in liberal market economies (Australia, Canada, New Zealand, the UK and the US). Among central European countries collective bargaining coverage has remained stable in some countries (Austria and Belgium), declined in others (Germany and Switzerland) and increased in the Netherlands. It has increased in mainland Europe (France, Greece, Italy, Portugal and Spain), as it has in northern Europe.

Within each group of countries, and within each country, joint regulation has probably not declined at a uniform rate. However, in liberal market economies the steep decline of joint regulation appears to have affected all industrial sectors, if not evenly. If we consider a third indicator of joint regulation, union recognition, in the UK for example, the number of

Table 8.2 Average union density (%) and density change in 20 OECD countries, 1980–2000

Region	1980	1990	2000	Change 1980–2000
Northern Europe	71.5	71.5	71	−0.5
Mainland Europe	35	25	22	−12.8
Central Europe	42	36	32	−10.6
Liberal market economies	47	38	26	−20.7

Source: Hamann and Kelly, 2008: 138.

Table 8.3 Average percentage of employees covered by collective bargaining in 20 OECD countries, 1980–2000

Region	1980	1990	2000	Change 1980–2000
Northern Europe	78	78	83	+5
Mainland Europe	73	78	83	+8
Central Europe	77	77	75	–2.5
Liberal market economies	55	47	36	–18.4

Source: Hamann and Kelly, 2008: 139.

workplaces recognising unions declined between 1980 and 2004 in all sectors but the decline was modest in the public sector compared to the private sector (Table 8.4).

What are the main reasons for the decline in joint regulation? Focusing on liberal market economies, because this is where the decline is most evident, and using the UK as an example, the decline in union recognition since the 1980s is mainly due to the failure of unions to organise workers and gain recognition for collective bargaining in new firms and new workplaces (Machin, 2000). Responding to heightened competitive pressures, managers have proved reluctant to recognise unions for fear of higher wages, and unions have found it difficult to recruit the growing numbers of female and service sector workers. As the number of large manufacturing plants and manual workers declined, the traditional habitat for adversarial collective bargaining was disappearing (Millward *et al.*, 1992). During the 1990s, these factors accounted for three-quarters of the decline in collective bargaining, although, in addition, managers in unionised workplaces were less likely to continue ongoing collective bargaining arrangements, with about one-quarter of the decline in the 1990s explained by abandoning collective bargaining in ongoing workplaces (Charlwood, 2007).

Trade union influence appears even lower than suggested by current levels of union recognition when we consider the scope and depth of joint consultation and bargaining. It is difficult to assess the extent to which managers rely upon collective agreements with trade unions in workplaces. Although formal collective agreements may include procedural arrangements for continued union influence in the workplace (Dunn and Wright, 1994), managers have increasingly exercised their prerogative to make important changes unilaterally, particularly in working methods (Geary, 1995). This suggests that although many employers retain agreements with unions, collective agreements have been hollowed out and in workplaces where union representatives are present only a modest level of joint regulation occurs. On average in British workplaces with recognised unions, for example, across seven different bargaining issues, employers report negotiating with union representatives in 10 per cent of workplaces, consult in 36 per cent, inform union representatives in 20 per cent, and neither negotiate, consult nor inform in 28 per cent of workplaces (Brown and Nash, 2008). Managers in many workplaces appear to regard certain HR issues as off-limits to union representatives and do not even provide information on these issues to unions. As a consequence, trade union influence in many workplaces has 'withered on the vine', and where union representatives remain in place this resembles a unionised approach to industrial relations which in fact is little more than a 'hollow shell' (Hyman, 1997).

Table 8.4 Average percentage of workplaces with 251 employees recognising unions, 1980–2004

	1980	1984	1990	1998	2004
Manufacturing	65	56	44	28	37
Private services	41	44	36	23	20
Public sector	94	99	87	87	88
All	64	66	53	42	39

Source: Blanchflower *et al.*, 2007: 288.

Unions have been denied influence by employers seeking greater freedom to choose employment practices. From the mid-1980s, this has been characterised as employers exercising an increasing degree of strategic choice in redesigning employment practices. The strategic choice theory of industrial relations marked a paradigm shift from unions making demands and employers conceding to those demands, to managers, rather than unions, becoming the central industrial relations actor in liberal market economies such as the US, and making demands to which unions had to accede (Strauss, 1984). At the core of strategic choice theory in industrial relations is the assumption that managers 'have discretion over their decisions; that is, where environmental constraints do not severely curtail the parties' choice of alternatives' (Kochan *et al.*, 1984: 21). However, declining union influence does not necessarily increase employer freedom of choice, for three reasons. First, the state has increasingly intervened to regulate employment practices to compensate for the decline of joint regulation between employers and unions (Piore and Safford, 2006). Second, intensive market forces have reduced employer discretion in employment practices in many instances. If all employers are, for example, forced to marginalise trade unions because they have to reduce employment costs then this is hardly a strategic choice but a market imperative (Lewin, 1987: for a broader review see Bacon, 2008). Third, the market for corporate control has increased pressure from financial markets to discipline managers to act in the interest of shareholders. As a result, economic returns to shareholders and senior executives have increased relative to the return for labour. Whether or not declining union influence reflects increased managerial strategic choice or not, declining union influence is associated with increased income inequality given wage redistribution is what unions do.

The implications of declining joint regulation

Trade unions have a range of beneficial effects, including forcing managers to improve human resource management practices (the 'shock effect' of unions requiring an improvement in management); increasing employee voice in the workplace to express the interests of employees, seeking the redistribution of outcomes and promoting equal opportunities (the 'sword of justice' effect); and increasing job satisfaction and reducing labour turnover. Union effects appear to have reduced remarkably in recent years; on some issues unions now appear to have no discernible effects and in other cases the effects only apply in specific circumstances (see Brown, 2008: 123). The long-term implications of the decline in joint regulation are potentially far-reaching.

According to the collective voice/institutional response model of unionism (Freeman and Medoff, 1984), unions express employees' views and have an impact on managers greater than the views expressed by individual employees, which are frequently ignored by managers. With this collective voice unions seek to raise employee wages and bargain for a range of beneficial policies for members, such as greater training. As a result, unionised workers traditionally received higher wages compared to non-unionised workers (the union wage premium) and, as described earlier, employees act rationally in joining unions for higher wages that outweigh the costs of membership. At a time when unions are less powerful, employers that recognise unions may resist pressure to provide improved terms and conditions. As a result, the union wage premium, calculated by comparing the wages of unionised and non-unionised workers, has reduced overtime (Blanchflower and Bryson, 2003). Nevertheless, in 2005 the union wage premium in Britain was 10 per cent of gross hourly earnings (Bryson and Forth, 2008). Trade unions also have a second important effect on wages by narrowing the pay distribution in attempting a fair redistribution of reward. It is therefore not surprising that declining unionisation results in increasing wage inequality (Charlwood, 2007) and the salaries of executive directors and managers have risen exponentially as unions have been less able to increase members' wages.

Moving beyond wages, declining unionisation has also affected training provision and the ability of unions to raise training levels. Trade unions raise training levels in a variety of ways.

Unions bargain directly for more training and increase wages so employers have to train employees in order for employees to contribute more and offset higher wages. In expressing and seeking to resolve employee grievances, unions also reduce employee turnover, thereby extending the period in which employers benefit from training investments. It appears, however, that the positive union effect on training is also in decline. Whereas training was higher in unionised workplaces throughout the 1980s and 1990s in Britain, by 2004 unionised workplaces in the private sector no longer provided more training than non-unionised workplaces in the private sector, and the union training premium in the public sector was weak (Hoque and Bacon, 2008). Even where unions have prioritised training (see the discussion of union learning representatives later in this chapter), and employers negotiated and bargained with union representatives over training, there is little evidence that employers respond to this pressure. In Britain at least, trade unions are currently not able to raise training levels above those provided in non-union workplaces in the private sector.

Trade unions also fulfil a 'sword of justice' role in promoting fairness and equality in the workplace. Unionised workplaces report more family-friendly policies and are more likely to have an equal opportunities policy (Noon and Hoque, 2001; Walsh, 2007). For example in Britain, whereas 63 per cent of non-union workplaces had an equal opportunities policy in 2004, 96 per cent of unionised workplaces had such a policy (Kersley *et al.*, 2006: 238). In the absence of union pressure and the willingness of employers to respond to this pressure, employers are less likely to adopt family-friendly and equal opportunities policies (Metcalf, 2004).

As the evidence reviewed so far suggests, unions are associated with many positive employment practices in the workplace, although employers are increasingly unresponsive to union pressure. There is also evidence that employers seek to offset the higher costs associated with unionisation by saving on employment costs elsewhere. For example, White (2005) reports that unionised compared to non-union workplaces not only report more high-performance work practices, fringe benefits and family-friendly practices, but unionised workplaces also report high levels of labour-cost-cutting policies such as reducing staffing levels, outsourcing and delayering management hierarchies. This suggests that where unions encourage managers to adopt expensive productivity-enhancing HR practices, employers look to reduce other employment costs by reducing staffing levels, or employing staff on inferior terms and conditions through contractors.

Earlier in this chapter the declining influence of unions on employer policy was shown by the significant number of unionised workplaces in which managers did not negotiate, consult or inform union representatives on key employment issues. Recent evidence suggests that trade unions are no longer as effective in raising the concerns of their members because managers are increasingly less willing to listen to concerns expressed through union representatives and prefer to deal with individual employees. Trade unions rely on the logic of collective action – expressing the collective voice of employees has more influence than an employee acting alone. Managers appear increasingly unresponsive to union voice, with evidence that unions are no longer able to shock employers into better practices to raise productivity (Bryson *et al.*, 2006). Trade unions find it increasingly difficult to resolve workplace grievances with unresponsive employers, and as a result find it increasingly difficult to increase the levels of satisfaction employees experience in their jobs. Guest and Conway (2004), for example, report that union members compared to non-union members report lower levels of job satisfaction, consistent with the suggestion that management unresponsiveness to union-expressed grievances and demands constrains union voice and increases the levels of dissatisfaction among union members. This is a worrying finding because job satisfaction is associated with turnover, and reduced turnover increases the incentive for employers to invest in commitment-enhancing human resource management practices, as the period over which they benefit from such investments is greater if fewer staff exit. Employer unresponsiveness to trade unions is gradually shutting off the productivity-enhancing impacts of trade unions.

Employers feel justified in avoiding unions or being unresponsive to pressure from unions because unions may damage productivity by exercising monopoly power to defend restrictive work practices and raise wage costs above market rates. These issues have been extensively debated by labour economists without clear resolution one way or the other. Metcalf (2004) summarising the data on the productivity effects of unions, the impact of unions on financial performance and the probability of firm closure, notes that there is no difference in the productivity, financial performance or likelihood of closure of union and non-union workplaces. It certainly seems likely that at a time of union weakness, any union impact on productivity is minimal, whether the impact is positive or negative. The declining impact of unions has, however, affected their ability to encourage employers to adopt sophisticated human resource management practices, improve employee terms and conditions, and raise job satisfaction levels at work. The joint regulation of industrial relations has certainly declined but what does this mean for the increasing number of workers who find themselves in non-union workplaces, and how effectively are the interests of non-union workers represented?

Non-union workplaces

In the classic account by Fox (1974), to maintain a non-union status managers enforce management prerogative by coercive power to justify a unitarist ideology. Managers have often used a wide-ranging web of defences against unionisation that in their more extreme variants in the US include 'sweet stuff' to make management policies more acceptable to employees, 'fear stuff' to discourage union joining and 'evil stuff' to demonise unions (Roy, 1980). Managers holding a unitarist frame of reference may adopt quite different approaches (Purcell and Ahlstrand, 1994): a 'sophisticated human relations' approach requires investment in staff development and use of a wide range of human resource management policies to substitute for the services unions provide for members (a union substitution approach or 'sweet stuff'); a 'paternalist' approach seeks to build the loyalty and commitment of staff through consideration for employee welfare ('sweet stuff'); and a 'bleak house' strategy involves minimising labour costs and aggressively avoiding union recruitment ('fear stuff' and 'evil stuff').

Several key commentators in the late 1980s predicted a growth in the non-union 'sophisticated human relations' approach (Sisson, 1989). A non-union environment appeared well suited to the demands of developing committed and flexible employees, as demonstrated by several large non-union US multinationals such as IBM, Hewlett Packard and Mars (Foulkes, 1980; Kochan *et al.*, 1986). For example, IBM had combined corporate success, a positive employee relations climate of low conflict, low labour turnover and long service, with good pay and conditions. In addition, the company provided procedures to fulfil many of the functions met by unions, including a complex array of alternative procedures (a no-redundancy policy, single status, equal opportunities policies, merit pay and performance assessments), a strong emphasis on internal communications and a grievance system. Most employees working at an IBM plant in the UK studied by Dickson *et al.* (1988) were positively attached to the individualistic ethos of the company and perceived little need for union protection. In the case of 'Comco', explored by Cressey *et al.* (1985), employees also identified strongly with the company and enjoyed 'greater benefits' and 'less disciplinary pressure'. Scott (1994) outlined a slightly different 'golden handcuffs' approach whereby employees in a chocolate works received good terms and conditions in return for accepting a high rate of effort and strict rules.

Despite this evidence, non-union companies with a sophisticated approach to managing employees appear to remain the exception. A study of high-tech companies in the southeast of England, where we might expect companies to reproduce the IBM non-union model, uncovered little evidence of sophisticated HRM, with companies either opportunistically avoiding unions or adopting the style of 'benevolent autocracies' (McLoughlin and Gourlay, 1994). Furthermore, the assumed benefits of a 'sophisticated human relations' approach may be illusory. Blyton and Turnbull (2004) suggest that Marks & Spencer, so often held up as an exemplar non-union company, simultaneously pursued a 'union substitution' strategy in retail outlets while forcing suppliers into a cost minimisation approach. In another example, a steel plant that had introduced apparently exemplary human resource and work organisation practices subsequently derecognised trade unions, with employees reporting that managers insisted on attitudinal compliance, work intensification and the suppression of any counter-balancing trade union activity (Bacon, 1999). It is also striking that among these cases, IBM lost its pre-eminence in its sector, Marks & Spencer now sources from Asian suppliers leading to the closure of many UK suppliers, and the steel plant mentioned above closed.

Given the comments earlier in this chapter about the positive impact of unions on the adoption of high-commitment management practices (the 'shock effect' of unions), it is not surprising that sophisticated HRM practices are to be found alongside union recognition mainly in larger workplaces and those in the public sector rather than non-union private sector workplaces (Cully *et al.*, 1999: 111; Machin and Wood, 2005; Sisson, 1993: 206). Furthermore, higher union density (the proportion of employees who are trade union members) is also associated with greater joint regulation and more high-commitment management (HCM) practices. There is also evidence that the combination of union recognition and high-commitment management practices has a powerful effect on workplace performance, with 'workplaces with a recognised union and a majority of the HCM practices … [performing] better than the average, and better than workplaces without recognition and a minority of these practices' (Cully *et al.*, 1999: 135). In private sector workplaces where managers withdrew from collective bargaining during the 1990s there was no compensating increase in high-commitment management practices, with lower productivity growth as a consequence (Charlwood, 2007). It is not clear, however, that these positive associations will continue, given the evidence presented earlier in this chapter showing that union effects on employers continue to diminish in unionised workplaces. If unions cannot force employers to adopt more HCM practices than non-unionised companies then the differences between working in the union and non-union sectors will gradually disappear and this inevitably reduces the incentive for employees to join unions.

Non-union employee representation

As many workplaces are effectively union-free, Towers (1997) suggests a 'representation gap' may have developed where managers operate without any independent employee voice. The representation gap is felt most keenly among workers who might join a union but a union does not exist in their workplace (Metcalfe, 2004). In Britain, for example, three-quarters of workplaces contain no employee representatives (either union or non-union employee representatives) and almost half of employees do not have an employee representative to speak up for them (Charlwood and Terry, 2007: 324). The absence of representation is important because dissatisfied workers who cannot effectively express their grievances may have little option but to leave the organisation (Hirschman, 1971). In the absence of union recognition managers can provide employee voice through direct channels by communicating with workers in team briefings and problem solving groups, and there is evidence that managers are more responsive to these communications than in listening to unions (Bryson, 2004). However, many organisations fail to provide either union channels or direct channels for employee voice.

Earlier it was mentioned that the state has increasingly intervened in industrial relations, partly to compensate for the decline in joint regulation through trade unions. The European Union Directive for informing and consulting employees provided rights for employees to be informed about the economic situation of their employer's business, employment prospects and substantial changes in work organisation or employment contracts (Hall, 2006). This imposes obligations on all organisations, including those without unions, to consult with employee representatives. Although workplace union representatives continue to have some effects on employer policies and employees' terms and conditions, the evidence to date reports that non-union forms of employee representation have no effects and are irrelevant (Charlwood and Terry, 2007). There is little evidence that non-union employee representation, even backed by legislation, meets the basic requirement of representing employee interests to influence employer practices.

Partnership with unions

What of other developments in the unionised sector? In organisations where managers continue to recognise unions, an important innovation in liberal market economies has been the signing of partnership agreements with trade unions, arrangements that may also be termed mutual gains enterprises (Kochan and Osterman, 1994). A central aim of partnership arrangements is to replace the notion of conflict between employers and trade unions with cooperation to introduce high performance work practices.

Managers and unions have contested the meaning of 'partnership' and at times it appears an inherently ambiguous industrial relations aim with no agreed meaning (Ackers and Payne, 1998; Undy, 1999). As Undy (1999: 318) has pointed out, 'What one party, or commentator, means by "partnership" is not necessarily shared by others.' Despite these different views, the Involvement and Participation Association (IPA), an independent pressure group, developed an influential definition of partnership with leading companies and trade union leaders (Involvement and Participation Association, 1992). This definition requires managers to make the following substantive and procedural commitments: declare security of employment as a key corporate objective; share the results of success with employees; and recognise the legitimacy of the employees' right to be informed, consulted and represented. In return, trade unions are required to: renounce rigid job demarcations and commit to flexible working; give sympathetic consideration to the continental model of representation of the whole workforce by means of election of representatives to new works councils; and recognise and then co-promote employee involvement methods.

Although critics of partnership agreements doubt whether a significant proportion of employers would sign such agreements, or that trade unions had much to gain by doing so (Kelly, 2004), employers and unions have signed significantly more partnership agreements than expected, with 248 partnership agreements signed in Britain between 1990 and 2007, covering almost 10 per cent of all employees and one-third of public sector employees (Bacon and Samuel, 2007). Furthermore, four-fifths of all agreements signed survived, suggesting that few employers and unions walked away from these agreements once signed in ongoing workplaces. However, the majority of partnership agreements have been signed in the public rather than the private sector, with private sector employers generally avoiding partnership agreements with trade unions. The growth of agreements in the public sector partly reflects union power in that sector compared to the private sector. In order to modernise public services, some governments have signed strategic agreements with unions and continue to work with them to meet the challenges of public sector expenditure restrictions.

Does the popularity of partnership agreements indicate that managers and unions are leaving conflict behind and are establishing the basis for a new industrial relations consensus? Careful study of the content of partnership agreements does not support such an optimistic interpretation. Few agreements conform to the IPA definition of partnership, mainly because few contain substantive commitments by employers to provide job security for employees, or to share the gains of productivity improvements with employees as suggested by the mutual gains model (Samuel and Bacon, 2008). Most partnership agreements in Britain are biased towards procedural rules over consultation and do not extend joint regulation or involve managers relinquishing control over unilateral determination of substantive terms and conditions. As employers relinquish so little in these agreements, more employers have signed partnership agreements than commonly appreciated.

Employers and unions signing partnership agreements have to deal with at least two critical issues. First, both sides have to commit fully to a single strategy of cooperative industrial relations throughout the organisation and avoid behaving in a short-term, contradictory or opportunistic manner. For example, at the Royal Mail several partnership initiatives have failed because not all managers in the company supported the partnership approach (Bacon and Storey, 2000). For some other employers, partnership agreements form part of a longer-term strategy to marginalise trade unions (Claydon, 1989; Gall and McKay, 1994; Kelly, 1996; Smith and Morton, 1993). Whereas one review of partnership agreements in six organisations reported that 'none gave serious consideration to ending recognition' (IDS 1998: 4), a study of management attempts to restructure industrial relations in ten organisations (Bacon and Storey, 2000) revealed that de-recognition had been more seriously explored. According to Oxenbridge *et al.* (2003), employers working in partnership with unions to implement organisational change are sometimes simultaneously excluding unions from bargaining over issues such as pay.

A second important issue for the future of partnership agreements is whether they deliver greater returns for managers and trade unions. If returns are not forthcoming for either party then enthusiasm for the partnership approach may wane. Kelly (1996) has argued, for example, that unions have more to gain from militancy than cooperation with employers. Partnership is associated by Kelly with eroding the willingness and capacity of union members to resist employers, inhibiting the growth of workplace union organisation and generating apathy among union members; it involves union 'give' and management 'take', results in attempts to drive down terms and conditions of employment, and fails to genuinely represent member grievances. The extent to which Kelly is correct and unions will not benefit from partnership agreements is an interesting question. Kelly (2004) compared similar UK companies with and without partnership agreements and found that partnership firms shed jobs at a faster rate than non-partnership firms in industries marked by employment decline. In contrast, however, partnership firms in expanding sectors created jobs at a faster rate than non-partnership firms. Partnership appeared to have no impact on wage settlements or union density. In another study of 54 companies, Guest and Peccei (2001: 207) discovered that the balance of advantage from partnership at work 'is skewed towards management', with improvements only in employment relations, quality and productivity. As few partnership agreements actually contain substantive clauses on job security or sharing gains with employees, gains for employees from partnership are particularly elusive (Samuel and Bacon, 2008).

Union organising and new types of union representatives

As many employers have preferred not to recognise unions, or negotiate and consult with unions even where they are recognised, it is not surprising that workers and unions have sought to defend their interests. Unions have increasingly focused on organising workers and recruiting new members as an alternative to partnership (Heery, 2002) and reversing falling membership levels and declining collective bargaining coverage. In training a new generation of union organisers to recruit members and organise workplaces (Fiorito and Jarley, 2008), it is not surprising to see unions learning lessons from the US in how to conduct effective recruitment drives when employers oppose unions (see Godard, 2008). Union avoidance techniques used by employers in the US (Logan, 2006) are also being learned by employers in other countries. A significant increase in new recognition deals has occurred in Britain, reflecting the work of union organisers and the backing provided by the statutory union recognition procedure of the Employment Relations Act 1999 (Gall, 2004). To date, however, this has slowed rather than reversed the decline of union recognition in Britain, as described in Table 8.4.

Such has been the pace of trade union innovation that unions in Britain have also developed and recruited new types of workplace union representatives focused on single issues. These include union learning representatives (ULRs) and equality representatives, although there are others such as environment representatives. The emergence of new types of workplace union representatives constitutes an important and strategic initiative by unions to service existing members, recruit new members and represent members' interests on specific issues. A key aim in recruiting members into single-issue union posts is to increase membership activity in workplace unions and to work with employers on issues that employers have recently regarded as areas of management prerogative. The impact of these new representatives will have an important influence in forthcoming years on whether unions are able to encourage employers to increase training provision and improve equal opportunities.

To assess the likely impact of these initiatives it is helpful to consider the case of ULRs in Britain as the most developed initiative, with 26,000 ULRs trained in 12 years by 2012 to improve training provision for their members. The Employment Act 2002 provided ULRs with statutory rights to paid time off for five key tasks: analysing training needs; providing information and advice on training; arranging training; promoting the value of training; and consulting the employer over these activities. Have ULRs been able to increase training provision? Research to date has failed to identify a consistent relationship between ULRs and training, with ULR presence not associated with training among any employee group with the exception of male non-managers in the public sector (Hoque and Bacon, 2008). The same research has, however, shown that ULRs may exercise a 'sword of justice' role. Employees who are traditionally less likely to report receiving training (for example, older workers, part-time workers, lower occupational groups, and workers with lower-level academic qualifications) are more likely to report training in workplaces with ULRs present. Whether ULRs are successful in raising training levels will depend on the extent to which employers value these new union representatives, employers are genuinely willing to consult and negotiate on these issues, and employers will provide paid time off from normal work duties for representatives to conduct these activities. A large proportion of ULRs in 2004, for example, did not spend any time on employee training in their role as a union representative and could therefore have little influence on levels of employer-provided training (Bacon and Hoque, 2008a). Employer support is essential if these new types of representatives are to be effective, as the amount of time spent on the ULR role is strongly related to the number of hours the employer pays for the ULR to spend time on the role (Bacon and Hoque, 2008b). Although other types of new union representatives are only just developing, it is anticipated that the degree of support from management for their role will affect whether unions are able to influence employer policies and develop workplace union representation through recruiting single-issue union representatives. Interestingly, initial findings concerning the impact of trade union equality reps suggest such reps are having a more significant impact on employer equality practices than ULRs have had on employer training practices (Bacon and Hoque, 2012). Whether this reflects the initial recruitment and impact of a particularly dedicated set of equality activists in workplaces with receptive employers is yet to be seen.

Conclusions

The aim of this chapter was to introduce the topic of industrial relations, outline some of the key contemporary developments in industrial relations and consider the implications. It covered management approaches to industrial relations, the reasons employees join unions, the decline of joint regulation and its implications, employer choice in industrial relations, non-union workplaces and employee representation in non-union workplaces, partnership with unions, union organising and new types of union representatives. Employers in liberal market economies and other countries are increasingly less inclined to support joint regulation of industrial relations. As a result, unions have found it increasingly difficult to represent effectively the interests of their existing and new members who continue to join trade unions. Employers avoid union recognition and influence in order to avoid the costs imposed by unions. The state has increasingly legislated on employment issues to protect employees from employer attempts to drive down terms and conditions and evade their responsibility for promoting equitable employment. The state is also the major sponsor of partnership agreements with unions as it attempts to reform public services. Employers also have to deal with more sustained attempts by unions to challenge employers by actively organising workplaces. New types of union representatives focused on specific issues are potentially helpful allies for employers seeking to increase employee participation in training and increase the effectiveness of equal opportunities policies. These new representatives are only likely to be effective, however, if employers are willing to concede management prerogative over these issues in the years ahead.

CASE STUDY 8.1

UNION–MANAGEMENT PARTNERSHIP AT NATBANK

STEWART JOHNSTONE

NatBank is a major UK bank with over 60,000 employees in the UK and over 100,000 employees worldwide. The partnership agreement at NatBank was born out of a very poor climate of industrial relations in the late 1990s, culminating in industrial action over pay in 1997. Union representatives and managers admitted that there was a need to end the hostile 'everybody out mentality' that prevailed within the bank whenever an issue arose, and that the 1990s situation of 'arm's-length adversarialism' was simply untenable. Improving employment relations was especially important as competition in the financial service sector was intense, and organisational performance had been disappointing. A formal partnership agreement was signed between NatBank and the recognised trade union in 2000, based upon an adaptation of six principles of partnership espoused by the Trades Union Congress:

The principles of partnership:

1 To secure and promote the long-term success of NatBank.
2 To promote the interests of employees, customers and shareholders.
3 To ensure that NatBank meets customer expectations by having people with the right skills in the right place at the right cost.
4 To facilitate the management of change.
5 To ensure employees are managed fairly and professionally.
6 To promote equality of treatment and opportunity for all, valuing diversity.

Partnership was described by senior managers as a modern and sensible approach to the management of industrial relations centred around a joint commitment to business success. In practice this was said to require greater dialogue and interaction with the trade union, and the ability to consider decisions from both an 'employee' as well as 'business' point of view. A senior manager contrasted this with a non-partnership approach, where the union may simply want what is best for the

union/employees, while the business simply wants what is best for the business. For local managers, partnership concerned a more proactive problem-solving approach, and achieving a clear understanding of the rationale behind decisions. It was made clear by the management team, however, that the union representatives and officials need not necessarily agree with decisions. Rather, the focus was on early consultation regarding developments and the opportunity for representatives to provide feedback and input while decisions are still at 'the design stage'. When local representatives had strong feelings on an issue and no agreement could be reached locally, there was the option of escalating it to monthly national consultation for further detailed discussion. However, it was clear that under partnership the business retained the right to make the final decisions.

Similarly, for a senior union official, partnership concerned problem-solving, mutual respect, transparency, and greater interaction between the union and the management team. However, he warned that the term 'partnership' for such an approach is perhaps inappropriate and potentially misleading. He suggested that the language of partnership often resulted in a debate regarding whether partnership suggests or requires an 'equal' relationship between unions and employers. He believed that such debates were actually unproductive, and that it is was better to view partnership in a more pragmatic way, as essentially an opportunity for unions to get 'inside the tent'. In turn, this was said to offer unions access to key business decision-makers, the provision of better information, and a greater respect for each party's point of view. He suggested that senior management now had a clearer idea of the operation and purpose of trade unions, and equally full-time officials now had a greater appreciation of business issues and decision making. He contrasted partnership with an 'institutional conflict approach', without any real dialogue or regard for the other party's point of view. It was suggested that partnership provided a framework by clarifying the rights and responsibilities of the employer and the union, and setting out the 'rules of the game'.

Overall, several benefits were identified compared to the adversarial approach of the 1990s. A key benefit concerned the ability of the union to influence decision-making. There was evidence to suggest that the union was involved across areas including pay and conditions, discipline and grievance, and organisational change. An example of this is the joint development of guidelines outlining various commitments regarding off-shoring practices. At the centre of this agreement were commitments to avoid compulsory redundancies and redeploy staff elsewhere in the business where possible, to provide early consultation, and to provide extensive support for employees who were ultimately displaced. With partnership it was suggested that the union now had a wider remit, especially in relation to organisational change issues, whereas prior to partnership much of the attention centred around pay and conditions. More generally, with partnership management were said to benefit from constructive feedback which assisted their decision-making, meaning that pre-emptive changes could be made and leading to the greater legitimacy and acceptance of decisions. For the business, it was suggested that the partnership dialogue also encouraged a longer-term perspective than may otherwise have been the case. On the other hand, the union was said to benefit from the opportunity to have a say, often being consulted at a very early stage in the decision-making process. Though the partnership process was not viewed as one of joint decision making per se, union officials and representatives believed that there was evidence of the consultation process having an impact, and this was also recognised by employees.

Another benefit of partnership was said to be more local decision-making and improved employment relations. The emphasis from the union had been on building a solid cadre of local representatives, and there was evidence to suggest that this had been successful. Representatives were active and knowledgeable, and appeared to be well respected by management and employees alike. Representatives described their role under partnership as one of questioning, challenging and persuading, as opposed to simply opposing management proposals. In this regard, a key issue was developing a strong basis on which to question proposals which took into account both business rationale as well as the impact on employees. There also appeared to have been an increase in union legitimacy. Prior to partnership, the union was said to have had few resources or facilities provided by the employer. Much of the work of a union representative was undertaken at home, and it was not unusual for vacancies for representative posts to be left unfilled. Since partnership, credible and active representative roles had been created, and all union committee positions were filled, and previously weak

trade union organisation was believed to have been revived. Representatives were now able to hold quarterly recruitment events, to distribute promotional materials, and to deliver a presentation at staff inductions for new staff. In addition, representatives were pleased with other arrangements in relation to the provision of sufficient time off for union duties, access to meeting rooms and use of office facilities.

In contrast to the frosty times of the 1990s, relationships between senior management and union officials, as well as between local management and union representatives, appeared to be very good. There was a belief that whereas prior to partnership relationships were best described as 'arm's-length legislative compliance', partnership relationships were characterised by a greater degree of trust and mutual respect. It was proposed that dialogue was now more concerned with business success, and trying to balance the needs of the business on the one hand and the likely impact for employees on the other. Building the necessary relationships was said to have been hard work, but was believed to be worthwhile. Again, this did not mean there had not been some significant disagreements between the union and management, but these were viewed as a natural part of any relationship. It also appeared that union representatives had a good relationship with employees. Though employee understanding of the exact nature of the union representatives' involvement and relationship with management was patchy, most employees perceived the union–management relationship to be generally healthy.

Nevertheless, some challenges remained. It was suggested that sometimes there was a lack of a clear understanding of partnership among actors, and what it means in terms of working relationships and decision-making. It was generally agreed to require both early consultation at the design stage and a genuine attempt to consider issues from both a business and employee point of view when making decisions. The emphasis was on an explanation of the rationale for decisions, and an opportunity for the union to comment, question and propose alternatives. However, the ultimate decision resided with management. Occasionally some management and union actors were said to have had difficulties with this style of arrangement, but overall most preferred a more collaborative approach compared with the more adversarial strategies of the 1990s. This related to the challenge of embedding a 'partnership culture' across the entire organisation, especially at middle-management level. Though relationships were said to be strong between senior management and union officials, as well as locally between business managers and representatives, tensions sometimes arose with line managers responsible for actually implementing decisions. It was believed that sometimes agreed procedures were inadvertently overlooked, and that some line managers were still uncomfortable with the requirements of the partnership style of working. Line managers also appeared to occupy a space outside the partnership system, which focused predominantly upon the relationships between senior/business managers and union officials/representatives.

An additional challenge was believed to be winning the buy-in of employees. There was a feeling that some employees had little interest in the union, although most employees did appear to trust the union to work effectively behind the scenes to protect their interests. A particular worry from some union representatives was the danger that they may be perceived to be 'in the bank's pocket', as employees only hear about the final outcomes of a decision, and not the actual process of consultation. Embargoes on information were believed to make it more difficult to demonstrate influence to members. As such, there was a feeling that with partnership it can be difficult to advertise the successes of

the union to members, and there was a perception that this may have been easier under traditional bargaining. The representatives stressed that there was a need for a great deal of trust from members that they were actively involved on their behalf and not just management poodles, as demonstrating their effectiveness to members was perceived to be more challenging through the low-key partnership approach.

A final concern was the sustainability of the partnership over time, and in particular the effect of a major organisational crisis such as an economic downturn. Equally, there were concerns if some of the key champions of partnership, both from management and the union, were to leave the organisation. Others also questioned the sustainability of partnership if there was a sudden change in government policy, away from the pro-partnership stance of the last decade. Nevertheless, it seems reasonable to conclude that, despite these challenges, a partnership approach appeared to be fairly well rooted, demonstrating a reasonable degree of success and delivering a variety of benefits to actors.

Questions

1   What were the main drivers for partnership at NatBank?

2   What did 'partnership' mean to managers and trade union officials/representatives?

3   What were the key benefits for management, the trade union and employees?

4   To what extent had partnership increased union effectiveness?

5   Why might line managers have found partnership particularly challenging?

6   What challenges might threaten the sustainability of partnership at NatBank in the future?

Bibliography

Ackers, P. and Payne, J. (1998) 'British trade unions and social partnership: rhetoric, reality and strategy', *International Journal of Human Resource Management,* Vol.9, 529–50.

Bacon, N. (1999) 'Union derecognition and the new human relations: a steel industry case study', *Work, Employment and Society,* Vol.13, No.1, 1–17.

Bacon, N. (2003) 'Human resource management and industrial relations', pp. 71–88, in Ackers, P. and Wilkinson, A. (eds) *Understanding Work and Employment:, Industrial Relations Transition*, Oxford: Oxford University Press.

Bacon, N. (2008) 'Management strategy and industrial relations', pp. 24–57, in Blyton, P., Bacon, N., Fiorito, J. and Heery, E. (eds) *The SAGE Handbook of Industrial Relations,* London: Sage.

Bacon, N. and Hoque, K. (2008a) 'Exploring the link between union learning representatives and employer-provided training in Britain'. Paper presented to WIAS, University of Sheffield.

Bacon, N. and Hoque, K. (2008b) 'Union learning representatives and training'. Paper for BUIRA Conference, University of West of England, 25–27 June.

Bacon, N. and Hoque, K. (2012) 'The role and impact of trade union equality representatives in Britain', *British Journal of Industrial Relations*, Vol.50, No.2, 239–62.

Bacon, N. and Samuel, P. (2007) 'Partnership agreement adoption, form and survival in Britain'. Paper presented to IIRA Conference, Manchester.

Bacon, N. and Storey, J. (1993) 'The individualisation of the employment relationship and the implications for trade unions', *Employee Relations*, Vol.15, No.1, 5–17.

Bacon, N. and Storey, J. (2000) 'New employee relations strategies: towards individualism or partnership', *British Journal of Industrial Relations,* Vol.38, No.3, 407–27.

Blanchflower, D.G. and Bryson, A. (2003) 'Changes over time in union relative wage effects in the UK and US revisited', in Addison, J.T. and Schnabel, C. (eds) *International Handbook of Trade Unions,* Cheltenham: Edward Elgar.

Blanchflower, D.G., Bryson, A. and Forth, J. (2007) 'Workplace industrial relations in Britain, 1980–2004', *Industrial Relations Journal,* Vol.38, No.4, 285–302.

Blyton, P. and Turnbull, P. (2004) *The Dynamics of Employee Relations* (3rd edn), Basingstoke: Palgrave Macmillan.

Brown, W. (2008) 'The influence of product markets on industrial relations', pp. 113–28, in Blyton, P., Bacon, N., Fiorito, J. and Heery, E. (eds) *The SAGE Handbook of Industrial Relations,* London: Sage.

Brown, W. and Nash, D. (2008) 'What has been happening to collective bargaining under New Labour? Interpreting WERS 2004', *Industrial Relations Journal,* Vol.39, No.2, 91–103.

Bryson, A. (2004) 'Managerial responsiveness to union and nonunion worker voice in Britain', *Industrial Relations,* Vol.43, No.1, 213–42.

Bryson, A. and Forth, J. (2008) 'The theory and practice of pay setting', pp. 491–512, in Blyton, P., Bacon, N., Fiorito, J. and Heery, E. (eds) *The SAGE Handbook of Industrial Relations,* London: Sage.

Bryson, A., Charlwood, A. and Forth, J. (2006) 'Worker voice, managerial response and labour productivity: an empirical investigation', *Industrial Relations Journal,* Vol.37, No.5, 438–55.

Budd, J. and Bhave, D. (2008) 'Values, ideologies, and frames of reference in employment relations', pp. 92–112, in Blyton, P., Bacon, N., Fiorito, J. and Heery, E. (eds) *The SAGE Handbook of Industrial Relations,* London: Sage.

Charlwood, A. (2007) 'The de-collectivisation of pay setting in Britain 1990–98: incidence, determinants and impact', *Industrial Relations Journal,* Vol.38, No.1, 33–50.

Charlwood, A. and Terry, M. (2007) '21st-century models of employee representation: structure, processes and outcomes', *Industrial Relations Journal,* Vol.38, No.4, 320–37.

Claydon, T. (1989) 'Union de-recognition in Britain in the 1980s', *British Journal of Industrial Relations,* Vol.27, 214–23.

Clegg, H. (1979) *The System of Industrial Relations in Great Britain,* Oxford: Blackwell.

Coupland, C., Blyton, P. and Bacon, N. (2005) 'A longitudinal study of the influence of shop floor work teams on expressions of "us" and "them"', *Human Relations,* Vol.58, No.8, 1055–81.

Cressey, P., Eldridge, J. and MacInnes, J. (1985) *Just Managing: Authority and Democracy in Industry,* Milton Keynes: Open University Press.

Cully, M., Woodland, S., O'Reilly, A. and Dix, G. (1999) *Britain at Work,* London: Routledge.

D'Art, D. and Turner, T. (1999) 'An attitudinal revolution in Irish industrial relations: the end of "them and us"?'. *British Journal of Industrial Relations,* Vol.37, No.1, 101–16.

Dickson, T., McLachlan, M.V., Prior, P. and Swales, K. (1988) 'Big Blue and the union: IBM, individualism and trade union strategy', *Work, Employment and Society,* Vol.2, 506–20.

Dunn, S. and Wright, M. (1994) 'Maintaining the "status quo": an analysis of the contents of British collective agreements 1979–1990', *British Journal of Industrial Relations,* Vol.32, 23–46.

Edwards, P. (1995) 'The employment relationship', in Edwards, P. (ed.) *Industrial Relations,* Oxford: Blackwell.

Edwards, P., Hall, M., Hyman, R., Marginson, P., Sisson, K., Waddington, J. and Winchester, D. (1998) 'Great Britain: from partial collectivism to neo-liberalism to where?', pp. 1–54, in Ferner, A. and Hyman, R. (eds) *Changing Industrial Relations in Europe,* Oxford: Blackwell.

Fiorito, J. and Jarley, P. (2008) 'Trade union morphology', pp. 189–208, in Blyton, P., Bacon, N., Fiorito, J. and Heery, E. (eds) *The SAGE Handbook of Industrial Relations*, London: Sage.

Foulkes, F.K. (1980) *Personnel Policies in Large Non-union Companies,* Englewood Cliffs, NJ: Prentice Hall.

Fox, A. (1966) 'Industrial sociology and industrial relations', *Royal Commission Research Paper No.3,* London: HMSO.

Fox, A. (1974) *Beyond Contract: Work, Power and Trust Relations,* London: Faber and Faber.

Freeman, R.B. and Medoff, J.L. (1984). *What Do Unions Do?,* New York: Basic Books.

Gall, G. (2004) 'Trade union recognition in Britain, 1995–2002: turning a corner?', *Industrial Relations Journal,* Vol.35, No.3, 249–70.

Gall, G. and McKay, S. (1994) 'Trade union de-recognition in Britain 1988–94', *British Journal of Industrial Relations,* Vol.32, 433–48.

Geary, J. (1995) 'Work practices: the structure of work', pp. 368–96, in Edwards P. (ed.) *Industrial Relations,* Oxford: Blackwell.

Godard, J. (2008) 'Union formation', pp. 377–405, in Blyton, P., Bacon, N., Fiorito, J. and Heery, E. (eds) *The SAGE Handbook of Industrial Relations,* London: Sage.

Guest, D. and Conway, N. (2004) 'Exploring the paradox of unionised worker dissatisfaction', *Industrial Relations Journal,* Vol.35, No.2, 102–21.

Guest, D.E. and Peccei, R. (2001) 'Partnership at work: mutuality and the balance of advantage', *British Journal of Industrial Relations,* Vol.39, No.2, 207–36.

Hall, M.J. (2006) 'A cool response to the ICE Regulations? Employer and trade union approaches to the new legal framework for information and consultation', *Industrial Relations Journal,* Vol.37, 456–72.

Hamann, K. and Kelly, J. (2008) 'Varieties of capitalism and industrial relations', pp. 129–48, in Blyton, P., Bacon, N., Fiorito, J. and Heery, E. (eds) *The SAGE Handbook of Industrial Relations,* London: Sage.

Heery, E. (2002) 'Partnership versus organising: alternative futures for British trade unionism', *Industrial Relations Journal,* Vol.33, No.1, 20–35.

Heery, E., Bacon, N., Blyton, P. and Fiorito, J. (2008) 'Introduction: the field of industrial relations', pp. 1–32, in Blyton, P., Bacon, N., Fiorito, J. and Heery, E. (eds) *The SAGE Handbook of Industrial Relations,* London: Sage.

Hirschman, A. (1971) *Exit, Voice and Loyalty,* Cambridge, MA: Harvard University Press.

Hoque, K. and Bacon, N. (2008) 'Trade unions, union learning representatives and employer-provided training in Britain', *British Journal of Industrial Relations,* Vol.46, December, 702–31.

Hyman, R. (1997) 'The future of employee representation', *British Journal of Industrial Relations,* Vol.35, No.3, 309–36.

IDS (1998) 'Partnership agreements', *IDS Study,* 656, October.

Involvement and Participation Association (IPA) (1992) *Towards Industrial Partnership: A New Approach to Management Union Relations,* London: IPA.

Kelly, J. (1996) 'Union militancy and social partnership', pp. 41–76, in Ackers, P., Smith, C. and Smith, P. (eds) *The New Workplace and Trade Unionism,* London: Routledge.

Kelly, J. (2004) 'Social partnership agreements in Britain: Labour cooperation and compliance', *Industrial Relations,* Vol.43, No.1, 267–92.

Kelly, J. and Kelly, C. (1991) 'Them and us: social psychology and the "new industrial relations"', *British Journal of Industrial Relations,* Vol.29, No.1, 25–48.

Kersley, B., Alpin, C., Forth, J., Bryson, A., Bewley, H., Dix, G. and Oxenbridge, S. (2006) *Inside the Workplace: Findings from the 2004 Workplace Employment Relations Survey,* Abingdon: Routledge.

Kochan, T.A. and Osterman, P. (1994) *The Mutual Gains Enterprise*, Boston, MA: Harvard Business School Press.

Kochan, T., Katz, H. and McKersie, B. (1986). *The Transformation of American Industrial Relations,* New York: Basic Books.

Kochan, T.A., McKersie, R.B. and Cappelli, P. (1984) 'Strategic choice and industrial relations theory', *Industrial Relations,* Vol.23, No.1, 16–39.

Lewin, D. (1987) 'Industrial relations as a strategic variable', pp. 1–41, in Kleiner, M.M., Block, R.N., Roomkin, M. and Salsburg, S.W. (eds) *Human Resources and the Performance of the Firm,* Madison, WI: Industrial Relations Research Association.

Logan, J. (2006) 'The union avoidance industry in the United States', *British Journal of Industrial Relations,* Vol.44, No.4, 651–75.

Machin, S. (2000) 'Union decline in Britain', *British Journal of Industrial Relations,* Vol.38, No.4, 631–45.

Machin, S. and Wood, S.J. (2005) 'Human resource management as a substitute for trade unions in British workplaces', *Industrial and Labor Relations Review,* Vol.58, No.1, 201–18.

McLoughlin, I. and Gourlay, S. (1994) *Enterprise Without Unions: Industrial Relations in the Non-Union Firm,* Milton Keynes: Open University Press.

Metcalfe, D. (2004) *British Unions: Resurgence or Perdition,* London: The Work Foundation.

Millward, N., Stevens, M., Smart, D. and Hawes, W.R. (1992) *Workplace Industrial Relations in Transition,* Aldershot: Dartmouth.

Noon, M. and Hoque, K. (2001) 'Ethnic minorities and equal treatment: the impact of gender, equal opportunities policies and trade unions', *National Institute Economic Review,* Vol.176, No.1, 105–16.

Oxenbridge, S., Brown, W., Deakin, S. and Pratten, C. (2003) 'Initial responses to the Statutory Recognition Provisions of the Employment Relations Act 1999', *British Journal of Industrial Relations,* Vol.41, No.2, 315–34.

Piore, M.J. and Safford, S. (2006) 'Changing regimes of workplace governance, shifting axes of social mobilisation, and the challenge to industrial relations theory', *Industrial Relations,* Vol.45, No.3, 299–325.

Poole, M., Mansfield, R., Gould-Williams, J. and Mendes, P. (2005) 'British managers' attitudes and behaviour in industrial relations: a twenty-year study', *British Journal of Industrial Relations,* Vol.43, No.1, 117–34.

Purcell, J. and Ahlstrand, B. (1994) *Human Resource Management in the Multi-Divisional Company,* Oxford: Oxford University Press.

Purcell, J. and Sisson, K. (1983) 'Strategies and practice in the management of industrial relations', in Bain, G. (ed.) *Industrial Relations in Britain,* Oxford: Blackwell.

Ramsey, H. (1975) 'Firms and football teams', *British Journal of Industrial Relations,* Vol.13, No.3, 396–400.

Roy, D. (1980) 'Fear stuff, sweet stuff and evil stuff: management's defences against unionization in the south', pp. 395–415, in Nichols, T. (ed.) *Capital and Labour: A Marxist Primer,* Glasgow: Fontana.

Samuel, P. and Bacon, N. (2008) 'Exploring the content of British partnership agreements signed between 1990 and 2007', Paper for BUIRA Conference, 25–27 June, University of West of England.

Schnabel, C. (2003) 'Determinants of trade union membership', pp. 13–43, in Addison, J.T. and Schnabel, C. (eds) *International Handbook of Trade Unions,* Cheltenham, Edward Elgar.

Schnabel, C. and Wagner, J. (2007) 'Union density and determinants of union membership in 18 EU countries: evidence from micro data, 2002/03', *Industrial Relations Journal,* Vol.38, No.1, 5–32.

Scott, A. (1994) *Willing Slaves?* Cambridge: Cambridge University Press.

Sisson, K. (1989) 'Personnel management in transition?', in Sisson, K. (ed.) *Personnel Management in Britain,* Oxford: Blackwell.

Sisson, K. (1993) 'In search of HRM', *British Journal of Industrial Relations,* Vol.31, No.2, 201–10.

Smith, P. and Morton, G. (1993) 'Union exclusion and decollectivization of industrial relations in contemporary Britain', *British Journal of Industrial Relations,* Vol.31, No.1, 97–114.

Storey, J. and Bacon, N. (1993) 'Individualism and collectivism into the 1990s', *International Journal of Human Resource Management,* Vol.4, No.3, 665–684.

Strauss, G. (1984) 'Industrial relations: time of change', *Industrial Relations,* Vol.23, No.1, 1–15.

Towers, B. (1997) *The Representation Gap,* Oxford: Oxford University Press.

Undy, R. (1999) 'Annual review article: New Labour's "Industrial Relations Settlement": the third way?', *British Journal of Industrial Relations,* Vol.37, No.2, 315–36.

Visser, J. (2003) 'Unions and unionism around the world', pp. 366–414, in Addison, J.T. and Schnabel, C. (eds) *International Handbook of Trade Unions,* Cheltenham, Edward Elgar.

Waddington, J. and Whitston, C. (1997) 'Why do people join unions in a period of membership decline?', *British Journal of Industrial Relations,* Vol.35, No.4, 515–46.

Walsh, J. (2007) 'Equality and diversity in British workplaces: the 2004 Workplace Employment Relations Survey', *Industrial Relations Journal,* Vol.38, No.4, 303–19.

White, M. (2005) 'Cooperative unionism and employee welfare', *Industrial Relations Journal,* Vol.36, No.5, 348–66.

CHAPTER 9
LINE MANAGERS AND HRM

Douglas W.S. Renwick

Introduction

Background

The involvement of Line Managers (LMs) in Human Resource Management (HRM) work seems such a common occurrence in work organisations today that it might be seen as an essential aspect of an HRM-based approach to employment relationships, in practitioner circles at least. If we work on the basis of logic, some reasons why LMs appear used in HRM seem perhaps straightforward: such managers occupy a leading operational role in the people-related elements of general management jobs, like motivating, communicating, rewarding, disciplining and releasing employees. In essence, LMs could thus be considered day-to-day managers of people – and hence key actors in enacting HRM workplace policies and processes. Devolution in HRM or 'assigning' HR work to LMs may (supposedly) release HR specialists from 'operational' HR tasks, and enable HR to undertake more complex HR matters (such as employment law and strategy), so HR can take a more holistic and/or longer-term view of managing people in organisations too.

However, research in the field of involving LMs in HRM also reveals that a number of developments, challenges and questions emerge from LM involvement in HRM, and as such, may ask us to re-evaluate the usefulness of LMs in HRM *per se.* This chapter aims to unravel some of these issues, and provides case studies to test the knowledge of learners on this topic. The chapter begins by outlining some definitions, rationales and problems regarding involving LMs in HRM, and then details developments on their role from the relevant global, European and British literatures. Some key issues that emerge from this literature base are then stated, and future research ideas specified. Thoughts about using theory more usefully in this field are then detailed, which are followed by some conclusions. The chapter ends with cases to test the knowledge of students.

Definition

Some commentators define LMs as enacting 'general management work – rather than being specialists in a particular functional area, like HRM, marketing or sales' (Legge, 1995). Here, relevant works differentiate between types of managers working at various levels in HRM, e.g. the role of middle managers (Currie and Procter, 2001;

Fenton O'Creevy, 1998, 2001), which 'are two levels below the CEO and one level above first-line supervisor' (Huy, 2002: 38), and who have direct responsibility over subordinates (Delmestri, 2006: 1523). Further, other works investigate the role of: Front or First-Line Managers (FLMs) (Leisink and Knies, 2011; Marchington, 2001; Purcell and Hutchinson, 2007; Storey, 1992), supervisors (Armstrong-Stassen and Schlosser, 2010: 375; Brunetto, Farr-Wharton and Shacklock, 2010: 206; Lowe, 1992), and production supervisors, i.e. shop-floor employees (Mason, 2000: 628). However, differences exist in the studies just mentioned on how managers enact HRM, as some authors use differing terms to define it, such as 'involvement' (Gibb, 2003; Marsh and Gillies, 1983; Renwick, 2009), or 'responsibility' (Larsen and Brewster, 2003; Thornhill and Saunders, 1998; Whittaker and Marchington, 2003).

Rationale

One reason why LMs seem to be involved in HR work is that such duties have been 'devolved' to them – a trend labelled 'HRM devolution' (Brewster and Larsen, 2000; Currie and Procter, 2001; Guest and King, 2001; Larsen and Brewster, 2003; Renwick, 2009; Storey, 1992, 2001). Here, while involving LMs in HRM may seem like a recent development, the relevant prior literature tells us that it is not. In the UK for example, many authors detail that LMs have been responsible and accountable in managing people for a long time (e.g. Guest, 1987; Legge, 1995; Marsh and Gillies, 1983; Poole and Jenkins, 1997; Storey, 1992). But it is the apparently increased involvement of such LMs in HRM via the use of HR devolution (and the related fanfare and transparency linked to it), which seems to hit the HRM headlines (in practitioner circles at least). In short, involving LMs in HRM appears, at present, *in vogue*.

Moreover, some British research studies also contend that the enhanced HRM role of non-specialist managers is a topic worth discussing (see Cully *et al.,* 1999; Millward, Bryson and Forth, 2000), and this idea is reinforced in the US literature, which reveals that some HRM outcomes occur through LMs implementing HR policies – as LMs have frequent contact with employees (Mishra and Bhatnagar, 2010: 414). Hence 'what happens' in HRM may be partly due to LM attitudes and behaviour too (Sanders and Frenkel, 2009), especially from an employee perspective, and is one reason why some researchers see the need to study the employee/LM relationship itself, e.g. Hyde *et al.,* (2006) (in Townsend *et al.,* 2011: 4). In essence, as HRM is part of many managerial jobs and LMs thus 'deliver' HRM to many workers (Renwick, 2009), there seems to be a 'critical role' for LMs as key actors in HRM (Townsend *et al.,* 2011: 12).

Problems arising

Authors also see problems from LMs having an HRM role, which are seen in Table 9.1 (below). From Table 9.1, there seems to be a key tension emerging in the relevant literature between espoused HR roles for LMs and the ones LMs seem to deliver (Teague and Roche 2011: 1). As such, consensus about 'devolving' or 'assigning' HR work to LMs appears to be 'an unresolved problem in many organizations' (Sanders and Frenkel, 2011: 1613). Overall then, while complexities may appear to be seen regarding the definition, rationale, level and practical application of 'devolving' or 'assigning' HRM to LMs (and which may potentially act to cloud our comprehension of it), some developments in the global, European and UK literatures on this topic are clear to see. Such developments are now detailed.

Table 9.1 Problems associated with involving LMs in HRM

Problem	Original work(s)	Cited in
LMs' resistance to accepting HR responsibilities	(Larsen & Brewster, 2003)	(Leisink & Knies, 2011: 1904)
LM ignorance of recent HRM developments	(Larsen & Brewster, 2003)	(Leisink & Knies, 2011: 1904)
LMs lacking consistency when implementing HRM	(Renwick, 2009)	(Townsend *et al.,* 2011: 4).
Views of senior managers and LMs sometimes differ about which HR responsibilities have been devolved	(Wright *et al.,* 2001)	(Teague & Roche, 2011: 1)
LMs are not always provided with adequate organisational support or training to complete assigned HR tasks	(Renwick, 2003)	(Teague & Roche, 2011: 1)
Time constraints lead LMs into making tradeoffs, which may mean some HR tasks are not completed properly	(Nehles *et al.,* 2006)	(Teague & Roche, 2011: 1)
Increased LM role ambiguity and conflict from HR being devolved to LMs	(Sanders & Frenkel, 2011: 1613)	(Sanders & Frenkel, 2011: 1613)
LMs lack commitment, competence and credibility in HRM	(Sanders & Frenkel, 2011: 1613)	(Sanders & Frenkel, 2011: 1613)
LMs 'bending' HR practices to meet their personal needs	(Sanders & Frenkel, 2011: 1613)	(Sanders & Frenkel, 2011: 1613)

 Developments in the literature

The global context

Research involving LMs in HRM have been seen in a number of countries globally, including studies in the People's Republic of China (PRC), Hong Kong (HK), Australia (Aus), New Zealand (NZ), the United States (US), Canada and Ireland. Findings from such works are now revealed.

In the People's Republic of China (PRC), Mitsuhashi *et al.*'s (2000) study investigated differing perceptions among an expatriate (survey) sample of top HR and line executives on the importance and effectiveness of HR practices in 25 multinational Chinese firms. They found that such Chinese-based executives perceive HR performance effectiveness as 'significantly lower' than HR executives do in terms of strategic (non-administrative) HRM, i.e. communications, measurements and responsibilities (Mitsuhashi *et al.*, 2000: 197). Their conclusions are that while their expatriate sample may have evaluated HRM on inappropriate 'strategic HRM' criteria (as HRM is still emergent in the PRC), some LMs there do not think that HR presently perform well enough to be considered a 'strategic partner' (Mitsuhashi *et al.*, 2000: 209, 211–212). Associations of social face and conflict avoidance have also been examined in the Chinese literature. Here, one interview questionnaire of 132 Chinese employees revealed that social face concerns and conflict avoidance were stronger among employees who interacted with Chinese managers, rather than employees working for Western managers (Peng and Tjosvold, 2011: 1031). Such findings seem to challenge traditional theories of social face leading to passive avoidance in China.

In Hong Kong (HK), Wai-Kwong, Priem and Cycyota (2001: 1325) studied the involvement of HR and LMs during strategy formulation and impact on performance. They argue that their findings are consistent with those elsewhere, e.g. Kanter (1982) in that middle managers encourage employee involvement (EI) programmes in the middle of re-designs to the production process, and works in the 1990s where alterations to middle management work roles (e.g. increased empowerment, speed and flexibility) saw LMs more committed to enacting changes in strategy at the operational level where they have most expertise (Wai-Kwong *et al.* 2001: 1341–2).

In Australia, one study based on 24 semi-structured interviews with ward staff at a medium-sized, private but not-for-profit hospital reveals that ward managers were frustrated with some aspects of their role. There, one ward manager states: 'you just end up being the sandwich in the middle sometimes' between upper and lower staff levels (Townsend *et al.*, 2011: 4–5, 9), which seems similar to McConville and Holden's (1999) picture of the HRM role of UK middle managers in the health sector as the 'filling in the sandwich'. This Australian case also found that ward managers seem to be 'a conduit' in providing employees with high levels of proximal commitment, as decisions on why some employees decide to stay 'comes down to . . . how well they get on with their manager'. Hence while many ward managers felt poorly prepared for their roles, 'according to their ward staff, they tend to be seen as good managers', and as some ward managers tend to develop themselves in people management 'almost through trial and error', there seems to be 'a lack of investment' in developing their HR knowledge and skills, meaning they are 'learning by doing' (Townsend *et al.*, 2011: 10–11, 13). Such findings may perhaps beg the question of whether LMs are learning HRM by doing it well (or not), and/or if LMs are being passed good (or bad) habits in HRM from other LMs too.

In New Zealand (NZ), Dewe and O'Driscoll's (2002) survey on stress management levels among 540 managers revealed that while stress management interventions encapsulate practices which may develop people and their well-being, many of them do not achieve such goals. They argue that this is due to such interventions offering only piecemeal solutions to stress problems, or not acknowledging overall issues of organisational structure and context within which stress interventions occur (Dewe and O'Driscoll, 2002: 143). Here, such managers seem uninterested in stress because of their perceptions of it, i.e. they view is as a 'high risk' issue and not one which organisations should manage, but one which individuals need to attend to instead (Dewe and O'Driscoll, 2002: 146, 153). They argue that managers should see stress as a transaction between individuals and their environment (as considering all staff as the same 'fails to capture the essential nature of the stress experience'), and conclude that many stress management techniques fail as they are superficial, and as some are used in an ad hoc way – because of a lack of managerial knowledge, attitudes and behaviour (Dewe and O'Driscoll, 2002: 162–3).

In the United States (US), Huy's (2002) three-year study of 104 middle managers in a large North American firm (Servico) found them showing varying emotion-management patterns to employees when major organisational change occurs. Huy states that some middle managers there establish continuing operations by enacting 'emotional balancing', i.e. catering to subordinates' psychological well-being, on issues like work/vacation scheduling, and exhaustion of young mothers from commuting. Such managers recognise that when organisations are reducing workforce numbers and moving their remaining staff onto one site, work and private feelings are difficult to separate and need attending to consciously. While Huy details an example of some managers being publicly hostile to some personal staff concerns during such change at one firm, he notes that other managers actively rejected firm rules on 'emotional display' to maintain subordinate continuity of experience (Huy, 2002: 49–50). Huy concludes that those middle managers who have a long tenure and know their subordinates well seem to attend to employee needs, and these factors may partially explain managerial efforts to help staff voluntarily (Huy, 2002: 61, 64).

Other US studies include George and Zhou's (2007) survey of 161 (matched) supervisors and staff in an oil field. They found that supervisors can support employee creativity by: handing employees developmental feedback, undertaking interactional justice displays to them, and in being trustworthy in their dealings with employees (George and Zhou, 2007: 605, 610).

Overall in the US, while some organisations seem to be assigning HR work to LMs, commentators also report 'reservations' regarding the HRM role of LMs too. This is because there seems to be: little LM training in HRM overall; less time to do it in the US (Perry and Kulik, 2008: 262–3); and more generally as some LMs appear to be 'unwilling partners in people management' there (Teo and Rodwell, 2007: 278). Additionally, HR frustration with LMs is also seen in the US regarding the inability of some LMs to manage women and black and minority ethnic (BME) staff in a professional manner (Dominguez, 1992: 385). Here, findings are of potential for BME staff there to experience 'unintended losses' from LMs appearing to take a reactionary stance towards diversity issues in particular (Fried *et al.*, 2001: 580).

Comparative studies connecting North American and European organisational contexts include McGuire *et al.*'s (2006) study on relationships between individual managerial values and HR decisions from a survey of 340 LMs in Canada and Ireland. They found that:

> The higher educated the person, the lower the perceived importance of health and safety issues... [where] the nationality of respondents proved to be the strongest predictor of the importance of employment equity [5.4 per cent]...with Irish respondents placing a higher importance on matters of employment equity...[and that] female respondents place a higher priority on employment equity than male respondents. *(McGuire et al., 2006: 263)*

McGuire *et al.*, (2006) state that 'too much' of the humanist-oriented HR discourse fails to comprehensively acknowledge that the realities of corporate life are where senior managers may be as likely to lay-off thousands of employees as they are to ask about their 'affective states or personal feelings'. Moreover, they argue that as many LMs enact operational HRM, such decision situations are where their individual values seem likely to influence the decision choices they make. Hence 'potential for conflict exists' between individual managerial values and organisational decision-making, which may be solved via: dialogue and discussion, managers ignoring, denying and suppressing it, or by managers exiting organisations altogether (McGuire *et al.*, 2006: 255).

The European dimension

Within Europe, Larsen and Brewster's (2003) study of 22 countries with 4,000 respondents reported the state of HR 'devolution' to LMs, and levels of LM responsibility for HRM. They found that HRM devolution to LMs in the UK and Ireland was low compared to other European Union (EU) states, and highest in Denmark and Finland. On HRM responsibility, while moves exist across the EU to hand LMs more responsibility for staff management, their study revealed that the extent of LM autonomy seems to be variable, depending on the HRM subjects examined. For example, they state that the most common pattern in Europe is one of shared responsibilities in HRM between HR and LMs (except regarding workforce expansion/reduction), and that many organisations remain very centralised in HRM overall.

Other pan-European works include Mesner-Andolsek and Stebe's (2005: 311) study of changes to the HRM function in 20 European and five non-European countries, which found some HRM tasks moved from HR departments to LMs. They found that country (as an institutional environment) seemed to both set limits to, and also encourage, devolution in to LMs in HRM, and also that while HR devolution seems to have developed in all areas there, it appears to be lower in large organisations with highly developed HRM teams (Mesner-Andolsek and Stebe, 2005: 326–7). They conclude that in HRM devolution processes, 'European organisations are gaining their autonomy through written HR policies', as such codified policies seem to be the strongest factor joining HRM practices in a common direction across the EU (Mesner-Andolsek and Stebe, 2005: 327–8).

Single-country European studies include works by Delmestri (2006), Brandl *et al.*, (2009) and Teague and Roche (2011). Delemestri (2006) surveyed 418 middle managers employed by 72 local and international organisations in Italy, and examined managerial identities as 'societal institutions'. Here, he found that:

The professional identity of the middle managers and their legitimacy, are based on either the capacity to personally solve technical problems (specifically German and Italian) or to demonstrate more managerial-like competencies (specifically British), whose identity is based on an idea of management as a mysterious mastery supported by the necessary personality traits and social skills. *(Delmestri, 2006: 1521)*

Delmestri's study also revealed that the incorporation of the HR department into global integration and identification with both a global and Anglo-Saxon culture are drivers of an 'Anglo-Saxon profile', and that national culture and exposure to local and foreign influence help shape espoused managerial beliefs (as ideal types) (Delmestri, 2006: 1531, 1537).

In a survey of 1,500 Danish managers, Brandl *et al.* (2009) found that they consider 'motivating others' to be their most important HR duty, whereas 'team-building', 'handling conflicts' and 'coaching' LMs consider least important. Here, they reveal that female top managers employed in the Danish public sector seemed to exhibit the greatest interest in HR, whereas men at lower managerial levels in the private sector there appeared to give the lowest priority to HR work.

Lack of LM 'confidence' to act independently regarding workplace conflict has also been seen in a study of HR manager's views of LM roles in Ireland by Teague and Roche (2011). Here, their survey of 360 enterprises reveals that line and supervisory managers' engagement in conflict management is 'most developed' in firms which have enacted commitment-oriented HR practices, and that LM 'engagement' in conflict management is 'positively associated with relative labour productivity, and relative absence rates' (Teague and Roche, 2011: 6, 14). Staying within the EU area, findings from the United Kingdom (UK) are now detailed.

UK findings

UK studies have historically seen chief production managers wanting to pass personnel and industrial relations (IR) activity to factory administrators; as such managers did not feel personnel/IR work to be an effective use of their time. While some production managers viewed IR work as part of their general work-load, they preferred to rely on personnel/IR specialists for advice regarding it – even though such managers were not keen to be subject to the direction of personnel/IR specialists (Marsh, 1971; Marsh and Gillies, 1983: 32–8).

More recently, UK research details LMs taking more responsibility for initial decision-making regarding recruitment, motivation, communication, discipline and employee counselling (Poole and Jenkins, 1997; Purcell *et al.*, 2003). Additionally, commentators detail 'partnerships' being formed between HR and LMs (Hutchinson and Wood, 1995), cost/benefit analyses of devolution in HRM (Sisson and Storey, 2000; Storey, 2001), and cases of LMs being encouraged to engage in boundary-spanning HR processes outside organisations, to 'experiment rather than being excluded from decision making' (Currie and Procter, 2001: 57).

LM enthusiasm to rely on advice from HR specialists is particularly apparent in the area of performance management and appraisal (PMA) in the UK. Here, Harris (2001: 1182–90) found that managers dislike the 'bureaucracy' of PMA, which could lead them to undertake an 'abdication management' approach to it, and Redman (2001) reveals that while some LMs seem to award themselves good ratings for their own (managerial) role in PA, they are not seen to complete subordinate appraisals very well. Further, Guest and King (2001: 36) argue that managers tend not to conduct PM properly, unless they get an encouraging 'kick' to do so.

In the training and development field, some UK LMs contend that they do not need training or development in HRM, because 'most of this' [HR work] 'is common sense anyway' (quoted in Cunningham and Hyman, 1995: 18). However, Gibb's (2003) analysis found that LMs may require specialist HR advice in an era of knowledge management (KM), as KM requires the re-alignment of work, organisation and management. Here, LMs may be required to move away from using 'control and direct' management styles to using ones based on tutoring, coaching and mentoring instead (Gibb, 2003). Understanding and developing the skills of employees and managers may also need to consider a possible gender dimension involved too, as Green and James (2003: 63) found that in instances where the LM is male and the employee female, potential exists for bosses to underestimate the skill level of such workers.

The UK literature on LM involvement in employment relations (ER) focuses on employee involvement (EI) schemes, and grievance and discipline (G&D) handling. On EI, Fenton-O'Creevy (1998: 67) found that 'resistance' among UK middle managers produced less positive outcomes in EI, and that senior managers may also blame middle managers for the collapse of failing EI schemes. Further, Marchington (2001) reveals some 'unintended impacts' from involving LMs in EI, such as deficiencies on LM ability in, and commitment to, EI; a lack of time and training to do it; and some doubt among LMs over why EI needs to occur.

The attitudes and behaviour of UK LMs in grievance and discipline (G&D) cases reveal some LM expediency in them occurring. Here, Rollinson *et al.* (1996) found HR managers having to 'sit in' on G&D meetings to 'police' LM practices (to maintain that useful results emerged), while IRS (2001) found LMs less involved than HR managers in taking responsibility for disciplinary procedures. The UK Chartered Institute of Personnel and Development (CIPD) claim that most operational managers take on less discipline handling than intended, mainly because of their 'attitudes and abilities' (CIPD, 2007: 21), and question if such managers 'are willing to, and capable of' enacting dispute resolution procedures (CIPD, 2008: 8) (in Jones and Saundry, 2011: 3–4). Additionally, findings from one study of seven UK organisations on discipline handling reveals perceptions among some HR practitioners that operational managers (especially those with less experience) tend to adopt a 'pragmatic and contingent approach' to it. This is because the threat of litigation and a lack of capability and experience has left many such managers 'increasingly dependent on HR advice and support', meaning that managers may need to develop 'confidence' to tackle such disciplinary issues (Jones and Saundry, 2011: 9, 14).

Other empirical UK work on 'devolving' specific HR tasks to LMs has seen problems emerging. For example, while some UK LMs seem to be being given more scope regarding making pay awards for their staff (Currie and Procter, 2001: 58–59, 63–6), research by Harris (2001: 1184) notes a lack of LM engagement with performance-related pay (PRP) schemes, and a lack of LM 'ownership' – this process, because some LMs see it as potentially overloading their job roles. Additionally, Cunningham and James (2001) reveal that some LMs seem unwilling to attend training courses to help manage long-term staff sickness and disability cases, and Dunn and Wilkinson's (2002: 245) study on absence management found that some organisations had an 'ad hoc' view of it, with unclear LM responsibilities, producing a 'muddling through' approach in some cases.

Further, Whittaker and Marchington (2003) found that some UK LMs requested help from HR specialists, as such LMs found doing HR work very hard when other high-priority business pressures emerged that LMs also needed to attend to, and Purcell and Hutchinson's (2007) survey of 608 employees in 12 'excellent' UK-based firms found both employee commitment towards their employer and job being influenced by the quality of leadership behaviour. There, older workers and those with longer service rated their managers as worse managers overall (Purcell and Hutchinson, 2007: 3, 5, 7, 9, 11).

UK research studies also describe the HRM role of LMs as one where LMs enact HR policies differently, thus providing an inconsistent workplace experience for their employee subordinates. Here, LMs do not always safeguard employee welfare (Hope-Hailey *et al.*, 1997: 15–17), gender management and equal opportunity provision (Guest and King, 2004; McDougall, 1998: 78), and 'deal with things in different ways' in discipline handling (Jones and Saundry, 2011: 12). Additionally, Renwick's (2010) interviews with 54 LMs in three organisations details LMs acting inconsistently towards employees.

Here, at UtilitiesCo Renwick (2010) finds LMs seemingly expedient in HR work, in asking 'What can I get away with in HRM?', which suggests such LMs might be experiencing value role conflict in performing HR duties (Caldwell, 2003: 993), or to generally lack 'enthusiasm, priority and interest' in HRM (Brewster, 2009: 385). Some LMs at LocalGov viewed 'layoffs, equal opportunities and race relations as add-ons' to their role, meaning potential may exist for a decline in professional HRM practice there, as some LMs seem to view HR responsibilities as a 'bolt-on' to their job (Purcell and Hutchinson, 2007: 13). At ManufactureCo, some LMs showed 'a lack of effort' when completing performance appraisals, and not 'identifying' employee development needs. Such findings suggest that LMs there do not always act as coaches to 'improve' or develop people (Buller *et al.*, 1991: 260; Fairbairn, 2005: 82; Ulrich and Beatty, 2001), and may need to focus more on their pastoral role with subordinate staff (Hutchinson and Purcell, 2007: 9). Renwick's (2010) work thus reinforces an identified 'implementation gap' in HRM (Cunningham *et al.*, 2004: 287), and risks where HR tasks are transferred to LMs, such as 'a serious loss in the quality of performance' (Brewster and Larsen, 2000: 204).

Summary

This review of the literature notes that the lack of capability in, and commitment by LMs to, HRM identified by Brewster and Larsen (1992) still resonates with research findings today, as do the costs arising from involving LMs in HRM too, such as a lack of consistency from LMs when dealing with employees (Renwick, 2009, 2010). The studies detailed [above] could be used to draw contrasting pictures of involving LMs in HRM, e.g. of LM willingness regarding, capability in and generally positive attitude towards HRM, or alternatively, one of LM resistance and cynicism to HR work, and a lack of LM knowledge and skill being applied to it. Additionally, they also reveal many factors which may limit LMs from conducting HRM duties well, such as: a lack of time and training to prepare; cross-cutting demands on LMs by others; a lack of clear help from HR managers; and LM needs to deliver business targets. Thus problems which may emerge from involving LMs in HRM are perhaps somewhat predictable, and not solely due to LM intransigence in HRM, but instead, partly arising from the organisational contexts they work in. I now outline some questions emerging regarding the involvement of LMs in HRM from the literature just detailed above.

Questions emerging

As LMs are now under pressure to work on the 'hard stuff', the 'numbers' (Whittaker and Marchington 2003), this circumstance has left some LMs needing to complete a large number of operational, as well as sometimes new, or additional HR tasks to a high-quality level. However, it is unclear if these non-specialist managers can deliver such conflicting requirements, and do all of them well. As such, questions may arise on which tasks LMs prioritise in HRM, and what impact their choices have on organisational performance, employee well-being, and ultimately, their own careers too. I now examine each of these aspects in turn.

Some research works seem fairly positive on the impact LMs seem to have on organisational performance. For example, large-scale UK survey research notes a key role for LMs in enabling HR strategies 'come to life' (e.g. Hutchinson and Purcell, 2003; Purcell and Hutchinson, 2007; Purcell *et al.*, 2003). Here, one LM at the UK firm Nationwide argues that:

> Our research has demonstrated that line manager behaviour has a significant impact on employee commitment, which has an impact on customer commitment, which has an impact on business performance. *(Lazenby* in *Hutchinson and Purcell, 2003: 55).*

However, other commentators argue that involving LMs in HRM seems to produce less effective organisational performance (Gibb, 2001), and some such as Gratton *et al.*, (1999) have long held the view that we need to consider the incentives LMs gain to develop staff, which may arguably disconnect causal chains if not considered. Hence questions arise on the exact role LMs play in contributing to organisational performance. Additionally, it is also apparent in UK studies that HR specialists do not always give useful advice to LMs in HRM (Guest *et al.*, 2001: 67), and that LM incapability, and lack of commitment/consistency in HRM can put a break on achieving such outcomes (Cunningham *et al.*, 2004; Harris, 2001; Redman, 2001), thus possibly disrupting such causal connections.

More recent international studies have started to investigate LM contributions to improving performance through the successful implementation of HRM policies and practices (Gilbert *et al.*, 2011), and their contextual and individual antecedents (Soens *et al.*, 2011). Here, studies reveal the impact of LM efforts on individual employee and collective work group performance outcomes (Han *et al.*, 2011; Kossek *et al.*, 2011), and that the more experienced HR subsidiary managers are, the more committed unit general managers are to their HR policies (Bjorkman *et al.*, 2011).

In terms of employee well-being (EWB), some studies find that LMs tend to 'marginalise, under-use and under-develop' part-time staff (Edwards and Robinson, 2001), and that LM incapability in HRM is one reason given by some employees as to why they are leaving their jobs – their 'poor boss' is, the 'last straw' (Taylor, 2002). Additionally, the LM role in taking HR-related decisions (such as increasing employee rewards and career development) are ones where LMs seem to need more skill to enable them as LMs to enact better choices overall (Marchington, 1999; Tyson and Fell, 1995). Here, auditing LM skills and knowledge in HRM may be one way of assessing the impact of LM interventions in HRM, and could tell us if LMs feel that completing HR work facilitates LM job and career progression, or is making LMs so generalist that they become easier to replace. For LMs themselves then, they may wish to assess if doing HR work makes them more or less employable, marketable and/or powerful in organisations today.

As the relevant literature varies in answering questions on whether involving LMs in HRM seems to enhance outcomes in terms of organisational performance, EWB and the general job/career prospects of LMs, we may want to question HRM models which include unitarist-based notions of HR–LM consensus or 'partnership' in HRM (e.g. Currie and Procter, 2001; Hutchinson and Wood, 1995; Jackson and Schuler, 2000). This is because findings from such works seem to be 'ideal types' when benchmarked against some of the more negative results seen from involving LMs in HRM above (especially in the UK), and as research is currently very mixed on whether LMs act professionally, consistently and fairly towards employees (Budhwar, 2000; Cunningham and Hyman, 1999; Marchington, 1999; Renwick, 2010).

Overall, the relevant literature seems divided on whether involving LMs in HRM is a positive development or not. On the one hand, some UK chief executives seem to be fairly enthusiastic about increasing LM involvement in HRM, as they view it as 'good people management' (Guest and King, 2001: 35). Here, some UK case data reinforces such thinking, as LM involvement in HRM has increased in some leading-edge UK firms (e.g. Hutchinson and Purcell, 2003; Larsen and Brewster, 2003; Purcell and Hutchinson, 2007; Purcell *et al.*, 2003). However, on the other hand, involving LMs more in HRM seems to be 'contested terrain' (cf. Edwards, 1979), as the contingencies of different organisational and work contexts seem to account for varying outcomes in it. For example, many of the more positive studies (just mentioned) are from 'excellent' firms where we might expect 'good' outcomes to occur (as they can invest significant resources to help and train LMs in HRM). But other organisations may not have such resources to support and develop LMs regarding HRM, and/or an HR presence on site to help either, such as small to medium-sized enterprises (SMEs) (Hunter and Renwick, 2009).

What data that does exist to assess the usefulness of involving LMs in HRM (especially in the UK and US, but also beginning to emerge more globally in the PRC and NZ now) seems to suggest that we be cautious when making such judgements. This is because one key finding emerging from *all* of the research studies in the relevant global literature (detailed above), is that more of them see problems arising from involving LMs in HRM than see benefits arising – for organisations, employees and LMs themselves. For example, with some exceptions being noted, such as single country case studies by Huy (2002) and Townsend *et al.*, (2011), very few quotes appear in this global literature from employees about 'my great boss', or from staff detailing how, and in what ways, their LM develops, motivates or generally inspires them at work. Instead, many more studies raise questions about the attitude, willingness, capacity and consistency of LMs in HRM, as detailed earlier. Some challenges arising from involving LMs in HR work are now examined.

Challenges arising

An initial challenge for LMs in HRM concerns how they can help deliver organisational outcomes, while also attending to employee needs and well-being. While organisations seem to require LMs to achieve such outcomes, LMs attempting to do them both may feel that they are the 'filling' in the HR sandwich (McConville and Holden, 1999). This is because such LMs arguably seem to be pushed from above, by senior managers (to achieve organisational goals), and also from below, by employees (to safeguard staff welfare). Hence LMs are asked, in essence, to reconcile the 'soft' (developmental humans) and 'hard' (resource-centred) elements of HRM in practice (Legge, 1995: Storey, 1992), or in Huy's (2002) terms, for LMs needing to engage in 'emotional balancing'.

A second challenge for LMs is that how they manage employees may impact on such staff careers overall (Walton, 1999), because LMs are the ones who are primarily being asked which employees they do, and do not, wish to recommend forward for pay awards or promotions. So, while LMs may make HR strategies 'come to life' (Purcell and Hutchinson, 2007; Purcell *et al.*, 2003), they may also possibly be instrumental in some employee careers floundering too. Hence there may be a potentially much 'darker' side to LM involvement in employee career development than is currently detailed in the relevant literature today. Here, although managing people well takes time and consideration, it is unclear from the relevant literature if LMs are given the scope and opportunity to motivate, develop and reward employees at work, or that such LMs wish to do so, in a fair and consistent way.

LMs may find making adjustments to develop employees at work difficult, as some LMs seem resistant to the changes involved, and as doing so requires some mental reflexivity from LMs to deliver it in practice (Renwick, 2003: 275). Additionally, LMs may also need to learn lessons from the strategy literature, such as: finding 'the right words' to talk to employees, 'in the right way – performing the conversation', and in building 'relationships, networks, and coalitions', to provide LMs with knowledge and credibility in HRM which may compensate for their lack of technical HRM expertise – 'setting the scene' (cf. Rouleau and Balogun, 2011: 960).

Some authors argue that when it comes to managing some aspects of HRM, e.g. workplace conflict, establishing 'organisational support structures is the most likely way' to facilitate LMs performing a useful HRM role (Teague and Roche, 2011: 15). However, producing useful outcomes from involving LMs in HRM also appears to rest on meeting a further (third) challenge – of *how* to provide internal (or external) HR support to LMs, and how HR staff can give such LMs good advice in HRM (Brewster and Larsen, 2000). One available option comes from Marchington and Wilkinson (2002), who suggest that the following steps could be taken:

How HR managers can support middle managers

- HR strategies should be composed of broad themes that can then be contextualised by middle managers at an operational level

- Middle managers should be encouraged to contribute towards an elaboration of these broad themes

- Opportunities should be provided for middle managers to span boundaries within the organisation through membership of project groups

- The HR function should be organised to allow HR professionals to work closely with middle managers at the point of delivery

- The development of middle managers is directed towards their contribution to strategic change

Source: Marchington and Wilkinson (2002) adapted from Currie and Procter (2001).

Nonetheless, it is unclear whether HR managers show adequate commitment, preparation, and support to LMs in HRM (Brewster and Larsen, 2000: 208), and if a 'simple, seamless transfer of responsibility' between HR and LMs is achievable, due to HR wanting to keep an operational role in HRM (Currie and Procter, 2001: 54).

If involving LMs in HRM is successful, then there arguably seems less need for organisations to employ many HR managers. Hence a fourth challenge – for HR managers – lies in how to increase the involvement of LMs in HRM without sowing the seeds of HR's own redundancy (i.e. reductions in HR manager headcount, the erosion of HR functions/departments, or increased use of HR outsourcing). Additionally for HR, studies from the European and Chinese literatures (above) may also imply that HR also need to assess a final (fifth) challenge – of how devolving HRM to LMs helps HR achieve increased organisational performance (Mesner-Andolsek and Stebe, 2005), and to what degree such HRM devolution supports a case from HR to become a 'strategic partner' in organisations overall (Mitsuhashi *et al.,* 2000). A research agenda for involving LMs in HRM is now detailed.

Future research

While many studies on involving LMs in HRM generally note the limitations surrounding it, some of them also appear somewhat enthusiastic about it too (e.g. Hutchinson and Purcell, 2003; Huy, 2002; Purcell and Hutchinson, 2007; Purcell *et al.,* 2003; Teague and Roche, 2011; Townsend *et al.,* 2011). However, a far higher number of research works detailed in this chapter appear to suggest that the limitations seen when involving LMs in HRM are more systemic and endemic, and thus arguably become serious points to note. To move research in this field forward then, we may initially benefit from more research studies being undertaken globally, so we can build clearer pictures on whether LMs seem capable of, committed to, and consistent when enacting HRM, or not. Here, a key requirement seems to lie in gaining the views of multiple HRM stakeholders (LMs, senior managers, union members and employees), so we can avoid the sort of single-respondent bias that exists in current data, and then triangulate the views of these stakeholders to produce greater validity and reliability in the generalisations and conclusions we draw.

It could also be useful to know much more from LMs themselves about their exact experiences of HR work. Here, we need data on how LMs: cope with conflicting job demands (Lynch, 2003); are recruited, selected, inducted, trained, appraised and rewarded in HRM; are assigned leadership roles to develop employees at work (Whittaker and Marchington, 2003); can, or do, utilise different management styles, such as tutor, coach or mentor (Gibb, 2003). Indeed, where using LMs in HRM is seen as a positive development, we could gain more evidence to add to that already seen on the capabilities and priorities of managers (Mesner-Andolsek and Stebe, 2005: 327), and on the role LMs play in inspiring or motivating employees towards achieving such high performance.

Additionally, we could research the possible centrifugal, situational forces that could pressurise LMs into acting in an automatic or spontaneous way which buffers, mediates or rejects employee needs and wishes. Here, it could be useful to understand (as per McGuire *et al.,* 2006) the impact some factors have on LM decision-making regarding employee interests, such as national culture, personality or institutional context. For example, a lack of managerial training, commitment, and general ad hoc management practice is seen to occur in the UK and to be longstanding (see McGovern *et al.,* 1997), which may partially explain less LM interest in employee demands and aspirations there. Such factors could be analysed comparatively, to build a more global view in this area.

Further, we might wish to explore the role factors such as education, nationality and gender may have on how LMs rate issues like employment equity and health and safety, and how they rank them in importance when compared to other HRM issues and other general management duties too (as per Brandl *et al.,* 2009; McGuire *et al.,* 2006). Lastly in this section, we could investigate LM decision-making processes (perhaps from using diary studies), to better understand why some LMs seem to treat employees inconsistently – which is seen in the UK (Renwick, 2003, 2010), and also in Canada (Rouleau and Balogun, 2011: 965). Before closing this chapter, some thoughts about using theory in this field are detailed.

Using theory to explain the HRM behaviours of LMs

If we accept some premises and assumptions made in the work psychology literature, we may be able to adapt them to connect individual LM attitudes to HRM informing LM intentions to HRM as a whole, and as such the HRM intentions of LMs then informing LM behaviour in HRM overall. If so, we may be able to use such links to explore the role of relevant theory to explain LM behaviour in HRM. Here, four such theories may be useful to consider. First, ability–motivation–opportunity (AMO) theory (Appelbaum *et al.,* 2000) provides one theoretical lens to view LM behaviour in HRM, as detailed by Purcell and Hutchinson (2007). Thus, AMO theory could be used usefully to detail LM capacity (ability) in, willingness (motivation) towards, and scope (opportunity) for, HRM, which are all very long-standing themes going back to original works in the literature such as Brewster and Larsen (1992). Second, leader–member exchange (LMX) theory (Gerstner and Day, 1997; Mueller and Lee, 2002; Uhl-Bien *et al.,* 2000; Yrie *et al.,* 2003) may help us understand LM relationships with employees. Such theorising has already been used to detail the role of FLM actions in the HRM-performance chain, most notably in Purcell and Hutchinson's (2007) concept of 'people management', which includes leadership behaviour based on LMX emphasising interpersonal relationships (Leisink and Knies, 2011: 1903, 1905).

Third, 'signalling theory' (Haggerty and Wright, 2009) could help explain signals HR managers give to LMs in HRM, and those LMs in turn pass on to employees. Here, connections between signalling theory and HRM systems theory (Bowen and Ostroff, 2004) may produce a comprehensive, multilevel and coherent framework for understanding the involvement of LMs in HRM, due to the focus made in it on HR processes and systems (Wright and Haggerty, 2005: 12, 14). This is because a 'strong' HR system could produce joint HR–LM ownership in HRM and a holistic HRM approach to benefit employees, while a 'weak' HR system may see little HR–LM ownership in HRM, and facilitate a piecemeal HRM approach towards employees instead. A key role exists then for LMs to create a 'strong situation' in HRM, to benefit all organisational stakeholders, and work already begun in this mode (e.g. Townsend *et al.,* 2011: 14) could provide an important addition to existing theorising on the LM contribution in HRM.

Other possible useful theoretical directions could include using more critically oriented power and politics theory (e.g. Lukes, 2005), fourth, as theoretical perspective by which to view the involvement of LMs in HRM. Here, the LM role in HRM may occur from HR managers 'devolving' HR work to LMs, or alternatively being 'dumped' on LMs by HR managers (Hall and Torrington, 1998; McConville and Holden, 1999), i.e. HR managers may be attempting to enact political, power-based strategies of advancement/dominance in HRM, as part of HR's quest to seek 'strategic' or boardroom status (Renwick, 2010).

However, while all of the four theories detailed above may offer some potential to usefully explain LM behaviour in HRM, caution is advised in using them, as they only seem to explain such behaviour in single cases (Townsend *et al.,* 2011), three cases (Renwick, 2010), and multiple, but best-practice cases (Purcell and Hutchinson, 2007), and also because *all* of these studies are single-country ones too. Hence studies using these theories appear to lack capacity to explain LM HRM behaviours across industries or sectors, and also across national cultures. Thus the general message here is that while the topic of involving LMs in HRM is not devoid of relevant, useful theorising, it does seem a little 'theory-lite', and somewhat case and country-based also. As such, developmental work on the role of theory to explain LM behaviours in HRM in a more general way across differing organisations globally may well be useful for interested researchers to engage in. Some conclusions are now offered forward.

Conclusions

Involving LMs in HRM today requires them to manage people in work environments often characterised by needs to meet high performance expectations set by many internal and external stakeholders, and where high levels of uncertainty and change also exist in both the internal organisational and external environment too. As such, LMs may have to deliver on financial criteria, e.g., cost-control, and also to take higher levels of responsibility for people management, i.e. to be seriously 'engaged' in HRM work, and to make key choices on how they manage their employee subordinates too. Coping with such demands may place great pressure and stress on LMs. Nonetheless, LMs themselves may well need to practise HRM in a more consistent and professional way no matter what demands are placed on them (as their expediency in HRM has long been understood), if they wish to become more credible people managers today.

In ending this chapter, it seems arguable to state that we may be at a crossroads on the topic of involving LMs in HRM, and need to ask important questions so as to chart the road ahead on it, in practical terms at least. For example, such questions may include: Do we want LMs to have an increased role in managing people at work? How do we want LMs to manage employees? What roles should non-specialist LMs and HR specialists take in HRM? Is involving LMs in HRM a positive development for multiple HRM stakeholders today? Answering these questions may help us comprehend if, how and why involving LMs in HRM is a development that employers are enacting to 'add-value' for organisations, pursuing as part of a cost-cutting strategy, or something different altogether. Here, prior historical trends on national and organisation culture in people management may come into play to help us answer such questions. For example, UK trends in managing people, e.g. of being opportunistic, ad hoc, and/or generally under-resourced (Legge, 1978; McGovern *et al.* 1997; Sisson, 1989) seem to suggest that involving LMs in HRM there may be part of an organisational or managerial 'efficiency drive'. More widely then, it may be interesting to see what rationales other organisations and managers use across the globe to explain why they involve LMs in HRM, and as such, whether the peculiarities of the UK experience regarding it (above) are a 'British disease'.

CASE STUDY 9.1

TRAINING LINE MANAGERS IN A CHINESE STATE-OWNED ENTERPRISE (SOE)

YUJUAN ZHANG* AND DOUGLAS W.S. RENWICK

This case concerns a state-owned enterprise (SOE), the Third Electronic Power Construction Company located in Shan Xi Province, China. This SOE was established in 1978, and is responsible for building thermal power plants across China focusing on quality construction. The Head Office of Third Electronic is based Shan Xi's capital, Tai Yuan, where 707 employees work, and their 12 subsidiaries of this SOE are distributed among other Chinese provinces, employing nearly 2,000 staff.

Increased competition from other Chinese SOEs, private companies and less government financial support are impacting on the operations of Third Electronic – who are responding to them by recruiting and developing technical experts and graduates. However, a key problem they face is with their existing Line Managers (LMs), who tend to be: older workers (mainly aged 46–55); whom have a lower than average educational level (up to Advanced Diploma level only); and who are not used to operating with Western concepts such as management development and HRM more generally. So, key challenges for Third Electronic lie in developing their existing LMs to meet competitive and financial pressures, and to recruit excellent new LMs to ensure managerial succession over time. To meet these HRM-based challenges, this SOE has produced an off-the-job management training course for LMs which includes some HRM-related elements, such as performance appraisal and communication skills. The module outline for this training course is detailed in Table 9.2.

The training programme lasts 11 days and contains some 80 hours of taught classes. What follows below are HR and LM views of this training course. Such managerial opinions are derived from data collected using semi-structured interviews with (all) 19 LMs working at Head Office in Third Electronic Power (China) in 2011.

Among the potential LM participants of the training course above, only four attended it, and such non-attendance figures contrast with findings from Yang (2003) of a 64 per cent attendance among managers in on-the-job training at other Chinese SOEs. When probed as to why this low take-up of training exists, the LMs interviewed state that the absent LMs want to 'go abroad' for such training instead, and/or are 'too busy' to attend this training course.

One senior manager at Third Electronic comments that the organisation do not generally provide enough training for LMs because 'the company care more about profit' than training, while another argues that this is not a problem, as such LMs can learn the practical skills they need 'on-the-job', or by themselves 'after work'.

Barriers to implementing LM training

LMs at Third Electronic identified a number of barriers to enacting LM training there. Initially, a lack of HR autonomy was seen, in terms of HR's ability to establish and deliver training programmes for LMs. Here, one HR manager argues that:

> All we can do is what the top manager wants. We cannot say 'no' to the training project, despite sometimes knowing that the training content is worthless. Most SOEs in China are like this. Additionally, when we designed the training proposal, the content, budget, time and place all need both manager and Party Committee approval. We can only implement the training after they all agree it.

Additionally, little training budget seems to exist for the HR department to fund such LM training. Here, another HR manager states that:

> The budget is too tight to invite outside training experts to come in, and it is not possible to implement training outside the organisation. Even if we have authority to do so, we cannot afford it.

---

*The case material above is derived from the Masters dissertation written by Yujuan Zhang at the University of Sheffield in 2011.

Table 9.2 Training course for LMs at Third Electronic Power Construction, China

Module	Topics	Taught Class Hours
Scientific thought of development – Party knowledge	Building and implementing Scientific thought of development	8
(16 class hours)	Analysis of current economy	4
	Electronic Power development	4
Leadership style construction	Honest and clean politics	4
(16 class hours)	Quality and ability of managers in SOEs	4
	Honour credibility	8
Managerial ability	Lean management	8
(44 class hours)	Electricity marketing	8
	Systems thinking and reallocating resources	8
	Performance appraisal	8
	Communication skills	8
	Calligraphy and painting appreciation	4
Others	Self-study	4
Total		80

Such a situation may perhaps seem odd to some observers of HRM in China, as the Chinese Vocational Education Law (of 1996) states that the lowest training investment for any worker is 1.5 per cent of individual total salary (Xie and Wu, 2001). Clearly, this 'law' is one that Chinese SOEs such as Third Electronic do not seem to rely on. However, other seasoned commentators in HRM may also note differences here between espoused HRM in theory, and enacted HRM in practice (as per Legge, 1995).

The LMs interviewed all also acknowledged that LM motivation plays a crucial role in the success of training processes. Here, one LM comments that:

I treasure training opportunities, as they could provide me with new knowledge and skills that I did not have before. It is really amazing for me, as my communication skills are improved through training, and now I have a rough knowledge about performance appraisal too.

However, a different LM added:

I do not value training. If training is designed better to cater for our daily work, it may be worthwhile to consider attending such training courses.

A lack of autonomy in choosing a training programme was also highlighted by LMs. Here, one LM argues that:

Usually I have no choice but to attend training, and HR would inform me in advance that I need to do so. I do not like being forced to attend, because I think sometimes the training is not suitable for me. I hope I can determine whether to attend by myself, however I do not think this can be realised in a hierarchy like an SOE.

This comment supports Yang's (2003) findings that some LMs in Chinese SOEs seem to have appreciably higher work motivation if they have the opportunity to determine their training participation.

In line with findings from Tsai and Tai (2003), all of the LMs interviewed mentioned top management commitment as an important driver of more positive LM attitudes to training, as:

If a senior manager said this training is worth attending, or something encouraging about it to me, then I am happy to go to it.

However, some other LMs had different, contrasting views about such top management support. On the one hand, one LM states that:

I think my top manager usually supports me. Because our company is an electronic power construction company, they focus more on safety. I have attended safety training twice this year.

While on the other, another LM comments that:

Top managers seldom support me. When I compiled the construction business plan for this year, he would not agree to give me the training I needed.

Further, LMs also mentioned training outcome expectancy as a factor which influences their attitude towards training. Here, one LM argues that:

I am very busy in my daily work, so if I take part in training, this is an opportunity not only to improve my knowledge level, but also to develop my career and may even lead to pay rise.

Or put more simply:

I think training is instrumental to career development, especially the political courses. For anyone who wants promotion, such courses are necessary to attend.

A final issue that LMs raised concerned the relevance of the topics they were taught. Here, regarding the modules on Party news, and knowledge and leadership style construction, one LM states that:

Every time in training it is essential to learn political knowledge. I know it may be important, but it cannot help improve my work. Also after this training, they test what you learnt about political knowledge, and we have to recite it after work as well. It is too hard to memorise.

Here, taught courses at Third Electronic seem more relevant to some LMs than to others!

While most 'cadres' in this Chinese SOE are Communist Party members, Party knowledge thus appears in organisational training, but some LMs at Third Electronic China also report that such political training may not always be seen as applicable to their daily work as LMs. Lastly here, and related to training relevance, it is also difficult to see (at least through arguably biased Western eyes) how training LMs in calligraphy and painting appreciation are relevant to LM work, or how they could be so in future.

Questions

1 What do you think Chinese organisations such as those in the case above can generally learn from the relevant literature on involving LMs in HRM?

2 Do you think that a rapidly developing country such as China is ready, or prepared for, training LMs in general terms? What evidence or arguments would you use to support your case here?

3 Reflecting on the case findings above, to what extent do you think Chinese LMs rate HR as a 'strategic partner'?

4 Do you think that Chinese LMs in the case above engage in either social face or conflict avoidance?

CASE STUDY 9.2

NORTH SERVICE GROUP (NSG): THE HRM ROLE OF LINE MANAGERS IN A BRITISH SME[*]

WILLIAM HUNTER AND DOUGLAS W.S. RENWICK

NSG is a recently created UK work organisation, consisting of two operating companies – Cook and Dickens Services – who enjoy an equal partnership while continuing to retain separate identities and operating locations. They provide personal services to residents of local communities in the north of England, which are similar, but the communities they serve are very different. Cook operates mainly in a metropolitan borough, and Dickens in a rural district authority. Cook was formed nearly 30 years ago, and Dickens was formed in July 2006 when 17 staff transferred to it from local authority control. NSG is a non-asset holding parent body, a charitable association governed by the regulations of the Industrial and Provident Societies Act (1965), and qualifies as a society run for the benefit of the community providing services for people other than its members. NSG's senior management team consists mainly of the Cook senior management team. NSG was created to bring together the skills, resources and values of Cook and Dickens Services to create a stronger body with clear vision of service provision for their service users.

The organisational culture of NSG is, according to the Chief Executive and Financial Director, to be 'open'. Line Managers (LMs) and staff are given their responsibilities and objectives, and then trusted to get on with their job. There is little or no 'checking up' or measuring of their performance. Due to its reputation and quality service, Cook has maintained continuous employment for almost all staff. The future of NSG is thought to be secure, though individual projects can be vulnerable to changes in government policies and public spending reviews. NSG hope that their growing size may help them survive, in addition to their good reputation. Cook has twice been awarded Charter Mark status and Investors in People (IiP) recognition. HR policies and procedures tend to be designed by the directors of NSG, as there is no specialist professional HR presence on-site. Cook use a number of consultancies to assist with policy development in HRM when required, e.g. in health, safety, appraisal, and recruitment, and LMs have also helped to develop some such HR policies.

Questions

1 If you have responsibility as a senior manager for some subordinate Line Managers (LMs) in a small to medium-sized enterprise (SME) such as NSG, where you knew there was either a very small or non-existent HR function, how would you advise, guide and support such LMs on a practical level in HRM?

2 If you were an LM at NSG, what changes would you like to see to help you deliver your role in HRM?

3 What lessons do you think can be learned from the relevant literature in terms of involving LMs in HRM in SME environments?

---

[*]A full version of this case study is detailed in Hunter and Renwick (2009).

CASE STUDY 9.3

LINE MANAGERS AND GREEN (ENVIRONMENTAL) HRM

DOUGLAS W.S. RENWICK

Considerable evidence exists that supportive managerial and supervisor behaviours in environment initiatives are important in developing employee engagement in environmental management (EM). For example, Ramus and Steger's (2000) study of European employee 'eco-initiatives' (defined as any action taken by an employee that they thought would improve the environmental performance of the company), found a strong relationship between managerial behaviours such as competence-building, communication, rewarding and recognising employees and their engagement with innovative environmental activities. Additionally, the UK Institute of Environmental Management (IEM) has established and delivered training workshops for environmental managers, including raising awareness and skills in EM (Bird, 1996), and managerial attitudes and norms are seen in the US wine industry to act as strong drivers for undertaking active EM behaviours in organisations there (Marshall *et al.*, 2005). Further, a self-report study of managers in China reveals that they have a 'strong disposition' towards taking environmental action, and that environmental knowledge and values are predictors of personal environmental behaviours there (Fryxell and Lo, 2003: 57) (See Renwick *et al.*, 2013 for details).

Questions

1 What evidence can you see of managers enacting green HRM practices in organisations today?

2 What factors do you think could help managers to enact 'eco-initiatives'?

3 Do you think that LMs are ready to embrace green HRM? What arguments would you make in support of them doing so, and what ones against?

Bibliography

Armstrong-Stassen, M. and Schlosser, F. (2010) 'When hospitals provide HR practices tailored to older nurses, will older nurses stay? It may depend on their supervisor, *Human Resource Management Journal,* Vol.20, No.4, 375–90.

Appelbaum, E., Bailey, T., Berg, P. and Kalleberg, A. (2000). *Manufacturing Advantage: Why High-Performance Work Systems Pay Off.* Ithaca, NY: Cornell University Press.

Bird, A. (1996) 'Training for environmental improvement', pp. 227–46, in Wehrmeyer, W. (ed), *Greening People: Human Resources and Environmental Management,* Sheffield: Greenleaf Publishing.

Bjorkman, I., Ehrnrooth, M., Smale, A. and John, S. (2011), 'The determinants of line management internalisation of HRM Practices in MNC subsidiaries,' *International Journal of Human Resource Management,* Vol.22, No.8 (April), 1654–71.

Bowen, D.E. and Ostroff, C. (2004) 'Understanding HRM–firm performance linkages: the role of the "strength" of the HRM system', *Academy of Management Review,* Vol.29, 203–21.

*Brandl, J., Madsen, M. T. and Madsen, H. (2009) 'The perceived importance of HR duties to Danish line managers', *Human Resource Management Journal*, Vol.19, No.2, 194–210.

Brewster, C. (2009) 'Changing roles in HRM', pp. 377–93, in Muller-Camen, M., Croucher, R. and Leigh, S. (eds) *Human Resource Management: A Case Study Approach,* London: CIPD.

Brewster, C. and Larsen, H.H. (1992) 'Human resource management in Europe: evidence from ten countries', *International Journal of Human Resource Management,* Vol.3, No.3, (December), 409–34.

Brewster, C. and Larsen, H.H. (eds) (2000) *Human Resource Management in Northern Europe: Trends, Dilemmas and Strategy,* Oxford: Blackwell.

Brunetto, Y., Farr-Wharton, R. and Shacklock, K. (2010) 'The impact of supervisor–subordinate relationships on morale: implications for public and private sector nurses' commitment', *Human Resource Management Journal,* Vol.20, No.2, 206–25.

Budhwar, P.S. (2000) 'Evaluating levels of strategic integration and devolvement of human resource management in the UK', *Personnel Review,* Vol.29, No.2, 141–61.

Buller, P.F., Napier, N.K. and McEvoy, G.M. (1991) 'Popular prescriptions: implications for HR in the 1990s', *Human Resource Management,* Vol.30, 259–67.

Caldwell, R. (2003) 'The changing roles of personnel managers: old ambiguities, new uncertainties', *Journal of Management Studies,* Vol.40, 983–1004.

CIPD (2007) *Managing Conflict at Work,* London: CIPD.

CIPD (2008) *Conflict management,* Survey Report, London: CIPD.

Cully, M., Woodland, S., O'Reilly, A. and Dix, G. (1999) *Britain At Work: As depicted by the 1998 Workplace Employee Relations Survey,* Routledge, London.

Cunningham, I. and Hyman, J, (1995) 'Transforming the HRM vision into reality: the role of line managers and supervisors in implementing change', *Employee Relations,* Vol.17, No.8, 5–20.

Cunningham, I. and Hyman, J. (1999) 'Devolving human resource responsibilities to the line: beginning of the end or a new beginning for personnel?' *Personnel Review*, Vol.28, Nos1/2, 9–27.

Cunningham, I. and James, P. (2001) 'Line managers as people managers: prioritising the needs of the long-term sick and those with disabilities', British Academy of Management Conference Paper, Cardiff University.

Cunningham, I., James, P. and Dibben, P. (2004) 'Bridging the gap between rhetoric and reality: line managers and the protection of job security for ill worker in the modern workplace', *British Journal of Management,* Vol.15, No.3, 273–90.

Currie, G. and Procter, S. (2001) 'Exploring the relationship between HR and middle managers', *Human Resource Management Journal,* Vol.11, No.1, 53–69.

Delmestri, G. (2006) 'Streams of inconsistent institutional influences: middle managers as carriers of multiple identities', *Human Relations,* Vol.59, No.11, 1515–41.

Dewe, P. and O'Driscoll, M. (2002) 'Stress management interventions: what do managers actually do?', *Personnel Review,* Vol.31, No.2, 143–65.

Dominguez, C.M. (1992) 'Executive forum – the glass ceiling: paradox and promises', *Human Resource Management,* Vol.31, 385–92.

Dunn, C. and Wilkinson, A. (2002) 'Wish you were here: managing absence', *Personnel Review,* Vol.31, No.2, 228–46.

Edwards, R. (1979) *Contested Terrain: The Transformation of the Workplace in the Twentieth Century.* New York: Basic Books.

Edwards, C.Y. and Robinson, O. (2001) '"Better" part-time jobs? A study of part-time working in nursing and the police', *Employee Relations,* Vol.23, No.5, 438–53.

Fairbairn, U. (2005) 'HR as a strategic partner: culture change as an American Express case study', *Human Resource Management,* Vol.44, 79–84.

Fenton-O'Creevy, M. (1998) 'Employee involvement and the middle manager: evidence from a survey of organizations', *Journal of Organizational Behaviour,* Vol.19, 67–84.

Fenton-O'Creevy, M. (2001) 'Employee involvement and the middle manager: saboteur or scapegoat?', *Human Resource Management Journal,* Vol.11, No.1, 24–40.

Fried, Y., Levi, A.S., Billings, S.W. and Browne, K.R. (2001) 'The relation between political ideology and attitudes toward affirmative action among African-Americans: the moderating effect of racial discrimination in the workplace', *Human Relations,* Vol.54, 561–84.

Fryxell, G.E. and Lo, C.W.H. (2003) 'The influence of environmental knowledge and values on managerial behaviours on behalf of the environment: An empirical examination of managers in China', *Journal of Business Ethics,* Vol.46, 45–69.

George, J.M. and Zhou, J. (2007) 'Dual tuning in a supportive context: joint contributions of positive mood, negative mood, and supervisory behaviours to employee creativity', *Academy of Management Journal,* Vol.50, No.3, 605–22.

Gerstner, C.R. and Day, D.V. (1997) 'Meta-analytic review of leader – member exchange theory: correlates and construct issues', *Journal of Applied Psychology,* Vol.82, No.6, 827–44.

Gibb, S. (2001) 'The state of human resource management: evidence from employee's views of HRM systems and staff', *Employee Relations,* Vol.23, No.4, 318–36.

Gibb, S. (2003) 'Line manager involvement in learning and development: small beer or big deal?', *Employee Relations*, Vol.25, No.3, 281–93.

Gilbert, C., De Winne, S. and Sels, L. (2011) 'Antecedents of effective HRM implementation by line managers'. Paper presented to the Academy of Management, San Antonio, Texas, USA, Session No.830.

Gratton, L., Hope-Hailey, V., Stiles, P. and Truss, C. (1999) 'Linking individual performance to business strategy: the people process model', pp. 142–58, in Schuler, R. and Jackson, S. (eds) *Strategic Human Resource Management,* Blackwell, Oxford.

Green, F. and James, D. (2003) 'Assessing skills and autonomy: the job holder versus the line manager', *Human Resource Management Journal,* Vol.13, No.1, 63–77.

Guest, D. (1987) 'Human resource management and industrial relations', *Journal of Management Studies,* Vol.24 (September), 503–22.

Guest, D. and King, Z. (2001) 'HR and the bottom line', *People Management,* 27 September, 34–9.

Guest, D. and King, Z. (2004) 'Power, innovation and problem-solving: the personnel managers' three steps to heaven?', *Journal of Management Studies,* Vol.41, 401–23.

Guest, D., King, Z., Conway, N., Michie, J. and Sheehan-Quinn, M. (2001) *Voices from the Boardroom*, London: CIPD.

Haggerty, J.J. and Wright, P.M. (2009) 'Strong situations and firm performance: a proposed re-conceptualization of the role of the HR function', pp. 100–14, in Wilkinson, A., Bacon, N., Redman, T. and Snell, S. (eds) *The SAGE Handbook of Human Resource Management*, London: Sage.

Hall, L. and Torrington, D. (1998) 'Letting go or holding on – the devolution of operational personnel activities', *Human Resource Management Journal,* Vol.8, No.1, 41–55.

Harris, L. (2001) 'Rewarding employee performance: line manager's values, beliefs and perspectives', *The International Journal of Human Resource Management,* Vol.12, No.7, 1182–95.

Hope-Hailey, V., Gratton, L., McGovern, P., Stiles, P. and Truss, C. (1997) 'A chameleon function? HRM in the 90's', *Human Resource Management Journal,* Vol.7, 5–18.

Hutchinson, S. and Purcell, J, (2003) *Bringing Policies to Life: The Vital Role of Front-line Managers in People Management*, London: CIPD.

Hutchinson, S. and Purcell, J. (2007) *Learning and the Line: The Role of line Managers in Training, Learning and Development,* London: CIPD, 1–24.

Hutchinson, S. and Wood, S. (1995) *Personnel and the Line: Developing the New Relationship*, London: Institute of Personnel and Development (IPD).

Hunter, W. and Renwick, D. (2009) 'Involving British line managers in HRM in a small non-profit work organisation', *Employee Relations*, Vol.31, No.4, 398–411.

*Huy, Q.N. (2002) 'Emotional balancing or organizational continuity and radical change: the contribution of middle managers', *Administrative Science Quarterly,* Vol.47, No.1, (March), 31–69.

Hyde, P., Boaden, R., Cortvriend, P., Harris, C., Marchington, M., Pass, S., Sparrow, P. and Sibbald, B. (2006) *Improving Health Through Human Resource Management: Mapping the Territory,* London: CIPD.

IRS Employment Trends (2001) 'Managing discipline at work', No.727, May, 5–11.

Jackson, S.E. and Schuler, R.S. (2000) *Managing Human Resources: A Partnership Perspective,* London: International Thomson Publishing.

Jones, C. and Saundry, R. (2011) 'The practice of discipline: evaluating the roles and relationship between managers and HR professionals', *Human Resource Management Journal* (online early), 1–15.

Kanter, R. (1982) 'Middle manager as innovator', *Harvard Business Review*, Vol.60, No.4, 95–105.

Kossek, E.E., Berg, P., Piszczek, M. and Petty, R. (2011) 'Work–life flexibility access by the line: linkages to group job context and individual effectiveness'. Paper presented to the Academy of Management, San Antonio, Texas, USA, Session No.830.

*Larsen, H. and Brewster, C. (2003) 'Line management responsibility for HRM: what's happening in Europe?', *Employee Relations*, Vol.25, No.3, 228–44.

Legge, K. (1978) *Power, Innovation, and Problem Solving in Personnel Management,* London: McGraw-Hill.

Legge, K. (1995) *Human Resource Management: Rhetorics and Realities,* Basingstoke: Macmillan.

Leisink, P.L.M. and Knies, E. (2011) 'Line managers' support for older workers', *International Journal of Human Resource Management,* Vol.22, No.9 (May), 1902–17.

Lowe, J. (1992) 'Locating the line: the front-line supervisor and human resource management', pp. 148–68, in Blyton, P. and Turnbull, P. (eds) *Reassessing Human Resource Management,* London: Sage.

Lukes, S. (2005) *Power: A Radical View* (2nd edn), Basingstoke: Palgrave Macmillan.

Lynch, S. (2003) 'Devolution and the management of human resources: evidence from the retail industry'. Paper presented to the Professional Standards Conference, Chartered Institute of Personnel and Development, University of Keele.

Marchington, M. (1999) 'Professional qualification scheme: core personnel & development exam papers & examiners' reports May 1999', Institute of Personnel and development. Paper given to the IPD Professional Standards Conference, University of Warwick, July, 1–12.

Marchington, M. (2001) 'Employee involvement at work', in Storey, (ed.) *Human Resource Management: A Critical Text* (2nd edn), London: Thomson Learning.

Marchington, M. and Wilkinson, A.J. (2002) *People Management and Development: Human Resource Management at Work* (2nd edn), London: CIPD.

Marsh, A.I. (1971) 'The staffing of industrial relations management in the engineering industry', *Industrial Relations Journal,* Vol.22, No.2, 14–24.

Marsh, A.I. and Gillies, J.G. (1983) 'The involvement of line and staff managers in industrial relations', as quoted in Thurley, K. and Wood, S. (eds) (1983) *Industrial Relations and Management Strategy,* Cambridge: Cambridge University Press, 27–38.

Mason, G. (2000) 'Production supervisors in Britain, Germany and the United States: back from the dead again?', *Work, Employment and Society,* Vol.14, No.4, 625–45.

*McConville, T. and Holden, L. (1999) 'The filling in the sandwich: HRM and middle managers in the health sector', *Personnel Review,* Vol.28, Nos 5–6, 406–24.

McDougall, M. (1998) 'Devolving gender management in the public sector: opportunity or opt-out?', *International Journal of Public Sector Management,* Vol.11, 71–80.

*McGovern, P., Gratton, L., Hope-Hailey, V. and Truss, C. (1997) 'Human resource management on the line?', *Human Resource Management Journal,* Vol.7, 12–29.

McGuire, D., Garavan, T.N., Saha, S.K. and O'Donnell, D. (2006) 'The impact of individual values on human resource decision-making by line managers', *International Journal of Manpower,* Vol.27, No.3, 251–73.

Mesner-Andolsek, D.A. and Stebe, J. (2005) 'Devolution or (de)centralisation of HRM function in European organizations', *International Journal of Human Resource Management,* Vol.16, No.3, (March), 311–29.

Millward, N., Bryson, A. and Forth, J. (2000) *All Change at Work? British Employment Relations 1980–1998, as Portrayed by the Workplace Industrial Relations Survey Series,* London: Routledge.

Mishra, S.K. and Bhatnagar, D. (2010) 'Linking emotional dissonance and organizational identification to turnover intention and emotional well-being: a study of medical representatives in India', *Human Resource Management,* Vol.49, 401–19.

Mitsuhashi, H., Park, H.J., Wright, P.M. and Chua, R. (2000) 'Line and HR executives' perceptions of HR effectiveness in the People's Republic of China', *International Journal of Human Resource Management,* Vol.11, No.2, 197–216.

Mueller, B. and Lee, J. (2002) 'Leader–member exchange and organizational communication satisfaction in multiple contexts', *Journal of Business Communication,* Vol.39, No.2, 220–44.

Nehles, A.C., Riemsdijk, M., Kok, I. and Looise, J.K. (2006), 'Implementing human resource management successfully: a front-line management challenge', *Management Revue,* Vol.17, No.3, 256–73.

Peng, A.C. and Tjosvold, D. (2011) 'Social face concerns and conflict avoidance of Chinese employees with their Western or Chinese managers', *Human Relations,* Vol.68, No.4, 1031–50.

Perry, E.L. and Kulik, C.T. (2008). 'The devolution of HR to the line: implications for perceptions of people management effectiveness', *International Journal of Human Resource Management,* Vol.19, 262–73.

Poole, M. and Jenkins, G. (1997) 'Responsibilities for human resource management practices in the modern enterprise', *Personnel Review,* Vol.26 No.5, 333–56.

*Purcell, J. and Hutchinson, S. (2007) 'Front-line managers as agents in the HRM–performance causal chain: theory, analysis and evidence', *Human Resource Management Journal,* Vol.17, No.1, 3–20.

Purcell, J. Kinnie, N., Hutchinson, S., Rayton, B. and Swart, J. (2003) *Understanding the People and Performance Link: Unlocking the Black Box,* London: CIPD.

*Ramus, C.A. and Steger, U. (2000) 'The roles of supervisory support behaviours and environmental policy in employee "eco-initiatives" at leading-edge European companies', *Academy of Management Journal*, Vol.41, 605–26.

Redman, T. (2001) 'Performance appraisal', pp. 57–95, in Redman, T. and Wilkinson, A. (eds) *Contemporary Human Resource Management,* Harlow: Pearson Education.

Renwick, D. (2003) 'Line manager involvement in HRM: an inside view', *Employee Relations,* Vol.25, No.3, 262–80.

Renwick, D. (2009) 'Line managers: text and cases', pp. 227–42, in Redman, T. and Wilkinson, A. (eds) *Contemporary Human Resource Management* (3rd edn), Harlow: Pearson Education.

*Renwick, D. (2010) *British Management Work Relationships: HR and the Line,* London/Saarbrucken: Lambert Academic Press/VDM Publishing.

Renwick, D.W.S., Redman, T. and Maguire, S. (2013) 'Green HRM: A review and research agenda*', International Journal of Management Reviews,* (forthcoming). Early view at: http://onlinelibrary.wiley.com/journal/10.1111/%28ISSN%291468-2370/earlyview

Rollinson, D., Hook, C., Foot, M. and Handley, J. (1996) 'Supervisor and manager styles in handling discipline and grievance: Part 2: Approaches to handling discipline and grievance', *Personnel Review,* Vol.25, No.4, 38–55.

Rouleau, L. and Balogun, J. (2011) 'Middle managers, strategic sensemaking, and discursive competence', *Journal of Management Studies,* Vol.48, No.5 (July), 953–83.

Sanders, K. and Frenkel, S. (2009) 'Call for papers/editorial: special issue on comparative perspectives on HR and line manager relationships and their effects on employees', *International Journal of Human Resource Management,* Vol.20, 501–3.

Sanders, K. and Frenkel, S. (2011) 'HR–line management relations: characteristics and effects', *International Journal of Human Resource Management,* Vol.22, No.8 (April), 1611–17.

Sisson, K. (ed.) (1989) *Personnel Management in Britain,* Oxford: Blackwell.

Sisson, K. and Storey, J. (2000) *The Realities of Human Resource Management,* Buckingham: Open University Press.

Soens, N., Buyens, D. and Taylor, S. (2011) 'High-performance work systems, cognitive and motivational mediators and performance: a reality check'. *Paper presented to the Academy of Management, San Antonio, Texas, USA, Session No.830.*

*Storey, J. (1992) *Developments in the Management of Human Resources*, Oxford: Blackwell.

Storey, J. (2001) 'Human resource management today: an assessment', pp. 3–20, in Storey, J. (ed.) *Human Resource Management: A Critical Text* (2nd edn), London: Thomson Learning.

Taylor, S. (2002) 'A poor boss can be the last straw', *Basingstoke Gazette*, 20 December, 56.

Teague, P.and Roche, W.K. (2011) 'Line managers and the management of workplace conflict: evidence from Ireland', *Human Resource Management Journal* (online early), 1–17.

Teo, S.T.T. and Rodwell, J.J. (2007) 'To be strategic in the new public sector, HR must remember its operational activities', *Human Resource Management,* vol.44, 265–84.

Thornhill, A. and Saunders, M.N.K. (1998) 'What if line managers don't realize they're responsible for HR? Lessons from an organization experiencing rapid change', *Personnel Review,* Vol.27, No.6, 460–76.

*Townsend, K., Wilkinson, A., Allan, C. and Bamber, G. (2011) 'Mixed signals in HRM: the HRM role of hospital line managers', *Human Resource Management Journal* (online early), 1–16.

Tsai, W.C. and Tai, W.T. (2003) 'Perceived importance as a mediator of the relationship between training assignment and training motivation', *Personnel Review,* Vol.32, No.2, 151–63.

Tyson, S. and Fell, A. (1995) *Evaluating the Personnel Function* (2nd edn), Cheltenham: Stanley Thomes.

Uhl-Bien, M., Graen, G. and Scandura, L. (2000) 'Indicators of leader–member exchange (LMX) for strategic human resource management systems', *Research in Personnel and Human Resources Management,* Vol.18, 137–85.

Ulrich, D. and Beatty, D. (2001) 'From partners to players: extending the HR playing field', *Human Resource Management,* Vol.40, 293–307.

Wai-Kwong, F.Y., Priem, R.L. and Cycyota, C.S. (2001) 'The performance effects of human resource managers' and other middle managers' involvement in strategy making under different business-level strategies: the case in Hong Kong', *International Journal of Human Resource Management,* Vol.12. No.8, 1325–46.

Walton, J. (1999) *Strategic Human Resource Management,* Harlow: Pearson Education.

Whittaker, S. and Marchington, M. (2003) 'Devolving HR responsibility to the line: threat, opportunity or partnership?', *Employee Relations,* Vol.25, No.3, 245–61.

Wright, P.M., and Haggerty, J. (2005) 'Missing variables in theories of strategic human resource management: time, cause and individuals. CAHRS working paper (WP05–03)', Cornell University ILR School, Ithaca, NY, USA, 1–17.

Wright, P.M., McMahan, G.C., Snell, S.A. and Gerhart, B. (2001) 'Comparing line and HR executives' perceptions of HR effectiveness: services, roles and contributions', *Human Resource Management,* Vol.40, 111–23.

---

*Useful Reading

Xie, J. and Wu, G. (2001) 'Training and development in the People's Republic of China', *International Journal of Training and Development,* Vol.5, No.3, 223–32.

Yang, X.H. (2003) *'Management Training in a Chinese State-owned Enterprise: A Neglected Aspect For Middle Managers'*. Unpublished MBA dissertation, University of Sheffield, UK.

Yrie, A., Hartman, S. and Galle, W. (2003) 'Examining communication style and leader-member exchange: considerations and concerns for managers', *International Journal of Management,* Vol.20, No.1, 92–100.

CHAPTER 10

ORGANISATIONAL AND CORPORATE CULTURE

Alistair Cheyne and John Loan-Clarke

Introduction

In the study of organisations and their management, the concept of organisational culture (sometimes referred to as corporate culture) has become increasingly important, and the quantity of research in the area has increased dramatically since the early 1980s (Siehl and Martin, 1990). This chapter outlines recent theory and research in organisational culture. In doing so, it outlines definitions and categorisations of culture, discusses the assessment of culture, investigates the links between culture and human resource management, and examines how organisations might attempt to manage culture.

The concept of culture

Culture as a concept derives from the fields of social anthropology and sociology. In general, its description has been used to characterise an organisation or group of individuals within a social structure. Culture is, however, not a well defined concept (Münch and Smelster, 1992); it describes roles and interactions that derive from norms and values in the socio-logical tradition, or from beliefs and attitudes in the social psychological field (Wunthow and Witten, 1988). In addition to these distinctions, there are at least two major approaches to the study of culture. The first views culture as an implicit feature of social life, and the second holds culture to be an explicit social construction (Wunthow and Witten, 1988), in other words culture as the structure of a sociopolitical group or culture as a product of that group.

In the same vein, two models of culture have been proposed: that which defines culture in terms of behaviour and that which defines it in terms of meaning. The second of these models is supported by Trice and Beyer's (1984) assertion that culture is a system of publicly and col-lectively accepted meanings operating for a given group at a given time.

Such views of culture have been incorporated into organisational theory to give rise to the concepts of organisational culture (Brown, 1998) and the similar corporate culture (Peters and Waterman, 1982). The term 'organisational culture' tends to refer to a naturally occur-ring phenomenon that all organisations possess, whereas corporate culture is held to be more management-driven, in an attempt to increase organisational effectiveness. Furthermore, it has been suggested (Shipley, 1990) that culture is central to the understanding and control of, and resistance to, change in society, organisations and social groups. For organisations, Yu (2007) suggests that having an appropriate corporate culture is held as a vital element of many companies' successes, and failures.

Organisational culture

As noted earlier, the study of culture has been influential in the field of organisational studies for over 30 years (Denison, 1996; Trompenaars and Hampden-Turner, 1997). Its importance stems, in part, from the notion that it provides a dynamic and interactive model of organising (Jelinek *et al.,* 1983; Smircich, 1983) and as such can help explain how organisational environments might be characterised, assessed and ultimately controlled (Deal and Kennedy, 1982; Schneider, 1990). Furthermore, a number of authors have proposed that successful organisations have a strong or positive corporate culture (Deal and Kennedy, 1982; Kilmann *et al.,* 1985; Peters and Waterman, 1982; Weick, 1985; Yu, 2007). The notion of culture can, therefore, imply a practical way of explaining how and why particular organisations enjoy differing levels of success (Brown, 1998; Trompenaars and Hampden-Turner, 1997). In the field of human resource management, organisational culture is increasingly held to be essential to success in organisations (see, for example, DeCenzo and Robbins, 2002). The suggestion that organisational effectiveness is heavily influenced by a positive corporate culture has been particularly influential for practising managers. A key influence for the formation of this assumption was the 1982 book by Peters and Waterman, *In Search of Excellence*:

> Without exception, the dominance and coherence of culture proved to be an essential quality of the excellent companies. Moreover the stronger the culture and the more it was directed towards the marketplace, the less the need there was for policy manuals, organization charts or detailed procedures and rules. *(1982: 75)*

However, some research (for example, Booth and Hamer, 2008; Kotter and Heskett, 1992) has indicated, the causal link between culture and organisational effectiveness is not necessarily easy to identify. We will come back to the potential link between culture and performance later in this chapter, after we consider what culture is, and how we might assess it.

Defining Organisational Culture

A number of definitions of culture have been proposed and it is possible to discern some common themes among these. Moorhead and Griffin (1995) suggest that organisational culture is a set of values that help people in an organisation to understand which actions are considered acceptable and which are unacceptable to the organisation and its members. Similarly, Schein (1985) has defined organisational culture in terms of employees' shared values and perceptions of the organisation, beliefs about it and common ways of solving problems within the organisation. Schein (1985) has also described organisational culture in terms of an ongoing process through which an organisation's behaviour patterns become transformed over time, installed in new recruits, and refined and adapted in response to both internal and external changes. Culture helps an organisation's members to interpret and accept their world, and so it is not so much a by-product of an organisation as an integral part of it, which influences individuals' behaviours and contributes to the effectiveness of the organisation.

Reviews of the concept of organisational culture (for example, Furnham, 1997; Rousseau 1990) have detailed the abundance of definitions that have developed over the years. Examples of the range of definitions are detailed in Box 10.1.

While it is apparent that there have been a number of disagreements over the precise nature of organisational culture, these definitions do bear some resemblance to each other. Several salient points emerge upon comparing these definitions. Emphasis, in many cases, is on values, beliefs and expectations that are shared within the group and/or organisation, and which, in turn, can help the members make sense of their environment, and direct behaviour. These shared values may be directly related to leaders' values within the organisation (Giberson *et al.,* 2009) or be the result of manager directed learning within organisations (Van den Steen, 2010).

Rousseau (1990) agrees that it is not really the definitions of organisational culture thaat vary widely but the approaches to data collection and operation. Pettigrew (1990) offers one explanation of the problem in defining organisational culture. He suggests that it is, in part, due to the fact that culture is:

> not just a concept but the source of a family of concepts (Pettigrew 1979), and it is not just a family of concepts but also a frame of reference or root metaphor for organisational analysis. *(1990: 414)*

BOX 10.1 HRM in practice   Definitions of culture

Kroeber and Kluckhohn (1952)	Culture consists of patterns of behaviour transmitted by symbols, embodied in artefacts, ideas and values
Bowers and Seashore (1966)	The best way of doing things around here
Becker and Geer (1970)	A set of common understandings
Geertz (1973)	The fabric of meaning which allows the interpretation and guidance of action
Van Maanen and Schein (1979)	Values, beliefs and expectations that members of organisations come to share

Swartz and Jordon (1980)	Shared patterns of beliefs and expectations that produce norms shaping behaviour
Ouchi (1981)	The set of symbols, ceremonies and myths that communicate the organisation's values and beliefs to its members
Deal and Kennedy (1982)	A system of informal rules that spells out how people are to behave most of the time
Louis (1983)	As having three aspects: (1) some content (2) specific to (3) a group
Martin and Siehl (1983)	The glue that holds together an organisation through shared patterns of meaning, consisting of core values, forms and strategies to reinforce content
Uttal (1983)	Shared values and beliefs that interact with an organisation's structures and control systems to produce behavioural norms

Pettigrew's explanation reflects two very different understandings of the concept of culture. Brown (1998) suggests that a clear distinction can be made between those who think that culture is a metaphor that helps us to understand organisations in terms of other entities (Morgan, 1986), and those who see culture as an objective entity that distinguishes one organisation from another (Gold, 1982). The view that culture is an objective entity can be subdivided, as pointed out by Rohner (1984), into something an organisation is (or its structure and meaning) or something an organisation has (for example, its behaviour), as embodied by most of the definitions summarised by Rousseau (1990) and detailed above.

Layers Of Organisational Culture

It may be that the use of culture as a concept can be seen to be too embracing, and some writers (Morgan, 1986; Rousseau, 1990; Schein, 1985) describe culture as having a series of different layers. Schein (1985) suggests that there are three levels of culture: artefacts, values and basic assumptions. Figure 10.1 shows a representation of these layers of

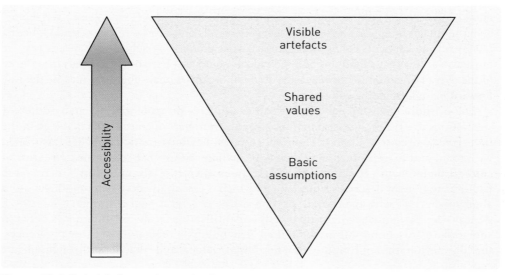

Figure 10.1 Schein's layer of organisational culture

culture, organised from readily accessible, and, therefore, more easily studied, to difficult to access.

At the most accessible level are visible artefacts, or products of cultural activity. These might include patterns of behaviour (Cooke and Rousseau, 1988), or the structures that reflect patterns of activity, observable to those outside the culture. Examples of these visible artefacts might include corporate logos and the physical layout of the organisation. The middle layer relates to values and priorities assigned to organisational outcomes. Such values might be reflected in group behavioural norms, or beliefs about what is acceptable and unacceptable behaviour within the organisation, similar to Moorhead and Griffin's (1995) definition of culture. This layer can be learned about through interaction with, and questioning of, group members. Patterns of unconscious assumptions (Schein, 1984) are the deepest of the layers of culture, and these may not be directly known by the organisation's members and therefore require a period of intensive interaction to uncover. An appreciation of layers of culture could, therefore, be important when considering whether culture can be managed (see below).

This type of representation of cultural layers has been further embellished, to present a more complex picture. Hatch (1997) has adapted Schein's (1985) original layers model to incorporate organisational symbols and processes in a more dynamic model. Similarly, Hofstede *et al.* (1990) have divided the manifestations (or more accessible elements) of culture into values, at the deepest level, through rituals and heroes, to symbols at the shallowest.

Subcultures

In addition to being layered, culture may also have different effects at different levels in the organisation. Subcultures might develop (Trice and Beyer, 1993) which can be associated with different roles, functions and levels in the organisation (Hampden-Turner, 1990). Schein (2004) agrees that cultures are found at every level of an organisation, as well as at the level of the organisation as a whole. There may also be differences in manifest culture between management and staff levels (Furnham and Gunter, 1993) and these differences should be consistent with the organisation's hierarchy (Deal and Kennedy, 1982). The status differences created by these hierarchies provide a basis for the formation of subcultures (Trice and Beyer, 1993). Adams and Ingersoll (1989) have proposed that the best way to conceive of organisational culture is in terms of its constituent subcultures. Indeed, organisations have been described as umbrellas for diffuse collections of subcultures, which may or may not cohere harmoniously (Martin *et al.*, 1985). It has also been argued that these organisational cultures and subcultures are nested (Pidgeon, 1991) and overlapping, being mutually influential across, and between, levels and groups. Morgan and Ogbonna (2008) suggest that conceiving of organisations as comprising subcultures means that we must also accept that subgroups and individuals could also have differing goals from those of the overall organisation, however the study of organisational subgroups may be the way forward in understanding culture.

The offshore environment provides an example of the potential for many different subcultures to exist on one installation, given the numbers of contractors involved in the industry (Mearns *et al.*, 1998). These subcultures may have particular beliefs associated with them and these in turn may dictate behaviour within that subculture. In terms of cultural maintenance it may be, therefore, more useful to talk of 'cultural alignment'. Cultural alignment describes a mechanism which is essentially designed to influence and align subcultures with the overall, or 'dominant', organisational culture (Thom, 1997). As a process, alignment might involve the identification of major differences between sub- and organisational cultures and then, depending on the nature of those differences, the promotion of appropriate organisational values and practices throughout the subcultures.

Categorisations of culture

In addition to the various definitions of culture and descriptions of level, several researchers have developed a number of classifications of organisational culture, allowing organisations to be described as different types of objective entity. Indeed, Balthazard *et al.* (2006) suggest that much of the research on organisational culture has focused on describing types of cultures and producing dimensions of culture. These allow us to compare and evaluate different organisations in terms of their culture, and allow types of culture to be associated with successes and failures within those organisations. There are many such categorisations; here we will examine three of the better known examples, those of Deal and Kennedy (1982), Harrison (1972) and Hofstede (1980, 1991).

Deal and Kennedy's Four Cultures

One of the most popular classifications of corporate culture was proposed by Deal and Kennedy (1982). Their categorisation of culture was the result of visiting hundreds of organisations and is based on two organisational environmental factors: the degree of risk associated with business activities, and the speed of feedback to the organisation and individuals about the success of those business activities. Deal and Kennedy (1982) identified four distinct culture types:

- **Tough-guy macho culture** – an organisation of risk takers who receive immediate feedback; examples include police, management consultants, media.
- **Work hard/play hard culture** – a low-risk, quick-feedback culture which encourages people to maintain high levels of activity; examples include sales companies, computer companies.
- **Bet your company culture** – the high-risk, slow-feedback culture, where ideas are given time to develop; examples include large multinationals engaged in research and product development.
- **Process culture** – the classic bureaucracy where feedback is slow and risks are low, so individuals focus on the processes; examples might include local government and heavily regulated industries.

Deal and Kennedy (1982) recognise that organisations might not precisely fit into these four types, or indeed perhaps not fit at all, but they propose that this model is still a useful tool for managers beginning to identify an organisation's culture.

Harrison's Typology

An early, relatively simple, yet extremely influential classification of organisational culture was suggested by Harrison (1972). This classification has been elaborated on by other scholars, including Handy (1978) and Williams *et al.* (1993), and, like the Deal and Kennedy model, includes descriptions of four main types of culture in organisations:

- **Power culture** – has a single source of power. Typically these types of organisation react quickly, but success often depends on those with the power at the centre and these organisations might be small, owner-managed businesses.
- **Role culture** – these types of organisations are more typically described as bureaucracies, with an emphasis on functions and specialities. These organisations are more likely to be successful in stable environments and could include public sector organisations.
- **Task culture** – the focus for these types of organisation is accomplishing goals; power is based on expertise and flexibility is important, for example management consultancies.
- **Person culture** – these types of organisation exist primarily to serve the needs of their members. Individuals are expected to influence each other through example and

helpfulness, and have almost complete autonomy. This type of culture may be evident in those in professional practice, such as lawyers or doctors, or those involved in a collective organisation.

National Culture Dimensions

The consideration of organisational culture is complicated further when the effects of societal and national cultures upon individual organisations' cultures are considered. Hofstede (1980) studied these influences in relation to IBM, the American multinational company, operating in over 40 countries worldwide. Hofstede collected survey data concerning work-related values from international affiliates and found evidence of national cultural differences. Hofstede (1991) demonstrated that managers in different countries varied in the strength of their attitudes and values regarding various issues. Four dimensions were identified, including:

- **power distance** – the extent to which members are willing to accept an unequal distribution of power, wealth and privilege;
- **uncertainty avoidance** – the manner in which individuals have learned to cope with uncertainty;
- **individualism** – the degree to which individuals are required to act independently;
- **masculinity** – related to dominant values such as success and money.

A fifth dimension, 'confucian dynamism' – the degree to which long-termism or short-termism is the dominant orientation in life – was added after further sampling and analysis of the data in an attempt to capture key aspects of Eastern cultural values. However, the core cultural values of Eastern nations have received much attention in their own right. For example, Wong *et al.* (2010) claim that there are five important values in Chinese culture:

- **collectivism** – a strong sense of group orientation;
- **harmony** – the need to maintain mutually respectful relationships and to show concern for humanity and morality;
- **respect for age and seniority** – the respect for and following of tradition and social hierarchy, such as rules, status and authority;
- **relationships** – *guanxi*, the importance of developing and maintaining interpersonal relationships or connections, including kinship to friendship, and politics to business;
- **face** – *mianzi*, related to status, ego or self-respect, this relates to the need to maintain reputation or value in the eyes of others.

The results of Hofstede's work suggest, for example, that organisations in the UK will have low power distance, be individualist, masculine and able to cope with uncertainty. Hofstede's work is not only deemed to be important for the identification of specific cultural differences (Hatch, 1997) but it has also shown that organisational culture is an entry point for societal influence on organisations. This notion has been developed further in the work of Fons Trompenaars (Trompenaars and Hampden-Turner, 1997). While Hofstede's work on national cultures has influenced much subsequent research, it has not been without criticism. See, for example, Kirkman *et al.* (2006) for a review of 25 years of research using Hofstede's framework. Gerhart and Fang (2005) have re-analysed Hofstede's original data and, using different statistical indicators, claim that organisational differences account for more variance in cultural values, than do country differences.

A number of similarities are apparent from these example classifications; for example, *tough guy, power, power distance* and *hierarchy* all seem to be tapping into similar types of culture, suggesting a degree of reliability in the observations of different research groups. However, while these typologies are a useful starting point in describing culture, as Deal and Kennedy (1982) acknowledge, we should remember that they represent ideal situations or models for us to compare actual organisations against, and no organisation will fit the types exactly. It is perhaps more useful for organisations to be able to describe the origin of their own cultures and the process by which they arise (Furnham, 1997), and how they can enhance organisational effectiveness. A first step in achieving this might involve the detailed assessment of organisational culture.

It is clear from the literature examined above that there are certain consistencies in the way culture is defined. Many researchers agree that organisational culture involves beliefs and values, exists at a variety of different levels, and manifests itself in a wide range of artefacts, symbols and processes within any particular organisation. Culture helps an organisation's members to interpret meaning and understand their working environment. It is an integral part of an organisation and, as such, can influence individuals' behaviour and potentially contribute to the effectiveness or ineffectiveness of the organisation. Furthermore, the more individuals identify with the key values of the organisation, the more important those values become and the stronger the culture (Booth and Hamer, 2008). Two examples of problems that can be encountered by individuals' interpretations of an organisation's culture and adherence to cultural norms are highlighted in Box 10.2.

A key issue for management is whether culture(s) will exist in the organisation irrespective of management action or whether management can proactively influence and change culture. These issues will be considered in more detail in the second half of the chapter; we now consider how an understanding of culture within an organisation can be acquired.

Box 10.2 HRM in practice   Problems of strong culture

The two instances which follow provide examples of the problems organisations and individuals can face when they feel bound by organisational culture to behave in a particular way.

Piper Alpha

An explosion and resulting fire destroyed the North Sea oil production platform the Piper Alpha on 6 July 1988, killing a total of 167 men. A leakage of natural gas condensate ignited, causing a massive explosion. The explosion ignited secondary oil fires and the released gas caused a second, larger explosion which engulfed the entire platform. The public enquiry (Cullen, 1990) pointed out a number of managerial and organisational issues in the development of the disaster. One aspect of the disaster which might give an insight into the culture in the organisation was the delay in shutting down feeds from other neighbouring platforms. The fire might have burnt out sooner had it not been fed new fuel from both the nearby Tartan and the Claymore platforms. Both platforms could see that Piper Alpha was burning, but, it has been suggested, felt they did not have the authority to shut down production. There may be many explanations for these actions, but they could suggest that the parent organisation's culture might be characterised as a role or process culture where individuals adhered to a strong hierarchy.

Japan Airlines, Anchorage

On 13 January 1977, a Japan Airlines DC-8 crashed shortly after take-off from Anchorage International Airport, Alaska, killing three crew members and two cargo-handlers and destroying the aircraft. The flight was captained by a 53-year-old American pilot with 23,000 hours' flying experience; his Japanese co-pilot was 31 years old, with considerably less experience (1,600 hours). The investigation into the accident found that the captain was around three times over the legal limit for driving a car. The National Transportation Safety Board held that a contributing factor to this accident was the failure of other flight crew to prevent the captain undertaking the flight.

Anderson and colleagues (2003) suggest that, while it is difficult to gauge exactly what happened on the flight deck, the incident might have had something to do with the perception of command relationships. Given Hofstede's categorisations of national cultural dimensions, we might expect an US culture to be low on power distance and individualistic, while Japan has a culture that has high power distance and is collective. As Anderson *et al.* (2003) point out, the co-pilot would have been conscious of his role within the cockpit and the seniority of the captain, and so might have questioned the captain in a discreet way rather than the more assertive challenge that would have been needed in this situation.

Assessing organisational culture

Meyerson (1991) has noted that:

> culture was the code word for the subjective side of organisational life … its study represented an ontological rebellion against the dominant functionalist or 'scientific' paradigm. *(1991: 256)*

In other words, organisational culture research came about in part as a reaction to the existing approaches to the study of organisations, focusing on systems (Brown, 1998). Despite this reaction, both quantitative and qualitative methods persist in the study of organisational culture (Brown, 1998; Rousseau, 1990). Moorhead and Griffin (1995) trace these differences back to the historical foundations, or antecedents, of current organisational culture research. These include methodologies influenced by economics as well as those from psychology, sociology and anthropology.

As we might expect from an examination of definitions, approaches to assessment vary widely. Rousseau (1990) argues that debates over organisational research methods are the result of the resurgence of qualitative methodologies, originally based in anthropology and sociology, and the perceived shortcomings of quantitative approaches. Smircich (1983) proposes that standardised, quantitative measures cannot describe a culture, which is essentially a frame of reference. Similarly, Schein (1984) suggests that, since each organisation is unique, it is difficult for an outside researcher to form *a priori* questions or measures to tap into its culture. Furthermore, Schein (1984) asserts that the use of such quantitative methods is unethical in its use of aggregated data and not the participants' own words. Given the definitions of culture discussed earlier, it is important for quantitative organisational culture research to address these criticisms.

Quantitative approaches to the assessment of culture are, however, still popular. Many similar dimensions appear on several culture assessment instruments, suggesting that values and behaviours can be expressed, and in turn assessed, in similar terms (Rousseau, 1990). Furthermore, Xenikou and Furnham (1996) found significant correlations between four instruments and went on to suggest a six-factor model based on the work of Cooke and Lafferty (1989), Glaser (1983), Kilmann and Saxton (1983) and Sashkin and Fulmer (1985; cited in Rousseau, 1990). The factors uncovered related to:

- openness to change;
- values of excellent organisations;
- bureaucratic culture;
- organisational artefacts;
- resistance to new ideas;
- workplace social relations.

Not surprisingly, these factors relate almost exclusively to the more accessible layers of culture outlined in Figure 10.1, and bear more than a passing resemblance to some of the categorisations discussed above. Comprehensive reviews of the plethora of quantitative measures used to assess organisational culture can be found in Ashkanasay *et al.*, (2000) and Sackmann (2006).

In addition to alternative research strategies and data collection methods, Pettigrew (1979, 1990) has identified several analytical issues, related to the complexity of the concept, that make the study of culture difficult. These include, among others, the fact that culture might exist at different levels (Schein, 1985), is pervasive across the organisation, can include subcultures and is interconnected with the organisational system, subsystems and the external environment. These kinds of issues, together with varying data collection and research strategies, would seem to make a comprehensive study of organisational culture almost impossible. Rousseau (1990) suggests that different approaches and strategies may suit the investigation of different levels and aspects of culture. Few empirical researchers claim to uncover everything about an organisation's culture in their investigations; they focus mainly on one or two of the elements discussed above, or the more accessible manifestations. The definitional and assessment issues discussed above have proved particularly problematic when seeking to understand any relationships between culture and organisational performance.

Culture and organisational performance

Of particular interest to organisations and managers is the (assumed) link between organisational culture and organisational performance. Silverzweig and Allen (1976) were probably the first to claim such a link. Based on eight case studies of organisations seeking to change their culture in order to improve effectiveness, they identified that six of the organisations improved their performance. However, the real spur to popularity of the culture–performance link was Peters and Waterman's (1982) *In Search of Excellence*. Several researchers have sought to define and assess the link between culture and various organisational outcomes, often in the hope of identifying or nurturing the 'best' culture associated with those outcomes. Lee and Yu (2004) point out that much research on the link with performance has focused on a search for particular shared organisational traits or values that result in superior performance. One example of theoretical links being drawn between culture and outcome measures is given by the role for organisational culture in productivity modelled by Kopelman and colleagues (1990). Their model is based on the influence of human resource management on productivity and individual satisfaction and motivation and illustrates how culture, management practices and climate can influence the outcome measure. Similarly, Bright and Cooper (1993) have proposed that quality management and organisational culture are closely aligned, with overall culture change being central to the development of quality management systems and essential to their functioning, although no empirical data is presented. Several attempts have also been made to link the assessment of organisational culture with financial performance (for example, Denison, 1984; Gordon, 1985; Gordon and DiTomaso, 1992). Gordon and DiTomaso (1992) suggest that the appropriate culture for achieving results in the insurance organisations they examined may not be best described only as 'strong' in terms of consistency, but also as flexible. The organisational culture related to effectiveness may, therefore, best be conceived as a combination of several characteristics, which facilitate enhanced performance.

Petty and colleagues (1995) have endeavoured to link the assessment of organisational culture with broader performance measures. Their assessment of performance incorporated evaluations of operations, customer accounting, support services, marketing and employee health and safety into one overall performance measure. This study found evidence of associations between the measures of performance and organisational culture, with the strongest indication of the link being evident in the correlations between 'teamwork' and performance. They conclude that a culture that fosters cooperation may be the most effective in the organisations included in their study. Similarly, Lee and Yu (2004) studied the link between organisational culture and a number of performance outcomes in various Singaporean companies. They found some evidence to suggest that the cultural strength of organisations was related to performance, but only in some of the cases they studied. However, Wilderom *et al.* (2000) are not convinced that meaningful conclusions can be drawn from the evidence available regarding culture–performance links. They argue that different measures of culture are used in different studies and that the operationalisation of performance is inconsistent and lacks validity. Certainly subjective measures of performance, for example as made by the chief executive of an organisation, in comparison to key competitors (e.g. see Chan *et al.,* 2004) seem to invite bias. This is particularly problematic in respect of the links between strong cultures supposedly leading to effective performance.

As well as an increasing number of subjective and objective performance measures, the last decade has seen an increasing emphasis on the role of intermediary variables in the culture–performance relationship. Garnett *et al.* (2008) suggest that communication has an indirect role by acting as moderator or mediator of organisational culture's influence on performance. Mohr *et al.* (2012) studying outpatient centres in healthcare, found that where a group-oriented culture existed it moderated the effect of employee turnover on customer service. However, the same culture did not have a significant effect on waiting times. Sackmann (2010) has emphasised the need for examining contingent, interactive relationships in order to better understand culture and performance. Taking up this theme, Kotrba *et al.* (2012) investigated whether consistent cultures (i.e. those with highly shared values) produced better market-to-book ratios; sales growth and return on assets. They found that consistent cultures interacted with higher scores on other cultural dimensions of involvement, adaptability and mission, to enhance market-to-book ratios and sales growth. Surprisingly, they found that high consistency, along with moderately low scores on the three other cultural dimensions, was associated with high profitability. As Yilmaz and Ergun (2008) point out, this highlights that different cultural dimensions are required to deal with contradictory business challenges.

 ## Organisational culture and human resource management

Having spent some time so far in this chapter outlining and debating conceptual issues relating to culture in organisations, this section of the chapter will seek to explore the impact of the interest in culture on 'people management' practices. Consistent with the trends within the people management literature generally, this chapter will consider human resource management to be the most contemporary, if not the most commonly used, general approach to the management of people in the workplace. As a number of commentators within the UK have noted, human resource management and organisational culture seem to be highly intertwined concepts. So, for example, Storey (1995) and Legge (2005) have articulated the centrality of organisational culture to the development and practice of human resource management. Storey (1995: 8) suggests that managing culture change coincides so much with the movement towards HRM that they 'become one and the same project'.

Fundamental assumptions which reflect managerial perspectives on organisational culture are also central to the beliefs and assumptions of human resource management. As Storey (1995: 6), observes, management does not merely seek compliance with rules and the implementation of procedures and systems as a way of controlling employee behaviour, but seeks to develop high levels of employee commitment through the management of culture.

As noted earlier in the chapter, there may be differences between the values that management espouses, and the values that employees consider to be enacted in the organisation. Howell *et al.* (2012) have recently explored the importance of employees' perceiving congruence between espoused and enacted values. They found that there was higher affective commitment in respect of the values of humanity and vision when espoused and enacted values were congruent. This shows that importance of management being considered to 'walk the talk'. Unfortunately, the values investigated across a range of Australian organisations were not company-specific, and future research exploring this important distinction will, ideally, be context-specific.

Mabey and Salaman (1995) comment that some have also welcomed the recognition that understanding culture changes the emphasis from focusing purely on formal/rational aspects of the organisation, for example organisational structure, rules, procedures and technical processes. However, like Sackmann (1991), they feel that 'managerialist' perspectives on culture are simplistic and ignore the complexities of the anthropological concept from which it is derived.

Some researchers consider that culture cannot be controlled by management within the organisation, whereas others tend to believe that it is at least possible. We shall return to this discussion later in the chapter. Nevertheless, there has been something of a convergence of approach to researching and understanding culture from those practitioners/consultants and academics who do believe that there is the potential to manage organisational culture. As Barley *et al.* (1988) have noted, both groups are interested in identifying how culture can be used as a mechanism to enhance performance.

There have been extreme concerns expressed by some academics regarding this approach to the management of employees. Whereas previous rational approaches overtly used rules, regulations and procedures as a way of ensuring behavioural compliance from employees, many see culture management as equally controlling but in a covert way. The difference is that culture management techniques focus much less on rational than on emotive approaches to employee management. Therefore, the winning of 'hearts and minds' and the legitimacy of seeking to manipulate employee emotions has been questioned by writers such as Casey (1995), Keenoy and Anthony (1992) and Willmott (1993), highlighting the ethical dimension.

Recognising that there are different perspectives in respect of the ethics and practicalities of manipulating culture within work organisations, we shall now assume that there is at least the potential for management to manipulate culture and explore how this might be done.

Culture Management and HRM Practices

It would seem logical that the human resources (HR) function ought to be centrally involved in attempting to influence organisational culture; however, this is not necessarily so in all organisations. A good example where it was the case is American Express. Fairbairn (2005) has outlined the role taken by HR in culture change. Particularly interesting in this account is the recognition that culture change was not necessarily problem-centred and focused on overcoming current deficiencies. The espoused approach was developmentally focused, seeking, in large part, to build on aspects of the culture which were considered positive. The CEO (2005: 81) 'believed that any change must reflect the realities and expectations of stakeholder groups, including employees . . . . 'Employees, through focus groups, were asked to envision what the organisation should be like in five years' time, and propose how it should get there. By using a consultative process that was not management imposed, it was recognised that leaders might actually be resistant to change, particularly as the organisation was performing successfully. This approach is rather different to management-imposed culture change. The area of mergers and acquisitions is one where culture clashes between organisations have not been given enough attention by senior management who tend to concentrate on financial issues. Marks and Mirvis (2011) have recently outlined a framework for the human resources role in attempting to manage culture in such situations.

Ngo and Loi (2008) investigated links between certain HR practices, culture and organisational performance. Performance was assessed by HR managers in various multinationals operating in Hong Kong, comparing their organisation to the industry 'average'. They found that employee behaviour flexibility, and HR practice flexibility had positive effects on adaptability culture. This culture had a positive effect on facets of HR performance e.g. morale, staff retention. This HR performance mediated the impact of culture on perceptions of organisational performance such as sales and profit. Chow and Liu (2009) studying 451 firms in China, found that organisational effectiveness is contingent upon linkages between appropriate cultures and HR systems, which must be aligned with business strategy. Both these studies, and others, illustrate the complexity of matching certain types of culture and HR practices in order to (potentially) influence organisational performance.

However, Alvesson and Karreman (2007) suggest that even where extensive HR systems and practices exist, they may not work as effectively, or rationally, as they purport to do. They studied an international management consultancy firm and found, for example, that despite the existence of systematised performance rating systems, structured selection processes etc., promotion decisions could still be subjective, politicised and biased. However, inside the organisation the prevailing beliefs were that excellent HR practices existed and the culture was one of objectivity and career progression based on performance criteria.

Various facets of HR activity might be used either to reinforce the existing culture within an organisation or to support management-initiated culture change efforts. We shall now consider what these might be.

Recruitment and selection

Traditionally, organisations have sought to match individuals' abilities to job requirements, commonly known as person–job (P–J) fit. Research has developed to focus on the fit between the person and the organisation (P–O), particularly in respect of the organisation's culture. In this sense the individual's abilities/competencies are considered less important than their attitudes/values and the match of these with the organisation's culture. This is an interesting development and implies that it may be easier to change/ enhance employees' abilities rather than their attitudes or values. Adkins and Caldwell (2004) explore whether the match of the individual with the subculture or group (P–G fit) of the organisation in which they are located may be more important to factors such as job satisfaction. They found that there were differences between groups (subcultures), even in an organisation seeking to maintain a strong overall organisational culture. This matching of the individual's values with the organisation's culture can be assessed, for potential employees, during the selection process. However, it is also important for individuals to assess whether the organisation's culture matches their own preferences. Dawson and Abbott (2011) highlight the importance of person–environment fit, that is, employees being hospitable in the hospitality industry. Examples of how the management of culture has been used to attract and retain employees are shown in Box 10.3. For multinational organisations a key staffing decision is the mix of parent country national (PCN) employees and home country national (HCN) employees. A number of factors, including cultural considerations, can influence the balance adopted. See Torbiorn (2005) for a useful discussion of this. Research shows, e.g. Harzing (2000), that north American multinationals tend to employ a greater proportion of HCNs, and Japanese multinationals tend to employ a greater proportion of PCNs, with European firms using more PCNs than US firms but fewer than Japanese organisations.

Box 10.3 HRM in practice   Managing culture to attract staff

Madame Tussauds, which runs waxworks and other visitor attractions in various countries, relies on seasonal labour for up to half its staffing, during peak periods. The company emphasises that it is a fun place to work as one of its mechanisms for (re)attracting staff. It uses beer and pizza evenings, Halloween balls and other events for staff to reinforce the culture it wishes to project (Arkin, 2004).

A study by Braddy et al. (2006) indicates that websites dedicated to recruitment can be useful in influencing potential applicants' perceptions of the organisation's culture. Perceptions of diversity (photos of staff from various ethnic backgrounds) and innovation (comments about how highly valued it was by the organisation, and the importance of risk-taking) were the culture dimensions most effectively communicated. The importance of a rewards culture was also communicated through reference to organisational policies regarding bonuses and other incentives for performance. Website design could also influence perceptions of attention to detail (required of employees) and professionalism. Explicit statements about organisational values and employee testimonials regarding their work experience in the organisation were also influential.

Research (Arnold et al., 2003) regarding recruitment and retention problems in the UK National Health Service (NHS) has also highlighted the importance of realistic job previews (Wanous, 1989). Arnold et al. (2003) identified that some potential employees were put off by what they saw as unrealistic advertising and promotion campaigns which portrayed NHS work as rather more positive and attractive than candidates perceived it to be, and underplayed difficulties. Therefore, key cultural values that participants wished to see associated with the NHS, such as honesty and integrity, appeared to be undermined by the recruitment campaigns which were simultaneously emphasising the high degree of expertise and professionalism expected of its staff.

A study by Van Vianen (2000) assessed new employees' perceptions of the organisational culture and whether this fitted with their personal preferences. Where new employees had a fit between their preference in respect of concern for people and this was shared with their supervisor, this was positively related to the newcomers' organisational commitment and (lack of) turnover intentions. However, general perceptions of the organisational culture had little influence on new employees' affective outcomes; thus it was less important that newcomers perceived the organisational culture in the same way as their supervisor/peers than that the culture fitted with the newcomers' preferences regarding value congruence.

Rather than seeking to ensure fit between applicants and the existing culture, Williams et al. (1993) identify the use of selection as a way of contributing to culture change. An electricity organisation increased the number of sales staff by 63 per cent over five years as part of a desired move from a technical to a sales culture. Iles and Mabey (cited in Stewart and McGoldrick, 1996) have identified British Airways' use of Egyptian cabin crew and incorporation of Egyptian 'culture' on the London–Cairo route. As they point out, this was done to attract more customers, not simply to introduce international diversification into the workforce. The evaluation by Iles and Mabey did not indicate complete success in either respect.

Employee induction

A key opportunity for the organisation to influence employee values is during the early stages of their employment, indeed Schein (1985) has described organisational culture in terms of how organisational behaviour patterns are installed in new recruits. Harrison (2000: 248), on the other hand, suggests that dialogic learning comprises a major component of induction programmes and 'should help [new starters] to understand and adapt to the vision of the organisation and its implicit values and norms'. For example, Dundon et al. (2001) have identified that an (unnamed) consultancy organisation employs a full-time culture manager, part of whose role is to ensure that new employees fit in with, and are committed to, the prevailing culture.

Trice and Beyer (1993) refer to different rites and identify induction and basic training as what they term a rite of passage, e.g. into the organisation. As they note, the manifest purpose of a rite of passage such as induction is to 'facilitate transition of persons into social roles and statuses that are new for them' (1993: 111).

The extensive socialisation literature has referred to the impact of the socialisation process on organisational newcomers. For example, Ashforth (2001) identifies that formalised collective socialisation, for example in induction programmes, can help reduce the anxiety of role/organisational entry for newcomers. Harris and Ogbonna (2011) found that the greater the extent of formalised socialisation activity the greater the extent of management-espoused cultural control over employees. In contrast, McMillan-Capehart (2005) emphasises that individualised socialisation efforts lead to a greater diversity of values and beliefs and a more heterogeneous organisation. Even if organisations commit considerable time and effort to the formalised socialisation process at the point of organisational entry, individuals will still, over time, be influenced by informal events which affect the newcomer's perspectives (for example, Ricks, 1997). Gundry and Rousseau (1994) have identified that new organisational entrants come to understand their organisation's culture by decoding 'critical incidents'. Harris and Ogbonna (2011) also found that individual needs can affect the extent to which employees internalise management espoused values. Those with strong need for social approval from immediate work colleagues showed a stronger relationship with organisational values. This did require that the workforce generally had incorporated management-espoused values.

Therefore, unless the formalised institutional socialisation represented by induction programmes is reinforced by the activities and contacts newcomers encounter in day-to-day organisational life, it may not necessarily achieve the desired effect (from the organisation's perspective).

Training and development

A traditional approach to training and development would tend to focus individuals on learning job-specific skills and knowledge rather than on personal development or broader career issues. However, Williams *et al.* (1993) indicate this may be a necessary first step as part of a culture change effort. For example, they suggest that it will not be possible to develop a customer-oriented culture if customer contact staff do not have the appropriate skills to interact effectively with customers. Legge (2005) reports the use of role-play exercises for Sainsbury's check-out staff, where they take on the role of the customer.

Lee (1996) proposes that learning and development activities can focus on different components of the individual. Some focus purely on the acquisition of knowledge ('head'), some focus on the development of skills ('hands'), whereas some focus on affective aspects of the self and their relationships with others ('heart'). Some activities seek to integrate all these components.

Williams *et al.* (1993) suggest that training focused on employee behaviour is likely to be necessary in seeking to change employee values and attitudes. Indeed, Kunda (1992) argues that explicit attempts to change values can lead to employees feeling manipulated or brainwashed and therefore becoming very cynical. Ogbonna and Wilkinson (1988) indicate that even behaviourally focused change efforts can lead to what they called resigned behavioural compliance. Hopfl *et al.* (1992) have followed British Airways' long-term programme of culture management and highlight the need for consistency of message and practice from the organisation if employees are to consider the message credible. Perhaps more significantly, they stress the differing reactions from individuals subjected to the same culture change process. Thus management cannot assume that all employees will respond in the way that management would wish. Similarly, Scheeres and Rhodes (2006) have identified that in-house training programmes which are explicitly designed to inculcate managerially desired culture are unlikely to succeed where, as one training programme participant put it: 'what management would say … with the core values and one thing and another, is at odds with how it really is on a day to day basis' (2006: 232).

In this study, where employees' work experience was not consistent with espoused core corporate values, they were not allowed to debate such issues during the course. They were required to get the 'correct' answers to confirm their intellectual understanding of (but not lived experience of) management-articulated values.

Caligiuri *et al.* (2005) provide a useful discussion of a range of issues associated with training and development in a multicultural workforce. For example, delivery methods may need to be adjusted to reflect national cultural preferences. Americans may enjoy debating issues face-to-face in a training course but Chinese employees would be more reticent to express their opinions. Charlesworth (2008) has identified evidence for a connection between national cultures and preferred learning styles, further reinforcing the complexity of training a multi-cultural workforce.

Fields *et al.* (2006) studied the responses of Hong Kong Chinese and US organisations to uncertainty in the supply of qualified labour. Hong Kong organisations increased training and development activity, whereas US organisations reduced it. Fields *et. al.* (2006) suggested that Hong Kong employees, in a collectivist culture, would perceive more training as both a reward, and an indication that the organisation was enhancing the value of the individual to it. In the individualistic US culture, less training occurred as, employees who have enhanced their skills, may seek a better job elsewhere.

In terms of corporate-level organisational learning and transfer across nations, Hong *et al.* (2006) have highlighted the importance of cultural considerations. In a study of Japanese subsidiary companies operating in south China, they noted that corporate values had to be taken into account as well as technical knowledge components. The use of parent company socialisation processes, as well as open plan factory and office designs, facilitated cross-border transfer of organisational learning systems.

Communication and integration activities

Communication is considered by many managers to be a central component of culture management (Williams *et al.,* 1993). Manipulation of artefacts and symbols, Schein's (1985) top or surface level of culture, is the focus here. For example, Unisys used publications and magazines as a way of reinforcing key cultural values such as customer orientation. Trice and Beyer (1993) identify two forms of rite which organisations may use to communicate culture. The rite of enhancement, for example the use of company newsletters, team briefings and employee of the month award schemes, can serve a number of purposes. It could be to spread good news about the organisation; equally, it could focus on individuals, and provide public recognition for their accomplishments. At the same time this recognition of individual achievement is designed to communicate to others what is expected of them and act as a stimulus for effort and motivation.

The rite of integration again uses non-work activities as a way of influencing employees' emotions. For example, organised social events, e.g. barbecues, visits to bowling alleys, etc., can be used to try to foster a sense of binding employees to the social system, i.e. the organisation. This may be particularly the case where the organisation seeks to foster a high degree of teamworking and team commitment. Williams *et al.* (1993) identify the way that Marley tried to break down formal divisions between functions within the organisation through the use of inter-functional social activities. Studying cross-functional integration, and the influence of national as well as organisational culture, Engelen *et al.*, (2012) have found that cross-functional integration is higher, and has positive impact on new product development, when the national culture dimension of collectivism is higher. The effect of this was enhanced when the organisation had a strong corporate culture as well.

Crumpacker and Crumpacker (2007) have highlighted the importance of an increasingly diverse workforce in terms of the age range of employees. Because of increasing life-spans and the pressure this puts on pension systems, some older employees are having to work beyond what were traditional retirement ages, e.g. age 65. This means there could be four generations represented in an organisation's workforce, potentially spanning up to a 60-year age range. Proponents of a generational understanding of the workforce, such as Zemke *et al.* (2000), argue that different generations hold different values, attitudes and lifestyle preferences. These influence employee perspectives on issues such as ethics, work–life balance, authority and leadership, and technology. Therefore, the organisation needs to consider whether it is desirable and feasible to develop a uniform/integrated culture or whether diversity, based on generational perspectives, is more relevant.

Cross-cultural integration

We mentioned earlier in the chapter Hofstede's (1980, 1991) work regarding the influence of national culture, and the way it can override management's preferred organisational culture. French (2010) reports that AXA, the insurance multinational, has attempted to overcome this in a number of ways. First, employees from various countries took part in focus groups to consider the relevance of the organisation's stated values in different cultures. Five key values were considered to best represent the organisation and potentially overcome cultural barriers. These values were then linked to behavioural traits, and staff were recruited, and appraised against these behaviours. Recognising, that even after translation, values and behaviours can be interpreted in different ways, AXA also uses pictures to communicate behavioural concepts and management styles. However, other research shows that national culture preferences can still prevail. Miah and Bird (2007) found that national culture in countries in South Asia (India, Pakistan and Bangladesh) was more influential in shaping HRM styles and practices in Japanese subsidiary and joint-venture activity in those countries. Auotocratic rather than participative approaches were preferred.

Dong and Glaister (2007) have studied Chinese parent firms involved in international strategic alliances (ISAs). Where corporate and national cultural differences are considered particularly important in their potential effects on ISA outcomes, proactive culture management is adopted, and reduces perceptions of cultural differences between ISA partners. Some caution needs to be attached to these findings as research participants only came from the Chinese organisations.

As Froese *et al.* (2008) discuss, there are various complex factors to consider when cross-national acquisitions occur. The type of strategy adopted by the acquiring organisation (e.g. assimilation, separation etc.), the cultural distance between the two organisations in respect of their existing organisational and national cultures, the expectations of the acquired organisation's employees in respect of degree of change, and the influence of contextual factors such as the prevailing economic conditions all need to be taken into account. Froese *et al.* (2008) found that Korean employees in firms acquired by Western organisations were more accepting of, and satisfied with, market-oriented reforms, because they expected them and saw the economic necessity of them in a Korean economy that was struggling. However, changes towards individualism which clashed with Confucian values were not well received.

Payment/rewards systems

Armstrong (1999) suggests that the organisation's remuneration policy can be used as a way of communicating organisational values. Williams *et al.* (1993) stress that consistency is important if the organisation is not to send mixed messages to employees regarding management's preferred cultural values. Emery (2004) has also highlighted the inconsistency of management espoused values of teamwork and the use of individualised assessment and reward.

Kuhn (2009) investigated the impact of the type of bonus an organisation mentions in recruitment adverts, on applicants perceptions of organisational culture. Bonuses based on individual performance led people to consider the organisation to have an individualist culture. Bonuses based on team or organisational performance created the impression of a more collectivist culture.

Lowe *et al.* (2002) studied reward practices across ten countries. Contrary to expectations, group or organisation-based performance incentives did not occur as much in 'collectivist' societies as would have been predicted. More consistent with Hofstede's (1991) dimension of masculinity, Schneider and Barsoux (2003) found that Swedish employees are likely to prefer time off from work, rather than a financial bonus, i.e. consistent with the country's higher preference for the femininity end of the dimension.

In multinational organisations the use of expatriate managers can be considerably more expensive than employing local managers. For example, Chen *et al.* (2002) have identified that employing expatriates in China can mean that they are paid up to 50 times more than local staff. However, Bonache and Fernandez (2005) note a number of reasons, including cultural ones, why the organisation may decide to incur these extra costs, for example if host country company-specific knowledge is required, possibly combined with the need to implement a global, rather than local, strategy.

Performance management/appraisal

Stiles *et al.* (1997) undertook a study of performance management and its impact on perceptions of values. This study occurred in a distribution company, a telecommunications company and a bank, all of which had recently introduced values statements. While managers were aware of the corporate values being espoused by their organisations, they still saw that their short-term demands were primarily focused around financial targets and the need to achieve other organisational objectives. In addition, the setting of objectives was imposed from senior management without any negotiation. Perceptions were also influenced by the fact that organisational downsizing left managers in doubt whether even achievement of their objectives would be enough to facilitate career progression or, at worst, even job security.

Hofstetter and Harpaz (2011) identified that the formal performance assessment system designed by senior management was operationalised and interpreted somewhat differently by middle and junior managers in the organisation. Considering the formal system to be a reflection of senior management's espoused cultural preferences, the authors considered that the 'norms in use' by other managers in the organisation were rather different.

We have already commented on the difficulty of identifying any relationship between culture and organisational-level performance. Research in the UK by Ogbonna and Harris (2000) suggests that cultures which are externally oriented incline towards risk-taking and readiness to meet new challenges and tend to be more strongly associated with organisational performance (which was operationalised using a range of measures) than cultures that are predominantly internally focused. However, as with other studies this work was cross-sectional and correlational and therefore it is difficult to identify whether culture was actually a cause of performance.

Williams (2002) suggests that the performance management process might be seen as a way of developing, at least in part, a 'performance culture'. However, certain advocates of performance management, e.g. Armstrong (1994), tend to associate performance management with a set of values reflecting openness, trust, employee participation, etc. in the performance management process. In contrast, a performance culture may not place any emphasis on these things and simply focus on increasing employee productivity, etc. For example, Fletcher and Williams (1992) identified that an organisation's performance culture placed particular emphasis on 'bottom line' results. Employees felt that fear was the driving force underpinning the performance culture rather than participation and openness. In the international setting Schneider and Barsoux (2003) note that performance assessment can be perceived negatively in some countries as character assessment, particularly in Asia and France.

Arkin (2007) reports an interesting example of the issues associated with seeking to introduce a standard approach to performance management in a multinational organisation. Kimberley-Clark, manufacter of Andrex toilet paper, and Kleenex tissues, operated in 68 countries around the world. Performance ratings were high but sales and share price were not good. There seemed a reluctance to rate anyone below average. An international project team was created to develop a new approach to performance assessment, and a 360 degree feedback system was agreed. However, because employees in Korea, South America and Asia were concerned about giving feedback on their managers, the compromise of anonymity was made, despite the reluctance of Western countries, who wanted to encourage openness and transparency. A web-based system, translated into each country's language, was introduced. Because of the process of consultation and adaptation, a survey of employees found that 95 per cent were confident in the new system's use. Milliman *et al.* (2002) have found that performance linked to pay is more common in individualistic countries such as the USA and Australia, although it is starting to become more common in China. In countries where teamworking and 'face' are considered important the link between pay and individualised performance is considered less desirable.

Leadership

The importance of leaders, particularly at the top of the organisation, as figureheads of, and role models for, preferred culture and values is seen as crucial. A new leader is often associated with a new approach to culture. Leaders at different levels in the organisation have influence and control over various organisational rites (Trice and Beyer, 1993). We have referred already to some of these rites. The rite of enhancement is a clear and generally public activity that enhances the status of an individual. Mechanisms that may be used here include employee of the month award schemes, articles in company newsletters and commendations at team briefings.

Schein (2004) identifies a number of mechanisms that leaders use to embed, and reinforce, beliefs, values and assumptions. Important among these are what leaders give attention to, and seek to measure and control. Allocation of resources, rewards and status by the leader is important. Equally, explicit role-modelling and coaching communicates what the leader considers important. Schein (2004) emphasises that formal mechanisms such as training are not necessary in order to communicate cultural values, as leader behaviour, observed in normal work activity, is sufficient.

Chatman and Cha (2003) give the example of Dreyer's Grand Ice Cream in the USA. At one point in time they experienced (a) their CEO getting a brain tumour; (b) a significant rise in raw material costs; and (c) the termination of their distribution contract by Ben and Jerry's. Rather than panic and embark on cost-cutting they continued their normal cultural practices such as openness in communication. They introduced free-phone calls for employees to hear pre-recorded updates by the CEO. They continued to invest in training activities. As one employee put it, (2003: 30) '...they reassured us by calling it straight ... they informed us of their game plan, and that they counted on us....you thought you'd run through a wall for this guy'.

Schein (2004) stresses the roles that leaders at all organisational levels have to play, and that this will vary depending upon the organisation's stage of development and require different types of culture management at different stages. He also stresses that different strategic issues lead to a focus on different cultural dimensions.

Research conducted in China by Tsui *et al.* (2006) identifies interesting variations on leader behaviour and its interaction with organisational culture. Leaders described as 'performance builders' tended to be young, with management qualifications. Their focus was primarily on external adaptation of the organisation to its environment. They gave little attention to internal processes to develop/reinforce values, and their organisations had relatively weak cultures. In contrast, 'institution builders' focused strongly on internal processes/systems to reinforce values but were much less charismatic as leaders. They also relied on the support of other managers to reinforce culture. These organisations had stronger cultures, and used human resource systems, such as selection, reward and training, to reinforce and sustain culture.

Is culture change feasible?

There is considerable scepticism regarding the feasibility of management proactively changing organisational culture, particularly at the deep fundamental levels. For example, Meek (1982) suggests that those who propose that culture change is feasible do not recognise that power differentials exist within organisations, that subcultures exist and that ultimately, in seeking to change culture, management is seeking to control employees. For example, within the healthcare sector Morgan and Ogbonna (2008) have identified that doctors and nurses (subcultures) may agree about certain core values of the National Health Service, but have different views about other issues. These are based on power, degree of expertise, desire for professional status and a range of other factors. Ogbonna (1992) suggests that the espoused aim of many culture change programmes, to enhance employee commitment, is not achieved. In many senses change is focused purely on employee behaviours and achieved through compliance rather than the commitment which is sought. Sackmann (1991) suggests that cultures are highly complex, dynamic systems with individual and group variability within them. Therefore, they are not really amenable to direct management. For some writers, attempts at culture management are ethically unacceptable. For example, Willmott (1993: 517), argues that managers may like the idea of greater control over employees by using culture management to 'colonise the affective domain ... promoting employee commitment to a monolithic structure of feeling and thought'. As he argues, the control has been transferred from managers to employees through high levels of self-monitoring and self-management. At one level employees are empowered to manage their own work, but in effect they have simply incorporated the organisation's desire for high standards of performance and behaviour and are only empowered to do what the organisation wants them to do. Thompson and McHugh (2002) reinforce this idea, suggesting that by managing the meanings and values of employees, management seeks to manipulate employees' internalised sources of control and commitment.

Despite the cynicism about both the ethics of attempting, as well as the feasibility of achieving, culture change, some writers have argued that culture change is feasible albeit with considerable difficulty. For example, Pettigrew (1990) has, on the basis of considerable research, proposed a number of factors for consideration in seeking to undertake culture change. He does note that this will be an arduous process and is more likely to affect surface levels of culture than core assumptions.

Harris and Ogbonna (1998) summarise the differing views on the feasibility of changing culture by suggesting three different perspectives: (a) culture can be managed, (b) culture cannot be managed, and (c) culture can be manipulated, but only under certain conditions. They also stress that little research effort has been directed at understanding employee reactions to managerial culture change attempts. Therefore, they conducted an empirical study in two contexts, one food and one clothing company in the British retail sector. They identified that employees could respond in a range of ways and that two key determinants seemed to be at play. One was willingness to change and the second was the existing strength of the particular subculture (for example, division of the organisation). Responses could range from active rejection through to active acceptance. Particularly interesting responses were reinvention and reinterpretation. Reinvention occurs where the attributes of the existing culture are recycled so that superficially, at least, they appear to be in line with the new culture being espoused by management. Reinterpretation occurs where employee values and behaviour are modified to some extent, but in a way which is consistent with both the existing culture and the desired culture. While there appears to be some adoption of the espoused culture, this is filtered through the understanding of the existing culture and in that sense is not necessarily a predictable response. As we commented earlier, individuals can and do respond to culture change efforts in widely different ways. As Harris and Ogbonna (1998) note, there can be a range of responses between outright acceptance and rejection. This unpredictability of response makes culture change difficult to manage. Therefore Harris and Ogbonna suggest that attempts at culture change should not seek radical and transformational change but work on an incremental basis.

Conclusions

Based on the evidence reviewed in this chapter, what can we say about organisational culture? First, drawing on the vast number of definitions and classification systems, we can describe organisational culture as a phenomenon that involves beliefs, values and behaviours, exists at a variety of different levels, and manifests itself in a wide range of artefacts within any particular organisation. It is also apparent that culture is difficult to assess directly, given the varying data collection methods and the multilevel nature of the construct. Furthermore, culture might provide a useful description of organisational environments, which facilitate their comprehension, interpretation, acceptance and control, and might, but only might, help explain their success in terms of performance. Finally, if organisational culture is to be of use to managers and organisations, they must be able to adapt and change their culture when necessary.

It is clear from the research discussed in this chapter, however, that while culture change and the management of it by the organisation may appear feasible, there are practical problems associated with it. A number of such issues can be identified:

- At what level is culture change occurring – is it at the artefacts level or at the level of fundamental assumptions?
- Even if behaviour is changed, is this really culture change? If employee values and assumptions have not changed, does this really matter, if management is primarily interested in employees demonstrating appropriate behaviours?

- Do organisations have unitary cultures, and, if so, is it feasible to change the culture of the whole organisation at once?
- If it is accepted that organisations comprise subcultures, are strategies for culture change sophisticated enough to recognise the differential approaches required?

Martin (1992, 2002) has suggested that three differing perspectives can be adopted in seeking to understand culture and therefore interpret ways to approach culture change and its effectiveness. The integration perspective is most typical of management in that it assumes an organisation-wide consensus within the organisation and that consistency is feasible. Cultural manifestations are interpreted in a consistent way i.e. reinforcing preferred themes. The differentiation perspective assumes that there are likely to be subcultures within the organisation. These have consensus within themselves but there is likely to be conflict between subcultures. Culture can be interpreted inconsistently e.g. managers say one thing but behave differently. The fragmentation perspective assumes that there is such a multiplicity of views with little or no consensus, and that managing culture will be immensely complex because of its ambiguity. As Rodrigues (2006) points out, the same organisation may experience each of these perspectives at different points in time. Indeed, Mathew and Ogbonna (2009) claim to have found the existence of all three perspectives simultaneously, when researching an Indian software company.

CASE STUDY 10.1
UNDERSTANDING THE CULTURE OF AN ORGANISATION

JOHN LOAN-CLARKE AND ALISTAIR CHEYNE

Think about an organisation you know. This could be one you have worked in full-time (now or in the past), temporarily (e.g. vacation work) or during an industrial placement. Consider the following two questions about that organisation:

CASE STUDY 10.2
LEVELS OF CULTURE

JOHN LOAN-CLARKE AND ALISTAIR CHEYNE

Various models of culture identify that it comprises a number of levels. For example, Schein's (1985) model comprises three. Choose one of these models and do the following:

Explain what each of the three levels means and what information would be needed to understand the culture at that level.

CASE STUDY 10.3

UNDERSTANDING CULTURE IN INTERNATIONAL HIGHER EDUCATION

XIAOZHENG ZHANG

Following the trend of internationalisation in higher education, there are an increasing number of European universities setting up international business schools in mainland China.

CBBS (Chinese-Based Business School) was co-founded by one British and one Chinese university in China, in 2010. The management of the school has been divided between the two partner universities along administrative and academic sectors. The Chinese university thus looks after the administrative aspects, dealing with issues such as student recruitment and registration; employing the administrative staff; providing administrative support such as logistics and supply of equipment and facilities. The academic work has been mainly taken care of by the British university, which is responsible for matters of learning and teaching, academic staff recruitment, evaluation of student academic performance, etc.

The administration is made up of native Chinese employees, who are required to be able to speak fluent English in order to communicate with the academic staff. In order to introduce British higher education standards into China, CBBS recruited all academic staff from the UK. These included both Chinese and British academics, who obtained their higher education degrees from a British university, and had at least five years, academic work experience in the British higher education sector. Working as expatriates in Shanghai, the academic staff were provided with accommodation and other assistance in terms of settling in China.

As part of their induction to the job, the academic expatriates were briefed about the structure of CBBS in China, the student entrance level and some basic knowledge regarding the Chinese cultural background. The key concepts of Confucianism were introduced, including Harmony, Face-saving, respect for age and hierarchy (Flynn *et al.*, 2007). Face-saving means to maintain an individual's positive self-image in front of others as much as possible (Merkin, 2006). Moreover, within the Chinese context, an individual is not only required to protect their own Face in the society, but also to pay great attention to caring for others' Face as well (Zhang, 2012). By doing this, people maintain harmonious relationships and avoid conflict with others.

After running for a year, the CBBS management identified some communication issues between the administrative and academic teams. The CBBS management requested the human resource department to evaluate the current situation and propose some practical plans to improve it.

Questions

1 Considering the potential influence of national culture, try to identify the main problems in communication between the administrative and academic teams.
2 What should be included as key themes in cultural training programmes for the academic expatriates?
3 In terms of recruitment and selection of academic staff, what are the important criteria that need to be considered?

CASE STUDY 10.4

MANAGING CULTURE AT BRITISH AIRWAYS

IRENA GRUGULIS, ADRIAN WILKINSON AND ASHLEA KELLNER

The British Airways story

Even by the standards of modern management myths, the British Airways transformation is impressive. At the end of the 1970s and the start of the 1980s BA was performing disastrously against almost every indicator. Its fleet was old, which meant journeys were uncomfortable and contributed significantly to the airline's record for unpunctuality; its productivity was considerably below that of its main overseas competitors; it was beset by industrial disputes; and it was recording substantial financial losses (£140 million or some £200 a minute in 1981). Staff discontent was more than matched by customer dissatisfaction and in 1980 a survey by the International Airline Passengers' Association put BA at the top of a list of airlines to be avoided at all costs. By the mid-1990s this picture was reversed. Not only had BA become the world's most profitable carrier, it was also voted the company that most graduates would like to work for and, in the year 2000, another survey declared it the second most admired company in Europe (Blyton and Turnbull, 1998; Corke, 1986; *Financial Times,* 9 July 1997; *Financial Times,* 18 March 2000; Warhurst, 1995).

Much of the management literature attributes this turnaround to BA's own cultural change which remodelled staff attitudes and set customer care as the primary focus of activity. As Doyle (1999: 20) noted:

> In the 80s BA had been transformed from a disastrous loss-making state enterprise – the British Rail of the sky – into the world's largest and most profitable international airline. It was a triumph for management, showing that Britain could produce world-class companies that could beat the best of the competition. Its success was the result of the process and strategy that management introduced. The process focused on creating a vision that would inspire the BA staff and gain their enthusiastic commitment.

It is certainly true that a great deal of effort and energy went into shaping BA's culture. At the heart of this was the 'Putting people first' (PPF) training programme launched by Colin Marshall, the company's new chief executive, in 1983. Originally intended for staff who had direct contact with customers it was, in fact, attended by all 40,000 employees by 1986 and it aimed to revolutionise their attitudes. In a direct challenge to the hierarchical and militaristic culture which existed in BA at the time, staff were instructed not to attend in uniform and, once on the course, put into cross-functional and cross-grade groups. Attendees were encouraged to take a more positive attitude to themselves, taught how to set personal goals and cope with stress, and instructed in confidence building and 'getting what they wanted out of life'. Lapel badges inscribed with the motto 'We're putting people first' provided a visible reminder of the course's message.

The approach was self-conciously 'indoctrinative' (Bate, 1994: 195). As Colin Marshall said

> We . . . have to design our people and their service attitude just as we design an aircraft seat, an in-flight entertainment programme or an airport lounge *to meet the needs and preferences of our customers.* (cited in Barsoux and Manzoni, 1997: 14: emphasis added)

However, the most impressive aspect of BA's cultural change was not so much the sophistication of the PPF programme itself, nor the commitment of executive time, but the extent to which other employment policies and practices were changed to fit the 'new' culture and the continued emphasis on these practices and programmes throughout the 1980s and 1990s. Three-quarters of the 100 Customer First teams, formed to propagate the message of PPF, survived into the 1990s. Not only were team briefings and team-working introduced, but these were developed and refined, with TQM, autonomous team-working and multi-skilling introduced in many areas. Direct contact with all staff was considered so important that 'down route' briefings were developed to ensure that mobile and isolated staff were not neglected, and in 1996 BA became the first company to make daily television broadcasts to its staff (Colling, 1995).

The way cabin crew were rostered was also changed. 'Families' of staff were created to work the same shift patterns. These were intended to provide mutual support, make cabin crew feel happier about their work environments and, as a result, facilitate the production of emotional labour (Barsoux and Manzoni, 1997). A new role of 'passenger group coordinator' was introduced and staff appointed based entirely on personal qualities. The importance of emotional processes was also reflected in the new appraisal and reward systems such that work was judged on the way in which it was performed as well as against harder targets (Georgiades and Macdonnell, 1998; Höpfl, 1993). Managerial bonuses could be as much as 20 per cent of salary and were calculated on a straight 50:50 split between exhibiting desired behaviours and achieving quantitative goals. 'Awards for Excellence' and an 'Employee Brainwaves' programme encouraged staff input. The personnel department was renamed 'human resources' with many decisions devolved to line managers and, in the first few years of the programme at least, a commitment was made to job security.

Closely following these developments, a 'Managing people first' programme targeted managerial employees and aimed to bring their behaviours into line with a list developed by two consultancy firms (see Table 10.1).

Other courses were developed to maintain the momentum created by 'Putting people first' and 'Managing people first'. These included 'Winning for customers', 'A day in the life', 'To be the best', 'Leading in a service business' and 'Leadership 2000' and, while each was different, they all shared a focus on shaping staff emotions. The most dramatic form of this was probably the 'love bath' exercise in one of the early courses in which delegates took it in turns to sit in the centre of a circle while their colleagues complimented them (see Höpfl, 1993). Nearly 20 years after the launch of PPF, BA managers attending a training course were still being told about understanding themselves and taking responsibility: 'understanding self is our starting point … That means that to make a change within the airline we need to start with you – what can *you* do differently.' In 1995, Bob Ayling, having newly taken over from Colin Marshall as chief executive, continued this active management of company culture and said of his staff:

Table 10.1 The four-factor menu of practices used in British Airways in 1984–5

The menu of practices	
Factor I	**Factor II**
CLARITY AND HELPFULNESS	**PROMOTING ACHIEVEMENT**
Establishing clear, specific objectives for subordinates	Emphasising and demonstrating commitment to achieving goals
Helping subordinates to understand how their jobs contribute to the overall performance of the organisation	Giving subordinates feedback on how they are doing
Clearly defining standards of excellence required for job performance	Communicating your views to others honestly and directly about their performance
Providing help, training and guidance for subordinates	Recognising people more often than criticising them
Giving subordinates a clear cut decision when they need one	Recognising subordinates for innovation and calculated risk taking
Factor III	**Factor IV**
INFLUENCING THROUGH PERSONAL EXCELLENCE AND TEAMWORKING	**CARE AND TRUST**
Knowing and being able to explain to others the mission of the organisation and how it relates to their jobs	Behaving in a way that leads others to trust you
Communicating high personal standards informally through appearance and dedication	Building warm, friendly relationships
Noticing and showing appreciation for extra effort	Paying close attention to what people are saying
Sharing power in the interest of achieving overall organisation objectives	Responding non-defensively when others disagree with your views
Being willing to make tough decisions in implementing corporate strategy	Making sure that there is a frank and open exchange at work group meetings

Source: [Reproduced with permission.] From *Leadership for Competitive Advantage* by Georgiades, N. and Macdonnell, R., 1998: 174. Copyright © John Wiley and Sons Ltd.

'I want them to feel inspired, I want them to feel optimistic, I want them to feel that this is a good place to be' ('Dangerous Company', BBC2 April 2000).

Such substantive change certainly seems to justify the plaudits heaped on it. But, as an account, it suffers from a number of flaws. Most significantly, as Anthony (1994) notes, together with other presentations of culture change it neglects structure. Yet the existence of cultural factors does not negate more material ones and there were certainly structural reasons for BA's success. Colin Marshall's emphasis on putting people first and caring for one another had been preceded by a rule of fear. BA's first response to its problems had been a massive series of redundancies, the largest in British history at the time, with staff numbers reduced by 40 per cent between 1981 and 1983 (albeit with generous severance).

More fundamentally, the company was well provided with slots in Britain's prestigious Heathrow airport and faced little competition on many of the routes that it served. European markets were still tightly regulated and market share often depended on negotiation skills rather than competitive success. In 1987, just before privatisation, BA controlled some 60 per cent of the UK domestic market and experienced competition on only 9 per cent of routes into and out of the UK (Monopolies and Mergers Commission, 1987). Post-privatisation its position was actually strengthened when it gained a 75 per cent share of domestic routes (Colling, 1995). Moreover, BA built up a series of alliances and mergers to consolidate this position.

While staff numbers were being drastically cut, the infrastructure was dramatically improved. The fact that new uniforms were provided is well covered in the human resource and marketing literature. Less commonly noted is that BA invested in control systems, terminal facilities and aircraft. Between 1980 and 1985 BA replaced over half its fleet (Colling, 1995). Computer reservations were introduced, a series of hub and spoke routes through first Heathrow and then Gatwick networked flights, and selectively focused competitive pricing served to limit what little competition the airline faced (Blyton and Turnbull, 1996). Nor was this the only strategy deployed against competitors. In 1993 BA used shared booking information to persuade Virgin customers to transfer to BA, informing them (incorrectly) that Virgin flights were no longer available. The subsequent court case fined BA £610,000 damages and £3 million costs. It raised questions about the extent of knowledge and involvement of Lord King, the chairman, Sir Colin Marshall, the chief executive, and Bob Ayling, the head of marketing, as well as criticising the impact of the BA culture itself.

Not only can much of the BA turnaround be attributed to structural factors, but also the extent of the company's cultural transformation itself is open to question. While cultural change interventions seek to influence the thoughts, values, attitudes and norms of others, employees are not cultural dupes. Cooperation may reflect ambition or pride in work as much as (or instead of) a belief in the organisation itself. Despite the claims of the prescriptive literature, the existence of 'culture management' does not ensure either that employees trust management, or that management trusts employees. So, in BA, 'new' management practices varied in the extent that they were introduced in departments and conflict between employees and management did not cease.

Nor was the much-vaunted job security quite as robust as it seemed. Alliances, mergers and franchising agreements with other airlines already supported what was, in effect, a 'tiered' system of terms and conditions, with employees based at Heathrow privileged over those in the regional airports. This emphasis on part-time, seasonal and subcontracted work was extended to most aspects of BA's operations. Its engine overhaul plant was sold off to GEC, data-processing work was moved to Bombay, and job security for existing staff questioned (Blyton and Turnbull, 1996; Colling, 1995; Warhurst, 1995). And all this at a time when BA was making record profits.

In short, BA, while putting a great deal of effort into encouraging certain behaviours from staff, did not base its employment policies and practices around the new culture in the way that many accounts suggest. Their array of human resource management techniques was certainly impressive, but not everyone benefited from them and those employed in partner, associate, merged or taken-over firms often experienced very different terms and conditions from those of the 'core' BA staff.

Staff reactions to 'culture change' included enthusiasm and acceptance but also doubt, concern, opposition and open cynicism. Such individual reactions were mirrored by the collective representations and the persistence of disputes even at the height of the 'cultural success'.

The 1997 dispute

By the end of the 1990s many of the structural factors that had provided the basis for the company's success were under threat. The emergence of low-cost carriers such as easyJet and Ryanair were undercutting BA's prices and, elsewhere, alliances between rivals Lufthansa and United Airlines ensured that cross-national traffic would be less likely to transfer to BA. The company's hold on Heathrow was also loosening under double pressure from Europe and the USA. In response, Ayling claimed that BA needed a second revolution. BA sought its own alliance with a different US carrier, American Airlines, as well as proposing £1 billion of cost savings from within the organisation, with the aim of doubling profits by the year 2000. Much of this was to come from staff savings, including 5,000 voluntary redundancies, with staff to be replaced by newly hired employees on lower pay (Blyton and Turnbull, 1998). In addition, BA established links with a charter airline called Flying Colours, intending to continue its policy of outsourcing to other operators.

This policy of reducing labour costs was also extended to 'core' BA staff. In early 1997, BA attempted to change the structure of payments to cabin crew. It was proposed that the existing employees would be 'bought out' of their series of allowances (petrol, overnight stay, etc.) by receiving a higher basic wage. BA offered a three-year guarantee that no crew member would earn less under the new system but nothing beyond that, and it was clear to cabin crew staff that the measure was launched with the explicit aim of saving money. When these negotiations failed, one union, the TGWU, threatened strike action (Cabin Crew 89, a small breakaway union, had already accepted management's offer). Despite 14 years of espoused policy of caring for one another and putting people first, the tactics deployed by BA's management were described by two such different sources as the TUC and *The Economist* as bullying (*The Economist,* 27 July 1997; Taylor 1998). Members of the cabin crew were warned not to strike and BA managers were instructed to tell discontented staff that anyone taking industrial action would be summarily sacked, then sued for damages. Any who simply stayed away would face disciplinary action, be denied promotion and lose both pension rights and staff discounts on flights for three years. BA were also reported to be filming pickets.

The subsequent strike ballot had an 80 per cent turnout, with 73 per cent of employees voting in favour of strike action. The TGWU called a series of 72-hour strikes, with the first action scheduled for 9 July 1997. In response, temporary staff and an alternative workforce of 'volunteer managers' were given training to perform the key tasks of the ground handling staff and BA threatened to take legal action over claimed discrepancies in the ballot. On the eve of the first day of action airline cabin crew were telephoned at home and warned that 'they had a duty to cooperate with their employer'.

These managerial actions certainly influenced the impact of the strike. On the first scheduled day of action fewer than 300 workers declared themselves officially on strike but more than 2,000 called in sick. The company's threats and 'replacement workers' notwithstanding, more than 70 per cent of flights from Heathrow were cancelled. It seemed that BA's macho approach had ensured only that collective action took the form of collective illness.

Ironically this 'mass sickie' served to make things worse for BA. Not only did the pre-strike ballots (conducted to comply with legislation designed to discourage union activities) compound the effects of the strike by providing customers with advance notice of it; but also those employees who had called in sick tended to stay away longer than the official 72-hour strike. BA insisted that sick employees provide a doctor's note within 48 hours instead of the normal seven days but many employees still stayed off for the full two weeks that their sick notes allowed and, throughout this period, services were cancelled and passengers turned away. The strike was costly. Airline seats are a particularly perishable form of consumer good and aircraft scheduling is easily disrupted. When Bill Morris, the General Secretary of the TGWU, announced that he had written to Bob Ayling, suggesting that they resume negotiations, Ayling agreed before even receiving the letter.

The TGWU promised to save £42 million over three years. Catering was sold off but existing staff kept earnings and BA staff discounts, while sanctions against strikers were withdrawn and the TGWU increased its membership by 50 per cent to over 10,000. BA's management fared less well, despite Bob Ayling's claim that this agreement marked a 'new beginning and spirit of a cooperation'. The gulf between the managerial rhetoric on culture and official actions during the strike had a predictable effect on employee morale. One undercover employee publication, aptly named *Chaos,* advised on ways of maximising payments by delaying aircraft. These included throwing duvet feathers into the engine, superglueing down the toilet seat and poisoning the pilot: 'a particularly obnoxious captain can be made to suffer all the symptoms of violent food poisoning by emptying eye drops from the aircraft medical kit into his salad or drink'.

Moreover, the agreement itself fostered further dissent. By the end of 1997, 4,000 staff had left, but 4,500 more were recruited, including 2,000 in 1998. By the terms of the agreement, these new staff were employed on different contracts to existing employees. As a result, cabin crew working the same shifts on the same aircraft were (increasingly) on different payscales. The impact of this on both labour relations and BA's much-prized team-working was problematic and problems were fuelled by suggestions that staff on new contracts were favoured by BA in promotion to purser (first-line manager).

Bob Ayling attempted to salvage the situation by placing more emphasis on managing the company's culture. Following Colin Marshall, he addressed staff training sessions and held question and answer forums with groups of employees. This time there were few positive reactions. The strike cost BA £125 million; morale never entirely recovered and profits suffered. Between 1998 and

1999 they fell by 61 per cent and in 2000 British Airways announced losses of £244 million on its main business. While gains from disposals succeeded in keeping the company out of the red, this was its worst performance (and first loss) since privatisation. The new logo Bob Ayling had launched (at great expense) during the 1997 dispute was unpopular and had to be withdrawn. These failures so coloured the public perception of the chief executive that even his attempts to refocus BA on to profitable routes and introduce a new seat for business class, long-haul passengers were not entirely welcomed. On 10 March 2000, Bob Ayling resigned as chief executive.

The next decade was characterised by ongoing disputes and the continued restructuring of the labour force to reduce costs. New CEO Rod Eddington replaced Bob Ayling but faced turmoil in the airline industry shortly after his appointment, following the tragic terrorist attacks on 11 September 2000. Like other airlines, British Airways suffered heavily in the period immediately following the attacks and their initial response was to announce 1,800 job losses, followed shortly by a further cut of 5,200 positions (Upchurch, 2010). In fact, between 2000 and 2005 the company cut 14,000 jobs, 7,000 of which were reportedly due to falling demand following 9/11 (Bamber et al., 2009).

While British Airways struggled, its low cost subsidiary 'Go', developed in 1998 in response to liberalisation of the airline industry, had grown rapidly and become highly profitable over just four years. The success of the subsidiary has been credited to adoption of a 'low-frills' rather than 'no-frills' approach, cutting costs on standard services but offering value to customers through quality surprises like flexible fares and premium coffee (Harvey and Turnbull, 2006). Another key contributing factor was the positive corporate culture developed in stark contrast to that at British Airways and attributed largely to the work of CEO Barbra Cassani. Cassani adopted a 'human asset' focus, which saw a strong emphasis on selecting applicants with the right cultural fit, developing and valuing staff and ensuring a collaborative management style rather than the more aggressive approach adopted by British Airways.

Although Cassani was encouraged by British Airways to adopt their staunch opposition to industrial activism, she was determined to ensure that Go staff were given the right to be represented by a union. Driven by her prior work experience in the US, she later explained her rationale for this strategy in a book about her involvement with Go. 'Develop an antagonistic relationship with unions and allow poor employee morale to eat away at your organisation? No thanks, I'd seen enough of that in the US airline industry' (Cassani and Kemp, 2003: 43). Cassani contrasted the short-term 'benefit' of confronting industrial involvement with the almost certain medium- to long-term deleterious effects that would surely have far harsher consequences for the organisation's performance. Her efforts paid off, with an employee survey in 2002 reporting that Go staff were far more satisfied with a range of aspects of work and conditions than employees at British Airways (Harvey and Turnbull, 2006). As Go began to compete with British Airway's short haul service in 2001, it was sold off and later acquired by easyJet.

The next few years saw a stream of ongoing industrial disputes and negative publicity for British Airways. In 2003, around 500 customer service employees went on strike at Heathrow airport in protest against a new automated attendance monitoring system. The largely female workforce was concerned that the new system would lead to losses in flexibility, control and security over hours of work. Although staff returned to work after two days, disruptions continued as the company scrambled to reposition aircraft and crew and ultimately cost £40 million. Industrial action escalated at the same time the following year when 3,000 check-in staff threatened a 24-hour strike over the busy Bank Holiday weekend. Although the strike was averted at the last minute, the threat still cost the company millions in lost profits.

In 2005, shortly after the company announced a healthy quarterly profit statement, the 'Gate Gourmet' dispute hit British Airways with a further revenue loss of £40 million. When Gate Gourmet, the outsourced catering function formed in 1997, announced the dismissal of 670 of its 2,000 employees, 1,000 British Airways ground staff promptly followed with a sympathy strike. The strike, which was deemed illegal, disrupted operations at Heathrow airport for two days, saw 700 flights cancelled and caused chaos for over 100,000 passengers. Again, in 2007, flight attendants called a strike in reaction to proposed reduction in pay, pensions and sick leave. Although the strike was averted at the last minute, the company's stock fell by almost £100 million.

Through the industrial turbulence, British Airways continued to deliver the same rhetoric to employees that brought them success in the 1990s, which was cutting costs while simultaneously developing and valuing their workforce. One-third of senior management positions were shed in a bid to 'remove duplication and complexity, provide greater accountability and reduce costs', and also, likely, in a bid to change culture (British Airways Corporate Responsibility Report, 2006: 3). This cost reduction measure was supported by a range of new programmes designed towards developing improvements through HRM. The 2008/09 Annual Report (p. 34) stated that 'to create a really high performing business we need to build an inspiring and rewarding workplace where talented people can work to the best of their ability and meet our customer needs'

British Airways introduced a range of new policies and programmes such as a High Performance Leadership Programme to identify talented employees and provide them with the tools and ongoing development opportunities to develop into future leaders. The company announced a renewed focus on providing extensive training, particularly utilising online learning. These programmes included advanced disability awareness, managing bullying and harassment, and programmes titled 'Dignity at Work' and 'Expect respect'.

Despite the company's focus on developing the workforce, the ongoing unrest was creating a reputation based on unreliability for customers. Until late in the decade, the management style demonstrated through these disputes was generally influenced by a traditional perspective, recognising the involvement of unions but supplemented with strategies designed to engage staff. Although management leaned towards a more aggressive approach in some instances such as the 1997 strikes, this style became increasingly predominant and was particularly evident in their reaction to the 2010 cabin crew strikes.

These were a response to an attempt by the company to restructure pay and working requirements for cabin crew staff. British Airways sought to create a 'new fleet' of cabin crew staff, with changes from seniority to performance based pay and restructured lines of authority. In the face of staff resistance and the overwhelming majority in favour of industrial action, the company sought an injunction from the High Court to prevent the threatened 20-day strike. Following the injunction, management sought to locate and reprimand all employees who even alluded to supporting further strike action within the company.

In the following months, British Airways suspended and disciplined over 45 cabin crew who indicated support for industrial action. According to Upchurch (2010), an indication of support was deemed to include personal comments on Facebook or other social media outlets, posts on the union website forum, text messages sent to colleagues, and even private discussions overheard in the corridor. However, it was the notifications of suspension and dismissal which were deemed to be particularly harsh and unreasonable: employees were marched out of meetings or met on the tarmac on disembarkation from their aircraft to be informed of their suspension; and the union reported that suspension notices were sent to the home of a pregnant woman on leave at risk of losing her baby, and another crew member recovering from surgery (Upchurch, 2010).

In this case and ensuing dealings with employees, British Airways have exhibited what has been termed by some observers as 'macho-management'. In the cabin crew dispute of 2010, management appeared to ignore traditional disciplinary methods and pursued a more aggressive stance by moving directly to suspension. The use of disciplinary action based on evidence as weak as hearsay and overheard private conversations was unprecedented and has been equated with 'the worse aspects of the methods used by the Stalinist secret police' (Upchurch, 2010: p.7). The main union for cabin crew also reported an increase in the use of bullying and harassment designed to isolate crew members and undermine the dispute. There appeared to be an emerging subculture of aggressive management coming from the top down, deliberately engineered to intimidate union members.

In summary, British Airways have experienced a series of significant cultural shifts over the past three decades. In recent years, their management style moved from a sophisticated approach, where industrial action was avoided through high quality HR practices, to macho-management, where union involvement was avoided through threats, intimidation, and general belligerence. Over the years it seems HR has been applied on a piecemeal basis in response to internal or external 'shocks', with limited consideration of a long-term strategy or outcomes. The results, particularly following recent events, appear to be the creation of a low-trust culture, with negative flow-on effects for staff satisfaction, morale, loyalty and commitment. Demoralised and resentful staff can be potentially disastrous to customer satisfaction, particularly in the case of cabin crew employees who serve as the front line for projecting the company brand.

From an organisational perspective, the extreme cost-cutting methods witnessed over the last three decades have been essential for survival of the company. British Airways' overall progress has been commendable, although there are improvements that could have been made to their management of employment relations and ultimately the firm's performance. The company has much to learn from Barbra Cassani's successful strategy at Go, where the right of employees to express their dissatisfaction and voice their perspectives was recognised and a positive culture ensued. The approach to managing employment relations exhibited by British Airways appears to be non-sustainable and counterproductive to producing the cultural climate required to achieve long-term business success.

Source: Adapted from Grugulis and Wilkinson, 2002.

Questions

1 Explain employee reactions to culture change initiatives in this case.

2 What lessons can managers learn from this case about managing culture?

Bibliography

Adams, G.B. and Ingersoll, V.H. (1989) 'Painting over old works: the culture of organisations in an age of technical rationality', in Turner, B.A. (ed.) *Organisational Symbolism*, Berlin: Walther De Gruyter.

*Adkins, B. and Caldwell, D. (2004) 'Firm or subgroup culture: where does fitting in matter most?', *Journal of Organizational Behavior,* Vol.25, No.8, 969–78.

Alvesson M. and Karreman D. (2007) 'Unraveling HRM: identity, ceremony, and control in a management consulting firm', *Organization Science,* Vol.18, No.4, 711–23.

Anderson, M., Embrey, D., Hodgkinson, C., Hunt, P., Kinchin, B, Morris, P. and Rose, M. (2003) 'The human factors implications for flight safety of recent developments in the airline indistry', *Flight Safety Digest,* Vol.22, No.3–4, 1–77.

Anthony, P.D. (1994) *Managing Culture,* Buckingham: Open University Press.

Arkin, A. (2004) 'Wax works', *People Management,* 25 November, 34–7.

Arkin, A. (2007) 'From soft to strong', *People Management*, 6 September, 30–3.

Armstrong, M. (1994) *Performance Management,* London: Kogan Page.

Armstrong, M. (1999) *Employee Reward* (2nd edn), London: Chartered Institute of Personnel and Development.

Arnold, J., Loan-Clarke, J., Coombs, C., Park, J., Wilkinson, A. and Preston, D. (2003) *Looking Good? The Attractiveness of the NHS as an Employer to Potential Nursing and Allied Health Profession Staff,* Loughborough: Loughborough University.

Ashforth, B.E. (2001) *Role Transitions in Organizational Life,* Mahwah, NJ: Lawrence Erlbaum.

Ashkanasy, N.M., Broadfoot, L.E. and Falkus, S. (2000) 'Questionnaire measures of organizational culture', in: Ashkanasy, N., Wilerom, C., and Peterson, M. (eds) *Handbook of Organizational Culture and Climate*. Thousand Oaks, CA: Sage.

Balthazard, P.A., Cooke, R.A. and Potter, R.E. (2006) 'Dysfunctional culture, dysfunctional organization: capturing the behavioral norms that form organizational culture and drive performance', *Journal of Managerial Psychology,* Vol.21, No.8, 709–32.

Bamber, G., Hoffer-Gittell, J., Kochan, T. and Von Nordenflycht, A. (2009) *Up in the Air*, New York: Cornell University Press.

Barley, S., Meyer, G. and Gash, D. (1988) 'Cultures of culture: academics, practitioners and the pragmatics of normative control', *Administrative Science Quarterly,* Vol.33, No.1, 24–60.

Barsoux, J.-L. and Manzoni, J.-F. (1997) *Becoming the World's Favourite Airline: British Airways 1980–1993,* Bedford: European Case Clearing House.

Bate, P. (1994) *Strategies for Cultural Change,* London: Butterworth Heinemann.

Becker, H.S. and Geer, B. (1970) 'Participant observation and interviewing: a comparison', pp.133–42, in Filstead, W. (ed.) *Qualitative Methodology,* Chicago, IL: Rand McNally.

Blyton, P. and Turnbull, P. (1996) 'Confusing convergence: industrial relations in the European airline industry: a comment on Warhurst', *European Journal of Industrial Relations,* Vol.2, No.1, 7–20.

Blyton, P. and Turnbull, P. (1998) *The Dynamics of Employee Relations* (2nd edn), London: Macmillan.

Bonache, J. and Fernandez, Z. (2005) 'International compensation costs and benefits of international assignments', in Scullion, H. and Linehan, M. (eds) *International Human Resource Management,* Basingstoke: Palgrave.

Booth, S.A. and Hamer, K. (2008) 'Corporate culture and financial performance: an empirical test of a UK retailer', *International Journal of Retail & Distribution Management,* Vol.37, 711–27.

Bowers, D. and Seashore, S. (1966) 'Predicting organizational effectiveness with a four-factor theory of leadership', *Administrative Science Quarterly,* Vol.11, 238–63.

Braddy, P.W., Meade, A.W. and Kroustalis, C.M. (2006) 'Organizational recruitment website effects on viewers' perceptions of organizational culture', *Journal of Business and Psychology,* Vol.20, No.4, 525–43.

Bright, K. and Cooper, C.L. (1993) 'Organizational culture and the management of quality', *Journal of Management Psychology,* Vol.8, No.6, 21–7.

*Brown, A. (1998) *Organisational Culture* (2nd edn), London: Financial Times/Pitman.

Caligiuri P., Lazarova, M. and Tarique, I. (2005) 'Training, learning and development in multinational organizations', in Scullion, H. and Linehan, M. (eds) *International Human Resource Management,* Basingstoke: Palgrave.

Casey, C. (1995) *Work, Self and Society: After Industrialization,* London: Routledge.

Cassani, B. and Kemp, K. (2003) *Go: An Airline Adventure*, London: Time Warner Books.

Chan, L.L.M., Shaffer, M.A. and Snape, E. (2004) 'In search of sustained competitive advantage: the impact of organizational culture, competitive strategy and human resource management practices on firm performance', *International Journal of Human Resource Management,* Vol.15, No.1, 17–35.

Charlesworth, Z.M. (2008), 'Learning styles across cultures: suggestions for educators', *Education and Training*, Vol.50, No.2, 115–27.

Chatman, J.A. and Cha, S.E. (2003) 'Leading by leveraging culture', *California Management Reviews*, Vol.45, No.4, 20–34.

Chen, C.C., Choi, J. and Chi, S.C. (2002) 'Making justice sense of local-expatriate compensation disparity: mitigation by local referents, ideological explanations, and interpersonal sensitivity in China–foreign joint ventures', *Academy of Management Journal,* Vol.45, No.4, 807–26.

Chow, I..H.S. and Liu, S.S. (2009) 'The effect of aligning organizational culture and business strategy with HR systems on firm performance in Chinese enterprises', *International Journal of Human Resource Management*, Vol.20, No.11, 2292–310.

Colling, T. (1995) 'Experiencing turbulence: competition, strategic choice and the management of human resources in British Airways', *Human Resource Management Journal,* Vol.5, No.5, 18–32.

Cooke, R.A. and Lafferty, J.C. (1989) *Organizational Culture Inventory,* Plymouth, MA: Human Synergistics.

Cooke, R.A. and Rousseau, D.M. (1988) 'Behavioural norms and expectations: a quantitative approach to the assessment of organizational culture', *Group and Organization Studies,* Vol.13, 245–73.

Corke, A. (1986) *British Airways: The Path to Profitability,* London: Frances Pinter.

Crumpacker, M. and Crumpacker, J.M. (2007) 'Succession planning and generational stereotypes: should HR consider age-based values and attitudes a relevant factor or a passing fad?', *Public Personnel Management,* Vol.36, No.4, 349–69.

Cullen, Hon. Lord (1990) *The Public Inquiry into the Piper Alpha Disaster*, London: HMSO.

Dawson, M. and Abbott, J. (2011) 'Hospitality culture and climate: a proposed model for retaining employees and creating competitive advantage', *International Journal of Hospitality & Tourism Administration*, Vol.12, No.4, 289–304.

*Deal, T.E. and Kennedy, A.A. (1982) *Corporate Cultures: The Rites and Rituals of Organisational Life,* Reading, MA: Addison-Wesley.

DeCenzo, D.A. and Robbins, S.P. (2002) *Human Resource Management* (6th edn), New York: Wiley.

Denison, D.R. (1984) 'Bringing corporate culture to the bottom line', *Organizational Dynamics,* Vol.13, No.2, 4–22.

Denison, D.R. (1996) 'What is the difference between organizational culture and organizational climate? A native's point of view on a decade of paradigm wars', *Academy of Management Review*, Vol.21, No.3, 619–54

Dong L. and Glaister K.W. (2007) 'The management of culture in Chinese international strategic alliances', *Asian Business and Management,* Vol.6, No.4, 377–407.

Doyle, P. (1999) 'From the top', The *Guardian,* 4 December.

Dundon, T., Grugulis, I. and Wilkinson, A. (2001) 'New management techniques in small and medium-sized enterprises', in Redman, T. and Wilkinson, A. (eds) *Contemporary Human Resource Management,* London: FT/Prentice Hall.

Emery, Y. (2004) 'Rewarding civil service performance through team bonuses: findings, analysis and recommendations', *International Review of Administrative Sciences*, Vol.70, No.1, 157–69.

Engelen, A.B., Brettel, M. and Wiest, G. (2012) 'Cross-functional integration and new product performance: The impact of national and corporate culture, *Journal of International Management*, Vol.18, No.1, 52–65.

Fairbairn, U. (2005) 'HR as a strategic partner: culture change as an American Express case study', *Human Resource Management,* Vol.44, No.1, 79–84.

Fields, D., Chan, A., Aktar, S. and Blam, T. (2006) 'Human resource management strategies under uncertainty: how do US and Hong Kong Chinese Companies differ?', *Cross Cultural Management: An International Journal*, Vol.13, No.2, 171–86.

Fletcher, C. and Williams, R. (1992) *Performance Appraisal and Career Development* (2nd edn), Cheltenham: Stanley Thomes.

Flynn, B.B., Zhao, X. and Roth, A. (2007) 'The myth of the dragon: operations management in today's China' *Business Horizons*, Vol.50, 177–83.

French, R. (2010), *Cross-Cultural Management in Work Organisations* (2nd edn), London: CIPD.

Froese, F.J., Pak, Y.S. and Chong, L.C. (2008) 'Managing the human side of cross-border acquisitions in South Korea', *Journal of World Business,* Vol.43, No.1, 97–108.

Furnham, A. (1997) *The Psychology of Behaviour at Work,* Hove: Psychology Press.

Furnham, A. and Gunter, B. (1993) *Corporate Assessment.* London: Routledge.

Garnett, J.L., Marlowe, J. and Pandey, S.K. (2008) 'Penetrating the performance predicament: communication as a mediator or moderator of organizational culture's impact on public organizational performance', *Public Administration Review,* Vol.68, No.2, 266–81.

Geertz, C. (1973) *The Interpretation of Culture,* New York: Basic Books.

Georgiades, N. and Macdonell, R. (1998) *Leadership for Competitive Advantage,* London: Wiley.

Gerhart, B. and Fang, M. (2005) 'National culture and human resource management: assumptions and evidence', *International Journal of Human Resource Management*, Vol.16, No.6, 971–86.

Giberson, T.R., Resick, C.J., Dickson, M.W., Mitchelson, J.K., Randall, K.R. and Clark, M.A. (2009) 'Leadership and organizational culture: linking CEO characteristics to cultural values', *Journal of Business and Psychology*, Vol.24, 123–37.

Glaser, S.R. (1983) *The Corporate Culture Survey,* Bryn Mawr, PA: Organizational Design and Development.

Gold, K.A. (1982) 'Managing for success: a comparison of the private and public sectors', *Public Administration Review,* Vol.42, November–December, 568–75.

Gordon, G. (1985) 'The relationship of corporate culture to industry sector and corporate performance', in Kilman, R.H., Saxton, M.J. and Serpa, B. (eds) *Gaining Control of the Corporate Culture,* San Francisco, CA: Jossey-Bass.

Gordon, G. and DiTomaso, N. (1992) 'Predicting corporate performance from organizational culture', *Journal of Management Studies,* Vol.29, 783–98.

Grugulis, I. and Wilkinson, A. (2002) 'Managing culture at British Airways: hope, hype and reality', *Long-Range Planning,* Vol.35, No.2, 179–94.

Grugulis, I., Dundon, T. and Wilkinson, A. (2000) 'Cultural control and the "culture manager": employment practices in a consultancy', *Work, Employment and Society,* Vol.14, No.1, 97–116.

Gundry, L.K. and Rousseau, D.M. (1994) 'Critical incidents in communication culture to newcomers: the meaning is the message', *Human Relations,* Vol.47, 1063–88.

Hampden-Turner, C. (1990) *Corporate Culture: From Vicious to Virtuous Circles*. London: Hutchinson.

Handy, C.B. (1978) *The Gods of Management*, London: Penguin.

Harris, L.C. and Ogbonna, E. (1998) 'Employee responses to culture change efforts', *Human Resource Management Journal,* Vol.8, No.2, 78–92.

Harris, L.C. and Ogbonna, E. (2011) 'Antecedents and consequences of management-espoused organizational culture control', *Journal of Business Research*, Vol.64, 437–45.

Harrison, R. (1972) 'Understanding your organization's character', *Harvard Business Review,* Vol.5, 119–28.

Harrison, R. (2000) *Employee Development* (2nd edn), London: Chartered Institute of Personnel and Development.

Harvey G. and Turnbull, P. (2006) 'Employment relations, management style and flight crew attitudes at low cost airline subsidiaries: the case of British Airways/Go and bmi/bmibaby', *European Management Journal,* Vol.24, No.5, 330–7.

Harzing, A.W. (2000) 'Structuring international organisations', pp.419–37, in Tayeb, M. (ed.) *International Business: Theories, policies and practices*, Harlow: Pearson Education.

Hatch, M.J. (1997) *Organizational Theory,* Oxford: Oxford University Press.

Hofstede, G. (1980) *Culture's Consequences: International Differences in Work-related Values,* Beverly Hills, CA: Sage.

Hofstede, G. (1991) *Cultures and Organizations: The Software of the Mind,* Maidenhead: McGraw-Hill.

Hofstede, G., Neuijen, B., Daval Ohayv, D. and Sanders, G. (1990) 'Measuring organizational cultures: a qualitative and quantitative study across twenty cases', *Administrative Science Quarterly,* Vol.35, 286–316.

Hofstetter, H. and Harpaz, I. (2011) 'Declared versus actual organizational culture as indicated by an organization's performance appraisal', *International Journal of Human Resource Management*. Available online 25 May 2011. DOI:10.1080/09585192.2011.561217. To link to this article go to http://dx.doi.org/10.1080/09585192.2011.561217.

Hong, J.F.L., Easterby-Smith, M. and Snell, R.S. (2006) 'Transferring organizational learning systems to Japanese subsidiaries in China', *Journal of Management Studies,* Vol.43, No.5, 1027–58.

Höpfl, H. (1993) 'Culture and commitment: British Airways', in Gowler, D, Legge, K. and Clegg, C. (eds) *Case Studies in Organizational Behaviour and Human Resource Management,* London: PCP.

Höpfl, H., Smith, S. and Spencer, S. (1992) 'Values and valuations: corporate culture and job cuts', *Personnel Review,* Vol.21, No.1, 24–38.

Howell, A., Kirk-Brown, A. and Cooper, B.K. (2012) 'Does congruence between espoused and enacted organizational values predict affective commitment in Australian organizations?', *International Journal of Human Resource Management*, Vol.23, No.4, 731–47.

Jelineck, M., Smircich, L. and Hirsch, P. (1983) 'Introduction: a code of many colors', *Administrative Science Quarterly,* Vol.28, 331–8.

Keenoy, T. and Anthony, P. (1992) 'Metaphor, meaning and morality', in Blyton, P. and Turnbull, P. (eds) *Reassessing Human Resource Management,* London: Sage.

Kilmann, R.H. and Saxton, M.J. (1983) *The Kilmann-Saxton Culture-Gap Survey,* Pittsburg, PA: Organisational Design Consultants.

Kilmann, R.H., Saxton, M.J. and Serpa, R. (1985) *Gaining Control of the Corporate Culture,* San Francisco, CA: Jossey-Bass.

Kirkman, B.L., Lowe, K.B. and Gibson, C.B. (2006) 'A quarter century of culture's consequences: a review of empirical research incorporating Hofstede's culture values framework', *Journal of International Business Studies*, Vol.37, 285–320.

Kopelman, R.E., Brief, A.P. and Guzzo, R.A. (1990) 'The role of climate in productivity', in Schneider, B. (ed.) *Organizational Climate and Culture,* San Francisco, CA: Jossey-Bass.

Kotrba, L.M., Gillespie, M.A., Schmidt, A.M., Smerek, R.E., Ritchie, S.A. and Denison, D.R. (2012) 'Do consistent corporate cultures have better business performance? Exploring the interaction effects', *Human Relations*, Vol.65, No.2, 241–62.

Kotter, J.P. and Heskett, J.L. (1992) *Corporate Culture and Performance,* New York: Free Press.

Kroeber, A.I. and Kluckhohn, C. (1952) *Culture: A Critical Review of Concepts and Definitions,* New York: Vintage Books.

Kuhn, K.M. (2009) 'Compensation as a signal of organizational culture: the effects of advertising individual or collective incentives', *International Journal of Human Resource Management*, Vol.20, No.7, 1634–48.

Kunda, G. (1992) *Engineering Culture: Control and Commitment in a High-Tech Firm,* Philadelphia, PA: Temple University Press.

Lee, M. (1996) 'Action learning as a cross-cultural tool', in Stewart, J. and McGoldrick, J. (eds) *Human Resource Development,* London: Pitman.

Lee, S.K.J. and Yu, K. (2004) 'Corporate culture and organizational performance', *Journal of Managerial Psychology,* Vol.19, No.4, 340–59.

Legge, K. (2005) *Human Resource Management: Rhetorics and Realities,* Basingstoke: Macmillan.

Lowe, K., Milliman, J., De Cieri, H. and Dowling, P. (2002) 'International compensation practices: a ten-country comparative analysis', *Asia Pacific Journal of Human Resources,* Vol.40, No.1, 55–78.

Louis, M.R. (1983) 'Organizations as culture-bearing milieux', in Pondy, L.R., Frost, P.J., Morgan, G. and Dandridge, I.C. (eds) *Organizational Symbolism,* Greenwich, CT: JAI Press.

Mabey, C. and Salaman, G. (1995) *Strategic Human Resource Management,* Oxford: Blackwell.

Marks, M.L. and Mirvis, P.H. (2011) 'A framework for the human resources role in managing culture in mergers and acquisitions, *Human Resource Management*, Vol.50, 859–77.

Martin, J. (1992) *Cultures in Organizations,* New York: Oxford University Press.

Martin J. (2002) *Organizational Culture: Mapping the Terrain,* London: Sage.

Martin, J. and Siehl, C. (1983) 'Organizational culture and counterculture: an uneasy symbiosis', *Organizational Dynamics,* Vol.12, No.2, 52–64.

Martin, J., Sitkin, S. and Boehm, M. (1985) 'Founders and the elusiveness of a cultural legacy', in Frost, P., Moore, L., Louis, M., Lundberg, C. and Martin, J. (eds) *Organizational culture.* Beverly Hills, CA: Sage.

Mathew, J. and Ogbanna, E. (2009) 'Organizational culture and commitment: a study of an Indian software organization', *International Journal of Human Resource Management*, Vol.20, No.3, 654–75.

McMillan-Capehart, A. (2005) 'A configurational framework for diversity: socialization and culture, *Personal Review*, Vol.34, No.4, 488–96.

Mearns, K., Flin, R., Gordon, R., and Fleming, M. (1998) 'Measuring safety climate in offshore installations', *Work and Stress*, Vol.12, 238–54.

Meek, V.L. (1982) 'Organisational culture: origins and weaknesses', in Salaman, J.G. (ed.) *Human Resource Strategies,* London: Sage.

Merkin, R.S. (2006) 'Uncertainty avoidance and facework: a test of the Hofstede model', *International Journal of Intercultural Relations*, Vol.30, 213–28.

Meyerson, D. (1991) 'Acknowledging and uncovering ambiguities', in Frost, P., Moore, L., Louis, M., Lundberg, C. and Martin, J. (eds) *Reframing Organizational Culture,* Beverly Hills, CA: Sage.

Miah, M.K. and Bird, A. (2007) 'The impact of culture on HRM styles and firm performance: evidence from Japanese parents, Japanese subsidiaries/joint ventures and South Asian local companies', *International Journal of Human Resource Management,* Vol.18, No.5, 908–23.

Milliman, J., Nason, S., Zhu, C. and De Cieri, H. (2002) 'An exploratory assessment of the purposes of performance appraisals in North and Central America and the Pacific Rim', *Human Resource Management*, Vol.41, No.1, 87–102.

Mohr, D.C., Young, G.J. and Burgess, Jr, J.F. (2012) 'Employee turnover and operational performance: the moderating effect of group-oriented organizational culture', *Human Resource Management Journal*, Vol.22, No.2, 216–33.

Monopolies and Mergers Commission (1987) 'British Airways plc and British Caledonian Group plc: a report on the Proposed Merger 247', London: HMSO.

Moorhead, G. and Griffin, R.W. (1995) *Organizational Behavior* (4th edn), Boston, MA: Houghton Mifflin.

Morgan, G. (1986) *Images of Organization,* Beverly Hills, CA: Sage.

Morgan, P.I. and Ogbonna, E. (2008) 'Subcultural dynamics in transformation: a multi-perspective study of healthcare professionals', *Human Relations,* Vol.61, No.1, 39–65.

Münch, R. and Smelster, N.J. (1992) *Theory of Culture,* Berkeley, CA: University of California Press.

Ngo H.N. and Loi R. (2008) 'Human resource flexibility, organizational culture and firm performance: an investigation of multinational firms in Hong Kong', *International Journal of Human Resource Management*, Vol.19, No.9, 1654–66.

*Ogbonna, E. (1992) 'Organisational culture and human resource management: dilemmas and contradictions', in Blyton, P. and Turnbull, P. (eds) *Reassessing Human Resource Management,* London: Sage.

Ogbonna, E. and Harris, L.C. (2000) 'Leadership style, organizational culture and performance: empirical evidence from UK companies', *International Journal of Human Resource Management*, Vol.11, No.4 766–88.

Ogbonna, E. and Wilkinson, B. (1988) 'Corporate strategy and corporate culture: the management of change in the UK supermarket industry', *Personnel Review,* Vol.18, No.6, 10–14.

Ouchi, W.G. (1981) *Theory Z: How American Business Can Meet the Japanese Challenge,* Reading, MA: Addison-Wesley.

Peters, T.J. and Waterman, R.H. (1982) *In Search of Excellence: Lessons from America's Best Run Companies,* New York: Harper & Row.

Pettigrew, A. (1979) 'On studying organizational cultures', *Administrative Science Quarterly,* Vol.24, 570–81.

Pettigrew, A. (1990) 'Is corporate culture manageable?', in Wilson, D. and Rosenfield, R. (eds) *Managing Organisations,* Maidenhead: McGraw-Hill.

Petty, M.M., Beadles, N.A., Lowery, C.M., Chapman, D.F. and Connell, D.W. (1995) 'Relationships between organizational culture and organizational performance', *Psychological Reports,* Vol.76, 483–92.

Pidgeon, N.F. (1991) 'Safety culture and risk management in organizations', *Journal of Cross-Cultural Psychology*, Vol.22, 129–40.

Ricks, T.E. (1997) *Making the Corps,* New York: Scribner.

Rodrigues S.B. (2006) 'The political dynamics of organizational culture in an institutionalized environment', *Organization Studies,* Vol.27, No.4, 537–57.

Rohner, R.P. (1984) 'Towards a conception of culture for cross-cultural psychology', *Journal of Cross-Cultural Psychology,* Vol.15, 111–38.

Rousseau, D.M. (1990) 'Assessing organizational culture: the case for multiple methods', in Schneider, B. (ed.) *Organizational Climate and Culture,* San Francisco, CA: Jossey-Bass.

Sackmann, S. (1991) 'Managing organisational culture: dreams and possibilities', in Anderson, J. (ed.) *Communication Yearbook,* Beverly Hills, CA: Sage.

Sackmann, S.A. (2006) *Assessment, Evaluation, Improvement: Success Through Corporate Culture*. Gütersloh: Bertelsmann Stiftung.

Sackmann, S.A. (2010) 'Culture and performance', pp. 188–224, in Ashkanasy, N., Wilderon, C. and Peterson, M. (eds) *Handbook of Organizational Culture and Climate*. Thousand Oaks, CA: Sage.

Scheeres, H. and Rhodes, C. (2006) 'Between cultures: values, training and identity in a manufacturing firm', *Journal of Organizational Change Management,* Vol.19, No.2, 223–36.

Schein, E.H. (1984) 'Coming to a new awareness of organizational culture', *Sloan Management Review,* Vol.25, 3–16.

Schein, E.H. (1985) 'How culture forms, develops and changes', in Kilmann, R.H., Saxton, M.J., Serpa, R. and Associates (eds) *Gaining Control of the Corporate Culture,* San Francisco, CA: Jossey-Bass.

*Schein, E.H. (2004) *Organizational Culture and Leadership: A Dynamic View* (3rd edn), San Francisco, CA: Jossey-Bass.

Schneider, B. (1990) *Organizational Climate and Culture,* San Francisco, CA: Jossey-Bass.

Schneider, S.C. and Barsoux, J.-L. (2003), *Managing Across Cultures*, (2nd edn), Harlow: FT/Prentice Hall.

Shipley, P. (1990) 'The analysis of organisations as a conceptual tool for ergonomics practitioners', in Wilson, J.R. and Corlett, E.N. (eds) *Evaluation of Human Work,* London: Taylor & Francis.

Siehl, C. and Martin, J. (1990) 'Organizational culture: the key to financial performance?', in Schneider, B. (ed.) *Organizational Climate and Culture,* San Francisco, CA: Jossey-Bass.

Silverzweig, S. and Allen, R.E. (1976) 'Changing the corporate culture', *Sloan Management Review,* Vol.17, No.3, 33–49.

Smircich, L. (1983) 'Concepts of culture and organizational analysis', *Administrative Science Quarterly,* Vol.28, 339–58.

Stewart, J. and McGoldrick, J. (1996) *Human Resource Development,* London: Pitman.

Stiles, P., Gratton, L., Truss, C., Hope-Hailey, V. and McGovern, P. (1997) 'Performance management and the psychological contract', *Human Resource Management Journal,* Vol.7, No.1, 57–66.

Storey, J. (1995) *Human Resource Management: A Critical Text,* London: Routledge.

Swartz, M. and Jordon, D. (1980) *Culture: An Anthropological Perspective,* New York: Wiley.

Taylor, R. (1998) 'Annual review article', *British Journal of Industrial Relations,* Vol.36, No.2 293–311.

Thom, G. (1997) 'SHAPE – The future of safety in the North Sea', *International Conference on Safety Culture in the Energy Industries*, Aberdeen, September.

Thompson, P. and McHugh, D. (2002) *Work Organisations: A Critical Introduction* (3rd edn), Basingstoke: Palgrave.

Torbiorn I. (2005) 'Staffing policies and practices in European MNCs: strategic sophistication, culture-bound policies or ad hoc reactivity?', in Scullion, H. and Linehan, M. (eds) *International Human Resource Management,* Basingstoke: Palgrave.

Trice, H.M. and Beyer, J.M. (1984) 'Studying organizational cultures through rites and ceremonials', *Academy of Management Review,* Vol.9, 653–69.

Trice, H.M. and Beyer, J.M. (1993) *The Cultures of Work Organisations,* Englewood Cliffs, NJ: Prentice-Hall.

Trompenaars, F. and Hampden-Turner, C. (1997) *Riding the Waves of Culture: Understanding Cultural Diversity in Business,* London: Nicholas Brealey.

Tsui, A.S., Zhang, Z.X., Wang, H., Xin, K.R. and Wu, J.B. (2006) 'Unpacking the relationship between CEO leadership behavior and organizational culture', *Leadership Quarterly,* Vol.17, No.2, 113–37.

Upchurch, M. (2010) *Creating a Sustainable Work Environment in British Airways: Implications of the 2010 Cabin Crew Dispute*, A Report for the Unite Union, Middlesex University.

Uttal, B. (1983) 'The corporate culture vultures', *Fortune,* Vol.108, No.8, 17 October, 66–72.

Van den Steen, E. (2010) 'On the origin of shared beliefs (and corporate culture)', *Rand Journal of Economics*, Vol.41, 617–48.

Van Maanen, J. and Schein, E. (1979) 'Toward a theory of organizational socialization', *Research in Organizational Behavior,* Vol.11, 209–59.

Van Vianen, A.E.M. (2000) 'Person–organization fit: the match between newcomers' and recruiters' preferences for organizational cultures', *Personnel Psychology,* Vol.53, No.1, 113–49.

Wanous, P. (1989) 'Installing a realistic job preview: ten tough choices', *Personnel Psychology,* Vol.42, 117–33.

Warhurst, R. (1995) 'Converging on HRM? Change and continuity in European airlines' industrial relations', *European Journal of Industrial Relations,* Vol.1, No.2, 259–74.

Weick, K. (1985) 'The significance of corporate culture', in Frost, P., Moore, L., Louis, M., Lundberg, C. and Martin, J. (eds) *Organizational Culture,* Beverly Hills, CA: Sage.

Wilderom, C.P.M, Glunk, U. and Maslowski, R. (2000) 'Organizational culture as a predictor of organizational performance', in Ashkanasy, N.M., Wilderom, C.P.M. and Peterson, M.F. (eds) *Handbook of Organizational Culture and Climate,* Thousand Oaks, CA: Sage.

Williams, A., Dobson, P. and Watters, M. (1993) *Changing Culture: New Organizational Approaches* (2nd edn), London: Institute of Personnel Management.

*Williams, R.S. (2002) *Managing Employee Performance: Design and Implementation in Organizations,* London: Thomson Learning.

Willmott, H. (1993) 'Strength is ignorance, slavery is freedom: managing culture in modern organizations', *Journal of Management Studies,* Vol.30, No.4, 515–52.

Wong, A.L.Y., Shaw, G.H. and Ng, D.K.C. (2010) 'Taiwan Chinese managers' personality: is Confucian influence on the wane?', *International Journal of Human Resource Management*, Vol.21, 1108–23.

Wunthow, R. and Witten, M. (1988) 'New directions in the study of culture', *Annual Review of Sociology,* Vol.14, 49–67.

Xenikou, A. and Furnham, A. (1996) 'A correlational and factor analytic study of four questionnaire measures of organizational culture', *Human Relations,* Vol.49, 349–71.

Yilmaz, C. and Ergun, E. (2008) 'Organizational culture and firm effectiveness: an examination of relative effects of culture traits and the balanced culture hypothesis in an emerging economy', *Journal of World Business,* Vol.43, No.3, 290–306.

Yu, L. (2007) 'Corporate culture in the numbers', *MIT Sloan Management Review,* Spring, 4–6.

Zhang, X. (2012) *Understanding Chinese and Western Cultures: An Exploration of the Academic Working Environment in Internationalised Higher Education*, PhD Thesis, Loughborough University.

Zemke, R., Raines, C. and Filipczak, B. (2000) *Generations at Work: Managing the Clash of Veterans, Boomers, and Nexters in Your Workplace,* New York: American Management Association.

PART 2
CONTEMPORARY THEMES AND ISSUES

CHAPTER 11
INTERNATIONAL HRM

Michael Dickmann

Introduction

International human resource management (IHRM) is distinct from purely domestic HRM. Dowling (1999) outlines a range of different variables that shape IHRM and provide a distinction to national people management approaches. Among these are primarily the higher complexity of organisations operating in diverse national cultures, embedded in distinct national business systems (Whitley, 1992), and having to cope with greater issues of distance, communication, control and coordination. In a simple form, IHRM concerns the strategies, structures, policies and processes used to manage people in organisations that operate in more than one country. Therefore, multinational corporations (MNCs), international governmental organisations (IGOs) and international non-governmental organisations (INGOs) and the people working within these are most often analysed. IHRM is to a large extent different from comparative HRM, which is devoted to understanding the people management approaches in different countries and to systematically analyse and compare these. Where there are overlaps, it often concerns issues such as the convergence of HRM in diverse countries as MNCs can be principal forces that diffuse standardised policies and practices. Comparative HRM issues are predominantly dealt with in another chapter in this book.

Given that IHRM is concerned with global approaches to people strategy, structure, policies and practices, this chapter will first trace the historical development of international organisations and the personnel challenges that these have faced. It will then present approaches that analyse the mindsets, strategic competitive considerations and structural consequences in MNCs. This is followed by a discussion of how organisations expand abroad and what shifts they experience in their HRM. This will lead us firmly into models of IHRM that depict the influencing factors, IHRM choices and goals of MNCs. Then the chapter will explicate a range of topics related to international working, balancing an organisational and individual perspective. In so doing we will develop a set of recommendations for the management of international workers.

Historical development of the multinational organisation

Several thousand years ago organisations operating in foreign regions existed. Some of the key international entities were armed forces – often invading other territories – and religious groups. Four thousand years ago Assyrian commercial organisations were active in several geographical regions, had overseas subsidiaries and employed foreigners. Therefore, it can hardly be said that IHRM is a recent phenomenon. And with large distances, the challenges of communication, transport, diverse norms and values, control and coordination became more stringent. The parallels to modern MNCs throughout history are quite strong which can be seen at the example of the great trading companies.

The English and Dutch East India companies or the Hudson's Bay Company had huge economic power and huge people challenges associated with their geographical expanse. Distance created a communication and control problem. The firms reacted by sending trusted staff to manage far-flung operations. These would strive to shape operations around their home country social norms and working patterns. In effect, their influence can be described as social coordination. But there were stronger control mechanisms. Goals were set in the head office and financial incentives were developed. Key performance measures were defined and financial measures – such as loss at loading of ship, ratio of capital to tonnage – existed. Stringent control approaches – such as the use of pursers on ships, sending agents to control local managers, even reading private letters – were implemented while head offices resorted to administrators and experts to run the organisation. The development of control mechanisms, superior communication, normative integration approaches and the professionalisation of management has some parallels to modern MNCs (Carlos and Nicholas, 1988).

Many of the drivers of international expansion have had precursors in history. Seeking resources, new markets and increasing power has been prominent throughout history, but especially after the Second World War the numbers and geographical expansion of MNCs increased dramatically. This was aided by technological advances in transport, communication and information processing. At the same time, trade barriers have reduced and the availability of capital to finance foreign ventures increased (Dickmann and Baruch, 2011).

 ## The mindsets of senior leaders

IHRM strategies and structures are intimately linked to the wider business literature and many approaches are based on the seminal works of Perlmutter (1969) and Hennan and Perlmutter (1979). These authors developed a typology that was originally intended to add to the general strategy literature and which was then most eagerly integrated into the IHRM discourse. Their thinking was based on the premise that organisational strategic and structural forms are shaped by administrative heritage and senior management cognitions. Their four types are outlined below:

Ethnocentric – 'One size fits all and head office knows best'.

In an ethnocentric company senior leaders are persuaded that their products and services are attractive both in domestic and foreign markets. In fact, based on their home-country values, norms and experiences they believe in their superior capabilities which leads to an export of their unadjusted corporate approaches. Overall, their way to compete is anchored to these perceived ownership advantages and the scale effects of large production runs. An example of globally integrated product markets would be the computer hardware industry. It is common for foreign subsidiaries to be set up by a trusted and experienced expatriate from the country of origin. The ethnocentric firm will have a shared company culture and integrated IHRM strategies, structures, policies and practices. Senior career patterns are bound to have intensive connections to the head office and country-of-origin nationals are most likely to be in key positions.

Polycentric – 'Foreign markets work differently and locals know best'.

Head office's top management is persuaded that markets around the world for their products and services vary substantially. Human food products, utilities and some professional services may be industries that can be seen as having a degree of polycentrism. Therefore, the polycentric firm tries to be as locally responsive as possible, which implies strong decision-making powers that are locally distributed. Each foreign operating unit is treated as a distinct national entity. This allows the polycentric to develop (or adapt) products and services that are locally attuned. Moreover, it can be responsive to the national environment (culture, legal context, key institutions) and its customers. Normally, foreign subsidiaries are set up and managed by locals who are rarely moved to the head office in the country of origin. In turn, only few expatriates go abroad to work in foreign affiliates and if they do, they tend to have a technical expert or financial control function.

Regiocentric – Geographical regions are different, professionals from diverse parts of the specific region know best, within region economies of scale are possible.

The regiocentric corporation has developed diverse management approaches in response to regional variations – it reflects the geographic structure and strategy of the globally operating entity. Within the regions (e.g. North America, Europe, Asia-Pacific, Africa) it is possible to find similar products and services so that some economies of scale are reaped. Regional managers may have driven the geographical expansion and start-ups in their regions. Talent is seen predominantly in regional confines which may lead to expatriation to countries within the same region but not across to other regions. There is some degree of regional autonomy but it is rare for European managers, for example, to be promoted to, say, the US head office.

Geocentric – worldwide approach where each part has unique contribution, ability not nationality counts, integration and scale economies where possible.

A geocentric organisation has a worldwide approach that leaves local autonomy to adapt where it is necessary and coordinates policies where it is beneficial. Therefore, it recognises both local differences and peculiarities (enabling responsiveness) as well as where product or service markets are integrated around the world (enabling efficiency through economies of scale). The geocentric recognises that each operating unit makes a unique contribution. This means that hierarchical structures are less important and that within this worldwide, integrated organisation ability is more important than nationality. The 'best talents' are sourced from wherever inside and outside the corporation and these rotate through head office and foreign subsidiaries.

The dualities of integration and responsiveness

The diverse mindsets of senior executives have a strong impact on the strategies, structures, policies and practices of an organisation. A theoretical approach aiming to explore these differences has been developed by Prahalad and Doz (1987). These authors link the decisions about MNCs' structures to the pressures to coordinate corporate activities, control and at times standardise them (integration) with pressures to react to local variations (responsiveness). If management cognitions are right, then a firm operating in an ethnocentric product market would need to have a high degree of *operational integration* in order to cope with highly standardised product and strong pressures for economies of scale (e.g. the automotive industry). Moreover, if the enterprise has many multinational customers with the ability to assess and compare prices and service levels around the world, its *strategic coordination* needs are high. If the company were to operate in a highly polycentric market then it needs to develop approaches to be able to *respond* successfully *to local variations*. For instance, a firm producing and distributing meats needs to be responsive to human preferences and religious implications (large-scale pork sales in the Middle East or beef sales in India are difficult etc.). Given that global firms are active in diverse industries and that they are exposed to a variety of pressures it is clear that there does not seem to be one best way to locate on Prahalad and Doz's integration–responsiveness grid.

Competitive challenges and international HRM configurations

Another milestone in the discussion of business and IHRM configurations – the strategies, structures, policies and practices of organisations – has been the ideas of Bartlett and Ghoshal (1989). They base their arguments on the competitive advantage arguments of Michael Porter, the integration–responsiveness distinction of Prahalad and Doz, Perlmutter's types as well as a range of other strategic literature ideas. Bartlett and Ghoshal present nine cases of large, multinational companies and analyse their worldwide strategies, structures and processes. On the one hand, the authors explore the cost advantages of highly integrated firms which suffer responsiveness challenges. On the other hand, highly responsive firms have a quality advantage due to more attractive solutions in the local market but are perceived to have a cost

Box 11.1 HRM in practice   **Integration and responsiveness**

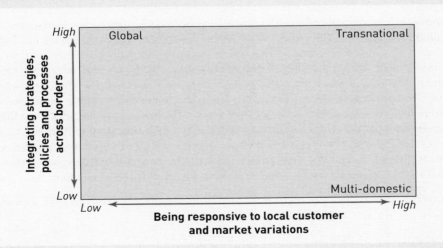

Figure 11.1 Integration and responsiveness

P. Almond and O. Tregaskis, International HRM in *Human Resource Management: A Contemporary Approach* 6 edn, (Beardwell, J. and Claydon, T., 2010) © Pearson Education Limited, 2001, 2011.

Questions

Taking your own company or an organisation with which you are familiar:

1 What does it most closely resemble? What factors did you take into consideration?

2 What are the pressures that push 'your' organisation into either integration or responsiveness?

3 Are there differences between global strategy, production, finance or IHRM? If so, what are they and why do they exist?

4 Where do you think your organisation wants to go with its IHRM in future? What external pressures would exert forces for this change? What will it gain from changing its IHRM approach?

disadvantage. Given that many corporations experience pulls into both the integration as well as the responsiveness direction, at the core of their discussion lies how to overcome this global–local dilemma. This was the dilemma that was underlying Prahalad and Doz's discussion, but Bartlett and Ghoshal expanded their ideas by introducing a further dimension – innovation. Porter (1985) had argued that competitive advantage can be derived through focus on key strengths: cost, quality or innovation. Equipped with these ideas, Bartlett and Ghoshal propose four configurations:

Multidomestic – polycentric strategy with a dispersed structure that has low degrees of integration and knowledge exchange.

The multidomestic (also called multinational) has only loose links between the country of origin head office and foreign subsidiaries. Given that markets and competitive environments are seen to vary substantially, there is much autonomy for local subsidiaries. Thus, integration levels – including bureaucratic control and social coordination – are low and the knowledge exchange across borders is moderate. This leads to little or no international HRM and personnel management mostly being domestic. This configuration is characterised by local responsiveness and some local innovation but little efficiency in production/management of worldwide operations. Cross-border innovation is low and outside the service sector the firm can only thrive in the long term if local national contexts are radically different.

Global – ethnocentric strategies, structures and integrated policies and practices with strong knowledge transfer from the head office outwards.

The global corporation is based on the belief that what works in the country of origin works around the world. Products and services are highly integrated and the corporate centre has developed sophisticated coordination and clear control mechanisms. This means that foreign subsidiaries have little autonomy – instead they have the function to learn from the perceived superior experience of the head office. All key decisions – including those with regard to strategy, product development, service delivery, finance, marketing, HRM – are taken in the corporate centre. Central HRM has manifold international functions for instance with respect to talent recruitment, selection, development, international careers or performance management. Corporate culture and communications are much more important than with the multidomestic enterprise. The global company competes on cost efficiency through economies of scale and can have highly successful, innovative products which were conceived and developed in the country-of-origin. Many companies in the IT, computer or engineering industries – e.g. Dell, General Electric – have strong global characteristics. The risks lie in the one-way innovation process that can stifle local innovation and responsiveness. This may be one of the reasons why Siemens announced in 2010 that it intends that in 2015 half of its products sold in India will be designed and produced in the subcontinent.

International – intense focus on worldwide innovation leads to high knowledge networking activities.

The international corporation is geared to worldwide innovation and is characterised by high knowledge flows through the network of foreign affiliates and head office. The degree of integration of these firms is less defined (Dickmann and Müller-Camen, 2006). IHRM would need to build a culture that creates space for innovation in all operations and mechanisms to identify and develop product or service ideas. As such, HR's role would be to source people from anywhere in the world who have a high creative potential. One of the firms that typifies such a culture is 3M. Control pressures may not be as strong as in the global firm since a reasonably high degree of autonomy encourages innovation. Among the risks of this approach are cost pressures through intense competition and the dangers of insufficient copyright protection in some countries as well as developments in knowledge exchange and focus that have led to shorter copying/reproduction times.

Table 11.1 Strategy, structure and processes in the four types of MNCs

Organisational characteristics	Multinational	Global	International	Transnational
Configuration of assets and capabilities	Decentralised and nationally self-sufficient	Centralised and globally scaled	Sources of core competencies centralised, others decentralised	Dispersed, inter-dependent and specialised
Role of overseas operations	Sensing and exploiting local opportunities	Implementing parent company strategies	Adapting and leveraging parent company competencies	Differentiated contributions by national units to integrated worldwide operations
Development and diffusion of knowledge	Knowledge developed and retained within each unit	Knowledge developed and retained at the centre	Knowledge developed at the centre and transferred to overseas units	Knowledge developed jointly and shared world wide

Source: Based on Bartlett and Ghoshal, 1989: 65, from *Managing Across Borders: The Transnational Solution*, copyright ©1989 by the Harvard Business School Publishing Corpn, all rights reserved.

Transnational – an ideal, networked organisation that has simultaneously high degrees of integration where possible, responsiveness where necessary and knowledge transfer.

While the multidomestic corporation competes on responsiveness (quality), the global firm on integration (price) and the international firm on innovation (new products or services), the fourth configuration, the transnational, achieves responsiveness, efficiency and worldwide innovation simultaneously. A central argument by Bartlett and Ghoshal is that MNCs need to achieve this ideal configuration over time if they want to survive. Going beyond Porter's argument, any firm is seen to be engaged in all three of these competitive arenas and will not prosper and thrive in the long term if it is not attractive on all these three accounts. In fact, some commentators even go beyond this nowadays in that they add other dimensions or factors such as social legitimacy and being perceived to act responsibly by customers, pressure groups and governments as a condition of survival (Dickmann and Baruch, 2011). In the transnational, knowledge and resource flows across borders are extensive – which includes frequent international working for staff. The transnational is a highly flexible organisation that operates in a network in which head office is *primus inter pares* i.e. has a similar role to that of other centres of excellence in the network. The table summarises some key strategy, structure and process considerations of the four types. One of the key roles of IHRM in a transnational is to further integration through creating and sustaining a strong and shared culture. Similar to the geocentric firm, the transnational remains largely an ideal that is difficult to empirically verify. Their ideas had a tremendous impact in that many academics embarked on research looking at these configurations (e.g. Harzing, 2000; Leong and Tan, 1993) and firms proclaiming a desire to become transnationals. Among the critique to the work of Bartlett and Ghoshal is that it underplays micro-political processes, power and individual agency (Edwards and Rees, 2006).

Dickmann and Müller-Camen (2006; 2009 with Kelliher) have built on Bartlett and Ghoshal's ideas and focused not on the general configurations but on strategies, structures and processes in international HRM. In so doing, they proposed that two key dimensions can be used to measure IHRM. The first, standardisation, is based on Harzing's (2000: 103) argument that there is a continuum of integration/coordination/globalisation advantages on the one side and differentiation/responsiveness/localisation advantages on the other side. In fact, this collapses the integration–responsiveness distinction into one dimension which assesses the 'uniformity' of IHRM approaches. The second dimension, knowledge networking, depicts

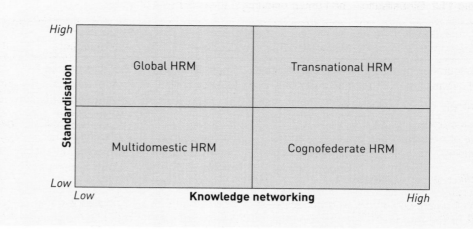

Figure 11.2
IHRM configur-
ations in MNCs

Source: Adapted from
Dickmann and Müller-
Camen 2006.

the communication flows, including control and coordination activities, in an MNC. Sophisticated communication and coordination is important for decisions where internationally
operating firms need to be responsive to the local context and where they can standardise. In
addition, it would allow worldwide innovation based on home and host-country nationals'
ideas. Dickmann and Müller-Camen showed that the international configuration was not
sufficiently specified and proposed a type they call 'cognofederate'. This resulted in a two by
two matrix of high or low standardisation and knowledge networking in IHRM. The matrix
is depicted in Figure 11.2 and Case study 11.1, at the end of this chapter, uses their approach.

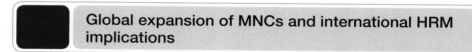

Global expansion of MNCs and international HRM implications

Adler and Ghadar's (1990) IHRM model illuminates changes in the role of culture and HRM
policies and practices based on the different stages of the product life cycle. Much of the discussion concentrates on exploring the shifting competitive pressures and resulting expatriate
effects. Moreover, the four identified stages explicate how HR activities change in response to
cultural and product requirements.

Phase 1: Domestic. In the domestic stage the product (or service) as well as HRM focus on
the home market. Products are assumed to be novel, unique and successful in the country-
of-origin market. This means that there is no organisational pressure to be culturally sensitive. If there are exports, the products or services will be delivered largely unadjusted. A
current example could be a German bakery producing specific dark (black) bread that may
be attractive to German expatriates or some highly health-conscious customers in the UK
precisely because of its different taste or high-fibre content. HR in a domestic firm is attuned
to the country of origin and there are very few international HR implications as expatriation,
frequent international flying or cross-cultural seminars will not be important. Given that the
head office is crucial (and foreign operations are not key), international work is not seen as
good for individuals' careers. If there are international workers, product or technical competencies will be important. Further HRM implications are outlined in Table 11.2.

Phase 2: International. Over time, competition increases in the home country so that
foreign markets become more attractive to the firm. Overseas plants and subsidiaries may
have been set up and divisional structures designed. Cultural sensitivity becomes more
important than before due to the larger foreign workforce. However, HR approaches are
designed in the corporate centre and aim to devise effective control mechanisms over the
international operations. Having superior experience with the production technology and

Table 11.2 Globalisation and human resource management

	Phase 1 Domestic	Phase II International	Phase III Multinational	Phase IV Global
Primary orientation	Product or service	Market	Price	Strategy
Strategy	Domestic	Multi-domestic	Multinational	Global
Worldwide strategy	Allow foreign clients to buy product/service	Increase market internationally, transfer technology abroad	Source, produce and market internationally	Gain global strategic competitive advantage
Staffing expatriates	None (few)	Many	Some	Many
Why sent	Junket	To see control or transfer technology	Control	Coordination and integration
Whom sent		'OK' performers, salespeople	Very good performers	High-potential managers and top executives
Purpose	Reward	Project 'to get job done'	Project and career development	Career and organisational development
Career impact	Negative	Bad for domestic career	Important for global career	Essential for executive suite
Professional re-entry	Somewhat difficult	Extremely difficult	Less difficult	Professionally easy
Training and development	None	Limited	Longer	Continuous throughout career
For whom	No one	Expatriates	Expatriates	Managers
Performance appraisal	Corporate bottom line	Subsidiary bottom line	Corporate bottom line	Strategic positioning
Motivation assumption	Money motives	Money and adventure	Challenge and opportunity	Challenge, opportunity, advancement
Rewarding	Extra money to compensate for foreign hardship		Less generous, global packages	
Career 'fast track'	Domestic	Domestic	Token international	Global
Executive passport	Home country	Home country	Home country, token foreigners	Multinational
Necessary skills	Technical and managerial	Plus cultural adaption	Plus recognising cultural differences	Plus cross-cultural interaction, influence and synergy

Source: Adapted from Adler and Ghadar, 1990; Beardwell and Claydon, 2010: 659.

processes, the international also strives to manage outwards knowledge transfer. Therefore, seminars to increase cultural sensitivity and adaptability are introduced. There is now more expatriation to get the 'job' done, but it is not integrated into general career planning so that re-entry to the country of origin is extremely difficult.

Phase 3: Multinational. The multinational stage takes place when the product (service) reaches maturity and is characterised by strong competition resulting in an intensive efficiency focus. An example here could be many computer hardware firms that source standardised components from a variety of sources and compete on price. Management's focus on cultural sensitivity relaxes because the cost reduction pressures lead to a strong focus on economies of scale. Therefore, the coordination of resources, production and supply-chains through integration has become paramount. HR approaches strive to establish a strong company culture and much of staff sourcing is predominantly linked to the seamless integration with the country of origin. As the foreign operations have become more important, the leadership of these is seen as more core to an individual's career. Very good performers who are culturally sensitive are selected as expatriates and 're-entry' after their global work is seen as less difficult than in earlier phases.

Phase 4: Global.   The fourth stage, global, is a theoretical speculation that assumes that, with increasing globalisation of business and higher competition, MNCs have to operate in all three earlier phases simultaneously, finding ideal solutions to global challenges. It has, therefore, some similarities with the geocentric mindset in terms of finding the right balance of integration and responsiveness. The firm needs to build sophisticated networks internally and externally to compete successfully. HR works towards global strategic competitive advantage which is linked to identifying, developing, deploying and performance managing the best individuals independent from their national origins. This is also seen to facilitate a rapid, globally responsive design of products and services at low costs. The global enterprise will have many expatriates from diverse countries and foreign experience becomes key for executive careers.

Adler and Ghadar's (1990) framework can be criticised for concentrating too heavily on expatriates, instead of on the whole staff of the organisation or other forms of international work. Moreover, issues of creating competitive advantage through responsiveness and innovation could be explored in more depth. Further, the distinction between the international and the multinational stage could be clearer. In addition, the international expansion of knowledge-intensive firms has sometimes been extremely fast and has happened simultaneously in diverse countries. For instance, some companies conducted their initial growth phases in the US and Europe simultaneously, thereby throwing the stage approach into doubt. Lastly, Milliman and Von Glinow (1990) propose an organisational life cycle model that takes into account the fact that modern firms have more than just one product or service.

 ## Strategic international HRM in MNCs

Schuler *et al.* (1993) have suggested what is probably the best-known model of IHRM. Their framework lists exogenous and endogenous factors and structural components of MNCs. It then depicts their link to strategic IHRM (SIHRM), distinguishing SIHRM, SIHRM functions, policies and practices. The strength of the framework lies in its broad, descriptive conceptual approach that also takes the concerns and goals of the MNC into account. While a criticism has been that the model does not explore micro-political processes between the head office and its foreign affiliates, it nevertheless provides a very broad picture of the elements and links of SIHRM. In 1999, De Cieri and Dowling simplified the SIHRM framework and added nuances in the areas of MNC structure and strategy.

 ## International HRM policies and practices – working abroad

Organisational and individual perspectives in international mobility

We have seen that international work is not a recent phenomenon, but working abroad is becoming increasingly common and varied (ECA, 2010; GMAC, 2009). The growing globalisation of markets and competitive activities as well as the broad political, economic, social and technological factors underlying this have been explored elsewhere in this book.

Harris *et al.* (2003) have suggested an expatriation cycle to outline the process of international work beginning with strategic considerations and ending with the return of the expatriate. Dickmann and Baruch (2011) have expanded this idea in two senses while focusing on global careers. First, their cycle explicitly distinguishes individual and organisational perspectives, embodying the dual dependency idea. Second, their timeframe goes beyond the immediate return to cover career effects over time. This model is taken up to guide the remainder of the discussion in this chapter. In so doing, it is slightly adjusted to take account of both international mobility and global career issues.

I Dimensions and patterns of international work

Peiperl and Jonsen (2007) argue that the variations in international working can be captured by a two-dimension matrix that outlines types of global careers. One dimension is time spent away from the individual's home culture or market, while the other is the amount of interaction across cultures and markets. Baruch *et al.* (2013) propose that context should be added to time, and content, resulting in seven dimensions: time spent away, intensity of international contact (from flexpatriates to expatriates); breadth of interaction (work-related or holistic), legal context of stay (illegal, legal), international work instigator (individuals themselves, their organisations), cultural gap (size of differences) and specific role differences (work with much or little need for local sensitivity and understanding). Their distinction resulted in 20 types of international work – of which the dozen probably most discussed in the literature are outlined in Table 11.3.

Much of the research on how to select, develop and manage expatriates has been conducted on traditional company-sponsored assignees and/or HRM leaders commenting on their international mobility approaches. While more insights relating to self-initiated expatriates have recently emerged, the discussion below reflects this information-asymmetry.

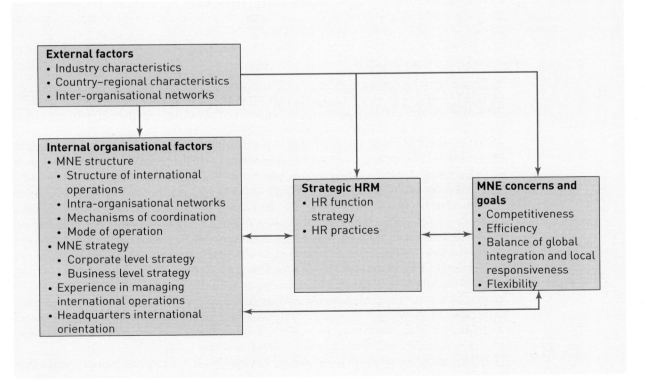

Figure 11.3 A model of strategic HRM in MNEs

Source: Adapted from De Cieri and Dowling, 1999.

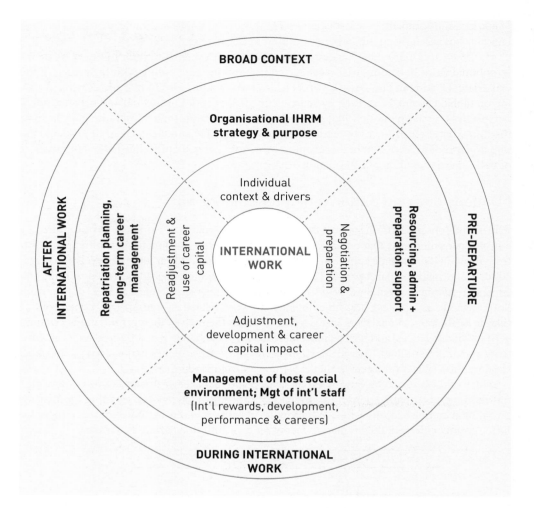

Figure 11.4
Individual and
organisational
areas of inter-
national work

Source: Adapted from
Dickmann and Baruch,
2011: 171, Fig. 7.2.

II The broad context: drivers of international work

There are few areas at work where the dependency of individuals on their employers and, in turn, the importance of staff performance for the organisation is so high. This is why Larsen (2004) calls this relationship one of 'dual dependency'. The key strategic drivers for organisations include control and coordination considerations, global leadership development aims, skills gap filling and knowledge creation, transfer and exploitation (Bonache and Dickmann, 2008; Edström and Galbraith, 1977). Above, we explained many of these factors in relation to corporate configurations. Below, the operational motives of quality of international resourcing (including acquisition, development and retention of talent), the speed of response to skills needs, the launching of new initiatives and the management of global careers will be discussed. First, however, we will explore individual drivers of working abroad.

Key antecedents include family and social background variables such as language command, friendship and familial ties with an impact on the willingness of individuals to live in geographical separation. Moreover, early experiences such as having lived or travelled overseas influence the decision about an international career (Tharenou, 2003). Finally, personality traits such as inquisitiveness or resilience have an impact on how successful individuals may be working abroad (Bird and Osland, 2004) and may influence their outlook.

Individual motivations to work abroad are manifold, but can be discussed under five broad headings. First, career and developmental motives are highly pertinent for foreign assignees, often being the most important driver (Dickmann *et al.*, 2008; Stahl and Cerdin, 2004).

Table 11.3 Key types of international work

Traditional, organization-sponsored long-term expatriation (longer than 1 year)	Short-term, organization-sponsored expatriation (shorter than 1 year)	Self-initiated expatriation to work in an organization, not sponsored by the employer
Inpatriation (organisation-sponsored, to the head office)	International project work	Flexpatriation (frequent flying to different countries)
Long-term legal/illegal immigration	International sabbaticals	Virtual global work
Cross-border commuting	Short-term voluntary work and work experiences	Self-initiated foreign study (schools or universities)

People often value the chance to acquire global business acumen, cross-cultural sensitivity, gather foreign experiences and learn unusual capabilities (Tung, 1998). While these drivers appear particularly strong for company-sent expatriates, they are also important for self-initiated foreign workers (Doherty *et al.*, 2011; Yan *et al.*, 2002).

A second important driver refers to individual interests, experiences and drives. These motivations seem to be particularly strong for self-initiated expatriates (Doherty *et al.*, 2011; Inkson *et al.*, 1997). They include drivers such as a thirst for adventure, travel or life change (Richardson and Mallon, 2005), personal challenge, a quest for understanding foreign cultures or a desire to live abroad (Doherty *et al.*, 2011).

The third, organisational, factor is sometimes key for assigned (company-sponsored) expatriates. Organisational drivers include the likely financial impact (Yurkiewicz and Rosen, 1995) but also non-financial incentives such as the expected length of stay, administrative support mechanisms and repatriation arrangements (Dickmann *et al.*, 2008).

The fourth set of decision influences, family and partner considerations, is often perceived to be a barrier to international mobility. For instance, the issue of dual careers – when the partner

Individual		Organisational	
Antecedents	*Individual motives*	*Operational considerations*	*Strategic drivers*
• Family and social background • Early experiences • Personality	• Career and development • Organisational factors and inducements • Individual interests and drivers • Family and partner considerations • National and location-specific factors	• Quality of resourcing • Speed of response • Management of global careers • Launching new initiatives	• Control • Coordination • Global leadership development • Knowledge creation transfer and exploitation

Figure 11.5 Individual and organisational drivers for international work
Source: Adapted from Dickmann and Baruch, 2011: 120.

has a career of their own and does not want to suspend it – is seen to be increasingly important and so authors argue that the willingness of the partner/family to relocate should be taken into account in the assignment decision (Harvey, 1995; Sparrow *et al.*, 2004). However, family considerations can also be an incentive to move abroad as in the case when parents regard the host country education system as superior (Dickmann and Baruch, 2011; Richardson and Mallon, 2005).

Fifth, national and location-specific considerations will have an impact on individuals' decisions to work abroad. The influence of host culture, history, language, climate and security considerations has been documented (Black *et al.*, 1992; Haslberger, 2008; Yurkiewicz and Rosen, 1995). Recent studies have also outlined specific location influences when analysing particular cities. Dickmann and Mills' (2010) study of London and Haslberger and Zehetner's (2008) research in Vienna identified factors such as the tolerance of citizens or the city's reputation for business/specific sectors that were regarded as attractive by expatriates and had influenced their decision to relocate.

The discussion above has shown a variety of drivers relating to why individuals go to work abroad. At times, we have distinguished self-initiated from organisation-sponsored assignees, but there are many more diverse forms of international careers. These are explored in the section below.

III Pre-departure: resourcing, administrative support and preparation

Once a decision has been made to fill a position in a foreign affiliate, a number of factors need to be considered. Just because the job has previously been done by a country-of-origin expatriate does not mean that this has to continue. The above discussion of organisational drivers, especially those relating to reasons of control, coordination, skills filling and knowledge transfer, can provide some guidance on where the new incumbent may come from and what capability set they need. It has become more common for companies to task their (traditional) expatriates with identifying and developing a local successor, which would in most cases be more cost-effective and would alleviate the problem of perceived 'glass ceilings' for local careers and mistrust between locals and foreigners (Hailey and Harry, 2008). Even self-initiated expatriates are suggested as a way to reduce the high costs of expatriation (as these tend to be on local contracts) and the reduction of some (mostly culture-shock-related, see below) risks (Howe-Walsh and Schyns, 2010). Moreover, other forms of international work – such as flexpatriation or virtual leadership – may be considered.

Assuming that traditional expatriation is selected, what factors and organisational approaches could impact on the success of the assignment? Table 11.5 outlines a whole range of issues. In the pre-assignment phase these include job design, selection (including negotiation and contracting), administrative and logistical support as well as further preparation. In terms of job design, factors that facilitate the expatriate's adjustment to the local culture are important. As such, individuals would benefit from autonomy and discretion as well as realistic job expectations. Adjustment is also facilitated when the individual is 'on top of the job', for instance when the position involves the use of capabilities that the person already possesses and/or when the job is similar to the job they have held previously (Dickmann and Baruch, 2011).

The selection of expatriates has been extensively covered in the literature. Dowling *et al.*, (2008) summarise the discussion on selection factors and link the decision to the following: technical ability, cross-cultural suitability, family requirements, country/cultural requirements, language and MNC requirements. Some of these requirements (such as the MNC drivers) have been discussed above. Technical ability is highly valued by MNCs (Sparrow *et al.*, 2004), but it is clear that technical competence is not enough in a foreign context. The way in which the person adapts to local processes and customs is often crucial. Furthermore, cross-cultural suitability also depends on the individual's personality. Caligiuri (2000) has linked these to the Big 5 personality theory and other authors have proposed cultural empathy, cultural intelligence, diplomacy, openness and adaptability as influencing cross-border work success (see, for example, Ang *et al.*, 2007). In reality, many MNCs do not employ highly sophisticated selection criteria in relation to the international work and adjustment – instead, they seem to use predominantly technical ability, performance, language ability and willingness to go (Dowling *et al.*, 2008; Harris *et al.*, 2003).

The international mobility selection systems can be categorised as either closed or open and either formal or informal (Harris and Brewster, 1999).

The less formal approaches have fewer defined criteria and measures and are linked by the authors to a 'coffee machine system' (Harris and Brewster, 1999: 497) in which chance encounters and word-of-mouth play a significant role in candidate identification and selection. Building international management expertise and global leaders becomes more important to MNCs (GMAC, 2008), a trend that may be associated with more closed selection systems if organisations identify their high potential and are keen to manage their global careers.

In terms of the individual, it is important to understand why they want to embark on a global career and to negotiate the monetary and non-monetary conditions. Key considerations are the expatriation salary, social and tax implications (see Dickmann and Baruch, 2011, Chapters 10 and 11 for an in-depth discussion). Moreover, family support (especially for a working partner or when there are health/care issues), security, travel, as well as a range of administrative and logistical help should all be clearly defined. Lastly, further pre-departure and post-arrival developmental help should be discussed. In many cases, the family of the expatriate should be involved in the discussions and negotiations. A 'look–see' visit can help to gain more realistic expectations.

IV During international work: host environment, individual adjustment, development, careers and management of international staff

Social environment and host-country national liaison role

The manner in which host country co-workers treat expatriates has an important bearing on their adjustment (Huang *et al.*, 2005; Toh and DeNisi, 2007). This can be linked to the host country national's role:

- Information-gathering role to help expatriates to understand the local organisation and local culture (Toh and DeNisi, 2007; Vance *et al.*, 2009)
- Social and emotional support role that helps expatriates to socialise and adapt to the host country's values, norms and behaviours (Toh and DeNisi, 2007).
- Training and coaching role to improve knowledge transfer (Toh and DeNisi, 2007) and to give career guidance (Vance *et al.*, 2009).
- Role of good liaison person to improve communication between host country nationals and expatriates which may help to avoid conflicts (Vance *et al.*, 2009).

These roles are normally not specified in the job description of the host country national and are to a large extent voluntary (Toh and DeNisi, 2007). Therefore, Templer (2010) argues that host country nationals can be unwilling to perform these roles for a range of reasons. Seeing expatriates not as members of one's own group (e.g. as an outgroup) would be one aspect influencing host country nationals if they fail to behave in a particularly constructive and helpful way (Toh and DeNisi, 2007).

How can this unwillingness to help expatriates be mitigated? Toh and DeNisi suggest that organisations could draw up policies and incentives to alleviate the situation and to encourage more helpful approaches. These could include an organisational culture that values support, rewards those who help foreign assignees and a fair salary level when comparing home and host compensation. In addition, MNCs could develop cross-border coordination approaches when selecting expatriates, moderate the pay differential between expatriates and locals, use more transparent promotion processes and criteria and prepare the host country nationals for the arrival of the foreign assignees (Bonache *et al.*, 2009; Leung *et al.*, 2009).

Training and development for international careers and expatriate work has been extensively discussed (Dowling *et al.*, 2008; Harris and Dickmann, 2005) and many MNCs make

Box 11.2 HRM in practice — Selection Systems

Table 11.4 Selection systems

	Formal	Informal
OPEN	• Clearly defined criteria • Clearly defined measures • Training for selectors • Open advertising of vacancy (internal/external) • Panel discussions	• Less defined criteria • Less defined measures • Limited training for selectors • No panel discussions • Open advertising of vacancy • Recommendations
CLOSED	• Clearly defined criteria • Clearly defined measures • Training for selectors • Panel discussions • Nominations only (net-working/reputation)	• Selectors' individual preferences determine criteria and measures • No panel discussions • Nominations only (networking/reputation)

Source: Adapted from Harris and Brewster, 1999.

Questions

1 What selection approach does your organisation/an organisation that you are familiar with use?

2 Why does it use it?

3 What are the advantages? What are the risks?

cross-cultural training available to their international assignees and to some extent to their families (GMAC, 2008). However, investment in these activities often remains quite low (Dickmann *et al.*, 2006; Doherty and Dickmann, 2012). As early as 1987, Mendenhall and colleagues drew up a model of cross-cultural training that distinguished training methods, their rigour and duration in relation to cultural novelty and interaction. They argue that in a situation where the cultural stretch is low and the length of stay is short *information-giving* approaches would be suitable. These would include area and cultural briefings, the use of books and films from the destination country and moderate, 'survival-level' language training. *Affective* approaches would be more suitable when there are moderate levels of cultural differences and the stay is planned to be up to one year. These could consist of role-playing, critical incident discussions, case work, culture assimilation activities, stress reduction training and more intensive, yet still moderate levels of language instruction. In these situations the training length would also be more extensive. The longest training is seen to be needed for people going to destinations which are culturally highly distinct and who will stay for long terms akin to traditional expatriation. Mendenhall *et al.* (1987) suggest an *immersion* approach that includes assessment centres, field experiments, simulations, sensitivity training and extensive language instruction.

Obviously, the expatriates openness to other cultures (see above) and their willingness to act upon the new insights and attempt to adjust to the new environment have a major impact on how effective the training is likely to be. Pre-departure and post-arrival training and experience-based learning is only one step in the process of working successfully abroad. In addition, learning and cultural adaptation is a process which benefits from monitoring and feedback by others (e.g. a host national liaison person).

Table 11.5 Some advantages and drawbacks of sending home country nationals to work abroad

Advantages	Drawbacks
• Efficient coordination	• Adaptation of expatriates uncertain
• Effective communication	• Selection procedures prone to errors
• Direct control of foreign operations	• High costs
• Diffusing central values, norms and beliefs throughout the organisation	• Difficulty in constant mentoring during stay abroad
• Broadening the view of expatriates and chance of growth for expatriates	• Complicated personnel planing procedures
• Rapid substitution of expatriates possible	• Government restrictions
• No need of well-developed international internal labour market	• Private life of expatriates severely affected
• Appropriate for entry into international business	• Reduced career opportunities for locals
• Country-of-origin innovation	• High complexity for tax and benefits possible
• Attractiveness for home country careerists	• High failure rates
	• Utilisation of career capital after return can be difficult
	• Potential home–host country frictions
	• Re-integration may be difficult

Source: Adapted from International Human Resource Management, London: CIPD (Harris, H. Brewster, C., and Sparrow, P. 2003) p. 146, with permission from the publisher, the Chartered Institute of Personnel and Development, London, (www.cipd.co.uk).

Adjustment to the local environment

The process of cultural learning when individuals are living in a foreign culture is called adjustment or cultural adaptation. In this sense it is akin to acculturation. The concept is key in the global mobility literature as highly adjusted individuals are seen to perform well at work (Bhaskar-Shrinivas *et al.*, 2005). Much research builds on the work of Black (1988) and Black and colleagues (1992) who proposed a model that consists of three facets of adjustment: interaction, general and work adjustment. Socialising successfully with locals would be an element of interaction adjustment. Coping with the general living context of aspects such as climate, health provision, banking, shopping, and outside work entertainment would be part of general adjustment. Successfully mastering the diverse demands of the job in terms of specific responsibilities and expectations is related to work adjustment. While this concept has aroused considerable interest in the academic literature, it has been critiqued by Thomas and Lazarova (2006). Their key points were that the Black *et al.* concept is not sufficiently rooted in theory (more a measurement of three loosely defined and partially overlapping dimensions), that it may have overlooked other facets of adaptation and that it assumes a one-dimensional concept. Haslberger (2008) picks up these points and develops a more nuanced view of adjustment.

   Haslberger (2008) distinguishes between three dimensions of adjustment. The first is cognitive confidence related to an understanding of the host culture. For instance, Akpos, an expatriate in England, may experience how courteous and conflict-avoiding people are (Fox, 2005). Even when he stepped on the foot of an Englishman in the London Underground they would apologise. But Akpos' confidence level was lowered once he tried to jump a queue for

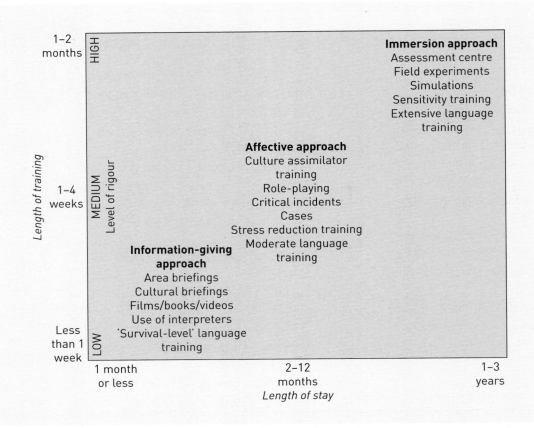

Figure 11.6 Cross-cultural training approach

Source: Adapted from Mendenhall *et al.*, 1987: 338.

a bus when he was in a hurry. Angry reactions made him rethink and adjust his behaviour. It took a while before he understood that fairness is a key value in English culture and that not queuing was a grave violation of this principle. Haslberger differentiates between the Akpos' cognitive confidence (not quite being able to explain the reactions to queue jumping) and the effectiveness of behaviour (not doing it again). His adjustment curve is depicted in Figure 11.7.

In addition, Haslberger suggests a third curve of emotions which often start off in a 'honeymoon phase' (Oberg, 1960). Over time, however, the novelty and excitement of living in a foreign, maybe even exotic, country wears off and the daily 'grind' of coping with differences that one may not fully understand affects emotions. Eventually, people surface from their 'culture shock' (Ward *et al.*, 2001) and both their emotions and cognitive confidence levels are likely to improve. Not everybody has to experience culture shock, in fact, if persons have had recent in-depth experience with the host culture their chances of avoiding culture shock are high (Takeuchi *et al.*, 2005). Overall, the individual adjustment patterns are likely to vary substantially and personal characteristics (Caligiuri, 2000), specific experiences, family influences and the host country context all have a strong bearing on the expatriate's adjustment.

International reward management

It is possible to have a variety of perspectives on the reward and performance elements in international mobility. In this chapter we will predominantly look at the individual and organisational issues. Employee pay and wider benefits can influence the sourcing,

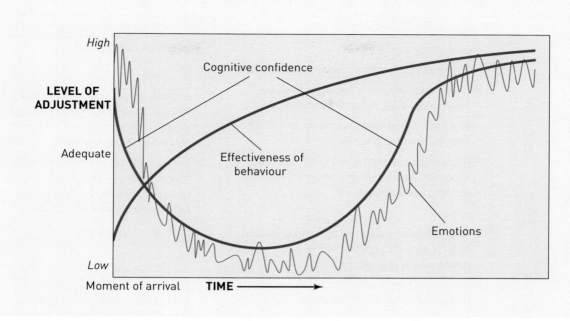

Figure 11.7 Adjustment curve with culture shock
Source: Haslberger, 2008.

performance management and retention activities and outcomes of companies (Beardwell and Claydon, 2010). In order to increase the chances of international assignees being motivated and productive, Suutari and Tornikoski (2001) suggest that mobility programmes need to have well-designed rewards programmes. MNCs have a range of choices when designing international compensation approaches. Organisations often want to achieve consistency, comparability and equity among their international staff group. Other considerations include cost-effectiveness of global transfers and ease of systems administration (Dowling *et al.*, 2008). As outlined above in the discussion on drivers of international work, expatriates often seek financial protection, location comfort and financial advancement.

Seven international reward approaches can be identified: negotiation/ad hoc, balance sheet, localisation, lump sum, cafeteria, regional systems and global (Briscoe and Schuler, 2004). All try to balance the conflicting pressures of attempting to be efficient and to save costs against the need to attract highly capable individuals to work abroad. The professional services firm Ernst and Young (2009) argues that companies increasingly tend to use either a home-based or a host-based approach. The home-based approach starts with exploring the salary, benefits and other remuneration elements of the individual in their current country of work. With the aim of not making the expatriate worse off, incentive components (such as housing allowances, hardship allowances, relocation money, educational grants) and equalisation adjustments (primarily cost-of-living adjustments, tax equalisation allowances and benefits adjustments) are factored in to reach the foreign compensation deal. The host country-based compensation approach can also be called the 'going rate approach' as it orients itself on the host country market rates of pay and benefits. The advantages of the home country-based approach lie in increasing the willingness of individuals to go on an assignment as they stand to benefit financially. It can, however, be administratively complex and is often highly costly for the organisation (Doherty and Dickmann, 2012). The host country-based approach has gained more popularity in recent times due to its cost-saving potential. However, it may struggle to find suitable candidates from high-wage countries to go to low-wage countries. A more specific discussion which models the diverse international remuneration approaches can be found in Dickmann and Baruch (2011).

Table 11.6 Organisational activities to foster successful international adjustment

Area		Organisational action	Some characteristics that would help
PRE-ASSIGNMENT	Job Design	• Give discretion in the job • Clarify job expectations and responsibilities • Gain agreement as to job objectives between individual, home and host country • Provide overlap with incumbent to facilitate 'hitting the ground running' • Align any other conflicting expectations regarding performance standards, job, working environment, etc.	*Job design choices:* • In most cases, choose a job that the candidate will find only a slight stretch. Adjustment to a new team and new culture is already a challenge • For earmarked top leaders the stretch might be larger. This might include changing divisions, functions or more radical job content alterations
PRE-ASSIGNMENT	Selection and negotiation	• Sophisticated selection factoring in personality factors, soft competencies, performance and potential • Involve partner in selection and consider extended family responsibilities • Use psychometric and other instruments and give feedback to candidate and partner regarding cross-cultural strengths and weaknesses • Match candidate's profile to inter-cultural job demands of organisation and international vacancies • Provide realistic job, local team and country previews (and also 'look–see visits')	*Individual characteristics:* • self-confidence • Willingness to learn about different cultures and business environments • Inter-personal orientation • Good communication skills • Willingness to critically review own values and norms • Willingness to critically review own values and norms • Openness
PRE-ASSIGNMENT	Administrative and logistical support	• Provide effective administrative support in relation to the international mobility framework, compensation and benefit questions • Provide good logistical support and high quality in terms of moving abroad, accommodation (abroad and at home), health insurance, banking, schooling, return visits etc. • Guarantee security as much as possible and provide protection in high risk areas • Monitor own and service provider activities and gain expatriate feedback for improvements	*Administrative issues:* • Set an end-of-assignment date in order to avoid assignments that 'drag on' • Consider periodically whether the assignment objectives have been fulfilled and, therefore, keep the option of early return open • Provide support through corporate sponsor, mentors and coaches who proactively approach the assignees at regular intervals

Table 11.6 (cont.)

Area		Organisational action	Some characteristics that would help
DURING ASSIGNMENT	Social environment	• Encourage local national employees to provide support to new assignees and families • Collect and provide information regarding social, religious, sport, cultural organisations and enable expatriates and their families to join these • Develop social support networks • Provide an Employee Assistance Programme (EAP) for people experiencing culture shock and train local managers to recognise symptoms	*Social facilitation:* • Consider setting up local 'buddies' for expats and partners • Support partners in carving out meaningful roles for themselves • Design organisational approaches that encourage host country nationals to view expatriates as 'ingroup' rather than 'outgroup' • Brief and prepare locals with liaison roles
DURING ASSIGNMENT	Training and development	• Provide rigorous training for increased job demands; ideally linked to organisational configuration • Provide inter-cultural training (pre-departure and post-arrival) and language classes • Include partner in the training • Provide team-building initiatives together with new team • Provide (where useful) extensive briefings to local employees regarding role and function of assignee • Enable interaction with repatriates from assignment region/area	*T&D considerations:* • Distinguish between local position requirements, global or international control, coordination and innovation responsibilities • Distinguish between general communication skills and development of personality of individual • Distinguish between work and social environment
DURING ASSIGNMENT	Reward management	• Create salary transparency and avoid large pay differentials between locals and expatriates • Understand individual drivers to link compensation and incentives to these • Minimise insecurity and tax exposure to both individuals and organisations • Understand the diverse social security and taxation systems and find a solution that balances organisational and individual needs	*Design considerations:* • Transparency if possible • Perceived equity within expatriates population • Balancing need for attracting highly capable individuals with cost-saving pressures • Minimise personal risks to individuals (tax, social benefits) • Minimise organisational risks (e.g. corporate tax) • Keep administrative complexity low

(Continued)

Table 11.6 Organisational activities to foster successful international adjustment (cont.)

Area		Organisational action	Some characteristics that would help
DURING ASSIGNMENT	**Career issues**	• Link selection to individual's long-term career plan and organisational career management (avoid 'out of sight, out of mind' syndrome) • Foster the acquisition of knowing how, knowing why and knowing whom capital • Design support mechanisms such as business sponsors, formal and informal networks, shadow career planning	*Career planning:* • The mutual dependency of individuals and organisation is especially strong during an international assignment. There is a case for more long-term career planning which looks likely to aid retention. • Consider NOT to promote on the way out – instead, actively consider to promote upon repatriation • Consider expatriation to centres of excellence and ways of applying insights and using social capital in the job upon return

Source: Based on Dickmann and Baruch 2011: 194–5 future developments.

Career capital during the assignment

One of the key aims for individuals working abroad is to advance their career. In order to assess this, authors have gone beyond the actual promotions to look at modern career theory. Using a resource-based view, DeFillippi and Arthur (1994) outline how to behave in order to acquire career capital. Career capital proponents such as Inkson and Arthur (2001) argue that individuals will benefit from investing in their skills, knowledge, abilities (know how), their social networks (know whom) and in mustering their inner drives and motivations (know why). International assignments have a substantial impact on these three ways of knowing with individuals and organisations devising strategies and interventions to increase career capital (Dickmann and Doherty, 2010).

This concept is also called the intelligent career and while it is likely that individuals will acquire new skills, knowledge and abilities when working abroad, and change their outlook on life (which is linked to their identity and knowing why) the social capital effects of foreign work may be less positive (Dickmann and Harris, 2005). Expatriates normally gain more international social contacts and are certain to acquire more host country connections. However, they are often 'off the radar' and, consequently, their home country networks may suffer. This is particularly damaging if the career system in their company is highly informal and if they are away from the head office where key promotion decisions are taken. This, then, can endanger their career path with a career 'wobble' upon return being likely (Doherty *et al.*, 2008). Therefore, designing support mechanisms such as business sponsors or mentors may help the expatriates to have a more positive experience and repatriation. Moreover, shadow career planning and the explicit acknowledgement and endorsement of the expatriate's need for home networking can help to reduce the risks for assignees (Dickmann and Doherty, 2010; Harris and Dickmann, 2005).

Overall, however, the large majority of expatriates state in interviews that they have acquired career capital and that they are confident they are more valuable to the organisation (Dickmann *et al.*, 2005). In turn, their employers devise systems to enable these expatriates to add to their career capital as this is seen to be positive for current performance and long-term leadership pipelines in organisations (Dickmann and Doherty, 2010). This makes it crucial, for both the individuals and the organisations, that repatriates can use their expanded skills, insights and networks in their home countries.

V After international work: repatriation, retention and long-term career issues

Repatriation is sometimes seen as the 'toughest assignment of all' (Hurn, 1999). The reasons relate to the problems that some individuals and organisations face when returning from working abroad and have been recorded in a range of surveys (GMAC, 2008) and articles (Lazarova and Cerdin, 2007; Stahl and Cerdin, 2004).

The organisational perspective

The employment and promotion perspective of repatriates is worse in times of economic hardship and slow growth (Huang *et al.*, 2006) so that the banking and sovereign debt crises of the early years of the third millennium decreased the positive prospects of returners. In addition, some firms have poor planning processes, so that they will not have assigned attractive positions for their returning assignees. This may be compounded when an enterprise is undergoing a restructuring as outlined by Dickmann and Doherty (2006) in the case of a tobacco firm that forced 40 per cent of repatriates to leave. In turn, many expatriates feel that they have become more marketable and may look for new challenges outside their organisations (Tams and Arthur, 2007). Overall, there is a repatriation and retention challenge. In order to alleviate these problems, Lazarova and Caligiuri (2001) suggested 11 HR practices:

1　Pre-departure briefings on what to expect during repatriation
2　Career planning sessions
3　Guarantee/agreement outlining the type of position expatriates will be placed in upon repatriation
4　Mentoring programmes while on assignment
5　Re-orientation programmes about the changes in the company
6　Repatriation training seminars on the emotional response following repatriation
7　Financial counselling and financial/tax assistance
8　Lifestyle assistance and counselling on changes likely to occur in an expatriate's life on their return
9　Continuous communication with the home office
10　Visible signs that the company values international experience
11　Communication with the home office about the details of the repatriation process.

In fact, many organisations admit that they are not effective at repatriation planning and support and many individuals consider leaving their employers (Dickmann *et al.*, 2005). However, if individuals stay longer than one year after returning, their retention rates over the next two years become very high with hardly any churn (Doherty and Dickmann, 2012). Companies that are seen as successful in retaining expatriates often heed the 11 factors outlined by Lazarova and Caligiuri and have integrated their international mobility with a general career system, managing the acquisition and utilisation of know how and social capital (Dickmann and Doherty, 2010; MacDonald and Arthur, 2005; Riusala and Suutari, 2004).

The individual perspective

In an ideal scenario, repatriates look forward to 'return' and are able to apply what they have learnt abroad. Unfortunately, the reality can look very different. A common occurrence is reverse culture shock. It arises out of changes in the repatriate's home culture and context, developments in the firm (head office) they are working in and because they themselves have changed during their experiences abroad. In addition, there is often an element of frustration arising from the loss of some of the perks of working abroad (financial, social, kudos) and moving from being a 'big fish in a small pond' to a more normal position of being a 'small fish in a big pond'. So, what could have been a 'honeymoon' of returning and re-engaging with friends and the wider context can be complicated by worries about the current job, progression opportunities, financial and social frustration. There are some parallels between how individuals cope in this phase and the culture shock when they move to work abroad. Some authors suggest that the 'career wobble' that may coincide with a reverse culture shock may last about a year for many people (Doherty *et al.*, 2008).

What can individuals do to increase their chances of successfully re-integrating both into their home countries and into their firm? One approach is to make oneself attractive to one's own or other employers as well as creating realistic expectations (within oneself and in others). Dickmann and Doherty (2010) outline a range of career capital activities that increase the knowledge, skills, abilities and insights that expatriates acquire when working abroad. It is crucial to explore early on (even at the pre-assignment, planning stage) how these can be used upon return. For instance, trying to go to a foreign centre of excellence can make the acquired know how more valuable for the organisation. Moreover, international workers and returnees should have a keen understanding of their social capital and consciously network with those who can help in the process of getting a good job upon return. In addition, discussions with mentors, sponsors, HRM and other stakeholders prior to return are important in terms of one's own realistic expectations as well as influencing the organisation's thinking towards a suitable repatriate position.

Table 11.7 outlines good practices in expatriate retention. It expands on work by Dickmann and Baruch (2011) and goes beyond the Lazarova and Caligiuri (2001) recommendations. The table is primarily based on what organisations can do and also covers individual activities to improve repatriation success.

Summary

This chapter has presented key considerations in international HRM. First, it has defined IHRM, in contrast to comparative HRM, as the IHRM configurations – strategies, structures, policies and practices – that are used to manage people in international organisations, be they for-profit or not. Second, from a competitive advantage, resource-based perspective we have identified a number of types of multinational organisation. The key rationale was linked to creating competitive edge in a variety of dimensions, most prominently in cost (global efficiency through integration), quality (local responsiveness through product/service differentiation) and innovation (worldwide knowledge networking). Third, the chapter introduced a number of IHRM models that charted the expanse of the global people management arena. Fourth, the text shifted its perspective towards more operational aspects of international working. In so doing, it has distinguished between pre-assignment, during the assignment and post-return issues of how organisations can manage their globally mobile staff. Crucially, we have also outlined the concerns, emotions, actions, identity and capability changes of global workers on their international journeys, leading to a longer-term perspective than normally taken. Many recommendations on how to manage international staff and how to behave as global careerists are summarised and presented in the chapter.

Table 11.7 After the assignment – good practices in expatriate retention

Area	Examples of policies and practices
Organisational strategy and structure	• Clear and attractive strategy to internationalise
	• Attractive degree of existing internationalisation
	• Little or no significant gap between statements of top management and implementation
	• Adequate organisational configuration
	• High kudos of international work

Table 11.7 (cont.)

Area	Examples of policies and practices
International mobility policies and practices	• Staffing policies are perceived to be fair or advantageous • Selection looks at a range of factors, including personality factors linked into adjustment and self-adjustment upon return • Pre-return preparation for the job • Ongoing support for time after return • Long-range planning for repatriation • Networking opportunities • Continuous communication with home
Career	• Long-term career planning • Re-entry planning • Career advancement • Mentor system/International work sponsor system
Development	• Systematic development of professional skills • Systematic development of personal skills • Systematic development of leadership skills • Repatriation seminars on the emotional response • Financial and tax counselling, advice and help for time after return
Job variables	• Job challenge • Ability to use new global capabilities • No reduced responsibility and autonomy
Financial impact	• Rewards for pursuing an international assignment • Rewards for developing an international perspective • Rewards for developing a worldwide network • Rewards for developing global skills, abilities and knowledge • Tie-over pay
Personal drivers and expectations	• Pre-return and after return dialogues to manage expectations/build realistic pre-return expectations • Briefing and update regarding organisational structure, goals, politics and changes in the new locations
Family	• Help for partner to find meaningful activity such as job and career re-entry • Help for family to (re-)settle
Individual activities	• Work on keeping social networks current and useful • Engage in work that takes place in the location of return so that knowledge remains current & expectations realistic • Reflect on personal/identity changes and what that means for life after return • Expect financial and status changes • Work on acquiring transferable capabilities and/or liaise with future expatriates in order to exchange insights • Balance perceived career capital management/return planning deficits in your organisation and proactively address these • Prepare, guide and help family through the repatriation transition

Source: Based on Dickmann and Baruch, 2011: 234.

CASE STUDY 11.1

AIMING TO PRACTISE TRANSNATIONAL PEOPLE MANAGEMENT, ACHIEVING COGNOFEDERATE IHRM

MICHAEL DICKMANN

InnovationCo was founded in the second half of the nineteenth century in Germany. It produces fast-moving consumer goods (FMCGs) and offers several thousand products in a variety of international markets. In the early twentieth century, the company founded its first foreign affiliate in Switzerland. In order to expand exports InnovationCo established operations in a further seven European countries before the Second World War. In the 1950s, production plants were founded in several countries in Europe, South America and Africa and the company started to sell in Asia. Over time, production was increasingly located abroad and the firm became more and more international to the extent of having two-thirds of staff located outside Germany at the turn of the millennium.

In its production processes, InnovationCo uses a pragmatic balance of global integration and local responsiveness. Growth had mostly been achieved through the acquisition of foreign and domestic companies. This created a status quo of differentiation which the firm wanted to shift towards more integration. The key driver to standardise production was seen to be in the increased scale effects and efficiency advantages. The diverse history of its acquired parts, their administrative heritage, different production technologies and customer insights, however, represented a chance to increase worldwide innovation.

IHRM Standardisation

InnovationCo's staff is widely spread geographically. InnovationCo's HRM combines a pragmatic use of local advantages and a German approach. InnovationCo's IHRM was described by its HRM board member as wishing to harmonise the philosophy while adapting to local methods. This integrated philosophy led to standardised international leadership guidelines, created and agreed by all European HR heads. Overall, IHRM principles and broad objectives were highly standardised. In contrast, InnovationCo chose only to cooperate in a few operational areas as these were deemed to be the methods that are best developed and applied locally (see Table 11.8). Overall, the degree of integration depended on the perceived importance of the area, its contribution to the company's success and the determination of the head office to shape worldwide policies according to its wishes. The motto was that it wanted to give local operations its freedom. This led to locally idiosyncratic HRM approaches which were tolerated by the head office.

IHRM knowledge networking

There was tight consultation and cooperation between the German head office and its subsidiaries in terms of IHRM policies and practices. This was facilitated through a conference of all HRM heads and six working meetings of all European HR top executives per year. The aim was to elicit local ideas that could be further developed and then introduced globally. The direction of knowledge exchange was multilateral and IHRM suggestions were derived from any part of the company network.

The open and intensive international communication made it hard to impose the head office view against joint resistance from foreign affiliates. In fact, a top HR manager from the head office argued that there was no intention to be the 'Vatican'– it was more seen as a heterarchical relationship that would lead to innovation on the road to transnationalism. However, there was a disadvantage to this system: higher knowledge networking did not mean that IHRM cross-border control became easier or more efficient. In the absence of strong international control, more informal, sophisticated integration mechanisms were needed. At least in terms of IHRM, InnovationCo did not achieve the transnationalism it aimed for – instead it had become a cognofederate with some development of local solutions that some HR top managers disliked. For instance, they wanted to have a more integrated training and development policy, but had encountered local resistance.

Table 11.8 IHRM in InnovationCo: philosphy/principles level

	Philosophy/principles level
Standardisation	
General HRM	*Leadership*: international principles and guidelines
	Security: guidelines related to healthy work environment, job security through standard work contracts
	Other – innovation: principle of international cooperation to elicit best ideas and learning
Recruitment and Selection	Search for global best talent
Training and development	Commitment to the development of staff, preference for dual vocational training to be used in local operations
Career management	International equality of career prospects, International assignment policy
Performance management	International principles and guidelines
Remuneration	Comparability of task and performance-related compensation
Knowledge networking	
General HRM	*Development and review*: concurrent international development of HR principles, multinational development of HR strategy, feedback on implementation from local units
	Control and coordination: little international coordination of HR budgets, no local HR budgets set or reviewed in headquarters, only basic local reporting of results (e.g. headcounts), one global meeting, bi-national monthly regional meetings, frequent visits
Recruitment and selection	International discussion of long-term international resourcing needs, no global committee (other than for board members)
Training and development	Cross-nationally coordinated long-range aims for future leaders developed, cultural cornerstones defined
Career management	Top career deciders drawn from headquarters, career principles sometimes formally discussed in European head of HR group
Performance management	General international performance management principles discussed cross-border
Remuneration	Headquarters HR management set guidelines

Sources: Based on Dickmann and Baruch, 2011; Dickmann *et al.*, 2009.

Table 11.9 IHRM in InnovationCo: operational level

	Operational level
Standardisation	
General HRM	Competency framework
Recruitment and selection	Resourcing local, using diverse criteria
Training and development	Some cross-cultural seminars and top management development integrated, dual vocational training not implemented everywhere
Career management	Integrated approach for upper/middle management (highest four levels); database of high potentials (some local units opted out)
Performance management	Standard processes and forms for top four management levels (management review and target dialogue)
Remuneration	Integration around Hay for upper five levels, lower management local; some local variation possible
Knowledge networking	
General HRM	Explicit feedback in European HR director committee on overarching systems and instruments every two months. Global competency framework designed in international (European) cooperation. High frequency of international HR meetings and visits
Recruitment and selection	International discussion of diverse selection instruments
Training and development	Head office design and international review of some international management seminars; a few have explicit cultural aims
Career management	Some cross-border exchange of data on high potentials; coordinated through more than 1 per cent of staff abroad on international assignments
Performance management	No international review of performance carried out
Remuneration	Central remuneration committee reviews rewards, formal cross-border discussion of experiences

Sources: Based on Dickmann and Baruch, 2011; Dickmann *et al.*, 2009.

Questions

1 Why do you think InnovationCo used the specific standardisation and knowledge networking approach in IHRM? What other options did it have?

2 What are the advantages and disadvantages associated with their IHRM?

3 Consider a worldwide operating organisation that you know well: how does its approach to international HRM differ from that of InnovationCo?

4 What are the possible effects on global careers for managers in InnovationCo? What would international HR careers look like?

CASE STUDY 11.2

GET ME READY, 'CAUSE HERE I COME: HR AND EMPLOYER PREPAREDNESS IN INDIAN MNCs

DHARA SHAH

TechIn Solutions is an Indian-headquartered consulting and IT (information technology) services multinational company (MNC) with its headquarters in India. It has operations in over 44 countries, an annual turnover of about US$1.13 billion, and more than 32,000 employees. The organisation has development centres in India, North America, the UAE, the UK, Hungary, Egypt, Singapore, Malaysia and Australia. Due to the escalating issues of overdependence on a single market and visa-processing restrictions for IT workers in the USA, the organisation has tried to diversify into new markets such as Singapore, Malaysia and Australia.

TechIn started its operations in the late 1980s by capitalising on the fast-growing demand for human resources in the IT sector. By the late 1990s, the company had moved up the quality ladder, offering software consultancy as well as other services. The deep domain-specific needs of its global customers required it to set up subsidiary operations in different countries. To meet the requirements of the new markets, it also had to send many software professionals to client sites to engage in technical work, onboard support, liaising and securing more business from the clients. Thus, the software professionals sent on international assignments became crucial to the company's success. However, the turnover rate of IT professionals was very high and costly for TechIn, due to competition with Western and other large Indian IT MNCs. It also delayed client projects, reduced quality and increased costs. Thus, retention of its IT professionals is a critical concern for the organisation and international staffing policies and practices of the company are important.

Senior managers claimed that TechIn adopted a geocentric approach, but more than 85 per cent of the employees at the Australian subsidiary were of Indian origin. The managers revealed that one of the major staffing challenges they faced in the Australian market was attracting people to work for them in Australia, as they did not have an established brand image here, and this was combined with the liability of the company's country of origin (the developing country of India). This had meant that they had to bring employees from India to work in Australia and these employees were vital for TechIn success. Thus, one of the main concerns for TechIn was retaining these IT professionals given their expertise and client knowledge.

TechIn also wanted to create an image as a global company and not be identified as an Indian company. Keeping up with the growing demands of the markets and competition, the Indian senior managers asserted that TechIn was trying to move away from being a hierarchical organisation to adopting a more decentralised structure in which the employees were empowered to act independently and the subsidiary offices were given the autonomy to adopt local HRM practices. However, given that the majority of the staff were of Indian origin, an Australian manager observed that Indian culture influenced the decision-making process and that there were issues with many Indian IT expatriates in relation to communication and misunderstandings caused by lack of cultural and communication knowledge. So what were the experiences of TechIn's Indian IT expatriates on international assignments in Australia?

The IT expatriates saw TechIn's expatriation process as client-driven and their selection for the assignment was usually rushed. The need to respond to clients meant their organisation had no control over when they had to leave for the assignment, with quite a number of them having had less than one week to prepare for the assignment. Expatriation and relocation were difficult, as this did not allow them to attend training sessions or provide them with the opportunity to mentally prepare themselves for the assignment. This they believed, in turn, impacted on their initial days in the host country.

The IT expatriates felt that little was done to prepare them for the host country; technical competence seemed to be the key, so that if there was a request from the client, an available person with the required technical skill set was sent on the assignment regardless of their potential ability to cope with the new context. One expatriate explained:

I felt that the initial phase could have been made better if organisations could have provided proper training and support and the expectations of the assignment were set out properly. It was bad enough with all the other stresses and then, lack of training actually lowered my self-esteem and I felt at a loss in every way.

Ranbir

This IT worker, along with many others asserted that it was extremely difficult during the initial stages to adjust due to lack of cultural or country knowledge or understanding of their expectations in the host country. This had a significant impact on the self-esteem and overall adjustment of most during the assignment. The issues in terms of language, accents, cultural differences and communication made them feel threatened, and sometimes they believed they had reacted in a way that was not acceptable, causing misunderstandings with the host-country managers. The organisation provided very little support in the initial settling-in period. While TechIn provided two weeks' accommodation, the IT expatriates were expected to find and move into their own accommodation thereafter. The organisation also expected them to start work within a day or two of landing in Australia. This only exacerbated the already difficult transition of moving to a host country.

For the workers going on their first assignment or travelling to Australia for the first time, establishing themselves at the client location and adjusting to a new country, the added pressure of looking for accommodation, opening bank accounts and organising contracts for phones, electricity and the like made it a stressful time for them. One reported:

It was very hard to concentrate on work and do everything. I used to search on the internet for the accommodation … so I just had one day, Saturday, to go and look for accommodation and I did not have the car and so had to walk to the different places from one lane to another, so the maximum you can manage is two houses in one day. And in Sydney, if you do not have rental history, it is quite tough to get accommodation; that was one of the major problems we all faced.

Raj

This is an interesting example of how lack of support can impede on the expatriates during the initial months, which can impact on their attitudes towards work. Organisational support was also highlighted as a significant factor contributing to the adjustment of the IT workers in the new environment and lack of support augmented the difficulties in the host country. Most of the respondents talked about how they felt neglected by their organisation. All of these factors caused dissatisfaction among the participants, many of whom considered leaving the organisation should the opportunity arise. The nature of IT work, added to the demands of living and working in a culturally new environment with a lack of preparation and support networks from employers, was found to influence their experiences and commitment to the organisation and their intentions to leave the organisation.

Questions

1 What are the implications for IHRM from the above case?

2 In regards to the literature, what lessons can the IT organisation in this case learn?

3 What issues can you identify in regards to the preparation and support provided to the IT expatriate/s going on an international assignment?

4 Would having enough time to prepare for the assignment resolve the issues that the IT expatriate will experience in the Australia? Or are there bigger issues that need to be considered?

Bibliography

Adler, N.J. and Ghadar, F. (1990) 'Strategic human resource management: a global perspective', pp. 235–60, in Pieper R., (ed.) *Human Resource Management: An International Comparison*, New York: de Gruyter.

Ang, S., Van Dyne, L., Koh, C., Ng, K., Templer, K., Tay-Lee, S. and Chandrasekar, N. (2007) 'Cultural intelligence: its measurement and effects on cultural judgement and decision making, cultural adaptation and task performance', *Management and Organization Review,* Vol.3, No.3, 335–71.

Bartlett, C. and Ghoshal, S. (1989) *Managing Across Borders*, London: Hutchinson Business.

Baruch, Y., Dickmann, M., Altman, Y. and Bournois, F. (2013) 'Exploring international work: types and dimensions of global careers'. *The International Journal of Human Resource Management.*

Beardwell, J. and Claydon, T. (2010) *Human Resource Management: A Contemporary Approach* (6th edn), Harlow: FT Prentice Hall.

Bhaskar-Shrinivas, P., Harrison, D.A., Shaffer, M.A. and Luk, D.M. (2005) 'Input-based and time-based models of international adjustment: meta-analytic evidence and theoretical extensions', *Academy of Management Journal,* Vol.48, No.2, 257–81.

Bird, A. and Osland, J. (2004) 'Global competencies: an introduction', pp. 57–80, in Lane, H.W., Maznevski, M.L., Mendenhall, M.E. and McNett J. (eds) *The Blackwell Handbook of Global Management,* Oxford: Blackwell Publishing.

Black, J.S. (1988) 'Work role transitions: a study of American expatriate managers in Japan', *Journal Of International Business Studies,* Vol.30, No.2, 277–94.

Black, S.J. and Stephens, G.K. (1989) 'The influence of the partner on American expatriate adjustment and intent to stay in Pacific Rim overseas assignments', *Journal of Management*, Vol.15, No.4, 529–44.

Black, J.S., Gregersen, H.B. and Mendenhall, M.E. (1992) *Global Assignments: Successfully Expatriating and Repatriating International Managers*, San Francisco, CA: Jossey-Bass.

Bonache, J. and Dickmann, M. (2008) 'The transfer of strategic HR know-how in MNCs: mechanism, barriers and initiatives', pp. 67–83, in Dickmann, M., Brewster, C. and Sparrow, C. (eds) *International Human Resource Management: A European Perspective* (2nd edn), Abingdon: Routledge.

Bonache, J., Sanchez, J. and Zárraga-Oberty, C. (2009) 'The interaction of expatriate pay differential and expatriate inputs on host country nationals' pay unfairness', *International Journal of Human Resource Management,* Vol.20, No.10, 21–35.

Briscoe, D. and Schuler, R. (2004) *International Human Resource Management* (2nd edn), London: Routledge.

Caligiuri, P.M. (2000). 'Selecting expatriates for personality characteristics: a moderating effect of personality on the relationship between host national contact and cross-cultural adjustment', *Management International Review,* Vol.40, No.1, 61–80.

Carlos, A. and Nicholas, S. (1988) 'Giants of an earlier capitalism: the chartered trading companies as modern multinationals', *Business History Review,* Vol.62, No.3, 398–419.

De Cieri, H. and Dowling, P. (1999) 'Strategic human resource management in multinational enterprises: theoretical and empirical developments', in P.M. Wright, Dyer, L.D. and Boudreau, J.W. (eds) *Research in Personnel and Human Resource Management: Strategic Human Resources in the Twenty-First Century,* 4th Supplement. Stamford, CT: JAI Press.

DeFillippi, R. and Arthur, M. (1994) 'The boundaryless career: a competency-based perspective', *Journal of Organizational Behavior*, Vol.15, 307–24.

Dickmann, M. and Baruch, Y. (2011) *Global Careers*, London: Routledge.

Dickmann, M. and Doherty, N. (2006). *Measuring the Value of International Assignments Report*, Cranfield: Research Report for PricewaterhouseCoopers.

Dickmann, M. and Doherty, N. (2010) 'Exploring organisational and individual career goals, interactions and outcomes of international assignments', *Thunderbird International Review*, Vol.52, No.4, 313–24.

Dickmann, M. and Harris, H. (2005) 'Developing career capital for global careers: the role of international assignments', *Journal of World Business*, Vol.40, No.4, 399–408.

Dickmann, M. and Mills, T. (2010). 'The importance of intelligent career and location considerations: exploring the decision to go to London', *Personnel Review*. Vol.39, No.1, 116–34.

Dickmann, M. and Müller-Camen, M. (2006) 'A typology of international human resource management strategies and processes', *International Journal of Human Resource Management*, Vol.17, No.4, 580–601.

Dickmann, M., Doherty, N. and Mills, T. (2005) *Understanding Mobility: Influence Factors in the Decision to Accept an International Assignment, Repatriation Issues and Long-term Career Considerations*. Report, Cranfield: Cranfield School of Management.

Dickmann, M., Doherty, N. and Mills, T. (2008) 'Exploring differences of drivers of company-sent and self-initiated expatriates'. Paper presented at the *Academy of Management Symposium,* 'New global nomads: examining diverse forms of international mobility', Anaheim, CA, August.

Dickmann, M., Johnson, A. and Doherty, N. (2006) *Measuring the Value of International Assignments*, London: PricewaterhouseCoopers and Cranfield School of Management.

Dickmann, M., Müller-Camen, M. and Kelliher, C. (2009) 'Exploring standardisation and knowledge networking processes in transnational human resource management'; *Personnel Review,* Vol.38, No.1, 5–25.

Doherty, N. and Dickmann, M. (2012) 'Measuring the return on investment in international assignments: an action research approach', *International Journal of Human Resource Management,* Vol.23, No.16, 3434–54.

Doherty, N., Dickmann, M. and Mills, T. (2011) 'Exploring the motives of company-backed and self-initiated expatriates', *International Journal of Human Resource Management,* Vol.22, No.3, 595–611.

Doherty, N., Brewster, C., Suutari, V. and Dickmann, M. (2008) 'Repatriation: the end or the middle?', pp. 174–91, in Dickmann, M., Brewster, C. and Sparrow, P. (eds) *International Human Resource Management: The European Perspective,* London: Routledge.

Dowling, P. (1999) 'Completing the puzzle: issues in the field of international human resource management', *Management International Review*, Special Issue No.3, 31.

Dowling, P., Festing, M. and Engle, A. (2008) *International Human Resource Management: Managing People in a Multinational Context* (5th edn), London: Thomson Learning.

ECA (2010) *Managing Mobility Survey*, London: Employment Conditions Abroad.

Edström, A. and Galbraith, J.R. (1977) 'Transfer of managers as a coordination and control strategy in multinational organizations', *Administrative Science Quarterly*, Vol.22, No.2, 248–63.

Edwards, T. and Rees, C. (2006) *International Human Resource Management: Globalization, National Systems and Multinational Companies*, Harlow: FT/Prentice Hall.

Ernst and Young (2009) *Expatriate Policy Survey*, Zurich: Ernst and Young.

Fox, K. (2005) *Watching the English: The Hidden Rules of English Behaviour*, London: Hodder & Stoughton.

GMAC (2008) *Global Relocation Trends Survey,* Woodridge, IL: GMAC Global Relocation Services.

GMAC Global Relocation Services (2009) *Global Relocation Trends: 2009 Survey Report*, Oak Brook, IL: GMAC Global Relocation Services.

Hailey, J. and Harry, W. (2008) 'Localization: a strategic response to globalization', pp. 19–38, in Dickmann, M., Brewster, C. and Sparrow, P. (eds) *International Human Resource Management: The European Perspective,* London: Routledge.

Harris, H. and Brewster, C. (1999) 'The coffee-machine system: how international selection really works', *International Journal of Human Resource Management*, Vol.10, No.3, 488–500.

Harris, H. and Dickmann, M. (2005) *The CIPD Guide on International Management Development*, London: Chartered Institute of Personnel and Development.

Harris, H., Brewster, C. and Sparrow, P. (2003) *International Human Resource Management*, London: CIPD.

Harvey, M. (1995) 'The impact of dual-career families on international relocations', *Human Resource Management Review*, Vol.5, No.3, 223–44.

Harzing, A.-W. (2000) 'An empirical analysis and extension of the Bartlett and Ghoshal typology of multinational companies', *Journal of International Business Studies,* Vol.31, No.1, 101–20.

Haslberger, A. (2008) 'Expatriate adjustment: a more nuanced view', pp. 130–49, in Dickmann, M., Brewster, C. and Sparrow P., (eds) *International Human Resource Management: A European Perspective*, London: Routledge.

Haslberger, A. and Zehetner, K. (2008) 'Cosmopolitan appeal: what makes a city attractive to expatriates and how do they benefit? The example of Vienna, Austria'. Paper presented at *4th Workshop on Expatriation, EIASM*, Las Palmas de Gran Canarias, Spain, October 2008.

Hennan, D.A. and Perlmutter, H.V. (1979) *Multinational Organizational Development*, Reading, MA: Addison-Wesley.

Howe-Walsh, L. and Schyns, B. (2010) 'Self-initiated expatriation: implications for HRM', *The International Journal of Human Resource Management,* Vol.21, No.2, 260–73.

Huang, T.J., Chi, S.H. and Lawler, J.S. (2005) 'The relationship between expatriates' personality traits and their adjustment to international assignments', *International Journal of Human Resource Management,* Vol.16, No.9, 1656–70.

Hurn. B.J. (1999) 'Repatriation – The toughest assignment of all, *Industrial and Commercial Training*, Vol.31, No.6, 224–28.

Inkson, K. and Arthur, M. (2001) 'How to be a successful career capitalist', *Organizational Dynamics,* Vol.30, No.1, 48–60.

Inkson, K., Arthur, M.B., Pringle, J. and Barry, S. (1997) 'Expatriate assignment versus overseas experience: contrasting models of international human resource development', *Journal of World Business,* Vol.32, No.4, 351–68.

Larsen, H.H. (2004) 'Global career as dual dependency between the organization and the individual', *Journal of Management Development*, Vol.23, No.9, 860–9.

Lazarova, M. and Caligiuri, P. (2001) 'Retaining repatriates: the role of organizational support practices', *Journal of World Business*, Vol.36, No.4, 389–401.

Lazarova, M. and Cerdin, J.-L. (2007) 'Revisiting repatriation concerns: organizational support vs. career and contextual influences', *Journal of International Business Studies*, Vol.38, No.3, 404–29.

Leong, S.M. and Tan, C.T. (1993) 'Managing across borders: an empirical test of the Bartlett and Ghoshal [1989] organizational typology', *Journal of International Business Studies,* Vol.24, No.3, 419–48.

Leung, K., Zhu, Y. and Ge, C. (2009) 'Compensation disparity between locals and expatriates: moderating the effects of perceived injustice in foreign multinationals in China', *Journal of World Business,* Vol.44, No.1, 85–93.

MacDonald, S. and Arthur, N. (2005). 'Connecting career management to repatriation adjustment', *Career Development International*, Vol.10, No.2, 145–58.

Mendenhall, M., Dunbar, E. and Oddou, G. (1987) 'Expatriate selection, training and career-pathing: a review and critique', *Human Resource Management*, Vol.26, No.3, 331–45.

Milliman, J. and Von Glinow, A. (1990) 'A life cycle approach to strategic international human resource management in MNCs', *Research in Personnel and Human Resources Management*, Supp. 2, 21–35.

Oberg, K. (1960) 'Cultural shock: adjustment to new cultural environments', *Practical Anthropology,* Vol.7, July–August, 177–82.

Peiperl, M. and Jonsen, K. (2007) 'Global careers', pp. 350–71, in Gunz, H. and Peiperl, M. (eds) *Handbook of Career Studies*, Thousand Oaks, CA: Sage.

Perlmutter, H. (1969) 'The tortuous evolution of the multinational corporation', *Columbia Journal of World Business*, Vol.4, No.1, 9–18.

Porter, M. (1985) *Competitive Advantage*, New York: Free Press.

Prahalad, C.K. and Doz, Y. (1987) *The Multinational Mission: Balancing Local Demands and Global Vision*, New York: The Free Press.

Richardson, J. and Mallon, M. (2005) 'Careers interrupted? The case of the self-directed expatriate', *Journal of World Business*, Vol.40, No.4, 409–20.

Riusala, K. and Suutari, V. (2004) 'International knowledge transfers through expatriates', *Thunderbird International Review*, Vol.46, No.6, 743–70.

Schuler, R.S., Dowling, P.J. and De Cieri, H. (1993) 'An integrative framework of strategic international human resource management', *Journal of Management*, Vol.19, No.2, 419–59.

Sparrow, P., Brewster, C. and Harris, H. (2004) *Globalizing Human Resource Management,* London: Routledge.

Stahl, G. and Cerdin, J.-L. (2004) 'Global careers in French and German multinational corporations', *Journal of Management Development*, Vol.23, No.9, 885–902.

Suutari, V. and Tornikoski, C. (2001) 'The challenge of expatriate compensation: the sources of satisfaction and dissatisfaction among expatriates', *International Journal of Human Resource Management*, Vol.12, No.3, 389–404.

Takeuchi, R., Tesluk, P.E., Yun, S. and Lepak, D.P. (2005) 'An integrative view of international experience', *Academy of Management Journal,* Vol.48, No.1, 85–100.

Tams, S. and Arthur, M.B. (2007) 'Studying careers across cultures: distinguishing international, cross-cultural, and globalization perspectives', *Career Development International*, Vol.12, No.1, 86–98.

Templer, K.J. (2010) 'Personal attributes of expatriate managers, subordinate ethnocentrism, and expatriate success: a host-country perspective', *International Journal of Human Resource Management,* Vol.21, No.10, 1754–68.

Tharenou, P. (2003) 'The initial development of receptivity to working abroad: self-initiated international work opportunities in young graduate employees', *Journal of Occupational and Organizational Psychology*, Vol.76, No.4, 489–515.

Thomas, D.C. and Lazarova, M.B. (2006) 'Expatriate adjustment and performance: a critical review', pp. 247–64, in Stahl, G.K. and Bjorkman, I. (eds) *Handbook of Research in International Human Resource Management,* Cheltenham: Edward Elgar.

Toh, S.M. and DeNisi, A.S. (2007) 'Host country nationals as socializing agents: a social identity approach', *Journal of Organizational Behavior,* Vol.28, No.3, 281–301.

Tung, R.L. (1998) 'American expatriates abroad: from neophytes to cosmopolitans', *Journal of World Business*, Vol.33, No.2, 125–44.

Vance, C.M., Vaiman, V. and Andersen, T. (2009) 'The vital liaison role of host country nationals in MNC knowledge management', *Human Resource Management*, Vol.48, No.4, 649–59.

Ward, C., Bochner, S. and Furnham, A. (2001) *The Psychology of Culture Shock* (2nd edn), London: Routledge.

Whitley, R. (1992) 'Societies, firms and markets: the social structuring of business systems', in Whitley, R. (ed.) *European Business Systems: Firms and Markets in Their National Contexts*, London: Sage.

Yan, A., Zhu, G. and Hall, D.T. (2002) 'International assignments for career building: a model of agency relationships and psychological contracts', *Academy of Management Review*, Vol.27, No.3, 373–91.

Yurkiewicz, J. and Rosen, B. (1995) 'Increasing receptivity to expatriate assignments', in Selmer, J. (ed.) *Expatriate Management: New Ideas for International Business*, Westport, CT: Quorum.

CHAPTER 12
COMPARATIVE HUMAN RESOURCE MANAGEMENT

Geoffrey Wood and David G. Collings

INTRODUCTION

This chapter is about ways of comparing human resource management (HRM)[1], from context to context. This raises a number of questions. First, in a world that is supposedly 'globalising', does this mean that HRM is likely to become more similar over time, regardless of context? Second, what makes HRM different in different places? Third, what are the key differences likely to be found in HRM in different places? Fourth, what ways have researchers used to study and understand such differences?

Let us start with the first question. A longstanding debate in the management literature concerns the extent to which management practices are converging or diverging across nation states. This is not a terribly new question, of course: even in the nineteenth century, scholars such as Durkheim and Marx sought to understand the nature of modernisation of societies and workplace practices, and the extent to which they were coming more alike. Over the past two decades, the debate about globalisation – the extent to which the opening of markets, more mobile investors, and the apparent homogenisation of global consumer taste has made the planet more unified – has rekindled all this. A key underlying consideration in this debate is the extent to which globalisation is facilitating the convergence of national economies and the HR and other management practices that encompass this, and the homogenisation of the modus operandi of multinational corroborations (MNCs) operating in the global economy (Brewster and Mayrhofer, 2011; Collings *et al.*, 2011; Ferner, 2010).

Discussion question

What factors do you think might retard the convergence of management practices in different countries?

---

[1]HRM has been defined in a number of ways ranging from 'a distinctive approach to employment management' (Storey, 1992: 5) with particular characteristics in regard to employee management to 'anything and everything associated with the management of employment relationships in the firm' (Boxall and Purcell, 2000: 184) (see also Chapter 1 of this text). In this chapter we adopt the latter definition and thus define HRM quite broadly and also incorporate issues external to the firm, such as the nature of the labour market, issues relating to trade unions and the like, which may have an impact on HRM policy and practice within the walls of the organisation.

Indeed, a good starting point in looking at the globalisation and HRM debate is in the latter area: surely firms that operate on a global basis are the pioneers of a common HRM practice? The issue of multinational HR practices is examined in Chapter 11. However, for the purposes of this chapter, it is worth noting that that multinational corporations, one of the principle agents responsible for foreign direct investment (FDI) (Hirst and Thompson, 1999), are the key drivers in the internationalisation process (Ferner and Hyman, 1998). Thus these corporations can be perceived as significant in transferring practices from their country of origin with them when they establish operations in foreign countries (Almond, 2011a; Ferner, 1997). Looking specifically at human resource management (HRM), there is broad consensus that dominant modern conceptions of the field are heavily influenced by US thinking (Brewster, 2007; Guest, 1990). Thus, there is a degree of expectation that these US models enjoy a hegemonic position in the global business contexts and that all HRM practice will converge on this US model. Writers such as Kidger (1991) and DiMaggio and Powell (1983) argue that US multinationals, business schools and consultants will contribute to global convergence on US conceptualisations of HRM, reflected in HRM practice across the world (see Brewster, 2007 for a recent review). In illuminating the convergence/divergence polemic in the context of cross-national management practice, we can point to a number of significant studies. For instance, Gunnigle et al.'s (2002) study found a clear variation between HRM practice in firms of different national origin (see also Gooderham et al., 1998). In a similar vein, Harzing and Sorge (2003) found that while internationalisation strategy was more closely related to industry and size than other variables, the country of origin of firms was significant in explaining differences in control mechanisms utilised by firms. Thus there was continued divergence in control mechanisms utilised in firms of different national origin and they argue that on balance divergence remains in place. Geppert and his colleagues also pointed to differences in the change management strategies pursued by organisations of different nationalities (Geppert et al., 2003). Thus, on balance, the literature suggests that management practices continue to be characterised by divergence across national borders (Brewster et al., 2004; Harzing and Sorge, 2003), and indeed Hirst and Thompson (1999: 95) go as far as to suggest that 'in many ways…[national business] systems are being reinforce and strengthened by the internationalization of business' (see also Hall and Soskice, 2001: 56–60; Whitley, 1999).

The debate is however a complex one and there are a number of theories advanced which posit a universalist (convergence) or continued divergence of business systems and management practices. These theories merit some discussion and the key debates are outlined below. Our discussion is framed in the arena of comparative human resource management, which is defined as 'about understanding and explaining what differences exist between countries in the way that human resources are managed' (Brewster, 2006: 68). Thus, comparative HRM stands in contrast to international HRM which Scullion (1995: 325) defines as 'the HRM issues and problems arising from the internationalization of business, and the HRM strategies, policies and practices which firms pursue in response to the internationalization of business': comparative HRM is about comparing what firms do in different national contexts, irrespective of whether they are multinational or not. While Boxall (1995: 5), writing in the mid-1990s, described comparative HR a poorly theorised, emerging field, there is little doubt that we have witnessed significant theoretical and empirical development in the field the past decade, and these developments inform our chapter.

There are two principal strands of literature on comparative HRM. The first draws on a range of different theoretical traditions to make assumptions as to the direction of national economies, supported by a mixture of case study evidence and macro-economic data – in short, top-down approaches. This area of study concerns itself primarily with what makes HR different from case to case, and what the general differences encountered are likely to be: in other words, the second and third questions with which we opened our chapter. In contrast, bottom-up approaches seek to shed more light on national commonalities and variations in human resource management through pragmatic empirical work. The primary focus of the latter school of thought is, hence, on cataloguing HRM practices, rather than trying to explain them in terms of a broader theoretical template. Again, it is about what distinguishes HR practices in particular national contexts. However, its bottom-up focus means that such studies often provide richer detail on precisely how HR is practiced in specific contexts – often enriched with case study evidence – although this may be at the expense of ease of comparative analysis. Finally, such studies draw on a range of different methods – be that surveys (economy, region, industry or firm wide), or more qualitative methods. This diversity makes for richness in detail, but, of course, makes direct comparisons between contexts more difficult!

CONVERGENCE OR DIVERGENCE IN HRM SYSTEMS

Universalists: the convergence debate

The key underlying philosophy of the universalists is the general applicability of a common system of social and economic organisation (Rubery and Grimshaw, 2003). In other words, they assume that a specific general model is of universal worth. Inspired by Francis Fukuyama's (2000) suggestion that the ending of the Cold War saw the 'end of history', such perspectives assume that all national economies will move towards the neo-liberal ideal, which would be mirrored by similar shifts in firm-level practices (see also Friedman 1999). Allowing space for individual self-actualisation and fair recognition in line with market incentives will unlock creativity and enterprise; firms will be able to operate without being reigned in by distortions (Fukuyama 2000: 320). While universalists do acknowledge that there may be variations between different countries, these are underscored by 'objective' economic or technological differences between societies or institutional barriers to the implementation of best practice as opposed to fundamental differences in what constitutes 'the best way' (ibid.). At an organisation-level convergence 'implies a relative degree of disembeddedness of practices and structures, overriding more regionally or nationally specific institutions or behavioural predispositions' (Harzing & Sorge, 2003: 188). Within the universalist school a number of distinct variations emerge. The most influential strand of this thinking are the so-called new-institutionalists (cf. Harbison and Myers, 1959; Kerr *et al.*, 1960; DiMaggio and Powell, 1983) and we focus on this as an example in this chapter.

New-institutionalism

New-institutionalism was popularised by the writings of Harbison and Myers (1959), Kerr *et al.* (1960) and DiMaggio and Powell (1983) among others, drawing on the works of Douglass North (1990). Underlying this broad tradition is a view of institutions as a provider of incentives to rational actors: institutions may help people make the right decisions, or deter them from making the wrong ones. Institutionalisation has been defined as the 'process by which social processes, obligations, or actualities come to take on a rulelike status in social thought and action' (Meyer and Rowan, 1977: 341). Organisations have a tendency to copy what is done elsewhere in an attempt to gain legitimacy or the support of external agencies within a society (Strauss and Hanson, 1997). While functional or technical criteria may be key determinants of adoptions of innovations at an early stage, the importance of these determinants become weaker over time (Tolbert and Zucker, 1996). In a similar vein, Meyer and Rowan (1977) argue that organisation may not conform to a set of institutionalised practices simply because they are taken for granted or 'constitute reality' but because they are rewarded for doing so through increased legitimacy, resources or survival capabilities. In other words, there are some external incentives which inform the organisation's decision to adopt the practices.

Organisations sharing the same environment are likely to demonstrate isomorphism (in other words, experience pressures to do similar things) as they are believed to become structurally similar as they respond to like pressures (Gooderham *et al.*, 1999). Broadly speaking, differences between economies are regarded as deviations from established 'best practice' and are expected to dissolve as nation states catch up to those countries higher up the technological or organisational ladder. The bulk of work in this genre makes the assumption that the US model of weak unions and a heavily deregulated labour market is the optimal model to be followed: all societies will inevitably move towards this model, if institutional distortions are removed. A central feature of the US model is strong rights for property owners, and weak ones for other parties: this is seen as a central prerequisite for the efficient operation of markets.

The implication for labour are quite profound and as Thelen (2001: 75) postulates, the convergence of human resource management and industrial relations systems is regarded by this school as:

> A seemingly inexorable, inevitable slide toward deregulation, as high unemployment and increased capital mobility allow employers to dispense with strategies based on accommodating labour and instead shop for the best (i.e. least restrictive, least expensive labour regime). The result is a convergence theory that sees changes in the 'strong labour' countries as moving them in the direction of the weak labour countries.

In practice, attempts to apply such theories to the management of people has two key characteristics. The first is its prescriptive nature: it aims to highlight best practices, aimed at what things should be – and perhaps, inevitably will be – rather than taking account of divergences from this model that are likely to manifest themselves even within the US context (Brewster, 2007). Second, it makes some very definite assumptions as to what best-practice HRM is likely to be like (Brewster, 2007). In practice, the type of HRM this will translate into is that where the employer has a relatively free hand to set the terms and conditions of the employment contract and work organisation without the 'interferance of extraneous parties such as trade unions, (ibid.). This may either translate into a type of 'soft HRM', where the firm emphasises communication and consultation – but little in the way of genuine co-determination by way of collective bargaining and works councils – or 'hard HRM' where the firm tightly monitors employee performance, tailoring pay to individual effort and outcomes, and where employees can be readily hired and fired according to day-to-day organisational needs. Such approaches, of course, ignore the fact that individual forms of communication tend to be primarily top-down – junior employees will be reluctant to express unpopular opinions or be seen as bearers of bad news, if this opens them to retaliation by the superiors. Again, weak job security may allow the firm to rapidly adjust its workforce size according to organisational needs and the relative demand for its goods or services, but it also weakens the commitment of employees to the organisation. In addition, such approaches discount the knowledge and wisdom employees may have accumulated over a time period of working for the organisation, which may be extremely difficult to accurately cost the worth of, and which will be lost forever, should they be arbitrarily dispensed with.

Finally, it is important to note that the dominance of particular economic models is somewhat cyclical resulting in punctuated recalibration of perception of successful economic models which should be replicated. For example, some might argue that while the heyday of such studies was the 1990s and early 2000s, when the US was doing rather better than many of the advanced societies of western Europe, the tables turned in the first decade of the twenty-first century when: to many, the US model appeared to be one of speculation, insecure living standards and labour repression, rather than that of a new better future. It was argued that the US model encouraged firms to create new jobs: this ignored the fact that in the US, unemployment is a lot worse than might initially seem apparent based on national statistics. These statistics obscure the fact that 6 million US workers hold highly insecure 'continengent' jobs, 15 million only work in part-time or reduced jobs without benefits, 3 million unemployed are not counted as such because they fail to qualify for benefits, 1.5 million are in the armed forces, and a further 2 million are in prison (Harcourt and Wood, 2007). What about in firm HR practices? Things are, again, a lot less efficient than might first seem apparent. While acknowledging that there is a good degree of heterogeneity in the nature of US industry, with some firms displaying paternalistic attitudes underscored by supportive welfare capitalist traditions (Jacoby, 1997) there is also a more dominant tradition in the US context which is less favourable to employees. None the less, US firms invest relatively large amounts in training, this is partially to compensate for an extremely poor vocational training system, and the recurring need to provide basic induction training to new staff in the case of firms that have high staff turnover rates (cf. Harcourt and Wood, 2007). Again, high levels of productivity in the US more reflect long working hours and fewer holidays: continental western European workers appear capable of producing similar amounts in significantly shorter periods of time, and thus are able to enjoy more leisure time, have better work–life balances, which, again, is likely to make them more useful when they are at work. Clearly the economic challenges which the European Union, and particularly the Eurozone is facing, at the time of writing (late 2011) have the potential to challenge the perceived superiority of the European system among some commentators.

At a theoretical level, new-institutionalism has been criticised from a number of perspectives since its emergence (cf. Sorge and Streeck, 1988; Sorge and Warner, 1986). For example, Sorge and his colleagues pointed to the fact that in the context of the UK and Germany, factories of similar size, producing similar products with similar technology could demonstrate dissimilar forms of organisation: there was no evidence that a US or US-like model was necessarily the best, or that it was driving out other models. They also pointed to the persistence of both corporate and free market models as responses to economic and technological change in different countries (see also Turner, 2006).

Divergence: the endurance of national systems

A key principle underlying most theories of divergence is that, contrary to management rhetoric, which is obsessed with efficiency, organisational life is heavily influenced by factors which have very little to do with organisational goals and, indeed, which may thwart these very goals. The wider societal collectives in which organisations are embedded are quite significant in influencing management practices in organisations (Sorge, 2004). The key schools which are generally associated with these arguments are broadly classified as culturists (cf. Hofstede, 1980; 2001; Trompenaars, 1993) and institutionalists (cf. Hall and Soskice, 2001; Whitley, 1999). We now look in turn at these schools.

The culturalists

Although there have been a number of studies which have attempted to classify different nationalities on the basis of cultural dimensions (cf. Schneider and Barsoux, 2003 for a synthesis of the literature), we focus on the work of Geert Hofstede, as the underlying premise of all of the studies is broadly similar and Hofstede's work is generally considered the seminal study in the field. Hofstede (2001: 9) defines culture thus: 'the collective programming of the mind that distinguishes the members of one group or category of people from another'.

Key to this definition, he argues, is the fact that social systems exist only because human behaviour is not random, but rather to a certain extent predictable. In developing his theory, Hofstede identifies three levels of human mental programming, the individual, collective and universal (2001: 2–3). While the universal level of mental programming is, as the name suggests, shared by almost all of human kind, 'a kind-of biological operating system', and the individual is unique to each individual, it is the collective level that is key to understanding national cultures. Most of our mental programming is learned at this collective level, this is illustrated by the fact that we share traits with people who have gone through the same learning processes but with different genetic makeup. This level of culture is shared by people belonging to a certain group. Examples of collective cultural similarities include language and deference shown to elders among other traits. Key to our discussion is Hofstede's (2001: 11) thesis that although societal norms reflective of the collective level of human programming originate in a variety of ecological factors, they have resulted in 'the development and pattern maintenance of institutions in society with particular structures and ways of functioning'. Examples of these institutions include the education system, political systems, legislation and the family. Hoftstede continues that although the institutions may change over time, the underlying societal norms prevail, reflecting the persistent influence of the majority value system. Any new institutions which emerge over time are smoothed by these underlying norms until their structures and functioning eventually adapt to the norms.

Hoftstede differentiated between national cultures on five different criteria. These criteria are outlined in Box 12.1 Hoftstede's study was based on a sample of some 116,000 IBM employees in 72 countries who completed pen-and-paper questionnaires between 1967 and 1973. In a latter stage, data from ten more countries and three multicultural regions were added (see Hoftstede (2001) Chapter 2 for further detail on the methodology of the study).

The key underlying premise of the culturist approach is that cross-national differences in industrial relations systems and in organisations and the management of human resources are rooted in strong values and beliefs of the people in a given country. Practices are sustained because people find it unappealing, unethical or even repulsive to do otherwise (Sorge, 2004). For example, individuals in countries which are classified as high on the collectivist dimension are more likely to be ideologically committed to the trade union movement, conversely where individualist preferences prevail individuals are likely to be less ideologically committed to the trade union cause.

Box 12.1 HRM in practice   Hoftstede's dimensions of cultural difference

1 **Power distance**, which is related to the different solutions to the basic problem of human inequality.
2 **Uncertainty avoidance**, which is related to the level of stress in a society in the face of an unknown future.
3 **Individualism versus collectivism**, which is related to the integration of individuals into primary groups.
4 **Masculinity versus femininity**, which is related to the division of emotional roles between men and women.
5 **Long-term versus short-term orientation**, which is related to the choice of focus for people's efforts: the future or the present.

Source: Hoftstede, 2001. *Culture's Consequences: Comparing Values, Behaviors, Institutions and Organizations Across Nations*, 2 edn, Thousand Oaks, California: Sage Publications © Geert Hoftstede B. V., quoted with permission.

Although quite influential, the culturalist approach has never been universally accepted and, indeed, the approach and specifically Hoftstede's work have been subject to a number of criticisms. Most notable is the argument that although the approach is useful in explaining differences between nationalities, it fails to account for heterogeneity within the citizens of a given country. Rather it represents a central tendency within a nation (Evans *et al.*, 2011). Although the culturalists point to the link between the evolution of a countries business system or institutional structures and the characteristics of a national culture, they generally fail to explore the relationship between the cultural values and the structural and institutional characteristics of national economic systems (Ferner, 2010; Ferner *et al.*, 2001). The results of Hoftstede's study have also been specifically criticised. Tayeb (1996) points to the limitation that the study is based on an attitude-survey questionnaire which she argues is the least appropriate way of measuring culture. His choice of dimensions of cultural difference (see Box 12.1) has also been criticised (McSweeney, 2002). A further significant criticism is the fact that the research is limited to a single organisation (IBM) and thus the sample may not be representative (McSweeney, 2002).

At a theoretical level, the perspective has been condemned as overly functionalist – i.e. that national systems work, and that they work as a coherent whole (Bacharach, 1989). It assumes that the culture both corresponds with national boundaries, and that national cultures are immutable. This raises the awkward questions as to whether some cultures are more conducive to doing business than others, and whether some nations are condemned to a particular path on account of their cultural heritage. Of course, this cannot explain why nations can reinvent themselves. Prior to the Second World War, Austria was a poverty stricken and unstable backwater, characterised by authoritarian and conflictual employment relations. Today, Austria is a highly prosperous country: Austrian employment relations are upheld as a model of cooperation between managers and workers. More recently, both New Zealand and Ireland have enjoyed strong economic recoveries linked to legal reforms that have promoted cooperation and mutual dependence, rather than conflict and 'winner takes all' relations at the workplace. However, the success of the Irish model has been subject to criticism with the economy's dramatic fall from grace during the global economic recession (2008 to time of writing in 2011) which highlighted the fragile foundations of the Irish 'economic miracle'. The access to cheap international capital, booming construction sector and other structural conditions masked the fragility on which the model was premised and the partnership model which underscored the Celtic Tiger era has come to an end.

None the less, Ferner (2010: 542) summarises the value of cultural approaches quite eloquently:

> This is not to say that cultural value differences are irrelevant, merely that by themselves they are inadequate form of explanation; they do not capture real differences in the ways in which economic activity is organised in different countries, and throw little light on processes of changes and evolution in business systems.

Recent years have witnessed the development of a less quantitative and more historical perspective on the divergence of modern industrial societies, the institutionalist perspective, we now consider the key arguments of this school.

Institutionalist perspectives

Rational–hierarchical approaches. The persistence of national diversity challenged new-institutional accounts of convergence. From within the economics and finance literature, new approaches – that again saw institutions as providers of incentives and constraints on rational actors – now sought to explain the persistence of national diversity. Such accounts focused on the relative strength of property (and hence, owner) rights, looking at the effects of law, constitutions and politics (Djankov *et al.*, 2003: 596). Roe (2003) argues that specific political contexts are likely to encourage co-determination at the workplace between managers and employees: in turn, this will make for poor managerial accountability to owners as the system will both divide supervisory boards and encourage collusion between workers and managers at the expense of owners. For example, many managers seek personal aggrandisement through running a disproportionately large organisation, which, in turn, encourages the inefficient use of labour: in turn, the workforce colludes in the myth of needed bigness.

In their work on the effects of judicial systems and corporate governance, La Porta and colleagues (2000) suggest that a country's legal tradition will determine investor rights. In common law countries, investor rights vis-à-vis other stakeholders are likely to be stronger, at the expense of other stakeholder interests; the converse is true in civil law countries (La Porta *et al.*, 2000). La Porta *et al.* further argue that national legal systems mould the regulation of labour (Botero *et al.*, 2004: 1379). In civil law countries, employee rights are more clearly delineated, while governments are more likely to directly regulate labour markets (ibid.: 1340). Hence, industrial relations will affect the manner in which a corporation is governed in the same manner as investor rights will (Botero *et al.*, 2004: 1379–80). When worker rights are strong, those of owners will be relatively weak, resulting in the 'bottom line' not receiving the same degree of priority as it would in a common law setting.

Paganno and Volpin (2005) propose a further variation on such accounts, and focus on the effects of electoral systems: proportional representation electoral systems are likely to promote coalition building, again constraining the rights of shareholders at the expense of other interest groupings: such systems also are likely to encourage neo-corporatist arrangements, promoting co-determinism at workplace level, again at the expense of owner rights. Both these schools of thought follow on a long tradition of 'property rights' approaches to understanding management: shareholders have ultimate authority, it is necessary for managers to follow their wishes, with owners rights taking precedence over the interests of all other groups in the firm (Rollinson and Dundon 2007: 73).

What this literature has in common is that it sees employee and owner rights as a 'zero-sum game' (Goergen *et al.*, 2009). If employees have rights, it must be to the detriment of owners and vice versa. Hence, in contexts where owner rights are stronger, one is more likely to encounter hard HRM policies geared to the bottom line: performance-based pay, close monitoring of output, effective performance appraisals, and insecure job tenure. In contrast, where employee rights are stronger, one is more likely to find strong unions, collective bargaining, high job security and, indeed, structures such as works councils that give employees a say in the organisation of work.

Varieties of capitalism approaches. This broad body of literature rejects the rational actor model: individuals make decisions not always on the basis of information, but also owing to commitments and relations with other actors. Hence, the varieties of capitalism literature locates the firm within a centre of relations with stakeholders: owners, employees, community and community associations, and government. The theoretical origins of this tradition are diverse, drawing on both functionalist and radical theories. Within the North American industrial relations literature, abiding influences have been Dunlop and Bendix's essentially functionalist accounts (see Bendix, 1956): national industrial relations practices constitute a coherent and incrementally developing system. Firms within a business system tend to adopt similar HR practices in the interests of familiarity, and because they are closely fitted to wider economic, social and cultural realities. Some of the criticisms levelled at cultural accounts can also be focused on this literature.

Within Europe, there are many different accounts, including Whitley (1999) and Amable (2003). However, probably the most influential account has been that of Hall and Soskice (2001): the 'varieties of capitalism' approach: this builds on earlier work by Dore (2000) and Lincoln and Kalleberg (1990), that pointed to the key distinctions both in firm-level HR practices and wider governance between Anglo-American liberal market economies (LMEs) and collaborative market economies (CMEs). Examples of the former would include the US and the UK, and of the latter, Germany, the Low Countries, Scandinavia and Japan. Hall and Soskice seek out national-level differences in the nature of capitalism and attempt to develop terms that classify these more generally than has previously been the case. They conceptualise political economies as terrains populated by political actors, each with a rational self-interest to advance their own interests. While acknowledging a multiplicity of actors, such as individuals, governments, trade unions, suppliers and others, firms are regarded as the critical actors in any capitalist economy. Firms are viewed relationally, in that the relationships which they develop with key internal and external actors are inextricably linked to the firms' ability to develop core competencies or dynamic capabilities, for developing, producing and distributing goods or services profitably.

The most significant characteristic of firms operating in LMEs in this regard is management's unilateral right to manage. This is reflected in the principle of 'employment-at-will' which dominates the US IR landscape. This places little obligation of firms to provide employees with a guarantee of employment and thus employees can be hired and fired 'at will' on the basis of business needs. This results in highly fluid labour markets characterised by the ease of release or hire of labour and the investment by employees is general, transferable skills as opposed to company-specific ones. This can be linked to the nature of corporate governance and the fact that the interests of shareholders are emphasised above those of any other stakeholder in the business relationship (Almond *et al.*, 2003)

Closely linked to the individuals' investment in general, transferable skills is the nature of the training and education system in LMEs. Vocational training is generally provided by institutions offering formal education emphasising general skills rather than company specific apprenticeships, as companies are unwilling to invest in specific training as there is no guarantee employees will remain with the firm. The imperative of employees gaining general training is further emphasised by the fluid nature of labour markets, where general, transferable skills determine employment potential. This high investment in general training lowers the cost of company-specific training, however, as firms generally focus on providing employees with in-house training not as expensive as traditional apprenticeship type programmes. Rather the focus is on further developing general, marketable skills (Hall and Soskice, 2001).

Conversely, in coordinated market economies industrial relations systems are characterised by strong industrial relations institutions. These institutions have evolved in response to companies' dependence on highly skilled employees with substantial work autonomy who could potentially hold their employers to ransom by moving to other firms, while employees may be exploited if they share information with management. In the German system many of these problems were addressed through the development of industry-level bargaining between employer organisations and trade unions. As Jacobi *et al.* (1998: 190–1) argue, while unions and employer organisations are in legal and formal terms independent, in reality they are mutually dependent, and should be considered 'reliable partners within a network of stable cooperation'. These provisions arguably protect employees against arbitrary management decision-making, including changes to working conditions and layoffs, thus encouraging employees to invest in company specific skills and extra effort.

Hall and Soskice link these differences to different national strengths. The pluralist HRM policies found in CMEs is likely to be conducive to high quality incrementally innovative production (exemplifiers of the latter including Toyota, Volkswagen, Siemens, etc). In contrast, the managerially dominant types of HRM found in LMEs are likely to be associated with either low-value-added service sector activity, or high technology innovation. This is likely to result in a number of key distinctions in terms of skills needs and HR practices. Incremental innovation requires good industry specific skills, high security of tenure (in order to encourage the development of firm-specific human capital) and cooperation and knowledge sharing through advanced forms of participation that genuinely empower employees (such as found through centralised collective bargaining and works councils) (Thelen, 2001). In contrast, hi-tech industry requires generic tertiary skills (e.g. university education), a mobile workforce and more individually oriented reward and incentives systems (Thelen, 2001). The low-value-added sweatshop paradigm requires little investment in people, with pay being tied to output, or being held at the lowest acceptable level. The fact that clusters of HR practices continue to be found within particular regions and nations points to the importance of understanding national context.

Hence, Locke *et al.* (1995: 143) point to the significance of the historical development of the employment relations system within a nation state, noting:

> [A]lthough a particular approach to employment relations has emerged in all the advanced industrial nations...[in their study]...the particular from [of the employment relations approach] it has taken and its extent vary considerably within countries, between firms, industries and regions, and between countries with different historical traditions and institutional arrangements.

This argument is articulated by a number of other authors based on empirical study. Sorge and Streeck (1988) have argued that there has been an explosive divergence in industrial relations, rather than an implosive convergence toward one central best practice. Morley *et al.*'s (1996: 652) study pointed to elements of convergence and divergence in European IR but concluded that overall, any coherent move toward convergence was 'a long way off'. Indeed, Hall and Soskice's argument that variance between the types of capitalism alluded to above will reinforce differences in national institutional frameworks seems to have significant merit based on the empirical evidence. This is a view shared by Geppert *et al.* (2003), whose case-based data suggests, that the more globalised the organisational strategy pursued by a firm, the more it perpetuates and reinforces cross national specifics. Thus they posit 'from this perspective one could argue that globalisation ultimately reinforces the importance of different national contexts' (2003: 833). Indeed, local variation is also something which multinational companies exploit in the context of the international division of labour and the global 'value chain' (Edwards and Kuruvilla, 2005; Wilkinson *et al.*, 2001). Such segmented coordination of value chains is premised on exploiting local differences in the way most effective to the MNC, by for example locating R&D in nations with high technical capability and production in nations where cost are low and lower levels of regulation allows greater flexibility (Ferner, 2010).

Discussion question

Which perspective do you find more persuasive – convergence or divergence?

EMPIRICAL WAYS OF UNDERSTANDING DIVERSITY

The preceding discussion has illustrated that we can see that diversity in HR practice may be understood from a range of different theoretical starting points. At an empirical level, there is a rich body of literature aimed at understanding variations in HR practices at a country level. While sometimes employing some of the above theories as a starting point, this literature is primarily concerned with documenting key HR practices within specific national contexts. Sometimes these have been consolidated into books about HRM in specific regions or continents, an example being Routledge's *Global HRM* series of edited books on HRM in specific regions, such as Europe (Holt Larsen and Mayrhofer, 2006), central and eastern Europe (Morley *et al.*, 2009), Africa (Kamoche *et al.*, 2003), Asia Pacific (Budhwar, 2004) and the Middle East (Budhwar and Mellahi, 2006), and the Wood and Brewster (2007) volume on industrial relations in Africa. These books have been distinguished by high-quality contributions by often locally based country experts, with the editorial team drawing out common themes and trends. A further recent innovation has been Morley *et al.*'s (2006) and Ackers and Wilkinson's (2003) contributions which take a regional perspective on the comparison of industrial relations systems.

Similar country-study-type articles have been published in a range of academic journals, most notably *International Journal of Human Resource Management*, and *Employee Relations*. These articles tend to focus on defining features of HRM either from a functional-areas or relationship approach. Articles in the former genre seek to document and explain national or regional practices in recruitment and planning, motivation and reward, industrial relations, and/or human resource development. In contrast, articles following on the latter approach tend to focus on issues such as the degree of employer–employee interdependence and the extent of delegation to employees (Whitley, 1999). The former would include job security, and the extent to which employers will invest in their people, and employees inclined to accumulate organisation-specific skills. Meanwhile, the latter would include the degree of participation and involvement. In practice, the comparative lessons of individual national experiences are often only briefly alluded to, or presented in a highly attenuated form, it being left up to the reader to decide what the experience of a particular nation or region reveals about the practice of HRM more generally.

A variation of such approaches are sub-national studies and supra-national studies. As Boyer and Hollingsworth (1997) note, institutions are nested at supra-, national and sub-national levels. In other words, although national setting heavily impacts on HR policies, institutions – be they rules (formal laws and informal conventions), training structures, development incentives and/or physical infrastructural provisions and support – may also vary within states, or may be shared between countries. For example, European Union directives governing labour standards have encouraged moves towards common continent-wide HR practices in many areas, an example being the treatment of elderly workers. This has led some commentators to suggest that a European-wide social model is emerging, associated with cooperative HR policies: other, more pessimistic writers have argued that Europeanisation has been associated with the introduction of more hardline management-oriented 'Anglo-Saxon' practices that have seriously damaged more cooperative continental European forms of HRM (O'Hagan 2002; see also Morley et al., 2006 section 2 for a discussion on these issues).

Within countries, regional development initiatives (and local training realities and historical legacies), have led to some regions pursuing distinct trajectories. An example of this would be the Grenoble hi-tech cluster in France: such regional concentrations of industry have encouraged firms to tailor their HR policies accordingly given specific sectoral needs and local skills realities. People management here centres on the efficient use of a relatively young incoming (from other parts of France, and abroad) workforce, with high levels of tertiary education, and the support of a number of excellent public research centres (Aniello, 2004: 314). In a 2004 edited collection by Colin Crouch et al. (2004), it was found that local production systems could be encountered in many countries across Europe, each bringing with them associated sets of HR policies and practices, in many respects different from national norms. More recently, the issue of sub-national governance systems has received increasing attention (see Almond, 2011b).

Discussion question

Consider the challenges of conducting research on differences in HRM and industrial relations across borders.

Conclusion

This chapter has aimed to introduce some of the major debates within the field of comparative HRM. A growing body of theoretical enquiry and empirical evidence points to the fact that individual nations and regions remain distinct in many areas. This would appear to vindicate the varieties of capitalism, and other similar institutional approaches. At the same time, in studying comparative HRM, we need to be aware that, even if countries and regions may not be coming more alike, they are all subject to change. In other words, in many respects we are studying a moving target. This would reflect the role of supra-national institutions such as the EU, technological changes, changes in laws and innovations in policy and firm-level practices and in some instances the impact of innovations introduced by foreign multinational companies operating in the host country (Ferner and Quintanilla, 2002; Gennard, 1974; Gunnigle, 1995). Hence, the new Irish HRM model, for example, is rather different from that encountered 20 years ago (see Collings et al., 2008; Gunnigle, 1995). This makes the empirically oriented studies that formed the focus of the second part of this chapter of particular importance: keeping abreast of innovations in practice is an essential part of being an excellent HR manager, and, indeed, an excellent student in HRM.

CASE STUDY 12.1

HRM IN MOZAMBIQUE

GEOFFREY WOOD AND DAVID G. COLLINGS

After almost 500 years of a particularly exploitative form of colonial rule, a failed socialist experiment and a bloody civil war, Mozambique underwent radical economic adjustment in the late 1980s and 1990s in line with the then prevailing neo-liberal orthodoxy. While the latter had severely adverse consequences for large areas of an already fragile manufacturing sector, it also led to an – albeit limited – increase in foreign investment and a partial revitalisation of the transport and tourism industries.

A nationwide survey of HR practices in Mozambique revealed little evidence of innovation or of leading edge practices. While most firms had a specialised people management function, the techniques employed remained personal, informal, but also top-down. At the same time, HRM techniques cannot be considered to be uniformally 'bleak house' or 'low road'; the 'low road' hypothesis is thus falsified. Rather, HRM practices seem to have much in common with those noted in other African countries; this would include a reliance on personal networks for recruitment, the use of informal training structures, and poor pay and working conditions being mitigated by a willingness by management to make informal concessions to workers in the event of personal difficulties. In contrast to the 'low road' model, Mozambican managers do not make use of rigid sets of rules, little communication, fixed bare minimum wages, and an unwillingness to depart from fixed procedures (cf. Taylor and Bain 2003). The dominant 'informal' managerial style is founded on autocratic partriarchialism, underpinned by personal ties. On the one hand, external shocks to the Mozambican economy have resulted in large-scale job shedding that must have done much to erode any sense of mutual commitment. On the other hand, managers retain close personal contact with the workforce – *inter alia*, through general meetings – and remain willing to adjust terms and conditions of service in response to individual need. The survey would thus provide further evidence to support Harrison (2000) and Pitcher's (2002) arguments that the Mozambican context is one characterised by long-term continuities, despite seemingly radical sociopolitical changes.

At the same time, the survey revealed evidence of a range of 'best-practice' techniques among a small minority of firms. While there is little doubt that the latter are likely to be best equipped to escape reverting to a low-wage, low-skill, low-value-added trajectory, it remains uncertain whether such a path is viable in a context of institutional weakness and cut-throat competition from abroad.

In summary, the survey revealed that relatively few firms make use of a full and complementary range of high-performance work practices. However, most firms have not reverted to the 'low road'/'bleak house' model that has become a feature of people management in specific sectors within the advanced societies. Indeed, many firms rely on traditional patriarchal–authoritarianism, and are reluctant to concede their workers even basic benefits such as paid vacations and sick leave. On the other hand, many are willing to grant leave at short notice and/or advances on wages, in the event of individual workers experiencing personal difficulties. Contact is maintained with the workforce through irregular meetings, both scheduled and ad hoc, while the mode of firms made use informal on the job training. The dominant Mozambican paradigm of people management shares these common features with that found in many other tropical African countries; such practices represent the product of both adverse external environments, periodic systemic shocks and colonial and/or precolonial traditions.

However, in Mozambique, the ability of this highly personal/patriarchal managerial paradigm to engender any sense of mutual commitment is likely to have been eroded by episodic rounds of redundancies, while firms are unlikely to systematically invest in their people through formal training programmes or systematic career planning given a highly competitive environment. Less principled rivals may not only gain a short-term cost advantage, but are able to poach staff from those firms who provide effective training and development. The diffusion of higher-value-added production paradigms is only likely in a more supportive institutional context that encourages firms to buy into mutually advantageous sets of rules governing fair play (cf. Marsden 1999), and which limits the rewards accruing to bad practice. While the more efficient enforcement of legislation may encourage the broader diffusion of 'high road' practices, their sustainability is, at least in part, contingent on the diffusion and reconstitution of supportive conventions (Dore, 2000); regrettably, this makes it extremely difficult to depart from the dominant existing paradigm.

Source: *Webster and Wood, 2005.*

Questions

1 *What are the key features of HRM in Mozambique?*
2 *Why do you think HRM in Mozambique has been characterised by many continuities?*

CASE STUDY 12.2
IRELAND AND THE MULTINATIONALS

DAVID G. COLLINGS AND GEOFFREY WOOD

Ireland is one of the most globalised countries in the world, owing to the significance of foreign owned MNCs which have established subsidiaries there. The scale of foreign direct investment (FDI) there is driven by a consistent public policy agenda, pursued by successive governments, of providing incentives to attract MNCs to invest in Ireland. This policy has proved very successful and recent research confirms that there are some 470[1] foreign-owned MNCs in Ireland (McDonnell *et al.*, 2007) employing over 140,000 people. US-owned multinationals are particularly significant players there, with 226 US-owned subsidiaries. These include large high-profile firms such as IBM, Microsoft, Dell, Google, Pfizer, Wyeth and the like. These firms are estimated to employ over 7 per cent of the private sector non-agricultural labour force and also contribute significantly through indirect employment through suppliers and the like and make a very substantial contribution to taxation revenues in Ireland.

Given the disproportionate significance of FDI and American FDI in particular in Ireland, combined with the expectation that HRM policies and practices are likely to converge on the US model, Ireland represents a very interesting context to study the convergence of HRM through looking at subsidiary practice in subsidiary operations. Further, if we do expect to witness convergence of HRM practice, Ireland would represent an interesting test case. The expected convergence would be even more likely to emerge in US MNCs owing to the fact that they tend to be quite ethnocentric in managing the foreign operations and display a preference for centrally developed, standardised policies in their foreign operations.

There is a broad consensus that MNCs have been an important source of innovation in management practices in Ireland, particularly in the application of new HRM/IR approaches and in expanding the role of the specialist HR function. For example, MNCs have been associated with innovation in areas such as the diffusion of so-called 'high-commitment' work systems and performance-related pay innovations which appear to have transferred to a degree at least indigenous firms. Further, US MNCs have been particularly strong in their resistance to recognising trade unions, a trend which stands in contrast to Irish traditions, which were generally supportive of trade union's role in the workplace. Recent research reveals that over time, as the country's reliance on the FDI sector has increased, MNCs have found it easier to establish and operate subsidiaries on a non-union basis.

However, we do still see evidence of divergence between US MNCs and indigenous firms suggesting that divergence remains important in the Irish context. For example based on Gunnigle *et al.*'s (2002) study, we see that US subsidiaries in Ireland put substantially more emphasis on performance appraisal and reward than did Irish organisations. Significantly, US

---

[1]This figure only includes all wholly or majority foreign-owned organisations operating in Ireland, with 500 or more employees worldwide and 100 or more employed in their Irish operations.

MNCs displayed a degree of adoption of HR practice to account to local standards. This study also unearthed differences between US firms and subsidiaries of other nationalities, providing further evidence of sustained divergence. More recently, Collings *et al*. (2008) argued for elements of an essentially hybrid system with regard to industrial relations in US MNCs, reflecting some particularly 'American' practices in these firms again suggesting divergence with indigenous firms.

Thus despite the relative power of US MNCs in the Irish context and the reliance of the Irish economy on the FDI sector, there is little evidence of complete convergence between US MNCs, other foreign MNCs and indigenous firms in the Irish context.

Questions

1 Consider the reasons why differences remain between foreign MNCs and indigenous firms in the Irish context.

2 What challenges may a heavy reliance on FDI have on a host government in terms of balancing the needs of powerful firms and employees in the host economy?

CASE STUDY 12.3

INSTITUTIONAL CHANGE, WORK AND EMPLOYMENT RELATIONS: THE CHANGING FORTUNES OF MERCEDES-BENZ IN SOUTH AFRICA

GEOFFREY WOOD

Cultural approaches to comparing HR between contexts tend to assume that countries do not readily change their defining cultural identities, and this will exert long-term effects on work and employment relations. While institutional approaches also assume some degree of embeddedness – that is that certain generally accepted ways of doing things are likely to persist – the recent literature on institutions has highlighted the manner in which institutional frameworks and associated rules can and do change. Such changes may be incremental, or they may involve significant ruptures at key historical moments from past forms of regulation and associated rules of conduct. In practical terms, this means that continuity cannot be always assumed in comparing work and employment relations within and between contexts. At the same time, major ruptures are relatively rare, and often carry over elements of the past order; changes in national systems are more commonly so incremental as to be invisible to all but a close observer.

In the 1980s, Mercedes-Benz's plant in East London, South Africa, was characterised by high levels of conflict. According to then HR Manager, Ian Russel: 'The union did not recognize management's right to manage. We had no structures to institutionalize conflict, no procedures, no recognition agreement' (quoted in Desai, 2008) Reflecting on events, then head of Mercedes-Benz South Africa (MBSA) Christoph Kopke acknowledged that 'Supervisors used to clock in and then lock themselves in their offices for the whole day. They didn't dare go out on the assembly lines.'

By the late 1990s, the situation had completely transformed. Reflecting this, in 2009, the plant was awarded the JD Power IQS gold quality award for the plant with the fewest defects and malfunctions of its product of any car plant in the world serving the US market, a feat that was repeated in 2010. 'To receive such an award despite the relentless pressure and stresses of the global recession over the past two years, points to the brilliant quality of our people and processes', said company representative Hansgeorg Niefer. In 2011, a worker at the plant of 30 years standing, Francois Waters, received Daimler's Laureate of Quality Excellence 2011. Waters said:

> I felt honoured to receive this award, and humbled to be rewarded for coming to work every day and just trying to achieve the best that I possibly can. It really is a combined effort as teamwork is critical to quality standards and we depend heavily on each other's strengths. It is important that everyone has the same mindset regarding quality, and that our targets are clear to everyone who has any input into the production process. Our processes are benchmarked, and it is vital that each employee ensures that they work strictly according to set standards, day in, day out.

What can account for the changes that took place in the Mercedes-Benz plant in South Africa? And, is this anything to do with institutions? Can we compare institutions and associated HR practices not only between countries, but also within the same country at different points in time?

So, although in looking at institutional approaches to comparing HRM, we tend to look at comparing different countries. However, it is also possible to look at how institutional changes have affected HR practices within a particular country.

South Africa underwent dramatic changes in both governmental structures and in terms of informal accepted rules of conduct as part and parcel of the end of apartheid in the early 1990s. Under apartheid, work and employment relations followed what is often called *racial fordism*, which may be defined as classic methods of mass production combined with institutionalised racism. Buoyed up by substantial gold revenues from the 1950s until the 1970s, the apartheid government had the financial resources to engage in both an active industrial policy and massive social engineering. Under apartheid, the South African domestic market was heavily protected. Moreover, the government provided a mass of subsidies to support sectors of manufacturing. Finally, large-scale infrastructural projects, including the electrification of the railway system and the expansion of port facilities greatly helped industry.

Apartheid was, in many respects, a contradictory system, which incorporated elements both to advance poor whites and to help big business, above all that which was Afrikaans-owned. However, the greatest contradictions concerned the usage of black labour. On the one hand, the apartheid regime had the long-term ambition of banishing the black majority to the rural periphery. On the other hand, large areas of industry and the mines were heavily dependent on cheap black labour. In practice, what happened was that the government sought to control the influx of black workers into the cities, linking temporary urban residential rights with employment. Moreover, job protection meant that many skilled trades were reserved for whites. In terms of labour legislation, blacks were denied access to the statutory industry-wide collective bargaining structures set up in the 1920s. Finally, the best universities and technical training institutions were reserved for whites. In practice, this led to the large-scale employment of black labour within inherently inefficient industries; institutionalised racism and low pay ensured that productivity generally low, and quality often poor.

Official propaganda notwithstanding, the African majority actively resisted the imposition and operation of apartheid through successive waves of resistance. There were many attempts to organise black workers in trade unions prior to the 1970s, but these failed to make much headway owing to a reliance on a few key activists and counterwaves of state repression. In the early 1970s, the situation changed dramatically. There were two reasons for this. First, the collapse of Portuguese rule in the southern African states of Mozambique and Angola led to the apartheid government seeking to wean itself off its reliance on ultra-cheap migrant labour from neighbouring states. High gold prices allowed for modest – but still significant – wage increases to entice greater numbers of black South Africans to work on the mines. This led to waves of spontaneous strikes in the urban centres of both Durban and East London, as workers sought similar wage increases for manufacturing jobs. Quite simply, after a long period of 'little hope', some change in material conditions finally seemed possible. Second, groups of liberal student activists established a number of worker services organisations, which soon developed into trade unions. Unlike earlier attempts at organising black workers, they adopted strong structures of shopfloor democracy, based on the British shop steward model.

The South African motor industry is concentrated in the Eastern Cape region. This was on account of the region's roughly equidistant location to the major urban centres of Cape Town, Durban and Johannesburg. In practice, a number of motor manufacturers set up plants to assemble knock-down kits in the Eastern Cape's port cities of Port Elizabeth and East London. As the apartheid regime gradually raised protective tariffs, most moved over to an ever-expanding of manufacturing activities. Mercedes-Benz even set up an engine manufacturing facility, at the time, the only Mercedes engine plant outside of Germany. Rather more sinisterly, its truck manufacturing facility supplied lorries and truck chassis that were used by the apartheid military. High local content helped circumnavigate sanctions.

Within the rural periphery, the apartheid government set about transforming the tribal reservations into 'independent' countries, with the ultimate aim of taking away South African citizenship from black South Africans. Adjoining East London, this involved the setting up of an 'independent' state apparatus, which transformed a particularly impoverished reserve into what ultimately became the 'country' of Ciskei, ruled with an iron fist by kleptocratic members of the Sebe family. Conveniently, for manufacturing firms in East London, a new township was established in the south-eastern tip of Ciskei within, an albeit long, commuting distance of that city. Pass laws meant that workers would have to endure long hours on public transport to return to the 'homeland' every evening. And, unencumbered by the remaining judicial checks and balances and civil society organisations in South Africa, the Ciskei authorities were free to brutally 'discipline' workers seen as troublemakers; the latter included union activists.

On the one hand, the Mercedes-Benz plant in East London was relatively unusual on account of the relatively higher wages offered and the relative quality of its products (most other locally made cars could charitably be described as unreliable rust buckets up until the early 1980s!). On the other hand, the relatively progressive reputation of management and the large workforce made it an attractive target for union activists. Soon, the plant established a reputation for strike proneness, with unions using the wage increases forced at Mercedes as a bargaining chip against employers elsewhere in the region. The brutality, greed and general antics of the Sebe family, and, more generally speaking, Ciskeian 'independence', further radicalised the East London workforce at large.

Reforms tabled in 1979 by the apartheid government deracialised centralised bargaining. This was with the intention of coopting increasingly effective unions, and drawing union leadership away from rank and file. On the one hand, this attempt generally failed: unions used centralised bargaining as a source of strength. On the other hand, workers for firms that already had a reputation for good wages naturally were suspicious of wage setting on industry lines. This led to ongoing tensions between union officials and the radicalised Mercedes-Benz workforce.

These tensions came to a head with the 1990 Mercedes-Benz strike. What happened was that groups of workers demanded that the firm withdraw from centralised bargaining, and rather bargain at plant level. Groups of workers occupied the plant, in defiance of union officials. After nine weeks, the occupiers were forceably evicted by the police, with the overt support of management, and to the relief of the union. While spectacular, this occupation represented only one example of an ongoing trench warfare between management and workers. This included threats of violence against foremen, the adoption of fake military garb (complete with fake weaponry) by sections of the workforce, and the large-scale theft of company property. Entire areas of the factory were reduced to no-go zones for management. Meanwhile, entire completed engines were going missing from the engine plant, and at least one finished motor car appears to have been mislaid.

The South African domestic market for luxury cars was not very large, and sanctions precluded sales to most other African states. Finally, during the 1980s, the South African economy experienced a deep recession. Given all this, the parent company in Germany seriously contemplated abandoning the enterprise in its entirety. However, whether because of altruism, a commitment to the region, and/or perhaps even guilt on having produced trucks employed by the apartheid military, Mercedes decided to stay in East London. In addition to further investment in workforce skills development, the somewhat disparate collection of factory buildings (interposed with public roads) was entirely enclosed into a large single walled complex. Not only did this reduce endemic theft, but it helped create a more uniform identity that was also helped through initiatives to beautify the factory environment and its surrounds. And, as growing numbers of Ciskei-based manufacturing firms collapsed (despite lavish state subsidies), jobs at Mercedes became increasingly desirable, not only owing to the good pay, but also through the growing dearth of meaningful alternatives.

However, relief arrived for the Mercedes plant from an unexpected quarter. The last hardline apartheid President, the dangerously stupid and narrow-minded P.W. Botha, suffered a stroke. Tired of his incessant bullying, a cabal of cabinet ministers ousted the temporarily incapacitated president. He was replaced by F.W. De Klerk, who, although having a conservative reputation, lacked Botha's close ties to the security establishment. Exiled to the political wilderness, Botha largely recovered from his stroke just in time to see his life's work being undone. On opening parliament in February 1990, De Klerk astounded the world by ending apartheid, and starting negotiations with previously banned black resistance organisations, most notably the African National Congress (ANC). While undeniably an act of great political courage, De Klerk was prompted by the fact that weak minerals prices meant that the apartheid government was running out of money. Cautious neo-liberal reforms were accelerated when, following democratic elections, the ANC came into power in 1994. Essentially, this included the abandonment of a range of subsidies for inefficient industries, privatisations and an end of most protectionist measures. All this led to wholesale job losses in manufacturing. However, the ending of the tensions caused by apartheid and the inefficiencies imposed by largely racial divisions of labour – and the ongoing skilling of the African labour force – meant that successful manufacturing firms could have far leaner staffing. In the end, all this meant that South Africa experienced a growth without jobs.

At Mercedes, many of the tensions of the past dissipated with the end of apartheid. The skilled Mercedes workforce valued the prestige and high pay that came with the job in an area of by now very high unemployment. Freed from racial discrimination governing where one could live, many workers could enjoy comfortable middle-class lifestyles. Furthermore, significant numbers of shop stewards moved into junior management positions. While Mercedes had recognised unions for many years, employee participation and involvement had now broadened to a new level. Employees directly or via their representatives had a say in the organisation of work, the introduction of new technology and a range of quality issues. Communication was much improved, supplemented by mature, centralised collective bargaining at industry level. Productivity rates soared, with a strong mutual commitment by all parties to the future of the enterprise.

Over 15 years since the end of apartheid, Mercedes in East London are today a model plant. The quality of production and the productivity of the workforce are among the highest of any car plant in the world. So many Mercedes cars are exported from the East London plant that an entire new car terminal has had to be constructed, necessitating a major expansion of East London harbour.

Questions

1 What happened at Mercedes-Benz in East London? What is the relationship between changes in the plant, and broader institutional transformation?

2 What are the limitations of cultural approaches to comparative HRM for understanding what happened at Mercedes-Benz?

3 Did the fact that the plant was owned by a large multinational have any affect on outcomes? If so, what were these?

CASE STUDY 12.4
REFLECTIVE CASE STUDY
GEOFFREY WOOD

Think of a company you know? Do its HR policies in any respect represent a product of the society in which it operates. And, do firms of a similar size in the same sector practise roughly similar HR policies? If so, why, and if not, why not?

Bibliography

Ackers, P. and Wilkinson, A. (2003) *Understanding Work and Employment: Industrial Relations in Transition,* Oxford: Oxford University Press.

Almond, P. (2011a) 'Re-visiting "country of origin" effects on HRM in multinational corporations', *Human Resource Management Journal*, Vol.21, No.3, 258–71.

Almond, P. (2011b) 'The sub-national embeddedness of international HRM', *Human Relations*, Vol.64, No.4, 531–51.

Almond, P., Edwards, T. and Clarke, I. (2003) 'Multinationals and changing national business systems in Europe: towards the "shareholder value" model?', *Industrial Relations Journal,* Vol.34, No.5, 430–45.

Amable, B. (2003) *The Diversity of Modern Capitalism*. Oxford: Oxford University Press.

Aniello, V. (2004) 'Grenoble Valley', in Crouch, C., Le Galès, P., Trigilia, C. and Voelzkow, H. (eds) *Changing Governance of Local Economies*. Oxford: Oxford University Press.

Bacharach, S. (1989) 'Organizational theories: some criteria for evaluation', *Academy of Management Review*, Vol.14, No.(4), 496–515.

Bendix, R. 1956. *Work and Authority in Industry*, New York: John Wiley

Botero, J., Djankov, S., La Porta, R., Lopez-de-Silanes, S. and Shleifer, A. (2004) 'The regulation of labor', *Quarterly Journal of Economics*, Vol.119, No.4, 1339–82.

Boxall, P. (1995) 'Building the theory of comparative HRM', *Human Resource Management Journal*, Vol.5, No.5, 5–17.

Boxall, P. and Purcell, J. (2000) 'Strategic human resource management: Where have we come from and where should we be going?' *International Journal of Management Reviews*, Vol.2, No.2, 183–203.

Boyer, R. and Hollingsworth, J.R. (1997) 'From national embeddedness to spatial and institutional nestedness', in Hollingsworth, J.R. and Boyer, R. (eds) *Contemporary Capitalism: The Embeddedness of Institutions*, Cambridge and New York: Cambridge University Press.

Brewster, C. (2006) 'Comparing HRM policies and practices across geographical borders', in Stahl, G.K. and Björkman, I. (eds) *Handbook of Research in International Human Resource Management,* Cheltenham: Edward Elgar.

Brewster, C. (2007) 'Comparative HRM: European views and perspectives', *International Journal of Human Resource Management*, Vol.18, No.5, 769–87.

Brewster, C. and Mayrhofer, W. (2011) 'Comparative human resource management', in Harzing, A.W. and Pinnington, A. (eds) *International Human Resource Management*, (3rd edn), London: Sage.

Brewster, C., Mayrhofer, W. and Morley, M. (eds) (2004) *Human Resource Management: Evidence of Convergence?,* Oxford: Elsevier Butterworth Heinemann.

Budhwar, P. (2004) *Managing Human Resources in Asia Pacific,* London: Routledge.

Budhwar, P. and Mellahi, K. (eds) (2006) *Human Resource Management in the Middle East ,* London, Routledge.

Collings, D.G., Gunnigle, P. and Morley, M.J. (2008) 'Boston or Berlin: American MNCs and the shifting contours of industrial relations in Ireland', *International Journal of Human Resource Management,* Vol.19, No.2, 240–61.

Collings, D.G., Lavelle, J. and Gunnigle, P. (2011) 'The role of MNEs', pp. 402–20, in Barry, M. and Wilkinson, A. (eds) *Handbook of Research on Comparative Employment Relations*, Cheltenham: Edward Elgar.

Crouch, C., Le Galès, P., Trigilia, C. and Voelzkow, H. (eds) (2004) *Changing Governance of Local Economies*, Oxford: Oxford University Press.

Desai, A. (2008) 'Productivity pacts, the 2000 Volkswagen strike, and the trajectory of COSATU in post-apartheid South Africa', *Mediations*, Vol.24, No.1, 25–51.

DiMaggio, P.J. and Powell, W.W. (1983) 'The iron cage revisited: institutional isomorphism and collective rationality in organizational fields', *American Sociological Review*, Vol.48, No.2, 147–60.

Djankov, S., Glaeser, E., La Porta, R., Lopez-de-Silnes, F. and Shleifer, A. (2003) 'The new comparative economics', *Journal of Comparative Economics*, Vol.31, No.4, 595–619.

Dore, R. (2000) *Stock Market Capitalism: Welfare Capitalism*, Cambridge: Cambridge University Press.

Edwards, T, and Kuruvilla, S. (2005) 'International HRM: national business systems, organizational politics, and the international diffusion of labour in MNCs', *International Journal of Human Resource Management*, Vol.16, No.1, 1–21.

Evans, P., Pucik, V. and Bjorkman, I. (2011) *The Global Challenge: Frameworks for International Human Resource Management,* New York: McGraw Hill/Irwin.

Ferner, A. (1997) 'Country of origin effects and human resource management in multinational companies', *Human Resource Management Journal,* Vol.7, No.1, 19–36.

Ferner, A. (2010) 'HRM in multinational companies', pp. 541–60, in Wilkinson, A., Bacon, N., Redman, T. and Snell, S. (eds) *The SAGE Handbook of Human Resource Management*, London: Sage.

Ferner, A. and Hyman, R. (1998) 'Introduction' in Ferner, A. and Hyman, R. (eds) *Changing Industrial Relations in Europe,* (2nd edn). Oxford: Blackwell.

Ferner, A. and Quintanilla, J. (2002) 'Between globalisation and capitalist variety: multinationals and the international diffusion of employment relations', *European Journal of Industrial Relations*, Vol.8, No.3, 243–50.

Ferner, A., Quintanilla, J. and Varul, M.Z. (2001) 'Country of origin effects, host country effects, and the management of HR in multinationals: German companies in Britain and Spain', *Journal of World Business,* Vol.36, No.2, 107–27.

Friedman, T. (1999) *The Lexus and the Olive Tree*, New York: Farrar and Strauss.

Fukuyama, F. (2000) 'One journey, one destination', in Burns, R. and Rayment-Pickard, H. (eds) *Philosophies of History*, Oxford: Blackwell.

Gennard, J. (1974) "The impact of foreign-owned subsidiaries on host country labour relations: the case of the United Kingdom", in Weber, A.W. (ed.) *Bargaining Without Boundaries*, Chicago, IL: University of Chicago Press.

Geppert, M., Matten, D. and Williams, K. (2003) 'Change management in MNCs: how global convergence intertwines with national diversity', *Human Relations,* Vol.64, No.7, 807–38.

Goergen, M., Brewster, C. and Wood, G. (2009) 'Corporate governance regimes and employment relations in Europe', *Industrial Relations/Relations Industrielles* , Vol.64, No.6, 620–40.

Gooderham, P., Nordhaug, O. and Ringdal, K. (1998) 'When in Rome, do they do as the Romans?' HRM Practices of US Subsidiaries in Europe, *Management International Review*, Vol.38, 47–64.

Gooderham, P.N., Nordhaug, O. and Ringdal, K. (1999) 'Institutional and rational determinants of organizational practices: human resource management in European firms', *Administrative Science Quarterly,* Vol.44, No.3, 507–31.

Guest, D.E. (1990) 'Human resource management and the American dream', *Journal of Management Studies,* Vol.27, No.4, 977–87.

Gunnigle, P. (1995) 'Collectivism and the management of industrial relations in greenfield sites', *Human Resource Management Journal,* Vol.5, No.3, 24–40.

Gunnnigle, P., Murphy, K.M., Cleveland, J., Heraty, N. and Morley, M. (2002) 'Localisation in human resource management: comparing American and European multinational corporations', *Advances in International Management,* Vol.14, 259–84.

Hall, P. and Soskice, D. (2001) 'An introduction to the varieties of capitalism', pp. 1–68, in Hall, P. and Soskice, D. (eds) *Varieties of Capitalism: The Institutional Foundations of Comparative Advantage,* Oxford: Oxford University Press.

Harbison, F.H. and Myers, C. (eds) (1959) *Management in the Industrial World: An International Analysis,* New York: McGraw Hill.

Harcourt, M. and Wood, G. (2007). 'The importance of employment protection for skill development in coordinated market economies', *European Journal of Industrial Relations,* Vol.13, No.2, 141–59.

Harrison, G. (2000) *The Politics of Democratization in Rural Mozambique,* New York: Edward Mellon Press.

Harzing, A.W. and Sorge, A. (2003) 'The relative impact of country of origin and universal contingencies on internationalization strategies and corporate control in multinational enterprises: worldwide and european perspectives', *Organizational Studies,* Vol.24, 187–214.

Hirst, P. and Thompson, G. (1999) *Globalisation in Question* (2nd edn). Cambridge: Polity.

Hoftstede, G. (1980) *Culture's Consequences.* Thousand Oaks: CA: Sage.

Hoftstede, G. (2001) *Culture's Consequences: Comparing Values, Behaviours, Institutions and Organizations Across Nations* (2nd edn). Thousand Oaks, CA: Sage.

Holt Larsen, H. and Mayrhofer, W. (eds) (2006) *Managing Human Resources in Europe: A Thematic Approach*, London: Routledge.

Jacobi, O., Keller, B. and Müller-Jentsch, W. (1998) 'Germany: Facing New Challenges', in Ferner, A. and Hyman, R. (eds) *Changing Industrial Relations in Europe,* Oxford: Blackwell.

Jacoby, S.M. (1997) *Modern Manors: Welfare Capitalism Since the New Deal,* Princeton, NJ: Princeton University Press.

Kamoche, K., Debrah, Y., Horwitz, F. and Nkombo Muuka, G. (eds) (2003) *Managing Human Resources in Africa*, London: Routledge.

Kerr, C., Dunlop, J.T., Harbison, F.H. and Myers, C.A. (1960) *Industrialism and Industrial Man: The Problems of Labour and Management in Economic Growth*, Harmondsworth: Penguin.

Kidger, P.J. (1991) 'The emergence of international human resource management', *International Journal of Human Resource Management*, Vol.2, No.2, 149–63.

La Porta, R., Lopez-de-Silanes, F., Shleifer, A. and Vishny, R. (2000) 'Investor protection and corporate governance', *Journal of Financial Economics,* Vol.58, 3–27.

Lincoln, J. and Kalleberg, A. (1990) *Culture, Control and Commitment: A Study of Work Organization in the United States and Japan,* Cambridge: Cambridge University Press.

Locke, R., Kochan, T. and Piore, M. (1995) 'Reconceptualizing comparative industrial relations: lessons from international research', *International Labour Review,* Vol.134, 139–61.

Marsden, D. (1999) *A Theory of Employment Systems,* Oxford: Oxford University Press.

McDonnell, A., Lavelle, J., Gunnigle, P. and Collings, D.G. (2007) 'Management research on multinational corporations: a methodological critique', *Economic and Social Review*, Vol.38, No.2, 235–58.

McSweeney, B. (2002) 'Hoftstede's model of national culture differences and their consequences: a triumph of faith – a failure of analysis' *Human Relations,* Vol.55, 5–34.

Meyer, J.W. and Rowan, B. (1977) 'Institutional organizations: formal structure as myth and ceremony', *American Journal of Sociology,* Vol.83, 340–63.

Morley, M., Brewster, C., Gunnigle, P. and Mayerhofer, W. (1996) 'Evaluating change in European industrial relations: research evidence on trends at organisational level', *International Journal of Human Resource Management,* Vol.7, No.3, 640–56.

Morley, M.J., Gunnigle, P. and Collings, D.G. (eds) (2006) *Global Industrial Relations,* London: Routledge.

Morley, M.J., Heraty, N. and Michailova, S. (2009) *Managing Human Resources in Central and Eastern Europe*, New York: Routledge.

North, D.C. (1990) *Institutions, Institutional Change and Economic Performance,* Cambridge: Cambridge University Press.

O'Hagan, E. (2002) *Employee Relations in the Periphery of Europe: The Unfolding of the European Social Model*, London: Palgrave.

Pagano, M. and Volpin, P. (2005) 'The political economy of corporate governance', *American Economic Review,* Vol.95, 1005–30.

Pitcher, A. (2002) *Transforming Mozambique: The Politics of Privatization*, Cambridge: Cambridge University Press.

Roe, M. (2003) *Political Determinants of Corporate Governance*, Oxford: Oxford University Press.

Rollinson, D. and Dundon, T. (2007) *Understanding Employment Relations*, London: McGraw Hill.

Rubery, J. and Grimshaw, D. (2003) *The Organization of Employment: An International Perspective,* Basingstoke, Palgrave.

Schneider, S.C. and Barsoux, J.L. (2003) *Managing Across Cultures* (2nd edn), Harlow: Prentice Hall.

Scullion, H. (1995) 'International human resource management' in Storey, J. (ed.) *Human Resource Management: A Critical Text,* London: Thomson Learning.

Sorge, A. (2004) 'Cross-national differences in human resources and organisation', in Harzing, A.W. and van Ruyssevekdt, J. (eds) *International Human Resource Management,* (2nd edn), London: Sage.

Sorge, A. and Streeck, W. (1988) 'Industrial relations and technological change: the case for an extended perspective' in Hyman, R. and Streeck, W. (eds) *New Technology and Industrial Relations*, Oxford: Blackwell.

Sorge, A. and Warner, M. (1986) *Comparative Factory Organization*. Aldershot: Gower.

Storey, J. (1992) *Developments in the Management of Human Resources*, Oxford: Blackwell.

Strauss, G. and Hanson, M. (1997) 'Review article: American anti-management theories of organization: a critique of paradigm proliferation', *Human Relations,* Vol.50, 1426–9.

Tayeb, M. (1996) 'Hoftstede' in Warner, M. (ed.) *International Encyclopaedia of Business and Management,* London: Thomson Learning.

Taylor, P. and Bain, P. (2003) 'Call centre organising in adversity: from Excell to Vertex', in Gall, G. (ed.) *Fighting for Fairness at Work: Campaigns for Union Recognition,* London: Routledge.

Thelen, K. (2001) 'Varieties of labor politics in the developed democracies', in Hall, P. and Soskice, D. (eds) *Varieties of Capitalism: The Institutional Basis of Competitive Advantage,* Oxford: Oxford University Press.

Tolbert, P.S. and Zucker, L.G. (1996) 'The institutionalisation of institutional theory', in Clegg, S. Hardy, C. and Nord, W.R. (eds) *Handbook of Organization Studies,* London: Sage.

Trompenaars, F. (1993) *Riding the Waves of Culture* (2nd edn), London: Nicholas Brealey.

Turner, T. (2006) 'Industrial relations systems, economic efficiency and social equity in the 1990s', *Review of Social Economy*, Vol.64, No.1, 93–118.

Webster, E. and Wood, G. (2005) 'Human resource management practice and institutional constraints', *Employee Relations*, Vol.27, No.4, 369–85.

Whitley, R. (1999) *Divergent Capitalisms: The Social Structuring and Change of Business Systems,* Oxford, Oxford University Press.

Wilkinson, B., Gamble, J., Humphrey, J., Morris, J. and Anthony, D. (2001) 'The new international division of labour in Asian electronics: work organization and human resources in Japan and Malaysia", *Journal of Management Studies*, Vol.38, No.5, 675–95.

Wood, G. and Brewster, C. (eds) (2007) *Industrial Relations in Africa*, London: Palgrave.

CHAPTER 13
UNDERSTANDING AND MANAGING CAREERS IN CHANGING CONTEXTS

Dulini Fernando, Laurie Cohen and Amal El-Sawad

When my children grow up I don't want them to have a job, I want them to have a career.

(Prime Minister Tony Blair on a visit to the Sheffield Job Centre,
Sheffield Star, 5 February 1998: 1. Cited in Mallon 1998: 48)

The word career is a divisive word. It's a word that divides the normal life from business or professional life, whatever that is. Everybody should have work they love, that's another story, but that's different from that word *career*, which says I will spend any number of hours pursuing this thing, which I may or may not be interested in even, to get somewhere, and the rest of my life is another story.

(Gracey Paley, from Bach and Hall, 1997: 228)

Life is what happens to us when you're busy making other plans.

(John Lennon, 'Beautiful Boy (Darling Boy)', 1980)

Introduction

This chapter is about career: how we can understand the concept of career, and how we might go about managing our own careers and other people's. Academics have examined careers in a whole range of ways: from psychological and sociological perspectives, as objective realities or subjective constructions, from individual and organisational points of view. Similarly, in everyday language, career has a number of different meanings and is used in a variety of contexts: the career of the footballer, the bureaucrat, the politician or the patient; career education, career breaks, career mentoring. If we were to analyse what career means in each of these cases, we would come up with a rich, diverse and probably ambiguous picture. In spite of this diversity, however, what many of these examples have in common is a relationship between individuals and organisations. The nature of this relationship is a fundamental issue within HRM.

This chapter has seven sections. The first focuses on the concept of career, considering a number of academic and popular definitions and usages, while the second explores the way in which academic thinking about career has developed, including traditional psychological and sociological approaches, as well as interpretive perspectives. A significant aspect of career is the notion of success and therefore section three examines how individuals make sense of this. Section four explores debates on the changing nature of careers focusing on some of the boundaries individuals encounter, while section five addresses the gendering of career, introducing some of the frameworks which have been developed to shed light on the particular ways in which women enact their careers. Section six examines the impact of ageing on careers. Finally, the last section turns to organisational interventions in career management, discussing these in the context of current debates about changing careers.

Diverse understandings of career

The term 'career' conjures up an array of images. We might use it to refer to a lifetime of service in a bureaucracy, or to a professional career such as law or medicine. In contrast, we could talk about the more temporary career of a professional sports person. In years gone by, 'career girl' was used to differentiate a woman in paid employment from housewives and mothers. We could refer to the career of a drug addict, a patient or a criminal. In contrast, we might also talk about the career of an academic subject, for example, the career of organisational analysis. In short, it is a term we use every day, unproblematically, in a whole variety of situations and contexts. But what do we actually mean by career? Is it just another way of talking about paid employment? Could any job be described as a career, or is the term exclusive to a particular type of position? And what role, if any, does one's life outside work play in the definition of career? An academic analysis of career and its management clearly requires some consideration of these questions.

A traditional view of career is illustrated in Wilensky's (1961: 523) classic definition:

> Let us define career in structural terms. A career is a succession of related jobs arranged in a hierarchy of prestige, through which persons move in an ordered (more or less predictable) sequence.

Implicit within this definition is the idea of career as paid work. The reference to 'hierarchy of prestige' suggests a bureaucratic context. Notably, Wilensky describes career as a structural phenomenon, that is, it seems to have its own existence independent of the individual. This view implies that careers are real things, prescriptions, available for people to take part in, in a particular, set way. This conflation of the concept of career with bureaucracy (with implicit notions of hierarchy and steady advancement) persisted through the mid to late twentieth century. Indeed, paths and ladders are familiar metaphors in talk about careers. While the path suggests career as a journey towards an ultimate destination, implicit in the ladder image is the notion of career as hierarchical and, again, oriented to a goal. Other popular metaphors for describing careers include tracks and arrows (and of course, the more cynical rat race).

In contrast are those definitions of career which extend beyond the domain of paid employment, to the sequence of an individual's life experiences more generally. Interestingly, although this more inclusive notion of career is becoming increasingly popular, its origins date back to the 1930s, when Chicago sociologist Hughes (1937: 413) explained:

> A career consists, objectively, of a series of statuses and clearly defined offices ... subjectively, a career is the moving perspective in which the person sees his [sic] life as a whole and interprets the meaning of his various attributes, actions, and the things that happen to him.

While acknowledging the structural, objective dimension of career, Hughes' definition also highlights the notion of the career as situated within the individual, thus emphasising its subjective dimension. Thus it is not the case that people simply act out prescribed career patterns; instead, they construct their career in dynamic negotiation with their social, economic and cultural context. Hughes' work stimulated research into career in a whole variety of social situations: from funeral directors to tubercular patients and marijuana users. Goffman (1961) further developed Hughes' notion of career, subverting conventional definitions which equated career with occupational advancement. More recent definitions, particularly those put forward by academics writing in the fields of HRM and career guidance, tend to reflect this broader, more inclusive approach: 'the individual's development in learning and work throughout life' (Collin and Watts, 1996: 393). Interestingly, Savickas (2002) has argued that this subjective element is not simply a way of looking at a career, but that it is fundamental to the career concept. In his words: 'the essential point is that career denotes a reflection on the course of one's vocational behaviour; it is not vocational behaviour' (2002: 384).

Box 13.1 HRM in practice   A challenge to bureaucratic notions of career

Traditionally the term 'career' has been reserved for those who expect to enjoy rises laid out within a respectable profession. The term is coming to be used, however, in a broadened sense to refer to any social strand of any person's course through life … Such a career is not a thing that can be brilliant or disappointing; it can no more be success than a failure. One value of the concept is its two-sidedness. One side is linked to the internal matters held dearly and closely, such as image of self and felt identity; the other side concerns official position, jural position and style of life and is part of a publicly accessible institutional complex. The concept of career, then, allows one to move back and forth between the personal and the public, between the self and its significant society. *(Goffman, 1961: 127)*

- How does this compare to other definitions introduced thus far?
- Would you say that Goffman places more value on certain kinds of careers?
- How might a researcher go about studying the 'two sides' of career

---

Finally, different subject disciplines lead to and often explain variations in definitions of career. For example, economists may define career as 'the vehicle through which human capital is accrued through a lifetime of education and experience' whereas those from the discipline of politics might understand career as 'the sequence of endeavours to maximise self-interest, through successive attempts to gain power, status and influence' (Adamson *et al.*, 1998: 253).

However, notwithstanding the 'elasticity' (Collin and Young, 2000) of the career concept and its diverse constitution within particular national – cultural, organisational and occupational contexts and from different disciplinary perspectives, we agree with Savickas (2002) who suggests that central to all of these are notions of development and movement through time.

Sociological and psychological approaches to the study of career

Career can be approached from a range of perspectives. Traditionally, scholars attempted to study careers through psychological or sociological disciplines. Psychological work on career focuses on the individual. From a psychological perspective, career theory can be separated into vocational literature and developmental literature (Gunz and Peiperl, 2007). The vocational literature on career is based on the notion of 'agency' (i.e. individuals' capacity to act). According to this perspective individuals should find out about their capabilities and match them to appropriate occupations. Holland's (1973) work on person–environment fit is a classic example of this view.

Box 13.2 HRM in practice   Person–environment fit

According to Holland, occupations have personalities as people do and therefore people who are in occupations which are *congruent* with their personality types will enjoy more satisfaction, success and stay in the occupation for a long period of time, while people in incongruent matches will change over to occupations that suit their personalities.

(Arnold, 2004)

Holland classifies personality types and work environments into six types which he labels as realistic, investigative, artistic, social, enterprising and conventional (often referred to by the acronym RIASEC).

Table 13.1 Personality type and work environment

	Description	Sample occupations
Realistic	Extremes of this type usually have good physical skills, but may have trouble expressing themselves or in communicating their feelings to others. They like to work outdoors and to work with tools and machines. They prefer to deal with things rather than with ideas or people. They enjoy creating things with their hands, and prefer responsibilities with a technical, mechanical or engineering focus	Farmer Carpenter Mechanical engineer
Investigative	This category centres around science and scientific activities. Extremes of this type are task-oriented; they are not particularly interested in working around other people. They enjoy solving abstract problems, and they have a great need to understand the physical world. They prefer to think through problems rather than act them out. Such people enjoy ambiguous challenges and do not like highly structured situations with many rules. They frequently are original and creative, especially in scientific areas. They enjoy responsibilities that offer opportunities for research and study	Chemist
Artistic	The extreme type here is artistically oriented, and likes to work in artistic settings that offer many opportunities for self-expression. Such people have little interest in problems that are highly structured or require gross physical strength, preferring those that can be solved through self-expression in artistic media. Investigative types in preferring to work alone, but have a greater need for individualistic expression, and usually are less assertive about their own opinions and capabilities. They describe themselves as independent, original, unconventional, expressive and intense. They enjoy responsibilities that provide opportunities to utilise their imagination and creativity such as writing, artistic design or dramatic performance	Painter Writer
Social	The pure type here is sociable, responsible, humanistic and concerned with the welfare of others. These people usually express themselves well and get along well with others; they like attention and seek situations that allow them to be near the centre of the group. They prefer to solve problems by discussion with others, or by arranging or rearranging relationships between others; they have little interest in situations requiring physical exertion or working with machinery. Such people describe themselves as cheerful, popular and achieving, and as good leaders. They enjoy responsibilities with a social emphasis that provide opportunities to help or relate to others	Social worker Counsellor

(Continued)

Table 13.1 Personality type and work environment (cont.)

	Description	Sample occupations
Enterprising	The extreme of this type has great facility with words, especially in selling, dominating and leading; frequently these people are in sales work. They see themselves as energetic, enthusiastic, adventurous, self-confident and dominant, and they prefer social tasks where they can assume leadership. They enjoy persuading others to their viewpoints. They are impatient with precise work or work involving long periods of intellectual effort. They like power, status and material wealth, and enjoy working in expensive settings. They enjoy challenging, enterprising tasks that result in organisational or personal growth and advancement	Sales representative Entrepreneur
Conventional	Extremes of this type prefer the highly ordered activities, both verbal and numerical, that characterise office work. People scoring high fit well into large organisations but do not seek leadership; they respond to power and are comfortable working in a well-established chain of command. They dislike ambiguous situations, preferring to know precisely what is expected of them. Such people describe themselves as conventional, stable, well controlled and dependable. They have little interest in problems requiring physical skills or intense relationships with others, and are most effective at well-defined tasks. They value material possessions and status. They enjoy organisational and routine responsibilities involving the manipulation of data, and prefer following established policies and procedures	Auditor Clerical staff Banker

Source: Based on from Holland, 1973.

Holland recognises that individuals are likely to represent more than one of these types. However, he argues that one type is usually evidenced most strongly. While there is support for person–environment fit models as a useful way of thinking about how individuals interact with their environments, some scholars have questioned the extent to which the degree of fit between personality types and occupational types is an effective predictor of vocational outcomes such as job satisfaction (see Tinsley 2000, Arnold, 2004). Holland later emphasized that vocational predictions for a person based on his theory works better when contextual variables such as age, gender and socioeconomic status are taken into account (Holland and Grottfredson, 1992). Holland's theory can be criticised for implying that people's personalities are stable over time and in doing so not leaving allowance for personal change. Moreover, scholars have raised questions about Holland's lack of attention to other life roles which impact on individuals' careers (Brown, 1987).

Development psychology presents a view of career as a dynamic and changing process that evolves and develops over time (Gunz and Peiperl, 2007). This perspective takes a micro-societal focus and emphasises individual development and self-actualisation. Donald Super's lifespan approach to careers can be taken as an example. Super (1980) argues that career development takes places across the individual's entire lifespan and therefore can be divided into five stages: growth, exploration, establishment, maintenance and disengagement.

Super postulated that not everyone progresses through these stages at fixed ages or in the same fashion, and that within each stage are tasks whose mastery allows people to function successfully within that stage while preparing them to move on to the next task. For example, before entering the maintenance stage, many individuals are in the process of asking the standard mid-life question, 'Do I want to do this job for the next twenty years?' eventually deciding to either hang on or let go. If they decide to hang on, they enter the maintenance stage. If they decide to let go and change job, company or career, they recycle back to earlier

Table 13.2

Stage	Age	Characteristics
Growth	*Birth–14*	Form self-concept, develop capacity, attitudes, interests and needs, and form a general understanding of the world of work
Exploration	*15–24*	
Crystallisation		Develop ideas about general field of work through trial and error
Specification		Turning developing preferences into vocational choices
Implementation		Making plans to enter and then entering
Establishment	*25–44*	
Stabilisation		Settling into occupation, including lifestyle
Consolidation		Making oneself secure in chosen occupation, demonstrating value and contribution
Advancement		Increasing earnings and level of responsibility
Maintenance	*45–64*	
Holding		Retaining position in face of changing contexts and competition
Updating		A more proactive version of holding, keeping abreast of changes in work demands and adapting goals
Innovation		Finding new perspectives and ways of doing familiar tasks
Disengagement	*65–*	
Decelerating		Reducing workload and pace, maybe by delegation
Retirement planning		In terms of finance and lifestyle
Retirement living		Learning to live without work

Source: Adapted from Super, *et al.*, 1988.

stages, adopt new career development objectives, and move forward from there. For those who hold on, they maintain what they have and update their skills and knowledge. One of Super's main tenets is that people seek career satisfaction through work roles in which they can express themselves and implement develop their self-concept (individual's understanding of the self). Therefore he argues that self-knowledge is the key to career choice and job satisfaction.

Super's model can be criticised for paying only little attention to the impact of social and organisational changes (Cohen and El-Sawad, 2009) which have the potential to shape individuals' careers. Moreover, it disregards factors that affect women's career choices such as gendered divisions of labour at home that often force women to take breaks in employment or undertake work on a part-time or flexible basis in order to harmonise home and work (Arnold, 1997). However, Super's theory has greatly influenced how we look at career practices. In addition to stages of the life cycle, Super has also highlighted several life roles a person might occupy; worker, home-worker, citizen, leisurite, student etc. He argues that any of these roles may occupy the majority of a person's daily life at any given time (Arnold, 1997). People can use Super's model as a framework to consider how to allocate their time between different roles in life and their current dominant career stage.

Traditionally, sociological perspectives of 'career' were based on the concept of 'career' being objective and external to the individual (Gunz and Peiperl, 2007). According to this view individuals' careers are constrained by a variety of factors and are therefore a representation of social structure rather than individual make up (Inkson, 2007). Early career theory which focused on social structural determinants of occupational choice such as social class background and parents' occupations grew from this perspective (Gunz and Peiperl, 2007). According to this view, however talented or motivated individuals are, their career progression could be constrained by larger forces beyond their control. An alternative view is that individuals can transcend social boundaries if they have the will to do so. Indeed, a number of scholars have taken this approach to study career by focusing on not only the social structures that constrain individuals' careers but also on how people perceive and engage with these structures. Stephen Barley's (1989) structuration model is one of the first attempts to look at career by focusing on the complex interplay between individuals and society. According to this model it is not the case that context determines people's careers nor do people have a free will, but rather career is about how people navigate their social structures.

Recently, scholars have developed Barley's (1989) work and used his approach to study individuals' careers. Duberley and colleagues (2006) applied Barley's structuration model of career to their study of how scientists in the UK and New Zealand developed their careers within organisational and other contextual settings. Their findings highlight the interrelationship of five institutional contexts which scientists saw as both constraining and/or enabling to them in developing a career: science, profession, family, government and national culture. The scholars proposed two modes of engagement: transformation-oriented and maintenance-oriented, which their respondents adopted to manage perceived contextual constraints on their careers. For instance, some scientists had worked towards change by means such as collaborating with campaign groups to widen women's access to scientific careers, while others had preferred to work within existing structures by means such as developing their disciplines in relation to opportunities available in the market. Scholars have developed Duberley et al.'s (2006) framework to investigate the careers of British academics pursuing careers across international boundaries (see Richardson, 2009) and self-initiated, highly skilled Lebanese migrants to France (Al-Ariss, 2010). These studies usefully highlight the various social contexts which impact on individuals' careers while illustrating how career actors navigate contextual barriers via different modes of engagement and with what implications.

Another sociological approach to exploring career, inspired by the work of the late French sociologist Pierre Bourdieu, is the application of field theory. Field theory, originally developed in relation to social class, comprises three components: field, habitus and capital. Field is the social context within which individuals are situated, while habitus refers to ways of thinking, feeling, evaluating, speaking and acting. Individuals continuously modify their 'habitus' (Duberley and Cohen, 2010) according to the context they are situated within. Fields and habitus are linked in a circular structure where they continuously influence and shape each other (Iellatchitch et al., 2003). Capitals are the resources valid within a particular field (Mayrhofer et al., 2004). When applied to the study of career, fields become the social contexts within which individuals' careers unfold and where they make career moves. Occupational sectors and organisations are examples of career fields. Habitus are the frameworks of thinking and action within career fields (Duberley and Cohen, 2010) while capitals are the resources individuals need to be successful within a particular career field. The aspect of field theory that has most captured careers researchers' interest is the capital dimension.

Box 13.3 HRM in practice   Career capitals

Pierre Bourdieu distinguished between four types of capitals; economic, social, cultural and symbolic capital (Mayrhofer *et al.*, 2004). Economic capital refers to convertible monetary resources, social capital involves resources based on social connections and/or group membership/affiliations (Mayrhofer *et al.*, 2004), and cultural capital is the accumulated result of educational and cultural effort undertaken by the individual and/or their ancestors (Iellatchitch *et al.*, 2003). Finally, symbolic capital, which Bourdieu introduced much later, is the combination of the three capitals above which is socially recognised as legitimate (Mayrhofer *et al.*, 2004). Each individual within a specific career field is likely to possess a unique portfolio of capitals.

The genetic disposition of the person and the social context they are born into shapes the career capitals they hold (Mayrhofer *et al.*, 2004). However, individuals are also likely to acquire career capitals through education, professional development and social connections. Bourdieu suggests that economic, social and cultural capitals are convertible with each other (Bourdieu, 1986). Only a few studies have investigated this in detail; however Postone *et al.* (1993) argue that economic capital is more easily converted into cultural, social and symbolic capital than vice versa.

Scholars have developed ideas about career capital in different ways. Examining career capital through a gendered lens Duberley and Cohen (2010) provide insights into constraints often missing in discussion of this concept. Based on their research into scientific careers, they show how women scientists experience a deficit of social capital due to being left out of male-dominated networks. Studies have also drawn attention to other forms of career capital apart from the ones Bourdieu proposed. For example, gender itself is a form of career capital where men are comparatively advantaged over women in their careers due to their gender (Duberley and Cohen, 2010; Huppatz, 2009). Likewise 'domestic circumstances', or rather having an understanding and supportive partner, could be an important form of career capital for women in particular (Duberley and Cohen, 2010). Career stage is a form of career capital where a relatively late career stage may allow individuals authority and legitimacy to do things that they could not do earlier on in their careers (Duberley and Cohen, 2010; Fernando and Cohen, 2011). Furthermore, Al-Ariss and Syed (2010) argue that for highly skilled Lebanese migrants in Paris, citizenship worked as a powerful form of career capital. They show how individuals possessing dual citizenship, i.e. Lebanese coupled with French or American citizenship, faced relatively easy immigration procedures to France in comparison to those with only Lebanese citizenship.

Overall, in this section we introduced psychological and sociological approaches to studying career. Under psychological work we discussed Holland's (1973) theory of person–environment fit which focuses on individuals' capacity to act, and Super's (1980) lifespan approach to career which addresses individual development and self-actualisation (see Super *et al.*, 1988). Under sociological approaches we looked at structuration models (e.g. Barley, 1989) and field theory (Mayrhofer *et al.*, 2004) which attempts to study career by focusing on the complex interplay between individuals and society. Psychological and sociological perspectives (and their combinations) continue to be widely used to explore contemporary careers.

Interpretivism

Recently, scholars have become increasingly interested in subjectivity in career – that is, how people perceive, account for and experience their career lives. These interpretive perspectives consider careers as unfolding stories, narratives which can vary according to the 'storyteller', their audience and the particular context in which they are situated at a given moment. Thus as Inkson has stated; 'when we talk about our careers, we tell stories about ourselves, any career is essentially a story' (Inkson, 2007: 277). Considering careers from a narrative perspective can be useful in a number of ways: first it enables the researcher to understand patterns of both change and continuity in a person's career over time; second, it illuminates contradictions, inconsistencies and ambiguities inherent to individual accounts and finally stories enable the researcher to understand peoples' relationships with their social worlds which is especially important since individuals do not construct their stories in a social vacuum (Cohen *et al.*, 2004). With regard to the last point, the issue of harmonising home and work is an emerging theme in people's reflections about their careers. Indeed, scholars have commented on how boundaries between home and work domains are becoming blurred where we find it incredibly difficult to define where one domain begins and the other ends (Cohen *et al.*, 2009; Nippert-Eng, 1995). Due to the interconnectedness between different life domains we cannot understand people's careers in isolation to their life worlds. According to Savickas *et al.* (2009), all career interventions should allow individuals to narrate a story which 'portrays their career and life with coherence and continuity (ibid.: 245).

Closely connected with this 'narrative turn' in careers research is a growing interest in the potential of social constructionism for illuminating aspects of career that are less easily accessed through other perspectives (Young and Collin, 2004). Social constructionism is based on the idea that 'reality' does not exist, 'out there' as an objective entity, knowable if one has the right instruments, but rather subjectively constructed through social interaction (Burr, 2003; Gergen, 2001). From this perspective, career is not a fixed set of occupations, roles or positions, but rather is a dynamic, 'elastic' construct, created by people through their social relationships as they move through time and space (Cohen *et al.*, 2004). We see three key implications of taking a social constructionist view to career research. First, social constructionism contextualises career (Young and Collin, 2004) by highlighting how individuals and their societies are deeply implicated with each other and continuously and iteratively impact on each other. This perspective therefore looks at career in relation to the various social contexts within which it is embedded such as organisational, familial and wider sociocultural contexts. Thus it highlights how individuals' careers are both enabled and constrained by the contexts they are situated within and offers insights into people's career meaning making in relation to their social contexts. Second, given its elucidation of the interplay of individual agency and social structures, social constructionism has the potential to illuminate how individuals contribute towards maintaining and/or redefining the contexts within which they operate through their career enactment. Third, social constructionism takes a critical stance towards taken-for-granted understandings and attempts to understand the processes by which understandings come to be seen as 'natural' (Young and Collin, 2004). Thus it encourages researchers to question conventional (bureaucratic) definitions of career (Gowler and Legge, 1989; cited in Cohen *et al.* 2004), assumptions about what constitutes viable career paths and notions of acceptable career behaviour (Cohen *et al.*, 2004).

Fernando and Cohen (2011) used social constructionism to explore professional women's careers in Sri Lanka. Their findings highlight how women are constrained by elements of organisational cultures such as ideal worker norms (Gambles *et al.*, 2006) which require employees to be present and visible within the organisation at all times. The scholars identify eight strategies the women in their sample used to overcome perceived contextual influences and climb up their organisations' hierarchies: adapting, compromising, manipulating, deceiving, explaining, networking, resisting and opting out. Their findings also reveal how women contribute towards maintaining and/or redefining elements of their organisations through their career enactment. For example, some women adapted their personal lives to fulfil their organisations' demands by working long hours. These women, however, contributed towards maintaining the long work hour cultures (see Lyng, 2010) which ultimately constrain women's career development (see Bolton and Muzio, 2007). That is, women who find it difficult to devote additional hours to work because of domestic commitments will continue to face challenges in developing their careers within organisational contexts.

Interpretive perspectives consider careers as unfolding stories which can vary according to the storyteller and their cultural milieu. With the increasing emphasis on hearing individuals' voices and the widespread recognition that we cannot understand people's careers in isolation from their life worlds (Savickas *et al.*, 2009), interpretive and constructivist approaches are becoming extremely popular methods through which to study careers.

Career success

Career success can be defined as 'the accomplishment of desirable work related outcomes at any point in a person's work experiences over time' (Arthur *et al.*, 2005: 179). The career success literature can be divided into two broad strands of research (Arnold and Cohen, 2008). The first strand focuses on predictors of career success where factors such as the number of hours worked, social capital and political knowledge and skills are examined (Ng *et al.*, 2005). However, one can argue that certain predictors of career success are outcomes of forms of career success themselves. For example, an individual may gain political knowledge and skills (predictors of career success), through their hierarchical advancement within an organisation which is a form of career success itself (Arnold and Cohen, 2008). Thus it is rather difficult to make clear-cut distinctions between variables in practice.

The second strand of research within the career success literature addresses the different ways people conceptualise career success and the degree to which they are related to one another (Sturges, 1999). In conceptualising career success, a distinction between subjective and objective career success is frequently made. Objective career success has been defined as 'an external perspective that delineates more or less tangible indicators of an individual's career situation' (Arthur *et al.*, 2005: 179). Verifiable attainments such as pay, promotions, rate of salary growth and hierarchical level attained in the organisation are examples. Subjective career success in contrast, is defined as an individual's evaluation of their career, across any dimensions important to them (Van Maanen, 1977; cited in Arthur *et al.*, 2005). However, the distinction between objective and subjective career success is less clear-cut than it may first seem (Arnold and Cohen, 2008). For example, although objective success criteria are often described as entities that are easily observable, things that are real are not always readily observable or measurable expect by asking people about their perceptions of them (Arnold and Cohen, 2008). Thus objective measures of career success such as promotions and salary increases can be taken as a mark of success only if the individual perceives it to be a mark of their success where this perception may be socially influenced (Burr, 2003). Studies highlight that men and women conceptualise career success differently.

| Box 13.4 HRM in practice | Do men and women make sense of career success differently? |

I think a spirit of generosity and kindness is extremely important. People forget that, in this day and age especially, with women wanting equality and sometimes, I think mistakenly, using male models of success. There are virtues that are oftentimes unique to women. Those are going to be important to the new kind of success. Success being defined not by how many billions of dollars did that company make, how many new products did you get out, but as something that makes a wonderful difference in the long term. When people measure their lives in those terms, the passion is there, the self-guidance is there, and the rewards are there. The success is always there.

(Amy Tan, Academy of Achievement, 1996)

Research suggests that women's conceptualisations of career success encompass a wide range of notions such as the degree to which their work is interesting and challenging and whether they gain recognition for their efforts (Cornelius and Skinner, 2008; Lirio *et al.*, 2007; Sturges, 1999). In contrast men's conceptualisations have been limited to hierarchical advancement (Cornelius and Skinner 2008; Sturges 1999). Research findings also suggest that women tend to be ethically value laden (Lirio *et al.*, 2007) in conceptualising career success. For example, most senior women HRM managers in Cornelius and Skinner's (2008) study in the UK had emphasised the importance of doing work they saw as worthwhile and none had been interested in the notion of promotion at any cost (see also Sturges, 1999). However, the men in this study had indicated interest in the notion of 'promotion at any cost'. Significantly, studies indicate that women describe career success in terms of achieving a state of balance in their jobs in contrast to men who are unbothered about home–work harmonisation (Sturges, 1999).

Cultural variations in the way individuals conceptualise career success have been noted.

Box 13.5 HRM in practice   Making sense of career success – cultural effects

Studies indicate that hierarchical advancement is a significant mark of career success to South Asian people (Budhwar *et al.*, 2005; Cohen *et al.*, 2009). For example, in contrast to women from more economically developed Western countries, professional and managerial women in India aspire to reach the highest possible level in their organisations' career structures (see Budhwar *et al.*, 2005).

Scholars also argue that the importance women place on work–life balance as a signifier of career success is culturally situated. For example Lirio *et al.*'s (2007) cross–national findings of high achieving women in Canada, Argentina and Mexico reveal that Argentinian and Mexican women did not have as strong feelings about striking a balance between work and family as did the Canadian women. The authors suggest that this may be due to parent and worker roles being more conflicting in Canada due to the lack of affordable domestic help (Lirio *et al.*, 2007).

Interestingly, some Mexican women in Lirio *et al.*'s (2007) sample referred to the importance of God in making their lives successful. Reference to God in individuals' conceptualisations of career success is yet to emerge in the Western literature. Indeed, these findings highlight that for individuals' career making is socially and culturally influenced.

The changing nature of careers?

There is an emerging consensus that in today's world of movement, diversity, flexibility and short-term relationships, careers are characterised by uncertainty and frequent change – of organisation, role, colleagues and required skills. While the causes and extent of change in today's world of work is still a subject of vigorous debate, scholars argue that bureaucratic careers are not only seen as less likely, but they are also perceived as less appealing. In the literature on emerging careers, organisations are frequently depicted as 'stultifying individuals' initiative and creativity and promoting an unhealthy dependence on organisations for the conduct of one's working life' (Cohen and Mallon, 1999). People have been encouraged to weaken their links with organisations, and to develop relationships based on short-term contracts and financial arrangements.

Scholars have argued for more embracing notions of career and have developed metaphors of boundaryless and protean careers (Arthur and Rousseau 1996; Mirvis and Hall 1996) to capture this changing landscape. While different in significant ways which we will discuss briefly below, both see careers as typically cyclical rather than linear, characterised by ongoing learning and development and involving movement and change. Although the notions of boundaryless and protean careers have sometimes been used synonymously, as a way of describing new kinds of careers and especially careers which do not conform to bureaucratic norms (Briscoe and Hall, 2006), in a number of recent articles scholars have sought to highlight their differences. Regarding the boundaryless career, introducing the concept for the first time Arthur and Rousseau (1996: 6) identified what they saw as its six key components:

1 Careers that transcend the boundaries of different employers.
2 Careers that draw validity and marketability from outside the present employing organisation.
3 Careers that are sustained and supported by external networks.
4 Careers that challenge traditional assumptions about career advancement and movement up through an organisational hierarchy.
5 Careers in which individuals reject opportunities for advancement for personal or family reasons.
6 Careers that are based on an actor's interpretation, who may see their career as boundaryless regardless of contextual constraints.

Central here is the idea of careers becoming less dependent on a single employing organisation, and more in the hands of individuals to develop as they see fit.

Whereas the boundaryless career is seen as involving both physical and psychological dimensions, the protean career is conceptualised more in terms of the latter – about individuals constructing their own careers, guided by their personal value systems and subjective notions of success. Coined by Hall in 1976, the metaphor has been developed (Briscoe and Hall, 2006; Briscoe et al., 2006) to describe careers in which 'the individual, not the organization, is in charge, the core values are freedom and growth, and the main success criteria are subjective (psychological) vs. objective (position, salary)' (Hall, 2004: 4).

While boundaryless and protean career metaphors are widely celebrated, questions have been raised about the concepts. For example, some scholars propose that these conceptualisations are a way of taking the responsibility for career away from organisations and putting the responsibility straight onto the shoulders of individual employees (Arnold and Cohen, 2008). Moreover, others have taken issue with this thesis itself (e.g. Bagdadli et al., 2003; Cohen and Mallon, 1999; Gunz et al., 2000; Mallon and Cohen, 2001), arguing that careers have not become completely boundaryless but rather there is a coexistence of choice and constraint in people's careers.

From boundaryless to reconceptualising boundaries

It is interesting that over the past couple of years some scholars have begun to turn their attention to the constraints which impact on individuals' careers, and the issue of boundaries, rather than boundarylessness has come to the fore. This could be a response to the criticisms noted above, but also to current economic conditions that raise questions about almost unfettered optimism which seems to characterise the concept of boundarylessness. Career boundaries are obstacles or constraints that people encounter when making transitions in their careers. For instance, in an organisation one might encounter boundaries in making hierarchical and/or functional transitions when specific work experience is necessary to progress upwards and across a particular organisation's hierarchy. Furthermore, people may confront boundaries in attempting to enter certain organisations when companies recruit people who have studied in prestigious universities or belong to particular ethnic groups. Drawing on both psychological and sociological perspectives Gunz et al. (2007) argue that career boundaries initially emerge as ideas 'in the heads of career owners and/or those with whom they interact. Here a striking example is an item on a UK BBC Radio 4 programme ('Today', BBC Radio 4 January 2012, 8:45 am) where a consultant neurosurgeon discussed how, in her view, women medical students perceive surgery as a male profession and thus see themselves as 'ineligible' for membership.

Having agreed that there *are* boundaries which have the potential to shape individuals' careers, we encounter the issue of how to understand them. Gunz et al. (2007) draw on Freud's psycho-analytic concepts of 'ego' and 'alter' to conceptualise boundaries. While the term 'ego' refers to career owners, 'alters' include those who interact with egos such as gatekeepers in organisations and occupations, networks of personal and professional contacts and recruitment consultants (Gunz et al., 2007: 477). According to Gunz and his colleagues, 'reluctance on the part of ego to consider a given option, perhaps because he or she is unaware that it exists, views it as unattractive for some reason, or sees it as unattainable' (2007: 482) will give rise to a 'reluctance to move boundaries'. Similarly, when alters who are gatekeepers in organisations, or occupations choose not to select the ego, the 'reluctance to select' boundaries occurs. Employers' hesitance to hire the middle-aged or people who do not have country specific work experience are examples of this boundary 'policing'.

The more reluctant an ego or alter is to consider a transition or make a particular selection, the more impermeable the subjective boundary becomes in their minds (Gunz *et al.*, 2000). The subjective boundaries which initially emerge in the heads of egos and alters become objective when ideas are shared among many actors and alters, and thus socially accepted patterns emerge as a result which become important shapers of labour markets and careers.

Gender and career

A persistent criticism of mainstream career theory is its exclusivity – its central concern with those most privileged in traditional career terms (Sullivan, 1999): white, middle-class and usually male-dominated occupational groups. As a consequence, career theory has been criticised for effectively constructing women as deviating from a dominant pattern (Marshall, 1989). With respect to gender, career theorists, mindful of the exclusion of women from the mainstream career canon, have sought to develop understandings which more adequately reflect women's lives. In recent years, research on gender and careers has focused on a whole array of issues, including constructions of career success (Höpfl and Hornby Atkinson, 2000; Perrewe and Nelson, 2004; Sturges 1999); family roles and responsibilities (Hakim, 2006; Hite and McDonald, 2003; Huang and Sverke, 2007); women's careers in management (Kottke and Agars, 2005; Wajcman, 1996; White *et al.*, 2003), experiences of career transition (Mallon and Cohen, 2001; Terjesen, 2005); work and leisure careers (McQuarrie and Jackson, 2002); and women's involvement in 'non-traditional' and new careers (Belt, 2002; Whittock, 2000) career decision-making (Smith, 2011). These studies offer illuminating insights into the day-to-day issues which women confront as part and parcel of their unfolding careers.

With respect to career development, contemporary scholars have developed career models especially for women. These models were developed in response to the new consensus that classic age/stage models of career development such as Donald Super's (1980) lifespan model noted under psychological career models are inappropriate for understanding women's career development because they are based on recurring patterns in men's lives (see Gallos, 1989; Marshall 1989; O'Neil *et al.*, 2008; Woodd, 2000). For example Super's (1980) life stage model was challenged for being linear in consisting of a sequence of eras which follows one another (Pringle and Dixon, 2003), conceptualising career progression as only upwards (Mirvis and Hall, 1996) and implying that a career involves unbroken employment in only one kind of employment with no significant conflict between work and family roles (Arnold, 1997). Such features were criticised as being unsuitable to explain women's careers, which are variable and non-linear (Pringle and Dixon, 2003), characterised by diverse occupational patterns rather than only upward mobility (Huang and Sverke, 2007). Thus scholars called for alternative career models for women and contemporary researchers responded to these calls. Joan Gallos (1989) was one of the first to throw down the gauntlet. She argued that traditional career development models, which are built on male models of work and success and supported by developmental beliefs of maturity and personal empowerment requiring separation from other people (Levinson, 1978), would not work for women whose identities, maturity and personal power are formed around ongoing processes of attachment to others. Gallos' (1989) basic point was that women are developmentally different to men and this idea should be applied to the study of their careers. Her arguments were influenced by ideas of women's psychological development over their lifespan especially the work of development psychologist Caroll Gilligan (1982). Contemporary women's career development models, which highlight women's preoccupations over age-based career phases (see Mainiero and Sullivan, 2005; O'Neil and Bilimoria, 2005; Pringle and Dixon, 2003), have emerged from ideas about women's psychological development over their lifespan.

In this section we will discuss two of the most widely used women's career models.

The Kaleidoscope career model (KCM)

The KCM explores career development by taking into account the particular ways in which women lead their lives. This model is based on the idea that women shift their career patterns by rotating different aspects of their lives to arrange roles and relationships in new ways in a similar manner to a kaleidoscope which produces changing patterns when the tube is rotated (Mainiero and Sullivan, 2005). The KCM comprises three parameters; authenticity, balance and challenge. Sullivan and Mainiero (2008) state that these parameters take different levels of importance depending on what is occurring in a woman's life at a particular point of time. The authors suggest that engaging in challenging work is likely to be the primary focus of women in early career phases (Mainiero and Sullivan, 2005), mid-career women would predominately be concerned about balance, while desire for authenticity would dominate the career and life decisions of late career women although they would be interested in addressing challenges in their own terms as well (Sullivan and Mainiero, 2008).

The KCM implies that women can shift their career patterns as they desire. However, studies have suggested that women's choices are often constrained by domestic (see Crompton *et al.*, 2005), organisational (see Gambles *et al.*, 2006), and labour market (see Burke and Nelson, 2002) structures. While we recognise the power of individual agency, as depicted in the KCM, we also emphasise that women cannot always make smooth transitions in and out of work as they desire. Significantly, studies highlight that women frequently associate their career development with the promise of increased remuneration (see Fernando and Cohen, 2012). Thus careers are not only about growth, development and learning, but also about material reward. It is notable that in our reading of the KCM career does not seem to be associated with earning a living. Moreover, work-related developmental tasks such as education, training and work experience that are central to individuals unfolding careers and crucial in their career outcomes have only a limited presence in the KCM. We would argue that these practices need to be more fully integrated into the model to make it more widely applicable.

O'Neil and Bilimoria's career development phases for women

O'Neil and Bilimoria (2005) likewise take issue with the androcentric nature of the dominant career development models and propose a model which more adequately embraces women's values and interests as they move through the life course. The first stage of their three-phased, age-linked model (idealistic achievement) comprises early career women aged 24 to 35. The second phase (pragmatic endurance) includes mid-career women aged 36 to 45 who are deemed to have a high relational context and are stated to be managing multiple personal and professional responsibilities. O'Neil and Bilimoria (2005) suggest that women in this phase are making choices about parenthood and career commitment given that their 'biological clocks are ticking'. The last phase (re-inventive contribution) comprises mostly late career women aged 46 to 60 who are suggested to take an active stance on issues such as justice and see their careers as learning opportunities and chances to make a difference to others.

Underlying O'Neil and Bilimoria's model is an assumption that women in similar age groups share similar interests. While this could be the case in certain instances, for us what raises most questions is the suggestion that women's age-based interests change drastically as they move from one age group to another. We would argue that it is not women's interests and values that change over their life but rather it is their preoccupations which shift due to organisational and domestic constraints which make home–work harmonisation difficult. Most importantly, as in the KCM we would argue that there is only very little about 'career development' in this model since it pays scanty attention to work-related developmental tasks which shape the sequence of occupations over an individual's life. Questions also arise about how the model would account for the careers of late starters or people who make career changes in mid-or late career.

In reflecting on extant women's career development models, we highlight three areas that we feel merit further examination and incorporation. First, we would argue that models of women's career development must engage not only with women's preoccupations and interests, but also on the actual, work-related developmental tasks such as education, training and work experience which shape the sequence of occupations in women's lives. Second, although these models highlight women's aspirations for life and career, they do not sufficiently accommodate the material and ideological challenges women face in realising their career aspirations. Third, these models seem to ignore the impacts of organisational, occupational sectoral (see Kaulisch and Enders, 2005), labour market (see Burke and Nelson, 2002) and economic contexts on women's career development.

Careers and ageing

Whereas twentieth-century theorists saw late career as a time of disengagement from the workforce and decline, now, with the abolition of the statutory retirement age and many people's decision to work beyond 65, the career experiences of older workers have become a highly salient issue. An array of studies highlights how older workers are stereotyped as having lower ability and being less motivated and productive than their younger counterparts (see Ali and Davies, 2003; Cuddy and Fiske, 2002; Kite et al., 2005). Moreover, older workers are also perceived to be harder to train, more resistant to change, less adaptable and flexible and as a result provided only few opportunities for training and development in their workplaces (Ali and Davies, 2003; Hedge et al., 2006). Stereotyping based on an individual's age and the discrimination which results from it (see Walker et al., 2007) is indeed a serious concern given that studies show very little evidence that job performance declines as employees grow older (see Ferris and King, 1992; Reio, et al., 1999), and there is virtually no research that examines the validity of the stereotypes that older workers are more resistant to change and less flexible than their younger counterparts (Posthuma and Campion, 2009). With respect to individual action, Clarke and Griffin (2007) draw attention to how older women workers invest in beautifying themselves in order to fight age-based discrimination at work.

While the Western literature indicates that youth is a form of career capital (Mayrofher et al., 2004) for individuals, a study of highly skilled women workers in Sri Lanka reveals that the situation of older workers in South Asia is starkly different. For instance, due to their superior statuses the late career women in Fernando and Cohen's (2012) sample were exempt from hectic work schedules and after-hours obligations which applied to their fellow employees in early and mid-career. Fernando and Cohen's (2012) findings highlight how organisations in Sri Lanka are characterised by norms of respect and compliance to superiors and how early and mid-career women struggled to comply with these norms, often ingratiating themselves with their bosses in order to advance upwards in their career structures. The privileged statuses of older workers in Sri Lankan organisations could be due to the emphasis placed on respect to elders within the wider Sri Lankan culture (Perera, 1991). Whatever the reasons may be these findings indicate that the declining older worker is not a universal phenomenon.

Organisational career management

Career management is an ongoing process of preparing, developing, implementing and monitoring career plans and strategies undertaken by the individual alone or in concert with the organisation's career system (Greenhaus *et al.*, 2000). The human resource management literature has stressed the importance of managing employees' career development, emphasizing that developing individuals is synonymous with developing the organisation's strength and capabilities (Sutaari, 2002). Some scholars have argued that traditional approaches to career management, based on notions of lifelong employment and hierarchical development, have become obsolete. However, others maintain that employees continue to attach real importance to managed career development initiatives, and certainly available evidence supports this (CIPD, 2003). Many organisations do make an attempt to intervene in individuals' career development. Drawing from an array of literature (e.g. Baruch, 2004; Derr, 1986; Noe *et al.*, 1996; Watts, 1989; Wils *et al.*, 1993), Kim (2005: 52) identifies a list of such interventions illustrated in Box 13.6.

Box 13.6 HRM in practice   Career development interventions

Personnel allocation systems

- Succession planning — Identifying and systematically developing high potential employees for certain key positions
- Career paths — Structuring sequences of jobs or positions related to specific career goals, such as managerial or technical career tracks
- Job posting/job matching — Internal announcing of vacant job positions and matching internal individuals' preferences with the job prior to external recruiting.
- Promotion/upward mobility — Advancement in position with greater pay, challenges, responsibility and authority
- Downward mobility — Moving to positions with a reduced level of responsibility and authority with an opportunity to develop skills and meet personal needs or interests
- Job rotation/lateral movement — Systematically transferring employees laterally to another function or area over the course of time, not necessarily involving increased responsibilities or compensation

Employee appraisal systems

- Assessment system — Evaluating and collecting data on employees to discover their performance and potential, feedback can be given to employees

Training/development systems

- Mentoring/coaching — Assigning mentors or coaches (often supervisors or superiors) to employees to help them develop their careers
- Training/development opportunities — Providing opportunities for career information workshops or training events that deal with career planning or transitions, self-assessment or other career issues, or supporting individual efforts to learn and develop

Career development support systems

- Career counselling/discussion — Providing counselling services and guides by profession (external or internal agency) or supervisors/managers to meet individual needs in employees' careers

- Career information system   Building a system for sharing information about career opportunities, such as various career paths or job vacancies, programmes and benefits offered through a variety of media

Employee compensation/benefits systems

- Individual compensation system   Adopting recognition systems for individual contribution to the organisation (e.g., merit pay, individual incentives, stock options)
- Flexible benefit plans   Allowing diverse, flexible options of benefits/rewards plans (e.g., insurance or pension provisions, retirement plans, flexible work schedule, part-time employment, child-care benefits, maternity and paternity leave)

Source: Adapted from Kim 2005: 52.

The benefits of career management interventions are said to include increasing employee commitment, satisfaction and motivation, increasing productivity, performance and person–job fit, identification of employees with most potential, identification of how well employees match organisational requirements, development of employees in line with organisational need and socialising employees into the organisational culture (Arnold, 2002: 127). However, in order to realise the above benefits it is important that career management interventions are implemented properly. The Chartered Institute of Personnel Development (CIPD, 2004) suggests that effective career management should adhere to a number of principles: consistency and coherency within organisations in messages about what career and career management is; proactivity; collaboration between employer and employee; and dynamism, requiring both 'flexibility and compromise over time as changing organizational and individual circumstances mean that each party wants and expects different things from the employment relationship' (2004: 8).

According to Arnold (2002), for career management interventions to run smoothly, everyone involved should see something in it for them. Managers should understand how precisely their departments would benefit by intervening in individual employees' career development, while employees should understand how exactly they will benefit from less direct interventions such as career counselling and career information systems. Arnold suggests that organisations should focus on a limited number of interventions 'with adequate resourcing and clear goals that are consistent with their culture and seen to benefit all parties involved, (2002: 128).

Significantly, interventions need to stay in existence long enough to become established. Moreover, the way in which these processes are managed and delivered is crucial. On a practical level, managers could be appraised on how well they carry out career interventions, and top management should be seen as actively supportive of such initiatives (Mayo, 1991). Here it is vital that career management programmes are seen as integrated in the organisation's daily practices, and consistent with its more general strategic orientation. Finally, it is essential that career management interventions are not perceived as only available to a select few (Tomlinson, 2004) rather, organisations should be seen to take an interest in the careers of all their employees, including minority groups.

It is important to consider HR interventions in career management in light of current debates on changing careers. As noted earlier, traditional approaches to career management were based on the notion of the career as lifelong, existing within and defined by the organisation, and sought to establish the right 'fit' between the person and the position. In this case, the role of the HRM practitioner 'became one of defining position requirements, identifying and selecting individuals capable of meeting those position requirements and assisting organizational members to progress through a sequence of positions within the organization' (Templar and Cawsey, 1999: 72). However, the emerging discourse on new careers sees the career as situated within the individual, focusing on individual choice, self-development and 'employability' (see Briscoe *et al.*, 2006). From this perspective, career management is contract-oriented, concerned with defining core competencies and identifying the 'core' workforce, and short-term in focus. Templar and Cawsey describe these, respectively, as 'position centred' and 'portfolio centred' career development procedures. Whereas the former sees HR practitioners as having a central role to play in the employees' long-term training and development, within a portfolio perspective individuals are responsible for their own training and career growth. In this case, HR managers must ensure that individuals have the requisite skills needed to fulfil the terms of a specific contract.

Given these two perspectives, we can then ask where the interventions outlined in Box 13.6 can be situated. Although certain interventions (such as career planning workshops and job assignment/rotation) are often associated with an individual's long-term relationship with the organisation, this does not have to be the case (Ball and Jordan, 1997). Taking opportunities for training and development as an example, such programmes could be offered by the organisation to help individuals prepare for promotion. However, in other cases individuals might opt into particular training courses as a way of updating their knowledge and skills – thus enhancing their personal portfolio. Thus, it is not the intervention per se which is significant, but the way in which it is understood and used.

Significantly, it is important to recognise informal shapers of careers (see Boseley *et al.*, 2009). In other words, the roles colleagues, friends, family members play in individuals careers which in the literature tend to be eclipsed by attention to formal organisational and guidance settings.

Box 13.7 HRM in practice   Informal shapers of careers

Drawing from life story research of 28 non managers in the UK, Boseley *et al.* (2009) identify five categories of career formal and informal career shapers: advisers, informants, witnesses, gatekeepers and intermediaries.

- **Advisers** offer opinions, suggestions or recommendations that shaped individuals' careers. The adviser group includes professional career advisers, managers, colleagues, family members and friends who help people clarify their career direction and/or take action in pursuit of a career idea or aim.
- **Informants** provide information about job vacancies and insight into occupations without intentionally promoting a particular point of view or seeking to influence participants. Informants are commonly friends, family, managers, colleagues and training staff. Only a few professional careers advisers were mentioned in this role.
- **Witnesses** communicate their perceptions of participants' skills and personal qualities. Both strengths and weaknesses. Witnesses were commonly managers, although education and training professionals, colleagues, family members and HR personnel were also mentioned. Witnesses conveyed their views of participants in relation to careers and played a part in shaping participants' career self-concepts, which in turn affected participants' career direction and/or aspirations. For example, participants raised their career aspirations as a result of greater belief in their capacity to take on unfamiliar roles that often provided challenges to their former career self-concept.
- **Gatekeepers** have power to provide or deny individuals access to jobs, internal promotions or developmental opportunities. Proactive gatekeepers approached participants with offers of jobs, promotions or developmental tasks, and were commonly associated with shaping participants' career direction. Responsive gatekeepers acted positively (or negatively) to requests for help in accessing jobs, promotions or developmental opportunities and were associated with shaping career action. Gatekeepers provided opportunities for participants to test and revise, or pursue their career self-concept. Gatekeepers typically included supervisors, managers and directors.
- **Intermediaries** exerted their influence with another person (usually a gatekeeper) on the individuals' behalf. Unlike gatekeepers, they lacked the power to enable or deny access to opportunities. Their influence was derived from their social or organisational position and they usually exerted their influence using informal social systems to circumvent formal ones. Colleagues and customers made up intermediaries.

Conclusion

This chapter began with three quotes about career. Together they raise some fascinating questions about what careers are, the relationship between personal and work–life, about where careers are located and the extent to which (and by whom) they can be managed. While not aiming to provide definitive answers, this chapter has explored these questions, considering, in particular, emerging debates on changing careers and the implications of these debates for HR practice.

At the outset of the chapter we discussed a number of popular definitions of career and their usages, while exploring the ways in which academic thinking about career has developed. We then introduced our readers to the notion of career success and explored debates on the changing nature of careers. While the precise nature and extent of change is still an open question we argued that it is important to consider both choice and constraint in individuals' careers. We also paid attention to the gender dimension of career by considering how particularly women develop their careers and looked into the careers of older workers. Finally, in the last section we addressed organisational interventions in career management, considering these in the context of current debates about changing careers.

CASE STUDY 13.1

UNDERSTANDING CAREERS AND REFLECTING ON CAREER EXPERIENCES

BRADLEY SAUNDERS

1 What do people talk about when they talk about careers?

2 On the basis of your answers above, construct a definition of career. Why do you think this is an appropriate definition at the present time? How does it compare to other definitions introduced in the chapter?

3 Make a 'time-line' of your career to date. Choose an appropriate shape, and include significant events, decisions, people and transitions. Should aspects of personal life be included? What about voluntary or community activities, education, training? Who have been the key stakeholders in your career development?

4 Consider this time-line in terms of the theoretical approaches introduced in this chapter.

- Do you see your career as objective or subjective? Who 'owns' your career?

- To what extent do sociological/psychological approaches shed light on your career experiences?
- Explore the relevance of field theory. What are the merits/weaknesses of this approach in relation to your own experience of career?
- To what extent can your career be described as boundaryless?

5 Describe any career interventions you have experienced (in terms of your own career, or in terms of managing the careers of others). Critically examine the apparent strengths/weaknesses of this intervention, for the individual and the organisation.

6 Based on your experience and observations, to what extent and in what ways do you think careers are changing? What are the implications of these changes for individuals and organisations?

7 Using the concepts of ego and alter, explore the boundaries you have encountered in your career.

CASE STUDY 13.2

A JOURNEY INTO THE UNKNOWN

BRADLEY SAUNDERS

Steve is 36, single, and originally from Newcastle. After university, he joined a major retailer as a trainee area manager in Leeds in a job which he described as 'an emotional roller coaster – total stress for a minimum of six days a week'. After only a few years, he felt disheartened by the 'sink or swim, dog-eat-dog mentality' and asked for a six-week vacation. 'Such a request was unheard of and friends warned me not to rock the boat, but I was at the end of my tether. Fortunately, my request was granted, but without pay.'

Steve decided to use his frequent-flyer miles to get as far away as he possibly could. After a short stay in Singapore, he took a boat to Sumatra in Indonesia. The boat developed engine problems and drifted for a few days and Steve found himself bonding with the other passengers, none of whom spoke much English.

On arrival, a family took him in and he was touched by their hospitality. One day he was passing by a building when he heard English being spoken so he walked in to what was an English class for young children. By the end of the day, Steve had accepted a post as English teacher there for a salary of 25 dollars a month and board and lodging. He returned to Newcastle to sell everything and set off, but then decided to look for similar work overseas but with a better salary. 'I knew I wanted a fresh start but I'd got used to a certain level of income and realised I couldn't live on fresh air.'

Steve decided he could make good money teaching English in Japan. Shortly after starting work there, he became convinced that teaching was definitely what he wanted to do as a career. 'Looking back, I'm so glad I quit the rat race when I did. Teaching English allows me to travel, to see other cultures, to feel them first hand and do something far more valuable than retail management, valuable in terms of contribution to the world.'

Over the next few years, Steve gradually realised that his lack of qualifications was holding him back from getting better jobs, 'so I enrolled on a one-year Master's degree back home'. He thoroughly enjoyed his year studying but was left with quite a substantial student loan to repay. Rather than return to Japan, he decided to go to the Middle East as he had heard that the salaries there were much higher. He found a job teaching male students in a college in Riyadh. He enjoyed the teaching but was not too happy with the administration of the institution. 'They smothered the creativity out of you. They didn't care about how well you taught, just about how thoroughly you completed all the paperwork.'

Steve was quickly able to get back on a good financial footing. After two years, despite being offered the chance to renew his contract, he returned to the UK and spent a year teaching freelance there. 'After being micromanaged for so long in Saudi, I wanted to make my own decisions. I wanted a bit of freedom. I had an enjoyable, if precarious, time but I got fed up with spending most of my time and effort on finding new business, rather than on becoming a better teacher. I missed the lifestyle in the Middle East and one day I just decided to apply for a teaching post at a university in Dubai.'

Steve soon settled into his new job. 'First and foremost, as a teacher, what makes you look forward to a day at school is the students' attitude. My students here are terrific. They're hard-working and respectful. Not angels, you understand, but they do want to learn.' He also found that the cosmopolitan nature of the population meant that he could meet a wide variety of people. 'Did you know that here at the university, we employ 32 nationalities? I've got friends and colleagues from all over the world here. It's great!' However, he disliked being on short-term renewable contracts. He explained

that he worried at times about the prospect of not being given a contract renewal every three years. 'I'm fairly confident my current contract will be renewed next year but I'd really like a bit more security. Then again, I suppose if I did lose this job for whatever reason, I could always find work elsewhere and be happy.'

Steve found Dubai an interesting place to be. 'Even though it's a big city, with all that entails, it's easy to grab a few minutes of peace and quiet. I love going into the desert at weekends. It's near to a number of places I've always wanted to visit – last year I saw the pyramids, a lifelong dream! And yet I can find anything I want here, from the latest blockbuster to Newcastle United live on the TV. And English is widely spoken, so there's no pressure to learn a new language.'

Steve often thinks about the unusual way in which he 'stumbled into teaching as a career'. Looking back, he wonders why he ever went into retail management when 'all my life my main desire was to help people who needed helping'. He attributes this decision partly to a desire to 'make my parents proud of me', adding that he was the first member of his family to go to university.

'It's strange,' Steve explained, 'that even though I didn't originally plan on leaving the UK for an extended period, a decade later I've spent only two years back in the UK apart from the odd visit. Unless my parents suffered a major health setback, I have no plans to return there to live and work in the foreseeable future.' One reason is the realisation that he would find it hard financially if he were to return to the UK and work there as an English teacher. 'I wouldn't want to do any other kind of work – especially not retail management! As a teacher I would either really struggle to make ends meet or work myself silly freelancing. But money isn't the reason I want to stay here. The real reason why I have no desire to return to the UK is that I learn so much more living overseas. When I'm in the UK I feel like I'm missing something.'

Steve sometimes thinks about looking for a teaching job in another country, such as Turkey, but is aware that the money he would earn there is far less than in the Middle East. Therefore, he wishes to stay for the next few years since he is making very good money there and is even able to start thinking about planning for his retirement. 'I really don't know how long I'll be able to stay here or where I'll be in 10 years' time. But, truly, I feel very fortunate in that I've had the freedom to do what I want to do when I want to do it. I know now that I'm doing what I want to do, what I need to do, and I hope in my old age that will give me satisfaction.'

Questions

Having read Steve's account, consider the following questions:

1 Would you say that Steve's career could be described as a 'boundaryless career'?
2 In what ways, if any, does Steve seem to reconstruct career boundaries, rather than break free of them?
3 In your view, could Steve's career be described as external, having an objective existence, or internal, subjectively constructed by Steve himself?
4 Is Steve's story more about change or continuity?
5 How does Steve conceptualise success in career?
6 From the information given in the case study which one of Holland's personality types does Steve fit into? To what extent does Holland's notion of congruence between personality and occupation apply to Steve?

CASE STUDY 13.3
A SRI LANKAN PERSPECTIVE ON WOMEN'S CAREERS

DULINI FERNANDO

Devika was a star student at school. However, she chose to opt out of university and get married to her long-term boyfriend instead. Six years lates she was a mother of two. Once the girls started their school career in a prestigious private institution in Colombo, Devika came to realise that most mothers were professionals. Indeed, this was different from when she went to school. In Devika's words:

I felt bad that I didn't have anything to say about myself. This is when I started to think about doing a degree.

After careful thought and consideration, Devika decided to read for the Chartered Institute of Management Accounting (CIMA) examination which is considered as equivalent to an undergraduate honours degree. She decided to do this since CIMA took only two years to complete as opposed to a three-year degree. Moreover, CIMA was very popular in Sri Lanka where most jobs on the paper were for CIMA-qualified accountants. Devika completed the CIMA examinations and decided to get into developmental finance since career paths in developmental finance are shorter than traditional management accountancy. In her words:

In management accounting you work for about two years as a trainee then another four to five years as an accountant before being a finance manager. In

developmental finance the structures are flat which is advantageous for late starters – you start as a project officer and get promoted to senior project officer based on your performance. I wanted to be a manager as soon as possible since I was 32 years old.

Devika secured a job as a project officer in a leading developmental finance company known as EFCC, through her uncle who knew the CEO of the company. According to Devika, most jobs in Sri Lanka were publicised through word-of-mouth and awarded on the basis of personal contacts. As project officer, Devika was involved in assessing prospective business ideas and recommending loans for them. Within a year she was promoted to senior project officer and transferred to the company's head office in Colombo. As senior project officer, Devika networked with the assistant director of the department maintaining a close relationship with him. In return, he put Devika in charge of projects of significance. In her third year at EFCC Devika came to a turning point in her career:

In my third year at EFCC a project they had funded – a plant manufacturing soft drinks – collapsed. EFCC had to decide whether to liquidate the plant or run it ourselves, develop it and sell it for a higher price. Anyway EFCC put together a team of people to evaluate this project. I was also assigned to this team. I recommended that we run this plant while all the others recommended liquidation. By talking to a few people, I found out that the owners hadn't paid the workers on time on many occasions, so most of the skilled workers had left. Basically they had experienced inefficiencies, delays and lost production orders due to lack of experienced personnel – this was a key insight I got from chatting with some of the workers in an informal manner. I wrote this on a report and the CEO was very interested in my synthesis. Although my recommendation was quite risky, he approved it. Soon afterwards EFCC put together a cross-functional team to turn this plant around. I was a made a member of this team. I wasn't the project manager, but I eventually took over that role. We spent nine months on this plant, turned it around and sold it for profit. The CEO instantly made me manager of special projects and moved me to corporate restructuring – this designation was made especially for me.

As soon as she got into management, Devika enrolled in a postgraduate master's programme, since this was vital for career advancement in Sri Lankan organisations. She completed the programme in two years, when she encountered another challenge in her career. EFCC took over the DEK bank and Devika was given the task of integrating the two hostile institutions.

The CEO appointed a special integration team – I was made the team leader. In the beginning we just concentrated on getting to know the DEK people, trying to get them integrated to the EFCC philosophy, but they weren't agreeable to anything we proposed. They had a lot of grievances with EFCC – I always listened to whatever they said. I let the DEK team do a lot of things the way they wanted to do it – delegated more authority than my team thought appropriate. Anyway this got the DEK team to cooperate with us. They were not like the citizens of conquered country who were bitter towards their conquerors, and they slowly got to trust me. We finally proposed both companies coming under a common philosophy – not EFCC or DEK bank – but the Nautica philosophy. Now this was successful. Although it wasn't too different to the EFCC philosophy – the name made a big difference. We slowly managed to build citizenship through the name Nautica – we got Nautica T-shirts, pens, bags, numerous things for everybody. I was involved in this project for almost two and half years.

Devika did this excellent work despite the extensive demands of her three teenage children and mother-in-law. While she was at work, Devika resolved regular clashes between her mother-in-law and domestic maids over the phone and checked up on her problematic younger daughter. She also took her work home often. Her effort was well recognised. As soon the integration team wound up, they were congratulated by the CEO and Devika was made director of special projects. Devika currently serves as a board director at EFCC. She is 46 years old.

Questions

Having read Devika's account, consider the following questions:

1 To what extent can extant women's career models such as the KCM and/or O'Neil and Bilimoria's (2005) model explain Devika's career?
2 How does Devika conceptualise career success? To what extent does her definition resonate with findings of women in the West?
3 What are the career capitals important for individuals to progress in career in the Sri Lankan context?
4 In your view, what is the most appropriate theoretical perspective from which to explore Devika's career? Justify your answer.

Bibliography

Academy of Achievement (1996) 'Interview with Amy Tan', 28 June, Sun Valley, ID. http://www.achievement.org/autodoc/page/tan0int-1.

Adamson, S.J., Doherty, N. and Viney, C. (1998) 'The meanings of career revisited', *British Journal of Management*, Vol.9, 251–9.

Al-Ariss, A. (2010) 'Modes of engagements: migration, self-initiated expatriation, and career development', *Career Development International*, Vol.15, 338–58.

Al-Ariss, A. and Syed, J. (2011) 'Capital mobilization of skilled migrants: a relational perspective', *British Journal of Management*, Vol.22, 286–304.

Ali, H. and Davies, D.R. (2003) 'The effects of age, sex and tenure on the job performance of rubber tappers', *Journal of Occupational and Organizational Psychology*, Vol.76, 381–91.

Arnold, J. (1997) *Managing Careers into the Twenty-First Century*, London: Paul Chapman.

Arnold, J. (2002) 'Careers and career management', pp. 115–32, in Ones, D.S. and Anderson, N. (eds) *Handbook of industrial, Work and Organisational Psychology*, Vol.2, Thousand Oaks, CA: Sage.

Arnold, J. (2004) 'The congruence problem in John Holland's theory of vocational decisions', *Journal of Occupational and Organizational Psychology*, Vol.77, 95–113.

Arnold, J. and Cohen, L. (2008) 'The psychology of careers in industrial and organizational settings: a critical but appreciative analysis', pp. 1–44, in Hodgkinson, G.P. and Ford, J.K. (eds) *International Review of Industrial and Organizational Psychology*, Vol.23, London: John Wiley & Sons.

Arthur, M. and Rousseau, D. (1996) *The Boundaryless Career*, Oxford: Oxford University Press.

Arthur, M.B., Khapova, S.N. and Wilderom, C.P.M. (2005) 'Career success in a boundaryless career world', *Journal of Organizational Behaviour*, Vol.26, No.2, 177–202.

Bach, G. and Hall, B. (eds) (1997) *Conversations with Grace Paley*, Jackson, MS: University Press of Mississippi.

Bagdadli, S., Solari, L., Usai, A. and Grandori, A. (2003) 'The emergence of career boundaries in unbounded industries: career odysseys in the Italian New Economy', *International Journal of Human Resource Management*, Vol.14, No.5, 788–808.

Ball, B. and Jordan, M. (1997) 'An open-learning approach to career management and guidance', *British Journal of Guidance and Counselling*, Vol.25, No.4, 507–16.

Barley, S. (1989) 'Careers, identities and institutions: the legacy of the Chicago School of Sociology', pp. 41–65, in Arthur, M.B., Hall, D.T. and Lawrence, B.S. (eds) *The Handbook of Career Theory*, Cambridge University Press: Cambridge, MA.

Baruch, Y. (2004) *Managing Careers: Theory and Practice*, Harlow, UK: Prentice-Hall

BBC Radio 4 (2012) 'Today', 4 January, 9:45 am.

Belt, V. (2002) 'A female ghetto? Women's careers in call centres', *Human Resource Management Journal*, Vol.12, No.4, 51–66.

Bolton, S. and Muzio, D. (2007) 'Can't live with "em": Can't live without "em": Gendered segmentation in the legal profession', *Sociology*, Vol.41, No.1, 311–26.

Boseley, S.L.C, Arnold, J. and Cohen, L. (2009) 'How other people shape our careers: a typology drawn from career narratives', *Human Relations*, Vol.62, No.10, 1487–520.

Bourdieu, P. (1986) 'The forms of capital', pp. 241–58, in Richardson, J.G. (ed.) *Handbook of Theory and Research for the Sociology of Education,* New York: Greenwood Press

Briscoe, J.P. and Hall, D.T. (2006) 'The interplay of boundaryless and protean careers: combinations and implications', *Journal of Vocational Behavior*, Vol.69, 4–18.

Briscoe, J.P., Hall, D.T. and De Muth, R.L. (2006) 'Protean and boundaryless careers: an empirical exploration', *Journal of Vocational Behavior*, Vol.69, 4-18, 30–47.

Brown, D. (1987) 'The status of Holland's theory on vocational choice', *Career Development Quarterly*, Vol.36, 13–23.

Budhwar, P.S., Saini, D.S. and Jyotsna, B. (2005) 'Women in management in the new economic environment: the case of India', *Asia Pacific Business Review*, Vol.11, No.2, 179–93.

Burke, R.J. and Nelson, D.L. (2002) *Advancing Women's Careers*, Oxford: Blackwell.

Burr, V. (2003) *Social Constructionism*, London: Routledge.

CIPD (2003) *Managing Employee Careers – Issues, Trends and Prospects,* London: Chartered Institute of Personnel and Development.

CIPD (2004) '*Career Management – A Guide*', London: Chartered Institute of Personnel and Development.

Clarke, L.H. and Griffin, M. (2007) 'The body natural and the body unnatural: beauty work and aging', *Journal of Aging Studies*, Vol.21, No.3, 187–201.

Cohen, L. and El-Sawad, A. (2009) 'Understanding and managing careers in changing contexts', pp. 317–42, in Redman, T. and Wilkinson, A. (eds) *Contemporary Human Resource Management*: *Text and Cases*, (3rd edn), Harlow: Financial Times/Prentice Hall.

Cohen, L. and Mallon, M. (1999) 'The transition from organisational employment to portfolio working: perceptions of boundarylessness', *Work, Employment and Society*, Vol.13, No.2, 329–52.

Cohen, L., El-Sawad, A. and Arnold, J. (2009) 'Outsourcing careers: western theories in an Indian context', pp. 182–214, in Thite, M. and Russell, B. (eds) *The Next Available Operator: Managing Human Resources in the Indian Business Process Outsourcing Industry*, London: Sage.

Cohen, L., Duberley, J. and Mallon, M. (2004) 'Social constructionism in the study of career: accessing the parts that other approaches cannot reach', *Journal of Vocational Behavior*, Vol.64, No.3, 407–22.

Cohen, L., Duberley, J. and Musson, G. (2009) 'Work–life balance; an auto ethnographic exploration of everyday home-work dynamics', *Journal of Management Inquiry*, Vol.18, No.3, 229–41.

Collin, A. and Watts, A.G. (1996) 'The death and transfiguration of career – and of career guidance?', *British Journal of Guidance and Counselling*, Vol.24, No.3, 385–98.

Collin, A. and Young, R.A. (2000) *The Future of Career*, Cambridge: Cambridge University Press.

Cornelius, N. and Skinner, D. (2008) 'The careers of senior men and women: a capabilities theory perspective', *British Journal of Management*, Vol.19, Iss.S1,S141–S149.

Crompton, R., Brockmann, M. and Lyonette, C. (2005) 'Attitudes, women's employment and the domestic division of labour: a cross-national analysis in two waves', *Work, Employment and Society*, Vol.19, No.2, 213–33.

Cuddy, A.J. and Fiske, S.T (2002) 'Doddering but dear: process, content and function in stereotyping of older persons', pp. 3–26, in Nelson T. (ed.) *Ageism: Stereotyping and Prejudice Against Older Persons*, Cambridge, MA: MIT Press.

Derr, C.B. (1986) *Managing the New Careerists,* San Francisco, CA: Jossey-Bass.

Duberley, J. Cohen, L. and Mallon, M. (2006) 'Constructing scientific careers: change, continuity and context', *Organization Studies*, Vol.27, No.8, 1131–51.

Duberley, J. and Cohen, L. (2010) 'Gendering career capital: a study of UK women scientists', *Journal of Vocational Behavior*, Vol.76, No.2, 187–97.

Fernando, W.D.A. and Cohen, L. (2011) 'Exploring the interplay between gender, organizational context and career: a Sri Lankan perspective', *Career Development International*, Vol.16, No.6, 553–71.

Fernando, W.D.A. and Cohen, L. (2013) 'A social constructionist perspective of women's career development: a study of professional and managerial women in Sri Lanka', in Patton, W. (ed.) *Conceptualising Women's Working Lives: Moving the Boundaries of Our Discourse*, Rotterdam: Sense Publications. (Forthcoming.)

Ferris, G.R. and King, T.R. (1992) 'The politics of age discrimination in organizations', *Journal of Business Ethics*, Vol.11, 341–50.

Gallos, J.V. (1989) 'Exploring women's development: implications for career theory practice and research', pp. 110–32, in Arthur, M.B., Hall, D.T. and Lawrence, B.S. (eds) *Handbook of Career Theory*, Cambridge: Cambridge University Press.

Gambles, R., Lewis, S. and Rapoport, R. (2006) *The Myth of Work–Life Balance: The Challenge of our Time for Men, Women and Societies*, Chichester: Wiley.

Gergen, K. (2001) Social Construction in Context, Thousand Oaks, CA: Sage.

Gilligan, C. (1982) *In a Different Voice: Psychological Theory and Women's Development*. Cambridge, MA: Harvard University Press.

Goffman, I. (1961) *Asylums*, New York: Anchor.

Gowler, D. and Legge, K. (1989) 'Rhetoric in bureaucratic careers: managing the meaning of management success', pp. 437–53, in Arthur, M.B., Hall, D.T. and Lawrence B.S. (eds) *Handbook of Career Theory*, Cambridge: Cambridge University Press.

Greenhaus, J.G., Callanan, G.A and Godshalk, V.M. (2000) *Career Management*, 3rd edn, New York: The Dryden Press.

Gunz, H., Evans, M. and Jalland, M. (2000) 'Career boundaries in a "boundaryless" world', pp. 24–53, in Peiperl, M., Arthur, M.B., Goffe, R. and Morris, T. (eds) *Career Frontiers: New Conceptualizations of Working Lives*, Oxford: Oxford University Press.

Gunz, H., Peiperl, M. and Tzabbar, D. (2007) 'Boundaries in the study of career', pp. 471–94, in Gunz, H. and Peiperl, M. (eds) *Handbook of Career Studies*, London: Sage.

Hakim, C. (2006) 'Women, careers and life preferences', *British Journal of Guidance and Counselling*, Vol.34, No.30, 279–94.

Hall, D.T. (2004) 'The protean career: a quarter century journey', *Journal of Vocational Behavior*, Vol.65, 1–13.

Hedge, J.W., Borman, W.C. and Lammlein, S.E. (2006) *The Aging Workforce: Realities, Myths, and Implications for Organizations*, Washington, DC: American Psychological Association.

Hite, L. and McDonald, K. (2003) 'Career aspirations of non-managerial women: adjustment and adaptation', *Journal of Career Development*, Vol.29, No.4, 221–35.

Holland, J.L. (1973) *Making Vocational Choices*, Englewood Cliffs, NJ: Prentice-Hall.

Holland, J.L. and Gottfredson, G.D. (1992) 'Studies of the hexagonal model: an evaluation', (Or, The perils of stalking the perfect hexagon.) *Journal of Vocational Behavior,* Vol.40, 158–70.

Höpfl, H. and Hornby Atkinson, P. (2000) 'The future of women's careers', pp. 130–43, in Collin, A. and Young, R. (eds) *The Future of Career*, Cambridge: Cambridge University Press.

Huang, Q. and Sverke, M. (2007) 'Women's occupational career patterns over 27 Years: relations to family of origin, life careers, and wellness', *Journal of Vocational Behavior*, Vol.70, 369–97.

Huppatz, K. (2009) 'Reworking Bourdieu's "capital": feminine and female capitals in the field of paid caring work', *Sociology*, Vol.43, No.1, 45–66.

Iellatchitch, A., Mayrhofer, W. and Meyer, M. (2003) 'Career fields: a small step towards a grand career theory?', *International Journal of Human Resource Management*, Vol.15, No.4, 256–71.

Inkson, K. (2007) *Understanding Careers: The Metaphors of Working Lives*, London: Sage.

Kaulisch, M. and Enders, J. (2005) 'Careers in overlapping institutional contexts: the case of academe', *Career Development International*, Vol.10, 130–44.

Kim, N. (2005) 'Organizational interventions influencing employee career development preferred by different career success orientations', *International Journal of Training and Development,* Vol.9, No.1, 47–61.

Kite, M.E., Stockdale, G.D., Whitley, B.E. and Johnson, B.T. (2005) 'Attitudes toward younger and older adults: an updated meta-analytic review', *Journal of Social Issues*, Vol.61, 241–66.

Kottke, J. and Agars, M. (2005) 'Understanding the processes that facilitate and hinder efforts to advance women in organizations', *Career Development International*, Vol.10, 190–202.

Lennon, J.(1980) 'Beautiful boy (darling boy)', John Lennon and Yoko Ono, *Double Fantasy.*

Levinson, D. (1978) *The Seasons of a Man's Life,* New York: Knopf.

Lirio, P., Lituchy, T.R., Monserrat, S.I., Olivas-Lujan, M.R., Duffy, J., Fox, S., Gregory, A., Punnett, B.J. and Santos, N. (2007) 'Exploring career–life success and family social support of successful women in Canada, Argentina and Mexico', *Career Development International*, Vol.12, No.1, 28–50.

Lyng, S.T. (2010) 'Mothered and othered: (in)visibility of care responsibility and gender in processes of excluding women from Norwegian law firms', pp. 76–99, in Lewis, P. and

Simpson, R. (eds) *Revealing and Concealing Gender: Issues of Visibility in Organisations*, Basingstoke: Palgrave Macmillan.

Mallon, M. (1998) 'From managerial career to portfolio career: making sense of the transition', Unpublished PhD thesis, Sheffield Hallam University.

Mallon, M. and Cohen, L. (2001) 'Time for a change? Women's accounts of the move from organizational careers to self-employment', *British Journal of Management*, Vol.12, No.3, 217–30.

Mainiero, L.A. and Sullivan, S.E. (2005) 'Kaleidoscope careers: an alternative explanation for the opt-out revolution', *Academy of Management Executive*, Vol.19, No.1, 106–23.

Marshall, J. (1989) 'Re-visioning career concepts: a feminist invitation', pp. 275–91, in Arthur, M.B, Hall, D.T. and Lawrence, B.S. (eds) *Handbook of Career Theory*, New York: Cambridge University Press.

Mayo, A. (1991) *Managing Careers in Organisations*, London: Institute of Personnel Management.

Mayrhofer, W., Iellatchitch, A., Meyer, M., Steyrer, J., Schiffinger, M. and Strunk, G. (2004) 'Going beyond the individual: some potential contributions from a career field and habitus perspective for global career research and practice', *Journal of Management Development*, Vol.23, No.9, 870–84.

McQuarrie, F.A.E. and Jackson, E.L. (2002) 'Transitions in leisure careers and their parallels in work careers: the effect of constraints on choice and action', *Journal of Career Development*, Vol.29, No.1, 37–53.

Mirvis, P.H. and Hall, D.T. (1996) 'Psychological success and the boundaryless career', *Journal of Organisational Behaviour*, Vol.15, 365–80.

Ng, T.W.H., Eby, L.T., Sorensen, K.L., and Feldman, D.C. (2005) 'Predictors of objective and subjective career success: a meta-analysis', *Personnel Psychology*, Vol.58, 367–408.

Nippert-Eng, C.E. (1995) *Home and Work,* Chicago, IL: University of Chicago Press.

Noe, R.A., Hollenbeck, J.R., Gerhard, B. and Wright, P.M. (1996) *Human Resource Management: Gaining a Competitive Advantage* (2nd edn), Boston, MA: Irwin McGraw-Hill.

O' Neil, D.A. and Bilimoria, D. (2005) 'Women's career development phases: idealism, endurance, and reinvention', *Career Development International*, Vol.10, No.3, 168–89.

O'Neil, D.A., Hopkins, M.M. and Bilimoria, D. (2008) 'Women's careers at the start of the 21st century: patterns and paradoxes', *Journal of Business Ethics*, Vol.80, 727–43.

Perera, M. (1991) 'The impact of macro-events on social structure in Sri Lanka' in Masino, E. and Stratigos, S., *Women Household and Change*, United Nations University: United Nations Press.

Perrewe, P. and Nelson, D. (2004) 'Gender and career success: the facilitative role of political skill', *Organizational Dynamics*, Vol.33, No.4, 366–78.

Postone, M., LiPuma, E. and Calhoun, C. (1993) 'Introduction', in Calhoun, C. LiPuma, E. and Postone, M. (eds) *Bourdieu: Critical Perspectives* (pp. 1–13). Chicago, IL: University of Chicago Press.

Postuma, R.A. and Campion, M.A. (2009) 'Age stereotypes in the workplace: common stereotypes, moderators, and future research directions?', *Journal of Management,* Vol.35, 158–88.

Pringle, J.K. and Dixon, K.M (2003) 'Re-incarnating life in the careers of women', *Career Development International*, Vol.8, No.6, 291–300.

Reio, T.G., Sanders-Rejo, J.and Reio, T. (1999) 'Combating workplace ageism', *Adult Learning*, Vol.11, 10–13.

Richardson, J. (2009) 'Geographic flexibility in academia: a cautionary note', *British Journal of Management*, Vol.20, S160–S170.

Savickas, M. (2002) 'Reinvigorating the study of careers', *Journal of Vocational Behavior*, Vol.60, 381–5.

Savickas, M.L., Nota, L., Rossier, J., Dauwalder, J-P., Edwarda Duarte, M., Guichard, J., Soresi, S, Van Esbroeck, R. and van Vianen, A.E.M. (2009) 'Life designing: a paradigm for career construction in the 21st century', *Journal of Vocational Behavior*, Vol.75, 239–50.

Smith, J. (2011) 'Agency and female teachers' career decisions: a life history study of 40 women', *Educational Management, Administration & Leadership*, Vol.39, No.1, 7–24.

Sturges, J. (1999) 'What it means to succeed: personal conceptions of career success held by male and female managers of different ages', *British Journal of Management*, Vol.10, 239–52.

Sullivan, S. (1999) 'The changing nature of careers: a review and research agenda', *Journal of Management*, Vol.25, No.3, 457–84.

Sullivan, S.E. and Maneiro, L. (2008) 'Using the kaleidoscope career model to understand the changing patterns of women's careers: designing HRD programs that attract and retain women', *Advances in Developing Human Resources*, Vol.10, No.1, 32–49.

Super, D.E. (1980) 'A life span, life space approach to career development', *Journal of Vocational Behavior*, Vol.13, 282–98.

Super, D.E., Thompson, A.S. and Lindeman, R.H. (1988) *The Adult Careers Concern Inventory*. Palo Alto, CA: Consulting Psychologists Press.

Sutaari, V. (2002) 'Global leader development: an emerging research agenda', *Career Development International*, Vol.7, No.4, 218–33. thesius.emeraldinsight.com/vl=1531447/cl=136/nw=1/rpsv/~1142/v7n4/s3/p218

Templar, A.J. and Cawsey, T.F. (1999) 'Rethinking career development in an era of portfolio careers', *Career Development International*, Vol.4, No.2, 70–6.

Terjesen, S. (2005) 'Senior women managers' transition to entrepreneurship', *Career Development International*, Vol.10, 246–59.

Tinsley, H.E.A. (2000) 'The congruence myth revisited', *Journal of Vocational Behavior*, Vol.56, 405–23.

Tomlinson, J. (2004) 'Perceptions and negotiations of the business case for flexible careers and the integration of part-time work', *Women in Management Review*, Vol.19, No.4, 412–20.

Wajcman, J. (1996) 'Desperately seeking differences: is management style gendered?', *British Journal of Industrial Relations*, Vol.34, 333–49.

Walker, H., Grant, D., Meadows, M. and Cook, I. (2007) 'Women's experiences and perceptions of age discrimination in employment: implications for research and policy', *Social Policy and Society*, Vol.6, No.1, 37–48.

Watts, G.A. (1989) *Identifying career orientations of female, non-managerial employees at Virginia Tech*.(Doctoral dissertation, University of Virginia Polytechnic Institute and State University, 1989.) Dissertation Abstracts International, A50, 05, 1223.

White, M., Hill, S., McGovern, P., Mills, C. and Smeaton, D. (2003) 'High performance management practices, working hours and work–life balance', *British Journal of Industrial Relations*, Vol.41, No.2, 175–95.

Whittock, M. (2000) *Feminising the Masculine: Women in Non-traditional Employment*, Aldershot: Ashgate.

Wilensky, H. (1961) 'Orderly careers and social participation: the impact of social integration in the middle class', *American Sociological Review*, Vol.26, 521–39.

Wils, T., Guerin, G. and Bernard, R. (1993) 'Career system as a configuration of career management activities', *International Journal of Career Management*, Vol.5, No.2, 11–15.

Woodd, M. (2000) 'The move towards a different career pattern: are women better prepared than men for a modern career?', *Career Development International*, Vol.5, No.2, 99–105.

Young, R.A. and Collin, A. (2004) 'Introduction: constructivism and social constructionism in the career field'. Special Issue on Constructivism and Social Constructionism and Career. *Journal of Vocational Behavior*, Vol.64, No.3, 373–88.

CHAPTER 14
MANAGING DIVERSITY

Catherine Cassell

Introduction

It is now over 20 years since human resource management writers and consultants started using the term 'managing diversity' as a way of addressing equal opportunity issues. A focus on diversity recognises that people differ in a variety of ways. Examples include gender; ethnicity; age; sexuality; religion; disability; and social status. Managing diversity encompasses a number of concepts and refers to the systematic and planned commitment on the part of organisations to recruit and retain employees from diverse demographic backgrounds (Thomas, 1992). Building on the notion that all differences between groups and individuals within an organisation should be recognised and valued, managing diversity presents a business case for equal opportunities. Noon and Ogbonna (2001: 1) suggest that the concept of equal opportunities is increasingly being replaced with the notion of management of diversity: 'It has been a gradual drift, emanating from writers and organizations in the USA, travelling across the UK and seeping into mainland Europe.' In linking individual employee differences and equal opportunities initiatives directly with business strategy, the concept of managing diversity is inextricably linked to strategic HRM, and therefore a focus of concern for the HR practitioner (Shen *et al.*, 2009).

The aim of this chapter is to outline the principles behind the managing diversity approach and examine some of the key issues and tensions around diversity debates. The chapter begins by outlining the context in which managing diversity has arisen. The principles of managing diversity strategies are then discussed, together with some of the techniques and tools that managers can use to this end. The challenges facing the creation of global diversity programmes are then considered. The chapter concludes by examining some of the key issues and debates within this field. These include a consideration of the evidence for the effectiveness of managing diversity initiatives and a critique of the business case within which managing diversity initiatives are located. Finally, we question whether the language of equality is on the move again, and highlight the increasingly common usage in this field of the term 'inclusion' as a way of addressing issues of fairness and equality in the workplace.

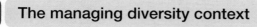

The managing diversity context

The management of diversity first emerged within the business literature towards the end of the 1980s. Therefore, in the history of personnel and HRM more generally, it is a relatively new concept. It is important to consider why the concept emerged when it did, and the currency that it currently has among HR academics and practitioners. By way of context, the triggers that led to a focus of attention towards diversity management are now considered. Two particular factors are important here: changing demographic trends and the emergence of the business case for the progression of equal opportunities.

Demographic trends

The development of managing diversity strategies is clearly located within the context of shifting demographic trends. The composition of the international workforce is changing dramatically. Prasad and Mills (1997: 4) pointed out the impact that these shifts initially had in North America:

> Few trends have received as much publicity or gained as much attention in management circles as the recent interest in managing diversity. It can be argued that much of this interest can be traced back to Johnston and Parker's [sic] [Packard] (1987) influential report, *Workforce 2000*, which alerted organizations to the dramatic demographic changes that were in the process of transforming the North American workforce . . . Confronted with the prospect of these major imminent changes, management practitioners, business educators, and organizational consultants quickly began preparing to meet the challenges of a new and diverse workforce in a number of ways.

Kandola (1995: 138), one of the pioneers of managing diversity initiatives in the UK and Europe, highlighted at the time that similar demographic changes to those that were occurring in North America were anticipated throughout Europe. Specifically, it was anticipated that there would be increasing numbers of women and ethnic minorities entering the labour market, and the overall age of the working population would increase. The argument was that such demographic trends had created the necessity to expand the labour pool to include those groups traditionally disadvantaged in the employment market. Roberson and Kulik (2007: 24) highlight how when these trends were first identified they were 'heralded as an opportunity for organizations to become more creative, to reach previously untapped markets, and in general to achieve and maintain a competitive advantage'. The key aim of diversity management therefore, was for companies to turn such demographic trends to their own advantage and make the most of the talents of the new diverse workforce that were now available to them.

The concern with changing demographic trends prevails. A recent report by the European Foundation for Improvement in Living and Working Conditions (2010) reviewed current and projected demographic trends in Europe and highlights three key developments: the ageing workforce; the increased feminisation of the workforce; and the increased importance of migration. As the authors suggest, 'the EU has become a major destination for global migration flows, surpassing even the USA, (EFWLC, 2010: 5). Similar trends have been highlighted in the United States and other parts of the industrialised world. Hence these demographic indicators point to the need to include and value those in the workforce who may traditionally have been excluded.

The emergence of the business case for equal opportunities

The development of managing diversity perspectives emerged at a time when there was considerable disillusionment among activists, practitioners and employers about the effectiveness and achievements of equal opportunities policies, particularly in the UK (e.g. Wilson, 1995). A number of concerns were expressed about the lack of success of equal opportunity (EO) initiatives ranging from their lack of attractiveness to employers (Ross and Schnieder, 1992) and the focus upon punitive measures for employers who refused to comply (Davidson and Fielden, 2003), to more general disappointment that equal opportunities policies were not delivering the intended outcomes for disadvantaged groups. Hence the business case for equal opportunities emerged at a time when some writers believed a re-think was required.

The business case focusses on the business benefits that employers accrue through making the most of the skills and potential of all employees. The argument is that the loss or lack of recognition of these skills and potential, usually as a result of everyday discriminatory practices, is very costly. Consequently, the business case is fundamentally linked to the principles of strategic HRM where the human resource and its full utilisation is seen to give a company the competitive edge (Storey, 1995). Additionally, it is crucial that equal opportunities initiatives are seen to tie in with the overall strategic direction of a company. A business case sees achieving equality as essential to achieving organisational goals. Again, in the same way that HRM is linked into the general strategy of a firm, so equal opportunities pervades every aspect of business policy, rather than being an add-on.

In 1995 the UK Equal Opportunities Commission launched a campaign to highlight the business case for equal opportunities. The aim was to demonstrate that in economic terms, equality made good business sense. A leaflet produced at the time outlines the 'Benefits of equality' and 'Costs of inequality'. The benefits of equality include:

- Best use of human resources
- Flexible workforce to aid re-structuring
- Workforce representative of the local community
- Improved corporate image with potential employees and customers
- Attracting ethical investors
- Managers can integrate equality into corporate objectives
- New business ideas from a diverse workforce.

The costs of inequality include:

- Inefficiency in use of human resources (high staff turnover; low productivity; and restricted pool of talent)
- Inflexible workforce limiting organisational change
- Poor corporate image with prospective employees and customers
- Management time spent on grievances
- Losing an industrial tribunal case.

These costs and benefits were linked in to the demographic trends outlined earlier. The business case blossomed as a rationale for the effective management of diversity within the workplace and became an important underpinning argument for furthering equality at work. This argument has remained. For example, more recently the British Chartered Institute of Personnel and Development (CIPD, 2011) have outlined three major benefits associated with the business case for equal opportunities and managing diversity that go beyond what is required by legislation. These relate to people issues such as drawing on a wider range of labour pool who will be more creative, innovative and happier in their work environment; market competitiveness where a diverse workforce can, for example, open up new market opportunities; and corporate reputation, where diversity and inclusion are linked into the wider issues of corporate social responsibility.

To summarise, it is worth examining the differences between the diversity model based on the business case and traditional social justice models of equal opportunity, though they are not necessarily mutually exclusive (CIPD, 2011). Kandola and Fullerton (1994) propose that whereas EO is externally initiated, legally driven and focuses on numbers and problems, diversity is internally initiated, business needs driven and focusses on qualitative and opportunity outcomes. EO approaches tend to assume assimilation and are reactive, whereas diversity approaches assume pluralism and are proactive. Finally, EO approaches focus on a particular set of differences, usually race, gender and disability, whereas diversity approaches focus on all differences. Therefore diversity approaches based on a business case theoretically represent a different way of looking at equal opportunities.

General principles and activities

A number of principles and activities characterise diversity management. Pitts (2006) provides a basic conceptualisation of diversity management that includes three inter-related components: recruitment and outreach, valuing differences, and pragmatic programmes and policies. The first: recruitment and outreach, focusses upon an organisation seeking out a range of different types of employees. Examples of activities here include a strategic plan for reaching out to typically under-represented groups (Pitts *et al.*, 2010: 869). This is based upon the assumption that greater staff diversity will lead to access to a wider range of talent and ideas, plus access to potentially novel markets. The second component identified by Pitts (2006) is valuing differences. Exponents of the management of diversity perspective (Cox, 1992; Jackson and Associates, 1992; Kandola and Fullerton, 1994; Montes and Shaw, 2003; Thomas, 1990) argue that all differences must be valued including those of white males. Kandola and Fullerton (1994: 8) provide a useful working definition of managing diversity which highlights the role of managing difference:

> The basic concept of managing diversity accepts that the workforce consists of a diverse population of people. The diversity consists of visible and non-visible differences which will include factors such as sex, age, background, race, disability, personality and work style. It is founded on the premiss that harnessing these differences will create a productive environment in which everybody feels valued, where their talents are being fully utilized and in which organizational goals are met.

Indeed, differences are not only valued but also potentially celebrated. As Prasad and Mills (1997: 4) suggest:

> Diversity is celebrated with the help of evocative metaphors such as the melting pot, the patchwork quilt, the multicolored or cultural mosaic, and the rainbow. All of these metaphors evoke enormously affirmative connotations of diversity, associating it with images of cultural hybridity, harmonious coexistence, and colorful heterogeneity.

A consideration of some organisational policies about diversity highlight some of the differences that need to be valued and managed. A typical policy will include differences such as gender, race, disability, spent criminal convictions, sexual orientation, religion and beliefs, socioeconomic background, age and potentially others such as personality differences and working styles. For example the general manager of global diversity and inclusion at Microsoft states that:

> Microsoft needs the insight, creativity and diverse perspectives that a range of employees can bring to the table. This means not only having a workforce balanced by race, ethnic origin, gender, sexual orientation, and gender identity and expression, but also having a workforce that embraces differences in approaches, insights, abilities and experiences.
> *(Microsoft, 2008)*

The third part of Pitt's (2006) model is pragmatic programmes and policies. These consist of a 'strategic set of management tools' (Pitts *et al.*, 2010: 870) that provide the means by which diverse groups can have their needs met. These could, for example, include family-friendly policies for those with dependents, or policies that enable religious minorities the opportunity to worship in the workplace.

Crucial to progressing diversity initiatives is some form of cultural change. Kandola and Fullerton (1994) suggest that managing diversity must pervade the entire organisation, if it is to be successful. They propose a **MOSAIC** vision, which summarises the key characteristics of the diversity-oriented organisation. MOSAIC is used here as an acronym for **M**ission and values, **O**bjective and fair processes, **S**killed workforce: aware and fair, **A**ctive flexibility, **I**ndividual focus, and **C**ulture that empowers. Therefore the HR professional should, in theory, have a key role in the implementation of such initiatives. Jackson (1992: 27) suggests that making the most of workforce diversity is a key challenge for HR professionals. She suggests that it is those professionals who are 'best able to educate business leaders about the strategic importance of working through diversity to mobilize them to take immediate actions'. She also suggests that HR professionals have a wide range of tools available to them for changing the attitudes and behaviours of their organisation's employees. Such tools include recruitment and selection systems, performance evaluation and appraisal, compensation and reward, and training and development. Celebrating diversity could, therefore, be reinforced through the use of these tools.

Implementing diversity initiatives

Given the range of different objectives that HR professionals seek to achieve through effective diversity management (Shen *et al.*, 2009), it is not surprising that a whole range of projects can be subsumed under the heading of diversity initiatives. Some are designed to encourage the voices of all individuals to be heard, for example advisory councils made up of different groups that can report to top management, and the creation of support groups for minorities such as women's or cultural minorities networks. An example comes from IBM who have created network groups for GLBT (gay, lesbian, bisexual and transsexual) employees in 12 EU countries. Externally, IBM also collaborates with various LGBT organisations, demonstrating both internal and external support for the LBGT community (EC, 2005). A further example is Dublin Bus's intercultural working group that involves staff and bus drivers from different origins and ethnic backgrounds. In both cases these network groups can raise key issues associated with the experiences of particular diverse groups that can then be addressed more generally at company level. Other initiatives ensure that attention is paid to the career development of particular minorities such as fast-track development programmes for targeted groups, or finding ways of rewarding managers on the basis of their record on developing those from targeted groups (Arnold, 1997: 179). For example in Adecco - a multinational recruitment business – skills gap training is offered to disabled candidates with the aim of ensuring long-term employment. Further, more detailed, examples of the use of different types of these interventions can be found in relation to DEC (Walker and Hanson, 1992); National Transportation Systems (Ellis and Sonnenfeld, 1994); American Express (Wolfe Morrison and Mardenfeld Herlihy, 1992); Pepsi-Cola (Fulkerson and Schuler, 1992); International Distillers and Vintners (Kandola and Fullerton, 1994); the construction industry (Gale *et al.*, 2003); BBC Scotland (Maxwell, 2003); Royal Mail (Foster, 2004); Rabobank (Subeliani and Tsogas, 2005); and Ericsson (Karabacakoğlu and Özbiglin, 2010) to name but a few.

A key element in most of these interventions is some form of diversity training. This usually focusses upon the importance of the successful management of diversity for achieving business benefits, and highlights how stereotypes of different groups may hinder their opportunities in the workplace. It also has the aim of seeking to enable the integration of minority groups into the workforce and provide other workers with the skills to be able to work productively alongside the members of such groups (Pendry *et al.*, 2007: 28).

It is apparent that specific diversity interventions will not work without a consideration of the environment within which they are being introduced. Other aspects of organisational processes are also important. For example Gilbert and Ivancevich (2000) identify five factors related to the success of diversity initiatives. These are the initiation and support of the chief executive; human resource initiatives; organisational communication; corporate philosophy; and measures of success. Wholesale organisational support needs to be available, as evidence suggests that individual one-off initiatives are not enough to make a noticeable difference. The processes by which the interventions are planned is also important as these are part of change strategies. Friday and Friday (2003), for example, provide a framework for using a 'planned change–corporate diversity strategy' based on Lewin's (1951) unfreezing model, arguing that any strategy needs to be carefully planned.

Research examining how diversity initiatives are being implemented internationally seems to indicate that much depends upon the cultural and historical context. Süß and Kleiner (2007) outline how in contrast to the USA, the starting point for managing diversity in Germany has been a focus on gender differences. They conducted a survey of 160 companies listed on the German stock exchange and found that 39.4 per cent had implemented diversity management; 18.2 per cent had heard of the concept; but 42.4 per cent knew nothing about it. The authors conclude that in the German context 'the concept is far from being a widespread and naturally employed management concept'. Similarly Meriläinen et al. (2009) in their research regarding diversity management in Finland suggest that diversity and its management are ignored on most Finnish corporate websites. Rather because Finland has had a long history of gender equality, there are instead many examples of gender equality discourse.

A key question here is what motivates companies to engage with or provide diversity initiatives. Some writers have drawn on institutional theory to suggest that organisations may create these programmes as a response to external expectations, in that it is expected that they will do so (e.g. Dobbin et al., 2011; Klarsfeld, 2009). In an exploration of the forces promoting six diversity programmes in a USA sample of 816 firms over 23 years Dobbin et al. (2011) suggest that corporate adoption of diversity programmes is 'spotty'. They contend that the key processes that lead to the adoption of diversity programmes are the institutional pressures from industry norms and internal pressures from identified groups, with white female managers seen as particularly influential in this latter process (Dobbin et al., 2011: 404).

Where implemented, organisations may also be using diversity policies to meet different strategic aims and objectives. Maxwell et al. (2003) examined the use of diversity policies in UK public service and hotel organisations and found that the public sector areas they examined seemed to be actively considering the intrinsic value of managing diversity such as treating the workforce fairly, whereas the hotel cases seemed more concerned with external organisational benefits. Foster and Harris (2005) reviewed the use of diversity management in the UK retail industry. Within that industry there are some well-publicised examples of companies claiming considerable business benefits from diversity policies. For example, Asda in a press release highlight the benefits of removing an age restriction to the employment of their workforce;

> We have always been really proud of the fact that we have such a diverse workforce with colleagues as young as 16, whilst others are in their 80's. We're in no doubt that this benefits everyone, especially our customers. We've understood for many years now that an older workforce offers maturity, commitment and knowledge which our customers value. Over the years we've found that some of our best colleagues are also some of our oldest, with loads of experience to share with younger colleagues – they make a massive difference to our stores. *(Asda, 2006).*

Foster and Harris's (2005: 14) research focussed on how line managers were interpreting the concept of diversity management in practice. They found that line managers in different companies were interpreting the concept in diverse ways. They also highlight an interesting tension that the line managers were experiencing:

> Growing numbers of organizations have corporate diversity statements that acknowledge the importance of employing a diverse workforce and valuing individual difference. Yet the

reported line management practice revealed that a standardized approach to dealing with employee differences was widely regarded as more sustainable and workable than the framework of the UK's present anti-discrimination legislation than more 'customized' approaches designed to accommodate individual diversity in the employment relationship.

Therefore it would seem then that there is increased evidence of the use of diversity initiatives in parts of the UK, Europe and the USA though coverage is still patchy. A complicating issue however, is the impact of increased globalisation. Individual companies may develop their own approach to diversity, but these approaches may be inappropriate within the different locations where a company is based. Global diversity management has therefore increasingly become the key challenge in this area.

Global diversity management

With the increased globalisation of the workforce, managing diversity across international borders has become an important issue. Sippola and Smale (2007) suggest that we know very little about how multinational firms are responding to the increasingly globalised nature of their workforce and operations. The extent to which diversity policies focussing on managing difference translate neatly across borders has been questioned. Nishii and Özbilgin (2007: 1883) suggest that 'American' labels regarding difference are 'simply ridiculous' outside the US context. They give the example of Canada where an important difference in the workplace regardless of ethnicity or gender is whether one is primarily English or French speaking. Other challenges about whether a US or Western model of diversity is appropriate have been posed with regard to India (Wilson, 2003); Australia (Strachan *et al.*, 2004) and New Zealand (Jones *et al.*, 2000). In research examining the extent to which Finnish companies have adopted managing diversity initiatives, Meriläinen *et al.* (2009: 231) summarise this problem neatly:

It has been difficult to root the diversity management concept outside Anglophone countries since its development has taken place in a specific multicultural context that is not directly comparable to other cultural contexts that have different histories of diversity.

Egan and Bendick (2003) also highlight that the US has different priorities about diversity due to the different legal, political and cultural environments. This raises the issue of whether global diversity initiatives should focus upon multidomestic approaches which are individual to each cultural location of the company, or focus on attempting to achieve a global strategy with a similar approach in all locations.

Nishii and Özbilgin (2007: 1886) suggest that global diversity initiatives based on the 'exportation of US based diversity programmes abroad have failed due to their lack of attention to local cultural and demographic differences'. They outline a conceptual framework that examines the leadership and cultural foundations and the organisational outcomes of global diversity management. The framework also includes four important components that need to be in place for successful global diversity management. First, global units need to be included in the decision-making processes of the company. This is in line with the strategies for inclusion that underlie diversity initiatives. Second, human resource management policies need to be designed flexibly in order to take account of local context. Third, although there needs to be locally defined goals for addressing particular forms of discrimination that take into account power differences between groups within a cultural context, the overall goals of the global diversity initiative need to be unified across global units. This prevents fragmentation of the overall company approach (Nishii and Özbilgin, 2007: 1888).

There is some evidence that multinational companies are adopting the kind of approach recommended. Egan and Bendick (2003: 723) examined how US multinationals were seeking to implement global diversity initiatives in European locations. They conducted a survey of

30 large US MNCs from a range of industries and services. They concluded that although diversity management is likely to become important in human resource management practices of US MNCs located in Europe, there is no one best approach. Rather 'for each company, the soundest approach is likely to be that which matches the degree of centralization that the firm applies to other important aspects of corporate operations'. They also draw attention to the issue that the business case may be different in different European contexts. A further point is that it may be difficult for diversity staff to cover both local and international work. Clearly there is the need more generally for the development of staff with expertise in international diversity management.

In summary, it would seem that the issues encountered with regard to global diversity management are similar to the debates about integration or national differentiation that characterise the nature of global HRM more generally (Sippola and Smale, 2007). Time will tell the extent to which global diversity initiatives manage to achieve their objectives.

Do diversity initiatives deliver?

A key question about managing diversity initiatives is to what extent do they actually work? The search for empirical evidence to validate the success of managing diversity programmes can be a frustrating exercise. One of the problems is that many of the case studies of diversity programmes that are reported in the literature do not contain any evaluative element. Indeed, sometimes these case study reports focus more on promoting a particular company approach with evangelical zeal, rather than assessing and evaluating the success of a given programme. An additional source of concern is that most of the studies that do look at diversity interventions are US-based. This in itself is not a problem, but, as highlighted earlier, there is the issue of how transferable the context is. Jones and colleagues (2000) point out the paradox that as managing diversity develops as a worldwide vocabulary for examining or celebrating difference, US cultural dominance may be reinforced by a US model of difference being applied globally.

It is notable however, that a number of firms do claim considerable business benefits from their engagement with managing diversity. In a survey of 919 European companies conducted by the European Union (EC, 2005), the strong message is that managing diversity does lead to business benefits. The authors suggest that the most important of these are the enhanced retention and recruitment of employees from a wider talent pool, improved corporate image and reputation, innovation and enhanced marketing. The case studies in the same report highlight some useful examples. For example Deutsche Bank's development of networks with gay and lesbian staff has led to an increase in their marketing activities to gay and lesbians and a ten-fold return on their initial investment. Tesco's 'Everyone is welcome' initiative has led to significantly more people from an ethnic minority background joining the company and a 250 per cent increase in sales of products tailored to the needs of different ethnic, religious and cultural groups. Despite these reported successes the report also states that 'one of the key findings is the lack of systematic monitoring and evaluation of the progress and benefits of diversity' with nearly 70 per cent of companies failing to monitor their impact (EC, 2005: 6).

A number of authors have drawn attention to some of the problems that emerge in seeking to evaluate diversity initiatives in organisations. Ellis and Sonnenfeld (1994) review three pioneering diversity programmes in USA companies. They conclude that although it makes sense that the benefits of such programmes may translate into higher productivity and lower turnover, few organisations actually measure the transfer of the educational interventions into actual changes in human resource practices such as recruiting, management development and promotion. Other evidence that diversity programmes are not being evaluated comes from the work of Kochan *et al.* (2003: 8). They argue that there are few studies that look directly at the impact of diversity policies on objective measures of organisational performance. They attempted to conduct research with over 20 large and well-known Fortune 500 companies who had expressed an interest in being involved in diversity research. However, the research team encountered difficulties in following through the research in these firms. As the authors outline:

> After often considerable discussion of the data, confidentiality, and time commitments, all but four companies declined to participate. In some cases, the diversity advocates and professionals in the company lacked sufficient influence to convince line managers to spend the time required to collect the necessary data. In other cases, these professionals were reluctant to examine the effects of their organization's policies, with a view that they had sufficient top management support for their current initiatives and did not need to demonstrate a business case to maintain this support.

As the authors suggest, one of the first interesting lessons from their research was that as well as managers not knowing the impact of diversity strategies on objective performance measures, few of them were interested in discovering this information. Within the four cases that were conducted the authors concluded that there was 'simply no evidence to support the simple assertion that diversity is inevitably either good or bad for business' (Kochan *et al.*, 2003: 17). Perhaps this was one of the reasons why the managers were unhappy about keeping data about the impact of their policies in this area.

There are a couple of studies that consider the financial benefits of diversity programmes. One such analysis is provided by Wright *et al.* (1995). Using data from 1986 to 1992, they examined the impact that announcements of US Department of Labor awards for exemplary affirmative action had upon the stock returns of winning corporations, together with the effects that announcements of damage awards from the settlement of discrimination lawsuits had on the stock returns of guilty corporations. Their results indicated that announcements of quality affirmative action programmes were associated with an increase in stock prices, and conversely, announcements of discrimination settlements were associated with significant negative stock price changes. The authors conclude from this study that:

> the prevalent organizational ethnic and gender bias (Hitt and Barr, 1989) should be eradicated not only because such bias is not ethical or moral, but also because it does not make economic sense. As the climate of competition becomes more intense, no enterprise can afford the senseless practice of discrimination. In fact, America's cultural diversity may provide a competitive advantage for unbiased US corporations over both domestic rivals that discriminate and European and Japanese companies in the world marketplace. *(1995: 284)*

More recently, research has begun to emerge that looks at the impact of a positive climate for diversity in an organisation on a range of business outcomes. For example Choi and Rainey (2010) measured the levels of diversity in 67 US federal agencies and then analysed how diversity management affects the relationship between levels of diversity and perceptions of organisational performance. Their findings suggest that the benefits of racial diversity among staff are enhanced with higher levels of diversity management. A particularly interesting study reported by Shen *et al.* (2010) looked at the effects of diversity management on organisational citizenship behaviours in the Chinese context. The authors point out that in China the key diversity issue is household registration status which differentiates rural peasants from urbanites, where rural peasants previously were forbidden from working in urban areas. Their results suggest that where there are effective diversity management practices in place, particularly in relation to selection and compensation, there is a greater likelihood in engagement in organisation citizenship behaviours from employees.

In their research on the implementation of diversity management programmes in public organisations, Pitts *et al.* (2010) suggest that management are the key players in ensuring that diversity management initiatives are successful, but the problem of evaluating the success of such initiatives is that diversity management is still an ambiguous concept which may be interpreted and therefore implemented differently across different companies. Overall then, it is hard not to agree with Klarsfeld (2009: 363) that 'the diversity–performance link advocated by respondents in organizations is a matter of belief or rhetoric more than scientific measurement'.

Critiquing diversity initiatives

Beyond the question of the effectiveness of diversity initiatives, a number of other critiques have emerged about the managing diversity approach. Cassell and Biswas (2000) suggest that much of the literature that exists on the subject is largely atheoretical and that there is a need to examine the extent to which diversity initiatives really have delivered positive outcomes for disadvantaged groups in the workplace. Indeed, there is a need to focus upon the different levels at which discrimination is experienced. Tatli (2011) suggests that single layer studies of diversity interventions which focus upon for example organisational processes or individual career outcomes are limited in their explanations. To address this Syed and Özbiglin (2009) instead propose a relational framework where account is taken of macro-level issues such as national structures and institutions; meso-level organisational processes such as rituals and routinised work behaviours; and micro-level work behaviours such as power and motivation. Such a framework produces a contextual and multi-level approach currently missing in the literature. It also draws attention to the importance of intersectionality in considering experiences of discrimination.

There is also some concern within the literature that managing diversity initiatives may be implemented as just another management fashion. Prasad *et al.* (2011), in their case studies of the design and implementation of diversity management programmes in six Canadian organisations, highlight a high level of fashion consciousness among those who supplied diversity programmes and those who consumed them. They draw attention to some of the difficulties this creates, for example a lack of local relevance in the initiatives introduced and a superficiality in programme design. Additionally, the bandwagon effect may lead to resistance from employees. As with any change initiative we would expect some resistance to managing diversity programmes. Yet this resistance is rarely addressed within the literature as managing diversity is promoted as being in the interest of all groups, regardless of their differences. Arnold (1977) suggests that one of the risks with diversity initiatives is the white male backlash. Wahl and Holgersson (2003) provide research evidence of male manager's reactions to gender diversity activities in Sweden. They argue that a number of factors impact on those reactions, including the numerical gender distribution, and the nature of job segregation in the companies concerned. Clearly there needs to be further consideration of the issue of resistance, why it occurs, and how it can be effectively managed, together with the consequences of that resistance for those traditionally disadvantaged groups who may be seen to gain from diversity initiatives.

A further important issue to consider is the extent to which the business case on which managing diversity is based is sustainable in the long term. The problem with a business case is that it is only persuasive within a given economic climate. Consequently, its impact in facilitating long-term change must be seriously questioned. A further issue is put forward by Richards (2001: 29) who highlights how the difficulties with employer driven equal opportunities agendas are that the priorities they usually support are those seen as important by the employer. These tend to address the more visible aspects of equal opportunities such as the number of women in senior positions for example. Therefore as Omanivic (2009: 355) suggests, although diversity management initiatives might seem an emancipatory concept, it is rather 'one that reproduces an established social order'. A further concern is that the links between valuing diverse skills and business success can be problematic. For example, Adkins (1995) in her analysis of gender relations in the tourist industry outlines how women workers were recruited to a variety of jobs at a theme park on the basis of their physical appearance.

Consequently, women deemed as sexually attractive were employed in order to please the clients, 'sexual servicing' as Adkins calls it. Similarly, Biswas and Cassell (1996) outline a case study of a hotel where the work was clearly divided on gender lines. It was argued that it was crucial that receptionists were physically attractive, as they were the first point of contact for the customer. In both these cases it could be argued therefore that accentuating the sexuality of women employees through styles of dress, etc. made business sense, hence drawing attention to some of the dilemmas that emerge when focusing upon a business case for equality alone.

A final point is that the business case may not apply equally to all diverse groups, and some groups might fit a business case more neatly than others. Woodhams and Danieli (2000) suggest that there is very little written within the diversity literature about the business case for employing disabled people. They suggest that the rationality underlying the diversity approach falters in relation to the employment of disabled people in a number of ways. As a considerably heterogeneous group who are not segregated within the labour market, a managing diversity approach based on the identification of group-based characteristics has little to offer. Furthermore, a recent CIPD report on disadvantaged groups in the labour market (CIPD, 2010) highlighted that the most disadvantaged group of workers in the UK were ex-offenders. Yet there is little, if any, mention of this group in the managing diversity literature. This discussion highlights the complicated nature of the processes through which issues of power, fairness and equality are reformulated into issues of competitive advantage. The potential for fundamental change within such an approach becomes questionable.

Conclusions

To conclude, four key issues emerge from this analysis of the managing diversity literature. The first is the extent to which there is evidence that organisations that manage diversity are more successful than organisations that do not. There is clearly the need for more research in this area. Ideally, research should focus upon the longitudinal assessment of diversity programmes, using a range of criteria from impact on economic performance to the attitudes of those groups that the interventions have been designed to address. Additionally, as stated earlier, there is a need to consider the various different levels of analysis where discrimination can occur. Only then can the claims made for the success of managing diversity approaches be properly evaluated.

Second, there is the question of the extent to which a movement that originated in North America translates easily into the distinctive HR contexts that exist in other parts of the world. It would seem that the business case for managing diversity is more partial in other economic contexts. A further issue is the problematic nature of universalistic notions of managing diversity. In practice the term does not have a unitary meaning, it means different things to different people, and can mean different things in different cultures or organisations in different international settings. Increasingly, there are challenges from other cultures about whether the Western model is appropriate. This is particularly important in relation to the development of global diversity initiatives and questions the international application of locally derived diversity policies.

A third issue is the extent to which managing diversity is really new. Kandola (1995) suggests that much that has been written under the heading of managing diversity is striving to make it appear to be a new area. He suggests that at best this is naïve, and at worst somewhat dishonest. He outlines how there has, for example, been generations of work looking at the impact of heterogeneity and homogeneity on the performance of groups in the workplace. Additionally, the work on diversity-focused organisations has produced very similar sets of characteristics to those identified as the characteristics associated with learning organisations elsewhere in the literature. It may be that the skills associated with managing diversity are no different from those of other skilled forms of managerial practice.

Finally, there is evidence that the language around equal opportunities may be changing again to move beyond managing diversity to a focus upon inclusion. Roberson (2006) suggests that there is a move from diversity to inclusion within the practitioner literature. Whether this represents something new or different from managing diversity is another issue. This move is still at an early stage indeed Shore *et al.* (2011: 1268) suggest that the inclusion literature is still in its infancy and similar to the managing diversity concept there is a disparity amongst researchers about its definition. Having said that, perhaps the labelling of the debate is of little significance, if, as an area of debate and intervention, managing diversity can offer hope for furthering equal opportunities in the workplace. More impetus is clearly needed to further moves for equality for those groups within the labour force who are traditionally discriminated against. What managing diversity approaches highlight is the economic costs to organisations of losing talented staff through discriminatory practices: surely a crucial issue for HRM policy and practice.

CASE STUDY 14.1

EDUCATE

CATHERINE CASSELL

David Nolan is the Chief Executive of Educate, a US based multinational publishing company. The company has offices worldwide, with large offices in the UK, Canada, Belgium, Australia, Singapore and the US. Currently the company is investigating the creation of two new offices in areas where there have recently been expanding markets: China and eastern Europe. David is proud that the company is seen at the forefront of contemporary educational publishing, a thriving market. Sales are good and the expansion plans have considerable support from the Board and shareholders. He is particularly proud that the company has just recently been rated as one of the USA's top 50 employers by the Diversity Digest. This is a survey read widely around the industry and the high rating at number 8 enables the company to attract the best employees from the range of diverse groups that make up the US workforce. Other accolades for the diversity friendly company have come from the US Union of gay workers, and the National Association of Women, both of which have rated Educate very highly in their annual awards as good places to work.

David Nolan knows, however, that a firm should not rest on its laurels. Recently, an issue has arisen at one of the subsidiary companies that may potentially threaten the good name of Educate. One of the senior managers at the UK subsidiary has recently emailed him to say that the women staff are unhappy with some aspects of their career progression, and that there is the potential for unrest within the firm about diversity issues. David realises that some of the good diversity policies that are currently practised in the US need to be also operating in the global wings of the business. His view is that it is time for him and the senior international team to intervene in the UK to try and ensure that statutory diversity requirements are being met.

The UK part of the business was initially established in 1902 as *Athertons Educational Publishers* a specialist publisher of educational textbooks. Starting off in a small printing press in a London back street, by the 1920s the firm employed 20 people in the selling and production of high-quality educational texts. After the 1944 Education Act the demand for educational texts increased and Atherton became one of the leaders in the market, with a name for commissioning and publishing language texts.

Initially focussing on English, the senior management team after the Second World War realised that there would be an increased demand for tuition in European languages. Their proactivity in addressing this new market led to the firm successfully developing a reputation as the leading publisher of foreign language texts. During the 1960s the senior management team predicted a growth in multicultural texts aimed at schools. In advancing in this direction Atherton took a large share of what was to be an increasingly important market. At the same time Atherton was taken over by Educate, by then a large multinational publishing corporation.

The economics of the international publishing environment have changed significantly during the last 20 years. A move has clearly occurred towards a more business-oriented and market-focussed culture with a reorientation in values away from an editorial focus towards marketing and sales. As one of the UK employees said:

> Publishing is about making sound commercial decisions about what people need and want. It used to be a gentleman's profession, but now we have had to tighten up our act – we need to publish things cheaply and quickly.

Currently, Dan Walker is the Managing Director of the UK Educate wing. He is a powerful, charismatic figure who is said to inspire his colleagues and staff. Currently, 4,500 employees are employed in the UK. Although 53 per cent of the UK managers in the company are women, only one woman is a member of the senior management team. Recently, there has been considerable dissatisfaction among the female staff who perceive that there is a glass ceiling at senior management level. There is a clear consensus among them that sexual discrimination at work is covert rather than overt. As one of them suggested:

> I've not directly experienced any prejudice, but I've seen evidence of it around. It's not easy to move higher in the organisation. If you're exceptional then you rise, but then women have to be a bit better than men in order to do that. It's still grey suits at the top.

Having children is one of the pertinent issues that is seen to influence the promotion prospects of women. Although the women managers recognise that Educate has good maternity policies, they feel that covert messages are given about having children and its impact on a woman's career. Most of the female managerial staff do not have children. Combining a successful career with motherhood is seen to be a difficult option, given the long hours and travel often associated with the work. Recent company evidence from the HR department suggests that talented female managers are leaving the company to work freelance, an option seen to tie in more favourably with raising a family. One of the female managers summed up this issue in the following way:

> Women are not promoted to senior editor positions and it's clear that women have often left due to frustration about this. It's difficult to see obvious cases of discrimination. My predecessor went on maternity leave: why didn't she come back? Women just become frustrated.

The vast majority of Educate employees in the UK are white. This creates issues with regard to selling multicultural texts in that region. In the last couple of years, Atherton have tried to recruit a number of ethnic minority publishers and sales people. Dan Walker's view is that they will serve to keep the company on top of the growing multicultural educational market, therefore employing a more diverse workforce would make business sense. Indeed, a number of clients purchasing multicultural texts have commented on the lack of ethnic diversity among UK Educate staff. This is particularly apparent in the schools market where sales staff meet regularly with multicultural education coordinators in schools. Despite actively trying to recruit ethnic minority staff, there has not been much success in both recruiting and retaining ethnic minority employees. Where ethnic minority workers have been employed, they have rarely stayed at Atherton long, commonly complaining about the lack of access to 'real' opportunities. One particular salesman expressed his feelings of tokenism in the following way:

> I'm sick of being the only Black face around the place, the guy who goes out just to get orders from the Black customers. There doesn't seem to be any other role for me here apart from that. This is not what I expected when I came to work with a big multi-national that wins awards for its diversity policies.

Dan Walker is concerned that some of the smaller, newer publishing firms are making inroads into the UK multicultural market, and are enticing away those customers who were previously loyal to the company. He wonders whether Educate UK actually has a problem with its image as an employer of the white, well-spoken, middle classes. He is also concerned that some of the older members of the workforce who have been around for a long time are reinforcing this traditional image of the firm by their very presence. In such a competitive market, where sales is a primary driver, Dan is concerned that the parent company is starting to ask questions about the image that the UK wing currently has and how it fits into the overall global profile. Although he knows that he has problems in this area, he is concerned that some of David Nolan's ideas about how to promote diversity may not go down too well in Educate UK. In particular the legislative context of the UK is different from the US where those who are different are more 'loud and proud'. His view is that a more specific diversity strategy is required for the UK Division of Educate. Yet David Nolan is demanding immediate changes. His view is that the implementation of a global diversity strategy will not only deal with the problems in the UK subsidiary, but also be useful in the expansion into the new Chinese and European markets. He thinks it is important that employees of Educate throughout the world toe the line with the progressive diversity policies currently at work in the USA.

Questions

1   What advice would you give to David Nolan about developing a global diversity strategy to cover Educate worldwide? What are some of the difficulties he may face in his attempts to implement a global diversity strategy?

2   What advice would you give to Dan Walker about how he can deal with the diversity issues currently faced in the UK part of Educate? What type of diversity interventions can be introduced locally that will both satisfy the staff that progress is being made and also satisfy David Nolan that the UK are coming into line with US diversity practices?

CASE STUDY 14.2

HINCHCLIFFE CARDS

CATHERINE CASSELL

Hinchcliffe Cards was started by William Hinchcliffe in 1874. Hinchcliffe had an artistic talent which he used for drawing individual greetings cards for his family and friends. As demand for the products he made increased, members of William's family joined him in creating the more intricately decorated cards. As the products of the firm grew in popularity, Hinchcliffe cards began to expand, investing in its first printing press in the early 1900s. The business continued to grow and moved into the mass production of greetings cards for the family market. William, who by then was managing director of the firm, was keen that some element of the origins of the company remained, and despite the focus on mass production, a small sideline in the design and production of handmade cards remained.

After William Hinchcliffe died in 1934 the firm remained in the family and is now managed by chief executive James Hinchcliffe, William's great-grandson. The company headquarters, warehouse and packaging plant are housed in the same Lancashire town in England where William originally started the business in his own home. Indeed, the firm prides itself on being a family firm and having a paternalistic culture. James Hinchcliffe is often to heard to say 'Now what would great-grandfather do in this situation', when discussing any key strategic or problem issues. Despite the paternalistic culture, James is keen that the company moves with the times. Having recently completed an MBA at a local business school, he is keen to hear about new ideas and new methods of working that he can introduce in to the company.

The company employs about 250 people. Seventy per cent of the workforce are women who work mainly on the production line and 10 per cent are from ethnic minority backgrounds. All the managers and senior management team, except the human resource manager (a white woman) are white males. Turnover in the company is generally low, though James Hinchcliffe suspects that there is a growing unease among the workforce about a number of issues.

The cards produced by the company feed in to two main markets. First, there is the mass production of greetings cards. In particular the firm recently won a couple of key contracts to produce Christmas cards for two of the larger chain stores which are internationally located. These contracts meant a considerable expansion of business which has caused some problems in terms of work scheduling as production needs to be far higher in the spring months to meet the Christmas demand. In particular, some of the more sophisticated machines that are used occasionally, for foiling for example, are in 100 per cent use at this particular time. Putting coloured or silver foil on a card is an expensive process and the two men who work that machine are highly skilled. Currently there is a shortage of such skills within the printing industry. To deal with the increase in output required at this time of year, the firm has tended to employ around 20 casual workers for the spring period when these cards are produced. There is evidence, however, that the permanent production workers display animosity towards the temporary workers. As one suggested:

> They're just here to make a quick buck, they don't seem bothered about the quality of what they do, their mistakes affect all of our bonuses.

The production workers have also recently been complaining about some other issues to do with their opportunities in the workplace. Some of the female workers have been asking why they haven't been trained on the more complex machines, which seem to be used exclusively by the male workers. Indeed, it is the production jobs based on those machines that carry the highest remuneration. Similarly a gendered division of labour also exists in other areas of the factory, for example the packing area where the cards are packed into boxes for distribution is populated exclusively with female workers. Additionally, there are concerns among the female workers that they are expected to work very long hours at short notice during peak production periods. This is seen to interfere with their family lives. As one suggested:

> They expect us to work into the evening at the drop of a hat but we don't get that flexibility in return. Cheryl, who recently left to have a baby, wanted to come back and work here part time, but they said they couldn't slot her in. It would be too difficult

to have one person working different hours from everyone else. The men may want to rake in the overtime payments but some of us can't just be in the factory every hour of the day.

Apart from these issues, the production workers are generally happy about their work. Hinchcliffe's has a good name in the local area for being a decent employer who pays the going rate for the job. They are almost an institution in the Lancashire mill town in which they are based.

The other market that Hinchcliffe's serves is the demand for handmade products. Orders for these cards come from all over the world. To tap these markets the firm has recently started an internet mail order business. In order to meet the increasing demand for handmade products, production has largely moved out of the factory. The cards are now made by a series of 50 homeworkers who make the cards in their own homes and are then sold to various specialist gift shops around the UK. These homeworkers are mainly women from ethnic minority groups. One issue that concerns the firm is the high rate of turnover among the homeworkers. They are generally perceived as having little loyalty to the firm and are unreliable in meeting agreed dates for production. There has been some talk within the firm of investing in a team of designers employed officially by the firm who can be based in the firm's headquarters. The plan is that some of the current homeworkers would be employed on this basis. Early evidence suggests that they may not be particularly interested in this option. Indeed, the majority of these workers are female who fit in their drawing work with looking after small children. Additionally, their view is that the company often treats them with little respect. An example of this is the common complaint that the materials needed to make the cards are often dropped off at their homes later than promised, sometimes with incorrect specifications. One homeworker has hinted that there may be some covert racism in the way some of the homeworkers are treated.

There is a recognition within the senior management team that the company is in a position to expand considerably through the internet side of the business. This means that there is an opportunity for the global emergence of the Hinchcliffe brand, something that James is keen to do. The firm already had some presence in European markets which had emerged from the entrepreneurial activities of a couple of the sales managers, however the Board are aware that in order to compete with other internet-based retailers, they need to become more efficient at producing the handmade cards more quickly and then delivering them on time. The regular publicly accessible ratings of firms on internet sites mean that just a couple of individual late deliveries could threaten the business of a firm seeking to expand in this way. Specifically, the good reputation of Hinchcliffe's may be at risk.

The prospect of this international expansion raises a number of issues for James Hinchcliffe. He is desperately keen to investigate the available avenues, but is also keen that the firm retains its Lancashire roots. He believes that the handmade products are just as good and as popular as the product his great-grandfather produced years ago. He recently arranged an away day with his senior management team where they had the opportunity to identify the potential strengths and opportunities in diversifying their business in this way. The management team identified that one of the greatest challenges required with such a strategy would be getting the homeworkers on board. As the production director stated:

> If we moved in that direction we could no longer deal with them dropping the cards off here at the factory a day late because the baby was sick or whatever. In fact we may have to abandon them altogether and go for an in-house design team. I know your great-grandfather was always keen to support the local community but maybe things have to change at some point. It's just very hard to get people like them working to our schedule.

Other members of the senior management team responded to this in a number of ways. One suggested that the company would lose considerably if the homeworkers were replaced:

> They have very different specialist skills. There is no way we could replicate those if we moved to just a couple of in-house designers.

There was also some debate about how the homemade cards were a unique selling point for Hinchcliffe's, and that these would be the key products sold over the internet. Therefore without these specialist workers, there would be little point in the firm attempting to address more international markets. The marketing director pointed out that it was this side of the business that needed some development

> Given the two big contracts we have recently got, we are clearly delivering what is needed internationally in the mass-produced part of the business. I know the staff moan a bit, especially some of those women, but we seem to be doing ok. It's those homeworkers we need to make more reliable.

He outlined how his internet-based research of competitors in the handmade cards business has indicated that most of the other outlets selling through the internet just had one or two people working for them. So for him:

> When you think of all the staff resources we have at Hinchcliffe's as a whole, there must be a way we can really take on that market – we just need to get all our people on board and involved.

At this stage of the discussion the HR director interjected. She said that she thought that some of the issues that were being faced at the company were managing diversity issues:

> What we are talking about here really is issues about how we manage diverse groups of staff in

order to harness the potential of all of our employees, both those who work in the factory and those who work at home

Other members of the management team were nodding at this point, agreeing that there may be something of interest in the idea of managing diversity. However, none of them felt that they were in a position to advise James about how to progress. At the end of the meeting the team agreed to approach a diversity consultant to ask them for any advice about resolving some of their diversity issues in order to progress the strategy of developing the business internationally.

Questions

1 What are the diversity issues currently faced by Hinchcliffe cards?

2 Imagine you are the consultant that has been approached by James Hinchcliffe to advise the company about how they can address each of the diversity issues you have outlined in number one above. What advice would you give them?

3 How do you think the advice you have provided in answer to question two will be received by:

   a. The homeworkers

   b. The male factory workers

   c. The female factory workers

   d. The senior management team.

4 Bearing in mind your answers to the above three questions, what advice would you give the company about how they can develop their international strategy?

CASE STUDY 14.3
EXERCISE IN DIVERSITY TRAINING

CATHERINE CASSELL

You are an HR manager working in a busy training department in a local government office. The department has a well-established managing diversity policy. Within that policy it is explicit that discrimination against certain groups within the workforce based upon any differences will not be tolerated. Your training department provides regular courses for line managers about areas such as recruitment, selection, assessment and appraisal. As part of these courses there is a focus upon the country's employment legislation. These parts of

the courses focus upon providing advice to managers about how to avoid inadvertently discriminating against staff as part of their general employment processes.

Recently, it has been suggested that there may be a need for diversity training in your organisation. Your manager has asked you to put together a one-day training event about managing diversity that is aimed at middle managers. She has also asked that you make some suggestions about how the impact of the diversity training can be evaluated.

Task

1 Provide an overview of the schedule for the days training session.
2 What is the aim of each of the sessions you have scheduled?
3 What kind of material will be included in each of the sessions?
4 What difficulties do you anticipate with the training you have suggested?
5 How will the impact of the training be evaluated?

Bibliography

Adkins, L. (1995) *Gendered Work: Sexuality, Family and the Labour Market*, Buckingham: Open University Press.

Arnold, J. (1997) *Managing Careers into the 21st Century*, London: Paul Chapman Publishing.

Asda (2006) 'DWP recognizes ASDA's continued good practice on age diversity'. Available at http://www.asda-press.co.uk/pressrelease/65. Accessed 21 January 2008.

Biswas, R. and Cassell, C.M. (1996) 'The sexual division of labour in the hotel industry: implications for strategic HRM', *Personnel Review,* Vol.25, No.5, 51–66.

Cassell, C.M. and Biswas, R. (2000) 'Managing diversity in the new millennium', *Personnel Review,* Vol.29, No.3, 268–74.

Choi, S. and Rainey, H.G. (2010) 'Managing diversity in US federal agencies: effects of diversity and diversity management on employee perceptions of organizational performance', *Public Administration Review*, January/February, 109–21.

CIPD (2010) 'Focus: disadvantaged groups in the labour market'. Available at http://www.cipd.co.uk/hr-resources/survey-reports/labour-market-outlook-focus-disadvantaged-groups.aspx. Accessed 17 November 2011.

CIPD (2011) 'Diversity in the workplace: an overview'. Available at http://www.cipd.co.uk/hr-resources/factsheets/diversity-workplace-overview.aspx. Accessed 17 November 2011.

Cox, Jr, T. (1992) 'The multi-cultural organization', *Academy of Management Executive*, Vol.5, No.2, 34–47.

Davidson, M.J. and Fielden, S.L. (2003) *Individual Diversity and Psychology in Organizations,* Chichester: John Wiley and Sons.

Dobbin, F., Soohan, K. and Kalev, A. (2011) 'You can't always get what you need: organizational determinants of diversity programs', *American Sociological Review,* Vol.76, No.3, 386–411.

Egan, M.L. and Bendick, M. (2003) 'Workforce diversity initiatives of US multinational corporations in Europe', *Thunderbird International Business Review,* Vol.45, No.6, 701–27.

Ellis, C. and Sonnenfeld, J.A. (1994) 'Diverse approaches to managing diversity', *Human Resource Management*, Vol.33, No.1, 79–109.

Equal Opportunities Commission (1995) *The Economics of Equal Opportunities*, Manchester: EOC.

European Commission (2005) 'The business case for diversity: good practices in the workplace'. Available at http://ec.europa.eu/social/main.jsp?catId=370&langId=en&featuresId= 25. Accessed 17 November 2011.

European Foundation for Living and Working Conditions (EFLWC) (2010) Demographic change and work in Europe. Available at http://www.eurofound.europa.eu/ewco/surveyreports/ EU0902019D/EU0902019D.pdf. Accessed 17 November 2011.

Foster, C. (2004) 'Royal Mail: delivering dignity at work', *Equal Opportunities Review,* No.132, August, 8–15.

Foster, C. and Harris, C. (2005) 'Easy to say, difficult to do: diversity management in retail', *Human Resource Management Journal,* Vol.15., No.3, 4–17.

Friday, E. and Friday, S. (2003) 'Managing diversity using a strategic planned change approach', *Journal of Management Development*, Vol.22, No.10, 863–80.

Fulkerson, J.R. and Schuler, R.S. (1992) 'Managing world wide diversity at Pepsi-Cola International', pp. 248–77, in Jackson, S.E. and Associates (eds) *Diversity in the Workplace: Human Resource Initiatives*, New York: Guildford Press.

Gilbert, J.A. and Ivancevich, J.M. (2000) 'Valuing diversity: a tale of two organizations', *Academy of Management Executive,* Vol.14, No.1, 93–107.

Hitt, M.A. and Barr, S.H. (1989) 'Managerial selection decision models: examination of configural cue processing', *Journal of Applied Psychology*, Vol.59, 705–11.

Jackson, S.E. and Associates (1992) *Diversity in the Workplace: Human Resource Initiatives* New York: Guilford Press.

Johnston, W.B. and Packard, A.H. (1987) *Workforce 2000: Work and Workers for the 21st Century*, Indiana, IN: Hudson.

Jones, D., Pringle, J. and Shepherd, D. (2000) '"Managing diversity" meets Aotearoa New Zealand', *Personnel Review,* Vol.29., No.3, 364–80.

Kandola, R. (1995) 'Managing diversity: new broom or old hat?', in Cooper, C.L. and Robertson, I.T (eds) *International Review of Industrial and Organizational Psychology,* Vol. 10, Chichester: John Wiley and Sons.

Kandola, R. and Fullerton, J. (1994) *Managing the Mosaic: Diversity in Action*, London: Institute of Personnel and Development.

Karabacakoğlu, F. and Özbilgin, M. (2010) 'Global diversity management at Ericsson: the business case', in Costanzo, L. (ed.) *Cases in Strategic Management*, London: McGraw-Hill.

Klarsfeld, A. (2009) 'The diffusion of diversity management: the case of France', *Scandinavian Journal of Management,* Vol.25, 363–73.

Kochan, T., Bezrukova, K., Ely, R., Jackson, S., Aparna, J., Jehn, K., Leonard, J., Levine, D. and Thomas, P. (2003) 'The effects of diversity on business performance: report of the diversity research network', *Human Resource Management,* Vol.42, No.1, 3–21.

Lewin, K. (1951) *Field Theory in Social Science,* New York: Harper and Rowe.

Maxwell, G. (2003) 'Minority report: taking the initiative in managing diversity at BBC Scotland', *Employee Relations,* Vol.26, No.2, 182–202.

Maxwell, G., McDougall, M., Blair, S. and Masson, M. (2003) 'Equality at work in the UK public-service and hotel organizations: inclining towards managing diversity?', *Human Resource Development International,* Vol.6, No.2, 243–58.

Meriläinen, S., Tierari, J., Katila, S. and Benschop, Y. (2009) 'Diversity management versus gender equality: the Finnish case', *Canadian Journal of Administrative Sciences,* Vol.26, No.3, 230–43.

Microsoft (2008) 'Message from Claudette Wilding, General Manager, global diversity and inclusion'. Available at http://www.microsoft.com/about/diversity/fromoffice.mspx. Accessed 21 January 2008.

Montes, T. and Shaw, G. (2003) 'The future of workplace diversity in the new millennium', pp. 385–402, in Davidson, M.J. and Fielden, S.L. (eds) *Individual Diversity and Psychology in Organizations,* Chichester: John Wiley and Sons.

Nishii, L.H. and Özbilgin, M.F. (2007) 'Global diversity management: towards a conceptual framework', *International Journal of Human Resource Management,* Vol.18, No.11, 1883–94.

Noon, M. and Ogbonna, E. (2001) *Equality, Diversity and Disadvantage in Employment,* Basingstoke: Palgrave.

Omanivic, V. (2009) 'Diversity and its management as a dialectical process: encountering Sweden and the US', *Scandinavian Journal of Management,* Vol.25, 352–62.

Pendry, L.F., Driscoll, D.M. and Field, C.T. (2007) 'Diversity training: putting theory into practice', *Journal of Occupational and Organizational Psychology,* Vol.80, 27–50.

Pitts, D.W. (2006) 'Modeling the impact of diversity management', *Review of Public Personnel Administration,* Vol.26, 245–68.

Pitts, D.W., Hicklin, A.K., Hawes, D.P. and Melton, E. (2010) 'What drives the implementation of diversity management programs? Evidence from public organizations', *Journal of Public Administration Research,* Vol.20, 867–86.

Prasad, A., Prasad, P. and Mir, R. (2011) '"One mirror in another": managing diversity and the discourse of fashion', *Human Relations,* Vol.64, No.5, 703–14.

Prasad, P., Mills, A.J., Elmes, M. and Prasad, A. (1997) *Managing the Organizational Melting Pot: Dilemmas of Workplace Diversity*, Thousand Oaks, CA: Sage.

Richards, W. (2001) 'Evaluating equal opportunities initiatives: the case for a transformative agenda', in Noon, M. and Ogbonna, E. (eds) *Equality, Diversity and Disadvantage in Employment,* Houndmills: Palgrave.

Roberson, Q.M. (2006) 'Disentangling the meanings of diversity and inclusion in organizations', *Group and Organization Management,* Vol. 31, No.2, 212–36.

Roberson, L. and Kulik, C.T. (2007) 'Stereotype threat at work', *Academy of Management Perspectives,* Vol.21, No.2, 24–40.

Ross, R. and Schneider, R. (1992) *From Equality to Diversity: A Business Case for Equal Opportunities*, London: Pitman.

Shen, J., D'Netto, B. and Tang, J. (2010) 'Effects of human resource diversity management on organizational citizenship behavior in the Chinese context', *International Journal of Human Resource Management,* Vol.21, No.12, 2156–72.

Shen, J., Chanda, A, D'Netto, B. and Monga, M. (2009) 'Managing diversity through human resource management', *International Journal of Human Resource Management,* Vol.20, No.2, 235–51.

Shore, L.M., Randel, A.E., Chung, B.G., Dean, M.A., Ehrhart, K.H. and Singh, G. (2011) 'Inclusion and diversity in work groups: a review and model for future research', *Journal of Management,* Vol.37, No.4, 1262–89.

Sippola, A. and Smale, A. (2007) 'The global integration of diversity management: a longitudinal case study', *International Journal of Human Resource Management,* Vol.18, No.11, 1895–916.

Storey, J. (1995) *Human Resource Management: A Critical Text*, London: Routledge.

Strachan, G., Burgess, J. and Sullivan A. (2004) 'Affirmative action or managing diversity: what is the future of equal opportunities policies in organizations', *Women in Managemant Review*, Vol.19, No.4, 196–204.

Subeliani, D. and Tsogas, G. (2005) 'Managing diversity in the Netherlands: a case study of Rabobank', *International Journal of Human Resource Management*, Vol.16, No.5, 831–51.

Süß, S. and Kleiner, M. (2007) 'Diversity management in Germany: dissemination and design of the concept', *International Journal of Human Resource Management,* Vol.18, No.11, 1934–53.

Syed, J. and Özbiglin, M. (2009) 'A relational framework for international transfer of diversity management practices', *International Journal of Human Resource Management,* Vol.20, No.12, 2435–53.

Tatli, A. (2011) 'A multi-layered exploration of the diversity management field: diversity discourses, practices and practitioners in the UK', *British Journal of Management,* Vol.22, 238–53.

Thomas, Jr, R.R. (1990) 'From affirmative action to affirming diversity', *Harvard Business Review*, Vol.68, No.2, 107–17.

Thomas, Jr, R.R. (1992) 'Managing diversity: a conceptual framework', pp. 306–18, in Jackson, S.E. and Associates (eds) *Diversity in the Workplace: Human Resource Initiatives*, New York: Guildford.

Wahl, A. and Holgersson, C. (2003) 'Male managers' reactions to gender diversity activities in organizations', pp. 313–30, in Davidson, M.J. and Fielden, S.L. (eds) *Individual Diversity and Psychology in Organizations,* Chichester: John Wiley and Sons.

Walker, B.A. and Hanson, W.C. (1992) 'Valuing differences at Digital Equipment Corporation', pp. 119–37, in Jackson, S.E. and Associates (eds) *Diversity in the Workplace: Human Resource Initiatives*, New York: Guilford.

Wilson, F.M. (1995) *Organizational Behaviour and Gender*, London: McGraw-Hill.

Wilson, E.M. (2003) 'Managing diversity: caste and gender issues in India', pp. 149–68, in Davidson, M.J. and Fielden, S.L. (eds) *Individual Diversity and Psychology in Organizations,* Chichester: John Wiley and Sons.

Woodhams, C. and Danieli, A. (2000) 'Disability and diversity: a difference too far?', *Personnel Review*, Vol.29, No.3, 402–17.

Woolfe Morrison, E. and Mardenfeld Herlihy, J. (1992) 'Becoming the best place to work: managing diversity at American Express Travel related Services', pp. 203–26, in Jackson, S.E. and Associates (eds) *Diversity in the Workplace: Human Resource Initiatives*, New York: Guilford.

Wright, P., Ferris, S.P., Hiller, J.S. and Kroll, M. (1995) 'Competitiveness through management of diversity: effects on stock price valuation', *Academy of Management Journal*, Vol.38, No.1, 272–87.

CHAPTER 15

WORK–LIFE BALANCE: NATIONAL REGIMES, ORGANISATIONAL POLICIES AND INDIVIDUAL CHOICES

Gill Kirton

Introduction

Paid work occupies a central place in the lives of most adults in developed countries. Paid work obviously provides the means for sustenance for the vast majority of people, but it is also said to contribute to a sense of identity, self-worth and usefulness in the context of society as a whole (Parent-Thirion et al., 2007). Indeed, government policies often reflect this idea, however ironical this may seem at a time when working lives have arguably been transformed for the worse and incomes and jobs have become less secure (McDowell, 2004). Yet increasingly, paid work is also seen to encroach on family and personal life to the extent that people's lives are often unbalanced with little time or energy left for other life activities beyond paid work.

Work–life balance concerns the reconciliation of work, private and family life. While many aspects of life can be included in work–life balance, such as time for leisure, community and citizenship activity, it is the decline of the nuclear family, an increase in the number of women in the labour market and in the number of households in which both partners work, that have pushed work–life balance higher up the agenda for individuals, organisations and governments. Women are a key focus of the work – life balance policy debate because of the greater likelihood of their taking primary responsibility for the home and family and the need for them to have access to work arrangements that allow them to combine work and home responsibilities. Nevertheless, behind the work–life balance discourses of many institutions lies the objective of encouraging men to play a greater role in the family and to share household chores.

This chapter first considers work–life balance discourses; it then moves on to explore the national context of work–life balance, next work–life balance and the workplace and finally individual choice and work–life balance.

Work–life balance discourses

While it is widely believed that discourses can influence practice as well as represent the world, it is important to recognise that discourses and practices are not the same thing and that there can be a rhetoric–reality gap. Discourses of work–life balance while part of national contexts are to a large extent globalised, in so far as work–life balance has made its way onto the policy agenda of many if not all industrialised countries. Policies that were once called flexibility and later 'family friendly' are now firmly located within the work–life balance discourse internationally. The shift in discourse and policy language is interesting to note. Work–life balance discourse originated in neoliberal contexts, particularly the USA and UK where there was a policy focus on enhancing competitiveness through minimal regulation (Lewis *et al.*, 2007). Writing from a UK perspective, Fleetwood (2007) argues that discourses and practices of flexible working became detached from one another from around the late 1990s. In the late 1980s and 1990s discourses and practices associated with the flexible firm model started to emerge in response to high levels of unemployment. For Fleetwood (ibid.), the kinds of flexible working practices that employers introduced in order to minimise the so-called rigidities of the labour market were employee-*un*friendly and the dominant discourses reflected this. For example, unions lobbied and campaigned against the 'casualisation of labour' – the creation of temporary, fixed-term jobs and the erosion of employment security.

In the late 1990s, in the context of a tight labour market, employers began to offer part-time work as a specific means of attracting women, particularly mothers, against talk of the 'demographic time bomb' and the need for employers to engage in the 'war for talent' in order to remain competitive. Political discourses began to emphasise the employee- or more specifically the family-friendly nature of flexible working, painting a win-win scenario. Fleetwood (ibid.) argues that although the representation of flexible working through political and public discourses became positive, the actual *practices* were still largely employee-*un*friendly in so far as part-time work, for example, was not necessarily temporally flexible and did not always fit well with family commitments.

Somewhere towards the end of the 1990s, family-friendly practices and discourses morphed into work–life balance in order to confront or perhaps side-step the criticism that family-friendly practices focused on women with children, excluding men and women without children. By now the public discourse of work–life balance was wholly positive while policies were more mixed with both employee-friendly and employee-*un*friendly elements, meaning that current discourses of work–life balance do not entirely match the realities. Even the unions have tended to adopt the positive discourse of work–life balance and tend to downplay the negative aspects of flexible working practices (Fleetwood, 2007).

Further, the change in language to work–life balance had the effect at the discursive level of making the policies *appear* gender-neutral when in reality practices remain highly gendered in terms of targeting and take-up. Despite the language of 'work–life balance' and the insistence of governments and employers that it is an issue 'for everyone', many of the policy initiatives (as discussed below) are implicitly aimed at women, especially mothers, and/or those with primary responsibility for children, just as 'family-friendly' policies were (Lewis *et al.*, 2007). Yet advocates of the new label argue that the language of work–life balance removes the discussion of the importance of achieving a better balance between home and work life from the ghetto of 'women's issues' associated with the now less popular family-friendly label. In this way, so the argument goes, work–life balance becomes an issue for everyone which employers will then take up more enthusiastically regardless of labour market conditions. The problem is that while we still have a marked gender pay gap internationally it will continue to make rational economic sense for most households to privilege the male career, so whether the work–life balance discourse can remove family-friendly work practices from the ghetto of women's issues remains questionable. After all, work–life balance discourses and policies do not confront structural gender inequalities such as segregation and the pay gap, which produce the material inequalities that push women towards privileging family roles and men towards privileging paid work.

Contemporary political discourses of work–life balance influence not only current employer policies and practices, but also popular perceptions. (Pocock, 2005) identifies four rationales for work–life balance:

- **the business case** – to help with the recruitment, retention and productivity of good staff
- **the social case** – workers who are satisfied with their work–life balance are likely to be happier social citizens, carers, parents
- **the political case** – industrialised countries are dependent on the paid work of women and workers with dependents
- **the personal case** – enhancement of individual well being.

These cases for work–life balance are reflected in political and popular discourses as well as in national and employer policies and practices. Political work–life balance discourses typically present a win-win scenario – employers benefit from greater employee flexibility (the business case), while workers get to organise their work, private and family lives in ways to suit their individual situations (the personal case). By extension, the demands of the social and political cases are also satisfied when workers experience work–life balance satisfaction.

While in some respects the prominence of work–life balance discourses might seem to represent a progressive turn that heralds greater gender equality, there is a more negative reading. Family and parental leave policies and flexible work arrangements contained within work–life balance discourses and policies might make life easier for individuals at particular phases of their lives, but they do not challenge the cultural and institutional norms that keep men tied to long working hours and women juggling work and family (McDowell, 2004). Instead, work–life balance discourses incline more towards ensuring women are kept marginalised within organisations as the ones who are perceived to be in need of special arrangements in the form of work–life balance policies. As we see later and in Case Study 15.1, being seen to be the ones taking up flexible work and other work–life balance arrangements can have negative consequences for women's careers.

Political work–life balance discourses also tend to focus on the perspectives of those in full-time employment, which is taken as the desirable norm (Bonney, 2005). Bonney, perhaps controversially, argues that flexible work arrangements for full-time employment have now taken priority over acknowledging and supporting part-time employment as a desirable solution to work–family conflict, particularly for parents (mostly mothers) of young children. He argues that part-timers and their lived experiences often get overlooked in popular discourses shaped by influential people in politics, the media and academia who more commonly regard full-time employment for all as the most desirable state. However, the career limiting nature and limited economic benefits of part-time work as it is currently configured in most countries (discussed below) should not be forgotten.

The national context of work–life balance

There can be no doubt that national institutional settings – including welfare, employment and gender regimes – matter for work–life balance. Sources of support for work–life balance can come from the state, market or family or from a combination of sources. Broadly, the state is the main provider of support in social democratic countries such as Sweden and in former socialist countries in central and eastern Europe (such as Bulgaria and Hungary). In conservative welfare states (Germany) and in southern European countries (Spain, Portugal), it is the family that provides support, while in liberal countries (the UK), the market is considered as the main provider of work–life balance support (Abendroth and den Dulk, 2011). Market (i.e. employer) policies (discussed later) are located within national regimes and while some employers might offer provisions beyond the legal minimum, others will only do what is required by law. Nevertheless, there is evidence to suggest that state support for work–life balance policies can stimulate workplace support because the state can both sensitise employers to the issue and encourage them to offer support (Abendroth and den Dulk, 2011). As important as national welfare regimes are for work–life balance, as a caveat it is important to state that there is some evidence that the variation in workplace support for work–life balance does not always correspond to Esping-Andersen's (1990) widely cited welfare regime typology. For example, despite post-communist countries having a strong tradition of state support, workplace support in Bulgaria and Hungary is found to be relatively modest (Abendroth and den Dulk, 2011).

Even though 'parental choice' is the avowed policy aim of nearly all countries (OECD, 2008), individuals make their choices about how to combine work, family and personal life against the array of institutional constraints and enablements. For example, national public and employer child-care and elder-care provision, the social and workplace organisation of time, gender roles in the home and family all impact on how individuals combine the work and non-work aspects of their lives. These institutional settings vary enormously from country to country and while there is not space here to go into detail, illustrative examples are given to underline the point that the work–life balance debate necessarily has to extend beyond the organisational and individual levels to the national.

National welfare and employment regimes

The main kinds of government policies that impact on work–life balance include tax and benefit systems, parental leave systems and child-care provision. Individualised tax systems, for example, mean that second earners (often mothers) pay a lower rate of tax than the primary earner, making it more attractive financially for them to work. However, tax relief for non-employed partners or family assistance systems that count both partners' incomes potentially reduce the financial incentive to work. Most OECD countries operate both systems. The extent of paid parental leave obviously makes a difference to how well mothers and fathers feel able to balance work and family, with at one end of the spectrum some countries offering up to three years of paid support (Austria, the Czech Republic, Finland and Hungary) and at the other end others offer very little or no universal paid leave (e.g. Australia, USA) (OECD, 2008). The main explanation for these stark cross-national differences is that some countries (i.e. the liberal welfare states such as the USA, UK and Australia) see care as a private family responsibility rather than as a matter for the state to make provision for (Craig et al., 2010). It is self-evident that greater access to formal state or employer subsidised child-care facilities helps parents to balance work and family and again this varies enormously from country to country. In most neoliberal social welfare regimes the costs of child-care are high (e.g. Australia, the UK) even with various tax benefits and in these countries there is a relatively high dependence on informal child-care often provided by for example grandparents. Nevertheless, increasing numbers of children use formal child-care. In Australia, for example, in 1996 of all children aged three to four years 22 per cent used formal child-care. This figure rose to 46 per cent by 2005 (Craig et al., 2010).

However, in general, there has been a move in the USA, Australia and some European countries towards neoliberal social welfare regimes which emphasise market-led provision, deregulation and the reduction of universal benefits (Craig et al., 2010; McDowell, 2004). In the USA, with its archetypal neoliberal welfare and employment regimes, work–life balance is certainly on the agenda of progressive 'think tanks', but minimal and patchy federal and state laws mean that employee rights are woefully inadequate for resolving work–family conflict and helping individuals achieve work–life balance. With no federal or state laws requiring that all employers even offer paid sick days (only about 50 per cent of workers in the US have access to paid sick leave), the USA trails well behind the UK and the rest of Europe in guaranteeing workers at least some opportunities to balance work–life responsibilities

(Boushey *et al.*, 2008). The USA is the only OECD country without a national parental leave policy although some states do provide leave payments (OECD, 2011). In the light of the currently weak institutional support for work–life balance, the US think tank *The Mobility Agenda* recommends that policy-makers and employers adopt four minimum work–life balance policies:

- guaranteed paid sick days for all workers
- paid family and medical leave
- right to request workplace flexibility
- scheduling flexibility.

At least some of the above policies are taken for granted in other countries – in many European countries for example – and are legal requirements in many. Institutional support for work–life balance is certainly far greater in the European Union than in the USA and is a key area of policy debate within the European Employment Strategy. Over the last 20 years, discussions at European Union level have focused on making work more flexible and facilitating shortening working hours to enable people to achieve greater work–life balance. In a 'roadmap' for equality between women and men, the European Union has the reconciliation of work, private and family life as one of its six priority areas of action for gender equality. The roadmap identifies three main areas for action: (i) flexible work arrangements for women and men; (ii) increasing care services; (iii) better reconciliation policies for women and men (e.g. parental leave, part-time work) (CEC, 2006). The Organisation for Economic Co-operation and Development (OECD) makes three recommendations for national policy – shown in Box 15.1. Not all countries measure up against these as shown by the OECD recommendations in Box 15.2 for selected countries.

Despite the prominence of work–life balance at EU level, actual national care services and reconciliation policies are highly variable across Europe. Sweden, for example, has much lauded subsidised child-care and mandated parental leave policies. On progressive parental leave policies, Norway stands out in so far as the parent on leave receives full pay in the form of social welfare benefits (Hardy and Adnett, 2002). Indeed, overall the most extensive national work–life balance policies are found in the Scandinavian countries (Abendroth and

---

Box 15.1 HRM in practice   **What should governments do on work–life balance? OECD recommendations**

- **Guarantee paid parental leave with employment protection**
  - Policy often helps parents take time off around the birth of a baby and sometimes provides some pre-school support. But, parents of older dependent children can also face significant barriers and they can require continuing support. The question for governments is whether caring for children at home should be subsidised.
- **Provide financial support for good, affordable childcare**
  - In many countries, good child-care provisions already exist, but they are not always affordable and do not always match working hours. Some countries need to give greater financial support for child-care either through capital investment in childcare facilities or through direct payments to parents. In addition to pre-school provision, adequate out of school hours/terms provision is also needed.
- **Grant employees the 'right to request' flexible working hours**
  - This emphasises the involvement of both employer and employee in determining working hours that suit both parties. It extends access to low-income workers who usually have little flexibility or autonomy to decide their working hours.

Source: OECD, 2008.

Box 15.2 HRM in practice	Improving government support for families – OECD recommendations on selected countries

Australia:

- extend child-care support programmes

Canada:

- strengthen investment in formal child-care
- improve affordability of child-care
- reduce child-care costs for low-income families

France:

- encourage a more equitable division of unpaid work within households via improved paternity leave
- improve access to labour market of mothers of young or large families via tax benefits and parental leave policy design

Germany:

- bolster child-care services
- reform tax/benefit system to encourage second earners in families with children

Netherlands:

- improve child-care facilities to enable women's participation in full-time work

New Zealand:

- do more to help parents of the youngest children
- provide better parental leave payment rates
- support sole parents into full-time work via provision of quality child-care

Spain:

- improve out-of-school hours child-care
- encourage a more equitable division of unpaid work within households

United Kingdom:

- provide affordable and good quality local child-care
- provide an effective child-care supplement for working parents

Source: OECD, 2011.

den Dulk, 2011). However, following recent reforms, Germany now has the most generous parental leave among OECD countries (OECD, 2011).

The length of the working week continues to be an issue discussed in relation to work–life balance even though weekly working hours have fallen among the full-time workforce in some countries. Research conducted in the European Union for example reveals that while the average length of the working week has fallen from 40.5 hours in 1991 to 37.5 hours in 2010, 12 per cent of the European working population overall – 18 per cent of men and eight per cent of women – continue to work long hours (in excess of 48 hours per week) (Parent-Thirion *et al.*, 2007). Meanwhile, Australia has the fourth highest proportion of people working 50 hours a week or more (20 per cent in 2000) and while the average length of the working week in Europe has fallen, in Australia the number of people working excessive hours is growing (Pocock, 2005). Against this working time context, some countries have started to legislate for flexible work arrangements. In the Netherlands, employees of enterprises with ten workers or more can change their working hours for whatever reason (OECD, 2008). In the UK parents with children under age 16 (or 18 in the case of a disabled child) and carers of adults (living at the same address) have the legal right to request flexible work arrangements (including shifting to part-time hours) to allow them to balance work and caring responsibilities. Employers can only decline the request if there are good business reasons for doing so. It is mostly women who take up this entitlement.

One form of flexible working – part-time work – is widespread. In all developed countries women have a far greater propensity to work part-time than do men. The European average for part-time working is about 30 per cent for women compared with about 7 per cent for men. In the UK, 43 per cent of women work part-time, similar to Sweden, Norway and Austria, but significantly lower than the Netherlands where 76 per cent of women work part-time. Although part-time working is more widespread among women with dependent children, many women never return to full-time work. Although the reasons for this are undoubtedly many and complex, it is clear that it is not always a simple matter of personal choice. Because part-time work is often segregated from full-time and found in specific occupations and industries and is often concentrated in low-paid, low-status jobs, many women end up either lacking the experience or skills for full-time jobs. This gendered employment pattern has far-reaching consequences for earnings even though it may offer a short-term solution to work–family conflict. For example, in the UK, the part-time gender pay gap – the difference between the pay rate of men working full-time and women working part-time – is around 35 per cent, compared with a full-time gender gap of around 12 per cent (EHRC, 2010). In the Netherlands a working mother with two adult children earns on average less than half the total working-life earnings of other female workers (OECD, 2011). Therefore, although again at the individual level and against institutional constraints that make full-time work for parents difficult, in many countries part-time work might seem like a solution to work–family conflict, it has quite dramatically negative consequences for women's pay and income equality in the short and long term. Certainly, when thinking about lifetime income, women pay in the longer term for what might seem like a temporary solution to work–life balance problems. In the USA, part-time jobs usually come without the health insurance that US workers depend on (the USA offering only minimal publicly funded health care). In the USA part-time work is therefore a far less attractive option, even in the short term, for dealing with work–family conflict and is far less widespread (Lyonette et al., 2011).

Gender regimes

It is argued that among the many aspects of national context that impact on work–life balance, the degree of gender equality is particularly relevant; that is the degree to which national cultures support women's development and achievements and recognise the importance of including women in all aspects of life (Lyness and Kropf, 2005). The allocation of gender roles in the home and family are indicative of national gender regimes that provide more or less support for women's employment participation/economic independence and for women's equality. Although studies identify a general trend towards a more equal gender division of paid and unpaid work, countries start from different baselines and still differ in beliefs about appropriate roles for women and men (Craig et al., 2010). In some countries women and men occupy highly sex differentiated roles (e.g. male breadwinner and female homemaker), whereas in other countries gender roles are more similar or overlap (Lyness and Kropf, 2005). The belief systems underpinning gender regimes then go on to permeate national and organisational policies described above and below on work–life balance and more specifically on work and family.

Despite some variation and against the increasing participation of women in the labour market, the evidence worldwide confirms that the traditional division of domestic responsibilities between women and men persists to one extent or another (EOWA, 2008b; Parent-Thirion et al., 2007). Working women continue to devote more time to household chores and caring (e.g. for children and elders) than do men. This is particularly the case for mothers, compared with non-mothers and men. The evidence from Europe shows that while men typically work longer hours in their paid jobs, when unpaid work in the home and paid work are combined women work longer hours than men. Men's work is generally confined to their paid jobs while women use the time freed up by their typically shorter paid work hours to carry out work in the home (Parent-Thirion et al., 2007). This unequal division of household and family work means that women are typically 'time poor' and obviously have less time to do other non-work activities including leisure or community for example. For women, work–life balance is very much about work–family balance and the presence of children tends to accentuate the gender division of labour, but the picture is more complex than formerly when the male breadwinner and female homemaker model was more prevalent. For example, Craig et al.'s (2010) study of the total (paid and unpaid) work carried out by women and men in Australia over 1992–2006, revealed that the total workload of both mothers and fathers increased over the period, although for mothers the increase was greater. At the end of the period, mothers were spending more hours on paid work and on child-care and the same on domestic chores. Fathers were also spending more hours on paid work and child-care, but less on domestic chores. Obviously the presence of children creates extra domestic chores (shopping, cleaning, laundry, cooking) and it is women who generally pick up the extra.

Further, the continuation of a traditional household gender regime inevitably restricts women's availability for paid work and goes some way to explaining their over-representation in part-time jobs in some countries. Therefore, it is in the more gender egalitarian countries that we see lower levels of women's part-time work (e.g. the Scandinavian countries). In a survey carried out in Australia by the *Equal Opportunity for Women in the Workplace Agency* (EOWA), nearly a third of women reported that if their partners carried out a larger share of domestic tasks, they would work longer hours. Equally, there is evidence that men would like to spend more time with their families. Sixty per cent of Australian men in the same survey reported that their jobs caused them to miss out on some of the rewarding aspects of fatherhood. The report highlights an experience that extends beyond Australia that many men have become trapped in the main breadwinning role and women in the domestic despite the fact that women have similar career aspirations to men and that men have similar family values to women (EOWA, 2008b). This underlines the interconnection between employment and gender regimes.

Work–life balance and the workplace

The business case

The idea that there is a business case for work–life balance policies is widely promulgated by governments in order to encourage employers to offer provisions. Before unpacking the business case, we must first ask why if there is a strong business case we would need national legislation as encouraged by the OECD and the European Employment Strategy (Hardy and Adnett, 2002). This caveat notwithstanding, employer benefits from work–life balance policies are said to include improved employee recruitment and retention, less employee ill-health/absenteeism and associated cost reductions, a more productive workforce and in turn a stronger financial/business performance (Boushey et al., 2008). However, research finds that employers often introduce work–life balance policies to attract and retain workers without a clear understanding of which specific policies are most attractive to their actual and potential workers (Thompson and Aspinwall, 2009).

Evidence does indicate that increased opportunities to balance work and life might lead to greater employee satisfaction, which is likely to yield significant benefits for employers. For example, while working long hours can have a range of negative effects (including health and safety) research finds that the greatest negative effect is on work–life balance. Eighteen per cent of workers in the EU27 are not satisfied with their work–life balance (Eurofound, 2010). Nearly half of all employees in the USA report conflicts between jobs and other responsibilities, more than a generation ago (Boushey *et al.*, 2008). Work–life balance satisfaction varies considerably between European countries with workers in Norway and Austria showing the greatest satisfaction and those in Greece the lowest. The longer the hours worked, the more likely people are to report work–life balance dissatisfaction in all countries (Parent-Thirion *et al.*, 2007). There are also gender differences – men in Europe are most likely to report dissatisfaction in the middle of their careers (between ages 30 and 49) when they are most likely to have dependent children. Twenty-seven per cent of men with dependent children under 16 reported that their working hours did not fit well with family and social commitments outside work, compared with 18 per cent of women (Parent-Thirion *et al.*, 2007).

Women are generally less likely to report work–life balance dissatisfaction, but those that do experience problems do so constantly over the entire course of their working lives (Eurofound, 2010). Given that women generally continue to take primary responsibility for the home and family in conjunction with increased participation in paid work, lower reported levels of WLB dissatisfaction might seem counterintuitive, but, of course, it is also the case that women are more likely to adapt their patterns of work to fit around domestic responsibilities. Flexible work arrangements and part-time work are the main means of doing this and employer policies on working time are therefore of critical importance to women.

Employer policies

Employers' work–life balance policies typically include arrangements such as parental and carers' leave, compressed hours, job-sharing, part-time work, flexi-time, working from home, childcare assistance and services. While potentially these arrangements give greater flexibility for work–life balance to a range of people with different life situations and at different stages of their lives, they very clearly target women and in particular women seeking to combine work and family. One study of the recruitment value of work–life balance benefits in the USA found that child-care benefits influenced the willingness to accept a job offer more than did flexi-time, telecommuting or elder-care benefits. Further, child-care was most attractive to women (Thompson and Aspinwall, 2009).

Evidence suggests that it is public sector and large organisations that tend to provide the most extensive work–life balance provisions (Abendroth and den Dulk, 2011; Lyness and Kropf, 2005; Pocock, 2005). However, it is significant that the fewer the national statutory requirements, the more variation there is in the work–life balance policies offered by employers within a country (Lyness and Kropf, 2005). Although many firms go beyond the minimum legal requirements, on the whole international evidence suggests that where national provision is low, private sector firms do not appear to fill the gap, particularly when it comes to family leave and child-care assistance (Hardy and Adnett, 2002). In many cases, employers' declarative statements on work–life balance and its importance seemingly substitute for actual action (Pocock, 2005).

One factor that points to the business case for flexibility if not for the whole package of work–life balance policies is that flexibility is usually offered on the employer's terms to suit the employer's needs. Part-time work and flexible hours are obvious examples of arrangements that suit many employers' needs in terms of opening hours, covering busy periods, etc. Research in Australia finds that by far the most commonly offered work–life balance initiatives are part-time work (offered by 95 per cent of organisations) and flexible hours (88 per cent). Less widespread are arrangements that might suit many employees, but that perhaps do not offer the same benefits to employers – working from home (offered by 59 per cent of organisations), job-sharing (57 per cent) and compressed hours (40 per cent). Only 12 per cent of organisations offer the more expensive work–life balance policy of child-care assistance and services, but 97 per cent offer family and carer's leave (EOWA, 2008a).

In the UK recent evidence indicates that the provision of work–life balance arrangements, especially flexible working and paid leave, has increased since the late 1990s and that a large number of employers now provide leave arrangements above the legal minimum. Seventy per cent of organisations participating in WERS 2004[1] offered the ability to reduce working hours, but flexi-time (flexible starting and finishing times) was available in only just over a third of workplaces (35 per cent). Rather worryingly, a substantial proportion of employees (between 16 and 37 per cent) were unaware of whether or not such arrangements were available to them (Walsh, 2007).

Walsh (ibid.) questions whether work–life balance arrangements in Britain genuinely cater for a diverse range of employee work and family needs. For example, leave for carers of older adults remains a relatively rare provision (offered by 6 per cent of workplaces) and workplace nurseries (3 per cent of workplaces) and child-care subsidies (6 per cent) are still relatively uncommon. Similarly, in Australia the EOWA notes the heterogeneity of employees and their different flexibility needs, for example, women who are pregnant or breastfeeding, employees with caring responsibilities, single parents, employees living in rural and remote areas, mature workers and employees with a disability. Employers are encouraged to consider this diversity in the design and implementation of their work–life balance policies in order to extend policies to a greater range of employees, but also to avoid the risk of flexible work arrangements becoming stigmatised and associated with inferior women's jobs (EOWA, 2008a). Other evidence from the UK indicates that employers generally have positive attitudes to work–life balance practices. When asked general attitudinal questions about work–life balance, 92 per cent of employers in a government survey agreed that people work best when they can balance their work and the other aspects of their lives. Sixty-seven per cent agreed that everyone should be able to balance their work and home lives in the way that they want. However, when asked questions relating more to actual experiences at the workplace, 73 per cent of employers also agreed that employees should not expect to be able to change their working pattern if it would disrupt the business and 67 per cent admitted that it is not easy trying to accommodate employees with different patterns of working (Hayward et al., 2007)

It is not just formal employer policies that matter for helping individuals balance work and family. Supportive organisational and work *cultures* are also important for encouraging employees to access the flexible work arrangements and other provisions that are available to them (Callan, 2007; Lyness and Kropf, 2005). Many workers do not have access to work–life balance provisions (beyond the legal minimum), but there is evidence that even those who do are either unaware of their contractual rights or fear the consequences for their careers particularly of taking up flexible work arrangements (EOWA 2008a; Walsh 2007). Employees generally understand that flexible work arrangements are a kind of special assistance to enable people (read women) who cannot conform to the inflexible and often long working hours' to work (Lewis et al., 2007). Thus, even seemingly generous employer policies are no guarantee that the workplace culture is sufficiently transformed to truly offer individuals all the flexibility that they appear to because they do not disrupt the dominant construction of the ideal worker (Callan, 2007).

Part of the explanation might lie in the fact that flexible work arrangements are not always introduced with work–life balance in mind despite the fact that they are usually packaged under the work–life balance rubric. Flexibility can be imposed by employers to suit their business and operational needs as well as actively sought by individual workers to suit their personal and family needs. Workers with fixed, regular, day-time work hours tend to report the greatest work–life balance satisfaction. Imposed flexibility that takes away choice and/or undermines the predictability of working hours is generally disliked by workers (Parent-Thirion et al., 2007). Unpredictable and imposed flexibility is obviously particularly problematic for those who need to make care arrangements for dependants. McDowell (2004) makes this clear by way of the example of an unofficial British Airways strike in 2003 over the

---

[1]WERS 2004 is the fifth Workplace Employee Relations Survey carried out in Britain since the 1980s.

introduction of new split shifts for the largely female check-in desk workers which threatened to disrupt the women's child-care arrangements.

Flexibility that extends choices to workers (e.g. flexi-time) is more favoured by workers themselves, but paradoxically perhaps, those with the greatest say in theory in the organisation of their work hours report the greatest work–life balance dissatisfaction (Parent-Thirion *et al.*, 2007). This is perhaps because those with greatest autonomy tend to work the longest hours (e.g. self-employed people and some professional occupations) so that the availability of flexi-time is less relevant. Evidence from Australia indicates that non-management staff is more likely to have access to flexible work arrangements than management. The difference is particularly marked for compressed hours, job-sharing and part-time work – the arrangements most likely to be taken up by those with child-care responsibilities. This hierarchical segregation of flexible and non-flexible jobs is problematic because managers need to be able to 'walk the talk' about flexible work arrangements otherwise flexibility risks being seen as and actually becoming damaging to career potential. The end result is that flexible work arrangements remain strongly gendered. The same study found that when job seeking 83 per cent of women and 73 per cent of men valued organisations that support work–life balance, indicating that there is an appetite for a less gendered model of flexible work. However, 17 per cent of women and 21 per cent of men believed that their employer offered no flexibility whatsoever (EOWA, 2008a).

Some forms of flexible work arrangements have been facilitated in recent years by technological advances, particularly the internet, allowing some people to work from home and/or the workplace in some sort of combination that accommodates outside commitments and activities. While at the individual level such flexibility might enable for example parents, particularly mothers, to continue to work full-time, the negative side is that improved communication technologies (email, broadband internet, mobile phones, smartphones etc) can also allow work to impinge on personal life in previously unimaginable ways blurring the boundaries between work and non-work time and space. Many people, particularly managers and supervisors, have extensive out-of-hours contact with their workplace which lengthens the working day and interrupts family and leisure time (Parent-Thirion *et al.*, 2007). There are now numerous internet blogs and even self-help books on the so-called 'crackberry' phenomenon – people addicted to checking email on their smartphones. If anything, rather than facilitating greater work–life balance, technology seems to have stimulated a greater addiction to paid work and a new kind of presenteeism involving always being contactable even outside of normal working hours. Thus, despite the positive rhetoric that typically surrounds the flexible work debate, it is not always the solution to work–life balance that it is held up to be.

Union action

In the UK, analysis of WERS 2004 found that unionised workplaces were more likely to have 'family friendly' policies (Kersley *et al.*, 2006). However, this association in itself does not prove that the unions have any direct involvement in work–life balance policy-making. That said, despite a chequered history internationally of involvement in equality issues, in many countries unions are now considered to play an important role in improving work–life balance provisions at the workplace. In Australia many unions have sought to increase paid maternity leave at enterprise level and have had some bargaining success. Other Australian unions have focused on control of working hours. The Australian Council of Trade Unions has lobbied for extended unpaid parental leave of 24 months, better rights to return to part-time work, the opportunity to 'purchase' extra weeks of annual leave, and a new right for parents to request a change in working hours to meet caring needs (as in the UK) (Pocock, 2005). The UK Trades Union Congress biennial equality audit similarly offers a fairly positive picture of union action. It found that 65 per cent of unions had up-to-date guidance/policy on flexible working and work–life balance and, more importantly, 44 per cent of unions reported negotiating successes on the issue. Further, 58 per cent of unions had up-to-date guidance/policy on working parents and carers and 51 per cent reported negotiating successes here (TUC, 2009).

In the context of converging union strategies in Europe, Gregory and Milner (2009) suggest that three opportunity structures encourage a shift towards work–life balance issues in union campaigns and bargaining:

- rise in the proportion of women union members and leaders
- national working-time regime
- union–management relations in specific organisations

On the first opportunity structure, it is argued that traditionally male-dominated unions have not seen the interface between work and family as a union issue. Female union negotiators are said to be more likely to bring issues of particular concern to women, such as work–life balance, to the table and that these issues are most likely to be pursued where women account for a significant proportion of membership (Kirton and Healy, 1999). National working-time regimes – the second opportunity structure – can provide an opening for unions to bargain on flexible work arrangements, for example in the European countries where working time is regulated. Union–management relations – the third opportunity structure – relates to the possibility for work–life balance to be presented as a mutual gains issue and an area for management–union partnership. This enables unions in the present era of relatively low membership and power to make progress on an issue where management and union interests could be seen to converge (Rigby and O'Brien-Smith, 2010). However, Gregory and Milner's (2009) study reveals unions to be relatively marginal actors in the process of introducing and implementing work–life balance policies in France and the UK not least because unions are forced into defensive positions by virtue of their weakened power bases. Nevertheless, they did find instances in the UK where unions had an influence in the early stages of policy-making and in France where negotiations on working time had led unions into negotiations on work–life balance. In contrast, Rigby and O'Brien-Smith's (ibid.) study located in the UK media and retail industry unions found unions to be fairly proactive on work–life balance issues. In neither sector did the unions adopt wholeheartedly a mutual gains stance, nor did they conceptualise work–life balance as positive flexibility. In the media sector there was little expectation of mutual gains and work–life balance was seen to be mainly concerned with the long hours working that characterises jobs in the sector. In retail, the main work–life balance issue was flexible work arrangements and neither did this fit a mutual gains stance because of inconsistencies in the employer approach insofar as seemingly good national policies were often undermined by unsympathetic line managers. Although the degree of impact unions can and do have on work–life balance policies and practices is variable, it is quite clear that unions in many countries are visible and active in the debate.

Individual choice and work–life balance

Although looking at work–life balance solely through an individual choice lens can obscure the structural and institutional constraints and enablements previously discussed, it is nevertheless worth considering how individuals seek to achieve work–life balance in order to avoid constructing individuals as nothing more than passive recipients of government and employer policies. This is particularly important given that a discourse of individual choice, autonomy and responsibility often pervades individuals' work–life balance narratives e.g. (Kirton, 2011; Lewis et al., 2007).

Although, as stated previously, the contemporary work–life balance discourse goes beyond the reconciliation of paid work and family responsibilities, the focus here is on the work–family interface. There can be no doubt that for individuals, particularly women, work–life balance comes into sharp focus when they become parents. As discussed above, it is women who still largely shoulder domestic and family responsibilities and adapt their career aspirations and behaviour to reconcile work and family (Windebank, 2001). In many countries, even highly qualified women in dual-career couples typically choose to prioritise the male partner's career and earnings potential once they have children (Hardill and Watson, 2004). Further, among such couples a traditional gender division of domestic labour remains strong with women overwhelmingly managing parenting arrangements (Windebank, 2001). Why is this?

There are in all likelihood multiple explanations, but Duncan et al., (2003) offer a compelling one. They argue that people make decisions about how parenting might be combined with paid work with reference to 'gendered moral rationalities': gender-based moral and socially negotiated views about what behaviour is right and proper (i.e. not just with reference to what child-care and parental leave are available) (Duncan et al., 2003: 310). While it is well established that gender matters for individual orientations to work–life balance, some research also finds that other aspects of identity such as class and race/ethnicity also matter. For example, research indicates that kinship and community are particularly salient for Asian communities who, it is argued, face a stronger sense of familial obligation that places pressures on individuals seeking work–life balance. Further, some 'migratory families' are spread around the world which can add to the difficulties individuals face in achieving balance (Dale, 2005).

Duncan et al's., (ibid.) UK-based study which included women of African-Caribbean background, found that ethnicity provided a 'major fault line' in mothers' understandings about combining motherhood and paid work. The African-Caribbean mothers, particularly those in professional and management jobs, were more likely than the white to regard substantial hours in employment as a component of good mothering, rather than of bad, neglectful mothering. On the other hand, mothers of Bangladeshi and Pakistani backgrounds are more likely to adopt a full-time homemaker model of motherhood compared with women of other ethnicities. However, it appears that generational change is also occurring in so far as highly educated British Bangladeshi and Pakistani women are much more likely to be in employment and less likely than their less educated counterparts to marry and have children at a young age (Dale, 2005). Further, in another UK study of young people, similar proportions and only a minority of all (ethnic) groups of girls said they would be happy to stay at home and look after children rather than have a career (Bhavnani, 2006).

There is also some evidence of *national* variation in conceptions of the 'good mother'. Based on a French case study it is argued that underpinned by relatively strong child-care provision, French women have 'a certain ability to not feel guilty about the social norms associated with the image of the "good mother" ', meaning that full-time paid work as a choice does not meet the same level of disapproval in France as in some other countries (Guillaume and Pochic, 2007). Further, conceptions of 'good' fatherhood are also changing. While the dominant breadwinning conception remains prevalent, there are also developing concepts of fatherhood as self-fulfilment and caring fatherliness, such that even though on average fathers work longer hours than mothers, some forgo other out-of-work activities to spend more time with their children (Bruegel and Gray, 2005). Further complicating conceptions of fatherhood, Bruegel and Gray (ibid.) identify a class effect in so far as men with more education and in managerial or professional jobs appear to spend more time on child-care than other men. Kirton's (2011) study of young black and minority ethnic (BME) graduates in the UK highlights the continuation of a male breadwinner identity, but at the same time some male respondents saw family life (beyond the nuclear family) and religious obligations as equally central to their lives and had the hope and expectation that work would be accommodating. A critical mass of male role models working flexibly has been heralded as a particularly effective way of challenging assumptions about gender norms and of providing legitimacy to work–life balance policies. Kirton (ibid.) considers that perhaps BME men will lead the way in this respect with a possibly stronger orientation in terms of obligations towards family, care and kinship.

Conclusion

The debate about work–life balance has permeated the discourses and policy-making of many countries. The aim of this chapter has been to highlight the myriad ways that despite there existing a somewhat globalised discourse, national context influences and impacts on employer work–life balance policies and on individual work–life balance orientations and choices. National welfare, employment and gender regimes and their interconnecting nature provide variable contexts in which people seek to combine paid work and other aspects of their lives. Gender regimes are particularly salient when it comes to work-family conflict, which is at the heart of work–life balance policy-making. Despite a globalised win-win work–life balance discourse, it is not at all clear that all industrialised countries are heading towards policy and practice convergence. Individual work–life balance choices are further complicated when we consider not just the availability of such polices as parental leave and childcare, but also 'gendered moral rationalities' in relation to parenting that bring gender and ethnic/race identities and their intersections into the frame.

CASE STUDY 15.1

WORK–LIFE BALANCE POLICIES AND CULTURE IN TWO CASE STUDY ORGANISATIONS – PHARMERGER AND ENGCORP

SAMANTHA CALLAN

PharMerger is a pharmaceutical company with significant global presence in six continents and premises in 45 countries. The UK has two research and development sites, one of which is the subject of this case study, and 14 commercial and production locations. The history of this site can be framed in terms of three distinct eras and it is these which have shaped the culture of the current organisation to a great extent. Founded in the mid-1970s, the original organisation was taken over by a foreign company at the end of the 1980s and then merged with a UK-based global giant in the mid-1990s.

However, there is not a clear starting point to the organisation's adoption of family-friendly working; the most senior HR respondent described the site's family-friendly emphasis as having 'grown progressively, it's not as if it "came in" at any point'. Employees have had flexi-time working arrangements since the early 1980s but specific and explicit family-friendly employment policies were not introduced until shortly after the merger with the pharmaceutical giant. These policies are perceived by employees to be indicative of the larger company's desire to control and systematise working patterns. Although employees were in agreement that PharMerger is more family-friendly than the original company, this was widely attributed to the passage of time, rather than to divergent approaches of the two companies. Any company aspiring to attract and retain the best employees (as PharMerger certainly does) now has to provide an environment which is more family-friendly than in previous decades.

Interviews with HR professionals revealed that, to some extent, competitors in the pharmaceutical industry whose employment packages include a high level of family-friendly provision, provide the impetus for ongoing improvement of PharMerger's policies. (This is also seen in other industries; McKee et al. (2000) found that oil and gas industry employers compete with each other when setting policies through a process informed by knowledge gathered through both informal and formal networking within the sector.) HR professionals were representative of the corporate perspective in their commonly held view that provision was generous, went beyond statutory requirements and employees *should* be satisfied with it.

Managers tended to concur, especially those with responsibility for several members of staff, rather than just one or two. Other research has examined the role managers play as gatekeepers to policy implementation (Bond et al., 2002; Dex and Scheibl, 2002; Yeandle et al., 2003) and this study confirmed previous findings about the decisive nature of their discretion. Respondents frequently described how it was 'down to the managers' and how they used policies and stated that the company itself had reached a limit in terms of policies that could be put in place. Managers described feeling constrained to a certain extent by policies, typically in the sense that policy provision was too generous in practice; if policies were fully implemented this threatened to affect their ability to deliver against somewhat inflexible and high targets.

Many employees were parents who needed their working patterns to fit around school hours; flexible working policies enabled them to leave the premises early and recommence work in the early evening. These opportunities, used almost exclusively by women, carried no penalty for administrative staff but it was typical for more senior staff to have to work in an officially part-time capacity if they wanted this level of flexibility. They also had to be willing to allow work to intrude their home life outside their contracted hours (e.g. they were expected to access email remotely and be available on the telephone). Individual employees also had demanding and inflexible targets to reach and these, in some cases, prevented them from taking advantage of policies. One scientist who occasionally needed to attend hospital appointments with a disabled child and thus required additional flexibility, reported that the pressure to reach her targets was a powerful disincentive to using policies. Her preferred option was to use annual leave instead. The pressure of targets strongly influenced her eventual decision to leave the company. This employee challenged key facets of the PharMerger culture, such as the 'ideal worker type', described elsewhere in the literature and evident in both organisations.

The ideal worker type is closely associated with beliefs about professionalism which 'sustain definitions of self-hood that elevate the workplace over home life' (Kerfoot, 2002: 93). Employees conforming to this type did not tend to structure their working day explicitly around family responsibilities and prioritised 'getting the job done' over keeping to fairly set working hours. Respondents appeared to accept that ongoing career advancement required conforming to this type and exhibiting willingness to relocate, travel and be available at home, outside working hours. In PharMerger the type was stronger (than in EngCorp), more evident and a source of workforce homogeneity but, common to both organisations, policies appeared to effect very little shift in this facet. This was because a) organisational survival was perceived to depend on it and b) the type is closely associated with the ideal worker *image*, how they want others to see them, and their preferred *identity*, how they see themselves (Hatch and Schultz, 1997; Whetten and Godfrey, 1998).

Significantly, female managers also contested the organisation's claim to be family-friendly on the grounds that career progression was impeded by taking up policies such as working slightly reduced hours. Career-oriented women whose working hours were routinely impacted by caring responsibilities (for example they worked on a part-time or flexible hours basis) considered that they had to minimise family concerns in order to conform to the 'ideal worker type' referred to earlier. This indicates to what extent this construct was bound up with stereotypically 'male' characteristics – although many men in PharMerger were also in frequent need of a measure of flexibility so they could undertake, albeit more limited, caring responsibilities.

The other case study concerned an engineering company, EngCorp, which also had an international presence. The two business units included in the study are both sited in the town regarded as the company's global headquarters. EngCorp has a reputation in the surrounding area of being a 'caring' company which 'puts people first', and many respondents considered their jobs to be the best they had ever had due to their employment conditions. Not all employees were familiar with the phrase 'family-friendly', however, most referred to the flexibility which was integral to working for EngCorp, and gave examples of the understanding repeatedly shown by the company for their family responsibilities. Parental leave policies enabled parents to negotiate nine-day fortnight arrangements (by using unpaid days) and annualised hours arrangements gave them more time away from work during school holidays.

Respondents were aware of a strong sense of company identity and many described the presence of a definable and pervasive culture which they attributed to shared and recognised values. It is important to make a distinction here between 'root' culture and more diffuse values. The 'emic' or insider view of culture tends to conflate and confuse these two terms whereas the role of the researcher in these case studies was to identify the unconscious and underlying assumptions that determine insiders' values about which, it is possible, few are aware. As was found in the PharMerger case study, several individuals clearly dissented to the recognisable majority view of the company. Managers and employees tended to hold somewhat different views of policy implementation and women's experiences could markedly contrast with those of their male counterparts.

The company described itself as 'male-dominated' and considered its family-friendly policies to be a significant aspect of its deliberative approach to attracting and retaining female engineers. (There is a parallel here with PharMerger's perceived need to maintain a high enough level of family-friendly employment provision to stay competitive in the global market for talent.) However, female employees who were ambitious in their careers judged their progression would be hampered, regardless of available policies, if they were not working according to the ideal worker type and following a different pattern to men in equivalent positions. The internalisation of this type was evident in interviews with women from both companies, even when work conflicted with their domestic responsibilities (and with men's who were primary carers, for example, widowers), given that work's intrusion into their home life went unchallenged, particularly if they were working part-time.

Source: Based on Callan, 2007.

Questions

1 What cultural changes would be necessary to make the work–life balance policies in the case study organisations truly deliver all they promise?

2 In what ways do the work–life balance cultures of the two case study organisations seem at odds with their policies?

3 How does the concept of the 'ideal worker type' help to explain workplace work–life balance cultures?

4 Discuss the implications of work–life balance policies and cultures for women's and men's careers and for the redistribution of household and family labour?

CASE STUDY 15.2

OBSTACLES TO COLLECTIVE BARGAINING ON WORK–LIFE BALANCE

GILL KIRTON

The following are obstacles that have been identified in the context of Spain. Discuss the extent to which these extend beyond one national context to other industrialised countries.

- The vast majority of members of collective bargaining commissions are men.
- Trade union culture at company level is rooted in traditional 'patriarchal' values.
- Progress in achieving work–life balance is sometimes hindered by workers since the demand for improvements in this area by some workers – mainly women – leads to disputes with the rest of the workforce among whom the company has to redistribute the workload. This situation is particularly clear in workforces containing a high proportion of women.
- Employers are reluctant to introduce work–life balance in bargaining because they feel it may disturb work organisation, working hours and the concept of working time itself.
- Employers consider that the development of work–life balance through leave arrangements may lead to an increase in labour costs, particularly in predominantly female sectors such as retail.
- The high proportion of workers on temporary contracts weakens the bargaining position of the trade unions.

Source: Artiles, 2005.

CASE STUDY 15.3

ATTITUDES TOWARDS WORK–LIFE BALANCE OF YOUNG UK BLACK AND MINORITY ETHNIC GRADUATES

GILL KIRTON

As part of a study of young, UK-based black and minority business graduates' career identities and aspirations, research participants were asked to talk about their future work-family balance. The following are selected quotations from the interviews.

Amer – British Pakistani male:

> ... work as hard as you can in your first 10 years because that's when your single. That's when you can make the most money. Like 21 to 30 that's where you make the most money you can. And work for a good company, save up, earn as much money as you can and then once you hit the age of 30 when you really know what you want to do in life, start up your own business. So once you start up your own business, you've probably more time to yourself. Like, I mean you got to run the business the first few years ... it's going to be tough but you can, like, balance it out because it's your business, you run the show so there'll be more time for

the kids, you can balance it out. When the kids are around you can spend more time with them and when they go to bed you can work. You can balance it out in that sense so…I think that's a good idea for a long-term plan. I think it's quite important to spend a lot of time with your kids. And so if I'm working for a big company and I don't have the time for my kids, I think I'd look for a better option.

Mohammad – British Pakistani male:

I know I've talked a lot about how important money is but I feel it's very, very important to spend time with my family. I would like to get home at a time where I can spend time with my kids. I wouldn't want to work 'til 8 o'clock say, get home at 9 and put my kids to bed. I would like to spend some time with them. I would be willing to make financial sacrifices.

Hamad – British Bangladeshi male:

Hopefully if I'm running my own business and the business grows then I should have some flexibility to take time off work that kind of stuff you know. Work a few days a week and then alternate … look after the kids some days and you know, hopefully the wife will do more of the looking after but, yeah something like that you know – a shared role basically. But making time for them [the children] otherwise they might end up as crack heads or something.

Sarina – British Indian female:

Life is so tough as it is and to have children on top of that … I mean, you need to be some sort of superwoman to be able to do everything. So my ambition really is to like do as much as I can now, do as much as I can with my husband, whether we can share a business or do some work together … That will be great and then have enough money by the time we have children to not work the long hours that we worked prior to having children. So I want to give my children … I feel so like I want have a baby now but, no I want give my children like a lot of time because in this day and age it's very hard, like you know you see the long hours culture and stuff and with the long hours culture you know your children get neglected and stuff. I mean even though there's like all these benefits around like maternity leave and pay and all of this …

Shahida – British Bangladeshi female:

Basically I am hoping to get all my experience, qualify as an accountant. And then I feel that once I have achieved that, qualified as an accountant, then I will have much more flexibility. You can demand it and make up the hours that you work, whereas at the moment because I am not qualified I will have to maybe work full-time. No, I think there are values and there are things that I'd like to, you know, teach my children and I don't feel that in a nursery environment they'd get that. But then my nieces and nephews they all went to nurseries and they have all ended up really, really clever. And if I send my children to nursery they might end up really clever as well. I mean I don't know …

Monira – British Pakistani female:

I don't think at this point I would need to go part-time as a teacher, just when I think about having kids as you work the same hours as your kids. You are on holiday with your kids, and there is a lot of help, in terms of child-care, and my mum looks after children so she would help out as well, so I don't think that would really be a big problem for me. And also my husband he has his own business as I have said before, so he would be more likely to help out in emergencies as opposed to my mum. So we have an understanding.

Questions

1 What kinds of attitudes to parenting do the above narratives reveal?

2 What kinds of orientations to work–life balance and the gender division of labour are revealed?

3 Do you detect any tensions and dilemmas among the young black and minority ethnic graduates?

Sources: Kirton, 2009, 2011.

Bibliography

Abendroth, A. and den Dulk, L. (2011). 'Support for the work–life balance in Europe: the impact of state, workplace and family support on work–life balance satisfaction.' *Work, Employment and Society*, Vol.25, No.2, 234–56.

Artiles, A. (2005) 'Work–life balance in collective bargaining examined'. European Industrial Relations Observatory Online ES0507204F. Available at http://Europa.eu/eiro/2005/07/feature/es0507204f.htm.

Bhavnani, R. (2006) 'Ahead of the game: the changing aspirations of young ethnic minority women', *Moving on Up? Ethnic Minority Women and Work*', Manchester: Equal Opportunities Commission.

Bond, S., Hyman, J., Summers, J. and Wise, S. (2002) *Family-friendly Working? Putting Policy into Practice*. Bristol/York: Policy Press/JRF.

Bonney, N. (2005) 'Overworked Britons? Part-time work and work–life balance', *Work, Employment and Society,* Vol.19, No.2, 391–401.

Boushey, H., Moughari, L. Sattelmayer, S. and Walker, M. (2008) *Work–life Policies for the Twenty-first Century Economy*, Washington, DC: The Mobility Agenda.

Bruegel, I. and Gray, A. (2005) 'Men's conditions of employment and the division of childcare between parents', pp. 147–69, in Houston, D. (ed.) *Work–Life Balance in the 21st Century*, Basingstoke: Palgrave Macmillan.

Callan, S. (2007) 'Implications of family-friendly policies for organizational culture: findings from two case studies', *Work, Employment and Society,* Vol.21, No.4, 673–91.

CEC (2006) *A Roadmap for Equality Between Women and Men*, Brussels: Commission of the European Communities.

Craig, L., Mullan, K. and Blaxland, M. (2010) 'Parenthood, policy and work-family time in Australia 1992–2002', *Work, Employment and Society* Vol.24, No.1, 27–45.

Dale, A. (2005). 'Combining family and employment: evidence from Pakistani and Bangladeshi women', pp. 230–45, in Houston, D. (ed.) *Work–Life Balance in the 21st Century*, Basingstoke: Palgrave Macmillan.

Dex, S. and Scheibl, F. (2002) *SMEs and Flexible Working Arrangements*. Bristol/York: Policy Press/JRF.

Duncan, S., Edwards, R., Reynolds, T. and Alldred, P. (2003) 'Motherhood, paid work and partnering: values and theories', *Work, Employment and Society,* Vol.17, No.2, 309–30.

EHRC (2010) *How Fair is Britain? Equality, Human Rights and Good Relations in 2010*, Manchester: Equality and Human Rights Commission.

EOWA (2008a) *Survey on Workplace Flexibility*, Sydney: Equal Opportunity for Women in the Workplace Agency.

EOWA (2008b). *Generation F: Attract, Engage, Retain*, Sydney: Equal Opportunity for Women in the Workplace Agency.

Esping-Andersen, G. (1990) *The Three Worlds of Welfare Capitalism*. Cambridge: Polity Press.

Eurofound (2010) *Changes Over Time: First Findings From the Fifth European Working Conditions Survey,* Dublin: European Foundation for the Improvement of Living and Working Conditions.

Fleetwood, S. (2007) 'Why work–life balance now', *International Journal of Human Resource Management*, Vol.18, 387–400.

Gregory, A. and Milner, S. (2009) 'Trade unions and work–life balance: changing times in France and the UK?', *British Journal of Industrial Relations,* Vol.47, No.1, 122–46.

Guillaume, C. and Pochic, S. (2007), 'What would you sacrifice? Access to top management and the work–life balance', *Gender, Work and Organization*, Vol.16, No.1, 14–36.

Hardill, I. and Watson, R. (2004) 'Career priorities within dual career households: an analysis of the impact of child rearing upon gender participation rates and earnings', *Industrial Relations Journal,* Vol.35, No.1, 19–37.

Hardy, S. and Adnett, N. (2002) 'The Parental Leave Directive: towards a "family-friendly" social Europe?', *European Journal of Industrial Relations*, Vol.8, No.2, 157–72.

Hatch, M.J. and Schultz, M. (1997) 'Relations between organizational culture, identity and image', *European Journal of Marketing*, Vol.31, Nos.5/6, 356–65.

Hayward, B., Fong, B. and Thornton, A. (2007) *The Third Work–Life Balance Employer Survey*, Employment Relations Research Series No. 86. London: Department for Business Enterprise and Regulatory Reform.

Kerfoot, D. (2002) 'Managing the "professional" man', pp. 81–98, in Dent, M., and Whitehead, S., (eds) *Managing Professional Identities: Knowledge, Performativity and the 'New' Professional*, London and New York: Routledge.

Kersley, B., Alpin, C., Forth, J., Bryson, A., Bewley, H., Dix, G. and Oxenbridge, S. (2006) *Inside the Workplace: Findings from the 2004 Workplace Employment Relations Survey,* Abingdon: Routledge.

Kirton, G. (2009) 'Career plans and aspirations of recent black and minority ethnic business graduates', *Work, Employment and Society,* Vol.23, No.1, 11–28.;

Kirton, G. (2011) 'Work–life balance: attitudes and expectations of young black and minority ethnic graduates', pp. 252–69, in Healy, G., Kirton, G. and Noon, M. (eds) *Equalities, Inequalities and Diversity,* Basingstoke: Palgrave.

Kirton, G. and Healy, G. (1999) 'Transforming union women: the role of women trade union officials in union renewal', *Industrial Relations Journal,* Vol.30, No.1, 31–45.

Lewis, S., Gambles, R. and Rapoport, R. (2007) 'The constraints of a "work–life balance" approach: an international perspective', *International Journal of Human Resource Management*, Vol.18, No.3, 360–73.

Lyness, K. and Kropf, M. (2005) 'The relationships of national gender equality and organizational support with work–family balance: a study of European managers', *Human Relations,* Vol.58, No.1, 33–60.

Lyonette, C., Kaufman, G. and Crompton, R. (2011) '"We both need to work": maternal employment, childcare and health care in Britain and the USA', *Work, Employment and Society,* Vol.25, No.1, 34–50.

McDowell, L. (2004) 'Work, workfare, work/life balance and an ethic of care', *Progress in Human Geography,* Vol.28, No.2, 145–63.

McKee, L., Mauthner, N. and Maclean, C. (2000) '"Family friendly" policies and practices in the oil and gas industry: employers' perspectives', *Work, Employment and Society,* Vol.14, No.3, 557–71.

OECD (2008) *Babies and Bosses: Balancing Work and Family Life*, Paris: Organisation for Economic Co-operation and Development.

OECD (2011) *Doing Better for Families*. Paris: Organisation for Economic Co-operation and Development.

Parent-Thirion, A., Fernandez Macias, E., Hurley, J. and Vermeylen, G. (2007) *Fourth European Working Conditions Survey*, Dublin: European Foundation for the Improvement of Living and Working Conditions.

Pocock, B. (2005) 'Work–life "balance" in Australia: limited progress, dim prospects', *Asia Pacific Journal of Human Resources,* Vol.43, No.2, 198–209.

Rigby, M. and O'Brien-Smith, F. (2010) 'Trade union interventions in work–life balance', *Work, Employment and Society,* Vol.24, No.2, 203–20.

Thompson, L. and Aspinwall, K. (2009) 'The recruitment value of work/life benefits', *Personnel Review,* Vol.38, No.2, 195–210.

TUC (2009) *TUC Equality Audit 2009. Progress on Bargaining for Equality at Work,* London: Trades Union Congress.

Walsh, J. (2007) 'Equality and diversity in British workplaces: the 2004 Workplace Employment Relations Survey', *Industrial Relations Journal*, Vol.38, No.4, 303–19.

Whetten, D.A. and Godfrey, P.C. (eds) (1998) *Identity in Organizations: Building Theory Through Conversations,* Thousand Oaks, CA: Sage.

Windebank, J. (2001) 'Dual-earner couples in Britain and France: gender divisions of domestic labour and parenting work in different welfare states', *Work, Employment and Society,* Vol.15, No.2, 269–90.

Yeandle, S., Phillips, J., Scheibl, F., Wigfield, A. and Wise, S. (2003) *Line Managers and Family-friendly Employment*. Bristol: Policy Press/JRF.

CHAPTER 16

DOWNSIZING

Tom Redman, Adrian Wilkinson and Alankrita Pandey

It was the best of times (for stockholders), it was the worst of times (for employees). The corporation was restructuring.

(DiFonzo and Bordia, 1998: 295)

Introduction

In this chapter we first introduce the subject of organisational downsizing by discussing its extent and potential for causing problems when mismanaged. The breadth and depth of organisational restructuring seen in the industrialised economies has been significant in recent years. Second, we review the methods by which downsizing occurs and consider a range of alternatives to its use. Third, we examine the processes involved and focus in particular on consultation, redundancy selection and support for those who are made redundant, and the survivors of downsizing. Lastly, we conclude by asking whether the costs of downsizing are worth it and whether downsizing translates simply into 'increased stress and decreased job security' (De Meuse et al., 1997: 168).

Downsizing: the reality of HRM?

Downsizing is the 'planned set of organisational policies and practices aimed at reducing the extant workforce with the goal of improving firm performance' (Datta *et al.*, 2010: 282). Since the 1980s, downsizing has gained strategic legitimacy (Boone, 2000; Cameron *et al.*, 1991; McKinley *et al.*, 2000). Indeed, research on downsizing in the US (Baumol *et al.*, 2003, see also the American Management Association annual surveys since 1990), UK (Chorely, 2002; Mason, 2002; Rogers, 2002; Sahdev *et al.*, 1999), and Japan (Ahmadjian and Robinson, 2001; Mroczkowski and Hanaoka, 1997) suggest that downsizing is being regarded by management as one of the preferred methods of turning around declining organisations, cutting costs and improving organisational performance (Mellahi and Wilkinson 2004). However, the impact of downsizing is mixed, with some studies revealing it to have positive results on organisations, (Baumol *et al.*, 2003; Bruton *et al.*, 1996; Espahbodi *et al.*, 2000; Wayhan and Werner, 2000). Other studies have revealed negative effects (Cascio, 1993; Cascio *et al.*, 1997; Caves and Kreps, 1993; Lee, 1997; Palmon *et al.*, 1997; Worrell *et al.*, 1991), while others show that downsizing has no impact on firm performance at all (Cameron *et al.*, 1991). Thus downsizing is a complex phenomenon in any organisation and should be understood as such.

Downsizing and restructuring are often used interchangeably, but organisations can restructure without shrinking in size and vice versa (Budros 1999). In the UK downsizing has been seen as an easy way to remedy management problems.

> The lack of labour market protection, the weakness of unions and the intense pressure on private and public sector companies alike to improve their profitability and efficiency have meant that the fashionable doctrine of downsizing has spread like a contagion. *(Hutton 1997: 40)*

The above comment from Hutton reflects that organisational downsizing is now firmly established as a central aspect of HRM practice in the UK. Equally, Guthrie and Datta (2008: 108) observe that millions of American workers have been laid off through downsizing over the last 20 years, a trend that shows no sign of abating (Mishra *et al.*, 2009). However, after a perusal of the growing numbers of textbooks on HRM, a reader could be forgiven for thinking that HRM practice is largely associated with a positively virtuous image within organisations. Righteous HRM managers recruit, train, devise strategies, manage rewards and careers, involve employees, improve labour relations, solve problems, etc. for the mutual benefit of the organisation and their workforce. Most management books take an upbeat tone, with little reference to the more unpalatable aspects of downsizing and redundancy. Revitalising change is seen as an entirely positive process to do with 'rooting out inertia', promoting efficiency and fostering innovation. Change is to be achieved not incrementally but through 'big leaps' (Hamel, 2000). Downsizing is more apparent in the Dilbert books (Adams, 1996), the Doonesbury cartoons (Anfunso, 1996) and Michael Moore's journalism (Moore, 1997). When managers do discuss downsizing it tends to be couched in very euphemistic terms (see Box 16.1). However, an examination of managerial practice over the past decade or so also finds a darker side to HRM in organisational downsizing. In 2000, Worrall *et al.* noted that there were over 200,000 notified redundancies in the UK each year and Cascio (2009) estimates 900,000 as the typical number in the US. This, however, pales in comparison with the 25 million laid off from state-owned firms in China between 1998 and 2001. Downsizing thus is not only a Western phenomenon. As we see stakeholder orientation being replaced by shareholder values as in Japan, there is now greater acceptability of downsizing even when cultural values suggest different terms are used. Thus, in Korea, redundancy is called an 'honorable retirement' – in keeping with the culture of the country.

Box 16.1 HRM in practice	The sanitisation of dismissal: sacking goes out of fashion

Redundancy and dismissal is an area of HRM practice that particularly suffers from euphemistic jargon. Some of the terms HRM managers use include:

building down	downsizing	re-engineering
career re-appraisal	exiting	releasing
compressing	headcount reduction	resizing
decruiting	involuntary quit	re-structuring
de-hiring	lay-off	retrenchment
dejobbing	letting-go	rightsizing
de-layering	non-retaining	severance
demassing	outplacing	slimming
de-selection	payroll adjustment	streamlining
disemploying	rationalising	termination
downscoping	rebalancing	wastage

The motor industry seems especially afflicted in this respect, perhaps as a result of the large scale of workforce reductions. For example, General Motors described one plant closure as a 'volume-related production schedule adjustment', Chrysler had 'a career alternative enhancement program', while Nissan introduced a 'separation program'. Two motor industry personnel managers interviewed about the effects of lean production methods talked of 'increasing the velocity of organisational exit' and 'liberating from our organisation' those who could not accommodate the new system. One also talked of getting rid of the PUREs (previously unrecognised recruitment errors). In contrast, the language of the shop floor is much more direct and includes being sacked, canned, given your cards, axed and being sent down the road.

Despite its importance and growing prominence, this aspect of HRM rarely merits treatment in the texts. In those few texts that recognise its existence the focus is usually on a discussion of how to avoid the legal pitfalls when reducing the workforce, or they provide a simple attempt to quantify its use. Much rarer is any discussion that examines the nature, significance and aftermath of making people redundant. This neglect is a serious and somewhat puzzling one. As Chadwick *et al.* (2004) note, successful performance following downsizing requires HR practices to continue to promote the discretionary efforts of employees, retain valuable human capital and reconstruct valuable organisation structures.

One possible explanation for the neglect of this issue lies in the view that workforce reduction is considered to be an isolated and unpleasant element of HRM practice and one that is best hurriedly carried out and quickly forgotten: the so-called 'Mafia model' of downsizing (Stebbins, 1989). The statistics for redundancy and dismissal in Britain would however suggest that as unpleasant as it may be, workforce reduction is not an isolated event; rather it has become a central aspect of HRM practice. What is particularly worrying here is the number of organisations downsizing who are actually making healthy profits. As Cascio (2002) points out, these are not sick companies trying to save themselves but healthy companies attempting to boost earnings. Organisational size is no longer a measure of corporate success. Western managers, it seems, have a propensity for sacking employees. Jack Welch, for example was known as 'neutron Jack' for his actions in getting rid of employees and leaving only the buildings intact (Haigh, 2004; Welch, 2001). 'Chainsaw' Al Dunlap managed to terminate 11,000 staff in two months, representing around 35 per cent of the workforce. Shareholder value was the banner under which these cuts were made (Lazonick, 2005: 594).

One trigger for increasing interest and attention for downsizing, above and beyond its greater extent and scale than in the past, is as Sennett (1997: 18) notes: 'downsizings and re-engineerings impose on middle-class people sudden disasters which were, under earlier capitalism much more confined to the working classes'. Effectively managing workforce reduction is thus of increasing importance in HRM practice, not least because of its greater scale and frequency but also because of the potentially serious negative effects of its mismanagement (Thornhill and Saunders, 1998; Wilkinson, 2004). The mismanagement of workforce reduction can clearly cause major damage to both the organisation's employment and general business reputation. Damage to the former can seriously affect an organisation's attractiveness with potential future employees by producing an uncaring, hire-and-fire image that affects the employer brand (Dewettinck and Buyens, 2002). Similarly, bad publicity over retrenchment can cause customers to worry that the firm may go out of business or give rise to problems in the continuity or quality of supplies and services, with associated reputational effects (Love and Kraatz, 2009).

There have also been increasing concerns about the organisational effectiveness of the post-downsized 'anorexic organisation'. The benefits, which organisations claim to be seeking from downsizing, centre on savings in labour costs, speedier decision-making, better communication, reduced product development time, enhanced involvement of employees and greater responsiveness to customers (De Meuse et al., 1997: 168). However, some writers draw attention to the 'obsessive' pursuit of downsizing to the point of self-starvation marked by excessive cost-cutting, organ failure and an extreme pathological fear of becoming inefficient. Hence 'trimming' and 'tightening belts' are the order of the day (Tyler and Wilkinson, 2007).

Research suggests that downsizing can have a negative effect on 'corporate memory' (Burke, 1997), employee morale (Brockner et al., 1987), destruction of social networks (Priti, 2000), increases in labour turnover (Trevor and Nyberg, 2008), and causes a loss of organisational knowledge (Littler and Innes, 2003). As a result, downsizing could 'seriously handicap and damage the learning capacity of organisations' (Fisher and White, 2000: 249). Further, given that downsizing is often associated with cutting costs, downsizing firms may provide less training for their employees, recruit less externally, and reduce the research and development budget (Mellahi and Wilkinson, 2010). Consequently, downsizing could 'hollow out' the firm's skills capacity (Littler and Innes, 2003: 93). It is interesting to note that the problems BA experienced in the summer of 2004 with angry travellers, people sleeping rough at airports, etc. was said by the unions to be the result of 13,000 redundant posts since 2001, leaving staff shortages in key areas (Inman, 2004).

Paradoxically, restructuring has also been seen as a sign of corporate virility, and stock market prices have boomed in the context of such plans. Barclays Bank shares soared after its announcement to axe 6,000 staff (Garfield, 1999). As Haigh observes (2004: 141), 'it remains the case that the quickest way for a CEO to obtain an ovation is to propose eliminating a layer of managers, as though dusting a mantelpiece or scraping off a coating of rust'. During the global financial crisis the number of unemployed in the US rose by 8 million between December quarter 2007 and December quarter 2009, more than doubling in the process, and in the EU 6 million were added to the unemployment rolls (Peetz et al., 2011). Equally, it is worth noting that organisations do face choices in the face of falls in demand – how much labour to dismiss, how much to hoard and how much to redeploy (Peetz et al., 2011). Employment decisions can also reflect different approaches to human resources, for example in the USA where they have an employment at will philosophy, labour was more likely to be shed in contrast to the EU, where there was more emphasis on finding alternatives. Peetz et al. (2011) provide examples of macho-style behaviour such as the European automobile equipment multinational, Continental, sending a letter to 600 out of 1,120 dismissed staff offering job relocations to Tunisia for salaries of 137 Euros a month, arguing that this complied with the legal obligation to relocate staff in existing operations within the company (soyoutv.com 2010). However, they also note other examples of employers using flexible reduction of working time or work-sharing with partial compensation of income losses financed by public funds (e.g. at Fiat and

Indesit in Italy, Scania and Volvo in Sweden, Daimler and Schaeffer in Germany, and Danfos and Grundfos in Denmark). There were others that focused on internal restructuring through redeployment of labour (e.g. Powertrain and Indesit in Italy). Some also restructured labour through training (e.g. Peugeot in France and Telecom Italia) (Glassner and Keune, 2010, see also Peetz *et al.*, 2011: 194–5).

Research on managing in Ireland during the global financial crisis reported that companies do not simply include 'hard' HRM policies aimed at cutting their pay roll and boosting productivity, but they also include 'soft' HRM policies aimed at maintaining employee commitment and loyalty via intensified communication and employee engagement efforts, retaining HRM initiatives and promoting fairness into their programmes to ensure that the impact is spread evenly across all groups of employees. Roche *et al.* (2011) concluded that HR managers appear to be trying to balance 'hard' and 'soft' people management policies in an effort to address short-term cost pressures while not eroding employee motivation or commitment.

Industrial conflict and workforce resistance (e.g. via strikes, sit-ins, work-ins, etc.) is also a potential problem that arises in periods of retrenchment (Contrepois, 2011; Cullinane and Dundon, 2011; Gall, 2011). For example, we have recently seen the return of factory occupations and a wave of 'bossnappings' in France as organisations closed down factories (Jefferys, 2011; Peetz *et al.*, 2011). However, given the unparalleled levels of workforce reductions, the relatively low level of disputes overall is perhaps more surprising. It may reflect not only reduced trade union and worker power, but also that redundancy is now so commonplace and woven into the fabric of industrial life that it is seen as an inevitable consequence of work in hyper-competitive times (Turnbull and Wass, 2004). The form of union resistance to redundancy has thus changed to one of attempting to secure the best deal possible for members via job security agreements which incorporate consultation mechanisms, severance payments and supportive measures, alongside a general lobbying and campaigning role, with industrial action as a rarely used last resort.

The potentially negative impact of downsizing is not restricted to those who leave but also has a major effect on the remaining employees. Such employees are now much more important to the employer, but are often overlooked in downsizing situations. The impact of downsizing on the remaining employees is such that commentators now talk of 'the survivor syndrome' (Brockner, 1992). This is the term given to the collection of behaviours such as 'decreased motivation, morale and loyalty to the organisation, and increased stress levels and skepticism' that are exhibited by those who are still in employment following restructuring (Doherty and Horstead, 1995). Studies also report how the health of surviving employees deteriorates after downsizing (Kivimaki *et al.*, 2000).

Cascio (2009) suggests that there are only two sets of circumstances where downsizing may be warranted. The first is when companies find themselves saddled with non-performing assets or consistently unprofitable subsidiaries. Here he states that they should consider selling these to buyers who can make better use of those assets. Then, employees associated with those assets or subsidiaries often move with them to the new buyers. The second case is when jobs rely on technology that is no longer commercially viable; for example, in the newspaper industry when after computer-based typesetting emerged, compositors were no longer required.

Complexity of downsizing

Figure 16.1 shows the complexity of downsizing. The decision to downsize is taken at the level of the organisation by the managers and the top management team. The organisation downsizes in response to economic or political forces. It may also be responding to market or technology changes. The impact of downsizing is felt at the organisational and individual

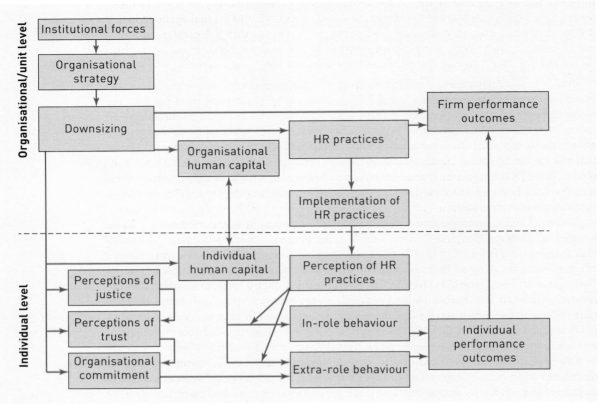

Figure 16.1 Impacts of downsizing on performance outcomes
Source: McMahan *et al.*, 2012.

levels. Downsizing directly reduces organisational human capital and also has an impact on HR practices such as selection and training, with an indirect impact on human capital. Downsizing negatively impacts on perceptions of justice, trust and commitment for individuals who are downsized and on those who remain. It therefore influences both in-role and extra-role behaviour and through them, individual and then organisational performance. Clearly, many organisations downsizing seek to mitigate these negative impacts.

Methods of downsizing

There are a number of ways that organisations can reduce the size of the workforce. In this section we first examine the strategies employers use the most. These include: natural attrition/wastage; voluntary redundancy; compulsory redundancy and early retirement. Second, we consider a range of alternatives to dismissing workers, in particular redeployment and wage reduction.

Natural attrition/wastage

Natural wastage is often preferred as the most positive and humane method of workforce reduction. It is seen as giving individuals a free choice in whether to leave or stay and thus reduces the potential for conflict and employee feelings of powerlessness. Evidence suggests that it is not the exact equivalent of normal labour turnover. It appears that in a redundancy situation both the rate and nature of labour turnover changes. Early research reported that labour turnover increases in retrenchment situations (Bulmer, 1971; Wedderburn, 1965), but this may reflect more on the nature of the labour market, with alternative jobs easier to obtain during this period. This form of workforce reduction poses problems for management in that it is unplanned and uncontrollable. Some evidence also suggests that it depresses workforce morale more than the short, sharp, shock approach of redundancy. Natural wastage is also a form of job loss that is much more difficult for employees and unions to resist because of its incremental nature.

Voluntary redundancy

This method has increasingly become most employers' preferred method of downsizing. Some common concerns are that it is expensive, as employees with long service find it attractive, and the best workers are more likely to leave because there is demand for their skills elsewhere, while poorer workers stay because they are less marketable. There is little evidence to make a judgement here, but Hardy's (1987) research suggests the reverse actually occurs in practice. Marginal performers are more likely to take up voluntary redundancy packages because of either disillusionment with the job or the fear of dismissal without any financial cushion at a later date. Savery et al. (1998) report that high absenteeism and low commitment are associated largely with those who have expressed an interest in voluntary redundancy. The main advantages are that at least employees are given a choice and this de-stigmatises, to some extent, the loss of the job. Although voluntary redundancy is much preferred to compulsory forms, it is sometimes seen by unions as 'selling jobs'.

There is, however, considerable evidence that voluntary redundancy is often far from a willing choice on the part of employees, with many reports of managers 'leaning' on targeted employees, leading to the question of did they jump or were they pushed? Research on teacher lay-offs, for example, found a wide range of informal and very threatening tactics used by managers to 'encourage' particular teachers to volunteer. In one case, this included a manager threatening to disclose to an employee's spouse his extramarital affairs if the employee did not 'volunteer' for redundancy (Sinclair et al., 1995).

Compulsory redundancy

Compulsory redundancy – where no choice is presented to the departing employee – this is normally a 'last resort' strategy for employers and is usually seen as the least acceptable face of downsizing. However, as it is based on managerial decision making, it gives employers the opportunity to design and implement criteria based on business needs. Compulsory redundancy is also more common where downsizings are large-scale or involve complete plant closures. According to WERS data, compulsory redundancy is also much more common in the private sector than in the public sector (Cully et al., 1999; Kersley et al., 2006). However, it has also been suggested that compulsory redundancy is rising in usage in the public sector as the potential for voluntary redundancy and early retirement has been exhausted and more generally because of doubts about the latter's effectiveness.

Retirement

Early retirement is usually utilised alongside other methods of workforce reduction, although it may often be sufficient to generate the required job cuts. It is often seen less as a method of redundancy and more as a way of avoiding it. The mechanics differ from other methods in one key respect; employees opting for early retirement are less likely to seek to re-enter the workforce. The increasing use of early retirement can be detected in surveys which measure the declining economic activity rates of older employees.

Ill-health is one cause for the increase in early retirement, but other developments at both company and national levels also lie behind the increase. There has been a major increase in the level of ill-health retirements in recent years. A commonly voiced argument is that this is a consequence of intensification of work and associated increases in stress levels which result in more long-term sickness.

At the national level there has been a desire by governments in the US and Europe, as well as other industrialised countries, to increase work opportunities for younger workers. At the company level, the expansion of occupational pension schemes and the inclusion of standard arrangements for redundancy retirement have facilitated the use of early retirement as a method of workforce reduction (McGoldrick and Cooper, 1989). The use of enhanced early retirement benefits makes it more palatable. It would also appear that many managers, usually with little supporting evidence, associate increasing age with declining levels of productivity and poorer-quality performance. Ageism in managerial circles, it seems, is rife, and some companies even had formal 'first in first out' redundancy policies until the advent of legislation on age discrimination throughout the EU. The view that older workers have critical experience and expertise with 'seasoning', as an asset not a liability, is not widely shared (Clabaugh, 1997). The main exception here appears to be senior managers themselves. The increasing age profile of directors has caused some to question whether there should be a 'sell-by' date for such a group (Weyer, 1994).

There are a number of advantages of early retirement ('downsizing with dignity' – Barbee, 1986); in particular, it is seen as carrying less stigma than other forms of redundancy; 'retired' is a much more socially acceptable 'r' word than 'redundant'. However, there are also a number of drawbacks. The decline of the last in first out (LIFO) redundancy selection criteria, which protected older workers by virtue of seniority, has left them disproportionately vulnerable to enforced early retirement under employers' labour-shedding policies. People are now living longer and retiring earlier and thus need sound financial provision if demeaning financial dependency is to be avoided. The adequacy of early retirement benefits is increasingly being questioned. It is now clear that the past trends in early retirement will not continue, not least because of uncertainty over the capacity of pension funds to sustain the costs and the end of default retirement ages in some countires, e.g. the UK. EU-wide legislation on age discrimination and a changing policy on mandatory retirement look set to radically alter early retirement trends.

Alternatives to redundancy

Employers are often encouraged to consider alternatives to redundancies, and to view compulsory redundancy, especially, only as a last resort. There is a wide range of possible alternatives to redundancy. These include redeployment, freezing recruitment, disengaging contractors and other flexible workers, reducing overtime, secondments, career breaks, and introducing more flexible working patterns such as job-sharing and part-time work.

However, despite such calls there is little evidence for any widespread development of redundancy alternatives in Britain. For some commentators an explanation lies in the ease with which British employers can dismiss their workers without having to consider alternatives. Turnbull and Wass (1997) argue that deregulation has made redundancy or what the European Union term 'collective dismissal', easier than other forms of workforce reduction. A consequence of a more protracted dismissal process is that it seems other countries have a much greater emphasis on avoiding redundancy. Japan and Scandinavian countries have the most developed forms of employment protection, with graded steps for cost reduction. In the case of Japan, this includes redeployment, relocation, retraining, transfer and even suspending dividends and cutting the salaries of senior managers. As Turnbull and Wass (1997) point out, this is the exact reverse of the British picture, where dividends and the bonus payments of senior managers are boosted by making workers redundant in the pursuit of short-term profit improvements.

Cascio (2009) points out that there is very limited research that examines the relative financial effects of these alternatives on firms, and the effects on individual employees, partly because there are few examples. He attributes this to the mental models that senior managers have about human resources. From his work he identifies two groups. One group of firms saw employees as *costs to be cut*. The other much smaller group of firms saw employees as *assets to be developed*. From here we can see a major difference in the approaches they took to restructure their organisations.

- **Employees as costs to be cut** – the downsizers. They constantly ask themselves, what is the minimum number of employees we need to run this company? What is the irreducible core number of employees the business requires?
- **Employees as assets to be developed** – the responsible restructurers. They constantly ask themselves, how can we change the way we do business, so that we can use the people we currently have more effectively?

As Cascio puts it, the downsizers see employees as commodities – like paper clips or light bulbs – interchangeable and substitutable, one for another. This is a 'plug-in' mentality: plug them in when you need them, pull the plug when you no longer need them. In contrast, responsible restructurers see employees as sources of innovation and renewal. They see in employees the potential to grow their businesses. A key issue is how HR can influence these mental maps and hence influence practice. Some of these main alternatives to redundancy are now briefly discussed.

Wage reductions

Wage cuts as an alternative to job cuts tend to be sparingly used, although there have been a number of prominent examples as a method of cost reduction in the UK and elsewhere, such as in Hong Kong. A particular use has been in the introduction of US concession-style bargaining arrangements wherein employees forgo a wage increase for some form of job security agreement. In the UK, Thomas Cook in 2001 cut jobs by 1,500 and asked staff to take pay cuts of 10 per cent as business collapsed in the wake of the terrorist attacks in the US. Senior executives cut their own pay by 15 per cent and those earning more than £10,000 had their salaries cut by 3–10 per cent (McCallister, 2001).

The phenomenon that wages are 'sticky' downwards, and labour markets respond to falls in demand by making employment adjustments is well established in economic theory. What Sullivan and Hogge term 'wage fix/employment flex' was found to operate widely with managers faced by a recession, seeking to control labour costs (via redundancies), to improve productivity, and maintain their employment reputation and workers' morale (Sullivan and Hogge, 1987). The mechanisms that best achieved this were adjustments to employment rather than wage reduction. Neither management nor unions sought to negotiate on maintaining employment as an alternative to real wages as this would damage the 'implicit contract' between workers and managers. An alternative might be to reduce hours, as VW did in the early 1990s as part of a large cultural change which involved removing layers of management, introducing teamwork and raising skill levels (Pfeffer, 1998: 189–92).

Redeployment

Although employers' attempts to secure more flexible workforces have been subject to a great deal of debate, the concept of spatial flexibility and the redeployment of workers has received little attention. In the US, redeployment – or 'inplacement' – is well established. In the recession of the mid-1970s, Japanese corporations maintained as many as 4 million permanent employees despite the lack of work for them to do. Redeployment made this easier because of the tendency to straddle employees across several industries (Hill, 1989: 51). Even in the 1990s, when Japanese weaknesses were identified, plant closure and sell-offs were rarely carried out. Even with the Japanese method of labour handling during a recession makes it difficult to instigate quick turnarounds; it also means that companies still have resources at hand for a rapid expansion.

Redeployment is not an easy option for managers. It requires considerable cooperation between different divisions, plants and departments within a firm and brings a number of often costly implications. A common need is for redeployed workers to be retrained and re-skilled. Relocation and/or travelling costs can be incurred. A key issue in supporting redeployment is the degree of pay protection given to such workers. The reality of redeployment is that most workers are redeployed to lower-graded posts. Many employers protect the existing income of redeployed workers for a specified period. Redeployment can also be problematic for the employee, and counselling, not least to help workers overcome a sense of loss, is helpful in such situations.

Box 16.2 HRM in practice   Redundant personalities

One controversial development in redundancy selection surrounds the use of psychometric tests, especially personality tests, in deciding who goes or stays. Tests have largely been used in redundancies involving white-collar jobs, for example at Anglian Water, Southwark and Brent Councils, Coventry Healthcare NHS Trust and Wyeth Laboratories. Their use has caused considerable concern among the employees and trade unions involved.

At Anglian Water around a third of the staff (around 900 employees) were to be made redundant. Instead of keeping the staff whose jobs remained, all employees undertook personality testing designed to measure conceptual thinking, innovation, teamwork, initiative, people-orientation and flexibility. The test was said to influence around 30 per cent of the final redundancy decision but the union believes it carried more weight. Whatever weight the tests were given in eventual termination decisions and despite their 'objective' nature, they became a focus of staff resentment. Unison (the public service trade union) claimed that the company determined the competencies to be tested before it identified what characteristics and skills were needed. Those dismissed felt unfairly deprived of their jobs and tribunal claims for unfair redundancy have ensued. Concerns about racial discrimination have also arisen with the use of tests for redundancy and downgrading. At the Coventry Healthcare NHS Trust five nurses won an out-of-court settlement from their employer on these grounds. A similar out-of-court settlement was also reached in the Brent case, where 53 workers lost their jobs after restructuring using aptitude tests. The particular tests used were found to be in error because they did not effectively take into account cultural differences.

A number of further concerns arise from the use of psychometric tests, which have been designed for other purposes, in downsizing decisions. Not least is the issue that effective testing relies on candidates behaving openly and honestly, and when some of the consequences of these tests are redundancy and downgrading, this is very difficult to achieve. Despite these problems, the use of tests for redundancy purposes is growing. It seems that managers like the idea of laying the blame for unpopular redundancy decisions on 'science' and the individual employee, rather than accepting responsibility themselves.

Sources: Rich and Dankin, 1994, *Financial Times* 14 December 1990: 10; Smith, 1996.

 ## The redundancy process

Redundancy, despite the practice that managers have had in undertaking it of late, is often badly managed, with many negative consequences. In part this may stem from the rarity of formal redundancy procedures. The large majority of employers do not have an agreed and written redundancy procedure. Recent interest in notions of labour-management partnerships have begun to take on such concerns. Some have embodied no compulsory redundancy guarantees in such agreements.

There is much to be gained from a humane, planned and strategic approach to downsizing (Wilkinson, 2004). According to Cameron (1994, 1998), the way downsizing is implemented is more important than the fact that it is implemented. He reports on three approaches to downsizing (see Table 16.1).

Workforce reduction strategies are focused primarily on reducing headcount and are usually implemented in a top-down, speedy way. However, the downside of such an approach is that it is seen as the 'equivalent to throwing a grenade into a crowded room, closing the door and expecting the explosion to eliminate a certain percentage of the workforce. It is difficult to predict exactly who will be eliminated and who will remain' (Cameron 1994: 197), but it grabs the immediate attention of the workforce to the condition that exists. Because of the quick implementation associated with the workforce reduction strategy, management does not have time to think its strategy through and communicate it properly to employees. This may result in a low 'perceived distributive fairness' (Brockner *et al.*, 1987). As a result, employees may be negatively affected by the stress and uncertainty created by this type of downsizing and may react with reduced organisational commitment, less job involvement, and reduced work efforts.

Work redesign strategies are aimed at reducing work (in addition to, or instead of, reducing the number of workers) through redesigning tasks, reducing work hours, merging units, etc. However, these are difficult to implement swiftly and hence are seen as a medium-term strategy.

Systematic strategies focus more broadly on changing culture, attitude and values, not just changing workforce size. This involves

> redefining downsizing as an on-going process, as a basis for continuous improvement; rather than as a programme or a target. Downsizing is also equated with simplification of all aspects of the organisation – the entire system including supplies, inventories, design process, production methods, customer relations, marketing and sales support, and so on. *(Cameron 1994: 199).*

Again, this strategy requires longer-term perspectives than that of workforce reduction.

Sahdev (2003: 72) suggests that the main focus of HR appears to be in implementing the procedural aspects of redundancy, including fair selection and provision of outplacement services for the leavers. While this is in keeping with the organisational justice approach, the contributions need to be directed towards managing the strategic aspects of decision-making processes with a view to managing survivors effectively. He suggests that HR practitioners

Table 16.1 Three types of downsizing strategies

	Workforce reduction	Work redesign	Systematic
Focus	Headcount	Jobs, levels, units	Culture
Eliminate	People	Work	Status quo
Implementation time	Quick	Moderate	Extended
Payoff target	Short-term payoff	Moderate-term payoff	Long-term payoff
Inhibits	Long-term adapt-ability	Quick payback	Short-term cost savings
Examples	Attrition	Combine functions	Involve everyone
	Layoffs	Merge units	Simplify everything
	Early retirement	Redesign jobs	Bottom-up change
	Buy-out packages	Eliminate layers	Target hidden costs

Source: Cameron, 1994.

need to be influential at both the strategic and operational levels, in order to manage survivors effectively and thereby enable the organisation to sustain competitiveness.

To what extent is such advice heeded in reality? Many problems relate to a low level of trust between those making decisions and those receiving them. A convincing rationale for downsizing is essential, and requires a degree of planning. 'Good HR practice' suggests that three elements of the redundancy process are often critical: consultation with employees, the selection decision, and pre/post-redundancy support for those made redundant as well as those who remain. We deal with each of these in turn.

Consultation

Consultation with unions and employees is emphasised in most accounts of downsizing. Employees need to understand the rationale for downsizing and also how the process will be managed. Breaks in communication are seen as sinister and lead to rumours (Kettley, 1995). Consultation with unions over redundancies can make a difference to the nature of the redundancy process used, and occasionally the number of jobs lost (Edwards and Hall, 1999). The downsizing process is often characterised by secrecy and swiftness and is thus often poorly planned and executed with little scope for employee involvement. To some extent this reluctance to consult over workforce reduction stems from it being seen as part of a deeply entrenched managerial prerogative about the right to hire and fire and close down businesses. The case of the deputies, supervisors and correction officers dismissed by the newly elected sheriff at Clayton County, Georgia is fortunately not that common. Staff who thought they were being invited to a swearing-in ceremony had their badges, guns and car keys removed, were then dismissed and escorted to a ride home (in police vans) under the watchful eye of rooftop snipers who were there 'just in case someone got emotional' (Younge, 2005).

Legislative restrictions on managerial prerogative in redundancy are extremely limited in the UK (CIPD, 2011). However, there is evidence that extensive consultation and employee involvement can help in smoothing implementation. US studies indicate that increased communication and participation of employees in the downsizing process were associated with improvement (Cameron, 1994; DiFonzo and Bordia, 1998).

Selection

Whatever methods are used to reach redundancy decisions, the notions of fairness and 'organisational justice' are key issues. Here the process of the decision making on redundancy is equally if not more important than the outcome. Research on the perception of organisational justice by employees has been found to be related to both how the decision was made and how much 'voice' they felt they had in the process. In general, there are fewer negative attitudinal and behaviour outcomes from employees when the decision to downsize is seen as more legitimate (e.g. because of a decline in sales, increased competition etc.), compared to a desire to increase profits, cut costs etc. The other important factors in the selection process, which also help increase employees' perceptions of fairness, are that they should be clear and appropriate.

There are some noteworthy general trends within selection criteria. First is the distinct move away from seniority and the reduction of LIFO and towards selection based on an assessment of skills and performance (CIPD, 2011; IRS, 2004). Despite the advantages of LIFO, which is according to ACAS, is an 'objective, easy to apply, readily understood, and widely accepted' criterion, it now tends to be used only as part of a wider range of selection criteria. However, with the introductions of age discrimination legislation, those with less service tend to be younger, so this makes it a risky method. There can also be problems of unfair discrimination in its application. The issue of employers using sickness absences as a criterion for redundancy has caused much concern among unions, not least because of the worry that employees will now be frightened to take time off work when genuinely sick. In the IRS survey of those employers who use attendance as a criterion (60 per cent of the sample), certified absence appears to count against an employee in the selection process almost as much as unauthorised absence. Most employers (81 per cent) said that leave covered by a doctor's certificate would count against a worker, and 87 per cent said that self-certified leave would (IRS, 2004).

Despite the outwardly 'objective' nature of many of these selection criteria and mechanisms, we can also find considerable evidence of subjective manipulation of a redundancy situation by managers. In the search for 'committed' workers, employers appear to use workforce reduction for a variety of ends. Often it seems a redundancy situation is used, or in some cases even engineered, to weed out 'troublemakers' and periodically get rid of 'deadwood'. Troublemakers are variously defined as the shirkers, union activists and the non-believers in new managerial philosophies and programmes. For example, the personnel director of Co-Steel Sheerness, a British-based but Canadian-owned steel mill, described how they dealt with employees who were unhappy with the new practices of 'total team culture' and union de-recognition thus:

> When it became clear that there were employees who became increasingly dissatisfied with our new philosophies. . . we bit the bullet with those employees and put in place termination programmes. About 5 to 6 per cent of employees were terminated. *(Guardian, 6 September 1995: 19)*

Employee support

A wide variety of post-redundancy assistance can be offered to dismissed workers. There is considerable evidence to suggest that such help can have a very positive impact on the management of redundancy at a relatively low cost (e.g. Guest and Peccei, 1992). The forms of support include redeployment centres, business start-up advice, training and loans, retraining, outplacement support, pre-retirement education, financial advice, job-search help and counselling, etc.

Redundancy counselling and stress management are emphasised to help employees overcome and come to terms with some of the intense feelings of damage to self-esteem, failure, loss of confidence, decreased morale, anxiety, bitter feelings of betrayal, debilitating shock and sense of loss that accompany downsizing. Real personal, social and financial problems also stem from redundancy situations. Studies of redundancy counselling and assistance programmes report it as being valued by the recipients but somewhat unproven in its actual benefits.

The availability of support is usually much greater the more senior the redundant employee is. Thus outplacement support is more often reserved for more senior grades, and where it is provided for all employees, senior managers usually receive external specialist services while lower-grade employees have in-house services. Surveys of outplacement, report that there has been considerable growth in the UK since its import from the US in the mid-1970s (Doherty, 1998). While most firms would claim expertise in wider career management advice, its main use is in downsizing situations. Its key aim is to help the redundant employee with the job-search process by providing practical services such as office support and specific counselling and advice. At more senior levels this is often provided on a one-to-one basis, involving psychometric tests and career counselling, while for other levels of employees, group programmes of CV construction and job-search strategies are provided.

The most common support for operatives is the statutorily supported one of time off to look for work. Some employers have even advertised the availability of redundant employees in national newspapers to facilitate their re-employment. The need for support in finding alternative work is a real one. Redundant workers suffer particularly in their search for a new job, the so called 'lemon effect' (Turnbull and Wass, 1997). Here recruiters become concerned about hiring an employee who has been discarded by another employer. Employers assume that a redundant worker must be of poor quality and potential. The labelling of redundant employees as inferior may well increase in the future as employers move to more performance-oriented selection criteria and away from seniority. Thus those most likely to be made redundant are least likely to follow a smooth path to re-employment.

Severance pay

Arguably, the acid test of support for redundant employees is the level of compensatory financial support or 'severance' pay (*Guardian*, 1989). Some companies provide little else in the way of support for redundant workers. For example, the financially oriented Hanson Trust did not use outplacement but were said to 'use pound notes to staunch the blood' with generous severance packages. Most employers offer better severance terms than the baseline required by statute, with the main exception being public sector employers, except for senior managers. In part this reflects the paternalistic nature of British employers but also the pragmatic need for a form of inducement to encourage employees to volunteer. Severance is usually paid in the form of a lump sum to facilitate a 'clean break' rather than staged payments. There is some debate about the labour market impact of severance pay. The main policy role in the introduction of compulsory severance pay in the UK was to help the efficiency of the labour market by ensuring redundant workers did not take the first job offered but took the necessary time to find work that fitted their skills and abilities. Research suggests that the payment of severance pay has either a negative effect on labour market outcomes such as unemployment and labour market participation rates (Lazear, 1990) or a more neutral one (Addison and Teixeira, 2005).

Survivors

The needs of those who remain post-downsizing appear to be often overlooked. For example, a survey of financial services found that 79 per cent of firms provided outplacement services for those employees who left but less than half gave support to the 'lucky' ones who remained (Doherty and Horsted, 1995). Yet we have increasing evidence that such forgotten employees are often in need of support and counselling. For example, there is considerable evidence that remaining employees feel shocked, embittered towards management, fearful about their future and guilty about still having a job while colleagues have been laid off. The effects of such feelings are not difficult to predict. Such employees are more likely to have lower morale and increased stress levels, be less productive and less loyal, with increased quit levels. Sennett describes survivors as behaving as though 'they lived on borrowed time, feeling they had survived for no good reason' (1997: 125). Indeed, the threat of further downsizing may create difficulties in that the most able seek alternative employment. Moreover, employees may be asked to do jobs they are untrained or ill qualified to do.

A number of downsized companies have recognised such problems by setting up training courses for managers in how to deal with downsizing effects, and have provided counselling programmes and help lines. One study found that the response of survivors is closely linked to the treatment received by those laid off (Brockner *et al.*, 1987). Survivors react most negatively when they perceive their colleagues to have been badly treated and poorly recompensed.

Devine *et al.* note that job control is important in terms of occupational stress and employee outcomes when dealing with downsizing (see also Niehoff *et al.*, 2001; Spreitzer and Mishra, 2002). Being laid off and having to attain new employment is not necessarily more negative than 'surviving' the downsizing as displaced individuals who gain new employment have a greater sense of control and, subsequently, fewer negative strains. Survivors feel less in control due to witnessing past layoffs and not knowing if they may be the next to go (Devine *et al.*, 2003: 121). Van Dierendonck and Jacobs (2012) report a positive relationship between fairness and affective organisational commitment for both survivors and victims.

Conclusions

The past decade or so has witnessed unmatched levels of workforce reduction in many industrialised countries. Most organisations have undergone some form of downsizing, however, a number of key questions still remain about downsizing. These are not so much about its nature or the effects on the redundant or surviving employees, rather they centre on whether organisations, and in turn whole economies, are now in better shape post-downsizing. Are such organisations leaner and fitter or understaffed and anorexic? Has downsizing resulted in increased competitive advantage for those companies who have undergone it? What are the drivers of continuing downsizing?

An increasingly popular view is that the effects of downsizing are the equivalent of an industrial nuclear war:

> Below the chief executive and his cheerleading human resources department, a number of companies resemble nothing so much as buildings blasted by a neutron bomb. The processes and structures are all there, but no human life to make them productive. (Caulkin 1995: 29)

There is thus mounting evidence that all is not well in the downsized organisational form. As Pfeffer states, 'downsizing may cut labour costs in the short run, but it can erode both employee and eventually customer loyalty in the long run' (1998: 192). As with all management tools, downsizing has unintended outcomes that could limit its presumed benefits such as cost reduction, removal of unnecessary layers of management, and better value for shareholders. Research has shown that downsizing has mixed effects on performance (Cascio, 2002) showing no long-term financial payoff to downsizing, on average, while shares of downsizing companies have outperformed the stock market for six months post downsizing, there is little evidence to suggest that long-run performance or stock prices are improved by job cuts (Hunter, 2000). A recent study by Said *et al.* (2007) called into question the economic legitimacy of major workforce reductions.

HRM clearly has an important role in the process. Indeed, Chadwick *et al.* (2004) confirm that downsizing is more likely to be effective in the longer term when accompanied by practices that reinforce the contribution of HR to financial success (e.g. extensive communication, respectful treatment of redundant employees and attention to survivors' concerns over job security). Trevor and Nyberg (2008) also find that supportive HRM practices buffer some of the negative employee attitudinal and behavioural consequences of downsizing.

A possible explanation for this increasingly reported negative relationship between downsizing and economic performance can be found in Hamel and Prahalad's (1993) analysis of competitive advantage via resource productivity, both capital and human. They suggest that there are two ways to achieve this; first via downsizing, and second, by the strategic discipline of stretch and leverage. This latter approach seeks to get the most from existing resources. Their view is that leveraging is mostly energising while downsizing is essentially the reverse, resulting in demoralised managers and workforces. In the jargon, it appears that to achieve economic effectiveness downsizing is far from always 'rightsizing'. Strategic decision-makers seem to have forgotten the benefits of growth strategies. Stephen Roach (chief economist, Morgan Stanley), the guru of downsizing business, has now disowned the practice of slash and burn restructuring (Carlin, 1996). According to Roach, 'if you compete by building you have a future . . . if you compete by cutting you don't'.

There are undoubted variations across industries. Downsizing may be more damaging to R&D or knowledge-intensive industries where human capital is a very significant contributor to success.

Given such a grim picture of the effects of organisational downsizing, why then do managers persist in continuing with it? A number of explanations have been put forward. First, it is increasingly argued that managers have simply become addicted to downsizing because being lean and mean is now fashionable in itself. Downsizing, according to Brunning (1996), has become a corporate addiction and the 'cocaine of the boardroom'. Farrell and Mavondo (2004: 396) suggest that:

> Managers resort to downsizing because it is simple, generates considerable 'noise and attention' in the organisation, and may be viewed by some managers as tangible evidence of their 'strong leadership'. However, managers that pursue a reorientation strategy must necessarily engage in the much more difficult intellectual task of deciding how to reorient the organisation, combined with the associated challenges of building support, generating commitment and developing a shared vision.

Second, rather than a more 'acceptable' and appropriate use of downsizing because firms are now more productive or better organised or too bureaucratic and over-staffed, managers are often forced to do so by the market's demands for short-term boosts in profits. Depressingly, it seems that downsizing acts as a reassuring signal to markets that managers are 'in control' and acting to put things right. Third, Hitt et al. (1994) suggest that the rage for 'mindless' downsizing (herd behaviour) is linked to the merger and acquisitions mania of the last decades as managers attempt to solve the problems associated with acquisitive rather than organic growth. Acquisition strategies are argued to promote conservative short-term perspectives among managers, hence downsizing as a solution rather than investing in human capital. Indeed, there is a case that with greater internal flexibility (e.g. wider jobs), there may be less necessity for external flexibility (e.g. via downsizing) as workers can cope more ably with adjustments and change. It is important to see security in the context of other policies. Workers are more likely to contribute ideas if they do not feel they are endangering their own colleagues' jobs, and both employer and employee are more likely to see investments in training as worthwhile.

Thus, despite the sufferings of many workers in an era of redundancy, there have been precious few long-term benefits to justify its level and severity, nor an overwhelming economic justification for its continuing blanket use. The redundant find meaningful, well-paid and stable work difficult to come by, while those who remain in employment are stretched thin, worried about their security and subject to considerable work stress in anorexic organisations. Questions may well be asked of MDs and CEOs who are still rewarded with high and increasing salaries and perks (Haigh, 2004), given it is not clear that reducing headcount improves performance. Lastly, it seems that the claim of HRM that people are an organisation's most valuable resource is difficult to sustain in this context. As Guthrie and Datta (2008) argue, rather than becoming lean and mean, organisations may well become lean and lame. It may be that the notion of strategic and non-strategic groups become important in that Lepak and Snell (1999) suggest that effects on different groups have different effects on the organisation. So if this is the case, downsizing non-core workers will be far less damaging to the organisation. In general, as Zatzick et al. (2009) note, that while there is no 'right' way to downsize and cut costs, organisations have used various best practices to mitigate the negative effects of downsizing on victims and survivors.

CASE STUDY 16.1

DOWNSIZING AT AIR AVIA

ALANKRITA PANDEY

'If people are your most important assets, why would you get rid of them?'

Attributed to the former head of HR in Southwest airlines.

One of the oldest airlines in the United States, Air Avia had withstood the test of time. Founded in the 1940s as a conglomeration and acquisition of several other airlines, Air Avia became an important image in US skies. In its early years, the management worked with aircraft developers and were able to develop and fly some of the best passenger transport aeroplanes. Air Avia expanded its business to Europe by acquiring other airlines. Then they expanded to Central and Latin America through a subsidiary. They managed to build and operate several airports there. It built up relationships with Hollywood offering free usage of its aircraft, and continued to gain in popularity, soon becoming one of the largest airlines in the world.

Air Avia proceeded to grow, expanding into jet travel though the offering of coast-to-coast non-stop flights. It then developed the first electronic booking system, the basis of online booking systems used today. It developed computer reservation systems and frequent flyer loyalty programs. It changed its routing to a hub-and-spoke system, opening hubs at different airports all over the US. The 1990s saw a period of low fuel prices and a very favourable economic climate, and Air Avia prospered making higher than average profits. Rumblings about low wages from the pilots union were quashed with the help of government intervention, and even while Airline deregulation had led to falling stock prices and bankruptcies for its rivals, Air Avia sailed through.

In the early 2000s, Avia bought the nearly bankrupt Worldways Canada and its hub in a contentious merger that resulted in a number of junior pilots from Worldways being furloughed. Over 50 per cent of Worldways pilots were moved to the bottom of the seniority list at Avia. Senior pilots from Worldways were integrated at the same level of seniority as Avia captains hired before them, however, Worldways pilots soon began to earn more than Avia pilots and Avia also inherited Worldways substantial debt. In the wake of this merger and the World Trade Center attacks on 11 September 2001, Avia began losing money. Owing to the extensive furloughs of World-

ways pilots, the former Worldways hub was soon staffed almost entirely by Avia officers. Cabin crews from Avia put former Worldways attendants on the bottom of their seniority lists and they were also furloughed. CEO, Doug Jenkins, tried to negotiate benefit agreements with unions but talks stalled because they found that executive compensation packages were being awarded at the same time. This revelation led to a severe undermining of trust, and Worldways' former hub was severely downsized.

Avia tried to cut costs by standardising its fleet at every other hub that they still maintained. They rolled back the intermediate classes of service to its customers, and they also expanded in several markets, especially in Asia, and were able to report a small profit by 2006. At this time, they were even achieving a 100 per cent rating on equality among employees – a rating they have since maintained.

However, the year 2008 brought a spate of further woes for Air Avia. April saw a mass grounding of aircraft and fuel prices were rising. By May, Avia, following the lead of other airlines, increased bag check fees to $15 for the first piece, then $25 for the second. They also instituted a steep $150 charge for domestic reservations. They also announced that they would retire several of their jets used for regional transport.

But the early summer, cost-cutting measures did not seem to be working. Avia decided to furlough about a 1,000 of their attendants in Texas and ground further aircraft. They truncated a few of their hubs, reducing the number of flights. They also began to concentrate their repair work to only one of their hubs, cutting down the repair capacity of the others. The city of Frontiersville, which was thus affected, offered to upgrade repair facilities on the condition that the airlines maintain 600 jobs, however the base was closed the following year.

Air Avia was accused of maintenance problems on at least 20 of their aeroplanes about a year later with such problems including faulty emergency slides, improper engine coatings, incorrectly drilled holes, and other badly done repair jobs. It was alleged that cracks in pressure bulkheads were also not repaired. This is a serious lapse since a ruptured bulkhead could lead to cabin depressurisation. The Federal Aviation Authority claimed that a plane was retired to keep the plane away from inspectors.

By mid-2011, Avia was in trouble again. A report showing a slowdown in air travel and cargo was released. There were fears of a weaker world economy. In addition, there was an announcement Air Avia had more than ten times the normal number of pilots retiring, a signal that they were afraid that the carrier was not going to last long. Avia shares tumbled by 33 per cent to a ten-year low. The stock exhibited such volatility that trading was halted several times. The price of Avia's stock fell by about 75 per cent that year compared to the rest of the industry shares that dropped by about 41 per cent. In addition it was the only major US airline that lost money that year.

Analysis revealed that Avia had an unusually large debt burden. They were also experiencing labour costs of about 30 per cent of their total costs. Unlike its rivals, Avia had never undertaken restructuring. They had also faced lower-cost competitors, and so, tried to deal with this through cutting their fares. While other legacy airlines had used bankruptcy to renegotiate labour contracts and slash costs in the past, Avia had stood firm, they had increased their borrowing and pledged all their assets. However, they were now dealing with a leaner and meaner market with former rivals now merging to form gigantic competitors. The company turned to its unions to discuss a solution. They wanted to change the structure of contracts with pilots, attendants and mechanics, but talks stalled when the pilots union did not send a proposal to its members to vote on.

In November, Avia filed for bankruptcy. US bankruptcy rules allow companies to reject contracts, so from this point, Avia felt it could better negotiate with unions. One of their aims was to reduce labour costs to competitive levels – 30 per cent was way too much. They also wanted to restructure and cut other costs to continue their operations.

Other carriers had gone the same route. The most benign form of cost cutting had always been replacing larger airplanes like 737s, A320s and MD80s with regional jets (RJs). This saves money on fuel costs for the aeroplanes and also because crews on these RJs are paid less, and customers would find these planes more cramped and uncomfortable. Other airlines had also tried reducing the number of flights in their hubs, and routes that were not making profits were cancelled and fewer flights were maintained on busier routes with higher loads, and while the popular routes were more likely to remain unaffected, there was a possibility that lighter routes could vanish altogether.

Avia then came up with a plan to reduce employee costs by about 20 per cent. In early 2012, they announced that they would eliminate 13,000 workers or about 16 per cent of their entire workforce. They would also cut back on the health benefits for current employees and retirees. They said that these cuts would reduce costs by about $2bn a year, $1.25bn of which came directly from employee cuts. The CEO claimed that it was the only sane move they could make when considering how their competition had restructured in the past. Thus, airlines that failed to change were no longer operationally viable.

The unions were angry. They felt that Avia had disregarded the provisions in their agreements. The 13,000 employees who lost their jobs would represent about 4,600 mechanics, 4,200 ground staff positions, 2,300 flight attendants and about 400 pilots. About 1,400 jobs would be cut for management and support services, though no specific numbers were given. Other proposals were for partnerships and more efficient use of Avia aircraft. Union officials felt that the company was downplaying the amount they were realising from their employees. Together with cuts in health and retirement benefits, employees such as flight attendants would be facing pay cuts up to about 18 per cent and faced working longer hours. In total, employees were likely to give back about $3bn annually.

Analysts note that Avia has shifted its policy of maintaining its aircraft in-house. They have decided to outsource repair work overseas as their competitors have done, achieving impressive savings. For instance, a multiyear contract with an Asia based repair shop is likely to save them hundreds of millions. However, there is still the disadvantage of foreign repair stations not complying strictly with US safety standards. The CEO, however feels that this 'near term' pain in cuts would result in an airline that once again ruled the skies.

Sources: Barrett and Farahany Justice at work Blog, 2012; De La Merced, 2011; Mouawad, 2012; Perkins, 2005; Peterson, 2012; Schlangenstein, 2012; Velotta, 2009.

Questions

1 What were the reasons for Air Avia to downsize for each time that it did so? Compare and contrast the reasons.
2 Like other airlines, Avia has options other than downsizing. Can it afford to reduce customer service and expectations at the cost of retaining its employees? Should the downsizing be accompanied with other changes to maximize its impact?

3 Do you think that the proposed downsizing in Avia is likely to be effective? Consider the changes to the workforce they propose. Have they learnt from past experience? Could they change their plan?

4 Air Avia has a contentious relationship with their unions. Could they have managed this relationship better to help them through their conundrum?

5 What are the likely long-term employee impacts of downsizing? Discuss how 'survivors' react to downsizing decisions, emphasizing their fears, concerns, feelings and long-term productivity. Will the reputation of Avia as an employer suffer?

Bibliography

Adams, S. (1996) *The Dilbert Principle,* London: Boxtree Press.

Addison, J.T. and Teixeira, P.(2005) 'What have we learned about the employment effects of severance pay? Further iterations of Lazear *et al.*', *Empirica*, Vol.32, 345–68.

Ahmadjian, L.C. and Robinson, P. (2001) 'Safety in numbers: downsizing and the deinstitutionalization of permanent employment in Japan', *Administrative Science Quarterly*, Vol.46, No.4, 622–58.

Anfunso, D. (1996) 'Strategies to stop the layoffs', *Personnel Journal*, June, 66–99.

Barbee, G, (1986) 'Downsizing with dignity', *Retirement Planning*, Fall, 6–7.

Barrett and Farahany Justice at Work Blog (2012) American Airlines considering extensive downsizing. http://www.atlantaemploymentlawattorney.com/2012/02/american-airlines-considering-extensive-downsizing.shtml.

*Baumol, J.W., Blinder, S.A. and Wolff, N.E. (2003) *Downsizing in America: Reality, Causes, and Consequences*, New York: Russell Sage Foundation Press.

Boone, J. (2000) 'Technological progress, downsizing and unemployment', *Economic Journal*, Vol.110, 581–600.

*Brockner, J. (1992) 'Managing the effects of lay-offs on survivors', *California Management Review*, Vol.34, No.2, 9–28.

Brockner, J., Grover, S., Reed, T., DeWitt, R. and O'Malley, M. (1987) 'Survivors' reactions to lay-offs: we get by with a little help from our friends', *Administrative Science Quarterly*, Vol.32, 526–41.

Brunning, F. (1996) 'Working at the office on borrowed time', *Macleans*, February, 8–9.

Bruton, G.D., Keels, J.K. and Shook, C.L. (1996) 'Downsizing the firm: answering the strategic questions', *Academy of Management Executive*, Vol.10, 38–43.

Budros, A. (1999) 'A conceptual framework for analyzing why organizations downsize', *Organization Science*, Vol.10, No.1, 69–81.

Bulmer, M. (1971) 'Mining redundancy: a case study of the workings of the Redundancy Payments Act in the Durham coalfields', *Industrial Relations Journal*, Vol.26, No.15, 227–44.

Burke, W.W. (1997) 'The new agenda for organisation development', *Organizational Dynamics*, Vol.26, 6–20.

*Cameron, K.S. (1994) 'Strategies for successful organisational downsizing', *Human Resource Management*, Vol.33, No.2, 189–211.

Cameron, K.S. (1998) 'Downsizing', in Poole, M. and Warner, M. (eds) *The IEBM Handbook of Human Resource Management*, London: International Thomson Press.

Cameron, K.S., Freeman, S.J. and Mishra, A.K. (1991) 'Best practices in white-collar downsizing: managing contradictions', *Academy of Management Executive*, Vol.5, No.3, 57–73.

Carlin, J. (1996) 'Guru of "downsizing" admits he got it all wrong', *Independent on Sunday*, 12 May.

Cascio, W.F. (1993). 'Downsizing: what do we know? What have we learned?', *Academy of Management Executive*, Vol.7, 95–104.

Cascio, W.F. (2002) 'Strategies for responsible restructuring', *Academy of Management Executive*, Vol.16, 80–91.

Cascio, W.F. (2009) 'Downsizing and redundancy', in Wilkinson, A., Redman, T., Snell, S. and Bacon, N. (eds) *The SAGE Handbook of Human Resource Management*, London: Sage.

Cascio, W.F., Young, E.C. and Morris, J.R. (1997) 'Financial consequences of employment-change decisions in major U.S. corporations', *Academy of Management Journal*, Vol.40, 1175–89.

Caves, R. and Krepps, M. (1993) 'Fat: the displacement of nonproduction workers from US manufacturing industries', *Brookings Papers on Economic Activity*, Vol.2, 227–88.

Caulkin, S. (1995) 'Take your partners', *Management Today*, February, 26–30.

Chadwick, C., Hunter, L. and Walston, S. (2004) 'Effects of downsizing practices on the performance of hospitals', *Strategic Management Journal*, Vol.25, No.5, 405–27.

Chorely, D. (2002) 'How to manage downsizing', *Financial Management*, May, 6.

CIPD (2011) *Redundancy Factsheet*, London: Chartered Institute of Personnel and Development.

Clabaugh, A. (1997) 'Downsizing: implications for older employees', *Working Paper*, Perth, Australia: Edith Cowan University.

Contrepois, S. (2011) 'Labour struggles against mass redundancies in France: understanding direct action', *Employee Relations*, Vol.33, No.6, 642–53.

Cullinane, N. and Dundon, T. (2011) 'Redundancy and workplace occupation: the case of the Republic of Ireland', Employee Relations, Vol.33, No.6, 624–41.

Cully, M., Woodland, S., O'Reilly, A. and Dix, G. (1999) *Britain at Work*, Abingdon: Routledge.

Datta, D.K., Guthrie, J.P., Basuil, D. and Pandey, A. (2010) 'Causes and effects of employee downsizing: a review and synthesis', *Journal of Management*, Vol.36, No.1, 281–348.

De La Merced, M.J. (2011) 'American Airlines parent files for bankruptcy', *New York Times*. http://dealbook.nytimes.com/2011/11/29/american-airlines-parent-files-for-bankruptcy/.

De Meuse, K.P., Bergmann, T.J. and Vanderheiden, P.A. (1997) 'Corporate downsizing: separating myth from fact', *Journal of Management Inquiry*, Vol.6, No.2, 168–76.

Devine, K., Reay, T., Stainton, L. and Collins-Nakai, R. (2003) 'Downsizing outcomes: better a victim than a survivor?', *Human Resource Management*, Vol.42, No.2, 109–24.

Dewettinck, K. and Buyens, D. (2002) 'Downsizing: employee threat or opportunity? An empirical study on external and internal reorientation practices in Belgian companies', *Employee Relations*, Vol.24, No.4, 389–402.

DiFonzo, N. and Bordia, P. (1998) 'A tale of two corporations: managing uncertainty during organisational change', *Human Resource Management*, Vol.37, 295–303.

Doherty, N. (1998) 'The role of outplacement in redundancy management', *Personnel Review*, Vol.27, No.4, 343–51.

Doherty, N. and Horsted, J. (1995) 'Helping survivors to stay on board', *People Management*, 12 January, 26–31.

Edwards, P. and Hall, M. (1999) 'Remission: possible', *People Management*, 15 July, 44–6.

Espahbodi, R., John, T.A. and Vasudevan, G. (2000) 'The effects of downsizing on operating performance', *Review of Quantitative Finance and Accounting*, Vol.15, 107–26.

Farrell, M. and Mavondo, F. (2004) 'The effect of downsizing strategy and reorientation strategy on learning orientation', *Personnel Review*, Vol.33, No.4, 383–402.

Fisher, S.R. and White, M.A. (2000) 'Downsizing in a learning organisation: are there hidden costs?', *Academy of Management Review*, Vol.25, No.1, 244–51.

Gall, G. (2011) 'Worker resistance and response to the crisis of neo-liberal capitalism', *Employee Relations*, Vol.33, No.6, 588–91.

Garfield, A. (1999) 'Barclays shares soar as city welcomes job cuts', *Independent*, 21 May.

Glassner, V. and Keune, M. (2010) *Collective bargaining responses to the economic crisis in Europe*. ETUI Policy Brief 1/2010, European Economic and Employment Policy, Brussels: European Trade Union Institute.

Guardian (1989) 30 July, 21.

Guardian (1995) 6 September, 19.

Guest, D. and Peccei, R. (1992) 'Employee involvement: redundancy as a critical case', *Human Resource Management Journal*, Vol.2, No.3, 34–59.

Guthrie, J.P. and Datta, D.K. (2008) 'Dumb and dumber: the impact of downsizing on firm performance as moderated by industry conditions', *Organization Science*, Vol.19, 108–23.

Haigh, G. (2004) *Bad Company: The Strange Cult of the CEO*, London: Aurum.

Hamel, G. (2000) *Leading the Revolution*, New York: Harvard Business School Press.

Hamel, G. and Prahalad, C.K. (1993) 'Strategy as stretch and leverage', *Harvard Business Review*, March-April, 75–84.

Hardy, C. (1987) 'Investing in retrenchment: avoiding the hidden costs', *California Management Review*, Vol.29, No.4, 111–25.

Hill, S. (1989) *Competition and Control at Work*, London: Heinemann.

Hitt, M.A., Hoskisson, R.E., Harrison, J.S. and Summers, T.P. (1994) 'Human capital and strategic competitiveness in the 1990s', *Journal of Management Development*, Vol.13, No.1, 35–46.

Hunter, L. (2000) 'Myths and methods of downsizing', *FT Mastering People Management*, 2–4.

Hutton, W. (1997) *The State to Come*, London: Vintage.

Inman, P. (2004) 'Flying right in the face of logic', *Guardian*, 28 August.

IRS (2004) 'The changing shape of work: how organisations restructure', *Employment Review*, No.794.

Jefferys, S. (2011) 'Collective and individual conflicts in five European countries', *Employee Relations*, Vol.33, No.6, 670–87.

Kersley, B., Alpin, C., Forth, J., Bryson, A., Bewley, H., Dix, G. and Oxenbridge, S. (2006) *Inside the Workplace: Findings from the 2004 Workplace Employment Relations Survey*, Abingdon: Routledge.

Kettley, P. (1995) *Employee Morale During Downsizing*, Brighton: Institute of Employment Studies, Report No.291.

Kivimaki, M., Vahtera, J., Pentti J. and Ferrie, J. (2000) 'Factors underlying the effect of organisational downsizing on health of employees: longitudinal cohort study', *British Medical Journal*, Vol.320, 971–5.

Lazear, E.P. (1990) 'Job security provisions and employment', *Quarterly Journal of Economics,* Vol.105, 699–726.

Lazonick, W. (2005) 'Corporate restructuring', in Ackroyd, S., Batt, R., Thompson, P. and Tolbert, P. (eds) *The Oxford Handbook of Work and Organization,* Oxford: Oxford University Press.

Lee, P.M. (1997) 'A comparative analysis of layoff announcements and stock price reactions in the United States and Japan', *Strategic Management Journal*, Vol.18, 879–94.

Lepak, D.P. and Snell, S.A. (1999) 'The human resource architecture: toward a theory of human capital allocation and development', *Academy of Management Review*, Vol.24, No.1, 31–48.

Littler, C. and Innes, P. (2003) 'Downsizing and deknowledging the firm', *Work, Employment and Society*, Vol.17, No.1, 73–100.

Love, E. and Kraatz, M. (2009) 'Character, conformity, or the bottom line: how and why downsizing affected corporate reputation', *Academy of Management Journal*, Vol.52, 314–35.

Mason, T. (2002) 'GSB top marketers exists as axe falls on budget', *Marketing*, Vol.31, 6.

McCallister, T. (2001) 'Thomas Cook cuts jobs and pay', *Guardian*, 1 November.

McGoldrick, A. and Cooper, C.L. (1989) *Early Retirement*, Aldershot: Gower.

McKinley, W., Zhao, J. and Rust, K.G. (2000) 'A sociocognitive interpretation of organisational downsizing', *Academy of Management Review*, Vol.25, 227–43.

McMahan, G.C., Pandey, A. and Martinson, B. (2012) 'To downsize human capital: a strategic human resource perspective on the disparate outcomes of downsizing', pp. 134-67, in Cooper, C.L., Pandey, A. and Quick, J.C. (eds) *Downsizing: Is Less Still More?*, Cambridge: Cambridge University Press.

Mellahi, K. and Wilkinson, A. (2004) *Downsizing and Innovation Output: A Review of Literature and Research Propositions*, BAM Paper 2004, British Academy of Management.

Mellahi, K. and Wilkinson, A. (2010), 'Slash and burn or nip and tuck: downsizing, innovation and human resources', *International Journal of Human Resource Management*, Vol.21, No.13, 2291–305.

Mishra, A.K., Mishra, K.E., Spreitzer, G.M. and DeGraff, J. (2009) 'Downsizing the company without downsizing morale', *MIT Sloan Management Review*, Spring 2009, Vol.50, No.3, 39–44.

Moore, M. (1997) *Downsize This*, New York: Harper-Collins.

Mouawad, J. (2012) 'American Airlines seeks 13,000 job cuts', *The New York Times*. http://www.nytimes.com/2012/02/02/business/american-airlines-seeks-job-cuts. html?ref=amrcorporation.

Mroczkowski, T. and Hanaoka, M. (1997), 'Effective downsizing strategies in Japan and America: is there a convergence of employment practices?', *Academy of Management Review*, Vol.22, No.1, 226–56.

Niehoff, B.P., Moorman, R.H., Blakely, G. and Fuller, J. (2001) 'The influence of empowerment and job enrichment on employee loyalty in a downsizing environment', *Group and Organization Management*, Vol.26, No.1, 93–113.

Palmon, O., Sun, H. and Tang, A.P. (1997) 'Layoff announcements: stock market impact and financial performance', *Financial Management*, Vol.26, No.3, 54–68.

Peetz D., Frost. A. and Le Queux, S. (2011) 'The GFC and employment relations', in *Wilkinson*, A. and Townsend, K. (eds) *The Future of Employment Relations: New Paradigms*, New Developments, Basingstoke: Palgrave MacMillan.

Perkins, E. (2005) 'Airline downsizing means more hassles, fewer choices for travelers', http:// www.smartertravel.com/travel-advice/Airline-downsizing-means-more.html?id=96416.

Peterson, B. (2012) 'The real story behind American's 13,000 job cuts', *Condé Nast Traveller*. http://www.cntraveler.com/daily-traveler/2012/02/American-Airlines-Job-Cuts.

Pfeffer, J. (1998) *The Human Equation*, Boston, MA: Harvard Business School Press.

Priti, P.S. (2000) 'Network destruction: the structural implications of downsizing', *Academy of Management Journal*, Vol.43, 101–12.

Rich, M. and Donkin, R. (1994) 'A testing time in the job market', *Financial Times,* 19 December, 10.

Roche W., Teague P., Coghlan A. and Fahy, M. (2011) *Human Resources in a Recession: Managing and Representing People at Work in Ireland*, Dublin: Labour Relations Commission.

Rogers, D. (2002) 'ITV digital culls staff to lure buyers', *Marketing*, 25 April, 1.

*Sahdev, K. (2003) 'Survivors' reactions to downsizing: the importance of contextual factors', *Human Resource Management Journal*, Vol.13, No.4, 56–74.

Sahdev, K., Vinnicombe, S. and Tyson, S. (1999) 'Downsizing and the changing role of HR', *International Journal of Human Resource Management*, Vol.10, No.5, 906–23.

Said, T., Le Lovarn, Y. and Tremblay, M. (2007) 'The performance effects of major workforce reductions: longitudinal evidence from North America', *International Journal of Human Resource Management*, Vol.18, No.12, 2075–94.

Savery, L.K., Travaglione, A. and Firns, I.G.J. (1998) 'The links between absenteeism and commitment during downsizing', *Personnel Review*, Vol.27, No.4, 312–24.

Schlangenstein, M. (2012) 'AMR unions seek arbitration in bankruptcy concession talks', *Bloomberg News*. http://www.bloomberg.com/news/2012-03-09/american-airlines-unions-seek-u-s-arbitrator-in-bankruptcy-giveback-talks.html.

Sennett, R. (1997) *The Corrosion of Character*, New York: Norton.

Sinclair, J., Seifert, R. and Ironside, M. (1995) 'Performance-related redundancy: school teacher lay-offs as management control strategy', Paper presented at BUIRA Annual Conference, Durham, July.

Smith, S. (1996) 'A fair test', *Personnel Today,* 1 January, 26–30.

soyoutv.com (April 1 2010) 'Continental propose des postes en Tunisie rémunérés 137 euros par mois: les députés dégoûtés!', Available at http://www.lepost.fr/article/2010/04/01/2014297_continental-propose-des-postes-en-tunisie-remuneres-137-euros-par-mois-les-deputes-degoutes.html.

*Spreitzer, G. and Mishra, A.K. (2002) 'To stay or to go: voluntary survivor turnover following an organizational downsizing', *Journal of Organizational Behaviour*, Vol.26, No.6, 707–29.

Stebbins, M.W., (1989) 'Downsizing with "mafia model" consultants', *Business Forum*, Winter, 45–7.

Sullivan, T. and Hogge, B. (1987) 'Instruments of adjustment in recession', *R & D Management*, Vol.17, No.4, 289–99.

*Thornhill, A. and Saunders, M.N.K. (1998) 'The meanings, consequences and implications of the management of downsizing and redundancy: a review', *Personnel Review*, Vol.27, No.4, 271–95.

Trevor, C. and Nyberg, A. (2008) 'Keeping your headcount when all about you are losing theirs: downsizing, voluntary turnover rates, and the moderating role of HR practices', *Academy of Management Journal*, Vol.51, No.2, 259–76.

Turnbull, P. and Wass, V. (1997) 'Job insecurity and labour market lemons: the (mis)management of redundancy in steel making, coal mining, and port transport', *Journal of Management Studies*, Vol.34, No.1, 27–51.

Turnbull, P. and Wass, V. (2004) 'Job cuts and redundancy: managing the workforce complement', Paper presented at the BUIRA Annual Conference, University of Nottingham.

Tyler, M. and Wilkinson, A. (2007) 'The tyranny of corporate slenderness: "corporate anorexia" as a metaphor for our age', *Work, Employment and Society*, Vol.21, No.3, 537–49.

Van Dierendonck, D. and Jacobs, G. (2012) 'Survivors and victims, a meta-analytic review of fairness and organizational commitment after downsizing', *British Journal of Management*, Vol.23, 96–109.

Velotta, R.N. (2009) 'Airline downsizing shifts passengers to smaller regional jets', *Las Vegas Sun*.

Wayhan, V.B., and Werner, S. (2000) 'The impact of workforce reductions on financial performance: a longitudinal perspective', *Journal of Management*, Vol.26, 341–63.

Wedderburn, D. (1965) *Redundancy and the Railwaymen*, Cambridge: Cambridge University Press.

Welch, J. (2001) *What I've Learned Leading a Great Company and Great People*, New York: Headline.

Weyer, M.V. (1994) 'The old men on the board', *Management Today*, October, 64–7.

Wilkinson, A. (2004) 'Downsizing, rightsizing and dumbsizing: quality, human resources and sustainability', invited Keynote Paper presented at the 9th World Congress for Total Quality Management, Abu Dhabi, UAE, September 2004.

Worrall, L., Cooper, C. and Campbell, F. (2000) 'The impact of organisational change on UK managers' perceptions of their working lives', in Burke, R.J. and Cooper, C.L. (eds) *The Organization in Crisis: Downsizing, Restructuring and Privatization*, Oxford: Blackwell.

Worrell, D.L., Davidson, W.N. and Sharma, V.M. (1991) 'Lay-off announcements and stockholder wealth', *Academy of Management Journal*, Vol.34, 662–78.

Younge, G. (2005) 'New black sheriff sacks opponents', *Guardian*, 11 January.

Zatzick, C.D., Marks, M.L., and Iverson, R.D. (2009) 'Which way should you downsize in a crisis?', *MIT Sloan Management Review*, Vol.51, No.1, 79–86.

*Useful reading

CHAPTER 17
EMPLOYEE PARTICIPATION

Tony Dundon and Adrian Wilkinson

Introduction

Employee participation has long been a central pillar of human resource management, with various practices often shaped by the different political, economic and legal context found in different countries. Contextual factors also influence the demand (among employees and unions) for participation as well as the desire (by managers and employers) for the types of mechanisms used. In different countries the terms employee participation and involvement can mean very different things, often with a lack of clarity surrounding the terms and practices used. The confusion of the terms 'involvement, participation or communication' is made worse as some methods (such as team briefings or quality circles) tend to coexist and overlap with other techniques (such as joint union–management consultative committees or collective bargaining). In a European context, collective voice remains significant in certain countries, notably Germany and Sweden. However participation is not exclusive to union-only channels and in these countries employee participation is increasingly set against an evolving regulatory (rather than voluntary) regime.

In considering these issues, the chapter first defines participation and considers the context in which participation has changed over time. We then review a framework against which to evaluate employee participation, and this is followed by an explanation of the types of schemes used in practice. Fourth is a consideration of the meanings and possible impacts on organisational performance and employee well-being. Finally, we review some of the current influences and policy choices in the area of employee participation.

Defining participation

The literature surrounding participation can be confusing (Heller *et al.,* 1998). Some authors refer to involvement as participation while others use empowerment or communications, often without fully extracting the key conceptual meanings or differences that are used in practice (Wilkinson *et al.,* 2010). For example, in one organisation the term 'involvement' may be used to identify certain practices that in another organisation are regarded as 'participatory'. There are further complications when considering employee participation in international terms. In European countries for example, government policy and legislation provides for a statutory right to participation in certain areas, among both union and non-union establishments. In other countries however, such as the USA or Australia, there is less emphasis on statutory provisions for employee involvement with a greater tendency to rely on the preferences of managers and unions, resulting in a complex web of individual and collective participation in many organisations. At the same time employees encounter participation at different levels, even within the same company (Wilkinson and Dundon, 2010). Differences can be further complicated depending on the presence or absence of a trade union (Benson and Brown, 2010). It is not uncommon for non-unionised companies to use the terms 'empowerment' or 'communications', even when they utilise representative forums such as European Works Councils (Ackers *et al.,* 2005). In Britain, the WERS surveys have shown that the majority of managers (72 per cent) prefer to consult with workers directly (Cully *et al.,* 1999: 88), with less than half of all establishments using any form of representative participation, such as a union, joint-consultative committee or even non-union employee representative (Kersley *et al.,* 2006: 132).

One way of making sense of the elasticity of the terms is to see participation as an umbrella term covering all initiatives designed to engage employees. However, there are two separate underlying ideologies behind the nature of participation. First, the concept of industrial democracy (which draws from notions of industrial citizenship), sees participation as a fundamental democratic right for workers to extend a degree of control over managerial decision-making in an organisation. Second, the economic efficiency model argues that it makes sense for companies to encourage greater participation. By allowing employees an input into work and business decisions can help create more understanding and hence commitment. Although these are two different perspectives toward employee participation they are not polar opposites. As Cressey *et al.* (1985) usefully reminded us, no one wants a 'democratic bankruptcy'. This perspective is also useful in helping us chart the changing patterns and arrangements to do with participation over time. Much more important is what certain practices actually mean to the participants and whether such schemes can improve organisational effectiveness and employee well-being (Dundon *et al.,* 2004). Brannen (1983: 13) adopts a broad definition in this regard, defining participation as the processes by which 'individuals or groups may influence, control, be involved in, exercise power within, or be able to intervene in decision-making within organisations'. We define employee participation in a similarly broad way, following Boxall and Purcell (2003: 162), as incorporating a range of mechanisms 'which enable, and at times empower employees, directly and indirectly, to contribute to decision-making in the firm'. As this chapter is also concerned with clarifying what is meant by different participation schemes, we will evaluate the extent to which various practices allow workers to have a say in organisational decisions. At times the extent of such a voice can be marginal, superficial and subject to managerial control; at other times it may be more extensive and embedded within an organisation. Informal dialogue between employees and their front line manager is significant for effective participation. Indeed, informal communications can be the glue that holds formal participation schemes together (Marchington and Suter, 2008).

The context for employee participation

Employee participation has a long history in most Westernised economies. Notwithstanding oversimplification, a number of distinct phases can be traced to help place the role of participation in a contemporary and international context. The 1960s was often preoccupied with a search for job enrichment and enhanced worker motivation. Managerial objectives tended to focus on employee skill acquisition and work enrichment, particularly in Britain and the US. In the UK, exemplar industries such as ICI and British Coal included semi-autonomous workgroups to promote skill variety and job autonomy (Roeber 1975; Trist *et al.*, 1963). In the US participatory management schemes were similarly concerned with employee motivation as an outcome, rather than as a system that allowed workers to have a say about organisational decisions (see Budd *et al.,* 2010).

The 1970s witnessed a shift in focus toward industrial democracy which emphasised worker rights to participate. Participation reached its high point in the UK with the 1977 Bullock Report on Industrial Democracy which addressed the question of how workers might be represented at board level (Bullock, 1977). This report emerged in a period of strong union bargaining power and the Labour government's 'Social Contact' of inclusion. The Bullock Report was partly union-initiated, through the Labour Party, and based on collectivist principles which saw trade unions playing a key role, although it was not without controversy (Brannen, 1983); in particular the general principle of employee rights established on a statutory basis (Ackers *et al.,* 1992). Experiments with worker directors were initiated in the Post Office and the British Steel Corporation, although along with the Bullock Report itself, soon abandoned with the new neoliberal agenda of the Thatcher government in 1979. Earlier, in the US, collective voice through unionisation gained some legitimacy with the Wagner Act (1935), designed to protect employees who sought union representation. However, in practice employers would go to extraordinary lengths to avoid collective participation, often by employing the services of union-busting consultants in order to undermine union certification and by-pass collective participation channels with managerial-led initiatives (Logan, 2006).

The 1980s saw a very different agenda for participation. Indeed, the vocabulary changed almost overnight. The term 'involvement' became more fashionable and associated with managerial initiatives designed to elicit employee commitment. During the 1980s the political climate was one of reducing union power and promoting more individualistic, anti-collectivist philosophies inspired by Thatcher in the UK; Regan and later Bush in the US, and Howard in Australia. Out went any idea of statutory support for greater industrial democracy and in came a new wave of financial deregulation, privatisation and managerial self-confidence for employee rather than union-centred communication channels. As Wedderburn summed-up the general climate at the time:

> Those who opposed the new polices increasingly ran the risk of being seen not as critics with whom to debate and compromise (the supreme pluralist virtue), but as a domestic enemy within, which must be defeated ... (quoting government spokesman). The mining dispute cannot be *settled*. It can only be *won*. (*Wedderburn 1986: 85*)

From the 1980s onwards the context for participation changed with a distinctive managerial agenda. The rationale for employee participation stressed direct communications with individual employees which, in turn, marginalised trade union forms of particpation. This new agenda was anchored on business improvements and enhanced market competitiveness as a route to employee commitment (Ackers *et al.,* 1992: 272). A reduced public sector workforce across many countries, coupled with privatisations, were accompanied by a shift from large-scale manufacturing industry to private services which shaped the preferences for more management-sponsored forms of employee participation. This wave of direct involvement was neither interested in nor allowed employees to question managerial power (Marchington *et al.,* 1992). In effect, this was a period of employee involvement on management's terms.

The 1990s saw a consolidation in the use of employee participation techniques. Tapping into employee ideas and drawing on their tacit knowledge was seen as one solution to the problems of managing in an increasingly competitive marketplace, in part due to global-isation and market liberalisation by governments, and also due to increasing customer demand for more choice, quality and design. The move to customised products with flexible specialisation, flatter and leaner structures was seen as the new route to competitive advantage which meant increasing attention to labour as a resource (Piore and Sabel, 1983; Wilkinson, 2002). Many of the specific mechanisms to tap into such a labour resource became crystallised in models of best-practice HRM and high-commitment management developed in the US (Becker and Huselid, 1998; Huselid, 1995; Pfeffer, 1998; Wood and De Menezes, 1998). In this way the objectives for employee participation can be seen as unitarist in approach, often moralistic in tone, and predicated on the assumption that 'what is good for the business must be good for employees' (Marchington and Wilkinson, 2012).

The twenty-first century witnessed another phase towards employee participation. Alongside the 1990s flavour for managerial-led employee involvement, the twenty-first century also saw the emergence of increasing state regulation, particularly at a European level. According to Ackers *et al.,* (2005), the significance of this has resulted in a continuing (and often complicated) policy dialectic that shapes management choice for employee participation. The broader environment now seems more sympathetic to trade union recognition, individual employment rights as well as emergent collective-type regulations, such as the *European Directive on Employee Information and Consultation* (Ewing, 2003). Arguably, the twenty-first century has ushered in a period of legal re-regulation, which can be divided between those policies that directly affect employee participation (European Directives for example) and those that indirectly alter the environment in which employee participation operates (the competitive environment and organisational strategies for HRM).

A framework for analysing employee participation

Before outlining various participation schemes, the purpose of this section is first to explain a framework that can be used to analyse the extent to which various schemes genuinely al-low employees to have a say in matters that affect them at work. What is important here is to be able to unpick the purpose, meaning and subsequent impact of employee participation (Dundon *et al.,* 2004). To this end a fourfold framework can be used: including the 'depth', 'level', 'scope' and 'form' of various participation schemes in actual practice (Marchington and Wilkinson, 2012).

First is the 'depth' to which employees have a say about organisational decisions (Marchington and Wilkinson, 2005). A greater depth may be when employees, either directly or indirectly, can influence those decisions that are normally reserved for management. The other end of the continuum may be a shallow depth, evident when employees are simply informed of the decisions management have made (see Figure 17.1). Second is the 'level' at which participation takes place. This can be at a work-group, department, plant or corporate level. What is significant here is whether the schemes adopted by an organisation actually take place at an appropriate managerial level. For example, involvement in a team meeting over future strategy would in most instances be inappropriate given that most team leaders would not have the authority to re-design organisational strategy. Third is the 'scope' of par-ticipation, that is, the topics on which employees can contribute. These range from relatively minor and insignificant matters, such as car-parking spaces to more substantive issues, such as future investment strategies or plant re-location. Finally is the 'form' that participation takes, which may include a combination of both direct and indirect schemes. *Direct* schemes

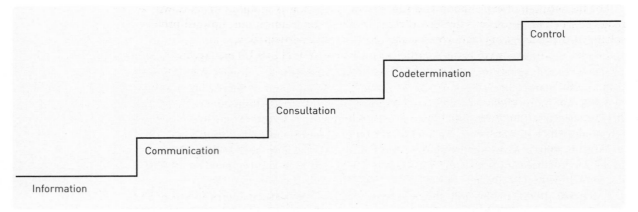

Figure 17.1 The depth of employee participation
Source: Marchington and Wilkinson, 2005.

typically include individual techniques such as written and electronic communications, face-to-face meetings between managers and employees (e.g. quality circles or team briefing). *Indirect* participation, in contrast, is via employee representatives, either union stewards or employee works council representatives in consultation with management. Another form of participation is task-based (or problem-solving) participation, where employees contribute directly to their job, either through focus groups or attitude surveys. There is also financial participation through variable pay and/or bonus schemes, such as profit sharing.

Taken together this framework allows for a more accurate description not only of the type of involvement and participation schemes in use, but the extent to which they may or may not empower employees (Marchington and Wilkinson, 2012). Figure 17.1 is more than a straightforward continuum from no involvement (information) to extensive worker participation (control). It illustrates the point that schemes can overlap and co-exist. For example, the use of collective bargaining and joint consultation does not mean that management abandon communication techniques. Central to this understanding of participation is power within the employment relationship, differentiated by the methods used (direct or indirect classifications), the level at which participation takes place (individual to boardroom level), and the extent to which any particular technique is employee- or management-centred (Wilkinson and Dundon, 2010).

 ## Employee participation in practice

The use of various employee involvement and participatory initiatives speeded up during the latter part of the 1980s and appears to have become more embedded and integrated with organisational practice during the 1990s (Marchington *et al.*, 2001). One of the most systematic forms of communication and participation is via the management chain of command. For example, regular meetings between managers and employees had grown over the last decade, as did suggestions schemes and newsletters (Kersley *et al.*, 2006). Evidence shows that direct employee involvement is typical through face-to-face meetings between management and employees (in 91 per cent of all UK workplaces), newsletters (45 per cent), suggestion schemes (30 per cent) and problem-solving groups such as quality circles (36 per cent). Only 14 per cent of British establishments had a workplaces level joint consultative committee (Kersley *et al.*, 2006).

For the purpose of explanation and subsequent analysis, it is useful to break down the range of schemes in use into five broad classifications: communications, upward problem solving, task participation, teamworking and representative participation.

Communication is a weak form of participation but is a means by which management share information with employees, ranging from written memos, email or informal face-to-face communications. These have increased substantially in recent years, and are often regarded as a precursor to deeper forms of employee participation (Marchington and Wilkinson, 2012). Of course, communication practices vary in frequency and intensity. Some companies rely on their own internal newsletter to report a range of matters, from profits, new products to in-house welfare and employee development topics. More sophisticated techniques found by Marchington *et al.*, (2001) included the use of electronic media, such as emails, company intranets and senior management online discussion forums.

The main problem with communications as a form of participation is a lack of objectivity. Given that information is often political and power-centred, the messages managers seek to communicate to workers may be used to reinforce managerial prerogatives. The way information is communicated can also be ineffective as many line managers responsible for disseminating corporate messages lack effective communication skills, or information is conveyed in an untimely manner (often when bad news has already passed to the media before employees are told).

Upward problem-solving techniques seek to go one step further than communications by tapping into employee ideas for improvements. As with communication methods, problem-solving practices have increased, often inspired by Japanese work systems which encourage employees to offer ideas (Wilkinson *et al.*, 2010). Upward problem-solving practices are designed to increase the stock of ideas available to management as well as encourage a more cooperative industrial relations climate. Specific techniques can be either individual or collective, and range from employee suggestions schemes, focus groups or quality circles to workforce attitude surveys (Wilkinson, 2002). The fundamental difference between these practices and communication methods is that they are upward (from employees to managers) rather than downward (managers disseminating information to workers).

In relation to the framework for analysing employee participation in the previous section, it is clear that upward problem-solving techniques do offer a greater degree of depth than

Table 17.1   Employee participation practices

	% of all workplaces	
	1998	2004
Face-to-face meetings between management and employees	85	91
Suggestion schemes	31	30
Regular newsletters	40	45
Problem-solving groups (e.g. quality circles)	28	36
Use of one or more employee share ownership scheme	15	21
Workplace level joint consultative committee	28	14
Any form of representative voice[1]	57	49

Source: Kersley *et al.*, 2006: 94; 127; 135; 191 (all workplaces with ten or more employees). The advice of the WERS 2004 Information and Advice Service (www.wers2004.info) is acknowledged in the compilation of the above figures.
[1]Representative voice is defined as the existence of: a recognised trade union; any JCC; union or stand-alone, non-union employee representatives (Kersley *et al.*, 2006: 132).

managerial communications. However, they have also been highly criticised as being inherently unitarist in nature (Sewell and Wilkinson, 1992). For example, the feedback given by workers in an attitude survey is essentially based on a managerial agenda as the information asked for tends to be set by employers. Furthermore, in organisations where quality circles have been introduced, the take-up and enthusiasm among employees has often been found wanting (Collard and Dale, 1989).

The third category of practices is *task-based participation.* The objective here has been to focus attention on the actual job rather than the managerial processes for participation. These practices have a longer pedigree in seeking to counter the degradation of work and associated employee alienation (Proctor and Mueller, 2000), of which many schemes formed part of a series of work psychology experiments in the 1960s and 1970s (e.g., Tavistock Institute, Quality of Work Life Programmes in the USA and Sweden). More recently, task-based participation is celebrated as a root to sustained organisational performance via employee commitment and motivation. The types of practices include job enlargement and job enrichment whereby employees perform a greater range of task with a greater degree of job autonomy. The criticisms levelled at task-participation are that outcomes often result in work intensification rather than job enrichment. Arguably, devolving more and more responsibilities to employees can increase stress levels. In other words, employees simply work harder rather than smarter (Delbridge *et al.,* 1992).

The fourth category is *teamworking.* Pfeffer's (1998) universal list of seven best practices includes, among other things, self-managed teams as integral to achieving better organisational performance through people. However, teamworking is one of the most imprecise of all the involvement and participation practices, and is often portrayed in an upbeat and uncritical way. For example, in the WERS98 survey, 65 per cent of managerial respondents indicated they have teamworking in their organisation, yet this figure reduced to 3 per cent when further questions probed the extent to which these teams were genuinely autonomous – such as deciding how tasks would be performed and appointing team leaders (Cully *et al.,* 1999: 43). Other commentators have reported a more subversive side to the effects of teamworking that result in forms of peer surveillance and control (Barker, 1993; Sinclair, 1992). For example, the pressure to conform to group norms and meet production targets is often policed by co-workers while simultaneously monitored by management (Geary and Dobbins, 2001).

The final category is *representative participation,* which can include joint consultation either via trade unions or, as is more typical these days, through forms of non-union employee representation (NER). Trade union participation in particular has experienced the most significant decline across most of the Westernised world in recent years. In Britain for example, the proportion of establishments with a recognised union has declined considerably with just 30 per cent recognising a trade union (Kersley *et al.*, 2006). The figure is even lower in the US, with around 12 per cent of the workforce enjoying union forms of participation (Dixon and Fiorito, 2009). Importantly, the use of joint consultation often varies by company size and particular organisational context factors, such as market pressure or technologically intensive industries. There are very few enterprises with fewer than 25 employees that have workplace-level joint consultative forums (Kersley *et al.*, 2006: 126).

It is often acknowledged that collective bargaining indicates a deeper and broader level of participation in organisational decision-making through the act of negotiation between management and employee (union) representatives (Pateman, 1970). However, the reality can be very different, as managers involve unions less and less as a legitimate participatory channel (Ackers *et al.,* 2005; Geary, 2003).

This may indicate that *representative participation* is not necessarily dependent on the existence of a trade union, but mediated through alternative NER systems (Dundon and Gollan, 2007). Dual or multiple mechanisms for representative participation point to a complex web of employer motives; in particular the simultaneous use of both union and non-union systems within the same organisation (Willman *et al.,* 2003). In Marchington *et al.*'s (2001) study into employee voice and management choice, it was found that non-union consultative committees were more common than a decade ago. In addition, these NER forums considered a range of organisational issues including working conditions, capital investment expenditure and disciplinary procedures. At the same time, others have commented that NER arrangements are often weak on power and shallow in depth (Dundon and Rollinson, 2004; Gollan, 2007).

However, debate remains concerning the efficacy of NER in relation to union-only channels and whether or not they function as a complement or a substitute to union methods of participation (Dundon *et al.*, 2005). While some scholars argue that managerial motives for participation is based around the desire to control employee actions (e.g. Ramsay, 1977), NERs may actually function for other reasons (Cullinane *et al.*, 2012). Indeed, it is probably wrong to view non-union employee voice as a single homogenous category of participation predicated only on the use of management power. Gollan (2007) argues that while NERs may be a complement to union channels, they do, on average, tend to be weaker than union participation.

Evidence indicates that NERs can be quite diverse in scope and coverage (Kaufman and Taras, 2010). One area of dual voice that has received relatively little scrutiny but appears to be on the increase is that of *double-breasting* employee participation (Cullinane *et al.*, 2012). The antecedents of double-breasting can be traced to the construction industry in the US (Lipsky and Farber, 1976). The practice was designed to marginalise union influence by having a unionised plant compete against a non-union site for work contracts. The objective was to award work to the plant with the lowest labour costs, typically the non-union plant (Donaghey *et al.*, 2012). Research indicates that double-breasting participation has increased globally and especially among multinational organisations operating in different industries and countries: for example in manufacturing and transportation in the US (Verma and Kochan, 1985); in Canada (Rose, 1986); Australia (Bamber *et al.*, 2009); Britain (Beaumont and Harris, 1992) and Ireland (Lavelle *et al.*, 2010). Donaghey *et al.* (2012) conclude that while double-breasting arrangements may be on the increase as a category within the area of representative participation, we do not know enough to comment on its effect and in particular the interplay of union and non-union participation regimes within a single organisation.

Inevitably, there are always dangers in seeking to locate discrete boundaries between certain practices. Some schemes are often unclear and ambiguous, ranging from the mechanistic descriptions of structures and procedures to more organic techniques that shape attitudes and behaviours. Other techniques limit participation to formal institutions and procedures, such as bargaining, a particular NER committee or joint consultation, while day-to-day interactions between employee and management may engender more informal dimensions to participation, particularly within the smaller workplace devoid of many formalised HR systems (Wilkinson *et al.*, 2007). At the same time, there are questions about whether informality can survive as a viable mechanism for independent employee participation in the absence of formal structures, especially if market conditions or senior management philosophies change (Wilkinson *et al.*, 2004). It is these dangers and uncertainties that warrant a consideration of the meanings and interpretations of how participation can impact organisational stakeholders.

 ## The meanings and impact of participation

There are a number of problems with the meanings and definitions of the schemes outlined above. For example, in some organisations the full range of mechanisms – both direct and indirect – may be used simultaneously, while in other companies one or two techniques may be employed. There is no reason to assume that more is somehow better. It is also quite common for a particular label to be ascribed to very different practices (Wilkinson *et al.*, 2004).

For example, a joint consultative committee which takes place on a monthly basis at plant level, involving senior managers and shop stewards, may have a more significant impact on decision making than a European Works Council that meets once a year, even though both are consultative and indirect in nature. There is the possibility that the latter is regarded by participants as 'bolted-on' to other organisational practices, with little substance or meaning in reality (Marchington and Wilkinson, 2012).

Arguably, the extrapolation of survey evidence about the use of various involvement and participation schemes tells us very little about the impact or extensiveness of such techniques within a particular organisation (Cox *et al.,* 2006; Marchington, 2005). Nor does this imply that certain schemes are an unwelcome intrusion into the lives of employees. For example, Geary and Dobbins (2001) suggest that while teamworking can lead to a reassertion of managerial authority this is not always as a brutal form of coercion. Geary and Dobbins (2001) found that team participation can be accompanied with autonomy and freedom, which served as a more placid form of employee control by granting workers a degree of discretion which ultimately protected managerial interests. In a study by Diamond and Freeman (2001), while employees tended to express satisfaction with the extent of involvement on matters such as the pace of work, a much wider participation gap was evident on a range of substantive employment matters, such as working hours or overtime rates. Donaghey *et al.* (2010: 63) adopt a different twist by examining not how much say employees may have, but explaining why employees can often remain silent. They highlight that management, through agenda-setting and manipulation of NER mechanisms, can engender a climate of silence which effectively manages employees out of the participation channel. Of course, management do not interpret employee participation schemes in a vacuum. Dietz *et al.,* (2009) show that when employees view involvement as little more than managerial rhetoric then trust and other so-called benefits soon diminish in the eyes of employees. In many respects, employee participation can become disjointed from other HR strategies and seen as something that is bolted-on, often depending on management latest fad or fashion.

The ambiguity and lack of trust about the meaning of involvement and participation schemes is evident in relation to the impact such techniques are claimed to have on enhanced organisational performance (Dundon *et al.,* 2004). First, it is practically impossible to isolate cause and effect and demonstrate that participation can lead to better organisational performance given the whole range of other contextual influences. For example, labour turnover is likely to be influenced by the availability of other jobs, by relative pay levels and by the presence, absence or depth of particular participation schemes. Second is the unease associated with the reference to benchmarking: of assessing the date at which to start making 'before and after' comparisons. Should this be the date at which the new participative mechanisms (say, a quality circle or consultative committee) is actually introduced into the organisation, or should it be some earlier or later date? For example, the claim that a quality circle saves money through a new work practice does not take into account that such ideas may have previously been channelled through a different and even better-established route. This also leads on to a third concern, that of evaluating the so-called impact and on whose terms. Should assessments be made in relation to workers having some voice (i.e., the process) or in terms of how things may be changed due to participation (i.e., the outcomes)? If it is the latter, then who gains? It remains the case that it is usually managers who decide what involvement and/or participation schemes to employ, at what level, depth and over what issues (Wilkinson *et al.,* 2010).

Employee participation and the EU

A more recent issue with regard to employee participation is the influence of European social policy. As noted earlier, the trend has been predominantly for employer-led schemes of a 'direct' nature, particularly since the 1980s. However the European Commission is beginning to promote what seems to be a favoured 'indirect' (i.e., more collectivist) route to employee participation. For example, the European Works Council Directive is to be re-caste to enable employee representatives in organisations of 1,000 or more employees (with 150 or more in two EU member countries) the right to consult with management. Further, the European Company Statute (ECS) sets-out a two-tier channel of participation for those companies that wish to avail of the EU Statute (which grants companies tax advantages), including works council type forum along with employee representative at board level. These are similar to a range of employee participation schemes that are currently more common in other EU countries such as Germany, Denmark, Sweden and the Netherlands. Of particular significance is the European Directive (2002/14/EC) on *Employee Information and Consultation*, recently transposed in Britain through the 2004 *Information and Consultation of Employees* (ICE) regulations.

These European regulations set out the requirements for member states to have in place permanent and statutory arrangements for employee information and consultation. The net effect is that workers in European countries will have a legal right to be informed and consulted on a range of business and employment issues. In countries such as Britain and Ireland, this marks a significant departure from the traditional voluntarist system of industrial relations (Gollan and Wilkinson, 2007). In Britain there is an important caveat here: the legal right is not automatic or universal. It excludes employees in establishments with less than 50 workers, and for those in defined organisations (e.g. 50+), employees 'have to trigger' the mechanism by requesting that management implement an information and consultation system.

The scope of the directive defines 'information' as the transmission, by the employer to employee representatives, of data in order to enable them to acquaint themselves with the subject-matter and to examine it. 'Consultation' means the exchange of views and establishment of dialogue between the employees' representatives and the employer, with a view to reaching agreement. Significantly, the explicit reference to 'employee representatives' in the directive is a clear indication of a preference for indirect (i.e., collectivist) forms of involvement and participation. However, the transposed ICE regulations allow for direct employee information and consultation practices, such as team meetings. Nor do the participation mechanisms have to incorporate or include unions, as the representative is defined as an 'employee' elected from and by the workforce (who may or may not be a union steward). Where the ICE regulations are likely to be contentious is among organisations that are either partly unionised, or have low union density levels. In all probability, companies that are highly unionised already have in place joint consultation arrangements that will suffice under the regulations. Similarly, in completely non-union companies, management and employees have the scope to design and implement information and consultation mechanisms in line with the regulations without a union/non-union dichotomy. More problematic is in organisations with partial union membership as it is unclear whether there have to be duplicate union and non-union employee forums, particularly if existing union representatives find it unacceptable to represent the interests of non-members. The regulations also state that organisations will have to inform and consult with employee representatives (whether union and/or non-union) on three general areas: the economic situation of the organisation; the structure and probable development of employment (including any threats to employment); and to inform and consult on decisions likely to lead to changes in work organisation or contractual relations (see Box 17.1 for a summary of the main features of the ICE regulations).

There are currently a range of debates and issues associated with employee participation contained in the regulations (see for example Gollan and Wilkinson, 2007). Article 6 (1) of the EU Directive ensures confidentiality in that employee representatives (and experts that may assist them) cannot disclose commercially sensitive information provided to them. Article 7 stipulates that each of the EU countries has to ensure that employee representatives have adequate protection from managerial reprisals when carrying out their duties. This is likely to be particularly important given that employee representatives may not have the support and protection of a recognised trade union. Under the ICE regulations in Britain, the Central Arbitration Committee (CAC) is charged with ensuring company compliance and has powers to impose penalties for non-compliance, amounting to fines up to £75,000. Under the regulations, management and employee representatives have the opportunity to define and negotiate their own voluntary arrangements that can vary from a statutory fall-back model; a principle that is not too dissimilar to voluntary arrangements contained in the European Works Council Directive.

| **Box 17.1 HRM in practice** | **Information and Consultation of Employees (ICE) Regulations 2004** |

- The regulations apply to undertakings in Great Britain with 50 or more employees. Equivalent legislation will be made in respect of Northern Ireland.
- The legal requirement to inform and consult employees is not automatic. A formal request has to be made by employees, or by an employer initiating the process (an employer notification).
- An employer must establish information and consultation procedures where a valid request has been made by employees.
- Such a request must be made in writing by 10% of employees in an undertaking (subject to a minimum of 15 and a maximum of 2,500 employees).
- Where the employees making the request wish to remain anonymous, they can submit the request to an independent body (such as the Central Arbitration Committee).
- The employer would have the opportunity to organise a ballot of employees to endorse or reject the initial request.
- An employer can continue with pre-existing information and consultation arrangements, provided that such arrangements have been agreed prior to an employee written request and:
  - (i) the agreement is in writing, including any collective agreements with trade unions;
  - (ii) the agreement covers all employees in the undertaking;
  - (iii) the agreement sets-out how the employer is to provide the information and seek employee views for consultation; and
  - (iv) the arrangements have been agreed by the employees
- Where a valid request (or employer notification) has been made, but no agreement reached, standard information and consultation provisions based on ICE Regulation 18 would apply.
- Where the standard information and consultation provisions apply, the employer shall arrange for a ballot to elect the employee representatives. Regulation 19 states that there shall be 1 representative per 50 employees, or part thereof, with a minimum of 2 and maximum of 25 representatives.
- Consultation should take place with a view to reaching agreement on decisions.
- Information must be given in such time, and in such fashion and with such content as are appropriate to enable the information and consultation representatives to conduct an adequate study and, where necessary, prepare for consultation.
- The maximum penalty for failing to comply with a declaration made by the CAC is £75,000.
- ICE Regulations 25 and 26 provide for the confidentiality of sensitive information given to I&C representatives.
- I&C representatives, and employees making a request, are protected against discrimination/unfair dismissal for exercising their rights under the ICE Regulations.
- I&C representatives are to be afforded paid time-off to carry out their duties.

Source: DTI, 2006 (see www.bis.gov.uk/files/file25934.pdf).

The ICE regulations differ from the original EU directive in a number of fundamental respects (Dundon and Rollinson, 2011). First, what the European directive defines as information and consultation is not the same as those contained in the ICE regulations. The former is a clearer indication for 'indirect' employee participation via elected employee representatives, whereas the language of the ICE regulations implies that direct information and communication channels are acceptable. Second, and referring back to the framework to analyse the depth of employee participation earlier in the chapter, the EU directive points toward a deeper and wider form of participation than the ICE regulations imply. It has been suggested that trade unions may become further marginalised because the ICE regulations apply to employee representatives, and consciously exclude any reference to recognised union officials (Gollan and Wilkinson, 2007). Third, the trigger mechanism for employees to avail of these new participation rights could result in fear or intimidation for those workers in non-union companies who do not have access to an independent trade union, employees who request these new rights might face managerial reprisals.

As a result employers, employees and unions have been adapting and reacting to what is an increasingly regulated environment for employee participation. It appears that these sorts of regulations have led to what Hall and Terry (2004) term 'legally prompted' forms of employee participation. In this scenario it is suggested that the law may encourage employers to be more creative by devising their own schemes for employee information and consultation, rather than rely on a legally imposed model of employee participation under the ICE regulations. A further possibility is that managers seek to avoid an extension of employee participation by following a minimalist strategy, in which a compliance attitude is adopted and managers do little more than tick the required boxes (Dundon *et al.*, 2006).

Conclusions

In this chapter we have outlined the context of employee participation over the last few decades in different countries and pointed towards future directions at a European level through a continuation of regulation. We have also considered the changing contours of management choice, public policy and that the adoption of various participation schemes is often uneven and complicated. While employee participation varies by context and across different countries, it is evident that a range of schemes often co-exist within an organisation and different forms of employee participation can be either complementary or contradict other management strategies and actions. A lot depends on the extent and depth of participation schemes and whether they are viewed as embedded or bolted-on to existing arrangements. Moreover, we have stressed that the meanings and interpretations of such schemes are much more important than the type or number of techniques adopted. What is important is the depth to which participatory mechanisms are integrated with other organisational practices, the scope to which workers have a genuine say over matters that affect them, and the level at which participation occurs.

These factors are now influenced and shaped by management choices as well as (in the context of Europe) increasingly regulations for employee participation. The case for industrial democracy in the 1960s and 1970s gave way to a neoliberal ideology dominated by global economic pressures, with an assumption that the state would remain largely absent from the employment relationship. The impact of such influences can be complex and uneven, belying simplistic dichotomies between state regulation and management choice for certain involvement schemes. Public policy neither represents a continuation of management-led involvement evident during the 1980s, nor a rolling-back to ideals premised on industrial democracy. Instead, elements of a new regulatory dialectic are beginning to emerge with its own dynamics (Ackers *et al.*, 2005).

At one level, the current practices of participation appear more embedded and less fragmented than they did a decade ago (Wilkinson *et al.*, 2004, 2010). Attempts have been made to consolidate and integrate different involvement and participation mechanisms over time (Marchington *et al.*, 2001). In some situations, the adversarial nature of shop floor relations appears to have partially diminished, with a new generation of union representatives willing and able to sit alongside non-union employee representatives on joint consultative forums. In other situations, particularly among multi-national organisations, plans for dual or double-breasted participation have marginalised and by-passed unions (Cullinane *et al.*, 2012; Donaghey *et al.*, 2012). The dualism in 1980s, of separated direct (individual) and in-direct (union) involvement channels seems to be more intermingled with a range of schemes that overlap and coexist at different levels.

According to Willman *et al.*, (2003), employers choosing voice regimes prior to 1960 did so in circumstances where union-based participation regimes were common exemplars and where there were normative and mimetic pressures to avoid non-union only regimes. The risk-averse option was a dual-channel of voice. However, over time, with the shift from manu-facturing to services and inward investments, non-union examples have become much more commonplace (Dundon and Rollinson, 2011). Where union participation exists it is highly likely to do so as part of a dual-channel voice regime (Bryson *et al.*, 2007). In terms of choice, employers can 'make' voice through HR professionals or 'buy' voice through unions. As HRM professionals become common the default option in the choice of voice regime has shifted over time to one dominated by non-union arrangements (Kaufman and Taras, 2010). Switch-ing costs, however, make the options for participation 'sticky', with radical switching (from union to non-union and vice versa) rare (Willman *et al.*, 2003).

Taken together, these developments suggest that the current policy environment holds bet-ter prospects for participation, partly as a result of greater EU regulation and partly because management has learned from the limitation of a weak form and a shallow depth to the par-ticipation initiatives of the 1980s. What remains problematic is that many managers find the European language of employment rights unpalatable and even alien to newer organisational cultures shaped by flatter and leaner market environments. This tension is significant as man-agers play a key part in interpreting legislative requirements into practice in the workplace. In this regard, employee participation is best understood not in terms of particular techniques or discrete typologies located along a static either/or continuum, but rather as a set of complex and uneven meanings and interpretations shaped by external regulation as well as internal stakeholder expectations for greater choice and voice. This incorporates informal dialogue as much as formalised structures and mechanisms. The challenges that lie ahead are how such a dynamic will be played out in practice, and whether existing multiple schemes for participa-tion will be integrated or the whether a new policy framework will result in another 'missed opportunity' for many managers (Wilkinson *et al.*, 1992).

CASE STUDY 17.1

RE-DESIGNING EMPLOYEE INVOLVEMENT IN A SMALL FAMILY-RUN BUSINESS

TONY DUNDON

Peninsula Lodge is a small boutique hotel close to the Great Barrier Reef in Queensland; a short distance from a national rainforest and within easy reach of beautiful beaches. It is a 3-star hotel with 85 rooms, a restaurant, bistro, banqueting and conferencing facilities. Peninsula Lodge currently employs 70 employees (full-time and part-time) comprising three senior managers, 16 function supervisors (such as housekeeping, catering, weddings, bistro etc.) and operational staff. Employees are not represented by a trade union.

The hotel is family-owned and two years ago a decision was made to add a leisure centre and market the hotel as a boutique wedding venue, offering a complete package and service to the wedding market. The addition of the leisure centre was described by a family owner as 'traumatic'. It was built at the same time as a new HR plan was rolled-out that sought to engage and involve staff. However, when the family owner attempted to introduce a new system to 'professionalise' supervisors and inject a new culture of customer service among employees, many quit, including long-service supervisors who were resistant of the changes. Further, a re-branded large hotel chain in the area intensified competition, resulting in growing economic pressure for Peninsula Lodge to compete in a wedding and leisure market dominated by large corporate hotels.

After observing other boutique hotels internationally, the senior management team decided to compete by offering a unique and differentiated service rather than on price alone. This involved the design and introduction of a new employee participation and engagement plan. Four 'core' elements to the engagement strategy were implemented. First, new communication channels were introduced that gave employees information about training possibilities in leisure, tourism and hotel activities. Employees were made aware and encouraged to apply for competency and work-related qualifications. Second, staff briefings were introduced so all employees were informed about work schedules, any changing shift patterns and particular special events coming up in the hotel or in the local vicinity. Third, new standard operating procedures were introduced and a weekly log of any faults, guest comments and employee ideas are fed back-up the management chain. Finally, important information is attached to individual pay slips.

Additional systems were developed around each of the four core participation elements. One of the most significant was functional area meetings and briefings which were used as a two-way communication channel. These were held every week and because staff work different shift patterns, minutes of the meeting were posted on bulletin boards. Employees who were not in attendance at a meeting had to sign to say they had received and read the minutes.

Senior management also introduced a system of 'self-directed' teamworking across seven key areas: customer service; human development; maintenance; cost control; quality; technology; and the environment. Employees from all functional areas could select to be part of a team responsible for one of the key seven areas, with management ensuring all areas were represented by staff. The team would then meet to discuss ideas and improvement. Prizes would be awarded on a monthly basis for the best ideas from staff. Half-day workshops were introduced on a bi-monthly basis so ideas of one group could be reported and proposed to the senior management team. Examples of employee ideas implemented included new gluten-free restaurant and bistro menus; new environmentally friendly technologies to help clean rooms; an information card issued to staff on weekly basis that provided up to date information for guests on local excursions or events.

The owners and senior managers of Peninsula Lodge feel they have started to promote a new culture of participation and engagement that was absent among staff previously. Business has picked up and anecdotally it appears new business has emerged from word-of-mouth recommendations. However, take-up of new training schemes by employees has been minimal. Furthermore, while there have been plenty of new ideas from staff, few have been implemented by senior managers. For employees, there has been a long tradition of informal dialogue and communication and some staff feel the new strategy is too structured for a small family-run hotel.

Questions

1 Why do you think some employees feel negative about the move to more formal types of employee participation initiatives at Peninsula Lodge?
2 How would you describe employee participation at Peninsula Lodge in terms of the framework explained in the chapter (e.g. depth, level, scope, form)?
3 Do you think the size of the Peninsula Lodge is an important factor in the nature of employee participation?
4 From reading the Peninsula Lodge case, why is it difficult to establish a relationship between employee participation and organisational performance?

CASE STUDY 17.2
ASSESSING PARTICIPATION

TONY DUNDON

Debating the case for and against participation

In Chapter 17 we reviewed the changing policy context for employee participation, in particular the on-going tension between management choices for employee participation and recent regulations for consultation rights, such as European regulations. Your task is to prepare an argument 'in favour' of a legal case for employee information and consultation. You will be required to explain your argument in a class debate with co-students, who will speak 'against' your position.

Advising on employee participation

Imagine you are a management consultant. Your services have recently been retained by a large multinational company employing 7,000 people overall (2,800 across four UK sites; 3,200 in two Germany plants; and 1,000 in one Italian location) to provide a report on the implications of the *Information and Consultation of Employees (ICE) Regulations 2004*. The company already has a European Works Council (EWC) and a union recognition agreement exists in Germany and for two of the four British locations. The remainder are non-union and different NER mechanisms exist. Management would like you to consider:

a. a brief explanation of what the ICE Regulations mean,
b. whether a double-breasting (union and non-union) employee participation plan is feasible and any potential drawbacks with a double-breasting voice arrangement for the UK plants, and
c. your considered opinion of any specific implications particular to this company.

Explain and justify the information you include in the report.

CASE STUDY 17.3

THE DURABILITY OF 'DOUBLE-BREASTING' VOICE IN A MULTINATIONAL ORGANISATION

TONY DUNDON

Introduction

Employee participation has retained a central role in HRM over the last two decades. It can be seen as a key component of best-practice HRM and high-commitment management leading to improved organisational performance. At the same time there has been a decline in union-channels of participation and an increase in Non-union Employee Representation (NER). The mix of dual union and non-union voice has also received widespread attention from scholars and researchers. Some view NERs as a form of union-avoidance: that is a mechanism intent on by-passing unions and removing any demand among employees for a trade union to represent their interests. On the other hand, arguments abound that NERs may function as a complement to union-channels that may coexist in tandem. This case study reports on double-breasting in one large multinational organisation, adapted from Cullinane et al., (2012).

The company and its context

BritCo is a former public utility that was initially privatised in Britain in the 1980s. It is now a multinational organisation with operations in over 170 countries. The case described here is the story of how BritCo entered the Irish market and proceeded to implement a double-breasting strategy for employee participation. BritCo entered the market in the Republic of Ireland through a process of commercial acquisition, which included the purchase of a non-unionised firm. Once established in the market place, BritCo management decided the company should operate on an all-island basis. This meant merging its operation in Northern Ireland (highly unionised, centralised and part of the UK management structure) with those in the South (exclusively non-unionised, decentralised and based on newer acquired operations).

The decision to structure BritCo on an all-island basis was not without its difficulties. To begin with, Brit Co (NI) has a deep history of collective representation and was a former State monopoly. There are two recognised trade unions in BritCo (NI) with over 90 per cent density, primarily operating through a UK industrial relations system with collective negotiations conducted centrally in London. In contrast, BritCo in the Republic is non-union and relations are locally rather than centrally based. The merger of BritCo across the island of Ireland resulted in negative repercussions as some functions moved from the South to the North. Significantly, redundancy caused problems as terms and conditions were much lower in the South than those that had been collectively negotiated for staff in the North. Indeed, no compulsory redundancy agreement exists for unionised staff from BritCo (NI); a legacy that remained post-nationalisation. Because of what appeared to be superior employment conditions for BritCo (NI) employees, a trade union organising campaign was instigated by some workers in BritCo in the South. Unlike UK law, there is no comparable statutory trade union legislation in the Republic of Ireland. In response to the union recognition campaign in the Republic of Ireland, management instigated a double-breasting strategy with union representation in BritCo (NI) and exclusively non-union participation channels for BritCo in the Republic.

Worker Participation in BritCo Northern Ireland

In Northern Ireland BritCo has a long history and tradition of collective participation through centralised negotiation and joint consultation and two separate trade unions are recognised for these purposes. At the same time the company has several other 'direct' forms of employee involvement, including staff/team briefings; weekly newsletters from management; regular use of the company's intranet for communications; and an annual company-wide survey. These direct employee participation techniques have increased at BritCo NI in recent years, with the CEO supportive of direct and transparent management communications. The newsletter, for example, provides staff with information on new business developments and how the company is performing. In addition, the intranet provides employees with direct access to a wide range of human resource policies (e.g. pension information and other company procedures, such as discipline).

Two recent employee engagement initiatives are also noteworthy. One is a weekly public 'phone call' in which all employees can listen in 'live' to the CEO talking about business developments. Employees can respond or just listen. Another engagement initiative is an annual 'engagement survey', which asks a series of questions about employee satisfaction and commitment on a company wide basis. The results can then be compared between regions and different business units.

In addition to the above are other '*indirect*' collective forms of participation, which have a much longer and deeper history across Northern Ireland operations. There is a company joint consultative committee (JCC), which includes the CEO, several functional heads (such as the HR, IT, Finance, Engineering Directors), local line managers and shop stewards, along with the full-time union official for each of the two unions. At these JCC meetings financial matters and company strategy, as appropriate to NI operations, are considered. Union officials or stewards do not have any input in terms of setting the agenda for the JCC, and typically do not know what issues will be discussed in advance of the annual meeting. However, union reps can and often do raise matters under 'any other business'. Other collective mechanisms that occur on a more regular basis include bi-monthly meetings between union stewards and senior managers to discuss any emergent issues of concern to employees. Running alongside the formal JCC and bi-monthly meetings is 'informal union–management dialogue', which tends to occur on a more regular albeit ad hoc basis. Issues pertaining to matters such as discipline, sickness or employee grievance representation will often be discussed informally or 'off the record' between union reps and managers before matters are progressed through the formal participation mechanisms.

While BritCo NI utilises both direct and indirect channels of employee participation at its NI operations, relations have not always been easy or smooth. Indeed, management say they have had to 'redefine' the union role so it can add value to the company (as well as its members). Newer roles have included how to deal with changes to work patterns in order to be more flexibly responsible to customer demands. Yet employees report a high degree of trust in management because they know that their union officials can and do call management to account when necessary.

Employee Voice at BritCo in the Republic of Ireland

As in the North, employee participation at BritCo in the Republic includes both 'direct' and 'indirect' mechanisms for workers to have a say. For the most part, direct employee participation converges across both BritCo NI and BritCo in the Republic (e.g. company intranet, newsletters etc). Regarding indirect employee voice, however, things are very different in the Republic with Non-union Employee Representation (NER) mechanisms used instead of union channels. These include, primarily, what is known as '*BritCo Vocal':* a non-union employee forum covering the whole of the Republic of Ireland. In addition, there is a '*Southern Works Committee' (SWC),* which is a collective employee council for Dublin-based engineers to deal with issues particular to that work group and location.

The NER arrangements at BritCo Republic had been established a couple of years ago in response to European information and consultation regulations. The NER system became inactive due to a lack managerial support combined with little employee interest. However, the forum was re-launched as '*BritCo Vocal*' in response to a union recognition campaign at BritCo in the Republic of Ireland. Employee reps were 'elected' when they were previously 'selected' by management. Within this, electoral constituencies exist for different business units so the forum represents all occupational groups. Furthermore, employee reps have an input into issues and agenda items, and afforded the opportunity to report back to their employee constituents (using email, intranet messaging and notice boards). The separate SWC emerged at the behest of management due to that group of engineers dominating the agenda of *BritCo Vocal* and because management wanted to isolate what they saw as a potentially militant and union supportive group of workers. In short, the SWC marginalised union sympathisers from the rest of the non-union workforce across Britco in the South.

While the existence of formal NER structures is important, it is necessary to assess the scope and depth of such employee participation in terms of the matters available for consultation. Perhaps the most immediate and significant issue was that of inferior redundancy conditions for employees in the Republic compared to those offered to workers in Northern Ireland. The discrepancy may be explained by long-established union agreement in the North that was not available to employees in the South. In response, management used the *BritCo Vocal* forum to review the situation and allow non-union employee reps considerable scope in redrafting the redundancy arrangements. The outcome was a revised policy handbook that incorporated key elements of the Northern Ireland redundancy scheme in the Republic.

While managers and employees were initially satisfied with *BritCo Vocal* and the amount of say employee reps had in changing policy and practice, over time things started to feel very different. Employee reps on the *Vocal* committee felt that once management attempted to resolve an issue, interest waned. In particular, management appeared to offer greater support and enthusiasm for the *Vocal* forum when the union organising campaign was at its peak. Consequently, some employee reps lost interest and dropped out of participating in *BritCo Vocal* forum meetings when management support waned. The way the SWC operated in practice was very similar. While it was initially active and dealt with concerns about performance management and the use of company vehicles for specific engineers at the Dublin South facility, activity diminished after about two years and when the union-organising campaign failed to secure recognition rights for workers in the Republic, employee reps felt that issues had declined in importance and management allowed minor, or what they called 'tea and toilet roll issues', to be dealt with at SWC meetings.

Summary: the durability of double-breasting employee participation

Employee participation in large, complex and multinational and global organisations such as BritCo are far from straightforward. The strategy for employees to have a say across the different sites and jurisdictions of BritCo Northern Ireland and BritCo in the Republic has been uneven and at times contradictory. With a new CEO and a belief in a culture of engagement and voice, direct employee mechanisms started to have a stronger and deeper hold. Yet at the same time, union channels of voice were supported and tolerated in the North, but actively discouraged in the Republic. To some extent this was because management could get away with such a strategy because of different employee participation regulations. Indeed, there is no comparative union recognition legislation in the South to that in the North. Likewise, both Irish and UK governments adopted a minimalist interpretation of European regulations for employee information and consultation that effectively downgraded collective voice in favour of direct involvement channels. Double-breasting employee participation at BritCo suited a managerial agenda of seeking to redefine (diminish) the trade union role for participation. How durable and extensive such a double-breasting strategy will be in the long run is of course a matter of some debate.

Questions

1 In the BritCo case, to what extent would you say that NER forms of employee representation are deep or shallow?
2 Does a strategy of double-breasting (union and non-union) participation serve managerial or worker interests?
3 Imagine you have been asked for your professional advice and opinion from the BritCo Ireland Board of Directors. They would like you to make a short presentation about the feasibility of a strategy of double-breasting voice in which one or two plants are unionised, and other sites have exclusive non-union employee participation mechanisms. What would you include in the presentation and why?
4 Given what has been described at BritCo, should trade unions be worried about the introduction of employee information and consultation regulations?
5 What implications are there from the BritCo case for the meaning of employee participation?

Bibliography

Ackers, P., Marchington, M., Wilkinson, A. and Goodman, J. (1992) 'The use of cycles? Explaining employee involvement in the 1990s', *Industrial Relations Journal,* Vol.23, No.4, 268–83.

*Ackers, P., Marchington, M., Wilkinson, A. and Dundon, T. (2005) 'Partnership and voice, with or without trade unions: changing UK management approaches to organisational participation', in Stuart, M. and Martinez Lucio, M. (eds) *Partnership and Modernisation in Employment Relations,* Abingdon: Routledge.

Bamber, G.J., Gittel, J.H., Kochan, T.A. and Van Nordenflycht, A. (2009) *Up in the Air: How Airlines Can Improve Performance by Engaging Employees*, New York: Cornell University Press.

Barker, J. (1993) 'Tightening the iron cage: concertive control in self-managing teams', *Administrative Science Quarterly,* Vol.38, 408–37.

Beaumont, P.B. and Harris, R.I.D. (1992) '"Double-breasted" recognition arrangements in Britain', *International Journal of Human Resource Management*, Vol.3, No.2, 267–83.

Becker, B.E. and Huselid, M.A. (1998) 'High performance work systems and firm performance synthesis of research and managerial implications', in Ferris, G.R. (ed.) *Research in Personnel and Human Resources,* Vol.16, Stamford, CT: JAI Press.

Benson, J. and Brown, M. (2010), 'Employee voice: does union membership matter?', *Human Resource Management Journal,* Vol.20, No.1, 80–99.

Boxall, P. and Purcell, J. (2003) *Strategy and Human Resource Management,* London: Palgrave.

Brannen, P. (1983) *Authority and Participation in Industry*, London: Batsford.

Brewster, C., Croucher, R., Wood, G. and Brookes, M. (2007) 'Collective and individual voice: convergence in Europe?', *International Journal of Human Resource Management*, Vol.18, No.7, 1246–62.

Bryson, A., Willman, P., Gomez, R. and Kretchmer, T. (2007), 'Employee voice and human resource management: an empirical analysis using British data', *PSI Research Discussion Paper No 27*, Policy Studies Institute, London.

Budd, J.W., Gollan, P. and Wilkinson, A. (2010), 'New approaches to employee voice and participation in organizations', *Human Relations,* Vol.63 (March), 303–10.

Bullock, A. (Lord) (1977) *Report of the Committee of Inquiry on Industrial Democracy*, London: HMSO (Cmnd. 6706).

Collard, R. and Dale, B. (1989) 'Quality circles', in Sisson, K. (ed.) *Personnel Management in Britain,* Oxford: Blackwell.

Cox, A., Zagelmeyer, S. and Marchington, M. (2006) 'Embedding employee involvement and participation at work', *Human Resource Management Journal*, Vol.16, No.3, 250–67.

Cressey, P., Eldridge, J. and MacInnes, J. (1985) *Just Managing: Authority and Democracy in Industry,* Milton Keynes: Open University Press.

*Cullinane, N., Donaghey, J., Dundon, T and Dobbins, T. (2012), 'Different rooms, different voices: double-breasting, multi-channel representation and the managerial agenda', *International Journal of Human Resource Management*, Vol.23, No.2, 368–384.

Cully M., O'Reilly A., Woodland, S. and Dix, G. (1999) *Britain at Work: As Depicted by the 1998 Workplace Employee Relations Survey*, Abingdon: Routledge.

Delbridge, R., Turnbull, P. and Wilkinson, B. (1992) 'Pushing back the frontiers: management control and work intensification under JIT/TQM factory regimes', *New Technology, Work and Employment,* Vol.7, No.2, 97–106.

Department of Trade and Industry (DTI) (2006) *The Information and Consultation of Employees Regulations 2004: DTI Guidance* (January 2006): www.bis.gov.uk/files/file25934.pdf.

Diamond, W. and Freeman, R. (2001) *What Workers Want from Workplace Organisations*: Report to the TUCs Promoting Unionism Task Group, London: Trades Union Congress.

Dietz, G., Wilkinson, A. and Redman, T. (2009) 'Involvement and participation', pp. 243–266, in Wilkinson, A., Bacon, N., Redman, T. and Snell, S. (eds) *The SAGE Handbook of Human Resource Management*, London: Sage.

Dixon, M. and Fiorito, J. (2009), 'Can unions rebound? Decline and renewal in the US labour movement', in Gall, G. (ed.) *Union Revitalization in Advanced Economies*, London: Palgrave.

Donaghey, J., Cullinane, N., Dundon, T. and Wilkinson, A. (2010), 'Reconceptualising employee silence: problems and prognosis', *Work, Employment and Society*, Vol.25, No.1, 51–67.

Donaghey, J., Cullinane, N., Dundon, T. and Dobbins, A. (2012) 'Non-union employee representation, union avoidance and the managerial agenda', *Economic and Industrial Democracy,* Vol.33, No.2, 163–183.

Dundon T. and Gollan, P. (2007), 'Re-conceptualising non-union voice', *International Journal of Human Resource Management*, Vol.18, No.7, 1182–98.

Dundon, T. and Rollinson, D. (2004) *Employment Relations in Non-Union Firms,* Abingdon: Routledge.

Dundon, T. and Rollinson, D. (2011), *Understanding Employment Relations* (2nd edn)*,* London: McGraw Hill.

Dundon, T., Curran, D., Maloney M. and Ryan, P. (2006), 'Conceptualising the dynamics of employee voice: evidence from the Republic of Ireland', *Industrial Relations Journal*, Vol. 37, No.5, 492–512.

*Dundon, T., Wilkinson, A., Marchington, M. and Ackers, P. (2004) 'The meanings and purpose of employee voice', *International Journal of Human Resource Management,* Vol.15, No.6, 1150–71.

*Dundon, T., Wilkinson, A., Marchington M. and Ackers, P. (2005) 'The management of voice in non-union organisations: managers' perspectives', *Employee Relations*, Vol.27, No.3, 307–19.

Ewing, K. (2003) 'Industrial relations and law', in Ackers, P. and Wilkinson, A. (eds) *Understanding Work and Employment: Industrial Relations in Transition,* Oxford: Oxford University Press.

Geary, J. (2003) 'New Forms of work organizations: still limited, still controlled, but still welcome?', in Edwards, P. (ed.) *Industrial Relations: Theory and Practice in Britain* (2nd edn), Oxford: Blackwell.

Geary, J. and Dobbins, A. (2001) 'Teamworking: a new dynamic in the pursuit of management control', *Human Resource Management Journal,* Vol.11, No.1, 3–23.

Gollan, P. (2007), *Employee Representation in Non-Union Firms*, London: Sage.

*Gollan, P. and Wilkinson, A. (2007) 'Implications of the EU Information and Consultation Directive and the Regulations in the UK: prospects for the future of employee representation', *International Journal of Human Resource Management*, Vol.18, No.7, 1145–58.

Goodman, J., Earnshaw, J., Marchington, M. and Harrison, R. (1998) 'Unfair dismissal cases, disciplinary procedures, recruitment methods and management style', *Employee Relations,* Vol.20, No.6, 536–50.

Hall, M. and Terry, M. (2004), 'The emerging system of statutory worker representation', in Healy, G., Heery, E., Taylor, P. and Brown, W. (eds) *The Future of Worker Representation*, Basingstoke: Palgrave Macmillan.

Heller, F., Pusic, E., Strauss, G. and Wilpert, B. (1998) *Organisational Participation: Myth and Reality*, Oxford: Oxford University Press.

Huselid, M. (1995), 'The impact of human resource management practices on turnover, production and corporate financial performance', *Academy of Management Journal*, Vol.38, No.3, 635–72.

*Kaufman, B. and Taras, D.G. (2010), 'Employee participation through non union forms of representation', in Wilkinson, A., Gollan, P., Marchington, M. and Lewin, D. (eds) *The Oxford Handbook of Participation in Organizations*, Oxford: Oxford University Press.

Kersley, B., Alpin, C., Forth, J., Bryson, A., Bewley, H., Dix, J. and Oxenbridge, S. (2006) *Inside the Workplace: Findings from the 2004 Workplace Employment Relations Survey*, Abingdon: Routledge.

Lavelle, J., Gunnigle, P. and McDonnell, A. (2010). 'Patterning employee voice in multinational companies', *Human Relations*, Vol.63 (March), 395–418.

Lewis, P., Thornhill, A. and Saunders, M. (2003) *Employee Relations: Understanding the Employment Relationship*, Harlow: Prentice Hall.

Lipsky, D.B. and Farber, H.S. (1976) 'The composition of strike activity in the construction industry', *Industrial and Labor Relations Review*, Vol.29, No.3, 401–28.

Logan, J. (2006) 'The union avoidance industry in the United States, *British Journal of Industrial Relations*, Vol.44. No.4, 651–76.

Marchington, M. (2005) 'Employee involvement: patterns and explanations', in Harley, B., Hyman, J. and Thompson, P. (eds) *Participation and Democracy at Work: Essays in Honour of Harvie Ramsay*, Basiagstoke: Palgrave.

Marchington, M. and Suter, J. (2008) 'Informal employee voice: filling the gaps or reinforcing the status quo', *Academy of Management Conference*, Anaheim, August.

*Marchington, M. and Wilkinson, A. (2005) 'Direct participation', in Bach, S. (ed.) *Personnel Management: A Comprehensive Guide to Theory and Practice* (4th edn), Oxford: Blackwell.

Marchington, M. and Wilkinson, A. (2012) *Human Resource Management at Work* (5th edn), London: Chartered Institute of Personnel and Development.

Marchington, M., Goodman, J. Wilkinson, A. and Ackers, P. (1992) *New Developments in Employee Involvement*, Research Paper No.2, London: Employment Department.

Marchington, M., Wilkinson, A., Ackers, P. and Dundon, T. (2001) *Management Choice and Employee Voice*, London: CIPD.

Northrup, H.R. (1995) 'Doublebreasted operations and the decline of construction unionism', *Journal of Labor Research*, Vol.16, No.3, 379–85.

Pateman, C. (1970) *Participation and Democratic Theory*, Cambridge: Cambridge University Press.

Patterson, M., West, M., Lawthorn, R. and Nickell, S. (1997) *Impact of People Management Practices on Business Performance*, London: IPD, Report No.22.

Pfeffer, J. (1998) *The Human Equation: Building Profits by Putting People First,* Boston, MA: Harvard Business School Press.

Piore, M. and Sabel, C. (1983) *The Second Industrial Divide,* New York: Basic Books.

Proctor, S. and Mueller, F. (eds) (2000) *Teamworking,* London: Macmillan.

Proctor, S. and Ackroyd, S. (2001) 'Flexibility', in Redman, T. and Wilkinson A. (eds) *Contemporary Human Resource Management: Text and Cases,* Harlow: Financial Times/ Prentice Hall.

Ramsay, H. (1977) 'Cycles of control: worker participation in sociological and historical perspective', *Sociology,* Vol.11, No.3, 481–506.

Roeber, J. (1975) *Social Change at Work,* London: Heinemann.

Rose, J.B. (1986) 'Legislative support for multi-employer bargaining: the Canadian experience', *Industrial and Labor Relations Review*, Vol.40, No.1, 3–18.

Sewell, G. and Wilkinson, B. (1992) 'Empowerment or emasculation? Shopfloor surveillance in a total quality organisation', in Blyton , P. and Turnbull, P. (eds) *Reassessing Human Resource Management,* London: Sage.

Sinclair, A. (1992) 'The tyranny of a team ideology', *Organization Studies,* Vol.13, No.4, 11–26.

Tebbutt, M. and Marchington, M. (1997) 'Look before you speak: gossip and the insecure workplace', *Work Employment and Society,* Vol.11, No.4, 713–35.

Trist, E., Higgin, G., Murray, H. and Pollock, A. (1963) *Organisational Choice: Capabilities of Groups at the Coalface Under Changing Technologies*, London: Tavistock Institute.

Verma, A. and Kochan, T. (1985) 'The growth and nature of the non-union sector within a Firm', in Kochan , T. (ed.) *Challenges and Choices Facing American Labor*, Boston, MA: MIT Press.

Wedderburn, K.W. (Lord) (1986) *The Worker and the Law* (3rd edn), Harmondsworth: Penguin.

*Wilkinson, A. (2002) 'Empowerment', in Poole, M. and Warner, M. (eds) *International Encyclopaedia of Business and Management Handbook of Human Resource Management,* London: ITB Press.

Wilkinson, A. and Dundon, T. (2010) 'Direct employee participation', in Wilkinson, A. Gollan, P., Marchington, M. and Lewin, D. (eds), *The Oxford Handbook of Participation in Organizations*, Oxford: Oxford University Press.

Wilkinson, A., Dundon T. and Grugulis, I. (2007), 'Information but not consultation: exploring employee involvement in SMEs', *International Journal of Human Resource Management*, Vol.18, No.7, 1279–97.

Wilkinson, A. Dundon, T. and Marchington, M. (2012) 'Employee Involvement and Voice', in Bach, S. and Edwards, M. (eds) *Managing Human Resources*, Oxford: Blackwell.

Wilkinson, A., Dundon, T., Marchington, M. and Ackers, P. (2004) 'Changing patterns of employee voice', *Journal of Industrial Relations,* Vol.46, No.3, 298–322.

Wilkinson, A., Gollan, P., Marchington, M and Lewin, D. (2010) 'Conceptualizing employee participation in organizations', in Wilkinson, A., Gollan, P., Marchington, M. and Lewin, D. (eds) *The Oxford Handbook of Participation in Organizations*, Oxford: Oxford University Press.

Wilkinson, A., Marchington, M., Goodman, J. and Ackers, P. (1992) 'Total quality management and employee involvement', *Human Resource Management Journal,* Vol.2, No.4, 1–20.

Willman, P., Bryson, A. and Gomez, R. (2003) 'Why do voice regimes differ?'. Paper presented at International Industrial Relations Association (IIRA) 13th World Congress, 8–12 September, Berlin.

Wood, S. and De Menezes, L. (1998) 'High commitment management in the UK: evidence from the Workplace Industrial Relations Survey and Employers' Manpower Skills Survey', *Human Relations,* Vol.51, No.4, 485–515.

---

*Useful reading

CHAPTER 18
KNOWLEDGE MANAGEMENT AND HUMAN RESOURCE MANAGEMENT

Donald Hislop

Introduction

The subject of knowledge management is arguably developing into a relatively mature academic topic, as there has now been a sustained interest in it since the mid-1990s. The focus of this chapter is on the linkages between knowledge management and the broad topic of human resource management. This is a not insignificant task, as a large body of literature now exists on both the sociocultural factors which shape workers' attitudes to knowledge management initiatives and also how HRM practices can be utilised to encourage workers to share their knowledge and participate in knowledge management initiatives.

The objective of this chapter is to illustrate why HRM issues are of central importance to the topic of knowledge management, and to give an overview of the way that the topics have been linked thus far in the literature. In doing so, the chapter will give a flavour of the many active debates and disagreements which still exist. Before proceeding any further, however, it is necessary to define the term knowledge management. At one level this is a simple task. Putting to the side the difficulties of defining such ambiguous terms as 'knowledge' and 'management', knowledge management can be defined as the attempt by an organisation to explicitly manage and control the knowledge of its workforce. However, the issue becomes more complex when it is recognised that there are a myriad number of ways by which this can be done. This can be illustrated by the number of typologies of knowledge management strategies that have been developed. One of the simplest, and most widely known is Hansen *et al.*'s (1999) distinction between personalisation and codification strategies, with a personalisation strategy focused on sharing knowledge between people, linked to a business strategy of knowledge creation. On the other hand, a codification strategy is focused on the codification of knowledge, linked to a business strategy of knowledge re-use. Hunter *et al.* (2002) and Alvesson and Karreman (2001) develop more complicated typologies, both of which produce four general knowledge management strategies. Of central significance to this chapter is that, as will be discussed in more detail later, the HRM implications of these different knowledge management strategies are quite distinctive.

The chapter begins by briefly examining the broad social context within which the growth of interest in knowledge management has occurred. Following this, subsequent sections consider how knowledge work is defined, why human motivation is key to making knowledge management initiatives successful, what general factors affect the willingness of workers to participate in knowledge management initiatives, and what specific HRM practices can be used to help persuade workers to participate in such initiatives.

 ## Social context: The growing importance of knowledge

The growth of interest in knowledge management that occurred in the mid-1990s can be to some extent explained by the growing significance of knowledge in contemporary economies. This has led many, both within and without the knowledge management literature to claim that we now live in a knowledge society. Thus, Littler and Innes (2003) suggest that the 'knowledge capitalism thesis' was one of the two dominant academic discourses during the 1990s and Tam *et al.* (2002) argue that such a belief has become 'conventional wisdom'.

Empirical evidence, to some extent backs up this claim, however, as will be seen later, this is one area of debate. The growing importance of knowledge to contemporary economies and organisations can be illustrated in a number of ways. First, since the 1950s there has been a growth in the proportion of knowledge workers in many economies. Reich (1991) showed that in the USA, between the 1950s and the 1990s, 'symbolic analysts' (his term for what contemporary writers call knowledge workers) grew from 8 per cent to 20 per cent of the workforce. Contemporary evidence from other economies also supports this (Frenkel *et al.*, 1999; Khatri *et al.*, 2010).

Critics, however, suggest that such claims and evidence provide only a partial and distorted view of the changes in the nature of work, neglecting the extent to which there has been a simultaneous growth in other types of work, such as low skilled, routine service work (Littler and Innes, 2003; Mansell and Steinmueller, 2000; Thompson *et al.* 2001). These writers suggest it is more accurate to talk of a bimodal trajectory in the contemporary evolution of work, with there being a simultaneous growth in highly skilled knowledge work, and low-skilled, routine service work. Thus, even if a sceptical perspective is taken to the 'knowledge society' rhetoric, it is undeniable that, to some extent, there has been a growth in the importance of knowledge in contemporary economies.

Arguably, the enormous numbers of organisations which have been attempting to develop and implement knowledge management initiatives are inspired by the idea that their competitiveness and innovativeness is derived and sustained from the way they manage, facilitate and control their knowledge base, and that neglecting to do so is likely to have negative consequences for organisational performance.

 ## Defining knowledge work

An enormous amount has been written on knowledge workers, and their growing importance is tied closely to the knowledge society perspective just discussed. Specifically, it is argued that for those societies that are evolving into knowledge societies, the number and importance of knowledge workers will increase significantly. Thus, as outlined, one of the key indicators used to establish whether a society can be characterised as being knowledge based is the proportion of knowledge workers employed in it. However, defining the types of work that can be considered to constitute knowledge work is by no means easy. This section therefore presents two contrasting definitions of the term.

The mainstream definition in the knowledge literature is that a knowledge worker is someone whose work is primarily intellectual in nature and which involves extensive and regular use of established bodies of formal, codified knowledge. From this perspective, knowledge workers represent an occupational elite: those workers who are in the vanguard of the knowledge economy, and whose work contributes significantly to the performance of their employers. Thus, as will be discussed later, they are typically regarded by their employers as workers who are worth retaining.

Based on such definitions, the range of occupations that are typically classified as knowledge work include:

- Lawyers (Hunter *et al.*, 2002)
- Consultants (Empson, 2001; Morris, 2001; Robertson and Swan, 2003)
- IT and software designers (Swart and Kinnie, 2003; Horowitz *et al.*, 2003),
- Advertising executives (Beaumont and Hunter, 2002)
- Scientists and engineers (Beaumont and Hunter, 2002, Benson and Brown, 2007)
- Artists and art directors/producers (Beaumont and Hunter, 2002).

Definitions of knowledge workers, therefore, overlap with and include the classical professions (such as lawyers, architects, etc.), but also extend beyond them to include a wide variety of other occupations (such as consultants, advertising executives, IT developers, etc.). Sometimes the term 'knowledge intensive work' is used to refer to such occupations due to the extent to which they involve the creation, and use of knowledge. However, the term 'knowledge intensive' has been criticised for being somewhat vague, making it open to interpretation which work constitutes knowledge intensive work (Alvesson, 2000).

However, embedded in such definitions of knowledge work is the privileging of certain forms of knowledge (abstract, theoretical, scientific knowledge) over other types of knowledge (tacit, contextual knowledge). Critics of the mainstream definition of knowledge workers, which ring-fences the term to refer to an elite range of occupations, argue that such definitions downplay, if not ignore the extent to which all forms of work involve the application and use of knowledge to some extent (Hislop, 2008, Thompson *et al.* 2001). Thus a second perspective on the definition of knowledge work is that in many ways all work can be defined as knowledge work.

Hislop (2008) outlines such a perspective through reconceptualising Frenkel *et al's* (1995) framework on knowledge work. Frenkel et al's (1995) framework provides a way of conceptualising all forms of work through taking account of three dimensions: knowledge, skills and level of creativity. The knowledge dimension takes account of the predominant form of knowledge used in work, with knowledge being characterised as being either theoretical, or contextual, with theoretical knowledge representing codified concepts and principles, which have general relevance, whereas by contrast contextual knowledge is largely tacit, and non-generalizible, being related to specific contexts of application. The skill dimension takes account of three types of skill: intellective, social and action based. Action-based skills relate to physical dexterity, social skills to the ability to motivate and manage others, while intellective skills are defined as the ability to undertake abstract reasoning and synthesise different ideas. Finally, the dimension of creativity (which is defined as a process of '*original problem-solving*', from which an original output is produced, (Frenkel *et al.*, 1995: 779) considers the level of creativity in work as varying on a sliding scale from low to high.

Using these dimensions, Frenkel *et al.* (1995) define a knowledge worker as anyone who firstly has a high level of creativity in their work, secondly, makes extensive use of intellective skills and finally, also makes use of theoretical rather than contextual knowledge. Thus conceptualised this framework is compatible with the mainstream, elitist professional knowledge work perspective. However, Hislop (2008) suggests that because it takes account of both contextual and theoretical knowledge, as well as the skill involved in work it can easily be reconceptualized to fit with the 'all work is knowledge work' perspective through defining knowledge work as any form of work involving the use of a reasonable amount of theoretical or contextual knowledge. This framework is illustrated at the end of the chapter through applying it to understand the character of two occupations, one of which fits the mainstream, elitist definition of knowledge work (management consultants) and one of which doesn't (office equipment service engineers).

Why worker motivation is key to achieving participation in knowledge management initiatives

As the knowledge management literature has evolved and developed there has been a growing awareness that taking account of sociocultural factors is key to the success of such initiatives. For example, a plethora of evidence shows how sociocultural factors such as levels of interpersonal trust, personality, national cultural values and organisational culture can play a crucial role in shaping the attitudes of workers to participating in knowledge management initiatives (Holste and Fields, 2010; Lam, 2005; Matzler *et al.*, 2011; Newell *et al.*, 2000; O'Dell and Hubert, 2011; Paroutis and Al Saleh, 2009; Teo *et al.*, 2011; Tong and Mitra, 2009).

Box 18.1 HRM in practice — Factors influencing knowledge sharing via Web 2.0 technologies

Paroutis and Al Saleh examined the factors that influenced people's decisions regarding whether to codify and share knowledge via Web 2.0 technologies within a single multinational corporation. They interviewed both users and non-users to understand their different rationales. In terms of the non-users, one of the main barriers which explained why they didn't use the Web 2.0 platform for knowledge-sharing was a lack of time, with it being perceived that using the Web 2.0 system could distract people from their main work activities. Second, they also had concerns about both the quality (*'it could come from a non-reliable source'*) and quantity (*'too much information'*) of knowledge that existed on the Web 2.0 system. Finally, people's unfamiliarity with the technology meant that they felt more comfortable sharing knowledge via traditional methods that they had always used.

In terms of the users of the Web 2.0 platform, a number of different benefits from using the system were articulated. First, it was regarded as both an effective way to communicate knowledge to other people, and also as a useful way of recording people's understanding and experiences (such as on a blog). Second, it was also regarded as a useful means by which to keep in touch with other people's latest ideas. Finally, it was felt that it could help people build and develop their social networks (*'I've built professional connections worldwide that would not otherwise exist'*) and their status (*'its helping to build a level of credibility'*).

Source: Paroutis and Al Saleh, 2009.

Part of the explanation for why workers cannot be assumed to be automatically willing to participate in knowledge management initiatives is due to structural factors which transcend individual organisations, including the power and status workers can typically derive from possessing specialist knowledge, the nature of employment relationship, and the potential for interpersonal/group conflict that exists in all organisations. First, not only is much organisational knowledge tacit and personal in character, being acquired and built up by workers over time, but the possession of knowledge can also be a significant source of power and status in organisations (Hislop, 2008; Horowitz *et al.*, 2003; Lam, 2005). This fact alone means that workers may be unwilling to participate in organisational knowledge management initiatives if they feel this involves 'giving away' a source of their power and/or status (Martin, 2006; Oltra, 2005).

Another structural factor affecting the willingness of workers to participate in knowledge management initiatives is the nature of the employment relationship, which results in the interest of workers and management not always being totally compatible. Thus, in relation to knowledge workers, there is potential conflict between workers and their employers over both who owns the knowledge of the worker, and how it is used. For example, Currie and Kerrin (2004) found that the knowledge management initiative undertaken by the large pharmaceutical company they researched, which occurred at the same time as a downsizing initiative, was relatively unsuccessful as many experienced managers were unwilling to share knowledge due to fears that it would be easier to make them redundant if they did so.

The potential for conflict in organisations also emanates from another structural factor: the real (and/or perceived) differences of interests between different workers and groups within organisations that inevitably exist (Marshall and Brady, 2001). In relation to knowledge management initiatives, the fact that, as discussed above, power and knowledge are closely inter-related, means that knowledge management initiatives can be used to play out what Storey and Barnett (2000) refer to as 'micro-political battles'. Thus, the attitudes towards and participation (or not) by workers in organisational knowledge management initiatives are shaped by the way such behaviours affect, and link into the political battles that are a part of the fabric of organisations.

This section has therefore shown how the participation of workers in organisational knowledge management initiatives cannot be taken for granted. The following two sections look at more specific factors within organisations which affect the attitudes of workers to knowledge management initiatives, and considers what HRM policies can be utilised to encourage the participation of workers in such initiatives.

The organisational climate and workers' attitudes to knowledge management initiatives

This section continues with the themes discussed in the previous section, why human motivation is key to the success of knowledge management initiatives, and why the participation of workers in knowledge management initiatives cannot be guaranteed. However, the focus here shifts from structural factors, which are to some extent beyond the control of organisational

Table 18.1 Research data on organisational factors affecting the attitudes of workers to organisational knowledge management initiatives

Factor affecting workers' attitudes towards participation in knowledge processes	Supporting evidence/analysis	Conclusions/findings
	Zhou *et al.* (2010)	Study of Chinese people which found that trust was positively related to knowledge sharing
	Holste and Fields (2010)	Study of managers within a not-for-profit organisation which found that trust was positively related to both the sharing and use of tacit knowledge
The existence of interpersonal trust and good working relations among co-workers	Cabrera *et al.* (2005)	Survey of a Spanish IT company which found that perceptions of support from colleagues was one of three key factors positively influencing workers' attitudes to knowledge sharing
	Lam (2005)	Case study of a failed KM initiative in an Indian IT consultancy company which showed workers were unwilling to codify and share knowledge due to the competitive, individualistic culture which existed

(Continued)

Table 18.1 Research data on organisational factors affecting the attitudes of workers to organisational knowledge management initiatives (cont.)

Factor affecting workers' attitudes towards participation in knowledge processes	Supporting evidence/analysis	Conclusions/findings
The existence of trust and good interpersonal relations between workers and their managers	Andrews and Delahaye (2000)	Case study of knowledge sharing among scientists which showed trust to be necessary for knowledge sharing to occur
	Li (2010)	IT-based knowledge sharing among US and Chinese workers positively related to the culture of knowledge sharing within the company
	Paroutis and Al Saleh (2009)	Knowledge sharing via Web 2.0 technologies found to be positively related to levels of organisational support
	Fong and Kwok (2009)	Study of constructions firms in Hong Kong found that the success of knowledge management activities was linked to management support for them
	Renzl (2008)	Survey of two companies which found that levels of trust in management were positively related to workers' attitudes to knowledge sharing
	MacNeil (2003)	Suggests the role of line managers in facilitating team/group-based knowledge sharing is key
	Ribiere and Sitar (2003)	The role of key leaders to success in developing appropriate knowledge cultures: leading by example, etc.
	Cabrera and Cabrera (2005)	Analysis suggests one key way to develop positive attitude to knowledge sharing is through developing a culture which regards knowledge sharing as a norm
Proper recognition and reward for work efforts and use of individual knowledge	Teo et al. (2011)	Case study of one division of Hewlett Packard which found that one key factor shaping participation in a knowledge management was recognition for knowledge sharing efforts.
	Han et al. (2010)	Study of workers in Taiwan which found that knowledge sharing was positively linked to participation in decision-making processes
	Robertson and Swan (2003)	Case study of a single consultancy showing how reward and recognition contribute to willingness by workers to participate in knowledge management initiatives
	McDermott and O'Dell (2001)	Knowledge management initiatives should be compatible with existing organisational culture

management, to factors affecting the general climate within organisations that are within the control of management. As outlined earlier, a lot of evidence shows sociocultural factors to be key in shaping the attitudes of workers to knowledge management initiatives. This section provides an abbreviated summary of this literature. While, this literature identifies an enormous diversity of factors that influence workers attitudes, these factors can be grouped into three general categories (see Table 18.1).

The overall, somewhat general conclusion from this evidence is that workers are most likely to be willing to participate in organisational knowledge management initiatives when the general organisational climate/culture is fair and positive, for example where people feel their efforts are fairly rewarded and interpersonal relations between workers, and also between workers and managers, are based on trust. The following section looks at the type of HRM practices which can be used to create such a climate, and which are thus likely to help facilitate organisational knowledge management initiatives.

HRM practices to support knowledge management initiatives

Before considering the way HRM practices can be used to help motivate workers to participate in organisational knowledge management initiatives, it is necessary to take account of the diversity of ways that organisations can manage their knowledge. As discussed earlier, a number of writers have developed typologies to categorise the range of knowledge management strategies that exist (Alvesson and Karreman, 2001, Hansen et al., 1999, Hunter *et al.*, 2002). Each particular approach to knowledge management requires different behaviours from workers. Thus, using Hansen *et al.*'s (1999) framework, a codification-based strategy requires workers to focus their knowledge management activities around the use of IT systems, where they should codify their own knowledge, and use IT-based knowledge repositories (such as searchable databases) to search for any knowledge they do not possess. On the other hand, a personalisation strategy requires workers to be willing to share their tacit knowledge directly with other people. Therefore, as each knowledge management strategy requires different behaviours, their HRM implications are distinctive.

The diversity of knowledge management strategies that exist means that it is impossible to develop a 'one best way' checklist of ways that HRM practices can be used to allow an organisation to effectively manage its knowledge. Ultimately, the way HRM practices are used requires account to be taken of the particular approach to knowledge management adopted by particular organisations (Haesli and Boxall, 2005).

HRM practices to facilitate knowledge management

In this subsection, consideration is given to how particular HRM practices can be used to motivate workers to actively participate in knowledge management initiatives.

Recruitment and selection

One way in which HRM practices can be used to underpin knowledge management initiatives is through using recruitment and selections processes to try and ensure that new staff have appropriate attitudes to organisational knowledge processes. The literature suggests there are two ways in which this can be done. First, recruitment and selection processes can be used to find people whose values and attitudes fit those of an organisation's existing culture and norms. For example, both Swart and Kinnie (2003) and Robertson and Swan (2003) found that the success of the knowledge-intensive firms they examined was partly related to their ability to recruit people who fitted in with the existing values of knowledge sharing and collegiality. Chen *et al.* (2011) reached similar conclusions in relation to the Taiwanese RandD engineers they examined.

How personality relates to knowledge sharing attitudes is a topic that is significantly under-researched. However, a number of studies in this area have concluded that certain personalities traits do appear to be positively related to knowledge sharing attitudes. Thus, the second way in which recruitment and selection processes could be used to facilitate organisational knowledge management efforts is through using personality tests to identify people who are likely to have positive attitudes to knowledge sharing. While all the studies in this area (Cabrera and Cabrera, 2005; Matzler *et al.*, 2011; Mooradian *et al.*, 2006) use the five-factor personality model, they come to different conclusions about which personality traits are related to positive knowledge sharing attitudes. Thus, Cabrera and Cabrera's (2005) research, which is based on a survey of a single Spanish organisation, found that the 'openness to change' personality variable was related to a positive knowledge sharing attitude. By contrast, Mooradian *et al.*'s (2006) study, which was also based on a survey of a single organisation found a link between 'agreeableness' and positive knowledge sharing attitudes. Finally, Matzler *et al.*'s (2011) study found that both agreeableness and conscientiousness were positively related to knowledge sharing attitudes. Thus, research in this area is in its infancy and does not come to firm conclusions regarding how personality is related to knowledge sharing attitudes. Therefore, the use of personality tests to identify positive knowledge sharing attitudes needs to be treated with caution.

Creating/sustaining appropriate cultures

One of the most common ways the literature suggests that HRM practices can be used to support knowledge management initiatives is through creating, developing and supporting an organisational culture that is conducive to knowledge sharing/use/development (Cabrera *et al.*, 2005; Robertson and O'Malley Hammersley, 2000). The general features of such a culture are that knowledge sharing is regarded as a norm and that people's knowledge sharing efforts will be well supported by colleagues, that staff have a strong sense of collective identity, that organisational processes are regarded as fair and finally, that staff have high levels of trust in and commitment to management. However, one of the weaknesses of much of this literature is that it is relatively vague on exactly what organisations need to do to create and sustain such cultures.

Further, within this literature there are debates which mirror those in the broader culture management literature (Mathew and Ogbonna, 2009). For example, there is a growing acknowledgement that organisations may not have coherent and unitary cultures, and that distinctive subcultures may exist which shape the characteristics and dynamics of organisational knowledge sharing processes. For example, Currie and Kerrin's (2003) study of knowledge sharing within the sales and marketing business of a UK pharmaceutical company found that the existence of strong sub-cultures within the sales and marketing divisions inhibited the sharing of knowledge between staff in them. Alavi *et al.* (2005–6), who examined how issues of culture shaped knowledge management practices in a US based global IT company found that some of the standard knowledge management tools utilised by the company were used differently within different sub-cultures. Thus, this research suggests that the utilisation of culture management practices to facilitate organisational knowledge management efforts needs to take account of the existence of any organisational subcultures that exist.

Job design

In the area of job design, there is virtual unanimity in the knowledge management literature about the best way to structure jobs to facilitate appropriate knowledge sharing attitudes. Fundamentally, work should be challenging and fulfilling, providing opportunities for workers both to utilise existing skills and knowledge, while also able to continuously develop their knowledge and skills (Robertson and O'Malley Hammersley, 2000; Swart and Kinnie, 2003). Thus, in Horowitz *et al.*'s (2003) survey of Singaporean knowledge workers and their managers, providing challenging work was ranked as the most important factor by managers for helping to retain their knowledge workers.

Further, as well as having work that is intrinsically interesting, the available evidence suggests that knowledge workers also typically regard having high levels of autonomy at work as important (Khatri *et al.*, 2010). For example, in the scientific consultancy examined by Robertson and Swan (2003), autonomy was found to be important to the consultants, and extended to areas as diverse as the projects they worked on (the consultants were free to pick and choose, so long as they reached their annual revenue targets), the selection of the training and development activities they undertook (it was the responsibility of the consultants to identify their own development needs, and funding was available to support this), work clothing and work patterns (a wide diversity of work patterns, personalities and clothing styles were apparent, and a culture of heterogeneity rather than conformity was developed and encouraged).

Finally, Cabrera and Cabrera (2005) suggest that if work is designed to allow the development of social capital between colleagues this can provide another way to facilitate interpersonal knowledge sharing within organisations. Two ways they suggest this can be done are through promoting and utilising team-based working (particularly cross-functional, interdisciplinary teams) and through encouraging the development of communities of practice.

Training

The previous section outlined the positive role that providing opportunities for self-development in work can play in motivating workers to participate in organisational knowledge management processes. While this can be done through the way jobs are organised, it can also be achieved through providing adequate and appropriate opportunities to undertake formal training. Research evidence suggests that knowledge workers regard the provision of such opportunities by their employers to be a crucially important way to help both motivate and retain them (Hunter *et al.,* 2002; Robertson and O'Malley Hammersley, 2000).

Various writers have suggested a number of more specific ways that particular types of training can facilitate appropriate knowledge behaviours. Thus, Hansen *et al.* (1999) suggest that the type of training provided should reflect the particular approach to knowledge management an organisation adopts, for example with IT-based training being suitable for those pursuing a codification-based strategy, whereas training to develop inter-personal skills and team-working being appropriate for organisations pursuing a personalisation knowledge management strategy. Further, Cabrera *et al.* (2005), whose study of a Spanish company found that self-efficacy (a person's belief in and confidence about their ability to perform a particular task) was related to positive knowledge sharing attitudes, suggest that investments in training focused on developing workers, self-efficacy levels may also benefit their knowledge management efforts.

Reward and performance appraisal

There is general agreement in the knowledge management literature that rewarding people for appropriate knowledge-related behaviours and embedding knowledge-related attitudes and behaviours in performance appraisal processes represents a potentially important way to use HRM practices to underpin organisational knowledge management efforts (Cabrera and Cabrera, 2005; Oltra 2005). Further, it is also agreed that such reward systems should reflect the particular knowledge management strategy adopted by an organisation and the type of knowledge processes associated with it. For example, Hansen *et al.* (1999) argue that if a codification strategy is pursued, the pay and reward systems should acknowledge employee efforts to codify their knowledge, and search for the knowledge of others, while with a personalization strategy, pay and reward systems should recognise the efforts of workers to share their tacit knowledge with each other.

However, at a more detailed level there is disagreement about exactly how reward systems can be used to facilitate positive attitudes and behaviours with respect to knowledge processes. Some research suggests that individually focused financial rewards can play a positive role. For example, Horowitz *et al.*'s survey of Singaporean knowledge workers found that providing a *'highly competitive pay package'* (2003: 32) was ranked as the second most effective way to help retain knowledge workers, with the lack of one being cited as the primary reason underlying the turnover of knowledge workers.

However, others suggest that such individually focused rewards can inhibit knowledge sharing through creating an instrumental attitude to knowledge sharing, and also through the way such reward mechanisms may undermine people's sense of team or community spirit and reduce the likelihood that people will share knowledge where the primary benefits of doing so are to the community or group (Fahey *et al.*, 2007). Such writers thus suggest that the best way to develop group-focused knowledge sharing is through making knowledge-related rewards group, rather than individually, focused (Cabrera and Cabrera, 2005; Chen *et al.*, 2011, Lam, 2005). Further, these writers suggest that non-financial rewards such as recognition can play an equally, if not more important role in facilitating and encouraging appropriate knowledge behaviours in people (Robertson and O'Malley Hammersley, 2000; Paroutis and Al Saleh, 2009, Teo *et al.*, 2011).

Box 18.2 HRM in practice — Integrating HRM practices to facilitate knowledge management

Chen *et al.* investigated how a range of different HRM practices affected the willingness of people within R&D teams in Taiwan to share knowledge. All the R&D teams surveyed were in high-technology industries (electronics, communications, precision machinery, semiconductors and optoelectronics). They analysed the surveys of over 200 employees from over 50 separate R&D teams. Overall, they found that most of the HRM practices examined did affect people's knowledge sharing behaviours. First they found that recruiting people who fitted with the existing culture and values of the teams promoted knowledge sharing. Second they also found that people's willingness to share knowledge was also positively related to the extent to which they perceived that their employer paid attention to their long-term career development. Finally, they found that performance appraisals which were focused on the individual inhibited people's willingness to share knowledge within teams. Thus, in the type of team-based contexts that they examined, team-focused, rather than individually focused performance appraisals are likely to facilitate knowledge sharing.

Source: Chen *et al.*, 2011

Retention: preventing knowledge loss through developing loyalty

Developing the loyalty of workers to their organisations represents another potentially important way for organisations to facilitate their knowledge management efforts. Having a high turnover rate of knowledge workers is a potentially significant problem for the organisations that employ them, due to some of the characteristics of knowledge workers outlined earlier (Alvesson, 2000; Beaumont and Hunter, 2002; Flood *et al.*, 2001). First, their knowledge is typically highly tacit. As outlined, one key source of knowledge possessed by knowledge workers is social capital, their knowledge of key individuals in client firms. Thus, when such workers leave, there is a risk for their employer that they will lose their clients as well. Second low retention rates may be a problem for knowledge intensive firms as the knowledge possessed by knowledge workers is often a crucial element in organisational performance. Thus, retaining workers who possess valuable knowledge should arguably be as important an element of an organisation's knowledge management strategy as motivating workers to participate in knowledge activities. This is because the tacit and embodied nature of much organisational knowledge means that when employees leave an organisation, they take their knowledge with them. As Byrne (2001: 325) so succinctly puts it, 'without loyalty knowledge is lost'.

However, some analyses suggest that many organisations have high turnover rates and find retaining knowledge workers difficult. This is to a large extent because labour market conditions, where the skills and knowledge of knowledge workers are typically relatively scarce, create conditions for knowledge workers which favour their mobility (Flood *et al.*, 2001, Horowitz *et al.*, 2003; Scarbrough, 1998). Benson and Brown (2007) present data from a counter-example where a large Australian research organisation did not suffer from such retention problems (see Box 18.3 below).

Alvesson (2000) argues that one of the best ways to deal with the turnover problem is to create organisational loyalty in staff, particularly through developing their sense of organisational identity. Alvesson identifies two broad types of loyalty: instrumental-based loyalty, and identification-based loyalty. Alvesson argues that the weakest form of loyalty is instrumental-based loyalty, which is when a worker remains loyal to their employer for as long as they receive specific personal benefits, with one of the most effective ways of developing such loyalty being through pay and working conditions. This conclusion is reinforced by the findings of Horowitz *et al.* (2003), as outlined in Table 18.2, which appears to present a general picture of knowledge workers displaying limited levels of organisational loyalty and being motivated to move jobs primarily by pay-related factors.

For Alvesson, the second, and stronger form of loyalty is identification-based loyalty, which is loyalty based on the worker having a strong sense of identity as a member of the organisation, and where the worker identifies with the goals and objectives of their organisation. There are three strategies for developing identification-based loyalty. First, there is an institutionally based strategy, where the organisation develops a particular vision or set of values that the knowledge worker identifies with. Second is what Alvesson refers to as a communitarian-based strategy, where workers develop a strong sense of being part of a cohesive team, which is achieved partly through the use of social events which allow bonding and the development of good social relations between workers. Finally, there is the socially integrative strategy, which is a combination of the institutionally based, and communitarian strategies. Joo's (2010) study on commitment and turnover intention with a large Korean firm provides support for the role that identification-based loyalty can play in facilitating commitment, as it found that people's levels of organisational commitment was positively related to the organisation's learning culture. This thus suggests that knowledge workers will be committed to their employers if they perceive that their organisation has an appropriate culture which supports knowledge and learning.

Table 18.2 Reasons for knowledge worker turnover

Reason for knowledge worker turnover	Percentage of organisations reporting this reason as most important
Better pay and prospects	39
Personal reasons	20
Career-related issues	13
Company-related issues	13
Market factors	10
Job-related issues	5

Source: Adapted from Horowitz *et al.*, 2003: 31, Figure 1.

Box 18.3 HRM in practice   **Loyalty and commitment among knowledge workers in Australia**

Benson and Brown (2007) report the findings of research on a large Australian organisation, which compared both the commitment levels, and its antecedents of some knowledge workers and routine workers. In contrast with their expectations, and with the findings of other studies into the loyalty of knowledge workers, they found that, when compared to the routine workers, the knowledge workers investigated had higher levels of attitudinal commitment.

Benson and Brown conceptualise commitment into two elements, attitudinal and behavioural commitment, with attitudinal commitment being related to a person's identification with their employer, while behavioural commitment relates to their loyalty and the extent to which they remain working for their employer. The literature on organisational commitment suggests that one of the consequences of workers having high commitment levels is that they are much less likely to leave their employer than workers with lower commitment levels. Thus, high levels of commitment aid retention.

Benson and Brown define knowledge workers in terms of three characteristics of the work they do. First, knowledge work involves variety and is typically non-routine. Second, knowledge work is highly interdependent, typically involving close collaboration with a number of work colleagues. Finally, knowledge workers typically have high levels of autonomy.

Based on the findings of existing published research they hypothesise that first knowledge workers will have lower levels of attitudinal commitment than routine workers and second that knowledge workers will have a higher intention to quit (lower level of behavioural commitment) than routine workers.

Benson and Brown's research was carried out in a large Australian 'semi-governmental, scientific research organisation' (2007: 128) which employed almost 7,000 staff. Its primary aim was to aid Australian industry and to encourage the development and application of scientific knowledge in industry.

Their analysis found that neither of the hypotheses tested were supported and they found the opposite of what they expected. Thus, in relation to their first hypothesis they found that 'knowledge workers had a significantly higher attitudinal commitment than routine-task employees', (2007: 132), and that in relation to their second hypothesis that knowledge workers had a lower intention to quit (higher levels of behavioural commitment) than routine workers.

Benson and Brown also investigated the antecedents of the knowledge workers' and routine workers' commitment, and found that there were different antecedents for each group. Of the four work organisation variables they examined, three (role ambiguity, co-worker support and supervisory support) were significant determinants of the attitudinal commitment of the knowledge workers, while only two were significant for the routine workers (role ambiguity and supervisory support).

To explain the unexpected finding that the commitment levels of the knowledge workers were higher for the knowledge workers than the routine workers, they argue that this may be due to one specific feature of the case study organisation, the prestigious international reputation that it had. Finally, the findings of their investigation into the antecedents of organisational commitment suggest that positive relations and support from co-workers crucially affected the knowledge workers' level of organisational commitment. Thus, developing good relations among colleagues represents one potential way to develop the commitment of knowledge workers.

Questions

1 Is the potential for conflict between workers and their employers over how the workers knowledge is used unavoidable? From a managerial perspective, what, if anything, can be done to minimise such potential conflict?

2 The dominant perspective in the knowledge worker literature is that to motivate and retain them their employers need to provide them with specific and privileged working conditions. Do the benefits of doing so outweigh the potential disadvantages that may occur, for example in creating resentment among other workers?

Further reading

Chen, W.-Y., Hsu, B.-F. and Lin, Y.-Y. (2011) 'Fostering knowledge sharing through human resource management in R&D teams', *International Journal of Technology Management,* Vol.53, Nos 2,3,4, 309–30.

Hislop, D. (2008) 'Conceptualizing knowledge work utilizing skill and knowledge-based concepts: the case of some consultants and service engineers', *Management Learning*, Vol.39, No.5, 579–97.

Hislop, D. (2009) *Knowledge Management in Organizations: A Critical Introduction*, Oxford: Oxford University Press.

CASE STUDY 18.1

DOMESTIC-POWERCO: SUPPORTING KNOWLEDGE SHARING AND USE AMONG DISTRIBUTED WORK TEAMS

DONALD HISLOP

This case study examines the way management and HRM practices are used to support the work and knowledge activities in an organisation whose workers are geographically dispersed and isolated, with few opportunities to interact and meet on a face-to-face basis.

ORGANISATIONAL CONTEXT

Domestic-Powerco is a UK-wide company whose main business is installing, repairing and servicing heating equipment in the homes of private individuals. During the 1990s, Domestic-Powerco management implemented a large-scale cost-cutting and restructuring programme, as such changes were believed necessary to allow the company to remain commercially competitive.

The research this case study is based on was carried out during the first half of 2003, with two colleagues of the author from Sheffield's Institute of Work Psychology. The research looked into the characteristics, knowledge sharing and communication dynamics of work that could be described as mobile telework, where people make extensive use of information and communication technologies as a central part of their work, and whose work requires geographic mobility between sites. The research study was small scale, and exploratory in nature, and in Domestic-Powerco involved extended, semi-structured interviews with six people who worked in the service, repair and installation division, in Lincolnshire and South Yorkshire.

Before the restructuring process it would have been inappropriate to describe the service engineers as mobile teleworkers, as while their work required them to be geographically mobile, the engineers were not required to use ICT's, and they all operated out of central depots, from which they started and finished their daily activities. During this period, while the engineers were required to work in customers' houses on their own, the fact that they began and finished work each day from a central depot, and had to return to the depot if they needed particular spare parts, meant that there were extensive opportunities to interact with, and share knowledge between engineers. This can be illustrated by the following quote, from one of the engineers interviewed,

> I can remember just before the depot shut, we had some outside assessors come in to look at our training, and ...the best training they saw was the informal training, with everyone stood around the locker, you know, and someone's got a part in their hand, and it's 'oh, don't take the right side off, do it from the left, it's a lot easier.

THE TRANSFORMATION OF SERVICE ENGINEERS INTO MOBILE TELE-WORKERS

The changes involved in the restructuring project were extremely radical in nature, and involved reducing the workforce from approximately 10,000 to 4,000. Further, there was also a programme to close an enormous number of the 450 depots that existed in the UK at that time, with offices and depots being rationalised into regional centres. As part of this process, the service engineers lost their bases in local depots. These workers no longer had any physical location at which they were based. While historically they had gone to the depot to be allocated jobs, under the new system this process was no longer necessary. Instead, each engineer, who had their own van and set of equipment, laptop and mobile phone, received their work instructions electronically. Thus, in terms of knowledge sharing, this change in working practices significantly reduced the opportunities for the type of interaction and knowledge sharing among peers illustrated by the first quote. This was summed up as follows by one of the engineers interviewed,

[Isolation] can be an issue. I think the one thing we have lost is the word-of-mouth to engineers, the group gathering in the morning. It is like taking a part of the social life off you. . . . A lot of the engineers would say the main thing they have lost is the contact with other engineers [about] this job.

As will be seen in the following section, Domestic-Powerco have recognised the consequences of these changes and have dealt with the loss of this informal means of knowledge sharing relatively successfully, through a number of mechanisms. However, among the engineers interviewed it was apparent that the organisational means to support interaction, communication and knowledge sharing did not totally satisfy their needs, and many of them developed their own informal means of doing this out of working hours, as illustrated in the following quotation,

We all go . . . to pick up our parts, and there's a canteen there and there's often four or five of us in the morning, so we'll go up and have a cup of tea and a chat, so we've gone together – we still do meet each other, you know go in half an hour before the shift starts.

MANAGERIAL AND HRM-RELATED SUPPORT FOR DOMESTIC-POWERCO'S SERVICE ENGINEERS

Domestic-Powerco was relatively successful at providing support for its service engineers. Despite the fact that many of the engineers felt their work did not give them adequate formal opportunities to interact with colleagues, which were substituted for by the type of informal meeting described above, those interviewed were relatively happy with their work. Further, there was no evidence that they were unwilling to do their work, utilise their knowledge and share their knowledge with colleagues where appropriate.

Categorising Domestic-Powerco's strategy for managing the knowledge of its workers is difficult, as it doesn't fall neatly into any of the categories developed by the academic literature. For example, in terms of Hansen *et al.*'s (1999) framework, as will be seen, there are elements of both a codification-based strategy, where electronic means are used to collect and disseminate codified knowledge, and a personalisation–based strategy, where means are used to facilitate and encourage interpersonal knowledge sharing.

There are three broad knowledge processes that Domestic-Powerco's engineers are required to utilise in order to be able to effectively do their job. First, they need to utilise and apply their acquired knowledge. For example, the diagnosis of problems is one important task they carry out, going into customers' homes with a vague description of a problem, which requires them to identify the precise problem and sort it out. Second, they need to continually acquire new knowledge, for example, learning how to install and repair new types of equipment. Finally, as with the photocopy engineers studied by Orr (1996), there is a need for engineers to search for and share knowledge with their peers. The following section outlines the range of processes Domestic-Powerco management utilised to facilitate and support these activities.

Training

There were a number of aspects to the training provided by Domestic-Powerco that supported the work activities and knowledge processes of their service engineers. First, there was a formal apprenticeship scheme, which was the basic training programme that new recruits with no previous experience were put on to learn the basic skills and knowledge of the job. This programme ran for a year with half of it being classroom-based, and half of it being on-the-job training in the region where the apprentices would finally be working. For the on-the-job part of the training apprentices went out with specific engineers and learned through both observing the engineers at work, and also by being allowed to do some tasks themselves.

The second aspect of Domestic-Powerco's training scheme, a buddy system, follows on immediately from the formal training programme, and is an extension and continuation of the engineers' on-the-job training with new engineers working full-time with experienced engineers. Thus in this period, new engineers do not visit any customers' homes without a more senior engineer with them. This process serves two purposes. First, it helps the new engineers develop their diagnostic skills in applying their formal learning to specific domestic situations. Second, it also allows new engineers to develop good working and social relations with a number of more experienced engineers, which helps them develop a network of people they can contact if they require support and advice in the future, as most engineers do.

Third, to provide the engineers with opportunities to update their skills and knowledge when necessary, there are a number of mobile training centres that tour the country, which groups of engineers take turns to go to. These centres are customised, articulated lorries, of which there are eight in the UK. For example, when a manufacturer launches a new piece of equipment, the mobile training centres may be used for this, as it allows the engineers to get hands-on experience looking at and working with the new equipment.

Finally, there is a system for providing staff with regular technical updates, in the form of codified knowledge and information that can be uploaded onto their laptops. This is discussed more below, in the section on codified knowledge.

Managerial support

An intrinsic element of the support system for the service engineers is provided by their managers. Groups of engineers are organised into geographically based teams of between 30 and 60, with one area manager being responsible for all the engineers in a particular area. For the 'small' areas that have only 30–40 engineers, the area manager is likely to have sole responsibility. For larger areas with over 50 engineers, the area manager will usually also have a supporting assistant manager working for them. With these supervisory ratios, the managers interviewed emphasised the importance of trust. Managers support and supervise their engineers through a combination of phone calls, team meetings (see below), and face-to-face meetings (close to customers homes, or when they are picking up parts from distribution depots). However, supervisory ratios mean that managers are only typically able to see and/or contact each of their engineers once a week. Therefore, a hands-off style of management is a necessity rather than a positive choice by managers. The day-to-day performance of engineers can be examined by managers via the performance management system that exists, which requires engineers to complete weekly, electronic activity sheets detailing what jobs they have been working on (see below).

Team meetings/social events

Another mechanism used to bring teams of engineers together, which offers the manager an opportunity to interact with them face-to-face, and allows the engineers to share relevant knowledge and information, and retain a sense of team spirit, are monthly team meetings. These are coordinated by the area manager, are typically relatively informal and ad hoc in nature, providing engineers with a forum to raise and discuss issues they regard as important. The staff interviewed also attended regular, team-based social events, organised outside working hours, but these were not a formal part of the management system, and were organised at the discretion of area managers.

Codified knowledge

A lot of codified knowledge was also used to support the engineers in their work. For example, their laptops had extensive, step-by-step lists of instructions, supported by relevant diagrams, for how to do most types of repair, on most types of equipment. Thus, theoretically, whatever model of equipment the customer had (with the exception of very old and outdated equipment), the engineer had, through their laptops, the resources to help them repair them. There were also regular (quarterly) updates of technical information sent to engineers on CD-roms. Finally, engineers also received some technical information as paperwork, via the postal system.

Technical support

The final form of support provided to the engineers 'in the field' was access to a 'technical helpline', which they could call up at any time if they found problems that they were unfamiliar with, or the information on their laptops did not cover. Thus, a lot of formal mechanisms existed to support the service engineers in their work, which acknowledged the isolated nature of their work, and provided mechanisms to search for and share knowledge and ideas when necessary

Pay/performance management

The final issue examined is the pay and performance management system that the service engineers had. While searching for, sharing and effectively utilising knowledge were key aspects of their work, there were no direct pay-related incentives or rewards for doing so. These activities were assumed to be an intrinsic element of the engineers' work, and it was therefore not deemed appropriate to provide bonuses for conducting such activities. The main aspect of variability in pay that existed was where extra pay was available for working weekends or holidays, and where engineers had to work overtime. The main way their performance was measured and monitored was on the quality of their work, and on their work-rate. Thus, each engineer had to complete a weekly activity sheet detailing all the jobs they had done. Every type of job they could do was allocated an amount of time to complete, and engineers had to ensure that they carried out enough jobs so that the time allocated to the total number of jobs they had done added up to the amount of hours they were meant to work in a particular week.

Questions

1 Is there more that Domestic-Powerco could have done with its payment and reward system to encourage/ reward appropriate knowledge sharing behaviours among engineers?
2 What would be the benefits and disadvantages of Domestic-Powerco providing formal support, within work time, for the informal, pre-work meetings that many engineers used to organise? Is it better to leave these meetings to be managed by staff informally, or for management?
3 Is the ratio of managers to engineers adequate, or too high? Reflect on the benefits and disadvantages of either increasing or decreasing this ratio, for both managers and engineers. Is changing this ratio significantly likely to have any impact on the knowledge sharing behaviours of the engineers?

CASE STUDY 18.2
OFFICE EQUIPMENT SERVICE ENGINEERS AND CONSULTANTS AS KNOWLEDGE WORKERS

DONALD HISLOP

INTRODUCTION

Hislop (2008) reconceptualised Frenkel *et al.*'s knowledge work framework to make it compatible with the 'all work is knowledge work' perspective. The utility of the revised framework was illustrated by using it to describe and understand the skills and knowledge involved in two different jobs: management consultants and office equipment service engineers.[1] Data on the engineers was collected via conducting interviews in three small office equipment servicing companies based in the same city in the English Midlands, while data on the consultants was collected via conducting interviews in two small HRM-focused management consultancies, from the north-west and south-west of England. Both these groups of workers were classified as knowledge workers, with the skills, knowledge and level of creativity involved in their work being summarised in Table 18.3.

OFFICE EQUIPMENT SERVICE ENGINEERS

The day-to-day work of the engineers involved visiting customers within a particular geographic area to repair, service and install office equipment such as copiers,

fax machines, printers and scanners. The number of clients visited per day typically varied from between two to seven dependent upon the complexity of particular jobs. For the service engineers, the level of creativity typically involved in their work was relatively low. This was because the majority of the jobs they did were relatively repetitive and required little diagnostic analysis, with most repair and service work involving dealing with similar types of repairs and tasks. In terms of the skill dimension of the framework, there was a reasonable need to make use of all three skill types. First, action-based skills were needed, as most jobs involved some amount of physically disassembling and reassembling equipment. Thus one engineer compared such work to carrying out a routine service on a car. Social skills were also necessary to allow effective communication not only with clients, but also with colleagues. The individualised nature of their work, which involved travelling to clients and working alone, required much of this communication work to be done by mobile phone.

The apparent simplicity of most jobs undertaken by the engineers was a little deceptive as it disguised the extent to which intellective skills were used. This was

---

[1]All the quotations presented in this case study are taken from Hislop, 2008.

Table 18.3 Characterising the work of management consultants and service engineers

		Management consultant	Service engineer
	Action-Based	Low	Medium
Skills	Social (including aesthetic and emotional)	Medium	Medium
	Intellective	High	Medium
Knowledge	Contextual	Important	Medium-important
	Theoretical	Very important	Low
Degree of creativity		High	Low–Medium

Source: From Hislop, 2008: 587, Table 2.

largely because these skills were relatively tacit, having been developed through experience. This process was summed up by one engineer as follows,

> You do the training course and they show you how the machine works: you take it apart. But when you get to that machine [on a job] it is when you start learning and obviously the first time you have a fault it might take you a couple of hours to figure out what it is and then the next time you go, because you have had it before you are straight in and sort it.

In terms of knowledge, the engineers made little if any use of theoretical knowledge, but their work did involve developing and utilising contextual knowledge. This consisted of an understanding, developed over time, of what the business needs of their client's office equipment were (the engineers covered specific geographic areas and over time visited the same clients many times), and how this impacted on the type of problems that typically developed. One engineer described this as follows,

> You get to know what they expect from the machine, which might be quite different from what someone else's identical machine expects.

Thus, the way their clients used their office equipment affected the type of faults that their equipment developed, and having an understanding of this constituted contextual knowledge for the engineers. They drew on this knowledge and combined it with the action-based and intellective skills they possessed in diagnosing and repairing these faults and carrying out their work.

MANAGEMENT CONSULTANTS

In contrast to the engineers, the work of the consultants involved a high level of creativity. The consultancy firms that were examined provided HRM-related advice to clients, primarily in the area of recruitment and selection. In the consultant interviews, one of the features of their work that provided the most job satisfaction was the level of variety involved in their work. For the consultants, no two client's needs and requirements were ever the same, thus every project the consultants worked on was different and involved developing a particular solution to the specific needs of each client.

In the skill dimension of the framework, while the consultants had negligible need to develop and use action-based skills, their work involved the frequent use of both social and intellective skills. As with the engineers, there were two features of their work which required them to use social skills, first in dealing with clients, and second in dealing with colleagues. The consultants needed to spend a significant amount of their time interacting with clients, face-to-face, by phone and email, as they needed to first work out what their requirements were, and then once they had developed a proposed solution they had to present it to their client, and if they were happy with this, they would help implement their solution. As with the engineers, the consultants spent much of their working day away from colleagues thus colleague-facing communication was mainly conducted by phone and email.

In understanding the nature of their intellective skills and how the consultants drew on them in their work it is useful to link them to the knowledge involved in their work. This is because all three were used simultaneously by the consultants in the key task their work involved: designing solutions to meet the specific needs of their various clients.

The work of the consultants involved the use of both theoretical and contextual knowledge. The need for theoretical knowledge and the intellectual character of the consultants' work can be seen in the fact that all the consultants are educated to at least degree level, with most having post-graduate qualifications. The contextual knowledge developed and used by the consultants related to the needs and requirements of their clients. Each client was different, and typically had diverse needs, thus with each project that the consultants worked on they had to develop their contextual knowledge of their client, largely through speaking to them and reading relevant documentation. The need for intellective skills in the work of the consultants involved bringing together their theoretical knowledge with the contextual knowledge they had developed of their client's needs to design bespoke solutions for each client. Thus, intellective skills were required in synthesising these two types of knowledge. This practical application of theoretical knowledge was another feature of their work they typically found rewarding. This process of using intellective skills to apply theory to particular situations was described by one consultant as follows,

I believe abstract theories are all very well but actually, really what you want is something that applies. It's good to actually put into practice theory and hopefully make a difference to some people.

CONCLUSION

From the perspective of the mainstream, professionally focused definition of knowledge work outlined earlier, only the management consultants would be labelled as knowledge workers. However, by taking account of both the contextual knowledge and intellective skills involved in the work of the engineers those adopting the 'all work is knowledge work' perspective consider it legitimate to label the work of both groups as constituting knowledge work.

Questions

1   Do you agree with the analysis that is presented, that due to the requirement of the service engineers to utilise contextual knowledge that they can be classified as knowledge workers?
2   If a knowledge worker is defined as anyone whose work involves the use of a reasonable amount of theoretical or contextual knowledge can you think of any occupations that it isn't appropriate to label knowledge work?

Bibliography

Alavi, M. Kayworth, T. and Leidner, D. (2005–6) 'An empirical examination of the influence of organizational culture on knowledge management practices', *Journal of Management Information Systems*, Vol.22, No.3, 191–224.

Alvesson, M. (2000) 'Social identity and the problem of loyalty in knowledge-intensive companies', *Journal of Management Studies*, Vol.37, No.8, 1101–23.

Alvesson, M. and Karreman, D. (2001) 'Odd couple: making sense of the curious concept of knowledge management', *Journal of Management Studies*, Vol.38, No.7, 995–1018.

Andrews, K. and Delahaye, B. (2000). 'Influences on knowledge processes in organisational learning: the psychosocial filter', *Journal of Management Studies*, Vol.37, No.6, 797–810.

Beaumont, P. and Hunter, L. (2002) *Managing Knowledge Workers*. London: CIPD.

Benson, J. and Brown, M. (2007), 'Knowledge workers: what keeps them committed; what turns them away', *Work, Employment and Society*, Vol.21, No.1, 121–41.

Byrne, R. (2001) 'Employees: capital or commodity?', *Career Development International*, Vol.6, No.6, 324–30.

Cabrera, E. and Cabrera, A. (2005) 'Fostering knowledge sharing through people management practices', *International Journal of Human Resource Management*, Vol.16, No.5, 720–35.

Cabrera, A., Collins, W. and Salgado, J. (2005) 'Determinants of individual engagement in knowledge sharing', *International Journal of Human Resource Management*, Vol.17, No.2, 245–64.

Chen, W.-Y., Hsu, B.-F. and Lin, Y.-Y. (2011) 'Fostering knowledge sharing through human resource management in R&D teams', *International Journal of Technology Management*, Vol.53, Nos.2,3,4, 309–30.

Currie, G. and Kerrin, M. (2003) 'Human resource management and knowledge management: enhancing knowledge sharing in a pharmaceutical company', *International Journal of Human Resource Management*, Vol.14, No.6, 1027–45.

Currie, G. and Kerrin, M. (2004) 'The limits of a technological fix to knowledge management', *Management Learning*, Vol.35, No.1, 9–29.

Empson, L. (2001) 'Fear of exploitation and fear of contamination: impediments to knowledge transfer in mergers between professional service firms', *Human Relations*, Vol.54, No.7, 839–62.

Fahey, R., Vasconcelos, A. and Ellis, D. (2007) 'The impact of rewards within communities of practice: a study of the SAP online global community', *Knowledge Management Research and Practice*, Vol.5, 186–98.

Flood, P., Turner, T., Ramamoorthy, N. and Pearson, J. (2001) 'Causes and consequences of psychological contracts among knowledge workers in the high technology and financial services industries', *International Journal of Human Resource Management*, Vol.12, No.7, 1152–65.

Fong, P. and Kwok, C. (2009) 'Organisational culture and knowledge management success at project and organisational levels in contracting firms', *Journal of Construction Engineering and Management*, Vol.135, No.12, 1348–56.

Frenkel, S., Korczynski, M., Donohue, L. and Shire, K. (1995) 'Re-constituting work: trends towards knowledge work and info-normative control', *Work, Employment and Society*, Vol.9, 773–96.

Frenkel, S., Korczynski, M., Shire, K. and Tam, M. (1999) *On the Front Line: Organization of Work in the Information Economy*, London: Cornell University Press.

Haesli, A. and Boxall, P. (2005). 'When knowledge management meets HR strategy: an exploration of personalization–retention and codification–recruitment configuration', *International Journal of Human Resource Management*, Vol.16, No.11, 1955–75.

Han, T-S., Chiang, H-H. and Chang, A. (2010) 'Employee participation in decision making, psychological ownership and knowledge sharing: mediating role of organizational commitment in Taiwanese high-tech organizations', *International Journal of Human Resource Management*, Vol.21, No.12, 2218–33.

Hansen, M., Nohria, N. and Tierney, T. (1999) 'What's your strategy for managing knowledge?', *Harvard Business Review*, Vol.77, No.2, 108–16.

Hislop, D. (2008) 'Conceptualizing knowledge work utilizing skill and knowledge-based concepts: the case of some consultants and service engineers', *Management Learning*, Vol.39, No.5, 579–97.

Hislop, D. (2009) *Knowledge Management in Organizations: A Critical Introduction*, Oxford: Oxford University Press.

Holste, J. and Fields, D. (2010) 'Trust and tacit knowledge sharing and use', *Journal of Knowledge Management*, Vol.14, No.1, 128–40.

Horowitz, F., Heng, C. and Quazi, H. (2003). 'Finders, keepers? Attracting, motivating and retaining knowledge workers', *Human Resource Management Journal*, Vol.13, No.4, 23–44.

Hunter, L., Beaumont, P. and Lee, M. (2002). 'Knowledge management practice in Scottish law firms,' *Human Resource Management Journal*, Vol.12, No.2, 4–21.

Joo, B.-K. (2010) 'Organizational commitment for knowledge workers: the roles of perceived organizational learning culture, leader–member exchange quality, and turnover intention', *Human Resource Development Quarterly*, Vol.21, No.1, 69–85.

Khatri, N., Baveja, A., Agarwal, N. and Brown, G. (2010) 'HR and IT capabilities and complementarities in knowledge intensive services', *International Journal of Human Resource Management*, Vol.21, No.15, 2889–909.

Lam, W. (2005) 'Successful knowledge management requires a knowledge culture: a case study', *Knowledge Management Research and Practice*, Vol.3, 206–17.

Li, W. (2010) 'Virtual knowledge sharing in a cross-cultural context', *Journal of Knowledge Management*, Vol.14, No.1, 38–50.

Littler, C. and Innes, D. (2003) 'Downsizing and deknowledging the firm', *Work, Employment and Society,* Vol.17, No.1, 73–100.

MacNeil, C. (2003) 'Line managers: facilitators of knowledge sharing in teams', *Employee Relations*, Vol.25, No.3, 294–307.

Mansell, R. and Steinmueller, W. (2000) *Mobilizing the Information Society: Strategies for Growth and Opportunity*, Oxford: Oxford University Press.

Marshall, N. and Brady, T. (2001), 'Knowledge management and the politics of knowledge: illustrations from complex product systems', *European Journal of Information Systems,* Vol.10, 99–112.

Martin, J. (2006) 'Multiple intelligence theory, knowledge identification and trust', *Knowledge Management Research and Practice*, Vol.4, No.3, 207–15.

Mathew, J. and Ogbonna, E. (2009), 'Organizational culture and commitment: a study of an Indian software organization', *International Journal of Human Resource Management*, Vol.20, No.3, 654–75.

Matzler, K., Renzl, B., Mooradian, T., von Krogh, G. and Mueller, J. (2011) 'Personality traits, affective commitment, documentation of knowledge and knowledge sharing', *International Journal of Human Resource Management*, Vol.22, No.2, 296–310.

McDermott, R. and O'Dell, C. (2001) 'Overcoming cultural barriers to sharing knowledge', *Journal of Knowledge Management*, Vol.5, No.1, 76–85.

Mooradian, T., Renzl, B. and Matzler, K. (2006) 'Who trusts? Personality trust and knowledge sharing', *Management Learning*, Vol.37, No.4, 523–40.

Morris, T. (2001) 'Asserting property rights: knowledge codification in the professional service firm', *Human Relations*, Vol.54, No.7, 819–38.

Neef, D. (1999) 'Making the case for knowledge management: the bigger picture', *Management Decision*, Vol.37, No.1, 72–8.

Newell, S., Scarbrough, H., Swan, J. and Hislop, D. (2000), 'Intranets and knowledge management: de-centred technologies and the limits of technological discourse', in pp. 88–106. Prichard, C., Hull, R., Chumer, M. and Willmott, H. (eds) *Managing Knowledge: Critical Investigations of Work and Learning*, London: MacMillan.

O'Dell, C. and Hubert, C. (2011) 'Building a knowledge sharing culture', *Journal for Quality and Participation*, Vol.34, No.2, 22–6.

Oltra, V. (2005) 'Knowledge management effectiveness factors: the role of HRM', *Journal of Knowledge Management*, Vol.9, No.4, 70–86.

Orr, J. (1996) *Talking About Machines: An Ethnography of a Modern Job*, Ithaca, NY: ILR Press.

Paroutis, S. and Al Saleh, A. (2009) 'Determinants of knowledge sharing using Web 2.0 technologies', *Journal of Knowledge Management*, Vol.13, No.4, 52–63.

Reich, R. (1991) *The Work of Nations: Preparing Ourselves for 21st-Century Capitalism*, London: Simon and Schuster.

Renzl, B. (2008) 'Trust in management and knowledge sharing: the mediating effects of fear and knowledge documentation', *Omega*, Vol.36, 206–20.

Ribiere, V. and Sitar, A. (2003) 'Critical role of leadership in nurturing a knowledge-supporting culture', *Knowledge Management Research and Practice*, Vol.1, No.1, 39–48.

Robertson, M. and O'Malley Hammersley, G. (2000) 'Knowledge management practices within a knowledge-intensive firm: the significance of the people management dimension', *Journal of European Industrial Training*, Vol.24, Nos 2–4, 241–53.

Robertson, M. and Swan, J. (2003) '"Control – what control?" Culture and ambiguity within a knowledge intensive firm', *Journal of Management Studies*, Vol.40, No.4, 831–58.

Scarbrough, H. (1998) 'Path(ological) dependency? Core competencies from an organizational perspective', *British Journal of Management*, Vol.9, No.3, 219–32.

Storey, J. and Barnett, E. (2000) 'Knowledge management initiatives: learning from failure', *Journal of Knowledge Management*, Vol.4, No.2, 145–56.

Swart, J. and Kinnie, N. (2003) 'Sharing knowledge in knowledge-intensive firms', *Human Resource Management Journal*, Vol.13, No.2, 60–75.

Swart, J. and Kinnie, N. (2010) 'Organisational learning, knowledge assets and HR practices in professional service firms', *Human Resource Management Journal*, Vol.20, No.1, 64–79.

Tam, Y., Korczynski, M. and Frenkel, S. (2002) 'Organizational and occupational commitment: knowledge workers in large corporation', *Journal of Management Studies*, Vol.39, No.6, 775–801.

Teo, T., Nishant, R., Goh, M. and Agarwal, S. (2011) 'Leveraging collaborative technologies to build a knowledge sharing culture at HP Analytics', *MIS Quarterly Executive*, Vol.10, No.1, 1–18.

Thompson, P., Warhurst, C. and Callaghan, G. (2001) 'Ignorant theory and knowledgeable workers: interrogating the connections between knowledge, skills and services', *Journal of Management Studies*, Vol.38, No.7, 923–42.

Tong, J. and Mitra, A. (2009) 'Chinese cultural influences on knowledge management practice', *Journal of Knowledge Management*, Vol.13, No.3, 49–62.

Zhou, S., Siu, F. and Wang, M. (2010) 'Effects of social tie content on knowledge transfer', *Journal of Knowledge Management*, Vol.14, No.3, 449–63.

CHAPTER 19
EMPLOYMENT ETHICS

Peter Ackers

> Ethics: The philosophical study of the moral value of human conduct and the rules and principles that *ought* to govern it.
>
> (*Collins Dictionary,* my emphasis)

Introduction

Employment ethics, as a subdivision of business ethics (see Chryssides and Kaler, 1993; Crane and Matten, 2004), involves the application of general moral principles to the management of employees' wages and conditions. In the same way as, say, sports or medical ethics, it begins with a concern about human relationships and how we treat other people. There are two dimensions to this: personal ethical issues at work and broader questions of business social responsibility. The first addresses the way you or I should behave, as responsible individuals, towards other employees and our employer. This might include questions like personal honesty in completing expenses forms, using the work telephone or internet facilities (see Mars, 1973), resisting the temptation of bribes, or simply kindness and consideration towards our workmates. Without a culture of personal ethics, high standards of business ethics are inconceivable. For this reason, many organisations now have an ethical code of practice to guide employee behaviour. The focus of this chapter, however, is on the second category, where you act as a management agent for the business organisation. In this case, while there is still scope for personal discretion, your approach to other employees will be heavily circumscribed by business policy. For instance, if 'the company' decides to close an entire factory or shop or make a group of employees redundant, you will be left, as an individual manager, to implement a decision whether or not you agree with it.

In this light, the chapter aims to guide the student through employment ethics as it applies to real business management practice, particularly in the Britain, past and present. As we shall see, this opens up a highly controversial, global public policy debate about the role and responsibilities of business in society, illustrated by recent British political arguments about the pay and bonuses of 'Bankers' (see Peston, 2008). Following some discussion of the complexities of applying ethics to business, various ethical theories are introduced by applying them to a real-life ethical problem. An employment ethics agenda is then established, contrasting, in broad economic policy terms, a right-wing emphasis on the free market with left-wing social regulation. These are then linked to two competing unitarist and pluralist conceptions of management as an ethical agent in employment relations. The next section sketches the history of ethical employment management, followed by an assessment of a critical development of recent decades, the advent of HRM as a new way of talking about labour management. The chapter closes by advocating an 'internal' stakeholder view of employment ethics as an antidote to three fallacies of recent HRM theory and practice (see Flanders, 1970).

To begin with, however, the process of translating ethics from personal behaviour to business practice is not straightforward. As we have seen, one initial complication to business ethics is that decisions about right and wrong are made by an impersonal organisation, rather than a single identifiable individual, as in some other spheres of moral decision making. A further apparent difficulty, compared this time to other fields of management activity, is that ethics is about what ought to be, rather than what is. In short, it involves value judgements and differences of opinion rather than just technical decisions. In truth, the same is true of almost all organisational policy affecting human beings; only elsewhere these value judgements are hidden behind technical-sounding words such as 'efficiency'. As Fox (1966) has argued, employment relations are always viewed through competing frames of reference leading to different interpretations of the situation. In this sense, 'ethics' should be seen as part and parcel of everyday personnel policy, not some entirely different realm of activity.

Employment ethics is still a highly problematic issue, for two further reasons. While modern business seeks the moral high ground, often for public relations purposes, sceptics retort that business ethics in general is an oxymoron, a contradiction in terms. Is not the main goal of business, after all, to maximise profits, with all other considerations, including the treatment of employees, coming a poor second? On the other hand, the employment relationship, between employer and employee, can become an especially deep-rooted and durable bond, evoking ethical notions of trust and loyalty. Paid work occupies many of our working hours and shapes our life chances, while HRM theory suggests that employees are a crucial resource to be nurtured, developed and retained by the business organisation (see Legge, 2004). Some argue that good ethics is, in fact, good business and, therefore, that no serious conflict exists between doing the right thing towards employees and improving business performance. This may be true for some businesses, some of the time. But more often 'being ethical' involves making difficult choices between expedience and principle.

While all ethics starts with common-sense claims about what is 'right' and 'fair', we soon find there are very different views about what these words mean. For this reason, we cannot say whether some employment policy is ethical or unethical, without referring back to which ethical theory we are applying. One central employment issue is how much we pay people. Let me imagine for a moment that I am the main shareholder and senior manager of a business organisation. A group of manual workers have asked for a 20 per cent wages increase, to provide 'a fair day's pay for a fair day's work'. Their language asserts an ethical claim. I want to act 'ethically', but how can I decide whether their claim is a just one? To take the matter further, we must enter what is popularly known as a 'moral maze'. While the detailed facts of the case are always important, the way we interpret them will be shaped by which ethical theory we choose to follow as the road to truth (see Chryssides and Kaler, 1993: 79–107; Winstanley and Woodall, 1999).

Ethical theories: enter the moral maze

One common-sense starting point is to look to the costs and benefits of awarding a pay rise and then to enter the passage into the maze marked 'Consequentialism'. Almost immediately, I begin to wonder how to weigh and measure these consequences. For instance, a pay increase will benefit these workers, but it will cut into my income as owner, perhaps reducing the amount I invest in new plant and machinery, spend on myself, or give to charity. How do I know which consequence is more beneficial? By now, however, my path has branched into another fairly wide thoroughfare entitled 'Utilitarianism', which claims to answer this question. Accordingly, whichever action gives the greatest happiness or utility is to be preferred. Since my employees are more numerous than me and on lower incomes, it may seem that a wage increase would be the most ethical course. But what of the broader consequences for happiness in society, if higher labour costs raise the cost of living for customers, or cut the incentive of entrepreneurs, like me, to establish business and create jobs? Another problem is that I do not know what the actual consequences will be, and can only guess. For instance, higher wages may benefit the business in the long run by improving employee performance and reducing labour turnover. Alternatively, higher labour costs may reduce competitiveness and lead to job loss. Thus, utilitarianism can nearly always provide good ammunition for both sides in an employment argument. More worrying, perhaps, it seems to provide a ready rationale for any employer seeking to wriggle out of social responsibility – which, of course, I am not.

A little discouraged, I retrace my steps to another, narrower passage, with the strange off-putting title of 'Deontology'. On closer inspection, however, we discover that this merely means that I should act out of duty and choose to 'do the right thing' irrespective of consequences. Indeed, this way purports to lead to a 'kingdom of ends' with two cardinal principles to guide my sense of duty. One is that I should be prepared to generalise or universalise my decision. So if I give these manual employees an increase, we will also have to consider the situation of office workers and whether they are being treated consistently. The second principle is that we must show a respect for persons, by treating them as an end in themselves and not a means to an end. In practical terms, this could mean that I should not sacrifice my present duty towards these employees – by rejecting their wage claim – in order to pursue the long-term best interests of my business and society. Indeed, one path branches off, called 'Human Rights', announcing that all employees have a 'right' to a decent living wage and so on. In this way, Kant's ethic of duty can appear so high-minded that it prevents business management from even considering economic factors, which may affect the long-term viability of the firm. Moreover, the assumption that we must act out of a sense of duty to be genuinely ethical appears to outlaw any considerations of economic self-interest. What happens, for instance, if my motive is disinterested, but I am also aware that granting an increase will solve the firm's labour turnover problems? Am I still acting ethically?

But how do I know that my primary duty lies towards these employees? Suddenly I notice two less obvious paths leading in diametrically opposite directions, each also departing from the deontological mainstream. The first 'Shareholder' way states boldly, 'Your primary duty is to the shareholders who own and invest in the company' (see Friedman 1993). Indeed, it turns out that their property rights can only be protected by keeping costs to a minimum, maximising profits and returning the best possible dividend. It is hard to see how a pay increase for employees can match these goals, unless it has a sound economic basis such as labour shortages or increased productivity. In this view, business efficiency must serve the shareholder, first and foremost. An alternative way, termed 'Stakeholding', argues that shareholders or investors are just one of several interest groups represented in the business corporation, including employees, customers, suppliers and the wider community. Accordingly, my ethical duty is to balance the needs of these different groups. Hence, if the pay and conditions of employees have been neglected in recent years, a pay award may be a justifiable piece of 'rebalancing'. On the other hand, if pay is already very high compared to elsewhere, and has been passed on in high prices to customers – as in Premier League football – this

Table 19.1 Fitting the ethical theories together

Consequentialist	Non-consequentialist
Utilitarianism	Kantianism
Happiness of the greatest number	Human dignity an end in itself
The end justifies the means	Universal moral rules
Language of economic utility	Language of human rights

will not be the right thing to do. The general problem remains of how to adjudicate ethically between the claims of the competing stakeholders. By this point, many passages have begun to merge and overlap, as stakeholding and shareholding each blur into utilitarianism on the one side, and human rights on the other, at some point on the way. As I have already begun to understand, the path to employment ethics is rarely easy.

At a clearing in the maze, however, a broad new passage begins, called 'Theories of Justice'. Yet within a few feet, this has divided in two completely different directions. The first route, 'Justice as Entitlement', eventually runs into the shareholder path on which we travelled earlier (see Nozick, 1993). This argues that human beings have a right to acquire and transfer property freely, providing they follow due process and avoid fraud and theft. Neither the government, nor any other organised pressure group, has a right to interfere in this free, and therefore fair, exchange. Seen in this light, my employees should conclude individual deals with me over wages and conditions, and accept whatever is the commercial going rate. Although I may pay them more, through kindness and charity – to borrow Kant's language – this is an 'imperfect duty' or an act of gratuitous generosity and it remains quite just to pay them the bare market rate. If, by banding together in a trade union, my employees are trying to 'force' me to pay a higher rate than I would from free choice, this is unjust and I would be right to resist their efforts. This view of justice neglects power inequalities in the employment relationship (see Colling and Terry, 2010), places little social responsibility on the business to protect the wages and conditions of employees and can lead to great economic inequality. It also demonstrates how far some ethical theories can depart from common-sense notions of fair treatment.

The other path, 'Justice as Fairness', leads to a table and chairs, where we all sit down, don blindfolds and think about what sort of society we would like to live in, without knowing what position we would occupy in it (see Rawls, 1993 and Case study 19.2). The conclusion drawn is that we would choose equal treatment except where differences work to the benefit of the worst off. We would not choose 'justice as entitlement' for fear that we might be born without talent or resources, and end up penniless and sleeping in the streets. Applied to my situation, this suggests that if the claimants are substantially poorer than I, or other shareholders and white-collar employees, I must either demonstrate that they benefit from these inequalities, or allow the pay claim. In defence, my unique skill and responsibility may be an adequate justification. Maybe to stay within the spirit of this social contract, I should give employees some say in the running of the business. This might involve establishing a consultation committee, including union representatives, having 'worker directors' or even turning the business into some sort of cooperative owned by the entire workforce, similar to the John Lewis Partnership. These options, if taken, lead into a common passage, shared with 'Stakeholding'. One linking way is 'Communitarianism' (see Etzioni, 1995), whereby we ponder not just the distribution of economic resources in terms of poverty and inequality, but also the impact on social cohesion. In short, will high manual pay contribute to a more tightly knit workforce and community?

After all this wandering in the moral maze, it is easy to become confused and disheartened. And there are three wide avenues radiating from a clearing, each promising a quick route to a satisfactory ethical conclusion. One, termed 'Divine Judgement', invites us to abandon all this confusion and buy a tried-and-tested set of moral rules, usually off the religious shelf. My problem is that rules like the Ten Commandments were devised long before the genesis of modern business, and are too general to tell me what to do in this precise situation. So while an ethical approach may be grounded in a religious tradition, this does not mean that there are easy, ready-made solutions to complex human problems. In a diverse modern society or workplace there is also the problem of appealing to others who have different religious beliefs or none, since employment ethics is also about dialogue and persuasion (see Fryer, 2011). In short, many of my employees have very different religious and ideological backgrounds, so I am searching for a broad language of ethics that will win their assent.

Another path, 'Ethical Relativism', runs in precisely the opposite direction, reassuring me that such diversity of opinion is unavoidable in our postmodern society, and recommending that I avoid the sort of universal claims made by the deontologists earlier (see Smith and Johnson, 1996). Far better to follow the shared opinion of my particular subculture, this approach suggests. I belong to many social circles, however, each with different ethical views, while my business friends simply press a shareholder view that is quite unacceptable to my employees. Finally, I encounter 'Enlightened Self-Interest', a way that reassures me that I worry too much (see Pearson, 1995). In the long term, good wages and conditions create loyal, productive, well-trained trustworthy employees, who, in turn, produce great rewards for all the stakeholders at the same time. This is the familiar human resource management (HRM) theory to which we return below. Yet still I wonder, how does this pay award help or hinder and what about the short term?

An employment ethics agenda

While the various ethical theories offer plenty of clues for what an ethical employment policy might look like, there are no straightforward and easy solutions that can be drawn from them. Moreover, most general ethical theories can be interpreted in very divergent ways. This said, the big debate in employment ethics concerns how far the state and social agencies, like trade unions, should be allowed to regulate the free market in order to protect workers' wages and conditions. And we can quickly see two main sides lining up and drawing together different elements from the above ethical theories.

The first, right-wing economic position stresses the utilitarian benefits of free-market capitalism, duty to the shareholder, justice as the entitlement to own and freely dispose of property, and a paternalist version of enlightened self-interest which renders state regulation unnecessary. The second, left-wing economic position emphasises the disutilities of short-term, free-market capitalism for society, employee rights, stakeholding, justice as fairness and a sceptical view of enlightened self-interest which presupposes the need for some state regulation to ensure good employment practices. In the USA, this division runs quite close to the right–left political and economic argument between Republican 'Conservatives' and Democratic 'Liberals'; whereas Europe, with its Social Democratic and Christian Democratic political traditions, leans more towards the second view. In these terms, the question of what is ethical employment practice transmutes into the question: how should employment be regulated and to what ends? But first, what sort of employment issues are we talking about?

Business ethics in general is already a major preoccupation of most large companies. Many corporate mission statements and ethical codes pay lip service to virtues such as integrity, fairness and loyalty and envision a variety of stakeholders, including employees. In some cases, this enthusiasm for ethics has been prompted by a scandal, which damaged a company's or industry's reputation, as with criticism of the banks for mis-selling pensions in the 1990s, the Enron case in the USA, or Shell's bad publicity over human rights in Nigeria. In other cases, ethics has been used as a marketing tool in a more proactive way. Hence, the Body Shop launched itself around a strong opposition to testing on animals for cosmetic purposes and has campaigned for fair trade with the Third World, while the Co-operative Bank has responded to customer objections to fur farming and investment in oppressive regimes (see Burchill, 1994). By and large, these companies have concentrated their attention on external public relations and the customer as a stakeholder, with the often undeclared assumption that stakeholding will work directly to improve the position of the shareholder. In all this, employees often appear as a poor relation in the family of stakeholders, such that companies can flaunt their ethics to customers while paying low wages and making thousands of workers redundant. Any distinctively employment ethics agenda will revolve around the damage caused to workers' wages and conditions by unregulated, flexible, free-market capitalism. In so far as customers and shareholders benefit from this regime – high dividends and low prices at the expense of low wages, for instance – it may reflect a clash of

Table 19.2 Capitalism and theories of justice – an interpretation

	Theory of justice	Corporate responsibility	Employment policies
Right wing	Nozick (entitlement)	Shareholder (unitarist)	Free market
Left wing	Rawls (fairness)	Stakeholder (pluralist)	Regulated market

stakeholder interests. As a consequence, employment ethics tends to deploy left-wing ethical arguments against free-market capitalism. Let us briefly rehearse four of these.

One points to fair pay and the enormous gap that has opened up between executive salaries and perks, on the one hand, and those of people in low-paid, temporary jobs on the other. The current British debate over 'Bankers' bonuses' is the latest instance of this. In deciding whether these are 'just' rewards we can apply Rawls' test – for example, senior management salaries are much lower in Europe and Japan than in Britain and the USA – and explore issues of 'merit' and 'need'. Likewise, the British national minimum wage is prompted by an ethical assessment that the 'market rate' is not always a fair rate and that the state has to intervene to regulate bad employers. On a global scale, this 'fair trade' argument applies not just to the price of fruit and vegetables, but to the wages and conditions of workers in the supply chain of large multinationals. Another issue related to the flexible labour market concerns individual and family welfare associated with working time. Some workers today are trapped in such sporadic, part-time and temporary work that they find it hard to support themselves, let alone a family. Other, better-paid salaried workers find it hard to draw boundaries between work and home life, such that they suffer stress and their relationships and children suffer neglect. In all these cases, as communitarians argue, the price for society may be family and community breakdown (see Ackers, 2002). Thus the European Union (EU) Working Time Directive, laying down a maximum 48-hour working week and minimum holiday provisions, rests on the assumption that in certain circumstances the free market can fail employees and society.

Two other issues are less directly economic in character. The first regards the right to employee participation, or the entitlement of workers (and the local community in cases of major plant closure), to have some say in the running of their business organisation. This relates to broader issues of corporate governance, and whose interests the business organisation should serve. Full-blown stakeholding or organisational pluralism demands some sort of representative structure by which workers can influence company decision making (see Ackers, 2010). In the past, trade unions played this role, and in many cases they still do. British legislation on statutory trade union recognition offers to bolster this union role. But this still begs the question of what happens across more than half of the economy where trade unions are completely absent. Within the EU, the European Social Chapter and various Directives have tried to entrench certain minimum standards for employee representation, information and consultations (see Chapter 17 on Employee Participation).

In addition to such positive rights, there is the issue of negative rights or civil liberties. For public sector workers in the EU these are now enshrined in the Human Rights Act. If left-wing thinking has often under-estimated the threat of the state to individual freedom, right-wing thinkers are equally blind to the threat posed by the large business. Equal opportunities issues around race, gender, disability and sexuality are already established in law and public policy. Measures against age discrimination have followed. But can an employer dismiss someone because they are fat, smoke, wear an earring or tattoo, or have eccentric religious or political views? In short, how far can a business, seeking to mould corporate culture, invade the private self of the individual employee or potential employee? This conundrum links to the question of whistleblowers or workers who expose unethical practices in their company. Does the business own their conscience because it pays the wages, or do they have a higher obligation to society?

Here again, a pluralist or stakeholding view of the corporation demands forms of external regulation to underpin these rights. Enlightened companies may address these issues of their own accord, through voluntary agreements, procedures and codes of practice. But, from this perspective, business as a whole cannot be trusted to do so. And firms with bad employment practices may gain short-term cost advantages and undermine the high standards elsewhere. In several of the above examples, recent British government or EU regulation has been prompted by the decline of trade unions and collective bargaining, leaving many employees exposed to the full power of the employer. Moreover, as we shall see below, employers in general have failed to fill this 'ethical gap' by voluntary action. This said, the state can only secure minimum standards, still leaving great scope for companies and managers to pioneer exemplary wages and conditions. Today, these may also include well resourced efforts to train and involve workers, as well as 'family-friendly' policies such as extended maternity and paternity provision, flexitime or nursery facilities.

Shaping an ethical workplace

If employment ethics is to mean anything in practice, we need to identify institutions or agencies capable of implementing it. Individual virtue is necessary, but not sufficient. Rarely does one person alone have the capacity to resolve an employment ethics dilemma, as in the wages scenario earlier. Economic life is highly complex and often beyond the scope of personal acts of goodwill. Only the state or substantial social institutions can impress some ethical pattern on the relationships that ensue. As Clegg's (1979) rule-making framework for employment relations suggests, three agencies can help to build an ethical approach into the very structure and process of economic life: from above, companies and their managers; from below, workers' own self-help organisations, most notably trade unions; and, finally, from without, the state as an expression of society's collective moral conscience. More recently, HRM academics have looked for new forms of social regulation – beyond the state and trade unions – by charities and civil society pressure groups (Williams *et al.*, 2011).

Let us turn now to the most pervasive rule-making agent in most contemporary employment relationships: employers and the professional managers who act on their behalf. Even where the state and trade unions play a central part in framing the employment relationship, the chosen style of employers and managers is crucial in defining the experience of work. While some good practices can be imposed from outside – as with racial and sexual discrimination or minimum wages – the devil is in the detail, and 'company culture' may become a major obstacle to the full realisation of an ethical workplace. In order to understand what role management can play, I will sketch the historical evolution of management practice, particularly in relation to the personnel function, and then look more closely at the experience of HRM; a management concept that has gained wider global currency since the 1980s (see Chapter 1). First, though, we need to understand what management is and what real capacity it has to shape the ethical tone of the enterprise.

Today, employer regulation is only rarely exercised by the single owner in person, except in the small business. Management is the collective name for a stratum of specialist, technical workers who act as the employer's (or shareholders') agents in day-to-day dealings with the workforce. As businesses grow in size, and as the personality of the individual owner fragments into the thousands of anonymous individual and institutional shareholders of the modern public limited company, managers become the visible hands and face of employer power. In line with modern rational–legal authority and scientific management, the extensive and ill-defined prerogatives of the individual master are broken down into a specialist management hierarchy. In large, complex organisations, this managerial division of labour is characterised by horizontal layers according to seniority, and vertical lines of function. At the apex, there are senior managers, headed by the managing director, who concentrate on business strategy; while, at the base, are line managers or supervisors who deal directly and regularly with ordinary workers. In between, lie various strata of middle managers who connect the two types of activity. Those at the two opposite ends of the management ladder tend to be general managers, but most of the intermediaries are allocated some specialist function, such as marketing, production or personnel. This management specialism is reinforced by some professional organisation and identity as is the case with groups like accountants, or more pertinently for us, HRM or personnel managers.

While few would dispute this general description of management, there is far greater controversy over who exactly managers are answerable to, and what their social responsibilities are. What we expect of managers in the business organisation depends largely on our chosen frame of reference and this is likely to dovetail with one of the competing ethical theories discussed above. For the unitarists, differences of management function and level are a purely technical issue, subordinate to their single purpose as the unquestioning agents of the shareholder owners. This 'stockholder' conception is enshrined in Anglo-American company law, though not in continental European stakeholder traditions. As the right-wing economist Milton Friedman (1993) argues, once managers or companies take on goals and responsibilities which do not serve their ultimate aim of higher profits, they betray their ultimate employers and endanger the whole future of the enterprise, indeed of capitalism itself. In short, absolute adherence to market principles outside the business and to the single line of authority within it, are but two sides of the same unitarist coin.

By contrast, pluralists are likely to perceive and welcome much greater diversity of allegiance and objectives among modern managers, for two main reasons. First, from a purely sociological point of view, this conforms to their image of the business as fractured by competing interest groups, including various management levels and functions. Thus, senior company directors often belong to the Institute of Directors, while line managers join supervisory trade unions. Personnel specialists seek professional status and accreditation through the Chartered Institute of Personnel and Development (CIPD) courses and exams – modelled on other professional bodies such as the British Medical Association and the Law Society. Second, from a more normative perspective, this view of managers also provides them with some scope to exercise independent ethical action, as is implied in the ethical codes of bodies like the CIPD. They are no longer just servants of the shareholders, at their every beck and call. Rather, they hold responsibilities to all the stakeholders in the organisation, including workers, customers and the local community, and to society as a whole. As always, observed fact and value judgement become intertwined. Post-war pluralist industrial relations thinkers such as Flanders (1970) found hope in the growing separation between the ownership and control of large public limited companies, precisely because it created new scope for professional managers to exercise a more spacious and socially responsible role. For them formal ownership no longer mattered, since *de facto* pluralism reigned even where, as in Britain, company law did not provide for this. In this they have been proved mistaken, for under Margaret Thatcher after 1979 a free-market government rolled back the blanket of state protection and trade union influence to reveal the short-term shareholder model beneath. For these reasons, the ethical role of management must be closely related to the responsibilities of business and the way in which society defines these.

The greatest burden of pluralist hopes lay upon the shoulders of personnel, the company function and department that specialises in dealing with employees and their representatives. This aspiring management profession seemed to personify the broader social concerns of management, as in the old conception of personnel managers as enlightened umpires, bringing management and workers together, and creating industrial relations concord. As we shall see, the history of personnel management has parallels with the growth of social work, beginning as a predominately female caring profession concerned with people. Below, I ponder whether the new title of HRM marks a rediscovery of this ethical mission, as some suggest, or an irrevocable break from any emphasis on workers as social beings, towards a calculating image of them as mere economic counters. But the management of people has never been the exclusive mandate of personnel. So it is important to set personnel's fluctuating role in the broader context of the overall management style adopted by the business towards employees, from the senior managers who attempt to shape the culture of the organisation, down to the line managers who actually conduct most relations between management and ordinary workers (see Fox, 1974).

A brief history of ethical employment management

In *History and Heritage* (1985: 1–30), Alan Fox identifies two competing systems of labour control as, from the eighteenth century onwards, British society adjusted to the modern, capitalist employment relationship. Each operated at the level of state policy and law and through the strategies of individual business units. In this, there is much that is familiar today, all over the world. The first strategy, paternalism, was carried over from the pre-industrial past, and combined notions of worker deference and a rigid social hierarchy with a sense of ruling-class social responsibility. Hence, for many years, wage levels and customary rights were underwritten by law, partly for fear that a desperate and dispossessed poor would prove dangerous to the rich and powerful. The second strategy, market individualism, was informed by the new capitalist economic order that was breaking free of these semi-feudal bonds. This challenged the notion of a fixed social order and focused on the rights of individuals in politics, while reinterpreting the employment relationship as a private economic contract. Either approach was a mixed blessing for ordinary working people. While paternalism locked workers into a position of permanent subordination, as a price for some moral concern and social protection; market individualism threatened to cast them adrift with no reliable source of income or living, in exchange for the opportunity to freely sell their labour at the best price and better themselves.

Today, the balance between these two strategies has been largely reversed, at least at the level of the firm, with market individualism being regarded as the normal economic relationship and paternalism a noteworthy and deviant one (see Ackers, 1998, 2001; Ackers and Black, 1991). None the less, the same tension in management strategy continues and connects with the central right-wing/left-wing ethical and economic divide outlined above. Should the business manage labour as an economic commodity, to be bought on the market at the cheapest possible price, or seek a long-term social relationship with their employees that transcends instant economic calculation? In most cases, the solution is a compromise between market and managerial relations, for, while labour may be hired in an outside marketplace, it can only be put to work in the social context of the workplace. For these reasons, though market individualism may be in the driving seat, it can rarely control the vehicle without some element of paternalism seated alongside. The development of management in general, and personnel management in particular, reflects this need to control and motivate the workforce as a social group, and passed through two main stages prior to the current era of HRM.

Stage one, roughly from the Victorian period to the Second World War in most large British companies, saw a new social hybrid, paternalist capitalism, emerge from the antisocial anarchy of early capitalism (see Ackers and Black, 1991; Greene *et al.,* 2001; Joyce, 1980). It is not surprising, therefore, that the birth of personnel management, as a distinctive profession, with its own authoritative body, code of practice and range of qualifications, coincided with the late Victorian movement towards a more socially conscious, if paternalist, employer style of management. As Britain settled down into more stable work communities, some large employers, influenced by Christian ideas about social responsibility, sought to shape a stronger social dimension to their businesses and the communities in which they operated. Many work towns of the early industrial revolution were merely factories surrounded by cheap housing for their workers – like the shanty towns of the developing world today. They lacked the most basic facilities, such as schools and sewage systems. To a large extent, the new working classes began to create their own civilisation through self-help bodies like trade unions, local religious congregations and cooperative societies.

However, enlightened employers also played an important part, for a mixture of motives including disinterested public service, personal self-aggrandisement and a concern for work discipline and social cohesion. Through involvement in local government or by personal direct donations, they sponsored the creation of social and cultural amenities like parks, chapels and libraries. At the turn of the century, the Quaker George Cadbury built the chocolate factory and garden city of Bournville, Birmingham for his workers and the local community. In the midst of acres of pleasant houses with large gardens stood the model factory, with its exemplary working conditions, splendid playing fields and welfare facilities. Bournville remains an impressive spectacle today, but the company has recently been acquired by an American multinational and thus Cadbury has followed the historical journey of many such firms.

Personnel management emerged from large-scale Victorian paternalist capitalism, as direct personal contact between master and servant declined, and the employer families sought more institutional expressions of their ethical calling. According to Torrington and Hall's (1991) rather idealised seven-stage taxonomy, social reformers were the first on the scene, notably the Quaker chocolate manufacturer's wife, Elizabeth Fry, who conducted social work outside the factory and campaigned for legislation to protect health and safety. Next, during the full flowering of Christian paternalism, on the Bournville scale, came the welfare officer, again usually a woman, who conducted industrial social work within the workplace. This brought social concern in line with the modern management division of labour then emerging in large factories. Thus, in 1913, the Institute of Welfare Officers was formed at Rowntree's York chocolate factory. In this respect, personnel began with the same high ideals of caring for employees as the best representatives of paternalist capitalism, and travelled with them from a personal to a professional and institutional expression of these values.

However, a number of factors began to unpick the fabric of paternalist capitalism, so that from the 1930s onwards a new modern bureaucratic company emerged associated with a more scientific and less moralistic personnel outlook (see Kynaston, 2008). By 1945 the sense of religious mission had entered into decline, as part of the general secularisation of mid-twentieth-century Britain. Trade unions had advanced during 'the people's war', which itself had eroded the spirit of worker deference. A comprehensive welfare state, meanwhile, superseded many company provisions. Otherwise, the main reason for the retreat of religious paternalism was the demise of the owner-manager and the private family company. This presents something of a paradox for pluralist advocates of social responsibility, since the growing separation of ownership and control destroyed the personal moral responsibility of individual or family ownership. Business owners moved away from the dirty towns they had created to live as country gentlemen, passed the running of the business completely to professional managers, and, ultimately, sold their shares to the highest bidder. Their children were educated at exclusive schools, and most preferred a genteel lifestyle to managing an ugly factory or busy store. As ownership of the new joint stock companies devolved to a multitude of passive shareholders and pension funds, only interested in a return on their investment, the guiding hand of employer paternalism slipped from view. To many employees this was welcome, since company beneficence had often gone hand in hand with a desire to interfere in and shape their private lives outside work (see Case study 19.1).

In this new era of rational–legal authority, when professional career managers ran the business and trade unions represented workers' interests, the religious language of calling and service appeared condescending and redundant. The emerging professions of teaching, social work and personnel reflected a new spirit of value-free social engineering. At work, social science theories of behaviour, such as scientific management and human relations, supplanted ethical idealism. During this phase, most employers withdrew from an active ethical role in both their business and the local community, as the welfare state and local government supplanted many of their earlier roles. Workers became more independent of their employers, preferring higher pay to cricket pitches, sermons and company picnics, and trade unions to consultative arrangements. In the long run, however, there would be a price to pay for this, as the business corporation was able to divest itself of any social responsibility beyond the efficient pursuit of profit.

Torrington and Hall (1991) identify four new and overlapping personnel roles which arose in this second period. The humane bureaucrat, a management specialist with skills in selection and training, first appeared during the inter-war years at public limited companies like the chemical giant, ICI. Later, after the Second World War, a company-level industrial relations role gained increasing importance. From the 1950s onwards, collective bargaining with trade unions was pulled down to the workplace, calling for negotiating expertise at that level. This saw the arrival of the consensus negotiator, or contracts manager, a tough masculine role, involving new skills of conflict resolution. At the same time, the organisation person was concerned with the effectiveness of the whole organisation, and not just employee welfare, linking together other management activities through their role in management development. Meanwhile, the manpower analyst set about quantifying human resources, for instance by measuring the cost of labour turnover and planning the labour supply. A concern for employee welfare still lingered on in these roles, though not as an end in itself, even in theory. Even the consensus negotiators restricted their relations with employees to the arm's-length, institutionalised relationship with trade union representatives. If the soul had gone out of personnel management, it seemed that at least a disinterested profession had been created, with an apparently social scientific knowledge base linked to practical skills.

Before turning to contemporary developments associated with HRM, it is important to qualify this generalised image of British business history. Sophisticated modern companies, such as Cadbury's, were far from the norm in the history of British industrial relations. What we have seen so far is the best parts of business putting their best face forward. For, as Fox (1985) argues, market individualism remained the dominant preference of British employers, tempered only by the often uninvited presence of trade unions that forced businesses to confront the collective nature of the employment relationship through detailed personnel policies. These standard modern employers embraced trade unions as a short-term and pragmatic response to organised labour, rather than as a principled, long-term social vision of the employment relationship (Fox, 1974). Most industrial relations commentators see this dual view of labour – a commodity in the external market and a cost within the firm – as conducive to a relatively low-skilled, low-waged and poorly trained labour force, in contrast to the best continental practice in economies like Germany. Many draw on Hall and Soskice's (2001) 'varieties of capitalism' framework to distinguish between 'co-ordinated' economies that invest heavily in labour and 'liberal market' economies, like the UK and USA, that tend not to (see Colling and Terry, 2010). Arguably, too, this latter mentality has denied personnel its proper status in the business organisation, creating a ragbag of low-status administrators and industrial relations firefighters, rather than a cohesive profession of influential employment architects (see Sisson, 1994). This, in turn, has stymied the development of distinctively ethical employment policies.

The advent of HRM

Britain offers an excellent historical laboratory for these theories, since radical Conservative governments revolutionised economic life between 1979 and 1997, transforming the country from a co-ordinated to liberal-market economy. This third period of employment management coincided with the absorption of US-style management concepts, such as HRM itself and Employee Involvement, presenting a remarkable opportunity for business to demonstrate its concern for employees, unhindered by state or trade union regulation. For two decades, the right-wing ethical perspective reigned supreme. During these years, management was cast as the principal agent of social change, and the rhetoric of the enterprise culture spoke eloquently of employee involvement and commitment, while remaining strangely silent about justice and rights at work (see Ackers, 1994). For personnel, HRM was the big new theme in management thinking that tied together these various initiatives and promised a new constructive role for people management in the workplace. It is to this that we now turn. Hitherto, the academic debate over HRM has revolved around the poles of 'rhetoric' and 'reality' (Legge, 1995). In other words, has business lived up to the promises it has made? We begin, therefore, with the claims of HRM in theory and then turn to what this has meant for the employment relationship in practice.

The ethical rhetoric of HRM is everywhere in contemporary business and society. Some variation on the phrase – 'this business regards employees as its number one resource' – has become part of the ritual of company reports and briefings, tripping easily from the lips of chief executives. The CIPD's magazine, *People Management,* is now subtitled '*the magazine for human resources professionals*'. The sleek new HRM model is boldly contrasted with the 'bad old days' of personnel past, much as born-again Christians sometimes celebrate their new creation by darkening their own past (see Ackers and Preston, 1997; Clark, 1993). Before, labour was a cost to be controlled; now, a resource to be nurtured. Before, personnel was a routine administrative activity; now, a strategic champion of people management for heightened business performance. Before, industrial relations was adversarial and arm's length; now, founded on consensus and employee consent. Before, personnel coveted people management; now, a human relations gospel for all. Rather than chase all these hares, as so many others have already, let us concentrate, first, on HRM's central claim – to have made human resources more central to today's businesses than they were a generation ago. This, after all, is one key test of the ethical employment credentials of contemporary business.

Sisson's (1994: 42) authoritative summary of the survey and case study evidence on the Conservative free-market experiment in Britain concludes that 'personnel management in many organisations in Britain is locked into a vicious circle of low pay, low skill, and low productivity'. This is surprising, as he recognises, since HRM had promised exactly the opposite, arguing that people are the key to competitive advantage for advanced economies where the low-cost labour is not an option. Old, rigid and authoritarian forms of management control were supposed to yield to 'the development of a highly committed and adaptable workforce willing and able to learn new skills and take on new tasks'. At face value, British business appeared to be placing a new stress on human resources, and this is the conventional wisdom taught in many business schools. However, much HRM research paints a more depressing picture. Following Fox (1985) and MacInnes (1987), this suggests that the enterprise culture has exacerbated the laissez-faire, short-term, cost-reduction employer attitudes to labour, endemic in the British employment relations tradition. Moreover, the definitive Workplace Employment Relations Surveys suggest that HRM in practice has not been so widespread (Cully *et al.,* 1999; Kersley *et al.,* 2004; Millward *et al.,* 1992). Yes, some HRM techniques, like employee involvement, are common in mainstream companies, often where trade unions remain a factor. Yet, where management has a free hand, in the now majority non-union sector, there is little evidence of a new 'ethical' HRM approach to managing labour.

The obvious conclusion is that union representation and effective joint regulation was often replaced, not by a new enlightened HRM, but by a tough 'bleak house' or 'low road' hire-and-fire employment policy. This tends to support the view of labour as a disposable commodity, a cost to be controlled rather than a resource to be developed. At this level, employment ethics is mainly about good public relations towards customers and staying on the right side of the law. Accordingly, this Anglo-American share or 'stockholder' model concentrates on short-term costs, profits and dividends, dictated by city and financial markets. As in the past, British capital is adjudged short-term and cost-minimising in outlook, failing to invest in labour as a resource; while management remains attached to crude, cost-effective, payment-by-results systems. Within this liberal-market framework, there is very little space for active employment ethics. Sisson (1994: 42–44) argued that for this to change,

> There would have to be a fundamental reappraisal of the way in which British companies are run .... A policy of laissez-faire not only sends the wrong signals, above all to small and medium-sized businesses, it also fails to take into account that, left to their own devices, many UK companies will find the 'high pay, high skill, high productivity' route quite simply beyond them.

He proposed the following stakeholding initiatives:

> overhauling the regulatory framework of companies and their relationships with the city; developing an appropriate training system; and introducing a legal framework of rights and obligations that would help to raise standards ... the kind of framework that our partners in Europe are anxious to introduce in the form of the Social Charter.

This is a powerful and influential analysis of HRM in practice, which Sisson and Purcell (2010) and others have recently restated, even after a further decade of 'New Labour Governments' (1997–2010), which appeared to move the UK away from the more extreme free market model (see Colling and Terry, 2010). There are two objections. The first is that this was always too sweeping a generalisation. Even within a liberal-market economy with large areas of low wage employment, there are still major sectors (public service, financial services, high-value manufacturing and so on) and many firms that take a more resource-based view, for instance through partnership relations with trade unions (see Ackers, 2012). This means that many companies and managers do still have the ethical choice of pursuing the 'high road' of good wages and conditions. Second, increased British and EU regulation since 1997 has created a regulatory environment that is more favourable than before to this high road – without transforming the world in the way Sisson had hoped. So a national minimum wage set a floor on falling wage levels; while statutory union recognition legislation and government encouragement of 'partnership' between employers and trade unions stabilising the decline of the latter; and policies on family leave and part-time work provided more protection for employees.

All this said HRM rhetoric still has to translate into a consistent, generalised management approach that values people, even in its own economic terms, as a resource. But if the reality of HRM has proved a disappointment so far, maybe the idea at least is worthwhile. It is to this that we now turn.

Conclusion: three fallacies of HRM ethics

Much of the above analysis presupposes that HRM has failed because British institutions have frustrated the managerial reforms that could have made it a reality; not that the management philosophy and language of HRM itself presents a positive barrier to any progress towards a more 'ethical' workplace. Only rarely has anyone asked whether the rhetoric, let alone the practice, offers an attractive and credible vision of the world of work and management's place in this (see Hart, 1993; Torrington, 1993). This brings us to the Kantian heart of the matter: how should we treat fellow human beings? Do we regard employees and thus the employment relationship as something of intrinsic human value, even when this operates within an economic framework; or do we regard workers like machines, as simply means to an economic end. Here the normative language of HRM matters as much as its practical consequences – though the two are never unrelated.

We might, for instance, regard HRM as some do as organised religion, and conclude that, despite all the bad things done in its name, there remains a valuable ethical essence that is worth retaining. Some academics and trade unionists have approached HRM in this spirit, arguing that we can 'play back' promises about 'people being our number one resource' and ask management to live up to these. In purely pragmatic terms, there is much to be said for this approach in a business environment where HRM is unlikely to go away, as we have argued elsewhere (see Ackers and Payne, 1998; Ackers and Wilkinson, 2003). On the other hand, if we do not go beyond such necessary opportunism, there is a danger of becoming ensnared within the HRM worldview. For once we peel away the layers of HRM hyperbole, we reach a hollow core: an impoverished ethical vision of the employment relationship. This rests upon three ethical fallacies, which I will term 'golden calf', 'enlightened self-interest' and 'happy family'.

The golden calf fallacy assumes that all human values should be subordinated to business considerations and calculations. At the heart of the HRM worldview stands the claim that the human resource is a business's most valued asset. This appears, at first glance, a noble belief, even if it flies in the face of the manner in which many employers actually treat their workers. In particular, it suggests a culture in which companies invest in workers' long-term development, instead of regarding them as merely costs, to be cut and controlled. Yet, there is a dangerous flaw in this ethical vision, and this relates to the broader stream of right-wing ethical thinking, which redefines human beings, with their complex social, spiritual and material needs, as mere rational economic categories, be these consumers or human resources. Such language assumes that business and its economic terminology should shape human aspirations, and not the other way round. From a practical management point of view, enlightened employment policies will always require a business case. Ethics should not be a recipe for economic suicide or ridicule. But to have a long-term competitive advantage at the back of your mind is not to subordinate every decision to short-term economic calculus, as HRM implies. For workers, the choice is between being a most valued economic asset and being a rounded human being whose dignity should be respected by all – in Kant's terms, a subject that should never become an object. This has grave implications for the role of managers, since they are asked to lead the worship at the altar of false values. They too are required to treat their subordinates as merely a means to economic ends, to count the cost of every act of kindness. To personnel management in particular, HRM offers a Faustian pact within the enterprise culture. The prize advertised is an ever-growing personnel influence inside the business organisation; the price is personnel's professional soul and its total commitment to goals defined by senior executives and large shareholders, over and above all other stakeholders.

The enlightened self-interest or 'business case' fallacy takes the heresy a stage further, by pretending that business considerations alone are sufficient for companies to look after their employees, without outside regulation from the state or trade unions. As Pearson (1995) argues, a business needs to build long-term trust relationships with employees, customers and other companies in order to thrive, and therefore it needs to behave with integrity towards all these groups. Thus HRM theory fosters the seductive economic idea that it is in the self-interest of business to treat workers well, and that, for this reason alone, they no longer need to fear for their own protection. Yet numerous businesses, large and small, thrive on short-term, one-sided relationships, as the evidence for the failure of HRM shows. Perhaps, as Sisson (1994) suggests, this is against the long-term interests of Great Britain PLC, but there is little reason why that thought should detain for long the mobile, well-rewarded, modern business executive. The significance for workers' pay and conditions is that their entitlements are entirely contingent upon what makes business successful. If profitability demands investment in the human resource, employers will undertake this; if it entails exploiting cheap disposable labour, and breaking trade unions to this end, they will do the same. Once more, an economic theory that makes the treatment of human beings entirely conditional on business convenience and puts a price on human dignity, lies at the heartless centre of HRM's view of the world.

The happy family fallacy assumes that the state and trade unions are unwelcome intrusions into a fundamentally harmonious, unitarist employment relationship. Most American-style HRM theory is unitarist in outlook and either silent about or actively hostile to trade unions as representative bodies (Guest, 1989). This approach to HRM claims to place the happy paternalist conjunction of self-interest and employee well-being on a new, harder, more calculative footing. However, it does so against all the evidence that the tradition went into decline long ago, and has collapsed in the post-war period. The way we live now, in post-industrial Britain, talk of company loyalty can be as specious and insincere as easy appeals to 'community' and calls for street parties to mark national anniversaries. The break-up of occupational communities, founded on steel, coal, cotton, tin, fishing or carpets, where large extended families all worked for the same firm, has created a much greater occupational and social fragmentation and a far more mobile workforce. When the HRM 'good news' hit British business in the early 1980s, most large companies had already shed their family benefactors, faded out the welfare provisions, sold off their leafy garden villages to middle-class professionals, turned their consultative committees into a branch line on which hardly anyone travelled, and begun building on their playing fields. Like the Cheshire Cat, too often all that remains of paternalism is the smile. Enlightened management can still make a central contribution in the creation of a more cooperative and cohesive employment system, through active policies like partnership (Johnstone, *et al.*, 2009). However, it will not do so by pretending that one exists already, if only we could see it.

The sheer ambiguity of HRM may pose the biggest ethical problem, leading to charges of misrepresentation and bad faith. What so often sounds like a species of left-wing ethical thinking, promising something extra for employees, turns out on closer examination to be a sugar-coated edition of right-wing moral and economic philosophy. Milton Friedman (1993), from the latter perspective, suggests that such spurious claims to added 'social responsibility' are better left unsaid and merely detract from the strong, unvarnished case for capitalism. And it is true that right-wing ethical thinking has a firm grounding in certain business, economic and social realities. Most of us recognise, to some degree, the utilitarian benefits of a capitalist economic system, wherein countless selfish, individual market transactions produce unprecedented living standards for most people. In our personal lives, we expect this 'hidden hand' (Smith, 1993 [1776]) to be allowed considerable freedom, in order to ensure that our pensions keep pace with inflation and our food, shelter and holidays are affordable. We also want to be free to use our own money and property as freely as possible without undue interference from the state. We probably regard this economic freedom from state control (including the freedom to change job when we wish) as one essential freedom in a liberal democratic society. For all these reasons, any framework of employment ethics which, like full-blooded socialism in the past, threatens to 'kill the goose that laid the golden egg' is likely to be unacceptable to us. The problem with right-wing ethical thinking is that it forces these genuine concerns to an extreme, so that only the most minimal, individual ethics, such as honesty and trust in contracts, is deemed either necessary or possible. By denying the reality of a long-term employment relationship and presenting the labour contract as a spot-market transaction, like buying a bag of apples, right-wing ethics sends HRM managers into the workplace naked. They either have to imagine new clothes, like the emperor, and hope their employees will believe them, or else they have to look elsewhere.

Perhaps the crucial distinction here, then, is between employment ethics as a public relations façade and rationalisation for what business already does out of short-term economic self-interest, and employment ethics as an active commitment to employees above and beyond this. Behind the necessary pragmatics of economic life lie deeper ethical questions about how we treat other human beings, which can never be simply 'set aside' so that managers can concentrate on business. In this view, managers can and should play a crucial role in constructing socially responsible business organisations at the heart of a decent society. This would require, however, what I have termed a *neo-pluralist* approach which places the long-term employment relationship and the wages and conditions of employees, alongside other stakeholders, at the heart of the business organisation (Ackers, 2001, 2012). In these circumstances, we could speak meaningfully of social partnership, loyalty and commitment. Within a framework of relationship capitalism, managers could regain their professional autonomy and integrity, as public servants with a stakeholder ethos, rather than simply the handmaidens of private capital (see Hutton, 1995). In communitarian language, the workplace would become a genuine 'moral community' responsive to society as a whole.

HRM presents us with a paradox, because it talks of developing people, while considering its subjects as human resources. The reversion to economic language and the decline of company-led welfare capitalism (see Jacoby, 1997), leads to the suspicion that when push comes to shove, the calculator will always take priority over the human being. Although the rhetoric of HRM contains elements that appeal to ethical employment principles, it fails to meet its promises on two counts. First, it bears little relation to the main developments in contemporary employment relations, and thus presents itself as a mystifying ideology, a false promise of a better life in another world which will never arrive. Second, it abdicates any autonomous, ethical role for management, beyond doing whatever makes large shareholders and senior executives richer.

CASE STUDY 19.1
EMPLOYMENT ETHICS AT A&B STORES

PETER ACKERS

Introduction

A&B is a chain of department stores, selling clothes, food and hardware. It employs 10,000 UK workers in retail, distribution and office positions, mostly on permanent, full-time contracts. In addition, around 1,000 manufacturing workers, employed by its main subcontractor, are highly dependent on A&B's success and employment policy. This case study presents an opportunity to assess the ethics of the business at all stages in its development (was it doing the 'right thing' towards employees?), and to address a major contemporary dilemma between remaining competitive as a business and retaining a reputation as an ethical employer. It allows you to explore various ethical theories and to consider this business dilemma as a choice between different ethical frames of reference.

In the beginning

A&B was founded in 1900 as a small store in a medium-sized Scottish town by an austere, very religious Presbyterian (with his elder brother as a 'sleeping partner'). In the early days, the founder knew all his employees by their first name and exercised a strong 'fatherly' influence over their lives in and out of work. This had both benign and harsh aspects. The company was generous at times of family sickness, with the founder often visiting in person, though sometimes employees wondered if he was really checking up on them. And any employees who were caught with the smell of alcohol on their breath at work, or even drunk outside work, were summarily dismissed. The founder also promoted a strong sense of family values, organising (alcohol-free) works picnics and providing a free hamper every Christmas and at the birth of any child (up to three in number) and 200 cigarettes to the 'employee of the month'. Christian prayers were compulsory before each morning's work began. He also initiated and contributed towards various 'self-help' savings and mortgage schemes. Wages were generally slightly above the industry norm, according to the discretion of the founder, who liked to quote the parable of 'The Workers in the Vineyard' and reward those whom he thought deserved and needed most. Women employees who married were required to leave, in order to fulfil their family duties, and all managerial positions were reserved for men with families. The firm promised lifetime job security for male employees and encouraged children to follow their parents into the trade. For many years, jobs were only rarely advertised externally.

Growth

The founder died in 1940 and ownership and control passed completely into the hands of his two sons. The boys had been educated at an English public school and lived in the Home Counties. But the founder's personal control had declined long before, as the company grew first into a Scottish chain in the 1920s, and then a nationwide chain during the Second World War. The founder had always strongly opposed trade unions as inimical to the family atmosphere of the firm, and in 1923 the firm fought off an organising campaign by the shop workers' union which was already well established in the stores of the strong Scottish co-operative movement. As a result, 20 'ringleaders' were dismissed. During the 'hungry thirties', A&B gained a good reputation for maintaining employment when other businesses were laying people off. This was partly due to good business performance, but it was also widely believed that the owning family accepted lower profits in order to continue both to keep the loyal workforce and invest in the expansion of the firm.

The workforce was now counted in thousands rather than tens, so it was impossible for senior managers to retain personal, face-to-face contact – though local store managers were encouraged to do so. In response, the company developed a professional personnel department to create a more systematic set of provisions and policies. These included a non-union, representative company council that operated monthly at store level, and biannually across the whole company. Representatives were elected from every work group, and both negotiated with management over wages and consulted over any issues affecting the welfare of the workforce. There was also a welfare and sports society, which was heavily subsidised by the company and provided local A&B social clubs – initially on a strict temperance basis. These organised competitions for football, cricket, ballroom dancing and so on. Company developments and these social activities were reported in *Voice of A&B,* a monthly company newspaper produced by the personnel department. The firm also pioneered a number of other welfare benefits, including a contributory pension scheme for all employees, and a seniority and promotion system called 'Growing our own', which meant that nearly all middle and senior managers were recruited from the shop floor. Following one year's service, all employees joined the company profit-sharing scheme, which, in most years, added a further 10 per cent to their income.

PLC

In 1965, A&B became a public limited company (PLC), and within a few years family shareholdings had been dwarfed by those of pension funds and other outside investors. No senior managers now belonged to the original family, and many were being recruited from outside the business, rather than rising through its lower ranks as they had in the past. A new graduate recruitment programme had short-circuited the old seniority systems, though most middle managers had still risen from below. The business had also had to adapt to outside social trends, such as legislation for sexual and racial equality, and relaxed social mores – leading, among other things, to the serving of alcohol in A&B clubs. A&B was still perceived by workers, customers and the general public as a family-run business with a strong ethical commitment to fair play. This was reflected in the trust and loyalty of long-service employees (and very low labour turnover), and of customers who repeatedly told surveys that they would not buy their clothes anywhere else. A&B continued to play a high-profile public charitable role, both in the town of its origin, where the head office remains, and in the wider community. In the latter case, the company sponsored a City Technology College in inner-city Glasgow during the 1980s and actively supported 'Business in the Community'. It also funded a professorship in Business Ethics at a leading British business school.

The company had developed another long-term business relationship since its first major expansion in 1920, with a large high quality clothing manufacturing firm based in the town – though 50 per cent of employment is now abroad – where the founder was born and A&B originated. Although Smiths & Co. is an independent firm, 70 per cent of its output is contracted to A&B – whose letters also prefix the name of the local football team. Company head office and the local store employ between them 750 people, while the founder had presented to the town a park and art gallery, as well as a row of cottages for long-service company pensioners. The founder's wife had played a prominent charitable role in the inter-war town, including organising youth clubs and holidays for children of the local poor and unemployed.

Today

A&B's personnel policy has remained fairly stable since the main structures were set in place in the 1930s. In line with 1960s and 1970s labour law and 'best practice', however, the company council system has been supplemented by a more formal (but still non-union) grievance and disciplinary procedure. Employees have shown no further interest in union membership, partly because wages and conditions are as good as those of most comparable unionised firms, and partly because they know A&B senior management are strongly anti-union and fear they might lose existing benefits if they push the issue. A new company interest in equal opportunities for women was partly inspired by the national policy mood, but also by labour shortages and recruitment difficulties in the post-war retail labour market. As a result, there has been a small influx of women graduates into managerial and supervisory roles, and the old distinction between 'men's' and 'women's' jobs has been replaced by a formally nondiscriminatory, A–G grading system. Equally, criticism that internal recruitment reproduced an 'all white' workforce, even in cities with large ethnic minorities, has led the company to advertise all vacancies in job centres and local newspapers, followed by a formal interview. Once again, outside policy influences have dovetailed with business concerns that its workforce should reflect the stores' potential customer base. Notwithstanding these developments, personnel policy still cultivates a long-term relationship with both the directly employed workforce and the manufacturing subcontractor. In the latter case, A&B has insisted on exercising substantial 'quality control' over the subcontractor's production process, while offering Smith & Co. employees access to its social clubs and welfare provisions (though wages and conditions are handled separately). The company's long-standing commitment to high-quality British-made products is a major attraction for its traditional customer base.

Until recently, A&B has interpreted the new wave of HRM thinking as largely an extension of its existing personnel practices. For instance, it has added team briefing, quality circles and a modest element of performance-related pay to its existing communications, consultation and reward structures. In some respects, like profit sharing, the firm was already a pioneer. Today, however, major changes in the retail market are forcing the company to reassess all elements of its activities. After years as a market leader, with steadily rising profits, A&B is now in some commercial difficulty. In particular, it faces competition from a new generation of fashion shops, which threaten its core clothing market. These firms source their products from low-cost Third World suppliers and are happy to switch these where and when the market justifies. They also employ a raw, if enthusiastic UK workforce of students and young people, almost entirely on short-term and temporary contracts. Their wages are close to the national minimum, often about 25 per cent less than A&B, and they spend far less on training and welfare. A&B has already responded to this threat by shedding 10 per cent of its workforce through natural wastage, early retirement and voluntary redundancy, while terminating one major contract with Smith & Co.

The ethical and business dilemma

A new managing director has been appointed to 'turn around' A&B. He has asked all the main functional directors to present a root-and-branch analysis of how the business can regain its market position and restore stock market confidence. These papers will be presented to and discussed at a 'Retail 2050: Future Directions' seminar, the outcome of which will determine the new business strategy to be presented to the next company AGM.

The recently appointed head of marketing has already stolen a march on the others by circulating radical plans for a new, marketing-led, customer-focused, flexible firm that breaks almost completely with the traditional shape of the business, including its much-vaunted ethical employment policies. She proposes a new 'culture of entrepreneurship' which will withdraw the 'comfort zone' and 'time-serving' of current employment practices. Using a cricket metaphor, she argues that the point is 'not to occupy the crease but to score runs'. This will include establishing specialist boutiques and other facilities (including restaurants) within the stores, run on a franchise basis, using external subcontractors wherever possible, transferring all remaining direct employees to part-time contracts, except for a core of 'enterprise managers and supervisors' who, in future, will be paid largely according to performance. In addition, she moots the closure of the Scottish company headquarters and complete withdrawal from the town to smaller, more convenient facilities in an English new town; and the ending of the contract with Smith & Co. to enable A&B to buy on the open market and benefit fully from low labour costs in southeast Asia. In the marketing director's view, the traditional paternalist approach is now completely archaic and untenable in the fast-moving retail market.

To further complicate matters, a whistleblower, within either senior management or the marketing department, has leaked these plans to the media. Rumours are circulating that A&B has been negotiating with a military dictatorship for access to its labour force. Concerns about the abandonment of existing employees and the exploitation of Third World 'cheap labour' have been tabled by the founder's family for the company AGM. There have been demonstrations by employees in the original 'company town', addressed by outside trade union leaders, who called for union recognition for A&B employees under the recent legislation and an effective European works council. A petition has been presented to the Scottish Assembly by local MPs and church leaders, describing A&B as 'the unacceptable face of capitalism' and urging a consumer boycott of stores nationwide.

Historically, the personnel function, now renamed HRM, has been seen as the custodian of the company's ethical employment policies. As we have seen, these centre on a long-term relationship with a stable workforce. Concerned at the bad publicity the business is attracting, the managing director has asked you, as personnel director, to frame an explicitly ethical employment policy which overcomes the difficulties you are facing and draws on some of the business' existing strengths. There are signs that the adverse publicity is affecting customers and undermining their trust and loyalty towards the company. No options are barred, but the managing director has asked you to consider specifically the following questions.

Note: While A&B is a fictional ideal-type company, it incorporates many real-life elements from a number of leading British manufacturing and retail organisations. These all began as paternalist family firms with their own ethical ideas about how employment should be managed and adapted, and developed these as they grew into large, modern businesses.

Questions

1 How far was A&B's original employment policy 'ethical' in modern terms? What sort of ethical principles did it draw upon? Which elements would be acceptable today, and which would not?

2 How justified was the decision to prevent trade union organisation and is it still appropriate today? Consider the arguments *for* and *against* and the principles involved.

3 Construct an ethical case in favour of the flexible firm solution proposed by the director of marketing, explaining which principles you draw on.

4 Devise an alternative, HRM-driven business and ethical case for maintaining the existing long-term relationship with employees, customers and subcontractors.

5 Which stakeholder groups should take priority when push comes to shove? What duty, if any, does the company owe to its employees and shareholders in a modern free-market society?

6 Design an up-to-date and realistic, *ethical employment code of practice,* consistent with your answers to the above questions, which can be issued by the personnel department to all employees and used for external public relations purposes. Begin with some general principles and then identify key areas of business and employee rights and responsibilities.

CASE STUDY 19.2
APPLYING THE 'VEIL OF IGNORANCE'

PETER ACKERS

1 In the spirit of Rawls' 'veil of ignorance', imagine how it would feel to occupy someone else's role in society. Consider the following roles:

a. carworker
b. black civil servant
c. hospital cleaner
d. female junior doctor
e. supermarket manager
f. social worker.

2 What workplace issues might concern you? What would justice mean to you? Think of both issues specific to your new situation, and more general issues affecting workers and employees.

Bibliography

Ackers, P. (1994) 'Back to basics: industrial relations and the enterprise culture', *Employee Relations,* Vol.16, No.8, 32–47.

Ackers, P. (1998) 'On paternalism: seven observations on the uses and abuses of the concept in industrial relations, past and present', *Historical Studies in Industrial Relations,* Vol.6, 173–93.

Ackers, P. (2001) 'Paternalism, participation and partnership: rethinking the employment relationship', *Human Relations,* Vol.54, No.3, 373–84.

Ackers, P. (2002) 'Reframing employment relations: the case for neo-pluralism', *Industrial Relations Journal,* Vol.33, No.1, 2–19.

Ackers, P. (2010) 'An industrial relations perspective on employee participation', Chapter 3 in Wilkinson, A., Gollan, P.J., Marchington, M., Lewin, D. (eds), *The Oxford Handbook of Participation in Organizations*, Oxford: Oxford University Press.

Ackers, P. (2012) 'Rethinking the employment relationship: a neo-pluralist critique of British Industrial Relations orthodoxy', *International Journal of HRM*. Online IJHRM2012, 1–18, iFIRST.

Ackers, P. and Black, J. (1991) 'Paternalist capitalism: an organisation culture in transition', in Cross, M. and Payne, G. (eds) *Work and the Enterprise Culture,* London: Falmer.

Ackers, P. and Payne, J. (1998) 'British trade unions and social partnership: rhetoric, reality and strategy', *International Journal of Human Resource Management,* Vol.9, No.3, 529–50.

Ackers, P. and Preston, D. (1997) 'Born again? The ethics and efficacy of the conversion experience in contemporary management development', *Journal of Management Studies,* Vol.34, No.5, 677–701.

Ackers, P. and Wilkinson, A.J. (2003) 'Introduction: the British industrial relations tradition – formation, breakdown and salvage', pp. 1–27, in Ackers, P. and Wilkinson, A.J. (eds) *Understanding Work and Employment: Industrial Relations in Transition,* Oxford: Oxford University Press.

Ackers, P., Smith, C. and Smith, P. (eds) (1996) *The New Workplace and Trade Unionism,* London: Routledge.

Burchill, J. (1994) *Co-op: The People's Business,* Manchester: Manchester University Press. (Reviewed by this author in *Review of Employment Topics,* Vol.5, No.1 (1997), 206–9.)

*Chryssides, G.D. and Kaler, J.H. (eds) (1993) *An Introduction to Business Ethics,* London: Chapman & Hall. (Reviewed by this author in *Human Resource Management Journal,* Vol.5, No.1, 103–5.)

Clark, J. (1993) 'Procedures and consistency versus flexibility and commitment in employee relations: a comment on Storey', *Human Resource Management Journal,* Vol.3, No.4, 79.

Clegg, H.A. (1979) *The Changing System of Industrial Relations in Great Britain*, Oxford: Blackwell.

Colling, T. and Terry, M. (2010) *Industrial Relations: Theory and Practice* (3rd edn), Chichester: Wiley. (See this author's review in *Work, Employment and Society* (2012) Vol.26, No.5, 879–82).

Crane, A. and Matten, D. (2004) *Business Ethics,* Oxford: Oxford University Press.

Cully, M., Woodland, S., O'Reilly, A. and Dix, G. (1999) *Britain at Work, As Depicted By the 1998 Workplace Employee Relations Survey,* Abingdon: Routledge.

Etzioni, A. (1995) *The Spirit of Community: Rights, Responsibilities and the Communitarian Agenda*, London: Fontana.

Flanders, A. (1970) *Management and Unions: The Theory and Reform of Industrial Relations,* London: Faber.

Fox, A. (1966) *Industrial Sociology and Industrial Relations*, Royal Commission on Trade Unions and Employers' Associations, Research Paper No.3, London: HMSO.

Fox, A. (1974) *Beyond Contract: Work, Power and Trust Relations,* London: Faber.

Fox, A. (1985) *History and Heritage: The Social Origins of the British Industrial Relations System,* London: Allen & Unwin.

Friedman, M. (1993) 'The social responsibility of business is to increase its profits', reprint of 1973 article in Chryssides, G.D. and Kaler, J.H. (eds) *An Introduction to Business Ethics,* London: Chapman & Hall.

Fryer, M. (2011) *Ethics and Organizational Leadership: Developing a Normative Model*, Oxford: Oxford University Press.

Greene, A.M., Ackers, P. and Black, J. (2001) 'Lost narratives? From paternalism to team working in a lock manufacturing firm', *Economic and Industrial Democracy,* Vol.22, No.2, 211–37.

Guest, D. (1989) 'HRM: its implications for industrial relations and trade unions', in Storey, J. (ed.) *New Perspectives on Human Resource Management,* London: Routledge.

Guest, D. (1999) 'Human resource management: the workers' verdict', *Human Resource Management Journal,* Vol.9, No.3, 5–25.

Hall and Soskice (2001) *Varieties of Capitalism*, Oxford: Oxford University Press.

*Hart, T.J. (1993) 'Human resource management: time to exorcise the militant tendency', *Employee Relations,* Vol.15, No.3, 29–36.

Hutton, W. (1995) *The State We're In,* London: Cape.

Jacoby, S.M. (1997) *Modern Manors: Welfare Capitalism since the New Deal,* Princeton, NJ: Princeton University Press. (Reviewed by this author in *Historical Studies in Industrial Relations,* Vol.8, 188–94.)

Johnstone, S., Ackers, P and Wilkinson, A. (2009) 'The British partnership phenomenon: a ten year review', *Human Resource Management Journal*, Vol.19, No.3, 260–79.

Joyce, P. (1980) *Work, Society and Politics: The Culture of the Factory in Later Victorian England,* Brighton: Harvester.

Kersley, B., Alpin, C., Forth, J., Bryson, A., Bewley, H., Dix, G. and Oxenbridge, S. (2004) *Inside the Workplace,* London: ACAS.

Kynaston, D. (2008) *Austerity Britain 1945–51,* London: Bloomsbury.

*Legge, K. (1995) 'Morality bound', *People Management,* 19 December, 34–6.

Legge, K. (2004) *Human Resource Management: Rhetorics and Reality,* London: Macmillan.

MacInnes, J. (1987) *Thatcherism at Work: Industrial Relations and Economic Change,* Milton Keynes: Open University Press.

Mars, G. (1973) 'Hotel pilferage: a case study in occupational theft', in Warner, M. (ed.) *The Sociology of the Workplace: An Interdisciplinary Approach,* London: Allen & Unwin.

Millward, N., Stevens, M., Smart, D. and Hawes, W.R. (1992) *Workplace Industrial Relations in Transition: The ED/ESRC/PSI/ACAS Surveys,* Aldershot: Dartmouth.

Nozick, R. (1993) 'Anarchy, state and utopia', (extract), in Chryssides, G.D. and Kaler, J.H. (eds) *An Introduction to Business Ethics,* London: Chapman & Hall.

Pearson, G. (1995) *Integrity in Organisations: An Alternative Business Ethic,* London: McGraw-Hill. (Reviewed by this author in *Employee Relations,* Vol.18, No.6 (1996), 97–8.)

Peston, R. (2008) 'A crash as historic as the end of communism', *The Times*, Tuesday, 9 December.

Rawls, J. (1993) 'A theory of justice' (extract), in Chryssides, G.D. and Kaler, J.H. (eds) *An Introduction to Business Ethics,* London: Chapman & Hall.

Sisson, K. (ed.) (1989) *Personnel Management,* Oxford: Blackwell.

Sisson, K. (ed.) (1994) *Personnel Management* (2nd edn), Oxford: Blackwell.

Sisson, K. and Purcell, J. (2010) 'Management: caught between competing views', in Colling and Terry (2010).

Smith, A. (1993 [1776]) 'The wealth of nations' (extract), in Chryssides, G.D. and Kaler, J.H. (eds) *An Introduction to Business Ethics,* London: Chapman & Hall.

Smith, K. and Johnson, P. (eds) (1996) *Business Ethics and Business Behaviour,* London: International Thomson. (Reviewed by this author in *Human Resource Management Journal,* Vol.8, No.2 (1998), 97–8).

Storey, J. (ed.) (1989) *New Perspectives on Human Resource Management*, London: Routledge.

Torrington, D. (1993) 'How dangerous is human resource management?: A reply to Tim Hart', *Employee Relations,* Vol.15, No.5, 40–53.

Torrington, D. and Hall, L. (1991) *Personnel Management: A New Approach,* Hemel Hempstead: Prentice Hall.

Williams, S., Abbott, B. and Heery, E. (2011) 'Civil regulation and HRM: the impact of civil society organizations on the policies and practices of employers, *Human Resource Management Journal*, Vol.21, No.1, 45–59.

Winstanley, D. and Woodall, J. (eds) (1999) *Ethical Issues in Contemporary Human Resource Management,* London: Macmillan.

CHAPTER 20
EMOTION AT WORK

Philip Hancock and Melissa Tyler

Introduction

Consider the following extract from a recent job advertisement:

> You will need to be full of energy and want to add to the fun … if you want to start work with a great cast of characters then telephone …

You might be forgiven for assuming that this advert is for a job in what Robin Leidner (1993) calls 'interactive service provision' – work involving direct contact with customers or clients. In fact, it is advertising vacancies for warehouse staff at a European distribution centre; for workers who handle 'things' rather than 'people'. Why is it important, then, for applicants to want to 'add to the fun', and why are potential colleagues and co-workers described as 'a great cast of characters'? Well, it would seem that emotion is now thought of as central to business success, whether that business is selling fast food or sorting boxes. As management writers such as Robert Cooper (1998: 48) have argued:

> Emotion has been rejected for many years as the messy, effeminate counterpoint to masculine logic and objectivity, but now it has become the latest business buzzword.

This raises the questions, then, why emotion, and why now (Bolton, 2004)? And of course, what exactly are emotions? Can they be managed, and if so, how and with what consequences? As sociologist Simon Williams (2001: 132) has observed, 'emotion is a moving and slippery target'. As he goes on to note:

> The very term emotion, it seems, is far from settled (being many things to many people); a trend exacerbated perhaps, by the recent upsurge of interest in this domain. What is fair to say, given these differing viewpoints, is that emotion is a complex, *multidimensional, multifaceted human compound,* including *irreducible* biological and cultural components, which arise or emerge in various socio-relationship contexts. [original emphasis]

Broadly speaking, emotions are human responses to a whole range of socio-relational events relating to how we feel and how we express and make sense of those feelings, either individually or socially. Emotions are largely intersubjective (experienced or made sense of with reference to others) and communicative (used to convey how we feel – see Crossley, 1998). They are often complex and contradictory – we might hear people saying that they have 'laughed until they cried' or 'wept tears of joy', for instance. As sources of (sometimes simultaneous) pleasure and pain, they are clearly central to who and what we are. Emotions can operate at many different levels, and can be highly reflexive or calculated strategies; they can be habitual or routine practices, as well as unconscious or involuntary responses, varying across time, place and culture.

Traditionally the province of psychology – with its emphasis on studying emotions largely as psychosomatic responses – it has been sociology that has dominated debates on the social nature of emotions in recent years, considering their expression and function, and also the way in which emotions are socially shaped and experienced. In this sense, sociologists have argued that no emotion is ever an 'entirely unlearnt response' (Elias, 1991), and that the emotional experiences of individuals – our ability to think about, feel and express emotions (relating to what sociologists call 'agency') – are linked to enduring social institutions and arrangements such as power and status (what sociologists call 'structure'). In this sense, emotions represent something of a juncture between society and the most personal aspects of our selves as individuals. They also straddle both the physical and mental realms of our existence as human beings. That emotions act as something of a 'pivot' in this respect, between the individual and the structural, the personal and the social, and the corporeal and the cognitive explains, at least in part, why management theorists and practitioners alike have begun to take such an interest in emotions in recent years, focusing on emotion as central to understanding and controlling organisations.

Because of their complexity, emotions are often thought about and expressed metaphorically – as if they were fluids in a container that might spill out or overflow at any moment. This fluid metaphor has been a strong theme in organisation and management studies, in which the workplace is often talked about as if it were an 'emotional cauldron' (Albrow, 1992) beneath the surface of which a toxic brew is thought to bubble away. Tracy and Tracy (1998: 390), in their study of a US 911 Emergency Centre use the metaphor of an emotional landscape, to describe 'the organization's emotion rules, and the communicative devices call-takers use to management their emotion'. Others have thought of emotions with reference to a weaving metaphor, arguing that emotions are 'woven' into the very fabric of organisational life (Fineman, 1994). For Fineman, the centrality of emotions is reflected, for instance, in the evocation of work organisations as families, communities or social groups; ideas perpetuated by managerial attempts to conflate formal and informal aspects of organisational culture, so that 'stage-managed meetings and reward ceremonies, "graduation" ceremonies and "away days" all have *a distinct evangelical tone, intended "to keep spirits high"'* (Fineman, 1993: 20, emphasis added).

Not that such allusions to the spiritual needs of employees are always entirely metaphorical, of course. Many organisations are increasingly supporting employees' participation in spiritually oriented programmes and events as a means of encouraging personal well-being and emotional contentment (Bell and Taylor, 2003). This is a trend which itself is likely to continue as more and more organisations embrace the idea that valuing employees' spirituality and the emotional benefits that this brings can also provide a powerful impetus to workplace identification and productivity (Konz and Ryan, 1999; Neck and Milliman, 1994).

It is significant that many such emotional and spiritual events occur outside of normal working hours and so blur the boundaries between work and non-work, between who and what 'belongs' to the organisation and what does not, and hence, many would argue, extends the scope of HRM into life outside of work (Fleming and Sturdy, 2009). Obligations on organisational members to participate in social events, outside the organisation's normal time and space, are often seen as opportunities to share 'real' (disorganised, unmanaged) feelings safely within a receptive audience of peers. Thus, 'apart from being individually cathartic, the social sharing of normally hidden feelings creates a subculture through which organisational members can emotionally bond and feel at one' (Fineman 1993: 21) – a central theme in HRM. In this sense, potentially anti-organisational emotions become subject to 'strategic renegotiations' (1993: 22) so that the possibility for emotional leakage (to continue the 'fluid' metaphor) *within* the organisation's time and space is minimised. For Fineman (1994), then, by effectively organising out 'bad' (unprofitable) feelings, by implication, the productive energy associated with 'good' feelings can be channelled into the labour process – a theme that has underpinned the turn to emotion in HRM.

The emotional turn: key concepts and issues

Although the presence of emotion within organisations has long since been recognised by management practitioners and academics, it seems to be only relatively recently (in the last three decades or so) that specific and sustained attention has been paid to the emotional aspects of organisation and its management. As Sharon Bolton (2000) has noted, emotions now seem to be 'here, there and everywhere'. Several reasons can be identified for this relatively recent turn to emotion in organisation and management studies.

Much of the academic interest in emotion was inspired by US sociologist Arlie Russell Hochschild's book *The Managed Heart,* published in 1983. As Bolton and Boyd (2003: 292) have put it, 'there is little that has been written concerning the subject of emotions and organizations … that does not take *The Managed Heart* as a reference point'. Crucially, Hochschild's intervention into the study of service work and its management in the early 1980s provided a conceptual framework within which to understand the nature and commercial value of social interactions involved in the delivery of customer service work, 'debunking the assumption that "real work" only takes place within manufacturing' (Lewis and Simpson, 2009: 56). Hochschild's (1983) introduction of the term 'emotional labour' to describe the ways in which emotions are incorporated into the labour process illuminated an aspect of paid work that has since been recognised as central to the lived experience of many workers, particularly those employed in the service sector, but that had been relatively obscured by dominant theoretical approaches both to management and to the study of management. Conceptualising some of the distinctive aspects of work in this way opened up fruitful avenues of investigation and analysis, and facilitated the ongoing reformulation of both academic and managerial conceptions of work necessary to keep pace with transformations in the nature of work, and in the economy in general.

One such transformation is that increasingly 'people's working lives are shaped overwhelmingly by the experience of delivering a service' (Allen and Du Gay, 1994: 255). This increase, over the past few decades, in the proportion of jobs in which people are employed specifically to work as front-line, customer-facing service providers has meant that sustained managerial attention has been paid to customer relations as a vital contributor to competitive advantage and hence particularly to the stage management of what Jan Carlzon (1987) called 'moments of truth': when customers interact with organisations through interpersonal encounters with sales-service providers. This recognition has increased the importance accorded to emotion and its management, particularly for those employees in direct contact with customers. Consequently, 'a key component of the work performed by many workers has become the presentation of emotions that are specified and desired by their organisations' (Morris and Feldman, 1997: 987). Johansson and Näslund (2009) document this process in their research on the design and management of customer experiences on board a cruise ship. Their study highlights the extent to which working in the so-called 'experience industry' places high levels of emotional demands on employees as the perceived freedom of the passengers to enjoy the experience on board the ship is dependent upon stringent managerial control of the emotional displays of service workers, and particularly of their interactions with customers and of the spaces in which these interactions take place.

Certainly in contemporary (what we might call 'post-Excellence') managerial discourse – that is, managerialism inspired largely by Peters and Waterman's (1982) *In Search of Excellence* and concerned particularly with the management of the cultural and subjective aspects of work – emotion has come to be viewed as an important resource that managers should harness in the service of organisational performance. In their book *A Passion For Excellence,* Peters and Austin (1985: 287) argued that organisational emotions (the feelings, sensations and affective responses to organisation) 'must come from the market and the soul simultaneously'.

In sum, the turn to emotion has been fuelled by various recent developments, including:

- **conceptual developments** in the way in which we recognise and understand the emotional aspects of work organisations and their management;
- **empirical changes** in the way in which we experience work and the context within which it takes place;
- **theoretical trends** in the way in which ideal forms of management are defined, largely in managerial texts and 'how to' guides.

Cumulatively, each of these developments has amounted to something of a challenge to the preoccupation with rationality in managerial theory and practice, underpinned by a largely instrumental interest in emotions and their expression. As we will now reflect, however, it is not the case that management and emotion have always been seen as ideal business partners.

Emotion in management theory and practice

Emotion, bureaucracy and scientific management

Rationality can be defined as the exercise of human reason in order to make decisions that are geared towards reaching an optimal resolution of a problem or ambition. As such, it is largely considered to be the opposite of following our feelings or instincts, which is subsequently deemed irrational. Modern organisations have been hailed since their inception as models of rationality and instruments of rationalisation. Bureaucracy – as the typically modern (advanced) mode of organising – has been defined largely according to an autonomous, impersonal, procedural rationality that has no place for emotion. What Rosabeth Moss Kanter (1977: 22) in her now classic critique of bureaucracy refers to as 'the passionless organisation', one that strives to exclude emotion from its boundaries, is an organisation that believes that efficiency should not be sullied by the 'irrationality' of personal feelings.

In her account of the development of this modern, bureaucratic organisation, Kanter (1977) argues that the 'corporation' began to emerge as the dominant organisational form in the late nineteenth century, when what she calls the 'administrative revolution' (the successor to the industrial revolution) took place. By this she means that an increasing number of organisational functions were brought together and merged into a single corporate administration in order to gain control over a range of disparate activities that would otherwise have continued to be subject to a high degree of uncertainty. Hence, the need to coordinate complex operations made management a specialised occupation and, as she notes, managerial skills began to be more rewarded in business than technical ones. However, as managers were neither owners nor a traditional 'ruling class', they were required to establish their legitimacy and did so through the language of rationality and efficiency.

Control by managers was therefore presented as the most 'rational' way to run a corporate enterprise. Early twentieth-century management theory – such as Taylor's (1911) 'principles of scientific management' – hence enshrined rationality as the central ideal of organisation, and defined it as the special province of managers. As Kanter (1977: 22, emphasis added) notes in this respect, 'the very design of organisations thus was oriented toward and assumed to be *capable of suppressing irrationality, personality and emotionality*'.

For Max Weber, whose sociological analysis focused largely on the rationalisation of Western societies, the suppression of emotion gave bureaucracies their advantage over other organisational forms. Indeed, Weber built his critique of the spirit of capitalism – 'that attitude which seeks profit rationally and systematically' (Weber 1989 [1904]: 64) – on the belief that it is anchored in deeply held religious and emotional attitudes of affect control; in other words, on the exclusion of emotions from organisational life. Thus, as contemporary commentators have noted, privileging rationality and marginalising or excluding emotion 'means that bureaucracy perpetuates the belief that rationality and the control of emotions are not only inseparable but also necessary for effective organisational life' (Putnam and Mumby 1993: 41).

Returning to Weber for a moment, it would be incorrect, however to say that his ideal type of bureaucracy is based on a total exclusion of emotion, (Albrow 1992). As the following passage from his book *Economy and Society* indicates, Weber's account does allow for emotions within modern organisations, but only in so far as their rational calculation is perceived as an intrinsic aspect of their constitution. It is not emotion per se that Weber admits into the organisation, then, but rationalised emotion, ensuring

> First, that *everything is rationally calculated, especially* those seemingly imponderable and irrational, *emotional factors* – in principle, at least, calculable in the same manner as the yields of coal and iron deposits. Secondly, devotion is normally impersonal, oriented towards a purpose, a common cause, a rationally intended. (Weber 1978 [1921]: 1150, emphasis added)

In sum, then, emotion was seen as irrational and unreasonable in Taylorism and bureaucracy, as the antithesis of organisation and in need either of exclusion or rational calculation on the part of managers as the personification of rationality.

Emotion and human relations

Yet, from the 1930s onwards management theorists and practitioners had begun to realise that even within the confines of organisational life, emotions cannot be excluded or ordered in any meaningful way. In management terms, this meant a significant shift from a view of 'ideal' organisations as based on the exclusion or rational calculation of emotion to an emphasis on the idea that work is meaningful and motivating only if it offers security and opportunities for achievement and self-actualisation (Herzberg, 1974; Maslow, 1943). In what came to be known as the human relations school of management, emotion therefore became 'in', so to speak, as affectivity began to be recognised as being of central importance to the pursuit of organisational performance. It became increasingly emphasised, therefore, that the management of work organisations should be based on 'articulating and incorporating *the logic* of sentiments' (Roethlisberger and Dickson, 1939: 462, emphasis added).

Elaborating on this recognition of emotions within organisational life, management theorist Chester Barnard (1938: 235) argued that 'feeling', 'judgement', a 'sense of proportion', 'balance' and 'appropriateness' are all vital attributes of the executive. Participative styles of management, deemed to engender loyalty and commitment and so increase worker satisfaction and productivity, increasingly perceived emotion as an important aspect of organisational life.

Elton Mayo (1933), for example, emphasised the importance for productivity of primary, informal relations among workers and developed the concept of the 'informal organisation' to include the emotional, non-rational and sentimental aspects of organisational behaviour. In Mayo's view, workers were controlled by their sentiments, emotions and social instincts – a phenomenon that he argued needed to be taken into account when devising, executing and evaluating management strategies. As Kanter (1977) notes in her critique, however, in emotional management terms human relations continued to rely on a relatively simplistic formula according to which managers were viewed as those who were able to control their own emotions as well as those of their workers, but not vice versa. According to a management training manual written in 1947 reminiscent of Rudyard Kipling's poem *If*, for instance,

> He [the manager] knows that the master of men [sic] has physical energies and skills and intellectual abilities, vision and integrity, and he knows that, above all, the leader must have emotional balance and control. The great leader is even-tempered when others rage, brave when others fear, calm when others are excited, self-controlled when others indulge. *(cited in Bendix 1956: 332)*

While the human relations emphasis on informal social factors may appear to diverge from those organisational traits considered important by scientific management, therefore, both approaches shared in common a similar conception of the role of heroism vis-à-vis emotion. This meant that in the HR movement management education continued to be thought of largely as a vehicle for learning how to master, not unleash, emotion. In other words, human relations may have 'modified the idea of rationality but preserved its flavour' (Kanter 1977: 22), often in highly gendered terms. As feminist writer Rosemary Pringle notes in this respect,

> While the Human Relations theorists added an informal dimension, they did not challenge the theorising of the formal bureaucratic structures. In some ways they reinforced the idea of managerial rationality: while *workers* might be controlled by sentiment and emotion, *managers* were supposed to be rational, logical and able to control their emotions. The division between reason and emotion was tightened in a way that marked off managers from the rest. *(Pringle 1989: 87, original emphasis)*

HRM: Management gets emotional

More recently, management practitioners and theorists have begun to emphasise that effective emotional management is a prerequisite for successful organisational interaction. Consequently, and for the reasons outlined above, recent managerial accounts of the importance of, say, successful service interaction place a considerable premium on the role of emotion and its contribution to organisational success. Many such approaches advocate the use of techniques that manage the emotions of service providers and consumers simultaneously, through the use, for instance, of particular symbolic techniques such as corporate slogans. Take, for example, the McDonald's 'I'm lovin' it' advertising campaign. Launched in 2003, and translated into several languages across the world, the aim of the campaign was to focus on the whole McDonald's 'experience' rather than simply its product range, and in doing so, to convey 'warmth' and 'passion' (according to the description on the McDonald's website at the time).

Examples such as these suggest that while broadly modernist approaches to management, including scientific management, bureaucracy and human relations, were concerned largely with the *organisation of emotion,* more contemporary managerial orientations are more preoccupied with the *emotion of organisation*; that is, with understanding and harnessing emotion as a human and therefore organisational resource. This recognition of emotion as an organisational resource produces what Vincent (2011) has described as 'an economy of feelings', a term which emphasises that while our emotions are highly personal, and central to who we are as individuals, they are also 'affected by managerial design and control systems that are intended to shape emotions displayed towards 'higher' organisational interests, such as increasing productivity, profitability and performance'.

Hence, management writers, consultants and practitioners have begun in recent years to advocate a less 'rationalistic' approach to the management of emotion and emphasised instead the extent to which

> emotions, properly managed, can drive trust, loyalty and commitment and many of the greatest productivity gains, innovations and accomplishments of individuals, teams and organisations. *(Cooper 1998: 48)*

According to Cooper (1998: 48) 'the ability to sense, understand and effectively apply the power and acumen of emotions as a source of human energy, information, trust, creativity, connection and influence' represents that 'really crucial ingredient' for organisational success in the contemporary era, or as Jack Welch (former chair of General Electric), has put it, 'soft stuff with hard results' (cited in Cooper, 1998). The 'proper' management of emotions, in this context, is often framed in terms of the deployment of *emotional intelligence.*

The term 'emotional intelligence' (EQ) is associated most notably with the work of Harvard psychologist Daniel Goleman (1999, 2009a,b) who has argued that the effective management of EQ involves:

- knowing one's emotions (emotional self-awareness);
- controlling one's emotions (emotional self-regulation);
- recognising emotions in others (social awareness);
- controlling emotions in others (relationship management);
- self-motivation.

Goleman (2009a) argues that emotions play a far greater role in decision making and individual success than is commonly recognised. In his best-selling book *Emotional Intelligence* he argues that *the* contemporary challenge is to manage our emotional life with intelligence. In other words, our emotions:

> when well exercised, have wisdom; they guide our thinking, our values, our survival. But they can easily go awry, and do so all too often . . . The problem is not with emotionality, but with the appropriateness of emotion and its expression. The question is, how can we bring intelligence to our emotions – and civility to our streets and caring to our communal life? *(Goleman 2009a: xiv)*

The answer, for Goleman, lies in effective emotional management. With the correct training and development, he argues, emotionally intelligent managers can achieve a high level of *emotional competence* which he defines as 'a learned capability based on emotional intelligence that results in outstanding performance at work' (2009b: 24). Goleman argues that EQ matters more to organisational performance than cognitive abilities or technical skills and impacts particularly, he argues, at the top of the 'leadership pyramid'.

In *Primal Leadership: Realizing the Power of Emotional Intelligence* (Goleman *et al.,* 2002: 3) Goleman and his colleagues emphasise that 'great leadership works through the emotions'. Echoing particularly Mayo's earlier writing on the importance of managing the informal organisation, he distinguishes between leaders who drive emotions positively (achieving *resonance*) and those who spawn emotional *dissonance,* 'undermining the emotional foundations that let people shine'. Here management is redefined as 'the emotional art of leadership' (ibid.: 13) and emotionally intelligent management is deemed to make effective use of the EQ competencies outlined above. The development of emotional intelligence skills has not simply been seen as the province of managers however. Prati and Karriker (2010) in their recent study of a large US-based retail organisation argue that emotional intelligence skills can be highly effective in moderating the relationship between an emotionally demanding work environment and voluntary turnover. Describing emotional intelligence skills as 'invaluable coping mechanisms' to defeat the adverse effects of organisational demands for a particular emotional display, they argue that 'emotional intelligence abilities can be useful resources in jobs where demands for the regulation of emotional display are excessive' (Prati and Karriker, 2010: 332).

Developing a similar theme, management writers Kandola and Fullerton (1995), known for their conception of the contemporary organisation as a 'mosaic', have also highlighted the organisational benefits of incorporating emotions into the management of diversity, including improved access to talent, enhanced organisational flexibility, promotion of team creativity and innovation, improved customer services, the fostering of satisfying work environments, enhanced morale and job satisfaction, greater productivity and sustained competitive advantage.

Not that such strategies are entirely without risk, however. Peter Frost (2003), for instance, has warned of the dangers of what he terms 'toxic emotions' and, in particular, the threat they pose to emotionally engaged managers whom he refers to as 'toxin handlers'. This concept refers to those managers (and other employees) who possess high levels of EQ, and are able to 'recognize the emotional pain in other people and in a situation' and as a result either absorb or deflect it 'so that people can get back to their work' (Frost 2003: 1). Yet while the endeavours of such figures are often vital to the success of an organisation, such individuals can themselves suffer from the absence of adequate support mechanisms or organisational recognition. Thus, as Frost (2003) observes, they are highly vulnerable to personal burnout unless they develop their own coping strategies or are provided with appropriate support from those within the organisation responsible for the well-being of its employees.

This concern notwithstanding, however, underpinning the championing of EQ is the broader perception that 'without an actively engaged heart, excellence is impossible' (Harris 1996: 18). In this respect, contemporary approaches share much in common with the earlier advocates of human relations and their concern to conflate what are perceived as artificial (and unprofitable) boundaries between the corporation and the individual. They have emphasised, perhaps most notably, that organisational stability comes at the price of losing originality, flexibility and creativity. The identification of innovative solutions that might emerge from processes that mediate and negotiate between diverse groups is thought to be foreclosed in more bureaucratic or scientific approaches to management that prioritise rationality over emotion.

Passionate commitment to organisational goals, to co-workers and to the organisation itself is also seen to be lost in the unemotional organisation, a theme that underpins the recent preoccupation within management theory and practice, particularly within the creative industries, with the promotion of workplace fun (Barsoux, 1993; Stewart and Simmons, 2010). However, critical accounts of workplaces in which fun is promoted emphasise (Fleming and Sturdy, 2009; Hunter et al., 2010; Warren and Fineman, 2007) the high levels of ambivalence engendered by HRM techniques designed to encourage employees to have fun at work. In their study of DIY Co. for instance, Redman and Mathews (2002) outline how the company's HRM practices were central to the promotion of a fun culture within the organisation. Their recruitment and selection process emphasised the employees' capacity for coping with the DIY Co. culture; employees were recruited less for their experience and more for their 'spirit' and 'heart'; customer service training was 'light-hearted' and intended to be humorous; staff reviews and development planning was linked to the fun culture and regular social and in-store events encouraged the promotion of fun (such as themed fancy dress days, for instance). However, many staff at DIY Co. found the compulsion to have fun oppressive and overwhelming, with participants in their study commenting 'sometimes you just don't feel like having fun', 'it's not really right that you should be told by management to have fun', and 'there is a limit to how much fun you can stomach sometimes'. So while it is not difficult to understand why 'fun at work' has become a popular managerial discourse, particularly given the current economic climate in most western economies, the demand for managed emotion is by no means unproblematic.

Critical perspectives on emotion

More critical perspectives on emotion have emerged primarily from the Marxist-inspired critique of capitalism and, particularly since the 1980s and inspired largely by Hochschild's *The Managed Heart* (1983), out of attempts to synthesise elements of labour process theory, feminism and organisational sociology. Such approaches tend to emphasise that employees are increasingly required to personify an emotional ethos prescribed by their employing organisation and have drawn attention largely to the alienating, degrading and objectifying consequences of this, particularly in relation to the control mechanisms and surveillance techniques used by organisations to prescribe and monitor the expression of emotion, and the ways in which the negation of the skills involved in the performance of emotional labour and the techniques used to manage it violate the right to dignity at work (Bolton, 2007). As Vincent (2011: 1383) has recently argued, the management of emotion through the deployment of high commitment HRM practices 'may simply intensify managerial control, rendering the experience of work more, rather than less, oppressive and alienating'.

Emotional labour

Coined initially by Hochschild (1979, 1983, 1990), the phrase 'emotional labour' refers, broadly speaking, to the commodification of emotions within the labour process. In *The Managed Heart,* Hochschild (1983) made a fundamental distinction between two conceptually different if empirically related ways of managing emotions; namely, emotion work and emotional labour. *Emotion work* describes the act of attempting to change an emotion and how it is displayed in everyday life. In everyday social interaction emotions are thought to be governed by what Hochschild termed 'feeling rules' – 'a set of shared albeit often latent, rules' (Hochschild 1983: 268) that define what is emotionally appropriate in any given situation (see Bolton, 2004 for a discussion of organisational, commercial and professional feeling rules). The effort involved in conforming to these rules is what she means by emotion work. So when we laugh at someone's unfunny joke, or express gratitude for an unwanted gift, we are engaging in 'emotion work', in Hochschild's terms. *Emotional labour,* however, is what occurs when a profit motive underpins the performance of emotion work within the context of the employment relationship – when someone pays us to manage our own emotions and those of others. As she puts it,

> by 'emotion work' I refer to the emotion management we do in private life; by 'emotional labour' I refer to the emotion management we do for a wage. *(Hochschild, 1990: 118)*

According to Hochschild, emotional labour 'requires one to induce or suppress feeling in order to sustain the outward countenance that produces the proper state of mind in others' (1983: 7). Drawing on the work of sociologist Erving Goffman (1959), Hochschild argues that producing the 'proper state of mind in others' involves techniques she describes as 'surface' and 'deep' acting. *Surface acting* involves pretending to experience emotions that are not genuine; 'faking it', in other words. *Deep acting* involves something more sustained and potentially intrusive – actually changing what, or rather, how we feel.

Hochschild argues that 'just as we may become alienated from our physical labour in a goods-producing society, so we may become alienated from our emotional labour in a service-producing society' (1979: 571). This sense of alienation may cause emotional labourers to feel false and estranged from their own 'real' feelings, an experience Hochschild (1983: 90) terms 'emotive dissonance'.

Example

In her account of the emotional labour undertaken by hospice nurses, Nicky James (1989) outlined the various skills involved in the performance of emotional labour. These include:

- being able to understand and interpret the needs of others;
- being able to provide a personal response to those needs;
- being able to juggle the delicate balance of individual and group needs;
- being able to pace work, and take account of other responsibilities.

Try to list other occupations in which these skills might be particularly important. Why might these occupations (and the skills they require) result in what Hochschild calls 'emotional dissonance'?

Research suggests that a wide range of organisational contexts exist in which employees are required to manage their own emotions and those of others in the service of an employing organisation. Empirical studies of emotional labour have appeared in a range of sociology and management journals in recent years. In sociology, the emphasis has primarily been on documenting the content of emotional labour, and to a large extent, noting its gendered aspects, focusing for instance on the high demand for emotional labour in nursing and other caring professions. In her study of police work, Susan Martin (1999) has also highlighted the extent to which women police officers are often assumed to be inherently skilled at the more emotional aspects of police work, such as providing support to victims of crime for instance, while men are assumed to be more suited to the 'real' police work of solving crime. Studies have also emphasised the impact of emotional labour on job satisfaction, and have drawn attention to the negative effects of performing work that involves managing one's own and others' feelings and to the ethical issues this raises. Such accounts have tended to examine jobs with the most obvious emotional labour content, particularly in interactive service work. These include studies of fast-food workers at McDonald's (Leidner, 1993, 1999), flight attendants (Hochschild, 1983; Tyler and Abbott, 1998), nurses (James, 1989; O'Brien, 1994), waiters and waitresses (Hall, 1993; Paules, 1996), hair stylists (Chugh and Hancock, 2009; Parkinson, 1991) and many others (see Fineman, 2008). Recent studies of customer service work in outsourced call centres in India have also highlighted the extent to which the intense demand for emotional labour, combined with the effects of identity management and working conditions, result in high levels of 'emotional burnout' (Agrawal and Sadhana, 2010; Surana and Singh, 2009).

In management journals the concern has largely been with highlighting the importance of managing emotion through effective recruitment, selection, socialisation and supervision in order to increase product or service quality and hence, raise profitability. Notable examples include studies of supermarket and convenience store cashiers (Rafaeli, 1989; Sutton and Rafaeli, 1988) and of ride operators at Disneyland (Van Maanen and Kunda, 1989). These studies emphasise that the successful performance of emotional labour typically requires 'a complex combination of facial expression, body language, spoken words and tone of voice' (Rafaeli and Sutton, 1987: 33). This combination seems to be achieved through a range of human resource management techniques, including recruitment and selection, training, supervision and monitoring of employee presentation and performance, to which we now turn.

Managing emotional labour

The importance accorded to emotion and particularly to emotional labour in recent years means that considerable efforts have been made to control both its experience and expression. Hence, whereas what Hochschild termed 'emotion work' is governed largely according to an informal network of rules, including social values, attitudes and expectations, emotional labour is subject to a complex range of direct and indirect management control techniques. The importance of recruitment and selection of individuals of appropriate emotional dispositions has been highlighted (Ashforth and Humphrey, 1995; Callaghan and Thompson, 2002), as has the role of induction and training in establishing group norms of emotional expression (Redman and Mathews, 2002). The importance of increasing group solidarity by creating opportunities for shared emotion during communal activities has also been emphasised (Morris and Feldman, 1997; Warren and Fineman, 2007). In particular, the rationalisation of emotion has been highlighted, particularly through the use of managerial attempts to introduce an element of routine and uniformity into the performance of emotional labour (Leidner, 1993, 1999).

Leidner's research suggests that employers introduce a variety of strategies aimed at reducing unpredictable elements, in order to standardise the behaviour of workers and service recipients. To overcome resistance to mass-produced service, for example, employees are often required to find ways to personalise routines, or to appear to do so. Further, where too much unpredictability remains to make it possible to dispense with worker flexibility entirely, employers often undertake what Leidner (1993) calls 'routinization by transformation' – changing workers into the kinds of people who will make decisions and interact with customers in ways that management desire and approve of. Indeed, the organisations in her research

(McDonald's and Combined Insurance) paid 'close attention to how their workers looked, spoke, and felt, rather than limiting standardization to the performance of physical tasks' (Leidner, 1993: 18).

Management writers Ashforth and Humphrey (1995: 104) identify four overlapping mechanisms for the management of emotion. These involve: *neutralising, buffering, prescribing* and *normalising* emotion:

> 'neutralizing' is used to prevent the emergence of socially unacceptable emotions, while the remaining means are used to regulate emotions that are either unavoidable or inherent in role performance; 'buffering' is used to encapsulate and segregate potentially disruptive emotions from ongoing activities; 'prescribing' is used to specify socially acceptable means of experiencing and expressing emotions; and 'normalizing' is used to diffuse or reframe acceptable emotions to preserve the status quo.

In her account of stories collected from members of various organisations in the US following terrorist attacks on 11 September 2001, Michaela Driver (2003) found that all four of Ashforth and Humphrey's measures were deployed as behavioural controls governing the expression of emotion. While buffering, prescribing and normalising seemed to have a positive effect on employee morale, the use of neutralising controls appeared to be somewhat damaging to employee commitment. Driver argues that it is useful to think of the range of reactions to organisational control attempts along a continuum (Figure 20.1).

In her research, buffering controls seemed to result in fairly positive reactions, somewhat above those that attempted to normalise emotion. Prescriptive controls, which 'refocused emotional expression from the horror of the events to acts of caring, seemed to result in the most positive reaction' (Driver, 2003: 542), as many employees were 'elated by how humane or family-like their organization appeared to be'. By the same token, employees perceived organisations that sought to neutralise or suppress emotional expression largely negatively, primarily because 'they would not grant space to express emotion but instead sought to return to business as usual'.

Driver's (2003) account highlights several themes in the management and study of emotion. First, it emphasises the importance of employee perceptions of the relationship between emotional control and organisational culture. As she puts it,

> if organizational members view organizational control behaviours as indicators of their organization's culture, then the selection of control behaviours may be a critical process.
> *(2003: 543)*

Furthermore, such measures may be an important means by which employees assess whether they 'fit' with the values and culture of the organisation, and hence are important in terms of recruitment, selection and retention (this illustrates the point made above that emotions often act as a 'pivot' between the individual and the social or organisational).

Second, employees seemed not only to accept but to expect some level of organisational control of emotional expression – 'none of the stories indicated that the storytellers resented their organizations for attempting to control their emotions' (Driver 2003: 544). Finally, her analysis emphasised the importance of developing a contingency approach to understanding the ways in which different employees respond to varying types of organisational controls on emotional expression in different circumstances and across different levels of organisational and occupational hierarchies.

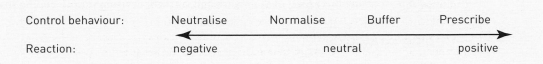

Figure 20.1

Source: Driver, 2003: 542, Fig. 1. Republished with permission, Emerald Group Publishing Limited (www.emerald.insight.com).

Developing this contingency theme, Sloan (2004) has recently highlighted the importance of occupational status for those who experience workplace frustration, noting how individuals in highly esteemed occupations are more likely than lower-status employees to deal with anger directly, and hence experience less anger-induced, work-related stress. A similar finding has emerged from recent research on the relationship between emotion, management and learning which has emphasised the tensions that can exist between individual and organisational learning. Vince and Saleem (2004), for example, have highlighted the tensions created through repeated patterns of caution and blame within organisations. Their study shows how these tensions actually inhibit emotional processes of reflection and communication, undermining the implementation and further development of strategies explicitly designed for organisational learning.

Such contingencies, status inequalities and tensions are relatively neglected themes in the highly functionalist literature on emotional intelligence, which tends to emphasise that the successful harnessing of emotion leads unproblematically to increased identification, commitment, productivity and manageability. Yet recent research on service work has suggested that managerial efforts to secure employee identification and commitment through training, in the use of scripted and set-piece dialogue techniques for example, can actually have the opposite effect, engendering emotional dissonance and disharmony (Lashley, 2002).

Many of the studies of emotional labour also highlight the ways in which it is managed through the design of systems and routines ('scripts', for instance – see Leidner, 1993), and through particular supervisory practices (Johansson and Näslund, 2009; Van Maanen and Kunda, 1989), often involving self-and peer surveillance (Tyler and Abbott, 1998).

Example

Consider the following instructions, given to flight attendants during a training course at an international airline:

Always walk softly through the cabin, always make eye contact with each and every passenger, and always smile at them. This makes for a much more personal service, and is what First Class travel and [we] as a company are all about. It's what we're here for. *(Cited in Hancock and Tyler, 2001b: 31)*

Why might these instructions have been given – what were the management team and the trainers trying to achieve?

How might the performance of emotional labour (through making eye contact, smiling and so on) have conflicted with other aspects of the flight attendant's job?

How might the flight attendants manage (or avoid) this potential conflict?

When combined with the various demands of the work involved, techniques used to manage emotional labour can result in its performance becoming especially problematic for the individual. Such demands can involve, for instance, the requirement that a particular emotional display – such as smiling for the entire duration of a long flight – be maintained over long periods of time, often in working environments that are entirely unconducive to maintaining such displays (Bain and Boyd, 1998). Similarly, emotional labourers tend to be required to maintain an appropriate emotional display to customers who are being rude or offensive (Filby, 1992; Hochschild, 1983), resulting in many emotional labourers experiencing difficulties in performing this aspect of their work and, as such, devising various coping strategies.

Coping strategies

At their simplest, coping strategies may involve employees making use of 'back stage' areas (where customers and possibly co-workers are not present) to let off steam or simply 'switch off' (Van Maanen and Kunda, 1989: 67). Whereas managerial approaches to coping with the demands of emotional labour tend to highlight the importance of HRM techniques such as enriching job engagement through career planning and re-design of work systems (see Agrawal and Sadhana's 2010 study of employee engagement in Indian call centres), more sociological approaches tend to focus on the development of what Korczynski (2003) describes as 'communities of coping', based upon the deployment of collective forms of emotion work. Respondents in Bolton and Boyd's (2003: 298) study for instance emphasised the importance of camaraderie in coping with the emotional demands of service work. According to one flight attendant in their research:

> The other crew are the best thing about this job and the only thing that keeps me going. We always manage to have a laugh during flights and that's what makes the long hours, annoying passengers and terrible working conditions bearable.

Similarly Åsa Wettergen (2010), in her study of workers involved in the processing of applications for asylum at the Swedish Migration Board, found that the men and women who took part in her research coped with the emotional demands of their work by developing interaction rituals that sustained an 'emotional regime' emphasising procedural correctness and professionalism. Similarly, in their study of 911 call-takers in a city-based Emergency Center in the US, focusing on the different ways in which feelings are understood, expressed and managed in an emotionally charged organisational setting, Tracy and Tracy (1998) emphasise the importance of communication in enabling co-workers to offer each other mutual support.

Humour also appears to be a particularly important mechanism for diffusing the potentially negative aspects of emotional labour – when police officers have to deal with major disasters, for instance, humour may be a way in which they can diffuse the emotional impact of their work on themselves and their colleagues (Alexander and Wells, 1991). In her account of humour as a coping strategy in the sex industry, for example, Teela Sanders (2004) argues that sex workers consciously manipulate humour as a social and psychological distancing technique; humour contributes to a range of defence mechanisms that are necessary to protect the personal and emotional well-being of sex workers. She identifies six types of humour among sex workers that probably apply to many other forms of interactive service work that require a range of emotional management skills and coping strategies. These are:

- private jokes used to ridicule clients;
- coded jokes that flow between sex workers in the presence of clients;
- stories and anecdotes of personal disclosure framed in terms of jocularity and jest;
- humour as a strategy to resist harassment and verbal aggression from community harassers and protesters;
- humour as a source of communication with professionals (healthcare workers and police officers, for instance);
- humour as a signifier of conflict and group membership.

An alternative strategy is to retreat into the routine. Leidner (1993, 1999) suggests that sales-service workers resort to their scripts as a way of separation and that scripting is not more alienating therefore, but less so, because 'routines may actually offer interactive service workers some protection from assaults on their selves' (Leidner 1993: 14). Another strategy identified involves a more empathetic form of deflection. For instance, in dealing with situations involving emotional conflict, Hochschild (1983: 105–8) reports that flight attendants are trained to perceive difficult or offensive passengers as people who are experiencing problems in their personal lives or who are afraid of flying, and to manage their emotions accordingly. Underlying this aspect of their training, however, is the requirement for attendants to respond positively to emotional conflicts and to manage them in such a way as to always 'think sales' and so, essentially, to rationalise an otherwise 'irrational' organisational interaction.

Emotional labour: a critique

In her critique of Hochschild's use of the term emotional labour – a concept she suggests 'has now been stretched to its very limits' – Sharon Bolton (2000) has offered a typology that distinguishes four distinct types of emotion management:

- **presentational** (emotion management according to general, social 'rules' – Hochschild's (1983) 'emotion work', see Bolton and Boyd, 2003);
- **philanthropic** (emotion management given as a 'gift');
- **prescriptive** (emotion management according to organisational/professional rules of conduct, but not necessarily in the pursuit of profit);
- **pecuniary** (emotion management for commercial gain – Hochschild's 'emotional labour', see Bolton and Boyd, 2003).

Bolton emphasises that emotional labour can be a source of pleasure as well as pain, and that many opportunities exist to engage in what Ackroyd and Thompson (1999) have called 'organisational misbehaviour'. For Yiannis Gabriel (1995), affective aspects of work are a fundamental part of what he calls 'the unmanaged organisation' – those spaces for resistance that are ultimately beyond the reach of managerial control. This may suggest, as Bolton argues, that an over-concentration on the 'pecuniary' category of emotional labour can lead to the neglect of vital parts of organisational life, in particular of 'the *emotional management skills* organizational actors possess' (Bolton and Boyd, 2003: 289, emphasis added), and of the potential for pleasure and job satisfaction in the performance of emotional labour.

Hence, despite its widespread and enduring influence, Bolton and Boyd (2003) note three central weaknesses in Hochschild's account of emotional labour. First, they argue, Hochschild over-emphasises the divide between public and private performances of emotional self-management, and tends to use the terms 'public' and 'commercial' interchangeably, creating an oversimplified dichotomy. Bolton and Boyd argue that here (and elsewhere) Hochschild operates according to the assumption that there is no room for 'emotion work' within organisational life.

Second, they argue that Hochschild mistakenly equates a physical labour process with an emotional one. However, Bolton and Boyd argue that unlike the factory worker in Marx's analysis, for instance, interactive service workers such as airline cabin crew 'own' the means of production (their bodies and emotions) and, therefore, ultimately control the capacity to present a 'sincere' or 'cynical' performance. What Hochschild fails to recognise, they argue, is that the indeterminacy of labour, and of managerial attempts to control it, is further exacerbated within the contested terrain of the emotional labour process as a result.

Third, Bolton and Boyd argue that 'Hochschild's concern with management attempts to seduce employees into "loving" the company, its product and its customers, creates an illusion of emotionally crippled actors' (Bolton and Boyd, 2003: 290). In contrast, they conclude that emotional labourers such as airline cabin crew demonstrate high levels of emotional dexterity as they are able to draw on different sets of feeling rules (commercial, professional, organisational and social) in order to match feeling to situation, thus rendering them multi-skilled emotional managers who are able to 'balance conflicting demands and still . . . effect polished performances' (Bolton and Boyd, 2003: 295).

Despite the efficaciousness of Bolton's critique, however, what remains the case is that emotional labour is relatively low-paid, low-status work. One of the main reasons for this is that it is predominantly carried out by women because women are deemed to be inherently skilled in its performance; in other words, the skill involved is 'essentialised'. In O'Brien's study of the UK nursing profession for instance, he argued that the skills possessed by nurses are often thought to derive 'not from the qualities of being a nurse, but from the qualities of being a woman' (O'Brien, 1994: 399).

Conclusions

In discussing emotion in organisations we have endeavoured to identify the various factors underpinning its emergence as an increasingly significant concern within HRM theory and practice. In sum, while traditionally emotion has largely been perceived as a relatively un-desirable appendage to organisational rationality and, as such, to be excluded from organised life, in more recent approaches, particularly those associated with HRM, emotions have become increasingly valued as organisational resources in themselves. A prime example of this can be found in the idea of 'emotional intelligence'. Yet, as Fineman has noted, although HRM 'aims to harness positive emotion as a "success" ingredient' (1994: 86), emotion is still regarded as being in need of careful managerial rationalisation. As Fineman (1994: 545) has put it, the dominant belief continues to be that

> Cool, clear, strategic thinking is not to be too sullied by messy feelings. Efficient thought and behaviour tame emotion. Accordingly, good organisations are places where feelings are managed, designed out or removed.

In the latter part of the chapter, however, we also outlined the insights of a range of more critical approaches to understanding organisations as 'emotional arenas' that demand the performance of emotional labour. Here, we drew largely on the work of those who have sought to understand organisational emotions in terms of their commodification. This approach has emphasised the extent to which the emotions of employees are considered fair game for employer intervention when self-presentation and interactive service style are integral parts of the labour process. As Simon Williams (2001: 112) has put it, the contemporary era is one in which emotions appear to be 'managed if not manipulated, and marketed if not manufactured, to an unprecedented degree'. Hence, the '(re)discovery' of the emotional has provided an important lever in terms of management practice and critique.

This led us to pay particular attention to the idea of emotional labour. While the definition first proposed by Hochschild over 20 years ago has endured, we acknowledged how subsequent research has not only demonstrated how the contours and experiences of emotional labour are now thought to be more complex than those described in her account, but how much more widespread it is becoming across the contemporary organisational landscape. For as Steinberg and Figart (1999: 23) have noted in this regard,

> As our economy moves increasingly toward the provision of services and as the public–private distinction further blurs, the skills, effort and responsibilities associated with emotional labour will become more central to our understanding of what it means to work.

In this chapter, then, we have tried to think critically about emotion in work organisations in terms of the management of emotion and the performance of emotional labour. In Case Study 20.1 (based on Russell and Tyler, 2002), we consider some of the concepts, ideas and debates introduced here with reference to the lived experience of emotion in the workplace, and reflect on some of the issues this raises for HRM theory and practice.

CASE STUDY 20.1

EMOTION MANAGEMENT AT GIRLIE GLITTER CO.

MELISSA TYLER AND PHILIP HANCOCK

The Girlie Glitter Co. concept and design

Girlie Glitter Co. is a UK-based chain of retail outlets whose products and services are marketed primarily at 3–13-year-old girls. The team who designed the concept took the theme of 'girl power' as their starting point, and aimed to create a retail format catering specifically for young girls. The idea was to develop a retail store that stocked not only a range of (largely dressing up and party) clothes, hair-styling products, cosmetics and fashion accessories, but also that provided the opportunity for girls to have a 'make-over' in store. The aim, as one of the co-founders of the company described it, was to create 'a girl friendly … pleasurable space … in which young girls could enjoy shopping together, and … mothers could enjoy shopping with their daughters'. In short, as the design team put it, the idea was to develop a retail experience that 'lets little girls live a dream'.

The format that was developed reflects a broader evolution in retail marketing towards stores as places to do more than just shop. With this in mind, a distinct design was developed – the stores are loud, bright and have a discernible colour and style theme that clearly differentiates them from other retail outlets in the shopping centres in which they are located. Indeed, colour was considered to be a vital component of their aesthetic and the design team decided that everything should be 'pink … and glittery, with lots of hearts'. This provided the style theme throughout the project and helped to bring to life the idea that the presentation of the products and services on offer should be a 'magical experience'. Much like other retail outlets and theme parks marketed particularly at children and families, the emphasis was upon the creation of an atmosphere of 'clean, wholesome, family fun'.

The Girlie Glitter Co. experience

Customers are enticed into the stores largely by the theatricality of what they have to offer. This is experienced through a combination of music, abundant use of glitter, bright lighting and white flooring, combined with distinctive chrome fittings, pink lettering and iconography (hearts and stars), as well as rows of sparkly costumes and make-up. Sales staff perform dance routines at the front of stores at regular intervals throughout the day creating 'an atmosphere of excitement', as one store manager put it. This reflects a broader performance ethos throughout the company that, at least in part, differentiates Girlie Glitter Co. from other retail outlets selling similar products. It has important implications for the recruitment, selection, training and monitoring of sales staff. As one of the co-founders of the company put it, 'staff don't see themselves as sales assistants but as performers'. Store managers are encouraged to think of themselves as 'co-ordinators of a leisure experience'.

In this respect, the marketing team developed a number of other features designed to differentiate the Girlie Glitter brand from other retail 'experiences'. As the store's publicity puts it, 'not only does Girlie Glitter stock all things feminine and girlie, it provides its young customers with the opportunity to be transformed into a fairy princess in store'. At the front of the stores are located spaces called 'Princess Studios'. These are hair-styling and make-up areas where customers can have their hair and nails done, as well as a range of themed make-overs.

Because of this aspect of their work, sales assistants (or 'performers') function not only as dancers but also as hairdressers, make-up artists and nail technicians. Instructed to 'have fun while thinking sales' on the shop floor, they are also told to just 'do what comes naturally' as one sales assistant put it. This means that sales assistants 'need to look right because we are there for the girls [customers] to copy'. In this sense, 'standard presentation is important because they are like role models, they influence the kids, much like characters in kids' cartoons or TV programmes, really', as one area sales manager said.

Aware of the potential pitfalls of standardisation and thematic repetition, however, the aim was to 'customise' the service provided, and to recruit staff capable of making individual customers feel special. Crucially, as the Girlie Glitter Co. marketing officer put it, 'this shop was not to be seen as an exploitation of children: it had to represent their dreams, and every girl who visited Girlie Glitter had to feel as though she had walked into a shop that was there just for her'. He goes on to say that this is because

> customers are no longer willing to accept that the shops they visit are just places to buy goods. They demand drama and deserve to be delighted by the experience. Shops have become destinations in themselves – not only a place to purchase, but as a place to be entertained, inspired and, in the case of Girlie Glitter Co., to have loads of fun. This means that the staff we select to work here, particularly on the shop floor, are absolutely crucial.

Recruitment, selection and training at Girlie Glitter Co.

Recruitment at Girlie Glitter Co. can be likened to the formation of an all-girl pop group; potential employees are asked to sing and dance. Recruitment sessions are described not as interviews but as auditions. When a number of sales staff are being recruited for a new store, group interviews (or 'auditions') are held, followed by individual ones. As the HR officer responsible for recruitment and selection put it, 'group auditions allow you to see who shines through above the rest … and that's what we're looking for, people who really shine through and have that extra special something to offer'. Applicants, even those with relevant work experience, are often rejected because they do not look, sound or perform right. This is largely because 'personality is so important to what we do. It is vital for staff to really believe in the concept, so we recruit the personality not just the person.'

There is no specific training as such for sales staff, more an informal process of socialisation that involves, for those not skilled in hairstyling and make-up techniques, learning largely from each other. The makeovers are taught and practised much like 'painting by numbers', according to colour-coded charts and a predetermined make-up palette. Dance routines are taught by store managers who act as choreographers, and are practised by staff mainly before and after store opening hours. All staff are encouraged to socialise together and it is routine practice for staff at new stores or new staff at established ones to be taken out to a local bar by the store or area manager on group social events. There is a lot of informal pressure to attend these social gatherings and anyone who does not go along is thought to be 'not much fun' and so not really a Girlie Glitter person.

The sales and marketing director at Girlie Glitter Co. likens her role to that of a theatre director or a stage manager: 'responsible for managing the performers who work together like a cast'. She also suggested that she sees herself very much as a script writer, involved in the production of Girlie Glitter Co. as a performance. This theatre metaphor carried through into other aspects of the format – store managers were likened to floor or 'front of house' managers, whose primary role is to stage manage those aspects of the store that are visible to the 'audience' [customers]; the till area was referred to by experienced staff as the 'box office', and the storerooms were described as 'backstage'. The opening of the store each day was called 'curtain call', and sales staff reported feeling 'stage fright' before the store opened and the 'performance' became subject to public scrutiny.

Emotional labour at Girlie Glitter Co.

Despite their nerves, staff were told it was 'more important to smile, and to look happy, than to be step perfect' in the dance routines. As one sales assistant put it, 'We're told it's more important to *look* happy than to *be* happy.' For many staff, this meant either faking it or as one described it, 'going into robot':

> Sometimes I just look in the mirror, smile, and remind myself to hold that position during the day. At other times, when we've got the music on and we're dancing, I start thinking about messing around with my mates the night before and then I start to smile anyway. So I daydream quite a lot. It looks like I am really enjoying myself there and then, and the customers don't know any different, so there's no harm done really. At other times you don't really have to try, because it is such good fun. You see these really cute little girls come in and do their hair and make-up and they look so pretty, really cute and it's just great. I think how much I would've loved that when I was their age, all the dressing up and stuff. Some days I really love it here. Other days, if we're busy, or there are kids that are playing up, or older girls are in here just messing about and being a pain then it's not so great and you have to just put it on because that's what we're being paid for … that's what we're selling, big smiles and loads of fun.

Some sales assistants coped with the embarrassment or 'stage fright' of the dance routines by relying on each other, and by 'having a laugh': 'It is scary when you're out there and it's a really busy day and you maybe see someone you know going by, or people are pointing and laughing and you just look at each other and giggle. I couldn't do it out there on my own, but at least together we can have a bit of a laugh, and I mean, to be dancing about with your mates and getting paid for it, you can't really complain can you?' New recruits particularly tended to feel anxious about performing in front of a crowd, however: 'I get very nervous before curtain call. But afterwards I get that coming off stage feeling and think, "Thank God, I did it", until the next time.'

Many of the staff are conscious that they are role models for their young customers, and realise the extent to which their uniform appearance (all shop floor staff wear fitted pink T-shirts with the Girlie Glitter logo on them – for sale in children's sizes in store, and black trousers) helped them to identify together as a group. The uniform appearance of staff is thought to be particularly important by the Girlie Glitter management team. One of the area sales managers (the only male employed by the company at the time of the research) also wore black trousers and a pink company T-shirt. He reflected 'I could wear a traditional suit and tie, but choose to wear the pink to fit in. It's not glittery and tight-fitting like theirs [the all-female sales staff], but at least we all look the same and that's important … so that we all fit in.'

Music is also particularly important to the management of Girlie Glitter Co., especially in terms of fostering employee and customer identification. Particular types of music (mainly by all-girl pop groups) or even specific songs come to be associated with the store, and these tend to provide a continuous soundtrack to the 'front stage' areas and, of course, to the dance routines performed at the store entrances. One particular store manager summed up the general effect of this when she said: 'Every time I hear one of the songs we play, I am immediately reminded of the company, wherever I am or whatever I'm doing.'

Some sales assistants had experienced really rude or aggressive customers – either children playing up, or their parents shouting and being abusive. When this happens

'you just think, 'Oh well, they're paying for it I suppose.' It's their kid's birthday or whatever, or maybe they're divorced Dads and this is their only day with the children and so you think, 'Just let them get on with it.' But it can be hard, sometimes. Some days when I've finished work all I can hear is the same music over and over in my head, and screaming, whining children saying 'I want this….' I don't think I'll ever have kids of my own, thanks very much. I've seen enough tantrums to last me a lifetime!

Questions

1 In what ways is gender relevant to the performance and management of emotional labour at Girlie Glitter Co.?

2 How might the concepts of 'surface acting' and 'deep acting' (Hochschild, 1983) be applied to the experiences of sales assistants?

3 Drawing on Bolton and Boyd's (2003) typology, identify the different types of emotion management performed by sales assistants at Girlie Glitter Co.

4 What techniques have the management team devised to encourage sales assistants to perform emotional labour?

5 What coping strategies do staff implement to alleviate the negative consequences of the emotional labour aspects of their work?

6 Draft a recruitment advertisement for sales assistants at Girlie Glitter Co. What key issues might you need to consider in recruiting, selecting and training new staff?

CASE STUDY 20.2

MANAGING FAMILY FUN AT THEME PARK CO.

PHILIP HANCOCK AND MELISSA TYLER

Jason is a section manager at Theme Park Co. He is responsible for managing 8 full-time and 14 part-time, largely seasonally employed workers, who work in the family section of a major theme park. This particular area of the park includes rides specifically designed for children who are under the minimum height requirement for the 'thrill' rides (the roller-coasters and so on), and many of the rides are based on familiar children's characters from television programmes, films and children's books. This section of the park has been experiencing recurring problems with unacceptably high levels of voluntary staff turnover, as well as escalating reports of customer dissatisfaction. The latter have been revealed as a result of verbal reports both to Jason himself, and to members of his team, as well as through customer exit surveys. These have suggested that both adult and child customers are particularly unhappy about excessively long waiting times, rides not functioning correctly and disappointment when children are refused entrance to a ride or attraction because it is being serviced or cleaned. The most stressful side of the job for Jason is balancing the need for 'throughput' (processing customers through the rides and attractions as efficiently as possible) with the demand for customer satisfaction, and the need to provide a quality, personalised service to children and their families. As he puts it, 'It's, you know, pushing people through but with a smile, so we do actually have to spend some time, to keep them coming back.' Through their staff development mechanisms, Jason and his line manager have reached the conclusion that while Jason is coping extremely well with the logistical aspects of his role, he would benefit from developing his skills in coping with the emotional side of the job, and in particular the competing demands placed upon him. They have identified a training consultancy that runs courses on emotional intelligence and need to outline what Jason feels he needs and how he is likely to benefit through developing his emotional intelligence.

Questions

1 Clarify what the term 'emotional intelligence' means and outline the kind of skills and abilities that Jason might improve as a result of developing his emotional intelligence.

2 What might be the main benefits of providing Jason with an opportunity to develop his emotional intelligence – for Jason, for Theme Park Co. as an employer, and for customers?

3 With reference to this particular example, what criticisms might be made of this approach, and of the concept of 'emotional intelligence'?

CASE STUDY 20.3
CHANGE AND EMOTION AT HOTEL CO.

MELISSA TYLER AND PHILIP HANCOCK

The senior management at Hotel Co., a large hotel in Singapore employing some 243 people at any one time, have recently introduced a computerised system that has fully integrated all aspects of customer service. The hotel's clientele are primarily Western business travellers and their families, and many of these are now able to make their own hotel bookings online. While all customer-facing and support staff have been fully trained in the more technical aspects of accessing and operating the system, this major change has impacted on staff in a number of ways that senior managers had not anticipated. First, staff who previously worked closely together even though they were formally part of different teams no longer have any reason to work together or to interact during the normal course of their work. This has caused a degree of disharmony and disappointment among some members of staff, particularly those who have been employed by the hotel for some time. Newer members of staff are also finding little reason to engage with their colleagues in any sustained way, as most forms of interaction and communication can be carried out electronically. Second, members of staff who have worked for the hotel for some time and had been happy with the old ways of working have resented not only the change itself, but also the way in which it has been introduced, with limited communication, consultation or explanation from senior management before, during or after the introduction of the new system. Third, the electronic booking system means that hotel guests can now book direct and request specific items for their room such as a room-service meal or even a particular type of pillow on their bed upon their arrival. However, as the system is relatively new and in the early stages of implementation, the hotel's staff are finding that they often have to intervene to correct or amend particular arrangements. Hotel guests are reporting that their rooms are not entirely what they expected when they booked and particularly front-line reception staff are finding that they have to increase the effort they put into providing a high-quality customer service. In recognition of some of the difficulties they face, the hotel's senior management team have enforced strict guidelines on uniform and grooming in order to convey a professional image of the hotel at all times. All staff have also been required to attend a one-day training course at which the '3 S's' of effective customer interaction are reinforced: 'smiling, sincerity and service'.

Questions

1 Why might Hotel Co., following the introduction of the new ICT system, be described as an 'emotional cauldron'? What does this mean – for staff, for senior managers and for customers?

2 What key aspects of managing change at Hotel Co. did senior management overlook?

3 What impact has this had on staff, and on customers?

4 In addition to the additional training courses they are offering, what measures might be introduced to address some of the difficulties the organisation faces in this current situation?

Bibliography

Ackroyd, S. and Thompson, P. (1999) *Organizational Misbehaviour,* London: Sage.

Agrawal, R.K. and Sadhana, J. (2010) 'Emotional labour and employee engagement in call centres: a study in Indian context', *International Journal of Work, Organisation and Emotion,* Vol.3, No.4, 351–67.

Albrow, M. (1992) '*Sine ira et studio* – or do organizations have feelings?', *Organization Studies,* Vol.13, No.3, 313–29.

Alexander, D. and Wells, W. (1991) 'Reactions of police officers to body handling after a major disaster', *British Journal of Psychiatry,* Vol.159, 547–55.

Allen, J. and Du Gay, P. (1994) 'Industry and the rest: the economic identity of services', *Work, Employment and Society,* Vol.8, No.2, 255–71.

Ashforth, B. and Humphrey, R. (1993) 'Emotional labour in service roles: the influence of identity', *Academy of Management Review,* Vol.18, No.1, 18–115.

Ashforth, B. and Humphrey, R. (1995) 'Emotion in the workplace: a reappraisal', *Human Relations,* Vol.48, No.2, 97–121.

Bain, P. and Boyd, C. (1998) 'Once I get you up there where the air is rarefied: health, safety and the working conditions of airline cabin crews', *New Technology, Work and Employment,* Vol.13, No.1, 16–28.

Barnard, C. (1938) *The Functions of the Executive,* Cambridge, MA: Harvard University Press.

Barsoux, J. (1993) *Funny Business: Humour, Management and Business Culture.* London: Cassell Publications.

Bell, E. and Taylor, S. (2003) 'The elevation of work: pastoral power and the new age work ethic', *Organization,* Vol.10, No.2, 329–49.

Bendix, R. (1956) *Work and Authority in Industry: Ideologies of Management in the Course of Industrialization*, New York: Wiley.

Bolton, S. (2000) 'Emotion here, emotion there, emotional organizations everywhere', *Critical Perspectives on Accounting,* Vol.11, 155–71.

Bolton, S. (2004) *Emotion Management in the Workplace.* London: Palgrave.

Bolton, S. (ed.) (2007) *Dimensions of Dignity at Work.* London: Palgrave.

Bolton, S. and Boyd, C. (2003) 'Trolley dolly or skilled emotion manager? Moving on from Hochschild's managed heart', *Work, Employment and Society,* Vol.17, No.2, 289–308.

Callaghan, G. and Thompson, P. (2002) 'We recruit attitude: the selection and shaping of routine call centre work', *Journal of Management Studies*, Vol.39, No.2, 233–53.

Carlzon, J. (1987) *Moments of Truth,* New York: Harper Row.

Chugh, S. and Hancock, P. (2009) 'Networks of aestheticization: The architecture, artefacts and embodiment of hairdressing salons', *Work, Employment and Society*, Vol.23, No.3, 460–76.

Cooper, R. (1998) 'Sentimental value', *People Management,* April, 48–50.

Crossley, N. (1998) 'Emotions and communicative action', in Bendelow, G. and Williams, S. (eds) *Emotions in Social Life: Critical Themes and Contemporary Issues,* London: Routledge.

Driver, M. (2003) 'United we stand, or else? Exploring organizational attempts to control emotional expression by employees on September 11, 2001', *Journal of Organizational Change Management,* Vol.16, No.5, 534–46.

Elias, N. (1991) 'On human beings and their emotions: a process sociological essay', in Featherstone, M., Hepworth, M. and Turner, B.S. (eds) *The Body: Social Process and Cultural Theory,* London: Sage.

Filby, M. (1992) 'The figures, the personality and the bums: service work and sexuality', *Work, Employment and Society,* Vol.6, No.1, 23–42.

Fineman, S. (ed.) (1993) *Emotion in Organizations,* London: Sage.

Fineman, S. (1994) 'Organizing and emotion: towards a social construction', in Hassard, J. and Parker, M. (eds) *Towards a New Theory of Organizations,* London: Routledge.

Fineman, S. (ed.) (2008) *The Emotional Organization: Passions and Power,* Oxford: Blackwell.

Fleming, P. and Sturdy, A. (2009) 'Bringing everyday life back into the workplace: Just be yourself!', in Hancock, P. and Tyler, M. (eds) *The Management of Everyday Life.* Basingstoke: Palgrave Macmillan.

Frost, P. (2003) *Toxic Emotions at Work: How Compassionate Managers Handle Pain and Conflict*, Boston, MA: Harvard Business School Press.

Gabriel, Y. (1995) 'The unmanaged organization: stories, fantasies and subjectivity', *Organization Studies,* Vol.16, 477–502.

Goffman, E. (1959) *The Presentation of Self in Everyday Life,* Harmondsworth: Penguin.

Goleman, D. (2009a) *Working with Emotional Intelligence,* New York: Bantam Books.

Goleman, D. (2009b) *Emotional Intelligence: Why It Can Matter More Than IQ,* London: Bloomsbury.

Goleman, D., Boyatzis, R. and McKee, A. (2002) *Primal Leadership: Realizing the Power of Emotional Intelligence,* Boston, MA: Harvard Business School Press.

Hall, E.J. (1993) 'Waitering/waitressing: engendering the work of table servers', *Gender and Society,* Vol.17, No.3, 329–46.

Hancock, P. and Tyler, M. (2001a) *Work, Postmodernism and Organization: A Critical Introduction*, London: Sage.

Hancock, P. and Tyler, M. (2001b) 'The look of love: gender and the organization of aesthetics', in Hassard, J., Holliday, R. and Willmott, H. (eds) *Body and Organization,* London: Sage.

Harris, J. (1996) *Getting Employees to Fall in Love With Your Company*, New York: Amacom.

Herzberg, F. (1974) *Work and the Nature of Man,* London: Crosby Lockwood Staples.

Hochschild, A.R. (1979) 'Emotion work, feeling rules and social structure', *American Journal of Sociology,* Vol.85, No.3, 551–75.

Hochschild, A.R. (1983) *The Managed Heart: Commercialization of Human Feeling,* Berkeley, CA: University of California Press.

Hochschild, A.R. (1990) 'Ideology and emotion management: a perspective and path for future research', in Kemper, T. (ed.) *Research Agendas in the Sociology of Emotions,* New York: SUNY Press.

Hunter, C., Jemielniak, D. and Postula, A. (2010) 'Temporal and spatial shifts within playful work', *Journal of Organizational Change Management*, Vol.23, No.1, 87–102.

James, N. (1989) 'Emotional labour: skill and work in the social regulation of human feeling', *Sociological Review,* Vol.37, No.1, 15–42.

Johansson, M. and Näslund, L. (2009) 'Welcome to Paradise: customer experience design and emotional labour on a cruise ship', *International Journal of Work, Organisation and Emotion*, Vol.3, No.1, 40–55.

Kandola, R. and Fullerton, J. (1995) *Managing the Mosaic: Diversity in Action,* London: Institute of Personnel Development.

Kanter, R.M. (1977) *Men and Women of the Corporation,* New York: Basic Books.

Konz, G.N.P. and Ryan, F.X. (1999) 'Maintaining an organizational spirituality: no easy task', *Journal of Organizational Change Management,* Vol.12, No.3, 200–10.

Korczynski, M. (2003) 'Communities of coping: collective emotional labour in service work', *Organization*, Vol.10, No.1, 55–79.

Lashley, C. (2002) 'Emotional harmony, dissonance and deviance at work', *International Journal of Contemporary Hospitality Management,* Vol.14, No.5, 255–7.

Leidner, R. (1993) *Fast Food, Fast Talk: Service Work and the Routinization of Everyday Life*, Berkeley, CA: University of California Press.

Leidner, R. (1999) 'Emotional labour in service work', *Annals of the American Academy of Political and Social Sciences,* Vol.561, 81–95.

Lewis, P. and Simpson, P. (2009) 'Centring and engendering emotions in service work: Hochschild's managed heart and the valuing of feelings in organizational research', *International Journal of Work, Organisation and Emotion*, Vol.3, No.1, 56–64.

Martin, S. (1999) 'Police force of police service? Gender and emotional labour', *Annals of the American Academy of Political and Social Science*, Vol.5, No.1, 111–26.

Maslow, A.H. (1943) 'A theory of human motivation', *Psychological Review,* Vol.50, 372–96.

Mayo, E. (1933) *The Human Problems of Industrial Civilization,* New York: Macmillan.

Morris, J. and Feldman, D. (1997) 'Managing emotions in the workplace', *Journal of Management Issues,* Vol.9, No.3, 257–75.

Neck, C.P. and Milliman, J.F. (1994) 'Thought self-leadership: finding spiritual fulfillment in organizational life', *Journal of Managerial Psychology,* Vol.9, No.6, 9–16.

O'Brien, M. (1994) 'The managed heart revisited: health and social control', *Sociological Review,* Vol.42, No.3, 393–413.

Parkinson, B. (1991) 'Emotional stylists: strategies of expressive management among trainee hairdressers', *Cognition and Emotion,* Vol.5, 419–34.

Paules, G. (1996) 'Resisting the symbolism of service', in Macdonald, C. and Sirianni, C. (eds) *Working in the Service Society,* Philadelphia, PA: Temple University Press.

Peters, T. (1989) *Thriving on Chaos,* London: Pan Books.

Peters, T. and Austin, N. (1985) *A Passion For Excellence,* New York: Random House.

Peters, T. and Waterman, R. (1982) *In Search of Excellence,* New York: Harper & Row.

Prati, L.M. and Karriker, J.H. (2010) 'Emotional intelligence skills: the building blocks of defence against emotional labour burnout', *International Journal of Work, Organisation and Emotion*, Vol.3, No.4, 317–35.

Pringle, R. (1989) 'Bureaucracy, rationality and sexuality: the case of secretaries', in Hearn, J., Sheppard, D., Tancred-Sheriff, P. and Burrell, G. (eds) *The Sexuality of Organization,* London: Sage.

Putnam, L. and Mumby, D. (1993) 'Organizations, emotion and the myth of rationality', in Fineman, S. (ed.) *Emotion in Organizations,* London: Sage.

Rafaeli, A. (1989) 'When cashiers meet customers: an analysis of the role of supermarket cashiers', *Academy of Management Journal,* Vol.32, No.2, 245–73.

Rafaeli, A. and Sutton, R. (1987) 'Expression of emotion as part of the work role', *Academy of Management Review,* Vol.12, 23–37.

Redman, T. and Mathews, B. (2002) 'Managing services: should we be having fun?', *Service Industries Journal*, Vol.22, No.3, 51–62.

Roethlisberger, F.J. and Dickson, W.J. (1939) *Management and the Worker,* Cambridge, MA: Harvard University Press.

Russell, R. and Tyler, M. (2002) 'Thank heaven for little girls: "Girl Heaven" and the commercial context of feminine childhood', *Sociology,* Vol.36, No.3, 619–37.

Sanders, T. (2004) 'Controllable laughter: managing sex work through humour', *Sociology,* Vol.38, No.2, 273–91.

Sloan, M. (2004) 'The effects of occupational characteristics on the experience and expression of anger in the workplace', *Work and Occupations,* Vol.31, No.1, 38–72.

Steinberg, R. and Figart, D. (1999) 'Emotional labour since the managed heart', *Annals of the American Academy of Political and Social Sciences,* No.561, 8–26.

Stewart, D. and Simmons, M. (2010) *The Business Playground: Where Creativity and Commerce Collide,* Harlow: Pearson Education.

Surana, S. and Singh, A. (2009) 'The effect of emotional labour on job burnout among callcentre customer service representatives in India', *Journal of Work, Organisation and Emotion*, Vol.3, No.1, 18–39.

Sutton, R. (1991) 'Maintaining norms about expressed emotions: the case of bill collectors', *Administrative Science Quarterly,* Vol.36, 245–68.

Sutton, R. and Rafaeli, A. (1988) 'Untangling the relationship between displayed emotions and organizational sales: the case of convenience stores', *Academy of Management Journal,* Vol.31, No.3, 461–87.

Taylor, F.W. (1911) *Principles of Scientific Management,* New York: Harper & Row.

Tracy, S. and Tracy, K. (1998) 'Emotion labour at 911: a case study and theoretical critique', *Journal of Applied Communication Research*, Vol.26, 390–411.

Tyler, M. and Abbott, P. (1998) 'Chocs away: weight watching in the contemporary airline industry', *Sociology,* Vol.32, No.3, 433–50.

Van Maanen, J. and Kunda, G. (1989) 'Real feelings: emotional expression and organizational culture', in Cummings, L.L. and Straw, B. (eds) *Research in Organizational Behaviour,* Vol.11. Greenwich, CT: JAI Press.

Vince, R. and Saleem, T. (2004) 'The impact of caution and blame on organizational learning', *Management Learning,* Vol.35, No.2, 133–54.

Vincent, S. (2011) 'The emotional labour process: an essay on the economy of feelings', *Human Relations*, Vol.64, No.10, 1369–92.

Warren, S. and Fineman, S. (2007) '"Don't get me wrong, it's fun here but …": Ambivalence and paradox in a "fun" work environment', in Westwood, R. and Rhodes, C. (eds) *Humour, Work and Organization,* London: Routledge.

Weber, M. (1978 [1921]) *Economy and Society,* Berkeley, CA: University of California Press.

Weber, M. (1989 [1904]) *The Protestant Ethic and the Spirit of Capitalism*, London: Unwin Hyman.

Wettergen, Å. (2010) 'Managing unlawful feelings: the emotional regime of the Swedish Migration Board', *International Journal of Work, Organisation and Emotion*, Vol.3, No.4, 400–19.

Williams, S. (2001) *Emotion and Social Theory,* London: Sage.

CHAPTER 21

FLEXIBILITY

Clare Kelliher

Introduction

Flexibility is a term which has become ubiquitous in business and political discourse in recent decades. However, it has been used in a number of different, albeit related, ways and in different contexts. It has been used to refer to labour market flexibility, concerned with the extent to which governments impose restrictions on employers (Lallement, 2011), organisational flexibility, where organisations are able to respond to changes in their environment (Legge, 2007) and flexibility in the organisation of labour (Kalleberg, 2003). Even within the context of flexibility in the organisation of labour the term has been used in different ways, which can be broadly divided into forms of flexibility which serve the interests of the employer and those which serve the interests of the employee (Alis *et al.,* 2006; Zeytinoglu *et al.,* 2009). Since this text is concerned with human resource management, the main focus here will be with flexibility in the way in which labour is organised. This chapter will examine these different forms of flexibility and while, to date, they have generally been discussed as separate activities and in different areas of the organisation and management literature, it will briefly explore the extent to which there may be potential for some synergy between the different approaches. The chapter begins with an overview of flexibility and will examine the factors which have influenced the growing use of flexible practices and calls for increased flexibility from governments, employers and employees in recent years. It then discusses the different approaches to flexibility in the organisation and management of labour in some detail and examines some of the consequences of alternative approaches to organising labour in different ways. Finally, the chapter will explore the potential for different interests in flexibility to be matched.

Background

Increased competitive pressure is commonly cited as the principal reason why organisations have sought to become more flexible in recent years (Olsen and Kalleberg, 2004). Flexibility as a response to competitive pressure is primarily concerned with an organisation's ability to respond to changes in their external and internal environment. This may require implementing different ways of operating and speed of response may be important in determining whether an organisation is able to take advantage of the opportunities that are available to them. For example, flexibility in this context might be concerned with an organisation responding to a new market opportunity, by being able to expand, or alter the nature of its output. Many changes of this nature will also have implications for the way in which labour is managed (Kalleberg, 2001). In order to be able to respond to a short term increase in demand, there may also be a corresponding short-term need to increase staff numbers. If an employer does not have the ability to increase staff numbers for the short-term only, they will need to weigh up the benefits of responding to the business opportunity, against the continuing costs of employing the additional staff when demand levels are lower.

Employers may also seek greater flexibility in the way in which labour is managed in times of more intense competition to allow them to reduce costs by managing labour more efficiently (Coe *et al.,* 2007). Organisations that experience variation in demand levels for their products or services may be able to increase efficiency by matching the supply of and demand for labour more closely. This is likely to be especially relevant to organisations that are labour intensive and where there is limited opportunity to store their product, as is the case with many services (Korczynski, 2002). For example, in the case of businesses with recognised peaks and troughs in demand, such as retail and hospitality, employers typically increase the numbers of employees in the periods of high demand to ensure that they can cope with the peak and decrease the numbers in periods of low demand, to ensure that they do not have too many staff in the troughs.

One of the primary factors influencing the intensification of competitive pressures in recent times has been greater global integration (Marquardt, 2005). Organisations in the developed world have increasingly faced competition from countries in the developing world, where the cost of labour is often lower. Consequently, this has put pressure on organisations in the developed world to look for ways of containing costs. Competing on the basis of wage rates in the developing economies is unlikely to be a realistic or attractive option for them and therefore they need to look at other means of competing such as innovation, management practices, including efficiency in the use of labour. Especially in those industries which are labour intensive, flexible work practices can open up a number of ways to use labour more efficiently, by for example employing labour only at the times, in the locations and in the quantities needed. Efficiency may also be improved by deploying labour more flexibly and moving away from traditional job boundaries. Increased global integration has also resulted in the need for greater flexibility over when work is carried out, since many organisations may need to accommodate working with colleagues and clients in different time zones.

Developments in information and communication technology (ICT) have also made a significant contribution, to enabling more flexible approaches to work and in particular spatial, or location flexibility (Van Dyne *et al.,* 2007). The availability of the internet has allowed some types work to be carried out away from the workplace, for example where employees can access electronic data remotely and in a similar way to when they are in the workplace. In addition, the pervasiveness of ICT into work and non-work life has also changed expectations associated the communication, availability and speed of response. In particular the use of mobile technologies has increased expectations about availability of people for and speed of response to communications (Matusik and Mickel, 2011), since they do not need to be physically present in a particular location (work or home) to receive, or respond to communications (Besseyre des Horst *et al.,* 2011; Brannen, 2005).

While flexibility is often considered as an organisational issue, it can also have more general relevance for how economies operate. Governments may take steps to promote labour flexibility by means of deregulating the labour market. A lightly regulated, or more flexible labour market, which places fewer legal obligations on employers, it is argued, will increase the attractiveness of an economy to inward investors (Legge, 2007). Flexibility in this context may go beyond the regulation of how labour is employed (e.g. fixed-term, part-time), or deployed (multitasking and multiskilling) and may include employers obligations in relation to issues such as health and safety, recognition and consultation with trade unions. In recent years there is some evidence that governments in Europe have responded to the economic crisis by attempting to make their labour market more flexible, by deregulating working conditions and rights (ETUI, 2012; Peck *et al.,* 2005).

At the same time as these developments in the business environment requiring organisations to become more flexible, we have seen a number of social and demographic changes which have resulted in employees expecting greater flexibility and choice in the way in which they work. In many countries employees seek greater flexibility over where, when and how much they work (Hall and Atkinson, 2006; Hooker *et al.,* 2007; Bloom and Van Reenen, 2006; Yanadori and Kato, 2009). Increasing participation of mothers in paid employment and growing concern among employees to be able to achieve a satisfactory balance between the work and non-work aspects of their lives has resulted in a desire for greater control over the way work is carried out. As such, employers seeking to be competitive in the labour market are likely to respond to employees desires for flexibility, in order to enable them to recruit high calibre employees (Rau and Hyland, 2002; Richardson, 2010). In circumstances where labour and/or skill shortages exist employers may be particularly keen to offer flexible working options, in order to increase their attractiveness to new recruits. See the Tata case study for an example of how a company has approached this. In addition, offering flexible options is seen to be an important tool in recruiting generation Y who are known to place high value on the ability to achieve a satisfactory work–life balance (Gerdes, 2009). Furthermore, in some countries (e.g. Australia, the UK) governments have introduced legal rights allowing employees to request flexible working arrangements. More generally the European Union have developed policy on promoting better jobs and this also includes the ability to combine work and non-work activities effectively (Eurofound, 2010).

Approaches to flexibility

The discussion about and study of flexible working in organisations can be broadly divided into so called flexibility *of* and *for* employees (Alis *et al.,* 2006). Flexibility *of* employees enables organisations to meet their needs for flexibility by using labour in non-standard ways. Flexibility *for* employees allows employees to exercise some degree of choice over how they work, in order to help them balance their work and non-work lives more effectively. Below each type is discussed in more detail.

Flexibility *of* employees

Flexibility of employees may include the use of temporary and part-time contracts; shift working; annual hours contracts; and/or deployment of staff across a range of tasks, crossing traditional job boundaries. This is normally used by organisations to help them to match the supply of and demand for labour more closely and assist with the management of uncertainty (Bryson, 1999).

Back in 1985, John Atkinson developed the model of the flexible firm, which was influential in shaping the debate about this approach to flexibility (Atkinson, 1985). The model identified various labour use strategies which employers might use in order to achieve organisational flexibility and is based on the idea of maintaining a stable core of employees, who are supplemented by a flexible periphery. In this debate a number of broad categories of flexibility are identified, most notably numerical and functional flexibility (Kalleberg, 2001) and, more recently, greater attention has been given to spatial and temporal flexibility.

Numerical flexibility allows for labour to be utilised at times when needed and disposed of when not needed and might involve using part-time employment, or the use of temporary staff, either employed directly or through a temporary employment agency.

Functional flexibility allows for staff to be deployed across different activities according to demand levels and might involve multiskilling and multitasking.

Temporal flexibility involves the time at which labour is used. Traditionally this has tended to involve shift-working, designed to allow labour input for a longer period of time than a standard working day, or to allow for continuous operation on a 24/7 basis as in for example a hospital environment.

Spatial flexibility is associated with the location of work and enables employers to deploy labour in different locations.

Although these forms of flexibility have tended to be distinguished as separate activities, they may also be combined in the context of one job. For example, part-time workers may also be shift workers as is sometimes the case in retail or cleaning work. Temporary employment may also be combined with spatial flexibility, for example with locum pharmacists or supply teachers.

These labour use strategies are likely to be of greatest use to employers who experience fluctuations in demand levels which have direct consequences for labour. Demand may vary on a predictable basis such as seasonal (in the tourism industries), weekly, daily or even within the working day (e.g. restaurants and fast food outlets), or may be unpredictable and influenced by factors such as the weather, or media coverage.

Numerical flexibility

Using numerical flexibility employers might choose to employ staff on part-time or temporary contracts, or to vary the number of hours worked by staff according to business patterns. Varying hours in line with demand levels might involve increasing and decreasing the number of hours worked by part-time staff, or alternatively might involve a longer-term arrangement for full-time staff, such as an annual hours contract. Under an annual hours contract the employer and employee agree a total number of hours to be worked in the year and the employer has the power to alter daily or weekly working hours, normally within an agreed maximum and minimum framework.

Employers who choose to use temporary staff may either employ them directly or may develop a labour supply relationship with a temporary employment agency. Temporary employment may be used to align staffing levels with fluctuations in demand, but may also be used to cope with uncertainty. For example, organisations developing a new product, or entering a new market may use temporary staff to reduce their risks until they feel able to forecast demand levels more accurately. See the BMW case study for an example of this.

Figure 21.1 shows the incidence of part-time work across the OECD countries. In Switzerland, Australia, Ireland and the UK part-time employment represents in the region of a quarter of total employment and in the Netherlands part-time employment represents more than a third (37.1 per cent) of total employment. By contrast, in countries such as Hungary and in the Czech and Slovak Republics part-time employment is much less common and represents less than 5 per cent of total employment. The figure also shows that in many countries there has been a marked increase in the incidence of part-time employment since 2000.

Figure 21.2 shows the proportion of employees with a temporary contract, or contract of limited duration across the European Union member states in 2010. Poland, Spain and Portugal all made relatively high use of this type of numerical flexibility, with in the region of one quarter of the workforce having a temporary contract. By contrast, in Romania, Lithuania, Estonia and Bulgaria the proportion was less than 5 per cent. In the EU as a whole in 2010, the number of employees with a contract of limited duration was 13.9 per cent. Differences

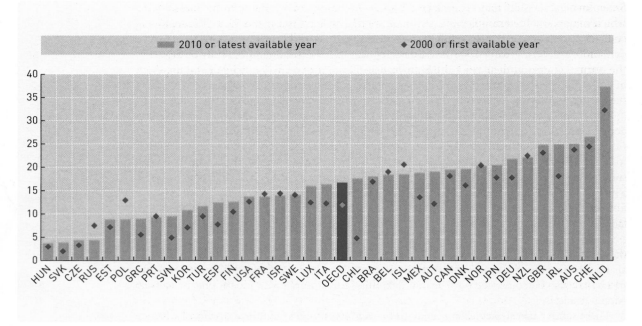

Figure 21.1 Incidence of part-time employment (as a percentage of total employment)

Source: OECD Factbook 2011–2012. *Economic, Environmental and Social Statistics*, OECD Publishing © OECD 2011.

in the use of flexible labour practices between member countries may reflect a number of factors, but are likely at least in part to be due to the ease with which employers can terminate the contracts of employment of permanent employees.

Functional flexibility

Functional flexibility refers to the deployment of employees across a range of tasks according to demand levels. Employees may be deployed across existing job boundaries, suggesting a more fluid approach to the management of labour than more traditional approaches where staff are normally engaged for a particular job, often defined by tasks and skill requirements.

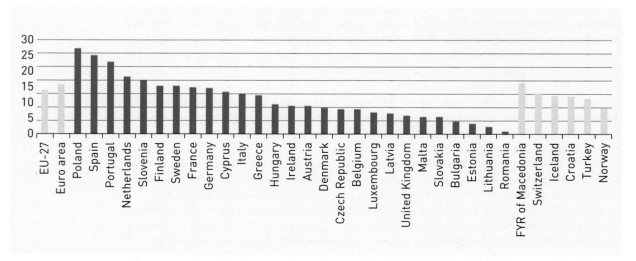

Figure 21.2 Proportion of employees with a contract of limited duration, age group 15–64, 2010

Source: Eurostat (online data code: lfs a_etpga).

Redeployment of staff may take place on an ad hoc basis, or in line with business cycles, which may occur for example on a seasonal, weekly or daily basis. The idea of redeploying staff across areas of work rests on the assumption that there will be variations in the nature of demand for different work tasks (Desombre *et al.,* 2006). Thus, if staff are fully occupied in the normal course of their work, little scope exists to improve efficiency by deploying them to other tasks. However, where variations in demand levels do occur this can create both periods of 'idle-time' for staff and also times when there is insufficient capacity to meet all demand. Redeploying staff who are multiskilled from areas of low activity to areas of high activity may reduce the need to hire additional staff and may also allow for greater speed of response to short-term and/or unpredictable fluctuations in business.

It is also argued that the use of functional flexibility can enhance quality in the provision of services. The use of trained multifunction staff can reduce the number of people a service user has contact with, thereby enabling a more holistic approach to be employed. For example, based on a study of nurses and nursing support staff, Desombre *et al.* (2006) suggest that using multiskilled staff who perform several tasks for the patient allows the experience to be more client- or user-centred, as opposed to a more traditional approach of being process- or specialism-centred.

In practice, functional flexibility can be implemented in a number of different ways and can be examined in terms of 'breadth' and 'depth' (Kelliher *et al.,* 2002). Breadth is concerned with the number of additional tasks an employee is deployed to do. This could range from a small number closely related to their main role, to an employee being deployed across a wide range of activities requiring diverse skills. Depth is concerned with the extent to which redeployed staff are able to take on an additional role. They may be expected and be able to take the role on fully, or may be able to only provide assistance with partial aspects of the role.

Evidence on the extent to which functional flexibility is used by organisations is less widely available than for some forms of flexibility (e.g. part-time or temporary contracts etc.), which in part is due to the difficulty in measuring it accurately as a result of the varied nature of activities grouped under this term. The Workplace Employment Relations Survey (WERS04) shows that in the UK 66 per cent of employers report that some core employees are trained to be functionally flexible (Kersley *et al.,* 2006), suggesting fairly widespread usage of the practice, even though it may only involve small numbers of employees in each organisation.

Temporal and spatial flexibility

While the above distinctions remain relevant, in a changing world these distinctions may not be sufficient to cover all types of flexibility that employers look for from employees, or how they interact with the types of flexibility employees may seek themselves. Developments in technology have had an important part to play in changing the way in which work is carried out (Kelliher and Richardson 2011; Zammuto *et al.,* 2007). Through the use of ICT, many employees can carry out work away from the workplace and it is argued that in some cases the boundaries between work and non-work activities have become blurred (Tietze and Musson, 2005). Although it is important not to lose sight that some roles still require employees to be physically present at the workplace and at designated times. For example, a doctor needs to be present to perform a surgical procedure and a call centre operators need to be available during operating hours.

Recent developments in the organisation of work have also resulted in labour being used in different ways. Although traditionally, temporary contracts have been used to cope with uncertainty, and/or known fluctuations in demand, an increased trend towards the organisation of work in project form has resulted in a corresponding increase in the use of temporary work, where staff are employed for the duration of a project, rather than on a permanent basis. While this approach has long been used in industries such as construction, this form of organisation has grown in the creative industries and in manufacturing (Packendorff, 2002).

Changes brought about by increasing global integration have also resulted in different employers looking for different forms of flexibility. Although it has always been commonplace for some employees to work outside of normal working hours (e.g. maintenance, security and cleaning staff), often through operating a shift system, employers who operate in different parts of the world and in different time zones may require employees to be available to work at different times to accommodate this. For example Sunday is a normal working day in the United Arab Emirates (UAE), therefore employees in other parts of the world who work closely with the UAE may sometimes have to work on Sunday to accommodate these different patterns. Similarly, people in Europe who collaborate with Asia or Australia may have to alter their working time to ensure an overlap in the working day with colleagues in these locations. For example, this might involve being available for additional, short periods of time to accommodate real time communication (one-to-one calls, conference calls) with other parts of the world (Kelliher and Anderson, 2010). The use of ICT often means that this additional, short-time availability can be carried out from a remote location, without the need for the employees to be present at the workplace.

Research on virtual teams who are geographically distributed, however, suggests that communication needs to be managed carefully to avoid negative outcomes both in terms of business outcomes and employee well-being, which may stem from too much connectivity. Collins and Kolb (2011) argue that an optimal balance between connection and disconnection needs to be achieved in order to secure benefits such as team creativity.

Notably, temporal flexibility has traditionally been subject to contractual arrangements (e.g. shift work, annual hours contracts). However, these more recent forms may be subject to rather subtler arrangements and expectations, which may effectively amount to an intensification of work (Kelliher and Anderson, 2010). The act of giving an employee a smart-phone may imply expectations of availability outside of work times and away from the workplace. For example, employees may be expected to engage in communication (phone calls, email, SMS messages etc.) with clients outside of designated working time and on non-work days. Wireless technologies such as smart-phones, which enable employees to stay 'in touch' have also created expectations of ever-availability (Besseyre des Horts *et al.,* 2011; Matusik and Mickel, 2011).

In addition, where ICT enables work to be done remotely, this may also yield cost advantages for employers, since this may allow them to reduce the amount of work space required. If employees work remotely for all or part of the time then the need for accommodation is likely to be reduced, either because no office space is required, or systems such as 'hotdesking' may be used which will allow higher occupancy rates for accommodation. However, it should be recognised that this may in turn raise a number of issues for employee performance. The chapter now turns to examine flexibility to meet employees' needs.

Flexibility *for* employees

Flexibility for employees covers circumstances where the employee is able to exercise some degree of control over where, when and how much they work. Typically, this might involve reducing the number of hours worked, working remotely from the workplace for all or part of their working time, or altering working times. In this context, organisations offer employees the opportunity to work flexibly in order to assist them achieve a more satisfactory balance between their work and non-work activities. Many organisations have flexible working policies which allow employees to make a request to change their working arrangements. In addition to accommodating individual requests, some organisations have standard policies such as flexitime available to all employees. Offering flexible working options to employees has often been seen as being a means to assist working parents and carers. Indeed when legislation was first introduced to support flexible working in the UK in 2003, the 'right to request' was restricted to parents of young or disabled children. However, employers have increasingly offered flexible working options to all employees (CBI/Harvey Nash, 2011) and the UK government have developed proposals to extend the legislative provisions to cover all employees (BIS, 2011). Offering flexible working options to all employees goes beyond a desire to be equitable on the part of the employer and is based on business reasoning (CIPD, 2005).

Many studies have shown that where employees have access to flexible working there are positive organisational outcomes, such as higher levels of job satisfaction (Gajendran and Harrison, 2007; Hooker *et al.,* 2007); organisational commitment (Chow and Keng-Howe, 2006; Harris and Foster, 2005); employee well-being (Redman *et al.,* 2009) and enhanced performance (Cranfield School of Management, 2008; Gajendran and Harrison, 2007). Over and above formalised arrangements which are subject to policy as described above, there is much evidence that informal arrangements for flexible working are prevalent in organisations (Healy, 2004; Kelliher and Anderson, 2010) and under these circumstances uptake of flexible working arrangements can be as high amongst men as women (Cranfield School of Management, 2008).

Remote working normally involves employees working at a different location for some, or all of their working time. This is often also frequently referred to as teleworking, since in practice many employees remain connected to their workplace by mean of some form of information and communications technology. Remote working often takes place at home, but may also include other locations.

Working at different times, or flexitime is where employees are able to exercise some degree of discretion over the timing when they work. This may be as an individual arrangement over working time, or as part of a flexitime scheme. Flexitime schemes are normally based around a framework of 'core' time, when all employees are required to be at work. Thus, essentially they offer some discretion over starting and finishing times, although some also allow employees to 'bank' additional time worked which can be taken as time off at a later period. Altering start and finish times may allow employees to accommodate the demands of their non-work lives more easily (e.g. taking children to school, healthcare appointments) and may also help employees avoid peak times when travelling to and from work.

Compressed working time also changes when work is done and involves employees working their contracted working hours over a shorter period of time than what is normal in the workplace. For example, this might involve a four-day week, or a nine-day fortnight instead of the normal five or ten days. This type of arrangement may be suitable for businesses with hours of operation which extend beyond a standard eight-hour working day for example, a retail outlet operating from 10am till 8pm each day may allow employees to work 4×10 hour days, in place of 5×8 hour days.

Reduced working hours represents a different type of change to working arrangements, since in these circumstances a change to the contract of employment is made and will have implications for the employee's pay and may influence their entitlement to benefits. As such this type of flexibility will always be subject to a formalised arrangement.

In practice, there may be considerable variation in how flexible working arrangements are actually enacted (De Menezes and Kelliher, 2011). For example, they may take the form of a regular arrangement, such as employee who always starts work at a different time on certain days of the week, or they may be more ad hoc, such as the employee who works remotely according to the demands of their work (for example, if they need uninterrupted concentration to complete a complex task) or non-working lives (wanting to be at home to accept a delivery). There may also be considerable variation in the percentage of full-time that a part-timer works, for example 50 per cent or 90 per cent. Notably, these different forms are not mutually exclusive and an employee might for example work reduced hours, partially from home and at different times from those that are normal for the workplace.

Implementation and outcomes

Changes to working arrangements, whether driven by the needs of employers or by employees, raise a number of issues for implementation. Looking first at those arrangements which allow employees to exercise a degree of choice over where, when and how much to work, the development of policy alone is insufficient to bring about change in the way in which work is carried out and for any benefits linked to their use to be gained. Employers also need to create an environment in which these policies are accepted and can be implemented without too many obstacles (Kossek and Ruderman, 2012). For example, in a workplace where there had been a traditional approach to work organisation and where employees would normally be expected to be physically present in the workplace during designated working hours, then unfamiliarity with different working arrangements may result in reluctance on the part of managers to agree to them. In other cases, employees who are aware that their manager is hostile to changes to working arrangements may be discouraged from making a request. Furthermore, in some organisations it may be seen as more acceptable for certain groups of employees (e.g. parents, employees in less responsible jobs) to request flexible working arrangements and so might deter more senior employees or non-parents from applying. As such it may be important to consider the context in which they are offered, since the mere existence of a policy may have little effect on their attitudes or feelings. Thus, not only does policy need to be developed, but organisations need to create an environment where employees believe they are available to them.

Perceptions of availability in addition to actual practice have been shown to be significant in relation to reaping the benefits associated with flexible working (Eaton, 2003). In practice the impact of this is potentially more widespread, since staff who have not taken advantage of flexible working arrangements may still place value on the availability, as they may foresee circumstances where they would like to have the opportunity to exercise some degree of choice over their working arrangements in the future.

Furthermore, in practical terms a workplace that operates with traditional working arrangements may need to consider what support is required to accommodate employees working according to different arrangements, at different times or in different locations. For example, security arrangements may need to be reviewed to allow employees to access and leave the workplace at different times. There may be a need to review support services such as IT and catering facilities. There may also be a need to manage remote workers and those in distributed teams in different ways (MacDuffie, 2007) and set up mechanisms to assist effective communication and maintenance of social relationships within the work environment (Mann et al., 2000). Furthermore, it may be helpful to provide some training to help employees and their managers and co-workers to transition to alternative working arrangements.

In some jobs arrangements such as compressed working time and reduced hours may be more difficult to implement. In jobs where employees are employed to fulfil a set of responsibilities, rather than for specific working hours (as in many professional jobs), the question arises over what is being compressed into fewer working periods, or less working time. Is it the time that the employee actually works in the week, or is it their contractual hours?

There has been much debate about the outcomes of offering employees some degree of choice over when, where and how much they work. In particular, there has been much interest in the question of whether or not a business case for flexible working exists. A business case needs to be judged in the light of why a policy was put into place. If the primary objective is to ensure that the organisation fulfils its legal obligations, it might be judged on whether legal cases are taken by employees and whether the organisation has had to pay compensation and/or suffered any damage to its reputation as an employer. However, if the objective of the policy goes further than this and is designed to contribute to organisational performance by creating favourable employee attitudes, then it needs to be judged in this context.

While individual studies, and particularly those conducted in recent years, do present convincing evidence for a business case, in terms of organisational performance, meta-analyses and reviews of the range of evidence suggest that an unequivocal business case for the offering of flexible working policies cannot be made (De Menezes and Kelliher, 2011). However, the diverse body of evidence which exists makes drawing general conclusions difficult. Many studies fail to distinguish between different degrees or frequency of flexible working. For example, it is likely that the experience of working on a 50 per cent contract will be a markedly different one from a 90 per cent contract. Similarly, the employee who works remotely on an occasional or ad hoc basis is likely to have a different experience from one who works remotely all of the time. It is perhaps not surprising that these different degrees are likely to raise different issues. As such care needs to be exercised in considering what has been examined in each case.

Furthermore, unlike many other HR policies which are effectively implemented by managers and may be imposed on employees (e.g. a pay policy linking pay levels to performance), this type of policy simply makes something available to employees and lays down a process for implementation. As a result, the relationship between this type of policy and performance outcomes may not be the same as those described in the HRM and performance literature (Paauwe, 2004).

In addition, as these types of policies become more commonplace in organisations and come to be considered as normal working conditions, then any positive effects on employee attitudes may be eroded by a growing sense of entitlement (Lewis *et al.*, 2001) where employees no longer see it as something that requires reciprocation (Kelliher and Anderson, 2010).

Turning to look at employer-driven approaches, such as numerical and functional flexibility, a number of issues are raised when they are introduced. An overriding concern is that, in order to be able to reap the benefits from these forms of flexibility, employers need to be able to forecast their labour requirements accurately. If the intention is to improve efficiency in the use labour, then employers need to monitor closely their business patterns and be able to translate these into labour requirements. They also need to be able to move sufficiently quickly to respond to unforeseen changes to demand. For example, in the case of part-time staff, employers need to be able to match the number and timing of hours with business activity at short notice. With temporary staff, if they are employed directly employers need to decide on the appropriate length of contract to be offered. If temporary staff are employed via a temporary employment agency, then their needs to be regular communication with the agency to agree the number of staff to be supplied.

It is noteworthy that temporary employment by its very nature promotes insecurity for staff (Legge, 2007). Many staff who take on temporary employment may be seeking the security of permanent employment and if permanent opportunities become available may leave in order to reduce job insecurity. As such, in some cases employers will pay temporary employees an enhanced rate of pay. A number of observers have noted the potential issues which may arise when temporary and permanent employees are employed side by side, but with different relationships with their employer.

In the case of functional flexibility, employers need to make decisions about the breadth and depth of their approach as discussed above. The use of functional flexibility raises questions about the skill requirements and the need for training for employees who are to be redeployed, which will be determined at least in part, by the actual way in which functional flexibility has been implemented. There are clear implications for training, but other factors which need to be considered may include whether employees who possess a greater number of skills and can be redeployed should receive some form of reward enhancement. There are also a range of issues which need to be decided upon in the day to day management of these multifunction staff, especially if they are redeployed within a working shift. Kelliher and Riley (2002) document details about how uniform changes and break times are accommodated.

There have been a number of studies which have attempted to investigate the relationship between various forms of numerical and functional flexibility and human resource management outcomes such as job satisfaction, organisational commitment and employee well-being. The evidence on numerical flexibility suggests that this type of flexibility often results in lower quality jobs (Green, *et al.*, 2010; Kalleberg *et al.*, 2000). Employees subject to temporary contracts in particular generally report lower levels of job satisfaction and well-being as a result of the job insecurity associated with this type of contract (see for example Aletraris, 2010; De Cuyper and De Witte, 2008; Mauno *et al.*, 2005). Part-time and shift working have also been found to be linked to higher rates of injury and ill-health (Robinson and Smallman, 2006). Since factors such as job satisfaction, organisational commitment and well-being have been shown to contribute to organisational performance (Boxall and Purcell, 2003; Paauwe, 2004), while numerical flexibility practices are designed to use labour more efficiently, in the longer term these practices may have the effect of indirectly inhibiting organisational performance.

In recognition of the consequences of using certain flexible labour practices for job security, the European Union has attempted to reconcile the objectives of increased competitiveness and job security by introducing a policy of flexicurity. Flexicurity attempts to combine flexibility and mobility of labour, alongside strong social security support, including unemployment benefits, pensions and healthcare (European Commission, 2007).

In contrast to the so called 'low road' approach to HRM which numerical flexibility is often seen as contributing to, functional flexibility is more commonly associated with a 'high road' approach, since it offers employees the opportunity to develop a greater range of skills and may increase job variety (Kalleberg, 2003) and can be seen as a way of humanising work (Friedrich *et al.,* 1998). The use of functional flexibility has been found to be associated with opportunities for learning (Lopez-Cabrales *et al.,* 2011) organisational commitment (van der Velde and van den Berg, 2003) and higher retention (Kelliher *et al.,* 2002). However, functional flexibility has also been shown to be linked to the intensification of work (Kahn, 1999; Kelliher and Gore, 2006) and in some cases increased stress has been reported (Allan, 1998; Kelliher and Desombre, 2005).

Matching employer and employee needs

The debates concerned with flexibility of and for employees have largely taken place in isolation and as separate areas of study (Zeytinolglu *et al.,* 2009). This separation has been reflected in practice also. In many organisations flexibility of employees is the concern of operations managers seeking to increase efficiency. Flexibility for employees tends to be led by the human resources department, or sometimes those responsible for diversity and inclusion. However, studies of implementation of these practices would suggest that, as described earlier, employers can gain benefits from employee-friendly practices, such as through increased organisational commitment (Chow and Keng-Howe, 2006; Harris and Foster, 2005) and job satisfaction (Gajendran and Harrison, 2007; Hooker *et al.,* 2007) and directly on performance (Kelliher and Anderson, 2010). Equally, studies have shown employees may sometimes perceive what are intended as employer-friendly approaches as being beneficial to them. For example, Kirkpatrick and Hoque (2006) report findings from a study of social workers, who voluntarily opted for temporary employment in order to increase their direct pay (akin to for example IT contractors); to acquire a greater range of skills and experience and to accommodate lifestyle preferences. However, it is noteworthy that this was generally considered a short-term approach and many indicated that they would look for permanent employment in the future. Kelliher and Gore's (2006) study of implementing functional flexibility in retail, healthcare and hospitality environments found that employees responded positively to functional flexibility, since although it often resulted in an intensification of work, it also resulted in their gaining new skills and experiences.

A number of more recent developments in spatial and temporal flexibility may also be seen as having beneficial outcomes for both employers and employees. For example, the ability to work away from the workplace, enabled by ICT may mean that employees are able to combine work and non-work activities more easily (Lim and Teo, 2000). Accessing work systems remotely may mean that employees can avoid time-consuming or stressful commutes, which may thereby leave them with more time and/or energy for non-work activities. Similarly, employees who are expected to participate in work activity outside normal working time, may also feel able to undertake non-work activities during normal working time. Ultimately, it may be who controls access to flexibility which determines whether benefits accrue to the employer, the employee or are mutual. Furthermore, in reality some of these practices may look similar (e.g. reduced hours), although they may be being used for different purposes. As a result it is not always easy to ascertain from published statistics whether the practice being reported is employee- or employer-driven (Zeytinoglu *et al.,* 2009).

Where different forms of flexible working look similar in practice, this raises the question over whether there may be scope for the interests of employers and employees to be matched in the way in which these practices are enacted (De Menezes and Kelliher, 2011). It could be argued that at least in some organisations there may be scope to match employer and employee interests. In large organisations it may be possible to match up employee preferences over working time with the needs of the organisation to have people working at different times. For example, in the stroke unit of Falu hospital in Sweden an electronic system for planning work schedules allows the needs of the organisation to be met, while at the same time allowing employees to exercise influence over their own work schedule (Eurofound, 2008). The use of working time accounts may allow both employers and employees to exercise some influence over when extra work is undertaken and when that time is taken off by employees. See Case study 21.3 at the end of the chapter as an attempt to do this. Practices such as allowing teams to self-roster around organisational requirements may help balance the needs of the organisation with those of individual team members. Given the pressure on organisations to be flexible in the face of growing competitive pressures, coupled with increased social pressures (in some countries backed up with legislative provisions), there is a real need for both researchers and practitioners to explore this possibility for a win-win situation further.

CASE STUDY 21.1

BMW: ACHIEVING FLEXIBILITY THROUGH THE USE OF TEMPORARY AGENCY STAFF

CLARE KELLIHER

Car manufacturers BMW have made extensive use of temporary labour since they began production of the Mini at their Oxford plant in the UK in 2001. Entering a different market segment from their existing business meant that they were unsure about how demand for the new car would develop and so were looking for some flexibility in their labour resourcing. In addition to maintaining a core permanent workforce, they decided to work with temporary employment agencies to supply labour. Maintaining an approximate 70:30 ratio of permanent to temporary staff was designed to help them adjust the number of people employed according to the level of demand.

In 2009, in response to volatile market conditions in automotive sales, a decision was made to switch from seven-day to five-day working. As a result the company announced that 850 agency workers would lose their jobs. The announcement was made just before the plant closed for a one-week holiday and at the end of the night shift. There were angry responses from many temporary workers when the announcement was made, some of whom had worked there for several years and had believed that if they worked hard and delivered good quality work they would eventually be given permanent jobs.

Sources: Milner, 2009; O'Brien, 2001.

Questions

1 Consider the advantages and disadvantages for companies like BMW of using temporary agency staff.
2 Do the agency workers have a case for feeling aggrieved at being laid off at short notice?

CASE STUDY 21.2

SECOND CAREERS INTERNSHIP PROGRAMME: THE TATA GROUP'S WAY OF ENTICING PROFESSIONAL WOMEN BACK INTO EMPLOYMENT IN INDIA'S DEVELOPING ECONOMY

One of the biggest challenges facing companies in developing economies is coping with the lack of skilled staff. In rapidly developing economies, such as India, companies need highly qualified talent now. While investment in education by governments can produce a workforce with the right skills for the future, companies facing skills shortages may look for other ways of accessing skills. One such way may be to entice those not currently in the labour force back into work. The Tata Group, one of India's largest conglomerate companies (their activities span IT, engineering, services, chemicals, energy and consumer products), has developed a scheme designed to persuade professional women to re-engage with employment, by offering an alternative, flexible, project-based approach to work.

In India, although women increasingly participate in higher education and well qualified female graduates enter the workforce, in the region of 40 per cent leave employment within a ten-year period, normally to take on full-time family responsibilities. The Tata Group scheme, the Second Career Internship Programme, was launched on International Women's Day in 2008. It is set up as a career transition management programme for women professionals who have taken between one and eight years out of employment. The scheme is designed to bring professional women back into work on a flexible basis. The scheme engages women to work on live business projects, but on a flexitime basis. The projects typically involve in the region of 500 hours of work input over a six-month period for companies in the Tata Group. Some project work may also be amenable to be being done partly from home. Participants in the scheme go through an induction programme to help them back into work and update them in their fields and they are provided with mentors for the project. The scheme is not designed to provide full-time, permanent job opportunities, but rather is designed to provide opportunities for professional women to work in different ways, on a short-term, project basis. Participants may, however, subsequently explore full-time, permanent employment with the company. Two years after the launch of the scheme about 30 per cent of the women who have participated are now working for the group on a full- or part-time basis.

Sources: Kazmin, 2011; Tata company website http://www.tatasecondcareer.com/about%20scip.aspx.

Questions

1 How well do you think a scheme like this actually helps in solving problems of skills shortage for large companies like Tata? Would it work for all companies?
2 What are likely to be the important factors influencing the successful implementation of a scheme like this?
3 Are there groups other than women who might be attracted by a scheme like this?

CASE STUDY 21.3

MEETING EMPLOYER AND EMPLOYEE NEEDS FOR FLEXIBILITY AT ENGCO?: THE CASE OF SMART WORKING

CLARE KELLIHER AND DEIRDRE ANDERSON

EngCo is a large UK headquartered engineering company which operates on a worldwide basis. It is structured into four main divisions and employs in the region of 39,000 people, located in 50 countries across the globe. Approximately 60 per cent of their workforce are located in the UK and are distributed across eight main sites. The company's workforce is predominantly male (only about 15 per cent of the workforce is female) and most are employed on a full-time, permanent contract. The majority of employees work a traditional 39-hour week, based around standard working times. Many employees have long service records and a significant proportion have never worked for any other employer. Here we examine the implementation of a new policy on flexibility, Smart Working, at one of the UK workplaces.

In recent years the company has become more concerned with the diversity of the workforce and has introduced a number of policies designed to attract a broader spectrum of employees. There has also been a growing recognition of the importance of work–life balance to employees and the need for the company to respond to this. As such they introduced a flexible working policy a few years ago, allowing employees to request flexible working arrangements (reduced hours, remote working, different hours etc.) in order to help them deal with the needs of their work and non-work lives more effectively.

The nature of the company's business means that there are 'ebbs and flows' over time in the level of activity throughout the company. Historically, this had tended to mean that the company used significant amounts of overtime working, in order to accommodate the 'peaks' in activity. (Beyond this some commentators suggested that evening and weekend overtime had become institutionalised in parts of the company and this represented a significant cost for the business.) However, in addition to the peaks, there were also 'troughs' in activity and during these quieter times employees, although present during normal working hours, were less occupied and therefore less productive. In an attempt to reconcile these variations in workload and reduce the cost of overtime, the company developed a new policy, Smart Working, which was also designed to give employees more control over their working time and help them improve their work–life balance.

The principal aim was to achieve greater flexibility and efficiency by moving from an environment which was attendance-driven, to one with an emphasis on performance delivery. This was seen as central to the company's strategy and acceptance of this new way of working was tied to future investment at the UK sites. The policy had been agreed with the trade unions representing the workforce and was being rolled out across the UK.

It was designed to reduce overtime costs by scheduling employees to work additional time at peak periods, but rather than paying them for this time, they would be able to recoup it at other less busy times. TOIL (time off in lieu) accounts were set up for employees so that a record would be maintained of time owing to each employee and which could be taken off at a later date. Recognising that the end of regular overtime would result in an income loss for some employees, the policy was introduced alongside a 6 per cent pay increase. This was seen by some as effectively incorporating overtime into basic pay.

In essence, Smart Working allows managers to match the supply of labour more closely with current workload. In practice, managers agree output targets with employees, or in some areas with self-directed work groups, for a set period of time. The thinking behind this was to move from a system which was time-based to one which is performance-based. The employee or work group then decide how the time

resources available to them need to be used in order to achieve these targets. If in peak times employees need to work longer than their normal hours and/or needed to come in at weekends, this additional time can then be 'banked' and taken off when the workload is less high. In addition, a flexitime system was introduced which removed the traditional starting and finishing times. Symbolically, this resulted in removal of the buzzer which signified the start and end of the working day across the workplace. The flexitime system is built around core hours (11.30–14.30) when all employees are required to be at work, but outside that period employees can choose start and finish times and these can be varied according to individual employee preferences.

In order to launch this new approach to working a series of training events was set up both for managers and for employees to help them understand the working of the scheme and how it was being implemented. On the whole, employees reported that they understood the scheme and that the regulations governing how it worked were clear. There was also a general view that it had been implemented fairly. The trade unions, who were involved in negotiating the agreement, also monitored its implementation to ensure that it was being run fairly.

Smart Working in practice
Flexibility over working time

Perhaps inevitably, views about how well it had worked in practice varied across the workplace. Many employees indicated that the opportunity to stagger start and finish times had been very useful to them. They welcomed the opportunity to accommodate non-work activities in their lives more easily by exercising some flexibility over working time. In essence, this type of scheme made it legitimate not to be at work outside of the core hours. In addition, the workplace was located close to a busy road network and there was often considerable congestion in the area. Having some flexibility over working time meant that employees could choose to travel at different times and avoid the stress of being stuck in traffic and not knowing whether they would make it to work on time.

Some work teams at this workplace liaised closely with their counterparts in North America and in India on a regular basis. Managers in these business areas indicated that they had encouraged employees to adopt different working times, since it meant they then had greater overlap with colleagues in different time zones – those who started earlier had a longer overlap with the working day in India and those who worked later had a greater overlap with North America. However, as a result it was acknowledged that internal meetings had to be concentrated into core hours, in order to secure maximum participation.

Nevertheless, some employees did suggest that in spite of the introduction of the new policy, many managers in the company had retained a traditional view of working time. Although in theory Smart Working made it legitimate not to be at work during traditional working hours, it was reported that some managers and co-workers, particularly those with long service records were still in a '9–5 mindset' and had not adjusted to the new approach. This resulted in some people feeling uncomfortable if, for example, they left the workplace early. One employee reported that if he wanted to leave work early he felt more comfortable leaving at 3pm, rather than say 4.30pm, because at 3pm many people assumed that he would be going to an off-site meeting rather than going home. This mindset of 9–5 working was felt to be unattractive to younger recruits and would impact on their retention.

Some managers reported that they preferred having their employees work a regular working pattern, even if they worked at different times. As one manager explained variation in hours could make planning more difficult,

'If you come in at half eight and then you come in at half eleven the next day, you might work your hours, but for someone trying to manage the team, there is a three hour difference between the two.'

Working extra time and banking hours

For some employees the Smart Working policy worked well and they were able to take TOIL at times that suited them, often for family and home-related activities. However, in certain parts of the business, the greatest concern expressed by employees was the lack of opportunity to take back any additional hours they had worked, since, as they saw it, the troughs never happened. Some indicated that their contracted hours were insufficient to achieve the required workload and as a result there were few opportunities for employees to take back time and attend to non-work activities. The seemingly constant number of 'rush jobs' meant that arrangements for greater flexibility could not always be honoured. In the longer term some employees reported that this discouraged people from putting in extra hours when workload was high, since they did not see the opportunity to take the time back. Managers acknowledged that there were some employees who had a large number of banked hours.

Although described by a senior director of the company as 'delivering a better work–life balance for employees and higher productivity levels when workload drops', there was some cynicism about whether or not the scheme really contributed to work–life balance in practice.

Where employees were able to take back time it was observed that Friday was a very popular day. Several years ago working time at this site had been adjusted to allow for the working day to finish one hour earlier on Fridays. Thus, Friday was attractive, not only because it extended the weekend, but also because employees needed to spend less of their banked time to take a day off. Lower staffing levels, together with people using flexitime to leave early on Fridays was seen to be problematic in those parts of the business that worked extensively with North America.

There was some debate over how working beyond normal hours was, or should be agreed. It was felt that any additional hours should be sanctioned when there was work pressure, or where it made sense to carry on working to complete a job in the working day, but not necessarily agreed when an employee just wanted the opportunity to finesse or 'gold plate' a piece of work.

There was also discussion about the detail of recording hours and how this worked in the spirit of Smart Working. In some departments there was little formal recording of hours, but rather if extra work hours were needed, then they were done, and then employees took other time away from the workplace to compensate. However, in other situations additional hours were recorded and taken back rigorously. As one employee put it 'Every minute is recorded and every extra minute is taken off'. The general feeling was that this was not in the spirit of the policy since the 6 per cent pay increase, linked to the implementation of Smart Working, was seen to be compensation for flexibility over time. Success of implementation was seen as being largely attributable to how individual line managers worked the policy with their staff. The introduction of Smart Working at this site had therefore met with some success, but there were some concerns over its implementation. The company was determined to build on what had been achieved, recognising the need to balance efficiency with a focus on work–life balance and employee well-being.

Questions

1 To what extent do you think employer and employee desires for flexibility can be reconciled by a scheme such as this one?

2 Are there certain circumstances that might make this more likely?

3 As a manager reviewing the introduction and implementation of this policy, what recommendations would you make to move the policy forward?

Bibliography

Aletraris, L. (2010) 'How satisfied are they and why? A study of job satisfaction, job rewards, gender and temporary agency workers in Australia', *Human Relations,* Vol.63, No.8, 1129–55.

Alis, D., Karsten, L. and Leopold, J. (2006) 'From Gods to Godesses', *Time and Society,* Vol.15, No.1, 81–104.

Allan, C. (1998) 'The elasticity of endurance: work intensification and workplace flexibility on the Queensland public hospital system', *Journal of Organisational Change Management,* Vol.23, No.3, 133–51.

Atkinson, J. (1985) 'Flexibility: planning for an uncertain future', *Manpower Policy and Practice,* Vol.1, 26–9.

Besseyre des Horts, C. H., Dery, K. and MacCormick, J. (2011) 'Paradoxical consequences of the use of Blackberrys? An application of the job demand–control–support model", pp. 16–29, in Kelliher, C. and Richardson, J. (eds) *New Ways of Organizing Work: Developments, Perspectives and Experiences,* New York: Routledge.

BIS (Department Business, Innovation and Skills) (2011) *Consultation on Modern Workplaces: Extending the Right to Request Flexible Working to All. Impact Assessment,* BIS, London.

Bloom, N. and Van Reenen, J. (2006) 'Management practices, work–life balance and productivity: a review of some recent evidence', *Oxford Review of Economic Policy,* Vol.22, 457–82.

Boxall, P. and Purcell, J. (2003) *Strategy and Human Resource Management,* Basingstoke: Palgrave Macmillan.

Brannen, J. (2005) 'Time and negotiation of work-family boundaries', *Time and Society,* Vol.14, 113–31.

Bryson, C. (1999), 'Managing uncertainty or managing uncertainly?', pp. 63–88, in Leopold, J., Harris, L. and Watson, T. (eds) *Strategic Human Resourcing,* London: Financial Times/ Pitman Publishing.

CBI/Harvey Nash (2011) *Navigating Choppy Waters: CBA/Harvey Nash Employment Trends Survey 2011,* London: CBI.

Chartered Institute of Personnel and Development (CIPD) (2005) *Flexible Working: Impact and Implementation – An Employer Survey,* London: Chartered Institute of Personnel and Development.

Chow, I.H. and Keng-Howe, I.C. (2006) 'The effect of alternative work schedules on employee performance', *International Journal of Employment Studies,* Vol.14, 105–30.

Coe, N.M., Johns, J.L. and Ward, K. (2007) 'Mapping the globalization of the temporary staffing industry', *Professional Geographer,* Vol.59, No.4, 503–20.

Collins P. and Kolb, D. (2011), 'Innovation in distributed teams: the duality of connectivity norms and human agency', pp. 140–59, in Kelliher, C. and Richardson, J. (eds) *New Ways of Organizing Work: Developments, Perspectives and Experiences,* New York: Routledge.

Cranfield School of Management (2008) *Flexible Working and Performance: Summary of Research,* London: Working Families.

De Cuyper, N. and De Witte, H. (2008) 'Volition and reasons for accepting temporary employment: Associations with attitudes, well-being, and behavioural intentions', *European Journal of Work and Organizational Psychology,* Vol.17, No.3, 363–87.

De Menezes, L. and Kelliher, C. (2011) 'Flexible working and performance: A systematic review of the evidence for a business case', *International Journal of Management Reviews,* Vol.13, No.4, 452–74.

Desombre, T., Kelliher, C., Macfarlane, F. and Ozbilgin, M. (2006) 'Re-organizing work roles in health care: evidence from the implementation of functional flexibility', *British Journal of Management,* Vol.17, No.2, 139–51.

Eaton, S. (2003), 'If you can use them: flexibility policies, organizational commitment and perceived performance', *Industrial Relations,* Vol.42, No.2, 145–67.

ETUI (2012) *How Has the Crisis Affected Social Legislation in Europe?* No. 2/2012, ETUI Policy Brief, ETUI, Brussels.

European Commission (2007) *Towards Common Principles of Flexicurity: More and Better Jobs Through Flexibility and Security,* Luxembourg: Office for Official Publications of the European Communities.

European Foundation for the Improvement of Living and Working Conditions (Eurofound) (2008), *Towards a Balanced Flexibility.* Available at www.eurofound.europa/eu.areas /qualityofwork/betterjobs/Bycategory6.htm.

European Foundation for the Improvement of Living and Working Conditions (Eurofound) (2010) *European Company Survey 2009: Flexibility Profiles of European Companies,* Luxembourg: Publications Office of the European Union.

Friedrich, A., Kabst, R., Weber, W. and Rodehuth, M. (1998) 'Functional flexibility: merely reacting or acting strategically?', *Employee Relations,* Vol.20, No.3, 504–23.

Gajendran, R.S. and Harrison, D.A. (2007) 'The good, the bad, and the unknown about telecommuting: meta-analysis of psychological mediators and individual consequences', *Journal of Applied Psychology,* Vol.92, No.6, 1524–41.

Gerdes, L. (2009) *Bad Economy Hasn't Changed Gen Y's Desire for Work–life balance.* Available at www.businessweek.com.

Green, C., Kler, P. and Leeves, G. (2010), 'Flexible contract workers in inferior jobs: reappraising the evidence', *British Journal of Industrial Relations,* Vol.48, No.3, 605–29.

Hall, L. and Atkinson, C. (2006), 'Improving working lives: flexible working and the role of employee control', *Employee Relations,* Vol.28, No.4, 374–86.

Harris, L. and Foster, C. (2005) *Small, Flexible and Family Friendly – Work Practices in Service Sector Businesses,* Employment Relations Research Series, No.47, London: Department of Trade and Industry.

Healy, G. (2004) 'Work–life balance and family friendly policies – in whose interest?', *Work, Employment and Society,* Vol.18, No.1, 219–23.

Hooker, H., Neathey, F., Casebourne, J. and Munro, M. (2007) *The Third Work–life Balance Employee Survey: Main Findings,* Brighton: Institute for Employment Studies.

Kahn, P. (1999) 'Gender and employment restructuring in British National Health Service manual work', *Gender, Work and Organization,* Vol.6, No.4, 202–12.

Kalleberg, A. (2001) 'Organising Flexibility: the flexible firm in a new century', *British Journal of Industrial Relations,* Vol.39, No.4, 479–504.

Kalleberg, A.L. (2003) 'Flexible firm and labor market segmentation', *Work and Occupations,* Vol.30, No.2, 154–75.

Kalleberg, A.L., Reskin, B.F. and Hudson, K. (2000) 'Bad jobs in America: standard and non-standard employment relations and job quality in the United States', *American Sociological Review,* Vol.65, 256–78.

Kazmin. A. (2011) 'Flexible work deals lure mothers from the home to ease India's skills shortage', *Financial Times,* 27 May 2011.

Kelliher, C. and Anderson, D. (2010) 'Doing more with less? Flexible working practices and the intensification of work', *Human Relations,* Vol.63, No.1, 83–106.

Kelliher, C. and Desombre, T. (2005) 'Breaking down boundaries: functional flexibility and occupational identity in health care', in Zeytinoglue, I. (ed.) *Flexibility in Workplaces: Effects on Workers, Work Environments and Unions,* IIRA/ILO, Geneva.

Kelliher, C. and Gore, J. (2006) 'Functional flexibilty and the intensification of work: transformation within service industries', pp. 92–102, in Askenazy, P., Carlton, D., de Coninck, F. and Gollac, M. (eds) *Organisation et Intensité du Travail,* Toulouse: Octares.

Kelliher, C. and Richardson, J. (2011) 'Recent developments in new ways of organizing work', pp. 1–15, in Kelliher, C. and Richardson, J. (eds) *New ways of organizing work: Developments, perspectives and experiences,* New York: Routledge.

Kelliher, C. and Riley, M. (2002), 'Making functional flexibility stick: an assessment of the outcomes for stakeholders', *International Journal of Contemporary Hospitality Management,* Vol.14, No.5, 237–42.

Kelliher, C., Gore, J. and Riley, M. (2002) 'Functional flexibility: implementation and outcomes', *International Industrial Relations Association Conference,* 25–28 June, Toronto, Canada.

Kersley, B., Alpin, C., Forth, J., Bryson, A., Bewley, H., Dix, G. and Oxenbridge, S. (eds) (2006) *Inside the Workplace: Findings from the 2004 Workplace Employment Relations Survey, Abingdon:* Routledge.

Kirkpatrick, I. and Hoque, K. (2006) 'A retreat from permanent employment? Accounting for the rise of professional agency work in UK public services', *Work, Employment and Society,* Vol.20, No.4, 649–66.

Korczynski, M. (2002) *Human Resource Management in Service Work,* Basingstoke: Palgrave Macmillan.

Kossek, E. and Ruderman, M. (2012) 'Work-family flexibility and the employment relationship', pp. 223–53, in Shore, L.M., Coyle-Shapiro, J. and Tetrick, L. (eds) *Understanding the Employee-Organization Relationship: Advances in Theory and Practice,* New York: Taylor and Francis.

Lallement, M. (2011) 'Europe and the economic crisis: forms of labour market adjustment and varieties of capitalism', *Work, Employment and Society,* Vol.25, No.4, 627–41.

Legge, K. (2007) 'Putting the missing H into HRM: the case of the flexible organisation', pp. 115–36, in Bolton, S.C. and Houlihan, M. (eds) *Searching for the Human in Human Resource Management,* Basingstoke: Palgrave Macmillan.

Lewis, S., Smithson, J., Cooper, C. and Dyer, J. (2001) *Flexible Futures: Flexible Working and Work–life Integration: Summary of Findings from Stage 2.* Available at www.workliferesearch.org.

Lim, V.K.G. and Teo, T.S.H. (2000) 'To work or not to work at home: an empirical investigation of factors affecting attitudes towards teleworking', *Journal of Managerial Psychology,* Vol.15, No.6, 560–86.

Lopez-Cabrales, A., Valle, R. and Galan, J. (2011) 'Employment relationships as drivers of firm flexibility and learning', *Personnel Review,* Vol.40, No.5, 625–43.

MacDuffie, J.P. (2007) 'HRM and distributed work', *Academy of Management Annals,* Vol.1, 549–615.

Mann, S., Varey, R. and Button, W. (2000) 'An exploration of the emotional impact of teleworking via computer-mediated communication', *Journal of Managerial Psychology,* Vol.15, Nos7/8, 668–91.

Marquardt, M. (2005) 'Globalisation: the pathway to prosperity, freedom and peace', *Human Resource Development International,* Vol.8, No.1, 127–9.

Matusik, S.F. and Mickel, A.E. (2011) 'Embracing or embattled by converged mobile devices? Users' experiences with a contemporary connectivity technology', *Human Relations,* Vol.68, No.8, 1001–30.

Mauno, S., Kinnunen, U., Makikangas, A. and Natti, J. (2005) 'Psychological consequences of fixed-term employment and perceived job insecurity among health care staff', *European Journal of Work and Organizational Psychology,* Vol.14, No.3, 209–37.

Milner, M. (2009) 'BMW accused of "scandalous opportunism" after scrapping 850 jobs at Mini factory', *Guardian*, 17 February.

O'Brien, J. (2001) 'BMW to get maximum from Mini contract workers', *Birmingham Post,* 15.

Olsen, K. and Kalleberg, A. (2004) 'Nonstandard work in two different employment regimes: The United States and Norway', *Work, Employment and Society,* Vol.18, No.2, 321–48.

Paauwe, J. (2004) *HRM and Performance: Unique Approaches for Achieving Long-term Viability,* Oxford: Oxford University Press.

Packendorff, J. (2002) 'The temporary society and its enemies: projects from an individual perspective', pp. 39–58, in Sahlin-Andersson, K. and Soderholm, A. (eds) *Beyond Project Management: New Perspectives on the Temporary-Permanent Dilemma,* Malmo: Liber.

Peck, J., Theodore, N. and Ward, K. (2005) 'Constructing markets for temporary labour: employment liberalization and the internationalization of the staffing industry', *Global Networks,* Vol.5, No.1, 3–26.

Rau, B.L. and Hyland, M.A. (2002) 'Role conflict and flexible work arrangements: the effects on applicant attraction', *Personnel Psychology,* Vol.55, No.1, 111–36.

Redman, T., Snape, E. and Ashurst, C. (2009) 'Location, location, location: does place of work really matter?', *British Journal of Management,* Vol.20, No.S1, 171–81.

Richardson, J. (2010), 'Managing flexworks: holding on and letting go', *Journal of Management Development,* Vol.29, No.2, 137–47.

Robinson, A.M. and Smallman, C. (2006) 'The contemporary British workplace: a safer and healthier place?', *Work, Employment and Society,* Vol.20, No.1, 87–107.

TATA. Available at www.tatasecondcareer.com. Accessed 2 March 2012.

Tietze, S. and Musson, G. (2005) 'Recasting the home-work relationship: a case of mutual adjustment', *Organization Studies,* Vol.26, No.9, 1331–52.

van der Velde, M. and van den Berg, P. (2003) 'Managing functional flexible in a passenger transport firm', *Human Resource Management Journal,* Vol.13, No.4, 45–55.

Van Dyne, L., Kossek, E. and Lobel, S. (2007) 'Less need to be there: cross-level effects of work practices that support work–life flexibility and enhance group processes and group-level OCB', *Human Relations,* Vol.60, No.8, 1123–53.

Yanadori, Y. and Kato, T. (2009) 'Work and family practices in Japanese firms: their scope, nature and impact on employee turnover', *International Journal of Human Resource Management,* Vol.20, No.2, 439–56.

Zammuto, R.F., Griffith, T.L., Majchrzak, A., Dougherty, D.J. and Faraj, S. (2007) 'Information technology and the changing fabric of organization', *Organization Science,* Vol.18, No.5, 749–62.

Zeytinoglu, I., Cooke, G. and Mann, S. (2009) 'Flexibility: whose choice is it anyway?', *Industrial Relations,* Vol.64, No.6, 555–74.

CHAPTER 22
WORKPLACE BULLYING

Sara Branch, Sheryl Ramsay and Michelle Barker

Introduction

Due to the important role managers play in the development and maintenance of vital, diverse and productive workplaces, understanding workplace bullying and its complexity is of great importance to organisations. As a complex phenomenon, workplace bullying presents significant challenges, including its theoretical conceptualisation, the identification of bullying behaviours and practical strategies for preventing and reducing its many negative facets. This chapter offers a comprehensive insight into each of these areas.

Described as a serious wrongdoing (Brown, 2007), research consistently shows that workplace bullying is a significant issue for organisations because of its relatively high rate of occurrence or prevalence (see Brown, 2007). In the management field, workplace bullying has been presented as an 'alarming issue' (De Cieri and Kramar, 2008: 625) that requires comprehensive understanding and management if the costs to individuals and organisations are to be alleviated. These costs include the significantly high emotional impacts on people and the associated economic losses that mount up (Einarsen et al., 2011b; McCarthy and Mayhew, 2004). This chapter aims first, to present a conceptual overview of workplace bullying, including its associated behaviours, impacts, risks and antecedents, and second, to discuss prevention and management strategies of relevance to the field of management. It includes examples of research findings (based largely on quantitative studies) to help explain particular points and also to demonstrate the type of research being conducted in the area.

Research into workplace bullying began in the late 1970s, largely growing out of Scandinavian investigations into schoolyard bullying (e.g., Olweus, 1978). Indeed, links between schoolyard and workplace bullying are evident. For instance, a study of 5,288 adults in Great Britain found that children who had been targets or perpetrators of schoolyard bullying were more likely to be targets of workplace bullying (Smith et al., 2003). Moreover, the nature of bullying is similar across school and work. For instance, verbal abuse and harassment represent the most common types of schoolyard bullying, followed by exclusion and social manipulation (Rigby, 2001), which is similar to the type of bullying behaviours identified in workplace bullying research (Bjorkqvist et al., 1994; Einarsen et al., 2011a; Keashly and Harvey, 2005; O' Moore et al., 1998). However, the formal power of the bully presents an interesting difference between schoolyard and workplace bullying because 'children are bullied for the most part by peers who have no formal organizational power over them, whereas adults are at least as likely to be bullied by managers and supervisors as by others who are lacking such authority' (Rigby, 2001: 5). Interestingly, recent research into up-wards bullying (i.e., a staff member bullying a supervisor or manager) supports the notion that those who lack formal sources of power within the workplace can actually bully individuals in positions of authority through various means, such as strengthening informal power-bases (Branch *et al.*, 2007a,b).

Throughout the world, a range of terms have been used in reference to negative social behaviour at work, including the terms mobbing, workplace bullying, workplace aggression, workplace incivility, workplace harassment, workplace deviance, social undermining, emotional abuse, abusive supervision and antisocial behaviour, with these terms often used inter-changeably (Einarsen *et al.*, 2011a; Zapf, 2004). Indeed the poster from mobbing.ca (see Figure 22.1) emphasises the different terms used to describe negative social behaviour at work. The term workplace bullying has been described as an umbrella term, as it can incor-porate harassing, intimidating, and aggressive or violent behaviours (Fox and Stallworth, 2005). In Scandinavia (the source of considerable research in this area), the term 'mobbing' was introduced by the late Heinz Leymann (1990), who referred to mobbing as a psychologi-cal phenomenon where repeated incidents, that are often minor, result in significant negative impacts for the target. As a result, the term mobbing is commonly used within Scandinavian countries in place of workplace bullying (Einarsen, 2000). In the United States, researchers often encompass bullying behaviours in the term 'emotional abuse' (Keashly, 1998, 2001; Keashly and Jagatic, 2011), which is usually characterised as a persistent and enduring form of 'workplace aggression' (Baron and Neuman, 1996, 1998; Keashly and Jagatic, 2011). Researchers within Australia and Great Britain (including Branch, 2008; Hoel and Cooper, 2001; Rayner, 2007; Sheehan *et al.*, 2004) tend to use the term 'workplace bullying', which is used throughout this chapter.

Figure 22.1 Poster highlighting the issue of workplace bullying

Source: mobbing.ca – http://www.mobbing.ca. Acknowledgements: Bobbie Osborne (Photographer) and Anton Hout (Designer).

> ## How is workplace bullying defined?

Despite increased research focus on workplace bullying in recent decades, considerable confusion exists as to what workplace bullying actually is and how it differs from, or is similar to, other forms of counter-productive behaviours in the workplace, e.g. harassment (see Figure 22.1). Indeed, especially given the range of terms in use and the complexity of workplace bullying incidents, an agreed upon definition of workplace bullying is yet to be developed (Saunders *et al.*, 2007). Within the bullying research community there exists a

> constant tension between the need to define a portmanteau term that would allow the inclusion of a range of phenomena from a range of cultural contexts and the need to retain key elements of the original concept. *(Fevre et al., 2010: 75)*

Some researchers even question whether it is possible to achieve a uniform definition of workplace bullying (Rayner *et al.*, 2002). Despite these different perspectives, agreement generally exists about the inclusion of and importance placed on several characteristics within the definition of workplace bullying (Branch, 2008; Nielsen *et al.*, 2008).

First, workplace bullying behaviours are often defined as *inappropriate* or *unreasonable behaviours* (Einarsen and Raknes, 1997; Einarsen *et al.*, 2011a; Hoel and Cooper, 2001; Saunders *et al.*, 2007). Examples of such behaviours include ridiculing people, keeping a constant eye on another's work, questioning another's professional ability, spreading damaging rumours and explosive outbursts and threats (Bassman, 1992; Rayner and Hoel, 1997; Zapf and Einarsen, 2001). However, due to different patterns and intensity of behaviours as well as contextual factors, consistent agreement as to what exactly represents a bullying behaviour has proven difficult (Rayner, 1997). Further muddying the waters is a person's 'subjective perception of being bullied', which can vary from one target to another (Agervold, 2007: 163). The difficulty of identifying workplace bullying behaviours will be discussed later in this chapter.

Second, definitions of workplace bullying emphasise that inappropriate *behaviours occur persistently or regularly over a period of time* (Einarsen *et al.*, 2011a; Keashly and Jagatic, 2011; Leymann, 1990). According to Hoel and Cooper (2001: 4), 'the long-term nature of the phenomenon is one of the most salient features of the problem'. In fact, some researchers have explained workplace bullying as a form of conflict escalation in which the intensity of the attacks escalates, with increasingly negative effects on the target (Einarsen and Skogstad, 1996; Keashly and Jagatic, 2011; Leymann and Gustafsson, 1996; Zapf and Gross, 2001). An important variation to the concept of persistent and possibly escalating behaviour proposed by some, is the notion of 'ongoing threat' (Zapf, 2004). For example, a verbal attack on someone may induce a long-lasting fear that it could re-occur. This variation is still open to debate.

Third, the existence of a *power imbalance* between the two parties (Keashly and Jagatic, 2011) is often regarded as an essential definitional component. Thus, when the two parties have an equal balance of power, a conflict would not be considered workplace bullying (Hoel and Cooper, 2001; Rayner *et al.*, 2002). Commonly, dependency on the part of the target is cited as a prime reason for a power imbalance developing, and for targets of workplace bullying being unable to defend themselves (e.g. because another person possesses greater formal, hierarchical power and/or informal power such as access to information or influence). Thus, a power imbalance between the two parties is an essential characteristic of the definition of workplace bullying (Einarsen *et al.*, 2011a; Keashly and Jagatic, 2011).

In summary, the important defining characteristics of workplace bullying appear to be the persistent use of inappropriate behaviours (be it regular use of these behaviours, or possibly an ongoing threat as a result of a single event), coupled with the inability of the target to defend themselves due to a power imbalance (Einarsen *et al.*, 2011a). Elements of these characteristics can be seen in the following widely accepted academic definition:

Bullying at work means harassing, offending, socially excluding someone or negatively affecting some-one's work tasks. In order for the label bullying (or mobbing) to be applied to a particular activity, interaction or process it has to occur repeatedly and regularly (e.g. weekly) and over a period of time (e.g. about six months). Bullying is an escalating process in the course of which the person confronted ends up in an inferior position and becomes the target of systematic negative social acts. A conflict cannot be called bullying if the incident is an isolated event or if two parties of approximately equal 'strength' are in conflict. (Einarsen *et al.,* 2011a: 22)

Furthermore, the concepts of power and inappropriate, persistent behaviours are included in the following practical definition. However, as mentioned earlier, differences in definitions of workplace bullying only begin to highlight the complexity of workplace bullying incidents (Rayner *et al.*, 2002).

Workplace bullying is

persistent unacceptable 'offensive, intimidating, malicious, insulting or humiliating behaviour, abuse of power or authority which attempts to undermine an individual or group of employees and which may cause them to suffer stress'. (UNISON, 2003)

You might like to explore the workplace bullying definition used by the University at which you are studying or organisation you are working in. Consider how their definition of workplace bullying is similar or different to the definitions provided here, and what elements are included in the definition.

The importance of power and dependency in workplace bullying

Power relationships within organisations have gained importance as work environments have become increasingly complex and unpredictable (Asch and Salaman, 2002). Power and how it is used constitutes a central concept when discussing relationships in organisations. Indeed, power is especially relevant to any discussion of workplace bullying (Hoel and Salin, 2003; Salin and Hoel, 2011), which often focusses on an imbalance of power between those involved and the defencelessness of the recipients (Keashly and Jagatic, 2011). As introduced earlier, one concept closely related to power is *dependency*. Importantly, it is the target's dependency on the offender that produces the power imbalance necessary for bullying to occur (Einarsen *et al.*, 2011a; Keashly and Jagatic, 2011). Bassman (1992: 2) even states, 'one common thread in all abusive relationships is the element of dependency. The abuser controls some important resources in the [target's] life, the [target] is dependent on the abuser'. For example, staff rely on managers for direction, resources and rewards, while managers are dependent on staff to be productive and fulfil the goals of the organisation (Cook *et al.*, 1997). If however, either party denies or hinders the other person in achieving their goals, power can be derived (Emerson, 1962).

Vulnerability to workplace bullying may also occur due to the characteristics of individuals or marginalised groups within society and workplaces (Ramsay, *et al.*, 2010). Einarsen and his colleagues (2011a), for example, suggest that being a member of a group which is considered to be outside the accepted dominant culture may be the only reason some people are bullied. Indeed, Zapf (1999) proposed that some group processes (e.g., scapegoating) are also related to workplace bullying. Ramsay and her colleagues (2010) recently expanded on this perspective using social identity theory (Tajfel and Turner, 1986) and social rules theory (Argyle *et al.*, 1985). Within this article the authors proposed that 'groups with negative social rules based on aggressive or anti-social behaviour (Gini, 2006) are more likely to promote and condone bullying within the group, particularly if it has a strong identity' (Ramsay *et al.*, 2010: 10). Group characteristics such as ethnicity (Fox and Stallworth, 2005), gender (Djurkovic *et al.*, 2004), age (Zapf, 1999 cited in Zapf and Einarsen, 2011) and organisational status differences (Hoel *et al.*, 2001), such as the division between management and staff (Jablin, 1986), have been found to be related to workplace bullying.

Identifying workplace bullying behaviours

A number of the specific behaviours that constitute bullying in the workplace have been identified. However, another demonstration of the complexity of workplace bullying is the various patterns of bullying behaviours in different work environments. For example, Djurkovic and colleagues' (2004) study of 150 undergraduate students found the most common bullying behaviours experienced were unjustified criticism, monitoring of performance, unfair pressure and comments or sarcasm. Alternatively, in an academic institution, Pietersen (2007) found that isolating the target or obstructing their work, as well as blocking career advancement were the most common bullying behaviours. There is also an indication that work-related bullying behaviours (e.g. withholding of information) are more common than non-work related behaviours (e.g. insulting remarks) in managerial ranks, where greater competition and significant work pressures may prevail (Salin, 2001). These differences in bullying behaviours may reflect the particular culture within different workplaces or environments.

There are, however, a number of difficulties with looking at the different behaviours that can constitute bullying in the workplace. Although some are observable and easy to label as bullying (such as irrational outbursts), other behaviours may be more covert and difficult to observe or describe. In fact, despite the assumption that bullying is physical in nature (Rigby, 2001), it has been recognised that most bullying behaviour tends to be psychologically based (Bjorkqvist *et al.*, 1994; Einarsen *et al.*, 2011b; O'Moore *et al.*, 1998; Zapf *et al.*, 1996). For instance, in a classic study of 460 male shipyard workers in Norway, threats of physical abuse and actual physical abuse were rarely reported (2.4 per cent), while the more covert behaviours of withdrawal of information (51.7 per cent) and dismissing a person's opinion (53.6 per cent) were reported more often (Einarsen and Raknes, 1997). Moreover, workplace bullying is not only about what someone does to another, but can also include what is not done (Rayner *et al.*, 2002), for example, the withholding of information or excluding the target from a relevant or significant work-related social event (Einarsen and Raknes, 1997). As a result, workplace bullying behaviours are not always easy to recognise or identify, again highlighting the complexity of workplace bullying.

Identifying bullying behaviours is also complicated by the fact that recipients of workplace bullying may not label it as such, often selecting other terms, such as aggression, harassment and intimidation (Hadikin and O'Driscoll, 2000). Moreover, the lack of recognition of particular behaviours as bullying may be the result of bullying behaviours becoming normalised in some workplaces (Archer, 1999; Hadikin and O'Driscoll, 2000; Rayner, 1997, 1999). This conclusion was reached by Lewis (2004) in relation to his interview study within the United Kingdom further and higher education context where bullying was sometimes difficult to identify as it appeared to have become a behavioural norm. Furthermore, with advances in technology, researchers and practitioners are becoming more aware of cyberbullying tactics. In one study in Australia it was found that 10.7 per cent of respondents experienced cyberbullying, with many of these targets also experiencing face-to-face bullying (Privitera and Campbell, 2009). It is expected that the area of cyberbullying will require ongoing examination.

Prevalence of workplace bullying behaviours and risk groups

Research indicates between 10–15 per cent of people are exposed to persistent inappropriate behaviours in the workplace (Zapf *et al.*, 2011). However, statistics on the frequency of workplace bullying can vary quite dramatically due to different definitions of workplace bullying and various approaches to measuring it. To demonstrate, Hoel and Cooper's (2000) questionnaire study of 5,288 individuals from 70 different organisations within the United Kingdom, found 10.6 per cent of respondents reported being bullied within the last six months, and 24.7 per cent of respondents reporting being bullied within the last five years. Notably, 46.5 per cent reported witnessing bullying within the last five years. However, consistent with other Scandinavian studies, Mikkelsen and Einarsen (2001) found lower levels of bullying (between 2.7 per cent to 8 per cent) in their research, which may be due to their use of a strict criterion of experiencing two negative acts per week during a six-month period. In addition, they found 17.7 per cent of respondents stated that they had witnessed bullying acts within the workplace. The authors concluded that the higher rates of witnessing may indicate that 'the real prevalence of bullying is higher than shown by the data' (Mikkelsen and Einarsen, 2001: 404).

You might like to consider if a strict criterion of experiencing two bullying behaviours a week for six months is a practical criterion for organisations to adopt?

Prevalence studies may also enable researchers to identify particular traits of targets and perpetrators. Accordingly, Zapf and Einarsen (2005) suggest most studies indicate that, of those targeted, the majority are women. For example, Lewis and Gunn (2007) found that women in the public sector (24 per cent) were bullied more than men (17 per cent). By contrast, Djurkovic *et al.*'s (2004) study of 150 undergraduate students found women and men were equally likely to be perpetrators of workplace bullying. Interestingly, they also found that the gender of the target and perpetrator often matched, suggesting that 'same-gender bullying occurs more frequently than between-gender bullying' (Djurkovic, *et al.*, 2004: 487). The authors indicate this may explain the concentration of bullying in either male- or female-dominated industries (Djurkovic *et al.*, 2004), such as in nursing (e.g. Quine, 2001) and the fire service (e.g. Archer, 1999).

While workplace bullying can be found in most organisations (Lewis and Gunn, 2007), research suggests that particular groups and industries may be more vulnerable. For instance, Lewis and Gunn (2007) found a higher occurrence of workplace bullying amongst non-white groups in the public sector in South Wales. Indeed, 35 per cent of non-white respondents indicated an experience of workplace bullying, compared with only 9 per cent of white respondents. This research may reflect the group processes that relate to the occurrence of workplace bullying (as introduced earlier). That is, belonging to a group which is considered to be outside the accepted dominant culture may be the only reason some people are bullied (Einarsen *et al.*, 2011a; Ramsay *et al.*, 2010).

Predominantly, research has examined downwards bullying (as perpetrated by a manager(s) against staff) and, more recently, horizontal bullying (one colleague bullying another) (Lewis and Sheehan, 2003). Notably, however, the voice of managers who feel they have been bullied by a staff member(s) has rarely been heard in this research data. Until recently, cases of upwards bullying have been reported rarely in the literature (Branch *et al.*, 2007a; Rayner and Cooper, 2003) and are often presented anecdotally or as a single instance (see Braverman, 1999, for example). Similarly, Scandinavian, UK and European research has identified the occurrence of upwards bullying as being between 2 per cent and 27 per cent, with a mean of 11 per cent (figures obtained from Table 5.5 presented in Zapf *et al.*, 2003: 116). Furthermore, Salin (2001) found that one-sixth of self-identified managerial targets of workplace bullying reported being bullied by a staff member. This led Salin (2001) to conclude that the power imbalance necessary for workplace bullying to occur can be created via means other than formal position, suggesting that it would be of interest to study further 'how superiors can be put into a position in which they cannot defend themselves and how bullying alters power relations' (Salin, 2001: 435).

A doctoral study by Branch (2006) into upwards bullying found that power and dependency appeared to play a role in the occurrence of upwards bullying. In an interview study it was found that managers (in discussing either their managerial work environment or a more direct experience of upwards bullying) were able to identify factors that could play a part in reducing a manager's positional power; factors such as lack of support and resources from upper management and particular dependency by the manager on the staff member(s). For instance, a number of managers interviewed indicated how a staff member being critical to the functioning of the workplace (e.g. highly advanced IT skills) created a dependency on that staff member which resulted in the manager being reluctant, at least at first, to take any action when the staff member demonstrated inappropriate behaviour. Interestingly, the majority of those who discussed dependency on a staff member were managers who reported a direct experience of upwards bullying (Branch, 2006). Further research into upwards bullying is needed to clarify this aspect but it again highlights the complexity of workplace bullying (see Branch, *et al.*, 2007a,b).

The effect of workplace bullying on targets

Bullying behaviours have the ability to negatively affect a person's health (Mikkelsen and Einarsen, 2002a,b) and ability to cope (Leymann, 1990), especially when they occur regularly over a period of time. For recipients of workplace bullying, the consequences can range from physical harm through to an increase in psychological stress for the recipient (Hogh *et al.*, 2011). In a study that demonstrates the severe impact that workplace bullying can have on an individual, Mikkelsen and Einarsen (2002a: 98) found that 80.5 per cent of participants reported that 'no other event in their life affected them more negatively than the bullying'. This was despite the reporting of experiences such as accidents, divorce, bereavement and serious illness. Furthermore, in a unique study into the metaphors that self-identified targets of workplace bullying used to describe their experiences, Tracy *et al.*, (2006) described targets' feelings of vulnerability and degradation (e.g. feeling like a slave or a prisoner isolated from others; being degraded like an animal; or being treated like a child). Indeed, for the individual experiencing workplace bullying, the impacts can be so pervasive that they may negatively affect not only their ability to function at work but other areas of life as well (Keashly and Harvey, 2006).

Examples of the wide-ranging impact workplace bullying can have on a person's life is demonstrated in its links to the occurrence of stress-related symptoms (Mikkelsen and Einarsen, 2001), depression (Niedhammer *et al.*, 2006) and post-traumatic stress disorder (PTSD) (Bjorkqvist *et al.*, 1994; Matthiesen and Einarsen, 2004; Mikkelsen and Einarsen, 2002a; Tehrani, 2004). For instance, researchers have found that as exposure to bullying increases so too does the risk of depressive symptoms (Niedhammer *et al.*, 2006). Of further concern, researchers found that 76 per cent of 118 targets of workplace bullying displayed PTSD symptoms, with 29 per cent fulfilling the full diagnostic criteria of PTSD (Mikkelsen and Einarsen, 2002a). Workplace bullying has also been associated with other psychological symptoms such as a higher risk of suicide attempts (O'Moore *et al.*, 1998) and clinical levels of anxiety (Quine, 1999). Finally, workplace bullying has been linked to greater long-term health risks through an increase in stress-related behaviours such as smoking, drinking and excessive eating (Quine, 1999; Savva and Alexandrou, 1998). Therefore, bullying in the workplace can have severe and enduring physical and psychological health consequences for those who experience it.

The effect of workplace bullying on witnesses

The complexity of workplace bullying can also be seen in the web of those drawn into incidents of bullying. For example, co-workers of those who experience workplace bullying have reported that workplace bullying impacts on them in a number of ways. In a British study of 761 public sector trade union members, 73 per cent of witnesses of workplace bullying reported an increase in their stress levels, and 44 per cent of respondents were concerned about being the next target (Rayner, 1999). In fact, it was found that those who witness workplace bullying and violence can be affected almost as severely as the actual target, which has vital implications for the loyalty of staff and productivity of organisations (Mayhew *et al.*, 2004). Understandably, such a *climate of fear* (Rayner, 1999) could flow on to an increase in absenteeism (Kivimaki *et al.*, 2000), which could place additional work demands on those who remain. Lowered work morale, increases in workplace conflict, and stress generated as a direct consequence of workplace bullying, are also seen as affecting others' well-being through the creation of an abusive work environment and culture (Hoel *et al.*, 2011; Hogh *et al.*, 2011; Parzefall and Salin, 2010). Thus, workplace bullying can have direct and indirect impacts on targets and witnesses, as well as others who experience the workplace climate more generally. These processes magnify the effects on the wider organisation.

You might like to think of how you would react if you witnessed a colleague of yours being bullied – keeping in mind the climate of fear that can be created when bullying occurs.

The effect of workplace bullying on the organisation

As would be expected, when the physical and psychological health impacts begin to be felt by targets and witnesses of workplace bullying, an individual's ability to function at work will also be affected (Bowling and Beehr, 2006). In general, bullying in the workplace can affect an organisation through loss of productivity, an increase in absenteeism and intention to leave, as well as the cost of intervention programmes (Einarsen, 2000; Hoel *et al.*, 2011; McCarthy and Barker, 2000; McCarthy *et al.*, 1995). For instance, a classic questionnaire study of 1,100 employees of a National Health Service Community Trust in the United Kingdom revealed that targets of workplace bullying not only had higher levels of job-induced stress, including higher levels of depression and anxiety, but also had lower levels of job satisfaction, and higher intention to leave than other workers (Quine, 1999). In addition, workplace bullying has also been linked to absenteeism within the workplace. Kivimaki *et al.*'s (2000) study of 5,655 hospital employees found a link between workplace bullying and an increase in sick leave taken. As well as the direct costs to the hospital, the financial impacts of lower motivation, impaired patient care, and the potential of staff leaving the workplace show the ongoing negative impact of workplace bullying (Kivimaki *et al.*, 2000). Indeed the cost of workplace bullying to organisations is staggering. Various studies have been conducted in an attempt to quantify the cost of workplace bullying to organisations and indeed whole countries. Kivimaki *et al.*, (2000) estimated that absenteeism due to bullying was

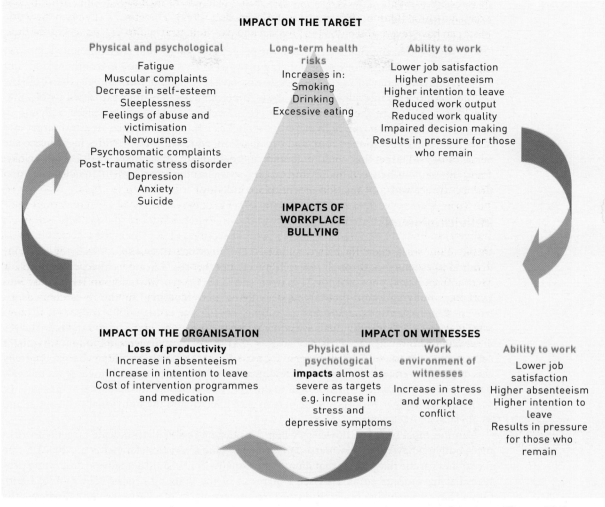

IMPACT ON THE TARGET

Physical and psychological

Fatigue
Muscular complaints
Decrease in self-esteem
Sleeplessness
Feelings of abuse and
victimisation
Nervousness
Psychosomatic complaints
Post-traumatic stress disorder
Depression
Anxiety
Suicide

Long-term health risks

Increases in:
Smoking
Drinking
Excessive eating

Ability to work

Lower job satisfaction
Higher absenteeism
Higher intention to leave
Reduced work output
Reduced work quality
Impaired decision making
Results in pressure for those
who remain

IMPACTS OF WORKPLACE BULLYING

IMPACT ON THE ORGANISATION

Loss of productivity
Increase in absenteeism
Increase in intention to leave
Cost of intervention programmes
and medication

IMPACT ON WITNESSES

Physical and psychological impacts almost as severe as targets e.g. increase in stress and depressive symptoms

Work environment of witnesses

Increase in stress and workplace conflict

Ability to work

Lower job satisfaction
Higher absenteeism
Higher intention to leave
Results in pressure for those who remain

Figure 22.2
The impacts of workplace bullying

costing the two hospitals who participated in the study £125,000 a year. Sheehan and colleagues (2001) estimated the cost of workplace bullying to Australian employers at between 6 and 13 billion dollars a year using a conservative prevalence estimate of 3.5 per cent and between 17 and 36 billion dollars per year if the prevalence estimate was increased to 15 per cent (see Hoel *et al.*, 2011 for a summary of the financial costs of workplace bullying). In conclusion, workplace bullying can have severe impacts on targets, witnesses and the organisation as a whole, as summarised in Figure 22.2.

Antecedents of workplace bullying

In an attempt to examine how the effects of workplace bullying could be reduced for individuals and organisations, researchers have explored the antecedents of workplace bullying. Research has examined individual factors, such as personality traits of the target or the bully (Ashforth, 1997; Coyne *et al.*, 2000; Douglas and Martinko, 2001; Zapf, 1999) and bullying as an interpersonal conflict (Einarsen *et al.*, 2011a). In addition, others have emphasised that bullying is a multifaceted and complex phenomenon and, as such, multiple causes, including organisational and group-related factors, need to be considered along with individual factors (Harvey *et al*, 2006; Heames and Harvey, 2006; Salin and Hoel, 2011; Zapf, 1999). For instance, Salin and Hoel (2011) suggest that, due to the complexity of workplace bullying, the actions and reactions of the target and perpetrator can only be understood within the context in which they occur.

In a further demonstration of the complexity of workplace bullying, Harvey and colleagues (2006) suggest that the characteristics of the perpetrator, target and environment all interact together in supporting workplace bullying processes. That is, if the environment does not support bullying behaviours, or if bullies do not have access to potential targets, then bullying will not occur. This interplay between these three elements is further explained by Heames and Harvey (2006) in their proposal of a cross-level assessment of workplace bullying. In their conceptualisation, the bullying event stretches beyond the perpetrator and target and has a flow-on impact to the group and organisation, which in turn provides feedback to the perpetrator and target that could potentially perpetuate or, alternatively, halt the behaviour. Thus, interactions between bullies and targets, as well as the environment are all involved in the occurrence and continuation of workplace bullying.

Individual level

In the main, researchers have conceptualised and investigated workplace bullying as an individual phenomenon, through research into the personality of targets and perpetrators, or as an interpersonal phenomenon (Einarsen *et al.*, 2011a). For instance, an Irish study into workplace bullying found that targets of bullying were identified by the researchers as introverted, conscientious, neurotic and submissive (Coyne *et al.*, 2000). Indeed, it is commonly suggested that individuals with low self-esteem may be more often targeted. Harvey *et al.* (2006) however, very elegantly suggest that there are five elements to an individual's self-esteem at work, any of which may increase the target's vulnerability. That is, the bully can direct their energies towards one or a number of these areas, which include an individual's: 1) cognitive ability; 2) emotional maturity; 3) personal and professional achievements; 4) organisational network (i.e., if the person is well liked) and the individual's character; and 5) physical characteristics.

Caution must be taken however, when considering results that indicate targets of workplace bullying have particular personality traits or characteristics (Rayner *et al.*, 2002). Some researchers argue that results that identify personality traits could actually be describing profiles that have occurred as a subsequent result of the bullying process (see Quine, 1999). Others have warned that researching the target's personality may be perceived as 'blaming the victim', rather than reflecting a more balanced approach to understanding the circumstances of the situation (Zapf and Einarsen, 2011). Indeed, in a recent study, Lind *et al.* (2009: 231) concluded that differences in personality were too small to 'differentiate targets of workplace bullying from nontargets', thus supporting the view that additional factors are at play. However, Keashly and Harvey (2006) suggest that because conflicts such as workplace bullying can be defined as a hostile relationship between target and perpetrator, exploring individual factors, including those of the target, is a valid approach in some circumstances.

In addition to research which has focused on the targets of workplace bullying, the personality of the perpetrator has also been investigated, although less so, due in the main to the reluctance of perpetrators to come forward (see Zapf and Einarsen, 2011 for summary). Counter to the common assumption that low self-esteem leads to aggression and violence, Baumeister and colleagues (1996), in a theoretical review of research into aggression, proposed that high self-esteem in combination with ego threat is a major cause of aggression and violence. In a study that tested Baumeister *et al.*'s (1996) conceptualisation, Stucke and Sporer (2002) explored the relationship between narcissism (individuals with an inflated but unstable self-esteem), self-concept clarity and aggression. The authors found that 'high narcissists, with low self-concept clarity reacted with anger and aggression', while less narcissistic participants displayed no aggression (Stucke and Sporer, 2002: 509). Despite the body of research into the personality of workplace bullying targets and perpetrators, Rayner and her colleagues (2002) suggest that using personality screening would not be useful in identifying potential targets and bullies. This is mainly due to the difficulty of identifying whether personality traits were a cause or effect of bullying and that factors other than personality alone, appear to influence the occurrence of workplace bullying.

Interactions between bullies and targets

As a further demonstration of the complexity of workplace bullying, research suggests that the reactions of targets may also play a part in the occurrence of workplace bullying (Keashly and Harvey, 2006). For instance, Zapf and Gross (2001) argue that the response of targets may further escalate the conflict between the perpetrator and themselves. Indeed, they found that those targets who successfully coped with workplace bullying were more able to recognise and avoid escalating behaviour by using less directly active strategies to defuse the situation (Zapf and Gross, 2001). Moreover, supporting the argument that workplace bullying incidents are complex, Tehrani (2011) suggests that the target–perpetrator relationship is not always simple to define, and that instead, an accusation of bullying is often 'triggered by the individual's responses to a series of interactions that are built up over a period of time' (Tehrani, 2003: 280). In fact, Tehrani (2003) proposes that during times of high stress and when a relationship is perceived as negative, small issues such as not saying hello in the morning, may be interpreted as an aggressive act. Alternatively, Einarsen (1999) suggests that some bullying cases may be predatory bullying (as opposed to dispute-related bullying), where the target appears to be bullied specifically because of particular characteristics such as their membership of a minority group (Einarsen *et al.*, 2011a; Zapf and Einarsen, 2005).

Environmental level

There have also been calls for researchers to move beyond the individual and dyadic levels of analysis and to consider group (previously discussed) and organisational factors in workplace bullying (Einarsen *et al.*, 2011a; Liefooghe and Davey, 2001; Ramsay *et al.*, 2010; Rayner *et al.*, 2002). Indeed, organisational factors, such as destructive and laissez-faire leadership, a negative social environment, poor job design, job insecurity, organisational change resulting in role conflict and job insecurity, high workloads, workgroup disharmony and acceptance of inappropriate behaviours have been associated with the occurrence of workplace bullying (see Agervold, 2009; Ashforth, 1997; Baillien and De Witte, 2009; Branch *et al.*, 2007b; De Cuyper *et al.*, 2009; Hauge *et al.*, 2007, 2009; Leymann, 1996; Rayner *et al.*, 2002; Skogstad *et al.*, 2007; Vartia, 1996). In addition to these factors, Harvey *et al.* (2006) have proposed a number of environmental factors that appear to be increasing and which they accordingly link to the increase in workplace bullying (see Table 22.1).

Perhaps again reflecting current work environments, research suggests that workplace bullying is associated with highly competitive workplaces (O' Moore *et al.*, 1998; Salin, 2003). For instance, Salin's (2003) study of 385 members of the Finnish Association of Graduates in Economics and Business Administration found a strong link between perceived organisational politics and workplace bullying. It was proposed that within the current organisational

Table 22.1 Organisational factors likely to be related to the increase in workplace bullying

Rate of change resulting in a high levels of uncertainty in the workplace
Lack of time to achieve tasks
Growing rate of diversity in the workplace
Downsizing/rightsizing resulting in concern for future longevity of survivors
Reduction of middle management resulting in an increased gap between management and workers
Lack of clearly outlined cultural norms within today's organisations

Source: Harvey *et al.*, 2006: 4.

climate of increased organisational pressures, bullying may be a rational response to the level of competition and 'need for survival'. Salin (2003) concluded that in some cases, workplace bullying may be perpetrated in order to promote some people's own self-interest, which is in turn rewarded by the organisation (e.g. given a promotion).

Branch and her colleagues (2007a), in a unique study into upwards bullying found that work environments characterised by high workloads, workgroup disharmony and acceptance of inappropriate behaviours appeared to contribute to upwards bullying. Indeed, it has been suggested that when stress in the workplace and interpersonal tension are not dealt with, they can eventually lead to workplace bullying (Skogstad *et al.*, 2007). Furthermore, Branch *et al.*, (2007a) found that change (e.g. an organisational restructure) appeared to play an important role in contributing to workplace pressures. In addition, it has been suggested that in a work environment of 'continuous change the potential for employees to project their fears and resentments into the construction of managers as bullies, whether deservedly or not, is high' (McCarthy *et al.*, 2002: 536). In other words, a 'victim-mentality' environment is created (McCarthy, 1999). Interestingly, it has even been proposed that staff may actually be using the term bullying as a way of voicing their dissatisfaction with organisational issues (Liefooghe and Davey, 2001). Similarly, McCarthy (2004: xv), suggests that the term '"bullying at work" has become a new signifier of distress that has acted as a solar collector of resentments'. Perhaps the above section better than any other demonstrates the complexity of workplace bullying and how a number of factors all work towards the occurrence of bullying in the workplace.

Prevention and management of workplace bullying

As noted by De Cieri and Kramar (2008), it is vital that the field of management clearly comprehends and strives to address the very serious issues related to bullying. In light of 'the emotional, physical, legal, reputational and financial costs' of bullying and its impact on individuals, unions and employers, they recommend a comprehensive approach whereby organisations articulate their stance on preventing and eliminating bullying and then develop and maintain appropriate processes to support this stance (De Cieri and Kramar, 2008: 626). Solutions, however, are not easy to identify. Indeed, given the complex and multidimensional nature of workplace bullying, no single approach is likely to provide organisations with the answer to solving the problem. As such, a number of researchers and practitioners have suggested a range of interrelated responses to prevent and manage bullying in the workplace. McCarthy and his colleagues (2002: 528) suggested that any effective response to workplace bullying needs to include 'prevention, redress/resolution, and support'. However, until recently the effectiveness of proposed interventions to address workplace bullying has been under-researched (Saam, 2010). This may be due to a lack of a suitable theoretical model explaining workplace bullying (Einarsen, 2000), or due to the complexity of the phenomenon. Nonetheless, the lack of research into this area means that relatively little is known about the success of proposed interventions. With this limitation in mind, the following section will now expand upon the framework proposed by McCarthy and colleagues (2002).

Prevention

Policy

Typical methods of preventing workplace bullying include a clearly articulated 'no bullying' policy, training which includes knowledge of responsibilities and obligations of employers and employees alike, as well as an effective risk identification and system for complaints (McCarthy *et al.*, 2002; Vartia and Leka, 2011; Vartia *et al.*, 2003;). When respondents were asked about how to deter workplace bullying in a questionnaire study of 512 Chartered

Management Institute members in the United Kingdom, four strategies were rated highly; training, a contact point for advice, the provision of an internal confidential counselling service and external mediation (Woodman and Cook, 2005).

Furthermore, Woodman and Cook (2005) provide additional insight into the use and possible importance of a workplace bullying policy. When asked to rate their organisation's ability to deter bullying, 70 per cent of respondents from organisations that had a formal policy addressing workplace bullying felt their organisation was quite effective or very effective at deterring bullying. The percentage of respondents rating the organisation as favourable was reduced considerably when the organisation had no formal policy (Woodman and Cook, 2005). Salin's (2008) research with HR practitioners also indicates their support for the incorporation of formal anti-bullying policies. However, later research by Salin (2009) suggests that the existence of formal anti-bullying policies neither increased nor decreased the reported likelihood of personnel managers taking action to address workplace bullying (i.e., reconciliation, transfer or punitive measures). Further research into this area is needed to clarify the efficacy of policies in either preventing or facilitating the management of workplace bullying. However, as important guiding principles in relation to policy, participants in the Woodman and Cook (2005) study identified the need to involve a wide range of stakeholders, including line managers and employees, in the development and implementation of the policy. It is also recommended that a workplace bullying policy be made widely available throughout the organisation and include clearly defined terms (Richards and Daley, 2003).

Training

As suggested by McCarthy *et al.*, (2002), a training programme that includes information on the responsibilities and obligations of employers and employees is one measure to prevent workplace bullying (see example in Figure 22.3). Awareness raising about what constitutes workplace bullying, its impacts, as well as what interventions can occur are vital steps in preventing workplace bullying and should take place throughout the whole organisation (McCarthy *et al.*, 2002). Awareness training about workplace bullying should outline the importance of clear objectives, roles and processes within the workplace, as well as the causes,

Figure 22.3 Workplace intervention poster

impacts and how workplace bullying is handled in the workplace (Vartia *et al.*, 2003). It is suggested that training should also be provided to managers on how to manage cases of bullying (McCarthy *et al.*, 2002; Richards and Daley, 2003; Vartia and Leka, 2011).

Capacity and resilience

The promotion of coping skills and resilience is also suggested as essential to assist targets to handle workplace bullying experiences (McCarthy *et al.*, 2002). In an earlier study, McCarthy *et al.*, (1995) found that training in interpersonal skills, conflict resolution and stress management assisted in helping targets of workplace bullying manage the behaviours of perpetrators better. Vartia and Leka (2011) suggest this type of training can be directed to all members of the organisation or targeted towards managers. Bystander training is also another approach being taken (see Mentors in Violence Program, Katz, 1995). Dispelling the myths of workplace bullying through awareness training may also assist in increasing targets' and potential targets' resilience to workplace bullying (McCarthy *et al.*, 2002). Moreover, training of this type could link into the broader organisational context, where a more positive climate of justice could ultimately reduce the prevalence of workplace bullying (Parzefall and Salin, 2010).

Redress or resolution

Due to the potential of workplace bullying to intensify if not dealt with early, the provision of early intervention measures is vital (McCarthy *et al.*, 2002). Early intervention is important not just in terms of assisting the target, but also in sending a clear message that inappropriate behaviours will be addressed within the organisation (McCarthy *et al.*, 2002). Redress can include informal (e.g., a contact officers' network to provide advice) and formal measures (e.g., a timely investigation process) (Richards and Daley, 2003). Similarly, an appropriate grievance procedure should include both informal and formal measures, such as informal mediation processes, disciplinary action, the provision of information about internal and external opportunities for redress, and compensation (McCarthy *et al.*, 2002). However, evidence suggests that informal discussions may make the situation worse for some targets because further retaliatory actions may occur (Woodman and Cook, 2005), indicating the need for great sensitivity and skill in these areas.

According to McCarthy and his colleagues (2002), it is crucial that perpetrators of workplace bullying, whether their behaviour is intentional or unintentional, are made aware of their inappropriate behaviours. This can occur, if suitable, at the point of the inappropriate behaviour, or through a performance review (McCarthy *et al.*, 2002). Importantly, it has been suggested that when approaching the perpetrator, managers should take a problem-solving approach, rather than adopt a punitive framework (McCarthy *et al.*, 2002).

If a formal complaint is lodged, Richards and Daley (2003: 254) advise that clear and specific information be provided within the complaint. This should include information as to the 'dates, times, and witnesses to incidents with direct quotes; factual description of events; indication of how each incident made the complainant feel; documentary evidence; details of any action the complainant or others have already taken'. Complaints of workplace bullying should be treated seriously and investigated in a timely manner while maintaining confidentiality (Victorian WorkCover Authority, cited in McCarthy *et al.*, 2002). However, due to the subtle nature of workplace bullying, a no-blame resolution approach is recommended as a first intervention, when appropriate (McCarthy *et al.*, 2002).

If an investigation is necessary, it should be fair and impartial (Richards and Daley, 2003). In cases where a serious allegation has been made, where the target does not want to work with the perpetrator, or pressure may be placed on witnesses, it is recommended that the alleged perpetrator (and target) be suspended with pay (Merchant and Hoel, 2003; Rayner *et al.*, 2002). Furthermore, the organisation should ensure that the complainant is protected from reprisals (Richards and Daley, 2003). In cases where the organisation does not have the capacity to investigate claims of workplace bullying, or if the alleged perpetrator is a senior manager, an external investigator is recommended (Merchant and Hoel, 2003).

Confidentiality throughout the investigation process should be maintained, however, it is recognised that it is difficult to stop the informal 'rumour mill'. Once the investigation has been finalised, discussions with members of the workgroup as to the outcome and reasons for the final decision may be necessary (Richards and Daley, 2003).

At the end of the investigation, a report should be provided to all parties, with the right to appeal for either party (Richards and Daley, 2003). Provision to manage malicious complaints, which can be related to revenge, should also be made within the procedure (Richards and Daley, 2003). In the case of a suspected malicious complaint, a motive must be shown (Merchant and Hoel, 2003). Referring to a policy from a local council, Richards and Daley (2003) indicate that if the investigator considers the complaint to be malicious, then disciplinary action should be taken. Similarly, disciplinary action should be taken in cases of substantiated complaints (McCarthy *et al.*, 2002). Despite the suitability of relocating the perpetrator in cases of substantiated bullying, often relocation of the target is the normal course of action, due to the willingness of the target to transfer (Richards and Daley, 2003).

Support

It is recommended that support via employee assistance schemes and human relations systems, such as counselling, be provided to both parties (McCarthy *et al.*, 2002; Richards and Daley, 2003; Tehrani, 2011). Indeed, 'support at work may function as a buffer against stress by providing resources to enable [targets] to cope' (Quine, 1999: 231). More recent results also suggest that high levels of perceived organisational support 'offset the effects of workplace bullying on intention to leave' (Djurkovic *et al.*, 2008: 415). On the other hand it has been suggested that lack of support is central to the ability or inability of targets to cope (Lewis and Orford, 2005; Leymann and Gustafsson, 1996; Matthiesen *et al.*, 2003). Seeking support, however, usually requires a proactive action, which is unlikely to be within the behavioural repertoire of someone who is feeling helpless and victimised, especially if they are worried this could damage their position further (Lee, 1997). For instance, by seeking help individuals may be concerned that they will appear incompetent (Lee, 1997), which may be especially relevant for managers who have been bullied by a subordinate (Branch *et al.*, 2007b). In an important interview study of 15 college and university lecturers who had experienced workplace bullying, Lewis (2004) found that targets often experience profound feelings of shame. Furthermore, despite the recognition that the provision of support is important in assisting targets to cope with workplace bullying (Djurkovic *et al.*, 2008; Lewis and Orford, 2005; Leymann and Gustafsson, 1996; Matthiesen *et al.*, 2003; Quine, 1999), research indicates that targets are particularly reluctant to seek support from an organisation that is perceived to be ineffective in addressing workplace bullying (Ferris, 2004; Hoel and Cooper, 2000).

Conclusion

Workplace bullying is a complex phenomenon which has increasingly become the focus of global research. Research, mainly using quantitative approaches (with more qualitative research occurring), has explored the behaviours, prevalence, groups who are most vulnerable within our workplaces, and the factors that contribute to the occurrence of workplace bullying. Research has consistently found that workplace bullying can have detrimental affects upon those who are targeted, those who witness it, and the organisations in which it occurs. Management processes are of utmost importance in articulating and managing workplace bullying issues. Commonly, a 'no bullying' policy, training and support are considered useful interventions in deterring and managing bullying in the workplace. Clearly, this is an area which demands urgent attention by researchers and practitioners alike.

CASE STUDY 22.1

MANAGING IN THE SHORT AND LONGER TERM AT GBD: A SECTION OF THE PUBLIC SERVICE

SARA BRANCH, SHERYL RAMSAY AND MICHELLE BARKER

Two years ago GBD had a major restructure. The client relations section, however, seemed to fall into the 'too hard basket' and was never assigned a permanent manager. The Section has had to make do with temporary managers who tended to stay for only a couple of months. However, for the last four months Chris (who has worked in client relations at GBD for a long time and in the public service for 30 years) has been taking on the temporary manager's role. Following your success in a public sector recruitment and selection process, you have been appointed to the role of manager and asked to 'clean up the area'. You have never worked for GBD but have had considerable experience outside of government. Your senior manager has told you that the area is lacking in transparent procedures, especially when dealing with clients, and that organisational policies are regularly not followed. You realise the task you are taking on is large but you are confident that your experience will guide you.

You first meet with each of the staff members to gain an understanding of what they do and of their expectations about their role, work tasks and management. Everybody seems willing to work with developing more transparent procedures. Even Chris, who you expected might be resistant (because you were informed that he had also applied for the permanent position) appears to be supportive. However, a couple of weeks after beginning to implement a number of processes, Lee, a client relations officer, begins to become very silent in meetings. This behaviour has now escalated into the occasional snide comment and you have heard 'on the grapevine' that Lee has been making some comments to others in the section about your ability to manage. This worries you as Lee is a staff member who you saw as being of central importance in the section, especially with regard to his expertise within a particular area of client relations. You ask to have a meeting with Lee to discuss his apparent withdrawal; but Lee says that everything is fine. You also try to raise the issue of whether Lee has any concerns about your ability to manage. Again Lee says everything is ok.

Another month passes and you are updating your senior manager, Robin, about how the workgroup is progressing:

Yourself: I have met with everybody and they all seem happy with the changes made. Everybody has submitted new position descriptions and we have negotiated and finalised them all....all but Lee who still refuses my requests for him to write a new position description. I have talked to him about this but he insists that his old position description is good enough. I explained to him that, given the restructure, it was no longer relevant given that his old role no longer existed as such. He insists that his old job remains very valuable and that he be allowed to continue doing it (with some very minor changes). I get the feeling that he is not happy with the changes I am making.

Robin: Oh Lee, he is so good at what he does and has been around here for so long, I guess he is having a hard time moving on.

Yourself: I agree he is a great source of knowledge and knows nearly everyone in the place but still that does not overcome the fact that he is refusing to do this task. He has also been refusing to do other small things as well.

Robin: Like what?

Yourself: Well there have been a few incidences but one recent but regular one is refusing to let me know where he is going when he conducts a site visit...and on top of that turning off his mobile phone. When I asked him about this he just said that he was out of range...but it is happening too often. He has also been behaving aggressively to me...nothing I can't handle but he often raises his voice to me when I ask him a simple question.

Robin: That is strange.

Yourself: And in meetings, when he eventually arrives, he is either silent or disruptive and makes snide comments about me or things I have said. I have tried to talk to him about it but he says he is fine and that he has no trouble with the way I am managing him. What would you suggest I do about it?

Robin: For now I would take it easy, and he will come around.

Yourself: Well I guess you know him better than I do, so ok, then.

Another couple of months go by, in which time Robin, despite your concerns, creates a new position for Lee. This position was not a planned change but it was felt that Lee, who had threatened to resign, had expertise they could not lose, and so he was accommodated.

A few more weeks pass and Lee seems to be inputting more into meetings. However, after a while the previous behaviours, such as being aggressive to you and making snide comments in meetings, return. You even begin to believe that he is starting to spread rumours about yourself, including your role as a manager being jeopardised because your marriage is 'on the rocks'. You only became aware of this when someone from another workgroup, whom you know personally, asked with concern how your marriage was.

At this point you start to become very wary about Lee and his behaviour. You believe that Lee is increasingly turning to Robin for advice. You also believe that Robin does not seem to take Lee's behaviour (against you) seriously. It is in one of your regular meetings with Robin that he lets it slip that Lee has been meeting with him regularly and this is what led to him gaining the new position. You start to feel like you are being undermined by Lee and that Robin won't do anything about it. It is mainly because of this you do not tell Robin about Lee's increasingly aggressive behaviour towards you. The last thing you need now is for Robin to think you cannot handle the situation.

You start to become careful about what you say to Lee. You also start to document what has been happening and details of interactions with Lee. Whenever you have meetings with Lee you make sure that someone else is present or the door is open. This however, has affected your ability to do your job effectively. You also notice a number of other staff sitting with Lee in meetings and making the same snide comments, while others in the group refuse to work with Lee. Importantly, for yourself, you have begun to feel less confident whenever Lee is around and often feel as if you are not so clear or even that you make mistakes in response to his comments. Work is no longer a pleasant place to be.

Things come to a head when two events occur in the same week. First of all an important report is due and Lee, whose knowledge is vital for a large part of the report, fails to produce any drafts and you need to pick up the slack at the last minute. On top of all of that, it has recently come to your notice that Lee has not been following the new procedures with clients. You only learn of this when one of Lee's clients contacts you directly with some concerns. The client also tells you that Lee has been talking about you in a very unprofessional manner to staff in their organisation. You decide to have a meeting with Lee about his failure to produce information vital for the report, the way he does not appear to be following the new procedures, and also the reportedly inappropriate comments he is making to clients.

Lee arrives at the meeting with Chris (the previous acting manager) who is there as a support person. You agree to this as you feel you have no other option at this point and besides your PA is there to take notes. Just after you begin to outline your concerns to Lee, Lee interrupts and begins to list to you all of the ways you have not been fulfilling your role as a manager. You perceive that Chris supports the interruption because he looks at Lee and nods; he makes no attempt to intervene. You state that this was not the purpose of the meeting and that these issues can be raised at another time if they would like. Chris then states that this is 'not good enough' and that you have 'picked on Lee', and that if you do not address these issues now they will 'file a grievance based on workplace bullying'. You are left feeling as if you are the one who has been bullied by Lee, with Chris's help.

Questions

1   Describe the behaviours displayed by Lee that could be considered as bullying.

2   Do you think that power played a role in this situation? In what way/s? You may need to think beyond the traditional formal power of a manager and to other sources of power.

3 What role did Robin, the senior manager, play in escalating the situation?

4 What impact is Lee's behaviour having on you in your manager role and your ability to do your job?

5 What impact do you think that Lee's behaviour is having (or could have) on the members of the group?

6 How do you think you, as the manager, could have handled the situation differently?

7 How do you think Robin, the senior manager, could have handled the situation differently?

8 Taking a strategic perspective, how could these types of situations be minimised or avoided in the future?

Epilogue

It has been eight months and although a lot has happened you seem to be in the same position trying to get Lee to follow your directions and requests.

Since the meeting with Lee and Chris where they stated they would file a grievance against you, accusing you of bullying Lee, there has been an investigation. It took all up seven months to finalise! Lee's grievance was lengthy – outlining a number of incidents that, while they occurred, were inaccurate with regard to the detail. There was, of course, no mention of Lee's snide comments in meetings. This in itself took you a week to respond to; more time away from your real job!

You were interviewed, by the independent investigator, at least three times for about two hours each time. About seven other people within the team and workplace were also interviewed over the grievance, which caused a lot of disruption in the workplace, took others away from their job, and worst of all upset a number of those who were interviewed. It seemed to you that the grievance process divided the workgroup into those who supported Lee and those who supported yourself.

Throughout this whole time you felt that you were unsupported by your manager. You understand that they had to be seen to be impartial but you really had no-one at work you could talk to. You felt very isolated at work. The only support you really felt was forthcoming was from home.

In the end, you were cleared of all of Lee's accusations, but your concerns about Lee's behaviour were not addressed by the organisation as too much time had passed since they had occurred. The outcome of the investigation was that yourself and Lee attend mediation together. You thought this was a good idea and may help you get to a point where the two of you could work effectively together. However, although you have attended three mediation sessions Lee only attended the first session. Lee made it very clear in this session that you are the one who needs the help. So it would seem Lee still thinks the problem is yours and there remains a lack of respect for your position and authority from Lee.

The crazy thing about the grievance investigation was that you were expected to manage Lee during the investigation! At issue here is the protection of all involved in the grievance investigation. If Lee's claims were legitimate, you could have very easily retaliated against Lee. Alternatively, as in this case, where the accusations were either malicious or frivolous, it placed you as manager in a situation of limited power in terms of managing Lee, especially until the investigation was concluded. It would seem for the safety of all parties involved in the grievance, there was a need to separate you and Lee or if this was not possible, implement safeguards until an outcome had been reached.

Questions

1 What disruptions did the grievance have on the workplace?

2 What would you do differently if you were the senior manager overseeing the investigation?

3 Did the investigation resolve the conflict that existed between Lee and yourself?

CASE STUDY 22.2

IS THIS A CASE OF PEER BULLYING?

SARA BRANCH, SHERYL RAMSAY AND MICHELLE BARKER

Ingrid: I cannot believe it has been a month since I took sick leave from Triple A. I am feeling so much better now but the thought of going back to work and working with Carmel terrifies me. Why, just the other day I had to go in and submit my doctor's certificate to HR and as I got closer to work I started shaking and crying uncontrollably and had to get off the train and go home. I ended up mailing in the doctor's certificate. When I went to see the doctor she was really concerned for my well-being. The headaches, not sleeping and panic attacks seem to be getting worse, not better!

I really don't understand what went wrong. Work use to be a great place, full of interesting people and projects that engaged and challenged me. But that all changed when Carmel arrived and started bossing everyone around, but more so me.

In the beginning I really liked Carmel and I thought she liked me. I thought, here we go, she will fit in really well here and spice up the place a bit. How wrong was I! She was employed at the same level as me in the same role but seemed to think she knew it all and that I knew nothing. After about three months she really started to boss me around, almost using me as her own private slave. It started with 'Can you get me that information?', using the excuse that she was new to Triple A and progressed to 'Where is that information I wanted! Why are you so useless?'

Everything I did was wrong, even the clothes that I wore to work she didn't like. It all came to a head when a report I was working on was sabotaged, making me look foolish and humiliating me in front of my manager and the client. What she did was take the report on the pretence of editing it and made changes that were not accurate. Why am I such a fool for trusting her!! After that I really felt like I was being set up all the time and strange things started happening. Nothing I could put my finger on but things like messages not being passed on to me, things going missing from my desk and then reappearing a day later. It wouldn't have been so bad if my colleagues had supported me but unfortunately most of them seem to have been talking to Carmel and think I am useless. They never felt this way before Carmel was here. I really feel as if I have been bullied.

Questions

1 Do you have the full picture?
2 What else would help you to have greater understanding of the case?

What other people in the workplace think

Jen: Ok Carmel sets high standards but what is wrong with that? Ingrid just needs to pull up her socks and get to work and stop worrying about Carmel. I really don't think that Carmel has been bullying Ingrid, I haven't seen her yell at her or anything like that; isn't that bullying?

Ross: Really Ingrid is just too sensitive. Carmel does a great job and helps out around the place a lot. She really seems to fit in nicely. If Ingrid has a problem with that then maybe she should not come back to Triple A.

Kate: Ingrid has had a difficult time lately. I know everybody around here seems to think that Carmel is great and she is as long as she likes you. I have been lucky and she seems to like me but I have noticed how she bosses Ingrid around. I tried talking to Ingrid on the side but she said that it was okay and that it would work out. Well it hasn't. I cannot say for sure if Carmel has been bullying Ingrid as I don't know what has been happening but I have worked with Ingrid for a long time and it is not like her to make mistakes such as the ones that were in the report.

Paul: As Ingrid's boss I take her accusations of bullying seriously but Ingrid didn't want to have a mediation session to try and get back to a working relationship. When I talked to Carmel about it she didn't seem to know what Ingrid was talking about. It is hard to know which way to go with this type of stuff, in a way you are dammed if you do something and dammed if you do nothing.

Questions

1 Imagine you are a HR professional employed by this organisation. You have been asked to provide a development programme for staff (in relation to the above scenario).

   a Where would you start?

   b What are the main issues you need to clarify before getting started?

   c Indicate the aims of such a programme and outline the most important elements that need to be addressed within the programme.

   d How would you evaluate such a programme?

CASE STUDY 22.3

REFLECTIVE EXERCISES

SARA BRANCH, SHERYL RAMSAY AND MICHELLE BARKER

Exercise 1

- In pairs reflect on the interpersonal conflicts you may have experienced, witnessed or heard about in the workplace and make a list of anti-social behaviours that occur in the workplace
- Consider if gender contributed to this conflict?
- Consider if power played a role in the conflict? If yes, then what power sources were being used.
- What is the potential affect on witnesses and what could they say or do?

Exercise 2

- Within small groups reflect on the contributing factors to workplace bullying and brainstorm three strategies at each level (i.e., individual, group and organisational) that you could use to address, and potentially reduce or prevent, workplace bullying.

Exercise 3

Judy receives a call from her old university friend Jan, who is now working as a support worker. Jan, in tears, relates to Judy the mean things her boss has been doing to her. He was nice enough when she first arrived at her job last year, but now he has become unbearable. Jan listed some of the things he had done that week: 'On Monday, he came in to work and told me in front of everyone that I was too slow and that I dragged down the whole department. The rest of the week he spent glaring at me each time he passed me in the hall. He threw a huge temper tantrum when I did not have a report ready two days before it was due. I snapped back and unfortunately that seemed to inflame the situation. I later found out that there had been a meeting involving all the support workers that he failed to tell me about. I even heard a rumour that I was sleeping with a client, and I am certain he started it. I just don't know what to do and who to turn to, especially as those around me just seem to keep their heads down. What do you think, Judy?'

- Discuss how the issues raised in this scenario could be addressed using the strategies discussed in Exercise 2.

Bibliography

Agervold, M. (2007) 'Bullying at work: a discussion of definitions and prevalence, based on an empirical study', *Scandinavian Journal of Psychology,* Vol.48, 161–72. doi: DOI: 10.1111/j.1467–9450.2007.00585.x.

Agervold, M. (2009) 'The significance of organizational factors for the incidence of bullying', *Scandinavian Journal of Psychology,* Vol.50, No.3, 267–76.

Archer, D. (1999) 'Exploring "bullying" culture in the para-military organisation', *International Journal of Manpower,* Vol.20, Nos1/2, 94–105.

Argyle, M., Henderson, M. and Furnham, A. (1985) 'The rules of social relationships', *British Journal of Social Psychology*, Vol.24, 125–39.

Asch, D. and Salaman, G. (2002) 'The challenge of change', *European Business Journal* Vol.14, No.3, 133–43.

Ashforth, B. (1997) 'Petty tyranny in organizations: a preliminary examination of antecedents and consequences', *Canadian Journal of Administrative Sciences*, Vol.14, No.2, 126–40.

Baillien, E. and De Witte, H. (2009) 'Why is organizational change related to workplace bullying? Role conflict and job insecurity as mediators', *Economic and Industrial Democracy* Vol.30, No.3, 348–71.

Baron, R. and Neuman, J. (1996) 'Workplace violence and workplace aggression: evidence on their relative frequency and potential causes', *Aggressive Behavior,* Vol.22, No.3, 161–73.

Baron, R. and Neuman, J. (1998) 'Workplace aggression: the iceberg beneath the tip of workplace violence: evidence on its forms, frequency, and targets', *Public Administration Quarterly,* Vol.21, No.4, 446–64.

Bassman, E. (1992) *Abuse in the Workplace*, Westport, CT: Quorum Books.

Baumeister, R., Smart, L. and Boden, J. (1996) 'Relation of threatened egotism to violence and aggression: the dark side of high self-esteem', *Psychological Review*, Vol.103, No.1, 5–33.

Bjorkqvist, K., Osterman, K. and Hjelt-Back, M. (1994) 'Aggression among university employees', *Aggressive Behavior*, Vol.20, 173–84.

Bowling, N. and Beehr, T. (2006) 'Workplace harassment from the victim's perspective: a theoretical model and meta-analysis', *Journal of Applied Psychology,* Vol.91, No.5, 998–1012.

Branch, S. (2006) *'Upwards bullying: An exploratory study of power, dependency and the work environment for Australian Managers'* PhD Thesis, Griffith University, Brisbane.

Branch, S. (2008) 'You say tomatoe and I say tomato: can we differentiate between workplace bullying and other counterproductive behaviours?', *International Journal of Organisational Behaviour,* Vol.13, No.2, 4–17.

Branch, S., Ramsay, C. and Barker, M. (2007a) 'Managers in the firing line: contributing factors to workplace bullying by staff: an interview study', *Journal of Management & Organization,* Vol.13, 264–81.

Branch, S., Ramsay, S. and Barker, M. (2007b) 'The bullied boss: a conceptual exploration of upwards bullying' pp. 93–112, in Glendon, A.I, Thompson, B.M. and Myors, B. (eds) *Advances in Organisational Psychology*, Bowen Hills, Qld: Australian Academic Press.

Braverman, M. (1999) *Preventing Workplace Violence: A Guide for Employers and Practitioners.* London: Sage.

Brown, A.J. (ed.) (2007) *Whistling While They Work: Enhancing the Theory and Practice of Internal Witness Management in Public Sector Organisations.* Draft Report.: Socio-Legal Research Centre, Griffith Law School.

Cook, K., Yamagishi, T. and Donnelly, S. (1997) 'Power and dependence in exchange networks: a comment on structural measures of power', in Szmatka, J., Skvoretz, J. and Berger J. (eds), *Status, Network, and Structure: Theory Development in Group Processes,* Stanford, CA: Stanford University Press.

Coyne, I., Seigne, E. and Randall, P. (2000) 'Predicting workplace victim status from personality', *European Journal of Work and Organizational Psychology,* Vol.9 No.3, 335–49.

De Cieri, H. and Kramar, R. (2008) *Human Resource Management in Australia* (3rd edn), North Ryde, NSW: McGraw Hill Irwin.

De Cuyper, N., Baillien, E. and De Witte, H. (2009) 'Job insecurity, perceived employability and targets' and perpetrators' experiences of workplace bullying', *Work & Stress,* Vol.23, No.3, 206–24.

Djurkovic, N., McCormack, D. and Casimir, G. (2004) 'The physical and psychological effects of workplace bullying and their relationship to intention to leave: a test of the psychosomatic and disability hypotheses', *International Journal of Organization Theory and Behavior,* Vol.7, No.4, 469–97.

Djurkovic, N., McCormack, D. and Casimir, G. (2008) 'Workplace bullying and intention to leave: the moderating effect of perceived organisational support', *Human Resource Management Journal,* Vol.18, No.4, 405–22.

Douglas, S. and Martinko, M. (2001) 'Exploring the role of individual differences in the prediction of workplace aggression', *Journal of Applied Psychology,* Vol.86, No.4, 547–59.

Einarsen, S. (1999) 'The nature and causes of bullying at work', *International Journal of Manpower,* Vol.20, Nos1,2, 16–27.

Einarsen, S. (2000) 'Harassment and bullying at work: a review of the Scandinavian approach', *Aggression and Violent Behavior,* Vol.5 No.4, 379–401.

Einarsen, S. and Raknes, B. (1997) 'Harassment in the workplace and the victimization of men', *Violence and Victims,* Vol.12, No.3, 247–63.

Einarsen, S. and Skogstad, A. (1996) 'Bullying at work: epidemiological findings in public and private organizations', *European Journal of Work and Organizational Psychology,* Vol.5, No.2, 185–201.

Einarsen, S., Hoel, H., Zapf, D. and Cooper, C. (2011a) 'The concept of bullying and harassment at work: the European tradition', pp. 3–40, in Einarsen, S. Hoel, H. and Zapf, D. and Cooper, C. (eds) *Bullying and Harassment in the Workplace: Developments in Theory, Research, and Practice* (2nd edn), London: Taylor & Francis.

Einarsen, S., Hoel, H., Zapf, D., and Cooper, C. (eds) (2011b) *Bullying and Harassment in the Workplace: Developments in Theory, Research, and Practice* (2nd edn), London: Taylor & Francis.

Emerson, R.M. (1962) 'Power-dependence relations', *American Sociological Review,* Vol.27, No.1, 31–41.

Ferris, P. (2004) 'A preliminary typology of organisational response to allegations of workplace bullying: see no evil, hear no evil, speak no evil', *British Journal of Guidance & Counselling,* Vol.32, No.3, 389–95.

Fevre, R., Robinson, A., Jones, T. and Lewis, D. (2010) 'Researching workplace bullying: the benefits of taking an integrated approach', *International Journal of Social Research Methodology,* Vol.13, No.1, 71–85.

Fox, S. and Stallworth, L. (2005) 'Racial/ethnic bullying: exploring links between bullying and racism in the US workforce', *Journal of Vocational Behavior,* Vol.66, 438–56.

Gini, G. (2006) 'Bullying as a social process: the role of group membership in students' perception of inter-group aggression at school', *Journal of School Psychology* Vol.44, No.1, 51–65.

Hadikin, R. and O'Driscoll, M. (2000) *The Bullying Culture: Cause, Effect, Harm Reduction*, Melbourne: Books for Midwives.

Harvey, M.G., Heames, J.T., Richey, R.G. and Leonard, N. (2006) 'Bullying: from the playground to the boardroom', *Journal of Leadership and Organizational Studies,* Vol.12, No.4, 1–11.

Hauge, L., Skogstad, A. and Einarsen, S. (2007) 'Relationships between stressful work environments and bullying: results of a large representative study', *Work & Stress,* Vol.21, No.3, 220–42.

Hauge, L., Skogstad, A. and Einarsen, S. (2009) 'Individual and situational predictors of workplace bullying: why do perpetrators engage in the bullying of others?', *Work & Stress,* Vol.23, No.4, 349–58.

Heames, J. and Harvey, M. (2006) 'Workplace bullying: a cross-level assessment', *Management Decision,* Vol.44, No.9, 1214–30.

Hoel, H. and Cooper, C. (2000) 'Destructive conflict and bullying at work', Manchester, UK: School of Management, University of Manchester, Institute of Science and Technology.

Hoel, H. and Cooper, C. (2001) 'Origins of bullying: theoretical frameworks for explaining workplace bullying', pp. 3–20, in Tehrani, N. (ed.) *Building a Culture of Respect: Managing Bullying at Work*, London: Taylor & Francis.

Hoel, H. and Salin, D. (2003) 'Organisational antecedents of workplace bullying', pp. 203–18, in Einarsen, S., Hoel, H., Zapf, D. and Cooper, C. (eds) *Bullying and Emotional Abuse in the Workplace: International Perspectives in Reserach and Practice*, London: Taylor & Francis.

Hoel, H., Cooper, C. and Faragher, B. (2001) 'The experience of bullying in Great Britain: the impact of organizational status', *European Journal of Work and Organizational Psychology*, Vol.10, No.4, 443–65.

Hoel, H., Sheehan, M., Einarsen, S. and Einarsen, S. (2011) 'Organisational effects of workplace bullying', pp. 129–48, in Einarsen, S., Hoel, H., Zapf, D. and Cooper C. (eds), *Bullying and Harassment in the Workplace: Developments in Theory, Research, and Practice* (2nd edn), London: Taylor & Francis.

Hogh, A., Mikkelsen, E. and Hansen, A. (2011) 'Individual consequences of workplace bullying/mobbing', pp. 107–28, in Einarsen, S., Hoel, H., Zapf, D. and Cooper C. (eds), *Bullying and Harassment in the Workplace: Developments in Theory, Research, and Practice* (2nd edn), London: Taylor & Francis.

Jablin, F. (1986) 'Superior–subordinate communication: the state of the art', *Psychological Bulletin*, Vol.86, 1201–22.

Katz, J. (1995) 'Reconstructing masculinity in the locker room: the mentors in violence prevention project', *Harvard Educational Review,* Vol.65, No.2, 163–74.

Keashly, L. (1998) 'Emotional abuse in the workplace: conceptual and empirical issues', *Journal of Emotional Abuse*, Vol.1, 85–116.

Keashly, L. (2001) 'Interpersonal and systemic aspects of emotional abuse at work: the target's perspective', *Violence and Victims*, Vol.16, No.3, 233–68.

Keashly, L. and Harvey, S. (2005) 'Emotional abuse in the workplace', pp. 201–35, in Fox, S. and Spector, P. (eds), *Counterproductive Work Behavior: Investigations of Actors and Targets*, Washington, DC: American Psycholocial Association.

Keashly, L. and Harvey, S. (2006) 'Workplace emotional abuse', pp. 95–120, in Kelloway, E., Barling, and Hurrell Jr, J. (eds), *Handbook of Workplace Violence,* Thousand Oaks CA: Sage Publications.

Keashly, L. and Jagatic, K. (2011) 'North American perspectives on hostile behaviors and bullying at work', pp. 41–71, in Einarsen, S., Hoel, H., Zapf, D. and Cooper, C. (eds), *Bullying and Harassment in the Workplace: Developments in Theory, Research, and Practice* (2nd edn), London: Taylor & Francis.

Kivimaki, M., Elovainio, M. and Vahtera, J. (2000) 'Workplace bullying and sickness absence in hospital staff', *Occupational and Environmental Medicine*, Vol.57, No.10, 656–60.

Lee, F. (1997) 'When the going gets tough, do the tough ask for help? Help seeking and power motivation in organizations', *Organizational Behavior and Human Decision Processes*, Vol.72, No.3, 336–63.

Lewis, D. (2004) 'Bullying at work: the impact of shame among university and college lecturers', *British Journal of Guidance & Counselling,* Vol.32, No.3, 281–99.

Lewis, D. and Gunn, R. (2007) 'Workplace bullying in the public sector: understanding the racial dimension', *Public Administration*, Vol.83, No.3, 641–65.

Lewis, D. and Sheehan, M. (2003) 'Introduction: workplace bullying: theoretical and practical approaches to a management challenge', *International Journal of Management and Decision Making,* Vol.4, No.1, 1–10.

Lewis, S. and Orford, J. (2005) 'Women's experiences of workplace bullying: changes in social relationships', *Journal of Community & Applied Social Psychology*, Vol.15, 29–47.

Leymann, H. (1990) 'Mobbing and psychological terror at workplaces', *Violence and Victims,* Vol.5, 119–26.

Leymann, H. (1996) 'The content and development of mobbing at work', *European Journal of Work and Organizational Psychology,* Vol.5, No.2, 165–84.

Leymann, H., and Gustafsson, A. (1996) 'Mobbing at work and the development of post-traumatic stress disorders', *European Journal of Work and Organizational Psychology*, Vol.5, No.2, 251–75.

Liefooghe, A. and Davey, K. (2001) 'Accounts of workplace bullying: the role of the organization', *European Journal of Work and Organizational Psychology,* Vol.10, No.4, 375–92.

Lind, K., Glasø, L., Pallesen, S. and Einarsen, S. (2009) 'Personality profiles among targets and nontargets of workplace bullying', *European Psychologist*, Vol.14, No.3, 231–7.

Matthiesen, S. and Einarsen, S. (2004) 'Psychiatric distress and symptoms of PTSD among victims of bullying at work', *British Journal of Guidance & Counselling*, Vol.32, No.3, 335–56.

Matthiesen, S., Aasen, E., Holst, G., Wie, K. and Einarsen, S. (2003) 'The escalation of conflict: a case study of bullying at work', *International Journal of Management and Decision Making*, Vol.4, No.1, 96–112.

Mayhew, C., McCarthy, P., Chappell, D., Quinlan, M., Barker, M. and Sheehan, M. (2004) 'Measuring the extent of impact from occupational violence and bullying on traumatised workers', *Employee Responsibilities and Rights Journal*, Vol.16, No.3, 117–34.

McCarthy, P. (1999), 'Strategies between managementality and victimmentality in the pressures of continuous change', pp. 22–3, in Fraser, C., Barker, M. and Martin, A. (eds), *Organisations Looking Ahead: Challenges and Directions*, Logan Campus, QLD: Griffith University.

McCarthy, P. (2004), 'Costs of occupational violence and bullying', in McCarthy, P. and Mayhew, C. (eds), *Safeguarding the Organization Against Violence and Bullying*, Basingstoke: Palgrave Macmillan.

McCarthy, P. and Barker, M. (2000) 'Workplace bullying risk audit', *Journal of Occupational Health and Safety: Australia and New Zealand*, Vol.16, 409–18.

McCarthy, P. and Mayhew, C. (2004) *Safeguarding the Organization against Violence and Bullying*, New York: Palgrave MacMillan.

McCarthy, P., Sheehan, M. Kearns, D. (1995) *Managerial Styles and their Effects on Employees' Health and Well-being in Organisations Undergoing Restructuring*, Brisbane: School of Organisational Behaviour & Human Resource Management.

McCarthy, P., Henderson, M., Sheehan, M. and Barker, M. (2002) 'Workplace bullying: its management and prevention', *Australian Master OHS and Environment Guide 2003*, Sydney: CCH Australia, pp. 519–49.

Merchant, V. and Hoel, H. (2003) 'Investigating complaints of bullying', pp. 259–69, in Einarsen, S., Hoel, H., Zapf, D. and Cooper, C. (eds) *Bullying and Emotional Abuse in the Workplace: International Perspectives in Research and Practice*, London: Taylor & Francis.

Mikkelsen, E. and Einarsen, S. (2001) 'Bullying in Danish work-life: Prevalence and health correlates', *European Journal of Work and Organizational Psychology,* Vol.10, No.4, 393–413.

Mikkelsen, E. and Einarsen, S. (2002a) 'Basic assumptions and symptoms of post-traumatic stress among victims of bullying at work', *European Journal of Work and Organizational Psychology,* Vol.11, No.1, 87–111.

Mikkelsen, E. and Einarsen, S. (2002b) 'Relationships between exposure to bullying at work and psychological and psychosomatic health complaints: the role of state negative affectivity and generalized self-efficacy', *Scandinavian Journal of Psychology*, Vol.43., 397–405.

Niedhammer, I., David, S., Degioanni, S. and 143 occupational physicians (2006) 'Association between workplace bullying and depressive symptoms in the French working population', *Journal of Psychosomatic Research,* Vol.61, 251–9.

Nielsen, M., Matthiesen, S. and Einarsen, S. (2008) 'Sense of coherence as a protective mechanism among targets of workplace bullying', *Journal of Occupational Health Psychology*, Vol.13, No.2, 128–36.

O'Moore, M., Seigne, E., McGuire, L. and Smith, M. (1998) 'Victims of bullying at work in Ireland', *Journal of Occupational Health and Safety: Australia and New Zealand*, Vol.14, 569–74.

Olweus, D. (1978) *Aggression in the Schools: Bullies and Whipping Boys*, New York: Wiley.

Parzefall, M.-R. and Salin, D. (2010) 'Perceptions of and reactions to workplace bullying: a social exchange perspective', *Human Relations,* Vol.63, No.6, 761–80.

Pietersen, C. (2007) 'Interpersonal bullying behaviours in the workplace', *SA Journal of Industrial Psychology*, Vol.33, No.1, 59–66.

Privitera, C. and Campbell, M. (2009) 'Cyberbullying: the new face of workplace bullying?', *CyberPsychology and Behavior*, Vol.12, No.4, 395–400.

Quine, L. (1999) 'Workplace bullying in NHS community trust: staff questionnaire survey', *British Medical Journal* Vol.318, No.7178, 228–32.

Quine, L. (2001) 'Workplace bullying in nurses', *Journal of Health Psychology*, Vol.6, No.1, 73–84.

Ramsay, S., Troth, A. and Branch, S. (2010) 'Workplace bullying through the lens of social psychology: A group level analysis', *Journal of Occupational and Organizational Psychology*. doi: 10.1348/2044–8325.002000.

Rayner, C. (1997) 'The incidence of workplace bullying', *Journal of Community & Applied Social Psychology*,Vol.7, 199–208.

Rayner, C. (1999) 'From research to implementation: finding leverage for prevention', *International Journal of Manpower*, Vol.20, Nos 1,2, 28–38.

Rayner, C. (2007) 'Preparing for dignity: tackling indignity at work', pp. 176–90, in Bolton, S.C. (ed.) *From Dimensions of Dignity at Work,* Oxford: Elsevier.

Rayner, C. and Cooper, C. (2003) 'The black hole in "bullying at work" research', *International Journal of Management and Decision Making*, Vol.4, No.1, 47–64.

Rayner, C. and Hoel, H. (1997) 'A summary review of literature relating to workplace bullying', *Journal of Community and Applied Social Psychology*, Vol.7, No.3, 181–91.

Rayner, C., Hoel, H. and Cooper, C. (2002) *Workplace Bullying: What We Know, Who is to Blame, and What Can We Do?,* London: Taylor & Francis.

Richards, J. and Daley, H. (2003) 'Bullying policy: development, implementation and monitoring', pp. 247–58, in Einarsen, S., Hoel, H., Zapf, D. and Cooper, C. (eds) *Bullying and*

Emotional Abuse in the Workplace: International Perspectives in Research and Practice, London: Taylor & Francis.

Rigby, K. (2001) 'Bullying in schools and in the workplace', pp. 1–10, in McCarthy, P., Rylance, J., Bennett, R. and Zimmermann, H. (eds), *Bullying: From Backyard to Boardroom* 2nd edn, Sydney: The Federation Press.

Saam, N. (2010) 'Interventions in workplace bullying: a multilevel approach', *European Journal of Work and Organizational Psychology,* Vol.19, No.1, 51–75.

Salin, D. (2001) 'Prevalence and forms of bullying among business professionals: a comparison of two different strategies for measuring bullying', *European Journal of Work and Organizational Psychology,* Vol.10, No.4, 425–41.

Salin, D. (2003) 'Bullying and organisational politics in competitive and rapidly changing work environments', *International Journal of Management and Decision Making*, Vol.4, No.1, 35–46.

Salin, D. (2008) 'The prevention of workplace bullying as a question of human resource management: measures adopted and underlying organizational factors', *Scandinavian Journal of Management,* Vol.24, No.3, 221–31.

Salin, D. (2009) 'Organisational responses to workplace harassment: an exploratory study', *Personnel Review*, Vol.38, No.1, 26–44.

Salin, D. and Hoel, H. (2011) 'Organisational causes of workplace bullying', pp. 227–44, in Einarsen, S., Hoel, H., Zapf, D. and Cooper, C. (eds) *Bullying and Harassment in the Workplace: Developments in Theory, Research, and Practice* (2nd edn), London: Taylor & Francis.

Saunders, P., Huynh, A. and Goodman-Delahunty, J. (2007) 'Defining workplace bullying behaviour professional lay definitions of workplace bullying', *International Journal of Law and Psychiatry*, Vol.30, No.4–5, 340–54.

Savva, C. and Alexandrou, A. (1998) 'The impact of bullying in further and higher education'. Paper presented at the Bullying at Work: 1998 Research Update Conference, Staffordshire University Business School.

Sheehan, M., Barker, M., and McCarthy, P. (2004) 'Analysing metaphors used by victims of workplace bullying', *International Journal of Management and Decision Making,* Vol.5, No.1, 21–34.

Sheehan, M., McCarthy, P., Barker, M. and Henderson, M. (2001) 'A model for assessing the impacts and costs of workplace bullying'. Paper presented at the Standing Conference on Organizational Symbolism (SCOS), Trinity College Dublin, 30 June–4 July.

Skogstad, A., Einarsen, S., Torsheim, T., Aasland, M. and Hetland, J. (2007) 'The destructiveness of laissez-faire leadership behavior', *Journal of Occupational Health Psychology*, Vol.12, No.1, 80–92.

Smith, P., Singer, M., Hoel, H. and Cooper, C. (2003) 'Victimization in the school and the workplace: are there any links?', *British Journal of Psychology,*Vol.94, 175–88.

Stucke, T. and Sporer, S. (2002) 'When a grandiose self-image is threatened: narcissism and self-concept clarity as predictors of negative emotions and aggression following ego-threat', *Journal of Personality*, Vol.70, No.4, 509–32.

Tajfel, H. and Turner, J. (1986) 'The social identify theory of intergroup behavior', pp. 7–24, in Worchel, S. and Austin, W. (eds) *The Psychology of Intergroup Relations* (2nd edn), Chicago, IL: Nelson-Hall Publishers.

Tehrani, N. (2003) 'Counselling and rehabilitating employees involved with bullying', pp. 270–84, in Einarsen, S., Hoel, H., Zapf, D. and Cooper, C. (eds) *Bullying and Emotional Abuse in the Workplace: International Perspectives in Research and Practice*, London: Taylor & Francis.

Tehrani, N. (2004) 'Bullying: a source of chronic post traumatic stress?', *British Journal of Guidance & Counselling,* Vol.32, No.3, 357–66.

Tehrani, N. (2011) 'Workplace bullying: the role for counselling', pp. 381–96, in Einarsen, S., Hoel, H., Zapf, D. and Cooper, C. (eds), *Bullying and Harassment in the Workplace: Developments in Theory, Research, and Practice* (2nd edn), London: Taylor & Francis.

Tracy, S., Lutgen-Sandvik, P. and Alberts, J. (2006) 'Nightmares, demons, and slaves: exploring the painful metaphors of workplace bullying', *Management Communication Quarterly*, Vol.20, No.2, 148–85.

UNISON (2003) 'Bullying at work: guidelines for UNISON branches, stewards and safety representatives', London: UNISON.

Vartia, M. (1996) 'The sources of bullying: psychological work environment and organizational climate', *European Journal of Work and Organizational Psychology*, Vol.5, No.2, 203–14.

Vartia, M. and Leka, S. (2011) 'Interventions for the prevention and management of bullying at work', pp. 359–80, in Einarsen, S., Hoel, H., Zapf, D. and Cooper, C. (eds) *Bullying and Harassment in the Workplace: Developments in Theory, Research, and Practice* (2nd edn), London: Taylor & Francis.

Vartia, M., Korppoo, L., Fallenius, S. and Mattila, M. (2003) 'Workplace bullying: the role of occupational health services', pp. 285–98, in Einarsen, S., Hoel, H., Zapf, D. and Cooper, C. (eds) *Bullying and Emotional Abuse in the Workplace: International Perspectives in Research and Practice*, London: Taylor & Francis.

Woodman, P. and Cook, P. (2005) *Bullying at work: The Experience of Managers*, London: Chartered Management Institute.

Zapf, D. (1999) 'Organisational, work group related and personal causes of mobbing/bullying at work', *International Journal of Manpower,* Vol.20, Nos 1,2, 70–85.

Zapf, D. (2004) 'Negative social behaviour at work and workplace bullying'. Paper presented at the Fourth International Conference on Bullying and Harassment in the Workplace, Bergen, Norway.

Zapf, D. and Einarsen, S. (2001) 'Bullying in the workplace: recent trends in research and practice: an introduction', *European Journal of Work and Organizational Psychology*, Vol.10, No.4, 369–73.

Zapf, D. and Einarsen, S. (2005) 'Mobbing at work: escalated conflicts in organizations', in Fox, S. and Spector, P. (eds) *Counterproductive Work Behavior: Investigations of Actors and Targets*, Washington, DC: American Psychological Association.

Zapf, D. and Einarsen, S. (2011) 'Individual antecedents of bullying: victims and perpetrators', pp. 177–200, in Einarsen, S., Hoel, H., Zapf, D. and Cooper, C. (eds) *Bullying and Harassment in the Workplace: Developments in Theory, Research, and Practice* (2nd edn), London: Taylor & Francis.